THE BANK OF ENGLAND

This history of the Bank of England takes its story from the 1950s to the end of the 1970s. This period probably saw the peak of the Bank's influence and prestige, as it dominated the financial landscape. One of the Bank's central functions was to manage the exchange rate. It was also responsible for administering all the controls that made up monetary policy. In the first part of the period, the Bank did all this with a remarkable degree of freedom. But economic policy was a failure, and sluggish output, banking instability, and rampant inflation characterized the 1970s. The pegged exchange rate was discontinued, and the Bank's freedom of movement was severely constrained as new approaches to policy were devised and implemented. The Bank lost much of its freedom of movement but also took on more formal supervision.

Forrest Capie is Professor of Economic History at Cass Business School, City University, London, where he was head of the Department of Banking and Finance. After receiving a Ph.D. at the London School of Economics, he taught at the universities of Warwick and Leeds. Professor Capie also has been a visiting professor at the University of Aix–Marseille and at the London School of Economics and a Visiting Scholar at the International Monetary Fund. He is an academician of the Academy of Social Sciences. He was editor of the *Economic History Review* and served on the editorial boards of other journals in the discipline. He is on the Academic Advisory Council of the Institute of Economic Affairs. Professor Capie has authored, co-authored, or edited more than 20 books and has written more than 100 journal articles for journals such as the *Economic Journal; Economica; Journal of Money, Credit, and Banking; Economic History Review; European Review of Economic History;* and *Business History.*

STUDIES IN MACROECONOMIC HISTORY

SERIES EDITOR

Michael D. Bordo, *Rutgers University*

EDITORS

Marc Flandreau, *Institut d'Etudes Politiques de Paris*
Chris Meissner, *University of California, Davis*
François Velde, *Federal Reserve Bank of Chicago*
David C. Wheelock, *Federal Reserve Bank of St. Louis*

The titles in this series investigate themes of interest to economists and economic historians in the rapidly developing field of macroeconomic history. The four areas covered include the application of monetary and finance theory, international economics, and quantitative methods to historical problems; the historical application of growth and development theory and theories of business fluctuations; the history of domestic and international monetary, financial, and other macroeconomic institutions; and the history of international monetary and financial systems. The series amalgamates the former Cambridge University Press series Studies in Monetary and Financial History and Studies in Quantitative Economic History.

OTHER BOOKS IN THE SERIES

(*Continued after the Index*)

To Dianna

The Bank of England

1950s to 1979

FORREST CAPIE

Cass Business School, UK

CAMBRIDGE
UNIVERSITY PRESS

CAMBRIDGE UNIVERSITY PRESS

Cambridge, New York, Melbourne, Madrid, Cape Town, Singapore,
São Paulo, Delhi, Dubai, Tokyo, Mexico City

Cambridge University Press
32 Avenue of the Americas, New York, NY 10013-2473, USA

www.cambridge.org
Information on this title: www.cambridge.org/9780521192828

First published 2010

Printed in the United States of America

A catalog record for this publication is available from the British Library.

Library of Congress Cataloging in Publication data
Capie, Forrest.
The Bank of England: 1950s to 1979 / Forrest Capie.
p.   cm. – (Studies in macroeconomic history)
Includes bibliographical references and index.
ISBN 978-0-521-19282-8
1. Bank of England – History.   2. Banks and banking,
Central – Great Britain – History.   I. Title.   II. Series.
HG2994.C37 2010
332.1′10941–dc22   2010014624

ISBN 978-0-521-19282-8 Hardback

Contents

List of Illustrations

List of Figures

List of Tables

Foreword

This volume is the latest in a series of 'official' histories of the Bank: it joins Clapham (1694–1914), Sayers (1891–1944), and Fforde (1941–58) and brings the story up to the end of 1979, which, for all sorts of reasons, proved a watershed for the Bank, as it did for the nation. The works in this series are official only in the sense that the Bank has sponsored their preparation and publication, providing access and research support: the selection of material and its presentation are the author's responsibility, and the Bank does not interfere. The benefits of this approach are, I believe, especially evident in this volume, and I am immensely grateful to Forrest Capie for providing such a thorough, perceptive, and (improbably) entertaining account.

The period covered is one of the least happy in our economic history, covering the series of crises that preceded the devaluation of 1967, the secondary banking crisis of 1973–74, and the great inflation of the 1970s. Neither the instruments of policy nor the policies themselves seemed capable of addressing the seemingly irreversible decline in our fortunes.

However, the Bank is at its best in adversity, and whatever private doubts might have been harboured, heroic deeds were done. Governor Cromer famously assembled $3,000 million of central bank credits to support sterling over the telephone on a single morning in 1964. Roy Bridge, the Head of Foreign Exchange, set and sprang traps for the sterling bears. Sir Jasper Hollom, the Deputy Governor, almost single-handedly saved the financial system in 1973: The vignette of Hollom taking a call from a Burmah shareholder is priceless.

And in the background there were those looking for a new policy framework. The prevailing orthodoxy had been that money did not matter. The Bank of the 1950s had almost forgotten what Bank Rate was for; both it and the Treasury became adept at using quantitative and qualitative credit controls as a substitute. In 1970, though, Goodhart and Crockett published 'The Importance of Money' in the *Quarterly Bulletin* – despite, it has to be said, attempts by the Bank establishment to keep such speculative material out. Steadily, and against opposition, the case was advanced for measuring money, for controlling money even, and for varying the price of money for reasons other than managing the market in gilt-edged securities.

Domestically, this was the time when the great departments of the Bank started to erode, whereas the policymaking part of the Bank expanded. In the early years, only a handful of senior people in the Bank had any connection with policy; the rest were part of a machine. By the end of the period, in the 1980 reorganisation, Richardson was able to reorganise the Bank into policy divisions, with the banking function in support rather than in command. Also over the period the Bank became more open, publishing (rather grudgingly at first) a *Quarterly Bulletin* and producing accounts for the first time in 1971.

Against this background of policy failure, therefore, and partly in response to it, the seeds of the modern Bank became discernible. While the Bank struggled, with exasperated loyalty, to hold a fractured system together, there were those who fixed their gaze on a more rational and stable system, in which the objectives of monetary policy were clear, and the central bank had the authority to deliver them. That story is for our next official history.

Mervyn King
Governor
July 2009

Preface

I undertook to write this book at the invitation of the Governor; it was an invitation I was delighted to accept. The book follows on from the works of Clapham, Sayers, and Fforde in the series of commissioned histories of the Bank from its foundation in 1694 to the recent past. The terminal date is determined by the implicit 30-year rule the Bank operates on its archives, although I have been given access to papers beyond that date. The starting date has been left open – the 1950s. That is partly because although John Fforde had a finishing date in his title of 1958, he chose a sometimes narrow focus in his book, and some topics therefore merited further development. In any case, though, each historian will have a slightly different approach, and several subjects require an introduction that involves some historical background. To begin with 1959 might lead to speculation that it was the establishment of convertibility that determined the starting point or indeed some other striking event such as the fact that Che Guevara became Governor of the central bank of Cuba that year. I have had access to all the materials available and every assistance in talking to current and former personnel. And I have been given complete freedom in the writing of this history. The long list of acknowledgements that follows indicates the extent of support I have enjoyed.

Readers may need to be reminded that a history of the Bank is not a monetary history of the period. Neither is it a business history nor an institutional or administrative history, although it does impinge on all of these. It is not an applied economics or econometric exercise that tests the propositions that economists would like to see. (That is the job of economists.) A history of the Bank is first of all a record of what the Bank did, how it did it, and if possible, an explanation as to why it did it the way it did. The focus is the Bank. In addition, it should be placed in the context of the times.

The writing of history requires two important things: perspective, that is, some distance from the events, and primary documents. There is no difficulty with the first. However, a caution is needed on the second. For twentieth-century history, a common problem is too much information, and the task is to try to distill it. However, this is not always a problem for the Bank. Perhaps it is the nature of banking and its concern with confidentiality that has meant that much is not written down. Of the Bank's handling of the 1914 crisis, Clapham wrote, 'The way hit upon – how and by whom is nowhere written down – was a great operation by the Bank....'[1] And of the key decisions on Bank Rate, Sayers complained, 'Despite the significance attached, through decade after decade, to this regular function of the Bank, there is not the slightest indication in the Court or Committee of Treasury records of the reasoning on which each week's action was based.... no minutes, files, diaries or letters contain regular explanatory notes bearing on this central question.'[2] These habits continued into the late twentieth century. A key meeting in the Bank was morning 'Books' (formerly 'Prayers'), where the Governor and his senior officials would discuss business and tactics across the range of activities in which the Bank was involved. There were no briefing papers, and no records were kept, at least not before the 1980s. Certainly, in the 1950s and 1960s, on the subject of Bank Rate there is almost no paper. The Governor might consult his deputy or another official before telling the Chancellor of his decision. There is some evidence of change in the 1970s, but not a great deal. Thus on key areas of the Bank's activity there are no papers.

Even where things are written down, there is no guarantee of survival. For a host of reasons, someone makes decisions on what should be kept. Generally speaking, though, there is no institutional policy and no particular responsibility. Some material simply might be disposed of before it reaches an archive. And even if it is kept for a time, for reasons of convenience or storage space or costs, it might not survive longer term. Material also could be destroyed by accident, and it remains a possibility that some will be destroyed on purpose. Thus there are some substantial gaps in the Bank's records, with material on important topics, such as the secondary banking crisis, lost to posterity.

On what appears, at least at first glance, the more positive side, there is a possibility, in carrying out comparatively recent history, of the chance to interview some of the participants. Oral history has flourished in the

---

[1] Sayers (1976), vol. III, p.41.
[2] *Ibid.*, vol. I, pp.28–9.

second half of the twentieth century for a number of reasons. Leaving aside the question of mechanics, of whether to tape or not or to tape with agreement to quote, or simply to have a conversation, interviewing participants offers an opportunity to better understand the people involved, and it can alert the writer to the existence of documents (although not necessarily their survival), and well-designed questions might elicit clues that are worth following up. That said, perceptions can differ greatly, and added to this, memory is a strange thing. And then the passage of time and the intrusion of other versions of the events can colour; and even where there is a strong desire to recapture the past, it is not always or perhaps ever successful. Seldom are two stories of an event the same from any two participants. There is, too, the subconscious at work, improving the contribution of the reteller of events in which he or she was involved. Moreover, there is another danger, and that is that a judgement made by the author based on written sources may get reconsidered when the author discovers the person to be charming and helpful – the usual stance of the interviewee – and likely to be around when the book is published. Despite all this, I am extremely grateful to all those who spared the time to talk about the Bank in the period.

A word on usage is needed. Should the 'Bank' be treated as singular or plural? 'The Bank' was an abbreviated version of 'the Governor and Company of the Bank of England' and therefore a plural noun. Formal documents such as court records and Bank publications such as the *Annual Report* and *Quarterly Bulletin* always used the plural. However, some internal notes referred to 'the Bank' in the singular, resulting in inconsistency. Outside writings, notably the press, referred to the Bank as singular. The issue was raised in the late 1970s, with some feeling that the plural use could be seen by critics of the Bank as 'an unnecessary and irritating self-conceit'.[3] In 1978, the Governor, Gordon Richardson, accepted that in legal documents the Bank should remain plural but wanted the singular in other uses because the plural often resulted in 'unnatural, contorted English which must seem strange or even pompous to readers who do not appreciate the reason for it'.[4] It was agreed that 'all concerned should exercise flexibility and good judgement, without the imposition of hard and fast rules'.[5]

A large number of people appear in this story. They are identified on first appearance by their full name and thereafter by their surname. On occasion,

---

[3] Colin Henderson (Secretary's Department) to Peter Brown/Geoffrey Gough (The Secretary), 'The Bank: singular or plural', 20 July 1977', 3A114/1.

[4] Chief of Establishments, Notice to Staff, 'The Bank: singular or plural', 18 December 1978, 3A114/1.

[5] Extract from 'Meeting of Heads of Departments', 7 February 1979, 3A114/1.

however, if there is a risk of confusion or if one mention is sufficiently far away from another, the full name is used.

A brief word on sources also might be useful. Apart from the number of archives that have been used (the references for which are all in the endnotes), the publications of several financial institutions, including the Bank – Annual Reports, Reviews, and so on – also have been used extensively. Again, the full references are in the endnotes and not shown in the Bibliography.

Acknowledgements

A work of this kind could not be accomplished without the help of a large number of people. I would like to say that the responsibility is partly theirs, but of course, I cannot. However, I do express my sincere thanks to all who took the time to talk or correspond with me about the Bank. It would be invidious to present these in any order that implied a degree of gratitude or hinted at the size of their contribution. So I begin with those closest to the project. I must start with my principal research assistant, Mike Anson, who was with the project from the beginning to the end and without whose industry and application the work would have taken a lot longer. His skills in tracking down material in the archives and providing summaries were a boon. I owe him a great debt of gratitude. He was ably supported by Will Goodfellow, and I had the secretarial support of first Chris Armbsy and then Shona Carswell. And then in the Bank directly supporting the project were the staff of the Bank's Archive: Sarah Millard, Jeanette Sherry, Jenny Ulph, Lara Webb, Ben White, and Hayley Whiting; followed literally closely by those in the Information Centre: Janet Adams, Kath Begley, Catherine Gardner, Maggie Hawes, Penny Hope, Shahid Nazir, Sarah Stevens, and Chris Thomas; and from the Museum: Richard Brigenshaw, Sue Jenkins, John Keyworth, and Lorraine Painter.

Other Bank staff who gave freely of their time included Andrew Bailey, Charlie Bean, Ian Bond, Alastair Clark, Roger Clews, Stephen Collins, Robin Darbyshire, Paul Fisher, John Footman, Joe Ganley, Sir John Gieve, Andy Haldane, David Ingram, George Johnston, Rachel Lomax, Mark Robson, Peter Sinclair, Paul Tucker, and Andrew Wardlow. I also was able to have informal lunches and discussions with a number of new entrants to the Bank in the 1970s who were still with the Bank in 2008: Stuart Allen, Chris Armsby, David Basterfield, Roger Beales, Sue Betts, Gail Bishop, Barbara

Carr, Laura Daniels, Sue Davidson, Julie Gallagher, Sandra Mills, Diane Moore, Pat Morgan, Debbie Nyman, Lesley Oughton, Sarah Pegg, Stephen Sabine, Russell Seddon, and Nick Stansfield. Former Bank staff who gave their time include Bill Allen, Tony Coleby, Leslie Dicks-Mireaux, Garth Hewitt, John Hill, David Mallett, Teresa May, Chris Parry, John Pullinger, John Rumins, and Tony Latter.

Some idea of the work of the Agents was gained from a visit to the Agents: David Buffham (North East) and Tony Strachan (Glasgow); and I talked to John Bartlett (Birmingham). On a fascinating visit to the Printing Works at Debden, I was given a complete tour and short history by Jim Biggs, Martin Wylie, Paul Lane, John Clark, and Fiona Dodd.

On a visit to Washington to the International Monetary Fund (IMF) and the Federal Reserve, I enjoyed the hospitality of and benefited from the guidance of current and former employees of the IMF and the Fed: Mark Allen, Jim Boughton, Mohsin Khan, Jens Larsen, Jacques Polak, Mahmud Pradhan, Tom Scholar, Dave Small, and Bob Solomon.

A long list of others includes Roger Alford, Mike Artis, John Atkin, Bob Aliber, Peter Bernholz, Michael Bordo, Alec Chrystal, Lord Cobbold, Tim Congdon, Christopher Fildes, Stuart Fleming, John Forsyth, Lord Griffiths, Lord Harris, David Henderson, Elizabeth Hennessey, Robert Hetzel, Harold James, William Keegan, David Kynaston, Allan Meltzer, Michael Oliver, Leslie Presnell, Robert Pringle, Lord Roll, Sir Patrick Sargent, Anna Schwartz, Martin Sheppard, David B Smith, Andrew Smithers, Sir Alan Walters, Sir Douglas Wass, Geoffrey Wood, and Jeremy Wormell.

Then there was the assistance of people from other archives and outside organisations: Andrew Riley, Churchill College Cambridge Archives; University of Glasgow Archive Services; Moira Lovegrove, Baring Archive; Karen Sampson, Lloyds TSB Archive; Edwin Green and Tina Staples, HSBC Archive; Jean Marcouyeux and Premela Isaac, IMF Archives; British Library staff; Kathleen Dickson and Vic Pratt, British Film Institute; House of Lords Record Office staff; Catharine Morris, *The Times*; The National Archives staff, Kew; and Michael Paige, British Broadcasting Corporation.

A number of people from the Bank, the City, Whitehall, and the press agreed to a formal interview (some more than one), and I express my sincere thanks to them all: Sir Nigel Althaus, Lord Armstrong, Roger Barnes, Sir George Blunden, Sir Samuel Brittan, Peter J. Bull, William Clarke, Lord Cobbold, Tony Coleby, Peter Cooke, Andrew Crockett, Lord Croham, Michael Foot, Rodney Galpin, Lord George, Malcolm Gill, Graeme Gillchrist, Charles Goodhart, Stuart Graham, David Green, Lord Healey, Sir Jasper Hollom, Sir Martin Jacomb, Peter Jay, Pen Kent, Graham Kentfield,

Lord Lawson, Sir Geoffrey Littler, Sir Kit McMahon, Leslie Dicks-Mireaux, George Morgan, Sir Jeremy Morse, Guy de Moubray, George Nissen, Willie Osborn, Oliver Page, Gordon Pepper, Sir Brian Pitman, Ian Plenderleith, Lionel Price, Brian Quinn, Lord Rees-Mogg, David Somerset, Sir David Walker, and Sir Nigel Wicks.

Further thanks must be given to those who read and commented on chapters or in some cases the whole manuscript: Peter Andrews, Roger Barnes, Michael Bordo, Alec Chrystal, Roger Clews, Stephen Collins, Peter Cooke, Christopher Fildes, John Footman, Charles Goodhart, Brian Griffiths, John Keyworth, Robert Pringle, Brian Quinn, Catherine Schenk, Anna Schwartz, and Geoffrey Wood.

Abbreviations and Acronyms

AAB	Allied Arab Bank
AMC	Agricultural Mortgage Corporation
BAMMS	Banking and Money Market Supervision
BEQB	*Bank of England Quarterly Bulletin*
BIS	Bank for International Settlements
BOCBA	British Overseas and Commonwealth Bankers Association
BOLSA	Bank of London and South America
BP	British Petroleum
CCC	Competition and credit control
CD	Certificate of deposit
CDFC	Commonwealth Development Finance Company
CLCB	Committee of London Clearing Banks
CWS	Co-operative Wholesale Society
DCE	Domestic credit expansion
DEA	Department of Economic Affairs
DTI	Department of Trade and Industry
EBH	Edward Bates Holdings
EBS	Edward Bates and Sons
EBSI	EBS Investments
ECI	Equity Capital for Industry Limited
EEA	Exchange Equalisation Account
EEC	European Economic Community
EID	Economic Intelligence Department
EPU	European Payments Union
FCI	Finance Corporation for Industry
FEC	Foreign Exchange Committee
FECDBA	Foreign Exchange and Currency Deposit Brokers' Association
FFI	Finance for Industry

FHA	Finance Houses Association
FNFC	First National Finance Corporation
FRBNY	Federal Reserve Bank of New York
G10	Group of Ten
GAB	General Agreements to Borrow
GATT	General Agreement on Tariffs and Trade
GDP	Gross domestic product
HMT	Her Majesty's Treasury
IBEL	Interest-bearing eligible liability
ICFC	Industrial and Commercial Finance Corporation
IFU	Industrial Finance Unit
IMF	International Monetary Fund
IRC	Industrial Reorganisation Corporation
ISC	Institutional Shareholders Committee
JSC	Joint Standing Committee
LDMA	London Discount Market Association
LSE	London School of Economics
MDHB	Mersey Docks and Harbour Board
MLR	Minimum lending rate
MPG	Monetary Policy Group
MSPs	Minimum sterling proportions
NATO	North Atlantic Treaty Organisation
NBPI	National Board for Prices and Incomes
NEDC	National Economic Development Council
OECD	Organisation for Economic Co-operation and Development
OEEC	Organisation for European Economic Co-operation
OPEC	Organisation of Petroleum Exporting Countries
OSA	Overseas sterling area
PSBR	Public-sector borrowing requirement
SAMA	South Arabian Monetary Agency
SARB	South African Reserve Bank
SCNI	Select Committee on Nationalised Industries
SCOOP	Scottish Co-Operative Wholesale Society
SDRs	Special drawing rights
SNB	Swiss National Bank
SSDs	Supplementary special deposits
SWL	Slater Walker Limited
SWSL	Slater Walker Securities Limited
TUC	Trades Union Congress
UDT	United Dominions Trust
WBB	Wallace Brothers Bank
WP3	Working Party Three

1

Introduction and Overview

No one invented central banking. The earliest central banks emerged from commercial banks. Any central bank that was a central bank from its inception was modelled on one of these ancestors. The Bank of England, founded in 1694, evolved as a central bank in the course of the nineteenth century. By the last third of that century it was carrying out the key functions of monetary policy (exchange-rate management in those days) and financial stability (lender of last resort). Most histories of central banks, perhaps because their births were so relatively recent, begin from their date of establishment. The Bank, however, has had a long history as a central bank, a longer one still as a bank of monopoly issue, and an even longer one as a banker to the government. All that history has been covered in volumes prior to this one, which starts with the 1950s and takes the Bank's history to 1979. The period thus covered was very mixed. At the outset, financial stability was taken for granted; it was always there without anyone apparently having to do anything to maintain it. And monetary policy was downplayed in importance. But monetary policy conducted by neglect failed, and financial stability was lost. A major rethink then took place. There were many forces at work in this process. Some perspective on these and on the world more widely will help to place the Bank in the context of its time.

Some Overview

Modern economic growth, the sustained rise in the rate of economic growth, began in the eighteenth century in Britain and northwestern Europe and accelerated and spread further afield in the nineteenth century. The first half of the twentieth century was a period of turmoil – of war, inadequate adjustment, economic depression, and war and adjustment again. Then growth rates accelerated in the second half of the twentieth century to the point where no previous era had known anything comparable in the levels of and rate of expansion in material well-being. By some measures, the world economy was as integrated in the 1890s as in the 1990s, but at the end of the nineteenth century, there was an emerging reaction against globalisation, and nationalism, together with its economic manifestation, protectionism, began to spread.[1] Indeed, much of this carries the blame for the collapse into war and depression that followed.

The developing world economy of the late nineteenth century came to an abrupt halt with the outbreak of war in 1914.[2] Trade, capital flows, migration, and the international monetary system all were seriously disrupted. The war was not without its economic advantages in terms of technological advances, and there were clear improvements in the fields of management and production. But the costs – even looking beyond the human suffering and loss of life – were enormous. All manner of problems were born, most of which were not to be resolved properly in the decade after the war. Some of them played a part in the coming of the depression that was so devastating for much of the world at the beginning of the 1930s. Apart from the disruption to trading patterns, huge war debts accumulated, and reparation payments were imposed on Germany. Hyperinflation and exchange-rate misalignment contributed to the distortions. The Great Depression that followed from 1929 to 1932 and beyond so severely damaged growth around the world that recovery was not achieved until the end of the 1930s.

Given this background, it is perhaps not surprising that following the Second World War there were very low expectations for growth in the world economy even on the assumption that there would be a relatively smooth political transition. In fact, a dominant theme was the likelihood of secular stagnation. Some fears went back to Hansen's belief that there would be an end to both rapid population increase and rapid capital-intensive technological change.[3] These fears increased in the later war years when it was believed that inevitably there would be high unemployment for some time after the war as millions of servicemen were demobilised and millions of other defence workers were put out of work. However, all this turned out to be yet another bad forecast by demographers and economists.[4] A legacy of the two world wars and the interwar depression was the view that governments could do better than markets. Indeed, the idea that markets failed

---

[1]   Bordo and Flandreau (2003).
[2]   Whether or not this was the end of globalisation is debatable, see James (2002).
[3]   Hansen (1938).
[4]   Fogel (2005).

became widespread, and the obvious response at the time was that governments intervened in or, more commonly, substituted for the market.

Throughout the Second World War, discussions were held among the
Allies (although most often that meant between the United States and
the United Kingdom) on the shape of the world economy after the war.
The principal objectives were to escape from the problems and the solutions of the 1930s – trade protection, currency devaluation, self-sufficiency,
and so on. Out of this came the International Monetary Fund (IMF) and
the General Agreement on Tariffs and Trade (GATT), which laid the basis
for a stable international monetary system and led to the increasing freeing of restrictions on trade. On the domestic front, however, there were
retrograde steps as the interpretation of the 1930s that markets had failed
and governments had to replace them resulted in the application of controls
and nationalisation. However, the most immediate threat in the 1940s was
the communist one. The rapid recovery of Western Europe was seen as one
means of containing that threat, and the Marshall plan was at the centre of
that effort.

There are seldom any clean breaks in history, and 1950 is not one
either. However, much of the postwar adjustment had taken place by then,
although no sooner had it than the Korean War broke out. Nevertheless, it
was from this juncture that much of the world began to embark on a period
of most striking economic progress. The world economy grew at a remarkable pace across the second half of the twentieth century, although there
were interruptions along the way. The period from 1950 to 1970 is increasingly referred to as a 'golden age', with many Organisation for Economic
Co-operation and Development (OECD) countries experiencing dramatic
improvements in their economic fortunes. Of course, the 'world economy'
was a much smaller one in 1950 in several respects. There were fewer countries and a very much smaller total population. The Soviet Union and its
satellites in Eastern Europe largely excluded themselves from the rest of the
world economy, and Communist China too was essentially closed.

Between 1950 and the end of the century, the world's population more
than doubled from 2.5 billion to almost 6 billion. Africa and Latin America
tripled in size, whereas Western Europe grew by less than a third. The growth
of income, though, was vastly greater. World gross domestic product (GDP;
in 1990 dollars) grew from $5.3 billion to over $33.7 billion. Growth was
fastest of all in Asia, where it rose by a factor of 12. In Western Europe
it grew fivefold. Even Africa grew fivefold.[5] The greatest period of growth

---

[5]   Maddison (2006).

was that from 1950 to the beginnings of the 1970s. Real GDP per capita in Europe grew at 3.8 per cent per annum in these years, more than twice as fast as any comparable previous period and more than twice as fast as the following 20 years. Economic growth in Japan was even faster. Explanations for such performance range over many factors. US aid was important in the early stages of recovery in Europe, although that varied greatly across countries. In the case of Japan and some others, there was undoubtedly technological catch-up. The improving international environment of freer trade played its part, as did the desperate need to restore capital equipment and raise consumption following a long period of neglect.

World trade grew even faster than output. World exports (in 1990 dollars) grew from $0.295 billion in 1950 to almost $6 billion by the end of the century, that is, by a factor of 20. In the golden age, German exports were growing at an annual rate of over 12 per cent, America's by over 6 per cent, and Japan's by more than 15 per cent. For the world as a whole, the figure was 8 per cent. All these rates slowed in the following quarter-century to 4.4, 6.0, 5.3, and 5.1 per cent, respectively, but that was from a higher base and still represented considerable growth.[6]

The explosion in capital flows came later. They were constrained under the Bretton Woods arrangements, but they were growing in the 1960s, and when they were completely freed, they grew rapidly, reaching their greatest rates in the 1990s. It is not easy to be precise about the scale of capital flows – distinguishing net and gross is just one problem – but there can be little argument that it was huge. One indicator is that foreign-exchange trading in the 1970s was of the order of $10 to $20 billion. By the mid-1990s, it was around $1,260 billion – close to 100 times greater.

In the Western world, there were two important political developments for the world economy. One was the end of empires, and the other was the formation of the European Economic Community (EEC) that would in time become the European Union (EU). A principal feature of the postwar world was the retreat from empire. European countries that had colonised the world in the late nineteenth century came under pressure to return sovereignty to what had been colonies. In some cases, some former dependencies simply declared independence. Since the war had been fought in terms of freedom and democracy, this was both to be expected and not seriously resisted. Some of the transfers were successful, and others less so. The British experience was on the whole successful, although there were many setbacks in the process. By 1965, all British colonies in Africa were independent

---

[6] OECD, *Annual Report*, 2003.

except Southern Rhodesia. Countries that gained their independence did not blossom immediately, for they were often not well equipped to direct their own affairs; in fact, they almost invariably regressed. The Colonial powers had not prepared the way for the transference of power – indeed, in many cases could not, given the pressing demands that were being made. Although suitable legal systems frequently were in place, education was not advanced, and there often was disagreement among the different domestic political parties, disagreement that too often ended in civil war, with the inevitable human and economic costs.

The second important feature was the emergence of the beginnings of the EU. Almost as soon as the war was over, schemes were devised and implemented to bring the countries of Europe together. This was motivated partly by politics and partly by economics. There was the desire on the part of some to offer competition to the United States and Soviet Union, who otherwise looked like they would be dominating the world. On the economic front, there were schemes for co-operation and the integration of some industries (e.g., coal and steel). In 1957, the Treaty of Rome created the EEC or Common Market. This marked the beginning of the process that would lead to ever greater co-operation and integration. A scheme for monetary union also was launched and was finally achieved for most of the EU in 2002 with the introduction of the euro. Many saw this as essentially politically motivated, for a monetary union really requires a fiscal union to support it, and that, in turn, requires increased centralisation of political power.

The end of the golden age came with the accelerating inflation of the late 1960s. There are several explanations for the inflation (to which I will return later), but it was in part a consequence of the financing of the Vietnam War and of large US government expenditures on the 'Great Society'. The pegged exchange-rate regime then transmitted the inflation around the system. The Vietnam War was an unpopular war and had to be financed by money creation rather than by taxing and borrowing. The resulting inflation was becoming clear towards the end of the 1960s and led inevitably to the breakdown of the international monetary system at the beginning of the 1970s. The world at that point moved to an entirely fiat monetary system for the first time in history, ensuring that inflation would persist for much longer – in fact, until people tired of it, and governments were obliged to take action to curb it.

Inflation was one of the striking features of the world economy in the second half of the twentieth century. Remarkably, most market economies in this period underwent at least one inflationary experience of more than

25 per cent per annum. The principal exceptions were West Germany and Switzerland. Many had inflation of more than 100 per cent that lasted for some years. In the 'transition' economies, the experience was far worse. Most of them had inflation of more than 400 per cent at some point in their transition. All of this had a damaging impact on economic performance. Thus the great achievements that were made might have been even greater.

Further, at the end of the golden age, there was a downturn in many economies, but there was a good deal of misinterpretation of the reasons for the downturn and confusion over how recovery might be effected. The response to the recession at the beginning of the 1970s generally was to turn to expansionary policies of a Keynesian kind. Under floating exchange-rate regimes, expansionary monetary policies could be used, it was believed, to boost incomes. Of course, as some leading economists had been pointing out for some time, these policies would produce inflation in the long run without any benefit to output. And inflation is what followed.

At least two contributory factors were involved. One was trade union power. It was widely believed that powerful unions were pushing up wages and producing 'cost-push' inflation. It is clearer now, although it could be seen then, that weak governments were giving in to union pressure and printing the money required to settle large wage demands. The second factor was oil price rises brought about by the Organisation of Petroleum Exporting Countries (OPEC) cartel. The first of these shocks came in 1973–74; the second, in 1978. Again, the price of one item rising does not produce, let alone cause, inflation, even if that item is a large one in the economy. What happened, and arguably with some justification in order to ease adjustment, was that governments again printed money to accommodate the increase in prices. These monetary expansions certainly contributed to the increasing inflation, in several OECD countries reaching annual rates of around 20 per cent.

However, the real economy did not improve. Instead, it languished in the doldrums, and the term 'stagflation' – stagnant output with inflation – began to be used. This was the point at which, at least in some countries, there was growing realisation and acceptance of the fact that there needed to be supply-side corrections. The real economy had become over-regulated and taxed and lacked the appropriate incentives to produce at its most efficient. Thus it was that in the recession in Britain at the end of the 1970s, policies were adopted that looked, to many, to be tightening rather than expansionary and widely condemned as such. In fact, however, they signalled the beginning of supply-side changes that would help to arrest the relative decline of the British economy.

The last 20 years or so of the twentieth century might be labelled the 'triumph of the market'. It was then that there was increasing recognition that while there might have been less than ideal market outcomes, there also were less than ideal government outcomes. In its crudest form, this could be seen from casual inspection of the two great competing systems – those of the centrally planned economies and those of the market or, more accurately, mixed economies. Even within these mixed economies, however, it was becoming clear that less intervention produced better results. Thus it was that around the world all kinds of markets were being deregulated, labour markets freed, barriers to trade reduced, capital markets liberalised, and so on. The growing divergence between the economic performance of the market economies and the centrally planned economies undoubtedly contributed to the demise of the latter.

The British Economy

The period covered by this study was one of mixed fortunes for the British economy (Table 1.1). For most of the period, there was better performance than there had been for a long time, although in the 1970s there was the worst experience with high inflation and sluggish growth. Despite of the good performance, though, there was a developing awareness that others were doing better, and the perception of decline began to take over. This notion of decline, as well as a growing desire for faster growth, became one of the principal features of the period. The other striking feature is high, accelerating, and volatile inflation.

Although the British economy was the first to experience modern economic growth, it has never been at a high rate. Even in the course of the industrial revolution in the second half of the eighteenth century, the economy grew at close to 1 per cent per annum.[7] It was not until the middle years of the nineteenth century that it reached annual rates of growth of close to 3 per cent. Data deficiencies preclude any precision in these figures. For the years after the middle of the nineteenth century, there are better data, although they are still far from ideal. The picture from that point on, however, is of a fairly steady decline in the rate of growth such that by the closing years of the century and the opening decade of the twentieth century, the rate was around 1 per cent per annum. Thereafter, it picked up, and in the 1920s and 1930s, the trend rate was again over 2 per cent, only for that to be interrupted by war in the 1940s. In the 1950s and 1960s, though, it was

[7] Crafts and Harley (1992).

Table 1.1. *UK macroeconomic variables, 1955–80 (%)*

Year	GDP growth (2002 prices)	GDP growth (1980 prices)	Inflation	Unemployment	Unemployment (contemporary)	Money growth (M3)	Bank Rate High	Bank Rate Low
1955	3.1	3.4	4.5	1.2	1.1	0.4	4.5	3.5
1956	1.0	1.6	4.9	1.3	1.2	−1.0	5.5	4.5
1957	1.7	2.0	3.7	1.6	1.4	2.2	7.0	5.0
1958	0.4	0.3	3.0	2.2	2.1	2.9	7.0	4.0
1959	4.4	4.0	0.6	2.3	2.2	4.1	4.0	4.0
1960	5.5	4.6	1.0	1.7	1.6	3.6	6.0	4.0
1961	2.5	3.3	3.4	1.6	1.5	3.2	7.0	6.0
1962	1.2	1.1	4.3	2.1	2.0	2.2	6.0	4.5
1963	5.1	4.2	2.0	2.6	2.5	4.1	4.5	4.0
1964	5.6	5.2	3.3	1.7	1.6	0.04	7.0	4.0
1965	2.3	2.3	4.8	1.5	1.4	11.9	7.0	6.0
1966	2.0	1.9	3.9	1.5	1.5	4.8	6.0	7.0
1967	2.5	2.8	2.5	2.3	2.4	4.0	8.0	5.5
1968	4.2	4.2	4.7	2.5	2.4	6.2	8.0	7.0
1969	2.1	1.3	5.4	2.5	2.4	2.1	8.0	7.0
1970	2.3	2.2	6.4	2.6	2.6	15.8	8.0	7.0
1971	2.0	2.7	9.4	3.4	3.6	11.7	7.0	5.0
1972	3.6	2.3	7.1	3.8	3.8	23.9	9.0	5.0
1973	7.1	7.9	9.2	2.7	2.7	26.9	13.0	7.5
1974	−1.3	−1.1	16.0	2.6	2.6	18.3	13.0	11.5
1975	−0.6	−0.7	24.2	4.0	4.2	9.5	11.5	9.8
1976	2.7	3.9	16.5	5.5	5.7	10.5	15.0	9.0
1977	2.4	1.0	15.8	5.8	6.2	9.4	12.3	5.0
1978	3.3	3.6	8.3	5.7	6.1	14.5	12.5	6.5
1979	2.7	2.1	13.4	5.3	5.8	11.6	17.0	12.0
1980	−2.1	−2.1	18.0	6.8	7.4	15.9	17.0	14.0

Source: GDP growth (2002 prices) calculated from *Economic Trends Annual Supplement* 2005; GDP growth (1980 prices) calculated from *Economic Trends Annual Supplement* 1985; inflation, Office of National Statistics (ONS); unemployment, Mitchell (1988); unemployment contemporary, monthly average from *Monthly Statistical Digest* (unemployment rate defined as the number registered as unemployed as expressed as a percentage of the estimated total number of employees); M3 calculated from Capie and Webber (1985); Bank Rate and MLR taken from *Bank of England Quarterly Bulletin*.

again between 2 and 3 per cent. Thus the picture from around the middle of the nineteenth century to about 1970 was a U-shaped one, with rates close to 3 per cent at the beginning, then falling fairly steadily to around 1 per cent in the middle, and then climbing to between 2 and 3 per cent at the end. Then it stalled in the 1970s so that, for instance, the level in 1976 was only about 5 per cent above that of 1972.[8]

Britain enjoyed rates of growth in the 1950s and 1960s that were better than they had been perhaps since the middle of the nineteenth century. If not quite a 'golden age', it seemed highly satisfactory in the 1950s. When the period 1950–73 is taken as a whole, GDP per capita in the United Kingdom grew at 2.4 per cent per annum. This rate dropped to 1.5 per cent per annum for the remainder of the 1970s (1973–79). Viewed from an international perspective, however, the picture looked less rosy, and indeed, by the end of the 1950s, it was evident that other European countries in particular were performing considerably better. For example, for the period 1950–73, the annual rate of growth per capita for a 12-country OECD median was 3.4 per cent, substantially higher than the British. And although that dropped in the period 1973–79, it was still 2 per cent and again considerably better than the British.[9]

Additional output can usually be produced with more inputs, so a better measure of performance is productivity, and labour productivity is one guide. The figures for Britain for 1950–73 are 2.5 per cent per annum as opposed to the 12-country median of 3.6 per cent; then the British figure fell to 1.3 per cent for the remainder of the 1970s, whereas the OECD average was 2.2 per cent.[10] Nevertheless, over the whole period, British output (GDP) per hour worked almost doubled. It is true that these figures did turn around over the next decade, and the British were marginally higher than the OECD for both output growth and labour productivity in the period 1979–88. From the 1950s onward, growth had become a policy objective, something to which most governments explicitly committed themselves. By the 1970s, growth had moved firmly to centre stage and dominated policy making. A range of policies was pursued, often misguidedly, as the drive for growth took precedence over all else.

These growth rates, of course, are the trend rates. As ever, the actual path of output growth was cyclical. For long periods in British economic history, the cycles were of roughly similar length – around seven to nine years from

---

[8] Matthews, Feinstein, and Odling-Smee (1982).
[9] Bean and Crafts (1986, p. 133).
[10] Ibid.

one peak to the next peak or from trough to trough. In the period up to the Second World War, the downturn in the cycle usually resulted in actual falls in output. After the war, actual falls disappeared, but nevertheless there were still cycles, although they had become growth cycles. The cycle became shorter too, and it was argued that it was more subject to political forces.

There has been much written on the dating of cycles, and several variants are available depending on the definition being used and the techniques employed to identify the cycle. According to one, though, our period began in 1958 with a trough followed by a sharp boom that peaked in 1960.[11] Then it was down to a trough in the winter of 1962–64 and a peak again in 1964. This short period cycle continued with another trough in 1967, followed by a peak in 1969 and a trough again in 1972. Another peak is given as 1973, and that is followed by a trough in 1975. The period then ends with a peak in 1979, following the longest and slowest recovery in the whole period.

There were fears at the time that the cycle was becoming more pronounced. And indeed in the mid-1970s there was a return to actual falls in output. There was a great deal of gloom at that time and some good reason for it. Falls in output had not been seen since the 1930s, and there were many comparisons made with that earlier experience. In the depression of the 1930s, output had fallen in total over a period of three years (1929–32) by 5.6 per cent. In the 1970s, there was negative growth in 1974, 0.6 per cent in 1975, and then a jump back in 1976 of 2.7 per cent.[12] The big difference between the two periods was in prices. In each of the three years of recession in the 1930s, prices fell by 5.7, 6.1, and 3.2 per cent, whereas in the 1970s, prices rose by 16.0, 24.2, and 16.5 per cent (see Table 1.1). Thus, as output was falling, prices were soaring, and that was the completely new experience that earned the name 'stagflation'.

The economy reached another peak in 1979 and then began a downturn that produced another deep recession. It was time then to resurrect the Kondratieff cycle, the notion that modern industrial economies move through long cycles as well as short cycles of around 50 years – 25 years of growth followed by 25 years of slowdown. The fact that timing seemed so precise, a peak in 1979 just as there had been a peak in 1929 and a trough in 1982 just as there had been a trough in 1932, encouraged a great burst of research activity and the revival of the idea of long cycles.

Aside from that cyclical experience, from the early 1950s, there was a growing awareness of the superior trend performance on the continent.

[11] Britton (1986).
[12] Capie and Collins (1983); *Statistical Abstract*.

There had been the Italian and German 'economic miracles' of the late 1940s and early 1950s. More generally, though, there had been steady out-performance of Britain. And a certain amount of gloom and some resignation seemed to settle over the country. In fact, the idea of British economic decline goes back much further – at least to the end of the nineteenth century when unfavourable comparisons began to be made with some European economies but notably Germany on everything from production methods through management techniques to education and training and much else. Thus began a small but robust industry in self-denigration. This gathered great pace in the third quarter of the twentieth century, and a flurry of titles appeared not only charting the decline but explaining it.[13] Most were of the view that the obvious industrial decline was synonymous with or at least indicative of overall decline. Some of the accounts got close to hysterical, forecasting not only continuing ailing but terminal illness. For example, one predicted that Greece would have overtaken Britain by 1987 and Portugal would have by 2008 and that Eastern Europe would have 'sailed past' Britain and within another generation Britain would be the poorest country in Europe with the possible exception of Albania.[14] Another wildly wrong forecast!

The explanations for the decline, as hinted at earlier, covered a range of possibilities. Distaste for trade and enterprise was encouraged by the class system and the accompanying education system. There also was the loss of empire for those who believed it was once profitable. There was the handicap of being the first to industrialise and so operating with outdated technology. However, central to many explanations was the role of the City of London and of finance. Investment was central to this particular story. It was being argued quite widely that growth was a straightforward function of investment, and the British investment rate was too low. British investment as a share of GDP was around 10 per cent, whereas on continental Europe rates were over 20 per cent and in Japan were close to 30 per cent. Apart from the failure to demonstrate a link between investment and growth – what kind of investment and so on – it could have been observed that the British rate had never been high at any time. That aside, though, the critics argued that the main reason the British rate was low was that the City of London had diverted funds abroad. There was supposedly a preference for safe overseas investment over domestic industrial investment.

[13] For example, see Kirby (1981), Sked (1987), and Weiner (1982).
[14] Pollard (1982, p. 6).

There is no room here to describe the rest of the economy in any detail nor to cover the myriad other reasons advanced for poor performance. However, it is worth bearing in mind that the period was one in which the public sector was growing and the private sector shrinking. Government spending rose as a percentage of total output from 36 per cent in 1950 to 46 per cent in 1980.[15] Numbers employed in the public sector rose from 1.8 million in 1960 to 3 million in 1980[16]. This in itself was the source of another serious explanation advanced at the time – 'too few producers'.[17] In fact, the superior economic performance of Europe and Japan can be seen with some perspective to have been mainly a catching-up phenomenon, and as remarked earlier, that began to go the other way in the 1980s. Even so, a considered view is that British growth in the period 1950–73 could have been better by about 0.75 to 1 per cent per annum had better policy choices been made.[18]

The British economy had always been extremely open when measured by the share of trade in total output. It also had for a long time been open in the other sense of free trade policies. However, that latter had come to an end in 1931–32 when a range of restrictive measures had been introduced together with the granting of preferential treatment for empire countries. After the Second World War, there was a desire, certainly on the part of the United States, for liberalising world trade and payments, and some steps were taken to promote that. But Britain persisted with many restrictions for a long time after the war. When these were at last being removed in the course of the 1950s, the main topic on the trade agenda was the formation of the European Common Market. Discussions were well advanced by the mid-1950s, and the Treaty of Rome was signed in 1957. Britain felt unable to participate at that point and instead was active in promoting the European Free Trade Area (EFTA) among a group of countries on the periphery of the core of six forming the Common Market.

Britain's trade as a share of GDP had been on the order of 30 per cent in the late nineteenth century. In the troubled interwar years, collapsing incomes in many of her trading partners, together with the erection of restrictive barriers to trade, meant that Britain's share fell to around 12 per cent. After the Second World War, it began to rise again with rapidly rising incomes and increasing liberalisation so that by the 1960s it was

---

[15] Calculated from *Economic Trends Annual Supplement* 2002.
[16] *Ibid.*
[17] Bacon and Eltis (1976).
[18] Broadberry and Crafts (2003, p. 719).

17 per cent. Protectionism was briefly on the rise again in the 1970s, and that, together with the fact that income growth had slowed sharply, was reflected in a slight fall in the trade ratio from 26 per cent in 1976 to 24 per cent in 1980.[19]

Britain had run a current account surplus from the Napoleonic wars until the 1930s. It turned slightly negative in the 1930s and then massively negative in the war years. Then, after the war, there was a perpetual concern over the current account and the fear that it would remain weak or in deficit. Although the account was still negative at the beginning of the 1950s, partly a consequence of the Korean War, it was generally positive from 1956 to 1959. Nevertheless, for the pessimists it was still too small to be able to replenish the lost reserves. Throughout the 1960s it persistently slipped into deficit, and talk of a balance-of-payments crisis was frequent. The worst years, however, came in the 1970s. In 1974, the deficit was 4 per cent of GDP.[20]

The role of labour was another dominant theme in this period. Ever since the white paper of 1944, priority had been given to full employment. The white paper was itself in part the result of a reading of interwar experience. On many fronts, as we will note, the policy making of the second half of the twentieth century was based on a particular interpretation of the interwar years. That experience was widely perceived to have been bad, and there are many images of the time still easily evoked to conjure up pictures of depression and poverty. Unemployment in the 1920s had been around 1 million and returned to that level after the recession years of 1929–32. During the recession, it had risen to around 3 million. However, the explanation for that rise is still debated. There had been no deep depression in Britain, as there had been elsewhere, and it certainly can be argued that the rise in unemployment between 1929 and 1932 was the consequence of fixed wage contracts and falling prices producing rising real wages, which, in time, brought rising unemployment.[21] In any case, after 1945, the consensus was that full employment should be pursued, and it was. And for many years, that pursuit seemed to be successful.

While the labour force grew quite steadily from 1950 onward, employment did too, and it continued to grow through to the late 1960s, with only one downturn in the late 1950s. And unemployment was at its lowest ever throughout the 1950s and 1960s before beginning to rise and then soar in

---

[19] Calculated from Mitchell (1988, pp. 454 and 830).
[20] Office of National Statistics.
[21] Beenstock, Capie, and Griffiths (1984).

the 1970s. Since labour was placed at the centre of the economic debate, it is not surprising to find trade unions beginning to have a major say in policymaking, and by the 1970s, unions had come to dictate terms in wage settlement. In the 1960s and 1970s, the *Financial Times* devoted a whole page every day to 'Labour'. Industrial relations were sour and got worse by the year and by the end of our period culminated in the 'winter of discontent' of 1978–79, in which unemployment reached 1.42 million, and the number of days lost in strikes reached 19.44 million compared with an average for the 1960s of 3.55 million.[22]

Monetary Background

The central feature of British economic life in the third quarter of the twentieth century was inflation. Never before in British history, not even in wartime, had inflation reached the heights that it did in the mid-1970s. This needs placing in a long run and to some extent international perspective. Inflation is best described as a sustained rise in the general price level. It is a relatively recent phenomenon in world history, belonging mainly, but with exceptions in a few rare episodes, to the twentieth century. There can be many pressures that produce price changes in the short term, but it is difficult to find examples of inflation in the absence of a corresponding growth in the stock of money. That growth was not easily achieved before technology allowed the production of a reliable paper currency, and that technology belongs in the twentieth century. This in itself is highly suggestive of the basic cause. For most of the world's history, the general price level was almost flat. Occasionally, the discovery of silver and gold or improved mining or production techniques would produce a period of rising prices, although these were generally modest – seldom much above 5 per cent per annum. There were one or two episodes before the twentieth century such as Britain in the Napoleonic wars when metallic backing for the currency was abandoned. Even in that period, though, inflation rates were quite low: 2 or 3 per cent at most over a 25-year period. Some other, more extreme cases such as the French Revolution and the American Civil War are good examples of the use/abuse of paper money and consequent rapid inflation. What changed after 1914–31 was that inflation became a common feature of economies. Certainly after the

---

[22] The annual figure for 1978 is quoted in the text. The annual figure for 1979 was 1,337,800. Both are taken from Mitchell (1988, p.128). The figure for the winter of discontent is the average of the 1978 and 1979 data taken from Mitchell (1988, pp. 146–147).

mid-1930s there was a relentless rise in the general price level for the rest of the century.

Prices rose sharply after 1914 until about 1920, and there was then a decade or so of hesitancy when major countries were pursuing deflationary policies in order to restore and then adhere to the new gold standard. After that attempt collapsed in the 1930s, however, the monetary discipline of a metallic base had largely gone, and prices rose almost without interruption. In the course of the twentieth century, there were some experiences of violent inflation and some others that were extremely serious.[23] The Second World War gave a boost to inflation even if there were all manner of attempts at containing it. After 1945, it appeared to become endemic and increasingly a problem. After 1971, when the world was for the first time exclusively on paper money, inflation accelerated almost everywhere. That 1970s experience concentrated attention on the problem, and there developed a widespread desire to contain and even kill inflation. In the last 20 years of the century, it seemed to be completely under control in most developed countries and was even declared dead.[24] There was even some concern that the opposite – deflation, a sustained fall in prices – might be emerging.

There have been two main explanations for the accelerating inflation that began in the mid-1960s. One has been labelled 'international monetarism', and the other 'wage-push' or 'sociological'. The first regards it as a monetary phenomenon. The second sees it as non-economic, pointing to supposedly spontaneous wage explosions of the late 1960s and early 1970s.[25] Thus, for the first explanation, the answer lies in the United States in the 1960s, which had embarked on a huge spending programme. The monetary expansion produced inflation, and that was transmitted to other countries through the exchange-rate system. The sociological explanation for inflation is that the cause was trade unions, the argument being that they exerted monopoly power and forced up wages. However, what this does is change relative prices – the wages of one union (or perhaps more) and not the general price level. It is unlikely that the majority of the labour force belonged to monopoly unions, but if they did, their effectiveness would depend on the relative strength of government in resisting the claims and not expanding the money supply. In any case, monopolies were less common than was supposed and less likely to last in an open world economy. Other explanations have focussed on the price of a major commodity – in the 1970s, oil. Again,

---

[23] Cagan (1956); Capie (1991).
[24] Bootle (1997).
[25] Jones (1973).

a price shock need not produce inflation. Where it is accommodated by the monetary authorities, it can shift the price level to a higher point. That is not inflation, however; it is a once-and-for-all change. Thereafter, the trend rate of inflation will carry on from where it was unless the authorities persist in monetary ease after having accommodated the shock.

Throughout history there have been attempts at controlling prices directly. This practice was given a great boost in the twentieth century in wartime. Price controls were imposed in many countries, including the United States and the United Kingdom. And in some respects, they did seem to work, supported by other factors such as patriotism, rationing, and subsidies. However, while price controls seem to have worked for a period, the common experience was that when they were removed, prices jumped up to where they would have been in the absence of controls. They may have served their purpose in wartime but not beyond that. Price controls were tried in peacetime too, but in the absence of these other factors. they invariably failed.[26] Also common in our period were attempts to control wages or incomes more generally. This followed from the belief that trade unions were the cause. These attempts were unsuccessful. Apart from being incompatible with a free society, there were simply too many ways of circumventing them.

With a return to the appreciation of the role of money in causing inflation, there developed a desire to control its growth. This began to emerge in the 1970s. There was much debate about how monetary control was best achieved, but whatever the conclusion, it became clear that it was only central banks that could do it, and increasingly it was seen that they should be given the independence to do this – to produce the particular kind of price stability that governments laid down.

There was a period when inflation was not the chief priority, but its increasingly observed negative impact brought a clearer understanding of the need to act. Inflation has damaging effects on the distribution of wealth, and while this might be thought of as a useful way of rearranging the distribution of wealth, the fact is that it is governments who are the largest debtors in the twentieth century. They were thus able to cheat their populations out of their savings in a number of ways. (This probably also damaged the trust in government and contributed to the lack of trust more generally, which, in turn, contributed to increasing regulation.) Further, as creditors suffer, that, in turn, dissuades saving and ultimately reduces investment. Inflation acts adversely on production in another way. When

[26] See Capie and Wood (2002).

producers detect an increase in demand for their product, they have difficulty in distinguishing between that and what might be a general increase in demand from the extra money that consumers are spending, and that is likely to result in plant overcapacity. Inflation distorts prices and interest rates. As inflation rises, it becomes more volatile, and this contributes to the difficulty in using prices as good signals – their key function. Different prices will be affected in different ways. Long-term contracts will suffer at the expense of short-term contracts and flexible arrangements. To this extent, inflation will discourage long-term contracts, and therefore, some activity will not be undertaken that otherwise would have been in conditions of less uncertainty.

British experience in these respects was among the worst in the OECD. Inflation was a concern from the 1950s onwards, although greater priority continued to be given to full employment. A look at the monetary aggregates provides a starting point for the explanation. From 1950 to 1960 there is not much to note on the path of £M3; just the most modest upward trend in the series that at minimum would be expected in a growing economy. The same could be said for the next decade, too, although there is a sharper rise right at the end of the decade. M3 grew 42 per cent from £10,194 million in 1960 to £14,795 million in 1969 and then jumped to £17,128 million in the following year, a growth of 16 per cent. The drama comes in the 1970s, however. From £17,128 million at the beginning of the decade, there was relentless growth such that M3 had reached £60,106 million in 1979 (a growth of 152 per cent) and then jumped even more dramatically to £69,672 million in 1980 (16 per cent). In percentage terms, after 1957, the change is always positive and, in the worst of the 1970s, in excess of 25 per cent per annum. (Figure 1.1). It was not just the result of the exploding money multiplier; the monetary base also was rising steadily in the first years of the period and then sharply in the middle and later years of the 1970s. For several years in the 1970s it was growing at around 15 per cent per annum.

Some Theoretical Positions and Prevailing Practices

The Bank had many functions in this period, and monetary and exchange-rate management/policy were two of them. An explanation of the part played by the Bank in their design and implementation can benefit from some knowledge of the framework within which they operated. An understanding of the Bank's operations requires a context within which to assess what objectives were and how they were pursued. If there was success, was it due to knowledge, technical ability, good luck, or some combination of these? If

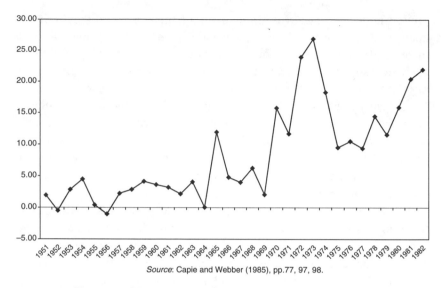

Source: Capie and Webber (1985), pp.77, 97, 98.

Figure 1.1. M3, percentage change on previous year, 1951–82.

there was failure, was it attributable to ignorance, technical incompetence, bad luck, or some combination of these? When the monetary authorities took some action (operating on some instrument), a number of responses might be noted, ranging from the view that it was a sensible action and in the circumstances should have been successful through to puzzlement over how it could have worked.

Some views on the working of the macro monetary economy also can help us to understand the context.[27] However, we need to keep in view the ideas that were available and widely accepted, for it is in large part against these that the actions of the time should be judged. Of course, many different strands of theory are available, but an institution such as the Bank might have been expected to have followed (insofar as it followed any at all) the dominant views of the time. Equally, some description of the institutional arrangements that were in place is also required. It cannot be a history of economic thought, although, of necessity, it will touch on that area. All that is being proposed is that the broad theoretical positions should be made clear. There is a vast amount of literature that covers a range of empirical economic research, and on occasion, it will be appropriate to note some of these results, but that is for later in the story.

[27] This is combined with a more traditional historical approach that addresses the primary material and discovers what was being discussed and how at the time.

How monetary policy, somehow defined, was viewed and indeed changed over time will be developed in due course. Whether attention was focused on the exchange rate in the 1950s and 1960s or on inflation directly – with the outcome for the exchange rate being a by-product of the relative success of that – leaves open the question of how powerful monetary policy might be under different exchange-rate regimes. The first thing, then, is to consider what monetary policy could achieve in the circumstances of the period between the mid-1950s and 1980.

After the war, most developed countries – those which would become the OECD countries – pursued similar objectives of full employment (variously defined) and economic growth with a pegged exchange rate, even if the emphasis varied a bit from country to country. The conventional framework of analysis in recent times has been a blend of Keynesian and new classical economics. Keynesian economics challenged classical theory, the monetary component of which was the quantity theory. In the simple quantity equation $MV = PQ$, velocity V was determined by institutional factors (payment arrangements and so on). Output Q was the outcome of whatever the real economy was capable of given labour, capital, technology, energy, and expertise. That left prices P to vary directly with the money stock M. Quantity theorists believe velocity V to be stable and predictable, although not constant, and output clearly was a slowly moving variable. Keynesian analysis questioned the fixity (not actually the stability) of velocity and of full-employment equilibrium. Furthermore, with sticky long-term interest rates, the ability of monetary policy to affect output was deemed limited.

In Keynesian analysis, financial assets are regarded as close substitutes for money, whereas goods and real assets are not. Thus, if there was a rise in the money stock brought about, say, by open market operations, an adjustment would take place in portfolios that redistributes the unwanted money balances into other financial assets. The distribution would reflect the changing returns on different assets. This would then lower the yield on certain financial assets, and there would be continuing effects across the spectrum of financial assets. At the end of the process, there would be a difference between the cost of capital and the return on capital. Thus any change in the money stock results in changes in interest rates on financial assets. If this line of argument is followed, monetary policy is better directed at influencing interest rates. Expenditure decisions did not seem to be affected much by changes in (nominal) interest rates, and it was concluded that monetary policy had little effect on the level of expenditure.

Keynesian economists had triumphed remarkably quickly. David Henderson, a young economist who entered the Treasury in 1957 wrote, 'In Britain, and increasingly in other countries too, the Keynesian revolution had taken hold. Its doctrines had established themselves with remarkable speed, not only within universities but apparently also as the basis for official policy.'[28] Thus the emphasis shifted to fiscal policy and demand management. For most of our period, Keynesian analysis was used, and it was accepted that monetary policy had little impact on aggregate demand. If the monetary authorities brought about a change in the money stock, interest rates would change. The belief was, though, and some empirical evidence further suggested that investment was not very sensitive to interest rates. The net result in *IS/LM* terms was a relatively flat *LM* curve and a relatively steep *IS* curve.

In the 1950s there had been an explicit challenge to Keynesian doctrine in Friedman's restatement of the quantity theory and general promulgation of what was said to be the long-standing Chicago School tradition.[29] For Friedman, the demand for money was expressed in terms of real balances and was a function of real income, wealth, and expected returns on a wide range of both financial and real assets. The elasticity of the demand for money with respect to interest rates was low. Changes in the money stock would affect the non-banking public's demand for real assets directly. This produced an opposite result in *IS/LM* terms to that above with the *IS* curve now relatively flat and the *LM* curve relatively steep. There was a further point. Changes in the money stock produced changes in real income only when unemployment was above the natural rate – more precisely, the non-accelerating inflation rate of unemployment (NAIRU). The natural rate was determined by an array of factors covering social mores, occupational and labour mobility, and so on. The argument ran that if aggregate demand was raised when unemployment was above this rate, then the result would be a rise in prices. And if that recurred, it would come to be expected and would be incorporated in agents' decisions and negotiating behaviour. Inflation then would accelerate. This latter part was not well known until Friedman's 1968 Presidential Lecture.[30]

Something that needs to be made explicit for the macroeconomic policy context is the government's budget constraint. The phrase may not have been used in the period, but the concept was at least implicitly understood

---

[28] Henderson (1986, p. 4).
[29] Friedman (1956).
[30] Friedman (1968).

in the Bank and, as will be seen in the next several chapters, was the basis for the constant nagging by Governors of Chancellors to try to contain government spending. Just as the individual consumer faces a budget constraint, so too does government. The present value of its consumption, current and future, must equal the present value of its income – tax collection current and future. A budget deficit can be financed by borrowing – from the commercial banks, the non-bank public, or the central bank. If the borrowing comes from the central bank, the debt is monetised. When the central bank buys government securities (usually Treasury bills in this case), it produces a change in the monetary base. Government expenditure must equal tax revenue plus new borrowing plus the change in the monetary base. There need not be a direct link between the budget deficit and the monetary base, and to some extent the connection will depend on the degree of independence from government the central bank enjoys, but constant borrowing almost invariably will show in an expanding money supply. The worst experiences of inflation around the world are testament to this. Weak governments, unable to raise taxes or borrow beyond a certain point, buy support or quieten opposition by agreeing to their demands, and this means spending, which, in turn, requires, in effect, printing money.[31]

For an open economy, other considerations need to be taken into account. Open economy macroeconomics rested heavily on the Mundell-Fleming extensions to the textbook *IS/LM* analysis. In a small (in the international trade sense), open economy, there is an external constraint. The balance of payments is the outcome of movements in exports, imports, and capital. These, in turn, are all products of domestic and foreign prices and hence of exchange rates. While much of this was appreciated at the time in an informal way, it was formalised in the early 1960s in the Mundell-Fleming model (essentially conceived in Keynesian terms). The principal thrust of this was to say that under fixed exchange rates and with low capital mobility, any attempted use of monetary policy to stimulate economic activity simply would result in a balance-of-payments deficit. And if there were fixed rates and total freedom of capital movement, monetary policy would be completely powerless to stimulate activity. Within our period, 1958–72 was one of pegged rates and limited capital mobility. With flexible rates and high capital mobility, monetary policy was potentially powerful and more powerful than fiscal policy, and in the remainder of our period, 1973–79, something closer to the obverse should hold, although it was not a clean float and there were still exchange controls in place and so less than free capital mobility.

---

[31] See, for example, Capie (1986).

The monetarist analysis developed independently of Mundell-Fleming produced a similar result – that under fixed exchange rates, rising money supply did not lead to inflation but to a growing balance-of-payments deficit.[32]

Operating in a fixed exchange-rate system implies the same inflation rate in all countries. With fixed exchange rates and the same inflation rates, there should also be the same nominal interest rates. It is possible that different monetary growth might be found in two areas if there were different output growth or if there were different income elasticities of demand for money. Inflationary expectations must be ruled out as a source of differences in interest rates because they must be assumed to be the same given the nature of the system. As we shall see, Britain had persistent balance-of-payments weakness in the 1950s and 1960s (the consequence of excessive monetary growth, which under the pegged exchange-rate system led not to inflation but to current account deficits).

Fixed and floating rates can be seen as alternatives that depend on the confidence there is in the monetary authorities to behave properly. For a small country, under a floating rate, there is no exchange-rate policy, and monetary policy can be used. Under truly fixed rates, the exchange rate is the target, and there is no monetary policy, with the monetary base determined through the balance of payments. Under either of these regimes, there are no balance-of-payments crises. Under pegged rates, however, there will be some attempt at monetary policy at the same time as the exchange rate is being targeted. With a pegged rate the monetary base has both domestic and foreign components. This last was effectively implicit in the working of the Exchange Equalisation Account (EEA). If capital inflows were considered excessive, there would be an attempt at sterilising the inflow. When the opposite happens and the central bank overcompensates, a balance-of-payments crisis would blow up. A further clarification is needed at this point. In this period, the word 'floating' often, but not always, was used in a restricted sense to mean 'wider bands'. Very few meant completely free floating. Another complication is that Britain had been a 'big' country and accustomed to operating an exchange-rate policy and a monetary policy. It was now an intermediate-sized country, further complicating the equation.

Another one of the building blocks that made up the generally accepted body of theory was the Phillips curve.[33] A. W. Phillips's examination of

[32]   Polak (1957).
[33]   Phillips (1958).

British data from the middle of the nineteenth century to the middle of the twentieth century seemed to show a trade-off between wage inflation and unemployment. This finding was soon converted into a plank of policy and later would take much of the blame for the subsequent inflation. (Phillips himself should be absolved of that[34]). Quite soon after Phillips's article was published, another appeared in the United States that embraced many of the same ideas and has been cited widely as being extremely influential in policymaking.[35] Samuelson and Solow reproduced Phillips with US data. They produced a neat downward-sloping graph of inflation against unemployment. They went on to suggest a 'menu of choice between different degrees of unemployment and price stability'. Thus, for example, there could be zero inflation with 5.5 per cent unemployment. Or if some inflation were tolerated, say 3 per cent, unemployment could be brought down to between 4 and 5 per cent. They did note that the trade-off held in the short run and could shift over time.

At almost the very same time as Phillips was publishing, so was Milton Friedman, whose huge empirical study with Anna Schwartz on the monetary history of the United States was well advanced. In 1960 Friedman published the Fordham Lectures, 'A program for monetary stability' that put forward the powerful case for money and monetary control.[36] He argued that it was clear that by 1958, when the lectures were given, that money did matter. The history of the United States was that major macroeconomic instability was brought about by monetary instability, and that came almost invariably from government intervention. He went on to argue that open market operations were sufficient for control of the money stock.

The Keynesian position nevertheless was dominant in Britain in our period. There developed a tension as the critics attacked it with growing confidence. The experience of rising inflation in the late 1960s and 1970s resuscitated interest in money generally and, in central banks, in technical aspects of monetary policy. It became increasingly clear what monetary policy could and could not do. At the centre of monetary theory is the principle that over time money affects the price level and not real variables. Money is said to be neutral in the long run. Furthermore, a basic principle of economics is that welfare is increased when uncertainty is reduced and so is increased most when uncertainty is reduced to a minimum. If price stability is the objective, it is then a case of deciding how best it can be

[34] Laidler (2000).
[35] Samuelson and Solow (1960).
[36] Friedman (1960).

achieved. Henry Thornton had in fact set out with the greatest clarity more than 200 years ago on how it could be done: 'To limit the amount of paper issued and to resort for this purpose, whenever the temptation to borrow is strong, to some effectual principle of restriction'. He explained that central banks should allow money to grow at the rate of real output growth, stand ready to act as lender of last resort, and avoid financing excessive government expenditure.[37]

There are one or two other strands of monetary theory that might be mentioned. First, there is the distinction between real and nominal variables, something that was in Henry Thornton but had largely disappeared from discussion and was not heard of much in the inflationary 1950s and 1960s. Second is the distinction between anticipated and unanticipated changes. It is only unanticipated changes in money that affect real variables, but unanticipated changes also need to be broken down into those that are seen as being temporary or transitory and not expected to last and those that are seen as being permanent or persistent or likely to last. Changes in technology or in the growth of the public sector, for example, could be regarded as permanent, whereas some harvest shortfall that affects relative prices is manifestly transitory. Of course, when changes occur, it may be difficult or even impossible to tell whether they are temporary or permanent. Also, it usually will be difficult to know the future path of money growth, so people make estimates based on some beliefs, and here, expectations enter the discussion. The examination of expectations has gone through various changes over time from extrapolative to adaptive to rational as more information has been made or has become more available and as improved models of the economy and a greater understanding of the economy have evolved.

A central bank may have an interest-rate target or a money-growth target. If all the shocks are transitory, it matters little which approach the bank takes. The interest-rate target naturally will be associated with less interest-rate variability and the money target with less money-growth variability. However, if there are permanent and transitory shocks, and the distinction between them cannot be made easily, then the difference between the two control strategies matters. Controlling money growth would let a permanent shock affect real interest rates but not money growth. Thus, for example, a new technology that had a once-and-for-all effect on productivity would produce a rise in real output and a fall in the price level. There would be a step shift in the trend of growth and converse in the price level

[37] Thornton (1802, p. 259).

while at the same time keeping the growth of money steady produces the same rate of inflation.[38]

If interest rates are controlled the central bank has to increase the money stock when there is a rise in real output and vice versa, and monetary policy becomes pro-cyclical. Mishkin argues precisely that for the 1950s and 1960s – that interest rate control led to pro-cyclical monetary policy. This argument requires that the central bank cannot know exactly where to set the interest rate. It would need to know about expectations, and the size of real and nominal shocks, among many other things. If monetary policy is directed at interest rates or exchange rates, these can be stabilised but only at a particular price level.[39] In the nineteenth century and for much of the twentieth century the exchange rate was the final target – a fixed rate under the gold standard and the restored gold exchange standard, and then the pegged rate of the Bretton Woods period. Under the gold standard flexibility of output, employment, and prices, brought about the adjustment.

Once it is accepted that the lasting effect of changes in the money stock is on the price level, monetary policy then should be implemented in ways that can achieve the desired result. That said, there remain problems of implementation of policy. For example, should it be done by rules or by discretion, even if these terms are difficult to use unambiguously. There is clearly a continuum that runs from a rigid rule to complete discretion. There are those who favour a strict rule, an example of which might be the gold standard, but even there, some scope was allowed the central bank for managing the exchange rate and even suspending the standard in times of crises.[40] At the other end of this spectrum are those such as Sayers for whom the very essence of central banking was discretion and, some would add, mystery.[41] Other problems in implementation might lie in lack of clarity in the objectives or in too large a number of objectives. These all lead to poor outcomes. The desire for simplification in monetary policy implementation returned, and the concentration on a specific target became popular even if different targets have appeared at different times.

In the writing of the history of central banking, it is also worth noting how some economic theoretical approaches to the analysis of central banks and price stability turn out to be less than useful in practice. For example, one examination of Federal Reserve behaviour in the 1960s and 1970s argued that two common ways of approaching the analysis were inappropriate. The

---

[38] King (1994), which draws on Poole (1970).
[39] Mishkin (2004).
[40] For a discussion of the Bank's experience of this, see Capie (2002, pp. 295–318).
[41] Sayers (1957).

first was time inconsistency. The second was public-choice analysis. And testing central bank reaction functions also was rejected.[42]

Time inconsistency applied to monetary policy uses models that produce different outcomes according to what is assumed about central banks' behaviour and about expectations formation. Unless it is known which of these sets of assumptions is applicable in practice, the theory is open ended as a guide to the world. A further weakness is the assumption of the model that an independent central bank cannot make a credible commitment to price stability.[43] A variant of the model is that central banks generate inflation to reduce unemployment in the short run. This certainly would seem to be closer to how central banks think, but there is a problem. If it is observed that a central bank targets an unemployment rate that turns out to be below NAIRU, has it tried to reduce unemployment (despite knowing that this will permanently raise the inflation rate) or has it underestimated NAIRU? Finally, in the period under review, it seemed unlikely to many scholars that time inconsistency was a major problem or that central banks or the monetary authorities thought in these terms.[44]

Public-choice theory is an alternative approach. Public choice has its origins in the United States and probably has had more applications to economic policy in that country than anywhere else. It has certainly been used extensively there in studies of banking regulation and commercial policy. Public-choice theory uses analysis of people behaving in their own interests. Everyone is an economic agent. The old political economy viewed governments as essentially altruistic and acting to provide the 'best environment' in which economic activity took place. This often meant trying to correct for what was seen as market self-interest. The new political economy, with which the term 'public choice' is sometimes used synonymously, shifted the ground and became a set of theories of government activity. Its application to monetary policy has been productive in some cases. It provides 'a useful explanation of certain characteristics of central banks, such as their penchant for secrecy and for particular operating targets'.[45] In terms of monetary policy, though, how do central banks gain from inflation? In the short run, they might escape the blame for unemployment, but in the longer run, they will be blamed for inflation and high interest rates. It might be argued that central banks did not really make monetary policy – and that would

---

[42] Mayer (1999, pp. 7–10).
[43] McCallum (1995, 1997).
[44] Mayer (1999, p. 87).
[45] *Ibid.*, p. 9.

appear to be in part justifiable in Britain for much of the period dealt with –
but it is still not clear how far their policies would have differed from those
of their political masters or mainstream economists of the time.

Another common approach to central bank behaviour has been to
estimate central bank reaction functions.[46] However, there are problems
here, too. First, can the regression coefficients in the reaction function be
interpreted as indicating the relative importance the central bank attaches
to different goals? A reaction function might explain why a central bank
raises its discount rate at a particular time, but it does not allow any inference to be drawn about the central bank's preferences and hence does
not explain its tolerance for inflation.[47] Second, the results that have been
obtained from such studies have been fragile, possibly because central
banks do not respond in a stable way to economic conditions. Or it might
be that they learn from experience, although that is difficult to model. More
likely, though, they have difficulty in identifying clearly what the conditions
were, a mixture of poor data and poor forecasts, and so on.

Monetary Growth Process

Within the macro monetary framework, how might money growth be
examined? While the roots of central banking lie in the nineteenth century, the idea of controlling monetary conditions belongs in the twentieth
century. By the second half of the twentieth century, it was widely accepted
that control of domestic monetary conditions lay at the centre of central
banking business. Before the First World War, Irving Fisher brought fresh
attention to the quantity theory of money.[48] After the war, Gustav Cassell
elaborated on this.[49] In 1920, C. A. Phillips developed the money-multiplier
model that linked the quantity equation 'to monetary policy implementation by building a bridge between broad monetary aggregates and the central bank balance sheet'.[50] For the rest of the twentieth century, that was the
model that dominated textbooks and was still central in Mishkin's (2004)
Economics of Money and Banking.[51] Furthermore, in the early 1920s, the
Fed was using open market operations to control money. British commercial banks developed their own cash and liquidity ratios in the nineteenth

---

[46] For a useful summary discussion, see, for example, Siklos (2002, Chap. 4).
[47] Mayer (1999, p. 10).
[48] Fisher (1911).
[49] Cassell (1922).
[50] Phillips (1926).
[51] Bindseil (2004).

century, and these continued to be the centre of focus in the twentieth century. The cash ratio may have had greater attention in the United States, but in England it was still important in the first half of the twentieth century, after which attention was drifting to the liquidity ratio.[52] By an agreement struck in 1946, the clearing banks agreed to hold a fixed 8 per cent cash-deposit ratio, and in 1951, they undertook to observe a liquid assets ratio in the range of 28 to 32 per cent. In 1957, the minimum ratio was made 30 per cent.

Broadly speaking, there have been two approaches to the money-supply process. One is the flow of funds between sectors, or the counterparts approach, and the other is the money multiplier. Each is useful in a different way. The counterparts approach, which was adopted explicitly in the 1970s, became known as the 'credit counterparts'. It was designed to link budget deficits and monetary growth. Batini and Nelson trace its origins back to a 1957 IMF staff paper by Marius Holtrop, Governor of the Nederlandsche Bank. He also set it out in evidence to Radcliffe the following year.[53] Advocates of this approach have been those who tended to believe that the best measure of money was one that moved closely with total credit. (Monetarist opponents insist on a clear distinction between money and credit.) The counterparts approach to determining M3 uses the flow of funds between sectors so that $\Delta M3 = \Delta$ currency $+ \Delta$ reserves $+$ bank lending to private sector $+$ bank holding of government securities $- \Delta$ non-bank liabilities. This approach derives in good part from viewing the change in money supply as the outcome of financing the government's budget deficits [public-sector borrowing requirement (PSBR)]. This can be thought of as made up of the change in currency plus borrowing from the non-bank public plus borrowing from banks less the change in foreign-exchange reserves. Thus $\Delta£M3 = $ PSBR $- \Delta$ borrowing from non-bank public $+ \Delta$ bank lending to private sector $+ \Delta$ foreign-exchange reserves $-$ non-deposit liabilities or $\Delta M£ = $ PSBR $-$ sales of gilts $+$ increases in bank lending $-$ external finance $-$ change in non-deposit liabilities.

The authorities seek to forecast the change in all these items and then consider the implications for monetary growth. If M3 were growing too rapidly, for example, the cause would have to be identified and some appropriate action taken. In fact, in the 1970s, the authorities believed that there

---

[52] Sayers (1972).
[53] Holtrop (1957) and Batini and Nelson (2005). Batini and Nelson point out that Holtrop's exposition included the key fallacious policy conclusion, 'borrowing by the Treasury from the commercial banking system has, by itself, exactly the same inflationary character as borrowing from the central bank'.

was a strict one-for-one relationship between a change in the PSBR and in broad money (M3) unless the PSBR was financed by selling securities to the non-bank private sector. Critics of the approach pointed to a range of faulty conclusions for policy.[54]

The money-multiplier approach provides a useful analytical framework within which growth of the stock of money can be examined.[55] The money stock is viewed as having three proximate determinants: high-powered money (or the monetary base); the non-bank public's cash-deposit ratio, which determines the distribution of the stock of monetary base; and the banking system's reserve ratio, which shows the banking system's preferred holdings of cash (i.e., till money and liquid balances at the Bank of England) relative to deposits. Broad money is the product of the monetary base and the money multiplier, with the latter the outcome of the banks' and the public's behaviour.

The approach can seem a contentious one for the United Kingdom, where it has been common (though not universal) to approach money-stock control through the counterparts identity outlined earlier. For example, for much of the post-1945 period, at least the attempted method of control was via interest rates. The authorities have some idea of the demand for money and how that changes with income and interest-rate changes. They then take income as given in the short run and operate on interest rates so as to lead the public to demand the amount of money that the authorities wish. This proved less than ideal, so the authorities went on to try to predict the growth of all those items in their own balance sheet and in the balance sheet of the consolidated system.

Whatever the merits of either approach as a control procedure for money growth, the multiplier approach can be useful for an investigation of both the short- and long-term behaviour of the money stock in the past. There is a sense in which the money stock, however defined, is always the result of the action of the monetary authorities – for they could always act to offset other influences. It is, however, useful to distinguish between changes in the money stock that were the result of action by the authorities and changes that were the consequence of their passiveness in the face of change originating elsewhere. The monetary base accounting framework is helpful in this distinction. Changes in the base usually are made by the authorities. Changes in the public's cash ratio are the result of private-sector decisions, although they can be decisions taken in response to actions by

[54] See, for example, Schwartz (1985).
[55] Cagan (1965).

the authorities. Changes in the reserve ratio of the banking system are again private-sector decisions (except on occasions when the authorities may decree a change or raise a minimum ratio) but ones that are highly sensitive to the activities of the authorities – banking law and the operation of the lender of last resort facility in particular.

The British banking system may not have operated on a cash base in the period under investigation. Nevertheless, there was close attention to the banks' cash reserve ratio for much of this period. And some would argue that for much of British monetary history it was generally thought that control of the money supply was carried out by the Bank of England through its control of the credit base. Banks were restricted in creating deposits by the need to observe some basic ratio of cash to deposits. They worked that out for themselves in the course of the nineteenth century, and then, for most of our period. the prevailing ratio was informally made a required minimum cash reserve ratio.

One reason why this view of the system nevertheless might have lost its central place was the growth and vast volume of Treasury bills and other short-term government debt in the Second World War, together with some changed priorities of the monetary authorities. An argument was that when banks found their cash reserves depleted through the open market operations of the Bank, they could offset this by allowing Treasury bills to run off.[56] This would mean control of the credit base had passed to the Treasury through control of the Treasury bill issue, something to which we will return later.

The framework nonetheless can be used to explore, in an accounting rather than causal sense, the determinants of the stock of money. It can help us to understand the relationships and changes in the relationships between the series. An example would be where we noted, say, a rapid growth of nominal money supply in some year; an examination of the determinants reveals whether or not this was a consequence of a change in the multiplier or in the base and, if the former, which element in the multiplier was responsible. It can also help to solve the question of the endogeneity of the money stock. Does money respond to the needs of the economy, or does the economy actually respond to money? The simple claim that British authorities pegged interest rates and therefore money must be endogenous is not satisfactory because interest-rate manipulation is, as noted earlier, a possible approach to money-stock control.[57] However, the approach has

[56] Sayers (1963, Chap. 8).
[57] Cagan (1965).

other advantages too. The United Kingdom has had a complex and vary-ing set of reserve requirements for its banking system. Have variations in the composition of reserve assets affected the behaviour of the stock of money in relation to the base? Have movements in the stock of reserve assets produced variations in the multiplier? Posing the question in this accounting framework avoids problems of conjecturing what the money stock would have been in the absence of these changes – conjectures that are necessary when the other identity, set out above, was used. The base/multiplier approach also has the advantage that it has been used as the basis for investigation in many other countries, so it facilitates direct comparison of findings for the United Kingdom with those for the United States and increasingly with those for other countries. In the end, the approach is an analytical/descriptive historical one.[58]

---

[58] See Mayer (1999) and Meltzer (2002) for fuller discussion of these points.

2

The Bank in the 1950s

The Bank in the 1950s had a recognisably similar structure to that at its foundation 250 years before. Perhaps the more striking feature, however, was that it was still in essence Montagu Norman's Bank, and that included the structural reforms of the 1930s. Most of the senior figures in the 1950s, and often into the 1960s and sometimes beyond (e.g., Cameron Cobbold, Humphrey Mynors, Leslie O'Brien, Jasper Hollom, Roy Bridge, Maurice Parsons, and Hilton Clarke) had joined the Bank in the 1920s and 1930s, and the very powerful personality of Norman left its mark. Hollom, for example, who joined the Bank in 1936 and was Deputy Governor through the 1970s, recalled going to listen to Norman speak to a group in the Bank soon after he joined. He was entranced as Norman spoke, using the recent difficulties of a firm called Huntley and Palmer to illustrate what he said. Hollom said that he felt that Norman was speaking only to him and that he had never understood anything so clearly before, 'that I was learning the innermost secrets of high finance and that this was him and him alone and he absolutely captivated one'.[1] It was not only the people on whom he left a mark but the building itself, which still bears the marks of Norman's reconstruction. Although the world had changed greatly and the problems facing the Bank had too, the approach to these problems can still be seen to be those of a previous era.

The Bank in part reflected the world in which it operated. It was hierarchical, it was stuffy, it was regimented, and yet it also had a relaxed atmosphere that allowed people time to do their work and to do other things as well. This was partly no doubt a reflection of the overstaffing. It is hard to imagine today that two Executive Directors could be sitting around with so little to do that they would idle away the afternoon writing their own

[1] Interview with Sir Jasper Hollom, 17 June 2005.

obituaries, but Mynors made a pact with George Bolton to do just that. It is worth quoting Mynors in full:

The death is announced of Mr X, an Executive Director of the Bank of England. Born on the 28th July 1903, he was the second son of the Reverend A. B. Mynors and was educated at Marlborough and at Corpus Christi College, Cambridge. Possessing considerable facility for passing written examinations, he took his degree at Cambridge with a first class in Part II of the Economics Tripos, and was therefore awarded the Wrenbury University Scholarship for research in economics, regardless of his lack of capacity for original work. Mr Mynors developed no bent for any useful or productive career & therefore drifted into teaching economics at his Old College, in which lotus-land he spent the next seven years, distilling to his pupils the ideas of others but acquiring none of his own.

In 1933 the Bank of England were anxious to defend themselves more adequately against the assault of professional economists whom they neither understood nor respected and were casting around for one of the tribe who had not yet committed the indiscretion of expressing in published work any point of view. Mr Mynors accordingly entered the service of the Bank & after five years in the Statistics Office became Secretary in 1939 & an Adviser in 1944. In 1949 he was appointed to the Court of Directors and became a full-time Director with special responsibility for staff questions.

Mr X's published work was confined to a few unsigned reviews of books which he had scarcely read: & having shown no early promise, his premature demise is the less to be regretted. He married in 1939 Lydia Marian, daughter of Professor Sir Ellis Minns, Litt.D., F.B.A., who survives him with three of their children.[2]

Not only is this revealing of Mynors himself, with his dry, self-deprecating sense of humour, and of the relaxed atmosphere at this level in the Bank, but it indicates their attitude to the role of economics; this had not changed from the 1930s to the 1950s, where it was still a case of being able to defend themselves against economists rather than in using them in the pursuit of improved policymaking.

Before any examination of the policies the Bank pursued in relation to domestic and external matters, though, we consider the structure, key personnel, and functions that were regarded as its remit as a central bank and conclude with an assessment of the Bank's finances and financial performance insofar as this can be done. This picture of the Bank provides the context for the following chapters, where we will discuss if/how the organisational capabilities evolved in order to deal with a changing world. It also gives a benchmark against which to compare the Bank at the end of the period.

[2] Mynors, 'Obit', 5 April 1949, ADM10/47.

Constitution and Structure

The constitution and powers of the Bank were determined largely by the Bank of England Act 1946 and the associated Royal Charter. Other Acts of Parliament contained further definitions, especially in relation to the public debt and the issue of Bank notes.[3] The 1946 Act, a slim piece of legislation comprising six clauses, was the first element in the post-war Labour Government's nationalisation programme. It transferred the whole of the Bank's capital stock of £14.553 million to the Treasury in exchange for the issue of government stock bearing interest at 3 per cent per annum. Stipulations were made concerning the number and means of appointing Governors and Directors and the persons who were disqualified from holding office. Also covered were relations between the Treasury and the Bank and between the Bank and other banks. Sections of existing enactments were repealed by the Act, while a new charter, dated 1 March 1946, revoked the provisions of existing charters, except where they incorporated the Bank of England. The primary purpose of the charter was to define the powers and responsibilities of the Court and Directors, and the document also contained sections relating to appointment and remuneration.[4]

Since the Bank already existed as a legal entity, the mechanics of taking it into public ownership were comparatively straightforward, and there was none of the pangs suffered during the birth of the other newly nationalised industries. During the drafting of the bill, the then Governor, Lord Catto, had been effective in lobbying Hugh Dalton, Chancellor of the Exchequer, and the bill went through smoothly. Dalton was keen to maintain the Bank's reputation for integrity and independence but wanted to wrest a degree of control over the business of banking. A second draft of the bill was entitled, 'Bank of England and Banking Regulation Act 1945', but Catto was adamant that such powers of financial regulation ought not to form part of a nationalisation bill, and in any case, the Bank felt that it already possessed sufficient authority over the banking system through existing informal mechanisms.[5] Catto did concede that the Treasury might seek a clear qualification on matters of policy and retain the option of being able to insert its own 'iron hand' into

---

[3]   For example, Bank Charter Act, 1844; Currency and Bank Notes Acts, 1939 and 1954.
[4]   Eleven enactments were repealed, see Bank of England 1946 Act, third schedule; the Charter of the Corporation and the Governor and Company of the Bank of England, 1 March 1946, revoked those of 1694 and 1892.
[5]   Chester (1975, pp. 879–884); Fforde (1992, pp. 9–11).

the Bank's traditional 'velvet glove'.[6] This was achieved through a clause that allowed the Treasury to give the Bank directions if this was deemed to be in the public interest. At the same time, the 'affairs of the Bank' would be managed by the Court. A further provision gave the Bank powers of direction over the commercial banks, again if thought necessary in the public interest. The Treasury had to consult with the Governor before exercising its power; likewise, the Bank had to have authorisation from the Treasury before making a direction. There was some ambiguity here. From its position as the ultimate authority in monetary policy, the Treasury could neither tell the commercial banks what to do nor direct the Bank to do the same. Furthermore, the Court could not be dismissed in the event of a policy failure.[7]

Complex drafting was required to specify the functions, powers, and purposes of the new public corporations, but in the case of the Bank, this was unnecessary because there was 'never any question that it should not continue doing what it had been doing for a very long time'.[8] While many countries had introduced legislation to create central banks with stated duties and responsibilities, there was no such need in the United Kingdom. The institution was already there.[9] Its operations were not laid out precisely or even imprecisely in the Act. Mynors, one of the Governor's Advisers in 1945, proposed a form of words for the Bank: 'to control the currency credit and banking system of the UK and maintain and protect the external value of the pound sterling'.[10] This was the only known attempt at such a definition, but it fell on stony ground, leaving the central act of Britain's monetary constitution 'eccentrically devoid of any reference to the wider purpose and responsibilities of central banking'.[11] The Bank retained a significant degree of autonomy in its operations, whereas its powers and position in the financial world were given a statutory footing that was based on a well-understood but largely ill-defined and unwritten status quo.

At the apex of the Bank's structure was the Court. Prior to nationalisation, there were 26 members of Court, and while initially the Chancellor had wanted to see that cut by half, he accepted a figure of 16, up to four to be full time and the rest part time. There was some debate as to whether there

---

[6] Cobbold to Edward Bridges (Permanent Secretary, HMT), 3 September 1945, quoted in Chester (1975, p. 884).
[7] Fforde (1992, p. 11).
[8] Chester (1975, p. 196).
[9] Fforde (1992, p. 5).
[10] *Ibid.*, p. 13.
[11] *Ibid.*, p. 13.

should be two Deputy Governors, but Catto argued, successfully, that two would only serve to confuse the lines of responsibility when the Governor was absent.[12] Thus the new Court was formed of the Governor, Deputy Governor, and the 16 Directors. The Court was still large compared with the boards of other public corporations.[13] When it came to appointments, the Bank was again an exception because these were made by the Crown rather than by the minister in the sponsoring government department. In effect, this meant the Prime Minister, advised by the Chancellor. As to the precise methods of selection, these were distinctly opaque, traditional informal contacts and connections remaining important. Prior to nationalisation, the Governor was chosen by the Court, although latterly, no decision could have been made without government approval. The proposal that Niemeyer be made Governor in 1944 was vetoed by Churchill.[14] On the other hand, it was unlikely that in the face of opposition from the Court, a Governor would be imposed on the Bank. In the years immediately before nationalisation, there was also increasing government involvement in choosing Directors.[15] After 1946, trade union representatives aside, there is little evidence that the seats on the Court were used in an overtly political manner.[16] The Governors were appointed for a five-year term, whereas the Directors served for four years. Overall, the changes to the Court were relatively minor, and beyond this, the 1946 Act made little difference to the structure and internal working of the Bank.[17]

The committee structure dated back to 1932 following the Peacock Committee's review of the Bank's organisation.[18] Meeting once a week, usually on a Thursday, the Court was the senior decision-making body, but the day-to-day management was undertaken through a number of standing committees that were appointed annually. Paramount among these was the Committee of Treasury, which dated back to the foundation of the Bank. Described by Sayers as a 'sort of inner Cabinet', it consisted of the Governor, the Deputy Governor, and five Directors who were elected by secret ballot.[19] Meeting every Wednesday, the Committee of Treasury was consulted on all important matters, and the Governor kept it informed about the

---

[12] *Ibid.*, pp. 9–10.
[13] Chester (1975, p. 493).
[14] Cobbold memoir; Sayers (1976, pp. 653–654).
[15] Sayers (1976, pp. 601–602).
[16] One reason, according to Laurence Cadbury, was that being on the court was 'not financially attractive'; Cadbury to Cobbold, 11 February 1949, G15/22.
[17] Hennessy (1992, p. 3); Kynaston and Roberts (2001, p. 198).
[18] Sayers (1976, pp. 597–601); Hennessy (1992, pp. 325–326).
[19] Sayers (1976, p. 632).

affairs of the Bank. Although it was the Court that formally ratified the decision on Bank Rate at its meeting on Thursday, it was at the previous day's Committee of Treasury meeting where any discussion occurred. This procedure was to come under close scrutiny following the Bank Rate 'leak' in September 1957. All reports to the Court from the other standing committees had to pass through the Committee of Treasury. Thus it held a central place in the management of the Bank as a whole, although the increasing use of Advisers had tended to erode some of its power.[20] There were six other standing committees. Two convened on a monthly basis: the Staff Committee dealt with employee matters, received reports from the Principals of the offices, and made regular 'visits of inspections'; the Committee on St. Luke's, renamed the Debden Committee from 1956, controlled the Printing Works. The other committees met quarterly: Audit, Expenditure, Premises, and Securities – the last being responsible for policy for the investment of certain internal funds, of which the pension fund was the most important. There was provision to appoint a special committee if a subject did not fall within the scope of an existing committee.[21]

Above the rest of the organisation and reporting directly to the Governors were a number of 'Advisers to the Governors'. Typically, in the 1950s, about five or six were employed in this capacity. The formal title had first been used in 1935, but the origins could be traced back to the appointment of Harry Siepmann and Walter Stewart as Advisers in 1926 and 1928, respectively. The Advisers provided expertise in specific areas, and Sayers saw them as 'not fitting at all into the traditional structure of the Bank'.[22] Together with the Executive Directors and the Chief Cashier, they formed a small coterie of senior staff gathered around the Governors.

Under the Court and the Governors lay a series of departments organised by function.[23] Figure 2.1 shows this organisation in 1955 when there were five departments: Cashier's, Accountant's, Secretary's, Establishment, and Printing Works. Another function, Audit, reported directly to the Court. The Cashier's Department had responsibility for a range of functions, and the Chief Cashier's Office was at the heart of it, if not the entire Bank. It carried out the tasks associated with the Bank's own market operations and also for overseas central banks and other customers. It also looked after the weekly Treasury bill tender, was responsible for the publication each

---

[20] *Ibid.*, p. 638.
[21] 'Internal administration of the Bank', various dates, 1936–70, G15/44.
[22] Sayers (1976, p. 620).
[23] 'The functions and organisation of the Bank of England', *BEQB* 6(3):233–245, September 1966; G15/44.

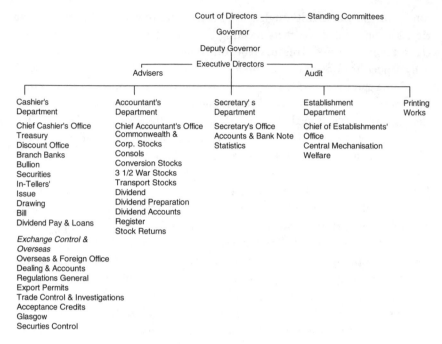

Figure 2.1. Bank of England organisation structure, 1955.

Thursday of Bank Rate, and prepared the daily 'books' for the Governor, which reported the market situation. Staff in 'Room 1' prepared the books, and those in 'Room 2' 'devilled' for the Chief Cashier. Work in these two rooms was undertaken in a hothouse atmosphere, in contrast to the sedate life in much of the rest of the Bank, and the capabilities of employees marked out for future promotion were tested there.[24] A link between Threadneedle Street and the Bank's eight branches was provided by the Branch Banks Office, while joint security control of assets was provided by a section called, confusingly, the Treasury.

The remainder of the Cashier's Department was divided into Banking and Exchange Control and Overseas. The most important office within Banking was the Discount Office, which maintained day-to-day contact with the money markets. It was where the discount houses discounted bills or borrowed. The Discount Office was also responsible for monitoring activities of financial institutions in the City, and the Principal often was referred to as the Governor's eyes and ears in the City. Operations in gold, foreign exchange, and foreign securities on behalf of the Exchange Equalisation Account (EEA)

[24] Interviews with Guy de Moubray, 15 June 2005; Sir Jasper Hollom, 17 June 2005; and Oliver Page, 21 October 2005.

and for other customers were carried out by the Dealing and Accounts Office. Physical handling of gold bullion and coinage was undertaken by the Bullion Office. The Issue Office controlled the supply of new notes and the withdrawal of worn notes, as well as dealing with forgeries. Customers' accounts were kept by the Drawing Office, the Bill Office oversaw the daily clearance of cheques and credit transfers through the London Bankers Clearing House, while the Dividend Pay and Loans Office paid coupons and dividend warrants and received subscriptions for new loans. The Exchange Control and Overseas section was created at the end of 1948. Monitoring of international economic and financial conditions and relations with international monetary authorities such as the International Monetary Fund (IMF) were conducted by the Overseas and Foreign Office. On exchange control, there were eight offices administering the regulations contained in the 1947 Exchange Control Act, but as restrictions were dismantled, the workload reduced, and offices were closed. At the beginning of 1957, the section was reorganised: Five Exchange Control offices survived and were retained within the Cashier's Department, while the Overseas and Foreign Office was instituted as a newly established and separate Overseas Department.[25]

Despite its name, the Accountant's Department was not concerned with financial matters, its duties being analogous to those of a company registrar. The department was responsible for management of the stocks domiciled at the Bank, including the bulk of the national debt and other government-guaranteed, Commonwealth, and corporation stocks. A substantial clerical support was required to maintain the accounts of stockholders.[26] All staff matters came under the control of the Establishment Department, as did management of the premises. The Printing Works was responsible for the production and destruction of bank notes, and in addition, it undertook general printing for other departments of the Bank.[27] The Secretary's Department supplied secretarial services to the Court, the Governors, and the committees. Secretary's also kept the Bank's accounts and drew up the balance sheet, compiled statistics, and had responsibility for a fledgling museum. In the 1950s, an exhibition room consisting of a miscellaneous collection of pictures, objects, and documents relating to the Bank was created in the Secretary's office. By the 1960s, more space was deemed necessary, and the collection was moved to the northeast rotunda in June 1965. Although not officially

[25] Committee of Treasury, 20 February 1957; Hennessy (1992, Chap. 9).
[26] Stock management at the Bank of England, January 1958, AC1/6.
[27] 'Bank note printing', *BEQB* 1(1):24–29, September 1961.

open to the general public, this 'museum' had about 90 to 100 visitors per week.[28]

Aggregate data on Bank employees are elusive. In 1949, there were 8,263 staff, 7,029 in the offices and 1,234 at the Printing Works. On the first occasion that such information was included in the *Annual Report,* in 1965, the total figure given was 7,000, of whom roughly 2,000 were at Debden. The largest department in 1949 was the Accountant's with 2,547 staff. At the same time, Exchange Control employed 1,537 and the Cashier's 1,100.[29] It is not possible to trace this breakdown through the 1950s, but by the mid-1960s, there were approximately 1,400 people in the Accountant's Department, 1,000 in the Cashier's, and 300 in Exchange Control.[30] There is greater certainty about the numbers of clerical as opposed to non-clerical grades. From a peak of 6,345 in September 1949, there was a steady decline: 5,415 in August 1952, 5,050 in August 1955, and 4,416 in June 1958. The trend continued into the 1960s, with 4,284 clerical-grade staff employed in 1962.[31] This fall of 2,000 in clerical staff was borne by the Accountant's Department and Exchange Control and is explained by a changing workload and mechanisation in the former and relaxation of controls in the case of the latter.

Most of the Bank's work was conducted at Head Office in Threadneedle Street. The original structure by Sir John Soane was rebuilt substantially in the interwar period, resulting in the well-known and iconic seven-storey facade. What could be seen from the outside was only the tip of the iceberg. The site covered three acres, and below street level lay 13 million cubic feet of vaults, corridors, and passage-ways that spread through three floors. Above ground, marble pillars lined the mosaic-floored entrance hall and corridors, while the elegant and decorated Parlours that housed the offices of Governors and the most senior staff occupied the core of the building.[32] In addition to Threadneedle Street, the Bank had a number of other premises in the City. The Accountant's Department had been based in Finsbury Circus since 1922, with additional accommodation at Regent Arcade House, Argyll Street, between 1948 and 1956 and then at the Bank's former Printing Works in Old Street. In 1958, the Department's entire staff moved into a £6 million development at New

---

28　Both ADM30/86 and 91 contain visitor figures to the Bank for this period.
29　F. W. R. Laverack (inspector of offices and branches), note, 12 January 1949, E4/3.
30　Bank of England, *Annual Report,* year ending February 1965, p. 19 and year ending February 1966, p. 23.
31　George Abell, 'Review of classification scheme', November 1957, G14/180; Howard Askwith to Cobbold/Mynors, 5 June 1958, G14/183; Abell to Cobbold, 29 May 1962, E3/7.
32　For more on the architecture, see Abramson (2006).

Change, facing St Paul's Cathedral.[33] On the top floor of the New Change premises, though not completed until 1960, was accommodation for official entertainment and a flat for the use of the Governor. Prior to this, the Bank had rented a property for Cobbold's use in Green Street, near Marble Arch.[34] Other offices were located at Bank Buildings and 19 Old Jewry, and there were dining facilities in Tokenhouse Yard/Kings Arms Yard.[35]

There was also a network of branches: Birmingham, Bristol, Leeds, Liverpool, Manchester, Newcastle, and Southampton; and the Law Courts branch in London opened in 1888 following suggestions by the Chancellor and various legal societies. The purpose of the provincial branches, the first of which dated from 1826, was to provide Bank services in the provinces for the convenience of banks and the general public, for example, note distribution and collection, local clearing accounts, and later, exchange control. The local branches also acted as a point of contact with local commerce and industry. An office in Glasgow, established in 1940, handled exchange control for Scotland and Northern Ireland, and again, it also acted as a point of contact.[36] The Agents working at the branches provided monthly reports that went to the Economic Intelligence Department in Head Office and formed part of a monthly report on industrial conditions presented to the Governors. Most of those who worked at the branches had either 'O' or 'A' levels, but no graduates were employed. The women were recruited locally, whereas most of the men were recruited in London.

Another important location was the Printing Works, which produced not only Bank notes but also many other documents and forms used in the Bank. Since 1920, operations had been based at St. Luke's, a converted former hospital for lunatics, in Old Street. However, by the end of the 1940s, capacity constraints, together with security and production difficulties, meant that an alternative had to be found. Only 14 miles by road from the Bank, served by the underground Central line, and in an area where many families traditionally associated with the printing trade lived, Debden in Essex stood out as the best location for the new site. In the summer of 1956, the Printing Works moved into its new purpose-built establishment. Situated on a 12.6-acre site, the works was massive and imposing, including

---

[33] The total expenditure on the New Change project, including furnishing and removals, was £6.26 million, Premises Committee, 24 June 1964, G26/42.
[34] Bernard to L. E. Peppiatt (Freshfields solicitors), 7 January 1949; Committee on Bank Premises, 24 March 1960, G26/42.
[35] On dining and 'club' facilities, see Hennessy (1992, pp. 361–363).
[36] 'Branches of the Bank of England', *BEQB* 3(4):279–284, December 1963.

an 800-ft production hall and a new 'Paid Note' building that was added in 1959. Debden was able to handle all the processes from the design, printing, checking, and eventual destruction of notes. Security was tight, and workers were watched closely from above through dark glass. For most of the staff, there was no contact with Threadneedle Street, and while the Printing Works may have been a department of the central bank, it was essentially a factory.[37]

Finally, there was the Bank of England Sports Club at Roehampton, which had been founded in 1908. Considerable damage was suffered during the Second World War, and a rebuilt pavilion was opened by the Governor in July 1956. Debden too had its own sports ground, complete with tennis courts, football, hockey, and cricket pitches. The Roehampton facilities were not used solely by Bank employees: England's 1966 football World Cup squad were invited to train there, and in return, the Bank received one or two tickets for the final, in which England famously lifted the Jules Rimet Trophy.[38]

Personnel

Throughout the 1950s, the Governor of the Bank was Cameron Fromanteel Cobbold. The Cobbolds were a family of Suffolk brewers and bankers (Bacon, Cobbold & Company, 'a sound Ipswich bank'), although Cobbold's father was a barrister.[39] Cobbold evidently was proud of the fact that his middle name provided a link to the early days of the Bank, a Fromanteel having been one of the original stockholders. In the early 1800s, a Martha Fromanteel married a Cobbold, and being sad about the name Fromanteel dying out, her husband agreed that all his male descendants would bear the name Fromanteel.[40] Like Montagu Norman, Cobbold had been educated at Eton, and both also spent a single year at King's College, Cambridge. After Cobbold left Cambridge in 1923, he spent a peripatetic decade trying his hand at accountancy and insurance until, in 1933, he joined the Bank as an Adviser specialising in 'Latin affairs'.[41] There has been some ambiguity in the accounts of how Cobbold arrived at the Bank. What is certain is that

---

[37] For exhaustive detail on Debden and the Printing Works, see Cubbage, *The Further History of the Bank of England Printing Works,* vols 1–3, PW6/ 9, 10, and 11. Also Hennessy (1992, pp. 186–192).

[38] Hennessy (1992, pp. 363–364); Bond and Doughty (1984, p. 223).

[39] Pressnell (1956, p. 169).

[40] Interview with Lord Cobbold, 24 October 2005.

[41] Note on 'Adviser to the Governors on Latin Affairs', 2 December 1932, G15/32.

in 1929, while working in Milan, he became involved in the operation to rescue the failing Banco Italo-Britannica. A number of major British banks faced exposure during this episode, and the Bank decided to intervene with some financial assistance and the nomination of a small investigative team. The investigators were looking for someone suitable in Milan to join the board of Italo-Britannica, and Cobbold was offered the position.[42] This brought him to the attention of the Bank. After this, it is generally assumed that, in his characteristic way, Norman spotted Cobbold and invited in the talented recruit, who later became a successor as Governor.[43] While an appealing story, the available evidence suggests that Norman was not involved. Indeed, when Norman and Cobbold first met, the appointment was all but sealed. It was Directors Edward Peacock, Patrick Ashley Cooper, and Charles Hambro who were instrumental in securing the position.[44] Ashley Cooper was one of the Bank's nominees on Banco Italo-Britannica, and Cobbold had close connections with the Hambros, being related to Charles Hambro by marriage and having travelled extensively after leaving Cambridge with Charles's second cousin, Jack. Later, in some personal recollections, Cobbold wrote that 'at first Norman was slightly suspicious and felt that I had been rather foisted on him by the others'. But they soon found common ground, with Norman especially pleased to discover that both men had lasted only one year at Cambridge.[45]

Cobbold was aged 29 when he entered the Bank; in a little over 15 years, he would became Governor. During this meteoric rise, in which he was an Adviser to the Governor, an Executive Director, and from 1945, Deputy Governor, Cobbold was involved in international financing, wartime planning, and post-war reconstruction. He was associated with the discussions that set up both the World Bank and the IMF and again was instrumental in the negotiations over nationalisation of the Bank. When he succeeded Lord Catto as Governor in 1949, he was only 44 years old, making him among the youngest ever holders of the post.[46] However, his appointment had by no means been assured. Dalton favoured either Lord Piercy, who had joined the Bank as a director in 1946, or Sir Clarence Sadd, chief executive and

---

[42] Sayers (1976, pp. 259–263).

[43] Sayers (1976, p. 263); Kynaston (2001, p. 28); Taylor (2004).

[44] Hambro to Cobbold, 4 January 1933; Norman to William Clegg (staff director), 14 January 1933, G15/32; Cobbold personal reflection on Norman, G15/19.

[45] Cobbold personal reflection on Norman, G15/19.

[46] For the early period, not all the ages of the Governors are known. Cromer was the youngest appointment since Kirkman Daniel Hodgson, who was aged 49 when appointed in 1863. Norman was aged 48 when he was appointed. Neatby to O'Brien, 24 May 1961, ADM30/1.

vice-chairman of the Midland Bank, though it would have been unusual if someone from a clearing bank had got the job. Stafford Cripps, Dalton's successor as Chancellor, offered the Governorship to Courtauld's chairman and member of Court, Sir John Hanbury-Williams, who after some consideration turned it down, leaving the field open for Cobbold.[47]

The new Governor may have lacked unanimous support from government, but he was well respected in the City, a critical attribute for his position. A pragmatist rather than an academic, he was well known for his suspicion of Keynesian economics. Fforde describes Cobbold as a commanding personality in the Bank and someone determined to maintain the authority of the Governor. Although his preference was for 'step-by-step adjustment of the existing system', once convinced of the need for change, Cobbold was not afraid to advocate more radical change and even demolition and reconstruction.[48] Known as Kim to his friends, Cobbold's family connections were strengthened by his marriage to Hermione Bulwer-Lytton. The two had met in India in 1925 when Cobbold was staying with her father, the Second Earl of Lytton, at that time Governor of Bengal.[49] When Hermione's father died in 1947, she inherited the ancestral seat, Knebworth House in Hertfordshire.

Cobbold's first Deputy was Dallas Bernard, a merchant who possessed a wealth of experience in the Far East. In 1954, when Bernard left the Bank, with a baronetcy, his place was taken by Mynors. In contrast to his predecessor, Mynors came from an academic background, and he also had held several senior positions in the Bank. An economics fellow at Corpus Christi College, Cambridge, between 1926 and 1933, Mynors joined the Bank as a Deputy Principal in the Statistics Section when the Deputy Governor was his uncle, Sir Ernest Harvey. Starting in 1939, Mynors had successive five-year stints as the Secretary, an Adviser to the Governors, and an Executive Director. Mynors was witty and self-deprecating about his abilities, and while Fforde notes that he exhibited great personal charm and a first-class mind, he kept his cards close to his chest and was keen to avoid disturbing the conventions and ambience of Norman's Bank. Trained in economics, Mynors was a very rare commodity at the Bank, but he 'thought along "banking school" lines' and was sceptical about the value of monetary statistics.[50] He made no effort to advance the use of economics in the Bank.

---

[47] Fforde (1992, pp. 366–367); Kynaston (2001, pp. 27–28); Dalton (1962, pp. 287–288).
[48] Fforde (1992, p. 268).
[49] Wilson and Lupton (1959, p. 39).
[50] Fforde (1992, p. 411); *Old Lady*, September 1980, pp.101–103.

Indeed, a contemporary remarked that Mynors had a horror of two words, 'economics' and 'research'.[51] Cobbold had made it clear to Mynors that he should have no expectation of eventually succeeding to the top job. Not that there was any doubt concerning Mynors' abilities, but it was necessary, in the minds of Cobbold and Senior Directors, for a future Governor to be 'a person with considerable practical experience of business and finance in the commercial field'.[52] Not everyone thought highly of Mynors. From the outside, he could seem a severe man intent on nothing but the highest standards.[53] One former employee felt the sympathetic portrait that hangs in the Parlours was a testament to the portrait artist's art.

Of the Directors in the 1950s, Charles Hambro was the most senior, having joined the Court in 1928. But Hambro was only 30 years old at the time of his appointment, and even in the 1950s, he was still younger than many of his fellow Directors. When he died in 1963, he had completed 35 years of service.[54] As an indication of Hambro's standing, in 1937, when 39 years old, he had been asked by Norman to take over the Governorship.[55] Of the four who became Directors in the 1930s, two, Cadbury and Hanbury-Williams, remained on the Court into the early 1960s, serving 25 and 27 years, respectively. The majority of the Court of the 1950s had been appointed in the immediate post-war years: 11 between 1945 and 1948. Eight new Directors joined during the 1950s. For the period 1918–44, Sayers calculated that the average age of the Directors on election to the Court was 47.[56] This figure had increased to 52 for those appointed between 1946 and 1959 but no doubt was skewed by the war. Under the Act, the Directors were appointed for a term of four years, and most served for two terms. Some gave very long service: 20 years or more in the cases of Cooper, Sanderson, Kindersley, Bolton, Babington Smith, and Keswick and 17 years for Pilkington and Eley. There was no provision in the 1946 Act or the charter for Directors to be dismissed, but they did have to retire at age 70, and of those included in Table 2.1, four stayed until age 70, whereas six left at either age 68 or age 69.[57]

[51] De Moubray (2005, p. 170).

[52] Cobbold to Bridges, 14 October 1953, G15/25.

[53] Interview with Peter Cooke, 27 March 2006.

[54] Hambro's father, Sir Everard Hambro, had himself been a Director for 45 years.

[55] Hambro declined because of his family business commitments, G15/24; Sayers (1976, pp. 652–653).

[56] Sayers (1976, p. 601).

[57] It was the intention of the 1946 Act that Directors would not be appointed if the period in office would take them over the age of 70. However, a private rule, adopted in 1918 after

Table 2.1. *Bank of England Directors of Court, 1950–60*

Director	Served	Age on appointment	Background
Executive directors			
Harry Siepmann	1945–54	55	Treasury/Bank of England
Sir George Bolton	1948–57	47	Bank of England
Humphrey Mynors	1949–54	45	Bank of England
Kenneth Peppiatt	1949–57	57	Bank of England
Sir George Abell	1952–64	47	Overseas service (India)
Sir Cyril Hawker	1954–62	53	Bank of England
Sir Maurice Parsons	1957–70	46	Bank of England
Sir John Stevens	1957–73	43	Bank of England
Part-time Directors			
Sir Charles Hambro	1928–63	30	Merchant banking (Hambros)
Patrick Ashley Cooper	1932–55	44	Commerce/trading (Hudson's Bay Company)
Laurence Cadbury	1936–61	46	Food (Cadbury Brothers)
Sir John Hanbury-Williams	1936–63	43	Manufacturing (Courtaulds)
Otto Niemeyer	1938–52	54	Treasury/Bank of England
Lord Sanderson	1945–65	50	Shipping (Shaw Savill)
Lord Piercy	1946–56	59	Economics/finance
Lord Kindersley	1947–67	57	Merchant banking (Lazards)
Lord Braintree	1948–55	63	Manufacturing (Critall windows)
Michael Babington Smith	1949–69	47	Clearing banking (Glyn Mills)
Geoffrey Eley	1949–66	45	Finance/stockbroking
Andrew Naesmith	1949–57	60	Trade union
William Keswick	1953–73	49	Commerce/trading (Jardine Matheson)
Lord Bicester	1954–66	56	Merchant banking (Morgan Grenfell)
Sir William Pilkington	1955–72	49	Business (Pilkington Brothers)
Sir Alfred Roberts	1956–63	58	Trade union
Sir George Bolton	1957–68	56	Banking (Bank of London and South America)

Source: Bank of England, *Annual Reports*.

A public school education was commonplace, with Eton and Rugby heading the list. In the latter half of the 1950s, five of the Directors, plus the Governor, were Old Etonians, rivalling the number found in the cabinet of the Conservative Government.[58] Oxford and Cambridge, particularly Trinity College at the latter, and Sandhurst featured prominently after school. Much has been made of the City as a gentlemen's club, and the Court reflected this.[59] This facet attracted particular attention in the aftermath of the Bank Rate 'leak', and a study of the social background and connections of the Bank's Directors revealed a large number of kinships and affinities.[60] There was little doubt that the Bank possessed the most well-connected board of any nationalised industry or, indeed, other financial institution, but this was scarcely surprising given the prominence and position of the Bank in the City.

The backgrounds of the non-executive, or part-time, Directors were predominantly in trade, commerce, and finance, with senior figures from well-known companies. Among the captains of industry were Laurence Cadbury, Managing Director of the confectioners, Sir John Hanbury-Williams, chairman of the artificial fibre manufacturers Courtaulds, Sir William Pilkington, of the glass makers Pilkington Bros., and Basil Sanderson, chairman of the Shaw Savill Shipping Line. Directors with experience in the banking sector included Sir Charles Hambro, of Hambros, Lord Kindersley, of Lazard Brothers, and Lord Bicester, of Morgan Grenfell. It was customary that representatives of the large clearing banks were not appointed to the Court, although Michael Babington Smith was Deputy chairman at the smaller institution, Glyn Mills.[61] Since nationalisation of the Bank, there had been a trade union representative on the Court, although the convention had no statutory basis.[62]

The duties of the part-time Directors included attending the weekly meetings of the Court and serving on the various standing committees. It was through the Committee of Treasury that the part-timers perhaps exerted their greatest influence: of the five elected seats available, at least four had to be from the non-executive ranks. During the 1950s, Hanbury-Williams,

the Revelstoke Committee, allowed Directors to resign in the February after reaching age 70. Cobbold to Piercy, 9 January 1954, G15/22.

58 *Tribune*, 21 August 1959, p. 1.
59 Kynaston (2001).
60 Wilson and Lupton (1959).
61 On this custom, see Bank of England, 'Constitution and functions', June 1957; Committee on Working of the Monetary System, *Memoranda*, vol. 1, 1960, p. 6.
62 Cobbold noted in 1962 that Sir Frank Lee had accepted that no seat on the court was earmarked for trade union representation; Cobbold note, 6 February 1962, G15/22.

Eley, Sanderson, and Bicester were the longest serving. The two senior part-time Directors on the committee also had to act as kingmakers in discussions concerning the appointment of Governors. This entailed consultations with colleagues, taking informal soundings from possible candidates, and relaying their findings to the Chancellor of the Exchequer.[63] As part of the Bank's evidence to the Radcliffe Committee, a memorandum described the interaction between the Directors and the Governors. The free exchange of ideas produced a 'constant two-way traffic and covers a wide variety of subjects'. Moreover, it was claimed that the relationship was one of 'intimacy, of confidence and of common thinking that has a special value to any councils in which any of them may take part whether inside or outside the Bank'.[64] No doubt the advice and intelligence were useful, but these aside, it is unlikely that the part-time Directors had more than an extremely proscribed role in the Bank's wider policy formulation.

By contrast, the Executive Directors played a central role in the running of the Bank. Despite their job titles, there were no formal executive lines of managerial responsibility; rather, the full-time Directors worked on specific areas determined by need and their particular expertise. Prior to appointment, all had seen at least some service with the Bank. At the beginning of the 1950s, the Executive Directors were Harry Siepmann, George Bolton, Kenneth Peppiatt, and Mynors. Both Siepmann and Bolton had considerable experience in foreign-exchange and external matters. Siepmann joined as an Adviser to the Governor in 1926 and was appointed Executive Director in 1945. Bolton had been employed in the Overseas Office since 1933 and assumed executive responsibilities in 1948. Soon after, Bolton was in the ascendancy on most questions of overseas policy.[65] Peppiatt had followed a traditional career path, entering the Bank in 1911 and then rising through the ranks to become Chief Cashier in 1934. He held the key post for 15 years before being appointed as the first Executive Director with specific responsibility for home finance. Although Peppiatt well understood the gilt-edged and money markets, he had little interest in the analysis of monetary policy, and reportedly, he avoided attending meetings at the Treasury.[66] After leaving the Bank in 1957, Peppiatt joined the board of Coutts and consequently had to remove his famous

---

[63] For detail of this procedure, see Dascombe (The Secretary) note, 6 November 1953, G15/25.
[64] Bank of England, 'Part-time Directors', 12 June 1958; Radcliffe, *Memoranda*, vol. 1, pp. 44–45.
[65] Fforde (1992, p. 196).
[66] *Ibid.*, p. 318.

moustache.[67] Facial hair was tolerated in the Bank, but bow ties were not looked on with favour.

George Abell became an Executive Director in 1952 after four years at the Bank. He had gained considerable administrative skills in the Indian Civil Service, and these were put to use overseeing the Bank's staff and premises. Abell's appointment took the number of Executive Directors to five, in contravention of the 1946 Act, and thus, at least in title, Mynors relinquished his executive responsibilities.[68] In 1954, Siepmann left to be replaced by Cyril Hawker. With more than 30 years of experience at the Bank, including spells as a Deputy Chief Cashier, Chief Accountant, and an Adviser to the Governors, Hawker was amply qualified by experience to assist Peppiatt on the domestic front. When Peppiatt retired, Hawker then took the lead, although he was less involved in the heavy workload generated by the Radcliffe Committee and did not appear as a witness. Not everyone had a high opinion of his abilities.[69] Hawker left in 1962 to take over the chairmanship of Standard Bank.

Executive matters on the overseas side were less straightforward. Bolton relinquished his executive responsibilities in February 1957, ostensibly because he was to take on the chairmanship of the Bank of London and South America (BOLSA). But there also appears to have been a struggle among several of the leading personalities. Bolton, a forceful personality, who might have been considered a candidate for Governor at one stage, was frustrated with the slow moves towards sterling convertibility.[70] His position was also seemingly usurped by Maurice Parsons and John Stevens, both of whom were overseas specialists. Known as 'the Pope' for his old fashioned style and very knowledgeable, Parsons began his career with the Bank in the 1920s, and between 1939 and 1943, he was private Secretary to Norman. He then had a spell at the IMF before becoming a Deputy Chief Cashier. Although passed over for the Chief Cashier's job in 1955, Parsons was marked out for a bright future, and he was instead made an Assistant to the Governor, with an equivalent grading and status to the Chief Cashier.[71] Stevens was a relative newcomer who joined the Bank from the army right after the war. He was seconded to the IMF in 1954, and on returning to the

[67] *Old Lady*, December 1979, p. 346.
[68] Mynors annotation on note, 19 September 1961, ADM10/47.
[69] Roger Alford diaries, 31 October 1960.
[70] Fry (1970, pp. 26–27). Kynaston (2001, p. 28) notes that it is unclear whether Bolton was ever seriously considered but that in Bolton's own mind it was a major disappointment to be passed over.
[71] Interview with Guy de Moubray, 15 June 2005.

Bank in 1956, he too was made an Assistant to the Governor. Although the Peacock Committee had considered the post of Governor's Assistant to be of the highest importance, it had been filled only intermittently, so the creation of two assistants looked odd.[72] Certainly, it appeared to undermine Bolton. Ten months before his resignation, it was clear to senior figures in the Bank that Bolton might give up his executive duties in February 1957, and since Peppiatt was due to stand down at the same time, the way was clear for both Parsons and Stevens to be appointed as Executive Directors. The former concentrated on exchange, exchange control, the IMF, the Commonwealth, and North America, whereas the latter dealt with the remaining countries plus the Bank for International Settlements (BIS)/European Payments Union (EPU) and, on the domestic front, statistics and audit. Neither was subsequently replaced as an Assistant to the Governor.[73] As for Bolton, he went on to lead BOLSA successfully, played a leading role in setting up the Eurodollar market, but did not, as is sometimes mistakenly claimed, chair a government enquiry into small firms.[74] He remained a part-time Director of the Bank until 1968.

During this period, there were usually five or six Advisers to the Governors. The longest serving in our period was Bernard Rickatson-Hatt, who held the post from 1941 to 1958. Arriving from Reuters, where he had been editor-in-chief, his background in financial journalism was put to good use. In effect, Rickatson-Hatt was the Bank's first press relations officer, although officially no such post existed.[75] Some were inclined to remark that his job was to keep the Bank out of the press and the press out of the Bank. This certainly was in line with the prevailing secretive attitude. Virtually all the other Advisers to the Governors in the period, John Lithiby, Frederick Powell, Lucius Thompson-McCausland, John Fisher, Max Stamp, Laurence Menzies, and Jasper Rootham, were concerned with external and foreign matters. Thompson-McCausland possessed the greatest experience, having attended, with Keynes, the negotiations over Lend Lease and Bretton Woods and, later, the conferences resulting in the General Agreement on Tariffs and Trade (GATT). There also were a number of other advisory posts,

---

[72] Hennessy (1992, p. 371); Abell held it between 1949 and 1952, and Parsons took the role from 1954.

[73] Cobbold, note, 29 July 1957, G15/223. The Assistant to the Governor post was reintroduced in 1965.

[74] Jones (2004). *The Committee of Enquiry on Small Firms* (Cmnd. 4811, 1971) was chaired by John Bolton, a chartered accountant.

[75] Hennessy (1992, p. 378) notes that he was careful to emphasise that he was not the Bank's press officer.

totalling ten in the mid-1950s, which again provided specialist knowledge of foreign issues.[76]

The one exception to this concentration of overseas expertise was provided by economist Maurice Allen. The need for an economics specialist had been identified in 1948, but filling the vacancy proved troublesome. After an unsuccessful attempt to lure Dennis Robertson away from Trinity College, Cambridge, an approach was made to Richard Sayers, who had recently caught the eye with a paper on central banking. Sayers reluctantly declined the offer because he had just taken a chair at the London School of Economics (LSE), although this was not to put an end to his future involvement in the Bank's affairs. He continued to correspond with senior staff and was later commissioned to write the official history. Attention then was directed towards Allen, a graduate of the LSE, who was assistant director of research at the IMF. He accepted the post and joined the Bank in 1950, initially as an Adviser and becoming an Adviser to the Governors four years later.[77] Allen's economics, like Mynors', were on 'banking school' lines, characterised as 'expectational, psychological, and non-quantitative', and assessments of the economic effects of policy were 'heavily judgemental and conspicuously reliant on qualitative, even anecdotal, information'.[78] The phrase 'banking school' derived from the nineteenth-century school whose views were focussed on money-market operations and interest rates rather than on monetary aggregates. And that was something that dominated the Bank's views for a long time. At the beginning of 1957, the number of professional economists at the Bank was increased to three with the arrival of John Fforde as an assistant to Allen. Aged 35, Fforde was a Fellow of Nuffield College, Oxford, where he had impressed John Hicks, and in 1950, he had received a Houblon-Norman grant to assist with the writing of a book on the United States Federal Reserve.[79] Fforde later would become Chief Cashier and an Executive Director.

Of the general hierarchy of salaried staff, the most senior was the Chief Cashier, in effect the chief executive and the only official of the Bank who had the ear of the Governor daily. Percival Beale, holder of the post during the first half of the 1950s, was, according to Fforde, a difficult character

---

[76] These posts were designated 'Adviser' and 'Adviser (Acting)'.

[77] Mynors to Allen, 7 October 1949, G15/32.

[78] Fforde (1992, pp. 411, 613).

[79] Hicks considered that Fforde displayed an impressive ability to deal with monetary and banking material but also noted that 'the book does suffer undoubtedly from excessive detail and a certain lack of digestion'; John Hicks to Allen, 28 May 1956, G15/32; Fforde, *The Federal Reserve System, 1945–1949* (1954) was based on his Ph.D. thesis.

who had been encouraged to leave the Bank and take a post in India. Most contemporaries held strong negative views on Beale. He was succeeded by Leslie O'Brien. O'Brien had joined the Bank in 1927, straight from school, and after gaining experience in the Cashier's and the Overseas departments, he became private Secretary to Norman and then Catto and became a Deputy Chief Cashier in 1951 and then Chief Cashier at the beginning of 1955. On his appointment, O'Brien had been told by Cobbold that it was the expectation of the Court that 'he should have a long tenure of office, perhaps for the rest of his Bank career, while others may move elsewhere and possibly higher.'[80]

The other leading officers included the heads of departments and their deputies and the Principals of some of the more important offices, such as the Dealing and Accounts, and the Discount. In March 1956, the most senior staff were men, with an average age of 52, and nearly all had been at the Bank for more than three decades. One person who did not match was Jasper Hollom, only just appointed as a Deputy Chief Cashier and not yet 40 years old. Other younger staff included Hilton Clarke (age 46) and Roy Bridge (age 44), Principals, respectively, of the Discount and the Dealing and Accounts Offices. O'Brien himself was 48 years old.

Like the clearing banks, the Bank operated an internal labour market.[81] Every entrant began his or her career at the bottom, and because below the level of Court the Bank was essentially a meritocratic organisation, it was possible for any male clerk to rise to the top. While grade and seniority were fairly rigidly imposed, it was, as the examples of O'Brien and Hollom demonstrate, possible for talented staff to make their way up the hierarchy. Nevertheless, the opportunities to become involved in high-level decision making were strictly limited because, as Mynors recognised, 'the bulk of the Bank's work raises few issues of policy and its management entails following well-trodden paths and handling people, not issues'.[82] O'Brien held similar views: The Bank was 'a big organisation, devoted in the main to routine tasks, a large part of which is rarely touched by policy at all'. Indeed some offices could function 'quite happily' if there was not a Chief Cashier in charge of the department.[83] It is probably reasonable to suggest that of the, say, 4,500 staff employed

---

[80]   Cobbold, 'For the record', 9 December 1954, G14/181.
[81]   Winton (1982, pp. 83–87, 150–152, 190–192); Ackrill and Hannah (2001, pp. 431–451); Billings and Capie (2004, pp. 324–325).
[82]   Mynors to Abell/O'Brien, 8 June 1955, E3/7.
[83]   O'Brien to Mynors, 'Recruitment and training', 28 June 1955, E3/7; Fforde (1992, p. 1) gives a similar characterisation of the Bank.

in the banking departments, at most two dozen were involved in serious decision making.

Almost the entire staff had joined from school, and there were very few university graduates at the Bank. Between 1910 and 1913, there had been an abortive attempt to recruit from Oxford and Cambridge, but Sayers notes that few were acceptable, hardly any stayed, and those who did received no special attention. He adds that, with the benefit of hindsight, the Bank's 'aloofness' might have been misplaced.[84] In September 1946, the Court took a decision to reintroduce graduate recruitment, and initially, six per year of these 'special entrants' were taken.[85] By 1955, there were 71 graduates at the Bank, a figure that had grown to 99 at the end of 1960.[86] Most of them came from Oxford or Cambridge and were generalists.[87] However, Hennessy points out that the proportion of 'quitters' was higher among the special entrants because the early years in the Bank did not live up to their expectations.[88] A common complaint was that abilities were not being used to the full. Although 142 graduates joined the Bank between 1946 and 1960, 43 of these left during the same period. Such a rate of attrition was not out of line with the experience of other employers, and the 99 who remained included a future Deputy Governor (George Blunden) and three future Chief Cashiers (John Page, David Somerset, and Malcolm Gill).[89]

Associated with the issue of the graduate entrants was a wide-ranging debate that embraced recruitment and retention, the quality and abilities of new staff, and training and development. In the climate of post-war full employment, there was greater competition for staff, and there was also a feeling that the City in general was struggling to attract quality recruits.[90] The Bank was not immune, although as Mynors observed, the 'prestige of this Bank should however be still considerable'. Notwithstanding the opportunities for travel and an exotic life abroad, the fundamental difficulty was career prospects, with the work being regarded as 'dull' and progress 'rather slow'. Rootham recognised that this initial experience had the virtue of

---

[84] Sayers (1976, pp. 609–610).
[85] Minutes of court, 26 September 1946, G4/169.
[86] Note on 'Special Entrants', 1 March 1955, E4/25; Note, 8 December 1960, E3/7.
[87] Abell to Cobbold and Mynors, 'Recruitment of graduates', 9 July 1954, G14/180.
[88] Hennessy (1992, p. 358).
[89] Note on 'Special Entrants', 8 December 1960, E3/7. Other names include Luce, Carlisle, Hillage, Wood, Kirbyshire, Whittome, and Coleby.
[90] Abell to Cobbold/Mynors, 'Recruitment of graduates', 9 July 1954, G14/180; 'Review of classification scheme – General background', November 1957, E3/7. In the 1960s and

promoting 'accuracy and quick figuring under pressure', adding that 'even if regarded as Purgatory [it] ought to be gone through by all'.[91]

Cobbold had expressed his dissatisfaction about the adequacy of training arrangements and questioned whether the Bank was getting the right material at the lower levels.[92] A debate followed, and a special committee was established to undertake a comprehensive review of training at all levels.[93] Mynors was deeply sceptical of training schemes if they merely entailed 'watching others and being talked to'. He was worried about promoting staff too quickly and emphasised the desirability of the technical proficiency of senior officials. There was also a danger of creating a 'race of Superior Persons who do not need to understand about Banking'.[94] O'Brien evidently shared these sentiments, declaring that 'I have no faith in elaborate schemes of training as a means of revealing the high fliers and ensuring that they are thoroughly well grounded'. What was most important was 'doing the Bank's work and being judged on performance'.[95]

Despite this preference for traditional methods at the senior level, and notwithstanding Cobbold's remark that the 'Bank of England is a bank not a study group', by the end of the 1950s, there was little doubt that greater resources would have to be devoted to economic and statistical analysis.[96] There was a paucity of specialist economists at the Bank, and there also were calls for an expansion in the number of professional statisticians. Principal of the Statistics Office James Selwyn argued that graduates in economics, mathematics, and statistics were required to meet the 'rapidly increasing demand for more information and more intensive analysis'.[97] In responding, O'Brien had to concede that high quality was needed in this field, and it was unlikely to come from ordinary recruitment.[98] There also were some interesting proposals for the creation of new offices in order to meet the changing demands being placed on the Bank. In 1955, Rootham suggested the formation of an 'intelligence section', based in the Chief

1970s, the Bank also employed 'supplementary staff', men and women between 40 and 54 years of age looking for stable employment. They had no prospect of promotion and conducted routine work. Male staff could continue as supplementary staff on retirement at age 60; see E3/11.

[91] Rootham, 'Some reflections on graduate recruitment', 31 May 1955, E3/7.

[92] Cobbold to Mynors, 13 April 1955, E3/7.

[93] Hennessy (1992, pp. 350–352).

[94] Mynors to Abell/O'Brien, 8 June 1955, E3/7.

[95] O'Brien to Mynors, 'Recruitment and training', 28 June 1955, E3/7.

[96] There is some uncertainty about the origins of this phrase. Cobbold used it in a speech to the Overseas Bankers Club in February 1958, *The Times*, 18 February 1958.

[97] James Selwyn to Abell, 15 November 1957, E3/7.

[98] O'Brien annotation on Allen to O'Brien, 2 December 1955, E3/7.

Cashier's Office, to provide information on developments in the domestic economic and financial spheres. This also would help to 'dissipate the false idea that the Chief Cashier's Office is nothing but a clock with a lot of little wheels of which only one or two men have the key'.[99] Similarly, Mynors, obviously aware of contemporary developments in business, was attracted by the potential of an 'Operational Research' section, again under the Chief Cashier. O'Brien was enthusiastic about the concept. Such a section, he argued, could 'draw attention to the way in which policy objectives were being achieved and to what might be necessary in the future to carry them through'.[100] Although nothing was to come of this straightaway, it was a discussion that presaged the Radcliffe Committee's pronouncements on the need for improved statistics by four years.

If poor prospects threatened to deter recruits, there was general agreement in the Bank that salary levels were not a serious impediment because they bore favourable comparison with other organisations. Differentials between the Bank and the clearing banks were monitored closely. In the early 1950s, the salary of a 28-year-old male clerk at the Bank was £662 per annum, compared with £583 at the Westminster Bank and £683 at Lloyds, where a new pay scheme had just been introduced. Overall, in 1951, the salaries of the Bank's male 'classed' staff were 22 per cent higher than those of their counterparts at other financial institutions. The gap was eroded to 16 per cent, before the Classification Scheme of 1958 restored the differential to the 1947 level of 24 per cent.[101] For senior staff, remuneration could be considered to be excellent. In 1956, the top 22 earned above £3,500, with heads of departments receiving £5,000 and more and the Chief Cashier, £7,500. Those attached to the Governors also were well rewarded. Ranging between £5,000 and £6,500, the pay of the assistants and the Advisers to the Governors was on a par with that of the Bank's chief officers. These Bank salaries can be compared with those in the Civil Service, where the three most senior grades, permanent Secretary, Deputy Secretary, and under Secretary, received £4,500, £3,250, and £2,600, respectively.

For members of the Court, the yearly remuneration was specified in the 1946 charter, and there was a clause that allowed the Court to agree to additional payments as deemed appropriate.[102] In the early 1950s, the Governor's salary was £8,000 and his Deputy, £6,500; in 1959, the sums were £14,000

[99] Rootham, 'Some reflections on graduate recruitment', 31 May 1955, E3/7.
[100] O'Brien to Mynors, 28 June 1955, E3/7.
[101] Bernard, note on 'salary scales', 20 November 1951, G14/183; Askwith to Abell, 14 May 1959, E12/75; Hennessy (1992).
[102] The Charter, 1946, section 12.

and £12,000, respectively.[103] In comparison, the pay of the chairmen of other nationalised industries was in a range between £4,500 and £8,500 per annum.[104] There was greater variation in the pay of the Executive Directors, largely a reflection of seniority. In the middle of the decade, Abell and Hawker were paid £6,500, Peppiatt £7,000, and Bolton £7,500. By 1959, Abell and Hawker's salaries had increased to £8,750, and the two more junior executives, Parsons and Stevens, both received £8,000. By any standards, these were highly paid jobs, particularly that of Governor. The rewards reflected the status and had to be capable of attracting the required calibre of person to the Bank. On the other hand, the sum of £500 received by the part-time Directors remained unchanged for 52 years, not being altered until the 1998 Bank of England Act. Cecil King, a member of the Court in the 1960s, reckoned that for him, the net value of the payment after tax was about £12.50 per annum, adding that the lunches were worth considerably more.[105]

It was not just salary levels that made the Bank a good place to work. There was a general feeling that it treated its staff extremely well. According to O'Brien, the Sports Club had been established 'to foster the feeling that in the Bank one is a member of a community and a service and not just an employee'.[106] The large array of clubs and societies, including the Rifle Club, the Horticultural Society, the Chess Club, the Operatic and Dramatic Society, and the Table Tennis Club, further added to the sense of 'belonging'. Indeed, the Bridge Club was an attractive prospect to future Governor Eddie George in joining the Bank.[107] Another society, although with a more secretive influence, was the Masonic Lodge, intended for the sole use of Directors and clerical staff of the Bank.[108] Of course, such paternalistic behaviour was not unique to the Bank, but certainly the organisation liked to think that it was special.

Objectives and Functions

The Bank was not charged with a specific set of objectives. Nowhere in the 1946 Act or indeed in any other official documentation was there a statement

---

[103] G15/222.

[104] For example, the chairman of the British Transport Commission received £8,500; the chairman of the National Coal Board, £7,500; the chairmen of area electricity boards, £4,000. *Top Salaries*, Appendix 2.

[105] Interview on BBC Money Programme, 'The Old Lady of Threadneedle Street', broadcast 26 November 1976.

[106] O'Brien to Parsons/Bailey, 'Sports Club', 3 August 1967, G14/336.

[107] Interview with Lord George, 8 February 2006.

[108] *Old Lady*, March 1921, p. 6.

of what the government expected the Bank to do. This gave the Bank a great deal of freedom. Despite the absence of explicit guidelines, after many years of evolution, the responsibilities and behaviour of the Bank were, at least implicitly, well understood. In any case, as Sayers observed in a lecture to the Institute of Bankers in 1953, the tasks of the Bank could not be rigidly defined. It was, he maintained, 'the very essence of central banking that it should be fluid and should adapt its ways to the needs of the time'.[109]

Contemporary accounts are useful on the functions of the Bank during this period. The fourth edition of Sayers's *Modern Banking* provides a clear exposition of the Bank's position and role in the banking world in the 1950s.[110] For Sayers, 'the fundamental business of a central bank is to control the commercial banks in such a way as to support the monetary policy directed by the State'.[111] To achieve this, the Bank had to be a source of cash, pursue open market operations, and stand ready to act as the lender of last resort. It also regulated the note issue. Other work, such as banker to the government or to private customers, was not essential to its basic function as a central bank. Neither was foreign-exchange business, which was conducted mainly as agent for the Treasury, 'indissolubly related' to the Bank's main functions.[112] While these other functions did receive some attention, Sayers was interested mainly in central bank operations and their impact on both the banking system and monetary policy. The experience of the latter during the 1950s led Sayers to conclude that 'it is probably fair to say that there has never been a time when there were so many unsettled questions of central banking as there are today'.[113] This was written in April 1957, one month before the announcement of the Radcliffe enquiry. Sayers was appointed a member of the Radcliffe Committee, and subsequent editions of *Modern Banking* were heavily rewritten in the light of the report.

The Radcliffe Committee contains a useful guide to the work of the Bank during this period. A memorandum on 'Constitution and Functions' was submitted by the Bank as evidence in 1957. Less concerned with theory than with practice, the paper drew attention to five areas: the note issue, operation of the EEA, application of exchange controls, management of debt, and banking.[114] The report itself divided the work of the Bank into three

---

[109] Sayers (1957, p. 33).
[110] The preface to the fourth edition was dated April 1957, and the book was published in 1958.
[111] Sayers (1958, p. 79).
[112] *Ibid.*
[113] *Ibid.*, p. 304.
[114] Bank of England, 'Constitutions and functions', June 1957; Radcliffe, *Memoranda*, vol. 1, pp. 4–5.

areas: external business, domestic business, and operations by which the Bank influenced the economy.[115] The Bank set out its functions and organisation in an article in the *Quarterly Bulletin*, where four main elements were highlighted: banking, agency work for the government, the Bank's advisory role, and operations in the financial and foreign-exchange markets.[116] A chapter on the Bank in a book published by the BIS, written by John Fisher, an Adviser at the Bank, can be taken as representing the official view. Fisher enumerated eight 'implicit' objects. Two – note issue and registrar for the public debt – were largely operational tasks. Three – defending the value of the currency, acting as lender of the last resort, and providing expert advice to government – were fairly specific. The remainder were more general in nature – 'to maintain the credit and reputation of the banking and financial system', 'to promote orderly financial and exchange markets', and 'to promote the orderly flow of capital in the capital markets'.[117]

The Bank's role in the conduct of monetary policy and the impact of its interventions in the money and foreign-exchange markets are clearly paramount. There was a range of activities, for example, operations in the discount market, changes in Bank Rate, and management of government debt via the gilt-edged market. We simply list them here, but they are central to the story. The Bank had a degree of autonomy in the day-to-day use of its instruments, but ultimately, tactics were directed towards attaining, or at least trying to attain, objectives that were set elsewhere. Policy was determined by the government, not the Bank. However, the Bank was no passive agent, merely implementing instructions from the Treasury; it was intimately associated with the formulation and application of monetary techniques.

The principal customers for banking services were the government, the commercial banks, and overseas financial institutions. There also remained a small, though 'obstinate', amount of private banking business.[118] As the government's banker, the Bank held the main accounts, including that of the Exchequer, the Paymaster General, the Post Office, and the National Debt Commissioners. These accounts were managed by the Bank on a day-to-day basis to ensure that sufficient funds were available to meet spending requirements and that large surpluses did not accumulate. In its role

---

[115] Committee on Working of the Monetary System, *Report*, August 1959 (cmnd. 827., paras. 321–367).

[116] Bank of England, 'Functions', p. 233.

[117] Bank for International Settlements (1963, p. 99).

[118] 'The Bank of England today', text of talk given by Bailey to the Institute of Bankers, 18 February 1964, E7/2.

as the bankers' banker, the Bank held accounts for the commercial banks, the discount houses, the accepting houses, and some of the overseas banks operating in London. There were nearly 100 accounts by the mid-1960s. The accounts of the London clearing banks were the most significant, and a large part of their total cash holdings was maintained in the form of balances at the Bank. Daily cheque and credit clearings were settled against these 'bankers' balances'. Through its lending to the discount houses, the Bank was lender to the banking system. Accounts were held for about 90 overseas central banks and other monetary authorities, the latter including the BIS, IMF, and International Bank for Reconstruction and Development (IBRD). Most of the central banks within the sterling area held the bulk of their reserves at the Bank of England, whereas others kept large working balances there. The Bank provided facilities for the management of these funds.[119]

A significant amount of the Bank's work was undertaken on an agency basis for government. Two principal tasks were the administration of exchange control and management of the EEA. Exchange-control restrictions were imposed under the Exchange Control Act 1947, itself an extension of wartime controls. The measures were designed to protect and conserve the gold and foreign-exchange reserves by making transactions outside 'scheduled territories' subject to the permission of the Treasury. These scheduled territories initially included most of the Commonwealth and some sterling area countries. The associated bureaucracy was significant. At its peak in 1950, the Exchange Control section employed more than 1,600 people, around a quarter of all clerical staff at the Bank. During the 1950s, there was a gradual relaxation of controls, and as a consequence, some of the Exchange Control Offices were abolished. Staff numbers were reduced to about 250 at the end of the decade, although this did not result in any redundancies. Management of the EEA was undertaken on behalf of the Treasury. The account was established in 1932 and was operated to prevent large fluctuations in the day-to-day value of sterling. This role continued in the post-war period, and the EEA was charged with ensuring that the exchange rate did not vary by more than 1 per cent either side of the $2.80 parity value dictated by IMF membership.[120]

One of the most visible aspects of the Bank's activity was the note issue. This was governed by several pieces of legislation. The 1844 Bank Charter

---

[119] Bank of England, 'Functions', p. 234.
[120] HMT, 'Exchange Equalisation Account', January 1958; Radcliffe, *Memoranda*, vol. 1, p. 105; 'The Exchange Equalisation Account', *BEQB* 8(4):377–390, December 1961.

Act stipulated that there should be separate Issue and Banking departments. In practice, the two were discrete only in an accounting sense, the split not being reflected in the departmental organisation. The Bank had, and has, the sole right to issue legal tender banknotes in England and Wales.[121] The notes themselves were issued to the Banking Department, which released them as required. In the mid-1950s, the number of notes in circulation, mainly in £1 denomination, was over 1,500 million, with a total value of £1,800 million.[122]

The entire note issue was fiduciary; that is, the paper currency was backed by government securities rather than gold. This had been the case since the Currency and Bank Notes Act 1939, when, except for a token amount, the gold backing the issue was transferred from the books of the Issue Department into the EEA. Under the 1939 Act, the size of the fiduciary issue was set at £300 million, but it could be exceeded with the authority of the Treasury. Temporary measures were introduced during the war, and the limit was increased subsequently to £1,575 million by the Currency and Bank Notes Act of 1954. There was provision to increase this if required, although a Treasury Order was required if the specified total was exceeded for more than two years; at the end of 1956, the fiduciary issue actually stood at £2,000 million. There was also the storage of gold, much of it held for other central banks; it was stored in the main gold vaults in sets of 1,000 bars, each set weighing just under 13 tonnes.[123] There was an important link between the EEA and the Issue Department. In order to maintain the book value of the securities, payments were made to and from the EEA depending on the results of the weekly revaluation. These movements could fluctuate quite markedly. However, the figures represented only a tiny proportion of the fiduciary issue. Indeed, even the £17 million that was wiped from the value of the Issue Department securities in September 1957 following the 2 per cent Bank Rate rise was only 0.9 per cent of the total. The government securities held in the Issue Department played a central role in the Bank's management of government debt. These securities were managed to meet

---

[121] Under the Bank Notes Act, 1954, notes of less than £5 were in fact legal tender in Scotland and Northern Ireland; see Byatt (1994, pp. 159, 163).

[122] 'The note circulation', *BEQB* 5(1):39–45, March 1965; 'Changes in demand of Bank notes', *BEQB* 5(3):248–249, September 1965; Bank of England, *Annual Report*, year ending February 1956, pp. 1–3.

[123] Unpublished article, 'The work of the bullion office', intended for September 1963 *Bulletin*, EID5/35. On 1 May 1967, gold to a value of £750,000 (140 bars) was stolen in the biggest robbery of the time. A van destined for Rothschilds loaded with gold from the Bank was overpowered by a gang before reaching its destination. Some of the gold was later found in Switzerland. See C43/152.

the requirements of the Bank's market operations and not with the intention of maximising income. Nevertheless, this income was substantial, particularly because of the extra interest earned owing to higher Bank Rate. From this, the Bank deducted its costs incurred in the note issue, leaving large profits that were passed back to the Treasury through the EEA.[124] These profits totalled £271 million between 1950/51 and 1959/60.

The Bank also acted as the registrar of government stocks, including those issued by nationalised industries. In 1958, these amounted to 160 different securities comprising over 3 million individual accounts. The annual workload included the processing of the millions of dividend payments and stock transfers. As with Exchange Control this operation was extremely labour-intensive, and the Accountant's Department, where the work was based, had a staff of between 1,500 and 2,500 in this period. This routine administration and paperwork associated with the registrar's function were a rather different matter than management of the government debt, a task that had important ramifications for monetary policy.[125]

The Bank's advisory and supervisory functions were diverse. Advice was given to the government on all aspects of domestic and external monetary policy. Relations with the Treasury are hard to pin down, but in its normal operations, the Bank experienced little interference. The 1946 Act, however, had made the Bank subordinate to the Treasury, and Radcliffe's recommendations served to reinforce this position. Yet the Bank was the representative of private-sector interests in the City, and it was also the normal channel of communication between the Treasury and the wider banking world. There were close links between the Bank and City institutions and with commerce and industry. During the 1920s and 1930s, the Bank had been active in financing industrial reorganisation, and after 1945, it was involved in establishing the Finance Corporation for Industry and the Industrial and Commercial Finance Corporation. In the 1950s, the Bank advised on denationalisation of the steel industry (1951), creation of the Commonwealth Development Finance Company (1952–53), and an unsuccessful attempt to prevent the takeover of British Aluminium (1958).[126]

The intelligence underpinning this advice was built up through the Bank's network of formal and informal contacts, from members of Court, from the Agents at the Branches, and from visits; this accumulated expertise had no

---

[124] Following the 1968 National Loans Act, the profits were paid to the National Loans Fund rather than to the EEA.
[125] 'Stock management at the Bank of England', January 1958, AC1/6; Bank of England, 'The Bank of England as registrar', *BEQB* 3(1):22–29, March 1963.
[126] Fforde (1992, pp. 704–749).

real public outlet. The Bank remained a secretive organisation, and the *Annual Report* was notoriously sparse. Sayers, a long-standing critic of the report, described it variously as 'the dullest central bank report in the world', and a 'bare and boring document' that was 'hardly worth printing'.[127] Radcliffe, too, was highly critical.[128] This contrasted with the extremely detailed and informative reports of other nationalised industries and the material produced by central banks, for example, in the United States, Canada, and Australia.

The provision of advice also extended to overseas topics, particularly on the establishment of central banks, in the main in the Commonwealth and developing countries. The Bank offered technical assistance to the fledgling institutions, and during 1959, the first of its courses on central banking was run.[129] In many cases Bank staff were seconded to overseas central banks, and on occasion, this went as far as supplying a governor. Also important was the development of relations with other international financial institutions, in particular the IMF and the BIS. Blunden and Page had spells as researchers at the IMF, and at the end of 1956, Guy de Moubray was appointed the personal assistant to the IMF Managing Director. The latter post was for many years thereafter filled by Bank staff.[130]

Banking supervision during this period was distinctly low key – to the point of invisibility. There were no formal mechanisms of control, and neither was there any statutory provision for oversight of the banking system. The Bank of England Act 1946 did allow the Bank, with the authorisation of the Treasury, to give directions to banks, but these were powers that remained unused. The Principal of the Discount Office had a pivotal role. By and large, the institutions responded to the warnings issued within this informal regime. However, much of it applied only to the acceptance and discount houses, with the clearing banks on the periphery of the Bank's influence.[131] As new forms of financial institution developed, such as secondary banks and finance houses, sometimes as a consequence of existing control measures, control became increasingly problematic. From the mid-1950s, there were moves to introduce a credit trading bill that would have given powers to control the acceptance of deposits. In a scheme devised

---

[127] Sayers (1957, p. 44); Sayers (1958, pp. 73, 313); Hennessy (1992, pp. 213–214).
[128] Radcliffe, *Report*, paras. 366, 859.
[129] Beale to Bernard, 'Staff for posts outside the bank', 15 October 1952; Overseas and Foreign Office, 'Posts abroad which are or may be filled by members of the staff of the Bank of England', 26 April 1955, E39/1. Hennessy (1992, pp. 308–311); 'The overseas work of the Bank of England', *BEQB* 7(4):374–378, December 1967.
[130] Horsefield (1969, Appendix A, pp. 620–621); Committee of Treasury Extracts in G14/167 (on IMF) and G14/163 (on BIS).
[131] Fforde (1992, pp. 749–760).

by Hollom, institutions other than some exempted categories would be required to register with the Board of Trade for an annual licence and demonstrate that they met prescribed financial conditions.[132] Lacking government support in 1957, the idea came to nothing, a missed opportunity in Fforde's opinion, and it was some time before the issue was revisited.[133]

Not surprisingly, for an institution that was 250 years old, tradition was strong. On entering the Bank, staff were greeted by a Gatekeeper either at the front entrance or at the Princes Street gate. The Gatekeepers' lavish traditional attire of a pink jacket, red waistcoat, robe, and hat with gold trimmings and wooden staff with a silver head dated back to the very beginnings of the Bank and were a striking reminder of the past. The procedure for announcement of Bank Rate was also long-standing. Indeed, O'Brien admitted that no one seemed to know when it had actually started, although it had been the same since he joined the Bank in 1927.[134] After the formal vote at the weekly meeting of the Court, the decision was announced at 11:43 a.m. to waiting officials from the door of the Courtroom by the most junior Director. The Principal of the Discount Office then arranged for a notice indicating 'No alteration in the rate of discount this day' or 'Bank Rate x%' to be displayed in the front hall at 11.45 a.m., where runners from around the City gathered anxiously for the news and immediately rushed out to deliver it to their offices. Meanwhile, having been informed of the decision by the Chief Cashier, the Government Broker made the short walk to the stock exchange, this journey being so timed that the announcement was indicated on the floor of the exchange simultaneously with it being displayed in the Bank.[135]

Another highly visible element of tradition was the guard that came to Threadneedle Street every night to 'act as a psychological deterrent to anyone with evil designs on the Bank'.[136] Established in 1780 to deal with the Gordon riots, the Bank Picquet marched from Wellington or Chelsea Barracks along the Embankment dressed in red coats and bearskins and armed with rifles and bayonets to protect the Bank until the following morning. The Picquet was usually provided by the Brigade of Guards.[137]

---

[132] Hollom to Peppiatt/Cobbold, 'Hire purchase', 16 March 1956, C40/721.
[133] Fforde (1992, p. 777).
[134] O'Brien to Mullens, 'Announcement of Bank Rate', 18 April 1961, C42/5.
[135] Hollom to Armstrong, 15 September 1959; Makins to Cobbold, 15 September 1959, G14/156.
[136] Reid to Hollom, 21 March 1963, E5/17
[137] Although during our period other units including Commonwealth contingents, the Gurkha Regiment, and the Royal Air Force were used. Bank of England, Press announcement, note to editors, 1 August 1973, ADM10/7.

The question of abolishing the guard was raised in *The Times* in 1963, and the debate carried over into the Commons, where 'its meaningless duties' were questioned.[138] Subsequently, the Bank reviewed the role of the Picquet, but Cromer (an ex-guardsman himself) was adamant that it was essential for the security of the Bank.[139] It was reduced in size, and its role became more tactical than ceremonial; from 1963 on, the guard came by army vehicle and in service uniform.[140] Improved security features such as closed-circuit television and the availability of armed police ultimately made the guard redundant: after nearly 200 years, the Picquet came to an end on the evening of 31 July 1973.

The Bank took great pride in knowing how financial markets operated. Its capacity to offer advice on economic theory of any variety, however, was extremely limited – indeed, it was to be avoided – and in a situation where maintenance of the exchange rate was paramount, neither did it have a fully developed appreciation of many aspects of monetary policy. Yet it was the failure of monetary policy that resulted in appointment of the Radcliffe Committee. Radcliffe gave the prevailing orthodoxy the official seal of approval, but as it transpired, the outcome of monetary policy continued to disappoint.

Financing the Bank and Financial Performance

While it is difficult to conduct an examination of the Bank's overall performance, something can be attempted on its financing. There are three principal ways in which a central bank can be financed: out of taxation, by retaining seignorage, and by levy on the financial institutions. The Bank had arrived at the last of these. There are some problems with the first two in terms of incentives and independence. The third raises fewer objections. At the beginning of the twenty-first century, with greater transparency in business and government, the Bank's financing is easily discovered. Under the 'Cash Ratio Deposit Scheme', the principal financial institutions are obliged to place non-interest-bearing deposits at the Bank. These deposits are invested by the Bank, and the income earned covers the costs of the Bank's monetary policy and financial stability operations. In addition, the Bank charges the government for the services it carries out.

---

[138] H. C. Deb, 24 April 1963, vol. 676, c191–193.
[139] Cromer to Profumo (secretary of state), 4 April 1963, C40/1043.
[140] Page to Downey, 23 July 1973, ADM10/7.

The roots of this scheme lie in the nineteenth century. In the early years, the commercial banks had a certain amount of understandable antipathy towards the Bank largely because of its privileged joint stock position. That gradually faded, however. Then, after the Bank had been given a monopoly of the note issue in the legislation of 1844 and it became the ultimate source of cash, conditions were in place for it being the lender of last resort. This role was one the Bank played imperfectly in the middle years of the century but then more or less ideally from the 1870s onwards. The Bank, by virtue of its position, could provide emergency liquidity to the banking system, effectively without limit. It was sensible, therefore, for banks to place their reserves with the Bank and facilitate, at reduced cost, the settlement of claims on each other. When any panic blew up, the banks would seek assistance from the central issuer. Ultimately, this could result in holders of central bank claims demanding gold from the Bank, but if confidence could be preserved in the banks, that also ensured the safety of the Bank. In the second half of the nineteenth century, bankers' balances started to become a significant part of banks' liquid assets. Some secrecy surrounded these figures from this period until well into the twentieth century.[141] Secrecy in the accounts was for a long time justified on the grounds that the Bank might, on occasion, provide support for a particular institution, and it was better for the system if details of such an operation were not known.

Bankers' balances stood at about £1.5 million in 1850 and had grown to around £10 million in the 1870s, and by the First World War, the normal order was about £60 million.[142] The Bank had called for increased balances following the Baring crisis of 1891, and the movement in them was something that the Governors watched very closely. The balances were also becoming important for another reason. By the late nineteenth century, there was an acceptance at the Bank that its public role took precedence over its private role, and as a consequence, it would have to forego some profitable commercial activity. Thus its income now was derived in large part from bankers' as well as government balances.

By the late 1920s, the balances were still in the range of £55 million to £63 million. After 1931, in the era of 'cheap money' when Bank Rate was held at 2 per cent, the balances gave less cause for concern for the Bank or the banks. However, a change came following the Second World War. It was agreed in 1946 that the clearing banks would operate with a cash reserve–deposit

---

[141] Clapham (1944, p. 307).
[142] These must be true in real terms as well because the price level in 1914 was more or less the same as it had been in 1870.

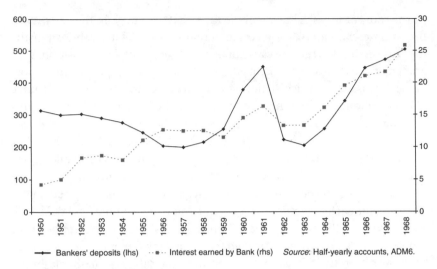

Figure 2.2. Bankers' deposits and interest earned by the Bank, 1950–68 (£m).

ratio of 8 per cent. The cash was to be made up of till money and balances held at the Bank, although it did not matter what the split was. The balances were non-interest-bearing, although this was of less significance while the era of cheap money continued. However, after the reactivation of monetary policy in 1951, interest rates were much higher than they had been in the preceding 20 years, and consequently, the Bank's earnings rose. Bankers' balances were larger, too. In the 1950s and into the 1960s, they were of the order of £250 million to £300 million. In the financial year 1950/51, total Bank income was £8.9 million, of which interest earned was less than half at £4.1 million. This rose steadily across the next two decades so that by 1969/70, while the Bank's income was £31.9 million, interest earned was now £25.8 million, more than 80 per cent of the total.[143] Figure 2.2 shows the path of interest earned and of bankers' deposits over the period.

The obligatory holding of cash meant that the banks were subject to an implicit tax, the recipient of which, in the case of bankers' balances, was the Bank. It would have been possible at the time to make an estimate of the cost to the banks by performing a simple calculation. The balances can be multiplied by a market rate of interest or the Treasury bill rate as a reasonable proxy in this instance. The numbers then provide rough orders

---

[143] This would be about £250 million in current terms (2007), whereas the costs of the Bank's monetary and financial stability operations are currently £106.2 million per annum; Bank of England, *Annual Report*, 2008, p. 32.

of magnitude indicating what the opportunity cost was to the banks (and the corresponding earnings of the Bank). These costs have been estimated roughly for the period 1951–71 as close to £500 million.[144]

For an interested observer in the 1950s, it was almost impossible to deduce much about the finances of the Bank other than by the kind of calculation just made. In the prevailing culture of secrecy, the Bank published very little financial data about itself, and the *Annual Report* was uninformative. The Bank was not alone in this lack of disclosure, it being a similar story for the commercial banks.[145] Half-yearly accounts were produced for internal use, the Bank being exempt from complying with the form of accounts under the Companies Act 1948. It was not until 1971 following a recommendation from the Select Committee on Nationalised Industries that the Bank started to publish its annual accounts (see Chapter 7). One document that was publicly available was the statutory 'Bank Return'. A requirement of the 1844 Act, it was published every week in the *London Gazette,* as well as being displayed at the Bank.[146] In the return, there was a clear distinction between the Issue and Banking Departments, but it was possible to see only a broad outline of securities, deposits, discounts, and advances, and it was an opaque source for anyone seeking to establish details of the Bank's true financial position. Certainly, nothing was revealed about the Bank's income and expenditure or profits and reserves.

Using the internal accounts, Table 2.2 shows the Bank's sources of income during the 1950s. For the reasons already described, interest derived from the bankers' balances was the dominant component. The other two significant sources, each bringing in more than £2 million per annum, were stock and bond services and sundry receipts. Both were tasks undertaken on behalf of government. Stock and bond services comprised the management of the funded and unfunded debt and the work connected with issues, conversions, and redemptions. Sundry receipts included the costs that the Bank recovered for the note issue, administration of exchange control, and operation of the EEA. For the decade as a whole, total income from these elements was £11.6 million for exchange control work, £8.2 million for note issue, and £1.8 million for the EEA. The remaining (smaller) sources of income were 'interest on bills discounted and advances', an item for which higher interest rates again were beneficial. In addition, smaller sums came from commissions, fees, and rents.

---

[144] See Griffiths (1970); Capie (1990, p. 135).
[145] Billings and Capie (2009).
[146] Hennessy (1992, pp. 193–194).

Table 2.2. *Bank of England sources of income, 1950–60 (£m)*

Year ending	Interest on British government securities[a]	Interest on bills discounted and advances	Stock and bond services[b]	Commissions, fees and rents	Sundry receipts[c]	Total
Feb. 1951	4.1	0.1	2.2	0.1	2.3	8.9
Feb. 1952	4.9	0.1	2.4	0.1	2.3	9.8
Feb. 1953	8.0	0.3	2.3	0.1	2.4	13.1
Feb. 1954	8.5	0.2	2.2	0.3	2.3	13.6
Feb. 1955	7.8	0.2	2.3	0.2	2.3	12.9
Feb. 1956	10.1	1.0	2.2	0.1	2.3	15.7
Feb. 1957	11.6	1.1	2.3	0.2	2.2	17.4
Feb. 1958	11.0	1.5	2.3	0.2	2.1	17.1
Feb. 1959	11.8	0.8	2.3	0.4	2.1	17.4
Feb. 1960	10.9	0.7	2.2	0.2	2.1	16.0

[a] Government securities and Treasury bills.
[b] Management of funded and unfunded debt; other stocks and bonds issue, conversion, and redemption.
[c] Fees for work undertaken by Issue Department, Exchange Control, EEA, and other.
Source: Half-yearly accounts, ADM6/93–7.

Table 2.3 shows the costs of running the Bank in the 1950s. The average yearly expenditure was £6.8 million. While the Bank's income almost doubled during the decade, expenditure grew by just 36 per cent, from £5.7 million in 1950/51, to £7.8 million in 1959/60. By far the largest single item was salaries and wages. This averaged £4.3 million over the 1950s, roughly two-thirds of total expenditure. With pension provisions and associated costs included, the figure was 77 per cent. The wage bill increased despite the fact that staff numbers were declining. In addition to the normal expenditure, some substantial capital investment, totalling over £10 million, was made during the decade. This included the new Printing Works at Debden (£2.5 million) and the office accommodation for the Accountant's Department at New Change (£6 million).[147] More that £8 million of this was met from annual income, with the rest coming from reserves.

[147] On Debden, see PW12/3, 4.

Table 2.3. *Bank of England gross expenditure, 1950–60 (£m)*

Year ending	Personnel wages[a]	Pensions	Total	General[b]	Premises[c]	Total
Feb. 1951	3.6	0.7	4.4	0.8	0.5	5.7
Feb. 1952	3.8	0.7	4.6	0.9	0.5	5.9
Feb. 1953	4.2	0.8	5.0	1.0	0.5	6.5
Feb. 1954	4.2	0.8	5.0	1.0	0.5	6.5
Feb. 1955	4.3	0.8	5.1	1.0	0.5	6.6
Feb. 1956	4.5	0.9	5.5	1.2	0.5	7.1
Feb. 1957	4.6	0.9	5.5	1.1	0.5	7.1
Feb. 1958	4.7	0.8	5.5	1.2	0.5	7.2
Feb. 1959	4.9	0.9	5.8	1.2	0.6	7.6
Feb. 1960	5.1	0.8	6.0	1.2	0.6	7.8

[a] Includes Governors' and Directors' remuneration.
[b] Operating and running costs.
[c] Rates and maintenance.
Source: Half-yearly accounts, ADM6/93–7.

With the growth of receipts easily outstripping the increase in expenditure, the Bank enjoyed a very comfortable level of profits. Not that this was widely appreciated: even in the Bank, the figures were a closely guarded secret. Over the course of the decade, gross profits, shown in Table 2.4, rose from £4.6 million to over £9 million. Gross profit has been calculated from normal receipts plus capital receipts less normal expenditure. From this it is also necessary to deduct the capital liabilities that were paid into the superannuation fund. These were made from 1952 onwards, following an actuarial review of the pension fund. The Bank was also liable for income tax and profits tax, and thus, while gross profit nearly doubled, so too did tax. The after-tax profit figures match those given in Hennessy and the historic data calculated in the Bank.[148] Once tax had been deducted, there was the statutory annual payment to the Treasury made under the terms of the 1946 Act. The sum of £1,746,360, paid in two annual instalments of £873,180, was equivalent to the interest payable on the government stock issued at the time of the Bank's nationalisation. The amount remained unchanged until 1972, when it was increased to £5.5 million.

[148] Hennessy (1992, Appendix A, pp. 221–223); Rumins (1995); David Best, working papers in G15/650.

Table 2.4. *Bank of England gross and net profits, 1950–60 (£m)*

Year ending	Gross profit[a]	Pre-tax profit[b]	Tax	Profit after tax	Profit after tax and dividend payment[c]	Distribution of profits		
						Write-off of capital expenditure	Provision for future expenditure	Transfer to other reserves
Feb. 1951	4.6	4.6	1.2	3.4	1.7	0.2	0.8	0.7
Feb. 1952	4.4	4.4	1.2	3.2	1.5	0.1	0.9	0.5
Feb. 1953	6.7	5.8	2.0	3.8	2.0	0.6	1.1	0.3
Feb. 1954	7.4	6.5	2.1	4.3	2.6	0.9	1.7	0.0
Feb. 1955	6.7	5.7	1.9	3.9	2.1	1.6	0.5	0.0
Feb. 1956	8.7	7.6	2.6	5.0	3.2	2.1	0.2	0.9
Feb. 1957	10.4	9.7	3.4	6.3	4.5	1.5	1.8	1.2
Feb. 1958	9.7	9.1	3.4	5.7	4.0	1.9	1.0	1.1
Feb. 1959	9.9	9.3	4.1	5.2	3.5	0.7	0.5	2.2
Feb. 1960	9.5	8.9	3.0	5.9	4.2	0.0	0.0	4.2

[a] Normal income and capital receipts less normal expenditure.
[b] After deduction of superannuation capital liability.
[c] 'Dividend payment' is the annual payment to the Treasury of £1.7 million.
Source: Half-yearly accounts, ADM6/93–7.

Net profits after tax and dividends were distributed over three areas. First, monies were used in writing off capital expenditure and writing down securities. Nearly £10 million was used for this purpose in the 1950s. The other two headings represented increases in the Bank's reserves. One covered the funds set aside to meet anticipated future expenditure, for example, on equipment, premises, and pensions, whereas the other included contingency reserve accounts: £8 million was paid into the former and £11 million into the latter. In all, the net increase in the Bank's reserves over the decade was £16.3 million, and the total, in February 1960, was £77.9 million. Table 2.5 shows the distribution and size of the various accounts.

How can the profitability of the Bank be assessed? The preceding tables provide a number of profit series, including pre-tax, post-tax pre-dividend (the measure favoured historically by the Bank) and post-tax, post-dividend that all show substantial increases. Another measure involves deducting from net profits the capital expenditure written off and the securities written down. Indeed, this was often the treatment adopted, albeit inconsistently,

Table 2.5. *Bank of England reserves, 1950–60 (£m)*

Year ending	No. 1 Account	Contingency	Central banking	Premises	Pensions	British Government Securities	Securities Management Trust	Rest	Total
Feb. 1951	14.5	5.0	1.5	3.3	3.1	28.8	1.7	3.9	61.6
Feb. 1952	14.6	5.0	1.5	4.0	2.5	29.0	1.7	3.9	62.1
Feb. 1953	15.2	5.0	1.5	5.1	2.5	29.3	1.7	3.9	64.0
Feb. 1954	16.0	5.0	1.5	6.8	2.5	29.3	1.7	3.9	66.6
Feb. 1955	15.9	5.0	1.5	7.2	2.5	30.0	1.7	3.9	66.9
Feb. 1956	16.1	5.0	1.5	7.2	2.7	30.0	1.7	3.9	68.0
Feb. 1957	16.4	5.0	1.5	7.9	3.7	30.0	2.7	3.9	71.2
Feb. 1958	16.7	5.0	1.5	7.9	4.7	30.0	3.6	3.9	73.3
Feb. 1959	15.4	5.0	1.5	7.3	5.2	30.0	7.1	3.9	75.4
Feb. 1960	16.5	5.0	1.5	5.6	5.2	30.0	10.2	3.9	77.9

Source: ADM6/197; ADM6/200.

in the commentary on the annual accounts presented to the Committee of Treasury. Profitability can be expressed in different ways, most commonly as a return on capital employed. The effective paid-up capital of the Bank was £14.6 million, but reserves also should be included. Using the gross profit figures gives a return of between 6 and 12 per cent during the 1950s, not a figure that that would have raised undue concern. These are crude results. Arguably, the reserves should comprise only of sums available to absorb losses, while the accounting conventions of the time gave no value to the buildings.[149] Thus the return should be taken as indicative and not much more. Of more interest is the fact that out of its income, the Bank could comfortably cover its normal running costs, as well as undertaking major capital expenditure and topping up the pension fund. For a monopoly supplier whose output cannot be measured easily, however, the profit figures, highly susceptible as they are to changes in accounting conventions, say little about actual performance.

What is clear is that the high level of profits was a concern to the Bank. In a note on the subject written in September 1960, Mynors warned that 'it may become increasingly difficult to justify the need for profits on this scale'.[150] By the late 1960s, the surpluses were much greater. These worries were linked to an ongoing debate concerning the relationships between the Bank's profits, the contribution to the Treasury, and the remuneration for agency work for the government.

The 1946 Act made provision for the dividend payment to be varied on agreement between the Treasury and the Bank. As early as 1950, Sir Wilfred Eady, a joint second Secretary at the Treasury, asked whether a procedure could be introduced to consider the amount of the half-yearly payment. Such a mechanism was felt to be necessary because of the level of the payments that the Treasury was making for various services. Cobbold was wary: 'I should certainly not be prepared to have any informal discussion with the Treasury on the subject.' One reason undoubtedly was the desire to maintain secrecy, with Cobbold observing that talks could not take place 'without going into the accounts as a whole'.[151] This came from a man who knew what he was talking about, who had made his name disentangling the accounts of an Italian insurance company. The Governor also rejected the implication that the Treasury was being overcharged. While the Bank was able to fend off the Treasury on this occasion, the amount of the annual

---

[149] For discussion of some of these issues in relation to commercial banks, see Capie and Billings (2001b).

[150] Mynors, 'The Bank's profits', 19 September 1960, G15/11.

[151] Cobbold, Governor's note, 17 March 1950, G15/11.

payment and the charges for agency work were to remain sensitive issues for another two decades.

The charges to government were calculated in a number of ways. Note issue and management of the EEA were the most straightforward, with the costs recovered in full. This position was relatively easy to defend because the tasks were seen as permanent features of the Bank's work.[152] Management of stocks and bonds was covered by a scale of charges agreed to in 1942. Under a tapering formula, the Bank received £325 per million for the first £750 million of stock (i.e., a total of £243,750), £150 per million on the next £5,250 million of stock (i.e., £787,500), and £50 per million on the balance. The fee for Treasury bills, which dated back to 1919, was set by a two-part scale, with no charge made for bills handled in excess of £550 million. Issues, conversions, and redemptions were charged on an ad hoc estimate of costs, and tax reserve certificates attracted a flat rate of 1s. (one shilling) per certificate.[153]

In the case of exchange control, the Bank recovered its costs under an agreement made with the Treasury in 1942. However, the calculation was 'a lengthy process quite outside the normal costing system'.[154] The figures included salaries and wages, rent and rates, premises charges, stationery, telephones and postage, machines, and other sundries. Complex apportionments were required because the work was undertaken across the entire Bank. In August 1952, 1,300 clerical staff were engaged on the task, but only 576 were located in offices wholly concerned with exchange control. The 'remaining 724 was calculated by aggregating fractions'.[155] Then, in 1953, Treasury Permanent Secretary Sir Edward Bridges asked whether the Bank might instead charge an appropriate annual fee for the provision of these services. This was because the Comptroller and Auditor General had expressed concerns that the figures provided by the Bank were not liable to audit or inspection. Cobbold agreed to Bridges' proposal and suggested a fee of £1.3 million.[156] Over the years, this was progressively lowered at the instigation of the Bank, and by the end of

---

[152] In 1953, the Bank had used this argument when rejecting a request from the Treasury for the costs of managing the EEA to be recovered through a fee. Burke Trend (HMT) to Dascombe, 4 May 1953, and reply, 11 May 1953, ADM6/48.

[153] Dascombe to Bernard, 'Management of British Government securities', 13 July 1951; O'Brien to Hawker/Cobbold/Mynors, 4 June 1959, G15/11.

[154] V. C. Coombs to Dascombe, 'Exchange control charge', 30 January 1953, ADM6/54.

[155] Coombs to Dascombe, 'Exchange control charge', 30 January 1953, ADM6/54.

[156] Bridges to Cobbold, 28 January 1953; Cobbold to Bridges, 2 February 1953; Dascombe, 'Note for record', 3 February 1953, ADM6/54.

Table 2.6. *Bank of England (profits)/losses incurred on work for the government, 1950–60 (£000)*

Year ending	Stock and bond services	Exchange control	Deposit banking	Total
Feb. 1951	(104)	216	366	478
Feb. 1952	10	221	370	601
Feb. 1953	250	294	399	943
Feb. 1954	306	381	369	1,056
Feb. 1955	321	372	233	926
Feb. 1956	513	390	112	1,015
Feb. 1957	611	451	29	1,091
Feb. 1958	577	330	124	1,031
Feb. 1959	758	376	155	1,289
Feb. 1960	860	354	139	1,357[a]

[a] Includes miscellaneous of 4.

Source: Costing Section, 'Comparative statement of profit/loss on the Bank's activities,' 18 June 1959; Mynors-Cromer, 28 June 1962, G15/11.

1959, the fee was £750,000.[157] This fall, of more than 40 per cent, was a consequence of lower costs, primarily owing to reduced expenditure on staffing, which was the largest component in the charge.

During the 1950s, it became evident that these charges were insufficient to cover the costs incurred by the Bank. Overall profits may have been rising, but when it came to the provision of specific services for government, the losses were mounting (Table 2.6). The deficit for stock and bond services accelerated in this period, totalling £4.1 million. Plainly, the existing scales did not adequately reflect current circumstances. Large additions to the national debt only produced revenue at the lowest marginal rate of £50 per million, and the cap on charging for Treasury bills over £550 million appeared restrictive when £5,000 million were in issue.[158] Losses on exchange control work fluctuated to a lesser extent, but the total still amounted to £3.4 million. Here, the fee was deliberately set below the charge that would have

---

[157] Cobbold to Bridges, 1 January 1955; Cobbold to Sir Roger Makins, 18 December 1956; Mynors to Makins, 29 December 1958; Mynors to Sir Frank Lee, 1 January 1960, ADM6/55.

[158] Dascombe to Eric Geipel (deputy secretary), 'Management charges', 24 September 1953; O'Brien to Hawker/Cobbold/Mynors, 4 June 1959, G15/11.

been made under the previous method, a figure that in any case did not capture the Bank's total costs in administering exchange control.[159] If deposit
banking activities for government are also included, then total losses on the
agency work during the decade were £9.8 million. This represents 12.6 per
cent of gross profits earned during the same period. In effect, the services
undertaken for government were subsidised by the interest that was earned
on the bankers' balances. Furthermore, this subsidy was supporting tasks
that, arguably, were not the core business of a central bank.

O'Brien reviewed the situation in the summer of 1959. He argued that
the losses were a consequence of maintaining stable charges and a reluctance to alter these at a time when 'high short term rates made the Bank's
other operations exceptionally remunerative'.[160] While he did not want to
provoke an annual renegotiation with the Treasury over costs and organisation, he wanted to put these elements of the Bank's work on a sounder footing. In order to achieve this, O'Brien maintained that charges would have to
be increased by approximately 60 per cent. There were, however, dissenting
voices. Mynors reacted by querying whether receipts for services necessarily
had to cover costs when the total activities of the Bank were profitable. He
conceded that 'the present arrangements are undoubtedly illogical, and to
that extent difficult to defend' but continued, 'I doubt whether they lead to
inefficiency or financial embarrassment for the Bank.'[161] Hollom had a similar reaction. Rather than immediately pursuing the issue with the Treasury,
it was decided first to undertake an exercise to establish what level of profits
the Bank as a whole required and how these would be made. This method
offered an alternative view of the Bank's financing, but changes towards this
remained some years away.

In summary, the Bank in its day-to-day operations was largely unchanged
by nationalisation, and despite its formalised subordination to the Treasury,
it retained a great deal of autonomy. Policy formulation and decision making remained in the hands of a tiny group of people. Analysis was based on
banking experience and a feel for markets, whereas there was little exposure
to economic theory. Indeed, there was scarcely a means to register developments in this area, let alone assess them. On the other hand, there was little
disposition on the part of the Bank to explain its actions. The Bank was

---

[159] For example, the fee for the year ending September 1956 was £1.1 million, whereas the
chargeable costs were £1.24 million, and the total cost was £1.54 million. The costs that
were not charged included supervision by Chief Cashiers and Directors and Advisers;
Coombs to Phillimore, 2 September 1949, ADM6/54.

[160] O'Brien to Hawker/Cobbold/Mynors, 'Stock and bond services', 4 June 1959, G15/11.

[161] Mynors, 'Management: first reactions', 8 June 1959, G15/11.

fortunate to find itself awash with revenues in the period – not that anyone else knew the details because even though the Bank was a public body, its culture of secrecy remained strong. Yet a changing financial and economic world, together with a growing dissatisfaction with the results of monetary policy, put the Bank under pressure. First, the Parker inquiry into the Bank Rate 'leak' and then the Radcliffe Committee served to put the rather private world of the Bank and its workings under close public scrutiny.

The Bank's long history in private banking left it heavily inclined to secretiveness.[162] In addition, following the nationalisation of 1946, it was on the defensive, particularly in relation to the Treasury, and this all added up on occasion to making it obstructive. The fact that discussion and decision making were in the hands of a very few meant that a common complaint among senior figures was that they had no idea what went on at the top. It was hardly the ideal setting for the conduct of monetary policy insofar as there was such a thing or even for carrying out its many agency functions, many of which were for the Treasury. Recruitment to the higher reaches generally came from a narrow social class and had a smack of nepotism. The Bank certainly was non-intellectual but possibly also anti-intellectual – a bank, not a study group. Much of this was about to change, but it is hard to say if the pace of change was equal to what was going on elsewhere, particularly in other financial institutions.

---

[162] Some attempt at countering this was made by making of a short film about the Bank in 1959. Two further films were released in 1966 and a fourth in 1974.

3

The Monetary Setting and the Bank

When the Governor Cameron Fromanteel Cobbold was being chauffeur driven in his Rolls Royce from his country seat, Knebworth House, to give evidence to the Radcliffe Committee, the car broke down. Cobbold and his chauffeur had to walk to the nearest railway station. Neither of them was carrying any cash. Cobbold approached the ticket clerk and said, 'Now look, I am the Governor of the Bank of England but I don't have any money.'[1] There would be those in the following years who would have wished that he and his successors had taken a similar line with the long list of Chancellors who knocked on their door. The Radcliffe Committee began taking evidence in 1957 and completed its report in 1959. It was the most important document on money and banking in the period. Its origins lay in dissatisfaction with how monetary policy was believed to be working in the 1950s. The findings and recommendations provoked immense debate and subsequent controversy. It set the scene for the next decade. For the Bank though, the enquiry had relatively little impact on the way in which it conducted its operations. It prompted a little more openness, more research, and the provision of statistics, even if it could be argued that the Bank was already moving in that direction.

Antecedents: Old and New Orthodoxy

Before the First World War, a considerable body of central banking theory and practice developed. Much of this took place either in the Bank or in response to actions the Bank was taking. The real origins lie with Henry

---

[1] As told to the author by Lord Armstrong, formerly Robert Armstrong Secretary to the Radcliffe Committee.

Thornton.[2] However, as Allan Meltzer has shown, subsequent to Ricardo, bankers and men of affairs became sceptical of the applicability of theory, and much was lost.[3] Also, by the late nineteenth century, monetary policy, sometimes called 'bank rate policy', had the relatively straightforward task of regulating the gold flow.[4] Thus Bank Rate was used to protect the exchange rate. The lender-of-last-resort function was developed for times of crisis. And there lingered the notion of accommodating the needs of trade – the real bills doctrine.

Unfortunately, Thornton's contribution was largely forgotten. His book, *Paper Credit*, written in 1802, contained a lengthy description of the current institutional environment, but soon after he wrote, the institutional arrangements were undergoing such rapid change that his work tended to be set aside and remained so for at least the rest of the nineteenth century.[5] However, in the course of the nineteenth century, Bagehot's principles – in clear linear descent from Thornton – gradually came to be accepted, particularly on how to behave in a panic.[6] The Bank, implicitly at least, adopted these principles and continued to follow that guidance well into the twentieth century. The one striking omission in central bank behaviour generally in the twentieth century was any recognition of the distinction between real and nominal variables, a distinction that had been present in Thornton and resurrected and developed again later by Irving Fisher in the 1890s.[7]

Under the gold standard, the original view was that there was considerable automaticity. Gold movements, a consequence of differential prices and reflected in current account balances, determined the monetary base. The banking system and the non-bank public held cash and deposits in a certain stable fashion, and so broad money was determined. What was added to that view was that support could be provided by a central bank. If the commercial banks were obliged to hold or out of convenience held some balances at the central bank, then the latter would be able to speed and smooth the adjustment process. It would watch for indications in the current account and work through open market operations. The evolution

---

[2]   Thornton (1802).
[3]   Meltzer (2002).
[4]   There were similarities in the 1950s and 1960s when the objective was to hold to a pegged exchange rate.
[5]   Thornton (1802). It was Hayek who began the revival of interest with a new edition in 1939.
[6]   Bagehot (1873).
[7]   Fisher (1896).

of the payments system had shown that it was convenient to settle balances in central bank money.[8] Discount houses had emerged as a buffer between the commercial banks and the Bank and proved effective in their role. In the middle of the nineteenth century, the discount houses had been given privileged access to the Bank, further facilitating operations. Bank Rate was made effective by keeping it above the rate at which the discount houses borrowed from the commercial banks so that borrowing from the central bank carried a penalty. Thus when pressure was applied it ultimately resulted in the commercial banks' reserves of cash falling and they had to cut their assets. Control was effective so long as continuous borrowing from the central bank was prevented and that was in effect done through the penalty rate charged. The transmission to the real economy is a separate matter. This was simply monetary control albeit a by-product of holding to a fixed gold parity.

Before the Great Depression at the beginning of the 1930s, it was generally accepted that the stock of money was an important determinant of the level of money income and of prices. But after it the view took hold that banks had played a big part in the failure and money had proved impotent in stimulating recovery. That soon became 'money does not matter' or that if it had any effect it was on a limited range of interest rates which themselves were of limited significance. So if monetary policy had a purpose it was to keep these interest rates low to avoid interfering with investment. After the Second World War the dominant view was that money did not matter much for anything and that included inflation. Writing of the immediate post-war years Alec Cairncross said, 'The influence of the Bank on monetary policy (so far as there was such a thing) was distinctly limited'.[9] The policy of 'cheap money' that was pursued in Britain and elsewhere in the 1930s and was continued after 1945 reflected these ideas. Bank Rate remained at 2 per cent for almost 20 years from 1932 to 1951 apart from a brief small rise at the outbreak of war. These views either derived from Keynesian economics or derived great support from Keynesian economics. Yet, as Meltzer reminds us, 'A wide gulf separates Keynes's views from familiar Keynesian policies and procedures. Keynes was opposed to the use of econometric models, opposed to attempted trade-offs between prices or inflation and output or employment, and generally opposed to countercyclical policies

---

[8] B. Norman, R. Shaw, and G. Speight, 'The history of interbank settlement arrangements: exploring central banks' role in the payment system', paper presented at the Past, Present and Policy Conference held at the Bank of England, 23–24 November 2006; and revised paper 2009.

[9] Cairncross (1987).

to stimulate consumption.'[10] After a dinner in Washington in 1944 with a group of American Keynesians, Keynes is said to have remarked, 'I was the only non-Keynesian there.'

In the course of the 1950s, a great debate blew up about adapting the traditional principles and mechanics of monetary control to the needs of the times.[11] The views emerging became known as the 'new orthodoxy' – in good part the application of Keynesian ideas to what was seen as changed circumstances and consequent changed priorities. The essence of the view was that open market operations were no longer effective in controlling banks' cash and deposits because the banks could easily offset any pressure applied. They could recall loans to the discount houses, or they could run off Treasury bills. The discount houses had automatic access to the Bank (the *right* to borrow at Bank Rate), and following the huge government borrowing of the war years, the system was awash with Treasury bills. Therefore, according to this argument, the system had, in effect, stalled, and the monetary authorities had lost the power of control over the cash ratio. Control of the money stock had atrophied in the course of the war and post-war years. Monetary policy could not work because of the large floating debt, so a large funding operation was needed.[12] The debt was so large that any shift out of it by the non-bank public would have produced a huge increase in the monetary base.

Thus, despite generations of experience, what was being argued was that the world had changed and that fundamental and established principles no longer worked. (This is never a good guide to action.) The cash-asset ratio on this view was outmoded. Attention should be directed instead to the liquidity-asset ratio, with the emphasis on funding. This would prove to be the only effective means of controlling bank deposits. There was a complication because wartime needs had seriously distorted the balance sheets of the commercial banks. The ratio of advances to total deposits had evolved from the late nineteenth century when advances were around 60 per cent of total assets. During the interwar years, the ratio fell to below 50 per cent. In the Second World War, though, advances were severely curtailed, and government stock took up much of the space. Advances fell to 16 per cent of total assets in 1944. After the war, the banks therefore were holding hugely inflated quantities of

---

[10] Meltzer (1998).
[11] See, for example, Hobson, *News Chronicle*, 18 November 1955, p. 2; King (1956); Dacey (1956); Smith and Mikesell (1957).
[12] Balogh (1956).

government debt, and they set out to restore the pre-war 'normal' position. Thus, through the 1950s, as the banks were trying to build their advances and reduce their holdings of debt, the monetary authorities were trying to cap or at least slow the growth of advances and at the same time sell increasing amounts of debt.

The minimum liquidity ratio (then 30 per cent) became the subject of much discussion: should it be a statutory requirement rather than a banking convention? Should it be a variable ratio to suit circumstances? There was close interest from the Treasury, with the Chancellor, Macmillan, going so far as to propose that he include the imposition of a higher liquidity ratio in his 1956 budget. All this had irked Cobbold, who argued that the ratio had been arrived at by the banks, for banking reasons, and it was not in any dispute: a different ratio, for different reasons, would 'raise every sort of new hare'.[13]

Assessments undertaken in the Bank were consistently unconvinced by the 'new techniques' for operating on the liquidity ratio largely because of the feeling that it would not address more fundamental ills.[14] The impact on monetary control of the size of the floating debt remained a particular concern. A memorandum in which O'Brien reiterated this point drew a response from Otto Niemeyer. Having left the Court in 1952, Niemeyer was now chairman of the Court of the London School of Economics but still kept an office at the Bank and acted as an informal adviser. He concurred with O'Brien's views, asking, 'is not the ultimate moral that the Government is still spending too much ... and letting the national [*sic*] industries one after another put out fantastic programmes?' The solution for Niemeyer was not to seek to 'anaesthetize' the floating debt by introducing new liquidity ratios, but to 'avoid the virus increase in Treasury bills'.[15]

In the apparent absence of effective monetary weapons, the Bank was left to resort to requests, controls, and exhortation. The requests to the banks highlighted a contentious issue between the Bank and the Treasury in that the Chancellor, both by convention and under the terms of the 1946 Act, could not issue direct instructions to the clearing banks but had to operate

---

[13] Cobbold to Mynors/Peppiatt/O'Brien/Allen, Governor's note, 29 December 1955, G1/73. Macmillan to Cobbold, 23 March 1956, G1/74.

[14] O'Brien to Peppiatt/Cobbold/Mynors, 'Internal credit policy', 15 February 1955; O'Brien, 'Credit policy', 22 April 1955; O'Brien to Peppiatt/Cobbold/Mynors, 'Credit policy', 17 November 1955, C42/12. Cobbold to Mynors, 25 October 1955, G1/73. O'Brien to Peppiatt/Cobbold/Mynors, 'Monetary control', 27 April 1956, C40/690.

[15] O'Brien to Peppiatt/Cobbold/Mynors, 'Monetary control', 27 April 1956, C40/690; Niemeyer to Cobbold, 2 May 1956, C40/691. On Niemeyer, see Fforde (1992p. 372).

through the Governor. In fact, in July 1955, Chancellor Rab Butler had made an indirect request to the clearers that they make 'a positive and significant reduction' in advances.[16] For their part, the banks complained about equity. They found it difficult to turn away what appeared to be justifiable business and were irritated that nationalised industries were not being forced to cut back on their spending programmes. This was to be a familiar complaint from the clearers over the next years, and the tensions and inconsistencies that reliance on controls brought also were to multiply.

Thus the belief was that government finance through Treasury bills had paralysed the conventional means of operating monetary policy. Many objections could be taken to this view and were taken on institutional and theoretical grounds. A key point was the belief that the Bank had lost its power because in its capacity as lender of last resort it had to accept bills tendered by the discount houses without limit. (The Bank appeared to go along with this view.) It is surely worth pointing out here that Bagehot's principles were designed to prevent liquidity panics. They contained no prescription for the continuous use of the Bank by the discount houses as a source of funds. How and where that confusion arose are interesting, but a subject for the historian of thought. The other important point was – At what price?

Not everyone accepted that the large volume of Treasury bills prevented control of the cash base. The view was that when the Bank sold securities to reduce bankers' deposits, the banks would counter by calling in loans to the discount market. There were those who argued that all that was needed for the sale of securities to be effective was a high enough rise in the rate of interest to induce the public to take up the Treasury bills or for Bank Rate to be sufficiently above the market rate to impose a significant penalty. The objection to this tended to be that the Bank had to maintain 'orderly markets', facilitate the financing of the exchequer, and support London as a financial centre. Additionally, there was a deep scepticism about the effectiveness of interest rates. This certainly applied to their use at low levels. However, at the same time, there appears to have been a fear that interest rates might rise too far and even overshoot (although this language was not used) and dreadful consequences might follow.

The 1950s, of course, were very different from the 1930s. Inflation had replaced deflation as the concern. And there was some recognition of the fact that interest rates might be better at containing inflation than they were

---

[16] Butler to Cobbold, 25 July 1955, G1/73; HC Deb, 25 July 1955, Vol. 544, c825; Fforde (1992, pp. 632–643).

at stimulating activity in depression. This was by no means straightforward, though, for the traditional method of using Bank Rate in conjunction with open market operations was said to be defective in the 1950s. However, while 'dear money' had replaced 'cheap money' in the 1950s, in many countries there was continued dispute as to its effectiveness in restricting credit because other measures were being employed simultaneously, such as rationing and hire purchase and other direct controls. Even aside from the role that interest rates could play, however, there was also disagreement over what credit restriction could achieve. The judgment of Cairncross was that while monetary policy was used four times between 1947 and 1957 to check inflation, 'None of them, with one possible exception, met with much success'.[17] Setting out the Court's view in early 1955, Cobbold told Butler that the contribution of monetary policy was not to be overestimated because inflationary pressure was mainly a result of the 'cost and wage structure' rather than monetary factors, and consequently, the battle must 'mainly be fought in the wider fields of economic policy'.[18] This was part of a general belief that inflation had non-monetary sources.

In the end, it was felt that the whole area of monetary policy was in need of scrutiny, and it was this that led to calls for an enquiry and the subsequent appointment of the Radcliffe Committee. The previous occasion on which such an enquiry had been held was the Macmillan Committee, which sat between 1929 and 1931. In November 1955, Francis Whitmore, City editor of *The Daily Telegraph*, wrote that there was an urgent need for a successor enquiry to Macmillan.[19] Greater political pressure came in March 1956, when Sir Bob Boothby, the maverick member of parliament (MP) for East Aberdeenshire, led a deputation to see the Chancellor, seeking a public enquiry into the monetary system.[20] The establishment of a high-profile committee may have held some attraction for Macmillan, who had arrived at the Treasury vowing to be a reforming Chancellor and whose ambitions included reorganisation of the Bank. He resisted the demands of Boothby and his colleagues, however, on the grounds that it was too early to judge the impact of the measures.[21] The Bank, too, wanted to avoid such a committee.

Although Macmillan declined to establish a public enquiry, he did agree to a Treasury suggestion for an internal review. A note outlining its

---

[17] Cairncross (1987, p. 2).
[18] Cobbold to Butler, 24 February 1955, G1/73.
[19] *The Daily Telegraph*, 1 December 1955, p. 6.
[20] Boothby to Macmillan, 6 March 1956, TNA T171/469.
[21] Horne (1989, p. 377).

proposed scope suggested that the government should take stock of the events in 1955 and draw lessons for the future.[22] The 'central question in all monetary policy is an understanding of the mechanics which determines the total of bank deposits and this involves the Central Bank control over cash and bankers' balances, and the answers to the various questions now being asked about liquidity ratios. In this connection we should look into the charge that floating debt issues (mainly on behalf of the nationalised industries) have offset steps taken in other directions.' The Treasury was keen to provide the Chancellor with an 'agreed doctrine about the views now being expressed, that control would be better and the cost of borrowing less if we prescribed liquidity ratios.' Cobbold evidently was nervous about this agenda. He sanctioned O'Brien and Allen's participation in the study, provided that it was on a 'personal' basis, that it was intended primarily to establish how far there was a 'meeting of minds', and that it allowed for further consideration.[23] More generally, Cobbold was annoyed by those who decried the banking system, complaining to Macmillan that it was a period of trial and error in the monetary field. While he was happy to receive criticism to keep the Bank on its toes, he asked, 'can we not start from the premise that our system is the best, and not the worst, in the world?'[24]

Sir Edmund Compton and Robert Hall, economic adviser to the government, represented the Treasury, with O'Brien and Allen from the Bank. The 'four wise men', as they were dubbed, first met in May 1956 following completion of the Bank's own assessment. The burden of work fell on Allen, and Cobbold was keen to limit Allen's report to a review of historical fact; it was not the place to make recommendations – 'the essence of monetary policy is flexibility. It would not be convenient for the Bank to deal with future policy operations in a joint report of this nature.'[25] Compton was less happy, pointing out that the Chancellor was expecting rather more in the way of explicit policy prescriptions.[26] Following some revisions in order to address these concerns, the final report, entitled, 'Monetary Organisation', was unanimously agreed and circulated at the end of June 1956.[27]

The report rehearsed the principles of monetary policy and examined the course of events during 1954–56. Surprisingly perhaps, it asserted that the

---

[22] Cairncross (1991b, p. 65); Compton to O'Brien, 11 April 1956, enclosing 'Study of the "credit squeeze"', 11 April 1956, C40/690.

[23] Cobbold to O'Brien, 12 April 1956, C40/690.

[24] Cobbold to Macmillan, 26 March 1956, G1/74.

[25] Cobbold to O'Brien/Allen, Governor's note, 1 June 1956, C40/691.

[26] O'Brien to Cobbold, 5 June 1956, C40/691.

[27] Compton/Hall/O'Brien/Allen, 'Monetary Organisation', 25 June 1956, C40/691.

monetary measures adopted had produced 'substantial' results, particularly given the adverse circumstances of government finance.[28] Less surprising was the finding that the high volume of Treasury bills made it difficult to use established financial techniques to control properly the volume of money. It examined alternative techniques such as direct regulation of the liquidity ratio and direct regulation of advances. Neither was felt to be a suitable tool, and the report concluded that existing techniques remained the most practicable and flexible way to influence the banks. This required a combination of 'balance-sheet pressures' that could be exercised when the floating debt (mainly Treasury bills) was under control and good relations between the authorities and the banks so that requests for restraint were heeded.[29]

Cobbold told Bridges that it was an 'admirable document' and, given its technical nature, 'surprisingly readable'. He then returned to a familiar litany: 'As a matter of history and of guidance for future policy I should like to record my view that it is not only monetary policy (with which this report is concerned) but general economic and financial policy which, as we can now see, should have been more restrictive at an earlier date.'[30] On the appearance of the report, Hall noted in his diary, 'I think it is the biggest advance in monetary policy since the Macmillan Committee in 1932 or whenever it was.'[31] The lustre soon faded, and seven months later Hall was questioning its value. Fforde said that the most that could be said for it was that it did not scare those who received it.[32] Clearly, it did not cause a fright at the Bank because it was written largely by Allen, and not only was it a distillation of the discussions that had been taking place between a handful of senior Bank figures over a period of 18 months, but it also was expressed in Allen's inimitable cautious prose. During this period, the nature of the tools and techniques was questioned frequently, but with the invariable conclusion that the existing arrangements were sufficient and that new controls should be viewed with some scepticism.

Thus, prior to Radcliffe, the Bank believed it knew how to operate monetary policy, although only if others – the government, the banks, and the general public – behaved as they had in the past. But the economic environment was changing, and Cobbold and his senior colleagues were left to hope that their existing approach, supplemented where necessary, ultimately would work. Either that, or there were fundamental flaws in the

[28] 'Monetary Organisation', para. 30.
[29] *Ibid.*, para. 55.
[30] Cobbold to Bridges, 27 June 1956, C40/691.
[31] Cairncross (1991b, p. 69).
[32] Fforde (1992, p. 665).

Bank's understanding of the monetary mechanism. There was little or no explicit discussion of real and nominal rates; it was sometimes implicit. When Cobbold said that he had qualms about a period of prolonged monetary constraint, Bridges retorted, 'I am not sure that I follow how the credit squeeze can have been so very severe if everyone is still able to act as if we were in a strong boom.'[33] Conditions were not as harsh as was read from nominal interest rates: with inflation of around 4½ per cent and a Bank Rate of 5½ per cent, the real interest rate was still very low.

Establishment of the Radcliffe Committee

At the beginning of 1957, the Bank appeared to be more receptive to the idea of a formal enquiry into the monetary system, although not entirely clear why. When he saw Sir Roger Makins, Treasury Joint Permanent Secretary, in January, Cobbold mentioned views that were 'floating around' about a new monetary committee. He went on to say that while, a year ago, the Bank had strongly rejected an enquiry as being premature, 'I personally see some advantage in the near future.'[34] In February, Cobbold spoke to the Chancellor, Peter Thorneycroft, about the matter, and a fortnight later, Makins reported that Thorneycroft had accepted the idea and was to raise it with the Prime Minister.[35] Meanwhile, the *Midland Bank Review* called for a fresh authoritative survey into the financial system, and Boothby was agitating again. Both these appeals cited parallel pressure for a study in the United States, where establishment of the Commission on Money and Credit was announced in November 1957.[36] Questions were also asked in the Commons, but Thorneycroft, knowing that an enquiry was in the offing, made suitably noncommittal replies.[37]

There were three issues that had to be addressed: (1) the remit, (2) the chairman, and (3) the other committee members. Initial thinking in the Bank was that the remit should be fairly broad, giving consideration to public finance and maintaining the internal and external value of the currency.[38] The Treasury was keen to avoid anything that ranged too widely

---

[33] Bridge to Cobbold, 28 June 1956, C40/691.
[34] Governor's diary, 31 January 1957, G3/10.
[35] Governor's diary, 1, 20, and 25 February 1957, G3/10; Committee of Treasury, 6 and 27 March 1957, G8/73.
[36] *Midland Bank Review*, February 1957, pp. 1–3; *The Times*, 28 February 1957, p. 9; Bloomfield (1959, p. 16); Aliber (1972).
[37] HC Deb, 5 March 1957, Vol. 566, cc168–169.
[38] Mynors, 'Draft', 5 February 1957 (sent to Makins, 15 February 1957), G1/131.

over the field of economic policy. Certainly, there could be no prolonged public discussion on fixed and floating exchange rates, and references to 'policy' were deliberately suppressed. The wording finally agreed to was 'to inquire into the working of the monetary and credit system, and to make recommendations'.[39] A suitable chairman was quickly settled on, namely, Lord Radcliffe, a lawyer who already had experience chairing two public inquiries.[40] In April, Thorneycroft announced the establishment of the enquiry, that Radcliffe had consented to serve as chairman, and that the names of the other members would be announced as soon as the appointments had been made.[41]

The interests and backgrounds of these remaining people were carefully balanced. After analysing the composition of the Macmillan Committee, Mynors had concluded that if a body was 'packed with politicians and interested parties it will not produce enough unanimity to command respect'.[42] This should be avoided. Radcliffe, too, was against 'anything suggestive of political background'.[43] The choice of economists was critical because it would be an important determinant of the committee's theoretical leaning. Two were selected: Alec Cairncross and Richard Sayers. Cairncross was professor of applied economics at Glasgow University with considerable experience of government, whereas Sayers was Cassel professor of economics at the London School of Economics. The latter's textbook, *Modern Banking*, was the standard work on the subject.[44] But the names of other economists had been in the frame.[45] Thorneycroft's preference was Lionel Robbins, but this would have created a London School of Economics bias, and in any case, Radcliffe was opposed. Another of Thorneycroft's suggestions was Anthony Crosland, an economics fellow at Oxford. However, Crosland's political ambitions – he had strong socialist tendencies and had been a Labour MP between 1951 and 1955 – counted against him.[46] Some

---

[39] Makins to Mynors, 26 February 1957; Mynors, 'Monetary committee', 1 March 1957, G1/131.

[40] In 1947, Radcliffe was appointed chairman of the Boundary Commission, responsible for dividing British India into India and Pakistan, separating 400 million people along religious lines. The partition was known as the 'Radcliffe line'. See also Heward (1994).

[41] Minutes of Court, 4 April 1957, G4/203; HC Deb, 9 April 1957, Vol. 568 c986.

[42] Mynors, 'Macmillan Committee', 1 February 1957, G1/131.

[43] This view reported in Mynors, 'Monetary committee', 8 April 1957, G1/131.

[44] Sayers (1938).

[45] 'Extract from Mynors's memo 15 February 1957'; Mynors, 'Monetary committee', 1 March 1957; Mynors, 'Monetary committee', 8 April 1957, G1/131.

[46] The suggestion was serious enough for some in the Bank to read Crosland's *The Future of Socialism*; Rootham to Allen, 19 February 1957 and Allen to Cobbold/Mynors, 21 February 1957, ADM12/3.

thought was also given to having three economists, with Shadow Chancellor Harold Wilson proposing David Worswick, a former colleague of his, from Oxford. Hall was worried about having too many economists: 'There is a danger that they will bewilder the remaining members by theological controversies.'[47]

The other appointees were more straightforward. Banking expertise was provided by Sir Oliver Franks, chairman of Lloyds Bank, and Lord Harcourt, a Director of Morgan Grenfell. Business interests were represented by Sir John Woods and Sir Reginald Verdon Smith. Woods, a Director of English Electric and a retired Permanent Secretary at the Board of Trade, told Cobbold, 'I think I ought to have my head examined.'[48] The trades union links were provided by William Jones, president of the National Union of Mineworkers, and George Woodcock, assistant general secretary of the Trades Union Congress (TUC). Robert Armstrong, who had risen quickly to the position of Principal at the Treasury at the age of 27, was secretary. Work began in May, and Radcliffe expected that the enquiry would last for one year.[49]

Ten days after the appointments had been announced, the Governor wrote a long private letter to Radcliffe in which he outlined some 'random' thoughts about the likely work of the Committee.[50] He enclosed extracts from his speeches relating to monetary policy and a copy of Clay's biography of Montagu Norman. Radcliffe confided that the latter would be more interesting reading than the 'austere books on monetary theory' to which he was introducing himself.[51]

The letter itself is an important document that in some ways is more revealing about the Bank's views than the mass of carefully considered submissions and evidence. Cobbold began with some wider observations about economic policy in the light of the need for future investment, the enormous national debt, and the burden of sterling balances. For Cobbold, the most fundamental question was 'how, with a policy of full employment, a strong tendency towards increasing public expenditure on current and capital account, and continuous pressure on wages, any credit or monetary measures can be devised which will prevent the inevitable result'. This might have been outside Radcliffe's remit, but Cobbold was convinced that

[47]   Telegram, Makins to Hall, 1 May 1957, copy in G1/131.
[48]   Woods to Cobbold, 15 April 1957, G1/131.
[49]   HC Deb, 3 May 1957, Vol. 569, c34W; *The Times*, 4 May 1957, p. 6; Mynors, 'Monetary committee', 8 April 1957, G1/131.
[50]   Cobbold to Radcliffe, 13 May 1957, G1/131.
[51]   Radcliffe to Cobbold, 14 May 1957, G1/131.

'unless we can get straight thinking on this problem, I fear that no credit or monetary techniques can help us'. The Governor went on to explain that over the past five years, monetary policy had been 'a conscious mix of technical measures (i.e., Bank Rate, pressure on liquidity ratios, etc.) and "persuasion"'. Unless taken to 'extreme lengths', he averred, technical measures could not do the job alone, whereas persuasion would work only if the technical measures were operating in the same direction.

Cobbold then highlighted two criticisms that had been levelled against recent monetary policy: funding should have been more vigorous, with lower prices for gilt-edged stock, and Bank Rate changes should have been 'better timed and more decisive'. The Governor defended the Bank's policy on the former, observing that experience had shown funding could only be carried out effectively on a rising market. No doubt, Cobbold argued, there was always a point at which the price of gilt-edged stock would be attractive, but 'we have always seen objections, both of morality and expediency, to the "authorities" selling down Government stock'. On Bank Rate, Cobbold did not claim that timing had always been correct, but his personal view was that it would have been 'wrong to try to force the issue by an extremely tough interest-rate policy'. He continued, 'My judgment remains that it was most unlikely to be successful against the general line of Government policy; and that, if by chance it had been effective, it would have led to a repetition of the 1920's and monetary policy would have been written off for another generation.' Moreover, 'the worst service the Bank could have given would have been to encourage undue reliance on monetary controls by themselves.' As to techniques, the present controls (requests and self-denying ordinances) were 'wearing thin' and were 'harmful' to the banking system. He told Radcliffe, 'it is here that we need the help and criticism of the Committee.' He hoped that the Committee would bear in mind three factors that were always on his own mind. First, governments were 'by nature more inflationary than conservatively-run banking systems', and thus anything that made it easier for them to borrow from the banks should be discouraged. Second, the British banking tradition was better suited to co-operation with the authorities than to compulsion. Finally, official influence over bank advances should be sparing. If used for long periods, it was a sign of a more general problem in economic policy, and, Cobbold warned, 'it will either break down or lead to a totalitarian control of the banking system.'

On other issues, the Governor did not want the Committee to delve deeply into relations between the government and the Bank: 'Though there is a mild blow up from time to time, the relationship is pretty smooth and pretty well defined.' Cobbold also felt that links between the Bank and banking system were good, although he cautioned Radcliffe that some banking economists felt that they were inadequately consulted. There would no doubt be calls for more information from the authorities, and the Bank was making some moves towards this. Cobbold did not want to go too far or too fast, adding, 'And Heaven protect us from a monthly "Federal Reserve Bulletin", a duplication of Government Economic Services, and a continuous spate of unreliable statistics and prophecies.' Pronouncements in public had to be made 'circumspectly and rarely' or they would cause more harm than good.

The Governor concluded by expressing his concern about how the evidence might be made available to the public. He hoped that it would be published at the end of the process and not provide a running commentary that might upset the markets. He also wanted an option for giving evidence in secret, explaining that he would find it awkward to talk 'with complete freedom for a 100 per cent published record about Issue Department operations and policy'. However, as the Bank was to discover, Radcliffe was a strong advocate of openness. There had already been some early hints of the chairman's views, and after an informal meeting with him on 15 May, Cobbold noted that the question of secrecy was one of the Committee's main preoccupations.[52] In any case, when Wilson pressed the matter in the Commons, Thorneycroft assured him that a full record of the evidence would be taken and published with the Committee's report.[53] By this time, Radcliffe and his colleagues had started work and were preparing to hear evidence from the first witnesses. We can only speculate on how the insistence on openness might have affected evidence given by reticent witnesses.

The Bank Rate Leak and the Parker Tribunal

More than two years elapsed between appointment of the Radcliffe Committee and the appearance of its report in August 1959. In the meantime, monetary policy continued to operate in much the same way as before. Indeed, had Radcliffe been published in 1957, it is unlikely that the general tone would have differed from that adopted in the report. One specific episode, however, that did have an impact on Radcliffe was the decisive increase in Bank Rate in September 1957. It was a critical decision, the implications of which went far beyond the purely monetary and economic. Allegations

---

[52] Cobbold, Governor's note, 15 May 1957, G1/131.
[53] HC Deb, 28 May 1957, Vol. 571, cc204–5.

of a 'leak' and the subsequent investigation put an unwelcome spotlight on the Bank, the manner in which Bank Rate was set, and the role of the part-time Directors. To this extent, Radcliffe consequently was diverted down a path it might not have followed otherwise.

In the summer of 1957, pressure was mounting on sterling, and reserves fell significantly. The Bank saw three possible remedies: two were familiar, a tougher fiscal stance and further restrictions on the banks; the third, an aggressive use of Bank Rate, was a new development. Since the beginning of 1955, the Governor had lost no opportunity to remind successive Chancellors about the need to keep government spending in check. During the buildup to the September crisis, he again suggested that appropriate fiscal measures were required.[54] While it was 'virtually impossible' to vary or postpone government current expenditure, Thorneycroft was keen to at least hold the level of capital investment to assert control over the money supply.[55]

Unsurprisingly, the further curtailment of advances found little favour in the Bank. In a private note to Thorneycroft, Cobbold argued that 'we have come to the end of what can be done by talking to the banks about advances.'[56] Neither did he consider that the alternatives, such as liquidity or advances ratios, offered much hope. This was entirely consistent with the previous views of the Bank. A new argument was that the recommendations of Radcliffe should not be prejudged. Nonetheless, the Treasury was still keen to pursue the use of more formal powers than hitherto, and the strategy was made explicit when Thorneycroft saw Mynors, together with Franks and David Robarts (chairman of National Provincial), from the Committee of London Clearing Banks (CLCB). While Thorneycroft recognised what had been achieved by voluntary means, he said that he now wanted to impose a limit on bank credit. The bankers were adamant that the policy was both inappropriate and unworkable. Undeterred, Thorneycroft wanted the average level of advances capped, and he warned if the outcome was not satisfactory, he was still prepared to consider introduction of a statutory provision.[57]

---

[54] Cobbold note, 22 August 1957, handed to Makins to show to Thorneycroft; Mynors, 26 August 1957, G1/75; O'Brien to Governor, 'A profits tax', 21 August 1957; Cobbold, unsent draft, 22 August 1957, C42/4.

[55] Mynors, 26 August 1957, record of meeting between Cobbold and Thorneycroft on 22 August 1957, G1/75.

[56] Cobbold, note, 22 August 1957, G1/75.

[57] Compton to Mynors, 10 September 1957, enclosing 'Note of a meeting on 9 September 1957'; 'Note of a meeting ... on 11 September 1957,' G1/75.

Mynors, in what was unquestionably his most important intervention as Deputy Governor, left the Chancellor in no doubt as to the Bank's position. He did not expect that the clearing banks would voluntarily accept a formal limit; moreover, 'it would not serve the purpose you have in view if you were publicly to express a wish to which they felt in honesty bound to demur or indeed to which they found themselves in fact unable to conform.' As to the Chancellor using powers under the 1946 Act, Mynors was unequivocal: 'I feel bound to advise you that I much doubt whether they [the Bank] would think it "necessary in the public interest" to seek your authority for issuing a direction under that Act, by which a formal limit of the kind under discussion was imposed on the clearing and other banks.' Mynors went on to caution against additional legislation because it would raise grave questions about the relationship between the banking system and government. Radcliffe, too, was a factor, but Mynors noted that it was not necessary to plead the existence of that committee as a reason for not pursuing new powers: 'One look at the exchange position is enough.'[58]

By now, Cobbold and his colleagues were increasingly convinced that there should be a sharp increase in Bank Rate, which since February had stood at 5 per cent. Perhaps they had little choice. In August the Governor told the Chancellor that the only remaining monetary policy weapon was 'a drastic increase in Bank Rate either in one move or in quick stages'.[59] The exchange position was the principal worry, and O'Brien conceded that the action might have to be harsher than the domestic situation demanded in order to convince opinion, particularly overseas, 'that we really mean business'.[60] Fforde, newly arrived as an economic adviser, was quickly into his stride advocating a steep rise in Bank Rate as a means of dealing simultaneously with several policy objectives.[61]

The situation was sufficiently frightening. In August the reserves had dropped by $227 million (10 per cent), one of the largest falls on record. During the first two weeks of September, $55 million was spent in support of sterling. When Cobbold returned from holiday in September, he saw Mynors immediately to discuss tactics. The outcome was a note to Thorneycroft warning that unless there was a complete turnaround in the exchanges, consideration should be given to implementing, on 3 October, a sharp increase in Bank Rate. For good measure, Cobbold reiterated that

[58] Mynors to Thorneycroft, 10 September 1957, G1/75.
[59] Cobbold note, 22 August 1957, G1/75.
[60] O'Brien to Mynors, O'Brien, 29 September 1957, G1/75.
[61] Fforde to Mynors, 30 August 1957, G1/75.

legislation in advance of the Radcliffe report would 'get us all into far more trouble than it would get us out of'.[62]

The following days were dramatic. Cobbold met the Chancellor on 15, 16, and 17 September and saw the Prime Minister on the 17th as well. Thorneycroft was due to make a statement on 19 September, and it was agreed that if there was to be a move in Bank Rate, it should come on the same day. Having taken soundings from colleagues, Cobbold's view was that the rate should be increased from 5 to 7 per cent. Clearly, there was unease at the Treasury, within the cabinet, and on the part of the Prime Minister. Treasury officials did not want to go beyond 6 per cent, whereas Macmillan saw no reason for a high Bank Rate at all.[63] However, on 18 September, the government had approved the decision. On 19 September, Bank Rate was raised from 5 to 7 per cent, the biggest jump (in terms of basis points) and the highest level since 1921.[64] The Chancellor told the Commons that the government was determined to maintain the internal and external value of the pound. There was, he said, no remedy for inflation that did not include control of the money supply. Consequently, public-sector investment, rather than rising as planned, would be held at its current level, and the clearing banks had agreed to co-operate in trying to contain the average level of advances. He said that the exceptional rise in Bank Rate was necessary because of heavy speculation against sterling, but, he continued, it was also required to support the measures that he had introduced.[65] In fact, the explanations of this crisis are varied, with problems identified on both the external and domestic fronts. Even though the causes may have been more imagined than real, severe measures were required. The lack of confidence in sterling can be interpreted as a lack of confidence in the domestic economy. The reaction to the increase was one of almost complete surprise: it had come as a 'thunderbolt' according to Cobbold and dominated the front pages of the newspapers. Overseas opinion interpreted the rise as a panic move or a sign that the government was going to tackle the inflation problem.[66]

---

[62] Cobbold to Thorneycroft/Makins, 15 September 1957; full details of events are in Cobbold, 'Bank rate 19th September 1957' and 'Chancellor's statement', same date; 'Notes of discussions – 14–20 September', 24 September 1957, G1/75.

[63] Macmillan (1971, p. 356).

[64] Bank Rate was reduced from 7 to 6½ per cent on 28 April 1921, G15/97. Basis points were not used in this period, and a movement from, say, 5 to 6 per cent would be described as a '1 per cent increase'.

[65] 'Press brief', 19 September 1957, ADM10/22; 'News summary', 20 September 1957, ADM10/22; HMT Press Office, 'Statement by the Chancellor', 19 September 1957, G1/75.

[66] Bridge to Parsons, 20 December 1957, G1/80.

For the Bank, there was a large degree of fallout from the September crisis. The episode did nothing for relations with the Treasury. Thorneycroft was neither able to instruct the clearing banks what to do nor could he force the Bank to act on his behalf. New legislation would merely have inflamed Bank-Treasury relations, and overseas it would have been viewed dimly. No sooner had the Governor, or at least Mynors as his representative, refused to tell the banks what to do than immediately he came back and recommended that Bank Rate should increase by 2 per cent! Thorneycroft wanted to sack Cobbold but then discovered that he did not have the necessary powers.[67] The Treasury solicitor advised that the 1946 Act prevented him from sacking the Governor or the Directors unless they 'went mad, became bankrupt or were convicted of an offence'.[68]

In addition to his frustration with the Bank, Thorneycroft remained unhappy with the monetary situation. Unable to wait for Radcliffe to report, he asked his economic secretary, Nigel Birch, to chair a secret working group to consider 'what steps are required to get effective control of the credit base'.[69] The group consisted of Hall, Compton, and Sir Thomas Padmore, from the Treasury, Mynors and Fforde as the Bank representatives, and Robbins as the external economist. There was some haste. The group first met on the day of the Bank Rate rise, and a draft report was presented to the Chancellor in early October. During the process, the Bank had tried to prevent the group from talking about new means of controlling the banks and the use of statutory powers, but to no avail. Robbins' contribution was wide ranging.[70] The group gave most attention to Robbins's idea for explicitly fixed minimum liquidity ratios, in conjunction with the temporary use of Treasury deposit receipts (TDRs).[71] In fact, the resurrection of TDRs or some other form of special deposit had already been the subject

---

[67] Cairncross (1991b, pp. 126–127).
[68] Padmore to Thorneycroft, 10 September 1957, TNA T233/1664.
[69] Padmore to Mynors, 17 September 1957, enclosing Thorneycroft to Birch, 'Monetary policy', 17 September 1957, G1/78.
[70] Padmore to Mynors, 26 September 1957, enclosing Robbins, 'Notes on the more general aspects of the exercise', 25 September 1957, G1/78. Called 'social' insurance contributions in the document.
[71] The TDR in June 1940 was a wartime expedient that allowed the Treasury to borrow directly from the clearing banks. They largely replaced Treasury bills, and the volume outstanding reached £1,700 million in 1944 but had fallen to zero by 1952. TDRs were not negotiable in the money market, so an increase acted as a squeeze on the banks. When introduced, interest was paid at 1⅛ per cent, slightly above Treasury bill rate, and reflecting the fact that the lending was for six months. See C40/431.

of discussion in the Bank.[72] Although the group came down in favour of Robbins' suggestion for set liquidity ratios and the compulsory holding of what were now termed 'stabilisation bills', the Bank reserved its position on the draft report.[73]

Cobbold clearly was stung by some of Thorneycroft's assertions, and he was prompted to mount a robust defence. He began a long letter to the Chancellor by denying that the Bank had lost control of the money supply; if this was the case, 'they would certainly have got busy about it and not sat and wrung their hands!' On the contrary, he maintained that since the war, control had been progressively regained. He accepted that the control of money could still escape through the 'automatic arrangements under which the Bank of England provides to the market the cash necessary to ensure that Government requirements are fully met'. While the Bank *could* interrupt the arrangements, Cobbold said, it would be 'an extreme and unsatisfactory measure'. He continued, 'in practice it is in the power of the Treasury and no one else to see that its demands for cash are not such as to force an increase in the money supply'. Still worried about the possibility of fresh legislation, Cobbold made three points. First, it would make Britain the only leading democracy where the Treasury, and not the central bank, was able to direct the commercial banks. Second, it would alter the powers and responsibilities of the Bank, a matter that was of 'grave concern' to the Court. Finally, it would give the government the potential to force the banks to lend to themselves. If such powers were ever assumed, then confidence in both the banking system and sterling would be seriously harmed.[74] Thorneycroft conceded, 'I see the force of your view that financing is too automatic to be healthy, and I would like consideration to be given to methods by which a statutory limit might be placed on the amount of Government short-term borrowing.' Conveniently, all this became subsumed within the Bank and Treasury's work on submissions to Radcliffe.[75]

There were other ramifications from the September Bank Rate rise, not so much monetary as procedural. The increase may have struck

---

[72] Niemeyer to Cobbold/Mynors, 15 August 1957; O'Brien to Cobbold, 16 August 1957, C42/4; Fforde (1992, p. 677).

[73] HMT, 'Note of meeting ... 27 September 1957', 30 September 1957; Downie to Mynors, 8 October 1957, enclosing Birch to Thorneycroft, 7 October 1957, G1/78; Fforde (1992, pp. 688–689).

[74] Cobbold to Thorneycroft, 9 October 1957, G1/75.

[75] Thorneycroft to Cobbold, 14 October 1957; Cobbold to Thorneycroft, 15 October 1957, G1/75.

as a 'thunderbolt', but some were seemingly able to avoid it. Prior to the announcement, there was some significant selling, and stories began to circulate in the press that the decision had been leaked in advance.[76] The allegations were serious, particularly if the source was traced to the Bank. Cobbold took soundings and in a personal letter to the Prime Minister asserted that, in his opinion, there was no evidence of any leak or irregularity.[77] That might have been the end of the matter but for politics. Charles Lloyd had reported 'inspired selling' in *The Times*. Although by this Lloyd meant that stockbrokers and jobbers had got it right, Wilson seized on this to mean selling based on inside information.[78] Wilson was persistent in his call for a full inquiry.[79] In the face of mounting pressure, Macmillan eventually relented.[80] Lord Justice Parker was appointed to head the tribunal, which had wide-ranging powers to call witnesses, with the remit to investigate whether there was any justification for the allegations that information about the raising of Bank Rate had been improperly disclosed, and if so, whether the information had been used for private gain. Mynors asked Court members to ascertain whether any businesses with which they had connections had sold stock before the increase was announced. This process brought the names of two part-time Directors to the fore: Lord Kindersley (Managing Director of bankers Lazards) and William Keswick (chairman of the Far East trading house Matheson & Co.).

There was intense public and media interest that threw light on the largely secret world of the Bank and the City. The affair was enlivened by stories of meetings on the grouse moors, conversations on trains, and gossip at cocktail parties. In all, 132 witnesses appeared, and 236 written statements were submitted. From the Bank, Cobbold, Mynors, Bicester, Bolton, Dascombe, and of course, Kindersley and Keswick all appeared in person. Cobbold was to admit subsequently that he found the tone of the proceedings very unpleasant.[81]

The Parker Tribunal report was published on 21 January 1958. It was clear and unconditional in its verdict: 'We have unhesitatingly reached the unanimous conclusion that there is no justification for allegations that information about the raising of the Bank Rate was improperly disclosed to

---

[76] See press cuttings file ADM38/99.
[77] Cobbold to Macmillan, 27 September 1957, G15/1.
[78] Private correspondence with William Clarke, March 2008.
[79] HC Deb, 14 November 1957, Vol. 557, cc1147–1172, 1265.
[80] HC Deb, 12 November 1957, Vol. 577, c766; 14 November 1957, Vol. 577, cc964–969; *Financial Times*, 15 November 1957, pp. 1, 14.
[81] Cobbold to Sir Norman Brook, 10 March 1958, G15/3.

any person.'[82] Kindersley and Keswick were totally exonerated. The former 'conducted himself with complete honesty and propriety'; the latter 'did not, either intentionally or unintentionally, disclose any information that the Bank Rate was about to be raised'.[83] The tribunal recognised that in some circumstances Directors of the Bank, who had other business interests, might find themselves in a difficult and embarrassing situation. However, 'this raises a general and very important question of policy with which we are clearly not concerned.'[84]

Newspapers headline writers found it hard to be original with such unequivocal findings. *The Times* ran with 'No Leak about Bank Rate Rise'; *The Daily Telegraph*, 'Tribunal Says No Bank Rate Leak'. Some managed to avoid the obvious words: the *News Chronicle* had '7% – Everyone Cleared'. Others remained sceptical. Predictably, for the *Tribune*, the tribunal was 'the great whitewash'. The outcome was also widely interpreted as a defeat for the Labour Party, which had been so vociferous in its demands for an inquiry.[85] All that said, the affair had left the Bank looking amateurish.

There was obvious relief at the Bank about the outcome. In a message to staff, Cobbold said that the report had given the Bank 'complete clearance', and he thanked everybody for their support and confidence during what had been 'a very worrying time for all of us'.[86] The new Chancellor, Heathcoat Amory, wrote to Mynors, in Cobbold's absence, reassuring him that the government were fully supportive of the Bank. It was a ringing vote of confidence, perhaps too effusive given the suggestion that the Governor might earlier have been sacked.[87] The only point in the report that required some action concerned the role of part-time Directors. If their position was not a matter for Parker, it was in Radcliffe's purview, and consequently, the Committee was asked by Amory to consider the implications.[88] Two weeks after the report was published, there was a debate in the Commons. It lasted two days, was unedifying, and achieved little. Dascombe, and Hollom from the Bank, went to sit 'in the box' and observe. They were distinctly unimpressed. The opposition lost no opportunity in attacking

---

[82] 'Report of the tribunal appointed to inquire into allegations of improper disclosure of information relating to the raising of Bank rate', January 1958, (Parker), para. 115.
[83] Parker, paras. 57 and 78. Despite Parker's findings, Kindersley's reputation in particular never fully recovered. See Orbell (2004b).
[84] Parker, para. 117.
[85] Press cuttings file ADM38/100–101.
[86] Cobbold, 'Message to staff', 22 January 1958, G15/2.
[87] Amory to Mynors, 10 February 1959, G15/3.
[88] Committee on the Working of the Monetary System, Command 827, para. 778; Amory to Radcliffe, 31 January 1958, G1/131.

the City, leaving Dascombe worried about a future when Labour might be in power.[89]

With not even a hint of scandal in Parker's report, journalists turned to general pieces about the Bank and its future. Members of Court found their portraits reproduced and their backgrounds and business interests closely scrutinised. This treatment ranged from the *Reynolds News* story 'Bank of Eton' to a sober assessment entitled, 'Bank of England', in *The Economist*.[90] The press concentrated on the nature of the part-time Directors, the apparent slowness of the mechanism to change Bank Rate, the relationship between the Bank and the Treasury, and the secrecy of the Bank.[91] Many solutions were proffered, including Professional Directors, greater control for the Treasury, and the provision of enhanced information and statistics by the Bank. These were all issues that were to be addressed by Radcliffe. Academics treated the subject from the perspectives of economics, political science, and sociology, the last examining social backgrounds and connections and revealing school, university, club, and family links among the main protagonists.[92]

Some internal discussion followed on the procedure for deciding and announcing Bank Rate. Cobbold told Mynors, 'I am just not prepared to expose the Bank to the risk of another Enquiry.' The aim was to 'protect the Bank and Directors from frivolous charges and innuendoes on future changes of rate'.[93] Proposals were put to Amory, but he wrote to Cobbold saying that to contemplate a change so soon after the Parker Tribunal might be seen as a 'sign of weakness', and it would 'revive a controversy that is at present quiescent'.[94]

The Governor's first public statement after the affair was widely reported.[95] After noting that the City would be grateful for the way in which Parker had

---

[89]   HC Deb, 3 and 4 February 1958, Vol. 581, cc815–948 and 985–1127. Interview with Sir Jasper Hollom, 17 June 2005; Dascombe, Aide memoire – 'Tribunal', 14 March 1958, G15/3.

[90]   *The Economist,* 25 January 1958; *Reynolds News,* 26 January 1958; also see 'The Bank of England from within', *The Banker* 108(386):162–171, March 1958.

[91]   Rickatson-Hatt to Dascombe, 'Summary of criticism of the Bank arising from tribunal evidence', 6 February 1958, G15/3.

[92]   Devons (1959); Hanham (1959); Wilson and Lupton (1959); a version of the article was also printed in the *Manchester Guardian,* 20 January 1959, p. 6.

[93]   At the beginning of February, the suggestion was Committee of Treasury at 5/5.30 p.m. on Wednesday; Court on Thursday at 9.30 a.m.; no announcement to be made unless there was a change in Bank Rate; any change to be announced on Thursday before 10.00 a.m. Cobbold, Governor's note, 5 February 1958, G14/156.

[94]   Amory to Cobbold, 12 February 1958, G14/156.

[95]   Speech to the annual dinner of the Overseas Bankers Club at Guildhall on 17 February 1958 in G13/1.

refuted the rumour, Cobbold went on to say that in recent weeks, suggesting how the Bank should be run had been 'a popular national pastime' and asking his audience 'for a few minutes perhaps I may play too'. He then made the remark with which he is most associated: 'The Bank of England must be a Bank and not a study-group.' Continuing, he argued, 'The prime requirement must be operational competence. ... With two former economics dons from Oxford on our senior permanent staff, not to mention the Deputy Governor, who may still remember something from his ten years at Cambridge, a charge that the Bank is bereft of professional economic thinking does not bear examination.' This did not wholly convince: 'Two economists for the whole bank!' exclaimed the *Manchester Guardian* the following day.[96] 'Our policy', he continued, 'has been to move gradually in the direction of saying more about what we are doing and giving more background.' As a result of the tribunal, Radcliffe was asked to look at some aspects that it might not otherwise have considered. The Court paid tribute to the fortitude that Cobbold had displayed during the Bank Rate leak episode by presenting him with a replica of the Houblon tankard; appropriately, part of the inscription on the original read, 'in token of his great ability, industry and strict uprightness at a time of extreme difficulty'.[97]

Standards in public life undoubtedly declined in the second half of the twentieth century, and in the early twenty-first century there is a tendency for the public to assume guilt in such cases. This was less likely to be the case in the 1950s, and the verdicts appear to have been generally accepted. Nevertheless, there was strong circumstantial evidence against Kindersley at least. He was on the board of British Match. In 1957, this company held around £250,000 of gilts and had done so for some years through the ups and downs of rate changes. However, it sold them the day before Bank Rate was raised dramatically. The tribunal cleared Kindersley on this point, finding that the sale was not made as a result of his knowledge.[98] For Nigel Althaus, however, a leading gilt broker of the time and later Government Broker, it seemed conclusive, 'they sold that stock and that seemed to me was the absolute clincher, and I think Lord Kindersley was very lucky'.[99]

---

[96] *Manchester Guardian,* 18 February 1958, p. 1. Richard Fry of the *Guardian* apparently also annoyed some friends in the Bank by declaring, 'I see that Maurice Allen has got an assistant'; Fry to Richardson, 25 March 1980, 7A127/1.

[97] Dascombe, 'For record', 27 March 1958, G15/3. The tankard was presented in 1696 to the first Governor, John Houblon. Replicas of the tankard were made in 1924, 1936, 1958, and 1966.

[98] Parker, para. 55.

[99] Interview with Sir Nigel Althaus, 3 October 2006.

Radcliffe: Proceedings

Although Radcliffe had anticipated that work would be completed within a year, by June 1958, he admitted that it might take another year.[100] In October, following a 'gossip' with Armstrong, Mynors noted that 'once the descriptive chapters are over, the Committee cannot think what to say.'[101] When publication finally came, in August 1959, more than two years had elapsed since the announcement of Radcliffe's appointment. During this period, the Committee had held 88 meetings, with formal oral evidence taken at 59. More than 200 witnesses were asked a total of over 13,000 questions, and written evidence received from 71 organisations and 41 individuals was published. The respondents included government departments, overseas central banks, banking and financial institutions, industrial and commercial associations, public corporations, and large industrial concerns. Individuals included former Chancellors, central bankers, businessmen, and economists.[102] While the Committee's proceedings were wide ranging, the focus here is on the Bank and its role in the workings of the monetary system.

The Bank spent a great deal of time on preparation of the evidence. A small working party was established, led by O'Brien, and it included Hollom, Allen, Fforde, and Michael Thornton (Deputy Principal of the Statistics Office).[103] Cobbold and Mynors were also closely involved. The Committee gave a list of 15 topics that it hoped the Bank would deal with in its memoranda. These ranged from general issues such as Bank-government relations and statistics to specific questions about current methods of monetary control and possible changes in technique.[104] There also were informal hints. Sayers privately told Mynors of two areas, the performance of the discount market and greater Bank openness, that the Committee would take seriously. 'And I guess he will prompt them to do so', noted Mynors.[105] By early June, the subjects of the Bank's papers had been finalised. Cobbold and Makins had agreed that there should be no 'party line', but the latter

---

[100] Extract from Mynors note, 10 October 1958, G1/131.
[101] Mynors, 'Radcliffe Committee', 3 October 1958, G1/131.
[102] Radcliffe, 'Report', paras. 1–2 and appendices I and II. In addition to those published, 81 other submissions were received but not reproduced.
[103] 'Report on the chief cashier's office for the year ended 30 September 1957', 28 October 1957, C40/42.
[104] Mynors, 'Radcliffe Committee', 31 May 1957, C40/897; R.C.(57) 3rd, 31 May 1957.
[105] Mynors, 'Radcliffe Committee', 23 May 1957, G1/131.

was anxious to ensure that both sides at least used 'the same history and geography books'.[106]

The Governor was keen that the Bank's memoranda be sent to Radcliffe, if possible, by the end of June.[107] Drafts were circulated internally and to a limited extent externally, and the feedback was largely constructive.[108] Bolton was characteristically forthright. He found the constitution and functions paper 'inadequate and so colourless as to cause suspicion', whereas that on current monetary policy was 'platitudinous and full of portentous solemnities'.[109] In fact, this latter memorandum had proved extremely difficult to put together. Cobbold and Mynors were heavily involved in its editing, the Governor, in particular, making numerous handwritten amendments.[110] This is most evident in paper 12 ('Current Monetary Policy'), which, of all the Bank's submissions, is the one where Cobbold's own thoughts are most strongly imprinted. With the exception of papers 8 ('Monetary System since 1931') and 13 ('Alternative Techniques'), the memoranda all had been forwarded to the Committee by early July.[111]

The memoranda were concerned almost entirely with the domestic monetary system, and external matters were covered to the extent that the position of sterling reacted on domestic problems. The two most important memoranda, both troublesome in preparation, were paper 12 on policy and paper 13 on possible modifications in technique. Subsequently, three more papers were added. Thoughts also were directed towards the formal oral evidence. The burden of that fell on the Governors and the Chief Cashier. The appearances were spread over a two-year period, but the majority occurred in the first six months of the hearings. There was then a six-month gap before Parsons and Bridge appeared with the Treasury during the Committee's discussion of the forward exchange market in June 1958. Then, in November, O'Brien accompanied Government Broker William H. J. de W. Mullens in order to avoid the embarrassment of an agent being questioned about his client's policy. The remainder of the Bank's oral evidence was given in 1959, once in January and on 30 April, which was the final day on which the Committee heard from witnesses.

[106] Cobbold to Makins, 14 May 1957; Makins to Cobbold, 17 May 1957, G1/131.
[107] Extract from Governor's note, 30 May 1957, G1/131.
[108] Hollom, 'General comments on Radcliffe papers', 26 June 1957, C40/898.
[109] Bolton, 'The Radcliffe Committee papers by the Bank of England, comments by Sir George Bolton', 24 June 1957, C40/906.
[110] These various drafts are in C40/918.
[111] Dascombe to Armstrong, 28 June and 4 July 1957, C40/898.

It might have been expected that the oral evidence would offer the opportunity for both the Committee and the witnesses to move away from carefully crafted scripts, but the Bank had made careful preparations to minimise being caught out.[112] More critically, the form of the hearings was predictable. Radcliffe's legal style was to examine the witnesses closely on their papers paragraph by paragraph, so the agenda on the oral evidence was, to a large degree, dictated by the content of the submissions. And, of course, the nature and content of these had been decided, albeit with some guidance, by the Bank.[113] There was some wrangling over the release of confidential information, but Radcliffe made it clear that it was intended that a full record of the evidence would be published.[114]

Cobbold's summary of the Bank's views on monetary policy stressed three points: (1) that the need to raise finance to meet government requirements, allied to the refinancing of maturing debt, had made monetary management difficult, (2) that monetary measures had been successful in containing bank advances, and (3) that the Bank was aware of the cost to the exchequer and to the balance of payments of high interest rates, and thus it had been cautious in the use of Bank Rate (the note was written before September 1957). Then he repeated his familiar point that 'unless carried to extreme and unacceptable lengths', increases in Bank Rate were effective only when there was supporting action by the government elsewhere.

In the debate between proponents of the old and the new orthodoxies, what could be achieved by the Bank through its operations in the money and the gilt-edged markets was a primary concern. What light did the evidence presented to Radcliffe shed on these activities?

As in other markets, the Bank's general objective in the money market was to maintain order. More specifically, it had two aims. One was to smooth the daily fluctuations of receipts and payments between the authorities and the banking system, and the other was to influence the short-term interest rate. These aims were pursued through the sale and purchase of Treasury bills and the provision of assistance to the market, including advances made to the discount houses. New bills were sold through the weekly Treasury bill tender, whereas other transactions were undertaken by the 'Special Buyer', a position analogous to the Government Broker in the gilt-edged market.

---

[112] Cobbold, Governor's note, 19 June 1957, C40/898; 12 dossiers were prepared; see C40/906–910.

[113] Armstrong to Peter Taylor, 16 August, C40/902; 18 November and 17 December 1957, C40/903; Committee on the Working of the Monetary System, 'Minutes of evidence', 1960, appendix.

[114] Radcliffe, 'Evidence', 26 July 1957, questions 750–751.

In this case, the firm involved was the discount house Seccombe, Marshall & Campion.

The working of the discount market during the 1950s and 1960s is well described in the literature.[115] For the Treasury bill tender, the number of Treasury bills to be offered at the Friday tender was announced by the Bank the preceding week. Under an agreement reached in 1934, the tender was underwritten by a syndicated bid from the 12 discount houses that comprised the London Discount Market Association (LDMA). Tenders also were received from the clearing banks, which, as part of the same agreement, did not bid on their own account but only on behalf of customers. Bids were also made by other bankers, brokers, and the Bank itself, again for its customers such as central banks. The completed tender form, which had to be at the Bank by 1 p.m., gave details of the requested date, quantity, denomination, and price of bills. The tenders were opened the same day in the presence of senior Bank officials and a representative from the Treasury. After sorting into price order, an allotment was made on the basis of the highest bidder first. Because the syndicate bid covered the tender, it set the price floor, with anything below that being rejected. Thus the success of the outside bidders depended on their ability to predict the syndicate bid, with the danger that they might have to pay too much for their bills. The average price determined the average percentage rate of discount on the bill, which was below Bank Rate but closely tracked its movements.

The number of bills on offer was largely determined by the needs of the exchequer, although it suited the Bank to create an initial shortage of money, thus providing greater control in daily operations. Assistance to relieve shortages of money in the market took several forms. The first was for the Bank, acting through the special buyer, to purchase Treasury bills. This could be done either from discount houses, thus providing them directly with cash, or from the clearing banks, which then reduced their call on the discount market. Each day the discount houses would try to cover their positions, and if they were unable to find the money required, they had the privilege of being able to borrow from the Bank. In its position as ultimate source of cash, the Bank would never refuse to make loans to the discount houses, although a penal rate of borrowing, Bank Rate, was charged. Houses would adjust their margins accordingly, and by this mechanism the Bank was able to influence the range of short-term interest rates. And the

---

[115] Scammell (1968); Fletcher (1976); 'The London discount market: some historical notes', *BEQB* 7(2):144–156, June 1967; see also King (1936).

Bank need not be passive because it could choose to engineer a situation whereby the market was forced into the Bank to borrow. In cases where there was surplus cash in the system, the Bank was able to mop this up by selling Treasury bills. While the Committee found itself unable to claim that the discount market was indispensable, it accepted that the market performed an important function in smoothing irregularities in the flow of funds within the banking system, and this work was carried out effectively and at minimal cost. Clarke, Principal of the Discount Office, was pleased that the references to the discount houses were 'on the whole favourable'.[116]

The gilt-edged market has been described as 'one of the great markets of the world, if not the greatest' – in terms of liquidity and commissions.[117] Management of the market and use of Bank Rate are together the principal means of executing interest-rate policy, that is, monetary policy. As with many asset markets, this one was highly sensitive to news, and the news that mattered was anything that was likely to affect interest rates and inflation. For the first part of this period, the likelihood is that the state of sterling predominated. Weak sterling raised fears that interest rates would be raised. On the domestic front, the expected path of inflation should be uppermost.[118]

The modern origins of the market lie in the nineteenth century. In the second half of that century, when Bank Rate was used to protect the gold reserve, money-market rates often were below Bank Rate, and the ability of the Bank to raise rates was weak. Some means had to be found to make Bank Rate effective.[119] The market somehow had to be made short of reserves, and these mostly took the form of bankers' balances at the Bank. Techniques were developed to force financial institutions to the discount window of the Bank; it was these techniques that came to be called 'open market operations'.[120] In 1889, when several rises in Bank Rate failed to produce a corresponding rise in market rates, the Bank reinforced the

---

[116] Radcliffe, 'Report', para. 180; Radcliffe, 'Evidence', 11 July 1957, questions 191–272, 16 July 1957, questions 355–361, and 23 January 1958; Discount Office, 'Report for the end of September 1959', C47/64.

[117] See Gordon Pepper, 'An account of analytical techniques developed in the 1960s and 1970s in the gilt-edged market', produced for circulation at 'The old gilt-edged market', witness seminar held at Bank of England, 22 March 2006. www.lombardstreetresearch. com/witness_seminars/2006_gilt-edged.html (accessed 13 November 2009).

[118] For descriptions of gilt-edged market, see Chalmers (1967) and Wormell (1985). Also, Pember and Boyle's 'British Government Securities in the twentieth century' and supplements.

[119] The following paragraphs draw on Capie, Goodhart, and Schnadt (1995).

[120] See King (1936).

borrowing operations by sales of gilt-edged securities. A problem was that the stock exchange market makers to whom the Bank sold these gilts were not reliant on the money market for funds and so approached the Bank for advances to finance their gilt purchases, and the Bank complied. Thus the Bank's sales did not always have the desired impact on bankers' balances or minimum rates. The use of Treasury bills was also growing at the end of the nineteenth century, and after the First World War, they became the main instrument through which the Bank regulated bankers' balances.[121]

Attempts were also made to reduce long-term interest rates. The major attempt had been the conversion of 5% War Loan stock in 1932 to '3½% 1952 or after'. In 1917, £2,553 million had been issued, and at the end of March 1932, there was still £2,100 million outstanding, more than a quarter of the entire national debt and equal in value to half the national income in 1932. The conversion was carried out successfully, and *The Economist* hailed it as a great triumph.[122] Later, Cambridge economist Nicholas Kaldor wrote: 'the new Chancellor … carried out the greatest conversion operation in history … which brought down the whole structure of long-term interest rates.'[123] And so the authorities' belief strengthened that they could influence the structure of interest rates.[124]

Whether they did or not is doubtful.[125] An early analysis argued that the most important explanation lay outside the control of the authorities: the economy was in recession after 1929, so there was a decline in the demand for transaction balances; abandonment of the gold standard in 1931, growing confidence in government, and the knowledge that there was an interest in conversion led to an expectation. This led to a purchase of gilts in anticipation of falling interest rates and capital gains. These all helped to bring about the anticipated outcome. There was also a substantial creation of credit.[126] A more recent statistical analysis shows that the bill rate was explained most easily by exchange-rate policy. And there is little evidence that the conversion brought about a dramatic fall in the consol yield.[127] At any rate, from our narrower perspective, the episode is, in the words of Sayers, 'illuminating on the ways of the Bank: its

---

[121] Sayers (1976, p. 55).
[122] *The Economist*, 20 August, 1932, p. 339.
[123] Kaldor (1982, p. 1).
[124] It also might help to explain why a favoured practice in the 1950s was conversion, perhaps also because there were still a majority of private holders.
[125] See, for example. Howson (1975).
[126] Nevin (1955).
[127] For a full discussion, see Capie, Mills, and Wood (1986).

determined exercise of all the power derived from its position in financial markets'.[128]

After the Second World War, bill operations with the discount houses became the main channel through which the Bank acted on the reserves of the banking system. Other pressures on interest rates could be applied, and the authorities' ability to support the gilt market was strengthened by virtue of the increased size of the departmental funds.[129] The low-interest-rate policy of the 1930s was pursued in the post-1945 era with even greater vigour. In the 1950s, the gilt-edged market was made up of the Bank, jobbers, money brokers, and stockbrokers. The market was in two parts: the primary market, where new stock was issued and subscribed, and the secondary market, where existing stock was traded. The Bank, acting as agent for the government, issued (through its Issue Department) new stocks to the market through the Government Broker – the firm of Mullens and Co. Most commonly, the Bank would place a new issue on the market at a price of its choosing and buy in any unsubscribed stock through its Banking Department. Thereafter, it would sell the stock slowly in tranches according to demand, that is, through the tap. In 1957, there were about 20 jobbers in the gilt-edged market,[130] but there were only three or four jobbers who mattered in the primary market.[131] On the other side, there were three stockbrokers who acted as money brokers, lending either stocks or money to the jobbers as required. The supply of gilts to the market came primarily from the government's financing requirement.

The essential characteristics of the market were easy marketability, accommodating very large amounts, and prompt delivery and payment. In the middle of the 1950s, the gilt-edged market had a total nominal value of approximately £20 billion.[132] Clearly, one of the main features of gilt-edged stock is that there is a high degree of security attaching to it because the good name of the British government was behind it. The reactivation of monetary policy at the beginning of the 1950s brought quite sharp rises in interest rates and meant a concomitant fall in the price of stock. Investors then had reservations on the wisdom of holding these stocks, and that was a reason for keeping the market stable that dominated after 1950. Avoiding too much fluctuation in interest rates became a central concern of the authorities. There is, though, a conflict with controlling money supply. The

---

[128] Sayers (1976, p. 431).
[129] See Chalmers (1968).
[130] Radcliffe, 'Evidence', 27 November 1958, question 11921.
[131] Pepper, 'Analytical techniques'.
[132] See Goodhart (1973) for 1957–58, and Revell (1966, p. 72).

principal long-term objective for debt management was to ensure that the exchequer could get all the finance it needed, so reducing or, better still, obviating the need to borrow from the banks and thus avoiding inflationary pressures. One of the skills of the Bank was in designing the right size of gilt issue, although this included the likelihood of holding some and releasing them when market conditions were more favourable – what was called the 'tap'. The tap became the principal means of issuing in the 1960s when the intention was to signal to the market that there would be stock available for the foreseeable future.[133]

The written and oral evidence taken by Radcliffe presented the definitive official public view of policy in the gilt-edged market during the 1950s. The Governor made a long statement about the Issue Department in which he said that the general objective was to 'maintain an orderly market in gilt-edged securities, sometimes by providing a market or meeting a demand for a particular stock, and sometimes by ironing out what seems an unreasonable fluctuation'. Occasionally, it might be necessary to intervene in order 'to give a lead or to steady the market, but it is no part of the general Issue Department policy to resist a definite trend of markets in one direction or the other'. Cobbold said that they would sell at firm or rising prices but would not force sales on a weak or declining market. Under the latter conditions, buyers would be scarce, and Cobbold was adamant that it would be a mistake to lower prices to attract them: 'The price might be a long way down, much damage might be done on the way to markets and to confidence at home and abroad (I need not remind you how closely the exchange markets and the gilt-edged market watch each other) and in the end buyers might be few and shy if they felt that a repetition of this process was likely.'[134] He then went on to stress the importance of expectations in the market: as the Committee was to note in its report, it was a view that dominated the thinking of the authorities.

The subject was discussed in greater detail when the Government Broker and O'Brien appeared before the Committee in November 1958. Tactics had changed slightly by this time. O'Brien began by saying that the policy previously set out by the Governor had been maintained, but with the significant caveat that on a rising market, 'restraint may have been more

---

[133] Part of the mechanism was the Bank granting the use of 'Z' accounts providing facilities to jobbers for same-day transacting in stocks rather than the three-day cycle. For details, see Cooke to Page/Fforde/O'Brien/Hollom, '"Z" Accounts', 28 January 1972, enc., 'Gilt-edged stocks: certifiable balance facilities and stock lending', 5A135/1.

[134] Radcliffe, 'Evidence', 25 October 1957, question 1762.

consciously exercised than in some earlier periods.'[135] He emphasised, however, that the Bank was not aiming at any particular range of rates. Given the sensitive nature of gilt-edged operations, this session was potentially very awkward: the Government Broker was suitably coy, giving short and guarded answers, whereas O'Brien was not entirely happy with one of his own answers. Nonetheless, Cobbold thought that both had performed very well. The change in stance was reiterated during the Governor's final summing up before the Committee in April 1959.[136]

A key concern of Radcliffe was the relationship between the Bank and the Treasury, the division of responsibilities for policy and operational matters, and questions about the statutory powers and constitution of the Bank. Cobbold emphasised that the principal relationship was, and had been for centuries, that of banker and customer: 'The Bank holds at the Treasury's disposal its banking services and its advice over the wide range of financial problems with which the Treasury deals.' Then Cobbold described the responsibilities of the Bank and the Treasury in domestic monetary policy:

The Bank have the first responsibility for the management of the money market, including the fixing of Bank Rate and the management of the Issue Department securities. By statute this responsibility lies with the Bank unless they are given directions by the Treasury: in practice, in recent times both before and since the Bank Act, it has been the policy of the Bank to accept this responsibility but to consult, and in the last resort to defer to, the Government. At the same time many decisions which directly affect the management of money (e.g., Government borrowing and debt management, the finance of public bodies and local authorities, control of hire purchase terms) are the direct responsibility of the Government. In these circumstances it is clear that the Treasury and the Bank must act (as in fact they do) in the closest consultation and in absolute confidence.

In some areas, for example, the Exchange Equalisation Account (EEA) and exchange control, the Bank was purely an agent, and policy was made by the Treasury, although, again, there was close consultation. Cobbold explained that this represented the general picture and that in many instances it was difficult to say exactly where an idea or an initiative had originated.[137]

Makins said that in most cases the ultimate decisions rested with the Treasury.[138] Sayers and Radcliffe were interested in which view would prevail in the event that the Bank and Treasury disagreed about making a direction to the commercial banks and whether additional powers then might

---

[135] *Ibid.*, 27 November 1958, question 11919.
[136] *Ibid.*, 30 April 1959, question 13416.
[137] *Ibid.*, 11 July 1957, question 260.
[138] *Ibid.*, 10 September 1957, question 974.

be required by the Treasury. The Permanent Secretary refused to be drawn. Although he was correct in saying that no direction had ever been issued, it was only the previous month when the Bank had refused the Chancellor's instruction to tell the banks to cut their advances.

More than a dozen other witnesses expressed views on the relationship between the Bank and the Treasury. Most dissatisfaction, unsurprisingly, came from voices on the left. The TUC wanted to see a greater measure of control over the Bank, and economist Thomas Balogh envisaged significant reforms. Balogh, a close adviser to Wilson, proposed that a senior Treasury official should be made chairman of the Court, with the Governor as a member only, and there should be a vigorous exchange of staff. 'The Bank', he argued, 'must regard itself as a part of the central government machinery.'[139] The Committee also took evidence from former Chancellors Butler, Dalton, Gaitskell, and Thorneycroft without consulting the Treasury, much to the latter's annoyance.[140] Ten questions were sent in advance on the subject of Bank-Treasury relations.[141] Butler, Dalton, and Gaitskell saw no case for Bank independence, although Butler preferred to speak of 'partnership' rather than the Bank being an instrument of government. Thorneycroft favoured an institution that was 'largely independent', and he was against any novel reconstitution of the Bank: 'In particular it would be wrong to turn it into what was virtually a Department of the Treasury.' Edward Bridges, a former Treasury Permanent Secretary, noted that monetary policy was likely to continue to provoke controversy and was bound to affect the statutory relationship between the government and the Bank. Consequently, he could see 'no prospect of success for any scheme which would confer autonomy on the Bank of England', but this was not to say that it could have no authority of its own.[142]

Cobbold made a further, and more expansive, statement to the Committee in January 1959, speaking in the light of public criticisms made after the Bank Rate tribunal. He argued that in a country with private enterprise and a market economy, direct control of the central bank by the Treasury would be a 'major weakness', and where, as in the United Kingdom, there was a reliance on international trade, it could be a 'disaster'. He was certain that it would be a mistake to blur the boundaries between the two

---

[139] Thomas Balogh, 'Memorandum of evidence submitted by Mr. Thomas Balogh', August 1958, paras. 14–17; Radcliffe, 'Memoranda', Vol. 3.
[140] 'Extract from DG's memo, 12 September 1958 ...', C40/922.
[141] Radcliffe, 'Evidence', p. 846.
[142] Bridges, Untitled memoranda, 30 December 1958; Radcliffe, 'Memoranda', Vol. 3, pp. 47–48.

institutions, although arguments could be advanced about precisely where these boundaries lay. 'But the fundamental question', he concluded, 'is whether the central bank should be a separate entity, albeit the servant of the Government of the day, or a sub-department of the Treasury. I hold that, in present and foreseeable economic conditions in the Western world, the former is undoubtedly right.'[143] The evidence to Radcliffe on this question presented widespread agreement that government held ultimate primacy over monetary policy but that the Bank had a particular role to play in the day-to-day management of monetary matters. Between these two positions lay diverse views about the freedom and responsibilities of the Bank and the Treasury.

In the aftermath of the tribunal, Radcliffe was specifically asked to consider the role of part-time Directors.[144] Hambro, Hanbury-Williams, and Roberts, part-timers and all members of the Committee of Treasury, argued that potential conflicts of interest were 'greatly exaggerated', rare, and easy to avoid.[145] In January 1959, Cobbold made a formal statement about the statutory position and organisation of the Bank that was explicit about the benefits of the part-time Directors; they were, he said, 'fundamental to the existence, the standing and the efficiency of the central bank as a separate entity'.[146] Several witnesses thought that one or two economists would be beneficial, but Thorneycroft worried that it could ally the Bank with a particular school of economic thought.[147] Nobody mentioned that Keynes had been a part-time Director from 1941 to 1946. Representatives of other central banks also presented evidence on the constitution and the division of responsibility between the monetary authorities and the executive, the methods of monetary control, the status and appointment of the governing body, the provision of statistics and reports, and the working of the sterling area arrangements.[148]

---

[143] Radcliffe, 'Evidence', 15 January 1959, question 12813.

[144] Radcliffe, 'Evidence', 11 July 1957, questions 249–253.

[145] 'Part-time Directors (memorandum submitted by the part-time Directors)', 12 June 1958; Radcliffe, 'Memoranda', Vol. 1, pp. 44–45; Radcliffe, 'Evidence', 27 November 1958, especially questions 12159–12185; Brand, 'I did not agree with one or two of my partners who told the Parker Tribunal that it was very difficult', 16 October 1958, question 10729.

[146] Radcliffe, 'Evidence', 15 January 1958, question 12813.

[147] Radcliffe, 'Evidence', 24 October 1958, questions 11294–11299; Gaitskell and Brand favoured economists.

[148] Cobbold, Governor's note, 6 January 1958; Radcliffe to Cobbold, 29 January 1958; Cobbold to Radcliffe, 30 January 1958; Armstrong to DC Ingram, 6 March 1958; Radcliffe to Cobbold, 2 July 1958, C40/899; Radcliffe, 'Memoranda', Vol. 1, pp. 245–308; Radcliffe, 'Evidence', 13 June 1958 (de Kock), 19 and 27 June 1958 (Riefler), 21 November 1958 (Holtrop).

The need for better provision of statistics was a key recommendation in the final report. The clamour for better data was nothing new, similar sentiments having been expressed by the Macmillan Committee.[149] The issue was also pressed by several bank and academic economists and raised wider questions about the adequacy of the Bank's *Annual Report,* its public relations, its openness, and its links with the economics profession. Harry Johnson felt that a greater interchange of ideas and staff between the Bank and professional economists would be an advantage, confessing to Radcliffe that 'talking to bankers is an experiment rather than a habit'.[150]

Cobbold preferred that statistical material should be published mainly by the government, although the Bank would help where it could.[151] But there were worries about both the immediate and the longer-term implications of Radcliffe in terms of the release of sensitive information and the dangers of creating an unwelcome precedent.[152] One instance was the market holdings of Treasury bills. Although Cobbold sent Radcliffe the required figures in broad terms, he said that he would only be prepared to show the Committee the holdings of the Banking Department on a confidential basis. Radcliffe suggested that further consideration be given to devising a statement that was both suitable for publication and not against the public interest, and that was agreed.[153] O'Brien suggested that 'we should be wise to take a stand against them only where we are on really firm ground.'[154]

The Bank's memoranda had been prepared, submitted, and subjected to oral questioning by the Committee in little more than a six-month period. It was then another 20 months before the report was published. Although much happened in the intervening period, Radcliffe posed remarkably few additional questions, and in the case of the special deposits scheme announced in July 1958, the Committee did not raise the matter with the Bank at all. Neither did the passage of time cause the Governor and his colleagues to modify their views. Speaking on the final day of oral evidence,

---

[149] CSO, 'Financial and economic statistics relating to the monetary system', June 1958; Radcliffe, 'Memoranda', Vol. 1, pp. 141–162; NIESR, 'The improvement of financial and monetary statistics', June 1958, 'Memoranda', Vol. 3, pp. 1–27.

[150] Harry Johnson, 'Memorandum of evidence submitted by Professor H. G. Johnson', April 1958, para. 9, Radcliffe, 'Memoranda', Vol. 3; Radcliffe, 'Evidence', 7 October 1958, question 10607. Johnson was Professor of economics at the LSE.

[151] Radcliffe, 'Evidence', 26 July 1957, question 753.

[152] O'Brien to Hawker/Cobbold/Mynors, 'Figures for the Radcliffe Committee', 23 May 1957, C40/907.

[153] Cobbold to Radcliffe, 25 July 1957; Radcliffe to Cobbold, 30 July 1957, C40/907; Cobbold to Radcliffe, 13 August 1957, C40/907

[154] O'Brien to Mynors, 11 September 1957, C40/909.

Cobbold stated, 'Had the papers been written in 1959 instead of 1957, the emphasis might therefore not have been quite the same; but I do not think that we should have wished to amend the general tenor of our evidence.'[155]

Radcliffe: Findings and Recommendations

The Committee's report was published in August 1959; the minutes of evidence and three volumes of supporting memoranda appeared in the following year. The report was a mixture of narrative, analysis, and prescription, and it is difficult to summarise. It was a most detailed and exhaustive description of the British monetary system. There were complaints that too many of its conclusions did not rest on rigorous examination of data. The Committee deliberately eschewed the usual summary of recommendations, arguing that that this 'would not do justice to the ideas which we wish to convey and in some cases would need to be stated with so much fullness and subject to so many qualifications that we should virtually be writing parts of some of the chapters over again'.[156] Thus the recommendations are to be found scattered throughout the body of the report. At least 60 specific points can be identified, although the difference between a proposal, an observation, and a suggestion is not always apparent. It was the section of the report on statistics written by Cairncross that contained the greatest number of identifiable recommendations.[157]

The report highlighted five main ideas that the Committee believed had emerged.[158] First, there were the unavoidable limitations caused by the complexity of aims in economic policy and the partial effectiveness of monetary measures. Second, the 'state of liquidity of the whole economy' was more important than the 'supply of money'. Third, monetary policy had to exert its influence through the structure of interest rates, and this could be achieved through management of the national debt. It was an instrument of 'singular potency' and something that Radcliffe felt was 'the fundamental domestic task' of the central bank. The authorities could not be neutral on this point: 'They must have and must consciously exercise a positive policy about interest rates, long as well as short, and about the relationship between them.'[159] Fourth, there should be no 'fixed order of

---

[155] Radcliffe, 'Evidence', 30 April 1959, question 13416.
[156] Radcliffe, 'Report', para. 978.
[157] *Ibid.*, para. 796.
[158] *Ibid.*, para. 980–985.
[159] *Ibid.*, para. 982. Similar views in the United States went under the name of 'Operation Twist'.

preferences' in the use of monetary tools. Aside from interest rates and prescribed ratios, the Committee thought that, in normal economic circumstances, there were only three other monetary regulators that deserved serious attention: control of international capital movements, control of hire-purchase terms, albeit used only sparingly, and control over lending by other financial institutions. Finally, the country's external assets and liabilities were an integral part of the economic and financial system, and their movements were not a separate set of problems but a different aspect of the total problem.

As far as the crucial issue of debt management was concerned, the report made three principal observations. Most critically, Radcliffe contested the Bank's argument that the demand for gilts could not be stimulated by dropping prices. It considered that expectations, which the Bank saw as being central to market behaviour, were over-rated. The Committee also found that the attitude of the authorities towards long-term interest rates had been 'entirely passive, indeed fatalistic'.[160] On the specific mechanics of new issues, Radcliffe disliked the practice of announcing that an issue had been fully subscribed when in fact unsold securities were taken up by the Issue Department for later sale. The announcement, said Radcliffe, 'is universally known to be a form without substance'.[161] Finally, the report bemoaned the fact that no statistics relating to transactions in the market were available. It sought quarterly data to be supplemented by publication of a Bank commentary on the previous year.[162]

Announcing that new government issues had been fully subscribed was something that arose immediately because a conversion operation was due to be completed at the time of the report's release. O'Brien thought that 'but for an occasional jibe', the current formula was 'of long standing and being generally understood as accepted'. He felt that Radcliffe had under-rated the advantages of not revealing how much had been taken up by the Issue Department, adding that the process of funding was difficult enough without 'announcing to the world the exact magnitude of the task'.[163] Hawker was unequivocal: 'I could not feel more strongly about this.' The Committee, he said, 'have no experience of markets; otherwise they would not have made the comments they have. Let us stick to custom.'[164] In the event, it was

---

[160] *Ibid.*, paras. 551–553, 563.
[161] *Ibid.*, paras. 578–580.
[162] *Ibid.*, para. 582.
[163] O'Brien to Hawker/Governors, 'Government loan operation', 5 August 1959, C40/475.
[164] Hawker annotation on O'Brien to Hawker/Governors, 'Government loan operation', 5 August 1959, C40/475.

decided, with agreement of the Treasury, that it would be unwise to make any change so close to the issue of the report. The question was again raised with the Treasury in October, when it was decided that the public interest would not be served by providing more detail about the subscription of stock. A new form of wording for announcements was agreed, although it still gave nothing away.[165]

While the market knew perfectly well that the Issue Department played a major part in these operations, there was no accurate idea of the scale. Monitoring of press and market gossip by the Bank indicated that speculation could be very wide of the mark, usually underestimating the amount of stock taken up by the Issue Department. The market 'would be thunderstruck', O'Brien told William Armstrong, 'to learn that the most we ever get from public subscription is about £30 million'.[166] Typically, it was less than 10 per cent of the issue.

On the contentious issue of selling gilts, the attitude at the Bank was unequivocal. In November 1959, when considering the maturities due in February and March 1960, O'Brien wondered whether it would be worth experimenting with a more attractive offer to the public. The Bank's view was clear: 'We did not accept in evidence, and still do not accept, the view of the Radcliffe Committee that the way to sell gilt-edged is to put prices down until the resulting yield attracts sufficient buyers.' Although O'Brien conceded that there might have been some truth in this, he feared the consequent and lasting damage to the market that such 'arbitrary action' would cause.[167] Nonetheless, a 'small bow' towards the Committee was a possibility. It was not evident during the next issue, the third tranche of 4½% Conversion 1964, in January 1960 when Hollom wrote that there was no scope for Radcliffe-style pricing below the market.[168]

Of the findings and recommendations of the report that related specifically to the Bank, three main issues were addressed: Bank-Treasury relations, the part-time Directors, and the gathering and dissemination of information. The Committee did not accept that the Bank should be completely independent from political influence, but neither should it be regarded as a 'rather exceptional government department'. Since 1946, it was observed, both sides had attempted to evolve an allocation of functions that recognised that the will of the government was paramount while

[165] O'Brien to Armstrong, 1 October 1959; Armstrong to O'Brien, 20 October 1959; O'Brien to Armstrong, 11 November 1959; Armstrong to Hollom, 28 January 1960, C40/627.
[166] O'Brien to Armstrong, 1 October 1959, C40/627.
[167] O'Brien to Hawker/Cobbold/Mynors, 'The next maturities', 19 November 1959, C40/483.
[168] Hollom to Hawker/Cobbold/Mynors, 22 January 1960, C40/484.

accepting at the same time the advantages of the Bank as a separate organisation that had 'a life of its own, capable of generating advice, views and proposals that are something more than a mere implementation of its superiors' instructions'. For Radcliffe, the function of the central bank was to act as 'a highly skilled executant in the monetary field of the current economic policy of the central government'. This being so, the problem was then to ensure that the exchanges between the two bodies were properly organised. To this end, there were two recommendations. In the Committee's view, the true responsibility for fixing Bank Rate lay with the Chancellor and not the Bank. It therefore would be preferable if the announcement of a change was made explicitly in the name of the Chancellor and on his authority.[169] Radcliffe was also concerned to secure in the relations between the Bank and the Treasury arrangements to ensure that changes in monetary policy took sufficient account of wider economic policy, and vice versa. Thus it was recommended that a standing committee be established with the remit of reviewing and advising the authorities on all matters relating to the co-ordination of monetary policy. The Chancellor and the economic secretary to the Treasury would be, respectively, chairman and Deputy, with the remaining membership consisting of the Governor, Deputy Governor, and officials from the Treasury, Bank, and the Board of Trade.[170] Radcliffe did not envisage that this would mean a reduction in the Bank's influence over policymaking, but it was recognition of the fact that monetary policy had become inextricably linked with wider issues, such as fiscal operations and debt management.[171]

The report included Radcliffe's thoughts on the subject of part-time Directors. Suggestions that either the post be abolished and replaced by full-time executives or that membership of the Court should be closed to those whose businesses operated in the money or capital markets were both rejected. In the Committee's opinion, there were clear advantages in retaining the office of part-time Director. Moreover, the changes that were proposed, particularly in terms of setting Bank Rate, would reassure the public that the part-time Directors would not be exposed to any future embarrassment because of their position.[172]

Clearly, the Bank had an important role to play in both the compilation and publication of statistics.[173] Radcliffe also thought that the authorities

---

[169] Radcliffe, 'Report', para. 771.
[170] *Ibid.*, paras. 773–774.
[171] *Ibid.*, para. 775.
[172] *Ibid.*, paras. 778–787.
[173] *Ibid.*, paras. 812, 817–821.

should make more regular comments on monetary and financial affairs. While it was appreciated that it might be awkward for the Bank to speak publicly, the report argued that this should not prevent the Bank from using its *Annual Report* 'to illuminate the problems of monetary management which confront the authorities'. The Committee wanted to see greater coverage given to topics such as the evolution of exchange control, movements in commercial credit, and fluctuations in business liquidity and the gilt-edged market. If the treatment of these were to go beyond the scope of the *Annual Report,* then two solutions were proposed – either the preparation of short monographs containing signed articles or, alternatively, the production of a quarterly bulletin. The purpose of the bulletin would not be to promote greater discussion about the workings of the monetary system – there was already an ample range of technical journals in existence – but to give opportunities for 'fuller and freer exposition by members of the staff of the Bank of issues which they are in a unique position to discuss'. Allied with this was the Committee's desire for a strengthening of research and intelligence within the Bank. There was a case for some interchange of staff with the Treasury, and another possibility was that academic economists could be recruited for limited periods in order to help with specific pieces of research.[174] Another recommendation was that the Head of the Bank's Economic Intelligence Department should have the rank of an Executive Director, something that would signify the greater weight attached to this field.[175] In general, Radcliffe sanctioned the prevailing monetary techniques and suggested that these could be improved with better statistics and a greater use of professional economists and economic research. The Committee proved no better than others in demonstrating the boundaries between the Bank and Treasury.

Reaction and Response

The report was published in August. In more recent times, it might have been suspected that the middle of the holiday period and a Parliamentary recess was a good time to hide something, but public trust at that point was not quite so badly damaged as it later became, and nothing sinister was (or should be) read into the publication date. The report had been widely anticipated, and speculation as to its content abounded. 'Bank of England May Have to Lift Veil of Secrecy' ran a headline indicative of the general

---

[174] *Ibid.,* para. 863.
[175] *Ibid.,* para. 777.

tone.[176] It was not exactly clear what the report was suggesting in terms of the execution of monetary policy, and there were some complaints that the Committee had declined to provide a summary of recommendations. As Charles Goodhart expressed it much later, 'None of these commentators seemed able to extract from the Report a clear, structured and workable account of how monetary policy could or should operate in the British monetary system; instead they produced a long list of doubts and loose ends.'[177]

There continues to be disagreement over the significance or influence of the report. Within hours of its publication, Lord Robbins was writing, 'It will be regarded as a document of historic importance' and one entitled to 'an outstanding place in the great series of reports which have moulded our financial tradition'.[178] Some six months later he told an audience at the University of Rome that Radcliffe 'would take its place as one of the most important publications of its kind in the long course of British monetary history'.[179] More than 25 years later, monetary economists were still describing it as 'extremely influential'.[180] Its significance for us lies first in its description of the working of the system and the basis for monetary policy that it set out and then in how the Bank changed or did not change its behaviour.

The general view in the press was that the report was extremely important, even 'epoch making'. And there was a common feeling that it was giving the City a kick, as a headline in the left-wing *Tribune* made explicit: 'A Swift Kick in the Striped Pants – Official.' The *Tribune* might have been expected to take this line, and it concluded that 'the shackles of tradition and outworn theory have been discarded … [and] The City of London will never be quite the same again'.[181] The left-inclined *Reynolds News* was equally approving, claiming that the report had 'blessed a whole batch of policies long urged by Labour spokesmen'.[182] Nicholas Davenport, writing in *The Spectator* in an article entitled, 'The Old Lady Snubbed', wrote, 'The outstanding feature of the Report is, I think, that it puts monetary measures and their managers in their places.'[183] But there were similar kinds of views to be found at the

---

[176] *Yorkshire Post*, 15 August 1959, p. 1. Further press cuttings are in ADM38/103–104.
[177] Goodhart (2004, p. 1074).
[178] *Financial Times*, 21 August 1959, p. 8.
[179] Robbins (1971b, p. 90).
[180] Allsopp and Mayes (1985).
[181] *Tribune* 21 August 1959, pp. 1, 9.
[182] *Reynolds News*, 23 August 1959, p. 4.
[183] *The Spectator*, 28 August 1959, p. 282.

other end of the spectrum. *The Daily Telegraph* had it: 'Put at its bluntest, the Radcliffe Report on the working of our monetary system is a blitzkrieg on the City.'[184]

Immediate reaction focussed on a few common aspects that are understandable in the context of the time. One was greater openness. For a long time there had been a deep suspicion surrounding the mystery, as it was seen, of the City in general and the Bank in particular. This reached something of a climax in the Bank Rate tribunal. Therefore, what the report had to say about how the business of the Bank and the City was conducted was welcomed, and by some reckoning, the most important achievement of the report was to create and spread understanding of how the monetary system worked. Most parts of the press picked up immediately on the idea of the new standing committee to co-ordinate monetary policy and the suggestions on the mechanism for changing Bank Rate. This also touched a nerve. There had long been the feeling that the autonomy enjoyed by the Bank in setting interest rates before the war had hardly been changed by nationalisation and that this was now the moment to achieve this. Much of the commentary thus focussed on the question of Bank Rate.

However, on what came to be seen as the report's central message on monetary policy, that it was the 'whole liquidity position' of the economy and not the money supply that required attention, there was less discussion. Perhaps this was so because there was limited understanding. It was this proposition on liquidity that came to be regarded as contentious at least and, for many, the basic defect of the report, but there was little criticism on this in the immediate press reaction. Economist Frank Paish did address it. He wrote:

The best word I can find for what I think they mean is 'unsqueezability'. ... The wider is the distribution of assets, and therefore of creditworthiness, and the more perfect the organization of the capital market, the more difficult it is to prevent people getting hold of money and using it as they want to. ... The right of the discount market to borrow unlimited amounts of money from the Bank of England has made it impossible for the Bank to prevent the discount houses, and through them the clearing banks, from obtaining as much cash as they want; all the Bank can do is to make it more expensive to turn non-cash assets into cash by raising [the] Bank Rate. Since the immense rise in the size of the government redeemable debt, this power of obliging the authorities to convert non-money assets into money has been extended from the discount market to the general public. ... In these circumstances, any attempt by the Government to limit the use of money by the public by making it generally scarce results merely in the attempted squeeze

---

[184] *The Daily Telegraph*, 20 August 1959, pp. 18–19.

being passed straight back to the Government; and, apart from physical controls, the Government's only defence is to offer sufficiently high interest rates to induce other existing borrowers to cut down their demands or holders of idle balances to release them.[185]

Economists continued to debate Radcliffe for many years, and even now use it as a source of explanation for the poor performance of policy in the 1960s.[186] But how was the report received by the economics profession at the time of publication?[187] The two economists on the Committee, Sayers and Cairncross, are usually referred to as belonging to Keynes' circle at Cambridge in the 1930s, although some say that Sayers was closer to Dennis Robertson.[188] Their views are clearly dominant in the report. Indeed, Cairncross said later that Sayers had written the two-thirds that had to do with money and that he, himself, had attended to loose ends.[189] Given that the approach of the report was regarded as the 'new orthodoxy', the gathering together of recently developing trends in war and post-war practices and ideas, it is perhaps not surprising that voices in support were less often heard or were more muted. It was those who felt that they were being dismissed or attacked who were more vocal.

Apart from Robbins, who had been a candidate for membership of the Committee, an important witness, and a commentator in both press and Parliament, there were many other economists who made their views known after publication of the report. Two who had been witnesses were Christopher Dow and Sir Roy Harrod. Dow, at that time Deputy Director of the National Institute of Economic and Social Research (NIESR) and later to become Executive Director for economics at the Bank in the 1970s, focussed on monetary policy. He was critical of Radcliffe's confusion over liquidity and of the suggestion that attention be moved from bank deposits to advances.[190] Harrod, an economist at Nuffield College, Oxford, was close to the Bank, often offering informal advice and lunching with senior staff. His immediate reaction was that Radcliffe lacked a theoretical framework. At greater length later in the year he took exception to the downplaying of money, 'the foundation stone of British monetary theory', replacing it with the 'whole liquidity position'. The report was profoundly sceptical about the potency of

---

[185] Paish (1959, p. 593).
[186] See, for example, Batini and Nelson (2005).
[187] For a detailed and dispassionate reaction, see Alford and Rose (1959).
[188] Cairncross (1999, p. 4).
[189] Cairncross (1991a).
[190] *Manchester Guardian*, 20 August 1959, p. 2.

monetary policy, and Harrod felt that it was too confused to derive any help from it.[191]

There were many early expressions of doubt over the unanimity that was a proudly claimed virtue by the Committee. Given that two economists are supposed to produce three views, how could two economists, a lawyer, a banker, a trade union official, etc. arrive at only one? *The Times* called it a great triumph that the Committee had produced a single report without a reservation. It did go on to say that some passages betrayed differences in emphasis and that 'there are some mutually compensating recommendations which might be part of a "package deal".'[192] Enoch Powell (who had resigned as financial secretary to the Treasury in 1958) had been more sceptical in the Commons, noting that the unanimity had led to ambiguity, 'to blurring and to downright contradiction'.[193] Financial journalist Harold Wincott was more blunt: 'Unanimity [was] achieved only by some rewriting of history.'[194] A group of economists who felt strongly about this published a short volume soon after the report appeared with the title, *Not Unanimous*.[195] They included Victor Morgan, Frank Paish, Wilfred King, and former Chancellor Thorneycroft. Again, all of them had given evidence. They took issue with the concept of liquidity and to the downgrading of money in policy and objected in the main to the idea of formalising Bank-Treasury relations.

Sayers was said to have been bitterly disappointed by the critical response. He said more than once, 'Two years of my life – two years wasted.'[196] There was certainly a bitter tone in his presidential address to the British Academy one year after the report came out. Referring to a point of detail in the report, he said, 'That in twelve months no one should, to my knowledge, have drawn attention to [this] is a sad commentary on the extent to which the arguments of the Report have been understood.'[197] The report was the subject of a series of seminars held in the Economics Department at the London School of Economics. Sayers sat at the back and did not participate but would mutter from time to time, 'That is not what we meant.'[198]

[191] Harrod (1959).
[192] *The Times*, 20 August 1959, pp. 5, 8, 13.
[193] HC Deb, 26 November 1959, Vol. 614, c650.
[194] *Financial Times*, 15 September 1959, p. 8.
[195] Seldon and Thorneycroft (1960).
[196] Cairncross (1991a, p. 554).
[197] Sayers (1960, p. 713).
[198] Private communication between author and Roger Alford.

The Committee on the Working of the Monetary System was not a Royal Commission. It was simply a Committee, although Cairncross claimed that it had the status of a Royal Commission.[199] Either way, there was no obligation on the part of the government to implement any recommendations that it made. The normal procedure in British policymaking, going back at any rate to the nineteenth century, was for a problem to be identified, an inquiry set up, and recommendations made to Parliament. Whether or not legislation followed depended on the debate in Parliament. Even then, of course, action could be frustrated by civil servants. In the absence of legislation, though, there was the likelihood that recommendations simply could get lost. There was certainly no formal monitoring procedure. The Treasury did not avail themselves of the recommendations to increase their power over the Bank: 'Officials were almost embarrassed about the kind of support that the Treasury received from the committee. They contented themselves with some concessions the Bank made regarding the improvement of statistics and the setting up of the special deposits scheme.'[200] And in some respects it is surprising that anything got done at all, but then again, many would feel that in an essentially conservative country, that is a satisfactory outcome. As it happened, some of the recommendations of Radcliffe were adopted – some, if not exactly with enthusiasm, quite happily and some more reluctantly.

Initially, the Bank was not enamoured of many aspects of the report. But the Bank largely achieved what it wanted in terms of retaining its relative independence. The monetary policy advocated in the report, insofar as it was advocated at all, was going to take time to find, let alone consider. In the Treasury, there was initial satisfaction, as Hall wrote in his diary: 'Generally speaking, the Report suits me very well and endorses all the things I have stood for in recent years.'[201]

The criticism of the Bank and the City was anticipated, and attempts were made to soften or deflect such criticism. There was agreement between the Bank and the Treasury that the time between the press getting the report and its publication should be used to spread the view that the suggestions about the Bank should be seen as logical developments of current practice. Hall wrote, 'I was to urge the same thing from my end and also use any influence I had with the newspapers to get them to take the same line.'[202] *The Times* appeared to comply precisely with such a request when it wrote,

[199] Cairncross (1999, p. 2).
[200] Ringe and Rollings (2000, p. 130).
[201] Cairncross (1991b, p. 209).
[202] *Ibid.*

'There are two proposed changes in the relations between the Government and the Bank which, although in practice they only recognise the present position and would make no change of substance in the way in which things are really done.'[203] The Prime Minister Macmillan was informed that the press would present the report in dramatic terms, drawing attention to the failure of the 1946 Act, and that steps should be taken to make government control more effective.[204]

The theme of Bank-Treasury relations was central and was seen as one cause of the failure of policy and of the need for a committee in the first place. The precise extent of the contact between the Bank and the Treasury is difficult to document, but it may have been more than Cairncross remembered: 'Up to the time of the Radcliffe Committee, contact between the Bank and the Treasury on monetary policy was almost exclusively through the Governor.'[205] The Bank had been preparing itself a defence well in advance. For the last quarter of 1958, Cobbold had asked for a record of Bank-Whitehall contacts, predominantly with the Treasury, to be kept. A table was compiled that showed that in that period there had been 301 meetings, 6,852 letters, and 9,964 telephone calls and conversations. This is roughly 5 meetings, 115 letters, and 160 phone calls and other conversations every working day! The table was headed 'Whitehall', but a note said it was essentially the Treasury, as would be expected.[206] Much of the contact undoubtedly had to do with exchange controls and routine banking matters, and the data have other weaknesses. Nevertheless, clearly long gone were the days when a Treasury official could say that he always took a taxi to the Bank because he wasn't quite sure where it was.[207]

The recommendations relating to Bank-Treasury relations proved controversial. At the end of July 1959, Cobbold drew Mynors' attention to what he called 'two damned silly specific proposals' that the Committee was making and that he would devise ways of getting out of.[208] These were the proposals on determining Bank Rate and the establishment of a committee to decide monetary policy. On the latter, Sayers told Leslie Pressnell that Radcliffe had slipped in the idea; Pressnell added that nobody bothered much about it, 'though the Bank's Court presumably had a frisson or

---

[203] *The Times*, 20 August 1959, pp. 8, 13.
[204] Timothy Bligh (Principal Private Secretary) to Macmillan, 18 August 1959, PREM 11/2668 TNA.
[205] Cairncross (1995, p. 78).
[206] 'Contacts with Whitehall, quarter ended 31 December 1958', 1 January 1959; note for use of Cobbold at Radcliffe evidence on 15 January 1959, G15/9.
[207] Sayers (1976, p. 14, fn. 1).
[208] Cobbold to Mynors, 31 July 1959, G15/9.

two'.[209] Mynors' first reaction on reading the draft chapters relating to the Bank was 'blank amazement'.[210] When Cobbold met Makins on 4 August, he expressed his concerns that any perceived downgrading of the Bank would worry foreign opinion, especially in the Commonwealth, and that could damage sterling. He was completely opposed to the standing committee, and Makins was sympathetic.[211] A fortnight later, Cobbold re-stated the view that monetary policy was a complicated subject that would require lengthy discussion between the Bank and the Treasury. He stressed his liking for the report's view on the continuity of the Court and its Directors, on the importance of the Bank remaining a 'body with a life of its own', and that proposals on Bank Rate would normally originate in the Bank: 'But they then proceed to make a specific suggestion which conflicts with this conception; that the full responsibility for Bank Rate decisions should be transferred to the Chancellor', and further that there should be a standing committee to deal with monetary policy. These two suggestions in their present form, judged Cobbold, would 'do much to damage the status of the Bank'.[212]

The question of Bank Rate setting was partly one of principle and partly symbolic. The Bank took a strong line from which it never deviated: this was an operating rate, and only the Bank knew how it should be moving. To a large degree, this was accepted by government. A briefing for the Prime Minister on the main issues arising from Radcliffe stated, 'It is their rate, is intimately bound up with their day-to-day operations and should be fixed by them – subject, of course, to the Government's approval.'[213] In any case, there does not appear to have been much enthusiasm in the Treasury for a strict adoption of Radcliffe's recommendation on Bank Rate; a compromise was struck whereby the Court would delegate its power to set Bank Rate to the Governors, with the Chancellor giving formal approval to any change.[214] Cobbold then informed the Court of the new scheme. The Governor would be free to discuss the question of Bank Rate with the part-time Directors, but no specific proposals would be put before the Committee of Treasury or the Court. After the usual informal talks with the Chancellor, the Governor would submit, on the day before an intended change in Bank Rate, a formal

---

[209] Private communication between author and Leslie Pressnell.
[210] Mynors to Cobbold, 31 July 1959, G15/9.
[211] Cobbold, Governor's note – 'Radcliffe', 7 August 1959, G15/9; Makins records a meeting with the Governor of the Bank of England on 4 August 1959, T233/2130, TNA.
[212] Cobbold to Makins, 17 August 1959, G15/9.
[213] Bligh to Macmillan, 18 August 1959, PREM 11/2668 TNA .
[214] Mynors, 'Radcliffe report', 21 August 1959; Cobbold, Draft, 21 August 1959, G14/156.

written proposal to the Chancellor, who, in turn, would convey his formal written approval. On the day of change, the Governor would report the matter to the Court, and the decision then would be announced by the Bank using the existing mechanism. Cobbold attached great importance to the fact that it would be clear that the initiative for changes normally would come from the Bank. Hambro expressed thanks to the Governors for reaching an acceptable solution that 'did not in any way reduce the standing and prestige of the Bank, particularly abroad'.[215]

Although not enamoured of the proposal for a standing committee, Cobbold did ask Mynors to give some thought to what such a body might do. It was a defensive move in case the government accepted the idea in principle. Yet he thought that there might be some use in a forum for keeping up pressure on government over-spending and general credit control. If a standing committee to co-ordinate monetary policy was established, then Cobbold wanted to 'make it as effective as possible and ensure that it gets its hands on the real sources of inflation'. Indeed, the Governor had heard in private from Harcourt that this was what some of the Radcliffe members had in mind when agreeing to the recommendation.[216] In the event, there was no need for Cobbold and his colleagues to worry because the Treasury suggested that the desired co-ordination could be achieved by giving the Bank formal membership of various official groups, in particular the Economic Steering Committee and the Budget Committee.[217]

The general election of October 1959 delayed the parliamentary discussion of Radcliffe. Among politicians, the report was received with a degree of ambivalence. Labour was enthusiastic enough; the Conservatives distinctly less so. The report was on the workings of monetary system, and while monetary economists have tended to focus on the model of monetary policy being explored and left aside the institutional framework, at the time, great attention was paid by non-economists to the conduct of business and its presentation. It is nevertheless impossible to escape the fact that deep antipathy existed on both sides of the political debate. The hostility to the Bank went back at least to the First World War when Governor Cockayne, in the critical year of the war, 1917, 'defied the government with impunity

---

[215] Neatby (Secretary), 'Informal statement of the Governor's statement to the Court of Directors held on 19 November 1959', 23 November 1959, G14/156; Minutes of Court, 19 November 1959, G3/202.

[216] Cobbold to Mynors, Governor's note, 21 August 1959, G15/9.

[217] Makins to Cobbold, 22 September 1959, enc. HMT 'Radcliffe Committee: relations between the Treasury and the Bank of England'; Mynors, 'Radcliffe Committee', 21 October 1959; Amory to Cobbold, 18 November 1959, G15/9.

over a Bank Rate decision while the nation was still at war'.[218] It was the next Governor, Norman, however, who was seen as the chief culprit for the perceived failings in the interwar years. Peter Jay, a financial journalist and son of Labour politician Douglas Jay, told how his father brought him up on the view that the Bank was 'not merely a negative force, but a somewhat ludicrous, grotesque and obscurantist force'.[219] In the 1960s, Jay's own view of the Bank was 'that it was deeply engrained in all sorts of ancient British and City traditions and mystiques, most of which I believed or presumed to be irrational, absurd and unmodern and standing in the way of intelligent and liberalising and progressive tendencies'.[220] Things obviously had changed by the time Jay became a non-Executive Director of the Bank in 2003. Such views of the Bank had become deeply entrenched in British economic historiography. For example, Pollard, blaming Norman for almost everything, wrote:

Yet that poor, tortured, and mentally unstable Governor, notoriously unable to collaborate with anyone on equal terms, going 'ill' whenever the difficulties brought on by his policies caused a crisis, inarticulate as to his ideas and a resounding failure as to his practice, was not dismissed. ... It is hardly conceivable that a political leader could have got away so easily with such a massive failure, and the fact that Norman did does not increase one's trust in the Central Banks as against the politicians.[221]

In the Lords, Pakenham (later Earl of Longford) was to plead for a better understanding of this divide. As both chairman of the National Bank and a lifelong Labour supporter, he felt that he understood the prejudice on both sides. But such deep-seated feelings were unlikely to be moved much by argument.

In the Lords' debate in November, the general view was that lavish praise should be expressed for all the useful information contained in the report, but there was disappointment on the lack of clarity (readability was not a problem) on what was meant and on what was being suggested should be done. Lord Pethick-Lawrence said that he was disappointed not because he was in opposition to its findings, 'but owing to the fact that, at the end, I was not quite sure of what the Report intended its findings to convey'.[222] Lord Boothby, who claimed credit for having the Committee set up, regarded it as a 'revolutionary document', and Lord Pakenham felt it debunked 'what

---

[218] Pollard (1970, p. 19).
[219] Coleby interview with Peter Jay, 13 May 1997.
[220] *Ibid.*
[221] Pollard (1970, p. 21).
[222] HL Deb. 11 November 1959, Vol. 219, c500.

might be called the orthodox view of monetary policy'.[223] Pakenham went
further than most in his criticism, but his background gave him a particular
perspective. He began politely, 'The collection of figures is monumental,
the labours past all praise', but ended with a sting: 'but when it comes to
conclusions they are slightly ridiculous.'[224] There were comments over the
lack of recommendations. Lord Beveridge complained that the report made
no recommendations of any kind, but since he admitted that he hadn't read
the report, he would not have known that recommendations were scattered
throughout.[225]

The debate was notable for the fact that it was the one in which Lord
Robbins made his maiden speech. Robbins was a considerable authority on the subject, but it was not simply his intellectual authority and
expository brilliance that so impressed their Lordships, but his diplomacy, humility ('The Report deals with matters which from time to time
I have been concerned.'), and unfailing courtesy.[226] Almost every subsequent speaker paid tribute to Robbins. Indeed, so delicately phrased
was his speech that Pakenham, his friend and former student, felt the
need to tell their Lordships that in fact Robbins really thought it was a
'rotten report'.[227] Robbins apparently shook his head in disagreement.
But Robbins tackled the serious central issues. Having first heaped
praise on the descriptive sections and noting his agreement on the
importance of debt management in the context of monetary policy –
though not a totally new discovery – then he turned critical. First, he
attacked the concept of the 'so-called liquidity of the system as a whole'.
He preferred the useful central guiding concept of money supply. On
the report's diagnosis on the effects of monetary policy, he found it very
difficult to follow what was being argued. He rejected the analysis of
recent monetary experience. He believed that the failure to act in 1955
and the success of action in 1957 vindicated his views. Robbins went on
to draw attention to the distinction between real and nominal variables
and particularly real and nominal interest rates, a distinction that was
commonly ignored and certainly was by the Committee. He felt that
the chief praise for the report came from those who hardly believed in
monetary policy at all.[228]

---

[223] *Ibid.*, c518.
[224] *Ibid.*, c506.
[225] *Ibid.*, cc523–525.
[226] *Ibid.*, c508.
[227] *Ibid.*, c516.
[228] *Ibid.*, cc508–514.

On the important question of Bank-Treasury relations, Pethick-Lawrence made some sensible observations to the effect that much depended on personalities. He had been a financial secretary to the Treasury and knew the workings of the Treasury. 'It is not simply a matter of who has the right or the theoretical responsibility. ... Certain Chancellors ... seem to me to possess powers ... which enable them to stand up to the Bank of England ... whereas other(s) have been largely mouthpieces of the Bank of England.'[229]

At the heart of the serious debate was the setting of interest rates. Labour wanted the Bank deprived of this task and wanted it made clear that the Chancellor took the decision. More than that, harping back to the Parker Tribunal, they wanted to establish that no part-time Director of the Bank got to know of the decision beforehand. In the closing speech for the opposition, Douglas Jay said that he was astonished at the way the Chancellor had treated the report, pushing aside its recommendations with 'paternal indifference'. For Jay, the report was 'much the best ... I have ever read'. Compared with Macmillan, he found it 'more lucid, more coherent, more balanced, and much more unanimous – if that be the proper way to put it – and more intelligent'.[230] He referred to Robbins fighting a rearguard action on the supply of money. He dealt at length with the main issues of monetary policy, the impact of Bank Rate, the idea of liquidity, and especially the nature of Bank-Treasury relations. Jay concluded by asking what was the point of setting up such committees only for government then to 'summarily reject all their main recommendations'.[231] Economic Secretary to the Treasury Anthony Barber wound up for the government. He reminded members that the report had a good deal to say about international aspects before dealing in turn with all the points in the proposed amendment and recommending that the amendment be rejected, as it duly was by 303 to 225 votes.[232]

Following the debate in the Commons, the press greatly revised its view. It looked like little in Radcliffe was to be adopted, and this was widely interpreted as a success for the Bank. *Reynolds News* said, 'It's surrender to the Bank.'[233] The *Financial Times* developed that line: 'One couldn't help feeling that, by taking on the Bank of England, Radcliffe was asking for trouble in a big way. And so it turned out to be. ... Though confident of victory, she [the Bank] had not expected such a complete rout of Radcliffe.' The explanation

---

[229] *Ibid.*, cc505–506.
[230] HC Deb, 26 November 1959, Vol. 614, c681.
[231] *Ibid.*, cc680–690.
[232] *Ibid.*, cc690–702.
[233] *Reynolds News*, 29 November 1959, p. 6.

offered by the *Financial Times* was that the Bank had been successful in persuading the Chancellor that the best protection against any future spendthrift government was to leave the Bank to look after the currency in the way it knew best.[234] This was a line that the Bank had consistently advanced and would continue to do so even more forcefully under the next Governor, Cromer.

Apart from the report's recommendations on Bank Rate, those that related directly to the Bank were less controversial. These were concerned primarily with the provision of statistics, commentary on monetary and financial conditions, and Bank-Treasury relations, although, of course, the last of these included the way in which Bank Rate decisions were taken and announced. The first two implied greater research capacity, and the report was explicit in suggesting that the Bank might recruit economists to undertake this work. These recommendations were readily accepted by the Bank. Indeed, it was already moving quickly in this direction, with Cobbold wanting to 'keep the initiative in our hands' and show that the Bank was 'willing and able to get on with this under its own steam'. He requested, by the end of September 1959, a scheme to merge the existing Overseas Department into a new Intelligence Department, the identification of potential 'economic assistants', and the laying of plans for a quarterly publication to begin in 1960.[235] Progress was such that Cobbold was able to allude to these developments during his Mansion House speech in October.

The reorganisation was speedily accomplished. In October, the Central Banking Information Department (CBID) was created. A positive spin was put on the change, saying that it had been under consideration for some time but that the Bank had thought it appropriate to wait until the Radcliffe Report.[236] There was some discussion over the name, and while Cobbold thought it 'a bit long-winded', it was 'the best we can think of', and the CBID was finally adopted.[237] Under this guise, it operated until February 1964, when there was a further reorganisation. Overseas once again became a separate area, and the new Economic Intelligence Department (EID) was established. Thus five years after Radcliffe, economics and research gained, for the first time, a separate and identifiable department in the Bank, headed by a senior member of staff. Roy Heasman, previously a Deputy chief in

---

[234] *Financial Times*, 30 November 1959, p. 3.
[235] Cobbold, Governor's note, August 1959, G14/125.
[236] 'Notes for seeing the press', 28 October 1959, ADM10/1.
[237] Committee of Treasury, 21 October 1959; Informal Court records, 22 October 1959; Cobbold, 26 October 1959, G14/125; Henessey (1992, pp. 319–323).

CBID, was in charge.[238] When Heasman became Chief Accountant in June 1967, Thornton took charge of EID. Thornton had joined the Bank in 1938 and spent most of his early career on the statistics side, although since 1962 he had been a Deputy Chief Cashier. He was the most junior member of the Bank to appear as a witness before Radcliffe.[239] He remained as head until his retirement in 1978, by which time EID had 250 staff.

There was also progress in recruiting some academic economists, although this came more slowly. The Bank already had a means of attracting and accommodating academic researchers, the Houblon-Norman fund, established in 1944 for this purpose.[240] A long list of academics benefited from the fund in different ways. Many, perhaps most, of the recipients of grants were engaged in research, however, that was somewhat removed from money and banking. When the young economist Alan Walters returned from a sabbatical in the United States in late 1959 and read the Radcliffe Report, he was prompted to do some work gathering monetary data and testing some hypotheses. He applied for a Houblon-Norman grant but was rejected on the grounds that money did not matter and that no one was interested in it as a research topic.[241] The Treasury clearly was ahead, recruiting many economists in the 1950s and attracting academics on secondment. The Bank's emphasis on market skills was fine up to a point, but it was being out-gunned intellectually by the Treasury, and that had to change. In the Bank, Allen wanted to build up his team with a recognised academic who ultimately might become a senior figure within the Bank and through the short-term employment of assistant advisers.[242] Mynors declared himself 'allergic' to the appointment of advisers because of his own experience of having 'nothing in particular to do'. However, he recognised that there was a case for 'discarding tradition and recruiting a small number of the right type – if we can get them – *as economists*'. What was needed, he concluded, was someone who was more 'gimlet'

---

[238] Mynors favoured 'Home intelligence department' because he was wary of 'anything that might suggest the herding of "economists" into a little corner where they take in each other's washing'; Mynors, Note, 13 December 1963; O'Brien suggested 'Economics and statistics office'; O'Brien to Cromer, 'CBID and Exchange Control', 13 December 1963; O'Brien, Note 'CBID and Exchange Control', 20 December 1963, G14/125; Selwyn to Rootham, 'C.B.I.D.', 14 November 1963, OV21/13.

[239] When the Treasury's paper on debt management was discussed, Thornton attended with Makins, Compton, and Hall in case there were queries on the figures that had been provided by the Bank; Radcliffe, 'Evidence', Vol. 3, December 1957.

[240] See EID 14/1 and EID 14/15.

[241] Walters (1986, p. 105).

[242] Allen to Cobbold/Mynors, 'Team', 23 July 1959, G14/125.

than 'junior John Fforde'.[243] Allen identified a number of potential targets. For the more experienced role, the name of Christopher (Kit) McMahon was proposed. An Australian with degrees in history and English from Melbourne University and philosophy, politics, and economics from Oxford, he was an economic adviser at the Treasury, but at the time, he was working at the British embassy in Washington. He was not approached at this stage but eventually was to join the Bank in September 1964. Among the names for the junior positions were a number with London School of Economics connections. One candidate was Roger Alford, a lecturer at the London School of Economics who had spent time working at Gilletts, one of the largest discount houses in the City. He was already known to O'Brien and Clarke, travelling regularly with the latter on the same train from Guildford to London, together with Professor Frank Paish, who provided a further London School of Economics link. Parsons was also on the train but travelled first class. In December 1959, Alford was offered a two-year post, making him the first academic economist to be recruited on secondment to the Bank. He started work on 16 April 1960. This marked the beginning of a steady stream of such people including Andrew Bain (Cambridge), Tony Cramp (University College London) and Brian Reading (Oxford). Another important appointment was Leslie Dicks-Mireaux, who joined as an Adviser in 1967. A statistician who had worked at the (NIESR), the National Economic Development Council (NEDC), and latterly the Organisation for Economic Co-operation and Development (OECD), Dicks-Mireaux was something of a prize for the Bank because Cairncross also had been keen to recruit him to the Treasury. He had the specific brief of building up the economics team. Graduates with backgrounds in economics and statistics were also recruited in greater numbers. Among these, in 1966, was Andrew Crockett, who had studied at Cambridge and Yale. Perhaps most significant was the secondment of Charles Goodhart. Educated at Eton, Cambridge, and Harvard, he had been a fellow of Trinity College, Cambridge, an economist at the Department of Economic Affairs (DEA), and a lecturer in economics at the London School of Economics. Goodhart came highly recommended by Sayers and Sir Frank Lee at the Treasury, but he had already impressed the Bank with a draft of a chapter on British monetary policy that he sent to McMahon in 1967. 'He clearly understands how we operate', noted Tony Carlisle in the EID.[244] Appointed

---

[243] Mynors to Cobbold, 'Economists', 24 July 1959, G14/125.
[244] Goodhart to McMahon, 25 September 1967; Carlisle, 'Paper on British monetary policy 1957–67', 5 October 1967, 6A50/3.

as an Acting Adviser for a two-year term from October 1968, he joined the permanent staff in February 1970.[245] Thus, by the end of the decade, the Bank's capacity for economic analysis had been greatly enhanced.

Radcliffe called for greater commentary on monetary conditions and explanations of the Bank's activities and operations. In fact, the report had gone further and suggested how this might be done in terms of publications, at one stage actually using the phrase 'quarterly bulletin' and going on to say, 'in which could appear either some of the more technical issues or signed articles on more controversial matters'.[246] This was an area in which the Bank was well prepared to proceed even if initially it was guarded over what would be said. As early as June 1958, though, Mynors said, 'We have accepted the proposition that the Bank should do more to explain'.[247] This was an illustration of the Bank acting, perhaps defensively, in advance of the Committee's publishing, allowing it to say that it was in fact already doing this sort of thing.

The Bank may have been greatly overstaffed, but the argument was that it needed to be sure that there would always be people available to carry out certain kinds of work at short notice. It also prided itself in doing a first-class job on whatever it did. There was to be a demonstration of this in the publication of what emerged as the *Bulletin*. First, there was an analysis of an array of other commercial and central bank publications.[248] The clearing banks all published quarterly reviews, and many central banks produced a variety of publications. All these were examined. At the end of November 1959, the title *Bank of England Quarterly Bulletin* had been decided. By December 1959, Fforde, who was very actively involved, wrote of the Bank's commitment to publish and noted that this had been endorsed by Radcliffe, thus encouraging the view that it was the Bank's initiative.[249] He attended to every detail of the proposed publication down to the finest detail of the decoration for the front cover. There was no need to find printers because the Bank had its own, the vast and expert printing establishment at Debden.

Agreement was quickly reached on what statistical information should be provided. Fforde was careful to note that the Bank did not want to step on the toes of the Central Statistical Office, especially when formal responsibilities were transferred to them on specific tasks when publication of the

---

[245] Details of appointments in G17/59.
[246] Radcliffe, 'Report', para. 861.
[247] Mynors to Cobbold, 18 June 1958, EID5/24.
[248] *Ibid.*
[249] Fforde to Mynors/Stevens/Watson, 15 December 1959, EID5/24.

Statistical Summary ended.[250] So advanced had the preparation become that it was possible to send the material for a dummy issue to Debden in June 1960 and to have a copy produced in August, barely 12 months after Radcliffe had appeared, carrying the date September 1960 and labelled 'Vol. 0, No. 0'. That issue was not circulated. The first issue circulated carried the date December 1960 and was labelled 'Vol. 1, No. 1'. Despite the fact that the commercial banks were circulating almost 20,000 of their quarterlies and of the fact that reprinting was then an expensive exercise, the Bank adopted a typically cautious approach and produced 6,000. The first issue contained two articles, unsigned, as they would continue to be with just an occasional exception that started in 1970, one on special deposits, and one on the financial surplus of the private sector. There was also the Governor's October Mansion House speech. The latter continued to be a feature, with the *Bulletin* reproducing speeches of Governors, Directors, and other senior officials. It began, though, with a 15-page commentary on the period April to September 1960 covering the whole range of monetary and financial conditions, domestic and external, and included an analysis of 'banking and Exchequer statistics'. It also contained a statistical annex of more than 30 pages providing in many cases annual data from 1951 and monthly from 1959.

Although Radcliffe had called for the publication of more statistics and envisaged the regular issue of a 'digest of financial and monetary statistics', it had not specified whether this should be done by the Bank or the Treasury.[251] Indeed, the role of the Treasury was left rather vague. At the time of the first *Bulletin,* Cobbold had declared that the Treasury should not be involved because 'he did not consider that the Treasury's relationship to the proposed *Bulletin* was such that they should or need concern themselves with details.'[252] Mynors agreed: 'We must formally maintain more freedom for a Quarterly, although in practice being very ready to show particular passages to them. They cannot escape having to take some of this on trust: and it will pay them to be able to deny any suggestion of censorship.'[253] During Cromer's Governorship in the first half of the 1960s, there were increasing calls for the control of public expenditure that spilled over into public speeches, and these found their way into the *Bulletin* and its commentary. This seems to have been what led to the loss of Bank discretion on the content. Looking back from the 1990s, Jasper Hollom said,

[250] Fforde to Mynors, 8 October 1959, EID5/24.
[251] Cairncross, (1985a, p. 381).
[252] 'Extract from Deputy Governor's memo dated 2 December 1960', EID5/24.
[253] Mynors, 'Publications: Mr. Fforde's note of 15 December', 18 December 1959, EID5/24.

'The *Bulletins* were always a matter of negotiation, they were drafted, the text went down the other end [the Treasury] and came back with amendments required, they weren't really our *Bulletins* at all, by the time they had finished they were a compromise.'[254]

The other publication that was under discussion was the *Annual Report*. It had long been seen as being meagre on information to the point of being unhelpful. There were some hints in Radcliffe that it might be beefed up and include some of the proposed commentary. Mynors, known for his miserly approach to the release of Bank information, wrote, 'the best we can do is – given an effective quarterly – to see how little we can get away with.'[255] Fforde went as far as advocating that the *Annual Report* should be reduced in size 'to a purely formal document if not kill it entirely.'[256] Mynors rejected this idea, and in fact, the 1960 *Annual Report* was more than twice the usual size with much more statistical content, although it then returned to 'normal' in the following year. [257]

The *Annual Report* was also the source of some strained relations with Whitehall. In 1963, the Bank sent a proof to the Treasury and received a letter back saying, 'We are, therefore, happy to give *formal* approval to its publication' [italics added].[258] Mynors replied in a distinctly irritable tone:

For the record, I think I should say that our *Annual Report* is not a statutory requirement but is laid before the House of Commons, as I understand, as the outcome of a remark made by Dr. Dalton, as Chancellor of the Exchequer, in the debate on the Bank of England Bill, 1946. We are therefore naturally at pains to put nothing in the Report which the Chancellor would find difficult to defend: but 'formal approval', as in the second paragraph of your letter, is not required.[259]

Whether anything at all, apart from cosmetic presentational features, changed after Radcliffe is less certain. Mynors never accepted that there had ever been a change. On 28 February 1964, the day before he retired from the Bank, Mynors wrote in a memorandum seen by the Governor and the Chief Cashier only:

The abortive Report of the Radcliffe Committee proposed the establishment in Whitehall of a Standing Committee on Monetary Policy, which was clearly impracticable. In order to make it appear that their recommendations were taken seriously,

---

[254] Coleby interview with Sir Jasper Hollom, 11 January 1995.
[255] Mynors, 'Publications: Mr. Fforde's note of 15 December', 18 December 1959, EID5/24.
[256] Fforde to Mynors/Stevens/Watson, 15 December 1959, EID5/24.
[257] Mynors, 'Publications: Mr. Fforde's note of 15 December', 18 December 1959, EID5/24.
[258] Goldman (HMT) to Mynors, 14 June 1963, G15/10.
[259] Mynors to Goldman, 18 June 1963, G15/10.

two new procedures were nominally introduced: (1) A new technique of setting Bank Rate which pretended that the Directors of the Bank were neither aware of nor had any responsibility for any change and (2) The appointment of the Deputy Governor for the time being to be a member of two existing Committees of Senior Officials in Whitehall. These arrangements, although neither is more than a façade, cannot be abolished because they are recorded in general terms in the pages of Hansard.[260]

Be that as it may, soon after Radcliffe appeared, Cobbold felt confident that he had secured the Bank's position, and he wrote to other central bankers effectively telling them this, stating, 'We here feel that this is a satisfactory outcome, which makes virtually no change in the reality of existing normal practices.'[261] There were several congratulatory replies.[262] Cobbold had stayed on as Governor to see Radcliffe through, and having done so successfully, he began to make arrangements to leave.

A Brief Assessment

Radcliffe may not have introduced any fundamental change, but it did contribute to the introduction of a more professional approach in the Bank in the gathering of data, the conduct of research, and the use of more economists and so on. And it was a step on the road to greater openness with its commentary on conditions and explanation of its operations. It has been described as one of the most important documents in Keynesian monetary economics and even as one of the most important publications in British monetary history.[263] The report was the most authoritative account of the working of the monetary system. It nevertheless should be remembered that it was produced in an interventionist climate and reflected the view that the wisdom of officials was a surer route to optimal outcomes than the operation of rules. Indeed, Sayers, one of the principal authors, remarked elsewhere that 'the essence of central banking is discretionary control of the monetary system.'[264] It was nevertheless a comprehensive description with some analysis of the British monetary system. And interestingly, Cairncross, the other key economist member of the Committee, remarked

---

[260] Mynors to Cromer/O'Brien, 27 February 1964, G15/10.
[261] Cobbold to numerous central bank Governors including Fussell (Reserve Bank of New Zealand), Coyne (Bank of Canada), Blessing (Deutsche Bundesbank), 27 November 1959, C40/901.
[262] Fussell to Cobbold, 5 January 1960, C40/901.
[263] Cobham (1992); Robbins (1971b, p. 90).
[264] Sayers (1957).

later that Radcliffe thought exclusively of the Bank as if the 'objective study of monetary and financial problems did not equally concern the Treasury'.[265]

Radcliffe either ignored much of what there was in monetary theory and analysis before Keynes or explicitly rejected it. This is quite striking. No comparable enquiry (and there had been several) up to the time of Macmillan (1931) had cast any doubt on the proposition that an excessive growth in the quantity of money – excess over the growth of output – would tend to raise prices and that any deficiency in relation to output would produce deflation. Macmillan is open to some interpretation on this but is certainly much closer to the quantity theory than to Radcliffe. Had the world changed? It might be difficult or even impossible to demonstrate that what was contained in Radcliffe was the approach that was used by the monetary authorities in our period, but it is fair to say that it presented the dominant view in Britain at the time, and given the significance attached to the Bank's evidence to the Committee, it must be taken to represent very largely the Bank's position. The core of the theoretical analysis is an attack on a simple quantity theory. The conception of the respective transmission mechanisms were roughly as follows: from money directly to income for the quantity theory and from money through interest rates and then to investment and finally to income for the Radcliffean view. But it was more than that. The objective was to influence aggregate demand: 'The immediate object to monetary action is to affect the level of total demand.'[266] And total demand depended on the overall liquidity position, which, in turn, depended on the whole structure of interest rates. So that was the focus of attention. But how could this whole structure of interest rates be manipulated? This was not clear, but debt management was to play a central part. The link between interest rates and investment was seen as being weak. In fact, neither consumption nor investment was seen as being responsive to interest rates – interest elasticities were extremely low. This view had its origins in a famous study in the 1930s at Oxford that involved a large number of economists but was overseen by Hubert Henderson and Roy Harrod. Members of the group included Maurice Allen, Robert Hall, and Richard Sayers, so it is not hard to trace the view or understand its strength. Their work was heavily influenced by the results of surveys of businessmen. Given the times, though, with Bank Rate fixed at 2 per cent year in year out and the Treasury bill rate almost invisible, the results were hardly surprising.[267] Thus, providing

---

[265] Cairncross (1985a, pp. 381–387).
[266] Radcliffe, 'Report', para. 397.
[267] Besomi (1998).

a case for monetary policy was difficult, for it had to circumvent the link between interest rates and investment. If the structure of interest rates is the main instrument of policy, then the role of the money supply is to set interest rates.

Radcliffe doubted that money could be operationally defined and repudiated the concept of velocity, the oft-quoted sentence being: 'We cannot find any reason for supposing, or any experience in monetary history indicating, that there is any limit to the velocity of circulation.'[268] Radcliffe believed that velocity could be changed at will by the private sector by altering payment arrangements, by changing the volume of direct lending, or most important, by increasing the amount of financial intermediation. Yet Friedman and others were at this time demonstrating in a rigorous way that velocity was indeed stable. Thus, instead of money-stock control, Radcliffe talked in terms of 'the whole liquidity position', and it was thus necessary for the authorities 'to regard the structure of interest rates rather than the supply of money as the centre piece of the monetary mechanism'.[269] Thus control of the money supply became no more than an important facet of debt management. The reason the volume of short-term government debt was so important was that if the commercial banks found their cash reserves depleted by the open market operations of the Bank, they could reverse that by allowing their Treasury bills to run off. The net effect was then that government borrowing from the Bank recreated the reserves of the joint stock banks.[270] This meant that control of credit had passed to the Treasury through control of the Treasury bill issue, and this led to concern with non-bank financial institutions because their activities were thought to offset or even nullify the effect of a change in the money supply or interest rates. All of this, it should be said, reflected the mainstream academic views of the period.

The old orthodoxy that dated to the nineteenth century and was still essentially alive in the Macmillan Committee regarded bank deposits as being determined by the cash base. It can be found later in the neo-orthodoxy as proposed, for example, in Crouch (1963, 1964).[271] The new orthodoxy of Sayers and of Radcliffe was that the monetary authorities operated to stabilise the Treasury bill rate, so the cash base became endogenous, and therefore, liquid assets became the crucial determinant. Yet, even if debt management was important (and the argument was that because of the scale of the debt, it was), the major objective in relation to monetary policy

---

[268] Radcliffe, 'Report', para. 391.
[269] *Ibid.,* para. 397.
[270] Sayers (1938).
[271] Crouch (1963, 1964).

should be the arrangement of short-term borrowing so as to harmonise the aims of the Bank with regard to the credit base.[272] For Radcliffe, it was not the supply of money but the long-term interest rate or the structure of rates that had to be the focus of attention.[273]

The report was cast in the mould of the new orthodoxy, where the importance of money was played down and the notion of credit was played up. While these were the dominant views, there were nevertheless some dissident views. Some, in fact, were quite hostile. For example, Ralph Hawtrey wrote in *The Bankers' Magazine* in September 1959, 'So far as the aims of monetary policy are concerned, the Committee leaves them in precisely the same state of confusion and ambiguity in which it found them.'[274] Sir Dennis Robertson made a scathing attack in *The Banker* on the core of the thesis, writing of confusion, non-sequiters, and double confusion.[275] But the basic philosophy of Radcliffe prevailed in the 1960s.

To summarise and to provide a broad basis on which to proceed, the picture in the 1950s and 1960s was broadly as follows: the monetary authorities at least accepted that inflation was a potential problem. They were committed to adhering to a fixed exchange rate or, in the language of the time, to guaranteeing the value of sterling. They also saw a link between inflation and the exchange rate. To some extent, it was further accepted that to control inflation, 'credit' had to be restricted. [There was some confusion between bank deposits (bank credit) and trade credit and total credit.] But inflation was seen as a consequence of wage bargaining, and it was believed that the main way of containing it was by incomes policy. More important, the authorities saw themselves as having a number of other objectives. They had to manage the national debt, and they felt an obligation to stabilise interest rates. There was the perceived constraint of having to satisfy the needs of London as an international financial centre. All this said, did the authorities have the appropriate techniques and institutional arrangements for carrying through all these objectives in the markets?

[272] For some contemporary observations, see Goodhart (1973).
[273] Sayers (1938, 1964).
[274] Hawtrey (1959, p. 172).
[275] Robertson (1959).

4

The Bank's External Responsibilities to 1964

In the nineteenth century, the Bank's principal function had been to maintain gold convertibility. In the 1920s, there was an attempt to restore the gold standard that had been disrupted by war and that was achieved somewhat unsatisfactorily as the gold exchange standard. And although central banks were in the main still private institutions, the discipline of maintaining gold convertibility was felt to be a sufficient check on their activity. After 1945, the desire was to return to something close to the nineteenth-century gold standard but with improvements. The Bretton Woods arrangements, however, were faulty and stumbled along uncertainly from their introduction in 1947 through their fuller realisation in 1958 to their demise at the end of the 1960s. The period sees sterling and the 'system' under constant pressure – sterling because it was one of the two reserve currencies, and if it went, pressure would shift to the dollar. Thus the background to the problems that were to dominate in international finance in the 1960s lies in the nature of the Bretton Woods arrangements. At the heart of the problem lay the scale and distribution of gold reserves and how they might change. At the end of the Second World War, the United States had gold reserves of $20 billion, about 60 per cent of total official gold reserves. That seemed more than enough to defend the dollar parity. In fact, US reserves grew and peaked at $25 billion in 1949. Thereafter, through the 1950s, they fell fairly steadily so that by 1960 they stood at $18 billion. US losses meant growing dollar holdings in foreign countries that were convertible into gold at the official price of $35 an ounce. In fact, between 1958 and 1960, Britain made purchases of gold of $1.86 billion, and in the Organisation for European Economic Co-operation (OEEC), gold and foreign-exchange holdings rose by $3.7 billion in 1958 and a further $1.4 billion in 1959. The dollar shortage was well and truly over.[1] In Britain, expansionary policy led to current account weakness, a fall in reserves, and pressure on sterling. This would then be addressed by tightening policy – both fiscal and monetary – with Bank Rate being considered useful in this context. A large deficit on current account and long-term capital account emerged in the second half of 1959 and persisted into 1961. Sterling then was in one of its recurrent crises or in a phase of one long crisis.

From the 1950s, holding the exchange-rate parity dominated the Bank's main purposes; it was the 1970s before domestic policy superseded external policy. Following the Second World War, the British economy was in a greatly weakened position compared with that of the 1930s and earlier. Many of the problems it confronted were related to its external position – its indebtedness, the exchange-rate regime, the prospects for the balance of payments, the sterling balances, and its capacity to cope with all these in the different world in which it found itself. It had moved from being the world's greatest creditor in the years before 1914 to being the world's greatest debtor after 1945 – by some reckoning with a debt-income ratio of around 300 per cent.[2]

The principal problems, as they were perceived after the war, were the exchange-rate regime that came with the International Monetary Fund (IMF); the loan/line of credit from the United States in 1946 ($3,750 million or £925 million) that came with conditions, particularly relating to convertibility of sterling; the persistent balance-of-payments difficulties in the first few years after the war but with problems stretching well beyond that; and sterling balances and the sterling area. These are all interlinked. Also at the end of the war, policymakers were more apprehensive about the likely slowness of switching from wartime to peacetime production and hence of being able to deal with the problems. And finally, there was the gloomy outlook for the world at large. What was to follow was a series of patching measures.

Origins of the Pegged-Rate System

The exchange rate and exchange-rate regime were arrived at after long negotiations, primarily with the United States, and resulted in the Bretton Woods

---

[1] A good coverage of this can be found in Bordo and Eichengreen (1993).

[2] Over the same period, the United States had moved from being the greatest debtor to being indisputably the greatest creditor, although that would change again to being the biggest debtor in the 1980s. See Goodhart (1999).

arrangements. Following the experience of the 1930s, there was a desire to return to the greater certainty of the gold-standard world of pre-1914, although it was believed that could be improved on. The gold standard, in its classical form, dates from around 1870, with the rich advanced countries on the standard by the closing years of the nineteenth century, along with some poorer countries. Belonging was seen as 'a Good Housekeeping seal of approval' and as a way of becoming accepted in the world and being able to borrow at the most favourable rates.[3] It required good behaviour on the monetary and fiscal fronts. Emerging economies endeavoured to behave in such a way as would allow them to become accepted and to join the club. There developed a core and a periphery, and international adjustment was different for both. The advanced countries were capital-rich, and the others were capital-poor. The key distinction between the core and the periphery was financial maturity, where that meant the ability to issue international securities in domestic currency. Before 1914, the core was on gold, and the periphery tried to be.[4] While that system could not go on working indefinitely, for a variety of reasons, after the First World War, the motivating force was still the desire to be accepted.[5] When it finally broke down, variations on managed floating followed until the Second World War. The failure of the restored gold standard, and the ineptitude of the Federal Reserve in the years 1928–32, initiated and exacerbated the Great Depression in the United States, which, in turn, had worldwide ramifications.[6] The resulting mixture of managed exchange rates in the 1930s provoked a series of competitive devaluations, something future designers of the international monetary system expressly wished to avoid.

The restored gold standard of the mid-1920s was a defective gold exchange standard. There was the continuing problem (continuing from the old gold standard) of asymmetric adjustment and the concomitant failure to play by the rules. There was compulsory adjustment for the debtors and voluntary adjustment for the creditors. There was, too, a fear that convertibility would be a problem, and that led to periphery countries reducing their holdings of foreign exchange. Additionally, in the 1920s there was a problem of confidence resulting from the shifting of currency holdings from a weak centre (United Kingdom) to the strong centre (United States). The fear was that this weakened the system.[7]

---

[3]   Bordo and Rockoff (1996).
[4]   Bordo (2003).
[5]   Bordo and Kydland (1995).
[6]   Friedman and Schwartz (1963); Brunner (1981); Meltzer (2002).
[7]   Bordo (2003).

An important element in the story was capital movements. The unsatisfactory resolution of many economic issues following the First World War created political uncertainty in Europe and stimulated a corresponding amount of capital movement. There also was a 'normal' change in the direction of capital flows when, for example, American investment in Germany in the mid-1920s began to be returned in the late 1920s as the New York Stock market boomed. The really large movements in capital, however, were provoked by the growing uncertainty at the turn of the decade. The spreading world depression, and political developments such as the emergence of the Nazis as the second largest party in the Reichstag in 1930, contributed to the uncertainty. In the summer of 1931, the Bruning government introduced exchange controls, and a standstill on short-term debt owed abroad was negotiated; not surprisingly capital flight increased. Many other countries followed suit soon after, producing a proliferation of exchange controls. There were fears that Britain would introduce similar measures, and in September 1931, it abandoned the gold standard.

After that, Britain endeavoured to manage the exchange rate through the Exchange Equalisation Account (EEA), announced in the budget of April 1932 and formally established on 1 July of that year. The EEA was designed to dampen or even eliminate the short-term fluctuations in the exchange rate but not to resist trend movements. That is, it should work to cushion the impact of balance-of-payments movements and in the process try to distinguish between current and capital account transactions – easier said than done. The EEA, the Treasury's but operated by the Bank, started with an initial capital of £170 million to deal in sterling and foreign currencies.[8] At the beginning, £50 million of foreign currency, which had been hidden away in the Issue Department as 'Other Securities', was transferred to the EEA in exchange for Treasury bills. In fact, from the end of 1925, Norman had been using 'Other Securities' to build up a secret reserve of US dollars.[9]

The aim of the account was the opposite of that of the gold standard. Under the gold standard, adjustment took place by allowing capital flows

---

[8] The initial capital was £150 million from the government's consolidated fund plus between £21 million to £25 million from the Treasury's exchange account. According to Sayers, £8 million then was deducted from the capital as compensation for Bank's losses incurred when repaying central banks in August 1931. Bank of England, 'The exchange equalisation account: its origins and development', *BEQB* 8(4):377–390, December 1968; Sayers (1976, pp. 427, 43)1; HMT, 'Exchange Equalisation Account', Radcliffe, 'Memoranda', Vol. 1, p. 105; Waight (1939); for an early and interesting account of the EEA and the secrecy involved in its early operations, see Hall (1935).

[9] Sayers (1976, pp. 217–218).

to enter domestic credit directly, and then price changes would bring about the needed correction in the external accounts. The EEA was designed to prevent capital flows from affecting domestic credit. To work well required techniques that provided insulation. The fund acquired foreign currency entering Britain in exchange for Treasury bills. This usually meant supplying the British banking system with Treasury bills, which in the early days was not the problem that it was later to become.[10] After the dollar left gold, the United States also established a stabilisation fund, in 1934, and it was a short step further for Britain, the United States, and France to negotiate the Tri-partite Agreement in an attempt to stabilise exchange rates more generally.[11] It was this agreement that Mundell regarded as the real beginnings of the Bretton Woods arrangements.[12]

These experiences, and others of floating and managed floating in the interwar years, were to matter greatly in discussions on the future of the international monetary system. Nurkse argued in an influential book that floating produced destabilising speculation. Friedman later refuted this interpretation, and later still, Eichengreen found no evidence of it in the 1930s. Neither did Eichengreen and Sachs find any evidence of the beggar-my-neighbour policies that were also said to be problematic. Nevertheless, the perception that gained acceptance at the time, a perception that took hold and lasted a long time, was largely based on Nurkse.[13]

Although Britain suffered comparatively modestly in the Great Depression (output fell less than 6 per cent across the depression years of 1929–32, against a fall in the United States of around 30 per cent), unemployment did rise steeply in those years, even if this was more readily attributable to real wage effects.[14] Britain did, nevertheless, behave as if it were severely affected. It reversed its free-trade policies of almost a century and introduced a general tariff. It saw in its empire a possible solution to trade and output concerns, for it contemplated turning the empire into a customs union. The Ottawa Conference of 1932 did something less than that, but nevertheless, a large number of trade agreements were signed with empire partners, and more significantly, preferential treatment was extended to empire countries – imperial preference.[15] This greatly upset the

---

[10] See Waight (1939).
[11] Clarke (1977).
[12] Mundell (2000, p. 331).
[13] Nurkse (1944); Friedman (1968b); Eichengreen (1992); Eichengreen and Sachs (1985, pp. 925–946).
[14] Beenstock, Capie, and Griffiths (1984).
[15] Capie (1983).

United States, Britain's biggest trading partner, and soon after the United States granted Lend Lease to the United Kingdom early in 1941, they presented the bill – 'a commitment was required from Britain to work with the U.S. towards elimination of trade restrictions … and in particular Britain's system of imperial preference.'[16]

The direct link with the 1930s begins to emerge more clearly. Given what was widely accepted would be Britain's balance-of-payments position after the war (little to export but a strong demand for imports), it was felt that some safeguards would be needed if Britain were to abandon the apparatus of imperial preference. To allow Britain to do this, Keynes drafted his proposal for an International Clearing Union, the basis of the 'Keynes plan', which he himself described as utopian. And Britain was keen to restore the position of sterling after the war in part to demonstrate its status as a leading power. Washington proposed, through US Treasury Department official Harry Dexter White, a more limited stabilisation fund, with the new institution's reserves being made up of national currencies and gold. The differences between the two schemes are sometimes overstated, but something that needs to be remembered is that there was undoubtedly a certain amount of American antipathy to Britain.[17] Against that, a measure of the support provided by the United States can be found in the extent of Lend Lease and the Marshall Plan, although these benefited others too. In any event, by the spring of 1944, the two proposals had been combined, and a scheme was developed to establish the IMF and the World Bank. Thus, following the upheavals of the interwar years, the aims were to have stable and 'realistic' exchange rates, with the countries experiencing difficulty having access to adequate international reserves to smooth out short-term problems. Good behaviour would be expected, and some codes of behaviour would be put in place. This ambition was to incorporate the good aspects of the past (the classical gold standard) with the removal of problems of the 1930s (trade restrictions and emphasis on domestic survival).

The IMF would assist member countries to manage their balance of payments in a manner consistent with stable exchange rates. The principal obligation of members was to allow free convertibility for current account transactions, whereas capital account controls were permitted. The IMF was established in 1945 and began operations in 1947. However, it immediately became apparent that there was going to be a longer transition period

---

[16] Pressnell (1997, p. 216).
[17] Skidelsky (2000). Skidelsky was inclined to see the whole Roosevelt administration as opposed to Britain.

than anticipated – convertibility could not be achieved quickly. The major industrial countries achieved some limited current account convertibility at the end of 1958, although most persisted with exchange controls on the capital account.

It is being recognised increasingly that the world never, or at best only for a very short time, followed the Bretton Woods rules. The rules were intended to apply to all equally, but since each was to be free to pursue its own macroeconomic policies, this could result in different inflation rates, hence the requirement for long-run flexibility in the exchange rate. This last feature was, of course, the opposite of the requirements of the pre-1914 gold standard. However, the United States emerged as the only country that could really behave autonomously, whereas 'other countries were caught in a straight jacket – that is a new and apparently unplanned international monetary standard – where the elbow room for exercising national macro autonomy was limited.'[18] Thus it was that a pegged-rate dollar standard emerged for the period 1950–70. The United States had to remain passive in the foreign exchanges, keep capital markets open, pursue an independent monetary policy, and maintain its position as net creditor by limiting fiscal deficits. All this was clearly very different from the original intention: '... the architects of the system created rules that appeared to be logically attractive but that were inapplicable in practice.'[19] Some argue that the Bretton Woods articles never came into effect for the very good reason that the impact of the Marshall Plan was not something that had been anticipated. The urgency of containing Communism prompted Washington to support recovery programmes in many countries, and recovery in Europe, particularly Germany, was viewed as essential. This also lay behind their desire for European integration that affected so many policies. The Marshall Plan was both a plan for recovery and an effort to promote European integration. It provided a mixture of grants, loans, and conditional aid, but its interest for present purposes lies in how it changed the basis of the international monetary system.

Part of the recovery project linked to the plan was the establishment of the European Payments Union (EPU) in 1950 to restore current account convertibility using the dollar as the unit of account for calculating credit balances. Each country had to declare an exact dollar parity and follow policies to keep that parity. The early form of the scheme began in 1948 as a means of trying to bring order to trade and financial stability in Europe.

[18] McKinnon (1993, pp. 601–602).
[19] Feldstein (1993, p. 615).

All the immediate and more or less predictable difficulties at the end of the war and other unanticipated problems meant that it was impossible for the IMF to behave as planned, and it was 'effectively sidelined until the Suez crisis of 1956'. [20] The failure of sterling convertibility in 1947, the big French devaluation of 1948 (with multiple rates for hard currencies), and Italy's use of multiple rates, followed by the British and other devaluations of 1949, all damaged any prospect of the system working as intended. And of course, the United States granting of loans and then the Marshall Plan changed the nature of the system. Thus the origins of the IMF can be found in the diverse international monetary experience of the preceding 50 years or so but in particular and proximately of the 1930s and 1940s. In fact, though, a different system came into being from the one intended, a system of pegged exchange rates. The IMF made a contribution to its working by providing short-term resources to countries with balance-of-payments difficulties. The arrangements are often thought of as running from 1947 (the agreement was signed on 18 December 1946) until 1971. Convertibility was not achieved until the end of 1958, and so the period might really be said to have started in 1959. And the finishing point probably needs to be revised back to early 1968 with the end of the Gold Pool and the beginning of a two-tier system, one private and one official. It was then that trading in gold began to take place, and the writing was on the wall for the Bretton Woods years.

What options could realistically have been considered by Britain after the war? The war had proved extremely costly for Britain. There was the loss of foreign assets of around £4,000 million. There were the huge sterling balances – estimated at £3,700 million in 1945 and £3,795 million in 1951. These had been useful in wartime, but they were about to constitute a particular kind of burden in peacetime. The sterling area had really come into being at the beginning of the war. There is a view that before 1931 it was coterminous with the whole world, but that is surely not very accurate.[21] Something that could loosely be called the sterling area was in existence in the nineteenth century. It was made up of most empire countries and some others that kept their currencies stable in terms of sterling, and of those countries holding some or even all of their international reserves, as claims on London.[22] On a stricter definition, a currency area suggests inconvertibility, and so long as sterling was a fully convertible currency, there was

---

[20] Presnell (1997, p. 214).
[21] Robertson (1954).
[22] Pressnell (1978, pp. 67–88).

no sterling area.[23] After 1931, when sterling was no longer convertible into gold, a period of confusion followed. After 1933, however, the countries of the loosely defined sterling area more formally became the Sterling Bloc, and in the period of floating rates, they kept constant the rate of exchange of their own currencies into sterling.

What happened after 1939 was different. Countries not involved in the war severed their connection with the Sterling Bloc. The introduction of exchange control in September of that year provided the conditions for the development of the sterling area. What followed was a complicated system of different degrees of transferability of sterling among members and with the outside world on both current and capital transactions. At the same time, though, import restrictions were frequently in place, so while there might be freedom to make a payment, there was not always freedom to make the purchase. Also, there were various provisions governing control of capital movements between some areas. And not all sterling owned by members was freely available. Thus there was a complex set of arrangements that was to persist and has a bearing on any discussion of the problem of sterling.

During the war, when closer co-operation between member countries was developing, a central reserve of foreign exchange was built up. Britain undertook to make dollars available to member countries to cover unfavourable balances on dollar transactions. The other member countries were obliged to make available any surplus gold or dollars they acquired. That system persisted after the war and is the reason sometimes given for viewing sterling's problems in terms of the area as a whole. During the war, the sterling balances had surged from the relatively modest levels in the 1930s: where they had been steadily on the order of £500 million, they jumped to £3.5 billion at the end of the war and would double again, at least in nominal terms, by the mid-1970s.[24] The balances were the result of British purchases in wartime when domestic production was turned almost exclusively to wartime needs. A major ambition after the war was to restore sterling to full convertibility, but conditions simply were not right, and it was necessary to suspend the attempt.[25]

The rate for sterling clearly had been a key question at the end of the war. James Meade was a lone, if distinguished voice arguing that sterling should be allowed to float. However, the main discussion was about the rate rather

---

[23] Sargent (1954).

[24] 'Overseas sterling holdings', *BEQB* 3(4):264–265, December 1963; 'Overseas sterling balances 1963–73', *BEQB* 14(2):162–175, June 1974; CSO, *United Kingdom Balance of Payments*, 1980 edition, Table 11.5.

[25] See Pressnell (1986, pp. 366–367).

than any question of floating. As in 1925, there was little debate on the parity and more on honouring obligations, so it was again after the Second World War. Several countries, most notably India, had maintained extensive sterling balances during the war, and there was concern to ensure that such countries did not suffer on account of this. The pegged rate chosen was $4.03, and that soon proved to be an overvaluation against the dollar.[26] A nominal 30 per cent devaluation eventually was agreed on in 1949 (about 10 per cent on a trade-weighted basis). The new rate had been agreed on quite quickly, and any idea of floating was dismissed.[27]

Floating reappeared in the form of 'Robot', the scheme advanced in 1952. It carried in its name a hint of automaticity but also took the initials of some of the leading advocates: Leslie Rowan and Otto Clarke from the Treasury and George Bolton from the Bank (ROwanBoltonOTto). It was prompted, in part, by the slow progress towards convertibility. Reserves at the beginning of 1952 were low and forecast to fall further, and parity was believed to be unsustainable; that led some in the Bank and the Treasury to conclude that only a drastic change in policy could bring about alleviation of the difficulties and that floating should be considered an option.[28] The idea was that the pound would float within some quite wide bands, although these would not be announced publicly. There is another view, one that shifts the emphasis considerably, that argues that the form in which the scheme was put forward by the Bank focussed not on the balance of payments but rather on the desire to protect sterling's position as an international currency. Those in favour in the Treasury may have seen it as the ideal solution to the pressing immediate problems, but not the Bank.[29]

The scheme was one in which floating was to be accompanied by convertibility for non-residents and the blocking of other sterling balances. Chancellor Butler was in favour, but the cabinet failed to approve the plan. Butler later regretted the failure, believing as he did that the 'absence of a floating exchange-rate robbed successive Chancellors of an external regulator for the balance of payments.'[30] He said this was not with the benefit of hindsight, but rather it was the view of experts at the time from the Governor of the Bank through most of Butler's Treasury team.[31]

---

[26] There was, for example, one in Portugal at the time.
[27] HC Deb, 27 September 1949, Vol. 468, c12.
[28] For example, Cairncross (1985b).
[29] Proctor (1993).
[30] Butler (1971), p. 158.
[31] Gilmour (2004). Ian Gilmour, however, claims that despite what Butler said in his memoirs, he later admitted that his opponents had been right all along. But people often give in to the moods of the time and renege on previous positions.

There were many reasons for the failure to get the plan adopted. They ranged from the organisational, to the grand political, to the moral. The scheme was clearly in breach of IMF articles, although that did not seem to have been regarded as an insurmountable problem. It also would have led to complications at least for the EPU, although that too seems to have been regarded with equanimity.[32] The view of the designers of Robot seemed to be that the EPU was coming to the end of its useful life anyway. That aside, there were other likely reasons for the failure of Robot, and one would have been that it would have involved the blocking of substantial sterling balances. This alone did not appeal to liberal economists.[33] More than that, it was devised and developed in secrecy and without proper discussion and consultation and, finally, presented in a great hurry. The immediate problem for sterling then seemed to resolve itself. Reserves grew in 1952. Instead of falling to a predicted $600 million to $1,000 million, they finished the year at $1,800 million, and the issue was effectively over for that year. The discussion did rumble on for a while before fading, and the question of floating did not disappear in the 1950s.

The whole approach to the question of the exchange rate and related problems was piecemeal, conducted on a day-to-day basis, responding to every change that appeared in the figures. This approach was characteristic of British political life in the third quarter of the twentieth century. Very rarely were there those prepared to tackle a large issue. There was insufficient resolve to grapple with the fundamental problem, a lack of political and institutional leadership that runs through much of the period.

The fundamental problem was the exchange-rate parity and the determination to pursue 'full employment'. While the decision on parity was an economic calculation in part – using purchasing-power parity – that calculation was based on defective price indices.[34] A solution would have been to let the exchange rate float, as Meade was arguing.[35] Could this have been one of those rare moments in history when an opportunity might have been seized? Britain might have been able to say:

In the course of this mammoth war effort we have disinvested hugely and become a huge debtor. We are in no position to hold to commitments that have been made in the past. This therefore is our only way out. But in any

---

[32] For details of the Bank's views on the operations of EPU, see Fforde (1992, pp. 212–214).

[33] For example, Boyle (1979, p. 7). Boyle said that Lionel Robbins would have been outraged at that.

[34] Capie and Wood (2002).

[35] Cairncross (1985b, p. 165); Pressnell (1986, p. 448). Canada did just this in the 1950s.

case it will prepare the way for a better world more quickly. It will facilitate the restoration of free trade and payments.

Indeed, a recent reassessment of the Robot plan makes some comments along these lines:

> In the midst of the economic crisis in February 1952, the British Government had a unique opportunity to take a bold, almost revolutionary, step in the external field which would have ... restructured Britain's domestic economy to tackle the long-standing productivity, export and labour market problems.

It would have re-established Britain as a leading power.[36] That probably goes too far. The opposite view was taken by the economist and civil servant Donald MacDougall, who believed that the British economy performed well in the 1950s and 1960s and that had Robot been implemented, this would not have been possible.[37] What would have happened obviously involves a huge counterfactual, and it might be argued that given the failure to implement policies to protect the exchange rate, the worst might be feared – a continuing downward spiral of exchange-rate depreciation and of ever-rising inflation. However, the possibility remains that Robot could have provided the environment in which a more rapid recovery was made with less need to attend to the balance of payments.

Convertibility

The ambition was convertibility, and Robot was one way of approaching that, although how 'convertibility' was defined is not clear. It was a term that was bandied about a lot without it always being clear what was intended.[38] It often was assumed that it meant the abolition of all restrictions, but it was certainly not that. There were many possibilities. Was it to apply to residents of the sterling area or to non-residents? Would it extend to all individuals or be restricted to central banks? Would it apply to sterling accumulated in the past or only to sterling accumulating after a certain date? Would it apply to transactions on current account or capital account? There was also the question of whether the freedom to exchange sterling was going to be accompanied by measures that would make it more difficult to acquire it. And there was still the question of whether it would be convertible at a

---

[36] Burnham (2003, pp. 2, 7).
[37] MacDougall (1987, p. 108).
[38] For example, Winder (1955) argued a very convincing case for floating exchange rates, but it did not bear on the convertibility problem of the time other than in the sense that a free float implied the abolition of all currency (and other current account) restrictions.

fixed or floating rate. Some of these questions could be dispensed with quite quickly. Richard (known as Dick) Sargent noted that at the IMF meetings of 1953 there was "'a strong and growing conviction" that the sterling rate would eventually be set free'.[39] The conviction was shared by Meade, and financial journalist Samuel Brittan judged that the pound could have been floated in 1957 'without rocking the international boat'.[40] Pressnell believes that the last real opportunity for floating was missed in 1955.[41]

At the end of 1952, the 'Collective Approach' was adopted that aimed at convertibility in co-operation with European countries and financial support from both America and the IMF, although that proved a false hope. A key element in the plan, and one that was favoured by the Bank, was a floating rate. While the Europeans went along with the plan, they did so without enthusiasm. They were more interested in discussing integration. The hopes of the Bank for a floating rate (and by some at the Treasury) were being bypassed at the OEEC discussions in Paris. And then at the Messina Conference in June 1955, the six principal European integrationists were devising a different kind of system. But a significant step in terms of convertibility was taken in late 1955: the Bank was permitted to support the transferable rate. Transferable sterling was not convertible into dollars, but it lay outside British jurisdiction, and unsurprisingly, there was a market in it where sterling traded at a discount. It also therefore could be used and was used for commodity shunting, that is, using foreign exchange to buy goods that were then sold to obtain the currency of a country in which it was desired to invest.[42] What the change of early 1955 meant was that any excess supply of transferable sterling would get official support. Dollars then could be obtained at the official rate, de facto convertibility.

As Alan Day put it at the time:

The meaning that should be attached to the idea of convertibility in the context of the next year or two is one to which much uncertainty attaches. About all that can be said with confidence is that an effective convertibility must give some additional rights to someone. The difficulty arises when one attempts to define these additional rights; it is much more easy to see who is the 'someone' to whom they are given. ... One thing is quite clear; sterling convertibility is not meant to give

[39] Sargent (1954, p. 55, fn. 3).
[40] Meade (1955); Brittan (1964, p. 194).
[41] Pressnell, personal communication with author based on his work on 'External economic policy since the war'.
[42] Seldon and Pennance (1965). For some discussion on shunting, see Dow (1964). This illustrates how difficult it was to control the system.

additional rights to citizens of the United Kingdom. For as far ahead as can be seen, exchange controls over both current and capital transactions are likely to continue. Nor does the British interpretation of convertibility seem to envisage substantial additional rights for sterling area residents. ... Convertibility, therefore, implies additional rights for residents of the other EPU countries.[43]

What looked possible was that convertibility could be allowed for current account transactions on sterling accumulating after a certain date, although whether this could be extended to both residents and non-residents of the United Kingdom was complicated by commercial policy considerations. Quantitative controls were in place at this time to protect the trade account. Exchange controls affected invisibles. The removal of the latter but not the former therefore would have discriminated in favour of invisibles, and there seemed little sense in that. Technically, it was not a difficult problem to solve because a sufficiently high *ad valorem* tariff could have been employed that would have produced a more efficient outcome. But that was not allowed under the General Agreement on Tariffs and Trade (GATT).[44]

Yet, at the end of the 1950s, and despite all that had been written on the subject of convertibility, the Governor expressed a widespread view when he wrote to the Chancellor on the eve of the introduction of convertibility: 'I am somewhat bothered by the way the word convertibility is being bandied about again. I have always tried to kill it, because nobody knows what it means – I suppose it really means that anybody with sterling could come to the Bank of England and demand gold and dollars or other currencies without question.'[45]

Cobbold had written to the Chancellor in April 1956 remarking that 'we have missed the boat for a flexible rate or wider spreads. ... In any event the one thing that we must absolutely avoid is further discussion or negotiation on the rate question. Sterling just will not stand it. We have discussed all this *ad infinitum* with Commonwealth, USA and Europe. We need now to decide what we want to do, and do it.'[46] Yet the question of a floating rate was back on the agenda the following year in an article by William Rees-Mogg advocating a flexible exchange rate.[47] The Treasury was preparing a

---

[43] Day (1956, p. 151).
[44] For example, see Sargent (1954).
[45] Cobbold to Heathcoat Amory, 22 September 1958, OV44/21.
[46] Cobbold to Macmillan, 12 April 1956, OV44/21.
[47] At this time, Rees-Mogg was the chief leader writer for the *Financial Times*. He had stood as a parliamentary candidate for the Conservative Party at a by-election in 1956 and was to stand again in the 1959 election – he was defeated on both occasions.

response on which they sought the Bank's views.[48] Again, the case for floating was to allow full convertibility.[49]

The Treasury reasserted the government's (and what it said was the Bank's)
position that the best interests were served by maintaining a fixed parity of
$2.80 to the pound.[50] In the Bank, Frederick Portsmore, an Adviser, and
Thompson-McCausland discussed it. Thompson-McCausland, generally
known as Lucius, was not a trained economist but self-taught, and 'he had
great confidence in his own intellectual powers ... and regarded the exposition and indeed the further creation of monetary economics as within
his capabilities.'[51] The Treasury paper was also seen by Bridge, Principal of
the Dealing and Accounts Office with responsibility for the Bank's day-to-
day foreign-exchange operations. Maurice Parsons, Executive Director, was
also closely involved. The Bank treated this seriously and did not want to be
misrepresented on it. Bridge commented:

The point on which I believe Rees-Mogg to be on the strongest ground is his argument that the present regime encourages and indeed increases speculation in times
of uncertainty. I believe that to be absolutely true and very difficult, if not impossible, to refute as an argument. ... Beyond that I doubt if it is possible to go since I
do not believe that a convincing case can in fact be built up at all for an indefinite
continuation of the present system.[52]

Bridge acknowledged that pegged exchange rates were open to speculative
attack, and if such an attack were successful, there could be a graver collapse
with more serious consequences than if a depreciation had taken place
under a floating regime. In June, Parsons replied to Sir Denis Rickett, third
secretary in Overseas Finance at the Treasury: 'If it is true, as I believe it is,
that there is a grave risk that the sterling area would not survive another
devaluation ... this by itself would, to my mind, be a complete and convincing answer to Mr Rees-Mogg.' The Bank feared that a big change in
the rate would lead to dissolution of the sterling area, and that would be
the end of sterling as an international currency. 'The effects of this would
not only be very serious as regards our own invisible earnings but would,
I believe, be disastrous for world trade. International liquidity would be

[48] Robert Williams (HMT) to Frederick Portsmore (Adviser), 28 May 1957, enc. Rees-Mogg,
      'British currency policy', April 1957, OV44/11.
[49] Rees-Mogg, 'British currency policy', April 1957, OV44/11.
[50] Williams to Portsmore, 'Exchange rate policy', 4 June 1957, OV44/11.
[51] Fforde (1992, p. 322). As a supporter of Robot in 1952, Lucius Thompson-McCausland
      had been christened 'Lucifer' in the Treasury.
[52] Bridge to Thompson-McCausland/Parsons, 'Mr Rees-Mogg on currency policy', 26 June
      1957, OV44/11.

very substantially reduced, with the consequent inability of other countries besides ourselves to maintain trade at anything like its present level.'[53]

Bridge and Parsons were key actors for the Bank in the overseas arena. They were both strong defenders of the pound. Bridge joined the Bank from Dulwich College in 1929.[54] His skills in foreign exchange led to him becoming a member of the team negotiating the post-war European Payments Agreements in Paris.[55] He made rapid progress and proved to be 'a highly accomplished monetary technician, readily conversant with the intra-European monetary complexities'.[56] Parsons, too, had joined the Bank straight from school, in 1928. As private secretary to Norman, he was marked out as a 'high flyer', and indeed, he had such a close relationship with Norman that when O'Brien took over the position, he found it impossible to replace Norman's 'lost love', and O'Brien was 'afflicted with nervous dyspepsia for the only time in my life'.[57]

In the late summer of 1957 another sterling crisis was flaring up. The precise cause is difficult to identify. It was not obvious that it was a balance-of-payments problem of the common kind. Indeed, Lionel Robbins, writing shortly after the crisis, said: 'This was *not* a crisis of the current account.'[58] The Suez crisis of late 1956 may have been dramatic in political terms, but it passed by without having great effects on the economy.[59] There was a big fall in reserves in November, but in the first half of 1957, there was a substantial surplus on current account – running at an annual rate of about £250 million. Nevertheless, there were continuing concerns over the state of the reserves. There had been a temporary upswing accompanying the current account movements in the first half of 1957, but from the summer onwards there was a sharp downturn. In August the loss was $225 million. In fact they reached their lowest point since June 1952 in the autumn of 1957. The authorities would really like to have seen an annual surplus on current account of between £400 million and £500 million to provide the boost to reserves that was felt to be needed. At any rate, the immediate trigger for the run on sterling in the summer of 1957 appears to have been changes in, and expected changes in, other currencies, the partial devaluation of the French franc, and the spreading rumours of an imminent realignment of

[53] Parsons to Rickett, 27 June 1957, OV44/11.
[54] *The Times,* 22 September 1969, p. 25.
[55] *Old Lady,* December 1969, p. 254.
[56] Fforde (1992, p. 186).
[57] O'Brien memoir, p. 21.
[58] Robbins (1958).
[59] Klug and Smith (1999).

European currencies.[60] There also were withdrawals of sterling balances by India to meet commitments under its development plan and some consequent outflows of gold. Thus it was the ever-present problem of the level of the reserves in relation to liabilities and the fact that any kind of disturbance made holders of sterling nervous. At the heart of the problem, however, was the fear among foreigners that the British authorities were not prepared to take the policy actions required to protect and enhance the reserve.

In other words, fears about sterling cannot be separated from the course and expectations of the course of inflation. While the proximate cause of the crisis may have been external, it was domestic policy weakness that lay behind external fears. Policy weakness was reflected in the apparent inability to contain public expenditure or wage increases, which for some was a failure to contain monetary growth, even if most of the monetary authorities did not see the latter that way. Inflation, however, was a serious reality and recognised by some. In an article for *Lloyds Bank Review*, Robbins reckoned that in the 1950s, inflation had averaged close to 6.5 per cent per annum.[61] It was against this background that the crisis measure of raising Bank Rate from 5 to 7 per cent was taken on 19 September. As *The Economist* put it, 'The Chancellor sets off for Washington this week with every cannon firing in defence of the pound.'[62] In his statement, Thorneycroft particularly stressed that there was no question of the pound's value being changed or indeed the width of the bands around the declared parity being widened.[63]

Yet the debate on floating rumbled on through 1958. In March, Rickett's main case against wider bands was that it was contrary to the obligations to the IMF and 'that on balance the arguments for maintaining our present policy of a sterling rate fluctuating only within narrow margins are overriding', to which Bridge had pencilled in the margin, 'a wrong one in my opinion' – a clear indication that he at least was a long way from agreeing with the Treasury.[64] When Rowan expressed his views on making the final move to convertibility, he was now opposed to a float and in the process brought out the continuing antipathy of Bridge. At the end of the piece, Rowan rounded off with 'It will be clear from this argument' – Bridge, who

[60] See Paish (1962, p. 152).
[61] That was based on the index rising from 100 in 1950 to 143 at the end of 1957; more accurately, this is a rate of 4.3 per cent per annum but still substantial.
[62] *The Economist*, 21 September 1957, p. 909.
[63] HMT Press Office, 'Statement by the Chancellor', 19 September 1957, G1/75.
[64] Rickett to Rowan, 24 March 1958, enc. 'Advantages and disadvantages of flexible exchange rates', OV44/21, and Bridge annotation.

disliked such phraseology, added 'Nothing is clear.'[65] Later, in March, the Prime Minister asked the Chancellor for clarification.[66] Sir Robert Hall, economic adviser to the government, noted Meade's important contributions in favour of floating, rehearsed again the theoretical arguments, and drew on some empirical evidence, including a potted history of the international monetary system. His interpretation of the experience of the 1930s, however, led him to conclude that floating rates brought instability. He also turned to the role of sterling as it was used to finance international trade and as a reserve currency. On the latter, he remarked that sterling was suspect as a reserve currency because there were doubts as to whether Britain was 'strong enough to maintain (sterling's) value against possible internal and external strains'.[67] And he went on to note that for these reasons, there were those who believed that Britain should cease trying to keep sterling as an international currency. This, as will be noted later, was not the Bank's view.

At the time Hall was writing, sterling's reserve currency status was in some ways only recently acquired and in many ways limited. It is true that sterling was used in much of the empire from the nineteenth century onwards and that much international trade was conducted in sterling. However, since Britain had run a current account surplus every year bar none from 1816 to 1931, there were limited possibilities for sterling acquisition other than for those who were able and prepared to purchase sterling. There was more opportunity in the small deficits of the 1930s, and then sterling balances built up hugely with the massive deficits of the war years. These last were the serious source of the sterling balances. However, sterling remained inconvertible until well into the 1950s, and that is a serious limitation for a so-called reserve currency. In any case, no sooner had it appeared as a serious reserve currency in the middle and late 1950s with de facto convertibility than there were those advocating a retreat from such status if possible.[68]

Thus at this point the Bank was still a long way from the Treasury. In a longer paper to Cobbold, Bolton made the case for bringing the different forms of sterling together and for the possibility of doing so with a floating rate. 'I suggest, therefore, that it would be prudent to organise monetary

---

[65] Rowan to Parsons, 26 March 1958, enc. 'The arguments against a move now', 26 March 1958, OV44/21, and Bridge annotation.

[66] Rowan to Parsons, 25 March 1958, enc. Macmillan (Prime Minister) personal minute to Amory, 21 March 1958, OV44/21.

[67] Rowan to Parsons, 28 March 1958, enc. Hall, 'Flexible rates', 28 March 1958, OV44/21.

[68] Thompson-McCausland to Parsons, 'Robert Hall's paper on flexible rates', 31 March 1958, OV44/21.

policy, both at home and abroad, on the probability that something like a unified floating rate policy is inevitable but to make no attempt to force the pace until it becomes more acceptable to the Western world as a whole.'[69] Cobbold expressed complete agreement. The Treasury continued to insist that there was no difference between the Bank and itself on this matter, but this was surely wide of the mark and only for external presentational purposes. There were some parts of the financial press that picked up on what was the developing mood in the City in favour of a floating rate. One in particular suggested that in the forthcoming budget of 1958, an announcement would be made of the introduction of a floating rate.[70] In the course of 1958, discussion centred on how to bring the rates for the remaining two kinds of sterling together.[71]

There was still no agreement on the meaning of convertibility. When the Chancellor asked the Governor to draft him something on 'what is meant by convertibility' for his Mansion House speech in October 1958, Cobbold replied:

Progress towards convertibility has been an objective of successive U.K. Governments. … But … I am not sure that the word 'convertibility' always conveys exactly the same meaning to everybody. Some take it to mean complete freedom from exchange restrictions, some take it even to include removal of all trade discrimination and some give it more limited application to technical moves in the foreign exchange field. We have made a good deal of progress in all these matters and we intend to make more. But it would be idle to pretend that we see as an early objective the complete removal of all exchange restrictions, more particularly those relating to capital transfers. … We have already advanced a long way in the process of amalgamating the many types of sterling which emerged from war-time controls. We shall move forward as fast as, but no faster than, our strength allows.[72]

Bolton had long been exasperated by the slow progress that was made on the road to convertibility, and some have gone so far as to suggest that this was part of the reason for his leaving the Bank in 1957, although he did continue as a non-Executive Director for another 13 years.[73] Progress indeed does look to have been slow. By early December 1958, though, almost everything seemed to be in place, and the final stages of 'operation unicorn', as it

[69] Bolton to Cobbold, 1 April 1958, OV44/21.
[70] *Reynolds News*, 30 March 1958, p. 4.
[71] Rowan to Parsons, 23 May 1958, enc. 'Exchange rate policy', 22 May 1958, OV44/21.
[72] D. C. Ingram (Superintendent, Establishment Department, working in Secretary's) to A. J. Collier (private secretary to Chancellor of the Exchequer), 6 October 1958, enc. Cobbold, 'What is meant by convertibility', 6 October 1958, OV44/21.
[73] Fry (1970, pp. 27–28.

had come to be called, were being reached. A timetable was drawn up for notifying Britain's trading partners, EPU members, Commonwealth countries, and the IMF. The assessment was that the conditions in the exchange markets were right, and the time had come 'to remove the anomaly by which transferable sterling is artificially held in a small discount and can only be dealt in foreign centres'.[74] Incidentally, and this is something that will run through the whole story, there was an exchange between the Bank and the Treasury that is fairly typical and is highly indicative of the relationship between them. On the foreign exchanges, Parsons wrote to Rickett explaining what the situation was and recommended a particular course of action. Rickett promised to report to Makins 'but felt disposed to leave the matter to our (i.e. the Bank's) judgement'.[75] This was certainly typical of questions on sterling.

Aside from technical details as to when the Bank would begin dealing and the like, it then remained only to make the announcement of convertibility on 28 December 1958. It was also clearly stated that there would be no change in the margins around parity and that exchange control would be retained. Further, the changes would not affect residents.[76]

Gold

One obvious way of detecting pressure in the international monetary system could be found in the changing price of gold in an open market such as existed in London. At the end of the 1950s, the shortage of gold was a consequence of its price being fixed in 1935 while the world price level had risen steeply between 1940 and 1960 and the fact that gold was the anchor for the US dollar. Furthermore, the leading industrial countries, Germany and Japan, had been building up their holdings of international reserve assets, which included gold, at a faster rate than gold was being produced. The United States then became the residual supplier of both gold and US dollars. It followed from this that the US Treasury would become a seller of gold.[77] The United States adopted a number of restrictive measures on both the current and capital accounts designed to reduce the flow of dollars to foreigners, even if that was against their basic principle of promoting open trade and payments. There were inevitably disturbances in the gold

---

[74] Draft press announcement, 1 December 1958, OV44/23.
[75] 'Extract from Parsons' memo dated 3 December 1958', OV44/23.
[76] For full details on the progress to convertibility, see Fforde (1992, pp. 566–605).
[77] For an excellent contemporary view, see Gilbert (1968).

market, and these came to a head in October 1960 when the price rose to over $40 in the London market. Almost immediately after the price rise, *The Economist* argued that 'the American authorities cannot ignore the psychological effect of the dollar premium on gold in London. At the least they should positively encourage the central banks to undertake the arbitrage that is necessary to bring the London market back into line'.[78] The following week, Robert Aliber, in an unsigned piece, argued similarly, pointing out that it was in the interest of all countries to defeat the speculators and, further, 'that the central banks and treasuries of the world have it in their power to set the price of gold where they choose'. He nevertheless accepted that the existence of free markets alongside the New York pegged price caused continual difficulty.[79]

The London gold market had reopened in 1954, having been closed at the outbreak of war in 1939, and the Bank intervened to steady prices and to keep orderly markets, something that was high on its agenda. However, this was not simply a desire for tidiness, for although the price of gold in the London market was primarily a matter of concern for the United States, it was a reflection of international sentiment on the dollar and so affected other currencies, of which sterling was invariably next on the list. The Bretton Woods system depended on the United States standing ready to buy and sell gold at $35 an ounce. The question was, would the US Treasury supply, either directly or indirectly through the Bank, sufficient gold to hold the price there? If not, and the price began to rise, holders of gold would be tempted to cash in. Yet, if the United States did supply the necessary gold, its reserves would fall even further. In July 1959, Roy Bridge, the dominant figure in the world of foreign exchange, had drawn attention to a *Princeton Essay in International Finance* by Miroslav Kriz that argued that current US inflation could lead to a flight from the dollar and that it looked like the dollar price of gold would rise. There were already hints of the pressure to come reflected in the rising price of gold.[80]

In 1959, the Bank's immediate concerns for the gold market lay in the activities of both the Bank for International Settlements (BIS) and the South African Reserve Bank (SARB).[81] Bridge was particularly upset by the behaviour of the BIS, and in a note to the Governor, he said:

[78] *The Economist*, 22 October 1960, p. 385.
[79] *The Economist*, 29 October 1960, pp. 475–477, and private conversation between the author and Robert Aliber, 9 November 2005.
[80] Bridge memo to Parsons/Cobbold, 'Gold policy: London market, BIS and SARB', 3 July 1959, C43/335.
[81] For a description of the peculiar features of the market, see 'The London gold market', *BEQB* 3(4):18, December 1963.

We cannot pretend to know where we are. Firstly, there is confusion between the BIS and ourselves as to what they may and may not do. Secondly, it makes a nonsense for them to pay fancy prices in order to muscle in on the South African gold; if they are prepared to pay higher than the market price they should tell us and only go elsewhere if we are not ready to deal with them. Thirdly they, as we too, are entitled to take whatever policy line they choose in relation to earmarks in New York[82]; but I think we are entitled to know a little more about what they are doing and why.[83]

The Bank was the agent for SARB in the London market, and later that month, the Governor wrote to Guindey at the BIS saying, 'I should like to repeat that we are most anxious that anything the BIS do affecting gold shipments from South Africa to London and the London gold market should take full account of our interests. I shall be bringing Bridge to Basle for the next meeting and I hope it may be possible to clarify things.'[84]

By the end of June, Bridge had been to Basle to discuss the situation, and some progress was made in resolving the issues. The following points were established: except after prior reference to, and agreement with, the Bank, the BIS would deal with the SARB only in gold loco London (i.e., in the vaults of the Bank of England), and the BIS was not at that point seeking to purchase more than a maximum of 100,000 fine ounces per week from South Africa and would give the Bank advance notice of any intention to raise that maximum figure.[85] It is clear from the exchanges that were taking place that the Bank's policy was to encourage the development of the London gold market by all available means, and the behaviour of the BIS and the South Africans threatened to disturb the equilibrium. By November 1959, however, not all the issues had been resolved. Bridge wrote:

Since all this comes to us confidentially from SARB it is difficult to suggest anything that could be said to the BIS which would not run the risk of creating bad blood, perhaps in South Africa as well as in Basle. But it does confirm our original suspicion that the BIS are deliberately offering an incentive so as to attract traditional business away from one of their members.[86]

---

[82] Earmarking was the practice that followed from the secretary of the Treasury granting the New York Fed the freedom to undertake transactions in gold for 'legitimate monetary purposes'. *The Economist* of the last week of September 1960 carried a piece that claimed the Fed welcomed earmarking, but Parsons said there was no foundation for the story.

[83] Bridge to Cobbold, 'BIS – gold', 17 June 1959, C43/335.

[84] Cobbold to Guillaume Guindey (GM, BIS), 25 June 1959, C43/335.

[85] Bridge to Parsons, 'Note on a Visit to the BIS Basle, 23/24th June 1959', 26 June 1959, C43/335.

[86] Bridge to Cobbold/Parsons, 26 November 1959, C43/335.

There is no sign here of the co-operative climate the BIS was supposed to be fostering.

George Preston (Principal, Dealing and Accounts), working for Bridge, met the South Africans in November 1959, at which point it seemed that they were more than a little reluctant to discuss their dealings with the BIS. 'I was told that the BIS had asked that the price basis of their operations with the SARB should be kept secret and to that end had arranged a settlement procedure which would preclude the Bank finding out prices at which business was actually done.'[87] What seemed to emerge was that the BIS had been systematically paying a price over the London market price in order to cut in on the South African gold and had committed themselves to take an open position – irrespective of the actual prospect of profit or loss – over a few days because the sterling to pay for the gold had to be bought in against dollars before the price to be paid for the gold was known. The debate on South African gold continued into 1960, with the Bank still of the opinion that the BIS were not playing by the agreed rules.[88]

The first serious test of the Bank's expertise in smoothing oscillations in the market and of American compliance in their activities came in March 1960 when the price began to push above $35. The Bank sold gold to exert some downward pressure, but the US Treasury did not co-operate in restoring the Bank's gold holdings. In the late summer of 1960, further signs of pressure appeared, and Mynors warned Alfred (Al) Hayes, president of the Federal Reserve Bank of New York (FRBNY), that if the price of gold continued to rise, a movement out of the dollar could be triggered.[89] Some fears on this were related to the progress Senator John F. Kennedy was making in the polls for the presidential election because it was believed that the Democrats would have a laxer approach to policy and were less concerned with the external account.

The annual IMF meetings were due to be held in Washington at the end of September. These were meetings around which a great deal of gossip commonly swirled, and the Bank cautioned against any open discussion of gold at the meetings because the slightest hint of such discussions could spark speculation. This also reflected the Bank's natural inclination to secrecy. (At the 1959 meetings of the IMF, when there had been some rumblings of discontent over the dollar, the United States had made a point of announcing that the official price of gold would be maintained.)

---

[87] Preston to Bridge, 'BIS operations in South African gold', 26 November 1959, C43/335.
[88] For example, see Parsons to Cobbold/Stevens/Bridge, 'Note of a conversation with Mr. Macdonald of the BIS', 2 February 1960, C43/335.
[89] Mynors to Hayes, 13 September 1960, G1/357.

In September 1960, Parsons was in the United States for the meetings. Parsons was a tall, distinguished figure who would always be noticed at international meetings and was regarded as the epitome of discretion. He talked to Hayes and Coombs at the Fed in New York as pressure on gold (and that meant on the dollar) mounted and showed no signs of lifting in the next weeks. On 12 October, there was some respite when the BIS told the Bank that it would not buy any sterling area gold,[90] action of the kind the Bank had been pressing for some time. It now expressed its gratitude because it was keen to acquire as much gold as possible from non-US sources. Parsons meanwhile had gone to Canada on separate business but had asked Stevens to prepare an update on gold for him for when he returned to Washington to meet the Fed again. Stevens duly reported to him that there had been a lot of buying the week of 17 October – possibly Swiss and possibly private, but they couldn't be sure, and it might be Eastern European. But things were moving fast, and Bridge wrote to the Governor on the 20 October to say that despite heavy Bank sales, the price had risen to \$35.34 on Tuesday, to \$35.65 on Wednesday, and to \$38 'today', that is, Thursday 20 October, and further that the price may well go over \$40 before the close.[91] There was a corresponding weakening of the dollar in European markets. The price did indeed reach \$40 that day – in fact, \$40.60 – and rumours of dollar devaluation spread.

When Parsons returned from Canada and met Hayes and Coombs in New York on 20 October 1960, they were still talking about the wisdom of having reopened the London gold market, but more to the point, they wanted to know if the Bank could have prevented the price rising as it had recently. Parsons reminded them of discussions he had had with Martin and Secretary Anderson in Washington and said that in view of the opinions expressed there, the Bank did not feel free to intervene on a 'massive scale'. Both Hayes and Coombs were surprised and disappointed at this. They deplored an article by Ed Dale in the *New York Times* of 21 October (presumably they had prior access) that said that the Fed and the US Treasury gave no encouragement to the Bank to take action to prevent the gold price rising.[92] Stories of dollar devaluation then were circulating ever more widely. Harrod felt compelled to write to the Governor on 21 October saying that while the Bank should help the Americans in any way it could, Britain should point out that there were limits and that 'we are convinced

---

[90] Stevens to Guindey, 12 October 1960, G1/357.
[91] Bridge to Mynors, 20 October 1960, G1/357.
[92] Parsons, Note for record, 22 October 1960, G1/357.

that the dollar price of gold will eventually have to be adjusted, and that, that being so, the sooner it is done the better.'[93]

The following day, again in New York, Parsons met Frank Southard, US Executive Director at the IMF, and explained the Bank's intervention policy. With the price having reached $40 an ounce, the US Treasury agreed that they would sell gold to the Bank and furthermore let the Bank decide on how and when it would intervene in the future. But fears of more serious pressure were being addressed, for by the following month the Bank was considering what might happen if the United States was forced to abandon the price of $35.[94] Although the price had settled back to close to its official level in December 1960, there was pressure to return more than once under the new Kennedy administration, which at the beginning appeared to be ignoring external considerations. In January 1961, the price was up to $35.80. When further gold losses followed, a raft of measures from capital controls to changed fiscal and monetary policies was introduced. It was in these exchanges of the autumn of 1960 that the origins of the Gold Pool lie – 'a kind of gentleman's agreement … with the aim of co-ordinating the gold operations in London of certain European central banks and the Federal Reserve Bank of New York'.[95] More immediately, in late 1960, Bolton was predicting turmoil in the currency markets – 'nothing less than a presidential announcement of an intention to intervene in the gold markets can help' – and even then, that would only postpone the crisis. 'I may easily be wrong', he concluded, 'but I feel quite convinced that major exchange troubles leading to chaotic conditions are now inevitable.'[96]

Central Bank and International Co-operation

These continuing problems prompted a lot of activity in central banks as they sought solutions, and the BIS had an opportunity to play the role originally envisaged for it. The first object of the BIS defined by its statutes is 'to promote the co-operation of central banks'.[97] It is difficult to define co-operation and impossible to measure. When some see it in action, others fail to. Some argued that there had long been central bank co-operation, ever since central banks came into being.[98] Others argued that central banks

[93] Harrod to Cobbold, 21 October 1960, G1/357.
[94] Parsons, Notes of 20 October, 21 October, and 30 November 1960, ADM 13/3.
[95] *BEQB* 1(5):10, December 1961.
[96] Bolton to Cobbold, 23 October 1960, G1/100.
[97] BIS, *Sixth Annual Report*, May 1936, p. 41.
[98] Eichengreen (1995).

were simply acting out of self-interest.[99] Some see the BIS in the 1930s as successful in this exercise, whereas others do not.[100] Certainly, the view of the Bank in the 1930s was that co-operation was negligible; as Siepmann, a leading figure in the recently established Overseas Department, put it in 1935:

Ten years ago, it seemed that Central Banking co-operation might become a factor of international importance and that the Bank of England had a leading part to play in promoting it. But when the Overseas and Foreign Department was established as an integral part of the Bank, our business relations with other Central Banks had diminished to insignificant proportions and practical co-operation, whether directly or through the B.I.S., was not a reality. This was due directly to our going off gold, which meant that the initiatives in monetary policy passed from the Bank to the Government; and monetary policy is the natural field of co-operation by Central Banks. It may be that we shall have a long time to wait before the opportunities for initiative are restored to us by a return to some international currency system.[101]

Although the BIS appeared to be redundant after the Second World War, and indeed came very close to being wound up, it reinvented itself, becoming the agent for the OEEC and managing the EPU. However, a case can be made that it was in the two years between 1960 and 1962 that the BIS did come into its own in its originally conceived role of promoter of central bank co-operation. It may have looked as some have described it as simply like a talking shop or a fire station with firemen sitting around playing cards, but in fact, they are learning about each other. When the fire comes, they know how to react and work together. Perhaps. The immediate problem in late 1960 was that foreign central banks held $US6 billion, convertible into gold at the US Treasury window. Speculation on currency revaluations duly followed, and sterling took the brunt of the selling.

There had been clear signs of these developing problems in the late 1950s, and some solutions were advanced.[102] One emerged in the course of 1961 when three changes were proposed on the operation of the IMF: (1)

---

[99] Flandreau (1997).
[100] Toniolo (2005); Cooper (2008).
[101] Siepmann to Frederic Powell (Overseas), January 1935, OV21/10.
[102] The Triffin Plan proposed to convert the IMF into a World Bank. Features of the proposal were (1) the reserves of each member country would include deposits at the IMF in terms of a new unit of account, (2) each country would hold 20 per cent of its official reserves in this form, (3) payment between members normally would be made in terms of these new deposits, and (4) while these deposits would be increased to meet the growing demands of world trade, the size of the annual increase in deposits would require the prior agreement of the member countries.

improve the ability of the IMF (contrary to a 1946 interpretation of the articles) to lend to members to offset payments problems owing to capital account problems, (2) the introduction of a policy on the use of currencies other than the dollar in IMF transactions, and above all, (3) some standing arrangement under which the IMF would be able to borrow currencies from members and so fortify it to perform (1). These ideas have been described as originating with the IMF staff and then were proposed by Managing Director Per Jacobsson.[103] However, there are suggestions that the ideas had their origins in the Bank. According to Jacques Polak, the IMF's Director of research, immediately after the September 1960 IMF meetings in Washington, Parsons asked to meet Polak and Joseph Gold to discuss a proposal. They met and discussed these very ideas, and there followed a lengthy discussion that went into great detail on how the changes might be brought about. Two days later, Polak and Gold sent a long memo to Jacobsson, who embraced the ideas with enthusiasm – they later became known as the 'Jacobsson proposal' – and in the course of 1961–62 he got them approved by the board and, in what became the General Agreements to Borrow (GAB), the 10 potential lenders. These latter agreed to stand ready, in special circumstances, to lend $6 billion to the IMF.[104]

The revaluation of the German and Dutch currencies that was carried out on 4 and 5 March 1961, respectively, was accompanied by further speculation against both the dollar and sterling.[105] The monthly meeting of central bank governors at Basle took place a week after the revaluations, at which point it was feared that the Bretton Woods arrangements were in grave danger. Unless the central bank governors 'took early and effective action, the whole stability of the foreign exchange structure, which had stood with certain modifications broadly steady since 1949, would be undermined.' What followed came to be known as the 'Basle agreement' or the 'Basle arrangements'.[106] A key contribution was the use of swaps. Swaps in foreign-exchange markets have a long history, at least back to the 1920s. These swaps involved 'the purchase (sale) of a currency in a spot transaction and the simultaneous sale (purchase) of the same currency for forward

---

[103] Solomon (1982, p. 43). Solomon uses Horsefield (1969, Vol. 1, p. 507), which does indeed provide that account.

[104] Private communication from Jacques Polak. There is no trace of the Polak/Gold memo in the IMF archives, and neither is there any trace in the Bank of England archive, including Parsons' papers, nor anywhere else. But Polak has the clearest recollection of it down to the finest detail. For a recent full and interesting account, see Polak (2006).

[105] Coombs (1976, p. 30).

[106] *BEQB* 1(4):9–10, September 1961.

delivery at a selected date.'[107] The price of the swap was largely a function of the interest differential between the two centres. However, the swaps that were being developed for use by central banks in the late 1950s and early 1960s were somewhat different. These are said to be in big part the brainchild of Max Iklé, a Director of the Swiss National Bank (SNB) and since 1956 head of financial market operations, the department that implemented monetary policy and conducted money market, foreign exchange, and gold operations.[108] The swaps have their origin in Swiss domestic finance and in the window dressing of the commercial banks.[109]

At the time of the Basle meeting in late March, when Bridge was there as head of the Bank's exchange operations, Iklé offered the Bank a three-month credit of $310 million. This provided the nucleus of a $1 billion bundle of credits that Cobbold and other Bank officials raised from continental European banks over the weekend.[110] It is this episode that is often cited as the real turning point in central bank co-operation. And Cobbold is often credited with the prominent part. Fforde, for example, refers to Cobbold in 1961 'just after he had helped inaugurate the epoch of central bank co-operation through exchange swaps'.[111]

While these arrangements are widely touted as significant evidence of central bank co-operation, they did not change fundamentals, and sterling was coming under pressure again in the summer of 1961. Cobbold told Martin that the Bank did not wish to go to the IMF yet, not until late July or August, but rather would persist with these arrangements and hoped that the Fed would take a hand in the arrangements to help tide over the next two months. He stressed the need to demonstrate central bank co-operation to the wider world.[112] Other co-operative moves included the OECD setting up two working parties or subcommittees, one for economic growth and the other for analysis of the effect on international payments of monetary and fiscal and other policy measures.[113] The second, Working Party 3 (WP3), was to detect problems at an early stage and, ambitiously, correct the causes of imbalance.[114]

These swaps that began to be discussed in the early 1960s were between central banks. (Others at other times might be between a central bank and

[107] Atkin (2004, p. 51).
[108] Bernholz (2007, p. 150).
[109] Bridge to Parsons on Switzerland, 15 December 1959, C43/368.
[110] *BEQB* 1(4):9–10, September 1961.
[111] Fforde (1992, p. 567).
[112] Cobbold to Martin, 7 June 1961, OV44/35.
[113] OECD, Economic Policy Committee, 'Agreed minutes', 19 April 1961, OV46/78.
[114] Tew (1970, p. 128).

the market.) They were essentially window-dressing arrangements and allowed a false picture of the reserves to be presented. Such was the lack of transparency at the time that it was acceptable to present only the asset side of the reserve position, and any sterling liability could be hidden. However, they could also be regarded as a standby that could be activated on demand. The transaction would not affect the exchange rate directly, at least not until one or another central bank sold its holdings of the other central bank's money. Some of the initiative for swaps came from the Americans.[115] An agreement in August 1962 followed Coombs' proposal for a dollar-sterling swap on which both parties would earn the same rate of interest. Bridge was opposed, describing it as an 'artificial transaction', but they went ahead in the interests of Anglo-American financial relations.[116] He also objected to the possibility of distorting the market:

We ought to be reluctant to facilitate their [Fed's] using sterling in support of the dollar: if the Fed come into the market selling sterling which we have provided at the same time as we are buying dollars to prevent the pound from rising too high we should, without doubt, get in one another's way and the only people to benefit would be the banks in the market who would be quick to make any arbitrage profits. ... Coombs proposal would produce an artificial increase to our reserves. ... We do not want that.[117]

Thus the Bank went along with a pilot scheme for $50 million, and mutual deposits were made ahead of being needed.[118]

Cobbold Leaves; Cromer Appointed Governor

In these kinds of times, there was seldom a good opportunity for a Governor to leave, but the summer of 1961 marked the end of Cobbold's term as Governor. Finding a suitable replacement proved a protracted affair. When Cobbold was reappointed as Governor in February 1954, he had made it clear that he would serve only one further term, expiring in February 1959. Senior non-Executive Directors met to consider the matter in 1956, and their favoured name for the Governorship was Lord Kindersley, already a member of the court. By October 1957, Kindersley had ruled himself out

---

[115] Bordo, Humpage, and Schwartz (2006).

[116] Bridge to Parsons, 'American exchange operations with European central banks, Governor's note, 11 February', 9 March 1962, C43/742.

[117] *Ibid.* I am grateful to Roger Clews for drawing my attention to this and to both he and David Ingram for guidance on swaps.

[118] Bridge, Note for record – 'Pilot Operation with the F.R.B.', 15 May 1962, C43/742.

because of business commitments, but in any case, the controversy surrounding the Bank Rate leak surely would have disqualified him. Another option was Franks, but Harcourt remained the favourite within the Bank.[119] There was a complication. Both were members of Radcliffe, and it would be difficult to join the court while that committee was still proceeding. When it became apparent that Radcliffe's work would take longer than expected, coupled with the fact that Harcourt wanted to wait until the dust had settled on the report before joining the Bank, Cobbold indicated that he would agree to carry on, although he had no wish to complete the full five-year term.[120]

Following publication of the Radcliffe Report, thoughts again turned to the subject of the new Governor. The names of Harcourt and Franks were still in the frame, but now supplemented by Lord Cromer, economic minister at the British embassy in Washington and UK Executive Director at the IMF. Of the three, Harcourt remained the clear preference in the Bank. For the government, Franks was considered the best candidate. While Franks would no doubt be excellent from a technical point of view, there were worries in the Bank about his judgement and his experience in the City, and his 'rather cold personality' might prevent people talking freely to him.[121] And there was the likely reaction from other clearing banks if the head of a joint stock bank became Governor.[122] Franks met the criteria, although Macmillan admitted that it was not known if he would agree to take the job.[123] In fact, Franks was offered it and rejected it. The reasons for this are not entirely clear, although it may be that he was aware of the opposition to him on the court.[124] The Bank appears to have accepted that the

[119] Dascombe, 'Note of meeting on 25 October 1957 between Cobbold, Hambro, Hanbury-Williams, and Sanderson', 25 October 1957, G15/25.

[120] Hambro, Aide memoire, 'The Governor: succession', 16 July 1958; Cobbold, 'Lord H', 22 July 1958; Hambro, 'Note of meeting on 25 July 1958 between Cobbold, Hanbury-Williams, Sanderson and Chancellor', 31 July 1958; 'Note of meeting on 2 October between Cobbold, Hambro, Hanbury-Williams and Sanderson', G15/25.

[121] Cadbury had confided to Hambro, 'It is clear that F. [Franks] does not automatically exude bonhomie'; Cadbury to Hambro, 14 October 1960, G15/25.

[122] In 1958, Mynors had indicated 'reservations' should Franks be chosen; Dascombe, Note, 4 June 1958, G15/25.

[123] Neatby (the secretary), 'Note of meeting on 11 October between Hambro, Hanbury-Williams, Sanderson and Selwyn Lloyd', 12 October 1960; Neatby, 'Note of meeting on 18 October 1960 between Hambro, Hanbury-Williams, Sanderson, and Macmillan', 19 October 1960; Neatby, 'Note for Record', 21 October 1960; Hanbury-Williams, 'Conversation between the Chancellor of the Exchequer and J.H.W', 1 p.m., 28 October 1960, at 16 St. Martins Le-Grand, 28 October 1960, G15/25.

[124] Kynaston (2001, pp. 252–3).

appointment was inevitable: draft press notices were prepared, and Franks visited the Bank on 21 October to discuss terms and conditions. Yet a week later the Chancellor told Hanbury-Williams that Franks had in fact declined the offer, and the way was left open for Cromer. Perhaps it was no bad thing. Harrod, who was close to the Bank, called Franks 'that dullest of dogs, that bum-faced purveyor of last year's platitudes'.[125]

At any rate, Cromer followed in Cobbold's footsteps, with 'considerable temerity'.[126] The appointment was made public on 10 November 1960. At age 42, Cromer was the youngest Governor for 200 years, (Cobbold was 44 when appointed). 'Rowley' Cromer, as he was known to his friends, came from a banking family (Barings) and gained other experience with directorships in companies such as Royal Insurance, Daily Mail, and General Trust. Time spent in New York with JP Morgan, Kidder Peabody, Morgan Stanley, and the Chemical Bank provided further experience. It also gave him useful insights into the United States and the opportunity to make friends, among whom were Martin and Hayes. In 1959, Cromer saw more of Washington when appointed economic minister, and he 'quickly made his mark there, fulfilling banking and social duties with great efficiency and charm'.[127] He was later the UK Executive Director of the IMF and the World Bank, and some feel that in this period he was already being groomed as Governor, although, according to *The Times,* the appointment came as 'a marked surprise to banking circles in the City'.[128]

When Cobbold left, he was the second longest-serving Governor after Norman and still only 56. He has frequently been seen as the natural successor to Norman and sometimes spoken of as though he had actually followed immediately after, without Catto's intervening term in office. The view that he could be ruthless and did not engender an atmosphere of personal warmth has been disputed and condemned.[129] Cobbold had great charm and a strong personality. He was a man of few words, but metaphors, especially sporting ones, were a favourite device in correspondence. He was a relaxed Governor and frequently took his family on the monthly trips to the meetings in Basle. It was doubtless no handicap that he had Knebworth House as a magnificent place for entertaining foreign dignitaries. Visiting

---

[125] Davenport-Hines (2006, pp. 290–291).
[126] Cromer to Cobbold, 4 November 1960, G15/25.
[127] *The Times*, 18 March 1991, p. 12.
[128] *The Times*, 11 November 1960, p. 12.
[129] *The Times*, 3 November 1987, p. 15. Many politicians and former colleagues and others who worked in different capacities with him wrote of how this was the antithesis of their experience. Puzzlingly, the obituary was written by George Bolton, a former close colleague whom Cobbold greatly admired.

central bankers often would find themselves playing family games with the Cobbold children.[130]

Cobbold seems to have been genuinely apolitical. He was a traditionalist but made the first television appearance by a Bank official when he agreed to be interviewed by the aggressive television journalist Robin Day in 1958.[131] He was a champion of the 'we know how markets work' approach that proved effective in retaining key operations under the Bank's control. It also gave him greater influence in the City. He wrote most of his own speeches and apparently could be found pacing the grounds at Knebworth an evening before, for example, the Mansion House speech.[132]

He argued the Bank's case personally with the many Chancellors he faced, 'on occasion making what tactical mileage he could out of the Bank's formal position and his own public status ... retaining some worthwhile degree of independence and authority for the bank and resisting encroachment from Whitehall'.[133] But all this had to be done without disturbing the delicate Bank-government relationship too much and provoking unwanted action from government. Any assessment has to grapple with the difficult question of just how much freedom of action the Bank had, and none more so than in the field of monetary policy. He was Governor during a period when policy is often said to have failed. Economics certainly was not his strength, and this was reflected in his Bank. His most well-known comment – that the Bank was a bank and not a study group – encapsulates the approach. He maintained the Bank's autonomy of operation where possible, even if his room for manoeuvre was limited.

From Crisis to Crisis

At the beginning of June 1961, his final month as Governor, Cobbold set out his view of the situation for the Chancellor. He warned that sterling was under heavy pressure and that it was likely to worsen as a consequence of rumours about a devaluation of sterling and a further revaluation of the Deutsche mark, as well as anxieties about whether there was something 'fundamentally wrong' in the United Kingdom that made it impossible to avoid recurrent crises. As to solutions, Bank Rate could, indeed, eventually might have to, be used. However, Cobbold was cautious. As he had often told previous Chancellors, raising Bank Rate or restricting credit

---

[130] Interview with Lord Cobbold, 24 October 2005.
[131] Independent Television News, Interview, 'Tell the People', 18 May 1958, G1/13.
[132] Interview with Lord Cobbold, 24 October 2005.
[133] Fforde (1992, p. 612).

'would not deal with the realities of the problem and would be regarded as again attempting to do by monetary action what should mainly be done in other fields'. He continued, 'This is not 1957 [when there was a balance-of-payments surplus], and the same remedies are not appropriate.' Cobbold proposed an immediate programme that covered international and domestic action. Assistance would have to be sought from other central banks and the IMF, whereas at home the Governor wanted an urgent review of government expenditure with a possible statement made in July. In addition, the clearing banks should be warned that action might be required to deal with continued expansion of bank credit.[134]

The same day (6 June), Cobbold and Cromer met the Chancellor and Financial Secretary Edward Boyle, along with other senior Treasury and Bank officials, including Cairncross, who had just taken up his post as economic adviser to the government in succession to Robert Hall.[135] Cobbold reiterated the serious concerns about sterling and explained that in the negotiations with other international financial institutions it would be imperative to be able to demonstrate that 'appropriate corrective action' was being taken. They all accepted that it would be inadvisable to raise Bank Rate and that there was no good case for increasing special deposits. Ideally, there should be an announcement that government expenditure in the coming year would be the same as or below the proportion of GNP as it currently was.[136] The Bank and Treasury then worked urgently on measures to deal with the emerging sterling crisis. Meanwhile, at his BIS meeting in June, Cobbold had arranged for a continuation of the assistance from central banks.[137] When the Chancellor outlined the main points that he intended to make in this statement and did not include putting up Bank Rate, or increasing special deposits, or tightening hire-purchase terms, O'Brien and Armstrong were unimpressed.[138]

Cairncross claims that the Bank was reluctant to increase rates and that it was the Treasury that made a good deal of the running.[139] Notwithstanding the Chancellor's apparent determination to leave things unchanged, there

---

[134] Cobbold to David Hubback (HMT), 6 June 1961, enc. Cobbold, 'Top secret note', 6 June 1961, G1/252.

[135] Cairncross (1999, p. 40).

[136] H. M. Treasury, 'Note of a meeting … 6th June 1961', 6 June 1961, G1/252.

[137] Cobbold, Governor's note, 7 June 1961; Mynors, 'Note', 14 June 1961; HMT, 'Note of a meeting … 15th June 1961', 19 June 1961, G1/252.

[138] HMT, 'Note of a meeting … Tuesday, 11th July, 1961', 12 July 1961, G1/252; O'Brien to Cromer/Mynors, 'Monetary measures', 11 July 1961, C42/5.

[139] Cairncross (1999, p. 37).

were certainly worries among his officials about the reaction if Bank Rate was not increased. Armstrong confided to O'Brien that overseas opinion would not understand such a decision, whereas at home it would be seen as an endorsement of what he described as the Radcliffe view that it was a 'costly and comparatively useless weapon'. Armstrong also felt that Bank Rate used on its own at a later stage, rather than now as part of a package, would appear to be a 'gesture of despair'. O'Brien gave a number of reasons why the Bank had only a little earlier been disinclined to adopt the weapon too quickly. The country's troubles were 'deep-seated' and necessitated 'difficult political decisions'; a higher Bank Rate was thought to be of little use and could give the impression abroad 'that we were trying to shelter behind a high Bank Rate because we could not bring ourselves to take the unpalatable action the situation really required'. He said sterling was 'more suspect abroad now than at any time since 1949', and anything less than a 2 per cent rise would be unlikely to arrest the situation. However, a change of this magnitude would have implications for international co-operation on interest rates, attract 'hot money' to London, increase the cost of debt servicing, and make capital investment more expensive. Finally, O'Brien wanted to hold something in reserve for possible later use.[140] His expectation was that any measures were likely to be equivocal and would not provide the reassurance required. This pointed to more drastic action. A rise of 1 per cent would be insufficient: 'My present feeling is that we have no option but to repeat the medicine of 1957. Whatever some critics may say, it was strikingly effective then. This time, however, we must make better use of the time one would hope that it would again give us.'[141]

Fforde, now a Deputy Chief of Central Banking Information Department (CBID), had been a strong advocate of the September 1957 move, but he was not entirely convinced about the present tactics. If tough measures were taken, then a crisis Bank Rate 'had a lot in its favour'; otherwise, Fforde asked, why throw it into a 'hopeless engagement'? Furthermore, in the event that another package was required in the autumn, 'Do we really think that we can go to 9 then if we go to 7 now?' Fforde then drifted into Machiavellian speculation that the 'horror' of Bank Rate at 9 per cent might enable stronger pressure to be exerted on the government. On the other hand, it might press the government 'to do exactly what we don't want – to devalue'.[142] It is clear from all this that psychological factors

---

[140] O'Brien to Cromer/Mynors, 'Monetary measures', 11 July 1961, C42/5.
[141] *Ibid.*
[142] Fforde to O'Brien/Allen, 13 July 1961, C42/5.

loomed large in the deliberations on Bank Rate as they did in much of what the Bank did.

Arriving in the middle of a crisis, Cromer was quickly into his stride, making it abundantly clear what he thought was required in support of any monetary measures. He was at Chequers on Sunday, 23 July when Macmillan, Lloyd, and senior Treasury officials grappled with the contents of the package prior to its discussion at cabinet the next day. Cairncross suggests that many of the personnel involved were either new to their posts or deputising for someone more experienced and had 'little doubt that a combination of Cobbold, Robert Hall and Frank Lee would have offered better advice and been more persuasive than we were'.[143] But was this really the case? Cromer had been shadowing Cobbold for some time, knew the international monetary system, and could scarcely have been more forthright in making his thoughts known to the Chancellor. O'Brien and Mynors provided the experience and continuity. The fact that there was a new Governor made little difference to the stance that the Bank adopted.

Satisfied with the proposals, Cromer then sent the formal letter proposing the alteration in Bank Rate from 5 to 7 per cent and an additional call for special deposits[144] (see Chapter 6). These moves were announced by the Bank on the afternoon of Tuesday, 25 July, timed to coincide with Lloyd's statement in the Commons. It was a rare instance of Bank Rate not being changed on a Thursday and thus only added to the sense of crisis. The package also included a proposed reduction in government expenditure, the imposition of the customs regulator, and a 'pay pause' in the public sector.

Aside from use of Bank Rate, special deposits, and the appeal to curtail lending, there were other elements in the Chancellor's proposals. One with implications for the Bank was the imposition of restrictions on private investment outside the sterling area. Its significance was that it marked the end of the process of gradually dismantling exchange controls. Introduced as emergency wartime measures in 1939, exchange controls then were established in peacetime in legislation of 1947. In the late 1950s, there was some relaxation in part a consequence of the introduction of convertibility. But the balance-of-payments difficulties witnessed a reversal of that. In the crisis of July 1961, severe restrictions were placed on outward investment.[145] Although that investment had produced returns in the long run, the

---

[143] Cairncross (1999, pp. 50–51).
[144] Cromer to Lloyd, 24 July 1961, C42/5.
[145] 'The UK exchange control: a short history', *BEQB* 7(3):257–258, September 1967.

complaint was that too frequently these returns had not directly benefited the balance of payments.

The Bank generally was opposed to exchange-control restrictions as a means of meeting a balance-of-payments crisis. And Frank Lee, the Joint Permanent Secretary, claimed that the Treasury disliked the policy intensely, but he thought that it could be justified as a temporary measure. Furthermore, he believed that having announced and put into effect the policy, it would be dangerous to go back on it straightaway.[146] This reinforcement of exchange controls to aid the balance of payments caused considerable alarm at the Bank. Parsons had told Rickett that the policy 'would do nothing but harm'.[147] The Bank also had to fend off a suggestion to introduce a travel ration of £100. It was impossible, the Treasury was told, to bring in such a major change in the middle of the holiday season because the administrative machinery of exchange control in the Bank had been run down.[148] The edifice was to be gradually reconstructed over the following decade.

The main focus at the beginning of the 1960s was the pound, and monetary policy, such as it was, was directed at maintaining the $2.80 parity. While that was the focus, the underlying problem was inflation differentials. So long as Britain's inflation rate was greater than that of its trading partners, the pegged exchange rate meant that pressures were likely to appear in the external accounts – in the trade account but more generally in the current account. The inflation problem was in part a consequence of actions taken based on the prevailing belief that the British economy was not growing as fast as it should. While growth was faster than in any previous period, it was relatively poor when placed alongside the performance of other European countries. Growth therefore was pursued in the vain belief that governments could adjust policies to achieve higher rates of growth – 'demand management'. It was these ideas that led to a desire for and implementation of different planning schemes.

Inflation was not helped by the fact that the authorities did not hold a monetary theory of inflation; indeed, they mostly rejected it and held instead what might be called a 'sociological theory' – inflation was caused by rising costs, with the major cost being wages, and behind that lay trade union power. The answer therefore was to hold wages under control by

---

[146] Piers Legh (Assistant Chief Cashier) to Hamilton and Parsons, 'Overseas investment', 23 August 1961, EC5/328.

[147] Parsons to Rickett, 12 June 1961; Stevens to Cobbold/Mynors/Cromer, 16 June 1961, G1/252.

[148] Legh, 'Note for record – exchange control restrictions', 28 June 1961, EC5/328.

some means. Incomes policy was the principal way of achieving the goal. It could be supplemented by attempts at containing the expansion of credit, and that was done primarily by a variety of direct controls.

However, the problem was not solved, and on the external front, Britain continued to suffer with weak trading performance that left reserves too low in relation to short-term liabilities. The external accounts had for long been characterised by a current account surplus made up of a negative visible trade balance but a strong positive invisible balance. (Invisibles were roughly half the current account.) That changed in the 1950s when there was a big change in the composition of invisibles. While government spending on both military and non-military items was rising, as were net earnings on foreign investment, against these, net earnings from shipping, insurance, and other services were in decline.[149] These latter stood at £250 million in 1952 and had fallen to £166 million in 1964. Net invisible receipts had fallen sharply between 1958 and 1960 from £285 million to £58 million, and at that point there was a deficit on shipping earnings.[150]

How could this be addressed? We leave aside policies that were the exclusive concern of government, such as reducing military expenditure, the imposition of trade restrictions, allowing an increase in the unemployment rate, and so on, and focus instead on what the Bank was involved in and on which it could reasonably offer expertise and techniques.[151] Exchange controls were already in place and were varied according to perceived need. Intervention in the foreign-exchange markets was used to influence expectations and then indirectly the rate. The Bank had long seen one of its functions as keeping orderly markets, but in foreign exchange, it went further than that. In most markets the Bank did not attempt to resist the trend – it simply tried to reduce volatility – but in the foreign-exchange market, tackling the trend was implicit in the obligation to preserve the parity under the IMF articles – a price had to be targeted. However, the way in which that was done, at least until 1964, was to try to influence expectations and by preventing wild fluctuations in the rate. Thus the Bank would move to protect the spot rate before it got near to its lower bound (the range was $2.78 to $2.82, but the Bank would move whenever the rate dropped to $2.7825) and so hope to alter expectations. For these reasons, the upward movements in Bank Rate tended to be large to provide unmistakable signals.

---

[149] 'Invisibles in the balance of payments', *BEQB* 1:(5):17–25, December 1961.
[150] CSO, *UK Balance of Payments, 1967*.
[151] For a discussion of the range of means of 'correcting' the deficit, see Cooper (1968).

The strong determination to hold to the parity was in part influenced by the view that devaluation was not an option on account of the obligation to holders of still substantial sterling balances. This was also seen as the Bank's responsibility as guardian of a reserve currency, albeit the junior reserve currency. At times of extreme pressure and in the absence of sound domestic policies, a number of resources had to be tapped. Borrowing from other central banks, the BIS, the IMF, and the new arrangements of the GAB were some of the options. The use of swaps also continued. While the Basle arrangements of early 1961 might be identified as the real beginning of central bank co-operation, much more was needed in the next few years.

Almost immediately on taking over as Governor on 1 July 1961, Cromer went on the attack. In a letter to the Chancellor on the 7 July, he echoed much of what Cobbold had written the previous month. He expressed his deep concerns on a number of points, but central was government expenditure. He said that Britain's economic position was considerably worse than other central bankers appreciated or than 'the speculators would guess'. Sterling was under pressure, 'and the imminent threat of devaluation is only being held in abeyance by massive short-term support from other Central Banks, but ... this support was simply to cover a speculative attack.' Sterling was currently lying at the bottom of its range at \$2.78½. The external situation was bleak. Net reserves at the end of June 1961 were, he calculated, £565 million. The likely drain on these over the next six months would be £360 million and a further £355 million in 1962. The resources for meeting this situation were limited to £340 million in US securities and drawing rights on the IMF – possibly £715 million and possibly a little more. A strong government statement on policy was urgently needed, 'certainly in the course of this month'. They needed to avoid short-term palliatives and to get to the root of the problem – government expenditure and wages. Government expenditure was too high both at home and abroad. Military expenditure 'is a heritage from the great days of our Imperial past, rather than related to the defence needs of the United Kingdom in the 1960s'.[152] Britain needed to become more competitive by attacking costs.

He wanted to stress that the problem that had emerged for sterling in the early months of 1961 had been resolved successfully by central bank co-operation but that this was only short term. Not only was immediate action required to repay the short-term indebtedness, but longer-term policies were required to deal with the deep-seated problem. In many ways this was par for the course for a central banker. Central bankers' anti-inflationary

---

[152] Cromer to Lloyd, 7 July 1961, G1/252.

inclination was almost a tradition. They usually saw government spending as too high and taxation as too low. There was a 'common, almost pathological preference of bankers and Treasury men for cuts, restrictions and sacrifices, as if they had some independent merit of their own'.[153] They surely had right on their side, for sound monetary policy can be conducted satisfactorily only if fiscal policy supports it.

Cromer followed up with another letter on 19 July explaining that he could not go to the court with proposals to raise Bank Rate and increase special deposits unless he could be sure that the rest of the package – the bit the Treasury was putting together – was convincing. There were two areas about which he was particularly concerned. The first was the need for a strong statement on wages, salaries, and restrictive practices. The second was a reduction in government expenditure. '... at the very least if your statement is to carry conviction I think it will be necessary that you state in unequivocal terms that you will ensure that Government expenditure for the next year or two will not rise in absolute terms at *current* prices' (italics in original). 'You will appreciate that I need to be able to say [to the court] that in my view the measures proposed have a reasonable prospect of achieving the object of defending the existing parity of sterling.'[154] Overall, Cromer's sentiments were little different from those of Cobbold, but they tended to be expressed more often and more aggressively. It was a pattern that was to be repeated throughout Cromer's Governorship.

That the external position was serious was not in doubt, although at the time the immediate position was not easy to assess with precision. Balance-of-payments figures were notoriously troublesome and subject to revision, often substantial revision. In January 1961, the estimated current account balance for the previous year was a deficit of £150 million to £175 million, but by April, the revised deficit had doubled to £344 million. Later figures put the actual deficit at around £200 million.[155] There was other evidence that also had to be interpreted carefully, but some of it was not encouraging. Following the capital outflow of March, reserves continued to fall and were falling still in July. The immediate need was to relieve pressure on sterling and try to improve the balance of payments. The package of measures announced in July was part of an overall strategy and linked to the approach that was being made to the IMF.

---

[153] Pollard (1970, p. 17).
[154] Cromer to Lloyd, 19 July 1961, G1/260.
[155] Blackaby (1978, p. 17).

What had become clear by the middle of 1961 was that it would be necessary to go to the IMF seeking substantial funds sooner rather than later. It is sometimes believed, possibly based on initial practice, that the IMF dealt almost exclusively with ministries of finance, or the Treasury in the British case. In fact, however, it deals with the nominated 'fiscal agent' of the government, and in Britain (although, as is common, ambiguity was present), that could be the Bank. In 1946, there was a formal appointment of the Bank as 'the normal channel of communication' with the IMF.[156] Partly as a consequence of this, itself in part a product of the Bank's expertise in the foreign-exchange markets and partly also inevitably because of the fact that the Bank had been responsible for securing the recent short-term accommodation, the Bank was closely involved in the preparation of the proposal for the IMF.

At the end of May 1961, a team from the IMF was in London on one of their regular missions, the origins of which lay in the need to examine the justification for continuing British restrictive exchange measures (required under Article XIV of the IMF agreement). However, with Britain's approval, the IMF board decided that there was great merit in periodic discussions with members and so were discussing a range of matters relating to the British economy. At the same time, they were pursuing their views on extending the IMF's lending capacity – what would come to be called the 'Jacobsson proposal'.[157] By the beginning of July, though, there had been informal discussions on a British drawing with Douglas Dillon, Secretary of the US Treasury, Roosa, and Southard in Washington, as well as between Parsons and Jacobsson. Jacobsson had thought in terms of $1.5 billion of drawing and a further $0.5 billion of standby, made up of three equal parts of US dollars, other currencies, and IMF gold.[158]

They then began to discuss a timetable. In July, Bridge made a first 'cockshy' at a proposal. He reckoned that they could get $1 billion quickly and without conditions but that that would not be enough, and it would be unsatisfactory to go to the IMF twice. If they went for $2 billion, which they probably needed, there might be an IMF mission to look at the programme, and there might then be conditions. Bridge felt that they should go for $1.5 billion drawing and $0.5 billion standby.[159] The submission had to be carefully worded to ensure that the United Kingdom was seen to be

[156] Letter from the Treasury to the IMF secretary, 18 August 1961, C40/569.
[157] Portsmore to Parsons, 'I.M.F.', 1 June 1961, OV39/12.
[158] Parsons to Cromer/Mynors/Stevens, 'Note of a conversation with Mr. Jacobsson', 3 July 1961, OV39/12.
[159] Bridge to Parsons, 'I.M.F.', 10 July 1961; Bridge to Parsons, 13 July 1961, OV39/12.

taking the necessary steps and moreover that this was being done voluntarily and not as a result of the IMF imposing conditions.[160] The whole proposal was considered and approved by the IMF's board on 4 August. David Pitblado, Cromer's successor as the UK Executive Director on the board, presented the case and outlined the extensive programme that had been put in place to help correct the longer-term problems. He was able to report home that the tenor of the discussion at the board had been friendly and that every member had spoken in favour of the application. There was nevertheless some uncertainty expressed by the European Directors as to what the longer-term measures really amounted to and therefore whether they really did address Britain's fundamental problems.[161] With the drawing approved, Britain then was in a position to repay the short-term accommodation arranged in March from the central banks. The IMF drawing would be repayable in between three and five years, and the standby was available until August 1962.[162] In fact, the scale of the drawing probably was greater than was needed at the time, but as Cromer wrote to Lee in September, 'Jacobsson and many countries in Europe felt that a massive drawing would be a demonstration of world determination to see that the pound was supported through the crisis and that one drawing would be more appropriate than two.'[163]

By September 1961, some assessments were being made as to whether the midyear measures had had the intended effect. Not much more than a month had passed when Cromer wrote again to the Chancellor specifically to outline how he believed the measures taken in July 'to deal with our chronic deficit on our balance of payments' had worked. While he recognised that certain measures took a long time to work through, he felt that he could say something on the specific monetary measures. He felt that the hike in Bank Rate had not had the same psychological effect on foreigners that it had four years earlier when there had been an identical rise. There was not yet the inflow of funds from abroad that might have been expected; that, he claimed, was because foreigners were adopting a 'wait and see' attitude. Nevertheless, he believed that the measures had helped to keep the pound above parity. There was, though, he asserted, still a lack of

---

[160] Pitblado to Rickett, 28 July 1961, OV39/12.
[161] Portsmore to Cromer, 'I.M.F. standby', 26 July 1961, OV39/12; Washington to Foreign Office, Telegram 197, 4 August 1961; Washington to Foreign Office, Telegram 156, 4 August 1961; 'Statement by Mr. D. B. Pitblado, Executive Director for the United Kingdom, at IMF board meeting on August 4, 1961', OV39/13.
[162] IMF, *Annual Report,* 1962, pp. 13–15.
[163] Cromer to Lee, 13 September 1961, G1/260.

confidence in Britain's determination to tackle the basic problem. Cromer, however, seldom deviated long from his main preoccupation, and he went on to remind the Chancellor of 'continuing indiscriminate wage demands, despite your plea for a pause' and that this would continue until government faced down such demands: 'Any climbing down ... will almost certainly start a new run on sterling.'[164] Thus, while monetary measures were helping to restore confidence in the pound, they could not correct the underlying balance-of-payments deficit. In a personal letter to the Chancellor at the end of the year, Cromer was blunt:

I deplore as much as you do the spivish sort of society ... [leading to] speculation and abuse of the expense account. I would question whether you realise the degree of bitterness and disillusionment ... during long years of Conservative rule. ... no real move has been made to reward effort and discourage opportunism. Successive Conservative governments have built up a vested interest in inflation ... which is today endangering our international position.[165]

By the end of the year, the Bank gave a more considered assessment on what the July measures meant for sterling. Between the end of July and the end of October, reserves were up after allowing for the large IMF drawing and the repayments of other short-term loans. However, the figures suggested that there was no large investment inflow in August and September, although there was some in October. Thus, while there had been some restoration of confidence in sterling, there was no immediate reverse of investment flows. The Bank noted that this also had been the case in 1957 and speculated that investment funds probably were invested for a given term in other financial centres in a form that was not quickly realisable. However, it also could have been affected by the reduction in Bank Rate on 6 October and the expectation that there might be further reductions. The rate for security sterling in New York rose in August from $2.77¾ to $2.79 9/16, but in October it rose steeply to $2.81½.[166]

Yet little of this is in evidence in the Governor's mood. He began the new year where he had left off the previous one and in a way in which he seemed certain to continue. In a letter to the Chancellor, he made the gloomiest prognosis: 'tentative indications of the Budget out-turn for this financial year, compel me to express to you my grave concern at the probable effect on sterling.' He estimated 'overspending' at £390 million as opposed to the April 1961 budget estimate of £69 million. 'For the Exchequer to find it

[164] Cromer to Lloyd, 6 September 1961, G1/260.
[165] Cromer to Lloyd, 19 December 1961, G1/260.
[166] *BEQB* 1(5):3–5, December 1961.

impossible on a year to year basis to limit expenditure to available financial and economic resources is, I would contend, bound sooner or later to
call in question the integrity of the currency.' The previous year's 'massive
borrowing' from the IMF, of which there was still $1 billion outstanding,
'was undertaken in the light of expressed intention as to the limitation and
control of growth of Government expenditure in the future'. If things went
wrong, it was unlikely, he contended, that the use of monetary measures
of the kind that had been used in the previous July would be successful.
The real need was to 'eliminate the inflationary element in Government
expenditure'. He went on to say that if things continued in this way, devaluation might not be a matter of choice. He finished dramatically: 'May I
seriously submit to you my considered belief that failure to act in this sense
will bring about from lack of confidence a severe crisis in the exchanges
during the course of this year which it may well not be within our power to
withstand.'[167]

In fact, the next two years were relatively quiet. It is true that there were
rumours circulating at the beginning of 1962 that the pound might be
devalued. The main source for the speculation seemed to be that it would
need realignment when Britain joined the Common Market. These rumours
were firmly rebuffed, and the middle of 1962 certainly looked much better
than the middle of 1961. Confidence in sterling had grown, the outflow of
funds had been reversed, and the current account had moved from deficit
to a small surplus. The large IMF drawing of the previous year was repaid
in full by the end of July, although standby arrangements were made for
£357 million for a further 12 months. The doubts about gold that surfaced
that month also led to some fears over both reserve currencies, but the fears
soon disappeared. Even the Cuban crisis of late October 1962 had limited
effect on sterling.[168] What activity there was took place in the gold market,
where demand was the heaviest it had been since the re-opening of the
market eight years earlier.

Sterling was less strong in January 1963 when fears began to arise that
Britain's application to join the European Economic Community (EEC)
would be unsuccessful. It then came under further pressure when the
breakdown in negotiations was announced on 29 January following the
French veto. However, since the current account had shown a small surplus in the last quarter of 1962 and a slightly bigger surplus in the first
quarter of 1963, sterling showed signs of strengthening again after March,

[167] Cromer to Lloyd, 22 January 1962, G1/260.
[168] See C8/23.

and the gold market went quiet. Sterling then was quite firm for most of the rest of the year. Markets even remained remarkably quiet into 1964 following the assassination of President Kennedy, with both sterling and gold steady.

There were always schemes of one sort or another floating about on how the international monetary system might be re-designed or improved. One of these had appeared in 1962 when new Chancellor Reginald Maudling announced that he would be advancing new proposals for the IMF. This took what would now be called the 'international financial community' by surprise. It also took some time for the 'Maudling Plan' to emerge, and when it did, it took longer to understand what it meant. It looked like 'a rather confusing, miniversion of the 1943 Keynes plan for a Currency Union, to be run side-by-side with ... the IMF'.[169] It seemed to take no account of the very recent difficulties in getting the GAB established. The IMF never discussed the plan formally, and it fell in to deserved oblivion. However, Polak says that it perhaps played a part in stimulating discussion that began a process that ultimately resulted in the creation in 1969 of the special drawing rights (SDR) facility.[170]

At any rate, with the short- and medium-term problems of sterling apparently taken care of after 1961, some attention began to be given to longer-term aspects of the problem. The two continuing issues were sterling's role as a reserve currency and the related sterling balances. Exchanges between the Bank and the Treasury on these matters went on throughout 1962 on the relative merits and demerits of a reserve currency with no strong conclusions emerging. A note by Allen concluded that no general answer could be given other than if a country was strong economically, having a reserve currency was a distinct advantage, whereas if it was weak, it could prove a further handicap, without elaborating on what was meant by 'strong' and 'weak'.[171]

In January 1963, Mynors prepared another paper on the subject, at the head of which he put a quotation: "I regard it as a major aim of policy to free the UK economy from the inhibitions of its reserve currency status." The initials 'R. M.' followed the quotation, along with the date '2/12/62'.[172] He was quoting Reginald Maudling, the Chancellor, revealing a marked difference of view between the Bank and the Chancellor and possibly the Treasury. While it is sometimes asserted that the Treasury and the Bank

[169] Polak (2006, p. 15).
[170] *Ibid.*, p. 19.
[171] Allen, 20 September 1962, OV44/13.
[172] Mynors, 3 January 1963, OV44/13.

were as one on this, there is considerable room for another interpretation.[173] Fforde sent a paper to Thompson-McCausland at the end of 1964 bemoaning the fact that lax policy was making operation of the reserve currency problematic. He speculated:

I do not think that at the highest levels in the Bank there would be dissent from the proposition that to get rid of reserve-currency status while maintaining our trading currency position would be a most desirable achievement. ... There remains ... the danger that if we once let it get about that we would like to wind up sterling as a reserve currency we should precipitate a disaster.[174]

Fforde had views on many subjects, and they did not always have wider support in the Bank.[175] More than this, though, Fforde explicitly defends sterling's reserve currency status at another point. In commenting on a working party report on sterling, he advanced his own views and added, 'It will be recognised that the strategy outlined would, if successful, preserve the reserve currency status of sterling. I believe this to be a correct objective, if an unfashionable one.'[176]

As far as the sterling balances went, the Chancellor was worrying over the proportion of sterling that was repayable on demand and raising questions over the possibility of giving a gold guarantee. His concern was motivated by what might happen in terms of withdrawals in a sterling crisis. Rootham went over familiar ground of it being difficult to say what the proportions were and of needing to run surpluses with the sterling area, but he ruled out completely the prospect of guarantees.[177]

Euromarkets

An important development in international finance, the emergence of the 'Euromarkets', needs mention and perhaps not least for the fact that one of the Bank's Directors, George Bolton, was instrumental in their development. It was in the late 1950s that the Euromarkets first made their appearance, initially referred to as the 'continental dollar market', but it

[173] See, for example, Schenk (2004, p. 551).
[174] Fforde to Thompson-McCausland, 2 December 1964, OV47/63.
[175] For another illustration, see Fforde's paper on reforming the banking system, which was politely slapped down by the Governor; Cromer, Governor's note – 'The banking system', 9 June 1965, ADM35/6.
[176] Fforde to O'Brien/Parsons, 'Report of Sterling Area Working Party', 30 January 1968, OV44/116.
[177] Rootham annotation on Rickett to Parsons, 16 October 1962, OV44/13.

soon became the 'Eurodollar market'.[178] The original impetus seems to have come from the desire of banks in Eastern Europe to keep their dollar balances in Europe – mostly in Paris and London – with correspondents rather than in their own names in the United States. The Banque Commerciale de l'Europe du Nord was a Soviet-owned bank in Paris that was used by Eastern European countries for trade finance and together with its London sister, the Moscow Narodny Bank, held large balances in dollars. The correspondent banks then found a number of outlets for the balances, providing them at lower rates than borrowers would have paid to US banks. There also had been a supply of dollars from the Marshall Plan for Western Europe, and many of the beneficiaries were content to keep the dollars outside the United States.

There was a stimulus to the market in 1957 when sterling was under pressure. When restrictions were placed on the use of sterling for the finance of non–sterling area trade, British banks could offer their customers dollars in its place. The Bank was always keen to promote London's interests as an international financial centre and encouraged the banks to acquire dollars for the purpose. Also, as US payments' deficits grew in 1957 and 1958, there was then an increasing supply of dollars to meet the growing demand. Further still, when convertibility of most countries' currencies was achieved in late 1958, that provided another stimulant because commercial banks could then take foreign-currency deposits and pay higher interest rates than their US counterparts. Coincidentally, in late 1958, rates paid in European banks for dollar deposits were well above those in the United States, where banks were restricted by Regulation Q.[179] The Bank saw Regulation Q as the main factor stimulating the market in these early years.

Certainly, in 1957 a 'broad active market for US dollar deposits began to develop in Europe in which US dollars were not reinvested in the United States but were instead re-lent to other European banks, corporations and individuals'[180] There is a claim that the Midland Bank was, in 1955, the pioneer in the business and a further claim that the market helped the British balance of payments and reserves because eurodollars were capital inflows.[181] However, the whole point of eurodollar markets was that they lay outside national systems. They could not enter any calculation of the

---

[178] For an excellent summary of the early market, see Holmes and Klopstock (1960).

[179] This was the Federal Reserve regulation that dated from legislation of 1933 and 1935, in response to perceived failings of the banking system in the Great Depression. It placed a ceiling on rates of interest paid by banks on their deposits.

[180] Clendenning (1970, p. 21). See also Schenk (1998) for a somewhat different story.

[181] Schenk (1998).

balance of payments. They did not feature as capital flows. Thompson-McCausland pointed out that if the recipient of the dollars decides to hold them and not convert them into their own currency, then they do not flow to the central bank's reserve. It was not impossible that they would convert, but that would depend on factors such as the interest rates and the exchange rates, and these were the factors that had launched and been responsible for the market in the first place. Rootham and Parsons both agreed that this succinct exposition was totally convincing and that the matter could be left there.[182] Many other currencies proved acceptable in the market, but the dollar was by far the most important, a consequence of its size and its role in the international economy.

Interestingly, in the early years, little attention was paid to the market, and the feeling seemed to be that its popularity soon would fade. Paul Einzig was one of the first to pick up on its importance and wrote one of the first full studies, pointing out in the Preface that while the market was thriving during the taking of evidence for Radcliffe (witnesses were being heard up to April 1959), none of the bankers or economists who gave evidence remarked on any aspect of the market, and no committee member asked any question on it.[183]

The market came under close scrutiny in the 1960s with all the discussion on international liquidity. At the Basle meetings in April 1961, Coombs had said that American views on the market had changed from indifference to hostility. They now felt that the market constituted a danger to stability and would like to close it down or see it reduced considerably in size.[184] The Bank's estimate at the time – although they stressed the huge difficulty of making estimates – was that the gross total of US dollar deposits taken by the London market had risen from $250 million at the beginning of 1960 to just over $500 million at the end of 1960, although they added that the surge had been in the first six months of the year, and the inference was that it might not grow at that kind of rate again. As to the Bank's attitude, it was at worst ambivalent but more generally favourable. Clearly, they argued, there were beneficiaries, and if the market served a useful function, it should not be suppressed. The dangers were harder to assess. In fact, all the Bank could manage was that 'the only real danger would appear to arise from events which we hope will not happen – i.e., revolution, moratorium,

---

[182] Thompson-McCausland to Stevens, 'Eurodollars', 9 May 1962, EID10/21.
[183] Einzig (1964).
[184] Parsons to Cromer/Mynors, 'Note of a conversation in Basle on 10/11 April', 14 April 1961, ADM13/4.

or war', and even so, normal banking prudence should take care of these.[185] Other dangers might arise if central banks entered the market and then withdrew large funds unexpectedly, but central bank co-operation should take care of that.

There were some exchanges within the Bank in early 1962, with O'Brien wanting to know who the principal operators in the market were and what the extent of the activity was. Preston had noted earlier that the most important operator was the Bank of London and South America (BOLSA), and the best place to start would be for Stevens to talk to Bolton. When Bolton had become chairman of BOLSA in 1957, he had immediately set up a new foreign-exchange department and encouraged dealers to look for deposits in foreign currencies. While others were involved, 'Bolton was one of the first to plunge headlong into the new medium, and for several years BOLSA was the largest single dealer in Euro-dollars in London', and that at a time when there were around 150 banks in the business.[186] Thus, in the early years of the market, the Bank had direct access to perhaps the single best authority on the subject, on the court, and was surely completely au fait with each development. While most of that contact is likely to have been informal and conversational, there is some evidence that Bolton was consulted more formally on issues related to the market.[187]

Regulation Q continued to provide stimulus to the Euromarkets in the 1960s. In 1959, Regulation Q prohibited interest being paid on deposits of less than 30 days, not more than 1 per cent on time deposits of between 30 and 90 days, and a maximum rate on time deposits between 90 days and six months of 2.5 per cent. After 1963, Regulation Q ceilings were raised.[188] And a similar stimulus came from the German and Swiss banning of the payment of interest on foreign-owned balances and so sent such balances in search of interest to be earned elsewhere. In 1963, the Interest Equalisation Tax was introduced in the United States and, in 1965, restrictions on US bank lending abroad with the Voluntary Foreign Credit Restraint. Also in 1965, limits were placed on US-financed foreign direct investment, the Office of Foreign Direct Investment Guidelines. While perhaps not sufficient to explain the great growth of the market in the 1960s, these elements were accommodating.

---

[185] Bank of England, 'The Euro-dollar market', 20 April 1961, EID10/21.

[186] Fry (1970, p. 30).

[187] For example, Parsons discussed his views on the reporting needs of the market with Bolton, Parsons to Cromer/Mynors/O'Brien/Hollom, 18 February 1964, 6A123/1.

[188] 'U.K. Banks' external liabilities and claims in foreign currencies', *BEQB* 4(2):103, June 1964.

There was still some confusion over what constituted a Eurodollar and how they came into being. Milton Friedman related how even as late as the end of the 1960s, he 'heard a high official of an international financial organization discuss the Eurodollar market before a collection of high-powered international bankers. The official estimated that Eurodollar deposits totalled some $30 billion. He was then asked: 'What is the source of these deposits?' His answer was partly US balance-of-payments deficits, partly dollar reserves of non-US central banks, and partly the proceeds from the sale of Eurodollar bonds. Friedman wrote, 'This answer is almost complete nonsense.'[189] Friedman instead described the markets in the same way as domestic banking, with growth essentially dependent on the multiplicative expansion of deposits resting on a cash base. There was quite a lot of talk about this in the period and a variety of estimates of the size of the multiplier.[190]

Closer to home, indeed, as close as was possible without actually belonging in the Bank, Harrod wrote, 'It must be stressed at the outset that Eurodollars are not a separate species of dollars; they are just plain dollars. ... Euro-dollars consist of deposits at some commercial bank located in the United states.'[191] This is all the more baffling because Harrod was a close friend of Maurice Allen and had in fact carried out a study of the Eurodollar markets with the help of introductions from Allen. In thanking Allen for his help, he wrote, 'I saw a good many people in the City about the Eurodollar last week. My main object, as I explained, is to get some sense of what actually happens.'[192]

In the view of one observer in 1961, 'The dimensions of the market are impossible to calculate with any degree of accuracy.'[193] Nevertheless, attempts were made, and the BIS played a leading part in the collection and dissemination of statistics, but it needed above all the contribution of the Bank because London was by far the most important centre of activity. When the IMF asked the Bank in 1962 for data on the markets, they replied that information at that point was inadequate but that they hoped soon to collect information.[194] By some reckoning, the annual volume in 1964 was $7.5 billion, and that would grow to $130 billion in 1973.[195] In

---

[189] Friedman (1970, p. 273).
[190] See, for example, Klopstock (1968).
[191] Harrod (1969, p. 320).
[192] Harrod to Allen, 11 July 1966, 6A123/3.
[193] Tether (1961, p. 399).
[194] Selwyn, 'Information on Euro dollars for the I.M.F.', 6 March 1963, EID10/22.
[195] BIS, *Thirty-sixth Annual Report*, June 1966, pp. 145–146: *Forty-fourth Annual Report*, June 1974, p. 172.

the early stages in the 1950s, there was little awareness of or interest in the market, and even as late as 1963, Armstrong, now Permanent Secretary at the Treasury, asked Cromer whether 'a brief could be prepared explaining how the market worked and what its implications were for monetary and exchange management'.[196] There was then growing interest among academics and in the Bank and increasing exchanges on the subject between the two.

Gold Pool

The disturbances in international financial markets in late 1960 and early 1961 provided evidence for some that the Bretton Woods arrangements were not sustainable in their current form. Two developments designed to cope with the problems, and already alluded to, were making progress. One was the General Agreements to Borrow (GAB) and the other the Gold Pool. There were also many proposals from academics and others. Some wanted the IMF to behave more like a bank, accepting deposits and creating credit. Robert Triffin belongs in this group. Most focussed on raising world liquidity. The least radical proposals were on ways in which the IMF could tap into greater resources – to reduce the need for more liquidity by redistributing existing reserves. Jacobsson was opposed to all these 'professors' and pushed ahead with his 'own' scheme, although the paternity is disputed.[197]

The second development was in gold operations. One solution to the shortage of gold at the beginning of the 1960s would have been to adopt floating rates when no reserves would be required, but that went against the whole ethos of the post-war consensus. Another idea was to raise the US dollar price of gold to something in the region of $70 to $100. Since two of the main beneficiaries of that would have been South Africa and the Soviet Union, that was politically unacceptable, and instead, the approach adopted was to manage the gold price through formation of the cartel that was the Gold Pool. During the autumn of 1961, when gold came under pressure, US

---

[196] Mynors, 'Talk with Mr Armstrong', 5 June 1963, G3/151.

[197] In fact, Jacobsson later identified the IMF meetings in September 1960 as the launching point for the ideas. In a letter to Cromer in August 1962, he wrote, 'I have been amused reading about Jacobsson's plans in parliamentary speeches and newspaper articles in your country. … It has taken nearly two years to get accepted what was started at the Annual Meetings in 1960 and put as a statement to the executive board in February 1961; it is now becoming part of the international monetary structure', Jacobsson to Cromer, 1 August 1962, G1/256. The IMF paper, 'Replenishment by borrowing', SM/61/34, was circulating from April 1961. See also Horsefield (1969, Vol. 1, pp. 507–516).

authorities feared a recurrence of the events of October 1960 and, anxious to avoid further American gold losses, suggested that either others shared with them the burden of selling gold to keep the price down or that central banks keep out of the gold market, agreeing to buy and sell gold exclusively between themselves at $35. The market would be left free to non-monetary operators without any attempt to hold the price around $35.

Dillon encouraged Roosa to work with the British and then secure the support of the other European countries of these ideas.[198] In October 1961, Coombs proposed a scheme for central banks to share the cost of controlling the price of gold in the London market. The premise was that the United States and the United Kingdom as managers of the reserve currencies bore too much of the burden of maintaining the traditional monetary system, and agreement was needed to hold the price at $35.20. The Bank would carry out the day-to-day operations to hold the London market price. The Bank was in any case keen to protect the free gold market in London. The procedure would be that the Bank would inform the Federal Reserve Bank of New York (FRBNY) at the end of the monthly period how much it had made use of the syndicate's gold and then would await instructions from the FRBNY as to whom it should look for reimbursement.[199] There was agreement on the broad principles of the scheme, although further details would have to be worked out at the next meeting at Basle. The British were perfectly willing to participate, but they wanted to leave open the possibility of withdrawal if circumstances changed for the worse. Indeed, Rickett noted, 'once we embark on an operation of this kind it will not be easy to break off.'[200]

There was an American suggestion of a ceiling price for gold, but Parsons objected because there might be a time when the price should be allowed to rise. And he also made it clear that the United Kingdom was already doing a great deal to make gold available. Between February 1961 and the end of July, $1,700 million of gold had been sold to other central banks in addition to the $500 million dollars that those banks had obtained from the IMF in connection with the UK drawing. This left the United Kingdom with a lower proportion of gold to total reserves than ever before. Despite a general consensus in favour of the plan, some at the Treasury remained sceptical. Derek Mitchell wrote to Allen, 'We are far from convinced that it will be practicable to translate Mr Roosa's ideas into a workable scheme or

---

[198] Toniolo (2005, p. 376).
[199] Parsons to Cromer, 'Brief for talk with Dr.Holtrop. Gold', 30 October 1961, G1/280.
[200] Rickett to Lee, 7 November 1961, G1/280.

that such a scheme would in fact be likely to achieve any useful results.'[201] Lee was also unsure: 'We cannot be certain that we shall know what we may be letting ourselves in for.'[202] Nevertheless, Rickett felt that if the rest of Europe was keen, it would be 'damaging that the UK alone should stand aside from this scheme'.[203]

The United States suggested that the scheme should run initially for a limited trial period of one month, and almost all the other countries agreed on this basis. Participating countries were the United States, the United Kingdom, Germany, Italy, France, the Netherlands, Switzerland, and Belgium. According to Toniolo, 'Cobbold (England), who had no option but to accept the scheme, was still not entirely convinced.'[204] This might not capture accurately the British position. It is true that there was some diffidence about the possible weakening of the Bank's position in the market (although the proposal in some ways strengthened that), there also were those who were concerned about damaging market forces.

The Gold Pool went into operation with an amount of $270 million. It was all done in great secrecy, as was the way of things at that time. No transparency; opaqueness where possible. In the first trial month it was claimed that the dollar price was not only prevented from rising but was lowered successfully to below $35.16. The trial was taken to prove that the mechanism worked well and could be activated whenever it was felt necessary. After the trial period, it was agreed that neither the international political situation nor the state of the gold market justified the continued operation of the scheme, and it was therefore decided that it should be put into 'cold storage' until the time came when the need would arise for it to operate again. Coombs thought that it had 'served a useful purpose'.[205] The Gold Pool would be reviewed at the periodic meetings at Basle.

In early 1962, the scheme was extended, and it was agreed that, in order to avoid the possibility of European central banks bidding against one another for gold on the London market, they should abstain from individual purchases and instead form a buying syndicate for gold for which the operating agent would be the Bank. The Americans offered to act as residual buyers of gold purchases by the Gold Pool and to waive for the central banks

---

[201] Mitchell to Allen, 6 November 1961, G1/280.
[202] Lee to Hubback, 7 November 1961, G1/280.
[203] Rickett to Lee, 7 November 1961, G1/280.
[204] Toniolo (2005, p. 377). Cobbold had left the Bank as governor in June 1961, and Cromer was in Basle, although Cobbold was still on the BIS board.
[205] Parsons to Rickett, 20 December 1961, G1/280.

members the ¼ per cent commission charged on gold purchases and sales of gold in New York.[206]

The Gold Pool thus consisted of two elements, a selling consortium and a buying syndicate. The selling consortium was in operation to prevent an undue rise in the London gold price when demand was strong. It had to be specifically activated by the members. Its operations did not affect the extent of intervention in the market, and the Bank continued to intervene in accordance with its own judgement. The buying syndicate operated automatically for the purchase on behalf of the group of any gold available at $35.08 or below. By the beginning of July, the scheme was deemed to be working satisfactorily. In a note for the Chancellor, Rickett wrote:

The Bank of England and the Treasury have felt that the arrangements proposed by the US were open to criticism on technical grounds. It was however difficult for us to go too far in opposing the arrangements in Basle, and we therefore accepted them in the interests of good relations with the United States. So far one cannot say that they have given rise to any serious difficulty.[207]

In a relatively early assessment by the BIS, in January 1963, it was reported that 'it is not possible to prove positively that coordinated action in relation to gold operations has brought additional stability to the international gold market for the simple reason that no one knows what the course of events would have been had the central banks not been working together as in fact they did.' Nevertheless, the report claimed that the Gold Pool had a key psychological impact. The knowledge that central banks were working together was deemed an important factor in inducing stability.[208]

Throughout 1964, the Gold Pool continued to operate effectively and apparently exert a stabilising influence on the market. Increased new production, plus substantial sales of gold by the USSR in the first three months of the calendar year, enabled the pool to share out the equivalent of approximately $600 million of gold to its participants. No contributions to the Gold Pool had to be made in 1964 by participating central banks.[209] Nevertheless, it was simply one of several patching measures used to paper over the defects of the system.

[206] The idea was first considered by the US Treasury in December 1961. Parsons was not so sure of the scheme and believed it would run into 'technical difficulties'. See 'Note of a meeting held at the US Treasury on Thursday, 4th January 1962', G1/280.

[207] Rickett to Hubback, 23 July 1962, G1/281.

[208] BIS, 'Co-ordinated gold operations – report of the group of experts on the experiences of the past year', 12 January 1963, G1/284. See too BIS, *Thirty-second Annual Report*, June 1962, pp. 125–127.

[209] IMF, *Annual Report*, 1965, p. 101.

In the closing months of 1961, the immediate problems of sterling had been resolved. The determination to hold to parity had been restated. Medium-term borrowing had been secured. And the satisfaction with that was reflected in the reductions in Bank Rate in October and November that meant it was at 6 per cent at the end of that year. In the opening months of 1962, progress on sterling seemed to be steady. There was an inflow of funds, the reserves had increased, and there had been a repayment of £75 million to the IMF.[210] There remained continued uncertainty over pay, the new planning body, and the forthcoming budget, but despite that, confidence seemed to grow, and by March, two further reductions in Bank Rate took it down to 5 per cent.

In the next few years, the measures used in support of sterling ranged over tightening exchange controls to short-term central bank assistance, usually through the BIS, to IMF drawings, and to trying to sort out sterling balances. There were discussions on the price of gold and searches for new kinds of liquidity. The possibility of devaluation appeared, and by the mid-1960s, positive planning for it was under way. The Bank was a great defender of the pound, possibly too great, but it disliked direct controls as a means of holding to parity.

The foreign-exchange markets had been relatively quiet throughout 1962 and 1963. But that was not to last. The stop-go policies that had been pursued from the 1950s continued, with short-term measures providing some temporary corrective, but by the 1960s, a view was gaining ground that such action was inhibiting long-term planning in the private sector, and hence investment was below optimal levels and, by extension, economic growth was less than it might have been. There then followed, after establishment of the National Economic Development Council (NEDC), a deliberate drive 'to go for growth'. The NEDC believed in 1963 that a rate of growth of 4 per cent per annum was feasible for the next four years. There was a belief and hope that growth would solve the balance-of-payments problem.

Bank Rate had remained unchanged for over 12 months, until it was increased to 5 per cent in February 1964. There was some prior discussion about whether ½ or 1 per cent was a more appropriate increase, and in the process, an old nostrum was revisited. Since 1900, rises of ½ per cent were unusual, a fact supposedly a result of the so-called Goschen Rule that the rate should go up by steps of 1 per cent and come down by steps of ½ per cent. Of the 140 changes between 1900 and 1963, only 29 did not comply with Goschen's dictum, but it is questionable whether this 'rule' actually was

---

[210] *BEQB* 2(2):83, June 1962.

used in decision making. However, there was undoubtedly a danger that, as happened in 1955, a ½ percent rise would appear to be insufficient and merely create the expectation that another one was imminent.[211] Thus, on 27 February 1964, Bank Rate was moved from 4 to 5 per cent. The Bank suggested that the change was required to check domestic expansion, and there was obvious irritation that on the same day the Chancellor, unbeknown to the Bank, called a press conference at which he gave the impression that the move had been made in the light of overseas factors.[212]

---

[211] George Joachim Goschen was a member of the court between 1858 and 1865. His rule was first propounded in Bageot's *Lombard Street*. There was no formal court minute relating to the rule. Sayers to Mynors, 25 March 1955, enc. "'The Goschen rule" in Bank rate changes'; Mynors to Sayers, 31 March 1955; 'Minimum rate of discount in London 1844–1934', extended to 1957, 19 September 1957, G15/97; Hollom to Cromer/Mynors, 'Bank rate', 14 January 1964, C42/8.

[212] Press briefing, 27 February 1964; Whittome to Parsons, 3 March 1964; Dudley Wynn-Williams to Hollom/Stevens, 'Bank rate and the press', 16 March 1964, C42/8.

5

From Crisis to 'Crucifixion'

The fragile nature of the international monetary arrangements and the delicate position of the two reserve currencies meant that there was increasing discussion and co-operation among the principal participants. The February 1964 Bank Rate rise, for example, was notable for the reason that it was the first occasion on which there was open consultation with US authorities. At the end of 1963, Cromer had told the Chairman of the Fed, Bill Martin that with the economy gathering impetus, his thoughts were turning to an increase. Cromer was keen to co-ordinate any rise with a similar move in the United States in order to leave interest-rate differentials unchanged.[1] In January 1964, the Governor pursued the matter with Hayes and Coombs in Basle, while the Chancellor discussed it with Roosa at a meeting in Paris.[2] Co-operation was perhaps desirable, but negotiations were awkward and required some delicate diplomacy. Telegrams were exchanged between President Johnson and the Prime Minister Macmillan. In Washington, UK Economic Minister Eric Roll was extremely active, whereas in London, only the day before the increase in Bank Rate was announced, Armstrong, Cairncross, Goldman, and Mynors held what was described as an 'exceptionally frank' discussion with representatives of the US administration. Although in the event US rates remained unchanged, the cooperation was deemed to have been a success.[3] The only negative was a concern that serious

---

[1] Cromer to Martin, 16 December 1963, G1/253.
[2] Cromer, Governor's note, 14 January 1964; HMT, 'Interest rate policy, 15 January 1964; HMT, 'Note of a meeting ... 20 January 1964', 21 January 1964; Rickett, 'Interest rates', 23 January 1964; 'Extract from the Deputy Governor's memo dated 24.1.64 ... ', G1/253.
[3] 'Extract from Deputy Governor's memo dated 3.2.64'; Roll to Armstrong, 4 February 1964; Armstrong to Roll, 7 February 1964; Mynors, Notes, 13, 18, and 21 February 1964; Cromer, Governor's note, 25 February 1964; HMT, 'Note of a meeting 26 February, 1964'; 'Extract from note of a meeting held at HMT 29.2.64. Visit of Mr. Roosa', G1/253.

risks had been taken with security, and there could have been another Bank Rate 'leak'.[4] All this was an indication of the growing significance of international monetary coordination and the wider sensitivities of monetary decisions taken in Britain and the United States. Mynors, for one, appeared to lament the developments, confiding to Martin, 'Thus, what when I was a boy was a purely domestic concern of this institution, now looks like being a matter of argument not merely between the City and its West End Branch, but even between our two governments.'[5]

The economy was growing strongly at the beginning of 1964, and the Bank Rate rise was in part to help moderate the growth of demand, although this was not quite in line with Radcliffean views. It is not always easy to follow the logic of some policy statements; on this occasion, it was said that the higher Bank Rate would encourage business confidence and sentiment in the gilt-edged market.[6] The emphasis was, as ever, on psychology – the Bank was addicted to psychological warfare – and presumably, the hope was that the rise would be taken as an indication of the resolve that unnecessary expansion would not be allowed to develop. Real output was forecast to grow at 5 per cent and personal disposable income at 7 per cent in nominal terms in the course of the year. However, the fear that resurfaced was that such demand inevitably would be accompanied by difficulties on the external account. At the beginning of 1964, however, all markets were relatively quiet. There was a brief period of pressure on sterling at the end of February when the spot rate fell from $2.7970 to $2.7945 in the space of a few days, and support was given to hold the rate there at a cost of $25 million.[7] That episode, however, was associated with the persistent rumours that the Deutsche mark (DM) was to be revalued. Of more concern was the fact that the British current account was at the same time slipping into deficit.

On the continent, there continued to be fears that Britain was not taking its reserve position sufficiently seriously. In a letter that reflected these fears, Frederick Conolly of the Bank for International Settlements (BIS) wrote to the Governor expressing such views. He began, 'It is unusual for me to write to you but I hope you will permit an exception.' And to add to the hint of conspiracy, he ended with a PS: 'No copies of this letter are circulated here, nor has anyone been told I am writing to you.'[8] Conolly had been a Bank employee in the 1920s, joined the BIS in 1933, and was currently manager

[4]   'Extract from the Deputy Governor's memo dated 4.3.64 … ', G1/253.
[5]   Mynors to Martin, 19 February 1964, G1/253.
[6]   *BEQB* 4(2):87, June 1964.
[7]   Cooke and Bull, 'A history of the sterling crisis', 1967, p. 8, EID1/24.
[8]   Conolly to Cromer, 23 January 1964, G1/560.

of the Monetary and Economic Department.[9] The thrust of his letter was that Britain's reserves were too low when compared with other countries or when expressed in terms of import coverage. Whereas they were about $3 billion, they should, by Conolly's reckoning, have been $5 billion. The $2 billion could be found by using $1.5 from US securities requisitioned during the war and $0.5 billion by borrowing from a 'surplus' country such as Germany (with $7 billion reserves) against UK government paper denominated in DM and for, say, 10 years. He finished by saying, 'This may seem to you rather naïve and I may have got into Continental ways of thought ... but ... no amount of "standbys" can compare with real cash in hand.'[10] The Governor was in Pakistan at the time, so Mynors, disregarding any implicit confidentiality, took it on himself to reply. He could not see anything wrong with the first suggestion, although he thought that there might be obstacles in terms of US politics and British Treasury ministers' indecision over how to regard the asset of US securities. Overall, though, he was not enthusiastic and in characteristically Mynors fashion said, 'To my purist mind, there is far too much borrowing about already without sufficient thought of repayment.'[11]

At any rate, while the authorities were ever watchful, in January 1964, there was no immediate concern in Britain generally or in the Bank over these questions. And indeed, one of Conolly's points was that action could be taken when things were as quiet, as they were then. However, as the weeks passed, it was becoming clear that there had been a substantial deterioration in the balance of payments. In May, the National Institute of Economic and Social Research (NIESR) predicted that in 1964 the overall deficit (current and long-term capital accounts) would be £300 million. By July, the official estimate of the deficit was £600 million, and at that point, the threat to sterling was being acknowledged. Between late May and late July, the spot rate had fallen from $2.8000 to $2.7875. The NIESR's *Review* in August gave a current deficit of £400 million and an overall deficit of £500 million. In fact, the current deficit, as published in 1965, turned out to be £374 million, and the latest revisions give the figure as £327 million.[12] It does not really matter greatly from a policy point of view. It was huge, one of the biggest ever.

---

[9] Toniolo (2005, p. 700).
[10] Conolly to Cromer, 23 January 1964, G1/560.
[11] Mynors, 30 January 1964, G1/560.
[12] NIESR, *Review* 28:10–11, May 1964 and 29:7, August 1964; Cooke and Bull, 'A history of the sterling crisis', 1967, pp. 9–10, EID1/24; Kahn, 'Enquiry into the position of sterling 1964–65', 1 June 1966, p. 14, EID1/20.

While no drastic action was being contemplated, as early as April 1964, there began to be talk of devaluation. Indeed, talk of floating or of devaluation never went away completely. However, Balogh expressed the view that was common in official circles: 'Devaluation and even more a floating rate could not in present conditions bring more than fleeting relief. Either would damage the dollar and embitter relations with America and the sterling area countries. They would also lead to a loss of available support credits for sterling when they are most needed.'[13] There were, of course, always rumours around somewhere on the topic, and most recently, they had been circulating at a high level in Europe. In April, however, it was being taken seriously in the Bank and in the Treasury, even if only to dismiss it as unacceptable. Rupert Raw, an Adviser to the Governors specialising in European matters (he earned some notoriety by swimming across the Rhine at Basle and being picked up by police[14]), cited the French devaluation of 1958 to make the point that only in the direst circumstances – in that case imminent civil war – should it be contemplated. In France for three years after devaluation, he said, the unions feared armed right-wing intervention and so remained compliant. Clearly, his argument was, nothing like this existed in Britain.[15] Allen added that the franc was not a reserve currency. More pragmatically, though, in the course of 1964, Britain was going to need short-term finance from abroad to see it through the balance-of-payments deficits. If there were a devaluation at that point, they could not expect to receive that financial assistance, and it also would put at risk the general spirit of international co-operation that had developed in the previous three years. He concluded, 'Economic and political consequences make it quite indefensible to recommend devaluation as a way of improving our earnings from exports and from invisibles.'[16] Parsons could not have agreed more: 'the devaluation of the currency of a major trading nation may be a necessity, but only as a confession of ineptitude and irresponsibility.'[17] This was very much the Bank line.

Nevertheless, the subject continued to receive increasingly serious treatment. In June, Cairncross said that it should be an important object of policy to avoid allowing the situation to arise in which devaluation would be inevitable. He went through the arguments for it and made calculations

[13] *The Times*, 19 March 1963, p. 9.
[14] *Old Lady*, August 1972, p. 189.
[15] Rupert Raw to Cromer/O'Brien, 13 April 1964, OV44/132.
[16] Allen, Draft on 'Devaluation', 15 April 1964, and Bank of England, 'Devaluation', 17 April 1964 (a copy was given to Armstrong at the Treasury on 20 April 1964), OV44/132.
[17] Parsons to Cromer/O'Brien/Allen, 24 April 1964, OV44/132.

based on a devaluation of 10 per cent (with the pound at $2.40, that would make a cent equal to a penny) and using export and import elasticities. It was the kind of exercise that had been done before at the Treasury from at least 1931.[18] On the first version of the Cairncross paper, O'Brien wrote in school-masterly fashion, 'Not a very happy effort', and added that if this was what was going to be annexed to Armstrong's report, then the Bank might want to prepare a separate paper along the lines of Maurice Allen's.[19]

The Next Sterling Crisis

While the policy of devaluation might have been seen as distasteful, it nevertheless was seen as something for which preparation needed to be made. There were, though, more pressing needs in the late summer of 1964. In the middle of August, the spot rate was still weak, whereas the forward rate was less so, and the interpretation was that the current account was worrying people but that no nervousness was developing over the longer term. However, with International Monetary Fund (IMF) meetings about to be held in Tokyo in September, there was growing concern in the Bank as to what action might need to be taken in the next month when central bank governors and finance ministers were absent in Tokyo. The Governors, together with Parsons and Hollom, called on the Chancellor on 28 August to put the question and were told that the US swap facility should be used rather than selling gold.[20] The swap facility, arranged in August 1962 with the Federal Reserve initially for $50 million, was created on a standby basis for periods of three months and renewed every three months until May 1963 and then annually. At the end of May, it was increased to $500 million.[21] The Governor suggested that Bank Rate might be raised, although he was in no hurry to do this, but the Chancellor doubted if it would help, without really pausing to consider what scale of problem was being anticipated. There were perhaps political considerations implicit on both sides, with the government unwilling to allow a Bank Rate rise just before an election campaign and with Cromer content with that, providing as it might

[18] Cairncross to Allen, 15 June 1964, C44/132; see, for example, Donald Ferguson to E. R. Forbes, 'Some notes on revenue tariffs', 4 March 1931, TNA T175/52, on the likely effect of a tariff.

[19] O'Brien, Annotation, 16 June 1964, on Cairncross to Allen, 15 June 1964, OV44/132. On balance-of-payments prospects, see HMT, 'Balance of payments prospects and policies. Memorandum by Sir William Armstrong covering the report of a group of officials on balance of payments prospects and policies', September 1964, TNA T230/639.

[20] Hollom, Note for record, 28 August 1964, OV44/123.

[21] Cooke and Bull, 'A history of the sterling crisis', 1967, appendix 1, EID1/24.

a better chance of continued working with them rather than with a new Labour Government.[22] At any rate, while nothing serious was concluded, they did agree that in Tokyo they might as well make it clear that they were going to need an IMF drawing soon.[23] In August 1964, the $1 billion IMF standby was renewed to cope with a run of 1961 proportions, which might well develop in the course of the coming election campaign. In September, though, further measures were taken. A $500 million facility was arranged with other central banks to be repaid at the end of December. By Friday, 11 September, there was more pressure on sterling, and it extended to the forward markets.

The problems of sterling could hardly have been expected to diminish in an election campaign, especially so with the opposition understandably drawing attention to the external account. In October Cromer expressed his concerns to the Chancellor, '... Mr Wilson is quoted as saying that the latest figures were going to "dominate the Election from now on."'[24] The prospect of a Labour Government aggravated fears too, for it was believed that they might abandon parity in a push for economic growth. (Against that, Labour had been in power on the occasion of the two previous devaluations in 1931 and 1949, and some believed that they needed to break that association to gain financial credibility.) On the day of the election, 15 October, it became clear quite early on that Labour had won, and Friday, 16 October was another bad day for sterling, with the spot rate at $2.7825, the lowest since 1955.

What followed was one of the worst sterling crises of the post-war years, in effect, a crisis not resolved that culminated in the devaluation of 1967. The crisis in 1964 might have been avoided if prompt and decisive action had been taken. The new government, however, dithered on all fronts. The new president of the Board of Trade, Douglas Jay, made a statement on 20 October to the effect that the government could solve the balance-of-payments problem without cutting back on domestic activity. This showed scant awareness of the way in which the British economy was seen at home or abroad. Another bad day followed on Friday, 23 October when £33 million was used to hold the rate at $2.7825.

Before the election, Labour had in fact decided against devaluation, although it is probably too strong to say that 'from the first day devaluation

---

[22] According to Ziegler (1993, p. 194), Cromer 'made little attempt to hide the low opinion' he had of Wilson (slippery).

[23] Hollom, Note for record, 28 August 1964, OV44/123.

[24] Cromer to Maudling, 1 October 1964, G1/260.

was dismissed ... and not mentioned again until July 1966'.[25] The option certainly was threatened in the first few weeks of the government. At a meeting at 10 Downing Street on the Saturday following the election, only MacDougall argued for devaluation,[26] although Cairncross and the Treasury Economic Adviser Robert Neild also were in favour in October.[27] Later, others accepted that the mistake in not devaluing distorted policy for the next several years.[28] However, there is no doubt that at the time, the dominant view was opposed to devaluation, and that included Cromer and officials at the Bank. There may have been a division of opinion among Whitehall economists, as former senior Treasury official Leo Pliatzky says, but there was none in the Bank.[29] More typical of the Bank's position was that of Bridge; when yet another note on the subject was being commented on in December, in his usual robust style, he wrote that he was in broad agreement with the note but was disappointed not to see 'mention anywhere of devaluation being tantamount to an act of armed robbery', adding 'but it was probably not considered politic to include that diagnosis'. At other times, Bridge had described devaluation as 'highway robbery'.[30]

The Americans were being kept fully informed of the developing crisis, and in October, the Prime Minister told President Johnson:

> We have considered and rejected two alternative courses of action: the first with all its repercussions on the international exchanges will be obvious to you, and this we have rejected now, and for all time (that was devaluation); the second an increase in interest rates, I am against in principle both because of its restrictive effect on the economy and because of its effect on your own problems, especially at this time.[31]

Did his opposition to an interest-rate rise because of its domestic impact mean that he now rejected the Radcliffe view that he had previously endorsed wholeheartedly? Wilson's remarks were, of course, the kind to be expected on such subjects: strong denials in an attempt at pre-empting any precipitate action in the markets. In 1964, though, it does seem to have been believed. *The Times* offered support: 'This (devaluation) was

[25] Morgan (1997, p. 212).
[26] MacDougall (1987, p. 152).
[27] Middlemass (1990, p. 114).
[28] Castle (1984, p. xiii).
[29] Pliatzky (1982, p. 66).
[30] Bridge to O'Brien, 14 December 1964, OV44/132. In September 1964, he wrote, 'Devaluation is an act of highway robbery upon one's overseas creditors in £'; Bridge, Note, September 1964, OV44/132. In June 1965, Bridge talked of 'highway robbery and piracy'; Bridge to Cromer, 'Mr. Fforde's three papers', 8 June 1965, OV44/133.
[31] Wilson to Johnson, 24 October 1964, OV44/123.

thought possible in 1961. It is not now.'[32] In October, the government set out its assessment of the economy.[33] The expected rise in Bank Rate, however, did not come, nor did it on the following Thursday. Cromer complained about remarks of the foreign secretary about Bank Rate. 'I am sure you will agree [that] this is not a subject for public discussion and if it is to be mentioned in public at all should only be done so by yourself or the Prime Minister, or conceivably myself, but in any event only after full consultation between us.'[34]

The Queen's speech of 3 November did nothing to allay fears and certainly nothing to lift spirits and nothing to address the problems of sterling. Worse, there was no change in Bank Rate on 5 November, and heavy selling of sterling began again. Things got so bad that on 6 November, a Munich newspaper carried a confident statement that sterling was about to be devalued. Thus the dithering continued. A mini-budget was presented by Chancellor James Callaghan on 11 November that set out some proposals for reducing the public-sector borrowing requirement (PSBR). It too failed to persuade users of sterling that the basic problem was being properly addressed. Moreover, on the following day, there was still no rise in Bank rate. On the next day, Cromer reported to the Chancellor that there was profound anxiety among other central banks. The Governor proposed a 1 per cent rise in Bank rate, but Neild and the Treasury felt that 'on domestic grounds a rise in bank rate would not be appropriate now.'[35] Sterling came under renewed pressure that day, and £20 million was spent supporting a rate of $2.7828. Almost unbelievably, there was no change in Bank Rate the following Thursday either, 19 November, and Friday, 20 November, proved the worst day to date as a further £63 million was spent defending the rate – this was more than on any day in the 1961 crisis.[36]

On 20 November Cromer wrote to the Chancellor to say that 'the situation of sterling is deteriorating disturbingly quickly. … we have now in the course of this month lost £147 million.'[37] Although the press speculated on the scale of support that was being given, they usually greatly underestimated, and very few did know. 'Not even [the] Cabinet were told the figures of the daily losses and I confided only in Harold Wilson and George Brown',

[32] *The Times*, 8 October 1964, p. 19.
[33] *The Economic Situation: A Statement by Her Majesty's Government,* 26 October 1964, HMSO.
[34] Cromer to Callaghan, 28 October 1964, G1/260.
[35] Neild to Armstrong, 16 November 1964, TNA T326/268.
[36] Cooke and Bull, 'A history of the sterling crisis', 1967, pp. 15–17, EID1/24.
[37] Cromer to Callaghan, 20 November 1964, G1/260.

the Chancellor recalled.[38] Cromer complained about the inadequacy of the budget and to say that borrowing alone could not get them through – no matter how much they borrowed. Wilson, in turn, complained of Cromer, 'we had to listen night after night to demands that there should be immediate cuts in government expenditure … we were being asked, almost at pistol point, to cut back on expenditure.'[39] But Cromer did not let up and at the end of November wrote, 'I must once again urge upon you and your colleagues that an early increase be made in Bank Rate. … I must give you notice that it is quite probable that I shall have to recommend to you a 2 per cent increase, i.e., to 7 per cent.'[40] Cromer, however, was still suggesting that the change be made on the following Thursday and the final decision taken on the Wednesday. Coombs was in the Bank that day, 20 November, and he said, 'That Friday night I left the Bank with the feeling that the Labor [*sic*] Government was about to throw in the sponge.'[41]

The continuing, and inexplicable, reluctance to raise Bank Rate could only mean that when it was raised in the midst of the flight from sterling, the only interpretation to put on it was that of a panic measure, as indeed it had become by then. A message from Washington conveyed complete support from the Americans for raising the rate and intimated that they would follow suit, although they were thinking in terms of ½ per cent regardless of whether Britain moved 1 or 2 percent. However, concern was expressed that negotiating an additional standby from the IMF might be difficult, and activation of the General Agreements to Borrow (GAB) could run into obstacles in the form of the Europeans who did not believe enough had been done to correct the balance-of-payments problem. At a meeting at Chequers with economic ministers and Advisers and the Bank's Governor over the weekend of 21–22 November, the decision was finally taken to raise Bank Rate to 7 per cent. The announcement was made on Monday, 23 October, at 10 a.m. rather than on the customary Thursday, thus adding to the sense of panic. That afternoon, the Chancellor told the Commons that 'the purpose of the move is to place beyond any doubt the Government's determination to maintain sterling at its present parity.'[42] When questioned about the impact of the rate increase, Callaghan replied that 'it was the unanimous conclusion of the Radcliffe Committee that an increase in Bank Rate had its first immediate effect on the international situation. … I hope

[38] Callaghan (1987, p. 168).
[39] Pimlott (1992, p. 134).
[40] Cromer to Callaghan, 20 November 1964, G1/260.
[41] Coombs (1976, p.114).
[42] HC Deb, 23 November 1964, Vol. 702, c914.

it will not work through to the domestic economy.'[43] If that was the belief, then it might legitimately be wondered why there had been such a delay in using it.

Another possible supplementary question considered was: 'Does the fact that the rise in Bank Rate is being announced on a Monday betray panic on the part of the government?' To which the predictable prepared answer was, 'No, certainly not'.[44] But panic there certainly was. On Tuesday and Wednesday, there was a massive run on the pound. Despite support of £87 million on Tuesday, the spot rate fell to $2.7860, and at that stage, 'the flight from sterling had got out of hand.'[45] Coombs recalled that Bridge rang him at 2 p.m. GMT to say that they were now losing reserves at a rate of $1 million per minute.[46] At 5.30 p.m. on Tuesday, 24 November, a crisis meeting was held in the Treasury with the Chancellor and the Governor. The Governor reported that 'we [are] now in a state of extreme crisis; all our credit facilities [have] been exhausted; we now [have] to sell gold.' When the Chancellor asked for the Governor's view as to the explanation for this state of affairs, the Governor replied unhesitatingly that it was a lack of confidence in the government's policies. The Deputy Governor added that many at home and abroad believed that there was a fundamental weakness in the economy 'for which no fundamental remedies had been put forward.'[47] They moved from the Treasury to continue the discussions with the Prime Minister at 10.30 p.m. at 10 Downing Street. The meeting had a distinctly edgy atmosphere. When a suggestion was made that there might be difficulties in raising finance from other central banks, Wilson announced dramatically, 'if central banks and their governments were going to impose a situation in which a democratically elected government was unable to carry out its election programme, then he would have no alternative but to go to the country.'[48] Michael Stewart gleefully recorded, 'The wily Yorkshireman spreadeagled Cromer's stumps with a googly.'[49] The Prime Minister went on to say that he thought some import prohibitions might have to be introduced, but the Governor pointed out that IMF Article XIII did not allow this. The Prime Minister and the Chancellor said that they were unaware of that! The Prime

[43] *Ibid.*, c916.
[44] HMT, 'Notes for supplementaries on Bank Rate', November 1964, c.22, in OV44/123.
[45] Cooke and Bull, 'History of the sterling crisis', 1967, p. 19, EID1/24.
[46] Coombs (1976, p. 115).
[47] HMT, 24 November 1964, 'Note of a meeting … 24 November, … ', OV44/123.
[48] Derek Mitchell [Wilson's PPS] to O'Brien, 25 November 1964, enc. 'Record of a meeting at No. 10 Downing Street at 10:30 p.m. on Tuesday, November 24, 1964', OV44/123.
[49] Stewart (1977, p. 35).

Minister, remarkably, went on to say that he was coming to the conclusion 'that an acceptable alternative to devaluation, in both political and economic terms, might be to let the rate float.' But then, as the meeting was concluding, he said that if it proved impossible to find short-term finance, 'there would be no alternative but to consider seeking a mandate for devaluation.' He may have been calling Cromer's bluff, although Cromer retorted that calling an election 'would mean putting Party before country'.[50] But Wilson cynically perceived that the last thing that central bankers wanted was turmoil in the international financial system and that he could be confident that Cromer could arrange a rescue package. He may not have liked Cromer, and even suspected him of undermining Labour, but he did admire his central banking skills. On Wednesday, 24 November, a further £92 million was spent to hold the rate at $2.7860.

In fact, from the previous morning, the Governor had been busy making telephone calls to other central banks, and at 7 p.m. on Wednesday, an announcement was made that a $3 billion package had been put together. It had been done largely at the personal initiative of the Governor. He had help in the United States from Coombs, who was at the same time calling his colleagues and telling them that if the pressure on sterling finally resulted in devaluation, there would then follow an attack on the dollar, and hence the international monetary system was under threat. Coombs urged them to support a package of the kind Cromer was organising.[51] The package was made up of swaps and deposits from 11 countries, the BIS, and the Eximbank. The largest contribution was a DM-sterling swap for $500 million; there was also an increase in the Federal Reserve Bank swap from $500 million to $750 million. Most of the facilities were available until the end of February 1965 and then renewable until May of that year.[52] The package brought to a halt the feverish speculation in the exchange markets, and it was thought to have finally removed the threat of imminent devaluation, even if doubts lingered over the long-term prospects for the economy. Cromer likened the operation to Dunkirk and warned the Chancellor that the victory had still to be won. With typical hyperbole he added, 'failure could be almost as calamitous to the position of this country in the world as would have been military defeat'.[53] However, the Governor was correct in his view that the package

[50] Mitchell to O'Brien, 25 November 1964, enc. 'Record of a meeting at No. 10 Downing Street at 10:30 p.m. on Tuesday, November 24, 1964', OV44/123.
[51] Coombs (1976, p. 114); Meltzer (2009, p. 757).
[52] Cooke and Bull, 'A history of the sterling crisis', 1967, annex 1, EID1/24.
[53] Cromer to Callaghan, 1 December 1964, OV44/132.

would not entirely restore confidence, as events over the next few weeks would show.

On 2 December, a $1 billion (£357million) drawing under the standby facility with the IMF was announced, the money being used to repay the short-term credits arranged earlier. This was repayable within three years. On 3 December, $80 million in Swiss francs was drawn under a bilateral credit. And yet, when O'Brien, deputising at short notice for Cromer, met the Chancellor on 4 December, he reported that, 'he [the Chancellor] was clearly losing confidence in the ability of the government to avoid devaluation'. To the rumours of devaluation that were circulating abroad, there now were added those of the government falling. The Chancellor on 4 December was still visibly shaken from his visit to Paris, and when O'Brien told him that there was no more money to be had, Callaghan replied that as he saw it, 'the Government would have to go to the country allowing the rate to float meanwhile'.[54]

Heavy pressure on sterling returned on 10 and 11 December when £75 million was spent defending the rate. And from there things got steadily worse. Such was the state of agitation that on 10 December Parsons wrote to the Governor to say that he had just been told

> … that for the first time since the 1930s a London bank had failed. Coming at the present juncture this could well mean that all the efforts of the past few weeks will have been wasted. This will be regarded by the foreign Press as an indication that the London banking system is not altogether reliable. … The responsibility for this deplorable state of affairs seems to rest between the Midland Bank, the Accountants and the Bank of England and I very much hope that if we manage to survive this new disaster there will be a very serious investigation into the question as to how this was allowed to happen and whether there are other potential failures in the offing.[55]

In fact, the firm in question was a relatively small private merchant bank by the name of Knowles and Foster. It was old (established 1828) and did a lot of foreign business and hence might have some overseas ramifications that would not be welcome at that time. The Bank had been keeping an eye on it for some time because it had suffered some serious fraud in 1962.[56] While it was not of great significance, the response of Parsons indicates the kind of edginess that had taken over. Indeed, on the same day, Cromer

---

[54] O'Brien to Cromer, 4 December 1964, OV44/123.

[55] Parsons to Cromer, 10 December 1964, ADM13/7.

[56] Fforde to Clarke, Note for record – 'Knowles & Foster', 9 October 1963; Clarke, Note for record – 'Knowles and Foster', 18 November 1964; Various press cuttings, C48/399.

told Armstrong of the dire impact of devaluation that the Bank predicted for the international monetary system, for trade, and for the domestic economy. Cromer had hoped that his views would be relayed to both the Chancellor and the Prime Minister, but Callaghan ruled that nobody else in the Cabinet, including Wilson, should be told.[57]

On Friday, 18 December, £71 million was spent in support of sterling and then a further £58 million on the Monday (21 December). Cromer told the Prime Minister that confidence was still diminishing, that rumours were rife, and that they had still not convinced markets that enough had been done. The strain on reserves was of unprecedented magnitude. Those in the sterling area had 'shown remarkable steadfastness', but if they lost confidence, then the day would be lost. 'We are close to the brink of the abyss.' He recommended a TV broadcast and cuts in public expenditure.[58] On 23 December, he and the Deputy Governor went to see the Prime Minister to follow up. The Prime Minister agreed that the situation was worrying, but he saw no point in taking action before a public holiday. He would make an announcement in the middle of January and a TV broadcast expressing 'a mood of resolute confidence' and include a number of positive measures aimed at boosting exports and possibly a substantial cut in defence expenditure. On 22, 23, and 24 December, £43 million, £97 million, and £74 million, respectively, were used in support of sterling. These amounts were unprecedented in size, and the greater part of all this was done in the forward markets.

The crisis called for the deployment of every available technique, and forward intervention was one of these. Forward intervention is a technique to support the exchange rate (usually covertly) of a weak currency and so to encourage holders of that currency to stay in the market. (The opposite might be done with a strong currency as a means of exerting downward pressure on interest rates.) When the Bank bought sterling forward, usually at a date of three months, the market counterparties might hedge by buying spot for later delivery. The forward purchase could be seen as a way of buying time, either waiting for some policy action to take effect or simply waiting for conditions to improve. The purchases might well be rolled over at the end of whatever date they were at, and

---

[57] Cromer to Armstrong, 10 December 1964, enc. Bank of England, 'Consequences of devaluation', 10 December 1964; O'Brien to Cromer, 14 December 1964, OV44/132. Reportedly, Callaghan told Armstrong that the note 'would not tell him [Wilson] anything that he did not already know, and his resolution on this topic needed no bolstering'; O'Brien to Cromer, 14 December 1964, OV44/132.

[58] Cromer to Wilson, 21 December 1964, G1/260.

possibly more than once, in which case there would be no consequences for the reserves. Only when the transactions were closed would they affect the reserves. Both the Bank's and the Treasury's evidence on the subject to the Radcliffe Committee was opposed to forward intervention on a number of grounds: limited experience of it during 1945–51 confirmed that it did not diminish speculation in a crisis; any possible interest arbitrage attraction might be negated in a crisis by fears of exchange-control restrictions; the potential liability could not be gauged, and public fear of undisclosed liability could have damaging effects on confidence – the opposite to that expected from a policy of intervention; and there was also the risk that other currencies might be revalued.[59] Radcliffe did give some support to forward intervention as a means of holding on to sterling holders, although not as a way of countering a speculative attack.[60] The circumstances of late 1964, however, changed all that, and every technique that could be used was used.[61] With devaluation rejected, the aim was to make forward cover cheaply available, and the scheme seemed to work well for about two months. Forward intervention had been carried out by the Exchange Equalisation Account (EEA) before, and certainly in the previous three years, but it was the scale that was relatively new at the end of 1964. And the form of intervention meant that the amounts formerly being spent in the spot market were now being pushed into the forward market.

The Governor thought that more losses would follow, up to New Year's Day, but he had every hope that the atmosphere would alter in January. Before the meeting on the 23 December ended, he wanted to discuss the reserve figures that would be published in early January. 'The real loss was £115m but £107m had been financed by borrowing; it would therefore be possible to announce a loss of only £8m during December. Clearly this would not carry conviction but neither would any other figure which was far short of the true one.' It was agreed to do that.[62] Cromer proved correct. Further substantial support was required in the last few days of the year, and there then followed a lull in the crisis in the first few months of 1965.

---

[59] 'Intervention in the foreign exchange market', 28 May 1970 (by Hallett/Sangster), enc. with Hall to O'Brien et al., 28 May 1970, 6A134/1.

[60] Radcliffe, 'Report', para. 707.

[61] *BEQB* 5(1):3–4, March 1965; 5(2):107–108, June 1965.

[62] Mitchell to O'Brien, 24 December 1964, enc. 'Note of a meeting at No. 10 Downing Street at 3 p.m. on Wednesday, December 23, 1964'; O'Brien, 23 December 1964 (note on the same meeting), OV44/123.

Continuing Crisis

What followed over the three years following the election of the Labour Government was a fight to save the parity, responding to each new phase in the crisis as it arose with ad hoc measures and then relaxing until the next phase appeared. In the Bank, the continuing line contained a strong desire for fiscal purity, almost begging the Chancellor on occasions to take action on government expenditure. It did not matter greatly who the personnel were; the line stayed steady. However, there were important changes in personnel. Mynors retired in February 1964 after 10 years as Deputy Governor. He may not have promoted serious economic research in the Bank, but he kept to a strong line on fiscal policy and had provided continuity at the top during the transition of Governors. His place was taken by O'Brien, Executive Director for home finance, thus following Catterns in advancing from clerk to Deputy Governor. At the same time, Cromer took the opportunity to alter the responsibilities of his executives, with international matters now placed entirely under Parsons and Stevens taking over O'Brien's previous brief on the domestic front. When Stevens left to head the Treasury delegation in Washington in 1965, Jeremy Morse, who joined the Bank the previous year, took his place. Aged 36 and a generalist with a clearing-bank background, Morse was later to play a leading role on the international side. So too would McMahon, an economist who had joined the Bank as an Adviser in September 1964 in part because of his expertise on sterling balances.[63] Personnel may have changed, but the story continued more or less unchanged. It seemed impossible to escape from the pressures on sterling long enough to adopt a longer-term approach to policy design. Instead, there is a series of responses to new information – on the balance of payments, the reserves, bank advances, international events, and so on.

At the beginning of 1965, there was a period of relative calm in the foreign-exchange markets. At the end of January, as if to capitalise on this, several strong statements were put out by the British, the IMF, and the Americans to the effect that there would be no devaluation of sterling.[64] Over the next few years, that was to be the pattern – strong public statements on the sanctity of parity, rumours abroad of sterling's imminent devaluation, and endless discussions with central banks and finance ministries on how sterling could be protected. The co-operation often went with conditions, usually of some action being taken to restrain demand through domestic policy with

---

[63] McMahon had written a small book, *Sterling in the Sixties*, published in 1964.
[64] Cooke and Bull, 'A history of the sterling crisis', 1967, p. 26, EID1/24.

action on wages, prices, and government expenditure. The conditions could hardly be enforced and in any case were at the time in conflict with government views on growth and escaping stop-go cycles.

While the foreign-exchange markets were relatively quiet at the beginning of 1965, this did not prevent Cromer from pursuing his usual line. He was permanently troubled by what he saw as the deeper malaise in the British economy, and before leaving for Basle in early February for the monthly meeting, he wrote to the Chancellor at length, as was common, and along familiar lines:

I feel it my duty not to leave you or your ministerial colleagues in any doubt that in my firm opinion Her Majesty's government will fail to maintain the parity of sterling unless overriding priority is given to the re-establishment of confidence in sterling through bold economic policy decisions appropriate to our situation. ... action taken so far inadequate ... The Budget that you are to present in all likelihood will prove crucial to the future of this country.[65]

On his return from Basle, where the central banks had agreed to extend the existing facilities for a further three months, Cromer followed up with another letter in even gloomier tones:

I should tell you Mr Chancellor, that there are very grave misgivings on the part of virtually all my colleagues as to the justification for renewing these facilities. ... grave misgivings were expressed as to whether the Budget would face up to the situation that exists. ... the future of sterling depends upon your Budget in early April.[66]

The following day a story appeared in the Gaullist *La Nation* that said the devaluation of sterling was inevitable. Given the source, it was widely taken to be official thinking.[67]

Each piece of news on reserves or trade figures or anything even tenuously connected was examined and acted on in the foreign-exchange markets. The commentary in the March 1965 issue of the *Bulletin* struggled to be positive but could only produce the anodyne, 'an active economy moving forward on a broad front'.[68] It was little wonder, then, that rumours about sterling persisted, and a German news agency reported in March that the devaluation of sterling would be announced that weekend or in the imminent budget speech. Immediate reaction to the April budget (6 April) was that

[65] Cromer to Callaghan, 2 February 1965, G1/260.
[66] Cromer to Callaghan, 9 February 1965, G1/260.
[67] Cooke and Bull, 'A history of the sterling crisis', 1967, p. 28, EID1/24.
[68] *BEQB* 5(1):14, March 1965.

it was deflationary, and as a consequence, it was moderately well received. However, some conflicting action was taken soon after when the import surcharge, which had been introduced in October 1964, was reduced from 15 to 10 per cent in April, and later in April, special deposits of 1 per cent were called. In early May, further domestic tightening was requested of the banks. Fears over the currency reappeared, and further measures were announced by the Chancellor in July specifically to improve the balance of payments.

Some temporary relief for the balance of payments might have been afforded by the import surcharge, but apart from that, the measures employed were increasingly regarded as insufficient. The voluntary wage restraint of February 1965 was regarded with proper scepticism, and indeed, wages surged ahead. In May, Britain was drawing $1.4 billion from the IMF. Anticipating further difficulties, in June the Fed's Open Market Committee (FOMC) authorised Coombs to begin fresh consultations with central banks on possible assistance for sterling.[69] In July 1965, a package of fiscal measures was implemented. As usual, they were designed to reduce demand substantially and, as was common, to persuade foreign investors that appropriate action had been taken. There was a tightening of hire-purchase arrangements, cuts and postponements in public expenditure, and specifically, and for immediate effect on foreign exchange, a tightening of exchange controls.

After some relaxation in the 1950s, exchange-control restrictions had been tightened in the July 1961 package, which can be seen as marking the beginning of a more active use of this device. The developing crisis of 1965 was another such occasion.[70] More restrictions came in July.[71] At the same time, steps were taken to siphon off some of the privately owned foreign securities pool into the reserves: 25 per cent of the proceeds of all sales of foreign-currency securities had to be sold in the official exchange market, leaving 75 per cent available for sale as investment currency or for reinvestment.[72]

In May 1966, further exchange-control measures were introduced, although the Bank doubted their usefulness in a crisis. The use of investment currency for direct investment was restricted to cases where substantial benefit to exports or the balance of payments could be shown to be likely to materialise in the short term and continue over the longer term. All other

[69] Solomon (1977, pp. 89–90); FOMC minutes, 15 June 1965.
[70] Chalmers (1968, p. 43).
[71] Atkin (2004, pp. 118–120).
[72] 'The U.K. exchange control: a short history', *BEQB* 7(3):258. September 1967.

investment had to be financed from foreign-currency borrowing. A further set of restrictions applied to Southern Rhodesia following their declaration of independence in November 1965.[73] Also in 1966, a £50 limit was imposed on cash gifts made by UK residents to non–sterling area residents. At the same time, it was announced that emigrants taking up residence in a country outside the sterling area would continue to be allowed to transfer up to £5,000 per family unit over the official exchange. Changes in travel expenditure were introduced in November 1966, something that had been unrestricted since 1959. Private travel outside the scheduled territories was restricted to £50.[74]

It is clear that the initiative for tightening exchange controls came from the government, with the Bank providing the technical advice and expertise. At the same time, though, the Bank had considerable freedom in interpreting the complex directives that made up the controls and were able to allow certain kinds of applications at their discretion. They might even give advice on how an applicant's chances could be improved. There also were some suggestions that pressure could be put on the Bank from people in high places, pressure that the Bank found difficult to resist.[75] And there was always the suggestion that the City lived quietly with the controls because there were ways around them, at least to a tolerable level. That and the knowledge that the Bank was unhappy with controls and allowed as much freedom as possible gave comfort. However, where the Bank thought that specific proposals were unworkable, they were not slow to raise objections, and alternative suggestions were made even when there was little sympathy for the different measure. Restrictions on foreign exchange for travel were a case in point. The details of the scheme announced by the Chancellor in 1965 came from the Bank. Nonetheless, while maintaining an open mind for the Treasury, the consistent view in the Bank was that exchange controls were inappropriate for dealing with a crisis and that if

---

[73] Bank of England, *Annual Report*, February 1966, pp. 22–23, and February 1967, p. 21.
[74] Bank of England, Press notice, 11 April 1967, EC5/667. The security sterling market and official exchange market were unified in 1967. Prior to that, the sterling proceeds of the sale of non-resident-owned sterling securities (other than certain short-term investments in, for example, Treasury bills, National Savings Certificates, and Defence or National Development Bonds) were not convertible over the official exchange but could be sold in markets abroad as security sterling at a discount. From April 1967 onwards, non-residents buying sterling securities from residents were no longer able to pay in security sterling but had to pay in foreign currency or in sterling bought at the official rate of exchange.
[75] Roger Alford diaries, 13 November 1961. Bank records of individual applications under Exchange Control regulations were destroyed, so there are no means of verifying any of these kinds of allegations.

such restrictions had to be introduced, then they should be the lesser element in a total package.[76] This had been the position in 1961, and there was certainly unease about many of the controls proposed in 1965 (and again later in 1966). Running through a Treasury list of possibilities in April 1965, Piers Legh, Deputy Chief of the Overseas Department, commented that none could be regarded as in the category designed to prevent devaluation; indeed, it was 'an illusion to suppose that in a situation where confidence and perhaps control of immediate events are nearly gone, Exchange Control measures could restore either of them.'[77] In July, Parsons expressed similar sentiments: 'The foreigner is not going to be impressed by these sort of pettifogging Exchange Control measures.'[78] On the question of travel, the Bank was, as a matter of principle, opposed to the imposition of restrictions on foreign currency and thought that the weapon should be used only as a last resort.[79] Cromer wrote to the Chancellor, 'No doubt the exchange control proposals will save some exchange but I cannot believe that they will be good for confidence or for exports.'[80] The following year, the proposals in relation to legacies were described as 'barrel-scraping', whereas Cromer was moved to tell Goldman that limits on the transfer of emigrants' assets 'amounted to a serious interference with the basic liberty to move and live where one liked.'[81] In private, the Governor noted that 'if well-to-do people decide to emigrate I see no reason why they should be expected to be denied their own assets to support the way of life these assets entitle them to.'[82]

There is no evidence of any direct influence from Hayek, who had written in 1944 that control of dealings in the foreign exchanges was 'the decisive advance on the path to totalitarianism and the suppression of individual liberty. ... Once the individual is no longer free to travel ... effective control of opinion is much greater than that ever exercised by any of the absolutist governments of the seventeenth and eighteenth centuries.'[83] But Cromer

---

[76] Legh to Rootham, 'Questions from Dr. Balogh', 24 December 1964, EC5/586; Legh, Note for record 'Overseas investment', 8 January 1965, EC5/586; Horace Stobbs to Hunter/Fenton/Rootham, 'Travel', 5 March 1965; Legh to Parsons, 'Exchange control', 26 April 1965, EC5/665; Rootham, Annotation on Legh to Rootham/Parsons, 'The proposed package', 21 July 1965, EC5/666.

[77] Legh, 'Exchange control', 22 April 1965, EC5/665.

[78] Parsons to Cromer/O'Brien, 'The proposed package', 21 July 1965, EC5/666.

[79] Legh to Rawlinson, 14 September 1965, EC5/666

[80] Cromer to Callaghan, 24 July 1965, OV44/133.

[81] Hunter to Rootham/Fenton, 'Legacies', 20 April 1966; Extract from Deputy Governor's memo dated 22.4.66 on a Governor's conversation with Mr. Goldman', EC5/666.

[82] Cromer, Annotation, 20 June 1966, on Rootham to Legh, 'Emigrants and legacies', 17 June 1966, EC5/667.

[83] Hayek (2005, p. 69).

certainly held views of that kind. In his long personal letter to William Armstrong at the Treasury in 1963, Cromer had complained about the slow progress in dismantling exchange control. 'I start from the basic belief that exchange control is an infringement on the right of the citizen. ... Except in a totalitarian state this infringement is only tolerable as long as the safety of the state in the widest sense is in jeopardy.'[84] This was in a line from the beginnings of exchange control at the outbreak of the Second World War. The exchange-control group was influenced from the top when Norman had put Siepmann in charge because the latter hated controls 'and would see that administration was kept within sensible bounds. ... Siepmann responded: in large letters on the wall opposite the door of his room was the inscription, "Freedom is in danger. Defend it with all your might." His assistants, having seen the words as they entered the room, left it with the injunction, "Find out why you shouldn't say Yes."'[85]

Yet the Bank also knew that a bonfire of restrictions was unlikely to be accepted by the Treasury on the grounds of cost. Assessing the situation in 1967, Legh reckoned that granting maximum concessions in four key areas would cost up to an estimated £160 million; the Treasury reportedly wanted less than £50 million. At that time, the current account surplus for the final quarter of 1966 was given as £157 million. In the specific case of controls relating to travel, there were plenty of arguments for relaxation: they breached international obligations; the allowances were barely adequate; there was a strong incentive to evade; and at £20 million, the benefit was small.[86] Even in an organisation generally opposed to controls, it was hard to dismantle the established bureaucratic machinery.

Some indication of the administrative burden of all these controls is given by the number of separate changes and amendments issued. There were just over 100 notices between 1960 and 1964 and then nearly 375 in the following five years.[87] Numbers employed at the Bank also rose, although to nowhere near the peak of 1,626 that had been reached in 1951. After falling to a low point of 232 in 1963, the figure was 500 by 1970. Costs of exchange control were largely a function of staff numbers, and since these were charged for, there was no pressing need for control. These costs remained on a plateau of around £1.4 million across the early 1950s and then fell to a

---

[84] Cromer to Armstrong, 30 April 1963, G1/260.
[85] Sayers (1976, p. 571); Hennessy (1992, p. 396, fn. 4) noted when she wrote in 1991 that the sign was in the official's dining room. It now appears to have been lost.
[86] Legh to Fenton/Rootham/Morse, 13 February 1967, EC5/667. *BEQB* 7(2):195, June 1967, table 19.
[87] See lists in 3A152/5–6

low of £0.6 million in 1963, after which they increased quite steeply to £1.8 million in 1970 (all figures in current prices). However, over the period, the Bank deliberately reduced the fee that it charged to the Treasury for these services, and from 1966, only £50,000 per annum was being recouped[88] (see Chapter 7).

While exchange controls were tightened with the intention of improving the balance of payments, another argument was put forward by the government's economic advisers. During the first half of 1965, Whitehall debated overseas investment policy and the relative merits of domestic and overseas investment. The economists favoured domestic investment and wanted to restrict overseas investment by taxation, exchange control, or both. From the Bank's standpoint, overseas investment, in the long run, benefited the British economy.[89] This reflected a long-running debate on the role of investment in economic growth. From the political left, there was the assertion that the British economy had been deprived of investment funds because investors preferred the returns available abroad; it followed that the City was complicit in this. Labour had for long favoured a National Investment Board that would restrict foreign lending and direct funds to deserving domestic activities.[90] That official exchange could not be used to finance overseas direct investment in the non-sterling area produced complaints from firms unable to reconcile the measure with the government's repeated requests to export more. Rootham (now Assistant to the Governors) wanted the 'absurd consequences of this rigid policy' pointed out to the Treasury.[91]

Washington Initiative

Whether or not the measures of July 1965 would prove effective did not stop action on other fronts. Some had their origins abroad and reflected the concern of the United States that pressure would move to the dollar. The July measures were better than expected in the United States, but fears were strong that the pressure on sterling was likely to increase over the

---

[88] ADM6/54–56.
[89] For example, Parsons to Rickett, 12 January 1965, EC5/586; Parsons to Rickett, 8 February 1965; Rootham to O'Brien-Parsons, 15 February 1965; Rootham, Note for record, 19 February 1965, EC5/664; Legh to Rootham/Parsons, 'Overseas investment', 11 January 1965, EC5/586.
[90] Turner and Williams (1987).
[91] Rootham, Annotation on Jack Hunter (Assistant Chief of Overseas Department) to Fenton, 1 December 1965; Legh to Rawlinson, 9 February 1966, EC5/656, EC5/656.

next few weeks and 'might cause HMG seriously to consider the possibility of sterling devaluation'. While some US economists thought that sterling was over-valued and should be devalued, others felt that parity could and should be defended.[92] The United States was prepared to try to do this, but only if the Europeans joined in. President Johnson's aide, McGeorge Bundy, emphasised too that the White House must have a say in any US Treasury plans for supporting sterling. The Governor felt that the idea would be worth following up 'on a purely central banking basis without saying anything to Whitehall for the time being'.[93] The Governor favoured placing a suggestion with Karl Blessing (Blessing had joined the Reichsbank in 1920 and became president of the Bundesbank in 1958), to give him the opportunity to think it over. At the beginning of August, when Cromer telephoned Martin, they agreed that 'things were not encouraging', and Martin felt that something was needed to 'reverse the psychological malaise in which sterling now found itself'. Martin said that he felt that any further assistance would be conditional on tough and dramatic measures to restore confidence and that 'a wages and prices freeze would probably do this'.[94] The Fed was of the view that at most what could be arranged would be $1.5 billion to $2 billion, with Europe providing $1 billion, and that such an amount could be arranged for three months but with no possibility of refunding.

Armstrong argued that what was wanted was a declaration by the US government and other Group of Ten (G10) countries that they regarded the 'maintenance of sterling at its present parity as of paramount interest in the world monetary system' and that they were satisfied that Britain had done what was necessary on her part for this and that they would be giving their full support to the objective.[95] In August, Martin effectively agreed to this with Cromer on the phone. Cromer, however, still worried about the kind of commitment the Bank might be taking on; as he expressed it to Armstrong, 'All Central Banks must under all circumstances be able to meet its obligations, no matter what the consequences of Government policies may be.' So worried was he that he asked Armstrong to 'affirm formally the basis on which the Bank of England acts as Manager of the Exchange Equalization Account', it being understood that the government would not establish any prior charge on assets that were held for the account. And

---

[92] Stevens, Draft 'Note of meeting at White House, Washington, D.C. at 10:30 a.m on Friday, July 30, 1965', handed to Cromer the next day, OV44/125.

[93] O'Brien, Note for record, 2 August 1965, OV44/125.

[94] Cromer, Governor's note, 3 August 1965, OV44/125.

[95] David Walker (HMT) to Rodney Galpin (GPS), 4 August, enc. Armstrong, 'Support for sterling', 4 August 1965, OV44/125.

he wanted further assurance that the proceeds from any drawing from Eximbank or the United States would be available to the Bank to meet obligations entered into for the EEA.[96]

Later that day, at a meeting at Downing Street, Cromer began by saying that since the July 1965 statement they had lost £146 million of reserves, which meant that net reserves were now down to between £500 and £600 million, enough for four or five days if things continued as they were. But Wilson resisted pressure to make a declaration on wages and prices in the absence of a clear statement from the central banks on the support they would provide, and he again used his threat to devalue and 'to appeal to the country'. He would be prepared to tell President Johnson that the only course open was devaluation and a general election.[97]

In August, US Treasury Secretary Henry (Joe) Fowler, who O'Brien called that 'lovable little gentleman', outlined a possible sterling rescue package that consisted of four main elements. There would be the commitment on a wage-price freeze, a statement by the co-operating countries expressing gratification at this, the accumulation by the latter of sterling balances for up to 5 per cent of their reserves, and some arrangement to safeguard those balances in a currency holding agreement managed by the Governor and guaranteeing the value of all such central bank sterling holdings under the agreement.[98] What was being proposed, as Coombs saw it, was an operation under which their exchange-market operators 'would mount a "massive bear squeeze"'.[99] The Bank wanted to get all the G10 including the French to participate because anything less would be seen as a vote of no confidence.

The government was of the view that the July measures were appropriate and would reduce demand by the amount intended, reduce the balance-of-payments deficit in 1965, and eliminate it entirely in 1966. However, the markets were clearly less sure, and sterling remained weak. Thus what was needed was a major demonstration of 'official' international confidence, and the proposals that were being worked on were seen as the best means of doing that. In late August, agreement was reached that the British should approach the Europeans, and the Americans would be ready to come in on the basis of Preston's letter to Coombs. A letter went out to the European central bank governors on 28 August proposing that the support operation

---

[96] Cromer to Armstrong, 5 August 1965, OV44/125.

[97] 'Note of a meeting at 10 Downing Street, SW1, on Thursday, 5 August, 1965 at 9:30 p.m.', OV44/125.

[98] Preston to Rootham/O'Brien, 10 August 1965, enc. 'Exchange protection on specially acquired sterling balances', 10 August 1965, OV44/125.

[99] O'Brien, Note for record, 27 August 1965, OV44/125.

could be announced in the week of 6 September and made to look like the G10 reaction to the most recent measures.

Coombs and O'Brien lunched at the Savoy on Sunday, 29 August when they had news that the French would participate, indeed would be offended if they were left out.[100] There were still obstacles to be overcome. For instance, Louis Rasminsky, Governor of the Bank of Canada, had said that he would need assurance that he would be able to convert sterling acquired on a specific date. Others such as Guido Carli (Banca d'Italia) and Holtrop wanted to see any solution for sterling linked to the wider question of international liquidity, and the Germans were reluctant because there was an election looming and there were strong feelings in some circles in Germany that sterling should be devalued. The Swiss had constitutional difficulties that prevented them holding sterling in their reserves.[101]

On the British side, there was the worry that the government would not deliver on the wages/prices front. Cromer suggested a meeting of the G10 Governors for 6 or 7 September and that they should go ahead even if one or more of the group who had participated in the previous package declined this time. In O'Brien's words, 'it was probably to be our last throw.' He stressed to the Chancellor that 'getting everyone in rested very largely on the Chancellor standing firm on the wages and incomes front.'[102] At the eleventh hour, even the Americans, the source of the initiative, had second thoughts. They felt that the 5 per cent figure for sterling reserves disadvantaged them in relation to the Europeans and wondered if the latter might take a slighter bigger amount. Roy Bridge meanwhile was at work in Switzerland visiting Walter Schwegler and Iklé at the National Bank, persuading them of the need to join, and then to Mandel and Macdonald at the BIS keeping them in the picture.[103]

At any rate, a meeting was arranged for Basle for Sunday, 5 September, and the promised statement on prices and incomes was made on Thursday, 2 September, in which the government proposed giving the National Board for Prices and Incomes statutory powers and committed to introducing legislation that required proposed price and pay increases to be deferred until the board reported on them.[104] On Friday, 3 September, Fowler

---

[100] Preston to O'Brien, 31 August 1965, OV44/125.

[101] O'Brien, Note for record – 'The initiative', five separate notes dated 1 September 1965, OV44/125.

[102] O'Brien, Note for record – 'The initiative', eight separate notes dated 2 September 1965, OV44/125.

[103] Bridge to O'Brien, 2 September 1965, OV44/125.

[104] O'Brien, Note for record – 'The initiative', eight separate notes dated 2 September 1965, OV44/125.

congratulated the Chancellor on the statement, saying that he 'thought we had pulled it off'. He added that the US representatives who would go to Basle would go with instructions to support 'any programme which was within the ambit of the "Martin/Cromer proposals"'.[105]

Yet the Basle meeting did not go well. Many felt that it was time to halt further support to finance the British deficit. There would be some further central bank assistance in the next few years, but in many ways this can be seen as the beginning of the end of the brief period of intense central bank co-operation. In the end, the French withdrew, and the proposed nature and scale of the proposal changed such that what finished up as support was for the amount of $925 million. The United States would make a sterling deposit of $400 million and the Germans one of $120 million. There were some other sterling deposits and some dollar deposits. Apart from the United States, the facilities were for three months with an option to extend for a further three months. The US facility had no time limit, something of which the others were almost certainly unaware. Apart from the names of the countries involved, no details on amounts were released, supposedly to enhance the psychological advantage. Nevertheless, after the announcement, sterling's fortunes began to improve quite sharply, and there was growing confidence that the measures had had a psychological effect without having been used. In the last months of 1965, the Bank was even on occasion able to acquire some sterling. But that hardly constitutes the success *The Times* painted: 'the most massive bear squeeze in the history of the foreign exchanges', with the Bank having 'the exquisite satisfaction of deciding when to let the market out'.[106] O'Brien, too, gives some credence to this view. He refers to it as 'one of the famous Bridge/Coombs bear squeezes in the exchange markets, in the success of which they both took such great delight.'[107]

Planning for Devaluation

At the same time as the elaborate bear squeeze was being planned in the foreign-exchange market in 1965, a small group of Treasury and Bank officials were undertaking contingency planning in the event of devaluation. It was a highly secret exercise, known only as 'FU'. The FU committee first met in March 1965, under Armstrong's chairmanship, and the idea was to

---

[105] Bancroft, Note for record, 3 September 1965, OV44/126.
[106] *The Times*, 25 November 1965, quoted in Browning (1986, p. 8).
[107] O'Brien memoir, p. 57.

produce a set of papers that could be presented to ministers should the need arise.[108] Thus, despite the public face of denial, plans were being made, even down to preparing a detailed timetable of events as if devaluation were imminent. Cromer told the Chancellor, 'it is possible that we may be faced with a flight from sterling of dimensions that could deprive us of any choice as to maintaining the existing parity of sterling.'[109] The FU committee's work related to straightforwardly administrative tasks that were set out in a 'Devaluation War Book'.[110] When FU met in October 1965, it was agreed that the war book was complete and that the exercise could be put on a care and maintenance basis. The next meeting of the committee was not held until November 1966.[111]

Arising from the FU work were some contentious and unresolved issues. Although the war book plans assumed that devaluation would mean a move straight to another fixed parity, not everybody agreed with this. In July 1965, Kaldor (special adviser to the Chancellor) raised the subject of flexible rates, as did Neild.[112] Both argued the benefits of floating, but neither impressed Cromer. If Neild's proposals were accepted, 'no banker would advise any client to hold one penny of £'; on Kaldor, he wrote, 'It is because Britain has followed policies diametrically opposite to the philosophy of this paper that £ became universally respected. I feel ashamed to read such a paper on HM Treasury stationery.'[113] Bridge, too, was predictably and immediately dismissive. 'As a serious practical exercise Kaldor's paper can be faulted in several places on lack of knowledge of history, or markets, of perspective and of people', he wrote. He felt that Neild was more aware of the dangers 'but has, I suspect, been sufficiently bewitched by Screwtape to believe that the pound is incapable of encountering a fate similar to that of the defunct pengo.'[114] Kaldor has been called many names, but Screwtape seems to be new. Bridge

---

[108] 'Sterling devaluation F.U.'; the FU stood for 'follow up', a suitably opaque term designed to hide what was actually being discussed. Some think that such was the dread of devaluation that FU stood for 'forever unmentionable', and there are other, less polite suggestions. Portsmore to Parsons, 'Contingency planning', 31 March 1965; FU (65) 4th, 13 April 1965, OV44/132.

[109] Cromer to Callaghan, 23 June 1965; Cromer to Callaghan, 6 July 1965, G1/260.

[110] Devaluation War Book, FU (65) 34 (2nd revise), 1 September 1965, OV44/133.

[111] FU (65) 13th, 22 October 1965; Fforde to O'Brien et al., 'F.U.', 25 October 1965, OV44/134.

[112] Walker, 'Note by the secretary', 23 July 1965, enc. Kaldor to Armstrong, 22 July 1965, 'Fixed or flexible rates' [FU (65) 48] and Neild, 22 July 1965, 'Fixed flexible rates' [FU (65) 47], OV44/133. FU (66) 1st, 11 November 1966, OV44/135.

[113] Cromer, Annotations, 26 July 1965, on Walker, 'Note by the secretary', 23 July 1965 (two letters of this date), OV44/133.

[114] Bridge to Rootham, 'Fixed or flexible', 3 August 1965, OV44/134.

was undoubtedly brilliant on the exchanges, 'alert to all the technical and psychological forces of the market', but he was, nevertheless, wayward in his prognosis that a floating rate would bring about a collapse in world trade. Bridge's initial conclusion was that 'the logical thing would be not to intervene in the market at all for a period', and this clearly went against the grain for someone who saw floating as an 'abdication of responsibility'.[115] At FU in October 1965, Parsons outlined the Bank's position. It rejected the exhaustion of reserves followed by a floating rate as an untenable alternative, and neither could it advocate interim flexibility within prescribed limits. The Bank's strong words did not entirely deflect opponents, though, and in this inconclusive atmosphere, Armstrong suggested that it might be better, for the time being, to leave the matter as it stood.[116] In the Cabinet, there was little knowledge of the FU exercise, although the Chancellor and the Prime Minister did see some of the material.

After the travails of 1964–65, there was an official examination of the pressures on sterling during this period. This highly secret work was initiated by the Treasury and undertaken by Cambridge economist Lord Kahn, together with financial journalist Richard Fry and Eric Woolgar, general manager (Overseas Department) at Lloyds Bank. A great deal of assistance was given by the Bank, with Tom Bell (EID) and Peter Cooke (Chief Cashier's Office) providing the secretarial support. The group was appointed by the Chancellor in November 1965 and completed its work in June 1966. The 'Kahn Report' assessed the underlying reasons for pressure on sterling and made suggestions as to the measures that might have been taken, together with detailed statistics.[117] In fact, all this went far beyond the initial remit. The origins of Kahn were to be found in Wilson's suspicions (prompted by Balogh, according to Bridge) that currency speculators were primarily responsible for the troubles of sterling. At one stage, the Prime Minister went so far as to propose a full-blown tribunal along the lines of that held for the Bank Rate leak, but officials instead were able to limit it to a secret investigation. The Bank was unhappy about either of these but reluctantly accepted the latter.[118] It soon became clear that the group was

[115] Bridge to Rootham, 5 August 1965, enc. Bridge, 5 August 1965, 'Strategy and tactics for a floating rate', OV44/134.

[116] FU (65) 13th, 22 October 1965, OV44/134.

[117] Kahn, 'Enquiry into the position of sterling 1964–65', 1 June 1966, EID1/20; interview with Peter Cooke, 27 March 2006.

[118] O'Brien to Cromer/Parsons, 7 September 1965 and Bridge annotation; O'Brien, Note for record, 4 October 1965, and Cromer annotation, 7 October 1965; 'I am not in favour but suppose there is little we can do'; Bridge called it an 'ill conceived initiative'; Bridge to Parsons, 12 October 1965, G1/538.

straying into wider areas, such as policy on forward-exchange operations and exchange control. At one stage, the Governor ordered that all cooperation be withdrawn, although this was quickly reinstated, and a wider remit was then agreed.[119]

Opinions on the report were mixed. Heasman (Head of the Economic Intelligence Department) thought that it would be useful to have as an authoritative study of the crisis. Bridge, writing two years later, was rather more dismissive: it was 'no doubt highly informative to the participants', but it had 'no favourable influence on government policy'.[120] These two views neatly sum up Kahn: it contains a full chronological description and data not readily available elsewhere, but it had little contemporary impact, even as sterling was in crisis again. Despite the existence of Kahn, the Bank prepared its own internal narrative, 'History of the Sterling Crisis', written by Cooke and Peter Bull of the Economic Intelligence Department (EID).[121] Later, in November 1968, Kahn was asked by the Treasury to prepare another report covering the period from January 1966 to February 1968. Typically, Bridge declared the exercise 'an almost complete waste of valuable time'.[122] In this case, assistance was provided by Malcolm Gill (Bank) and David Walker (Treasury). Much to his embarrassment, Kahn did not complete the task until August 1971.[123]

Following the bear squeeze in the foreign-exchange markets in September 1965, there was a period of relative calm that lasted until February 1966. Some argued that the performance of sterling was more solidly based than previous recovery periods. The rate never fell below $2.80 in those months, even if some support began to be given in the second half of February. Reserves rose by almost $1 billion, although there were some special reasons for that. At any rate, the belief was that the support operation had

[119] Cooke to Parsons, 'The Kahn Committee', 26 January 1966 and annotations by O'Brien and Parsons; Parsons to Cromer/O'Brien, 26 January 1966; Cromer, Governor's note, 27 January 1966, G1/538; Cromer to Neatby, Governor's note, 1 February 1966, Galpin to Neatby, 11 February 1966, Cooke to Kahn, 11 February 1966, G1/496.

[120] Heasman to Rootham et al., 'The Kahn Committee Report', 30 June 1966, EID1/23; Bridge, Annotation, 23 August 1968, on Richard Balfour (Deputy Chief Cashier) to Bridge, 23 August 1968, G1/498. For the Bank's response to the recommendations in Kahn, see Heasman to Workman (HMT), 30 December 1966, EID1/23.

[121] Heasman to O'Brien, 'The history of the exchange crisis', 15 December 1966; Cooke to Preston, 'The history of the sterling crisis', 9 January 1967, C43/126; Cooke and Bull, 'A history of the sterling crisis', 1967, EID1/24; Bridge's copy with some entertaining comments is in C20/6.

[122] Bridge, Annotation, 23 August 1968, on Balfour to Bridge, 23 August 1968, G1/498.

[123] Kahn, 'Enquiry into the position of sterling January 1966–February 1968', 12 August 1971, Vol. I, EID1/6, vol. II, EID1/7; Interview with Malcolm Gill, 14 February 2006.

worked. This tended to be the response after a crisis had been surmounted, and it meant that no serious attack on the fundamental problem was made. That, of course, must be tempered with the knowledge that the monetary authorities operated with different beliefs in a different climate, one that led them to believe that controls were a necessary part of the armoury and certainly that controls could contain inflation (even if doubts remained over the political will to use them). They also operated in the belief that growth through planning would deliver them from the balance-of-payments problems.

The markets seem to have been persuaded that there was sufficient international desire and clout to support sterling and the system. However, the psychological case was strengthened by the contemporaneous improvement in trade performance in both visibles and invisibles, as well as in the capital account, where foreign domestic investment (FDI) in Britain was rising. The following few months were the doldrums, though, and it was not long before the old pattern was emerging again. Whereas over the closing months of 1965, news had been absorbed and potential minishocks had been negotiated, from February 1966, old doubts resurfaced, and sterling showed signs of weakening again. However, it did not happen suddenly. An election had been called for March, which Labour were expected to win. In the run-up to this, Cromer had recommended an increase in Bank rate, something that resulted in an intense row with Wilson. The Prime Minister saw it as an attack on democracy, and the Governor made repeated threats to resign.[124] There was no increase in Bank rate, and Labour won the election. The budget that followed almost immediately was generally accepted as satisfactory but then, after a little consideration, disappointing. April trade figures and reserve losses in May had an effect, and by the beginning of June 1966, pressure was mounting. Support of almost £100 million was necessary on Monday and Tuesday, 5 and 6 June.

Sterling Balances and Gold

With yet another stage in the crisis brewing, central bank assistance was being considered for sterling balances, with a proposal that sought to take a longer view of the problem. This should not be overstated because what began to be discussed was referred to initially as 'Basle credits' to replace the 10 September 1965 measures. These were due to expire in March 1966 but

---

[124] Derek Mitchell (No. 10), 'Note of a meeting at 10 Downing Street, at 10:00 p.m. on Wednesday, March 9, 1966' (the meeting finished at 12:30 a.m.), PREM 13/3153 TNA.

were being extended by three months pending possible alternative arrangements. In fact, as early as September 1965, discussions were under way on what might be done, and an early idea was that central banks might accumulate sterling with a guaranteed exchange rate. Holtrop told O'Brien that it was a silly idea. However, as O'Brien noted, at least it turned everyone's attention to the problem of the sterling balances.

Ideas of long-term funding which had been kicking around for many years were at last seen for the nonsense they were. These sterling assets were the liquid foreign exchange resources of governments, central banks and private holders. Their ebb and flow greatly exaggerated our recurrent exchange crises but what to do about them we did not know. They continued to haunt us for a number of years.[125]

Cromer sent Ferras, now general manager at the BIS, and Holtrop the Bank's views for discussion at the November Basle meeting. These were that after convertibility in 1958, it became possible to attract to London private non-sterling area (NSA) short-term capital by using interest rates and holding sterling steady. After 1961, there were the various arrangements with the central banks and the IMF that allowed containment of the problem while they waited for the underlying balance of payments to improve. The latter had not happened. With sterling important to the international monetary system, something different therefore was needed.[126] At the Basle meeting it was agreed that Ferras and Milton Gilbert, Head of Economics at the BIS, should be commissioned to write a paper. Gilbert called on the Bank soon after (12 November) for discussions and got the impression that 'facilities of the order of $1–$1.25b in addition to the existing Fed swap would be about right'.[127] The essence of Gilbert's paper was that a facility should be available to cover any fall in sterling balances. It got a lukewarm response.[128]

Nevertheless, discussions did get under way, with the initial intention being to establish a swap network for the United Kingdom to draw on to offset certain specified movements in sterling balances and a line of credit of $1 billion for a period of a year.[129] Over the next several months, discussions covered a variety of possibilities, including that of issuing British 'Roosa' bonds.[130] The February BIS board meeting was devoted entirely

---

[125] O'Brien memoir, p. 58.

[126] 'The problem of sterling balances', 1 November 1965, OV44/152.

[127] Fforde, 'Note for record, visit of Milton Gilbert, 12 November 1965', 15 November 1965, OV44/152.

[128] Toniolo (2005, p. 392).

[129] Sterling balances draft, 22 December 1965, OV44/152.

[130] Roosa bonds were short-term (1 to 2 years) denominated in dollars and foreign currencies at special rates of interest.

to a discussion of the proposed new facility.[131] At this point, the facility was being proposed for nine months, after which some operation through the IMF or BIS was to be considered. The American share was to be $300 million possibly converted into a long-term asset such as a reverse 'Roosa' bond – a long-term sterling claim on the United Kingdom denominated in dollars. A further $500 million would be converted into claims on the IMF and $200 million by the BIS.[132] What was becoming clear was that the new arrangements were being designed specifically to exclude providing support for the pound for balance-of-payments purposes.

When the next stage in the crisis came in July 1966, it was the worst of all. The pressure that had been growing through June worsened with every bit of adverse news that flowed in. Forecasts for the balance of payments were bleak for a long way ahead. An incomes freeze was being proposed and was regarded as central to the package of measures, but there was little confidence that the proposed policy would deliver. There was deep scepticism that such a freeze could be implemented. Cromer reported that 'sentiment towards sterling over the medium and longer term is poor in the extreme' and gave the scepticism over the incomes policy as a principal reason.[133] Talk of devaluation began to be heard, and the press was beginning to ignore patriotic-type appeals to remain quiet on the subject, *The Observer* saying, 'The sooner sterling topples, the better.'[134]

The incoming Governor was every bit as pessimistic and gloomy as the outgoing one. On 12 July, O'Brien wrote at length to the Chancellor. He went over the extent of the cumulative deficit on current account over the previous three years and the apparent lack of resolve to get to grips with the basic cause. All manner of stop-gaps had been tried from import surcharges to restrictive exchange controls to very little effect.[135] Only three days later he wrote again opening with, 'No one embarks willingly on discussion of devaluation of sterling.' O'Brien was deeply opposed to devaluation. But he argued that there had been a complete failure to control demand, and until there were signs of a sensible relationship between productive capacity and demand, devaluation would not achieve 'its purpose at home nor be understood and accepted abroad'.[136] He argued passionately against

[131] Parsons, 'Basle meeting 12th–14th February', 15 February 1966, OV44/153.
[132] Parsons, 3 March 1966, OV44/154.
[133] Cromer to Callaghan, 15 June 1966, G1/260.
[134] Cooke and Bull, 'A history of the sterling crisis', 1967, p. 52, EID1/24.
[135] O'Brien to Callaghan, 12 July 1966, G41/1.
[136] O'Brien to Callaghan, 15 July 1966, G41/1.

devaluation, feared it would become inevitable, and pleaded yet again for stricter policy.

Then July was disastrous. The losses to reserves in the month totalled almost $1 billion, and the total cost of supporting sterling was over $2 billion. The published loss for July was shown as £25 million, but £331 million had been drawn under different facilities, most of them secret, such as the overnight swap with the United States and the BIS gold swap. Just as in late 1964, there were bad days and less bad days in the course of the month. Even with support pouring into the market, the authorities struggled to get the rate above $2.7865. In the middle of the month, Bank Rate was raised to 7 per cent and other deflationary measures introduced, and an announcement was made that even more measures would follow. August also began badly, and in the first two days, £85 million in support was given. It was not until September that there was any sign of recovery, but given the long period of crisis that ran from the end of 1964, no one was getting overly excited. It was not until the end of the year that it could be said that the markets were calm.

Throughout the crisis for sterling in the mid-1960s, the gold market remained relatively calm. The Gold Pool took much of the credit for that. Throughout 1964, the Pool appeared to operate effectively and to exert a stabilising influence on the market. There was increased production, plus substantial sales of gold by the USSR in the first three months of the calendar year, that enabled the pool to share out the equivalent of about $600 million of gold to its participants. No contributions to the Gold Pool had to be made in 1964 by participating central banks.[137]

In 1965, the Gold Pool engaged in considerable activity in its two capacities of selling consortium and buying syndicate. In early January 1965, the sales consortium was reactivated, and from this point until the end of February, the Bank sold gold equivalent to $151 million. In October, substantial amounts of Russian gold became available, enabling the selling consortium to clear its books. The buying syndicate started operating again and held the equivalent of $34 million by the end of October.[138] Throughout 1966, the selling consortium was in almost continuous operation. In September, it was agreed that the Pool should be increased by $50 million from $270 million to $320 million. If the Bank got through this quickly, it was decided that another $50 million could be negotiated. The Americans

[137] IMF, *Annual Report*, 1965, p. 101.
[138] Medcraft to H. L. Jenkyns (HMT), 'Basle Gold Pool operations in 1965', 11 January 1966, TNA T312/1735.

originally wanted an increase of $100 million, but this was reduced to $50 million at the request of the French, who were beginning to show signs of anxiety. The Americans, however, reserved their right to come back for another $50 million. Early in 1967, Colin Peterson (Principal at the Treasury) commented to William Ryrie (Assistant Secretary in International Monetary Affairs) that the Gold Pool had 'worked successfully' and had probably 'helped to protect the market from the kind of flurry which took place in 1960'.[139] At the end of May, all participants agreed to the second 'rallonge' of $50 million, thus ensuring that the Pool total was increased to $370 million. The French did not want to be committed for more than two months. Arising out of heavy demand for gold caused by the Middle East crisis in the middle of 1967, it was agreed that the limit of the commitment of the Gold Pool's selling consortium should be raised to $420 million. In the following month, this was raised another $50 million to $470 million. The French saw this as a step too far and refused to participate.[140]

Cromer Leaves

In the midst of the long-running sterling crisis of the mid-1960s, Cromer's term in office came to an end. Speculation that he would not be reappointed developed at the end of 1965, and in March, he had made known his intention not to seek a second term.[141] In April, following the election, Cromer told Callaghan of his decision. It was not because of the crisis but rather the impossibility, as he saw it, of working with the new Labour Government.

Cromer's relationship with both Conservative and Labour governments during his term was turbulent, but it was with Wilson that 'bruising confrontation' occurred.[142] Perhaps Cromer's main contribution as Governor was his skillful use of central bank contacts in raising financial support when confidence in sterling was low. Cromer's actions managed to prevent a forced devaluation at a time when government policy was to hold the rate at all costs. The feud over interest rates led to a warning from Cromer that the Bank had a statutory right to act independently, and if overruled, it

---

[139] C. V. Peterson to William Ryrie (HMT), 7 February 1967, TNA T312/1735.
[140] The exact date is not clear. In the nature of things, there is great secrecy attached to a member behaving in their own interests. Certainly, on 27 November 1967, Bridge stated that France no longer participated in the Gold Pool; see 'Extract from Mr. Bridge's note for the record dated 27/11/67', G1/285. Toniolo says that France had pulled out in June 1967 (Toniolo, 2005, p. 679). According to the *Bulletin*, France 'had ceased to take an active part in the Pool in July', *BEQB* 8(1):5, March 1968.
[141] Cromer to Kindersley, 8 March 1966, 4A10/1.
[142] Orbell (2004a).

would say so publicly. Wilson retorted, 'In that case, the history of the Bank of England, which had begun with Governor Houblon, would end with Governor Cromer.'[143] Cromer found Wilson 'slippery and unsound and made little attempt to hide the low opinion he held', and Wilson viewed Cromer as 'hectoring and bigoted'.[144] Sayers once wrote, 'in the words of an outstanding Governor of the Bank of England the central bank has "the unique right to offer advice and to press such advice to the point of nagging."'[145] There was no greater nag than Cromer. Labour was relieved to see him go. He was deemed a 'right-wing reactionary in Labour circles, in the direct line of descent from Montagu Norman'.[146] Like most Bank officials of his time, Cromer would never have claimed to be an intellectual and saw himself as essentially pragmatic.[147] He returned to Barings in 1967 but found his role there an anticlimax. He went to Washington as British Ambassador to the United States between 1971 and 1974. Back in Britain in 1974, he returned to his attack on inflation and the need for sound currency.[148]

Cromer was vigorous and open in defence of sound money and City interests. He encouraged foreign banks to set up in the City, promoting London's role as an international financial centre. He did not like City institutions communicating directly with government departments rather than proceeding through Bank channels.[149] To some, Cromer was 'an accessible figure who brought a welcome, indeed novel degree of verve and imagination to the job; to others, he seemed self-important, and in an unacceptably patrician way, lacking in sympathy for life's toilers in the ranks'.[150]

As to Cromer's successor, there were two main candidates; Herbert Coombs, Governor of the Reserve Bank of Australia, was well regarded by Wilson, whereas John Stevens was the Court's favoured candidate.[151] *The Economist* wanted to see 'a figure as strong as Lord Cromer himself, but one who was acceptable to both City and Government, and who – in modern conditions – should preferably be something of an economist', and Sir Eric Roll was, according to the magazine, 'the best man in Britain for the job'.[152] Parsons also had featured as a possible candidate. Coombs

---

[143] Mitchell, 'Note of a meeting ... March 9, 1966', PREM 13/3153 TNA.
[144] Ziegler (1993, p. 194).
[145] Sayers (1963, p. 67).
[146] Morgan (1997, p. 205).
[147] *Old Lady*, Summer 1991, p. 100.
[148] *The Times*, 18 March 1991, p. 12.
[149] *Ibid.*
[150] Kynaston (2001, p. 257).
[151] *Ibid.*, p. 316.
[152] *The Economist*, 30 April 1966, p. 450; 4 December 1965, p. 1047.

decided to stay in Australia, and in early February, Cecil King came into O'Brien's office announcing that the Deputy Governor was now the front-runner. According to King, they had already offered him (King) the Governorship, but he had turned it down. This was the kind of thing King said. The Chancellor favoured someone from the Bank, and they all approved of O'Brien. Callaghan told Wilson, who agreed that this was the right choice, and O'Brien was appointed for five years from 1 July 1966. In his memoir, O'Brien accepted that if Labour had not been in power, he would not have been Governor. The fact that he had been in the Bank for 39 years, together with his good working relationship with Callaghan, certainly helped.[153] His appointment was seen by some to be a compromise and essentially a safe choice; *The Economist* criticised 'the petty motives underlying his appointment'.[154] Parsons, Executive Director, was appointed deputy, although this was not O'Brien's preference.[155]

Central Bank Assistance

The period of Cromer's Governorship covers the key years of central bank co-operation. He did not inaugurate this; if credit were to go to one person, then it was more correctly attributable to Cobbold and to the pressing needs of the system at the turn of the 1960s. But Cromer's undoubted skills carried it through. And when he had gone, the intense co-operation began to fade. Again, this was not so much because of his departure as the wider dawning realisation that sterling could not be saved and the growing reluctance of central banks to contribute in the face of the unrelenting and probably irresistible pressure. Cromer had kept up his own pressure on governments so far as he could, warning, threatening, cajoling, and nagging constantly that only prudent policy could deliver sound money, and that was the prerequisite for stability in the exchange rate. He was also at pains to stress that the short-term central bank finance that he was able to arrange was simply that. Swaps and similar instruments were generally for three months, renewable for a further three months and on rare occasions for slightly longer. They were definitely not for more than a year. (On occasion, if they were not fully used, they might be placed on standby and in effect

---

[153] O'Brien memoir, pp. 60–62.
[154] *The Economist*, 30 April 1966, p. 450.
[155] O'Brien memoir, p. 62. O'Brien does not say, but there were rumours then or soon after that Parsons' health was not good. He may have been suffering from the first signs of an ageing disease. Despite being Deputy Governor and having specialised in international monetary matters, he seems not to have played much part in devaluation.

become a line of credit.) But they were arranged only to provide time to organise longer-term support from the IMF or elsewhere. However, neither was a long-term solution to deep-seated problems.

The essence of the swap network that revolved in the main around the Federal Reserve was to provide, in the case of the Bank, dollars for intervention purposes and the Fed with sterling with which it could purchase dollars that otherwise might be converted into gold. Britain's experience in the first half of the 1960s tended to be of continual renewal. In November 1964, $1 billion of credit arranged earlier in the year had been exhausted and was repaid in December with a $1 billion IMF drawing. But Cromer had raised that extraordinary central bank assistance of $3 billion at the end of November 1964, and in February 1965, that was renewed for three months. In May, there had to be a further drawing from the IMF and a further renewal of the Fed swap of $750 million, in this case for a year. At the beginning of 1966, short-term facilities available to the United Kingdom consisted of the Federal Reserve Bank swap of $750 million and the central bank package of September 1965 of about $900 million. In February 1966, the liquefied dollar portfolio ($885 million) was brought into the reserves, and the Federal Reserve Bank swap was repaid. In June 1966, a $1.2 billion credit with the BIS replaced the September 1965 arrangements, and this was further extended for a year in May 1967. A new swap with the Fed for $1.35 billion was arranged in September 1966, and at the end of 1967, that was increased to $1.5 billion. By the end of April, $2 billion had been repaid in eight months, and the Federal Reserve Bank swap was completely reconstituted. The borrowing was all carried out at relatively low interest rates, and Kahn estimated that in broad terms, the cost of the assistance in 1966 and 1967 probably totalled around £50 million.[156]

Figure 5.1 shows the amounts of assistance outstanding at month end from 1961 until the end of 1967. It brings out how the assistance had peaked at $1.6 billion during the 1961 crisis before falling to zero by mid-1962. It stayed close to zero until the middle of 1964, when the figure grew rapidly to $2 billion at the beginning of 1965 and further steeply to around $3.5 billion at the peak of the 1965 crisis and then on to more than $4 billion in the mid-1966 crisis. There was some relief in 1967, but that proved to be brief before the even greater assistance followed swiftly after devaluation. By this time, borrowing from central bank sources was greater than that from the IMF.

---

[156] Kahn, 'Enquiry into the position of sterling, January 1966–February 1968', 12 August 1971, Vol. II, p. 207, EID/7.

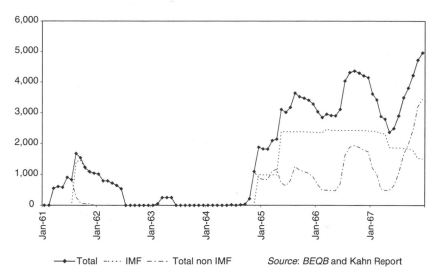

Figure 5.1. International assistance, monthly, 1961–67 ($m).

Assistance was intimately bound up with the position of the reserves, the centre of much attention across the whole period, but perhaps never more so than in the mid-1960s. However, it was by no means easy for outsiders to interpret the figures. The published figures were massaged. After all, the 'basic issue of reserves policy [as the Chancellor saw it] was to handle it in such a way as to maintain and strengthen confidence in sterling.'[157] Quite apart from massaging, there were questions over how to treat the many items and kinds of assistance in the accounts. Figure 5.2 shows the course of the published reserves from 1959 to 1967. Having been at a low point of around $2 billion in 1957, they were over $3 billion in 1959. Thereafter, while there is quite a lot of movement, the trend is gently downward until mid-1965. Then there is a sharp upward move-ment at the beginning of 1966, followed by a downward path to September 1967. What is to be made of this? There seems on the face of it little to get excited about in what is generally thought of as a period of great turmoil for the pound. For a number of reasons, though, the published series is not an entirely reliable guide. Figure 5.3 shows that all was not as it might have seemed.

Table 5.1 helps to illuminate. Column 1 gives the published reserves monthly from mid-1964 to April 1968. Column 2 shows the short-term

---

[157] Ian Bancroft (HMT), Note for record, 7 January 1966, C43/49.

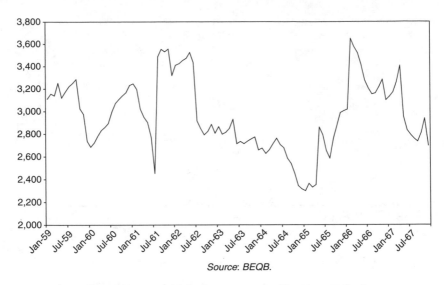

Source: BEQB.

Figure 5.2. UK published reserves, monthly, 1959–67 ($m).

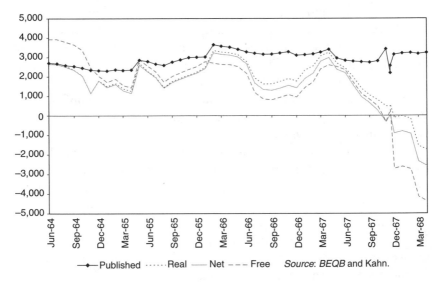

——♦——Published ······Real —— Net – – – Free   *Source: BEQB* and Kahn.

Figure 5.3. Measures of UK reserves, monthly, 1964–68 ($m).

central bank assistance – negligible at the beginning but significant for most of the rest of the period. These figures were sometimes not available at all or were not available until after some time had elapsed. The authorities themselves were ambivalent at best on how to present them. As one note put it in the middle of 1966:

Table 5.1. *UK total gold and convertible currency reserves, June 1964–April 1968 ($m)*

Month end	(1) Published reserves	(2) Short-term assistance	(3) Real reserves	(4) Net reserves	(5) IMF/GAB	(6) Dollar portfolio	(7) Free reserves
Jun 1964	2,705	14	2,691	2,649	0	1,280	3,928
Jul 1964	2,677	0	2,677	2,635	0	1,296	3,931
Aug 1964	2,584	14	2,570	2,509	0	1,282	3,791
Sep 1964	2,540	199	2,341	2,341	0	1,310	3,651
Oct 1964	2,453	414	2,038	2,038	0	1,319	3,357
Nov 1964	2,344	1,201	1,142	1,142	0	1,324	2,467
Dec 1964	2,316	526	1,789	1,789	1,078	1,322	2,033
Jan 1965	2,299	801	1,498	1,448	1,061	1,327	1,714
Feb 1965	2,363	706	1,658	1,607	1,061	1,333	1,879
Mar 1965	2,330	941	1,389	1,282	1,061	1,338	1,560
Apr 1965	2,352	1,098	1,254	1,148	1,061	1,344	1,431
May 1965	2,859	148	2,710	2,604	1,061	1,350	2,892
Jun 1965	2,792	510	2,282	2,257	1,061	1,355	2,551
Jul 1965	2,652	675	1,977	1,952	1,061	1,361	2,251
Aug 1965	2,584	1,140	1,445	1,420	1,061	1,366	1,725
Sep 1965	2,755	1,000	1,756	1,708	1,061	1,372	2,019
Oct 1965	2,873	949	1,924	1,876	1,061	1,378	2,192
Nov 1965	2,988	899	2,089	2,041	1,050	1,383	2,374
Dec 1965	3,004	773	2,232	2,184	1,050	1,386	2,520
Jan 1966	3,018	538	2,481	2,422	1,036	1,389	2,775
Feb 1966	3,648	300	3,349	3,231	1,036	504	2,699
Mar 1966	3,573	300	3,273	3,156	1,022	498	2,632
Apr 1966	3,520	288	3,231	3,114	991	498	2,621
May 1966	3,413	280	3,133	3,016	991	498	2,523
Jun 1966	3,276	496	2,780	2,663	986	498	2,176
Jul 1966	3,206	1,271	1,935	1,672	986	0	1,184
Aug 1966	3,153	1,532	1,621	1,338	983	0	854
Sep 1966	3,161	1,532	1,630	1,296	983	0	812
Oct 1966	3,217	1,470	1,747	1,408	977	0	930
Nov 1966	3,282	1,380	1,901	1,551	977	0	1,072
Dec 1966	3,100	1,330	1,770	1,420	966	0	952

(continued)

Table 5.1 *(continued)*

Month end	(1)	(2)	(3)	(4)	(5)	(6)	(7)
	Published reserves	Short-term assistance	Real reserves	Net reserves	IMF/GAB	Dollar portfolio	Free reserves
Jan 1967	3,130	804	2,327	1,901	963	0	1,436
Feb 1967	3,170	627	2,542	2,173	949	0	1,722
Mar 1967	3,259	202	3,058	2,786	893	0	2,391
Apr 1967	3,405	160	3,245	2,976	871	496	2,601
May 1967	2,954	260	2,694	2,366	350	496	2,512
Jun 1967	2,834	400	2,433	2,195	342	493	2,346
Jul 1967	2,792	809	1,982	1,562	342	493	1,714
Aug 1967	2,758	1,369	1,389	960	325	490	1,126
Sep 1967	2,733	1,691	1,042	644	314	490	820
Oct 1967	2,808	2,016	792	244	255	490	479
17 Nov 1967[a]	2,195	1,722	473	25	249	490	266
17 Nov 1967[b]	2,559	2,005	554	31	291	571	311
Nov 1967	3,424	2,940	484	−328	0	0	−328
Dec 1967	3,144	3,248	−104	−904	1,806	0	−2,710
Jan 1968	3,206	3,220	−14	−798	1,806	0	−2,604
Feb 1968	3,231	3,396	−165	−927	1,806	0	−2,733
Mar 1968	3,175	4,726	−1,551	−2,341	1,806	0	−4,147
Apr 1968	3,234	4,981	−1,747	−2,570	1,806	0	−4,376

Note: 'Real reserves' are published reserves less short-term assistance; 'Net reserves' excludes guaranteed sterling, special swaps, and other loans, as well as short-term assistance; 'Free reserves' are net reserves less IMF/GAB plus the dollar portfolio.
[a] Old parity.
[b] New parity.
Source: Bank of England, 'Gold and convertible currency reserves', 4A98/1.

The next issue of *Economic Trends,* which is due out 29 or 30 June, will contain the balance of payments analysis for the first quarter. In this the details of financing are apparently being deliberately suppressed on the grounds that nowadays there are so many operations of so many different sorts that it is no longer practicable to distinguish between what is and what is not 'central bank assistance'.[158]

[158] Bridge, Note for record – 'Conversation with Sir Denis Rickett Friday afternoon, 24 June', 27 June 1966, C43/49.

In order to obtain a clearer picture of the position, however, this amount for assistance should be deducted. When it is, we get what might be called 'real reserves', as shown in column 3. There were some other much smaller forms of assistance such as BIS swaps and Swiss loans that also should be deducted to give what is shown in column 4 as 'Net reserves'. Drawings from the IMF also need to be taken out. The end-month position for these is shown in column 5. There were no drawings at the start of this period, and they had all been repaid by the end, but in between, they were large. Thus, as an example of the kind of discrepancies that could appear, for January 1965, the published reserve figure was $2.3 billion, whereas, in fact, net reserves less the IMF drawing totalled only $387 million.

It was only a couple of years after this, when Cecil King, a non-Executive Director of the Bank and editor of the tabloid newspaper The *Mirror*, embarked on a major assault on the Labour Government that the question of the reserves was brought to the attention of a much wider public. His attack appeared on the front page of the paper on Friday, 10 May 1968. It argued that Britain was facing its greatest ever financial crisis that was 'not to be removed by lies about our reserves'.[159] In his diaries, King had written the previous day, 'It necessitates resigning from the Bank Court and I am sending a letter this evening to that effect'.[160] In the Bank, a note was prepared: 'The reserve figures themselves are, of course, accurate. … What is really at issue is our policy on non-disclosure of the use of central bank credit facilities'.[161]

But there is one other complicating factor, and that is the dollar portfolio shown in column 6. This was described at the time as a third line of defence. The origins of the dollar portfolio lie in the compulsory acquisition under wartime emergency legislation of certain dollar securities owned by British residents in order to provide foreign exchange to support the war effort.[162] In 1940, the government had to resort to the outright sale of vested securities to finance the war. There had been previous suggestions that this should be transferred to the reserves, but there was some unease over what could be construed as the use of long-term assets to pay short-term debts.[163] Some of the dollar securities held by British residents and taken over by the authorities in 1941 were pledged as collateral for a loan from the American Reconstruction Finance Corporation, a loan of $425 million in July 1941 at

[159] *Daily Mirror*, 10 May 1968, p. 1.
[160] King (1972, p. 192).
[161] C. J. Wiles (EID assistant seconded to HMT), Note for record, 15 May 1968, 4A98/1.
[162] 'British Government's holding of dollar securities', 3 March 1966, C94/167.
[163] Conolly to Cromer, 23 January 1964, G1/560.

3 per cent, of which $390 million actually was borrowed.[164] The securities pledged as collateral were not released until the loan was finally repaid in October 1951. They consisted of three groups of stocks: shares of British insurance companies' subsidiaries in the United States (about 40 in total), shares of companies in which the British interest was controlling or substantial, and a wide range of US preference and equity stocks – which included large blocks of equities such as Shell Oil, General Motors, and Standard Oil. All these groups of securities were either vested or pledged with the Treasury in 1941. Most of the first two groups were pledged, whereas most of the third group were vested. The difference between pledging and vesting is the distinction between a temporary and permanent loan.[165] When the collateral was returned by the Reconstruction Finance Corporation to the Treasury in 1951, most of the securities pledged were sold back to their former owners, but the greater part of those vested formed the basis of the portfolio. In 1949, the value of marketable securities was over $335 million. On 31 December 1959, the value was $961 million, and by 1966, it was estimated roughly at $1,250 million (£445 million), the changes simply the result of market movements.

At the end of 1963 it was decided to liquefy the portfolio up to a total of $500 million. The liquefying programme began at the beginning of 1964, and by November 1965, a substantial part of the portfolio had been switched out of common stocks into more liquid holdings, mainly of US government short bonds.[166] By February 1966, the liquefied portion stood at $880 million, or 64 per cent of the total value of US dollar securities of nearly $1,400 million (£500 million).[167] The portfolio included US Treasury bonds and notes, BIS deposits, certificates of deposit (CDs) of less than 1 year at issue, US Treasury certificates, and Federal Reserve Bank and current accounts at the Bank.[168] In February 1966, H. L Jenkyns (Assistant

---

[164] The Reconstruction Finance Corporation was established by President Hoover in February 1932 as one response to the Great Depression and was financed through the US Treasury. One ambition was to recapitalise the nation's banks. Its responsibilities increased under Roosevelt. It financed the construction and operation of war plants, provided protection against war and disaster damages, and interestingly, made loans to foreign governments. In 1953 it was abolished as an independent agency, and in 1954 it was transferred to the Department of the Treasury and finally disbanded in 1957.

[165] C. D. Butler, 'Draft: Britain's overseas investments, redraft of British Government holdings of dollar securities', 18 February 1966, pp. 29–30, C40/167.

[166] Rickett to Hubback, 4 February 1966, C94/167.

[167] Butler to Kelley, 'Mr Wingfield Digby's P.Q. for answer on Tuesday, 22 February', 11 February 1966, C94/167.

[168] Butler, 'Changes in the composition of HMG's dollar portfolio', 23 February 1966, C94/167.

Secretary at the Treasury) wrote to the Governor requesting the transfer of cash and securities of the value of $880 million and Canadian $5 million into the reserves.[169] The Deputy Governor told Hayes of the intention to take the liquid portion of the portfolio into the reserves, and Hayes felt that this would be 'a sensible and constructive move' and would 'clean things up considerably' although he would have gone further.[170] The Bank was in favour of liquefying the remainder of the portfolio because large-scale borrowings from the IMF had made it 'virtually inevitable that the whole portfolio would be needed to help repay those borrowings'.[171] At the beginning of 1966, the rise in reserves is simply the result of bringing in a portion of the dollar portfolio. There is a similar rise late in 1967 for the same reason.[172]

From Figure 5.3 it can be seen that real, net, and free reserves all follow a remarkably similar path, one that was much more volatile than the published figure but, more interestingly, falling away steeply from April 1967 onwards and in the case of free reserves reaching minus almost $3 billion at the end of 1967. Where the published reserves are almost flat throughout, the 'true' position was increasingly serious and in the end calamitous.

Preparing for the Inevitable

The period from the middle of 1966 until devaluation in November 1967 had an air of inevitability about it. The remorseless slide of sterling continued – intermittent crises, short lulls, and preparation for the end. In July 1966, Bridge wrote, 'The smell of the start of another crisis – like November

---

[169] The breakdown was as follows: US Treasury notes $254.4 million, US Treasury certificates of indebtedness $325.0 million, Federal agency bonds $35.5 million, IBRD bonds (American issue) $3.5 million, time certificates of deposit $75 million, Bank for International Settlements deposits $160 million, Eximbank sub-participation certificate $7.9 million, funds awaiting reinvestment on deposit with US Treasury $18.8 million.

[170] Wood, Note for record, 'Conversation with Mr. Al Hayes', 28 February 1966, C94/167.

[171] Rickett to Jenkyns, 17 March 1966, C94/167.

[172] For the dollar portfolio, see C94/139, 140, 166, 167, and 171. There had been a scheme running in 1967, code named Jason, concerned with reconstituting the dollar portfolio. It went through many versions and had little support in the Bank. Bridge wrote: 'I continue to regard these idiotic proposals with grave concern and must again warn against the effect which their adoption could have upon confidence in the UK's intention to maintain the existing parity.' O'Brien took this line too and advised Armstrong against Jason of any sort. Bridge also wrote that: 'This idea is so ridiculous as to be almost incredible. Let us hope the PPS can be relied upon to kill it – if the Bank cannot do so ... ', Bridge to Rootham, 'Jason', 15 May 1967; O'Brien to Armstrong, 23 May 1967; Bridge annotation on Legh to Morse, 'Jason', 20 July 1967, 3A53/2.

1964 or March or July/August 1965 – is unmistakable.'[173] By the end of the month, Stevens was reporting from Washington that 'opposition to devaluation at the highest levels may be changing.'[174] A feeling was developing that if it had to come, then the sooner the better. In the Cabinet, Brown insisted on raising the topic of devaluation in the middle of 1966, and from that point on, the Cabinet was alive to the issue.[175]

There were apparently fears around in August 1966 that devaluation could be carried out during the IMF meetings of the following month. In the Bank, the talk was of trying to change market psychology, and the most promising line of strategy was to operate on the forward exchange. Allen argued that there was no reason to fear an abnormally large oversold forward-exchange position vis-à-vis the market when confidence was low, hedging prevalent, leads and lags moving against the Bank, and the prospects for the balance of payments favourable: '... our strategy should be to *maximise,* and be seen to be *ready* to maximise the size of our oversold position' (italics in original).[176] This, it was reckoned, would demonstrate confidence, protect the spot reserves, and reduce the financing problem with only marginal risk. Yet it might be wondered from where came the belief in the strength of the underlying balance of payments. It did not extend across the Channel, for the following day the Governor of the Belgian central bank, Hubert Ansiaux, telephoned O'Brien to say that rumours were rife in his market.[177]

By the end of 1966, the Bank was discussing a reduction in Bank Rate from 7 per cent, and on balance, the Governor felt that there was a case for a minimal reduction of ½ per cent, with another ½ per cent soon to follow.[178] It was March, though, before the further ½ per cent was considered again. By then, a cautious optimism was creeping back in some quarters, and while the Governor remained anxious, he recommended the further cut in his letter to Armstrong.[179] While the later months of 1966 and early months of 1967 had shown some promising signs, and by March the Bank had repaid the outstanding swaps and short-term borrowing from the United States and others, it was a false dawn, and the gloom was to close

---

[173] Bridge to O'Brien, 'For Treasury meeting 5 p.m. Friday, 15 July', 15 July 1966, OV44/124.
[174] Stevens to Armstrong/Trend, Telegram 2165, 26 July 1966, OV44/124.
[175] Tew (1978b, p. 313).
[176] Allen to O'Brien, 'Forward operations of EEA', 4 August 1966, OV44/124.
[177] O'Brien, Governor's note, 5 August 1966, OV44/124. See Cairncross and Eichengreen (1983) for estimates of oversold position and loss at devaluation.
[178] O'Brien to Callaghan, 29 December 1966, OV44/124.
[179] O'Brien to Armstrong, 9 March 1967, OV44/124.

in again before long. There did follow in April some discussion of reducing Bank Rate further to 5 per cent in the course of the summer, the only fear being that it would be interpreted as the 'go' signal.[180] The rescue operation that had been carried out in July 1966 with new arrangements for sterling was renewed in September 1966. The following months were devoted to discussion of further renewal and extension.

In the second quarter of 1967, however, there were several reversals of fortune. The growth in world trade began to slow, and while British export growth slowed, imports remained high. Foreign exchange flowed out, and sterling weakened in May. It was in that month that a new application was made to join the European Economic Community (EEC), and immediately there were suggestions that that inevitably would require devaluation. There were, nevertheless, sufficient resources available under existing arrangements to cope with these kinds of ups and downs. A bigger blow came with the Middle East crisis and closure of the Suez Canal. The fall in reserves that was showing in May then continued through the summer. With the situation looking grim, a letter for the Governor to send to the Chancellor was prepared. It outlined possible actions, including devaluation. O'Brien said that he could appreciate the force of the arguments for altering the exchange rate, but he had to reject them: 'I, like you I know, abhor the very idea of devaluation.' In conclusion, O'Brien apologised that the letter was depressing, but the outlook was bleak, and there were 'not many shots left in the locker'. In the end, the letter was not sent, but it reveals his sombre mood.[181]

Against this background, the FU Committee also had started meeting again regularly, updating the Devaluation War Book.[182] The question of fixed versus floating exchange rates again came to the fore. McMahon had by this time taken Fforde's place on the committee. On devaluation, McMahon was a pragmatist, having, the previous year, made a plea that the matter at least should be elevated from 'unthinkable last resort' to 'explicit possible policy'.[183] However, on the matter of fixed versus floating, he was firmly allied with the Bank's position. An FU document circulated in September 1967 presented the Bank/Treasury view against a floating or flexible rate, but McMahon told the Governor that it did not make the case well enough.

---

[180] Fforde to O'Brien, 6 April 1967, OV44/124. We begin to see more evidence of discussion in written material about this time.

[181] Draft letter to Callaghan, 11 July 1967, OV44/136.

[182] McMahon to O'Brien, 'F.U', 16 May 1967; Stanley Payton (Deputy Chief, Overseas) to Parsons, 'The war book: state of play', 24 August 1967, OV44/136.

[183] McMahon to Cromer/O'Brien, 'Economic policy', 18 March 1966, OV44/123.

Indeed, he thought that much of it was 'straight Kaldor'. McMahon reckoned that if there were a devaluation in the near future, the Prime Minister 'will be hot for floating' and that Douglas Allen (permanent under-secretary at the Department of Economic Affairs) might lend his weight.[184] The Bank's original position was that 'The weight of opinion is against a flexible rate', but the revised opinion was that 'Although some economic advisers have advocated a floating rate, at least as a temporary measure, official opinion in both the Treasury and the Bank of England is strongly against it.'[185] There were still some Treasury dissenters, however. Recently appointed Economic Adviser Michael Posner favoured a float together with an announcement to re-peg at a later stage.[186] With the dock strike that began in the middle of September, the picture turned even gloomier. Reserves tumbled, even if that fact was obscured by central bank borrowings. Over the summer period from May to September, borrowings reached $1.7 billion. There was further talk of central bank support in September, but it did not come to anything, and reserves fell further in October.

As the position of sterling deteriorated, thought was given to an increase in Bank Rate for 12 October. In the event, no move was made, but four days later Fforde admitted that he had changed his mind and advocated a rise of ½ per cent, to 6 per cent, on 19 October. The size of the increase was dictated by Fforde's view that a full 1 per cent rise would leave inadequate room for manoeuvre given the 'risks and dangers' that had to be taken into account; that is, Bank Rate would have to be increased again.[187] For public consumption, it was explained that the move was designed to ensure that sterling was not adversely affected by short-term rates in other markets. Sure enough, by the end of the month Fforde had produced a note weighing up the case for another rise. With events moving quickly, he cautiously proposed a further ½ per cent on 9 November. Clearly, the situation was awkward. Hollom observed that the previous move had 'tied our hands' and that it would be difficult to move up 'unless we are demonstrably following someone else'.[188] Fforde's note drew a typically sharp response from

[184] FU (67) 5 (revise), 'A fixed or floating rate'; McMahon to O'Brien, 'F.U', 14 September 1967; FU (67) 5th, 14 September 1967, OV44/137.
[185] McMahon to Parsons, 22 September 1967, enc. 'Fixed or floating rates', 22 September 1967, OV44/137; FU (67) 5 (2nd revise), OV44/138.
[186] Posner to Armstrong, 25 October 1967, enc. 'Fixed and floating rate', 25 October 1967; McMahon found Posner's attitude on the subject 'more reasonable and less intransigent' than Kaldor; McMahon to O'Brien/Parsons, 2 November 1967, OV44/138.
[187] Fforde to O'Brien/Parsons, 'Bank rate', 16 October 1967, C42/9.
[188] Hollom annotation on Fforde to O'Brien/Parsons, 'Money rates in London', 27 October 1967, C42/9.

Bridge. Looking from his 'particular window', Bridge thought that use of Bank Rate over the previous two years had appeared 'ham-handed and occasionally disastrous'. The October increase, he said, 'was obviously too late' and should have occurred two weeks, if not two months, earlier. Bridge went on to dispute Fforde's assertion that the recent move had established 'credibility' in policy; it might apply to the discount market and the stock exchange but 'certainly does not go for most of my more sophisticated "customers", who sometimes wonder whether we have a policy, because we seem never to do what is required until it is overdue'. These were strong criticisms given that Bank Rate was used primarily for external reasons. As to the immediate future, Bridge agreed that there should be a move as soon as possible, but he warned that anything more than ½ per cent would be dangerous because it would 'encourage those Americans who are betting on the £ being devalued before 15 November'.[189] Bank Rate accordingly was increased ½ per cent to 6½ per cent on 9 November. The press guidance explained that it was necessary because of pressures towards higher interest rates in other international markets. In a supplementary note, Bridge used the analogy of putting on a raincoat before the rain begins to fall rather than waiting 'until you are really wet before donning it'. Making a further sideswipe at policy, he commented that the latter had been 'our customary posture over recent years'.[190]

As to the timing of a devaluation, there now was talk of making a pre-emptive strike. In early October, Cairncross told Armstrong that the government would be abdicating its responsibility if it just waited until events forced it to devalue. They must make a judgement on future prospects and act accordingly. On a copy of this note that appeared at the Bank, O'Brien wrote 'very much my own line of thought'. There was now an air of inevitably surrounding devaluation. Planning had moved beyond vague contingency to detailed planning, and Armstrong told the FU meeting on 9 November that they were in the 'amber light zone'.

In these final months before devaluation, the Bank had concentrated its efforts on garnering international support for sterling in order either to avoid devaluation or, if it occurred, to ensure that it was successful. On the latter, the Bank was keen to establish the attitude of other countries if the parity was changed and, in particular, whether others would follow suit. In September, Bridge had noted three possibilities for additional financing: a consortium of Swiss banks, the BIS, and the holding of additional

---

[189] Bridge to O'Brien/Parsons, 'Money rates in London', 3 November 1967, C42/9.
[190] Press guidance, 9 November 1967; Bridge, 'Bank rate. Supplementary note for talking to the press', 9 November 1967, C42/9.

guaranteed sterling by the US Treasury.[191] These were all pursued. Sterling's plight had been the subject of much discussion in September 1967 when all the key international participants were in Rio de Janeiro for the IMF/World Bank annual meeting. O'Brien and McMahon took the opportunity to have talks with Pierre-Paul Schweitzer (Managing Director of the IMF), Martin, J. Dewey Daane, Hayes, Coombs (United States), and Blessing (Germany). Later, in Buenos Aires, they saw BIS President Jelle Zijlstra. The outcome of all this was a $450 million loan from the Swiss, $25 million from Japan, and the likelihood of $250 million to $300 million through the BIS. The last of these was discussed at an 'experts' meeting in Basle at the end of October and was on the agenda for ratification at the BIS board meeting on Monday, 13 November.[192]

On Friday, 10 November, McMahon produced a 'hurried and tentative' note for the Governor on how much assistance might be available in the event of devaluation. His estimate was that total facilities could reach $2.3 billion, plus a $400 million standby.[193] The same day, O'Brien and Morse met Callaghan. O'Brien was about to go to the BIS monthly meeting in Basle, and Morse, along with Rickett, was heading to Washington. They discussed tactics for the various negotiations. An approach to the United States was being formulated that would seek financial support, either through a long-term loan or by increasing the holdings of guaranteed sterling. Whether they would have been prepared to take such long-term credits has been doubted by some. It was perhaps a way of giving advance notice.[194] Draft letters, including one that could be passed to President Johnson, emphasised how critical the situation had become. It was now known that the October trade figures, due out on the following Wednesday, would be extremely poor, and although it was argued that the impact of the docks strike made these figures 'meaningless', a run on the pound was anticipated. In response to O'Brien's query about what line to take with his colleagues in Basle, the Chancellor suggested that the Governor might emphasise the international, political, and economic consequences if Britain had to devalue.[195]

During the weekend of talks in the United States, Rickett told the Americans that a support package totalling $3 billion would be needed, and how this could be achieved was discussed. One element would be a

---

[191] Bridge to Fenton, 'Additional financing', 14 September 1967, OV44/143.
[192] Bridge to O'Brien/Parsons, 'B.I.S. assistance. Meeting of experts 30/31 October at B.I.S., Basle', 31 October 1967, OV44/143.
[193] McMahon to O'Brien, 'Assistance', 10 November 1967, OV44/139.
[194] Solomon (1977, p. 95).
[195] Peter Baldwin (HMT), Note for record, 10 November 1967, OV44/143.

$1.4 billion standby from the IMF, and later the same day the British officials raised this matter with Schweitzer. The Managing Director was supportive but emphasised that there would have to be overwhelming backing from the Europeans.[196] Morse telegrammed O'Brien to tell him that the reception had been friendly and co-operative. He outlined the package that comprised guaranteed sterling holdings of $1.3 billion (United States $500 million, Germany $250 million, Italy $250 million, and others $300 million), the $1.4 million standby from IMF, and $300 million of medium-term loans from commercial banks.[197] However, on Sunday, O'Brien reported from Basle that his fellow Governors were not impressed with the proposals and had instead suggested that the operation should take the form of an IMF standby of $3 billion (unique in the IMF's history by going over 200 per cent of quota). The British officials told Schweitzer, who apparently received the idea calmly and not unfavourably. On Sunday evening, Morse dined with Martin and Daane and, when quizzed about the Governor's views, said that O'Brien now doubted whether the position could be improved without a change of rate but that if other countries thought that it was important to avoid a devaluation and put together a large support package, then the Governor would 'gladly accept it'. Later that evening, after 11:00 p.m., Schweitzer phoned to say that having given the matter further thought, he had to reject the $3 billion proposition as unfeasible. Morse relayed all this to O'Brien, calling him at 1:00 a.m. (Washington time, 6:00 a.m. in Basle).

In Basle, the Governor found central bank opinion divided on whether Britain should devalue and be lukewarm on the support package. He reported developments to Callaghan by phone on Sunday and again on Monday morning. O'Brien then attended the BIS board meeting, where the $250 million cover was ratified, before flying back to London for a meeting with Callaghan that afternoon. O'Brien ran through the views of the central bank representatives: Ansiaux for devaluation, Per Åsbrink (Sweden's Riksbank) against, Blessing against, Jacques Brunet (Banque de France) for, Carli against, Edwin Stopper (Swiss National Bank) against, and Hayes and Coombs against. Nevertheless, O'Brien advised Callaghan that devaluation was inevitable and ought to be undertaken.[198] Most American officials realised, too, that a change of rate was inevitable, and the ensuing discussions

---

[196] Telegrams 3533 and 3535, 11 November 1967; Evan Maude, 'Record of a discussion at the US Treasury on 11 November 1967' and 'Record of a talk with Mr. Schweitzer, on 11 November 1967', both 11 November 1967, OV44/143.

[197] Telegram 3536, 11 November 1967, OV44/143.

[198] Baldwin, Note for record, 13 November 1967, OV44/143.

were largely about planning for it rather than trying to avoid it. Schweitzer confirmed that a standby of $1.4 billion would quickly be negotiable in order to support a new rate. At the Fed on early Monday evening, Morse was told by Martin that President Johnson would prefer that devaluation should not happen, but if it was necessary, then Britain could count on US support.[199]

Late on Monday, 13 November, Wilson and Callaghan took the decision to devalue, and this was made known to a small group of ministers, the 'Tuesday Club', the following day. Even at that late date, the New York Fed had not given up on a support package, reportedly having grown more anxious that Britain should not devalue. The centre of negotiations had now moved to Paris, where officials were gathering for meetings of the G10 and Working Party Three (WP3). The United States was still pursuing the idea of increasing its holdings of guaranteed sterling by $500 million if the European central banks took a corresponding amount. On Wednesday, 15 November, at 10:30 p.m., Callaghan met O'Brien, Morse, Armstrong, and Posner and said that this was possibly the final time for them to make their views known. O'Brien said that he now favoured devaluation, but only if the package of measures was right.[200] The formal decision to devalue was taken by the Cabinet on Thursday, 16 November, and the administrative juggernaut set out in the Devaluation War Book rolled into action.

Even then, matters did not go entirely to plan. Despite the considerable detail contained in the war book, there was little provision for action in the event of a leak or sudden pressure on sterling during the countdown period. And that, in effect, was what happened. All sorts of rumours were circulating in the newspapers, and the fact that the $250 million BIS loan had already been correctly predicted added credence to stories that a $1 billion support package for sterling was being negotiated in Paris. When, on the Thursday, a parliamentary question was put to the Prime Minister about such a loan, the question was referred to the Chancellor, and he gave a far from satisfactory answer.[201] The immediate reaction in the market was to sell sterling heavily. On Friday, the markets were in turmoil. Sterling suffered disastrously, and by the day's end, a total support of $1,450 million had

---

[199] Morse to O'Brien/Parsons, 'Washington, Friday, November 10–Monday, November 13', 14 November 1967, OV44/143.

[200] Telegrams flagged in Morse to O'Brien/Parsons, 'Washington, Friday, November 10–Monday, November 13', 14 November 1967, OV44/143; Baldwin, Note for the record, 16 November 1967, OV44/140.

[201] HC Deb, 16 November 1967, Vol. 754, cc632–635.

been used, almost all in the spot market. Robert Solomon of the Fed wrote later that on that day the Bank 'paid out more than a $1 billion of reserves in support for sterling at a rate that was to be abandoned the next day'.[202] He was close but still some way short of the actual figure. On Saturday, 18 November, the government announced that the par value of sterling would be reduced from $2.80 to $2.40, a devaluation of 14.3 per cent against the dollar. By that time, however, it was hardly news. (The amount was in line with the IMF's calculation that 15 per cent was required.) Bank Rate went up by 1½ per cent to 8 per cent, then the highest level that had been reached since the outbreak of war in August 1914. A package of emergency measures was also introduced. A few days later, a $1.5 billion central bank support package was announced to defend the new parity, and on 29 November, an IMF standby arrangement was organised.

Questions remain over whether devaluation might have been carried out earlier and at less cost. Certainly, the immediate timing was poor even apart from the mess of the Chancellor's response to the parliamentary question. The end of October would have allowed a more orderly process. By mid-November, it was increasingly costly and difficult to stick to the planned timetable. However, it might have been done as early as July 1966 instead of embarking on that date on another round of support for sterling. By the middle of 1967, 'it was indefensible to refrain from acting'.[203] Kahn judged the delay 'to have been a gross error',[204] and estimated that had it taken place at the end of June 1967, then by the end of 1968 'the external position would have been better by at least £400 million'.[205] Of course, it might have been done in November 1964.

One of the principal failings in the operation as far as the Bank was concerned was their obsession with psychological warfare. Their pride in market skills and the lack, for so long, of serious economic input contributed to a concentration on manipulating the market. There was no economic model employed in the discussion of devaluation in the Bank. There was no mention of the monetary approach to the balance of payments.[206] The analysis used was the elasticities and absorption approach that had been used in the analysis for the 1949 devaluation.

---

[202] Solomon (1977, p. 95).

[203] Cairncross and Eichengreen (1983, p. 216).

[204] Kahn, 'Enquiry into the position of sterling January 1966–February 1968', 12 August 1971, Vol. I, p. 99, EID1/6.

[205] Kahn, 'Enquiry into the position of sterling, January 1966–February 1968', 12 August 1971, Vol. II, p. 217, EID1/7.

[206] One relatively early example of which could be found in Polak (1957).

The costs included the losses on forward intervention, which had contin-ued to be significant in scale from the end of 1964. The technique was useful so long as there was a credible rejection of devaluation.[207] Indeed, it could be profitable, and experts in the Bank recommended maximising the over-sold position, that is, the sale of dollars. There was a risk, however, that once engaged in, it could be difficult to withdraw if the crisis of confidence did not abate. That said, there were two occasions on which the Bank reduced its forward position by $1 billion, one in early 1966 and the other in the first quarter of 1967, when presumably profits were taken.[208]

In early 1965, the Bank prepared a paper on the subject for the Treasury. O'Brien wanted to be sure that Bridge was happy with it. He was not. He replied:

I would be a little doubtful as to the wisdom, at the present time, of the Bank send-ing to the Treasury a paper of this nature. Dissertations on forward exchange, like books on sex, tend to stimulate unduly the imaginations of those less experienced in the subject and, amongst recent temporary recruits to Whitehall, there are a number of such.[209]

(He might have had Balogh, economic adviser to the Cabinet, in mind, for the previous day he had dismissed Balogh's views on an aspect of the subject as ridiculous.[210])

The Bank entered into forward contracts on a huge scale, managing them to keep the forward discount down.[211] And in the mid-1960s, a minidebate on the activity blew up.[212] A question was how forward dealing affected confidence; it seemed it could go either way. The activity ended, at least temporarily, as devaluation became increasingly likely, 'affording almost unlimited opportunities for bear speculation with the Bank not daring to withdraw' for fear of that appearing to be a signal that the authorities were about to devalue.[213] From January 1963 to November 1967, forward

---

[207] Aliber (1962) argued that it could in fact be profitable even in the absence of credible rejection.

[208] 'Intervention in the foreign exchange market', 28 May 1970 (by Hallett/Sangster), enc. with Hall to O'Brien et al., 28 May 1970, 6A134/1.

[209] O'Brien to Parson/Bridge/Thompson-McCausland, 18 February 1965; Bridge to Parsons/ O'Brien, 'Forward transactions in exchange', 22 February 1965; for the final version of the paper, see Bank of England, 'Forward transaction in exchange', 26 February 1965, C43/676.

[210] Bridge, Annotation, 21 February 1965 on Heasman to Allen, 'Breakdown of forward pur-chases and sales between residents and non-residents', 15 February 1965, C43/676.

[211] 'The Euro-currency business of banks in London', *BEQB* 10(1):39, March 1970.

[212] Oppenheimer (1966); Einzig (1967).

[213] Tew (1977, p. 84).

sterling was always at a discount and at its largest discount in the year from November 1964 to November 1965.[214] Figures were not published, and that made it difficult for commentators to discuss its extent. However, in 1970, the balance-of-payments statistics revealed a figure for the loss on the forward transactions of £105 million in 1967 and £251 million in 1968, a total of £356 million.[215] That was approximately one-third of reserves. Tew and, later, Cairncross and Eichengreen made estimates based on this information that suggested forward contracts of over £2 billion.[216] Since devaluation was 14 per cent, the loss of £356 million ($854 million at $2.40) implied that outstanding forward commitments on the eve of devaluation were $5,981 million (£2,136 million at $2.80) – equal in value to more than twice total reserves. Table 5.2 and Figure 5.4 show the forward position as reported monthly by the Bank to the Treasury. In September 1966, the oversold position with the market was $3.2 billion, and in November 1967, it was $4.4 billion. Bank sources show that on 17 November the oversold position was actually £1,640 million (£1,913 million after devaluation). There was a loss to the reserves of £273 million – the figure used in the second Kahn Report. Kahn thought that given the situation, it would be unreasonable to criticise the Bank's tactics too severely, but he was critical of the fact that after devaluation the Bank decided to withdraw from the market and allow maturities to run off rather than take advantage of what he thought to be favourable conditions to make profits out of the discount on forward sterling.[217]

Another remarkable thing about all this was that the Bank dealt on this huge scale with close to total freedom. There was no correspondence on the subject with the Treasury in 1964. This did not surprise Roy Bridge, for, as he said, 'operational policy is usually developed quite quickly ... and agreed orally between the Bank and the Treasury – in the case of a major decision like this one, usually at the highest level.' Thereafter, the Bank sent an end-month letter to the Treasury notifying them of what had been done. There is no evidence of any complaint from the Treasury or of any hint of direction. Bridge went on to say that there was at that time no indication of what the costs were likely to be, but that 'The decision to intervene virtually without limit ... would not in all probability have been taken had there not been an unequivocal intention to maintain the exchange rate.'[218]

[214] Bordo, McDonald, and Oliver (in press, figures 1 and 2).
[215] *UK Balance of Payments 1970*, table 3 and p. 82.
[216] Tew, (1978b, p. 342); Cairncross and Eichengreen (1983, p. 184).
[217] 'Gold and convertible currency reserves', 4A98/1; Kahn, 'Enquiry into the position of sterling January 1966–February 1968', 12 August 1968, Vol. I, pp. 126–127, EID1/6.
[218] Bridge to Hubback, 5 December 1968, C43/667.

Table 5.2. *Forward exchange oversold position, October 1964–December 1967 ($m)*

Month end	Oversold position	
	Market	Total
Oct 1964	188	602
Nov 1964	249	1,448
Dec 1964	1,879	2,484
Jan 1965	2,103	2,982
Feb 1965	2,033	2,817
Mar 1965	2,190	3,209
Apr 1965	2,229	3,405
May 1965	2,282	2,402
Jun 1965	2,268	2,750
Jul 1965	2,346	2,993
Aug 1965	2,859	3,870
Sep 1965	2,419	3,548
Oct 1965	2,122	3,200
Nov 1965	1,851	2,878
Dec 1965	1,803	2,705
Jan 1966	1,560	2,229
Feb 1966	1,355	1,784
Mar 1966	1,372	1,826
Apr 1966	1,383	1,831
May 1966	1,397	1,834
Jun 1966	1,439	2,092
Jul 1966	2,304	3,735
Aug 1966	3,153	4,844
Sep 1966	3,220	4,914
Oct 1966	2,738	4,371
Nov 1966	2,548	4,091
Dec 1966	2,545	4,038
Jan 1967	2,780	3,746
Feb 1967	2,495	3,284
Mar 1967	2,148	2,514
Apr 1967	2,013	2,338
May 1967	2,268	2,615

Month end	Oversold position	
	Market	Total
Jun 1967	2,531	3,018
Jul 1967	2,817	3,713
Aug 1967	2,758	4,214
Sep 1967	2,800	4,578
Oct 1967	3,406	5,506
Nov 1967	4,392	7,012
Dec 1967	4,298	7,183

Source: Monthly report to the Treasury, 6A152/1 and C43/121.

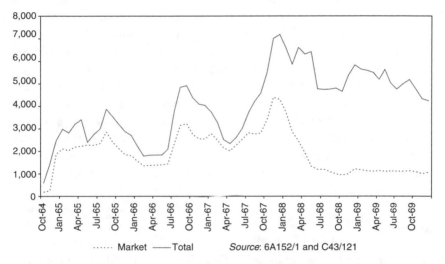

Figure 5.4. EEA forward position, month end, 1964–69 ($m).

A charge that surely can be made against the Bank was that it delayed devaluation. The Bank was committed to defending sterling. But did it go too far? In Bridge and Parsons it had two of the most able defenders, and they were determined to hold the rate. And they were strongly supported by similarly minded central bankers in the Fed and in Europe. As the date approached, Bridge's comments on the daily foreign-exchange markets report grew ever more despondent: Friday, 13 October was a 'real shocker'; the Bank Rate increase on 19 October, 'too little too late'; 2 November was 'just a depressing Thursday'; 6 November was 'disagreeable'; on Friday, 17 November, Bridge wrote one single word, 'Crucifixion.' He took the event badly, later describing the period as the 'most miserable' of his career.[219] Both he and Parsons left the Bank soon after.

The international monetary system continued to stumble along in the course of the 1960s as doubts persisted over the long-run viability of the two reserve currencies. A range of ad hoc measures grew up as different responses were made to plugging the dyke when holes of different kinds appeared. Thus there was the gold pool to stabilise the market in monetary gold, the central bank swap network in currencies, the Basle arrangements for central bank co-operation in short-term credits (itself a stop-gap measure until IMF drawings and standbys could be arranged), and a broader form of Organisation for Economic Co-operation and Development (OECD) co-operation on monetary and financial matters in the WP3. Short-term credits were used essentially to deal with episodes where it was believed there was a sudden lack of confidence reflected in a 'speculative attack' on a currency. Recourse to the IMF was a medium-term solution for repaying the short-term credits but was also more focussed on the balance of payments – a primary concern of the IMF. All these measures arose in the early 1960s and continued for the remainder of the decade as the struggle to save the system went on. In addition, in Britain, apart from general economic policy, whose first concern was the exchange rate, there were the specific measures such as exchange controls. These were used by most countries to act directly on the exchanges, but they were probably most severe in Britain.

As far as sterling was concerned, by 1963 or 1964, there were many who felt that it was over-valued.[220] For a variety of reasons, however, some domestic and political and others external, a defiant stance was adopted that there would be no devaluation. Of the former, the most important was the fact that the newly elected Labour Government was determined not to be seen as the party of devaluation. It is difficult to recapture at a distance the powerful feeling of the time that the strength of the currency was a clear reflection of the strength of the economy. The performances of the external accounts together with that of sterling were used as ready-made indicators of British 'decline', an idea that had taken hold and was even popular at the time. As Manser wrote in 1971:

---

[219] 'Foreign exchange and gold markets', dealers' daily reports in C8/35. *The Times*, 22 September 1969, p. 25.

[220] See Middleton (2002).

The balance of payments is the English sickness. This is not because the British have a balance of payments that is any different from any other. It is because only the British make it a point of national conscience. ... The UK's self-revulsion over the balance of payments is only part of a larger, and more long-lived process. For many years, ... Britain has seen herself to be on a gentle slide. ... Into this atmosphere erupted ... the post-war balance of payments problem.[221]

Well, Britain's balance-of-payments problem was somewhat different from that of other countries, but Manser reflects accurately the obsession with it and the misuse of it for purposes of illustrating terminal decline. Sterling's performance was more and more regarded as a virility symbol, and that, in part, lies behind the desperate and ultimately foolish attempt to hold to the parity of $2.80 after 1964. In the Bank, there was greater concern than elsewhere for the holders of sterling and a related concern for the welfare of the City. External pressures came in the main from the United States (and in particular the New York Fed), who saw sterling as a line of defence for the dollar, but more widely, it came from those who wanted to see the Bretton Woods arrangements survive.

All that said, the crisis of 1964 had stunned Labour and left them with the feeling that Britain could no longer afford the 'burden' of an international currency, and this gave fresh impetus to consideration of the part played by a reserve currency. The trouble lay in large part in the confused views on growth and the belief that the way to address inflation and domestic demand was through a prices and incomes policy. The failure to discern the problem was appreciated in some quarters at least. In January 1965, *The Banker* fumed, 'No international monetary system could save a currency from the repercussions of the indifference and (later) ineptitude of Britain's economic policies in this past year.'[222]

Reflecting on the trials of the pound in the years since the war, Hirsch in 1965 identified eight sterling crises. There was that associated with convertibility in 1947, the devaluation of 1949, the summer of 1951, the summer of 1955, Suez in the autumn of 1956, the late summer of 1957, the summer of 1961, and that of the end of 1964.[223] Had he postponed writing for another two or three years, he could have added another two or three crises. Or should he? Are most of them, at least after 1957, not better seen as one long crisis with the same fundamental cause and explanation? Hirsch did try to distinguish between speculative attacks and serious current account deficits, but not surprisingly, he frequently found both at work.

[221] Manser (1971, pp. 178–179).
[222] *The Banker* 115(467):11, January 1965.
[223] Hirsch (1965, pp. 48–49).

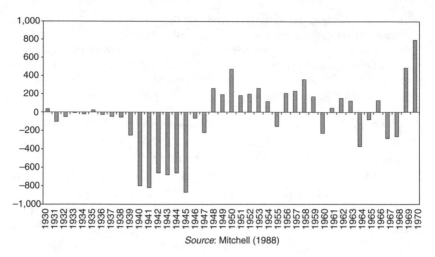

Source: Mitchell (1988)

Figure 5.5. UK balance of payments, current account, annual, 1930–70 (£m).

The balance of payments was the proximate cause of sterling's problem and, it could be said, vice versa. There is a small literature on the conceptual and statistical difficulties in presenting balance-of-payments figures. I abstract from these and simply present the data available to policymakers at the time and revisions to show how perceptions later changed. Figure 5.5 shows Britain's balance of payments in this period in a longer context. What stands out is that while the position had clearly changed in the 1930s and 1940s, in the 1950s and 1960s, the current account, while slipping into deficit from time to time, mostly bobbled along just in positive territory. The government of the day, however, had to deal with the problem as it was perceived at the time. There was no doubt a problem, but the scale of the problem was not always so clear. To the Labour Government of 1964, the visible trade deficit was believed to be in excess of £800 million, a truly staggering figure when total foreign-exchange reserves were around £2,300 million. To put it in two other ways, the deficit was 3 per cent of GDP, or there were reserves sufficient to cover 5½ months of imports. The balance-of-payments figures used at the time have since been revised many times such that the figure now being used for 1964 is down to £543 million.[224] This is still a substantial deficit. However, for some purposes, it is necessary to use the figures that were available at the time to appreciate what the nature of the problem was perceived to be. Douglas Allen (later Lord Croham), a Treasury official and Permanent Secretary between 1968 to 1974, later observed:

[224] Thirlwall and Gibson (1994, pp. 230, 232–233, tables 9.3 and 9.4).

Anyone trying to recount the history of a period in which he was active, relying on memory and the material available at the time, would be totally astonished to find that most of the figures for the same period produced by other people twenty or thirty years later were quite unrecognisable. ... It might well be, therefore, that many of the things that happened in the 1960s took place because of inadequate guidance and information.[225]

The revised figures show that the deficit on current account for 1964 was £358 million. These kinds of deficits were to continue for the next few years, with a new record being set for the trade balance in 1967 of £599 million, only to be surpassed the following year with £712 million. The respective current account figures were better at £269 million and £244 million, but they still indicate the scale of the problem.[226]

Why did the balance-of-payments problem persist as it did? There are many strands to a full explanation. Nevertheless, the question can be expressed quite simply, as Dennis Robertson did: 'What are politely called "balance of payments difficulties" do not necessarily drop like a murrain from heaven, but ... any nation which gives its mind to it can create them for itself in half an hour with the aid of a printing press and a strong trade union movement.'[227] There was simply a lack of resolve to address the basic issue. The fact was that with the pegged exchange-rate system, all the monetary authorities could do was to manage domestic 'credit expansion'. This term did not enter their lexicon until the late 1960s, but the concept was around. The core of the problem, as the Bank seldom let up on saying, was that public-sector borrowing was excessive. That could have been offset by debt management, but the Bank's failure was its treatment of the gilt-edged market. If monetary policy was to be consistent with maintaining the exchange rate, there would need to have been a significant positive relationship between reserve changes and domestic assets held by the Bank. But there was no trace of such a relationship even after allowing for various lags.[228] The analysis needed was far from new; it was in fact old and reputable and had been restated by Nurkse in 1944 and by Meade in 1951.[229]

---

[225] Croham (1992, p. 92).

[226] McMahon (1964, p. 20). For another contemporary assessment of problems in reading the balance of payments, see also R. L. Major, 'Appendix: errors and omissions in the balance of payments estimates', *NIESR* 19, pp. 57–59.

[227] Robertson (1954, p. 56).

[228] Fausten (1975), especially Chapter 7.

[229] Nurkse (1944); Meade (1951).

6

Domestic Monetary Policy after Radcliffe

The Bank's main policy goal in the 1960s was to maintain the exchange-rate parity. Apart from this, a prime function was to ensure the smooth financing of the exchequer, and of lesser importance was the control of bank advances. To these ends, the Bank pursued order (nowhere defined) in the money and gilts markets. As Radcliffe saw it, debt management and funding were central in monetary policy. The containment of inflation was seldom explicit, but concern was frequently expressed over the expansion of credit or the growth of bank advances. However, it should be stressed that monetary policy at the time was neither remotely like that of previous periods nor of later ones, nor did it bear much resemblance to what was found in textbooks.[1] The monetary authorities, especially the Treasury, had for some time been uncertain as to the effectiveness of conventional monetary policy for controlling the domestic economy. The views found in the Radcliffe Report were not far from those of the Treasury, and it was these kinds of ideas that gave rise to the enquiry in the first instance. That is, it was the reading of the experience of the years 1955–57 in particular that suggested that monetary policy did not deliver or certainly not quickly. Thus monetary policy became instead a collection of devices intended to work on both the domestic and external variables: 'It was neither aimed at controlling the stock of money nor was it much relied upon to combat inflation.'[2] Bank Rate was used, but of more importance were direct controls: directives to banks, ceilings on advances, and special deposits. Varying the liquidity ratio was also considered, and at one point it was adjusted. In addition, hire-purchase controls and incomes policies of different types were used. There were open market operations, even if the phrase was not

[1] Except perhaps in Sayers (1958).
[2] Cairncross (1996).

in use, but they were seen as vaguely supporting the other main measures. However, the story is in large part about controls of one kind or another and the search to find better control techniques, as well as continual tinkering with the range of devices used.[3]

New Techniques: The Special Deposits Scheme

The removal of existing controls in the autumn of 1958 was accompanied by the announcement of a completely new control measure – special deposits, the origins of which lay in the search for alternative monetary tools, the proceedings of Radcliffe, Thorneycroft's desire to see new controls, the Bank's dislike of existing controls, and relations between the government and the banks. From the mid-1950s, the Bank had periodically given thought to measures that would act on the liquidity of the clearing banks in the expectation that advances consequently would be contained. Invariably, the conclusion was that such measures would be ineffective. In May 1957, work began on a submission to the Radcliffe Committee on ways of restricting bank credit.[4] Cobbold was unhappy with it because it looked only at 'different forms of the same *fundamental* technique'. He wanted to present Radcliffe with real alternatives and saw a choice between maintenance of a system that was the 'most efficient in the world' at providing painless and automatic financing of both commerce and government and the restriction of rediscount facilities and/or the sterilisation of deposits so that the automatic arrangement was broken and the government was forced to ask for money. Cobbold, O'Brien, and Niemeyer had discussed 'sterilisation', or some form of 'special deposit', but the conclusion was that the concept was 'unsafe' and little different from Treasury deposit receipts (TDRs). 'In the long run we shall regret action on these lines more than inaction', argued O'Brien, and Cobbold agreed 'for now' but warned that 'we must think seriously about these real alternatives'.[5] Within a year, he had developed a 'very definite conviction' that the introduction of special deposits would be in everyone's best interest.[6]

In the draft of the paper for Radcliffe that appeared in early November 1957, a scheme for special deposits had been inserted. Mynors sent copies

---

[3] For useful surveys of this period, see Griffiths (1970 pp. 23–29); Hodgman (1971); Goodhart (1973); and for an overall survey across the period, see Middleton (1996).

[4] Hollom, 'Possible alternative methods of restricting credit in the UK', draft, 23 May 1957; 'Some possible modifications in technique', draft, 11 June 1957, C40/917.

[5] Cobbold to Mynors, 21 August 1958, C40/917.

[6] Cobbold to Tuke et al., 25 June 1958, G1/76.

to Robarts and Peppiatt, commenting to the former, 'We dislike all the suggestions in it very much: and generally have found difficulty in writing a hypothetical paper on such a subject', and to the latter, 'we are not proud of our homework'.[7] Senior people in the Bank had qualms. John Fisher, Adviser to the Governor, was apparently disorientated, not being sure 'at what door I came out on the memorandum'.[8] Parsons questioned the effect on relations with bankers if special deposits were introduced: 'bad, undoubtedly', added Mynors.[9]

The picture presented to Radcliffe highlighted eight monetary 'techniques': liquidity, advances, investment, and cash ratios; advances limits; ways and means advances; TDRs; and special deposits. There was little enthusiasm for any. None was free from serious drawbacks owing to the elements of compulsion and the introduction of rigidities into the banking system. All would prejudice co-operation between the banks and the authorities. If it became necessary to change the present system, the Bank argued, then none of the options could be definitely recommended, although special deposits came closest to meeting objectives and avoiding objections: 'The role of special deposits would be to adjust the liquidity of the banking system. ... but they would be explicitly designed to be a general monetary regulator operated by the monetary authorities, not an alternative and facile method of short-term financing.' In practice, the cash that the clearing banks required to make the necessary deposits would be provided through the purchase of Treasury bills by the Bank, thus reducing the floating debt. The special deposits would not count as part of bankers' cash or liquid assets, and so did not 'constitute a base for the superstructure of bank credit'.[10] Thus described, it was a way of operating on the liquidity ratio.

By November 1957, the pressure for change was greater in the aftermath of the September crisis, and Thorneycroft had asked the Bank and Treasury to draw up a plan of action in light of the report of the economic Secretary's group (see Chapter 3). When the plan appeared, it was not based on Robbins-inspired prescribed liquidity ratios and stabilisation bills but on special deposits. Although the concepts were similar, the officials argued that there was an important difference in emphasis between the two. The stabilisation bill represented direct borrowing by the government from the clearing banks and had only a secondary role as a regulator of liquid assets.

---

[7] Mynors to Robarts and Mynors to Peppiatt, both 8 November 1957, C40/917.
[8] Fisher to O'Brien, 11 November 1957, C40/917.
[9] Parson to Mynors, 11 November 1957, C40/917.
[10] Bank of England, 'Some possible modifications in technique', September 1957; Radcliffe, *Memoranda*, Vol. 1.

Special deposits, on the other hand, could be presented as a general instrument of monetary policy to act on the liquid assets of the banks. The Bank was always keen to avoid new legislation or amendments to the 1946 Act and cited Radcliffe as an effective defence.[11] The plan was a Thorneycroft initiative, and following his resignation in January 1958, it looked likely that it would be shelved. Nevertheless, O'Brien agreed with the Treasury that in order to keep things 'tidy', the Bank would return their revised draft.[12]

That might have been it, but for the fact that in February 1958 Radcliffe asked for 'a full technical explanation' of special deposits, necessitating some additional work and refinements.[13] More critically, there was a change in thinking at the Bank. By mid-April 1958, Cobbold had decided that it might be 'opportune' to introduce a scheme for special deposits, and work began on an aide memoire that was to be used to test the water with the bankers.[14] At meetings in June, Cobbold told Robarts and Franks of the Committee of London Clearing Banks (CLCB) that if a scheme was not prepared, something less satisfactory might be imposed.[15] The banks' representatives were cool about the plan, being sensitive to the fact that it might be interpreted as a criticism of their past conduct, and there were also concerns with some of the technical aspects. The Radcliffe Committee was another factor. Robarts thought that the scheme might be seen either to 'steal its thunder or to be torpedoed if they recommended something else'.[16] But Cobbold had already taken the precaution of clearing the way, assuring Radcliffe that if special deposits gave the appearance of 'bouncing' the Committee, or there was no support for the idea, then there would be change. In response, Radcliffe saw no reason for not going ahead.[17]

Cobbold used his considerable powers of persuasion with the clearing bank chairmen.[18] He gave them the good news that the credit squeeze was to end: requests would not be renewed, and targets for advances would be scrapped after July. As to the future, Cobbold's preference was to wait until necessary to do something, keep things informal, and then rely on co-operation. Radcliffe was another reason for doing nothing at present. Despite all this, the Governor went on to argue that an alternative

---

[11] Mynors, Note, 23 December 1957, C40/704.
[12] O'Brien to Mynors, 8 January 1958, C40/704.
[13] O'Brien annotation on Compton to O'Brien, 17 January 1958, C40/704.
[14] O'Brien to Cobbold, 'Special deposits', 15 April 1958; O'Brien to Cobbold, 'Special deposits', 5 May 1958, C40/704.
[15] Mynors, 'Credit policy', 22 May 1958, G1/76.
[16] Mynors, 'Credit squeeze', 10 June 1958; Mynors, 'Special deposits', 12 June 1958, G1/76.
[17] Cobbold, Governor's note, 4 June 1958, G1/131.
[18] Cobbold to Tuke et al., 25 June 1958, G1/76.

scheme had to be implemented now. The 'self-denying ordinance', the 'voluntary' limits, and agreements not to compete for business were highly unsatisfactory, and Cobbold would be hesitant about requesting such action again. Also, in order that the credit relaxation was not interpreted as a change in policy towards sterling or inflation, it was important that the current controls were not abandoned without other measures being put in place. The final and conclusive argument related to 'banking politics' and the relationship between the banking system and government. Cobbold was certain that if there was another exchange-rate crisis, the government, of whatever political persuasion, would insist on a new instrument rather than rely on informal co-operation. It would be better to fill the vacuum with a special deposits scheme now, so minimising the disturbance to current arrangements, than to wait and see it filled with something 'even less attractive'. The bankers were persuaded and agreed that although the proposals were inevitably unwelcome, the scheme would be accepted.[19] The next day, Cobbold flew to Edinburgh to meet representatives of the Scottish clearing banks. They too were disappointed but fell into line.[20]

The way was then clear for an exchange of letters between the Governor and the Chancellor.[21] In July 1958, Amory announced the end of the squeeze on bank credit. Control would be retained through normal monetary measures reinforced, if need be, by a new device, special deposits. This was to be 'a temporary arrangement pending the recommendations of the Radcliffe Committee, to whom we look for advice about any permanent changes'. Wilson claimed that Labour had pressed for a similar idea in May 1956; if they had, it was done in a very oblique manner.[22]

The Bank explained that the role of special deposits would be to adjust the liquidity of the banking system by acting on the conventionally observed minimum liquid assets ratio of 30 per cent. The scheme, in principle, could apply to the 'whole domestic banking system', but initially its scope would be limited to the London and Scottish clearing banks. This was no doubt a convenience because while an extension was possible, 'if the need arose', it would raise many difficult questions of definition and coverage and possible legislation if other financial institutions were to be included. The call would not be made on individual banks but against groups of banks, for example,

---

[19] Mynors to O'Brien, 26 June 1958, enc. 'Cobbold speaking brief'; Mynors, 'Credit policy', 27 June 1958, G1/76; Hollom, 'Special deposits', 30 June 1958; Minutes of meeting of chief executive officers of the clearing banks, 30 June 1958, G1/76

[20] Hollom, Note for record, 3 July 1958, G1/76.

[21] Amory to Cobbold, 1 July 1958 and Cobbold to Amory, 3 July 1958, G1/75.

[22] HC Deb, 9 May 1956, Vol. 552, cc227–1364.

all the London clearing banks in one and the Scottish clearing banks in another. Different ratios could be applied to each group. A percentage of the total gross deposits of the group would be called. For the clearing banks, a 2 per cent call equated to £120 million to £140 million. Since the banks had differing liquidity positions, the impact of the call would not be uniformly felt. The reason for the grouping was to avoid any detailed discussion of any bank's position and particular liquidity ratio and to emphasise that special deposits were a general monetary device. Interest would be earned on the deposits at a rate adjusted weekly to the nearest 1/16 per cent above or below the average tender rate of discount for Treasury bills. In the Bank Return, special deposits would be shown under a separate heading.[23]

In *The Banker*, King drew attention to what he saw as some of the difficulties. Without other measures, a call by itself might not cause any fall in bank deposits. If the banks' liquidity ratios were 34 to 35 per cent and a call of 2 per cent was made, they might not adjust liquidity. The special deposit would have diminished the excess but achieved little else. In any case, the banks might preempt a call by adjusting their liquidity downward, for instance, by purchasing investments. King concluded by asking whether the scheme was intended as a reinforcement of existing techniques or a substitute.[24] He thought the latter, but for the time being, it remained to be seen whether special deposits would be used and how effective they would be.

The subject was revisited following the Radcliffe Report, which had recommended that the 30 per cent liquidity ratio should be made explicit, if not statutory, and furthermore, it had an inclination towards the authorities having power to raise the ratio if necessary. This reopened yet again the debate about prescribed liquidity ratios versus special deposits. The Bank remained adamant that the special deposits scheme was the right option.[25]

Crisis to Crisis, 1957–1961

The boom that developed after 1955 was broken with the steep increase in Bank Rate in September 1957, and the economy duly turned down, reaching

---

[23] 'Credit control: plan of action', December 1957, C40/704; Aide memoire, June 1958; 'Special deposits', August 1958, C40/705.

[24] King (1958).

[25] Radcliffe, 'Report', paras. 505–511; HMT, 'Restraints on lending', MC(59)16, 23 September 1959; O'Brien to Armstrong, 9 October 1959, enc. 'Prescribed liquidity ratios or special deposits', 9 October 1959; Armstrong to Hollom, 25 January 1960, enc. revised draft, 'Special deposits scheme'; Hollom to Armstrong, 12 February 1960, enc. revised draft, 'Special deposits scheme', 12 February 1960, C40/705.

its next low point in 1958. Demand management then dictated that there should be reflationary measures, and between March and November 1958, Bank Rate was reduced progressively in five stages from its high of 7 to 4 per cent, ceilings on bank advances were removed, and hire-purchase restrictions were lifted (Table 6.1) This was followed by an expansionary budget in April 1959, when taxation was reduced sharply, an action not unconnected to the general election later that year. The predictable result was an increase in output, on this occasion by over 6 per cent. Unemployment fell to 320,000 (1.3 per cent according to prevailing measurement), the level at which it had been immediately prior to the Bank Rate increase of September 1957. The Conservatives were duly re-elected. The current account had been in record surplus in 1958 but then deteriorated to a substantial deficit in 1960. A peak in this short cycle was reached in the spring of 1960, by which time action was being taken to apply the brakes again.

Having raised Bank Rate to 7 per cent in September 1957, consideration then turned to bringing it down. In February 1958, Cobbold's objective was to get it down to 5 per cent by 'mid-summer', most likely in two stages.[26] O'Brien noted that but for the previous year's exchange crisis, it was doubtful whether Bank Rate would have been raised at all. With the crisis surmounted, the case for a reduction was strong. On the other hand, he conceded, 'Whether we like it or not, Bank Rate has become a symbol both at home and abroad of H.M.G.'s determination to fight inflation at all costs.'[27] This might seem confusing, but there were still central bankers abroad who held to the old orthodoxy, and for those like O'Brien who had been in the Bank since the 1920s, the old orthodoxy may have left some marks. In March, Cobbold proposed to Amory a reduction on the 27th, or possibly a week earlier if events moved quickly.[28] He then told Mynors, before leaving on a visit to Libya, 'If you decide to move on [the] 20th, O.K. by me.'[29] In fact, the Deputy Governor did implement the cut, reducing Bank Rate to 6 per cent.[30] Another four cuts, each of ½ per cent, took Bank Rate to 4 per cent in November 1958, where it then stayed until January 1960.

In a speech to the Machine Tool Trades Association in March, the Governor made a number of observations about monetary policy. He welcomed the fact that the previous week's reduction had not been interpreted as a reversal in policy but was accepted at its face value as being an

---

[26]   Compton, 'Note of a meeting at the Treasury … 7 February 1958', C42/4.
[27]   O'Brien, to Cobbold/Mynors/Hawker, 'Bank rate', 28 February 1958, C42/4.
[28]   Cobbold, Copy of note left with Chancellor, 10 March 1958, G1/76.
[29]   Cobbold to Mynors, 10 March 1958, C42/4.
[30]   Mynors to Cobbold, 21 March 1958, G1/76.

Table 6.1. *Bank Rate changes, 1957–70*

Date	Change (per cent)	New rate (per cent)
7 Feb 1957	−½	5
19 Sep 1957	+2	7
20 Mar 1958	−1	6
22 May 1958	−½	5½
19 Jun 1958	−½	5
14 Aug 1958	−½	4½
20 Nov 1958	−½	4
21 Jan 1960	+1	5
23 Jun 1960	+1	6
27 Oct 1960	−½	5½
8 Dec 1960	−½	5
26 Jul 1961	+2	7
5 Oct 1961	−½	6½
2 Nov 1961	−½	6
8 Mar 1962	−½	5½
22 Mar 1962	−½	5
26 Apr 1962	−½	4½
3 Jan 1963	−½	4
27 Feb 1964	+1	5
23 Nov 1964	+2	7
3 Jun 1965	−1	6
14 Jul 1965	+1	7
26 Jan 1967	−½	6½
16 Mar 1967	−½	6
4 May 1967	−½	5½
19 Oct 1967	+½	6
9 Nov 1967	+½	6½
18 Nov 1967	+1½	8
21 Mar 1968	−½	7½
19 Sep 1968	−½	7
27 Feb 1969	1	8
5 Mar 1970	−½	7½
15 Apr 1970	−½	7

Source: BEQB.

adjustment from a rate that was 'required at a moment of high crisis' to one more appropriate now that the immediate crisis was over. He went on to say that the decision had to be made on the balance of advantage and concluded, 'whether the decisions are exactly right, approximately right, or entirely wrong will be for the judgment of history – and even then history can unfortunately never tell you just what would have happened if something had been done rather differently'.[31] The speech was also notable for the fact that it revealed something of the thinking on Bank Rate. It was brief, but it was a sign that the veil of secrecy over policymaking was slowly being lifted. Indeed, Cobbold made seven speeches that year, the highest number since he became Governor.[32]

In the 1950s and early 1960s, the decision-making process for Bank Rate was less than clear. Before Radcliffe, there was the formal process of voting at the Committee of Treasury, with behind-the-scenes informal discussion, the Governor talking to senior colleagues in the Bank and, more critically, after 1946, to the Chancellor. In evidence to Radcliffe, Cobbold said that 'a Bank Rate decision is not made by the Chancellor acting on my advice, but made by the Court of the Bank of England'. But, he added, 'I think I could say that normally, certainly invariably in recent practice, it has been made by the Court after I had assured myself that the Chancellor would approve the decision'.[33] Of course, the procedure was put under the spotlight after the Bank Rate leak. The immediate interpretation after Radcliffe was that power had shifted, and it should be seen to have shifted from the Bank to the Treasury. There was an excited column in the *Evening Standard* that highlighted this supposed change. Alongside the cutting in a Bank file, O'Brien scrawled, 'Should we call it the Chancellor's Rate?'[34] However, while there may have been presentational changes, little else appears to have changed.

Cobbold also admitted to Radcliffe that there was little paperwork detailing the pros and cons of each decision.[35] What documentary evidence there is confirms the importance of the contacts between the Governor and the Chancellor and the fact that the initial moves appear always to have been made by the Bank. Indeed, in his television interview in 1958, Cobbold said 'by and large the initiative on all market

[31] Speech by Cobbold at the annual dinner of the Machine Tool Trades Association at Grosvenor House, 26 March 1958, G13/1.
[32] See speeches in G13/1.
[33] Radcliffe, 'Evidence,' 11 July 1957, question 262.
[34] *Evening Standard*, 26 August 1959, cutting in C42/5.
[35] Radcliffe, 'Evidence,' 11 July 1957, questions 263–264.

management matters, which includes Bank Rate, will come from us'.[36] There were a few instances where the Chancellor did query a proposal, most obviously in September 1957. The November 1958 reduction was delayed by a week, at the Chancellor's request, because he was apprehensive about 'inflation talk'.[37] Amory told Mynors in 1959, the election year, that if Bank Rate was reduced by ½ per cent, 'he would welcome it', but he did not press.[38] Indeed, there was no change in 1959. None of these can be construed as major interference by government. The November 1958 cut was the final change in Bank Rate where the formal decision was made by the Court.

By the time that Bank Rate was raised from 4 to 5 per cent in January 1960, the new procedures had been implemented and the Court stripped of its formal rate-setting powers. Even in this post-Radcliffe era, though, the Bank was to remain at the forefront of Bank Rate decisions. It went through the familiar routine, surveying the domestic economy – there might be a case for 'a slight pull on the reins' – looking at the external situation – reserve losses and interest rates abroad. Cobbold set out the general view of the Committee of Treasury and the consensus of the Court that there was a case for a rise. A letter then went to the Chancellor on the 20 January proposing a rise to 5 per cent, and on the same day, a reply came back from the Chancellor, 'I approve the proposal.' On 17 February, notice was given of a parliamentary question that was going to be put to the Chancellor the following day: 'What directions did the Chancellor give to the Bank of England in connection with the recent increase in Bank Rate?' The Treasury told the Bank that the answer would be, 'None, Sir.' And that was the pattern that followed thereafter.[39] In January 1961, the Bank again considered the need to raise rates, and again, it is clear that it was their initiative. Cobbold wrote, 'I made gentle murmurings both to Sir Frank Lee and the Chancellor that we might be beginning to think about a further small adjustment sometime in the second half of February. ... I left it with both of them that I may (or may not) come back to the subject in two or three weeks' time.'[40] He did not.

Of course, the Chancellor and the Treasury had views on what Bank Rate should be, and these were communicated to the Bank. For example, Amory had pressed strongly for an increase in December 1959, but the

[36] Cobbold interview with Robin Day, broadcast ITN, 'Tell the people', 18 May 1958, G13/1.
[37] Mynors, Notes, 13 and 24 November 1958, G1/77.
[38] Mynors to Cobbold, 13 February 1959, G1/77.
[39] Hollom to Hawker/Cobbold/Mynors, 17 February 1960, C42/5.
[40] Cobbold, Governor's note, 26 January 1961, C42/5.

Governor, and indeed Amory's own Treasury officials, resisted.[41] So there was dialogue, but nowhere is there any evidence, at least up to the early 1960s, that a change in Bank Rate was actually dictated or denied by the Treasury. After that, it appears from the surviving evidence that there was a shift in the way movements in Bank Rate were discussed. Aside from the formal letters and the announcement made in the Bank's name, there was now some dialogue with the Treasury where in Cobbold's time there had been little or none. The matter was discussed at meetings attended by the Governors, Chief Cashier, the Chancellor, Treasury ministers, and some senior Treasury figures. It may just be a reflection of the surviving paperwork in the 1960s, but there are far more documents recording the opinions of the Prime Minister, the Chancellor, and their officials about Bank Rate. But there were still no clear examples of blatant government interference in the process until March 1966.

At the end of 1959, the Chancellor had asked the Governor about the possible use of the new special deposits scheme, even though the details still had to be finalised. Cobbold replied that if restraint was required, then Bank Rate was the first course of action to consider.[42] Then, in February, Lee, who had recently replaced Makins as Treasury permanent Secretary, asked whether a corrective measure might be required before the budget and, if so, could special deposits be called without delay. The Bank said that the mechanics were straightforward but that it would be hard to obtain acceptance by the clearing banks unless action was also taken to restrain lending by other financial institutions.[43] Later that month, Bank and Treasury officials discussed how to address the problem of the other institutions. Given the inherent difficulties of extending controls, the only solution was to make a call in tandem with the re-imposition of hire-purchase controls.[44] At one stage, the Chancellor wanted to move before the budget but was dissuaded by his officials. The timetable prepared by the Bank assumed that the decision would be announced in the budget on 4 April, although in fact the Governor's preference was to wait until the effects of the budget could

[41] Makins, 'Interest rates', 3 December 1959; Mynors to Maudling, 6 December 1959; Mynors to Heathcoat Amory, 8 December 1959; Armstrong, Note for record, 24 December 1959, G1/77; Cairncross (1991b, pp. 221–222).

[42] 'Extract from William Armstrong note for record dated 24.12.59', C40/705.

[43] Lee to Cobbold, 2 February 1960; Cobbold to Lee, 4 February 1960, C40/705.

[44] Anthea Bennett (HMT) to G. K. Willetts (central clerk CBID working in Cashier's Department), 22 February, enc. HMT, 'Special deposits scheme', 16 February 1960; HMT, 'Note of a meeting … 24 February, 1960', 29 February 1960'; Bank of England, 'Special deposits – possible timetable', 3 March 1960; HMT, 'Note of a meeting … 3 March 1960', 7 March 1960', C40/705.

be judged. He was also keen to keep monetary measures distinct from fiscal ones.[45] Then, at the end of March, Cobbold and Amory agreed that they would give serious consideration to introducing the scheme towards the end of April.[46]

Given the antipathy of the clearers towards special deposits, the Bank went to considerable lengths to avoid any accusation that it had not given adequate notice for the scheme. Robarts said that there would be a great deal of complaint on the grounds of equity unless something was done to restrict hire-purchase lending and, in the longer run, to extend similar controls to fringe financial institutions.[47] The Governor and Mynors attended the monthly meeting of the CLCB, after which Cobbold was able to tell the Chancellor that the clearing banks were now 'conditioned' to the idea of the scheme.[48] Within a week, O'Brien and Hollom handed the clearing bank chief executives a draft press announcement and suggested that the call might be made on 28 April.[49]

Even at this stage, there was still confusion over quite how the scheme would work. When the clearing banks were being briefed, they pointed out that they would need time to rearrange their portfolios, and they would have to sell gilts, but after the special deposits had been made, they might wish to buy gilts. O'Brien suggested that some special deposits could be released to allow the banks to do this, but Mynors objected that this would 'falsify the scheme'. He continued, 'The size of Spl. Deps is under our control – both ways: if we let them be exchanged into gilt-edged the banks concerned then have an asset the size of which is at their option, not ours.'[50] And there was still no agreement on the percentage to be called from the Scottish clearers. Hawker reported from Scotland that they would accept half the rate based loosely on the observation that as a group they had shown a lower rate of expansion in deposits and advances than had the London clearers.[51] Even

---

[45] Cobbold, Note, 19 March 1960; HMT, 'Note of a meeting … 16 March [1960]', C40/705.

[46] Cobbold, Governor's note, 31 March 1960, C40/705.

[47] Mynors, 'C.L.C.B. meeting: 4 February 1960', 5 February 1960; Cobbold to David Robarts (CLCB) and Cobbold to W. R. Ballantyne, 16 February 1960; Cobbold, Governor's note – 'Special deposits', 22 March 1960, C40/705.

[48] 'Notes for the Governor's meeting with clearing bank chairmen, 29 March 1960', 29 March 1960; Cobbold, Governor's note, 7 April 1960, and Governor's note – 'Special deposits', 8 April 1960, C40/706.

[49] Hollom, Note for record – 'Special deposits: clearing banks', 14 April 1960, C40/706.

[50] O'Brien to Hawker/Cobbold/Mynors, 'Special deposits. The Governor's note of the 8 April', 12 April 1960, and Mynors annotation, 12 April, C40/706.

[51] Hawker to Cobbold, 26 April 1960, enc. 'Special deposits: Scottish banks', 26 April 1960, C40/706.

less was made of the fact that the Northern Ireland banks were being left out altogether.

In April it was agreed to make the first call for special deposits, and an announcement was made: a call for 1 per cent of gross deposits from the London clearers and for ½ per cent from the Scottish clearers (deposits of £70.8 million and £3.7 million, respectively) to be placed with the Bank by 15 June 1960 (Table 6.2). Amory spoke in the Commons at 2:30 p.m., where he also unveiled the re-imposition of hire-purchase controls. The Bank's own statement was released at 3:35 p.m., after the markets had closed, and formal letters requesting the deposits were sent to the banks. Other financial institutions were informed of the decision and asked to consider framing their own lending policy accordingly.[52] The second call soon followed, and with little advance notice, on 23 June 1960, the same day that Bank Rate was increased from 5 to 6 per cent. A further 1 per cent was to be deposited, half by 20 July and the other half by 17 August. The Bank said that it was 'desirable to maintain the restraint on bank lending'.[53]

It was a characteristic of the City across this period, and testament to the Bank's informal power, that the clearers accepted what was, after all, a voluntary scheme. And following the etiquette of the time, their general managers replied with grateful thanks for being told that they had to make the deposits.[54] Yet the clearing banks remained deeply unhappy. Franks made a plea on behalf of the CLCB that the scheme should be extended to a wider range of institutions. Cobbold copied Franks' letter to Lee and reminded him that the Bank was sympathetic to these claims for equity and wrote to the Chancellor in a similar vein.[55]

Hire-purchase controls were seen as another way of reinforcing credit control. They could be altered by varying the minimum deposit required or the length of period allowed for repayment. And these also could be varied for different classifications of goods depending on where it was thought the pressure was greatest. They were first imposed by the Board of Trade in

---

[52] Cobbold to Amory, 27 April 1960; Amory to Cobbold, 27 April; 'Special deposits: programme', C40/706. 'Special deposits. Announcement by the Bank of England', 28 April 1960; 'Background brief for the press', 28 April 1960; Edward de Rudolf (Principal, Cashier's Department), Note for record – 'Special deposits', 28 April 1960; letters to individual clearing banks and other organisations and cables to central banks, 28 April 1960, C40/707; HC Deb, 28 April 1960, Vol. 622, cc395–396.

[53] Press announcement, 23 June 1960; Wynn-Williams to Hollom, 23 June 1960, C40/708. Also see 'The procedure of special deposits', *BEQB* 1(1):18, December 1960.

[54] See replies in C40/707.

[55] Franks to Cobbold, 10 May 1960; Cobbold to Lee, 11 May 1960; Cobbold to Franks, 11 May 1960, C40/707.

Table 6.2. *Special deposits, 1960–64 (per cent)*

Date of announcement	Amount		Cumulative		Date and amount by which call/ release to be made
	London	Scottish	London	Scottish	
28 Apr 1960	1	½	1	½	15 Jun 1960
23 Jun 1960	1	½	2	1	20 Jul 1960 (½)
					17 Aug 1960 (½)
25 Jul 1961	1	½	3	1½	16 Aug 1961 (½)
					20 Sep 1961 (½)
31 May 1962	−1	−½	2	1	12 Jun 1962 (½)
					18 Jun 1962 (½)
27 Sep 1962	−1	−½	1	½	8 Oct 1962 (½)
					15 Oct 1962 (½)
29 Nov 1962	−1	−½	0	0	10 Dec 1962 (½)
					17 Dec 1962 (½)

Source: Press notices in 4A153/3.

1952, removed in July 1954, only to reappear again six months later, then lasting until October 1958. As another boom got under way at the end of 1959 and beginning of 1960, hire-purchase controls were back on the agenda. Macmillan wrote that if deflationary measures were to be taken, the best weapon was special deposits and 'if you like, add hire purchase to taste'.[56] In April 1960, minimum deposits were imposed (20 per cent for cars and domestic appliances and 10 per cent for furniture) together with a maximum 24-month repayment period. The restrictions were to remain a constant feature of domestic credit control until July 1971.[57]

To what extent were gilt operations used in support? The conventional view of policy in the 1960s is that the Bank would 'lean against the wind' in both directions. This marked a change from the practice, as outlined to Radcliffe. It was the approach to buying that had changed. In the months after the Radcliffe Report, the Government Broker apparently set a floor below which gilt prices could not fall, allowing the banks to sell all the gilts they wished and so increase advances and, they believed, provide stimulus

---

[56] Macmillan (1972, p. 221).
[57] Alford (1972, pp. 331–335); Tew (1978a, pp. 226–227); Board of Trade, Press notice, 28 April 1960, C40/727.

to the economy.[58] After the end of February 1960, policy seems to change. At this point, Lloyds had been a 'persistent seller' in the 1965–69 bracket, and on 25 February, in order 'to get them out of the way', the Bank offered ⅛ per cent below market and bought £10 million. The following day, Barclays appeared as a large seller, and the Bank bought £6 million nominal short-dated at ⅛ per cent below market and £14 million nominal in the 1965–69 range at ⅝ per cent below market. When the next day Midland wanted to sell £25 million, the Bank offered 1 per cent below market and bought £29.75 million nominal 1967–69.[59] In fact, 1 per cent was a heavy penalty, and Midland did not accept the price until almost 3 p.m. on the day, but it later emerged that Midland had sold another £10 million of short-dated to Union Discount at ½ per cent below.[60] There seems, therefore, to have been no floor at this point.

Following these quite spectacular sales, Lee met Mynors and accepted that the Bank's actions were 'market tactics' that did not require 'elaborate explanation beforehand'.[61] There had been no announcement of any change in policy stance, and many were upset at what they saw as the removal of support for the market. In the Lords, Pethick-Lawrence asked whether the government had been informed by the authorities (meaning the Bank) of the intention to withdraw support from the gilt-edged market and whether a floor was in operation. He was told that 'withdrawal of support' was an exaggeration and that the government approved of the action taken. No indication could be given as to the floor below which they would not be prepared to allow security prices to fall. Furthermore, the government did not have any responsibility for the profits or losses in the market. Anyway, since 24 February, the market had steadied.[62] The issue was again pressed in the Lords in March, Boothby asking if the 'policy of the Governor of the Bank of England of withdrawing support from the gilt-edged market had been allowed by the Chancellor'. He received a similar answer to the earlier one.[63] Allen maintained that the Bank had not withdrawn support from the market but merely 'shifted the level at which they were prepared to deal', while Mynors stressed to Lee and Armstrong that the root cause of funding difficulties was the overall

[58]   Radcliffe, 'Evidence,' paras. 12029–12033; Tew (1978a, p. 231).
[59]   'Gilt-edged market', 25 February 1960, C42/13.
[60]   Allen, 'Gilt-edged market: 19 February 1960 onwards', 3 March 1960, C42/13.
[61]   'Extract from Deputy Governor's memorandum dated 25.2.60', C42/13.
[62]   HL Deb, 29 February 1960, Vol. 221, c489.
[63]   Hollom to Hawker/Mynors, 'Interest rates', 2 March 1960; HL Deb, 8 March 1960, Vol. 221, c861.

budget deficit. Lee replied that elimination of the deficit was not practical politics.[64]

Shortly after this episode O'Brien set out the state of the gilt-edged market and the prospects for funding. He reaffirmed the Bank's belief that large sales could be made only on a rising market. Further, 'the more substantial sales are, the slower the market will rise. It was not enough for the market to wish to rise but to be prevented by our sales. It must be seen to rise, even if only a little, or the buying will stop.' O'Brien added, 'With all respect to various commentators, they can have no experience, as we have, of trying to sell without limit.' Because of the need for both heavy refinancing and funding new government borrowing, the threat of inflation, and the rise of equity markets as a hedge against inflation, O'Brien thought that the outlook for the gilt-edged market and for funding was 'somewhat bleak'. His suggested four-point strategy was that no attempt should be made to raise yields officially 'a la Radcliffe'; it would be unwise, 'even immoral', to allow a substantial fall in yields; in the interests of funding, 'we should not tread on every sign of a rising gilt-edged market, but allow a gentle rise from time to time'; in view of the previous point, there should be no new issue of stock for the moment. O'Brien added that he did not think it had been a mistake to push in the direction of lower prices earlier in the year and to then let the market down with 'something of a bump' when the banks were heavy sellers. It was correct, given what was known about the future, and was a 'reasonable reinforcement' of the January rise in Bank Rate.[65]

During the rest of 1960, the trend was towards higher long-term interest rates, with the average yield standing at 6 per cent at the end of the year. The Bank was happy to see this: 'For some long time past now we have clearly acquiesced in the rise in the gilt-edged long-term rate and indeed by our actions we have encouraged it.' This had been done, according to O'Brien, because the results achieved by funding at the existing levels of rates had been inadequate. In addition, there was a feeling that higher gilt-edged rates in the long term were needed to compete with the growth appeal of equities. O'Brien did not see appreciably lower rates ahead, and actions had to be designed to make this belief evident, in particular, 'to discourage any view that because short-term rates come down, long-term rates must necessarily do so'.[66] To help achieve this, a large issue of long-dated stock (£500 million

[64] Allen, 'Gilt-edged market: 19 February 1960 onwards', 3 March 1960; Hollom, Note for record, 4 March 1960, C42/13.
[65] O'Brien to Hawker/Cobbold, 30 March 1960, C40/457.
[66] O'Brien to Mynors, 'Government loan operations', 9 September 1960, C40/448.

5½% Treasury 2008/2012) was made in early October 1960, while at the end of the month, Bank Rate fell from 6 per cent to 5½ per cent.

The budget of 1961 was meant to be neutral, but since sterling remained weak, it is perhaps surprising that the Bank was suggesting that there might be an early release of special deposits.[67] O'Brien was keen to demonstrate that special deposits were not fixed indefinitely, and unless released whenever possible, the impact of future calls would be lessened. Cobbold agreed, but Lloyd and his officials thought that a release would create the wrong impression in light of the budget.[68] With sterling under pressure in the summer, officials developed a package of measures to support an increase in Bank Rate. In his final month as Governor, Cobbold warned Franks that action on bank advances might be needed.[69] Nonetheless, O'Brien was incensed to hear in July that, with echoes of 1957, the Chancellor wanted to ask banks and other financial institutions to restrict their lending, under the threat of direction or legislation. For O'Brien, 'these are the words of a man who has little faith in the ordinary measures of credit restraint or in the City machinery for enforcing them.'[70] Hire-purchase repayment periods had been relaxed to 36 months in January 1961, and because the Chancellor did not want to reverse his decision only six months later, he firmly resisted the recommendations of the Governor (now Cromer) and senior Treasury officials that hire-purchase terms should be tightened as part of the package.[71]

The Bank was clear that there should be a call for special deposits, and O'Brien considered that in any restrictive package, restraint on bank advances must have a place. However, such action should not be indiscriminate but should be directed towards advances for consumer purposes. The mechanism by which special deposits were supposed to work was far from clear, and even if some pressure was exerted on liquidity, there might be no impact on the purposes to which bank lending was put. Not to use special deposits, O'Brien wrote, would give the impression 'that we no longer have

[67] Blackaby (1978, pp. 16–17); the Economic Section calculated the total measure of restraint as about 1/3 of 1 per cent of total domestic expenditure; Bretherton (1999, pp. 25–26).

[68] O'Brien to Hawker/Governors, 'Release of special deposits', 22 March 1961; O'Brien to Hawker/Cobbold, 'Special deposits', 20 April 1961, C40/708; Informal Court record, 20 April 1961, G14/149; 'Note of a meeting … 21st April, 1961', G1/252; Committee of Treasury minutes, 26 April 1961, G8/79.

[69] Cobbold, Governor's note, 7 June 1961; Mynors, Note, 14 June 1961; HMT, 'Note of a meeting … 15 June, 1961', 19 June 1961, G1/252.

[70] HMT, 'Note of a meeting … 12 July 1961, G1/252; O'Brien to Cromer/Mynors, 'Monetary measures', 11 July 1961, C42/5.

[71] O'Brien to Hawker/Cromer/Mynors, 14 July 1961, C40/1209.

any faith in them'. He advocated a deferred call of 1 per cent, possibly paid in two instalments during August and September. This would take special deposits to a total of 3 per cent. But the call would have to be associated with an 'understanding' with the banks: the banks should not seek to evade the squeeze by selling gilts; neither should they resort to an expansion of bill finance with the same aim; there should be clear evidence of progress; that is, total advances in December should be no higher than in June; the banks would restrict advances for consumer purposes; and if the necessary results were not achieved, then the Bank would have to advise the Chancellor to make a formal and public request, such as that made by Thorneycroft in 1957.[72] O'Brien's recommendations were apparently accepted by his colleagues without demur. Certainly, nobody chose to highlight the fact that special deposits had been introduced in the first place in order to escape from requests, voluntary limits, and informal pressures.

On the same day that the July measures were unveiled, Cromer called for a 'substantial intensification of previous efforts to restrain the rise in bank advances', saying that he expected to see results by the end of the year. However, the banks were asked to keep in mind the importance of exports and 'productive industry' that would strengthen the economy: property development and other speculative transactions, loans for hire purchase, and personal consumption were all frowned on.[73] Franks pledged that the banks would co-operate but predictably added that they attached great importance to the need to bring other bodies under the 'same discipline and to the same extent as ourselves'. He specifically mentioned insurance companies, merchant banks, acceptance houses, overseas and foreign banks, and above all, finance houses. Finally, said Franks, in order to achieve the aims set by the Bank, it would be necessary for the clearers to restrict competition between themselves.[74] O'Brien had already foreseen trouble from the CLCB if other lending institutions were not similarly asked to limit their credit, particularly because of the Chancellor's refusal to impose greater restrictions on hire purchase as part of his July measures.[75] Thus 10 other organisations representing financial institutions were also sent either a copy of the CLCB letter or received an indication of how they were expected to assist. And to meet the concerns about finance houses, letters were, for the first time,

---

[72] O'Brien to Hawker/Cromer/Mynors, 'Bank advances and special deposits', 5 July 1961, C40/708.

[73] Cromer to Franks (chairman, CLCB), 25 July 1961, C40/700.

[74] Franks to Cromer, 27 July 1961, C40/700.

[75] O'Brien to Hawker/Cromer/Mynors, 'Bank advances and special deposits', 5 July 1961, C40/708; O'Brien to Hawker/Cromer/Mynors, 13 July 1961, C40/1209.

sent to the chairmen of the Finance Houses Association (FHA), and the Industrial Bankers Association (IBA).[76]

The 'pay pause' in the public sector, also announced as part of the July measures, was something that the Chancellor hoped others would follow. It was the precursor to a more formal incomes policy, an element that was to become a permanent feature of economic management in the 1960s.[77] It was based on the notion that inflation resulted from rising costs, particularly wages. Lloyd's pay pause was intended to remain in force until spring 1962, by which time the government hoped to have formulated a long-term policy for wages. It eventually consisted of a 'norm' or 'guiding light' prescribing the permissible annual incomes increase, a set of criteria by which wage claims could be judged, and the establishment of the National Incomes Commission (NIC), an independent body appointed to pass judgements on particular cases. No powers were taken to enforce the recommendations of the NIC, and in the absence of support from the trade unions, it failed to make an impact. Macmillan had placed great store in the policy, telling the Commons that it was 'necessary as a permanent feature of our economic life ... an indispensable element in the foundations on which to build a policy of sound economic growth'.[78] However, there was a distinct lack of support and guidance from the Chancellor and the Treasury, a factor that might have influenced Macmillan's decision to dismiss Lloyd later in the year.[79] Yet Maudling, his successor, proved no more successful, and by the end of the Conservative's period in office, the policy was in considerable disarray. Although Cromer would have welcomed the efforts to control wages, there is nothing in the files to suggest either that the Bank was consulted over incomes policy or even that it was monitoring developments at this stage.

Brakes Off, 1961–1964

After the crisis in the summer of 1961, the main concern, as in 1957–58, was having put Bank Rate up to 7 per cent to bring it down without it appearing that a mistake had been made in the first place. Although with a degree of hindsight O'Brien was sure that the move had been correct, he was also

[76] Cromer, Letters to various banking organisations, 25 July 1961; Hawker to J. Gibson Jarvie (chairman, FHA), 25 July 1961; Hawker to G. F. Corber (chairman, IBA), 28 July 1961; Hollom, Note for record – 'Finance Houses Association', 27 July 1961, C40/700.

[77] Dorey (2001, p. 55).

[78] HC Deb, 26 July 1962, Vol. 663, c1757; Dorey (2001, p. 59).

[79] Blackaby (1978, pp. 21, 362).

acutely aware of the harmful effects of high rates. The Treasury, too, wanted to see Bank Rate down quickly, albeit not as quickly as the Bank. As well as timing, there was also the question of extent. The Bank favoured ½ per cent and the Treasury 1 per cent.[80] At the beginning of October, O'Brien thought that key indicators were moving in the right direction: pressure on sterling had abated, consumer demand was 'sober', and the reduction in bank advances in September was the largest on record. Yet perceptions remained critical, and the likely reaction, at home and abroad, to any cut was still a major consideration. O'Brien was convinced that there should be an immediate ½ per cent reduction. He conceded that it might appear 'cautious or even timid', but a 'willingness to move, even if only a little, as soon as possible should be welcomed'.[81] The Chancellor agreed that the rate should be reduced as soon as possible (it was expensive for the exchequer), and the government did not want to be accused of 'toughness for its own sake'. Consequently, on 5 October, a ½ per cent reduction in the Bank Rate was announced, a move that took the City by surprise; the *Evening Standard* asked, 'Is this the green light?'[82] This was definitely not the intention, and the Bank was extremely sensitive about showing such a signal.[83]

Within weeks, thoughts had turned to a further reduction partly driven by worries of 'hot' money flowing into London because rates were out of line with those in other financial centres. Indeed, O'Brien told the Governors that the October Bank Rate reduction had 'accelerated rather than stemmed the inflow'.[84] As to the amount, surprisingly, the Bank's foreign-exchange experts advised that a cut of ½ per cent 'might even intensify it [the inflow] due to a feeling that further reductions were bound to be made'.[85] The explanation presumably was that the money was going into gilts, and there were expectations of further capital gains. At any rate, there was consensus about the appropriate response. Allen, Hawker, and O'Brien all favoured moving by 1 per cent and quickly. Cromer even felt strongly enough to write to the Chancellor suggesting that a quid pro quo for a substantial cut in Bank Rate would be an increase in special deposits. But the letter was not sent.[86]

[80] O'Brien, 27 September 1961, C42/6.

[81] O'Brien to Cromer, 'B.R.', 2 October 1961, C42/6.

[82] *Evening Standard*, 5 October 1961, p. 1.

[83] Cromer to Mynors/O'Brien/Hawker, 11 October 1961, C42/6; Mynors, 'Bank Rate', 16 November 1961, G1/252.

[84] O'Brien to Mynors/Cromer, 'The Governor's note of 11th October', 17 October 1961; Fforde to O'Brien/Allen, 'Hot money', 19 October 1961, C42/6.

[85] O'Brien, 'B.R.', 31 October 1961, C42/6.

[86] Cromer, Governor's note, 11 October 1961; O'Brien to Mynors/Cromer, 'The Governor's note of 11th October', 17 October 1961; Allen, 'Bank Rate', 30 October 1961; O'Brien, 'B.R.',

At the beginning of November 1961, Cromer told the Chancellor that he was inclined towards a cut of 1 per cent, either immediately or the following week. Lee worried that if it appeared that the Bank was heading rapidly back towards 5 per cent, it might give the impression that the July increase was an error and, worse, that the need for restraint had ended. The Governor replied that he had no objection to ½ per cent, provided that it was done quickly, and the following day, the Bank Rate was reduced by ½ per cent, taking it down to 6 per cent.[87] The move was justified by the continuing strength of sterling, although it was reiterated that the credit restrictions were still to be maintained.[88] In 1962, with sterling remaining firm, there were three successive ½ per cent reductions in the space of two months: 8 and 22 March and 26 April. Again, there were tensions between the Bank and the Treasury on timing and scale. The Governor backed down from proposing a ½ per cent reduction at the start of the year.[89] Then, in early March, Cromer told Lloyd, 'if only it were possible to wake up one morning to find the Bank Rate had gone down to 5 per cent, that would be an excellent state of affairs.'[90] However, worried that a full point cut might be 'overdramatised both at home and abroad', Cromer favoured two ½ per cent reductions instead. Lee supported this, and with the Bank Rate down to 4½ per cent, Cromer and Lloyd agreed on no further reductions.[91]

Consideration had also been given to a release of special deposits to coincide with the reductions in Bank Rate, but it was rejected in case it looked like a policy reversal. In May, the Governor professed to finding himself 'in a quandary' over the matter because, on the one hand, he wanted to demonstrate flexibility and, on the other, avoid the impression of easing up at home, before export figures had improved. He floated the idea that the letters of direction that had been issued as part of the July measures should be rescinded.[92] Mynors conceded, 'The general argument persists that this weapon is not now doing much good and is in danger of rusting.'[93] At the

31 October 1961, C42/6; Hawker to Cromer, 28 October 1961; Cromer, 'Top secret draft', 30 October 1961, G1/252.

[87] Hubback to Smallwood, 3 November 1961, enclosing 'Note of a meeting ... 1 November 1961', G1/252.

[88] 'Press guidance', 2 November 1961, C42/6.

[89] Hubback to Smallwood, 25 January 1962, enc. 'Note of a meeting ... 23 January, 1962', G1/253.

[90] Hubback to Smallwood, 2 March 1962, enc. 'Note of a meeting ... 1 March 1962', G1/253.

[91] 'Note of a meeting ... ', 28 May 1962, G1/253.

[92] Cromer, 'Special deposits', 4 May 1962, C40/1207.

[93] Hollom to Stevens/Parsons/Cromer/Mynors/O'Brien, 'Special deposits', 9 May 1962; Mynors, 'Special deposits', 11 May 1962; Parsons to Mynors, 'Special deposits', C40/1207.

end of May, Cromer and Lloyd decided that there would be a release of 1 per cent (½ per cent for Scottish banks). Lending for speculative purposes was still to be discouraged.[94] In other words, there was endless tinkering.

At the same time, the president of the Board of Trade was calling for a further easing of hire-purchase terms.[95] Remarkably, this was referred to the highest level. In a cryptic note, Mynors described a meeting with the Chancellor: 'He mentioned refrigerators but as a private thought, not for repetition. I made discouraging noises.'[96] Nonetheless, in June 1962, it was announced that the minimum initial deposit on all goods, except motor vehicles, would be reduced from 20 to 10 per cent. There were then no further alterations until 1965. The Board of Trade actually thought that the instrument was an unsatisfactory one and should be abolished. Surprisingly, the Bank was opposed to this. If the control went, asked O'Brien, 'Do we really think that we have anything equally effective to put in its place?'[97] The Treasury, too, was nervous, and hire-purchase controls were retained.

In the July 1962 'night of the long knives', Macmillan sacked Lloyd as Chancellor and appointed Reginald Maudling. Maudling is remembered as a Chancellor who pursued reflation and growth, and in September 1962, only a few months into office, he sought both a reduction in Bank Rate and a complete release of the remaining special deposits. Parsons recorded that Maudling was 'obsessed with the idea that the international obligations of sterling act as a direct restraint on economic growth and is therefore somewhat impatient of the argument that external considerations have to be taken into account'. He continued, 'I have been trying to persuade him, and incidentally some of his officials, that no country can ignore the external implications of domestic policy, but he is not altogether convinced.'[98]

On special deposits, both the Bank and Treasury officials were opposed to Maudling's desire to release the remaining 2 per cent in one go.[99] The Bank was particularly nervous that returning the deposits in their entirety

---

[94] 'Release of special deposits: letters to banking associations, etc.', 30 May 1962, C40/1207.

[95] Errol to Lloyd, 18 April 1962; Hollom to O'Brien/Cromer/Mynors, 'To-day's meeting with the Chancellor', 25 April 1962, C40/1209.

[96] 'Extract from Deputy Governor's memo dated 18.5.62 on his conversation with the Chancellor', C40/1207.

[97] O'Brien annotation on Hollom, Note for record – 'Hire purchase', 13 February 1963, C40/1210.

[98] Parsons to Cromer, 25 September 1962, G1/253.

[99] Extracts from Deputy Governor's memos on conversations with Mr. W. M. Armstrong, 4 and 11 September 1962, C40/1207.

would unleash a rapid expansion in advances.[100] Instead, it was announced in September that they would be reduced to 1 per cent and that the requests to exercise restraint in particular areas were to be withdrawn, although the Governor hoped that priority would continue to be given to activities that promoted exports and overseas earnings and gave assistance to business in areas of the country where resources were unemployed.[101] Then, at the end of November 1962, it was agreed that the general economic position permitted the release of the outstanding balances.[102]

It is not easy to say what special deposits achieved because a number of factors were at work. For example, the clearing banks were under-lent when compared with their pre-war position and had been gradually rebuilding advances during the 1950s and 1960s.[103] Even where advances did fall, as they did after July 1961, special deposits were only one element in a package. It is also difficult to disentangle the precise reasons for a decision. For instance, looking back on the call of July 1961, Cromer thought that this had been made because of the requirement for an imposing package rather than the need to act on the banks' liquidity position.[104] One thing seemed clear: in order to meet the early calls for special deposits, the banks had sold investments. Since advances were not being contained, it was then necessary to issue direction as to the response that was expected by the authorities. This also meant that there were implications for the Bank's operations in the gilt-edged market if government securities were being sold as a result of special deposits. Despite the attention the authorities gave to this technique, its use hardly rates a mention in the clearers' histories.[105]

Some of the explanation for this might lie in their lack of impact. In the Bank, Allen estimated that without the calls in 1960, the liquid assets of the banks would have been £29 million greater than they in fact were, 'a small mouse for 143 [£million] of Special Deposits!'[106] The Treasury concluded that the verdict on special deposits was 'not proven', and while O'Brien did not contest this, he professed himself 'a little less lukewarm'. He accepted that the major influence on banking liquidity had in fact been funding

[100] Hollom to I. de L. Radice (HMT), 5 October 1962, C40/1207.
[101] Cromer speech at the Lord Mayor's dinner, 3 October 1962, *BEQB* 2(4):261, December 1962.
[102] Mynors, 'Special deposits', 8 November 1962; Extract from the Deputy Governor's memo dated 23.11.62. on a conversation with the Chancellor of the Exchequer; Hollom to Radice, 28 November 1962, C40/1207.
[103] O'Brien to Armstrong, 19 December 1960, C40/708.
[104] Cromer, Governor's note – 'Special deposits', 4 May 1962, C40/1207.
[105] See, for example, Ackrill and Hannah (2001); Green (1979).
[106] Allen, 'Effect of special deposits', 14 September 1960, C40/708.

operations. Indeed, if special deposits had not been called, 'funding might have been even more successful and have achieved results, at least in terms of figures, as satisfactory as have been obtained by a combination of both weapons.' Despite this, O'Brien thought that Armstrong had under-rated the 'psychological impact' of special deposits, arguing that 'the knowledge that they [the banks] were always liable to have to make a further deposit has acted very strongly on the banks and has much intensified their efforts to restrain the growth of their advances.' Overall, he judged that despite harbouring reservations about the prolonged use of such devices, special deposits had 'so far made as effective a contribution to our objective as we had hoped.'[107] Equally, when special deposits were removed, it was difficult to be sure of the effect, and the impact of the 1962 releases proved hard to determine.[108]

Looking back on the events from some distance, Hollom, one of the authors of the special deposits scheme, believed it to be a quantitative control 'and a control which would operate by affecting costs, which was the only way we saw it working.'[109] Looked at like this, it was a squeeze on profits. But there was nothing in the discussion at the time to this effect. However, this does seem to be an accurate assessment of the outcome of the scheme. That being so, how big a squeeze was it, and why squeeze profits? If we take the biggest of the banks, Barclays, and take the worst possible case – the 3 per cent level of special deposits (in place for almost a year) – then Barclays would have had to place deposits of approximately £50 million. They received the Treasury bill rate of approximately 4 per cent rather than a longer rate of, say, 6 per cent, and so it cost them £1 million. Given that Barclays' profits that year were roughly £18 million, we might judge the squeeze to have been relatively small.[110] Or if it were argued that the banks as a cartel were earning monopoly profits, then they may have happily accepted such a loss. In any case, it hardly compared with the squeeze on profits that the cash ratio of 8 per cent represented. Cash earned no interest, and at this point, 1961–62, left to themselves, the banks might have chosen a ratio of closer to 4 per cent rather than the 8 per cent imposed. This meant that on 4 per cent of their balance sheet they

[107] Armstrong to O'Brien, 14 December 1960, enc. HMT summary and paper, 'The special deposit scheme', 7 December 1960, C40/708.
[108] HMT, 'The special deposit scheme: did it work?', January 1963; Thornton to Hollom, 21 March 1963, C40/1207.
[109] Coleby interview with Sir Jasper Hollom, 12 January 1995.
[110] Ackrill and Hannah (2001, p. 200). This is based on unpublished profits before realised gains or losses.

were losing around 4 or 5 per cent interest, and that was every year.[111] The more important point to make about the special deposits, however, is that if the banks found their profits being squeezed, surely a likely response would have been to attempt to recover the loss, and one way of doing that would have been to increase the size of their balance sheet – in other words to increase advances. This being so, the special deposits scheme was perverse. If, however, special deposits were equivalent to raising the banks' cash-deposit ratio, albeit with interest being paid on a portion of it, then that acted as constraint on the balance sheet.

Notwithstanding the external situation, with unemployment rising and output virtually stagnant, the state of the domestic economy remained a preoccupation for the government. In November 1962, William Armstrong, who had taken over from Lee as joint permanent Secretary, confided to Mynors that the Prime Minister was poised for a reflationary drive, 'much of which might doubtless come home to roost in subsequent months'.[112] Possible moves on Bank Rate were aired, but Mynors said that the Bank would prefer to wait until the turn of the year. On 3 January 1963, the sixth successive ½ per cent cut in Bank Rate was announced, taking it to 4 per cent, its lowest level since 1958. The official line was that it reflected the domestic economic situation and was consistent with the strength of sterling. It then remained unchanged until the rise to 5 per cent in February 1964.

At the time of the January 1963 rate cut, it was also announced that in future the Bank might on occasion charge above Bank Rate for loans to the discount houses. This, it was explained, would add flexibility to the Bank's operations. More specifically, it would 'widen the range within which, at any given level of Bank Rate, the average cost of the Market's money can fluctuate'; that is, short-term rates, and especially the Treasury bill rate, could be pushed up without raising Bank Rate.[113] The decision had its antecedents in a debate about differential interest rates that began in 1961 after President Kennedy proposed that the United States offer favourable interest rates on dollar deposits by foreign governments and monetary authorities.[114] Dusting off the response to the Treasury, Hollom found little reason to alter the earlier view. He did suggest that a 'harmless' counter to the proposal would be

---

[111] See Griffiths (1970) for some discussion.

[112] Mynors, 22 November 1962, G1/253.

[113] Hollom to Radice, 2 January 1963; 'Brief for interviews with the press 3.1.63'; Mynors to Lord Monckton (chairman, CLCB), 3 January 1963, C42/11.

[114] Sir Frank Lee to Tom Caulcott (Maudling's PS), 31 August 1962, enc. Maudling to Lee, 29 August 1962, C42/11.

to revert to the pre-1951 rule that advances should be made at not less than ½ per cent above Bank Rate. O'Brien was in favour because 'it somewhat increases our power to influence market rates at any level of Bank Rate' and went some small way towards meeting the Chancellor's point.[115] In October 1962, Cromer reiterated the Bank's scepticism about differential interest to Armstrong and also mentioned the 'technical device' of lending to the discount market at above Bank Rate, suggesting that this be announced and implemented the next time that Bank Rate was changed.[116] After further discussions, it was decided to hold the higher rate back as a threat, ready for use when the Bank wanted to exert an upward pressure on rates, rather than to apply it on the day of announcement.[117] Thus the device was unveiled in January 1963 and then applied for the first and only time on 19 March 1963, when £15.75 million was advanced at 4½ per cent. The move came following pressure on sterling and the fact that the average Treasury bill rate had fallen (from £3:11:3 on 4 January 1963 to £3:7:11 on 15 March) as the market sought to increase its allotments by increasing the tender price. The measure would appear to have enjoyed some success. Its immediate impact was seen at the next tender, when the average rate jumped to £3:15:8, exceptionally high in relation to a 4 per cent Bank Rate.[118] Thereafter, this rate was broadly maintained until the increase in Bank Rate in February 1964.[119] Looking back on the episode, Cromer thought that the device had been effective in a 'limited way' and that the Bank would use it again if the circumstances were appropriate.[120] In the event, its further use was not required.

There was one aspect of the Treasury bill tender that Radcliffe had been slightly uneasy about, and that was the apparent deliberate manipulation of the discount house bid in order to discourage outside tenders. To achieve this, the Committee noted, the syndicate had 'jumped its bid up and down'. The consequence was that rival bidders were either allotted

---

[115] Hollom to O'Brien/Cromer/Mynors, 'Differential Bank Rate', 10 September 1962, and O'Brien, Annotation, 11 September 1962, C42/11.

[116] Cromer to Armstrong, 18 October 1962, C42/11.

[117] Hollom, Note for record – 'Differential interest rates', 5 November 1962; Armstrong to Cromer, 16 November 1962, enc. HMT, 'The Governor's "technical device"', 12 November 1962; Hollom to O'Brien/Cromer/Mynors, 'Lending to the discount market at a rate other than Bank Rate', 19 December 1962; O'Brien to Cromer/Mynors, 'Lending to the discount market at a rate other than Bank Rate', 19 December 1962; HMT, 'Note of a meeting … 20th December, 1962', 21 December 1962, C42/11.

[118] Hollom to Stevens, 5 April 1963, C42/11.

[119] Bank of England, *Annual Report*, year ending February 1964; Register of bill and bond issues by tender, C10/3.

[120] Cromer to Armstrong, 16 November 1964, C42/11.

nothing or had to pay a high price for their bills. While this did happen, the data showing the proportion allocated to the discount market reveal that the syndicate did not always dominate, and this was increasingly true. Between 1961 and 1964, there were eight occasions on which the houses received less than 20 per cent of the available bills, whereas between 1965 and 1967, there were 23 occasions. In several instances, 10 per cent or less was allotted to the discount market (Figure 6.1). At any rate, for most of the 1960s, the Bank was happy to remain complicit in the arrangements. From the mid-1950s, demand for Treasury bills had grown, particularly from oil companies and industrial concerns attracted by the higher rates of interest available. The clearing banks tendered on their behalf. A number of fringe banks also had become involved, and although the Discount Office recognised their right to tender, they were subject to weekly fixed limits. Hilton Clarke felt that what he described as a 'highly competitive "outside" tender' was in the interests of all concerned.[121] O'Brien agreed that discouraging others from tendering would place the London Discount Market Association (LDMA) in too privileged a position, but he was not arguing for an entirely free tender. Critically for him, the existence of the syndicate, and the banks' agreement not to bid on their own account, 'make for rigidity which suits us, however much it may be criticised, because it helps us to influence short rates and keep them reasonably stable.'[122] Cromer opined that the arrangements were 'a masterpiece of British compromise', although he suspected that the 'creaky edifice' would require reconstruction.[123]

During the 1950s, great attention had been paid to liquidity, and the Bank monitored the position of the clearing banks, both individually and as a group. The Radcliffe Report devoted much space to the issue, and it continued to be prominent in the early 1960s.[124] At the beginning of 1963, the Bank started to worry about the 30 per cent liquidity ratio. The concern was not with restricting credit but with what could be done if a rise in lending was desired and the banks were already operating at the 30 per cent minimum ratio. This led to a re-examination of the case for special deposits

[121] Clarke to O'Brien/Cromer, 'The Treasury bill tender', 13 December 1962. Similar arguments resurfaced in 1967; Galpin to Keogh, 'Treasury bill tender', 25 May 1967, C47/53.

[122] O'Brien, Note, 13 December 1962, added to Clarke to O'Brien/Cromer, 'The Treasury bill tender', 13 December 1962, C47/53.

[123] Cromer, Annotation, 20 December 1962, on Clarke to O'Brien/Cromer, 'The Treasury bill tender', 13 December 1962, C47/53.

[124] Bank of England, 'Bank liquidity in the United Kingdom', *BEQB* 2(4):248–249, December 1962.

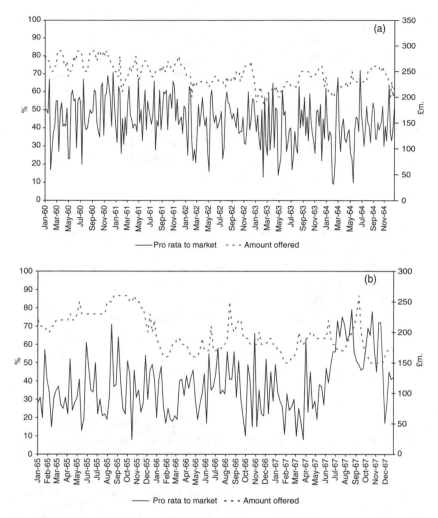

Figure 6.1. (*a*) Weekly pro-rata allocation of Treasury bills, 1960–64. (*b*) Weekly pro-rata allocation of Treasury bills, 1965–67.

as opposed to the use of variable liquidity ratios, something that had, of course, already been the subject of extensive debate.[125]

---

[125] Allen to O'Brien/Hollom, 'Below-zero special deposits', 21 January 1963; Paul Brader (Chief Cashier's Office) to Thornton, 'Variable liquidity ratios versus special deposits', 24 January 1963; Hollom to O'Brien/Cromer/Mynors, 'Special deposits versus variable liquidity ratios', 7 February 1963; Fforde to O'Brien, 'Special deposits v variable liquidity ratios', 11 February 1963; Allen to Hollom/O'Brien, 'Liquidity ratio', 13 February 1963, C40/1203.

At the beginning of March 1963, the Bank did not want a rise in bank advances, especially those for industrial purposes, to be inhibited by liquidity constraints, but neither did it want to see the gilt-edged market affected by the banks selling their investments. Therefore, other means of improving the banks' liquidity were required. Moreover, while the current situation might only be temporary, Hollom thought that something more permanent should be considered. On the question of special deposits versus variable liquidity ratios, the earlier arguments still were pertinent, but an additional benefit of the former was that they were now accepted and operated by the banks: 'For a voluntary scheme that imposes some financial penalty on the banks, this must be counted a considerable advantage.' Overall, Hollom saw no reason to change the previous verdict. He then considered whether the prevailing ratio of 30 per cent should be reduced, on either a temporary or a permanent basis. Since the figure had its origin 'in the mind of the prudent banker', any alteration would have to commend itself to the same mind. Temporary changes would be 'indistinguishable' from a variable liquidity ratio and thus should be opposed. Moreover, temporary fluctuations did not fit well with the prudent banker concept. Therefore, the move had to be permanent, and Hollom thought that the banks should be asked what they considered to be an appropriate figure. He wanted to dissuade them from suggesting a figure lower than 25 per cent, and 27½ to 28 per cent would suit the Bank.[126]

Cromer and O'Brien were keen not to push the banks in a particular direction. O'Brien wrote, 'If as I think we should, we are to continue to base our control of banking liquidity on the bankers' own convention, we should make sure that it still is their convention. If they want to reduce the minimum ratio for their own purposes, I think we should accept that as our basis too.' The Governor added that he was prepared to sound out the CLCB, 'but I have no desire to influence them on the ratio.'[127] At the same time, the situation was such that the banks were given permission to go below the minimum liquidity ratio in March, a dispensation that was extended subsequently into April and May.[128]

Both O'Brien and Cromer wrote independently to Armstrong reiterating that the case for retaining special deposits was 'pretty conclusive', although Cromer proposed asking the banks whether they wished to see

---

[126] Hollom to O'Brien/Cromer/Mynors, 'Banking liquidity', 7 March 1963, C40/1203.

[127] O'Brien to Cromer/Mynors, 'Banking liquidity', 21 March 1963; Cromer, Annotation, 8 April 1963, C40/1203.

[128] Extract from Deputy Governor's memo dated 8.3.63; Cromer, Note, 12 March 1963; O'Brien, Note for record, 12 March 1963, C40/1203.

a reduction in the minimum liquidity ratio and suggested that a move as far as 25 per cent would be acceptable.[129] Mynors threw an additional idea into the pot by arguing that the minimum ratio should be abolished altogether. If it became necessary to reapply special deposits, Mynors said, then the necessary fulcrum could be provided by introducing whatever minimum liquidity percentage seemed appropriate at the time.[130] Although attracted to the simplicity of this proposal, Hollom thought that in the absence of a minimum ratio, the banks would react by setting a figure. While Hollom conceded that there were disadvantages to the fixed ratio, 'on the whole my inclination would be to opt for the devil we know.'[131] Allen, too, was wary. He feared that removing official limitations on bank lending would give an 'undesirably large boost now', and more important, re-imposition at a later stage would appear as a major policy reversal.[132] Others went further, suggesting that if the banks were at, or close to, their chosen minima and near fully lent, there would be no need for a precise and agreed minimum liquidity ratio. Its practical value would be 'tiny', whereas a squeeze via interest-rate and funding policy would be more powerful.[133] Thomson told Cromer that the banks were unanimous in wanting to see the continuation of the present system based on convention rather than legal requirement. They disliked the notion of a variable liquidity ratio because it would create uncertainty, and they were against suspension of the fixed ratio, although they did want to see it reduced in a decisive way and not one that appeared to be 'nibbling' at 30 per cent. All the clearers agreed that a figure of 25 per cent would not be imprudent.[134] Cromer reported the CLCB stance to the Treasury and proposed an announcement, that month, of a revision of the liquidity ratio to 25 per cent.[135]

The Treasury suggested a compromise of 25 per cent and then applying special deposits to give an effective ratio of 28 per cent, something O'Brien described as 'silly'.[136] When Cromer sounded out the CLCB representatives about a figure of 28 per cent, Robarts complained that this would afford them virtually nothing because they would have to aim for

---

[129] Cromer to Armstrong, 11 April 1963, C40/1203.
[130] Mynors to Cromer, 24 April 1963, C40/1203.
[131] Hollom to O'Brien/Mynors, 'Liquidity conventions', 24 April 1963, C40/1203.
[132] Allen, 'Liquidity ratio', 25 April 1963, C40/1203.
[133] Fforde to O'Brien/Mynors, 'Liquidity conventions', 25 April 1963, C40/1203.
[134] Hollom, Note for record – 'Liquidity conventions', 8 May 1963, C40/1203.
[135] Cromer to Armstrong, 10 May 1963, C40/1203.
[136] Hollom, Note for record – 'Banking liquidity', 22 May 1963; O'Brien, Annotation on Radice, 21 May 1963, C40/1203.

29 per cent or higher.[137] When Maudling reconsidered, he was prepared to see a fall to 28 per cent, but 25 per cent was 'far too much'. 'I see no reason for reducing the figure by such a dramatic amount which might give the impression that we are embarking on a period of inflationary finance.'[138] Agreement was reached for the banks to continue to work to 28 per cent only until April 1964, and it was decided not to give any 'undue emphasis' in public.[139] In March 1964, Cromer proposed that the banks should carry on working to 28 per cent for the time being, although the Bank still saw a 25 per cent ratio as the ultimate goal. This continuation was agreed to by the Treasury, and again, there was no formal public statement.[140] What had begun as a potentially radical rethink on controlling bank liquidity had quickly given way to ad hoc and informal tinkering. And it was not the last occasion on which the relative merits of such monetary weapons would be debated exhaustively. In this instance, the Bank (and the banks) found that an informal and legally unenforceable figure, which was supposed to be determined by banking convention, could not be altered to what was thought to be appropriate because the Chancellor viewed the liquidity ratio as an instrument of credit control.

Just prior to these discussions in 1962, the Bank was seeking to give some guidance that lower rates were desired in the gilt-edged market, but not to be reached, of course, in a disorderly manner. The policy was 'to keep any tendency for prices to move upwards under firm restraint so that the pace of the movement remains modest (long-term yields have fallen about 6s. per cent [roughly 0.3 per cent] since the end of July [1961], which seems fully fast enough)'.[141] Cromer agreed that 'a gradual fall over a period of, say, 18 months–2 years to a level of about 5½ per cent might be regarded as a broadly desirable aim.'[142] A further tranche of 5% Treasury 1986/89, issued in May, was deliberately priced three-eighths above the prevailing market price in order to give a 'sharp nudge', whereas the June issue of 5% Exchequer 1967, a short designed to appeal to the banks in the light of releases of special deposits, was also priced to give a 'hint' to the market that

---

[137] Hollom, Note for record – 'Banking liquidity', 23 May 1963, C40/1203.
[138] Maudling to Cromer, 5 June 1963, C40/1203.
[139] Cromer to Thomson, 17 September 1963, C40/1204; Cromer speech at the Lord Mayor's dinner, 16 October 1963, *BEQB* 3(2):295, December 1963.
[140] Cromer to Armstrong, 12 March 1964; Armstrong to Cromer, 18 March 1964; Cromer to Viscount Monckton of Brenchley (chairman CLCB), 20 March 1964, C40/1204.
[141] Hollom to O'Brien/Cromer, 'New issue', 13 March 1962, 5A44/13.
[142] Hollom, Note for record – 'New issue', 15 March 1962, 5A44/13.

the authorities favoured a rather lower pattern of interest rates.[143] This kind of communication often failed.

In the summer of 1962, the question of long-term rates was considered by the Treasury, initiated as a result of the Prime Minister's interest in the subject. O'Brien was not amused: it was 'ridiculous for the Treasury to put in a paper on interest rates (of all things) to the Chancellor without pretty full discussion with the Bank beforehand'.[144] The Treasury argued that there would be clear advantages, in terms of the cost of borrowing, if the downward trend in long-term rates continued. In market operations, the Treasury claimed, 'we are doing nothing to interfere with a decline ... and indeed a number of things to encourage it.' These included reductions in Bank Rate and a tight budgetary policy. The Treasury also stated that 'we are no longer engaging in active funding – that is, selling long-term securities in order to redeem short-term debt and lengthen the debt as a whole.' The demand for capital in the economy, especially from local authorities, was pushing in the other direction. Finally, emphasis was put on inflationary expectations. It was the fear of inflation that had forced up long rates, whereas the measures taken in July 1961 had persuaded the public that the government was determined to keep inflation in check and resulted in a decline in rates. Budgetary and incomes policies were felt to be crucial in this. 'It is probably no exaggeration to say', concluded the Treasury, 'that nothing could be more helpful to a continued decline in the long-term rate of interest than government policies which convinced people that inflation would be stopped.'[145]

The Bank had two main reservations. First, there was unease about the analysis of funding policy. It was wrong to suggest that there was no interference with the decline in long rates, or that there was no engagement in active funding, or that the strength of the budgetary position meant there would be no need for funding. To withdraw completely from funding, interpreted either as net sales of stock or lengthening the maturity of the holdings without altering the total amount, would be a 'major act of policy which would immediately become headline news'. Likewise, a subsequent reversal would be just as conspicuous. The Bank could do no more than 'choose between allowing an upward market movement to be reflected primarily in the rate or primarily in more funding. At present we are leaning towards movements in rate, while continuing to fund in

[143] Whittome to O'Brien/Cromer/Mynors, 14 June 1962, C40/1159.
[144] O'Brien, Annotation on Whittome to O'Brien/Cromer/Mynors, 13 June 1962; Armstrong to O'Brien, 15 June 1962, C42/7.
[145] Armstrong to Padmore, 3 July 1962, C42/7.

slow time and at rising prices.' Whatever the budgetary position, though, the Bank would increase sales if it saw a rapid rise in bank advances and bank deposits. In short, the net effect was to 'permit market forces slowly to bring down long-term rates but without any loss of control'. The second concern was over the complete absence of any references to external considerations: 'There may be a conflict between the movements in interest rates which are desirable in the light of events at home and those desirable in the light of events abroad.' In particular, balance-of-payments troubles could influence the pattern of international rates, and there also could be an effect if Britain gained membership of the European Economic Community (EEC).[146]

The Bank's views on what was an 'essentially market operation' were sent to Lee in July 1962.[147] While agreeing that the current trend towards lower rates should be allowed to continue, the Governor warned that the fall in rates had to be sustainable; otherwise, the current interest in gilt-edged securities might be destroyed. There were uncertainties over the future strength of sterling, the likely success of incomes policy, and the level of public-sector borrowing. Even with optimistic assumptions about these variables, Cromer thought that it would be difficult to maintain a downward trend in rates unless the authorities were prepared to become net buyers of stock 'probably on an ever increasing scale'. Similarly, trying to hold a rate at a particular level would be equally troublesome because Cromer was convinced that the difficulty of disengaging from a policy of lowering interest rates was even greater than embarking on it. Sudden reversals of direction would leave the gilt-edged market 'demoralised and friendless' and in no condition to absorb sales of stock, even those required to match forthcoming maturities. Thus the Bank's view was that in order to avoid obvious manipulation of the market, and to try to allow for future uncertainties, official operations should continue along present lines. This approach would 'allow an appropriate gradual fall in rates while preserving to the authorities full freedom of manoeuvre to assess what is appropriate or feasible as time goes on and inconspicuously to vary their tactics accordingly'.[148] Much of this was incorporated into a note that Lloyd then sent to Macmillan.[149]

---

[146] Hollom to O'Brien/Cromer/Mynors, 'Long-term interest rates: comments on the draft note by Mr. William Armstrong', 5 July 1962; also Cromer, 'Long-term interest rates', 9 July 1962; Hollom to Cromer/Mynors, 9 July 1962, C42/7.
[147] 'Extract from the Deputy Governor's memo dated 6.7.62 ...', C42/7.
[148] Cromer to Lee, 9 July 1962, C42/7.
[149] HMT, 'Long-term interest rates', 10 July 1962, C42/7.

Long-term rates continued to fall through 1962; it was a trend that the Bank had 'expected, wanted and encouraged', although the pace had been moderated by raising the price of the tap more slowly. However, Deputy Chief Cashier Alan Whittome told Cromer and O'Brien that because of the outlook for the balance of payments and the growth in demand, the Treasury was speaking of halting the decline in rates. Such talk was misplaced, according to Whittome: 'If it were clear that we were determined to prevent any further fall, rates would inevitably begin to rise, the more so if the reasons we had in mind were suspected.' He believed that long-term rates certainly would rise if balance-of-payments problems emerged, but this was not to argue that they should not fall further now. The Bank would be content with something around 5 per cent by early 1963, but there should be no steps to encourage this.[150] When this was being written, in October 1962, the Cuban missile crisis had just erupted, and gilt prices had fallen sharply.[151]

The subject resurfaced in February 1963, this time prompted by the Bank, when O'Brien thought it desirable to get the long-term rate down as soon as possible.[152] The gilt-edged market had not regained the strength that it had shown prior to the Cuban crisis, and it was likely that in 1964 there would be upward pressure on rates. To prepare for this, it was suggested that the gilt-edged market could be nursed into as good a condition as possible before cyclic events moved against it. But no action should be taken that would result in the belief that prices were settled by official intervention. Unless the rise in prices could be brought about by 'encouragement' rather than 'coercion', it was 'an enterprise which had better not be attempted'.[153] Whittome did not think that there were many differences of substance between the Bank and the Treasury, although the latter over-emphasised the role of market management in influencing the long rate. 'We know', said Whittome, 'that the Treasury think that we speak with two voices on this question. We do. As we see it, the truth is that, according to circumstances, any attempt on our part to influence rates may either be very successful (even over-successful) or largely ineffective (even negative). The role ascribed to us in the paper may be flattering but it could be embarrassing if the record were left unamended.'[154] It is not difficult to see how the markets had a problem understanding the Bank's actions.

[150] Whittome to O'Brien/Cromer, 16 October 1962, C40/1160.
[151] Hollom to O'Brien/Cromer/Mynors, 20 December 1962, C40/1160.
[152] O'Brien to Rickett, 27 February 1963, C42/7.
[153] Bank of England, 'Monetary policy: long-term rates of interest', 27 February 1963, C42/7.
[154] Whittome to O'Brien/Cromer/Mynors, 22 July 1963, C42/7.

What the Bank took great exception to was the claim that it had been agreed in March that the Bank would attempt to bring the long rate down from 5¾ per cent to 5½ per cent. On days when the market was weak the Bank would take all the stock offered to it at prices just below prevailing levels; when the market was firm, selling prices would be moved up more rapidly than usual. By these tactics, the Treasury stated, 'The Bank have been able to bring the rate down to about 5¼.' Whittome noted that the entire passage should be rewritten because the Bank had no recollection of what had supposedly been agreed to, and the analysis of the tactics and results was both crude and exaggerated. He was backed by de Moubray (Assistant Chief of Central Banking Information Department [CBID]), who asserted that the Treasury had to accept that the while the Bank can influence the rate, it 'cannot with impunity reverse the trend'.[155] Cromer's subsequent letter to Armstrong stressed the Bank's opinion that the Treasury had seriously over-emphasised the part that market tactics had played in bringing about a lower rate in the last few months. Tactics had been a factor, but the underlying causes were more important. In any case, the Governor questioned whether a detailed discussion of the Bank's tactics was appropriate: 'What matters is, I believe, the aim, not the precise techniques used to achieve it.' It surely would be preferable, he continued, if the paper merely noted that 'the Bank's market operations were designed not to discourage the fall in rates that was already occurring.'[156]

The Bank obviously was keen to maintain its hold over operations in the gilt market, just as it enjoyed freedom of action in its daily money-market operations, although this latter was primarily a banking matter. Treasury bills continued to be of central importance, although there was a decline in the amounts offered for tender. In the year that the Radcliffe Report was published, the total value of 91-day Treasury bills *offered* was nearly £13 billion, an average of £246 million per week. Every week, there were, typically, around 300 *applications* for £400 million of bills. Over the following years, these figures gradually fell, and in 1967, the weekly averages were £191 million offered for tender, with 231 applications, for a total of £346 million of bills (Figure 6.2). A senior Treasury official was present when the tenders were opened, which took about half an hour, and he thus knew the basic results.[157] However, towards the end of 1963, the Treasury asked

[155] Guy de Moubray to O'Brien, 'Long-term rates of interest', 22 July 1963, C42/7.
[156] Cromer to Armstrong, 23 July 1963, C42/7.
[157] J. V. Ormsby to Moule, Draft 'Treasury bill tender', 2 February 1968, C40/1466; 'The Treasury bill', *BEQB* 4(3):187–189, 1968.

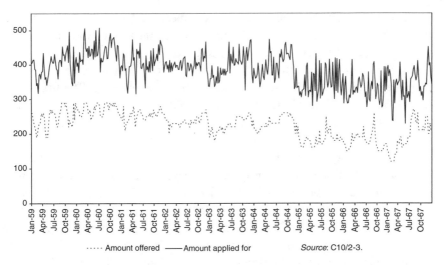

Figure 6.2. Weekly Treasury bill tender, 1959–67 (£m).

whether it could be provided with more information about the tender, in particular, details relating to the allotment of bills and what was taken up by the Banking Department. Radice said that this would help the Treasury in its understanding of the bill market and especially the role of outsiders. The Bank was doubtful. Aside from being regarded as a banking matter, and involving confidential information about customers, such disclosures likely would lead to further questions and, ultimately, to discussions of money-market tactics. It was argued that the Treasury would not gain by 'diverting their energies in this direction, and we strongly suspect that our own operations will suffer if any form of prior consultation were ever to be requested or if operations had subsequently to be justified'.[158] In any case, Clarke had difficulty understanding the value of such information to the Treasury, pointing out that once the bills were taken up, they changed hands with great rapidity.[159]

In the mid-1960s, the LDMA was worried that the syndicate arrangements for the tender would come under official attack as a restrictive practice, and there were concerns among the discount houses about the size of the outside tender. Also, moves by Clive Discount to purchase a controlling interest in Guy Butler & Co., a broker specialising in the inter-bank market, had caused unease and rumours that as a result, the syndicate, and even the

[158] Radice to Hollom, 28 November 1963; Anon. note to O'Brien/Mynors, enc. Unsent draft letter to Radice, filed 29 November 1963, C40/1154.
[159] Clarke to Whittome, 'The weekly Treasury bill tender', 30 January 1964, C47/53.

association, might break up. The LDMA had established a sub-committee, which Discount Office Deputy Principal Blunden termed a 'mini-Radcliffe', to review market functions and practices. Judging by the 'indiscretions' of committee members, Blunden thought it unlikely that anything radical would emerge. For the Bank, there were three general issues. The first was to ensure that the weekly tender was covered. Blunden foresaw no difficulty here because it was likely that the discount houses would still try to maintain their non-competition agreement with the clearing banks. In any case, it was probable that freed from a syndicate that sharply reduced individual bids, discount houses would increase the size of their weekly tender. Second was the problem of the Bank obtaining bills on behalf of its own customers. Under the existing arrangement, the Bank got all it required by bidding 1d. above the market rate; in the future, it might have to enter the market competitively and therefore sometimes be outbid. Finally, and for Blunden most important, the disappearance of the syndicate would tend to lead to a lower Treasury bill rate because greater competition for bills would bid up the price. If the Bank wanted either to steady or increase the rate, it would be necessary to resort to more vigorous use of lending at the Bank Rate or above. Blunden concluded that the syndicated bid was a 'convenience' for the Bank and that there probably should be no encouragement towards its abandonment. However, its demise would not be such a disaster that the Bank should press to keep it alive.[160] Hollom and O'Brien agreed.[161] Although the LDMA floated a number of ideas, the Bank had little enthusiasm for any of them, and it was agreed that the Governor should tell the LDMA that the clear preference was for no change to the existing arrangements. This Cromer did at the end of March 1966, and the houses agreed to maintain the status quo.[162] While O'Brien and others in the Bank were unwilling to declare the syndicate bid indispensable, it was not until competition and credit control (CCC) in 1971 that the arrangements were swept away.

---

[160] Clarke to Hollom/Morse/Cromer/O'Brien, 'London Discount Market Association', 5 April 1965, C47/32; Morse to Hollom, 'Discount market's syndicated tender', 8 October 1965; Blunden to Hollom/Morse, 'Syndicated tender', 13 October 1965; also see Blunden's postscript, Blunden to Clarke, 'Syndicated tender', 6 December 1965, C40/1466. On Clive Discount, see Clarke to Hollom/Morse/O'Brien, 13 December 1965, C40/1466 and Discount Office file, C47/6.

[161] O'Brien, Annotation, 4 January 1966 on Hollom to Morse/Cromer/O'Brien, 'Syndicated tender', 21 December 1965, C40/1466.

[162] LDMA, 'Report of the sub-committee', LDMA1/82; Hollom to Morse/Cromer/O'Brien, 'Syndicated tender', 21 December 1965; Clarke to Hollom/Cromer/O'Brien/Morse, 'Syndicated tender', 2 February 1966; Morse to Cromer/O'Brien, 'Money market operations', 18 March 1966; Hollom to Morse/Cromer/O'Brien, 'Syndicated tender', 30

The tender attracted some academic interest, for instance, when Andrew Bain took issue with Crouch's model (included in the latter's attack on the new orthodoxy) and argued that the allocation of bills in the tender did not determine the volume of bills available as liquid assets to the banks. Other than for short periods, the discount houses would not be allowed to bid too far out of line from the Bank's desired rate. For example, if the syndicate raised its price, with a consequently lower rate of discount, the Bank could force the market into the Bank to borrow at Bank Rate. Bain concluded that the syndicate was not a cartel but 'the residual buyers' who paid a price that was determined by the authorities.[163] This was close to the Bank's view. Later, in 1971, Griffiths argued that normal price theory could be applied to the tender and that the syndicate were acting to maximise their long-run profits. Griffiths thought that 'nods and winks' and 'obvious wishes of the authorities' were 'irrelevant as well as confusing'.[164] In fact, in the month that this was published, the mechanism was about to change.

In addition to 91 days, Treasury bills of 63-day duration also were made available periodically. Introduced in 1955, they were intended to smooth the effect of heavy revenue inflows in January and February on the maturity distribution of Treasury bills while allowing the Bank to retain its control of the money market. The 63-day bills were made available only in November and December in comparatively small amounts of between £30 million and £60 million a week, and there was a good deal of debate about their value and effectiveness.[165] O'Brien admitted they had not been an unqualified success, but they did appear to have played some part in smoothing out distortions. Consequently, he recommended that their use should continue, albeit with a reduction in the amount on offer.[166] Hollom argued that 'several of the features that led to the introduction and annual use of 63-day bills have in the past few years lost much of their force', and with the market's reaction to the bills 'persistently unfavourable', the Bank could manage without them that year.[167] No further issues were ever made. It was an instrument that the market did not particularly

---

March 1966; Blunden to Hollom, 'The Bank's operations in the discount market', 27 April 1966, C40/1466. LDMA Minute Book, 17 and 24 January, 1 and 7 February, 22 April 1966, LDMA1/2; LDMA notes, 1 April 1966, LDMA1/15.

[163] Bain (1965, pp. 62, 68–69); Crouch (1964, p. 918).

[164] Griffiths (1971).

[165] J. V. Bailey (Deputy Chief Cashier) to O'Brien, '63-day Treasury Bills', 4 May 1960, C40/1154.

[166] O'Brien to Hawker/Cobbbold/Mynors, '63-day bills', 14 September 1960, C40/1154.

[167] Hollom to O'Brien, '63-day bills', 30 April 1963, C40/1154.

like or want, but for some time the Bank thought that it worked, without being able to demonstrate exactly how. In this regard, 63-day bills were not unusual.

Back to Ceilings, 1964–1967

In the domestic economy, the mid-1960s were characterised by Labour's new approach to economic management: the drive for modernisation that placed a high importance on planning and centralised control that could do away with the 'stop-go cycle' (no red lights or green lights, so 'forever amber'). There had long been an admiration for the apparent success of French, and even Soviet, planning. The Conservatives had established the National Economic Development Council (NEDC). The first step in establishing the new institutional environment was the creation of a new ministry, the Department of Economic Affairs (DEA), intended as a counterpoise to the Treasury. Its responsibility was the preparation and implementation of the 'National Plan', which was intended to increase investment, expand exports, and replace inessential imports in order to boost growth. The basic projection was a 25 per cent increase in national output over the six-year period 1964–70. It was not a success and was closed in 1969.[168] Douglas Jay regarded the entire scheme as a disaster created solely to appease the rival personalities of Callaghan and Brown and said that in the Treasury the initials stood for 'Department of Extraordinary Aggression'.[169] The final element in the new apparatus was the National Board for Prices and Incomes (NBPI), established in April 1965, originally as a royal commission but reconstituted on a statutory basis in 1966. It was abolished by the Conservatives in 1970.[170]

Evidence of the Bank's views of these long-term initiatives is sparse, and in any case, there was little involvement with their implementation or operation. Of the 'National Plan', Cromer complained, 'The general difficulty is that a five-year plan, however well devised, must be setting out an expansionist, long-run approach to our problems. … only speedy, visible progress towards restoring our external position will halt the resumed loss of confidence in sterling.' They should make it clear that 'the overwhelming priority is given to prompt restoration of our external position, that developments outlined in the plan will have to be deferred if events

---

[168] Morgan (1997, p. 185); Stewart (1977, pp. 36, 120); Wilson (1971, p. 3).
[169] Morgan (1997, p. 210); Jay (1980, p. 166).
[170] Murphy (1979, p. 794); Fels (1972, pp. 138, 258–267); Mottershead (1978, p. 428).

do not turn out as we hope, and that no figures about the balance of payments are more than illustrative of one possible course.'[171] He only partly got his way.

There was a degree of enthusiasm, though, for incomes policies inside the Bank. Allen had advocated a 'Wages Board' that would establish a minimum wage and approve differentials and a 'Price Review' body to 'investigate, and pillory if need be, price increases'; McMahon also approved.[172] Even after nearly two years of limited success for the NBPI, O'Brien remained an advocate. In February 1967, he told Aubrey Jones, the board's chairman, 'I have long felt that in our kind of society a reasonably strong incomes policy in some form was necessary and, on balance, desirable.' The Governor did not feel himself qualified to comment on the specific recommendations contained in a paper by Jones but assured Jones of his 'warm personal support' for the general thesis.[173] Such views were entirely in line with the prevailing view that the way to check inflation was to limit wage increases and that this was best achieved through incomes policies.

Given the criticisms that Wilson had made at the time of both the Parker Tribunal and the Radcliffe Report, it might have been expected that on becoming Prime Minister there would be changes in the statutory or formal nature of Bank-government relations. None was forthcoming, although there was an attempt by the Chancellor to revive Radcliffe's idea for a standing committee on monetary matters. Callaghan was dissuaded by his own officials, and the Bank was spared the need to prepare a defence. Instead, the Chancellor implemented a series of joint Bank-Treasury seminars on a variety of topics in monetary policy.[174] The Bank was not entirely happy with the way that this idea had emerged, and Rickett conceded that it should have been put to the Governor first. Cromer was reluctant to take part at all, but O'Brien persuaded him that it would be prejudicial to his position for the Chancellor to chair a meeting at which representatives of the Bank were present but not the Governor.[175] The first meeting took place in October 1965, when a Treasury paper on the outlook for interest rates was tabled, and the next two topics to be discussed were debt management (in November 1965) and credit control

---

[171] Cromer to Armstrong, 6 August 1965, G3/146.

[172] Allen, 'Next round', 13 October 1964; McMahon to Allen, 'Next round', 14 October 1964, G1/253.

[173] Aubrey Jones to O'Brien, 1 February 1967, enc. Jones, 'The prices and incomes policy after mid-1967', 27 January 1967; O'Brien to Jones, 3 February 1967, G1/254.

[174] Hollom, Note for record, 2 June 1965 and 22 June 1965, C40/1252.

[175] Morse, Note, 22 June 1965, and O'Brien, Annotation, 28 June 1965, C40/1252; 'Extract from Mr. Morse's memo dated 13.7.65 … ', C40/1253.

(in February 1966).[176] There is little evidence that this initiative achieved anything.

Despite the high hopes for this long-term planning machinery, crisis quickly intervened, and the debate on economic management returned to the familiar territory of emergency financial measures, cuts, and restrictions. The budgets of 1965 and 1966 were both restrictive, with Callaghan introducing new taxes, including capital gains tax, corporation tax, and a selective employment tax. In the monetary field, controls in the form of requests and ceilings on lending were firmly back on the agenda despite the fact that special deposits were supposed to end all this. In fact the requests returned with a vengeance: the restrictions were tighter and had a wider application.

In the 1964 sterling crisis, the authorities eventually had raised Bank Rate by two percentage points to 7 per cent. Although it was forecast that clearing bank liquidity would be tight in early 1965, there were sufficient uncertainties for the Cashier's Office to propose a Governor's letter, and Hollom agreed that such a letter would 'suffice to apply a gentle brake'.[177] In the second week of December, the letter went out to the CLCB chairman. Cromer told Thomson that it was now an aim of official policy that the rate of increase in advances should decline. The extent was not quantified, but Cromer highlighted areas where action was required: to advances that promoted exports, manufacturing industry, and the government's regional development policy. Those to be avoided were property development, personal and professional uses, and advances for hire purchase.[178] The extent of this bureaucracy had not quite reached the point, as it had in the early 1950s, where there was a control covering the 'production of inessential goods', but in essence, that was what was now being requested.[179]

As on previous occasions when Bank Rate was at a 'crisis' level, the ambition was to bring it down as soon as possible. On this occasion, it was agreed that this should not occur before the 1965 budget (which was scheduled for 6 April), although not everyone was convinced. Morse said that there was

---

[176] HMT, 'The Chancellor's group on monetary policy. 'Note of a meeting ... 29 October, 1965 ... ', 8 November 1965; HMT, 'The Chancellor's group on monetary policy. Note of the meeting ... 22 November 1965 ...', 6A50/1; HMT, 'Chancellor's group on monetary policy' Note of a meeting ... 3 February 1966 ...', C40/1254.

[177] CCO, 'Restriction of bank credit', 9 November 1964; Hollom to Stevens/Cromer/O'Brien, 'Restriction of bank credit', 2 December 1964; 'Extract from the Deputy Governor's memo dated 2.12.64 ...'; Stevens to Goldman, 2 December 1964; Thornton, Note for record – 'Governor's letter on credit restraint, 8 December 1964', 9 December 1964, C40/1205.

[178] Cromer to Thomson, 8 December 1965, C40/1205.

[179] Alford (1972, p. 353).

no economic logic for relating Bank Rate to the budget, arguing that 7 per cent was a medicine that was required only for a short-term crisis, whereas it was for the budget to provide a cure for the balance-of-payments problem. Allen agreed on the crisis rate but appreciated the difficulties of timing and the likely interpretation of signals. A cut before the budget might be seen as confirmation that the Governor approved of its contents.[180] The Treasury also suggested that the re-imposition of special deposits could be announced during the budget as a means of reinforcing the other measures. It was not an idea that the Bank found attractive: the budget should 'stand on its own feet'.[181] After the budget, Callaghan and O'Brien discussed the possibility of combining the reduction in Bank Rate with an increase in special deposits. The Deputy Governor was worried that this could present contradictory messages, but circumstances might make it justifiable. Callaghan asked that officials examine the matter further, but in the event, the call for special deposits was made separately on 29 April 1965, after the disappointing figures for advances in April. The call was for 1 per cent from the English and ½ per cent from Scottish clearing banks.[182]

This still left Bank Rate. In early May, there was the slightest whiff of interference when Armstrong told Cromer, in a secret and personal letter, that the Chancellor had calculated that a reduction on 20 May would make the current period of a 7 per cent Bank Rate slightly shorter than the one in 1957–58.[183] The Bank, however, was not pressured, and no change took place, thus depriving Callaghan of the opportunity to make political capital. At the end of the same month, the exchange position meant that Cromer still viewed a Bank Rate reduction with some trepidation, and he maintained that any move would have to be associated with 'some worth-while presentational measure of a restraining character'.[184] However, Armstrong also reported that the Prime Minister favoured Cromer's

---

[180] Morse to Cromer/O'Brien, 'Future course of Bank Rate', 8 February 1965, G1/254; Hollom, Note for record, 28 January 1965; Allen to Cromer, 'Bank Rate', 8 March 1965, C42/9.

[181] Hollom to Allen/Parsons/Cromer/O'Brien/Morse, 'Monetary policy', 25 March 1965, C42/9.

[182] Hollom, Note for record – 'Meeting with the Chancellor on the 13 April', 13 April 1965; Extract from HMT, 'Note of meeting in the Chancellor of the Exchequer's room', 13 April 1965; 'Extract from Mr. Morse note dated 27.4.65 ...', C42/9; Cromer to Callaghan, 28 April 1965; Hollom to Morse/Cromer/O'Brien, 'Special deposits – market response', 29 April 1965, C40/1207.

[183] Armstrong to Cromer, 11 May 1965, C42/9; 19 September 1957 to 20 March 1958 was 183 days; 23 November 1964 to 20 May 1965 would have been 178 days; to 3 June it was 192 days.

[184] 'Extract from the Deputy Governor's memo dated 26.5.65 ...', C42/9.

advice of a 1 per cent reduction in Bank Rate, together with a simultaneous tightening in hire purchase, to be made that week, if possible.[185] On the
evening of Wednesday, 2 June, Cromer and Callaghan, along with seven
other Bank and Treasury officials, weighed up the pros and cons of the
double move. The Treasury recorded that the penalty of failure was great;
the Bank's view was more explicit, with Cromer saying that if the change
was badly received, 'we might end up with an 8 per cent rate'. Hollom also
noted that the Treasury officials 'displayed anxiety', whereas Callaghan
reluctantly agreed to a move largely because 'so conservative a body as
the Bank thought the chance worth taking'.[186] According to Wilson, it
was Callaghan who had to persuade the Bank to come down by a whole
point. This was not the end of it because there was then a furious political row with Brown over the hire-purchase changes, which ended in the
early hours of Thursday morning. Later that day, the two elements were
made public: Bank Rate announcement followed in the usual manner, and
the Chancellor spoke in the Commons. Press guidance issued by the Bank
stated that the rate still remained high and that the move did not imply any
relaxation in the restriction of credit.[187]

The Governor's letter of December 1964 was judged to have had an immediate impact because the January 1965 figures showed a fall, but thereafter
things were less satisfactory, with the February and March figures up. The
Bank's monitoring suggested that, at least as far as the clearers were concerned, there had been a good response. With the figures for April showing
another upward move, a letter went out to the CLCB on 5 May 1965, the
week after the call for special deposits had been made, requiring clearing
bank advances to the private sector to increase at an annual rate of no more
than 5 per cent for the 12 months to March 1966.[188] Further, the banks
ought to introduce a more frequent, probably monthly, breakdown of the
direction of their lending, and the use of commercial bills should be limited
in order to comply with the same objectives as those applied to advances.
For good measure, Cromer reminded the banks that the call for special
deposits should not be mitigated by the sale of investments.[189] Letters also
were sent to other banking and financial institutions, but there was greater

---

[185] Hollom to Cromer, 'Bank rate and hire purchase', 31 May 1965, C42/9.
[186] Hollom, Note for record – 'Bank rate and hire purchase', 3 June 1965; for the Treasury version, see Ian Bancroft (HMT), Note for record, 2 June 1965, C42/9.
[187] HC Deb, 3 June 1965, Vol. 713, c1973; 'Press guidance', 3 June 1965, C42/9; Cairncross
(1996, pp. 124–125); Wilson (1971, pp. 106–107).
[188] 'Extract from the Deputy Governor's memo on a Governor's conversation with Sir Denis
Rickett, 30.4.65', C40/1205.
[189] Cromer to Thomson, 5 May 1965, C40/1252.

difficulty in translating the Chancellor's objective into the required constraint.[190] In July, another letter was sent in which the Governor exhorted
the banks to scrutinise ever more closely requests for credit where there was
evidence that it might be used to pay for imports.[191]

Problems remained. One was how to deal with the rise in holdings of
commercial bills; another was the question of how to treat businesses that
lay beyond the reach of the Governor's letters. After a steady decline from
the mid-1920s, the use of bill finance experienced a resurgence in the
1950s and 1960s. Banks' and discount houses' commercial bills holdings
rose from £300 million in 1952 to £800 million by the end of 1964. There
were several reasons for this growth: competition for acceptance business
from overseas banks in London had affected commission rates; the periodic restrictions imposed on bank advances had led to the greater use of
bill finance; and a reduction in stamp duty in 1961 had taken the cost of
bill finance below that of bank advances. In addition, expectations of rising
interest rates gave an advantage to holding a fixed three-month bill over an
advance, and there had been a shortage of Treasury bills. Discount market
holdings had declined, and the discount houses had responded by increasing their business in commercial bills.[192] The Bank reminded the banks that
bill finance should not be used to avoid the requests for restraint.[193] In May
1965, the Governor also wrote to the chairman of the LDMA stressing that
the discount houses should keep in mind the aims of official policy and
limit their holdings of commercial bills on the lines that banks had been
asked to observe.[194] The limit, the LDMA suggested, should be placed on
the total of their commercial bills, that is, holdings plus re-discounts, and
the Bank relented.[195]

Even so, requests still did not cover everyone. At the end of June 1965,
letters went to eight firms drawing attention to the Governor's requests and
asking that they exercise comparable restraint.[196] Objections were made,

[190] Cromer, Letters to various banking organisations, 7 May 1965, C40/1252.
[191] Cromer to Thomson, 27 July 1965, C40/1253.
[192] Morse to Goldman, 5 July 1965, enc. Bank paper on 'commercial bills', nd, C40/1253.
[193] Thornton, Note for record – 'Request to the clearing banks for restriction of commercial
bill holdings', 18 May 1965, C40/1252.
[194] Cromer to C. C. Dawkins (chairman, LDMA), 7 May 1965, C40/1252.
[195] Dawkins to Cromer, 14 May 1965; Hollom to Allen/Cromer/O'Brien, 'Credit control and
the discount market', 19 May 1965; Clarke, 'Credit control in the discount market', 25 May
1965; Cromer to Dawkins, 31 May 1965, C40/1252.
[196] Morse, Letters to the chairmen of the Hodge Group, Wagon Finance Corporation, Capital
Finance, Ford Motor Credit, Vauxhall & General Finance Corporation, Western Credit,
F. C. Finance, Goulston Discount, 28 June 1965, C40/1252.

but no allowances were conceded.[197] A particular problem was Ford Motor Credit, which was trying to build up its hire-purchase business. It was told that the Bank would regard it as having exercised the appropriate level of restraint if their 'gross receivables' in March 1966 did not exceed £10 million (compared with £4.3 million that the 105 per cent implied).[198] Over the next few years, Ford was to remain an irritant.[199] Yet, behind this was a serious worry in the Bank about enforcing the requests. As Morse noted, Ford simply could refuse to conform and thus 'expose the formal weakness of our control'.[200]

In September 1965, there was alarm at the increases shown by accepting houses, and Cromer invited the chairman of the Accepting Houses Committee to see him, while Clarke dealt with the individual accepting houses whose figures were unsatisfactory. Discount Office staff also would visit any 'aberrant' British overseas and Commonwealth bankers. Two subsidiaries of clearing banks were reminded by Hollom to 'behave themselves properly', and the Moscow Narodny Bank were advised to ensure that their figures 'were not such as to invite our attention'. Figures for the discount houses also were disappointing, and Hollom was adamant that whatever pressure the houses were put under by others (i.e., by the flow of acceptances from the accepting houses), they must comply with the Bank's requirements.[201] Two months later, when the overall position was reviewed again, Hollom found the results 'not too discouraging', although there was agreement that it was necessary for the Bank to keep up its strong pressure.[202]

The letters, and their contents, serve to demonstrate that controlling bank credit was a confusing business and distorted by notions of equity. Also, it was no longer simply a matter of trying to plug a hole marked 'clearing bank': new holes would appear, and the Bank was running out of fingers. The Bank did not enjoy having to implement these controls or monitor their efficacy. An annotation of Cromer's to a memo discussing credit policy in

[197] Thornton, Note for record – 'Vauxhall & General Finance Corporation Limited', 16 July 1965, C40/1253.
[198] Keogh (Deputy Chief Cashier) to Morse, 'Credit control, 23 July 1965; J. N. R. Barber (Director of finance, Ford) to Morse, 26 July 1965; Morse to Barber, 18 August 1965, C40/1253.
[199] Hollom to Fforde, 'Ford Motor Credit', 30 September 1966; Keogh to Fforde, 'Ford Motor Credit Company, Ltd.', 20 October 1966, C40/1282.
[200] Morse to Thornton, 'Ford Motor Credit Company', 27 July 1965, C40/1253.
[201] Hollom to Morse/Cromer/O'Brien, 'Credit control', 9 September 1965, C40/1253.
[202] Hollom to Morse/Cromer/O'Brien, 'Banking sector credit', 3 November 1965; Morse to Cromer/O'Brien, 'The 105% limit', 3 November 1965, C40/1254.

the summer of 1965 commented, 'I trust the day will never come when the B of E assumes the responsibility of running the banks.'[203]

In June 1965, the Treasury decided that special deposits had been a 'comparative failure', and their 'epitaph may now have been written … as a primary or sole means of controlling credit', although they might still have a role if used in conjunction with a control on advances.[204] An internal committee, chaired by Morse, was established to set out, yet again, the Bank's views on credit control.[205] It began with Allen identifying four types of monetary action: psychological, credit rationing, control over the quantity of money, and operations on the structure of interest rates. Allen believed that psychology was important; rationing should be used sparingly for fear it would drive people away from banks and make control more difficult in the future. Radcliffe was used in support. Radcliffe had dismissed controlling the quantity of money and had stressed that it was the structure, rather than the level, of interest rates that mattered. Given Allen's rank, these views can be taken as a good indication of the Bank's line.[206]

In contrast to the Treasury, the Bank remained determinedly upbeat about special deposits, concluding that it was 'very probable' that the calls in 1960, 1961, and 1965 had kept the growth of advances below what it otherwise would have been. Nonetheless, it was conceded that their use was more effective when accompanied by a request not to sell investments.[207] It is hardly a surprise that the Bank thought the main impact to be psychological. Special deposits (and the imposition of liquidity ratios) represented an indirect control over asset ratios, but there was also the idea of a direct control through a 'private-sector credit' or 'lending' ratio. This idea had found some favour with Radcliffe, its main attraction being that it left little scope for banks to evade a squeeze by selling investments or resorting to commercial bills.[208] A suggestion that asset ratios also might be applied to finance houses found Allen dissenting: 'Why should we start particularising to the banking system just how much, and to whom, credit may be provided?' He had no quarrels with the technical merits of the conclusions, 'I merely regard them as misapplied.'[209] Morse highlighted the fact that the

---

[203] Cromer, Annotation, 4 August 1965, on Thornton to Morse/Allen/Cromer/O'Brien, 'Credit policy', 30 July 1965, C40/1253.
[204] HMT, 'Credit Control', June 1965, C40/1252.
[205] Hollom, Note for record – 'Credit control', 22 June 1965, C40/1252; Morse to Goldman, 5 July 1965, C40/1253.
[206] 'Note of meeting in Mr. Morse's room on 8 July', 9 July 1965, C40/1253.
[207] 'Credit control', 29 October 1965, C40/1254.
[208] Radcliffe, 'Report', para. 527.
[209] Allen to Cromer/O'Brien, 'Credit control', 10 November 1965, C40/1254.

private-sector lending ratio and the asset ratio control for finance houses were the only aspects that pointed to any major change in current policy.[210] Little then happened: ceilings continued to the fore, and further controls were applied during the sterling crisis in 1966.[211]

Towards the end of 1965, thoughts turned again to ceilings and the future of the 105 per cent limit. Morse felt that there was little option but to continue with a similar limit for the coming year and that that would be welcomed by the International Monetary Fund (IMF), and Cromer agreed.[212] Like Morse, McMahon thought that ceilings were unsatisfactory but argued that 'while we have got the policy, it is no use in shying away from making it effective.'[213] The CLCB were told in February 1966 that the ceiling would continue indefinitely.[214] Morse believed that it was working, and the Bank remained determined that the limit should be observed.[215] In May, there was even a suggestion that offenders should have to report to the Bank with weekly figures and explanations, but O'Brien had 'considerable doubt' about that, and Heasman thought that visits to the Parlours might be devalued if they were to assume a routine nature. Cromer added a characteristic reprimand: 'CCO [Chief Cashier's Office] should remember that the Banking system is not a Sunday School but a business.'[216]

One problem with this kind of control was that minor changes in policy could introduce distortions in liquidity needs. A case arose with the introduction of a selective employment tax (SET) in September 1966. There was a potential impact on the credit ceiling because company liquidity would come under pressure as the tax became due.[217] O'Brien advised Armstrong that it would be useful if there was an early statement to dispel any expectations that, in the context of SET, the ceiling would be relaxed.

[210] Morse to Cromer/O'Brien, 'Credit control', 1 November 1965, C40/1254.
[211] Morse to Rickett, 15 December 1965; HMT, Note of meeting on 3 February 1966, C40/1254. A Treasury note was sent to the Bank in May 1966 that elicited many scribbled comments but no formal response; HMT, 'A continuing system of credit control based on a private sector lending ratio', 23 May 1965, C40/1281.
[212] Morse to Cromer/O'Brien, 'The 105% limit', 3 November 1965, C40/1254.
[213] McMahon to Morse, 'Credit restraint in 1966/67', 3 January 1966, C40/1254.
[214] Cromer to Thomson, 1 February 1966; C40/1254.
[215] Morse to Cromer/O'Brien, 'Possible tightening of credit squeeze', 29 April 1966, enc. Wood (EID), 'The clearing banks and 105', 29 April 1966, C40/1282; Extract of CLCB minutes, 5 May 1966.
[216] Cromer annotation on Heasman to Morse/Allen/Cromer/O'Brien, 'The banks and the 105% ceiling', 20 May 1966, C40/1281.
[217] Price (1978, pp. 150–151); Hollom to Morse/Cromer/O'Brien, 'The C.L.C.B. and the credit squeeze', 4 May 1966; Morse to Cromer/O'Brien, 'Adjustment of the credit ceiling for S.E.T.', 17 June 1966; 'Extract from Mr. Hollom's memo dated 1.7.66 ...', C40/1281.

Callaghan announced in the Commons that there would be no offset for the tax, and the advances ceiling was to remain in place until March 1967.[218] Two days later, with sterling once again under pressure, Bank Rate was raised to 7 per cent, the fourth time since 1957 that this 'crisis' level had been reached, although on this occasion the shock value was perhaps diminished because it was a 1 per cent rather than a 2 per cent step. At the same time, there was a further call for special deposits, again 1 per cent and ½ per cent, taking the totals for the English and Scottish clearing banks to 2 and 1 per cent, respectively. The following week, Wilson announced a deflationary package in the Commons.

In 1966, the Bank for the first time lent money overnight to the discount market, a technique that had been proposed originally by the LDMA in 1960 as a way of easing conditions in the money market. Hollom believed it had a 'superficial attraction' where shortages of money were in prospect and there were no bills of close maturity available for the Bank to buy in. On the other hand, it would be taken as a signal that a shortage was expected, and rates would move in the light of this 'advice'. If the anticipated shortage did not materialise, and Hollom pointed out that conditions in the money market were not entirely predictable, then 'confusion and recrimination' might result. Thus, while he thought it could introduce an 'undesirable ambiguity' into market operations and that it was 'not really a suitable technique for everyday use', he did suggest that it could be tried for the half-year and year ends (30 June and 31 December) and possibly extended if the experience was satisfactory.[219] O'Brien liked the idea of greater flexibility and added that 'the management of the market with elegance and finesse should be a matter of pride with us.' This was a determinedly old-style Bank view, but O'Brien also warned against complacency and wanted to encourage 'intelligent innovation'; thus overnight lending held some attraction.[220] On 21 and 22 June 1966, the market was forced to borrow for seven days because the Bank wanted to see some hardening of the Treasury bill rate. Then on 30 June the Bank allowed overnight borrowing. As intended, this was supposed to combat distortions common at the end of the half-year. However, it was not long before the Bank was regularly forcing overnight borrowing at

---

[218] Thornton to Fforde/Hollom/O'Brien/Parsons, 'Selective employment tax and the 105% ceiling', 4 July 1966; Allen to O'Brien/Parsons, 'Selective employment tax', 4 July 1966; O'Brien to Armstrong, 7 July 1966, C40/1281; HC Deb, 12 July 1966, Vol. 731, c1198.

[219] Hollom to Morse/Cromer/O'Brien, 'Money market operations', 15 March 1966, C40/1466.

[220] O'Brien, 'Money market', nd but draft dated 21 March 1966, C40/1466.

Bank Rate in order to ensure that money remained tight and short-term rates high.

Difficulties of keeping within the 105 per cent brought increasing tensions. A Bank press notice, heavily pruned by the Treasury to remove references to the Chancellor's previous utterances on the subject, emphasised both the need for restraint and the need to meet priority borrowing.[221] Callaghan then contradicted this in answering questions in the Commons. This necessitated a hastily arranged meeting with the CLCB and the Governor at which Callaghan explained that the original statement took precedence over an unprepared response made in the heat of a parliamentary occasion.[222] Then the September 1966 figures for advances, down by £90 million (seasonally adjusted), raised anxieties that the squeeze was too drastic.[223] In October and November, these discussions went on, with Treasury interference and commercial bank dismay. Cromer had gone and with him his dictum that banking was a business, and relations between the Bank and the Treasury suffered further.

All this served to highlight what a crude instrument of policy the imposition of ceilings was. At one point the Bank found itself adjudicating on the plight of Guernsey's tomato growers and hoteliers, a measure of how far action had drifted from what might be considered conventional monetary policy.[224] Fforde deprecated such interference: 'The Chancellor and other Ministers may be under the impression that they can sit around a table and decide to allow so much money for this industry and so much for that', but it was 'impossible to achieve such a degree of selectivity'.[225] Yet Fforde still held to ceilings and argued that their occasional use could never be fully renounced; when a 'firm clampdown' on bank lending was required, 'nothing is so good – so effective, so simple, so easily understood – as a ceiling'.[226] But this was only the case for short periods, perhaps a year at a time, after which their operation became problematic. How, then, could

---

[221] CLCB, 'Note of a meeting held at the Bank of England at 3:00 p.m. on Wednesday, 27 July, 1966', C40/1281; Wood, Note for record – '105%: meeting with the clearing banks 27.7.66', 3 August 1966; Fforde to O'Brien, 'Draft press notice about credit restriction', 8 August 1966; Bank of England, Press announcement, 9 August 1966, C40/1282.

[222] Roger Lavelle (HMT) to Hugh Harris (Governor's secretariat), 15 August 1966, enc.losing Lavelle, 'Record of meeting ... 11th August', 15 August 1966, C40/1282.

[223] Thornton, Note for record – 'Clearing bank advances – September 1966'; 'Extract of Deputy Governor's memo on a conversation with Mr. Goldman, dated 28.9.66', C40/1282.

[224] F. J. Roper (EID) to Thornton, 'Guernsey: credit restriction'; Thornton to Lovell (HMT), 28 November 1966, C40/1283.

[225] Fforde to O'Brien/Parsons/Allen/Hollom, 'Possible relaxation of restrictions on bank credit', 17 October 1966, C40/1282.

[226] 'Credit control after the 105% ceiling', 12 January 1967, C40/1283.

credit be regulated when ceilings were removed? Fforde took it as read that special deposits provided the answer in the case of the clearers, so the issue was to devise an arrangement for the others. When special deposits had been unveiled in 1958, the option of widening their coverage had been left open. Now it was concluded that the arrangements should be extended to the non-clearing banks. In this instance, Fforde envisaged that special deposits would be used without any formal minimum liquidity ratio, but an understanding would be necessary with the banks on their lending. He believed that this would give the Bank all the influence it required because of the penalty of reduced income that would be inflicted; that is, the rate paid on special deposits would be less, possibly substantially less, than the marginal rate these banks earned on liquid assets in the form of local authority temporary money. He felt that these other banks would accept the proposal because it was free of complicated formulae, and their eagerness to see the end of ceilings would bring a co-operative attitude to negotiations.[227]

There were some qualms. One was that the penalty of reduced income was a new concept for special deposits, and it would make it 'a very different animal' from the scheme levied on clearing banks, which was supposed to draw off excess liquidity.[228] To use the term 'special deposits' for what was really a different scheme would mislead and confuse public opinion, and he suggested that the scheme might have to be modified into a cash-ratio or reserve-requirement scheme.[229] However, the Treasury was receptive to the idea, going as far as to alter its 1965 view that special deposits were a failure; indeed, it had gone 'overboard' in Hollom's opinion.[230]

The Chancellor then decided that he wanted to announce the abandonment of the 105 per cent limit in the budget.[231] A key point was that special deposits would no longer have a 'sensational significance' and that under the new arrangements, 'the signals of the authorities would be less dramatic but more frequent.'[232] In the April budget, Callaghan announced that while there was to be no change in the guidance on lending, the 105 per cent limit was forthwith being removed for the London and Scottish clearing

[227] Hollom to Rickett, 3 February 1967, enc. 'Credit control after the ceiling', 3 February 1967, C40/1283.

[228] Heasman to O'Brien/Allen/Hollom, 'Credit control after the 105% ceiling (the Chief Cashier's memorandum of 12th January)', 13 January 1967, C40/1284.

[229] Hollom, Note for record – 'Credit control after the ceiling', 13 February 1967, C40/1283.

[230] Rickett to Hollom, 16 March 1967; Hollom to O'Brien, 20 March 1967; Fforde to O'Brien/Parsons, 'Credit control', 21 March 1967, C40/1284.

[231] Goldman to Armstrong, 'Credit policy after the ceiling', 30 March 1967, copy in C40/1284.

[232] Lavelle, 'Record of a meeting … 4th April 1967 …', 6 April 1967, C40/1284.

banks. In the future, special deposits would be used in a 'new and more flex-ible manner', and a call 'should no longer be regarded as a crisis measure, but as a routine adjustment to conditions as they develop'. Other banking institutions would continue to be subject to the 105 per cent ceiling until new arrangements for securing restraint had been developed. As for finance houses, they presented a special problem, so ceilings might be required for a longer period while this was examined.[233] Callaghan's budget was neutral and intended to show that the economy was back on track in the first quar-ter of 1967. Indeed, balance-of-payments forecasts also were encouraging, and against this background, Bank Rate was lowered in January, March, and May 1967, on each occasion by ½ per cent, leaving it at 5½ per cent. All this proved to be yet another false dawn.

In the summer of 1965, Hollom had pointed out that since the most recent long tap (5¾% Funding 1987/91) had run out in January 1965, operations had been conducted by the use of other than tap stocks in the Issue Department portfolio. He argued that the means of controlling upward movements at the longer end of the market were now 'extremely limited'. In pressing for a new long tap, he noted that if jobbers were left without access to a reserve of tap stock, this could result in 'frustration and depression' for dealers and a contraction in the number of jobbing firms, which could 'permanently damage the market's structure'. In addition, recent experience had shown that short bursts of institutional demand for long and undated stocks led to 'exaggerated price movements and mark-edly wider quotations'. Furthermore, it was necessary to take advantage of any opportunity for funding that circumstances allowed. Hollom referred to the undertaking given to the IMF to limit the increase in clearing bank deposits over the year to March 1966 to 5 per cent and emphasised that 'every effort should be made to maximise sales of Government stock to non-bank holders.'[234]

From this evidence and the other files on new issues in the remainder of the period, we see the approaches of successive Chief Cashiers towards the gilt-edged market: O'Brien, uncomplicated and pragmatic; Hollom's, measured caution; Fforde's, lengthy speculations and fear of loss of con-trol. The essential message that emerges, though, is the same: control of the long-dated end of the market, encouraging where necessary, dampening were necessary, selling on gently rising markets where this could be brought

---

[233] HC Deb, 11 April 1967, Vol. 744, cc1000–1001. The details were confirmed by the Bank at the same time; Bank of England, 'Credit restraint in 1967/68', 11 April 1967, C40/1284.

[234] Hollom to Morse/Cromer/O'Brien, 'The case for a new long-dated Government issue', 31 August 1965, 5A44/40.

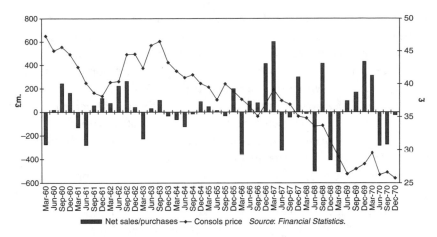

Figure 6.3. Gilt-edged net quarterly sales/purchases and consols price, 1960–70.

about, and no behaviour untoward or out of line. Above all, severe fluctuations were to be avoided. Protecting the gilt-edged market and ensuring
order were paramount.

So what was the outcome? Net quarterly sales/purchases of gilt-edged
stock during the 1960s are shown in Figure 6.3, together with the price
of consols. This confirms that sales generally were made when the market was rising. The most successful period, from this point of view, was
from mid-1961 until September 1963, when there were net sales in eight
of nine quarters. Substantial sales also were achieved at the end of 1966
and the beginning of 1967. In total, between 1960 and 1967, net sales were
£1.2 billion despite the fact that the overall trend was for prices to fall quite
steeply. Over the decade, there were net purchases from the banks of £644
million, while net sales to the non-bank sector totalled £1.6 billion. This
gives an overall net sales figure of £961 million in favour of the non-bank
sector. Of 25 new issues that were made between 1958 and 1967, only one,
a small issue of a short in October 1962, was fully subscribed, whereas a
couple of other shorts also attracted market interest. 90 per cent or more of
each long-dated stock that was issued ended up in the Issue Department.
The total of all these new issues was £10.6 billion; redemptions over the
same period were £9.8 billion.

Radcliffe noted that in the post-war period, 'the dominant motive of the
authorities in the management of the debt has been the desire to "fund",
i.e., to lengthen the average life of the securities outstanding.'[235] The Report

[235] Radcliffe, 'Report', para. 533.

provided some evidence of the maturity structure of gilt-edged securities. In the mid-1930s, 86 per cent of government securities were either undated or had more than 15 years to run until maturity. This figure had fallen to 63 per cent in 1952 and 49 per cent in 1958. By contrast, bonds of less than five years had grown from 3 per cent in the 1930s to 21 per cent at the time of Radcliffe, whereas medium stocks then formed 30 per cent of the total. The Report recognised that the huge supply of short bonds, a wartime legacy, had been a 'constant source of embarrassment to the authorities' and went on to reiterate the importance of funding.[236] No explicit data on the average age of the debt were given, but a year after publication of the Radcliffe Report the Chief Cashier's Office made a startling admission about the average length of the debt. Despite all the efforts to increase it, it had 'decreased from 14.2 to 12.7 years over the period 31 March 1953 to 31 March 1960'.[237] Thereafter, there was no improvement, and the average life to maturity remained close to 12 to 13 years.[238]

The Bank's position in the market had gradually become more interventionist. In early 1964, Hollom admitted, 'We have gradually come to be the lynchpin round which the market works'. When the Bank was out of the market, the jobbers lacked the 'reassuring guide to prices and turnover which our activities provide despite the fact that we may be intent on following, not leading, the market'. As a consequence, 'the market easily becomes lost and uncertain; momentum may then not be readily be regained'.[239] He expressed similar sentiments in 1965 when he wrote that the development of the market in recent years owed a good deal to the 'readiness of Issue to act as jobbers of last resort'.[240] Over the next few years, the degree of intervention used with the intention of protecting the marketability of gilts would increase further. That this may have then gone too far was to be conceded by the Bank when policy was changed under CCC.

Operations and tactics in the money markets are more difficult to discern. At core, the money markets catered for the residual financial needs of government. The day-to-day shortfall between receipts and payments would be covered by an issue of Treasury bills, and in order to make Bank Rate effective, the authorities would create a slight shortage in the market. The

[236] *Ibid.*, para. 549 and table 26.
[237] 'The gilt-edged market', 20 September 1960, C42/13. The same exercise was attempted in the United States under the name of 'Operation Twist'.
[238] This trend continued in the 1970s, with the exception of 1973, when the figure jumped to 14.5. Downton (1977, p. 320); Wormell (1985, p. 18).
[239] Hollom to Cromer/Mynors, 20 January 1964, C40/1170.
[240] Hollom to Morse/Cromer/O'Brien, 'The case for a new long-dated Government issue', 31 August 1965, 5A44/40.

discount houses could always get cash from the Bank, but at a penal rate. Some aspects of money-market operations were covered in the commentaries in the *Bulletin,* and these can be taken as evidence of how the Bank pursued its desire for an orderly market. They were only partially illuminating, as might be expected given that they were published, and in many cases the narrative amounts to little more than what had happened to bill rates. Occasionally, the files offer insights into what was happening. For example, in the winter of 1966–67, a sharp reduction in the amount of bills offered at the weekly tender coincided with increased competition between the discount market and the outside tenderers. Against this background, the Bank had experienced some problems in its daily market operations. To halt a fall in money rates, the Bank found it necessary to 'indulge in penal lending on an heroic scale'. Fforde later voiced his 'distaste' that this experience might be repeated the following winter, as did James Keogh, who had taken over from Clarke as Principal of the Discount Office.[241] Frustratingly, the trail goes cold. Neither do data on the Bank's intervention in the money markets present a clear picture. Figure 6.4 shows the amounts each month, the frequency of intervention, and the yearly totals. The greatest intervention, both in frequency and amount, was through the purchase of Treasury bills. And these activities both increased to the end of 1967. The absorption of surplus cash through selling Treasury bills was not so common, less than once a week, although, again, the total amount did grow. Treasury bills were central to the Bank's operations in the money market and were the means of creating or relieving shortages of cash. With so much going on in the market, however, it is impossible to draw much from the data, even where available daily. Assistance in the form of advances at or above Bank Rate also presents a fluctuating picture. What is most notable is that in 1964, apart from a small number of advances to meet the needs of midyear balance sheets, there was no lending in this form at all. The same was true in the early part of 1966. The use of overnight lending, as opposed to advances, from 1966 is also apparent. Again, it is hard to discern much about market tactics from these aggregate-level data, and it was another of these things that was not written down.

New Techniques: The Cash Deposits Scheme

The remaining issue in the 1960s was how to extend control to the 'other' banks. When Callaghan announced in his 1967 budget that there would

---

[241] Fforde to Keogh/Page, 'Treasury Bills', 24 November 1967; Keogh to Page/Fforde, 'Treasury Bills', 4 December 1967, C40/1466.

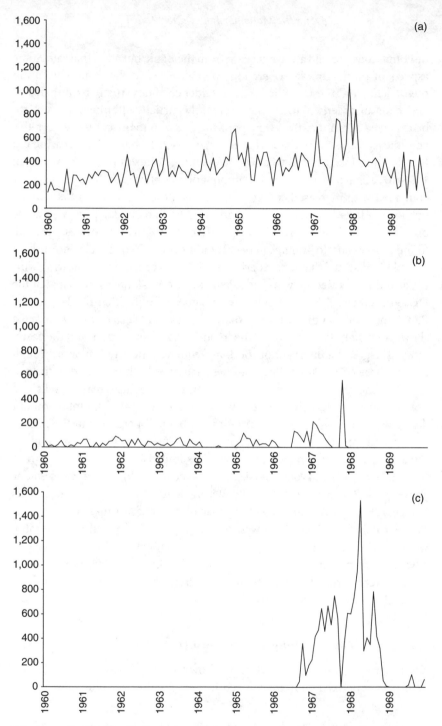

Figure 6.4. Bank of England intervention in the money market, 1960–69 (£m), (a) purchase of Treasury Bills; (b) advances at or above Bank Rate; (c) other advances.

be new arrangements to control these other banks, it was little more than a general idea. But Fforde went to work on a scheme and was soon circulating a paper that had the typically prolix but undeniably informative title: 'Proposals for New Arrangements to Secure a More Effective Official Influence over Bank Lending to Customers in the U.K. Private Sector and Overseas, in Situations Where a Degree of Restraint Is Required but Where the Imposition of a Rigid Quantitative Ceiling Is Not Necessary.'[242] By mid-May, it was simply called 'The Control of Bank Lending.'[243] It was, in essence, a cash/deposit scheme, and questions addressed included which banks to cover, whether the deposits should bear interest, and to what these deposits should be related: liabilities or assets. The latter had the attraction that it would allow the weapon to be related directly to the object of restraint. On the other hand, given the diverse nature of the banks in question, targeting assets could prove inequitable, and that led Fforde to favour deposits.

The new scheme was designed to secure a degree of official influence over other banks because their importance had increased since the scheme for special deposits was originally conceived in 1958. Lending had risen from £200 million to £800 million and accounted for 20 per cent of the growth in the entire banking sector. It might have been added that this was in part a reaction to controls. As to coverage, in the absence of a definition of a bank, it was proposed that the scheme should apply to the 125 institutions, other than clearing banks, recognised as banks for the purpose of banking statistics. An overriding factor was that the scheme should be straightforward and fair, and the Bank had concluded that this could best be achieved through 'a system of mandatory but variable Cash Deposits to be placed by the other banks with the Bank of England'. Like special deposits, the new scheme would relate to the banks' deposit liabilities. However, unlike special deposits, which the paper described as an 'asset freezer', cash deposits were to be an 'earnings squeezer'. Therefore, rather than pay a rate of interest, such as the Treasury bill rate that special deposits attracted, the rate on cash deposits had to carry 'a significant interest penalty'. Allen had argued for a zero rate, but others thought that half Bank Rate was better. This was the threat, but it was argued that because cash deposits were potentially more painful than special deposits, it would be important that the authorities issued clear and unambiguous guidance about their objectives for credit policy.

---

[242] Fforde to Parsons/Allen/Hollom, 13 April 1967, 5A171/1.
[243] Bank of England, 'The control of bank lending', 19 May 1967, 5A171/1.

The banks ought not to be penalised for doing something that they did not know was wrong.[244]

An initial round of consultations followed and was completed in September. The first lesson Hollom drew from the exercise was that 'we seriously under-estimated the difficulty of communicating a novel idea to them' and that in the future greater efforts should be made to ensure understanding. Many took it as an unwarranted attack on profits. This aside, the main point to emerge was that most of the banks would prefer something that acted on assets rather than deposits, yet Hollom and Fforde remained convinced of the superior-ity of a deposit-based scheme.[245] Fortunately, the Bank did not have to press the issue because the dissenters fell into line.[246] The findings of the consulta-tion process were conveyed to the Treasury at the end of October 1967, by which time the more pressing issue was devaluation.[247] As part of the pack-age of emergency economic measures, ceilings for the clearing banks were re-imposed: total sterling lending had to be held down to the level reached on 15 November 1967 (i.e., a ceiling of 100 per cent). Identifiable finance for export transactions was given an exemption, although this brought an additional administrative burden in the form of a monthly return detailing exempt lending.[248] There was no end date for the new ceiling.

It was several months before the Treasury sent a formal response to the Bank's letter of October 1967 on cash deposits. This was, as Goldman understatedly put it, 'owing to the change of Chancellor and the pressure of other events'.[249] Nonetheless, the Treasury accepted the ideas, and the Bank was authorised to consult again on the amended plans; by April, Page (First Deputy Chief Cashier) considered that the Bank was in a posi-tion to publicise the scheme, and this was done in the June 1968 issue of the *Bulletin*.[250] As formulated, cash deposits were a typical Bank device.

---

[244] *Ibid.*

[245] For material relating to the consultations, see 5A171/2; Wood to de Moubray/Hollom, 'Cash deposits', 5 September 1967, 5A171/2; Hollom to O'Brien, 'Credit control over "outside" banks', 15 September 1967, 5A171/3.

[246] John Read (Deputy Chairman, BOCBA) to O'Brien, 11 September 1967; Hollom, Note for record – 'Control of bank lending', 20 October 1967,

[247] Hollom to Goldman, 27 October 1967, 5A171/3.

[248] Bank of England, Notice on 'Credit restriction', 19 November 1967; O'Brien to Stirling (CLCB) and others, 19 November 1967; Hollom to various banks (over 40 in total), 19 November 1967, C40/1291.

[249] Goldman to Hollom, 25 January 1968, 5A171/3.

[250] Letter, 8 February 1968 in 5A171/3. Page to Fforde/Hollom/O'Brien/Parson, 'The cash deposits scheme', 3 April 1968, 5A171/4; Bank of England, 'Control of bank lending: the cash deposits scheme', *BEQB* 8(2):166–170, June 1969; copies of the article also were sent to the banks; see Letters in 5A171/4.

Evolutionary in nature and built on existing mechanisms, no major over-haul was required, legislation was avoided, and 'bank' did not have to be defined. And the whole scheme was developed in co-operation and consul-tation with the banking sector. As with special deposits, it was not perhaps entirely clear how the new instrument would work, and their impact cannot be assessed because the scheme was never put into operation. The economic situation was such that the scheme was shelved and ceilings were to remain in use for far longer than the maximum of one year that Fforde had thought desirable. There was no mention made in any of the discussion on the sub-stantial profits such a scheme would produce for the Bank, and that at a time when their surpluses were 'embarrassing'.

In the 1960s, following Radcliffe, there was considerable confusion as to what monetary policy was, what it could achieve, and how it might be implemented. The authorities had difficulty seeing beyond the use of direct controls. Bank Rate was reserved essentially for external purposes. For domestic purposes, there was little agreement over the efficacy of the tools available. For example, how the newly designed control technique, special deposits (which were supposed to replace existing controls), was expected to work was not set down and nowhere explained. Was it meant to work on the liquidity ratio or on the cash-reserve ratio or simply be an indicator – another psychological weapon? The aim was never precisely stated, and it was not long before its effectiveness was being questioned. And despite it being supposed to replace other controls, it was not long before the other controls were re-imposed and continued to be used. There was also a return to an examination of liquidity ratios, and they were changed. The Bank's operations in the money market were handicapped by their lack of belief in or their reluctance to use interest rates as was necessary. The main objective was to finance the daily needs of government and to leave the market short of funds. However, the right of the discount houses to get the necessary cash from the Bank left open the rate at which it could do that and left open the possibility that the penal rate might be too low. The Bank's operations in the gilt market frequently left the market confused. The Bank did have a substantial task in ensuring that the exchequer's needs were met smoothly and without interruption. In order to do this, it set out to make the market sufficiently attractive to investors, and that meant assuring them of ready sales at close to market prices. It therefore aimed for 'orderly' markets, although this was never defined. In seeking order, the Bank tried to influ-ence expectations and engaged in psychological warfare. It gave dark hints and by a variety of means nudged or indicated or otherwise tried to suggest the outcome it wanted. The coded messages, however, frequently baffled market participants. At a seminar held in the Bank in 2006 on the working of the 'old' gilt market, the Bank explained what it was trying to achieve, and market participants from the 1960s and 1970s revealed that they now understood for the first time.[251]

Given the varied and often vague objectives being pursued by a variety of means, it is difficult to say how much was achieved. Inflation certainly was not dealt with, and that was reflected in rising long rates and collapsing gilt prices. While there was extensive discussion on most of the possibilities and an openness of mind was demonstrated, these in themselves produced further problems in so far as there were frequent changes of mind leading to confusion outside. All this was to continue into the 1970s. And all the while the principal problem was the failure to use interest rates. It might be useful to remind readers that at the morning meeting of the Governor, called 'Books', business matters and tactics were discussed; it was an extremely important meeting. But no records were kept.

---

[251] 'The old Gilt-edged market', witness seminar, 22 March 2006 www.lombardstreetresearch. com/witness_seminars/2006_gilt-edged.html (accessed 13 November 2009).

Plate 1. Cameron Cobbold (Governor 1949–61) in 1959.

Plate 2. Humphrey Mynors (Deputy Governor 1954–64).

Plate 3. The Bank of England, Head Office, Threadneedle Street, in the mid-1950s.

Plate 4. The Earl of Cromer (Governor 1961–66) arrives at the Bank in 1961, with senior Gatekeeper at the entrance.

Plate 5. Leslie O'Brien (Governor 1966–73) when an Executive Director in 1963.

Plate 6. Maurice Parsons (Deputy Governor 1966–70).

Plate 7. Roy Bridge, pictured when Assistant to the Governors (1965–69).

Plate 8. The Bank of England Printing Works, Debden.

Plate 9. Jasper Hollom (Deputy Governor 1970–80) when Chief Cashier in 1962.

Plate 10. John Fforde as Chief Cashier in 1966.

Plate 11. Jeremy Morse (Executive Director 1965–72).

Plate 12. The Bank's New Change building.

Plate 13. Sorting bills at the weekly Treasury bill tender.

7

Other Activities and Performance

In the 1950s and 1960s, the Bank performed a number of functions that would no longer be considered central bank business and might even baffle a student of modern central banking. For example, a legacy of the interwar years, it continued to participate in organising and, on occasion, supplying industrial finance. It also took a keen interest in anything that affected the City; it oversaw all merger activity. It became heavily engaged in anything it felt was for the greater good of central banking and spent time and money on promoting central banking abroad. In addition, it had direct responsibility for a range of things such as note issue, and it frequently would be called on to give advice, often extensive in its coverage, on subjects such as decimalisation. This chapter describes its activities in some of these fields and concludes with an assessment of the Bank's financial position at the end of the 1960s. The results of other assessments, one by management consultants that the Bank appointed and the other by a select committee to which they agreed to submit, are also noted.

Industrial Finance

The Bank had been closely involved in the financing of industry from the 1920s. Montagu Norman had engaged in it as one way of deflecting interference from the state, and then, following the Macmillan Report, the Bank established an Industrial Finance Division that continued until late in the twentieth century. Immediately after the Second World War, a number of initiatives was taken with a view to enhancing the access to finance for different kinds of users and resulting in a confusion of acronyms. In most of these the Bank played an enthusiastic role, taking equity stakes in several bodies, as well as making loans at low rates of interest and providing other kinds of support.[1]

[1]   Sayers (1976, pp. 314–331).

The Commonwealth Development Finance Company (CDFC) was established in 1953 with the object of using private-sector funds to promote projects in developing countries within the Commonwealth, particularly where this might strengthen the sterling area's balance of payments.[2] The initial authorised capital was £15 million (increased to £30 million in 1959), with the shares held by various industrial, commercial, mining, shipping, and financial concerns. But the Bank was the major shareholder; it had made an outlay of £3.4 million by 1956, and an additional £2.1 million was paid when the capital was increased. Predictably, CDFC's *Annual Reports* wrote in glowing terms of its achievements, but the Bank was never very impressed with the running of the organisation. In 1963, Hollom declared performance to be 'modestly respectable rather than inspiring', scarcely a ringing endorsement.[3] Two years later, with the company's finances in an 'awkward muddle', Hollom found it hard to be sympathetic with a company whose financial performance 'has been a very poor advertisement for private enterprise'. Over the course of 13 years CDFC had paid only two dividends and had built up a reserve of just over £1 million.[4] The main concern was that it was too cautious and always seemed to look to the Bank to raise its capital. Such suggestions were rejected. In 1964, O'Brien told the company that it had been given an easy 10-year ride and that he saw no reason for the Bank to spoon-feed CDFC indefinitely, although they were still saying the same thing three years later.[5]

One of the main problems was senior management. The chairman, Frederick Godber (later Lord Godber of Mayfield) had been at the Head of CDFC since its inception. Well known for his achievements in the petroleum industry, Godber was less dynamic at CDFC. In any case, he was well into his seventies. The Managing Director since 1956 was Stanley Hoar. Although once Deputy Principal of the Overseas and Foreign Office at the Bank, he did not appear to inspire confidence in his former employers.[6] Godber and Hoar both stepped down in 1968. Typically, George Bolton, the

[2] 'The Commonwealth Development Finance Company', *Reserve Bank of New Zealand Bulletin,* July 1959; 'Memorandum to the board of directors: finance for development within the commonwealth', 21 December 1960, C40/565.

[3] Hollom to O'Brien 'C.D.C./C.D.F.C.', 16 August 1963, C40/1179.

[4] Hollom to Bailey, 'C.D.F.C.', 27 October 1965, C40/1601.

[5] Dudley Allen to Hollom, 'C.D.F.C.', 22 January 1964, C40/1179; G. L. Wheatley to Hollom, 'C.D.F.C. – financing', 10 August 1965, C40/1601; Colin Condren to Andrews, 'C.D.F.C. dividends', 9 November 1967; Andrews to Bailey, 'C.D.F.C. dividends', 13 November 1967, C40/1602.

[6] Hoar left the Bank in 1946 and went to the International Bank before joining the CDFC in 1955; Godber to members of CDFC, 14 February 1956, C40/559.

new chairman, immediately injected a sense of urgency into CDFC. Plans were drawn up for a strategy that would increase the corporation's activities both inside and outside the Commonwealth, attempt to raise foreign-exchange resources in association with German and Swiss partners, and might even take a new name. In outlining these ideas to O'Brien, Bolton warned that the only realistic alternative that he could see was liquidation.[7] However, after all the complaints about CDFC's undue caution, the Bank now found these proposals 'too radical'.[8] Eventually, in March 1969, O'Brien told Bolton that there could be some enlargement in the company's scope but that this should not go against the government's exchange policies. Shortly afterwards, it was confirmed that CDFC would widen its field to other countries, including the nonsterling area, and that there would now be greater emphasis on equity rather than loan capital.[9] Nevertheless, it was not long before the Bank again had to help the CDFC; in 1970, a loan of £1.25 million, at 3 per cent per annum for five years, was agreed. This was when Bank Rate was 7 per cent, and the commercial 'blue chip' lending rate was 1 per cent above this.[10]

The origins of both the Finance Corporation for Industry (FCI) and the Industrial and Commercial Finance Corporation (ICFC) can be found in Norman's final months as Governor, when he gave much thought to how, in the post-war period, industry should be re-built.[11] The Bank played 'a central role within a group of interests which determined the form which ICFC and FCI took in 1945'.[12] Both were established with the objective of providing finance to companies who found it difficult or impossible to raise money through normal commercial channels.[13] As it transpired, FCI became associated primarily with financing for the steel industry. Its authorised share capital was £25 million, with the Bank subscrib-ing 30 per cent, and the rest being taken by insurance companies and

---

[7] Dudley Allen to Fforde/Bailey/Parsons, 'C.D.F.C.: new policies', 26 June 1968; Bolton to O'Brien, 4 July 1968, C40/1602.

[8] Dudley Allen to Fforde/Parson, 'C.D.F.C.: new approaches', 12 July 1968, C40/1602.

[9] O'Brien to Bolton, 19 March 1969; CDFC, 'To all shareholders', 22 April 1969; CDFC, *Report and Accounts*, year ending 31 March 1969, C40/1603.

[10] The loan was to enable the company to meet potential losses arising out of non-repayment of loans to the Central Africa Power Corporation in Rhodesia. Page to Fforde/O'Brien, 'C.D.F.C.: Rhodesia', 6 October 1970; Page to Berkoff (MD, CDFC), 16 October 1970, C40/1604; Cawley to Mayes, 'Commonwealth Development Finance Corporation', 19 September 1977, C40/1608.

[11] Fforde (1992, pp. 704–727).

[12] Coopey and Clarke (1995, p. 13).

[13] *The Financial Times*, 27 June 1959, p. 5.

investment trusts. Paid-up capital was £500,000, so the Bank's share was £150,000.[14] A capitalisation of reserves in 1968 raised the total paid-up capital to £2.5 million and increased the value of the Bank's holding to £750,000.

While the Bank had been reluctant to assist CDFC, it proved to be far more generous in the case of FCI. After financial difficulties in 1957 and into 1958, a three-stage agreement was struck in August 1958. First, £5 million was paid in advance of a call on the Bank's shareholding. Provided that any dividend paid did not exceed 6 per cent, the £5 million would be free of interest for a period of five years (worth approximately £1 million). Second, FCI could draw on a Bank advance of a further £5 million once total advances from other lending banks exceeded £50 million, on the basis of £1 for every £5 clearing-bank money. This gave a total lending limit of £80 million (£50 million + £25 million from the clearers and £5 million from the Bank). The Bank's loan was treated as an ordinary advance of the Banking Department and subject to Bank Rate plus ½ per cent with a minimum of 4 per cent. The same terms were applied by the clearing banks. Finally, provision was made for another £5 million of emergency lending, related to the possible future needs of the steel industry.[15] After Mynors retired as Deputy Governor, he took over as chairman of FCI. He was later to express his irritation with the Bank's £5 million loan, which he saw as 'a constant reminder of a last-ditch rescue operation without which we would probably not have survived'.[16] What remains unclear, though, is why the Bank thought it necessary to intervene.

In the mid-1960s, steel re-nationalisation had returned to the political agenda, and the uncertainty surrounding it apparently made it difficult for the privately owned steel companies to raise finance in the market. Mynors pointed this out to O'Brien in September 1965 and suggested that FCI's current lending limit of £80 million might be insufficient to meet this demand. He asked whether the £5 million provision for steel contained in the 1958 agreement was still available. O'Brien wrote on top of the letter, 'I guess we shall wish to be helpful.'[17] Mynors also had approached the clearing

---

[14] Piercy, 'Memorandum for the Governor from Lord Piercy: a short note on I.C.F.C', 16 August 1961, C40/532.

[15] Agreement between FCI and Bank of England, 12 August 1958; O'Brien to Hawker/Cobbold/Mynors, 'Finance Corporation for Industry Limited', 16 September 1958, C40/536.

[16] Kinross, 'FCI and the Bank of England: the crisis of 1958', 18 February 1980, NLS 8699/3; cited in Coopey and Clarke (1995, p. 107).

[17] Mynors to O'Brien, 23 September 1965, C40/1173.

banks, and they agreed to increase their lending by £10 million subject to matching funding by the Bank. This was forthcoming, thus increasing FCI's lending limit to a total of £100 million (£85 million from the clearers, £15 million from the Bank).[18] In fact, the £10 million facility with the Bank was not utilised.

Steel re-nationalisation clearly presented problems for FCI because it lost its main source of business; the steel industry accounted for 57 per cent of the corporation's loans outstanding.[19] In his chairman's speech to the annual general meeting (AGM) in June 1968, Mynors was cautious about the future prospects for FCI; by the end of the year, he was highly pessimistic. He confided privately to O'Brien that 'after nearly five years I do not see how FCI can go on as it is.... the staff may sit for weeks, even months, on end with nothing really to do.'[20] This marked the beginning of talks over the future of FCI that culminated in a merger with ICFC to form Finance for Industry in 1973 (see Chapter 15).

ICFC was set up to provide finance assistance for the expansion or development of small and medium-sized industrial and commercial concerns.[21] The intention was that it would 'supplement, but not supersede, the activities of other lenders and financial institutions'.[22] ICFC financed shipbuilding as well as technological developments and the leasing of plant and equipment: from a minimum of £5,000 to a maximum of £300,000. The Bank subscribed £500,000, 3 per cent of the total share capital of £15 million. The remainder was undertaken by the clearing banks (86 per cent) and the Scottish banks (11 per cent).[23] In 1962, the share capital was increased to £20 million and 167 of the new £1,000 shares were allotted to the Bank. Further shares were allotted to the Bank in 1964 when the share capital increased to £22.5 million, and by 1966, the Bank held £1.2 million of the £40 million share capital. ICFC also had loan capital of £22.5 million, with the Bank initially holding £750,000, which was then increased to £1 million

---

[18] Hollom to Morse/O'Brien, 'Finance Corporation for Industry', 30 September 1965; 'Extract from minutes of meeting of Committee of London Clearing Bankers held on the 7 October 1965'; O'Brien, Note for record – 'F.C.I.', 7 October 1965; Cromer to Mynors, 14 October 1965, C40/1173.

[19] Coopey and Clarke (1995, p. 108) gives the figures as £56 million out of £99 million.

[20] FCI, 'Chairman's speech at the twenty-third annual general meeting held on Wednesday, 26 June, 1968'; Mynors to O'Brien, 24 December 1968, C40/1423.

[21] Thornton, 'Industrial and Commercial Finance Corporation Limited: historical material for the Deputy Governor's speech at the 21st anniversary dinner', 9 September 1966, C40/1172.

[22] Keogh to Crick/Lambert, 'F.C.I. and I.C.F.C.', 29 May 1958, C40/532.

[23] Lord Piercy, 'A short note on ICFC', August 1961, enc. with Piercy to Cromer, 16 August 1961, C40/532.

in 1959. By 1969, ICFC's loan capital totalled £70 million, consisting of six separate issues of debenture stock.[24] In 1959, ICFC converted from a private to a public company and so could, for the first time, raise money in the market. By 1960, it had provided over 900 companies with permanent capital or long-term loans.[25] Coopey and Clarke see the Bank as essential to the survival of ICFC:

> It had been the Bank which had engineered the Corporation at the outset and, under duress, had persuaded the clearers to participate. Similarly the Bank, using the same arguments about avoiding further government intervention in the financial sector, had staved off the intermittent attempts by the clearers to relinquish their obligation to support the Corporation.[26]

They also maintain that although the management methods of Piercy and Kinross ensured ICFC's longevity, 'without the guardianship of the Bank of England this would certainly not have been enough.'[27] That said, the Bank was not called on to assist ICFC in the same way that it had been with other corporations.

Another financial institution linked to the Bank was the Agricultural Mortgage Corporation (AMC), established in 1928 for making long-term loans on first mortgages on farm property. AMC's share capital was held by the Bank and principal clearing banks. On the setting up of AMC, the Bank contributed £200,000 to its capital. The bulk of AMC's resources came from publicly issued debentures. AMC also received financial help from the government in the form of interest-free loans 'to provide a guarantee fund as additional backing for the Corporation's debentures, and an annual subsidy towards expenses'.[28] In 1968, the Bank managed 13 debenture stocks totalling £98 million.[29]

The Bank's shares for the CDFC, FCI, and ICFC were held in the Securities Management Trust (SMT), the Bank's wholly owned subsidiary established in November 1929 as the 'channel through which the Bank itself would provide funds for the schemes supported by the Bank'.[30] With the establishment of FCI and ICFC in 1945, the original need disappeared,

---

[24] See C40/532 and C40/1172.
[25] *The Financial Times*, 22 June 1960, p. 10.
[26] Coopey and Clarke (1995, p. 74).
[27] *Ibid.*, pp. 74, 79–82.
[28] Bank of England, 'Principal changes in the British monetary system since 1931'; Radcliffe, 'Memoranda,' Vol. 1, p. 21.
[29] Somerset to Andrews/Hollom, 'Agricultural Mortgage Corporation stocks management and issue charges', 5 February 1968, 1A140/5.
[30] Sayers (1976, p. 325).

but SMT continued as a vehicle for holding certain investments on the Bank's behalf. In December 1964, the shares were transferred to the control of the Bank. and no further dividends or interest were received by SMT.[31]

In 1966, the Industrial Reorganisation Corporation (IRC) was set up to encourage and facilitate industrial reorganisation. The Labour Government believed that such an organisation was needed to stimulate reconstruction, rationalisation, and mergers to improve efficiency and raise productivity.[32] In essence, the IRC was a government body, but the Bank, being in favour of assistance to modernise industry, ensured that they had representation on the various committees formed to establish the IRC. The Bank also provided a small degree of assistance to help with the early costs of establishment. Typically, the Bank was also asked for its view on selection of the chairman. Sir Frank Kearton, chairman of Courtaulds, was the front runner. Although Kearton possessed the relevant experience and enthusiasm, Cromer was not convinced, and Morse, too, had doubts, believing him to have 'an abrasive attitude which has made him many enemies within industry and a tendency to act by himself rather than lead a team'.[33] Cromer and Morse both favoured Reay Geddes, and it was Geddes who eventually secured the role.[34] Since legislation for the IRC was slow to pass, the Bank made an advance of £50,000 to enable it to meet initial expenses. Furthermore, the indemnity that was required when the lease for the premises was signed was provided by the Bank because there were then no powers for the Treasury to do so.

Just as the Bank had a say in the setting up of the IRC, they also were consulted about its winding down. The Conservatives had always disliked the IRC, and it was no surprise when Barber, the new Chancellor, announced in October 1970 that it would be abolished.[35] A month later, O'Brien, at the ICFC 25th anniversary dinner, expressed his regret at the disappearance of the IRC.[36] A merger among the IRC, FCI, and ICFC was considered, but the Bank did not think it a good idea. There was also the question of who should look after the assets of IRC following its dissolution. The Bank

---

[31] Cromer, 'Minutes of a meeting of directors ... 2 December 1964 ...', SMT1/8.
[32] L. Petch to Sir Richard Clarke, 'Industrial Reorganisation Corporation', 30 September 1965, 5A164/1
[33] Morse, 'Industrial Reorganisation Corporation', 16 December 1965, 5A164/2
[34] Cromer to Roll, 3 January 1966; Morse, 'Industrial Reorganisation Corporation', 12 January 1966, 5A164/3.
[35] Hague and Wilkinson (1983, p. 3).
[36] 'Extract from the Deputy Governor's memo on the Governor's conversation with Mr. Rawlinson, 4 November 1970', 5A164/4.

did not want to take the IRC's portfolio into the Banking Department, and neither did they want to take on the job of handling IRC's business through the mechanism of an organisation such as a revived securities trust.[37] In the end, Rothschilds advised the Department of Trade and Industry (DTI) on the management and disposal of the assets until 1973, when the IRC eventually was wound up.

In addition to the indirect assistance to industry offered through various corporations, the Bank also intervened directly, albeit with government prompting, with Fairfield Shipbuilding and Engineering, an integral part of shipbuilding on the Clyde, with a long history of troubles. It was not the first time that the Bank had assisted the company. In 1932, it provided borrowing facilities and made an advance of £150,000, of which £45,000 was taken up. This loan was transferred to the Bank of Scotland in 1935.[38] By the mid-1960s, the company had suffered four consecutive years of losses, and a receiver was appointed in October 1965. At the same time, the Geddes Committee was in the process of considering what changes might make British shipbuilding competitive in world markets.[39] After many meetings, with Morse representing the Bank, Geddes concluded that it was in the national interest that the future of Fairfields should be held open at least until the Committee's findings had been reported. In November 1965, the Chancellor announced that the Bank would make an advance of no more than £1 million to be given to the receiver at Bank Rate (6 per cent) to ensure continuation of the shipyard until the following spring. The Bank was guaranteed against loss under Section 2 of the Borrowing (Control and Guarantees) Act of 1946, a power that had not been used before.[40] The money was to be advanced in stages through the Bank of Scotland. Cromer was not happy with this scheme and had advocated a variant whereby the Treasury guarantee was given to the Bank of Scotland directly, thereby leaving the Bank out of the affair. He argued that the Chancellor's scheme would imply for the Bank a degree of commitment that it could not accept.[41] The Bank also felt strongly that since the proposed support operation did not make financial or economic sense, it

---

[37] 'The Dissolution of the IRC', 24 November 1970, 5A164/4.

[38] Extracts from minutes of the Committee of Treasury, 29 January 1936, G14/59; Saville (1996, p. 595).

[39] The committee was appointed in February 1965 and reported in March 1966, *Shipbuilding Inquiry Committee 1965–1966*, cmnd. 2937 (HMSO, London, 1966).

[40] This gave the Treasury power to guarantee loans 'for the purpose of facilitating the reconstruction or development of an industry or part of an industry in Great Britain'; HC Deb, 4 November 1965, Vol. 718, c1235.

[41] Walker, Note for record – 'Fairfields', 3 November 1965, C40/517.

would be a pity if the Bank's name was linked with it, even though supported by a government guarantee.[42] Callaghan was not persuaded and went ahead and announced the Bank's advance.

It quickly became apparent that the loan would not achieve the objective of maintaining Fairfields in operation until Geddes reported, and without assurances over the yard's ability to carry construction to completion, several contracts were under threat.[43] An urgent decision was required as to whether to run down the yard or try to keep it going. To maintain the operation, the government set up a new company Fairfields (Glasgow) Ltd., that took over the shipyard in January 1966. Of the £2 million capital, the Board of Trade subscribed to half the £1 million ordinary shares, and all the £1 million unsecured loan stock. The Bank's £1 million advance was treated as a revolving fund, and involvement with Fairfields and its subsidiary Fairfield Rowan continued throughout the late 1960s and into the 1970s, with the government guarantee being renewed several times. The complicated process of financial transactions and repayments between the Bank and the Bank of Scotland finally came to a close in the mid-1970s when the capital and interest outstanding were paid off in the summer of 1974.[44]

What is to be made of the Bank's involvement with these bodies? It is clearly in a line that had been established by Norman, and the Bank had been instrumental in their establishment. Moreover, the Bank's presence persuaded other financial institutions to participate. While at the time of their birth there may have been a perceived need to fulfill the functions intended, by the 1950s and 1960s, the world had changed. Hence Mynors' gloomy prognosis for IFC or Rickett telling O'Brien in 1969 that the CDFC certainly would not be set up now. As to the Bank's interventions and assistance, it may have been, although this was never stated explicitly, that it did not want to be associated with a failed business. Also, for whatever reason, the Bank had been intimately involved from the start, so perhaps there was some feeling of moral obligation. And it is difficult to ignore completely the fact that people such as Bolton and Mynors had close links with the Bank. Perhaps, in an era when the Bank had such a diverse range of interests, nobody thought that it was a strange thing for a central bank to do.

---

[42] 'Extract from the Deputy Governor's memo on a Governor's conversation with Mr. Goldman, 3 November 1965', C40/517.

[43] Note of a meeting, 16 November 1965, C40/517.

[44] See C40/521.

The Bank and the City

The Bank's desire to oversee and speak for the City is more understandable. One aspect where this was particularly apparent was in merger activity, in the banking sector first, but also more widely. Since the Colwyn Report of 1918, there had been relatively few bank mergers, and both the government and the Bank had made it clear over the years that they were against any amalgamations involving the 'Big Five'. However, by the 1960s, opposition had diminished, and there were certainly some in the Bank who advocated some amalgamation as a means of producing a more efficient banking sector[45] (see Chapter 9).

One of the most notable mergers involved Barclays and Martins. Although Martins had been courted many times, notably by Lloyds, it had always resisted. In 1967, though, the possibility of an amalgamation looked increasingly likely. By September, Martins had received approaches from all the 'Big Five' except National Provincial, and these were discussed when Sir Cuthbert Clegg, the chairman of Martins, saw the Governor. O'Brien declared that a link between Martins and a foreign or overseas bank was out of the question, and he also explained that 'while we would not bless any union between two members of the big five, we would not in general oppose other link-ups'.[46] O'Brien was particularly unenthusiastic about a link between Martins and either Barclays or the Midland because this would create too large a bank.[47] A month later he changed his mind and decided that there was no reason for prohibiting such an amalgamation 'if an acceptable proposition is made'.[48] Keen to avoid a public takeover battle, O'Brien brought together Martins and representatives of the 'Big Five' to discuss the rules of the takeover procedure. Cooper Brothers & Lybrand, Martins' accountants, would furnish full details on a confidential basis of the profits, assets, reserves, and other relevant information to the banks who expressed an interest in acquiring Martins' shares. The banks then would submit offers, and the three best would be chosen for consideration.[49] Bids had to be received at the Bank by 26 January 1968.[50] Public announcement of the sale was made in

---

[45] Fforde to Parsons, 'Draft P.I.B. report', 10 May 1967, C40/1654.

[46] O'Brien, 'Governor's note', 15 September 1967, G1/490.

[47] *Ibid.*

[48] O'Brien to Armstrong, 26 October 1967, G1/490.

[49] 'Draft press announcement to be issued after hours on Monday, 12 February, 1968', 15 January 1968, G1/490.

[50] Ackrill and Hannah (2001, p. 174).

December, and by the January closing date, only two offers (from Barclays and Lloyds) were received.

Meanwhile, the two smallest of the 'Big Five', National Provincial and Westminster, announced their intention to merge on 26 January 1968. At the time, this was the biggest merger in British banking history. Remarkably, talks had been going on for only 10 days before the announcement. The two banks had decided that it would not make sense for them to make a bid for Martins, given the share price, but that they should merge. O'Brien viewed the union favourably, and the Treasury raised no objection either.[51] With these blessings, there was no need to refer the case to the Monopolies and Mergers Commission. For many in the City, a takeover of Martins by Lloyds now seemed a certainty. Indeed, some suggested that agreement in principle had already been reached.[52] Aware that only Barclays and Lloyds had put in offers for Martins, Peake (Lloyds) and Thomson (Barclays) met and proposed a three-cornered merger among Barclays, Lloyds, and Martins. Size was clearly an issue. The increasing strength and size of the American banks had to be met. From Barclay's perspective, Lloyds' involvement could be used to further its overseas contacts and would ensure Barclays could meet 'the very large demands of very large customers'.[53] The three banks argued that the merger would provide 'a bigger stature to compete with foreign banks' and increase efficiency through better resource utilisation and the development of new techniques.[54] According to Winton:

There was a need for larger units in banking to match those in industry; that savings would be gained by closing branches and from economies in administration and in computer work; that the co-ordination and development of the three banks' overseas interests would provide a wider coverage to meet British traders' varied and world-wide needs; that international banking and competition overseas required large units.[55]

Winton also suggests that in the face of news of the National-Westminster proposal, Lloyds simply did not want to be left behind.[56]

The announcement on 8 February shocked the City. *The Banker* expressed serious doubts and concluded, 'Their proposal would create a top-heavy banking structure without helping to remove the restrictions that have

---

[51] O'Brien, 'Governor's note', 23 January 1968, G3/267.
[52] *The Times*, 27 January 1968, pp. 11, 21.
[53] Ackrill and Hannah (2001, p. 179).
[54] 'Summary of the report of the Monopolies Commission on the proposed bank mergers', 12 July 1968, G15/102.
[55] Winton (1982, p. 197).
[56] *Ibid*.

distorted bank competition in Britain hitherto.'[57] Not keen on the move, the Prime Minster decided that the case should be referred to the Monopolies Commission, and O'Brien said that he would not be prepared to entertain any mergers until the commission had reported and the government had made its position clear.[58] In fact, the Governor was in favour of the merger but confirmed that 'if the Cabinet decided otherwise, I would not feel it necessary to go to the stake about it.'[59] The commission opposed the proposal,[60] but there was not a two-thirds majority, and the issue went back to Whitehall, where there was reportedly little consensus either.[61] The chairmen of the three banks, along with their chief executives and O'Brien, met the Chancellor Roy Jenkins and Anthony Crosland, president of the Board of Trade, in July, and a week later Crosland announced that the government agreed with the commission that a merger would be contrary to public interest. It was also felt that the merger might lead to pressure for further concentration, resulting in an eventual highly undesirable two-bank system.[62] The government, however, had no objection to Martins joining another bank, and because Barclays had made the highest bid, this offer was accepted. The merger came into effect on 15 December 1969.[63]

Mergers were not limited to the London clearing banks. In 1967, the Royal Bank and the National Commercial Bank of Scotland, both already members of the National and Commercial Banking Group, agreed to merge under the name of the Royal Bank of Scotland Limited. The Governor was kept informed throughout proceedings and had no objection, believing that 'Scotland had been over banked for a long time.'[64] In 1970, the British Linen Bank, owned by Barclays, was incorporated into the Bank of Scotland, and in the same year, the National, Williams Deacon's, and Glyn Mills merged to form Williams and Glyn's Bank. Hollom viewed this as 'a useful small move in the direction of further rationalisation of our banking system.'[65]

[57] *The Banker* 118(55):196, March 1968.
[58] O'Brien, 'Governor's note', 9 July 1968, G3/268.
[59] O'Brien, 'Governor's note', 10 July 1968, G3/268.
[60] Monopolies Commission, *Barclays Bank Ltd, Lloyds Bank Ltd and Martins Bank Ltd, a Report on the Proposed Merger*, 15 July 1968.
[61] Kenneth Andrews to Fforde/O'Brien/Parsons, 'Monopolies Commission Barclays/Lloyds/Martins amalgamation', 4 July 1968; Hollom to O'Brien/Parsons, 'Bank mergers', 16 July 1968, 7A108/4.
[62] HC Deb, 25 July 1968, Vol. 769, c991.
[63] Tuke and Gillman (1972, p. 18). According to Ackrill and Hannah, Barclays paid more for Martins than it was worth; Ackrill and Hannah (2001, p. 182).
[64] O'Brien, 'Governor's note', 13 December 1967, G1/490.
[65] Hollom to Sir Antony Part (permanent Secretary, Board of Trade), 11 March 1969, G1/490.

The clearing banks also built up their interests in financial institutions such as finance houses and other banking subsidiaries. In September 1967, the Midland announced that it had bought one-third of the equity capital in Montagu Trust, one of the City's leading merchant bankers.[66] It was the first time that a clearing bank had bought a share in a merchant bank and was, according to *The Banker*, 'a notable milestone in the gradual blurring of the traditional "demarcation lines" between clearing and merchant banking'.[67] Midland paid £8.7 million for its share in the firm, a holding company established in 1963, consisting of the merchant bankers Samuel Montagu, the Swiss Guyerzeller Zurmont Bank, and two insurance broking companies.[68] The press reported that the Bank had known about the negotiations and had clearly not raised any objection.[69] This was not the case, and news of the agreement left O'Brien fuming. Although Howard Thackstone, Midland's chief general manager, had made a vague passing reference to the link-up during an informal chat with the Governor in December 1966, O'Brien had heard nothing subsequently until he was shown a draft press announcement after lunch on the day of its release. An alliance between Montagu and Midland had been under consideration for a while, and the fact that neither side had consulted him left O'Brien extremely displeased.[70] In a later conversation with Cromer and Charles Hambro, O'Brien said that 'although the Midland-Montagu deal had created a precedent as far as British banks are concerned, he would not be prepared to accept that a foreign bank should acquire a shareholding of more than 10/15 per cent in a London merchant bank'.[71] In September 1970, another merger was on the horizon, this time between Lloyds Europe and Bank of London and South America (BOLSA). BOLSA wanted to expand as an international bank and desired more adequate representation in Europe. Fforde believed that the combination would 'add some useful diversity' and would overcome the problem of BOLSA's relatively weak capital position. It was seen as a 'desirable development', and the Bank adopted 'a mildly encouraging attitude during its gestation'.[72] The new firm, Lloyds & BOLSA International, was formed in May 1971. Parsons, chairman, was invisible in all this and

---

[66] O'Brien, 'Governor's note', 19 September 1967, G3/266.
[67] *The Banker* 117(500):831, October 1967.
[68] Homes and Green (1986, p. 238).
[69] *The Daily Telegraph*, 20 September 1967, p. 2.
[70] Kynaston (2001, p. 343).
[71] Parsons, 'Note of the Governor's conversation with Lord Cromer and Mr. Charles Hambro', 12 October 1967, G3/266.
[72] Fforde to R. R. D. McIntosh (Department of Employment), 10 September 1970, G1/491.

stood down in December 1970. Gordon Richardson was approached as a successor but declined.[73]

Why had the Bank's long-running opposition to mergers changed? One possibility is that the American banks were becoming more powerful and that size was seen as being part of their strength, while mergers were also seen as a way of improving the commercial banking system.[74] Cromer was not taken with the size argument, but others in the Bank, most obviously Fforde, certainly were in favour of some rationalisation. And there were other considerations. The desire to promote London and the City as an international financial centre was strong, and if the Bank could not go against the trend towards bigger units, at the very least it wanted to be informed of developments so as to be seen to be retaining its protective role.

The Bank also took an interest in other merger activity, primarily through the establishment, in March 1968, of the City Panel on Takeovers and Mergers. This body was to supervise the operation of the new 'City Code on Takeovers and Mergers'. The first code, published in 1959, was the product of a City Working Party formed on the initiative of Cobbold to ensure fair and equal treatment of all shareholders in relation to take-overs. It was revised in 1968, and the panel was set up to supervise the tougher code. O'Brien claimed entire responsibility for the panel's birth.[75] This was typical of the Bank's desire to maintain the reputation of the City and more specifically reflected O'Brien's desire for the Bank to remain the 'guardian of the city's morals'.[76] The panel dealt with specific problems of interpretation of the City code, both before a bid and during the period it was open for acceptance. Where it felt that action was required, the panel took up matters relating to the conduct of the bid. It was not concerned with the merits of any particular takeover or merger, only with the manner in which it was undertaken. The panel also heard progress reports, considered questions of policy and appeals against rulings, as well as various disciplinary cases.[77]

Members were drawn from the bodies represented on the City Working Party. At the Governor's request, Mynors agreed to serve as the first chairman, and Peter Cooke was appointed its first Secretary. Neither knew much about takeovers and mergers, and Cooke admitted that 'it was the

---

[73] Hollom, Note for record – 'B.O.L.S.A.', 30 December 1970, G1/491.
[74] Ackrill and Hannah (2001, pp. 172–173).
[75] O'Brien, Memoir, pp. 86, 88.
[76] Interview with Peter Cooke, 27 March 2006.
[77] The Panel on Take-overs and Mergers, *Annual Report,* year ending 31 March 1969, pp. 7–9, 10; year ending 31 March 1970, p. 4.

blind leading the blind for a while'.[78] Mynors served for little more than a year before he was succeeded by Lord Shawcross. In a letter to Michael Bucks, chairman of the panel, O'Brien emphasised that the Bank was 'wholeheartedly behind this exercise and will give any necessary support to secure its effective implementation'.[79] Arrangements were made to credit the account of the panel in the Drawing Office with the sum of £3,500 in May 1969 and with £1,000 at the end of each quarter.[80] This sum was increased to £1,450 per quarter in August 1969. The Bank bore the cost of the panel's work up to 1972, when it was decided that half the total expenditure would be met by other bodies. The Bank also provided temporary premises for the panel at New Change, costing approximately £4,500, before it moved to the London Stock Exchange in September 1970. The Bank met the cost of rent of the new suite and spent £6,500 in preparing the premises for the panel's use.[81]

Despite a rocky start, by 1971, the panel had become 'an established part of the City scene', and its authority was generally accepted.[82] The level of activity was high. In the period 1968–74, the panel dealt with over 2,000 proposals and opposed a number of bids – 41 in 1970, 47 in 1971, and 50 in 1972. It is difficult to assess the panel's achievements. Perceived breaches of the City code could cause uproar from the interested parties, and such controversy often made its way into the press.[83] It was a non-statutory body, and this left it open to criticism. The panel's regulatory weakness was the cause of much comment; in particular, it had no powers to obtain information.[84] Indeed, in the face of a refusal to co-operate or a threat of libel, the panel's authority was undermined. Consequently, in 1971, the panel considered seeking some statutory backing with the right to call for information, to subpoena witnesses, to call for oral evidence on oath, and immunity from defamation or libel suits. But, there was also a belief that securing statutory rights and privileges would not be possible without surrendering much of the panel's existing flexibility and informality.[85]

---

[78] Interview with Peter Cooke, 27 March 2006.
[79] *The Times*, 27 March 1968, p. 21.
[80] Balfour to Ian Fraser (Panel on Take-overs and Mergers), 13 May 1969, C45/80.
[81] Balfour to P. R. Frazer (Bank of England secondment to the panel), 17 December 1969, C45/80.
[82] Fforde to Sir Charles Whishaw (Freshfields), 27 May 1971, C45/80.
[83] For a fuller account, see Kynaston (2001, pp. 375–383).
[84] Fraser to O'Brien, 'Some notes on the future of securities regulation', 10 March 1971, C45/80.
[85] Whishaw to Fforde, 14 July 1971, C45/80.

By late September, Shawcross felt that an approach for legal powers was unnecessary, and the Bank agreed that the matter need not be pursued.[86] Three years later it still remained an issue. In the Foreword to the panel's 1974 *Annual Report,* Shawcross sternly rejected any criticism that a lack of statutory backing meant a lack of teeth. 'It would be a brave firm or individual', he argued, 'and also a very foolish one – who defied the Panel's decision.' This in fact seems to be mere rhetoric, and the only damage the panel could really inflict was on a company's reputation.

The reputation of the City was again a factor in 1968 when the Bank offered financial assistance to commodity traders who faced heavy losses and, it was feared, possible bankruptcy as a consequence of devaluation. As Chief of Overseas Roy Fenton noted, the Bank usually would expect traders to carry such losses, but the circumstances here were 'exceptional'. Companies had entered into binding purchase contracts in the local currency of sterling area countries, with the corresponding sales contracts in sterling. The potential losses were a result of the fact that the local currency did not devalue. In fact, some traders had recognised the risk and tried to obtain forward cover for these contracts, but this had been refused under exchange control regulations. A range of commodities was involved, including coffee, raw cotton, and oilseeds, and greatest difficulties were experienced in Nigeria. Representatives of the firms held meetings with the Bank, lobbied the government, received press coverage about their plight, and questions were asked in Parliament. An initial estimate of anything up to £30 million for prospective losses proved wide of the mark, it being quickly scaled back to less than £10 million and then £5 million.[87]

The Bank's willingness to intervene in this case was based on two considerations. First, there was the lack of forward cover, about which Hollom conceded, 'we are not altogether free from responsibility for a situation in which exchange cover was unobtainable.' The second and more compelling point was the risk of serious damage to the London commodity markets and the reputation of the City in general. At least, this put the case within the Bank's generally accepted sphere of influence. In a reference to Fairfields, Hollom asserted that 'I should have thought there was a fair argument for

---

[86] Shawcross to O'Brien, 24 September 1971; Cooke to Whishaw, 29 September 1971, C45/80.

[87] Fenton to Morse/O'Brien/Parsons, 23 November 1967, 24 November 1967; Anthony Nicolle (EID), Note for record – 'Commodity markets: devaluation', 29 November 1967; McMahon to Hollom/O'Brien/Parsons, 'Commodity dealers' losses', 7 December 1967, 6A351/1; newspaper cuttings in 6A351/2; HC Deb, 7 December 1967, Vol. 755, c378W.

suggesting that this area of invisible earnings was of as direct interest to us as, for example, a Scottish shipyard.' He suggested that the Bank might make loans on reasonably 'soft' terms. Fforde agreed because it would keep the traders in business and oblige them to meet their losses.[88] There followed two months of intensive negotiations with the traders and liaison with Whitehall before the Bank made its formal offer of commodity market loans at the end of January 1968. The Bank would make available a sum of up to £5 million to be divided pro rata, and in each case, the loan was not to exceed 80 per cent of net expected losses. Applications were received from 18 firms with combined losses of over £4 million. After verification of accounts, the Bank advanced £3.2 million; the smallest sum was £4,000 and the largest £663,000. The loans were at 5 per cent and repayable in 10 equal six-monthly instalments. There was no secrecy on this occasion, the support being detailed in the *Annual Report*.[89]

Promoting Central Banks Overseas

The Bank did not limit itself to City matters. It had a long history of encouraging the establishment and development of central banks around the world, and that continued by various means in the 1950s and 1960s and beyond. The Bank sent staff to work overseas, provided courses at the Bank for overseas central bankers, and offered advice on the establishment and running of new financial institutions. During the 1960s and 1970s, the Bank widened its scope of assistance most notably to parts of Africa and was involved in the banks of over 50 countries.[90] The promotion of central banking abroad was not new. Again, the link was with Norman. He encouraged the founding and development of central banks in the 'Dominions' and other territories in the 1920s and 1930s and promoted close relations with them. Authoritative advice and help on specific problems were offered. The interwar years witnessed the Bank's close involvement with the South African Reserve Bank and the Commonwealth Bank of Australia, as well as a more 'passive but opportunist' role in establishment of the Bank of Canada and the Reserve Bank of New Zealand.[91] It provided Governors

---

[88] Hollom to O'Brien/Parsons, 'Devaluation – commodity markets', 30 November 1967; Fforde to O'Brien/Parsons, 'Commodity markets', 1 December 1967, 6A135/1.

[89] Bank of England, 'Commodity market loans', 25 January 1968; list of applications dated 5 February 1968 and other correspondence, C40/1600; Bank of England, *Annual Report*, year ending February 1968, p. 24, year ending February 1969, p. 16.

[90] Eric Haslam (1979), *Central Banks in the Making: The Role of the Bank of England 1948–74* (private circulation).

[91] Sayers (1976, pp. 209, 513).

for some. Norman's enthusiasm for international financial cooperation was continued by Cobbold, who fostered good personal relations with central banks abroad.[92]

The most extensive study of this activity is that of Eric Haslam, an Adviser to the Governors between 1965 and 1972. In 1974, Haslam was asked by McMahon to write an historical survey of the part played by the Bank in the formation of new central banks.[93] *Central Banks in the Making: The Role of the Bank of England 1948–74* was the result. Running to three volumes, it examined the history of the Bank's participation in the creation and development of currency boards and central banks in more than 50 countries in Africa, the Near and Middle East, Asia, and the Caribbean.[94] Haslam lists nearly 300 overseas posts in central banks and other financial institutions that were filled between 1945 and 1974 by men and a few women from the Bank. *Central Banks* only had a limited private circulation because it was felt that its sometimes critical commentary and general lack of censorship could cause distress to some individuals discussed in the book.

The Bank was frequently asked to help with the staffing or management of new or young financial institutions. Bank employees were chosen to go out on a variety of assignments; the majority of positions were for men, although some women were seconded. Secondment of Bank staff to overseas posts had gone on since the end of the First World War, but the numbers involved were relatively small compared with those after 1945. As colonies acquired their independence, the old currency boards were seen as symbols of colonialism, and the financial instruments that had served the Colonial Empire were unlikely to remain acceptable to the newly independent countries. Yet, while the colonies pressed for their political freedom, the Bank's expertise was still needed for the creation of a stable financial system. The Bank believed that it was important that newly independent countries should get off to a good start in financial matters and thus made efforts to find suitable people to assist. Secondment was not only beneficial in putting relations between the countries and the Bank on a good footing, but also the knowledge and experience gained by secondees could be of considerable advantage on their return.

[92] Haslam, *Central Banks*, p. 1102. In this period, Richard Hallett was Governor, Bank of Northern Rhodesia, 1964–68; Stanley Payton, Governor, Bank of Jamaica, 1960–64, and succeeded by Richard Hall; Rodney Cunnell was Deputy Governor, National Bank of Libya, 1958–60, E39/5–6. These files contain an alphabetical listing, by country/institution, of all the Bank's overseas appointments.

[93] *Ibid.,* p. vii.

[94] *Ibid.,* pp. 1119–1145. For an account of a secondment to the Qatar and Dubai Currency Board in the early 1970s by Paul Tempest, see *Old Lady*, December 2004, pp. 148–149.

The terms on which staff were made available for overseas appointments were divided into two categories: those who were sent abroad while still members of the Bank and employees who were required to leave the Bank but had the option to return within three months of the end of the contract with the overseas employer. This applied to those who took senior policy-making posts, such as Governor or Deputy Governor, and therefore had to demonstrate loyalty to the new institution. In most cases, secondment did not involve resignation from the Bank. Appointments could last from six months to 10 years and range from Governor to secretary.[95] As might be expected, a high proportion of staff seconded came from the Bank's Overseas Department, although some also were from the branches. They had mostly been at the Bank for over 15 years and generally were in their mid-thirties or early forties.

The decision to accept an offer of secondment was not necessarily an easy one. While valuable experience could be gained, and there was the possibility of working at a higher rank, there were disadvantages, as Fenton told Morse in 1971: 'The general expansion of activity within the Bank, the feeling that promotion prospects are better served by remaining in London, together with the more demanding attitude of junior staff, have made them less amenable to the suggestion that service overseas would benefit their careers.'[96] Wives and children could complicate matters further, for secondment could mean considerable family upheaval. John Smallwood, who had once been Governor's Private Secretary (GPS) covering the transition from Cobbold to Cromer, turned down the invitation to become Deputy Governor of the new Central Bank of Uganda for family reasons. Shortly afterwards, he was moved sideways to another department.[97] The Bank therefore tended to target bachelors. Having served as alternate Executive Director for the International Monetary Fund (IMF) from 1972 to 1976, Peter J. Bull returned to the Bank to be quickly asked whether he would serve in Singapore. Bull did not have a family but felt that he would miss out on London life if he took the post and thus declined. He was subsequently sidelined in the Bank to working on the less than glamorous Eastern Bloc. Bull later recalled that if he had accepted the Singapore job, he might have eventually made Deputy Chief Cashier. It was not always wise to say 'No' to these requests.[98]

[95] Hennessy (1992, p. 306).
[96] Fenton to Morse, 17 March 1971, E39/2.
[97] Obituary, *The Independent*, 21 December 2007, p. 40.
[98] Interview with Peter J. Bull, 29 February 2008; Haslam, *Central Banks*, p. 18.

Experiences of the expatriates varied greatly according to their posting. Some had an easier and more fulfilling time than others. Conditions were not necessarily easy and in certain cases were dangerous.[99] Although the candidates were given a brief introduction to the country they were about to go to, this was not sufficient to give a real insight into daily life because the Advisers had little first-hand experience themselves. The individuals therefore faced considerable uncertainty. Most proved 'well adapted and capable, surprisingly so when it is considered at what short notice they were pitched into completely alien surroundings'.[100] Local nationalists might have displayed some 'anti-British bias', but for the most part, the men were left to get on with their jobs with little interference. Despite the fact that expatriates were expected to transfer their loyalty to their new placement, it was sometimes difficult to abandon a 'London' way of thinking, and where conflicts of interest arose, the secondee, unless he trod carefully, could be caught in the crossfire.[101] Life was perhaps a little less easy for the second-ees' spouses. The Bank gave little consideration to the employees' wives; indeed, 'much was taken for granted of wives and families; they deserved rather more recognition than they received.'[102] This contrasted with the experiences of wives of Hongkong and Shanghai Banking Corporation (HSBC) staff who worked abroad.[103]

On finishing their placement, expatriates almost invariably returned to the Bank. Stanley Payton, previously an acting Adviser, returned from his Governorship of the Bank of Jamaica in 1965 and rose to become chief of the Overseas Department 10 years later.[104] MacGillivray, Deputy Governor of the Bank of Rhodesia and Nyasaland, and Fenton, Governor of the Central Bank of Nigeria, also returned to Threadneedle Street and became Deputy and Chief of the Overseas Department, respectively.[105] Yet many of those who returned to the Bank found adjustment difficult. Frustration could arise from the fact that the nature of the work at the Bank was not as interesting or demanding as that of their placement. This also applied to those who went to Washington. David Somerset, for example, on returning to the Bank after working as Jacobsson's personal assistant at the IMF, found his role as a GPS quite mundane.[106] Faced with a step back, some left the

---

[99] Haslam, *Central Banks*, p. 2.
[100] Hennessy (1992, p. 308).
[101] Haslam, *Central Banks*, pp. 1107, 1113.
[102] *Ibid.*, p. 22.
[103] Kinsey and Green (2004, p. xiii).
[104] See G17/45.
[105] See G17/14 and G17/34.
[106] Interview with Pen Kent, June 2005.

Bank to pursue opportunities elsewhere; some stayed with the institutions they joined. Andrew Crockett was one of these. Having gone as the personal assistant to the Managing Director in 1972, he did not return, remaining with the IMF, much to Richardson's annoyance.[107]

The assistance given to Commonwealth countries that gathered momentum during the 1950s peaked in the mid-1960s. Indeed, in 1964, Parsons said that the Bank was 'stretched pretty much to the limit in finding people'.[108] Secondments began to tail off in the late 1960s and reached a low of 13 in 1975 as appointments at all levels began to be taken by locals. And yet, although the criteria for secondment were tightened up in the 1970s, levels of secondment began to rise again after 1975. In 1978, the Bank seconded 25 staff, a similar figure to that of 10 years earlier.[109]

It is difficult to judge the overall success of the Bank's role abroad. In the period 1955–78, the Bank appointed six Deputy Governors and eight Governors to a variety of foreign central banks, but mostly in Africa, with periods ranging from one to five years. They also managed to extend the geographical spread of their assistance. There were sometimes difficulties, and the experience in creating separate central banks in East Africa was 'neither particularly happy nor fruitful'.[110] Some expatriates stayed too long in their post, and the Bank could have withdrawn some of them earlier than they did, and as a result, 'often their time and talents were, to say the least, underutilised'.[111] Despite such comments, Haslam's view is essentially a positive one: 'In the limited, practical but nonetheless fundamental areas of currency provision, management of government funds and short-term debt, bank clearing, exchange control and the provision of basic statistical information and analysis, most of the ventures in which the Bank of England participated produced creditable standards of performance, often in the face of daunting manpower shortages'.[112]

Throughout this period, central bank staff from the Commonwealth also visited Threadneedle Street to improve their understanding of central banking and the institutional setting in London. There was an annual conference of sterling area central bank Governors that went back to Norman's time. The Bank welcomed them as part of its policy of central banking

---

[107] He later returned to the Bank as an Executive Director in 1989 and was also general manager, BIS, 1994–2003.

[108] Parsons, 'Note', 15 October 1964, E39/1.

[109] Haslam, *Central Banks*, p. 1099. It is not clear why this rise occurred.

[110] *Ibid.*, pp. 1108–1109.

[111] *Ibid.*, p. 1111.

[112] *Ibid.*, p. 1109.

co-operation. Visitors arrived throughout the year and were given tours of the Bank that proved extremely popular; these increased sharply from the mid-1960s to mid-1970s. In 1965, there were 300 overseas visitors, and in 1974, there were over 1,000 visitors from 90 countries.[113]

A more formal system developed in the latter half of the 1950s. In 1956, Guy Watson suggested that a Commonwealth Central Banking Summer School should be held at the Bank. The pace at which many of the colonies were moving towards independence indicated an urgent need to assist them in training people to run their new central banks. Watson believed there was a need for both 'education and propaganda (although not of an overt kind)'.[114] Crawshaw echoed this view: 'We want to sow the proper central banking doctrine early in Colonial minds.'[115] It was in Britain's interest to promote a clear understanding of the sterling area mechanism and the facilities offered by London. The courses also gave the Bank a good opportunity to lay the foundations for co-operation with future senior officials. Speakers were drawn mainly from the Bank, with others from the City, universities, government departments, and the Institute of Bankers. The study of London as a financial and commercial centre with special reference to the Bank occupied a large part of the curriculum, but there also were sections on central banking in Commonwealth countries and on problems in territories without a central bank.[116] Lectures, largely devoted to the structure of the monetary system in Britain, constituted the backbone of the course. The lectures were supplemented by visits to markets and other institutions in the City and to offices of the Bank.

A trial for the course was held over six weeks in April and June 1957. Thirteen people attended, with 10 from the Commonwealth and three from the Bank. The course was deemed a success, although Sayers, a lecturer and guest speaker, failed his appraisal – was reportedly, 'a disappointment to most people and was not well liked. ... he appeared aloof, uninterested and condescending.'[117] An increasing number of enquiries came from non-Commonwealth countries, and in considering extending the coverage, de Moubray argued, 'courses are fashionable to-day, and if we do not cater for the fashion, others will.'[118] But, the idea was rejected on the grounds that it would make the numbers unwieldy. Furthermore, the alternative of running

---

[113] Bank of England, *Annual Report*, year ending February 1974, p. 23.
[114] Watson, 'Commonwealth central banking summer school', 1 October 1956, OV21/26.
[115] Crawshaw, 'Central banking course – colonial candidates', 1 November 1956, OV21/26.
[116] 'Central banking course syllabus', 14 June 1957, OV21/26.
[117] Crashaw, 12 June 1957, OV21/26.
[118] De Moubray, 'Central banking courses', 31 March 1960, OV21/26.

a separate course for non-Commonwealth students was not thought to be feasible because of the burden it would place on senior officials. Nevertheless, the Bank extended invitations beyond the Commonwealth to South Africa and Eire in 1963 and further in 1973 when Italy, France, and Germany attended. The courses were held biennially, alternating with the South East Asia, New Zealand, and Australia (SEANZA) central banking courses, to which the Bank sent experienced officers as visiting specialists.[119] The courses were later incorporated into the Centre for Central Banking Studies (CCBS), established in 1990 in response to growing demands for training from central banks in Eastern Europe and former Soviet Union countries embarking on the transition to market economies.[120]

The Note Issue and Decimalisation

In the public mind at least, the Bank's most visible function was the printing and distribution of bank notes, something it had carried out since its foundation in 1694.[121] The note issue was a vast undertaking and in terms of staff numbers was by far the Bank's biggest operation. The fiduciary issue rose from £2,000 million in 1956 to £2,800 million in 1966, and by the end of the decade, it stood at £3,200 million. The number of notes in circulation increased from 1,197 million in 1950 to 1,539 million by 1969. Bank note production had moved to the huge purpose-built Debden site in 1956, and in the first half of the 1960s, the Bank produced, on average, between 6 and 8 million notes every working day. At Debden, over 1,600 people worked in the production, checking, and packaging of new notes, as well as the destruction of worn notes. To guard against fault, every note was examined; each examiner was expected to deal with a minimum of 15,000 notes per day, although the average was higher. At Threadneedle Street, the Bank stored new notes to provide a reserve against seasonal fluctuations and possible interruptions in the supply from the Printing Works. Forecasting the

---

[119] On SEANZA courses, see OV21/44.

[120] See 4A73/1.

[121] For a more detail, see Duggleby (1994); Hewitt and Keyworth (1987); Byatt (1994) provides a full account of the designing of new notes in this period, and Hennessy (1992, Chap. 4) also takes that up to 1960. Articles on various aspects of Bank notes, including printing and circulation, as well as the history of the Bank of England note, can be found in the *Bulletin;* see 'Bank note printing', *BEQB* 1(2):24–28, September 1961; 'The note circulation', *BEQB* 5(1):39–45, March 1965; 'The growth in demand for new bank notes', *BEQB* 6(1):3–39, March 1966; 'Changes in demand of bank notes', *BEQB* 5(3):248–249, September 1965; 'The Bank of England note: a short history', *BEQB* 9(2):211–212, June 1969.

life of a bank note and analysis of the movement of note circulation also took place at head office.[122]

At the beginning of the 1960s, 'Series C' bank notes were released, featuring for the first time an image of the Queen. The Chancellor had received a proposal from a Member of Parliament (MP) in 1954 that the image of the Queen should appear on bank notes, and O'Brien strongly supported that when he became Chief Cashier in January 1955.[123] The announcement that the Queen had agreed was made in July 1956, but it was almost four years before the image appeared on the £1 note in March 1960. An informal committee of Directors advised the Chief Cashier on bank note design, but the task of designing the portrait was undertaken by Robert Austin, president of the Royal Society of Painter-Etchers and Engravers. It proved to be a difficult task. Numerous attempts were made, and Austin found the job at times frustrating, especially when faced with the design of the watermark.[124] In a note on Austin's drawing of the Queen's head, O'Brien commented that it was good, but 'the lower half of the face seems slightly too "chubby". ... these first efforts are clearly not good enough to be shown by the Governor elsewhere within the Bank and still less outside it.'[125] When Austin resigned in 1961, he told O'Brien that although he enjoyed the job, some aspects were puzzling, and 'time-tables often seemed more important than the job'.[126] In his history of Debden, Cubbage notes that 'the controversy attendant upon his work must have been an unhappy disappointment to him.'[127] It had been proposed originally that the 10s, £1, £5, and £10 notes all would be the same size, but representations from the blind ensured that the size of the notes increased with each denomination.[128] Cobbold had also been in favour of a £2 note, but this was rejected by the government in November 1959.[129] When the new £1 note finally was released, it met considerable criticism on aspects that ranged over the placement of the serial numbers to the image

---

122 'Bank note printing', p. 24; 'Functions and organisation', p. 235; 'Growth in demand for new bank notes', pp. 37, 39, 41; Cubbage, 'A further history', para. 18.7, PW6/9; interview with Oliver Page, 21 October 2005.

123 Extracts from the minutes of the Committee of Treasury, 22 December 1954, G14/28; Hennessy (1992, p. 150).

124 *Ibid.,* p. 155.

125 O'Brien, 'Queen's head £1 note', 19 October 1956, G14/28.

126 Austin to O'Brien, 13 October 1961, G14/28.

127 Cubbage, 'A further history', Vol. 2, para. 30.3–13, PW6/10.

128 Hewitt and Keyworth (1987, p. 126). Before 1928, all Bank of England notes were the same size regardless of denomination.

129 Extracts from the minutes of the Committee of Treasury, 18 November 1959, G14/28. Interestingly, the $2 note in the United States, with Jefferson's portrait, has never been widely used and in fact is rarely seen outside Jefferson's home in Monticello.

of the Queen for its poor likeness.[130] The second note in the series, the 10s, was produced in October 1961, followed by the £5 note in 1963 and the £10 note in 1964. Both the £5 and £10 notes were the work of Reynolds Stone and included a new design of the Queen's portrait. This was the first time in 20 years that £10 notes had been issued since denominations of £10 and above had been withdrawn in 1943 following the appearance of German forgeries.[131]

In March 1968, another new series was announced that included a new portrait of the Queen, a new design of Britannia, and a historical figure on the reverse. Designed by Harry Eccleston, a skilled engraver, draughtsmen, and painter, the first of the pictorial 'Series D' notes was the £20 note in July 1970, featuring Shakespeare and a version of the balcony scene from Romeo and Juliet.[132] Other images in this series included the Duke of Wellington on the £5 note (November 1971), Florence Nightingale on the £10 note (1975), and Isaac Newton on the £1 note (1978).[133] Series C £1 and £10 notes ceased to be legal tender on 31 May 1979, and the final note in Series D, the £50 note depicting Christopher Wren and St. Paul's, was issued in 1981.[134]

Counterfeiting was a problem, and there were always concerns about specific forgeries. In 1963 and 1964, there had been 'anxieties over a particularly skillful forgery of the £1 note', and in October 1968, O'Brien told the Committee of Treasury that there had been 'a noticeable increase in the number of forgeries received in the past year', the most problematic being the Series C £5 note.[135] The increasing complexity of the note designs was a result of the need to prevent counterfeits. The inclusion of an engraved portrait was a useful element in challenging forgers because the smallest variation would noticeably change the expression.[136]

The sole supplier of paper for the notes was a firm called Portals that had been associated with the Bank since 1724. The Bank held an equity share in the company. In 1947, so as to make the Portal family shareholdings marketable in case of death duties, Portals became a public company. This raised the question of whether the Bank should itself take an increasing shareholding in the event that large numbers of Portals shares came onto

---

[130] Hennessy (1992, p. 158).
[131] Duggleby (1994, p. 61).
[132] Hewitt and Keyworth (1987, p. 129).
[133] Duggleby (1994, p. 62).
[134] This was the first multicoloured intaglio note for the Bank.
[135] 'Forgeries', 2 July 1969, G14/27.
[136] 'Bank note printing', p. 25.

the market. Peppiatt expressed the view that it would be 'inconvenient' if control of the firm were to get into 'unfriendly, or maybe even neutral, hands'.[137] The death of Lord Portal and another large holder led to the Bank buying several blocks of shares in 1949 and 1950. These transactions gave the Bank a stake of 17 per cent. Bought at prices of between 12/- and 13/6, the shares were written down to a nominal value of 10/-, at a total cost to the Bank of £668,000. A small reduction in the Bank's stock was made in the mid-1950s, and Portals also capitalised part of its reserves, so by 1963, the Bank held 1.5 million shares, 14 per cent of the total.[138] At this time, the Portal family were considering selling a significant part of their equity in the company, and Hollom recommended that the Bank again should increase its own holdings in order to protect its interest.[139] Thus a further 500,000 shares were bought at a cost of £651,856. Subsequently, there were more acquisitions that took the Bank's holdings to £3.3 million by 1968, a 30 per cent stake, and at that stage, the Committee of Treasury decided that further substantial additions would be unnecessary.[140] These putative strategic shares had been bought with an outlay of at least £2.5 million to £3 million. In 1989, the Bank disposed of its interest in Portals, realising a profit of £42 million.[141]

An illustration of the way in which the Bank was called on for advice can be found in the discussion on decimalisation. Interest in decimalisation went back to the seventeenth century, but the early attempts bore no fruit.[142] In the 1950s, an increasing number of countries were decimalising, and by the beginning of the 1960s, it looked as if Britain would be one of the few not to.[143] Indeed, O'Brien said, 'If we do not adopt a decimal currency, we are likely in a fairly short space of time to find ourselves the only independent country of any standing without one.' It was less clear why he thought that being the 'sole possessor of a non-decimal currency' would be

---

[137] Peppiatt, Annotation, 12 July 1949 on Bernard, Deputy Governor's note, 'Portals', 11 July 1949, G29/83.

[138] 'Portals' shares', 14 April 1954; O'Brien to Hawker/Cromer/Mynors, 'Portals Limited', 7 November 1958; Mynors, 'Portals', 4 November 1963, G29/83.

[139] Hollom to Cromer/Mynors/O'Brien, 'Portals Limited', 6 November 1963, G29/83.

[140] Thornton to Bailey, 'Portals (Holdings) Limited', 26 April 1967; Committee of Treasury, Note, 9 August 1967, 3A26/1.

[141] Only the prices for 2.5 million of the shares purchased can be verified (£2.53 million). This figure excludes the cost of writing down. The profit was shown as an exceptional item in the accounts; Bank of England, *Annual Report*, year ending February 1989, p. 22.

[142] For a discussion of attempts made in the nineteenth and early twentieth century, see 'The Bank of England and earlier proposals for a decimal coinage', *BEQB* 10(4):454–458, December 1970.

[143] Moore (1973, p. 24).

'a considerable handicap'.[144] He argued that after the transitional difficulties were over, the savings would outweigh the costs in a relatively short time. The claimed savings included simplified teaching of arithmetic in schools and benefit to routine business operations, and there would be a reduction in errors because some of the steps involved in money calculations would be eliminated. Moreover, a failure to decimalise would handicap the business machine industry in export fields and impose higher costs and limit choice for all users of business machines.[145] Not everyone was convinced by these arguments. Niemeyer, for example, was hesitant about tinkering with the pound. He saw 'many conveniences in a multiple of 12' and was sure that 'a change would not, however illogically, lead to a scaling-up of conventional prices, tips, etc.'[146] Allen, too, was opposed, being unimpressed with the alleged advantages and not being able to see any real demand for it. 'Business machines', he claimed, 'can deal perfectly well with the present system', and he was 'at a loss to understand how use of a decimal coinage would "simplify education"'.[147]

In May 1960, the British Association for the Advancement of Science and the Association of British Chambers of Commerce, which had investigated the costs and implications of a change to decimal coinage, produced a report, "Decimal Coinage and the Metric System: Should Britain Change?" – the first authoritative study for 40 years.[148] Later that year, the Treasury set up the Decimal Currency Working Party to consider the desirability and practicability of changes. There were representatives from the Treasury, the Bank, the Royal Mint, the Board of Trade, and the Post Office, and a vigorous debate followed. The three main proposals were (1) keeping the pound and dividing it into 1,000 units, (2) keeping the pound and dividing it into 100 units, and (3) adoption of a 10-shilling system whereby the 10s would act as the basic unit and a cent would be worth just over 1d. This would mean dropping the pound and adopting a new name such as the 'Crown' or 'Crown Sterling'.[149] In the Decimal Currency Working Party, the Bank was the sole supporter of keeping the pound, whereas the rest recommended the 10s system.[150] However, O'Brien commented, 'If we must keep the £

---

[144] O'Brien, 'Decimal currency', 4 November 1960, G14/31.
[145] O'Brien to Armstrong, 'Decimal currency', 16 November 1960, G14/31.
[146] O'Brien, 'Decimal currency', 4 November 1960, G14/31.
[147] Allen to O'Brien, 'Decimal coinage', 31, May 1960, C40/196.
[148] Moore (1973, p. 24).
[149] The 10-shilling system was later used by South Africa (February 1961), Australia (February 1966), and New Zealand (July 1967).
[150] Hollom, 'Decimal currency', 4 May 1961, C40/197.

sterling, we shall not decimalise, but I do not think that the importance of keeping the former justifies foregoing the latter.' He thought that decimalisation on the 10s unit should be accepted, professing that 'Much as one is wedded to the £ sterling, partly on sentimental grounds, I cannot believe that, if the change were made, it would be long before the past were completely forgotten and we should have obtained the very real benefit of the most simple possible transition (at least so far as the general public is concerned, which is the most important aspect) from our system to a new decimal one.'[151] Cromer shared the Chief Cashier's view.[152] Thus opinions were divided as to whether to accept a pound-cent or 10s system. Bridge, although believing the case for a 10s system was a strong one, did not want to abandon the pound. He contended that if a 10s system were to be adopted, the pound would either be lost or would have to be devalued by 50 per cent, and as might be expected, Bridge argued that the pound had a considerable psychological importance.[153] Furthermore, a departure from the pound might disturb foreign confidence in sterling.[154]

With the successful transition to a 10s-cent system in South Africa and increasing public interest in decimalisation, the Chancellor Selwyn Lloyd announced in December 1961 the appointment of Lord Halsbury, a scientist, administrator, and businessman, to lead a committee of inquiry on decimal currency.[155] An 'assessor' from the Bank, as well as one from the Royal Mint and the Treasury, assisted the committee.[156] On a Bank draft expressing an opinion for the committee, Cromer wrote, 'I would like to see an argument for retention of £ put more strongly. Is there no documentation we can add to provide further substance?'[157] The Bank's official stance was approved by the Court on 26 April 1962: it re-emphasised the importance of the international position of sterling and the position of London as a vital financial centre as crucial factors for backing the pound.[158] Reporting in September 1963, the Halsbury Committee recommended by a majority of four to two retention of the pound as the major unit and adoption of a

---

[151] O'Brien, Annotation on Hollom, 'Decimal currency', 4 May 1961, C40/197.

[152] Hollom, Note for record – 'Decimal currency', 9 May 1961, C40/197.

[153] 'Bank views on question of a decimal currency', 27 July 1960, C40/197.

[154] When flying to London with Per Jacobsson in the summer of 1962, Peter Cooke was asked whether the United Kingdom should decimalise on the pound or on ten shillings. Cooke responded, 'I really don't know, but the Bank of England think the UK should decimalise on the pound and not ten shillings.' Jacobsson said, 'Well, that's what I'll tell the Chancellor', and he did. Interview with Peter Cooke, 27 March 2006.

[155] Moore (1973, p. 26); HC Deb, 19 December 1961, Vol. 651, c1134.

[156] Moore (1973, p. 27).

[157] Cromer annotation on Hollom, 'Decimal currency', 6 April 1962, G14/31.

[158] Bank of England, 'Decimal currency memorandum', 26 April 1962, G14/31.

pound-cent-½ cent system. It was estimated that it would take at least three years to prepare for the change, and the cost, if there were to be no delays, would be £100 million.[159] On 1 March 1966, Callaghan announced that the pound would be retained as the major unit but should be divided into 100 units each worth 2.4 of the old pence. Five years were left to prepare for the changes.

The Decimal Currency Board was set up as an advisory body in December 1966 and was given statutory functions the following July when the Decimal Currency Bill received Royal Assent.[160] The preparatory period, which included familiarising the public with the new system, was co-ordinated by the Decimal Currency Board in close consultation with government departments. Six decimal coins were to be issued: three copper (½p, 1p, and 2p) and three silver (5p, 10p, and 50p). To alleviate the problems of coin distribution, 5p and 10p pieces were issued in 1968 and could be used alongside shillings and florins. The current £1, £5, £10, and £20 bank notes were kept but, the 10s note was replaced by the 50p coin, although the two circulated side by side after the controversial coin's introduction in October 1969.[161] Britain officially decimalised on Monday, 15 February 1971 ('D Day'). To prepare for the switch, all banks were closed for normal business for four days from Thursday, 11 February until Monday, 15 February. In the Bank, extensive training was given in preparation, and in the end, the transition in the Bank was conducted smoothly and efficiently. Since the pound was retained, the Bank's role in facilitating the change was minimal. Coinage issues were the responsibility of the Royal Mint, which bore most of the work. In the Bank, stock registers and drawing account balances were converted, stocks of coin exchanged, and accounting machines altered. Overall, decimalisation meant carefully considered and organised administrative changes rather than major disruption.

The Bank's Financing

The Bank's financing in the 1960s follows smoothly from the 1950s. As in the 1950s, income in the 1960s grew steadily – and for the same reason,

---

[159] Cromer, 'Decimal currency – Sent to Governors of foreign banks', 24 October 1963, ADM1/25.

[160] Appendix C, 'Press conference – 15 February programme and press release', note by the public relations officer, 31 January 1968, C40/1455.

[161] There was some debate as to whether the 10-shilling note should be replaced by a coin. The Governor was slightly wary of the coin, but he thought that if it were decided to have one, it should be started side by side with the note, and then whichever turned out to be less

higher interest rates. Total income between March 1960 and February 1970 was £234 million, of which £149 million (64 per cent) came from interest on British government securities bought with the bankers' balances. Interest on bills discounted and advances also grew significantly, from £1.7 million to £6.5 million, and over the decade accounted for 16 per cent of the total. The income derived from the provision of stock and bond services for the government remained static at £2 million per annum, whereas that from other agency services (e.g., Exchange Equalisation Account and Exchange Control) fell from £2 million to around £1.5 million per annum. At £30 million per annum, total income at the end of the 1960s was over £10 million per annum higher than at the start. Over the same period, expenditures increased by around £6 million per annum, primarily a result of wages, although general operating and premises costs also grew. Profits remained more than comfortable; the post-tax average was £6.9 million per annum. After deduction of the dividend payment, a total of almost £50 million was transferred to the reserves in the course of the 1960s (Tables 7.1 through 7.4).

Major capital expenditure during the decade included the redevelopment of some of the Bank's provincial branches. Liverpool was modernised at a cost of approximately £300,000, and the bullion yard at the Southampton Branch was rebuilt with an authorised expenditure of £52,000. 'Modern requirements', the Bank said, made it necessary to rebuild Bristol, Birmingham, Manchester, Leeds, and Newcastle. These branches, which dated back to the middle or latter part of the nineteenth century, were considered to be 'completely inadequate to deal with their job in the present day', and with limited prospects for enlargement or redevelopment, they had to be rebuilt on new sites.[162] The building of some of the new branches caused a stir. Locals protested against the construction of the Bristol Branch because it was on a historic site, and the building was criticised for its dull appearance. The Bank's decision to use Portland stone and Swedish granite in the Newcastle office was also criticised for snubbing northern industry.[163] The new Bristol Branch opened in 1963, and those in Manchester and Birmingham were completed in 1970.[164] Leeds and Newcastle were finished the following year. While the exact costs of the branches are not clear, the

popular should be eliminated; 'Extract from the Deputy Governor's note 11 November 1966 ...', C40/1453.

[162] *First Report from the Select Committee on Nationalised Industries. Bank of England* (SCNI 1970), 5 May 1970, 258, question 2110, p. 290.

[163] See press cuttings in G26/11–13.

[164] For a greater discussion on the Bristol Branch, see Hennessy (1992, pp. 284–289).

Table 7.1. *Bank of England sources of income, 1960–70 (£m)*

Year ending	Interest on British government securities[a]	Interest on bills discounted and advances	Stock and bond services[b]	Commissions, fees, and rents	Sundry receipts[c]	Total
Feb 1961	12.9	1.7	2.1	0.3	2.0	19.1
Feb 1962	12.9	3.2	2.4	0.2	2.0	21
Feb 1963	11.3	2.0	2.2	0.3	1.8	17.7
Feb 1964	11.2	2.1	2.2	0.1	1.8	17.7
Feb 1965	13.5	2.6	2.1	0.3	1.9	20.5
Feb 1966	16.2	3.3	2.1	0.3	1.7	23.8
Feb 1967	17.0	4.0	2.2	0.3	1.3	25.0
Feb 1968	15.4	6.3	2.5	0.5	1.3	26.2
Feb 1969	19.2	6.7	2.4	1.3	1.4	31.3
Feb 1970	19.3	6.5	2.6	1.7	1.6	31.9

[a] Government securities and Treasury bills.
[b] Management of funded and unfunded debt; other stocks and bonds issue conversion and redemption.
[c] Fees for work undertaken by the Issue Department, Exchange Control, EEA, other.
Source: Half-yearly accounts, ADM6/97–100, 202–203.

Table 7.2. *Bank of England gross expenditure, 1960–70 (£m)*

Year ending	Personnel			General[b]	Premises[c]	Total
	Wages[a]	Pensions	Total			
Feb 1961	5.0	0.8	6.0	1.2	0.6	7.9
Feb 1962	5.3	0.9	6.4	1.3	0.7	8.4
Feb 1963	5.5	0.9	6.5	1.4	0.8	8.7
Feb 1964	5.6	1.0	6.7	1.5	0.9	9.1
Feb 1965	6.4	1.1	7.7	1.6	1.0	10.3
Feb 1966	6.6	1.2	8.0	1.8	1.2	11.0
Feb 1967	6.9	1.2	8.2	2.0	1.2	11.4
Feb 1968	7.3	1.3	8.8	2.6	1.3	12.7
Feb 1969	7.8	1.3	9.3	2.8	1.4	13.5
Feb 1970	8.3	1.4	9.9	3.2	1.5	14.6

[a] Includes Governors' and Directors' remuneration.
[b] Operating and running costs.
[c] Rates and maintenance.

Table 7.3. *Bank of England gross and net profits, 1960–70 (£m)*

Year ending	Gross profit[a]	Pre-tax profits[b]	Tax	Profit after tax	Profit after tax and dividend payment[c]	Distribution of profits		
						Write-off of capital expenditure	Provision for future expenditure	Transfer to other reserves
Feb 1961	11.7	11.0	4.6	6.4	4.6	0.0	0.5	4.4
Feb 1962	12.6	11.9	5.4	6.5	4.8	0.0	1.5	3.3
Feb 1963	9.0	7.8	3.3	4.5	2.7	0.0	2.1	0.6
Feb 1964	8.7	7.4	3.1	4.4	2.6	0.9	1.5	0.3
Feb 1965	10.2	8.8	3.8	5.1	3.3	0.1	1.8	1.5
Feb 1966	13.5	12.0	5.2	6.9	5.2	0.0	2.9	2.3
Feb 1967	14.1	12.7	4.2	8.5	6.8	0.2	5.8	0.8
Feb 1968	14.0	12.7	4.4	8.4	6.6	1.4	5.3	0.0
Feb 1969	20.0	18.6	7.3	11.3	9.6	0.0	6.5	0.0
Feb 1970	12.9	11.4	4.3	7.1	5.3	0.4	4.3	0.6

[a] Normal income and capital receipts less normal expenditure.
[b] After deduction of superannuation capital liability.
[c] 'Dividend payment' is the annual payment to Treasury of £1.7 million.
Source: Half-yearly accounts, ADM6/97–100, 202–203.

Table 7.4. *Bank of England reserves, 1960–70 (£m)*

Year ending	No. 1 account	Contingency	Central banking	Premises	Pensions	British government securities	Securities Management Trust	Rest	Total
Feb 1960	16.5	5.0	1.5	5.6	5.2	30.0	10.2	3.9	77.9
Feb 1961	17.0	8.0	1.5	4.3	5.3	30.0	11.0	3.9	81.1
Feb 1962	17.0	11.3	1.5	3.8	6.3	30.0	11.0	3.9	84.8
Feb 1963	17.6	11.3	1.5	3.7	7.3	30.0	11.0	3.9	86.3
Feb 1964	17.9	11.3	1.5	4.2	7.3	30.0	11.0	3.9	87.1
Feb 1965	19.4	11.3	1.5	5.5	7.4	32.0	12.3	3.9	93.2
Feb 1966	23.7	11.3	1.5	7.8	7.4	32.0	12.3	3.9	99.8
Feb 1967	24.4	11.3	1.5	11.6	7.4	32.0	12.3	3.9	104.4
Feb 1968	24.4	11.3	1.5	13.6	7.4	32.0	12.3	3.9	106.5
Feb 1969	24.4	11.3	1.5	15.5	10.5	32.0	12.3	3.9	114.4
Feb 1970	25.0	11.3	1.5	16.4	10.5	32.0	12.3	3.9	116.0

Source: ADM6/197; ADM6/200.

files give final estimated expenditures: Bristol came to just over £500,000, Birmingham £1.7 million, Leeds another £2.5 million, Manchester £3 million, and Newcastle £2 million, thus totalling £9.7 million for the new branch buildings.[165]

There was also rebuilding work at Roehampton. The Sports Club was not being used as much as had been hoped, and it was therefore proposed that a swimming pool and indoor sports hall should be built to attract more staff. The new complex was approved, with an estimated cost of more than £500,000, in the summer of 1968 and completed in 1970.[166] This new development also meant amalgamation of the previously separate men's and women's sports clubs. In anticipation of increased membership, the pavilion was altered to provide improved accommodation. Bull suggested to the Governor that 'it was remarkable that the Court had felt able to sanction the expenditure' during a period of national economic restraint, and the Governor replied that 'if one had to wait for a better economic climate, the building would have never got built.'[167] O'Brien was a strong supporter of the club; apparently, at least one member of the Court in the 1960s suggested that it should be wound up and the land sold.[168]

Modernisation extended to increasing the role of computers in the Bank. Widespread use did not happen overnight – by 1970, the Bank was still using only four computers. Nevertheless, spreading technology was an important factor in the reduction in staff numbers. Transfer of the stock registers to magnetic tape, for example, reduced the number of staff in the Accountant's Department from 1,700 to 1,350 in the space of five years. Preparation of dividend payments by computer had begun in 1960, and by 1965, all dividends issued by the Bank were prepared by computer, saving nearly 200 staff. After 1968, current account banking and cheque-clearing operations and the payment of salaries and other banking and statistical work were transferred to computer.[169]

The whole question of the Bank's profits and the relationship between the dividend payment and the charges to the Treasury for agency work remained contentious. Losses on stock and bond operations continued to mount, and shortfalls also were incurred on exchange control. In the

---

[165] See G26/7, 9, 11–13, and 16.
[166] Extracts from minutes of the Committee of Treasury, 22 December 1965 and 11 September 1968, G14/336.
[167] Interview with Peter J. Bull, 29 February 2008; Bond and Doughty (1984, pp. 279–282); Tempest (2008, pp. 113–116).
[168] *Old Lady*, December 1982, p. 158.
[169] Bank of England, *Annual Report*, year ending February 1965, p. 16; year ending February 1966, p. 20; year ending February 1967, p. 24; year ending February 1969, p. 47.

Table 7.5. *Bank of England (profits)/losses incurred on work for the government,
1960–68 (£000)*

Year ending	Stock and bond services	Exchange control	Deposit banking	Other	Total	Surplus if loss eliminated
Feb 1960	860	354	139	–	1,357[a]	4,855
Feb 1961	938	160	1	21	1,120	5,492
Feb 1962	934	192	(68)	39	1,097	5,284
Feb 1963	1,145	239	128	50	1,562	3,441
Feb 1964	1,778	352	247	53	2,430	3,726
Feb 1965	2,045	429	207	90	2,771	4,542
Feb 1966	2,050e	800e	120e	300e	3,351	7,167
Feb 1967	n/a	n/a	n/a	n/a	4,171	9,249
Feb 1968	n/a	n/a	n/a	n/a	4,540	9,226

[a] Includes miscellaneous of 4.

Source: Neatby to Hollom/Morse/O'Brien, 'Profits', 9 November 1965; Hollom to O'Brien, 'Bank profits', 1 January 1969, G15/12.

financial year 1967–68, the total loss on these services had reached £4.5 million (Table 7.5). This was the result of a deliberate strategy by the Bank to reduce gradually the level of charges made to government. Thus, while the actual costs of exchange control had doubled to £1.8 million, the bill presented to the Treasury was reduced from £688,500 to £50,000; nothing was charged for the Exchange Equalisation Account (EEA), although the running costs were £350,000 in 1968–69.[170]

The strategy was designed to ward off Treasury interest in the Bank's financial position and avoid any changes to Section 1(4) of the 1946 Act. The Treasury was not entirely deflected. In April 1962, Lee asked Cromer whether the subject should be reviewed. A measure of the sensitivity was that the letter was strictly personal and confidential and was not to be referred to in any correspondence, internal or external. Cromer responded by telling Lee that he had initiated an exercise on the matter.[171] O'Brien, for one, was deeply unhappy at the prospect of revealing any details about the Bank's profits, but he conceded that things had been allowed to run on 'until we are caught on the wrong (?) [*sic*] foot

[170] On exchange control costs, see ADM6/54–56; for EEA, see ADM6/49.
[171] Lee to Cromer, 9 April 1962; Cromer to Lee, 10 April 1962, G15/11.

by F. G. L.[Frank Lee][172] The investigation was undertaken by Mynors, O'Brien, Hollom, and Neatby, who prepared an exhaustive dossier on 'Bank profits'. Their conclusions were that any regular review of the dividend payment ultimately would result in having to disclose a profit and loss account. It would constitute a 'fundamental change in the relation of the Bank and Government as established in 1946' and should be resisted; further, the policy of doing work below cost should be continued, but not so quickly as to appear to have been stimulated by Lee's approach, with the best candidates for further reductions being exchange control and the EEA.[173] When the Governor and Lee discussed the subject again in July 1962, it was agreed that there should be an exchange of letters. Armstrong, Lee's successor, made a couple of attempts to follow this up before being told by Cromer in April 1964 that there was at present no need to change the existing arrangements. This was accepted.[174]

The advent of corporation tax prompted a further review in 1965. Neatby proposed that this might present the opportunity to increase the annual payment to the Treasury, and he was supported by Hollom and Morse. The latter, who was something of a progressive when it came to long-established procedures, complained that he did not like the way in which time at a senior level in the Bank was wasted trying to minimise windfall profits.[175] However, O'Brien remained opposed to change. For a start, he thought that there were still reasons to build up the reserves, citing the plans for rebuilding bank branches and unexpected demands, such as Fairfields, as examples. O'Brien then argued that although the £1.7 million payment to the Treasury had remained unchanged for 20 years, the full notional benefit, after taking into account the losses incurred on work for the Treasury, was £4.5 million. He thought that this benefit could be increased by further reducing the cost of services: a nominal fee of £50,000 for exchange control and no charge for management of the EEA. Why this approach? O'Brien accepted that one day the statutory payment would be reviewed and changed and that inevitably the Treasury would demand to inspect the Bank's figures. If the Bank refused this request, there might then be a move to change the 1946 Act, and revisions would not be confined to 'this particular bone of contention'. For

[172] O'Brien to Mynors, 25 April 1962, G15/11.
[173] Mynors to Cromer, 'Bank profits', 28 June 1962, G15/11.
[174] Neatby, 'Bank profits', 27 July 1962; Armstrong to Cromer, 4 October 1962, G15/11; Armstrong to Cromer, 13 March 1964; Neatby to Cromer/O'Brien, 'Bank profits', 18 March 1964; Cromer to Armstrong, 30 April 1964; Armstrong to Cromer, 5 May 1964, G15/12.
[175] Neatby to Cromer/O'Brien, 'Banking Department profits', 23 September 1965; Neatby to Hollom/Morse/O'Brien, 'Profits', 9 November 1965; Morse and Hollom annotations, G15/12.

the time being, then, O'Brien was keen to avoid precipitating any changes in the 1946 Act.[176] The subject was raised intermittently after this. In 1967, Morse was still pressing to charge the full cost for services and to vary the dividend payment, but O'Brien again declared that there was no reason to change.[177]

Then, at the beginning of 1969, when Hollom summarised the position over two decades, he showed that the Bank had never lacked an adequate surplus. Quite the reverse in fact, 'under the combined effects of inflation in building up the bankers' balances which are our main source of income and high interest rates on our earning assets' wrote Hollom, 'our surpluses have tended towards embarrassing levels at times' and would have been even higher if the losses had not been incurred on the work for government.[178] There were now external pressures for change: a parliamentary select committee was about to embark on an enquiry, management consultants had been appointed to start work at the Bank, and financial disclosure by the clearers was under discussion. The debate would move quickly from whether to increase the annual payment and introduce full charging to how these should be done.

The amount spent by the Bank on these extra activities, which include its support for industry in the form of Fairfields, the IRC, the CDFC, ICFC and FCI, and the City panel, and the re-building of the Bank's branches, comes to approximately £25.5 million. Not all of this represents expenditure because the loans were repaid. Also, it should be taken only as a very rough estimate and in all probability does not take account of all the hidden support. Nevertheless, it is still a strikingly high figure and represents 60 per cent of the £50 million that was transferred to reserves during the 1960s. Unfortunately, the nature of the Bank's accounts makes it difficult to trace the sources of all this money.

External Investigations

The question over how well the Bank was performing was never far away in the 1960s, and in line with the fashion of the times, it was decided to invite an investigation by management consultants. O'Brien's decision to bring in consultants in 1969 was a momentous one. Although the Bank

---

[176] O'Brien to Cromer, 'Profits', 25 November 1965, G15/12.
[177] Morse to Neatby, 22 May 1967; O'Brien, Annotation, 21 December 1967 on Neatby to O'Brien/Parsons, 'Bank Act 1946', 31 October 1967, G15/308.
[178] Hollom to O'Brien, 'Bank profits', 1 January 1969, G15/12.

had been employing specialist computer consultants since 1966, never had a full-scale examination by outsiders been permitted.[179] In February 1968, James Selwyn, an Adviser, had noted that there was an 'increasing desire of various groups to put the Bank under the microscope', and the Bank's vulnerability ensured that it needed to be in a 'stronger position to repel outside criticism'.[180] Selwyn maintained that an investigation by consultants would lead to a 'clearer picture of ourselves'.[181] In addition, a fear of outside criticism, coupled with the fact that a large number of companies and nationalised industries were at the time calling on the expertise of consultants, may well have contributed to the Governor's decision.

The Court agreed in August 1968 that McKinsey be invited to examine the Bank, and the appointment was announced in October. Staff were told that although the Governors were satisfied that work was being performed competently within the existing structure, they wanted to ensure that the Bank was 'properly adapting to changes in the nature and range of work and taking full advantage of current developments in the field of management organisation'.[182] The choice of McKinsey was controversial. Selwyn had suggested that because of recent questions in Parliament about government departments and nationalised industries using American consultants, it would advisable to avoid such a firm unless it was 'markedly superior' to the best British one. In a later note, he added, 'The Bank has a world image ... and to choose American consultants in the present state of economic uncertainty could attract a lot of adverse comment'.[183] While the Bank considered a range of firms including DPRM and Urwick, Orr and Partners, McKinsey were judged most suitable. It had already dealt with other corporate giants such as Imperial Chemical Industries (ICI), Shell, British Petroleum (BP), and Lever Brothers and public bodies such as the Post Office, the British Railways Board, and the British Broadcasting Corporation (BBC).[184] Indeed, by this time, McKinsey had become 'the recognized brand name in management consultants'.[185]

The choice of McKinsey evoked a flood of publicity and comment, the decision deemed to have undermined confidence in British consultancy

---

[179] Coleby interview with Alcon Copisarow and Peter Taylor, 5 June 1996.
[180] Selwyn to Bailey, 26 February 1968, G39/1.
[181] Selwyn to O'Brien, 7 May 1968, G39/1.
[182] 'Notice to staff, management consultants', 25 October 1968, G39/1.
[183] Selwyn to Fforde, 31 May 1968 and 22 July 1968, G39/1.
[184] The four biggest companies were Associated Industrial Consultants, P. A. Management Consultants, P. E. Consulting Group, and Urwick, Orr and Partners.
[185] McKenna (2006, p. 182).

firms.[186] This was the time of the 'I'm backing Britain' campaign. Not surprisingly, British management consultants were at the forefront of criticism, and their representatives sought a meeting with O'Brien. The Prime Minister was also asked to intervene.[187] When cross-examined in the House of Commons in November 1968, the Prime Minister expressed doubts over the Bank's choice of consultants, but their decision was final.

McKinsey began work in February 1969, and the project lasted a year. Costs were originally estimated at £170,000, but the total fees actually came to just £142,900. Led by Dr. Alcon Copisarow, McKinsey were asked to examine the organisation and management processes to determine what changes might allow the Bank to operate more effectively and efficiently. With the exception of the Printing Works, all the Bank's activities, including the branches, were covered. The investigation consisted of a 'diagnostic phase' that looked at broad issues in order to highlight areas that needed more detailed investigation and a second phase that undertook further examination of the suggested areas.

At the end of September 1969, the report on the first phase was submitted, the conclusions of which were generally accepted by the Bank. McKinsey found that the quality of the Bank's work and the calibre of the staff were high but that the effective use of resources could be improved by changes in organisation, policy, and method. It suggested that the Bank should take steps to relate responsibilities more closely to major activities, improve procedures for formulating policy advice, and upgrade the management of resources by better financial control and personnel management. The main changes arising were to set up a formal Policy Committee chaired by the Governor; to introduce a more comprehensive system of budgetary and cost control; to form of a separate department to deal with computer developments, method study, work measurement, and job evaluation; and to develop improved methods of career planning, management training, and appraisal of performance.[188] A report on the second phase was produced in early 1970 and focused on, among other things, committees of the Court, common service departments, economic intelligence, note issue, and activities of the branches.

Initially, there had been unease in the Bank about bringing in consultants, mainly the fear that it would lead to a reduction of staff numbers. O'Brien admitted later that his decision was received with 'something

---

[186] Anthony Frodsham (chairman, Management Consultants Association) to O'Brien, 29 October 1968, G39/1.
[187] Frodsham to Wilson, 30 October 1968, G39/1.
[188] 'Press notice', 28 January 1970, G39/3.

approaching horror by a number of my close colleagues'.[189] Lord Robens, a part-time Director, had been suspicious of the effectiveness of management consultants and believed that a good internal team would be more capable.[190] Overall, though, the investigation was seen as a positive move. O'Brien told Copisarow how the Bank had 'much enjoyed' its association with the firm.[191] The Bank was 'well pleased with McKinsey's efforts on our behalf and much impressed by the calibre of the team that Copisarow gathered together and directed'.[192] The Bank accepted McKinsey's suggestions and acted accordingly. In fact, the speed of response came as a surprise to the City.[193] In May 1970, the Bank advertised for positions of 'Management Services Adviser' and a 'Controller of Budgets and Management Accounting'. The advertisements, according to *The Times*, demonstrated just how fully the Bank had accepted the McKinsey recommendations.[194]

The actual impact of McKinsey, however, was limited. The only notable change brought about by the report was the formation, in June 1970, of a new Management Services Department, headed by Heasman, to provide computer and general managerial services. Reorganisation also took place in the Economic Intelligence Department (EID). McKinsey argued that the production and collection of information and its analysis and interpretation, as well as the methods in which the information was communicated to users inside and outside the Bank, could be improved. The scope of economic information should be expanded through creating a separate research division in the EID, and the sector finance group as well as the analysis group should be enlarged. Thus, in March 1970, Dicks-Mireaux, an Adviser, became Deputy Chief of EID and headed a newly formed Economic Section to develop economic advice in the Bank. At the same time, Goodhart was appointed an Adviser and also became a member of the new section.[195] Some reorganisation of the Chief Cashier's and Establishment Department was also adopted. Also in March 1970, a Management Development Division was formed under a newly appointed management development manager to formulate the best methods of career planning, performance appraisal, and management training. de Moubray (former Deputy Chief of the EID)

---

[189] O'Brien, Memoir, p. 98.
[190] 'Extract from the informal court records', 8 August 1968, G39/1.
[191] O'Brien to Copisarow, 13 August 1970, G39/3.
[192] Draft, 23 December 1975, G39/3.
[193] *The Times*, 24 February 1970, p. 18.
[194] *The Times*, 12 May 1970, p. 25
[195] 'Press announcement', 19 February 1970, 5A78/1.

was appointed to this post.[196] The post of financial controller was created to introduce and maintain a budgetary control system and was filled by John Rumins.

While McKinsey was carrying out its investigation, the Select Committee on Nationalised Industries (SCNI) was also conducting an enquiry into the Bank. The Committee had long pushed to examine the Bank, and despite initial resistance from Callaghan when he was Chancellor, his successor, Jenkins, gave the go-ahead in 1969. Its aim was to contribute to the public understanding of the relationship between the government and the Bank in light of the developments since the 1946 Act. Leslie Pressnell, an economist with interests in money and banking at the London School of Economics, was appointed as the specialist Adviser. The Committee examined functions and organisation, the financial relationship between the Bank and the government, and the Bank's accountability. Its terms of reference meant that the Committee was not supposed to stray into questions of economic or monetary policy, exchange control, the EEA, or the role of the Bank as banker. Jenkins did not want to give the Committee carte blanche and felt that the Bank's confidential relations with the Treasury had to be protected.[197] There were 26 witnesses in total, five from Whitehall, six from the Bank, eight from the City, four from the press, and three from academia. Evidence was taken during an 11-month period from April 1969 to March 1970. O'Brien appeared on nine separate occasions, usually accompanied by Hollom and at some points by Peter Taylor, the Bank's Secretary, and the Bank also submitted a number of papers.

One of the main criticisms in the report released in May 1970 was the Bank's lack of published accounts. The *Daily Mirror* stated on the following day, 'The Old Lady of Threadneedle Street has been told to strip her bonnet and shawl and put on a see-through dress.'[198] The Bank had long been shrouded in mystery, and the call for it to be more open was welcomed by outsiders. While the Committee recognised that changes had taken place since Radcliffe, notably with introduction of the *Bulletin*, it felt that the level of material published still was insufficient. The Bank certainly lagged behind other central banks in terms of its publication of information.[199] According

---

[196] Bank of England, *Annual Report*, year ending February 1970, p. 41.
[197] *The Financial Times*, 7 February 1969, p. 17.
[198] *Daily Mirror*, 29 May 1970, p. 25.
[199] During its work, the committee had visited the United States and also conducted informal investigations into the central banks of the Netherlands and the Federal Republic of Germany.

to the Committee, the Bank should publish accounts comparable with other nationalised industries, and thus figures of assets and liabilities, incomes and expenditure, and profit and loss were expected to be included in an expanded *Annual Report*. The suggestion that the Bank should become a little less secretive reportedly caused the Governor alarm.[200] He had argued that the Bank's secretive nature meant that it could achieve 'good by stealth', as indeed had Norman, and greater publication would threaten its independence.[201]

'Is Pope Leslie infallible?' asked another newspaper headline.[202] Not according to the Committee: it was 'wholly inappropriate that a public body should be accountable to nobody'.[203] The Bank should, it was argued, be answerable to Parliament in much the same way as other nationalised industries. Despite its desire to think of itself as different from other industries, mainly owing to its history, the Committee believed that the Bank should be treated in the same way as other public corporations. There was also concern over the Bank's efficiency. The Treasury was unsure about it but recognised that nobody was in a position to assess it properly. The report argued that the Bank could have been operating inefficiently for years and could continue doing so.[204] Although the Committee believed this not to be the case, it warned that 'any institution which is protected by secrecy and shielded from scrutiny is in danger of becoming unself-critical and complacent.'[205] Other suggestions were that capital expenditure should be subject to the same kinds of tests as the capital expenditure of other publicly owned bodies. The Bank should pay over the profits of the Banking Department to the government after agreed provision for reserves and working capital and should charge the full costs of services performed for government, including the administration of exchange control and management of the EEA and the national debt. The new regional branch buildings, so-called Taj Mahals, also were under fire because they had been built with little regard to cost. Furthermore, the Committee supported Lord Radcliffe's views that the balance of the Court should be weighted much more towards the Executive Directors. The idea that the part-time Directors provided a channel of communication for the Governor was no longer valid.[206] They were not an adequate substitute for public accountability and failed to

---

[200] Garvin (1970, p. 1186).
[201] SCNI 1970, 'Report', para. 254.
[202] *The Daily Mail*, 29 May 1970, p. 13.
[203] SCNI 1970, 'Report', para. 269.
[204] *Ibid.*, para. 266.
[205] *Ibid.*, para. 267.
[206] *Ibid.*, para. 128.

fulfill a useful role.[207] The Bank should also be examined in the future from time to time by the Nationalised Industries Committees.

A press conference in May was told that 'the Bank had never opposed the enquiry and could not have been more helpful. The Governor himself had always been immensely courteous and had gone out of his way to provide the Committee with what they wanted.'[208] The following month, O'Brien professed that he was 'not too unhappy with the report and its reception.'[209] Looking back with more distance, he found the questioning process 'both stimulating and enjoyable', and his relations with the Committee's members were 'most harmonious'. He believed himself to be especially skilled in this area. Although Mikardo was deemed to be 'intelligent and perceptive besides being most courteous at all times', his harsh comments towards the Bank at the press conference led the Governor to conclude 'the vulgar political animal had won the day'.[210]

Outside views as to whether the report was a success were mixed. *The Banker* was positive, believing that a 'good deal of useful light has been thrown' on the Bank. Relations between the Bank and the Treasury had been made a 'great deal clearer than they were before', and despite fears from within the Bank, the report failed to 'drag out something embarrassing or discreditable'.[211] The *Financial Times* believed that the report would have a considerable influence on the future role of the Bank and its relationship with the government, whereas *The Sunday Times* argued that the Committee's recommendations would not make any difference to the aspects of the Bank's affairs that really mattered. The Committee was criticised for approaching the Bank without great knowledge of financial and monetary affairs and for not pushing hard enough.[212] Nevertheless, it did have some impact on the Bank. Following the Committee's recommendations, the Bank started publishing its accounts in its *Annual Report* in 1971, and new charging arrangements took effect from March 1971.

Internal Organisation and the Court

From the 1950s to the 1970s, there was little change to the basic organisational structure of the Bank: a series of departments lying beneath the

---

[207] *Ibid.*, para. 129.
[208] Morgan to Taylor, 29 May 1970, 5A7/1.
[209] 'Extract from the Deputy Governor's memo on the Governor's conversation with Sir Douglas Allen, 4 June 1970', G38/5.
[210] O'Brien, Memoir, p. 97.
[211] *The Banker* 120(533):691, July 1970.
[212] *The Financial Times*, 29 May 1970, p. 12. *The Sunday Times*, 31 May 1970, p. 60.

Court, the Governors, and the Executive Directors. What changes there were, were relatively minor and had little impact on the way that the Bank operated. Aside from the greater recognition given to economic research, the Chief Cashier's empire remained at the heart of the Bank. In the first half of the 1960s, the Bank was organised into six main departments: Cashier's, Accountant's, Central Banking Information Department (CBID), Secretary's, Establishments, and Printing Works. When the CBID was disbanded in March 1964, the number of departments increased to seven with the re-establishment of Overseas and the formation of Economic Intelligence. Figure 7.1 shows that by the early 1970s, the number of departments had increased to eight with the addition of Management Services. A ninth department was created in 1973 when exchange control was moved out of the Overseas Department. There were further changes in 1976 with the formation of the new Administration Department, which brought together the Secretary's, Management Services, and Audit Departments with part of the Establishment's Department. Within these departments, there were also changes through the period. The Discount Office disappeared, and supervision grew. The Overseas Department and the EID also were reorganised to give a clearer organisational distinction between analytical and statistical work.[213] Still, the general structure of the Bank remained unaltered. However, it was not long before thoughts were to turn to developing a new organisational form that would be very different from the one that had served virtually since the foundation of the Bank (see Chapter 16).

Aggregate staff numbers for the early 1960s are difficult to establish but are more readily available from the middle of the decade. Total numbers at the head office in the mid-1960s fluctuated around 4,000. The Accountant's Department was the largest, although numbers did fall – from 1,600 in 1964 to 1,200 in 1970. Next was the Cashier's Department, with 1,000 people. The number of full-time banking staff was around 4,500, whereas the total number of employees, including technical and services and those at Debden, was about 7,000. There was also a large number of part-time women, between 800 and 900, working in the Accountant's Department and the Printing Works. Debden aside, the largest department in the Bank was now the Cashier's Department, with an average of 1,250, of which 345 were in the branches. The Chief Accountant's Department also employed more than 1,000 throughout the decade.[214] Exchange control numbers in the 1960s,

---

[213] Bank of England, *Annual Report*, year ending February 1976, p. 20.
[214] For traces of staff numbers, see files C6/7, E27/1, E27/2, and 1A179/23, and from 1970, Bank of England, *Annual Report*.

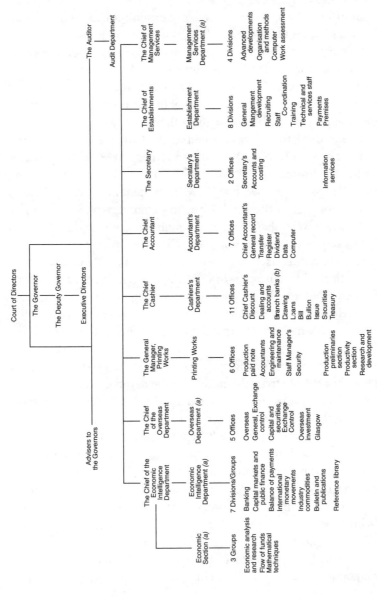

Figure 7.1. Bank of England organisation structure, 1970.

Note: A Financial Controller has yet to be appointed, and is not shown on this chart.

(a) Advisers are attached to the Economic Section and the Economic Intelligence, Overseas and Management Services Departments.

(b) Branches are maintained at Birmingham, Bristol, Leeds, Liverpool, Manchester, Newcastle upon Tyne, Southampton, and Law Courts (London).

doubling from around 250 in the early 1960s to over 500 by 1970 and then to around 750 at the end of the decade.

The 1970s witnessed an increase in the employment of graduates, with the intake doubling from 24 in 1972–73 to 48 in 1975–76. Then, after abolition of exchange controls, overstaffing saw recruitment fall to 18. By the middle of the 1970s, more graduates came from universities other than Oxford and Cambridge. On joining the Bank, graduates had nine weeks of basic training and induction with courses in banking and economics. Typically, they then spent two to three years either in the EID or the Overseas Department, engaged in the collection and analysis of financial and economic data. Development courses were offered, with those deemed to have potential for senior posts selected for an 'advanced training scheme', and entrants who showed considerable promise had the option of taking a post-graduate degree.[215] Graduates were expected to have reached junior management (supervisory) rank in their mid-twenties and administrative (middle management) rank in their mid-thirties. Not all, however, were satisfied. In March 1970, a note listing grievances was signed by 31 graduates who felt that far too much of their time was engaged in 'wasteful and frustrating' routine work for which graduate qualifications were not necessary. Furthermore, the pay structure was deemed 'inadequate and short-sighted'. Outside the Bank, salaries tended to increase rapidly in the first few years, levelling off later; inside the Bank, the opposite occurred. The graduates also believed that they received inadequate feedback on their performance.[216] The response from the chief of establishments was that the Bank provided 'an interesting and rewarding career for the graduate who is prepared to accept the natural constraints of the system'.[217]

The Bank continued to pay well throughout the 1960s. By 1968, senior staff earned between £7,000 and £10,000, whereas heads of departments could earn more (Table 7.6). The position of Chief Cashier remained the best paid among bank staff at £16,000. Remuneration for the Governors and Directors was examined and adjusted every four years. In 1961, the Governor's salary was £15,000 and the Deputy's £13,000. These were increased to £20,000 and £16,000, respectively, in 1964, and by 1968, the figures were £25,000 and £18,000. These figures were well above those for chairmen of nationalised industries, where the range was from £11,000 to

---

[215] Bank of England, 'Careers for graduates', 1975, 6A247/11.
[216] Various signatories to Davies, 9 March 1970, 8A314/1.
[217] Kenneth Andrews to Davies, 'The graduates' note of the 9 March 1970', 20 March 1970, 8A60/1.

Table 7.6. *Bank of England senior staff, March 1969*

Name	Joined	Position	From	Salary, £
John Fforde	1957	Chief Cashier	July 1966	15,325
Roy Heasman	1932	Chief Accountant	May 1967	12,374
Peter Taylor	1939	Secretary	March 1968	10,217
Charles White	1928	Chief of Establishment	May 1963	11,125
Gordon Fortin	1932	General Manager, Printing Works	March 1964	9,876
Geoffrey Tansley	1928	Agent, Law Courts Branch	April 1961	7,776
Kenneth Andrews	1939	Deputy Chief Cashier	April 1967	10,800
Richard Balfour	1935	Deputy Chief Cashier	April 1965	10,400
John Page	1941	Deputy Chief Cashier	April 1967	8,514
James Keogh	1937	Principal, Discount Office	October 1964	10,400
Roy Fenton	1929	Chief of Overseas	March 1965	11,352
Michael Thornton	1938	Chief of EID	July 1968	11,250
Guy de Moubray	1943	Deputy Chief of EID	July 1968	9,600
George Preston	1939	Principal, Dealing and Accounts	March 1967	8,032
James Humphrey	1928	Deputy Secretary	March 1968	7,379
Basil Maunder	1928	Deputy Chief Accountant	March 1963	8,628
Aphra Maunsell	1936	Deputy Chief of Establishments	July 1968	9,400
Clinton Smith	1932	Deputy Chief of Establishments	July 1968	9,200
Stanley Blackler	1939	Principal, Drawing Office	August 1966	5,506

Source: 1969 House List, E20/178.

£16,000.[218] Executive Directors on appointment received £14,000 and on re-appointment £15,250.

This situation did change somewhat in the early 1970s, when higher rates of pay for similar jobs elsewhere in central London were the main reason for staff leaving the Bank. In an assessment of young female staff, one manager wrote, 'Breaking into the Bank of England may have an initial glamour appeal, but it rapidly tarnishes if the booty does not match up, in cash terms.'[219] In 1973, it was recognised that the Bank would continue to lose young clerical staff because earnings were higher elsewhere.[220] Equal pay was introduced into the Bank in July 1972, ensuring that all women had equal treatment when employed on work of the same or similar nature to that of men. It was something that had been sought since 1964. In 1968, the Bank conceded equal pay in five instalments (although female staff later agreed to defer the implementation until 1969), and the scheme was implemented fully three years later.

Conditions for employees remained favourable. Recruitment brochures highlighted the array of sports and social activities that were available. *The Old Lady*, with its quarterly update on how the numerous sports teams faired and reports on theatrical productions, is testament to the numbers who took advantage of these facilities. There also were fringe benefits, something that was to come in for criticism from the 1976 Select Committee. These included housing and educational loan schemes, interest-free advances for travel season tickets, subsidised lunches, and unsecured personal loans for 'approved purposes'. Rates of interest on the loans were 2 to 3 per cent. In addition, there was a generous non-contributory pension scheme. Of course, the Bank was not unique among financial institutions in offering such facilities to its staff, but bearing in mind contemporary rates of inflation, the interest rates were extraordinarily low – over minus 20 per cent in real terms at times. The Select Committee suggested that in the prevailing financial climate it was time to bring such benefits into line with the sorts of charges that the public had to bear.[221] The *Daily Mirror*'s headline

---

[218] See G15/222.

[219] A. W. Miller, 22 October 1973, 6A61/3.

[220] Goodman to Thomas, 'Miss G. B. Hancock', 18 May 1973, 8A60/4.

[221] The calculation for housing loans was complex and based on a number of factors including rank. The 1976 Select Committee referred to mortgages of seven times salary. A 2 per cent mortgage in the rapid inflation in the 1970s was a powerful reason for staying at the Bank. *Seventh Report from the Select Committee on Nationalised Industries. The Bank of England* [SCNI 1976], 20 October 1976, 672; 'Report', paras. 122–123, and discussions with Bank employees. For more details, see Bank of England, 'Fringe benefits', SCNI 1976, 'Evidence', Appendix 4.

read, 'Chop Those Perks, MPs Attack Bonanzas for the Bank Staff'. George Morgan, the Bank's press officer, complained that the issue had been blown out of perspective by the newspapers, although it was inevitable that changes would come eventually.[222] Following an internal review in 1978, a revised housing loan scheme was implemented in 1979, by which new entrants had to finance their house purchase from a selected group of building societies with the interest rate subsidised by the Bank down to 5 per cent.[223]

When Cromer took over as Governor, the membership of the Court had been unchanged since the mid-1950s. Indeed, when Cromer joined the Bank as a part-time Director in January 1961, he was the first new appointment in four years. During the sixties and seventies, nine Executive Directors were appointed. The Executive Director with responsibility for establishments was George Abell until 1964, when James Bailey, formerly the Chief Accountant, took over. In 1969, Jack Davies succeeded Bailey. As Secretary of the Cambridge University Appointments Board since 1952, Davies had been instrumental in recommending graduates to the Bank, but his claim to fame was to have bowled the famous Australian batsman Donald Bradman for a duck during a cricket match between Cambridge University and the Australians in 1934.[224] Davies retired in 1976 and was replaced by Blunden.

The non-Executive Directors during the 1960s and 1970s remained the familiar mix of financiers, industrialists, and trades union representatives (Table 7.7) Some companies, notably Cadbury and Pilkingtons, had successive family members on the Court. The appointment of Ronald Thornton, who had been a member of the Halsbury Committee on decimalisation, signalled the first time that a Director had been chosen from one of the 'Big Five' and represented a significant break with the past: Morse had come from a clearer, Glyn Mills, as well, but they were small. In 1967, Gordon Richardson was appointed to replace Lord Kindersley, who, having been a Director since 1947, did not wish to be considered for reappointment. Richardson, the future Governor, then aged 51, was chairman of Schroders. A year later, newspaper baron Cecil King famously resigned following his article in the *Daily Mirror* on 10 May 1968 attacking the Prime Minister and the government and claiming that the country's reserve figures were cooked. Sir Eric Roll was a rare instance of a non-Executive Director who was an economist; reputedly tipped as a candidate for Governor on more

---

[222] Morgan, Note for record – 'Select committee report', 8 December 1976; Morgan to Taylor/ Page, 14 December 1976, 5A7/1.

[223] 'Housing assistance scheme', May 1978, 8A282/2, and other papers in 8A282/1–3.

[224] *The Times*, 10 May 1934, p. 6.

Table 7.7. *Bank of England Directors of Court, 1958–79*

Director	Served	Age on appointment	Background
Executive Directors			
Sir George Abell	1952–64	47	Overseas service (India)
Sir Cyril Hawker	1954–62	53	Bank of England
Sir John Stevens	1957–65	43	Bank of England
Maurice Parsons	1957–66	46	Bank of England
Leslie O'Brien	1962–64	54	Bank of England
Maurice Allen	1964–70	55	Bank of England
James Bailey	1964–69	55	Bank of England
Jeremy Morse	1965–72	36	Banking
Jack Davies	1969–76	57	University administrator
John Fforde	1970–82	48	Bank of England
Christopher McMahon	1970–80	42	Treasury/Bank of England
Christopher Dow	1973–81	57	Treasury/OECD
George Blunden	1976–84	53	Bank of England
Part-time Directors			
Sir Charles Hambro	1928–63	30	Merchant banking (Hambros)
Laurence Cadbury	1936–61	46	Food (Cadbury Brothers)
Sir John Hanbury-Williams	1936–63	43	Industry (Courtaulds)
Lord Sanderson	1945–65	50	Shipping (Shaw Savill)
Lord Kindersley	1947–67	47	Merchant banking (Lazards)
Geoffrey Eley	1949–66	45	Finance/stockbroking
Michael Babington Smith	1949–69	47	Banking (Glyn Mills)
Lord Bicester	1954–66	56	Merchant banking (Morgan Grenfell)
Sir William Pilkington	1955–72	49	Industry (Pilkington Brothers)
William Keswick	1955–73	51	Commerce/trading (Jardine Matheson)
Sir Alfred Roberts	1956–63	58	Trade union

(continued)

Table 7.7 *(continued)*

Director	Served	Age on appointment	Background
Sir George Bolton	1957–68	57	Bank of England
Lord Cromer	1961–66	42	Merchant banking (Barings)
Lord Nelson	1961–87	44	Industry (English Electric)
Sir Maurice Laing	1963–80	45	Building and construction
Sir William Carron	1963–69	61	Trade union (AEU)
Sir Henry Wilson Smith	1964–70	60	Treasury/industry (Powell Duffryn)
Cecil King	1965–68	64	Journalist
Lord Robens	1966–81	55	Politics/mining (National Coal Board)
Sir Ronald Thornton	1966–70	64	Banking (Barclays)
Gordon Richardson	1967–73	51	Investment banking (Schroders)
Sir Eric Roll	1968–77	60	Economist
Sir John Stevens	1968–73	55	Bank of England
Sir Val Duncan	1969–75	56	Mining/industrial (Rio Tinto)
Sir Sidney Greene	1970–78	50	Trade union
Sir Adrian Cadbury	1970–94	40	Food (Cadbury Schweppes)
Leopold de Rothschild	1970–83	42	Banking (N.M. Rothschild)
Lord Weir	1972–84	38	Engineering (Weir Group)
John Clay	1973–83	45	Merchant banking (Hambros)
Sir Hector Laing	1973–91	49	Food (United Biscuits)
Sir Alastair Pilkington	1974–84	54	Business (Pilkington)
Sir Robert Clark	1976–85	52	Merchant banking
Geoffrey Drain	1978–86	59	Trade union
Sir David Steel	1978–85	61	Oil (BP)

Source: Bank of England, *Annual Report*.

than one occasion, he left in 1977. Many of the Directors were long serving. On retirement in the 1960s, Cadbury, Hambro, Hanbury-Williams, and Sanderson had been on the Court for a total of 107 years.

The appointment process for the Court was no more transparent in the 1960s and 1970s than in previous decades and no clearer than the appointment of Governors (see Chapter 5). Both the Court and the government had names in mind as the Governor's term was coming to an end, but it is not obvious how the short list of candidates was drawn up. Senior non-executive members of the Court met the Chancellor to discuss the individuals, but thereafter the initiative rested wholly with the Treasury.[225] The Chancellor discussed the prospective candidates with the Prime Minister, and once the decision was reached, the appointment was made by the Crown. With other appointments to the Court, the Governor, after consulting the Committee of Treasury, approached the Chancellor with names in mind. According to a note, 'If the Governor is questioned separately about the selection of the Deputy Governor and Executive Directors, the formal procedure regarding the appointments is no different, but these being the Governor's "full time colleagues", it is natural that, in practice, the Governor's wishes should carry very special weight.'[226] This perhaps seems odd given O'Brien's uncertainty when Parsons became his Deputy, and matters appear to have changed little since then. In a speech in 2005, Howard Davies, Director of the London School of Economics and former Deputy Governor of the Bank, claimed that 'the procedures for identifying a new Pope, or a new Dalai Lama, are less opaque than those which precede the appointment of a chairman of the Federal Reserve, a Governor of the Bank of England or a President of the ECB.'[227]

Dating back to the Parker Tribunal and Radcliffe Report, the subject of the non-Executive Directors on the Court had been contentious, and it was raised again by the Select Committee in 1970. In evidence to the Committee, Lord Radcliffe, who was forthright about the role of these Directors, thought that the balance between the numbers of executives and non-executives was 'not very happily conceived today', and there should be more of the former and fewer of the latter. Radcliffe also deprecated the internal rule whereby there had to be a majority of part-time Directors on the Committee of Treasury; it was a 'relic from the old days'. The Select Committee endorsed these views in its report and suggested that the

[225] Anthony Loehnis, 'The Bank's non-executive directors', 29 March 1979, ADM10/49.
[226] *Ibid.*
[227] Howard Davies, 'What future for central banks?' lecture delivered at the London School of Economics, 24 November 2005.

1946 Act was too inflexible and should be, at a convenient time, amended to allow the balance of the Court to be weighted in favour of Executive Directors. It was not clear to the Committee that the part-time Directors exercised much influence, and there was scepticism about whether they fulfilled any essential role.[228]

Questioned by the Select Committee in 1976 about the role of the part-timers, Richardson said that he disagreed with the sentiments expressed in the earlier document. In the Governor's opinion, they performed a useful role: 'They give us a valuable and most useful spread of information – a sounding board, which I think we get in a most convenient and, if I may say so, extremely cheap form.' This final comment was a reference to the fact that the non-executives were still paid only £500 per annum, the amount specified in the 1946 Act. These comments were taken on board in the report, which stated that while the situation had not changed materially since 1970, 'the previous criticisms appear over-weighted, and we feel that we should redress the balance.' Bearing in mind the level of remuneration, the Committee felt that it had a duty to 'record with appreciation the services rendered by the twelve part-time Directors of the Bank at so little cost to the State'.[229]

The Wilson Committee had given brief consideration to the question of company boards and non-Executive Directors in general. Its main argument was that non-executives had their value but that the recruitment range should be as wide as possible and not limited to the great and the good. As shadow Chancellor during the saga of the Bank Rate leak Wilson had been less than impressed with the Bank and its part-time Directors. More than two decades later, he was not so critical. These Directors performed useful roles by sitting on internal committees, providing the sounding board for the Governors, and importantly for Wilson, supporting the Governor's position of 'quasi-independence from government'. However, while there was much to be said for the present system of appointing non-executives for their talents, the Committee felt that the present circle from which individuals were drawn was too limited. The makeup of the Court was little changed from the time of the Radcliffe Report, and insurance, building societies, and even non-business representatives were cited as notable absentees. There were two relatively muted recommendations: that non-executives should come from a wider range of backgrounds and that the maximum period of service

---

[228] SCNI 1970, 'Report', paras. 120–129, 134; 'Evidence', question 1737.
[229] SCNI 1976, 'Report', paras. 134–138; 'Evidence', question 555.

should be set at two four-year terms, with the appointment of Directors staggered in order to achieve both continuity and 'the infusion of new blood'.[230] If this rule had been in place at the end of the 1970s, then five Directors would have been disqualified.[231]

---

[230] Committee to Review the Functioning of Financial Institutions, 'Report' (Wilson Report), June 1980, cmnd. 7937, paras. 918, 1294–1300.

[231] The Bank of England Act 1998 changed the term to three years, whereas good governance practice means that generally only a maximum of two terms is served.

8

Sterling from Devaluation to Smithsonian

Whereas the devaluation of 1949 appeared to offer some resolution of the currency difficulties, that of 1967 did not, and sterling continued to struggle. In addition, the possibility of further devaluation and other drastic measures arose almost immediately. At the same time, there were other international monetary problems that were worsening. In the United States, as domestic policy increasingly took precedence over international considerations, further pressure developed on the dollar and hence on other currencies. Gold also felt the pressure. Sterling could not readily be separated from these problems, and in the years after devaluation, the developing tensions were such as to engulf the whole system. New sets of arrangements followed in the early and mid-1970s that owed less to design and more to the consequence of failing to find solutions to the problems. Sterling's devaluation was followed by the related collapse of the Gold Pool. The International Monetary Fund (IMF) pressure on the United Kingdom to accept conditions under the new standby and the tightening of policy were accompanied by continuing attempts to settle the sterling area questions. The debate on floating persisted, as did the use of exchange controls to stem both outflows and inflows, and there were, too, the attempts at reforming the international monetary system.

The immediate reactions to sterling's devaluation were largely predictable. When the Governor made his first speech in public following devaluation, he spoke with feeling of the frustrations that had been building over the previous years. He disposed of the myths of speculators or foreign bankers being responsible. There may have been bad luck in 1967, but essentially, the fault lay in poor policy and inadequate performance in the economy.[1]

---

[1] O'Brien, Speech at the Overseas Bankers Club, 5 February 1968; *BEQB* 8(2):171, June 1968.

He also expressed deep regret that devaluation had caused disappointment and embarrassment to overseas holders of sterling. Callaghan resigned, and Roy Jenkins became Chancellor on 30 November 1967. Sterling devaluation marked the beginning of the end for the international monetary arrangements of Bretton Woods, but from November on for the next several years, attention focussed on making devaluation work, and the first six months were the most difficult of all.

In 1967, most macro variables looked bad, with the possible exception of unemployment, the control of which continued to be a central objective. Even that was not at the level desired. It stood at 2.3 per cent in 1967, which was a rise over 1966, and this at a time when anything over 1.5 per cent was anathema to policymakers, and it continued to rise over the next five years to reach 3.8 per cent in 1972 (Table 1.1). The current account had deteriorated to a deficit in 1967 of £284 million and showed little signs of improvement until 1969, when it did eventually move into surplus and continued in surplus in 1970. Reflecting this, the exchange rate was under pressure in the early part of the period, staying close to $2.38 in 1968 and 1969, although only with considerable support, and then getting above $2.40 and staying moderately strong for the remainder of the short period. The reserves further reflected the external difficulties but continued to be distorted in the ways described in Chapter 5. Inflation had been a growing pressure, too, and while it had dropped to 2.5 per cent in 1967, it rose to 4.7 per cent in 1968 and further to 5.4 per cent in 1969. (It was then to go on rising until it peaked in the middle of the 1970s, when it reached annual rates of close to 30 per cent.) However, it was obviously of great concern in the three years after devaluation. There was a continuing belief among policy advisers and policymakers in a Phillips curve, whereby a little more inflation could be tolerated if it held down unemployment. (This, of course, was the time when there was serious academic challenge to the Phillips curve analysis.[2]) Added to that, though, was the belief that inflation could be contained by operating a prices and incomes policy. Such hopes were unfulfilled.

Following devaluation, there were mixed initial reactions both at home and abroad. There also were different views on both the early effects and what was seen as a lack of necessary supplementary measures. These latter were the principal concern of the IMF in the first consultations. And these concerns produced intense discussion of monetary control and, ultimately, led to a shift in policy from orderly markets with a focus on nominal interest

[2]   Friedman (1968); Phelps (1967).

rates to closer attention to monetary aggregates. It took some time before any of the promised benefits of devaluation could be detected, and in the meantime, there were other threats to the international monetary system. Of the questions that were framed at the time – of confidence, liquidity, and adjustment – the first was manifest in the gold market, where the crisis soon resulted in abandonment of the Gold Pool and establishment of a two-tier gold price. The second – liquidity – provoked increasingly urgent attention to reform of the international monetary system and in particular to the schemes for raising world liquidity. This was realised ultimately through the introduction of special drawing rights (SDRs), although by the time they were introduced the need had all but disappeared. The question of adjustment was addressed but not resolved in the extensive debate on monetary reform. For Britain, there was the further urgent need to do something longer term on the sterling balances, and this was achieved in large part through the Bank for International Settlements (BIS). Finally, there was continuing growth and continuing confusion over the Euro-currency markets. These had appeared in their modern form in the 1950s but became of increasing concern with their huge growth in the 1960s when they supposedly brought threats to both liquidity and inflation.[3]

Sterling Devaluation and Beyond

On Saturday, 18 November, the day of the announcement of devaluation, Morse visited Schweitzer at the IMF at 9:30 a.m. An executive board meeting was timetabled for 3:00 p.m. to discuss the possible IMF/General Agreement to Borrow (GAB) package that Britain required. It was hoped that a GAB meeting would follow soon after to agree to the principle of the standby and to approve the package that was required. The proposal was for an IMF $1.4 billion facility, very similar to that of 1965, made up of $400 million gold sales, $525 million borrowing under GAB, and $475 million use of existing IMF holdings.[4] Intensive negotiations went on over the next several days, with much depending on the content of the letter of intent required from the Chancellor and whether or not Britain would accept any conditions. The consultations with the IMF began immediately on Sunday, 19 November, where Cairncross outlined the likely impact of the announced measures. These contained insufficient inflationary control

---

[3] See Chapter 5 for origins and early development.
[4] Maude to Armstrong, Telegram, 18 November 1967; Peter Edgley to Fenton, 'I.M.F.: activation of G.A.B.', 18 November 1967, 4A160/5.

measures for the IMF.[5] Richard Goode, Director of fiscal affairs, headed the IMF's team, and he said that Schweitzer specifically wanted to know about HMG's 'monetary objectives'. In an IMF briefing paper of 17 November 1967, in anticipation of the visit to London, quantitative targets were set out for total net bank assets to be backed by specific restrictions on both private and public borrowing.[6] On the British side, however, there was deep scepticism over any kind of money-supply target, and Cairncross spoke in Radcliffean vein: 'The "liquidity position" of the economy was, in this country, largely a function of uncertainty.'[7] Goode pressed for a commitment to 'his version' of a monetary objective, and some indication of the gulf that existed between the parties can be detected in Thornton: 'I doubt if he is open-minded enough to be persuaded of its absurdity.'[8]

This division was to be the source of some wrangling and indeed almost brought the talks to a complete halt. Armstrong was so opposed to quantitative targets that he advised the Chancellor to reject them and, if necessary, forego IMF help. In the circumstances, this was hardly realistic. Goode suspected that the British were bluffing and reported to his superiors that the British were confident that the IMF could not afford not to lend.[9] The British team found the IMF's draft of the letter unacceptable: 'You will have seen the Fund mission's own draft – which we simply cannot accept.'[10] It meant that progress on the letter of intent was slow. Talks, however, did continue until Sunday evening, at which point it was arranged to draft the letter overnight.

A timetable then was drawn up for the IMF that would see them leave London on the Wednesday to have a board meeting on Friday, with approval sent to countries on the Saturday and a Group of Ten (G10) meeting in Paris on the following Monday. It was important that the programme should not slip for fear of a leak and the idea spreading that the proposed standby was running into difficulty.[11] The final version of the letter of intent was sent to the IMF on 23 November 1967. It contained strong intent and listed some

---

[5] Hubback to Rickett, 19 November 1967, 4A160/5; De Vries (1985, pp. 433–437); Cairncross (1997, pp. 247–255).

[6] Richard Goode and Albin Pfeifer (IMF Deputy Director, European Department), Paper, 17 November 1967, IMF C/UK/810 missions.

[7] Thornton to Hollom/Parsons, 19 November 1967, 4A160/5.

[8] *Ibid.*

[9] Thornton to O'Brien, 22 April 1968, 5A175/1; Alan Whittome (IMF Director, European Department) to Schweitzer, 22 November 1967, IMF C/UK810; Schenk (2010, Chapter 5).

[10] Hubback to Rickett, 'Letter of intent', 20 November 1967, 4A160/5.

[11] Morse to O'Brien/Parsons, 'Fund mission', 21 November 1967, 4A160/5.

objectives in terms of balance-of-payments surpluses and cutting public expenditure but was nevertheless less than was wanted by the other side. According to the letter, the government's main objectives remained a strong balance of payments, a high rate of economic growth, and full employment. More specifically, on the balance of payments, they were looking for an improvement of £500 million per year and for a surplus in the latter part of 1968 of £200 million. The public borrowing requirement was to be held down to £1 billion. The steps already taken meant that the expansion of 'bank credit' would be such as to 'ensure that the growth of the money supply will be less in 1968 than the present estimate for 1967 both absolutely and as a proportion of GNP'.[12]

A few months later, Thornton wrote on the subject of the money supply, saying that the words used in the letter of intent were 'carefully chosen to make it clear that we did not have "control of the money supply" as an explicit aim'.[13] They did not give a precise forecast for money supply but aimed for around £600 million for 1968, which included an optimistic assumption on the outcome for the balance of payments. This would have given a domestic credit expansion (DCE) of £300 million. The IMF felt that in order to get an outcome of £300 million DCE, interest rates would be needed at a level that would not allow the gross national product (GNP) contained in the forecast. They would have been prepared to see a higher forecast for the money supply, provided that the balance of payments was really going to be in surplus. In the event, the money supply did rise by about £600 million, but there was no balance-of-payments surplus. So much for the intentions immediately after devaluation.

When the new Chancellor made his statement to the House of Commons on 30 November 1967, his opposite number, Iain Macleod, replied, 'We recognise that there are nothing so crude as conditions attached to this. ... Is there a common view of desirable policies?' Jenkins replied, 'In spite of misleading reports to the contrary, the Fund has not attached conditions to this credit'.[14] Other countries were infuriated by the lenient treatment that Britain seemed to be receiving and by Britain's refusal to countenance any kind of conditions.[15] Remarkably, there were no strict conditions. But why, after all the problems of the 1960s and the failure to address the basic problem, is surely a puzzle. It was, after all, the normal procedure

---

[12] Hubback to Peter Baldwin (HMT), 23 November 1967, enc. Callaghan to Schweitzer [the letter of intent], 23 November 1967, 4A160/5.

[13] Thornton to Raw, 22 April 1968, 5A175/1.

[14] HC Deb, 30 November 1967, Vol. 755, cc643–644.

[15] James (1996, p. 190).

for the IMF to lay down conditions, and in the second half of the sixties, that meant negotiating domestic credit ceilings when providing standby or credit facilities. The origins of conditionality lie as far back as 1952, when the standby arrangements were developed. When in 1958 conditions were applied to Paraguay, the UK Executive Director wanted it recorded that this should not be regarded as a precedent. Yet, for Britain in late 1967, there were no provisions for phasing, no performance clauses, and relatively little in the way of credit ceilings. There were simply strong suggestions as to what was required, and there were plans for monitoring. This gave rise to discussions in the IMF that resulted in the principle of conditionality being given explicit legal sanction (in 1969).[16] However, in accordance with the undertakings given when the standby was negotiated, and more generally with IMF convention, an IMF consultation was planned to take place in February 1968, and it was hoped that some assessment of progress could be made at that time.

At the same time as the IMF standby was being negotiated, in late November 1967, a support facility of over $1.5 billion was organised through the BIS for a three-month period. This was much easier to arrange and was done without the long process that characterised the negotiations with the IMF. It was made up of $700 million from European central banks, $100 million from Canada, and $50 million from Japan; the BIS put in $250 million, and the Federal Reserve Bank (FRB) added $500 million to its swap line. This facility was renewed several times during the course of 1968 and 1969, but it finally lapsed in March 1970.[17]

On several occasions in the three years before devaluation, when the subject had arisen, there were some who pointed out that it was not a substitute for severe contractionary measures. As soon as O'Brien took over as Governor in the middle of 1966, he set out his ideas in a long letter to the Chancellor. In line with the mood of the time, he did not want to contemplate devaluation. However, like his predecessors, and against the general tide, he did at least implicitly challenge the growth and full-employment objectives by recognising that adjustment was also needed through what was called 'deflation'. Even if devaluation were to be discussed, however, O'Brien insisted that it would need to be accompanied by harsh measures. Adjustment could not take place solely through the exchange rate. Strict

---

[16] See Dell (1981).

[17] For various reasons, the actual amount of the facility was lower than the headline figure; for details, see EID3/297 and 1A155/1, and Bridge to O'Brien, 'Central bank credit facilities November 1967/March 1968', 4 September 1968, OV53/39.

monetary and fiscal policies would be needed too. O'Brien felt that deflation had not been sufficiently tried

... devaluation gives us no escape from the severities of deflation, severities which,
accompanied by statesmanship of the order this situation demands, might alone see
us through. Devaluation, unless so accompanied – indeed, even so accompanied –
means inflation of prices. ... Devaluation in a context of already-established control
over domestic demand and capacity to produce is one thing. Devaluation without
such pre-conditions is disaster.[18]

While there was some hesitancy in introducing such 'deflationary' measures, there nevertheless were some in November. Bank Rate was raised
from 6½ to 8 per cent, hire-purchase terms were tightened, ceilings on bank
lending were held at 15 November 1967 levels, and there were cuts in public expenditure and some raising of taxes. These measures were followed
by quite severe public expenditure cuts in January 1968 (£700 million to
take effect over the following year) and then a tough budget in March 1968.
Yet the balance of payments continued to deteriorate, and in the middle of
1968 (19 June), Britain made the drawing of $1.4 billion from the 1967 IMF
standby.

Reactions to sterling's devaluation in other countries were mixed but
largely predictable. Although there was a sense of betrayal, there was also a
lot of sympathy and a lack of surprise – it had been in the cards for so long.
Some were certainly hurt more than others and took it less kindly. While
the Fed had long been opposed to devaluation, Martin now realised it was
inevitable. However, Hayes and Coombs in New York were dismayed and
thought that Britain should have continued to rely on short-term money to
hold the rate. Coombs saw it as the first step on a road that would lead to
general chaos, and in certain senses, he was right.[19] Haslam visited the Far
East, and while his explanatory mission was appreciated, he nevertheless
reported that 'everyone feels let down [Bridge wrote in the margin predictably, 'So do we'] ... and the losses to their reserves will not be forgotten. ...
they are quite sceptical about the strength of the medicine we have declared
we intend to swallow [again Bridge wrote in the margin, 'So are we'].[20] The
Irish were sad but not surprised and had decided in advance to follow sterling. The Zambians were 'incensed'. There were no recriminations from
New Zealand or Australia. And so on.

[18]   O'Brien to Callaghan, 15 July 1966, G41/1.
[19]   Kirbyshire, Note for record – 'U.S.A and Canada', 22 November 1967, OV44/144.
[20]   Haslam, 'Devaluation, visits to Kuala Lumpur, Singapore and Hong Kong 19–24 November',
      1 December 1967, OV44/144.

In Britain in the weeks following devaluation, there was considerable gloom and fears that further devaluation would be needed. Just over two weeks after the devaluation, Aubrey Jones addressed the American Chamber of Commerce in New York and warned that sterling would be devalued again within two years.[21] Not surprisingly, the pound came under heavy pressure the next day. In the daily market report, Bridge remarks, 'Another nervous day. Little Aubrey [Jones] the talk of the town.'[22] At the end of November, Cromer, now back at Barings and in a private capacity, had met Dr. Herman Abs (a former Managing Director of Deutsche Bank and at the time a spokesman for the bank) with an influential group of bankers and businessmen, including Holtrop, Wilfrid Baumgartner (former Governor of the Banque de France), Wilfried Guth (Kreditanstalt fur Wiederaufbau), and Gianni Agnelli (Fiat), to talk about sterling and the Common Market. However, the conversation immediately turned to devaluation, on which the consensus was that not nearly enough had been done in support by way of tough measures to curtail demand – a view that Cromer communicated to O'Brien, even though, as he said, there was nothing particularly new in the view.[23]

In the Bank, there was gloom with defiance. On 20 December, McMahon wrote to Fenton and Morse to say that there was every chance that we would be pushed off the present exchange rate and that, if so, there would be no alternative to floating. The question then was, Should we plan for that? The answer was no:

We should be breaking IMF rules, could expect nothing from them and would therefore presumably want to do little more than give them a day or two's notice. Much the same would apply to the United States. We should very likely be toppling the dollar by our action and could expect no sympathy or help from them. Nor should we particularly wish to ask for it.[24]

This was not really like McMahon, who was normally calm and dispassionate, and it may have reflected the kind of stress they had been working under and the apparent lack of support from a government that was not rushing to take the needed measures.

However, it was not simply a knee-jerk response to the disaster, as some saw it. At the end of January 1968, Maurice Allen told Cecil King that he

---

[21] Kahn, 'Enquiry into the position of sterling January 1966–February 1968', 12 August 1971, Vol. I, p. 41, EID1/6.

[22] Market report, 7 December 1967, C8/35.

[23] Cromer to O'Brien, 1 December 1967, OV44/144.

[24] McMahon to Fenton/Morse, 'Contingency planning', 20 December 1967, 7A114/1.

thought the chances of a further devaluation in February were 50–50. And when King had Cromer to dinner two weeks later, the former Governor expressed the view that they would not get to budget day (19 March) without collapse of the pound.[25] Interestingly, when the Sterling Area Working Party reported in late January 1968, generally in platitudinous terms: 'restoration of confidence in sterling vital', 'try to contain pressures for diversification', 'build up surpluses and repay debt', and so on, it too had serious doubts. But it also considered more extreme measures, such as abandoning the $2.40 parity – this was not to be discussed outside the working party, although Morse agreed that the report could be circulated to Allen, Hollom, Bridge, Fforde, Leslie Crick (Adviser to the Governors), and John Kirbyshire (Adviser), the latter two experts on Latin America and North American, respectively.[26] Therefore, as early as January, at a serious level in the Bank, talk was around of further devaluation.

And yet, soon after devaluation, there appeared an assessment of the British economy by the distinguished American think tank, The Brookings Institution, in which Richard Cooper warmly endorsed the devaluation of 14 per cent, believing it to be more than enough to provide the required surplus on the balance of payments.[27] The surplus, or even any move in the direction of a surplus, however, took longer to appear than most had expected. There was a good deal written about this slowness of any improvement to appear, and there was some contemporary analysis in terms of the J-curve. This was the supposed shape of the time path of the balance of payments following devaluation. The pattern to the trade account was that there was a worsening before evidence of strong recovery appeared. The explanation for the empirical phenomenon was that it was a result of an immediate change in the tradable prices and a lag in trade volumes. Imports therefore rose in value and exports declined, and the current account worsened. Writing in 1969, Harrod noted that the 'likely course of the merchandise balance … should be represented as a J-shaped curve.' He also noted that Britain had been on the downward-sloping section for an unexpectedly long time and that there was still no sign of moving to the upward-sloping section in May of 1969.[28] The curve was much debated. For those who found it, the duration was of between one and three years. In Britain's case, it was mid-1969 when the trade figures began to move into

[25] King (1972, p. 171).
[26] Sterling Area Working Party, 'Report', 25 January 1968; Fenton, 'Sterling Area Working Party', 30 January 1968; Fenton to Morse, 30 January 1968, OV44/116.
[27] Cooper (1968, pp. 188–195).
[28] Harrod (1969, p. 265).

surplus, and by the end of that year, the current account surplus was £415 million. Also in 1969, though, there was a contractionary budget in April, and there was a monetary squeeze, a result of pressure from the IMF.

Before the budget of March 1968, there was the follow-up IMF meeting in February. For the first time, the Organisation for Economic Co-operation and Development (OECD) was to be included in the talks, mainly to help it prepare a paper for Working Party Three (WP3), although it would not be given much of the paperwork that was regarded as sensitive, such as balance-of-payments forecasts. The IMF was unenthusiastic about OECD participation, the more so because the Treasury wanted Dow, the OECD chief economist, to attend. Dow, formerly of the Treasury, had recently completed his study of the British economy – *The Management of the British Economy, 1945–60* – seen by his former employer as the final word on the subject. In his Stamp Memorial Lecture in 1968, Sir William Armstrong reviewed post-war economic policy and considered that the previous 10 years had demonstrated that economic policy clearly had been a success. The evidence for this could be found in Dow – you 'can't do better than turn to a book published in 1964 by Christopher Dow'. The book was a straightforward Keynesian analysis, so it is scarcely surprising that the Treasury was happy and the IMF was unhappy. In the event, Dow did not attend, although other OECD representatives did.[29]

It was anticipated that at the consultation a lot of attention would settle on the government's borrowing requirement and on monetary growth.[30] There were inevitably difficult areas, but broad agreement as to what was required was reached, and Goode's closing statement was thought fair, if predictable. The IMF was concerned about the rate of growth of consumption and worried about some of the assumptions lying behind the balance-of-payments forecasts. And the IMF pressed hard on the borrowing requirement, and it wanted action on the monetary aggregates. It was dubious about the sales of gilt-edged to the non-bank sector. The recommendations included that the March budget should aim to reduce final expenditure by between £400 million and £500 million and that the resulting borrowing requirement should be in the region of £500 million to £700 million.[31]

[29] Kirbyshire, Note for record – 'I.M.F.: U.K. consultations', 19 January 1968; Evan Maude (UKTSD) to Hubback, 24 January 1968; Kirbyshire to Morse/Fenton, 'I.M.F.: U.K. consultations', 26 January 1968; Hubback to Goldman, 26 January 1968; Hubback to Maude, 1 February 1968; HMT, 'I.M.F./O.E.C.D. consultations, February 1968', 9 February 1968, 4A160/6; Armstrong (1968, p. 15); Dow (1964).

[30] Callaghan to Schweitzer, 23 November 1967, 4A160/5.

[31] Kirbyshire to Morse/Parsons, 'I.M.F.: U.K. consultations', 28 February 1968, 4A160/6.

Even before the budget, though, there was need for action. At the beginning of March, confidence in sterling was precariously low, and the time was spent by the authorities searching for short-term credits. There is a story that on 7 March 1968, Jenkins warned his colleagues of a second devaluation within three months in such terms that they were never recorded in Cabinet minutes.[32] The developing gold crisis is an essential part of this story. At the Washington meeting to discuss the Gold Pool in mid-March, further central bank assistance of more than $1 billion was agreed in support of sterling. This included a further increase in the FRB swap facility, taking the total to $2 billion.[33]

In mid-December 1967, the Governor had written to the Chancellor saying that Britain had $1 billion in foreign-exchange reserves, of which roughly half were 'our own property'. By the following month, that position had changed, and the respective figures were $800 million and $300 million, while our debts to central banks, the BIS, Swiss banks, and the IMF totalled nearly $5 billion. Furthermore, debt to the IMF was due for final repayment in 1970, which meant that a start had to be made in repaying it in the course of 1968. The forecasts for the balance of payments for 1968, however, were showing no surplus at all. Additionally, there was the potential problem of countries diversifying out of sterling. O'Brien's message was that if Britain did not manage to persuade the world that it would deal adequately with the problem, 'I do not see how we can avoid bringing the international monetary system into chaos.' He added, 'The crisis in our affairs is such that I feel duty bound to ask you to be good enough to show this letter to the Prime Minister.'[34] Both the Governor and the Deputy Governor followed this up with accounts of how difficult it would be in the next two years to finance the debt, and in March, O'Brien told Douglas Allen that all the IMF standby of $1.4 billion should be drawn straightaway.[35] A small increase ($79 million) in published reserves had been shown for the first four months of 1968 but was possible only by increasing net borrowing by $1,489 million.

At the March 1968 meeting in Basle, the Governor secured some room for manoeuvre when the BIS agreed to release the Bank from commitments relating to the unused drawing rights on the IMF standby.[36] However, the

---

[32] Middlemass (1990, pp. 193–194), citing Crossman's diary.
[33] Details in EID3/297; Roper to Page et al., 'Bulletin article: "special assistance for the reserves: 1964–70"', 23 April 1971, 6A179/1.
[34] O'Brien to Jenkins, 11 January 1968, G41/2.
[35] Parsons to Armstrong, 7 March 1968; O'Brien to Allen, 21 March 1968, G41/2.
[36] Gabriel Ferras (BIS) to O'Brien, 22 March 1968 (telegram), and 8 April 1968, OV44/160.

short-term liabilities to central banks were such that something was needed quickly. A letter was drafted by officials for the Chancellor to send to Fowler at the US Treasury suggesting that $500 million of the Bank's drawings under the Fed's swap arrangements could be paid off but that a further £500 million might be funded through two-year Roosa bonds, which 'would give us a badly needed breathing space'. If that were arranged and it was announced that the Fed swap arrangement had been fully reconstituted, it would be good for confidence. Because of the gold crisis, the Bank had suggested certain modifications, but then the gold market closed on 15 March, and the letter to Fowler was not sent.[37] In Washington, a number of proposals were made, including that of blocking of sterling balances.[38]

On 18 March, Preston told the Governors, 'We are in need of quite a lot of money', and he proposed drawing the whole of the standby ($1,400 million) 'forthwith'.[39] The Governor told Armstrong that and explained that dollar resources were extremely low – 'we have less than $100m to play with' – and there was no sign of any inflow of exchange. It was also necessary to repay some central bank swaps.[40] O'Brien had been in close contact with Schweitzer and made all the necessary arrangements. But Schweitzer had made it plain to O'Brien that if Britain was forced off the new rate for sterling, the standby would no longer be available. This was one good reason for acting quickly. There were some complicating factors, though, and the need for some window dressing at the end of the month, so O'Brien's recommendation was that the drawing should be made in April.[41] The Treasury had doubts about how this might be presented and its effect on confidence, and instead, it sought to revive the suggestions in the Chancellor's aborted letter to Fowler.[42] In May, O'Brien wrote to Allen at the Treasury in the gloomiest of terms. He outlined at length the dire debt and foreign-exchange position: 'Our total indebtedness incurred since 1964 [was] $6,496m.' With the published reserves at $2,773 million but with market forwards of $1,922 million, the plight was clear. Some negotiations were going on with the Fed and US Treasury for a renewed swap, but optimism was not high. And it was in this context that O'Brien continued to see the need for an early IMF

[37] Bank draft, 13 March 1968; Fenton to Hubback, 14 March 1968, 4A160/7.
[38] Armstrong to Jenkins, 16 March 1968, OV53/38.
[39] Preston to Bridge/O'Brien/Parsons, 'I.M.F. drawing', 18 March 1968, 4A160/7.
[40] Extract from the Deputy Governor's memo dated 27 March 1968 … ', 4A160/7.
[41] O'Brien to Armstrong, 21 March 1968, G41/2; 'Extract from the Deputy Governor's memo dated 20.3.68 …', 4A160/7.
[42] Morse, 'Talk with Sir Denis Rickett and Mr. Goldman: Friday 22 March', 25 March 1968; Jenkins to Fowler, 25 March 1968; 'Extract from the Deputy Governor's memo dated 27.3.68 … '; 'Extract from Mr. Hollom's memo dated 10.4.86 … ', 4A160/7.

drawing.[43] Pressure was building, and at the April meeting in Basle, central banks were keen that some of the debt should be funded as soon as possible. The drawing finally was made in June, and the proceeds were used to repay some outstanding central bank debt and the whole of the FRB swap, but not before considerable ground had been ceded on the need for monetary control of the kind the IMF had suggested.[44]

In the middle of all this, the budget measures were announced on 19 March, and they were generally approved of. The pound strengthened on the back of the measures and strengthened further following the Stockholm agreement on SDRs. And in the ways of the past, with the immediate crisis over, Bank Rate then was reduced from 8 to 7½ per cent. However, heavy losses at the end of June and early July meant that the Bank again had to resort to the Fed swap arrangement, and by the end of July 1968, drawings amounted to $350 million. Although this was reduced to $300 million in August, it had increased to $400 million in early September.[45] Then heavy support for sterling in November required further drawings on the FRB, and by the end of 1968, $1,150 million of the $2,000 swap facility had been utilised.[46] This figure fluctuated during 1969, and it was still £1 billion in September. It was not until February 1970 that it was all repaid.

A picture of the changing foreign-exchange and reserve position across these few years can be seen in Figure 8.1, and market intervention is shown in Figure 8.2. The rate began well enough, above the new parity of $2.40, but then fell in March 1968 from $2.41 to $2.39. On some days, more than $200 million was being spent in support. Some recovery then was effected before further falls in the middle of the year to below $2.3850. There was then further substantial support and some recovery in the rate. The rate was to weaken again at the end of the year, and support, concentrated in two weeks in November and December, was greatest of all at over $1 billion, and the rate was held at $2.3850. Bridge anticipated this on 15 November when he wrote, 'Trouble brewing'. The following day was a 'shocking day'. Things got worse on 20 November, and the London market was closed. On 10 December, after the Basle meeting, *The Times* carried a headline, 'No More Credit for £', and the following day there was a 'bear attack from Continent'. But then that turned around quickly because trade figures were extremely good.[47]

---

[43]   O'Brien to Allen, 6 May 1968, G41/2.
[44]   Bruce MacLaury (FRNBY) to Bridge, 'Sterling', 14 February 1969, 6A83/3.
[45]   Coombs (1969, p. 51).
[46]   *BEQB* 8(4):356, December 1968.
[47]   Bridge annotation, 'Foreign exchange and gold markets, Tuesday 10 December 1968', 11 December 1968, C8/36.

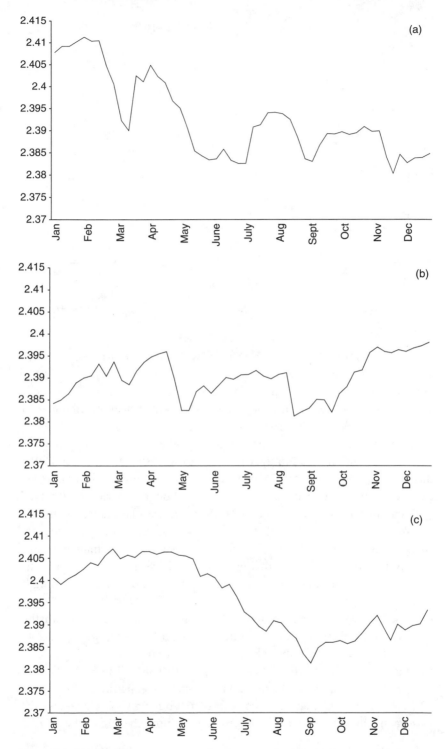

Figure 8.1 *(continued)*

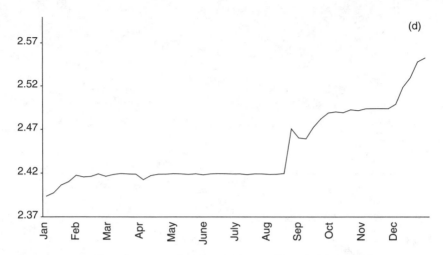

Figure 8.1. Weekly exchange rate (US$ spot) (a) 1968; (b) 1969; (c) 1970; (d) 1971.
Source: BEQB.

1969 was in some respects less eventful, with the rate more stable, albeit at a lowish level, almost always below $2.39, and there were two periods in May and August of that year when substantial support was given. On these occasions, Bridge was typically acerbic. On Monday, 5 May, he wrote of the previous Friday, 'a nasty Friday'. Two days later, he saw 'clouds gathering' but then made no comment on the worst day of all Friday, 9 May. In the middle of the year, 'flabby' and 'puddingy' were Bridge's words for the market. On the day after the French franc was devalued, Monday, 11 August, the market was more orderly than expected. By Wednesday, though, the view in the Bank was that the Chancellor's intervention [in exchange-rate management] was ill-timed, and we 'were forced to sell dollars massively until near the close'. Bridge added, 'Irresponsible political interference in rate management.'[48] However, in the last quarter of 1969, the signals were improving, with the balance of payments at last moving into surplus, the exchange rate strengthening, and dollar reserves being partially rebuilt. The first half of 1970 saw this continue, with the rate remarkably steady and above $2.40 and further substantial acquisition of dollars. Life in Foreign Exchange was quiet for a change. After June 1970, though, the rate went into decline, falling steadily through to September, when it reached a low of $2.3813. The fall in the third quarter, however, seems to have been regarded with equanimity. But then as $2.38 was once again approached, substantial buying took place, and that was again followed by a steadily improving rate until the end of the year.

---

[48]   See foreign-exchange market reports, C8/37; Jenkins (1991, pp. 280–281).

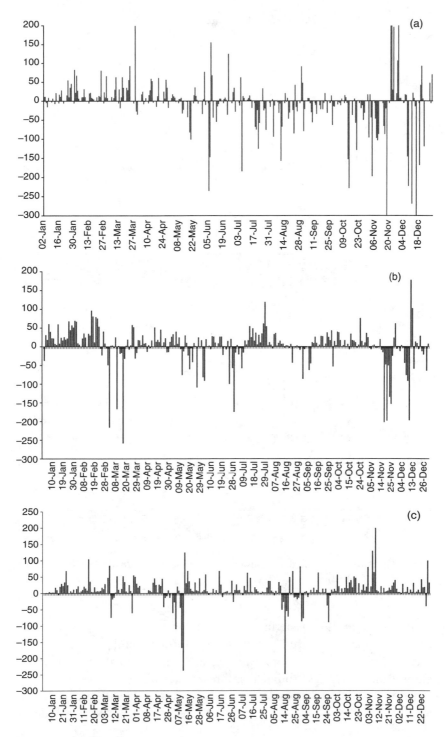

Figure 8.2 *(continued)*

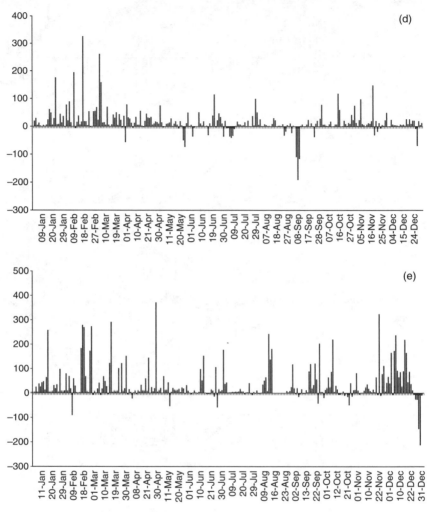

Figure 8.2. Bank of England daily transactions in the foreign-exchange market, (a) 1967;
(b) 1968; (c) 1969; (d) 1970; (e) 1971.
Source: Dealers' reports, C8 various.

The next year, 1971, is perhaps the most remarkable. The rate was almost completely flat and above $2.41 all the way through until August. This was a reflection of a vastly improved and improving external account, and it allowed the authorities to build their foreign-exchange reserves even further. After August 1971, when dollar convertibility into gold was suspended, the rate jumped sharply to $2.47 and strengthened steadily in the remainder of the year, even as the authorities built further their exchange reserves. After the Smithsonian Agreement setting new rates, the pound was fixed at $2.60, and the charts reveal the picture of stability until the middle of 1972, when the pound floated.[49]

It would be convenient if we could now turn to the reserves and see precisely what all this meant for the changing reserve position. Unfortunately, for a variety of reasons, this is not possible, as has already been discussed to some extent in Chapter 5. The published reserve figures are shown in Figure 8.3 for what they are worth. They must be worth something because they are what the markets looked at, although even that should be qualified. Roy Bridge, who knew better than most, said that the reserve figures 'mean nothing now since they have been consistently cooked since October 1964, and this is universally recognised'.[50] They certainly do not give a true account. In the 1960s, the published figure hovered around $2.5 billion to $3 billion. Immediately after devaluation, they stood at $2.7 billion (December 1967). They fell slowly through 1968 and into 1969 to reach a low point of $2.4 billion in May of that year. Thereafter, recovery saw the figures move to $3.5 billion by mid-1971 and $6.6 billion at the end of 1971. In the first half of the 1960s, the reserves were held almost entirely in gold – seldom less than 90 per cent and as high as 96 per cent in late 1964. However, the extensive borrowing of foreign currencies saw this change. In November 1967, the gold share hit a low point of 36 per cent, but it was back to around 60 per cent by the end of 1969 and stayed there until the third quarter of 1970; after that, the path was downwards and was well below 20 per cent by late 1971.

This changing composition of the reserves in the 1960s (Figure 8.4) has a fairly straightforward explanation. One part had to do with the existence of two reserve currencies, and the other had to do with the fact that gold did not earn anything. Until 1964, the Bank maintained that a reserve currency should be backed by an independent asset rather than by the other reserve currency. The following few years put paid to this argument. By 1971, the view was that a change in the price of gold was remote and that while the possibility of a US dollar devaluation existed, its timing was likely to be several years off. Therefore, it was concluded, hold dollars and repay the outstanding BIS swap with gold rather than dollars. In any case, in the first half of 1971, the Bank felt that it could not get more gold, even if it wanted it, and there was not undue worry about that. Furthermore, in view

---

[49] On one calculation of the real exchange rate (where January 1974 = 100), the rate stood at 111 in June 1966; then, following devaluation, it was 94, slipped to 93 in January 1968, but strengthened to 95 in the middle months of 1969 and then was 100 in the middle months of 1971. The numbers should be treated with due caution.

[50] Bridge to Morse, 12 December 1968, 7A114/8.

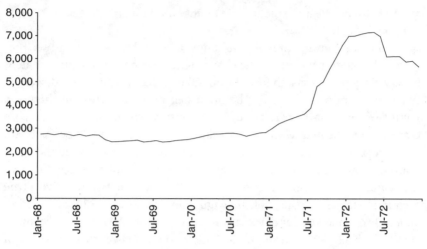

Source: Calculated from *BEQB* and *Economic Trends*.

Figure 8.3. UK published reserves, monthly, 1968–72 (£m).

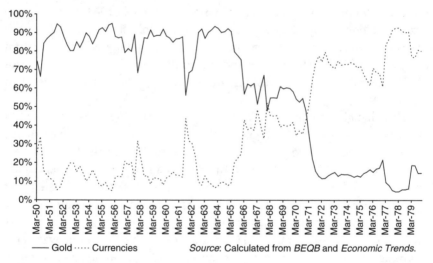

—— Gold ····· Currencies   *Source*: Calculated from *BEQB* and *Economic Trends*.

Figure 8.4. UK gold and convertible currencies as a percentage of reserves, monthly, 1950–79.

of the possible entry into the European Economic Community (EEC), the percentage of gold-based assets should be maintained at around the present level of 50 per cent.[51] When these ideas were discussed at the Policy Committee in early May, the Governor said that the only option open to

[51] 'The disposition of reserves', 24 March 1971 (written by Sangster and Hallett), 6A134/1.

them was to reduce the gold-based element in the reserves, but he did not want to take that option.[52] The explanation for the fall in 1971 was that most of the gold went to international organisations: to the IMF settling charges on previous borrowings and for the quota increases in gold sub-scriptions, as well as to the BIS to repay a £500 million gold swap from the late 1960s. Interestingly, in terms of freedom of action, the Bank appears to have made all the calculations and used its judgement as to how best to hold the reserves, and this was accepted, with limited consultation, by the Treasury.[53] It also demonstrated, for Treasury official Mary Hedley-Miller, that 'on things which the Bank would rather keep as "their" preserve, it is better to try to discuss with them than to write: they deliberately keep their letters pretty short.'[54]

The published reserve figures are of some use, but they are misleading in many ways. Not only were they routinely window-dressed, but they were inevitably distorted by the differing treatment given to the different types of borrowings and drawings. It is probably impossible to provide a 'true' picture. It is not always clear what path these borrowings took through the accounts. The overall position of Britain's indebtedness is shown in Table 8.1. There had been no net indebtedness in 1963, but it grew in the following three years and stood at $5 billion in late 1967. It was then to increase steadily to peak at over $8 billion at the end of 1968. Thereafter, the decline was relatively gradual, coming down to $2 billion in early 1971 and $1 billion in mid-1971 and, excluding public-sector foreign-currency borrowing, was repaid completely in April 1972. There were three main sources of funds: the IMF, the BIS and other central banks, and some foreign-currency deposits. Initially, the bulk came from the second group, and the third was relatively small. After devaluation, the bulk of the debt outstanding was to the BIS and other central banks, and this remained the case until the middle of 1970. The debt to the others was then repaid completely by February 1971. There were some other small debts in that local authorities were borrowing in foreign currency under special arrange-ments with Exchange Control, although that did not develop greatly until after 1972.

In a somewhat uncharacteristic display of transparency at the end of 1968, the Bank expressed the hope that it would be able to tell the story

---

[52] Peter J. Bull, 'Policy Committee. Meeting of 6 May 1971', 27 May 1971, 6A134/1.

[53] Alan Bailey (HMT) to Peter Gregson (No. 10), 18 October 1971, enc. 'The composition of the United Kingdom's reserves', 15 October 1971, T312/3302; Hedley-Miller to Rawlinson, 13 November 1969, T312/3416 TNA.

[54] Hedley-Miller to Rawlinson, 13 December 1971, T312/3302 TNA.

Table 8.1. *UK total assistance outstanding, quarterly, December 1967–72 ($m)*

Month end	IMF	Other borrowing with a sterling counterpart	Foreign-currency deposits placed with overseas monetary authorities	Public-sector foreign-currency borrowing	Total
Dec 1967	1,508	2,990	463	0	4,961
Mar 1968	1,508	3,957	768	0	6,233
Jun 1968	2,908	3,573	965	0	7,446
Sep 1968	2,823	4,039	674	0	7,536
Dec 1968	2,723	4,842	506	0	8,071
Mar 1969	2,400	4,692	374	0	7,466
Jun 1969	2,700	3,958	585	50	7,293
Sep 1969	2,675	3,987	684	113	7,459
Dec 1969	2,650	3,384	360	120	6,514
Mar 1970	2,400	1,570	0	120	4,090
Jun 1970	2,381	1,125	0	120	3,626
Sep 1970	2,364	1,502	0	120	3,986
Dec 1970	2,328	958	0	120	3,406
Mar 1971	1,639	0	0	243	1,882
Jun 1971	1,620	0	0	316	1,936
Sep 1971	996	0	0	316	1,312
Dec 1971	1,081	0	0	366	1,447
Mar 1972	1,055	0	0	366	1,421
Jun 1972	0	2,608	0	366	2,974
Sep 1972	0	0	0	366	366
Dec 1972	0	0	0	366	366

Source: BEQB.

of central bank and other assistance from the beginning of 1966. It was not entirely without prompting because journalists had been complaining that since 1965, the *Bulletin* had been uninformative. By the summer of 1969, the proposal was that there should be a *Bulletin* article that would tell the whole story from 1963 when there was no debt outstanding. Work began on the article, and a correspondence developed with the Treasury as the article went through several drafts. Finally, the proofs were ready in

November 1969 and duly went to the Treasury for clearance. The Treasury was in fact supportive, but the initiative failed at the last hurdle when the Chancellor vetoed it. He was opposed to providing the brief history because it would show that at the end of September 1969 debt outstanding was well above what it had been in March 1968, the time of his first budget when he could reasonably be said to have been in control of affairs. Jenkins wanted fuller disclosure postponed until better figures were available, and at that point, he would make the disclosure himself. Work, in fact, continued until the middle of 1971, but at that stage, with different people involved, there were other kinds of questions being raised in the Bank, such as should it not be cleared with the counterparties who had not always acted with the full knowledge of their governments.[55] The article never appeared.

Crisis in Gold

Before the IMF proposals on monetary control began to be discussed, there were still more damaging events in the international sphere. Of greatest immediate significance was the crisis in the gold market that led quickly to the collapse of the Gold Pool. It was late 1967 and early 1968 that saw the beginning of the end for that arrangement. In the immediate aftermath of sterling devaluation, attention had shifted to other currencies, and that, in turn, meant gold. And what was happening in the gold market gave rise to considerable anxiety for the wider system.

The Gold Pool, designed to bolster confidence, was put to its most severe test following devaluation, when there was the biggest ever rush into gold. Gold Pool losses in the week after devaluation were $578 million, making a total of $836 million for the month of November and more than $1 billion before the end of the year.[56] By the end of 1967, it had become clear that if the gold price were to be brought under control at minimum, the Gold Pool needed to be reinforced. A number of contributing participants could not go on indefinitely putting gold into the market. The French had in fact

---

[55] Morse to O'Brien, 'Disclosure of central bank assistance', 25 November 1969; Figgures to Morse, 26 November 1969; Francis John Roper (EID), 'Bulletin article: "Special assistance for the reserves: 1964–1970"', 23 April 1974; John Sangster to Hallett/Thornton, 'Bulletin article "Special assistance for the reserves 1964–1970"', 29 April 1971, 6A179/1.

[56] Meltzer (2009, p. 702). The US loss of gold was partly hidden by a British purchase: 'What the market did not know, of course, was that only a $250 million purchase of gold from the United Kingdom saved the United States from a still larger loss.' FOMC, Memorandum of discussion, 12 December 1967, *http://www.federalreserve.gov/monetarypolicy/fomchistorical1967.htm*.

withdrawn from the Gold Pool in June 1967, news of that inconveniently leaking out on the Monday following the British devaluation. The *Bulletin* put it diplomatically: France 'had ceased to take an active part in the pool in July'.[57]

A number of schemes emerged to try to solve the crisis, such as Solomon's 'gold certificate plan'.[58] In late 1967, the option of closing the London gold market came under consideration, but the Bank was not in favour, believing that it would damage confidence in the dollar. Ryrie supported that.[59] Furthermore, the Governor believed that as long as the United States wanted to go on with the Gold Pool, the United Kingdom should support it. He felt that the market had been 'a powerful stabilising factor'.[60] Other options included raising the price of gold, O'Brien's own preference. But the United States frequently and strenuously denied that they would do this. Devaluation was as unthinkable in the United States as it had been in the United Kingdom.[61] This remained the position for the succeeding administrations for the rest of the 1960s. The main argument against raising the price was the inflationary consequences, but in O'Brien's view, the Americans 'were more concerned with the sanctity of the almighty dollar and could not bear the shame of devaluing it against gold'.[62] Some in the 1960s argued for a doubling of the nominal price of gold to $70 per ounce, but even a more modest rise of half that in the middle of the 1960s would have raised US gold reserves to more than $20 billion and probably allowed the system several years more of life. The Americans also were opposed to any action that could benefit the Soviet Union, one of the largest gold producers, or the apartheid regime in South Africa, the other large producer. There was, too, the additional concern that raising the price would lead to the belief that it might well be raised again. In late November there was a huge movement of gold from the United States to London to ensure that there would be a sufficient supply to meet the sales to the market. In the event, though, none of this was sufficient.[63]

[57] *BEQB* 8(1):5, March 1968.
[58] Solomon (1982, p. 115).
[59] Parsons, 'Note of discussions in Frankfurt on November 26', 27 November 1967, G1/285; Ryrie to Rickett, 23 November 1967, T312/1735 TNA.
[60] O'Brien to Rickett, 14 August 1967, T312/1735 TNA.
[61] Sorensen (1965, p. 408).
[62] O'Brien, Memoir, p. 74.
[63] There was a huge airlift of gold from the United States, co-ordinated by the US Air Force, the Federal Reserve, and the Treasury; FOMC Minutes, 27 November 1967; and then stories of trucks pouring along the highway from Heathrow to the Bank.

At the beginning of January 1968, the United States removed gold cover from the dollar, and the writing then was on the wall. In order to hold to the official price of gold in London, the Gold Pool sold more than $3 billion of gold between November 1967 and mid-March 1968. Although as late as 10 March members of the Gold Pool were still maintaining that they would keep the Pool going, the strains were proving too great. On 14 March, 300 tons of gold ($385 million) were sold from US reserves, and it was anticipated that the same would be required on the following day. Before that happened, the gold market was closed on 15 March 1968 at the request of the United States. At an emergency meeting on 16 and 17 March 1968 in Washington, it was decided to end the Gold Pool's operations. A two-price system that permitted the price in private markets to be determined by the market without official intervention was proposed. The Bank was opposed, but, while no one regarded the dual-price system a complete solution, the proposal had the support of most delegates.[64] The London market remained closed until 1 April 1968, and on reopening, the private purchase and sale of gold was carried out at free-market rates, and two daily price fixings were established. This arrangement stuttered along for another two years.

A full assessment of the achievement of the Gold Pool is still awaited. What stability was achieved and at what cost, and who bore it? Was it a 'perfect example of multilateral cooperation facilitated by the existence of the BIS ... The Pool performed well in smoothing price gaps as long as the underlying fundamentals did not undermine its credibility as a price setter'?[65] In the early years, some fortuitous circumstances distorted the picture of success. In the first three years, the supply of gold was greater than demand, and the participants found themselves acquiring gold to the tune of $1.3 billion. After 1966, though, a combination of declining confidence in the two reserve currencies and a fall in production saw net sales total $3.5 billion. Furthermore, some of the participants did not share the view that it was in the common interest to preserve the system. The French in particular, although there were others, saw the use of the dollar as an international reserve as promoting inflation. And there were no disciplinary procedures for those who broke the rules.[66] It was a cartel, and cartels break up when some member(s) tries to escape before others when danger signals appear. On this occasion, it was the French who led the way out. As soon as news of French gold purchases was out, the game was over.

---

[64] McMahon, 'Top secret note', 14 March 1968, OV53/38.
[65] Borio and Toniolo (2005).
[66] Eichengreen (2007, pp. 64–66).

IMF Conditions – DCE Targets

The collapse of the Gold Pool was just one of the inevitables of the decade. It drew further attention to deficiencies, but addressing the basic question of monetary control was needed. From the IMF's point of view, the British responses to their strictures on monetary control at the time of devaluation were insufficient. It therefore proposed a seminar at which the questions could be discussed. The IMF began with the 'correct' definition of the money stock for an open economy as domestic credit creation, or domestic credit expansion (DCE). There was considerable resistance in Britain to any talk of monetary control, and the resistance extended to this particular version. The IMF believed that the British required educating and proposed a seminar at which DCE would be the central topic.[67] Unfortunately, yet again, the Bank's papers are missing, and there is no record of the preparations for the seminar, of its conduct, or of follow-up and outcome. The Treasury provided some papers, including the minutes of the meetings, and so an outline of the events can be told.

Although defining DCE proved problematic, the essence of the concept was relatively straightforward. For a closed economy, DCE would be roughly equivalent to changes in a broad monetary aggregate. In an open economy, however, credit expansion could leak abroad through a payments deficit. Thus a high rate of credit expansion accompanied by an external deficit could be consistent with a low rate of money growth. (This in fact appears to be what had happened in 1968.) It thus was a measure of domestic money supply adjusted for some external transactions. Any rise in domestic money supply therefore would be reduced by whatever the external spending was. The attraction was its usefulness when the balance of payments was the preoccupation and there was a pegged exchange rate.

The first meeting of the seminar was held in October 1968, and among others, there were from the Treasury, Cairncross, Kaldor, Posner, and Lovell; from the Bank, Allen and McMahon and Crockett on the secretariat; and from the IMF, Polak. They met over four days and considered a range of papers, and on the final day, 21 October 1968, Polak gave an admirable summing up.[68] Tew claims that the seminar was one of the chief catalysts of official thought for the Bank and the Treasury.[69]

---

[67] Thompson-McCausland to Allen, 29 May 1968, 7A136/1; between 1965 and 1968, Thompson-McCausland was a consultant to the Treasury on international monetary matters.
[68] Edwards, MS(IMF)1st–4th, 'Monetary seminar (International Monetary Fund) minutes of proceedings', 2 January 1969, 7A353/1.
[69] Tew (1978a, p. 247).

There had been a growing awareness in the Bank of the need to adopt a position on money supply (see Chapter 9). But this was certainly given an extra fillip following devaluation and the IMF consultations. At the beginning of 1968, Thornton, who happened to be among the most sceptical on monetary aggregates, prepared a note on money supply, and that prompted Hollom to propose wider discussion. Maurice Allen, one of the more sympathetic, followed up immediately, writing to Cairncross, 'We need to do something if we are to provide the IMF with coherent material on money in the UK.'[70] Wider interest in the subject was beginning to be shown, too, as evidenced by Conservative MP John Biffen putting down a parliamentary question on 27 March 1968: 'By what amount does the Chancellor expect to increase the money supply during the financial year 1968–69?' The prepared answer was to be: 'the growth of the money supply is not determined by government action alone; but I expect the increase to be smaller in 1968–69 than in 1967–68'. Harold Lever, Financial Secretary to the Treasury, however, answered for the Chancellor, and he departed from his script and said that monetary growth was affected by 'a great many factors outside our control' – an answer that was highly approved of in at least some quarters in the Bank.[71] Thornton sent a note to Fforde and Allen: 'You may like to share in the EID rejoicing over Mr Lever's unscripted Supplementary Answers. ... We certainly did not expect that we had such an ally in Mr. Lever.' Allen wrote on the note, 'I can only recommend that Mr. Lever should read more extensively in the works of Sir Ralph Hawtrey.' And O'Brien added, 'WMA, CC, CWM, MJT [Allen, Fforde (Chief Cashier), McMahon, and Thornton] had better have a talk with me about this.'[72]

In October, Conservative MP 'Jock' Bruce-Gardyne put down another parliamentary question that went back to devaluation and the IMF: 'Will the Chancellor make a progress report on the fulfilling of paragraph 11 of the Letter of Intent?' The answer was that the paragraph gave no undertaking, only an expectation, and that there was no need to revise that expectation.[73] It was, though, clearer than ever that the Bank needed to do something, and finally, in October, a working party on the subject was proposed by Allen to be made up of Morse, Dicks-Mireaux, and Goodhart,

---

[70] Allen to Cairncross, 16 February 1968, 5A175/1.
[71] HC Deb, 2 April 1968, Vol. 762, c164.
[72] Thornton to Fforde/Allen, 'Money supply', 5 April 1968, and Allen and O'Brien annotations, 5A175/1.
[73] Andrew Edwards (HMT) to Lovell, 'PQ on letter of intent and money supply', 10 October 1968, 5A175/1; HC Deb, 15 October 1968, Vol. 770, c72W.

with Crockett as Secretary. This marked the beginning of serious work on money in the Bank.

And yet there must have been considerable separate preparation within the Bank specifically for the IMF seminar, which had been known about for a long time. Indeed, the Bank provided three papers (of 23) for the meetings.[74] One of these was entitled, 'Defining the Money Supply', unsigned, but smacking much more of Thornton than Allen. It complained of how difficult it was to define money and how hard it was to reach any agreement on definition. It harked back to Radcliffe when it argued, 'Many would probably regard the money supply as measuring the funds "available" for spending. … But what is meant by "available"?'[75] Much time and discussion were given to the institutional factors and practices and what they allowed.

Two key papers from the IMF, both written by the Australian economist and IMF chief of the Special Studies Division, Victor Argy, focussed on the central issues.[76] The first began with a discussion of the money-supply process using the money-multiplier model of the kind the Bank deplored. One can only imagine (in the absence of papers) the reaction of the Bank. It also cited extensively and favourably the work of Crouch, the Bank's least favourite monetary economist, on one occasion referred to rather harshly in the Bank as 'an ass'.[77] It further reviewed the open markets operations debate that had run through the 1960s in England and included among its contributors Crouch, Newlyn, Cramp, and Zawadzki. Someone from within the Bank has scribbled over both papers in negative and even sarcastic terms.[78] When Polak summed up at the seminar, he was critical of the British monetary statistics and called for a greater effort to be put into their collection. He also regretted the fact that it had been the differences in view on the role of DCE that had been responsible for many misunderstandings in the frequent IMF consultations. He wondered why it was that the Bank had operated on liquidity rather than cash ratios since the war. And he asked why the Bank had not used open market operations in Treasury bills as a means of operating directly on the banks' cash reserves. Thornton's answer

---

[74] The Bank papers were MS(IMF)(68)14, 'The effect of interest rates on demand', 8 October 1968; MS(IMF)(68)19, 'Defining the money supply', 14 October 1968; MS(IMF)(68)20, 'Some observations on official operations in the gilt-edged market', 15 October 1968, 7A353/1.

[75] MS(IMF)(68)14, 'Defining the money supply', 14 October 1968, 7A353/1.

[76] MS(IMF)(68)2, 'Monetary instruments, the money supply and interest rates in the United Kingdom'; MS(IMF)(68)3, 'The impact of monetary policy on expenditure – with particular reference to the United Kingdom'.

[77] Goodhart annotation on Gibson to Burman, 30 January 1970, 2A128/3.

[78] For example, see MS(IMF)(68)2 and 3, 7A353/1.

was that it dated back to the Macmillan Report and that the liquidity ratio system had then become established, and further, 'There had been little general interest in monetary policy after the War'.[79] The seminar's concentration on DCE was a consequence of the IMF's views, and the bias was therefore to the monetary aggregates; liquidity in the Radcliffe sense was discounted. British officials continued to complain that there were problems of definition, of statistics, and of policy adjustment. They argued that a DCE target posed operational problems. And crucially, they said that if they adopted a target, they would be committed to an interest-rate policy that probably would be at odds with domestic economic and social objectives. It was this that had to change. And it began to in 1969. The growing emphasis on the money supply prompted a rethink and a change in behaviour in the Bank's tactics in the gilt-edged market. [80]

In the week following the seminar, Thornton resuscitated the idea of a working party in the Bank and suggested that Goodhart would be central. McMahon was in agreement, and the proposal was that work should get started in mid-November.[81] At the beginning of 1969, the Bank had begun to embark on serious work on these lines, testing the IMF hypotheses on credit creation and so on. In February 1969, Goodhart defined 'net domestic credit creation' and made some calculations for Allen. The latter took exception to the definition – 'it is, I submit, wrong' – and there followed fuller analysis and explanation as to how it was arrived at.[82] Later in the month, both Bell and Edwards at the Treasury prepared separate papers on DCE, the latter's for the Chancellor so that he could see what was involved in accepting a target for DCE before the matter was taken any further with the IMF.[83] There were still big differences between the Treasury and the Bank on what constituted the correct definition of DCE and indeed how the relationships were connected. And even in early 1969, there was no agreement as to what could be divulged to the IMF in the way of figures. Nevertheless, the definition of DCE agreed with the IMF and set out in a 'Memorandum of Understanding' in May 1969 was 'all lending by the banking sector

[79] MS(IMF)4th, 'Monetary seminar (International Monetary Fund): note of proceedings on final day of seminar', 21 October 1968, 7A353/1.

[80] Althaus (1969, p. 1176).

[81] Thornton to McMahon and Allen, 'Money supply: how to get there', 30 October 1968, 5A175/1.

[82] Goodhart to Allen, 'Quick calculations of net domestic credit creation', 7 February 1969; 'The tautologies of net domestic credit expansion', 10 February 1968; Allen to Goodhart, 'Tautologies: N.D.C.C.', 11 February 1969, 5A177/1.

[83] Geoffrey Bell to Figgures, 21 February 1958, enc. 'Thoughts on domestic credit expansion'; Edwards, 'IMF standby and overall credit ceiling', 21 February 1969, 5A177/1.

(including the Bank of England Banking Department) to the public and private sectors (including lending in sterling to non-residents but excluding foreign currency lending to the private sector for investment overseas), *plus* the change in domestic non-bank holdings of notes and coin *plus* overseas lending to the public sector'.[84]

When in the first half of 1969 it seemed that a new standby agreement with the IMF would be required, it was also acknowledged that it would not be forthcoming without acceptance of stricter conditions than had applied in November 1967. The IMF undoubtedly would require definite commitment on a DCE target. This would have to be convincing. The authorities would need to produce a quarterly figure and be prepared for the fact that if that deviated too much from the annual target, they would need to take action. And indeed in the May agreement with the IMF there was a commitment to provide 'an appropriate quarterly path of domestic credit expansion consistent with the intended result for the financial year 1969/70'.[85] The type of action considered was still essentially operating on the ceiling on bank lending. However, they added to that action on the public-sector borrowing requirement (PSBR) or on lowering sales of public-sector debt to the non-bank public. Edwards at the Treasury argued that so long as they retained the freedom to act on any one of these three possibilities, then they, the Treasury, would be quite happy.[86] In the Bank, Goodhart's only cavil was that Edwards had implied that changes in money supply (or DCE) caused changes in income. Since, he argued, the Bank's emphasis had long been on orderly markets, 'we have allowed changes in economic conditions ... to result in certain related changes in money supply.' If there were to be a radical change in strategy in financial markets (particularly the gilt-edged market), the previous relationships may no longer hold.[87]

In Jenkins' budget of April 1969, he put stress on restraining DCE, and this was in part in preparation for seeking further standby facilities from the IMF. In May 1969, he addressed his second letter of intent to the IMF in seeking $1 billion. The letter restated the April budget measures and objectives and explicitly accepted the IMF's target for DCE:

---

[84] Edwards, 'Domestic credit expansion and the central government borrowing requirement. Final agreement reached with the IMF staff on target and ceiling figures and on definitions', 16 June 1969, Annex C, 22 May 1969, 5A177/2.

[85] Edwards, 'Domestic credit expansion ... ' 22 May 1969, Annex B, 5A177/2.

[86] Edwards, 'IMF standby and overall credit ceiling', 21 February 1969, 5A177/1.

[87] Goodhart to Allen, 'Overall credit ceiling', 24 February 1969, 5A177/1. Was this an early intimation of Goodhart's law? See Chrystal and Mizen (2003).

The Government's objectives and policies imply a domestic credit expansion for the private and public sectors in the year ending 31 March 1970 of not more than £400 million compared with £1,225 million in 1968–69. It is the Government's policy to ensure that the course quarter by quarter of domestic credit expansion as a whole, and of the central Government borrowing requirement within it, is consistent with the intended result for the year as a whole, and to take action as appropriate to that end.[88]

The $1 billion standby facility was approved by the IMF on Friday, 20 June.[89] In his statement to the house on 25 June, Jenkins again stressed the need to comply with DCE targets and announced that he was persuaded that DCE was a better indicator of monetary stance than money supply.[90]

Work on DCE continued in the Bank through 1969, and in September, a supplement to the *Bulletin* on the subject was published. From the monetary authorities' perspective, DCE was best set out in terms of the counterparts approach. The Bank produced some figures for the percentage change in DCE together with percentage change in total final expenditure for the years 1952 to 1968, as well as graphs that showed a reasonably close correspondence between the two.[91] In fact, although not reported in the *Bulletin* article, Crockett and Price had done some further statistical work and produced correlation coefficients that revealed a poor connection between the series.[92] At any rate, the experience in 1968 had demonstrated to contemporaries to their own satisfaction the value of the concept. In that year, money supply rose according to their figures by almost £1,000 million. However, the deficit on the external accounts contributed almost another £1,000 million to government financing. Thus money supply rose by £1,000 million, whereas DCE rose by £2,000 million. DCE was deemed the better indicator. As Goodhart expressed it:

The DCE hypothesis is that an external deficit can only be financed by (1) increasing DCE, thus allowing money supply to remain constant, or (2) holding DCE constant so that the money supply falls. The purpose of a DCE target is to force the authorities to ensure that alternative 2 is followed.[93]

There was still a great deal of scepticism. In the middle of 1969, Crockett made the important point that when domestic credit was created it might add

[88] HC Deb, 23 June 1969, Vol. 785, c1010.
[89] De Vries (1985, pp. 348–349).
[90] HC Deb, 25 June 1969, Vol. 785, c525.
[91] 'Domestic credit expansion', *BEQB* 9(3):363–382, September 1969.
[92] Crockett/Price to Goodhart, 'The relationship between T.F.E. and D.C.E.' 24 July 1969, 5A177/2.
[93] Goodhart, Annotation on Clews to Boulter, 13 April 1970, 5A177/3.

to the money stock or it might leak abroad. If the former, then it continued in future years to generate spending, and if the latter, it did not. He added, 'It is not, finally, a logical extension of the teaching of Milton Friedman.'[94] In August, John Boulter added his complaints. He said the handy rule of thumb that was being used was that DCE was equal to any increase in the money supply plus the balance-of-payments deficit. But, he argued, credit is not money ('DCE comes from Polak not from Friedman'), and importantly, it was not the balance of payments that mattered but rather the external finance obtained by the public sector. Those two, he pointed out, could differ by hundreds of millions of pounds and move in different directions. These kinds of points continued to be made through 1969 and 1970 not only within the Bank but also in correspondence with outsiders who were taking an interest.[95]

Fforde was sceptical and facetious. In early October 1969, he wrote:

The Governor and the Chancellor are both intending to include in their Mansion House speeches some very commendatory remarks about DCE as an indicator, a warning signal, and so on. This 'Concept of the Year', which is supposed to go one better than the money supply, will be described as something which the authorities are now convinced they must 'keep an eye on' or pay heed to whenever it suggests that we may be 'off course'. The public is being asked to accept, on the highest authority, that we have paid insufficient heed to this magnitude in the past, have been heeding it ever so well in the current year and will go on keeping an eye on it in the future.

He went on to say that DCE had been several hundred million short of target in the first half of 1969 (although the Governor's speech said that it was satisfactorily on target), thus indicating a distinctly cool climate for 1970, so that they were in danger of making the opposite mistake to the one they had made the previous year. 'If this accusation is valid, we remain guilty of the charge of conducting monetary policy so as to destabilise rather than stabilise the economy.'[96]

The events of late 1967 to 1969 resulted in important changes to the way in which monetary policy was viewed. There was rising inflation after devaluation and a growing number of critics who felt that policy was not sufficiently restrictive. It may have seemed so by looking at nominal interest rates, but something that the inflation and academic discussion did

---

[94] Crockett to Goodhart, 'D.C.E.: a dissentient view', 30 June 1969, 5A177/2.
[95] Boulter to Dicks-Mireaux, 'Money supply, the balance of payments and D.C.E.', 29 August 1969, 5A177/2.
[96] Fforde to O'Brien/Parsons, 8 October 1969, 5A177/3.

was bring out the need to distinguish between real and nominal rates. More than that, the policy stance might be better judged by looking at monetary aggregates. It undoubtedly was the beginning of an intellectual conversion.

Personnel Changes

At the end of the 1960s, the Bank lost two of its most distinguished 'overseas' people, Parsons and Bridge, both of whom left the Bank soon after, and not unrelated to, devaluation. In November 1969, it was announced that Parsons would retire from the Bank slightly prematurely at the end of February 1970. He became chairman of the Bank of London and South America (BOLSA), succeeding Bolton there in July 1970. Both Parsons and O'Brien were due to end their terms in June 1971, and this troubled O'Brien. When Bolton suggested that Parsons could become his successor at BOLSA, O'Brien agreed, and Parsons accepted the offer.[97] It may be, however, that the position at BOLSA was created to move Parsons on. He was appointed KCMG in 1970, having been knighted in 1966, and later became Director of John Brown and Co. from 1970–72.

Parsons had a strong reputation as a leading international monetary diplomatist.[98] He had possibly had that key role in the establishment of the General Agreements to Borrow (GAB). He combined 'to an exceptional degree a charm of manner, an air of authority, a knowledge of his subject and a power of lucid exposition, a combination which put him in the front rank of international negotiators'.[99] There was no one who could beat Parsons at talking round a hardened Swiss or German central banker who was not interested in economic argument.[100] As Executive Director from 1957 and Deputy Governor from 1966, he was concerned mainly with external matters.[101] Yet, as Deputy Governor, he had a low profile. He was badly shaken by devaluation in 1967, and his 'heartfelt remorse' over the event left him in 'a state of virtual denial'.[102] After devaluation, his absence from affairs is striking, particularly given the active role of previous Deputy Governors and given his expertise in both external and domestic matters. O'Brien and Parsons had long been rivals. There was

[97] *The Times*, 21 November 1969, p. 21.
[98] *Old Lady*, December 1978, pp. 190–191.
[99] *Ibid.*, p. 191.
[100] Brittan (1964, p. 63).
[101] *The Times*, 26 July 1978, p. 16.
[102] Kynaston (2001, p. 361).

only a two-year difference in age between them, and they had joined the Bank within a year of each other. Both were private Secretary to Norman, served in senior positions in the Chief Cashiers Office, and been Executive Directors.[103] Samuel Brittan was a supporter of Parsons, writing, 'When he warns in a deeply serious but unpompous voice of the profound risks one might be running in some suggested scheme, he really does know his subject matter and sounds as if the candles of monetary civilisation may go out at any moment. It is not his fault that there is no one on the radical side a fraction as impressive.'[104] It could be that Parsons' diminished role in the late 1960s was the result of illness. He seems to have been suffering from an ageing disease, and his deteriorating mental state may have meant that he was kept out of major decision making. Hollom recalled an occasion when the Governor was away and Parsons was due to go to a meeting in Whitehall and someone said, 'We can't let him go by himself, can we?' At what stage his illness became serious and more widely known is unclear. O'Brien claims that no one in the Bank realised even before he left to take up the chairmanship of BOLSA that he was ill. However, Hollom certainly recalled that as Deputy Governor, Parsons was 'clearly very much in decline'.[105]

After 40 years in the Bank, Roy Bridge retired on 18 October 1969 and took up advisory appointments in the City.[106] The Bank lost not only the master of foreign exchange but also a considerable character. *The Times* described his knowledge of market psychology as 'immense'.[107] According to Coombs, throughout the successive sterling crises that shook the international currency markets in the 1960s, Bridge was 'alert to all of the technical and psychological forces of the market, as he took decisions whether to hold a certain rate level, at possibly heavy cost, or to retreat and risk even heavier losses'. Furthermore, he was a 'suave, imperturbable negotiator' and trustworthy in the eyes of foreign central bankers.[108] Internationally, he was held in the highest respect. His biggest challenge, and the one that ultimately defeated him, was avoiding devaluation. He was vehemently opposed to it, and as with Parsons, devaluation took its toll, leaving him deeply disheartened. He saw it as his duty to protect the pound at all costs, and thus by the end of November 1967, he felt that he had failed, letting not only himself

---

[103] O'Brien, Memoir, p. 100.
[104] Brittan (1964, p. 63).
[105] Coleby interview with Sir Jasper Hollom, 11 January 1995.
[106] *The Times*, 7 November 1969, p. 27.
[107] *The Times*, 20 September 1969, p. 11.
[108] *Old Lady*, December 1969, p. 224.

down but also his country. He was made CMG in 1967 in recognition of his role in international affairs.

Bridge was a popular figure with an engaging personality, 'infectiously enthusiastic', as Fforde put it.[109] Highly sociable and rarely seen without a cigarette in his hand, Bridge was full of amusing stories that he could tell in several languages.[110] While Bridge was at the Bank, Rootham had never 'laughed so much at my place of work before or since'.[111] He was missed. With Bridge and Parsons gone, McMahon and Morse came to lead on international topics.

Sterling Agreements

Even after devaluation, the pressing problem still was the exchange rate, and the main contribution that the Bank made was in tackling the continuing 'problem' of the sterling balances. If the overseas sterling area (OSA) portion of these could be stabilised, that would greatly diminish the problem of holding to the new parity, and it would obviate the need for more drastic action such as floating. Thus, while there was a need to bolster confidence and for longer-term plans for the international monetary system, Britain's more immediate concern in early 1968 was sterling balances. These balances, which had stood at £3,863 million at the end of 1962 (official £2,312 million and private £1,551 million), had grown by almost 50 per cent to £5,934 million in nominal terms in 1973, that being the highest level they had ever reached (Figure 8.5). In real terms, they had fallen to about £3.3 billion.[112] It became clear that a revised arrangement for sterling balances was required, and in the spring of 1968, discussion began with the BIS and other central banks. In July 1968 at Basle, agreement in principle was reached on a $2 billion facility for a period of three years to protect against reserve losses brought about by sterling area countries 'diversifying' out of sterling. There were more than 60 of these countries, and they had to be persuaded to hold.[113]

The Bank's Sterling Area Working Party, which had been in place for some time, was reconvened in December 1967 with Fenton in the chair. When it had last reported in late 1966, it had concluded on the need to develop the 1966 Basle facilities into a longer-term arrangement. Following

[109] Fforde (1992, p. 186).
[110] Coombs, 'R. A. O. Bridge'.
[111] *Old Lady*, December 1978, p. 190.
[112] 'Overseas sterling balances 1963–73', *BEQB* 14(2):162–175, June 1974.
[113] For these negotiations, see OV44/160–88.

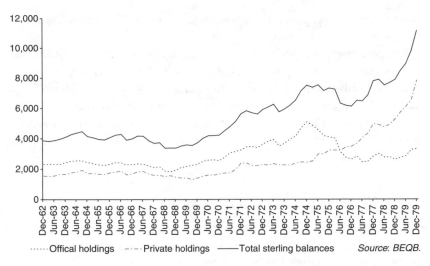

····· Offical holdings　　– – – Private holdings　　——Total sterling balances　　　*Source*: BEQB.

Figure 8.5. Sterling balances, 1962–79 (£m).

devaluation, with less trust and less confidence in British policy statements, it was recognised that there was likely to be increased pressure arising from OSA reserve diversification. The approach was to be primarily diplomatic: 'When we learn of any intentions, we must be prepared to use all our powers of persuasion, if necessary at a high level of representation, to discourage them.'[114] However, the working party also considered at great length what other possibilities there were, and it was forced to consider increased exchange control, although it went against the grain.[115]

Devaluation did not alter the Bank's view of sterling as a reserve currency; in fact, if anything, it strengthened it. At the beginning of 1968, Fforde was pessimistic about building up large enough surpluses to repay debt and favoured obtaining a long-term loan as part of a sensible strategy – an economic policy that would allow repayment to be made. He argued that if this strategy were successful, it would 'preserve the reserve currency role of sterling. I believe this to be a correct objective, if an unfashionable one.' He went further and in the context of the EEC negotiations argued that there was a good case for preserving sterling as a reserve currency if Britain were to join the EEC. 'The General may object, Rueff may scoff, Triffin may pontificate, Benelux authorities may turn blue with apprehension,

---

[114] Draft, Sterling Area Working Party conclusions, 9 January 1968, OV44/116. The final report referred to 'intensive financial diplomacy'.

[115] Sterling Area Working Party, 'Report', 25 January 1968, OV44/116.

but a properly developed Common Market will need to include, as part of its economic equipment, a reserve currency which the outside world can hold, and can use as a vehicle for international transactions.'[116] And that currency, according to Fforde, could be sterling. McMahon agreed. 'I think most people (at least in the Bank) would agree that it would be wrong to try really to "wind up" sterling's reserve role, let alone the vehicle currency role.'[117] Morse fully endorsed these views. In terms of the two key problems facing them in 1968, the danger of a run-down of OSA balances and the need to refinance short-term central bank debt, Morse preferred a loan to protect against a run-down and getting by on the central bank debt by use of the IMF and renewed central bank credit. In doing so, though, he posed the question: should we be deliberately working for some reduction in the reserve role of sterling or not? His answer was no: 'I think that we should not deliberately work for a reduction of the reserve role of sterling.'[118] When the suggestion was put to Morse that the Bank in the 1960s had favoured reducing sterling's reserve currency role, he completely rejected it.[119] And McMahon, too, explicitly rejected the idea. When it was put to him that there was a mood developing in the 1960s against sterling as a reserve currency and that the Bank was part of that, he said, 'That very much surprises me. ... I don't think that in the Bank in general there was anything, any belief that we should be getting rid of it' (sterling as a reserve currency).[120]

In the spring of 1968, the Bank had proposed a facility for sterling balances either through the BIS or the IMF, with the former preferred, being deemed more flexible and 'accessible'.[121] The essence of the proposals was that sterling area countries would agree to hold a certain percentage of their reserves in sterling and that, in return, they would receive a guarantee for that portion that would maintain the value of those reserves in terms of US dollars. Both the Bank and the Treasury had long been opposed to such guarantees, and while the subject had arisen again after devaluation, it was rejected on the grounds of expense and the likelihood that it would affect confidence in sterling that was not so guaranteed. The Sterling Area Working Party had raised the question of a guarantee when it reported in January but in the circumstances felt that it was scarcely credible. From March 1968,

---

[116] Fforde, 'Report of Sterling Area Working Party', 30 January 1968, OV44/116.
[117] McMahon, 'Note for the Governor', 1 February 1968, OV44/117.
[118] Morse to O'Brien/Parsons, 1 February 1968, OV44/117.
[119] Interview with Sir Jeremy Morse, 1 June 2005.
[120] Interview with Sir Kit McMahon, 6 July 2005.
[121] Morse, Note for record – 'The extension of the Basle arrangements', OV44/159; Morse to Ferras, 5 March 1968, enc. 'The future of the sterling balances', OV44/160; Toniolo (2005, p. 424).

however, the subject was back on the agenda as efforts to solve the problem were intensified. To start with, only a safety net was being discussed. Then Fforde proposed guarantees instead of a safety net, and Morse argued for both.[122] In May 1968, when McMahon reported on the experts meeting in Basle, specifically on a sterling area safety net (others in the group were Morse, Raw, and Preston), he noted that Sven Joge from the Swedish central bank and Fritz Leutweiler, a Swiss central banker, argued strongly for OSA guarantees.[123] The previous day, Parsons had met Van Lennep, who had expressed the view that if the sterling area countries used their sterling balances solely for meeting balance-of-payments requirements – in other words, treated sterling in the same way as had been laid down for SDRs – 'they would be entitled to demand a guarantee for their sterling'. Possibly, was Parsons view, but Britain, in turn, would need help to provide any such guarantee.[124] By June, however, things had changed, and there was general agreement that the risks of not offering guarantees were now greater than those of offering them.[125] The proposal that was being formulated at the BIS with other central banks would provide a medium-term facility that could be drawn on when required. The BIS annual general meeting in June discussed the $2 billion facility, and there was talk that an announcement might be made after the June meeting. That proved premature, however, and the hope became that the July meeting would reach agreement.[126]

Reaching agreement on the $2 billion facility had been relatively straightforward (it was, after all, what the BIS did, almost its raison d'etre), although the central banks wanted some assurances on the contribution sterling area countries would make to the stabilising process. The facility would 'offset fluctuations below an agreed base level in the sterling balances of sterling area holders'.[127] The net amount drawn on the facility at the end of the three-year period then should be repaid over the following five years. But agreement rested on restraint being shown by sterling area countries and the facility being used only to finance falls in reserves brought about by genuine balance-of-payments problems. The BIS also wanted some sterling area countries to deposit part of their non-sterling reserves with

---

[122] Fforde to O'Brien/Parsons, 'Safety net', 17 May 1968, and Morse annotation, OV44/161.
[123] McMahon, 'OSA safety net', 29 May 1968, OV44/162. According to one story, Raw apparently solved the problem of sterling balances during three hours spent escaping from a crevasse; see Tempest (2008, pp. 85–86).
[124] Parsons to O'Brien, 28 May 1968, OV44/162; Schenk (2010, Chapter 8).
[125] McMahon, 'O.S.A sterling balances', 5 June 1968, OV44/163.
[126] Dowler, Note for record, 21 June 1968, OV44/164.
[127] Bank of England, *Annual Report*, year ending February 1969, p. 13.

BIS. The second part of the problem, that of persuading sterling holders, was potentially much greater. Although it was a relatively small number of countries who dominated the sterling area (Australia, Singapore, Malaysia, New Zealand, Hong Kong, and the Republic of Ireland did the major share of business, and fewer than 10 countries in total held around half of all the sterling balances at the time), agreements were negotiated with 64 countries in the summer of 1968.[128] Twenty-nine countries struck agreements for five-year periods and 35 countries for three years in the first instance but extendable for a further two years. In 1971, 33 of the 35 did extend.[129]

Persuading the sterling area countries to participate by holding a substantial proportion of their reserves in sterling proved difficult, however. Negotiations sometimes were bitter and protracted. Interestingly, the Treasury (Douglas Allen) had already accepted the Bank's suggestion that the Bank should provide the negotiating teams.[130] The negotiations centred on the minimum sterling proportions (MSPs) that the countries would hold as reserves and the extent of the guarantee and the charge to be paid for it. Although the MSPs negotiated were lower than desired, there were some informal agreements that they would operate with slightly higher levels of holdings. For the more important holders, the MSPs generally were 40 per cent. At the beginning of July, there was still some insistence that there should be a charge for the guarantee and that it should be kept as high as possible; otherwise, unguaranteed sterling would be encouraged to flow in, and even dollars might be switched into guaranteed sterling.[131] Guaranteed sterling holders were, in effect, holding dollar assets, but they were getting the interest rate payable on sterling, which was higher than that on dollars. Any movement of balances would depend on how these relative rates moved. By the middle of July, there were many drafts of agreements ready and even some negotiations concluded.[132] From the end of July, though, efforts were being concentrated on three key areas: Australia, Kuwait, and Malaysia.

The Australians, who were among the most important holders, were among the most deeply opposed to the proposals and stubborn. Frank

---

[128] Of total sterling balances in September 1968, of £2,778 million, Australia held £329 million, Hong Kong £306 million, Ireland £288 million, Kuwait £194 million, and New Zealand £120 million, so these five alone held almost half; Bennett to Fenton, 6 September 1968, 7A114/5.

[129] 'Overseas sterling balances 1963–1973', *BEQB* 14(2):162–175, June 1974.

[130] O'Brien to Morse, Handwritten note, 25 July 1968, OV44/164.

[131] Morse to Figgures, 2 February 1968, OV44/166.

[132] Donald Macdonald (manager, Banking Department, BIS) to Raw, 19 July 1968, OV44/168.

Figgures, second permanent Secretary at the Treasury, spent some weeks in the summer of 1968 in Australia negotiating without success. When on 23 August it was reported from the British High Commission in Canberra that again no progress was being made, at the last minute O'Brien took on the job of resolving the differences and securing agreement himself.[133] He describes how he and Raw left for Australia on 29 August 1968, travelling in great secrecy because any knowledge of a mission that resulted in failure would have been hugely damaging and probably disastrous for the scheme. They travelled under false names and were smuggled aboard the aircraft through the freight-loading room. (This was not an entirely new Bank procedure, having been pioneered by Montagu Norman, alias Professor Clarence Skinner, on a trip to New York in August 1932 – 'a cloaked figure, bearded, and wearing a soft, black, wide-brimmed hat, appeared on the mist-enshrouded quayside at Southampton.'[134]) O'Brien and team left on a Friday and had to be back by the following Wednesday in order to get to Basle for a meeting on the Friday after that, which would tie up the whole scheme. They met Prime Minister John Gorton and Finance Minister Billy McMahon on the Sunday evening (without Figgures) and struck an agreement. When they returned to London, they were spirited away from the aircraft without being seen.[135]

O'Brien was enormously proud of his, and the Bank's, contribution, so when on the following Monday *The Times* carried a story by Peter Jay that the whole thing had been masterminded by Harold Lever, O'Brien blew up.[136] 'I went up like a lunar rocket, simply gibbering with rage. ... The injustice to the Bank, let alone myself, was insupportable.' He complained to the Chancellor, who then dined with him at No. 11. He rang *The Times* and demanded that Rees-Mogg, the editor, call on him immediately. (He called, but not immediately, which was probably just as well.) The offer of a peerage helped to placate him, even if he did put that on hold for the time being.[137]

Finally, agreement was reached at Basle, announcement of that was made on 9 September 1968, and the agreements became effective on 25 September 1968. No further drawing would be made under the 1966 arrangements,

---

[133] Fenton to O'Brien/Parsons, 'Sterling negotiations', 13 and 16 August 1968, OV44/169; Dudley Allen (at British High Commission, Canberra) to Fenton, 23 August 1968; Fenton to O'Brien/Parsons, 'Sterling negotiations', 27 August 1968, OV44/170.

[134] Hargrave (1937, p. 1).

[135] O'Brien, Memoir, pp. 79–80. Raw was taken because he had been at Brasenose, Oxford with the Australian Prime Minister and had even rowed in the same boat.

[136] *The Times*, 9 September 1968, p. 1.

[137] O'Brien, Memoir, p. 81.

and the outstanding debt would be repaid over a two-year period ending in June 1971.[138] There were still several loose ends to tie up, but the basis was firm. There even were some countries such as Yemen and Malaysia who had still to sign. O'Brien asked Morse to tell all those involved over the previous six months of his gratitude. The Bank had never before been involved in negotiations with so many countries at one time, nor so many of the Bank's staff preoccupied. This was another implicit vindication of the over-staffing, or emergency staffing, as it was sometimes called, that character-ised the Bank in the sixties. There always were enough good-quality people to call on in a crisis. Two days later, Allen wrote to O'Brien conveying the Chancellor's congratulations and spoke of 'the vital role performed by the Bank of England, and by you personally'.[139] Work then turned to producing a white paper that the Bank had a hand in drafting.[140] A further problem that needed to be addressed was how the guarantee would be implemented if, for example, sterling had to float. At the beginning of 1969, concern was such that the Bank sought an indemnity from the Treasury for the ster-ling agreements. The guarantee then was linked to the highly secret Bank-Treasury plan 'Hecuba'.[141]

The Basle facility for $2 billion allowed Britain to draw US dollars when sterling area countries' reserves fell below an agreed base of £3,080 million. In fact, at the time of the announcement, the balances already were below that level, and drawing started almost immediately. By the end of October 1968, $600 million had been drawn. However, improvement set in thereafter, and it was possible to repay the $600 million by September 1969. Moreover, there was no need for any further drawing. The Bank regarded the agree-ments as 'the major development' of the year.[142] Following the success of these negotiations and some other factors, the position improved, and from late 1968 to 1972, there were uninterrupted inflows so that sterling holdings

---

[138] Unpublished *Bulletin* article, 'Use of credit facilities with foreign monetary institutions', 20 November 1969, 6A179/1.

[139] Allen to O'Brien, 12 September 1968, OV44/172.

[140] Draft of the white paper is in OV44/174. *The Basle Facility and the Sterling Area*, October 1968, cmnd. 3787; Treaty Series No.118 (1968), *Exchange of Notes and Letters Concerning the Guarantee by the United Kingdom and the Maintenance of the Minimum Sterling Proportion by Certain Overseas Sterling Area Governments*, November 1968, cmnd. 3834, and Miscellaneous No.20 (1968), *Exchange of Despatches and Letters Concerning the Guarantee by the United Kingdom and the Maintenance of the Minimum Sterling Proportion by Certain Overseas Sterling Area Governments*, November 1968, cmnd. 3835.

[141] R. S. Symons (HMT) to Pyaton, 12 March 1969, enc. 'Hecuba. Sterling agreements: imple-mentation of the guarantees', 12 March 1969, OV44/179 12/3/69.

[142] Bank of England, *Annual Report*, year ending February 1969, p. 12.

were up by £2,700 million in these years. But the sterling agreements struck in September 1968 were for three years in the first instance and due to expire in September 1971, with repayment due between 1973 and 1978.[143] In 1970, attention had to turn to what might be needed before 1971.

At the beginning of 1971, preparations began to be made in earnest for renewal of the sterling agreements. Initially, this was discussed in terms of a straight renewal of the three-year agreement for a further two years. However, complications arose on both sides of the arrangements. On the Basle facility, Paul Volcker, the under-secretary for monetary affairs at the US Treasury, wanted the French included in the renewal. The Bank rejected this as a dangerous idea and wanted to avoid renewal of the facility becoming involved with the future of the sterling system.[144] The United States was also proposing to reduce its own contribution, and the fear in the Bank was that if that happened, the Canadians and the Japanese would pull out, leaving it looking like a European problem. And yet, sterling balances were £650 million above the starting figure, so the need for a withdrawal looked distant.

In February 1971, the Prime Minister was unconvinced that renewal was a good thing and worried about having to pay a large sum to sterling holders in the event of devaluation. The Governor insisted that the case for renewal was overwhelming, his main point being that if the guarantees were allowed to lapse, it would be assumed that we were going to devalue and that would provoke withdrawals. He further argued that the arrangements had made an important contribution to the stability of the international monetary system in the previous three years.[145] There was a geopolitical factor involved, too, for it was feared that there would be heavy withdrawals from some major holders if Britain went ahead with a controversial sale of arms to South Africa. Singapore was one likely withdrawer. Nevertheless, in March 1971, a proposal was made to all sterling area countries to renew without modification. As Raw put it, renewal was felt 'to have great presentational value as a general confidence inspirer'.[146] Yet, given the state of the foreign-exchange markets in March 1971, it was not surprising that two of the big holders, Singapore and Malaysia, were worried about a guarantee

---

[143] Morse to Figgures, 12 September 1968; Donald Harry Curzon (EID) to Hawkins, 'New Basle arrangements', 13 September 1968, 6A83/3. The 1966 short-term facility was progressively liquidated, with $600 million repaid in 1969–71; *BEQB* 8(4):357, December 1968.

[144] Fenton to O'Brien, 10 February 1971, OV44/189.

[145] Ryrie, Note, 23 February 1971, OV44/189.

[146] Raw to O'Brien, 2 March 1971, OV44/190.

in dollars and proposed some other currency such as the Deutsche mark (DM) or the yen. Malaysia was particularly reluctant, fearing a US devaluation. By July, of the 36 three-year agreements that had been made, 23 had indicated that they would be happy with the original offer of straightforward renewal, including, importantly, Australia. Some of the others wanted to negotiate lower MSPs.

And then the US bombshell landed in August and threw the whole process into confusion. The possibility then was that sterling might be revalued and wider margins introduced, and the guarantee would have to be at a new rate. Even so, at the beginning of September, there were 30 acceptances and only six outstanding, and on 17 September 1971, it was reported that 34 of the 36 countries had agreed, Singapore included. Malta and Libya declined, not a great loss.[147]

Measures for Protecting Sterling

In addition to work on the sterling balances prompted by fear of a further devaluation, effort was devoted to planning action in case of such an event. In the Bank, almost all the work was done by McMahon and Morse, both of whom were relatively new recruits to the Bank in 1964 and 1965, respectively. There followed in the next few years a number of highly secret plans devised to cope with all the foreseeable possibilities. The Treasury began to make preparations for the most drastic action, the blocking of sterling balances, a scheme that the Bank vehemently opposed. The chief alternative was floating, but both were described by the Bank as 'desperate acts'.[148] The Bank preferred floating to blocking, but for many, the one implied the other. Several schemes came under consideration by joint Bank and Treasury teams hidden under code names to address different contingencies. Operation 'Brutus' was the first and was underway in March 1968. It became known as 'Cranmer' and was for the blocking of sterling balances in the event of official reserves running out. This was essentially a Treasury position, and it was resisted by the Bank. 'Hecuba' got underway in July 1968, a contingency plan for a situation in which reserves ran out and the authorities were forced to float rather than making that choice. 'Priam' was for floating temporarily to protect sterling as a result of any realignment of exchange parities. 'Telemachus' was a scheme to combat the withdrawal of sterling balances by individual countries by means of exchange-control

---

[147] Allen to Coleby, 17 September 1971, OV44/193.
[148] This story is told in some detail from Treasury papers in Oliver and Hamilton (2007).

restrictions on the convertibility of sterling holdings. 'Polonius' was for the control of inflows. 'Brandon' and 'Mini Brandon' were schemes for the introduction of exchange control against countries of the sterling area. There was one called 'Bootstrap', renamed 'Androcles', for the mobilisation of British-owned foreign-currency assets (vesting). Additionally, there were 'Orestes', provided for substituting quantitative restrictions on a range of imports that could be introduced without legislation, to support 'Hecuba'; 'Baytown', not fully developed until 1971, to devalue; 'Palinurus' to float sterling by choice; and 'Proteus' to deal with a US gold embargo.[149] One called 'Conqueror' dealt with special support from the IMF. Another, 'Galileo', planned for German revaluation. As Samuel Brittan wrote, 'The letters of the Greek alphabet were nearly exhausted in devising contingency plans for different types of emergency.'[150] Changing circumstances rendered some of the schemes redundant quite quickly.

From as early as December 1967, there was talk of floating. McMahon argued that if pushed off the present rate, there would be no alternative to floating, but he did not think that there was any need for contingency planning. Armstrong could not agree that nothing should be done, and he expressed the wish for joint Bank-Treasury action. McMahon was asked to talk to Ryrie and so began a long, intensive, and at times tedious conversation on all aspects of the problem.[151] Throughout 1968, discussions were closely linked to what was happening to the negotiations with the sterling balance holders and what might be needed if these negotiations failed. To some extent, the problem was resolved when agreement was reached and signed with sterling area countries, but the continuing threat of a sterling crisis from some other source meant that contingency planning continued. At any rate, in February 1968, McMahon and Ryrie got underway, and new papers were commissioned to deal with the circumstances in which Britain might be forced to float, as well as one paper on the consequences of floating.[152] In March 1968, when a degree of panic appeared, McMahon wrote to the Governor setting out three possibilities. The first was to hold the rate for sterling and arrange the credit required to do that. The second was to block sterling. And the third was to float. The first was attractive to

---

[149] See 2A105/2.

[150] Brittan (1970, p. xii).

[151] McMahon to Fenton/Morse, 'The question of planning for floating', 20 December 1967; O'Brien to Parsons/Morse/McMahon, Governor's note, 3 January 1968, 7A114/1.

[152] McMahon to O'Brien/Hollom, 'Floating', 8 February 1968; Ryrie to Michael Hawtin (HMT), 28 February 1968; HMT, 'Note of a meeting in Sir William Armstrong's room on Tuesday, 5 March 1968 at 5.00 p.m.', 7A114/1.

the Americans, who would press support on Britain. The second would no doubt provide a breathing space but would be very damaging in the longer term. Employment of the third option at least would mean that Britain would stop losing reserves.[153] At a meeting in the Treasury on Sunday, 17 March, where Parsons, Hollom, Bridge, and McMahon were present, the Treasury strongly opposed floating, preferring instead the first option.[154]

By March, the plan had acquired the code name 'Brutus I'.[155] The Chancellor Roy Jenkins claimed that he was the architect of the plan. When revealed in *The Times* in 1999, the headlines were that 'Brutus' banned foreign holidays, imports of luxury goods – French wine, Swiss watches, and out-of-season strawberries, to name just a few. According to this story, only Harold Wilson and a handful of Cabinet ministers were aware of the plan. One of the many sillinesses of these kinds of measures is illustrated by the fact that Wilson 'agonised over the inclusion of tinned salmon being on the list'.[156] Discussions seemed endless and made little progress over the next two years.[157] If the United States were to go off gold, McMahon suggested that the European currencies should devalue by 50 per cent against gold and present the dollar with a fait accompli.

By July 1968, McMahon was exasperated, and he wrote to the Governor to say that contingency planning was 'now out of control':

There is a group on blocking which has produced a very elaborate plan for the end of the world. ... Despite all the intellectual effort that has been put into it, it is clearly unworkable and disastrous. At the same time, there has been a different working party on floating, one of whose assumptions is that we should thereby try to avoid blocking. ... There is a so-called 'gold and dollar group' ... which considers a number of external disasters of varying improbability. There was another group considering import deposits. ...[158]

And there was much more and many more groups. When Bridge was asked to comment on what was coming out of the Treasury, he was typically cutting. He thought it possible that there might be some instance tucked away in Latin American history where exchange control had been used with a floating rate, but they were, of course, mutually incompatible. 'If the UK were ever forced to float, the only course which I believe would make any sort of sense would be – (a) to make no interventions in the exchange

---

[153] McMahon to O'Brien/Parsons, 14 March 1968, OV53/38.
[154] Hollom, Note for record, 18 March 1968, OV53/38.
[155] Bennett to Fenton, 16 March 1968, 7A114/1.
[156] *The Times*, 1 January 1999, p. 4.
[157] McMahon to Morse, 20 March 1968, 7A114/2.
[158] McMahon to O'Brien, 18 July 1968, 7A114/5.

market for at least a fortnight and quite possibly not for a month; (b) to remove all exchange controls immediately; [and (c) of course, to throw out publicly any government advisers with Central European names.]' The Treasury's ideas were completely wrong. To float and then impose all the measures being talked about would 'smell so strongly of Schacht as to lead to an expectation of £1 being worth ultimately one cent or less'.[159] No prizes were offered for identifying the government advisers.

Following the successful conclusion of the sterling agreements or Basle arrangements in early September 1968, the Bank was hoping to 'put Cranmer to bed'. It really should have been dead at that point. Not that the Treasury had given up. Morse wrote of a Treasury paper that it had 'too much of the horrific detail, such as Douglas Allen has a taste for'. New schemes were sprouting. McMahon was tiring. In October, he wrote to the Governors, 'I am afraid I must trouble you again over this Trojan pair (Priam and Hecuba)'. In November, 'There was another confused and dreary meeting on this subject yesterday' – at the Treasury.[160] At the beginning of 1969, Morse suggested conflating the mass of contingency papers, and Allen seemed receptive, but nothing came of it.[161] In the course of 1969, although there were signs of improvement in the desired variables, discussion rambled on. 'Temporary floating' was reviewed but slapped down by Morse, who 'put the familiar Bank view that the concept did not exist'.[162] When the story reappears in the archival record in late 1970, attention had turned to managing a floating rate.[163]

British economic performance had begun moving in the right direction from mid-1969 onwards, at least temporarily, with three budget surpluses in 1969, 1970, and 1971, the last of which was at record levels, and there were improvements in the external accounts. Of the many measures under discussion, that on exchange-rate flexibility was receiving more attention; one of the least appealing was the resort once more to exchange controls.

The debate on flexible exchange rates had never gone away entirely. From Meade in 1945 through Robot in 1952 and Meade again in 1955 and on through Rees-Mogg at the end of the 1950s, there were still rumblings in the 1960s. However, it then reached another high at the end of the 1960s. In 1969, publication of an Institute of Economic Affairs (IEA) pamphlet

---

[159] Bridge to Morse/O'Brien, 18 July 1968, 7A114/5.
[160] McMahon to O'Brien/Parsons, 14 October 1968, 7A114/6.
[161] Morse, 'Hecuba', 29 January 1969, 7A114/10.
[162] McMahon, Note for record – 'Contingency planning', 11 July 1969, 7A114/11.
[163] For a full description of each of the various contingency plans, see J. W. Harvey (HMT), Note for record, 6 January 1971, T312/2908 TNA.

by Harry Johnson, 'The Case for Flexible Exchange Rates', stimulated further debate.[164] Although there was often ambiguity in the use of the word 'flexible', Johnson was using it to mean free-floating. It is clear from the discussion in the Bank from 1968 that Johnson's views were now falling on slightly more fertile ground.[165]

Johnson, next to Meade, was probably the most distinguished international economist in the country and had a history in British public intellectual life. (He gave evidence to Radcliffe in 1958 and was a frequent contributor to the economic debate in the press.) His views therefore were likely to be taken seriously, and they were expressed at a time when the intellectual climate was changing and the worldwide turbulence in the foreign-exchange markets was forcing a reassessment of existing regimes. Part of Johnson's argument was the common one – that central banks were always likely to prefer fixed exchange-rate regimes because it gave them prestige and political power over national governments because they are entrusted with managing the system and 'they naturally credit themselves with exercising more responsibly than the politicians would do and which they naturally resisted surrendering.'[166] Johnson's main point, however, was that floating removed the balance-of-payments constraint and so provided an extra degree of freedom in policy. His case was not simply academic, for he tackled the feasibility of floating in the circumstances of the time. The argument against sterling floating was that sterling's role as a reserve currency precluded it or that the IMF rules did not allow it, but the decline of sterling and the 1968 sterling agreements that gave a guarantee to holders of sterling allowed Britain to float 'without fear of recrimination from its official holders.'[167]

At the beginning of 1969, the Bank and the Treasury had in fact begun secret talks with the Fed on exchange rates. Interestingly, Nixon had appointed three proponents of floating rates to his Council of Economic Advisers (Hendrik Houthakker, Paul McCracken, and Herbert Stein). But the talks disintegrated and marked a change in UK-US monetary relations.[168] There was a further meeting in Washington in April, but the British came

---

[164] Johnson (1969). Johnson's title acknowledged the indebtedness to Friedman's 'modern classic essay, "The Case for Flexible Exchange Rates"', written as a memorandum in 1950 and published in 1953. Friedman was consulting for the US agency handling Marshall aid in 1950 and felt strongly about the restrictions on capital flows in Europe at the time. His solution was floating rates that would remove the need for exchange controls. Friedman, though, did not dismiss fixed rates in the way that Johnson was inclined to.

[165] Middleton (2002).

[166] Friedman (1968b, p. 12).

[167] *Ibid.*, p. 36.

[168] Oliver and Hamilton (2007, p. 499).

away with the feeling that Volcker was not interested.[169] Nevertheless, following the French devaluation of 11 per cent in August 1969 and the German revaluation of 9 per cent in September, in October the Fed proposed another study of exchange-rate flexibility. Once again, the word was used in a restricted sense. The study was to range over wider margins and crawling pegs, but it excluded outright floating.[170] Coombs had warned the Federal Open Market Committee (FOMC) earlier in the year that the international situation 'was the most dangerous of any yet encountered'.[171] No action was taken, however, but in any case, events would soon overtake these discussions.

Exchange controls were used from time to time to help support sterling, and in the middle of 1968, when sterling negotiations were still precariously balanced, the 'Hecuba' plan specifically dealt with introducing extensive exchange control in the sterling area in the event of a crisis. If 'Hecuba' failed, existing balances would be blocked. Brandon also had specific proposals on exchange control, but using them at the beginning of the 1970s was complicated with the proposed entry to the EEC and the changing exchange-rate regime. Morse cautioned that changes should be linked to requirements for joining the EEC.[172] This became reality quite soon, for there was an announcement in May 1972 that British residents who were going to take up employment in an EEC country (or Norway or Denmark) 'would be allowed to transfer sterling assets to the country concerned in excess of the normal allowances to the extent that this might be necessary to fulfill their intention'.[173] And yet, for some time, their use continued as before, tightening here, relaxing there. All manner of tinkering went on through the years 1969–72: restricted assets of emigrants, amalgamation of the property currency with the investment currency market, some relaxation on export paperwork, permission to use cheque guarantee cards abroad, and so on. In 1969, they were mostly bound up with the discussions on the various secret schemes to protect sterling given different contingencies.

Following the US measures of August 1971, there was the more general problem of what to do when several countries were about to float their currencies. It was believed that new measures would be needed to discourage inflows. Since the reserve figures published for August 1971

---

[169] *Ibid.*, pp. 500–502.
[170] Meltzer (2009, pp. 734–9).
[171] *Ibid.*
[172] Bennett to Fenton/Morse, 'Exchange control relaxations', 8 December 1969, 4A112/4.
[173] Bank of England, *Annual Report*, year ending February 1973, p. 21.

were good and balance-of-payments forecasts were favourable, speculative inflows became likely. (Moves to lower Bank Rate were also being considered.) In September, the pound/dollar rate that was felt to be consistent with the interests of British competitiveness was resulting in the accumulation of dollar reserves that was regarded as excessive. 'Our only sensible posture would be to decide where our sticking point vis-à-vis the dollar is – say, 2.52 – and then be prepared to hold the rate there.'[174] By October, Exchange Control had second thoughts on the usefulness of asking banks to report foreign-exchange deals – there were so many ways of disguising transactions that the returns 'would be virtually meaningless'.[175] By this time, however, the focus was on the exchange rate, and the discussion was about what rate they were prepared to tolerate and then accept all the dollars that might flow.[176] In the middle of 1972, Cairncross, then retired from the Treasury, produced an analysis of the impact of exchange controls. He asked why controls were tighter in 1972 when there was a floating rate than they had been in 1971 when there was not and why they were tighter in 1971 when there was a large balance-of-payments surplus than they had been in 1961 when there was a large deficit. Paradoxically, the tighter the controls became, the larger was the outflow of capital.[177]

International Monetary Reform

While a number of measures had been taken in the late 1960s to bolster confidence in the international financial system, it was acknowledged that more fundamental action was also needed.[178] Recognition of the need for international monetary reform was gaining some momentum from the beginning of the 1960s, when the focus was on a new international reserve asset. In 1963, when the G10 undertook a study, they were sanguine for the immediate future but felt that in the longer term the supply of gold and foreign-exchange reserves may prove inadequate. In 1965, the Ossola Group was set up to pursue this enquiry. Solomon was a member and was encouraged by Martin to pursue 'an open-minded exploration of the

---

[174] Sangster to Fenton, 'External monetary policy', 7 October 1971, 4A112/4.
[175] Thornton to O'Brien, 8 October 1971, 4A112/4.
[176] There were two separate exchange-control measures taken to deter inflows: one on 31 August 1971 and another on 7 October 1971, but then they were removed on 19 December 1971.
[177] Cairncross, 'UK capital controls', 18 July 1972, 4A112/5.
[178] Bordo (1993).

question of reserve creation'.[179] President Johnson appointed a Commission on International Monetary Arrangements and, secretly, a study group (the Deming Group) of senior officials to consider means of providing relief of pressure on sterling.[180] In August 1967, agreement was reached on a contingency plan for the creation of SDRs in the IMF. It was the culmination of long negotiations and finished as something of a hybrid with elements of a reserve asset (the British and American objective) and a line of credit (the EEC objective).[181] SDRs were allocated in proportion to existing quotas, and all transactions were conducted through special accounts in the IMF. The first allocations were made on 1 January 1970 and were followed by two more in the next two years.[182]

In the early months of 1968, political revolution was in the air, and political uncertainty spread across much of Europe. This was accompanied by turmoil in the foreign-exchange markets, and sterling weakened once again. So serious was the position that the Governor had told the other central bank governors at their regular meeting in Basle in November that if there were to be a French devaluation without a German revaluation, the British government would be obliged to take some step such as letting the rate float or introducing quantitative restrictions on imports.[183] As the DM strengthened and the French franc weakened, consideration was given to closing the foreign-exchange markets. The Germans were resisting outside pressure to revalue, most Germans having been unhappy over the 1961 revaluation, but by 1968, the Bundesbank was in favour, and Blessing, Otmar Emminger, and Heinrich Irmler all argued for revaluation on the Central Bank Council. However, Karl Schiller, the German minister of economic affairs, dismissed the idea as 'an absurdity'.[184] The Germans proposed an urgent conference in Bonn. The British agreed and seemed to play a very big card when they said that if sterling were forced to float and there was damage to the UK economy, the British 'contribution to NATO [North Atlantic Treaty Organisation] and the defences of the West would be bound to be seriously affected'.[185]

---

[179] Solomon (1982, p. 81). The group was named after Rinaldo Ossola from the Bank of Italy.
[180] The Deming Group was led by Fred Deming, under Secretary for monetary affairs.
[181] 'Post war monetary and economic policy', September 1967, OV38/90.
[182] Williamson, (1965). The Bank was also aware of work by Hirsch in 1969 on the crawling peg; Peter Hayward (Overseas Office), 'The crawling peg', 6 February 1969. It also saw a paper by Tew on deciscion making at the IMF, written following introductions made for him by Maurice Allen; see Tew to Allen, 21 January 1969, OV38/94.
[183] David Hancock (HMT), 'Note of a meeting ... 18 November 1968', 7A114/7.
[184] Holtferich (1999, p. 385).
[185] HMT, 'The Bonn conference', November 1968, OV44/130.

In Britain, the immediate response to sterling weakening was the introduction of yet another package of 'deflationary' measures.[186] Morse then had a telephone call from Coombs, who was in the office of Johannes Tüngeler (Bundesbank) in Frankfurt, to say that there would be no German revaluation. The US desire for a G10 meeting was made urgent by this refusal of the Germans to revalue. The Germans had given steady support to the dollar through the 1960s as part of the implicit deal with the United States whereby Germany got American military protection in exchange for absorbing large dollar liabilities.[187] The French, who had withdrawn from NATO in 1966, were antipathetic at best and hostile at worst and saw no need to cultivate good relations with the United States.[188] Fowler, already in Germany, wanted to close the major markets for the remaining three days of the week, the 20th to the 22nd, but O'Brien strongly resisted on the grounds that it would be a 'disastrous magnification' of the issue and that Britain would be most exposed to the speculation that would follow. In fact, O'Brien was not keen on the meeting at all. The Bank believed that the announcement of no revaluation would have 'catastrophic effects on sterling'.[189]

The G10 meeting, however, did go ahead, with a primary objective being to prevent the French from devaluing by too much. The meeting was unsatisfactory for a host of reasons. As Morse reported, it was ill-conceived, badly conducted, and should not have been held. O'Brien thought it a 'deplorable event'. Animosities quickly surfaced, and when the British Chancellor (Jenkins) proposed a 7.5 per cent revaluation of the DM, which he claimed had been agreed 'by a consensus of Governors at Basle', he 'provoked a storm and clamour of disapproval'. It was necessary for the Governor to step in and say that he believed a 5 per cent revaluation would not be enough and that he thought that some other Governors agreed with him.[190] Morse remarked that Professor Schiller in the chair had been 'petty, mischief-making, and garrulous' and 'the main source of an under-current of "Ministers versus Governors" feeling'. The press were constantly briefed, sometimes apparently in an anti-British way; 'on one occasion the German spokesman even suggested that the U.K. ought to devalue.'[191] Blessing had left the meeting in

---

[186] Morse, 'The course of events on Tuesday, 19 November', 19 November 1968, OV44/130.

[187] Eichengreen (2004, p. 8).

[188] For a fuller account of these geopolitical issues, see Gavin (2004).

[189] HMT, 'The Bonn conference' November 1968, p. 6, OV44/130.

[190] Morse to O'Brien/Parsons, 'Bonn meeting: 20–22 November', 25 November 1968, and O'Brien annotation, 26 November 1968, OV44/130.

[191] HMT, 'The Bonn conference' November 1968, p. 11, OV44/130.

anger 'because he didn't want to listen to the complaints of his colleagues any longer'. Emminger took his place but considered the meeting the most unpleasant monetary conference he had ever attended.[192] The communique issued at the end of the meeting reiterated the Germans' determination not to revalue, announced a $2 billion facility for the French, and that was it. The meeting may have been a failure, but it did mark another step on the road to recognising the need for parity changes. After a long battle and Schiller's conversion (in March 1969), revaluation eventually was carried through at 9 per cent in September 1969.

The Bonn meeting of 1968 undoubtedly marked a low point in international monetary affairs in the post-war era. And there was little recovery in relationships over the next few years. The unilateral changes in parities in 1969 simply continued the poor feeling that pervaded the atmosphere. In May 1970, the Canadian dollar floated – again. The United States pursued its own domestic agenda, and in March 1971, following a rush into both the DM and the guilder, the German Bundesbank cut its discount rate. The Europeans converted large proportions of their dollar reserves into gold. The Germans followed with a unilateral float in May 1971. At the end of May, the United States was still proclaiming that it would not devalue, not change the price of gold. However, when a US Congress Joint Economic Committee published a report in August 1971 that said the dollar was overvalued, there was no way out, and later that month the United States was forced to suspend the convertibility of the dollar into gold. The Nixon measures of 15 August 1971 effectively brought the system to an end.[193]

In the autumn of 1971, there followed intensive discussion among the major participants, with the case for floating being put with greater conviction. However, there was still reluctance on the part of many and still a belief that without the discipline of a fixed-rate system, inflation would assert itself more strongly. Finally, in mid-December 1971 at the Smithsonian Institute in Washington, an agreement was struck that established new parities with wider bands around them. A variation of 2.25 per cent rather than the 1 per cent of Bretton Woods was permitted so that European currencies could fluctuate by 4.5 per cent against the dollar and so by 9 per cent against one another. In its *Review*, the National Bank of Belgium remarked that 'this was more like floating currencies than a system of fixed exchange rates'.[194] But the United States was still a reluctant participant and determined

---

[192] Holtfrerich (1999, p. 385).
[193] For an excellent full account of these events, see James (1996).
[194] Quoted by Buyst et al. (2005, p. 208).

'not to let international objectives stand in the way of domestic economic objectives'.[195]

Euromarkets

The Euro-currency markets were never far away from central bank discussion in the 1960s on the questions of international liquidity and domestic monetary policy. There was worried discussion over the markets' alleged abuses or dangers. A common criticism was that they created a huge volume of world liquidity that would produce inflationary pressure. There is no doubt that they eased financing in trade and elsewhere. It is less clear where the inflationary pressures came from. And it is surely odd to complain about the creation of private liquidity at the very time there was a search for international liquidity for governments and central banks; the former made the latter redundant. A second complaint was that the large international movement of Euro-currency frustrated individual countries' ability to control their own money supply.[196] This was perhaps the most widely stated and accepted claim. Even the BIS seemed unsure: 'So far as inflation is concerned, borrowing in the Euro market by a country may enable the private sector to circumvent a domestic credit squeeze'.[197] But the criticism does not stand up. Apart from anything else, the funds would not normally be included in any definition of the money supply up to M3. While knowledge of the final use of the funds was sketchy, the common understanding was that the bulk was used in trade finance.[198] Maurice Allen recognised this when writing to Cairncross on the money supply in 1968. He said '*Financial Statistics*' failed to distinguish between sterling deposits and currency deposits, 'as if Euro-dollars owned by residents were part of the British money supply'.[199]

---

[195] James (1996, p. 238).
[196] See Bell (1973, pp. 8–12). Geoffrey Bell had been on secondment from the Treasury to the Fed in St. Louis in 1963 and published an article on the subject in the Fed's review, on which Parsons had commented, 'I'm afraid he gives me the impression of not really understanding his subject'; Parsons, Annotation, 9 January 1964, on Selwyn to Parsons/Bridge, 'The Euro dollar market', 6 January 1964. Later that year, Bell had an article published in *The Banker* [Bell (1964)], something Bridge thought was 'quite out of order' for someone from the Treasury: 'He might be presumed to have specialised knowledge'; Bridge annotation on Selwyn to Bridge/Parsons, 'Euro dollar market – paper by Bell (H.M.T.)', 23 June 1964, 6A123/1.
[197] BIS, *Thirty-fourth Annual Report*, June 1964, p. 141.
[198] See, for example, Tether (1961, p. 399).
[199] Allen to Cairncross, 16 February 1968, 5A175/1.

The criticism often took the form that if the US authorities conducted a tight monetary policy, as they did in 1966 and 1968–69, US banks simply could repatriate balances held in their overseas (largely London) branches and so defeat the authorities' attempt. In a succinct analysis and terse refutation, Wood and Mudd demonstrated how wrong this claim was. They concluded:

The net effect of transactions in the Euromarkets on the US money supply is virtually negligible. Transactions in the Eurodollar market cannot have contributed significantly to the recent growth of M1. Further, ... the US monetary authorities have the ability to offset whatever effects on M1 Eurodollar transactions may have. The existence of that market has not reduced the ability of the Federal Reserve System to control the US money stock.[200]

No one denies that the US banks could repatriate funds, but that did not mean that the Fed lost its ability to control the money supply. It mattered greatly how much capital mobility there was and what the exchange-rate regime was. The Bank left an element of ambiguity on this when it referred to commercial banks in the United States having found the market 'an increasingly convenient source of funds, particularly during times of domestic credit stringency'.[201] Insofar as there was a problem, it simply highlighted the difficulty of conducting monetary policy in a world with high capital mobility.

Another complaint was that international financial stability was damaged because the pressures that normally would be placed on deficit countries to adjust were weakened. Defining financial stability has proved more than troublesome for economists and central banks. International financial stability may just be a concept too far.[202] Countries could borrow in the Euromarkets without the kinds of conditions that normally would attach to IMF loans, and a complaint was that the necessary adjustment would not take place. It was sometimes suggested that banks might lend to doubtful customers. But the answer to that is surely, Why? There was also the fear that banks would borrow short (at call) and lend long (one to three months), but this is what banks do. Cromer had expressed the general position of the Bank when he wrote:, 'Let us be cautious without becoming agitated.'[203] The main response to these kinds of complaints was that the Euromarkets should be regulated. Even if this were a sensible response, the

---

[200] Wood and Mudd (1977). Most of the same points had been made by Friedman (1970).
[201] 'The Euro currency business of banks in London', *BEQB* 10(1):34, March 1970.
[202] Wood (2003).
[203] Jardine to Stone, and Cromer annotation, 20 November 1963, EID10/22.

question was, Could it be regulated? The market was born to escape regulation, and it tended to move to less restrictive jurisdictions.

Interestingly, the Bank showed little concern about regulation during the emergence and rapid development of the market. It did not believe that anything could or should be done other than 'a hint from the Governor that we were watching the market and requests for more detailed and more regular information'.[204] At the beginning of 1963, Charles Hambro, a non-Executive Director of the Bank, had expressed concern to Mynors over the rate of growth of the market. Mynors acknowledged that there were risks but played these down, relying on prudent bankers to steer the right course, and argued:

It is natural enough that London banks – and merchant banks in particular – with their expertise and international connections, should not only have become involved but have also sought to participate actively in this business. It is par excellence an example of the kind of business which London ought to be able to do both well and profitably. This is why we, at the Bank, have never seen any reason to place any obstacles in the way of London taking its full and increasing share. If we were to stop the business here, it would move to other centres with a consequent loss of earnings for London.[205]

While the Bank published several surveys of the Euromarket in the *Bulletin*, the first public pronouncement came as late as 1971, when the Governor spoke to the Bankers Club of Chicago.[206] O'Brien presented an entirely relaxed view. A few years later, McMahon took a similar position. He broadly favoured the contribution the market made to capital market integration and the provision of finance that had allowed the expansion of world trade and financed international payments imbalances. Neither could he see any threat to domestic monetary management. The problem simply was that of capital flows.[207] Not everyone shared the relaxed view of the Bank. The United States worried about it and from time to time considered how to control it. In February 1969, Governor Brimmer wanted controls on the grounds that Eurodollars were not subject to reserve requirements.

---

[204] Selwyn to Stevens, 'Currency deposits [meeting held on 7 August 1962]', 16 August 1962, EID10/21.

[205] Mynors to Hambro, 29 January 1963, EID10/22.

[206] 'U.K. banks' external liabilities and claims in foreign currencies', *BEQB* 4(2):100–108, June 1964; O'Brien speech to the Bankers' Club of Chicago, 27 April 1971, *BEQB* 11(2):224–231, June 1971.

[207] 'Controlling the Euro-markets', *BEQB* 16(1):74, March 1976. This was a slightly expanded version of a speech given by McMahon in February 1976 at the 'The Euro-markets in 1976' conference run by the *Financial Times/Investors Chronicle*.

Most governors in the Fed agreed. By the middle of 1969, US banks were borrowing $1 billion a week in the Eurodollar markets, and in August, regulations were introduced.[208] The Europeans saw it as a problem in many of the ways described, especially in increasing dangerous capital flows and undermining the effectiveness of domestic monetary policy, so placing at risk the international monetary system.

The BIS had for long taken an interest in the markets' growth, encouraged collection and dissemination of data, and provided occasional description and analysis of the markets in its *Annual Reports*. When there was a particularly dramatic growth in 1969–70, the BIS provided a forum for further discussion, and in 1971, a G10 Standing Committee on Euromarkets was set up 'to consider policy problems arising out of the existence and operations of the Euro-currency market'.[209] The committee discussed possible means of controlling the market: domestic restrictions on the entry of Euro-currencies, establishment of reserve requirements for Eurobanks, and adoption of a joint open market policy on the Euro-currency market.[210]

The fundamental problem, in Britain in particular, as has now been said in many different ways, was the pursuit of full employment and economic growth with a pegged exchange rate and governments that found it impossible to contain their own expenditure. Some countries did much better than Britain, and there are many reasons behind that. But the British pursuit of full employment, expansionary policy, and consequent excessive government expenditure must rank high in the explanation for pressure on the balance of payments and inflation. Given the frequent conflict between domestic and external objectives, choices had to be made between, essentially, inflation and rigid controls in foreign exchange. As it was, payments problems were regarded either as temporary or to be solved by first short-term and then longer-term borrowing. The big lesson of the 1960s was what was called the 'trilemma' – the impossibility of having an independent monetary policy, capital mobility, and fixed exchange rates. Britain's position was complicated by it being an intermediate-sized country with a history of being a large country and with sterling a reserve currency and the ever-present question of sterling balances. In addition, there was a pegged-rate regime and not a fixed one.

---

[208] Hackly, Board minutes, 19 February 1969. p. 11; Meltzer (2009, p. 740).
[209] Toniolo (2005, p. 465).
[210] *Ibid.*, p. 466.

9

The Road to Competition and Credit Control

When the intention to introduce 'Competition and Credit Control' (CCC) was announced in May 1971, it presaged the biggest change in monetary policy since the Second World War. Moreover, when announced, it marked a decisive shift in policy rather than the gradualism that generally characterised the Bank. Several strands came together. There was a growing dissatisfaction with controls and a developing interest in the need for greater competition in banking. And the work on money that suggested a stable demand function pointed to a greater role for interest rates in the control of money growth. There was some acceptance, under pressure, of the need to use open market operations. However, the road from the mid-1960s to 1971 was far from even.

Disaffection with Controls

Over the course of the 1960s, the Bank had become increasingly disaffected with controls and particularly with ceilings on advances. At base, it did not believe in them: they were inequitable, they were difficult to enforce, there were simply too many loopholes, and they soured relations with the banks and the Treasury. All of this had been demonstrated before 1967 and would continue up to 1970, when controls remained the main weapon of domestic monetary policy.

Lending ceilings for the clearing banks had been lifted in April 1967, only to be re-imposed at the time of devaluation when the clearers were asked to cap advances at the 15 November 1967 level. Other banks, which had been working to a ceiling of 105 per cent of March 1965, were required to cap the 31 October level. Credit for the finance of exports was exempt.[1]

---

[1] Bank of England, Notice on credit restriction, 19 November 1967; O'Brien to Stirling (chairman, CLCB), 19 November 1967 and letters to other banking organisations and banks, C40/1291.

The non-clearing banks complained about starting again at 100 per cent, but Fforde argued that there was no room for exceptions. If devaluation was to be made to work, 'the authorities must adopt a tough attitude towards anomalies and inequities and must not weaken their ability to be tough over the period ahead by making concessions at the outset'.[2]

Moreover, following devaluation, Fforde took a bleak view of the impact of Bank Rate: 'As things are now, the 8 per cent Rate is more a sign of failure rather than a useful element of current policy'.[3] It had not attracted short-term funds to London, although it had done much to restrain domestic demand for credit and was an important symbol of the fact the devaluation was not a painless option. While the Bank wanted to lower the rate, domestic and external conditions recommended 'a cautious and gradual approach'.[4] There was a reduction of ½ per cent following the restrictive budget of March 1968 and a further ½ per cent cut to 7 per cent in September 1968, tied to the Basle arrangements of that month and improved trade figures.[5]

The level and direction of bank lending continued to worry the authorities. In May it was decided that there would be a 'public admonition' if the figures were out of line, but it was agreed on 21 May that no action was required.[6] Then there was a dramatic shift when the next day the Treasury advocated a further tightening through a new ceiling that embraced all lending, including that for export purposes.[7] Why the sudden change? The visit from the International Monetary Fund (IMF), worried about the forecast money supply, was significant. Also, the latest issue of the National Institute for Economic and Social Research *Review* predicted a current account deficit until mid-1969 and called for the introduction of import controls. Thus the Chancellor and the Governor agreed to an immediate tightening of credit.[8] A new ceiling of 104 per cent based on November 1967 was set, and the previously exempt categories now would have to be met within the ceiling.[9]

---

2   Fforde to Hollom, 'Credit restrictions', 14 December 1967, C40/1291.
3   Fforde to O'Brien/Parsons, 'Bank rate', 30 January 1968, C42/9.
4   Fforde to Morse, 'Money rates', 1 March 1968, C42/9.
5   Press guidance, 21 March and 19 September 1968, C42/9; *BEQB* 8(4):341, December 1968.
6   Goldman to Sir Douglas Allen, 17 May 1968, enc. Lovell/Goldman, 'Policy on bank credit', 17 May 1968; Fforde to O'Brien, 'Credit policy', 22 May 1968, C40/1293.
7   Radice to Michael Hawtin (private Secretary to William Armstrong), 22 May 1968, enc. 'Policy on bank credit', 22 May 1968, C40/1293.
8   Radice to Hawtin, 23 May 1968, C40/1293; NIESR, *Review* 44:10–13, May 1968.
9   Robert Armstrong, Note for the record – 'Control of bank credit', 24 May 1968; O'Brien to David Robarts (chairman, CLCB), 23 May 1968, enc. Bank of England, Notice on credit

The clearing banks were furious. O'Brien recorded, with some under-statement, that Robarts and Sir Archibald Forbes of the Committee of London Clearing Banks (CLCB) were 'pretty put out' about the speed with which new restraints were introduced, the lack of communication, and their severity. They also raised a familiar complaint that restrictions were being placed on the private sector, when the public sector was still at lib-erty to borrow freely.[10] The Bank, too, was frustrated with the haste that had been dictated by the government's desire to take the headlines away from the National Institute for Economic and Social Research (NIESR), and Fforde hoped that the next change in credit policy would see a return to normality.[11] As to any suggestion that the clearers should have more direct contact with government, O'Brien was forthright: 'I will not tolerate the banks trotting off to Whitehall at regular intervals. Both the Chancellor and the banks know how I feel about this.'[12] If the clearers were upset by events in May, things were to become much worse.

In the middle of August 1968, O'Brien wrote to them saying that the period of grace in which to adjust to the new ceiling should now be regarded as over. Although the ceiling had not been breached, the underlying trend of lending was upward. He was sure that they would agree on the importance of demonstrating that voluntary methods of control were effective, but if not, he warned, 'more formal methods of control' could not be excluded.[13] Robarts disputed whether enough time had elapsed and appealed for more time, but no concession was obtained.[14] Parsons, acting in O'Brien's absence, replied that given limited progress since devaluation, 'we simply cannot afford to let the position run on to see to what extent your present efforts are succeeding'.[15] Even though the August figures were acceptable, a

---

restriction, 23 May 1968. Letters also were sent to nine other banking organisations. The FHA was asked to bring previously exempt lending within the ceiling of 100 per cent of 31 October 1967; O'Brien to A. Victor Adey (chairman, FHA), 23 May 1968, C40/1293. This version of events is at odds with Cairncross, who claims that the Bank initiated the squeeze 'contrary to official advice'; Cairncross (1996, p. 212).

[10] Hollom to O'Brien, 'Credit restraint', 24 May 1968; O'Brien, Governor's note: 'Credit restraint', 27 May 1968; R. T. Armstrong, Note for record, 30 May 1968; Sir Archibald Forbes to O'Brien, 6 June 1968, enc. Robarts/Forbes to O'Brien, 6 June 1968, C40/1293.

[11] Fforde to O'Brien, 'Credit restrictions: prior consultation with banks', 4 June 1968, C40/1293.

[12] O'Brien, Annotation, 4 June 1968, on Fforde to O'Brien, 'Credit restrictions: prior consul-tation with banks', 4 June 1968, C40/1293.

[13] 'Extract from Mr. Hollom's memo dated 9.8.68 ...'; O'Brien to Robarts, 13 August 1968, C40/1293.

[14] Robarts to O'Brien, 16 August 1968, C40/1293.

[15] Parsons to Robarts, 20 August 1968, C40/1293.

public announcement was made that the current credit restrictions must be 'rigorously enforced', and the needs of borrowers had to be met by reductions in lending for less essential purposes.[16]

Hire-purchase terms were tightened in November, although Allen doubted whether this would be sufficient and recommended more action on bank lending. He wanted fixed-rate finance for exports and shipbuilding to be re-exempted from the restrictions and suggested that the banks be asked to limit personal lending to make the restraint bear more heavily on consumption. However, the co-operation of the banks was 'sorely strained', and they might simply 'go through the ceiling'. Nevertheless, O'Brien believed that the high levels of demand and imports warranted greater severity and called for a revised ceiling of 98 per cent of mid-November 1967, some £100 million below the equivalent of the current ceiling. For discount houses and others with virtually no fixed-rate export lending, a ceiling of 102 per cent was proposed. O'Brien wanted to avoid drastic measures such as import controls, but he conceded that they might be inevitable anyway.[17] Following the turmoil in the international monetary system in November, the Chancellor announced an emergency package of deflationary measures that included tightening bank credit, increases in indirect taxes, and as the Governor had feared, controls in the form of 'import deposit scheme'.[18] The new ceiling would be 98 per cent of mid-November 1967 for the clearing banks, whereas the ceiling for the finance houses was reduced to 98 per cent of end-October 1967.[19]

Some notice had been given on this occasion. O'Brien had warned the clearers in early November that something was likely to happen, and on 19 November he gave them formal notice of the proposals.[20] The prior notice of the measures did little to diminish dissatisfaction. They complained that the burden of credit restriction would fall unfairly on the private sector. The *Evening News* gave coverage to the letter under the headline 'Banks

---

[16] 'Extract from Mr. Hollom's memo dated 29.8.68 ... '; Bank of England, Press announcement, 30 August 1968, C40/1293.

[17] O'Brien to Sir Douglas Allen, 15 November 1968, 3A8/1.

[18] 'Mechanics of import deposit scheme', filed as 22 November 1968, 3A8/1; *BEQB* 8(4):342, December 1968.

[19] Parsons to Robarts, 22 November 1968, enc. Bank of England, 'Notice: credit restrictions', 22 November 1968. A similar letter was sent to nine other organisations. Parsons to Adey, 22 November 1968. A supplementary note was issued in December; see Bank of England, 'Credit restrictions: explanatory notice to banks', 17 December 1968, 3A8/1.

[20] Hollom, Notes for record – 'Credit restraint: the big five', 'Credit restraint: the clearing banks', 'Credit restrictions: banks other than the clearing banks', 'Credit restrictions: visit to Northern Ireland', 25 November 1968, 3A8/1.

Slam Government Clamp on Lending' and speculated that the letter certainly would be discussed when the Governor and the Chancellor met, as it was.[21]

In February 1969, Bank Rate stood at 7 per cent, but the monetary authorities wanted a rise specifically to temper the expansion of the domestic economy, in itself a move away from Radcliffe principles. The case for a rise for external reasons was not particularly strong, but for the domestic economy, O'Brien felt that the arguments were much firmer: Bank Rate was abnormally low in relation to other short-term yields, an increase could provide a useful reinforcement of the credit squeeze, and the case would be even greater if the forthcoming figures for advances revealed little progress by the clearers towards achieving their lending target by March. O'Brien argued for a 1 per cent rise. Anything less, he thought, would be seen as too little and merely result in damaging expectations that another rise was imminent.[22] Bridge dissented, warning that because of its association with devaluation, a rate of 8 per cent would sound alarm bells, and internationally, there could be an adverse reaction to a cut.[23] However, in the wake of disappointing advances figures, Bank Rate was raised to 8 per cent on 27 February. That afternoon, Jenkins and O'Brien had a tetchy meeting with the clearing bank chairmen where it was explained that domestic factors, not external, had made the rise necessary. Heavy press briefing, including a meeting between the Chancellor and City editors, emphasised the point.[24]

Most of 1969 was taken up with trying to get the clearing banks to meet the 98 per cent ceiling. At the beginning of the year, the clearing Banks' advances were more than £140 million (3 per cent).[25] Everything from cajolery, exhortation, threat, and penalty were tried, but with little success. Regular warnings were given by the clearing banks that despite their best endeavours, the target would not be met.[26] Of course, bankers always complain about

---

[21]   Robarts to O'Brien, Draft, 27 November 1968; Robarts to O'Brien, 28 November 1968; 'Extract from Mr. Morse's memo dated 4.12.68 ...'; *Evening News*, 2 December 1968, cutting in 3A8/1.

[22]   Fforde to O'Brien/Parsons, 'Bank rate', 11 February 1969; HMT, 'Note of a meeting ... 17 February at 3:00 p.m.', 19 February 1969, C42/10.

[23]   Bridge to O'Brien, 'Bank rate', 25 February 1969, C42/10.

[24]   Armstrong to Dowler, 'Meeting with selected City editors', 26 February 1968; Press guidance, 27 February 1969, C42/10; HMT, 28 February 1969, 'Note of a meeting ... 27 February at 4:30 p.m.', 3A8/2.

[25]   'Clearing banks', 18 February 1969, 3A8/2.

[26]   Hollom to O'Brien/Parsons, 'Clearing bank advances', 9 January 1969; O'Brien, Governor's note – 'Bank advances', 9 January 1969, 3A8/2; Wood, Note for record – 'Meeting with the chief executive officers 27 February 1969', 3 March 1969; Fforde, Note for record – 'Credit

how difficult it was to meet imposed limits, but this time there was evidence to suggest that they were not bluffing. They claimed particular difficulties because their customers were making use of existing advances facilities, which greatly exceeded total advances outstanding, so restriction of new business was insufficient. As Fforde remarked, unless the banks were to be wholly disbelieved, 'one has to conclude that 98 per cent may well have been an impossible target'.[27] At the Treasury, Figgures had asked that less emphasis be placed on 98 per cent so that it would be easier to modify the figure at a later date. More important, the Treasury was keen to avoid a confrontation with the clearers.[28] For its part, the Bank stubbornly continued to insist on compliance, not accustomed to its targets being missed.

There was the usual disquiet from the Finance Houses Association (FHA), with its chairman, Victor Adey, making a number of representations to the Bank. He also had bent the ear of Figgures at a lunch and vented his frustrations in front of the Chancellor at the FHA's annual dinner in January 1969. The general thrust of these complaints was that imposition of the ceiling was inequitable.[29] While the Bank offered no prospect of any exceptions, there was some sympathy there.[30] It was inevitable, as Carlisle admitted, that ceilings would work unfairly both within and between groups of institutions: 'That is why the Authorities would like to give them up as soon as ever they can.'[31] This was one of a growing number of explicit expressions of dislike of controls.

After several years of heavy use, 'top hat' letters and calls to the Parlours were weapons that were becoming blunted and ineffective. At the other end of the spectrum from these traditional methods was the possibility of issuing a formal directive. These powers, contained in the 1946 Act, had never been used, but in January 1969, O'Brien briefly raised the spectre of a directive, only to draw back quickly, not wanting to provoke a challenge from the banks, fearing that it would achieve little apart from permanently changing

restrictions', 14 March 1969, 3A8/3; O'Brien, Governor's note, 26 March 1969 (on a visit by Sir Archibald Forbes [Midland Bank]), G3/269.

27 Fforde to O'Brien/Parsons, 'Special deposits', 11 February 1969, 3A8/2.

28 Hollom to Parsons, 'Credit restrictions', 28 January 1969; Pen Kent (GPS), Note for record – 'Credit restrictions', 30 January 1969, 3A8/2.

29 Adey to Parsons, 24 December 1968, 3A8/1; Edwards (HMT) to Page, nd, enc. Armstrong to Lovell, 3 January 1969; Adey to Parsons, 12 February 1969, 3A8/2; *Credit* 10(1):2–7, March 1969.

30 Parsons to Adey, 14 January 1969; O'Brien to Adey, 25 February 1969; Fforde to chairmen of various finance houses, 26 February 1969, 3A8/2; Hollom, Note for record – 'Finance Houses Association', 26 March 1969, 3A8/3.

31 Carlisle to Page, 'Finance Houses Association's complaint about ceiling controls', 10 January 1969, 3A8/2.

the nature of the relationship between the Bank and the banks.[32] His great worry was that the banks might fail to hit the target even after a directive had been issued. Such an outcome could bring the Act into disrepute and provoke a political clamour for tougher legislation: 'One very much doubts whether this is either what the banking community would like or what the Bank would consider desirable.'[33]

Another avenue was punitive action. In March, Morse asked what penalties there were in other countries and learned that in the Netherlands fines were imposed on each bank's lending in excess of a requested total. Fforde was not convinced.[34] But O'Brien was attracted, and after talking to the permanent Secretary, he wrote, 'Allen, like me, hankers after some device which could place additional restraint on the banks which failed to keep within the ceiling.'[35] At the beginning of April, the Governor told CLCB representatives that if there was not sufficient progress towards achieving the ceiling, then there would be immediate action to reinforce control.[36] This came in May when, following poor figures – still 2 per cent above the ceiling – the rate of interest paid on special deposits was halved with effect from 2 June.[37] In the CLCB's written response, Robarts claimed that the move would have 'no effect whatsoever on the level of advances', and he dismissed it as 'irrelevant' to the situation where the banks were trying to do everything to support government policy.[38] Nonetheless, the banks still effectively volunteered to be fined. Several months later, Fforde wrote that the move was supposed to give the banks a financial incentive to get within the ceiling, but in retrospect, he admitted that it was a 'tactical move designed to sustain the momentum of a tough credit policy, in the eyes of the public, at a difficult and delicate time.'[39]

---

[32] Parsons, 'Note of the Governor's conversation with Mr. Robarts', 14 January 1969, and O'Brien, Annotation, 16 January 1969, 3A8/2.

[33] Fforde to Parsons, 'Your meeting with the C.L.C.B. on Monday, 27 January', 23 January 1969, 3A8/2. The issue was considered again in September 1969; Page, Note for record – 'Use of Section 4 of the Bank of England Act 1946', 9 September 1969; Lovell to Page, 19 September 1969, 3A8/5.

[34] Michael Balfour (Adviser) to Morse, 'Credit controls – penalties', 12 March 1969; Fforde to O'Brien, 'Credit controls – penalties', 18 March 1969, 3A8/3.

[35] 'Extract from the Governor's memo date 19.3.69 ...', 3A8/3.

[36] Note for record – 'Meeting with clearing bankers, 31.3.69', 1 April 1969, 3A8/3.

[37] Hollom, Note for record – 'Bank advances', 29 May 1969, 3A8/3; Wood, Note of record – 'Meeting with the chief executive officers, 29 May 1969', 5 June 1969, 3A8/4; O'Brien to Robarts et al., 30 May 1969, 5A148/1.

[38] Hollom to O'Brien, Note for record – 'Bank lending' 29 May 1969; Robarts to O'Brien, 3 June 1969, 5A148/1.

[39] Fforde, 'Rate of interest on special deposits', 19 November 1969, 5A148/1.

Another problem was loopholes. In 1967 and 1969, the Bank was made aware of allegations that stockbrokers were borrowing money at call or short notice from banks and using it to avoid credit restrictions. 'Other money at call' was not subject to restraint because the Bank considered that its provision was necessary 'to ensure the efficient technical operation of the various financial markets'.[40] The Bank moved quickly to stop the practice.[41] When the matter was investigated again in 1969, Fforde found little reason to think that the position had deteriorated.[42] Concerns about commercial bills dated back to 1965, and reminder letters were issued on several occasions.[43] The Bank had always recognised that there was a potential leakage if the clearing banks were to reduce their purchases of commercial bills from the discount market and then offset the fall in bills by an increase in advances. By early 1969, the extent of the bill leak was a worry because the clearing banks' holdings of commercial bills had fallen by £100 million since summer 1968, and although warned, bills holdings continued to decline.[44]

The 'Irish leak' was essentially an offshore banking device whereby banks diverted sterling lending through subsidiaries or associates in Dublin. First reported to the Bank in March 1969, the claims took some months to investigate because the business was not reflected in British statistics, whereas the Irish central bank was unable to offer much assistance. It was left to Keogh, Principal of the Discount Office, to visit the mainly American banks with Irish connections to ascertain the extent of their involvement. Unsurprisingly, these banks assured Keogh either that they were not engaged in such business or that it would not grow any further in the future.[45] Fforde

[40]   Fforde to Radice, 10 January 1968, C40/1292.
[41]   Fforde to O'Brien/Parsons, 'Call money lent by banks to stockbrokers', 19 December 1967, C40/1291; Fforde to O'Brien/Parsons, 'Credit restriction: other call money', 4 January 1968; Hollom to CLCB and others, 10 January 1968; Fforde to Radice, 10 January 1968; Fforde to 48 banks, 10 January 1968, C40/1292.
[42]   Wood to Blunden, 'Money at call', 12 March 1969; Fforde to Armstrong, 14 March 1969, 3A8/3.
[43]   Fforde to Robarts, 22 July 1968; Hollom to Robarts, 9 August 1968, C40/1293; Wood to Thornton/Fforde/Hollom, 'Commercial bills and the discount houses', 18 February 1969, 3A8/2.
[44]   Wood to Thornton/Fforde/Hollom, 'Commercial bills and the discount houses', 18 February 1969; Wood to Fforde, 'Brief for meeting with the chief executive officers, 27 February 1969', 27 February 1969, 3A8/2; Wood, Note for record – 'Meeting with the chief executive officers, 27 February 1969', 3 March 1969; Fforde to Michael Wilson (chairman, CEOs of the London clearing banks', 6 March 1969; Fforde to Hollom, 'The "bill leak"', 11 March 1969; Wilson to Fforde, 14 March 1969, 3A8/3.
[45]   Morse to Hollom, '102 per cent ceiling/leaks from Ireland?', 26 March 1969; Fforde to Hollom, 'Offshore banking', 8 May 1969; Wood, Note for record – 'The Irish banks. Mr. Hollom's visit to Dublin and Belfast, 19–21 May 1969', 9 June 1969, 3A8/3.

reckoned that this had brought the situation under control, although he also cautioned that there should be no delusions that such offshore banking would not grow further. Hollom added, 'I am afraid this is a "fingers in dykes" exercise, where one cannot hope really to win.'[46]

The fledgling Barclaycard also prompted concern, with suspicions in the Treasury and the Board of Trade that the extended credit facilities offered by the card might flout hire-purchase controls and the Bank's notice on credit restriction. The Bank could not accept a situation whereby the country's largest clearing bank was acting in contravention of the guidance note, and shortly after, Barclays agreed to modify the scheme.[47] Overall, none of the leakages could be said to have caused a significant breach of credit restrictions. They operated at the margins but were nonetheless indicative of the problems of operating with ceilings. As long as there was a ceiling in place, ways of circumventing it would be sought. Investigating and policing this required resources, and the actions taken to close the loopholes could have unintended consequences. Often, though, there was little that could be done other than to issue a warning.

The Imposition of the 'fine' in May 1969 can be seen as a last attempt to get the clearers to fall into line. There was no sense of any coherent policy. The latest advances figures were indeed 'extremely bad', with the clearers on average almost 5 per cent over the target, and 'all the big banks culpable'.[48] The Governor delivered further exhortations to the clearers, while Bank and Treasury officials attempted to formulate a statement that would put a positive gloss on the figures.[49] It was a similar story in September. Again, the authorities held back and relied on a carefully worded statement.[50] There also were signs of increasing tensions between the government and the

---

[46] Fforde to Hollom/O'Brien/Parsons, 'Offshore banking: the Irish leak', 3 July 1969, and Hollom annotation, 3A8/4.

[47] Robert Armstrong (HMT) to Kenneth Andrews (Deputy Chief Cashier), 6 December 1967; Page to Fforde/Hollom, 'Credit restrictions – Barclaycards', 14 December 1967; Fforde to Hollom, 'Credit restriction – Barclaycards', 15 December 1967; Wilde to Fforde, 20 December 1967; Fforde to Hollom, 'Barclaycard', 20 December 1967; Fforde to Wilde, 22 December 1967, C40/1291; Ackrill and Hannah (2001, pp. 184–191).

[48] Hancock, 'Note of a meeting … 27 August 1969', 3A8/4.

[49] Fforde, Note for record – 'The Governors' meeting with the clearing bank chairmen: 29.8.69'; Hollom to O'Brien, 'The banking figures', 29 August 1969, 3A8/4; Unsigned [but is Figgures] to Hancock, 'Implications of the latest bank lending figures', 2 September 1969, 3A8/5.

[50] Armstrong to Hancock, 'Bank advances', 25 September 1969; Fforde to O'Brien, 'September banking figures', 26 September 1969; 'Extract from the Deputy Governor's memo dated 26 September 1969 …'; Hancock to Hayles (HMT), 29 September 1969; 'Extract from the Chief Cashier's memo dated 30.9.69 …', 3A8/5.

banks, with an awkward meeting of Jenkins, O'Brien, and the chairmen of the 'Big Five'. According to Fforde, the banks were worried that if they had to push the credit restriction further, their own management would be seen as too politically identified with the government.[51]

October 1969 finally witnessed a shift in policy. In the first half of the month, the Treasury was making strong hints that it wanted to see some relaxation of the 98 per cent target by accepting some excess over the ceiling, or by setting a revised figure, or by exempting short-term export finance at Bank Rate. Adopting the last of these would take out £125 million from the restricted category, but O'Brien was not in favour of such a move, and neither would it be liked by the IMF. He thought that the banks could be told that the present level of advances was acceptable and that the authorities were no longer seeking a reduction.[52] The Treasury was trying to find a means of abandoning 98 per cent without putting another number in its place.[53]

In November it was announced that the import deposit scheme would continue and that the credit squeeze would be reviewed over the autumn.[54] O'Brien told Jenkins, 'We must now recognise that the clearing banks will not get any nearer to the 98 per cent target without a further and fairly drastic tightening of the restrictions that they at present impose on their lending.' Indeed, he admitted that the authorities had known this for some time, while in public running a 'holding operation. ... We have certainly had our fill of numerical targets; and our experience with 98% makes one hesitate to adopt another one.' On the other hand, without a ceiling, implicit or explicit, was a risk that the banks would relax their efforts, and the Bank would have no clear criterion against which to judge performance or take action. The Governor was reluctant to commit himself at this stage, although he said that he was inclined towards a new ceiling.[55] Yet, while he wanted to maintain restraint, he also wanted to see some flexibility, and this would be difficult with a new target. What would be 'clearly undesirable' would be to 'conceal the dilemma by fudging'.[56] But the decision was

[51] Hancock, 'Note of meeting ... 11 September 1969', 12 September 1969, 4A116/8; Fforde to O'Brien, 'September banking figures', 26 September 1969, 3A8/5.
[52] Fforde to Hollom, 'Credit restrictions', 6 October 1969; Fforde to O'Brien, 'Credit restrictions', 14 October 1969; 'Extract from Mr. Morse's memo 16.10.69 ... '; Lovell to Neale, 16 October 1969, enc. Lovell, 'Bank credit policy', 16 October 1969; 'Extract from Mr Hollom's memo 20.10.69 ...', 3A8/5.
[53] Armstrong to Hancock, 20 October 1969, 3A8/5.
[54] HC Deb 21, October 1969, Vol. 788, cc952–954, 957.
[55] O'Brien to Armstrong, 22 October 1969, 3A8/5.
[56] 'Extract from Mr. Morse's memo 22.10.69 ...', 3A8/5.

fudged. The clearers were told in private that they no longer had to cut back their advances to 98 per cent. In public, the Bank's statement made no mention that the ceiling had effectively been abandoned.[57] The Bank was tired of controls and justified the abandonment in terms of technicalities. With advances for November and December satisfactory, the Treasury was keen to make a formal announcement that the 98 per cent had been withdrawn.[58] The Bank, however, remained cautious, and nothing was announced until the budget in April 1970.[59]

In the autumn of 1969, the Chancellor had asked officials to consider urgently alternative methods of compelling the banks to restrict credit. A Bank-Treasury working party chaired by Sir Douglas Allen (who had taken over from Sir William Armstrong as permanent Secretary at the Treasury the previous year) was immediately set up with the aim of producing preliminary results within two weeks. This informal body was quickly transformed into a fully fledged committee called the 'Group on Monetary Policy'.[60] Its remit was broader, too. As McMahon told Fforde, 'Allen's group is obviously going to range more widely and attempt to discuss more basic theoretical issues than it originally appeared.'[61] Hollom, Fforde, and McMahon represented the Bank, but the group was dominated by the Treasury, with a large membership of senior personnel, including Allen, Figgures, MacDougall, Posner, and Robert Armstrong. The group's task was to produce an interim report before Easter 1970, which it did, although no radical proposals were offered.[62] Control would continue to be based firmly on the existing fixed liquidity ratio, with guidance as a vital feature, and the use of special deposits (which had been unchanged, at 2 per cent, since July 1966). There

[57]   Hollom to O'Brien, 'Credit restrictions', 23 October 1969; Hancock, 'Note of a meeting ... 27th October 1969', 27 October 1969; O'Brien, Governor's note – 'Clearing bank advances', 27 October 1969; Bank of England, 'Note for guidance on October banking figures', 27 October 1969, 3A8/5.

[58]   'Extract from Mr. Morse's memo 3.12.69 ...'; 'Extract from the Deputy Governor's memo 17.12.69 ...', 3A8/5; Fforde to O'Brien/Parsons, 'Credit restriction', 22 December 1969; Armstrong to Fforde, 22 December 1969, 3A8/5.

[59]   'Extract from Mr. Hollom's memo dated 1.1.70 ...'; 'Extract from Mr. Hollom's note dated 9.1.70 ...'; O'Brien to Jenkins, 9 January 1970; 'Extract from the Deputy Governor's note 14.1.70 ...', Armstrong to Fforde, 15 January 1970; 'Extract from Mr. Hollom's memo dated 16.1.70 ...'; Hollom to O'Brien, 27 January 1970, 3A8/6.

[60]   Hancock, 27 October 1969, 'Note of a meeting ... 27th October 1969'; Fforde to Hollom, 'Credit control', 28 October 1969; Hollom to O'Brien, 'Bank credit', 29 October 1969, 3A8/5.

[61]   R. P. Culpin (HMT), 'Working part on control of bank credit ... Friday 28 November ...', 9 December 1969; McMahon to Fforde, 'Monetary policy', 5 December 1969, 6A74/1.

[62]   MP(70)15(final), 'Interim report on controlling bank lending to the private sector', 25 March 1970, 6A74/3; Interim report, para. 13.

appeared to be no case for retaining the interest penalty on special deposits. Indeed, the Bank had questioned whether the scheme, which it said was designed to be voluntary and non-penal, could be used further in this way without new legislation.[63] For the other banks, the only instruments available were ceilings and the as yet unused cash deposits scheme. In summary, then, the recommendations were: abolish the existing ceiling for clearing banks; control lending to the clearers through guidance, both private and public, and frequent use of special deposits; for other banks, issue guidance backed by the threat of a cash deposits scheme; and for all banks, issue no immediate call for special or cash deposits, but the interest penalty on the former should be removed. There was still no serious consideration of using interest rates as a means of control.

The Chancellor wondered, no doubt with thoughts of the impending general election, about announcing a Bank Rate cut in the budget.[64] Leaving aside this impertinence for a moment, according to O'Brien, the arguments for and against a ½ per cent reduction were 'evenly balanced', although he was worried that the budget should not appear overly relaxing. To offset this, he now proposed a small 'nominal' call for special deposits. Jenkins was keen to see Bank Rate at 7 per cent and was also attracted to the idea of making a call for special deposits at the same time. Both agreed that interest payments on special deposits should be restored because the 'offence' for which they were imposed was no longer regarded as an offence. In O'Brien's view, the package would be welcomed by the banks, and Jenkins said that he was inclined to announce all three elements in the budget.[65]

Reviewing monetary policy in the budget in April, Jenkins said that it 'was very tight by any standard'. For the coming year to March 1971, bank lending would be allowed to rise by 5 per cent. But the Chancellor was at last able to say that ceilings were to be abandoned for the clearing banks and special deposits to be used 'as freely as is required', and a call should not be regarded as a crisis measure. The additional ½ per cent call (¼ per cent for Scottish banks) was announced. Finally, the Chancellor turned to interest rates and, in a somewhat blatant piece of political theatre, said that Bank Rate would be reduced to 7 per cent with effect from the following day. The only other occasion on which this had happened was the reactivation of monetary policy in November 1951, but this was the first time that a

[63] MP(69)6, Bank of England, 'Rate of interest on special deposits', 19 November 1969, 6A74/3.

[64] Hancock, 'Meeting … 25th March 1970', 26 March 1970, 3A8/6.

[65] William Ryrie (Principal Private Secretary, HMT), Note for record – 'Bank Rate and credit policy', 3 April 1970, 3A8/6.

Bank Rate change had appeared in a budget speech. A press announcement was made by the Bank at the same time.[66] Despite all these measures, over the next six months, advances grew more quickly than requested, and at the end of October 1970, the Bank made a further call for special deposits, taking them to 3½ per cent for the London clearers and 1¾ per cent for the Scottish banks.[67]

Touted as a change of policy, the April 1970 announcement was merely a restatement about the use of existing tools and little different from what Callaghan had said in 1967. Options were clearly limited, and as Fforde noted, 'it would not make much sense for us to announce that the Cash Deposit scheme, negotiated with such pain in 1967, was now considered so ineffective by the authorities that it was being replaced by something else.' In any case, no other instruments had yet been developed.

The Clearing Banks: Mergers, Competition, Cartels, and Reform

Alongside the growing dislike of controls was a recognition that a more competitive banking sector was desirable. The Governor, in a widely reported speech in 1963, raised some important concerns relating to the behaviour of the clearing banks.[68] In the summer of 1965, when Fforde was an Adviser to the Governors, he produced a two-part report on the banking system. The first section, written in conjunction with John Luce and John (Jack) McDowall from the Economic Intelligence Department (EID) and Morse, was a review of developments in the sector since the 1950s. It was a seemingly uncontroversial narrative, backed with statistical analysis, that showed that the clearing banks had led a comfortable, though in many ways inefficient existence, whereas the merchant banks had tended to be innovative, and overseas banks had expanded rapidly on the business in Eurodollars. The second part was Fforde's work alone and displayed some of his more maverick tendencies. In particular, he argued that in the public interest there was a case for Bank intervention to promote greater efficiency. He accepted that this would be 'a near-revolutionary change of

---

[66] HC Deb, 14 April 1970, Vol. 799, cc1221–1236. Bank of England, Press announcement, 14 April 1970, C42/10.

[67] Page to O'Brien, 27 October 1970; Bank of England, Press announcement, 29 October 1970; Page to various banks, 29 October 1970, 5A148/1.

[68] 'Speech by the Rt. Hon. the Earl of Cromer, Governor of the Bank of England, at the 400th anniversary dinner of Martins Bank Limited on Thursday, 25 April 1963', G13/2; cuttings in ADM38/122.

emphasis' and that it was very delicate ground. He thought that the Bank might encourage the formation of larger, but independent merchant banks even to the extent of contemplating offering temporary financial help through direct equity participation. At the other extreme, the Bank could employ sanctions to prevent 'undesirable' mergers. Fforde admitted that the Bank knew almost nothing about the efficiency of the clearing banks, but he suspected that they were 'uneconomic users of resources' and especially that the country was 'over-banked' (i.e., had too many branches). In his opinion, this 'waste' had to be addressed. Rationalisation was the answer: he envisaged the optimal outcome as a 'Big Three', competing with each other and with the enlarged merchant banks. In order to bring this about, he saw a strong case for an independent enquiry, something that might happen anyway given the Labour Government's monopolies and restrictive practices legislation.[69] Fforde's views were undoubtedly radical and perhaps deliberately provocative, but they connected with wider preoccupations in planning and efficiency outside the Bank. Not that the paper ever went that far because Cromer was highly uncomplimentary about it, professing that he would be 'profoundly disturbed' if it was ever regarded as the Bank's appraisal of the banking system 'as it exists in reality' or used as the basis for discussing reform. His main complaint was that the paper 'lacks a "feel" of the City and the wide variety of inherited characteristics and traditions'. He deprecated the use of 'arbitrary compartments' to produce statistics 'either for our own edification or for the benefit of those who would like to run the national economy at the dictates of a computer'. Furthermore, Cromer was unconvinced that size was in itself an asset because it was 'enterprise and initiative', not rationalisation, that would 'continue to justify the City in the eyes of the world'. He concluded by describing the paper as 'an interesting theoretical study', but what was needed was further study 'based on extensive experience of practical banking in the City of London'. This implied less Fforde and more Cromer.[70]

Yet it was Fforde who was proved correct as mergers and the banks' putative monopoly power came to the fore in the next few years. Amalgamation had reduced the number of London clearers from 11 at the time of Radcliffe to six by 1970. However, the blocking of the Barclays-Lloyds merger had prevented the step to Fforde's preferred 'big three'. The clearing banks also

---

[69]　Fforde to O'Brien/Morse/Hollom/Clarke, 'The banking sector', 14 April 1965, enc. 'Implications of changes in the British banking system', parts I and II, ADM35/6.

[70]　Cromer, Governor's note, 9 June 1965, ADM35/6. Also see Fforde's recollection of this episode; Fforde to Richardson, 'Secondary banking: the antecedents', 20 January 1978, 7A149/2.

were put under the spotlight by a National Board for Prices and Incomes (NBPI) investigation into dividends, charges, and services. Questions of monetary policy, such as Bank Rate and the general level of interest rates, were not in the remit, but the inability of the NBPI to stay within its terms of reference proved to be an irritation for the Bank. In fact, Cromer was furious that the government had even made a referral in the first place. He was in his final month as Governor, and he sent a blistering letter to Callaghan defending the position of the City, the banks, and sterling and criticising the government. He saw the referral as a decision that would be interpreted as being taken for political motives, with no relevance to the present state of the economy; it would be seen as 'an attack, for political reasons, on the City'. Not only that, but it was a waste of resources and was likely to be inconclusive. Callaghan was reminded that the banks had co-operated in every way to implement the government's financial policies so as to sustain sterling, and this referral gave the impression that the government did not recognise this. At the same time, he claimed that the bill to renationalise the steel industry, which was about to be introduced, would be damaging to sterling and that the two pieces of news together would 'aggravate uncertainty in the exchanges'. His parting shot was vintage Cromer: 'I must leave you in no doubt, Mr. Chancellor, that, in my belief, such a step at this time may well yet further impair the national financial position.'[71]

While the new Governor did not behave quite as dramatically as Cromer, he was nevertheless keen to see that there was no straying into the field of monetary policy.[72] The NBPI took both oral and written evidence from the banks, whereas the Bank and the Treasury submitted written evidence. By the end of 1966, the Bank, the Treasury, and the clearers were expressing dissatisfaction with the way matters were progressing, and there was also annoyance about the fact that the investigation was to look at the question of disclosure of profits and reserves. O'Brien had warned Armstrong that there would be trouble if the report 'encroached on the Governor's own territory', and after a meeting with Aubrey Jones in December 1966, he noted, 'I think we probably have a not very easy task of instruction and persuasion on our hands.'[73] Several months later Morse observed that Jones was a man

---

[71] Cromer to Armstrong, 28 March 1966; Rickett told Morse that the reference was 'intended to gratify the Trade Unions'; 'Extract from Mr. Morse's note dated 14.6.66 … '; Cromer to Callaghan, 15 June 1966, C40/1652.

[72] 'Extract from Mr. Hollom's memo dated 6.7.66 …', C40/1652.

[73] 'Extract from Mr. Hollom's memo dated 2.12.66 …', C40/1652; O'Brien, 'Governor's note', 20 December 1966, C40/1652.

who 'inclines to megalomania', and while sound in some areas, he tended to 'strike out into the deeper waters of monetary policy, where he was obviously out of his depth'.[74]

Initial reactions to the draft report were far from positive.[75] A few days later, Maurice Allen quipped, 'Even if Mr. Jones's report be left to self-combustion, three or four of its features had better be modified, or else some of its mistaken ideas may persist injuriously into the public's mind.'[76] When Jones visited the Bank, O'Brien told him that the draft report left itself open to considerable criticism because there were too many assertions and not enough reasoned arguments. Again, Jones was urged not to stray beyond his terms of reference and to keep away from monetary policy. The Governor added that he did not want Jones to make the same mistake as had the Radcliffe Committee in taking a considerable amount of evidence and publishing a long report 'without making any attempt to test their opinions and conclusions in informed circles'.[77]

The report, published in May 1967, found that the banks had not been over-charging, but it concluded that the whole financial system could be better organised. The main recommendations were that there should be a widening of the area of competition between the clearing banks, they should diversify their role as lenders and in particular enter directly the fields of mortgage loans and instalment credit, banks should make full disclosure of profits and reserves, unrestricted expansion of the branch network had been uneconomic by militating against economies of scale, a considerable saving of clerical staff could be secured, and banks should experiment with more flexible opening hours.[78]

The Bank and the Treasury attempted to quell rumours in the press that they disapproved of the document, but they did. A press release said that the report provided valuable, previously unpublished information on total profits, costs, and profit margins of the clearing banks, and it made proposals of considerable importance for changing many of the existing practices in relation to the rates and charges.[79] In his Mansion House speech in October, O'Brien stated that 'the banks and authorities are giving

---

[74]   Morse, 16 March 1967, C40/1653; Morse to O'Brien, 1 February 1967, C40/1653.
[75]   Fforde, 'Prices and Incomes Board', 5 April 1967, C40/1654.
[76]   Allen, 3 April 1967, C40/1654.
[77]   O'Brien, 'Governor's note', 6 April 1967, C40/1654.
[78]   Allen, 'Report No.34 of the National Board for Prices and Incomes', 31 May 1967, C40/1655; 'The Committee of London Clearing Bankers Comment on the Report of the National Board for Prices and Incomes on Bank Charges', October 1967, C40/1655.
[79]   HMT, Press notice on P.I.B report on bank charges, 24 May 1967, C40/1655.

careful study to a thought-provoking report.'[80] However, by January 1968, silence made it clear that the report had been a failure. Cromer's initial doubts, voiced in his final letter to Callaghan in 1966, proved to be well founded.[81]

Yet the criticisms levelled at the clearing banks by both the NBPI, and the Monopolies Commission required some response from the authorities. It was decided to constitute a small group to consider the matter and that Brian Tew, professor of economics at Nottingham University, be asked to join as an Adviser. This 'Banking Study Group' (not widely known about) first met at the Treasury in September 1968 and continued to meet to consider the case for terminating the cartel or, more precisely, the collective agreements on rates for deposits, advances, and call money. At the time the group was deliberating, an agreement of 1964 was still in place on the structure of rates[82] (Table 9.1). One difficulty was that there was a conflict between rescinding the agreements and ceilings because the banks would be unable to increase their profitable lending.[83] Thus any longer-term thinking on the cartel was derailed by short-term considerations.

In October 1968, amidst all this discussion about the clearing banks and competition, a new financial institution, the National Giro, was set up. The idea of a Giro, a centralised money-transfer system to enable people without bank accounts to cash wages cheques, settle bills, and send money, had been around for some time. Radcliffe proposed that the Post Office could operate it, and the idea was taken up enthusiastically by the new Labour Government in 1964. The Bank played little part in this, although it was consulted. It was dubious about the estimates of the demand for services and other optimistic assumptions and was concerned that it might be a

---

[80] 'Speech by Sir Leslie O'Brien, G.B.E., Governor of the Bank of England, at a dinner given by the Lord Mayor to the Bankers and Merchants of the City of London on Thursday, 26 October 1967', C40/1655.

[81] 'Extract from Mr. Hollom's memo of 5.1.68 ... ', C40/1655.

[82] Neville Nagler (Assistant Principal, HMT), 8 October 1968, enc. 'The case for terminating the clearing banks' agreement'; Bank of England, 'The clearing banks' collective agreements', 20 August 1968, C40/1324; CLCB, 'Extract from minutes of meeting of chief executive officers of clearing banks held on the 18 June 1964', C40/1089. For another perspective on the historical origins of constraints in banking competition, see Pressnell (1970); Wood to Fforde, 'Banking Study Group. Revised draft report of 11 March', 13 March 1969, C40/1225.

[83] HMT, 'The clearing banks' cartel. Report of the Banking Study Group, 12 May 1969; Neale to Dowler, 'The control of bank credit and the clearing bank cartel', 20 June 1969, C40/1325.

Table 9.1. *Clearing banks agreed lending rates, as at August 1968*

Type of customer	Rate charged	Details
Nationalised industries (guaranteed by Treasury)	BR, with minimum 4 per cent	Some lending BR + ½ per cent reflecting use of funds in HP business
Local authorities	BR + ½ per cent with minimum 4½ per cent	The 'blue chip' rate
Building societies	BR + ½ per cent with minimum 4½ per cent	
Insurance companies	BR + ½ per cent with minimum 4½ per cent	
Other first-class industrial and commercial	BR + ½ per cent with minimum 4½ per cent	
Hire-purchase companies	BR + 1 per cent with minimum 6 per cent	Minimum rate
Export loans (guaranteed by ECGD)	(1) BR, minimum 4½ per cent	For loans up to 2 years
	(2) 5½ per cent fixed rate	For loans for 2–15 years
Other industrial and commercial and all private customers	At discretion, but above the 'blue chip' rate	
Medium-term shipbuilding finance (guaranteed)	5½ per cent fixed rate	For loans up to 8 years (10 in exceptional circumstances) by the Ministry of Technology

Source: Bank of England, 'The clearing banks' collective agreements', 20 August 1968, Appendix 1, C40/1324.

'costly experiment'.[84] This proved to be so: levels of business were disappointing, and the Giro struggled into the mid-1970s, when legislation was introduced to alter its capital structure and extend the range of services that could be provided.

The issue of disclosure raised questions about efficiency, costs, definitions of a bank, and the relationship between banks and the authorities. Historically, banks had created and maintained inner, or hidden, reserves

[84] Radcliffe, 'Evidence', 23 January 1959, questions 13105–13136, and 'Report, paras. 960–964; Morse to Goldman, 12 July 1965; Keogh to Morse/Cromer/O'Brien, 'Post Office giro', 29 July 1965, C40/1234.

that they used to smooth fluctuations in profits and so presented the appearance of greater stability. In 1945, the Cohen Committee had judged that confidence in the banks was of such importance that the practice be allowed to continue.[85] It was incorporated as Schedule 8 of the 1948 Companies Act. The committee on company law, under the chairmanship of the senior judge Lord Jenkins, which reported in 1962, also came down in favour of retaining the exemption, for similar reasons as Cohen. Jenkins, though, did feel that the climate of opinion was changing, and a note of dissent argued that exemptions were wrong in principle and that the case of the banks was based purely on expediency.[86]

The Bank observed all this from the sidelines, having decided to offer assistance but not to submit evidence to the committee.[87] At this stage, senior figures such as Hawker, O'Brien, and Clarke thought that things should be left as they were, but over the next few years, opinion in the Bank moved towards disclosure.[88] Hollom and Whittome argued that the case for exemptions was extremely weak, and by February 1963, O'Brien had accepted that view.[89] Morse came to the Bank from a clearer, already having a dislike of exemptions, partly on principle, but also 'because from my own experience I believe that they have had positive disadvantages for the banks. ... the need to keep true profits secret from all except a few inside each bank has hampered costing and other assessments and so reduced efficiency and profitability.'[90] Cromer agreed that there should be some reform.[91] Against them, Clarke was still opposed, arguing in 1966 that 'the need for the banking system as a whole to have hidden reserves is still a strong and valid one.'[92] Meanwhile, the Board of Trade and the Treasury,

---

[85] *Report of the Committee on Company Law Amendment*, June 1945, cmnd 6659, para. 101; Capie and Billings (2001a).

[86] *Report of the Company Law Committee*, June 1962, cmnd. 1749, paras. 399–407; Note of dissent, pp. 211–216. Gordon Richardson was a member of the committee.

[87] Hollom to O'Brien/Hawker/Cobbold/Mynors, 'Company law committee', 10 May 1960, C48/304.

[88] Clarke to O'Brien, 'Jenkins Committee – hidden reserves', 7 December 1960; O'Brien to Hawker/Mynors, 'Jenkins Committee – hidden reserves', 19 December 1960; Hawker, Annotation, 21 December 1960, on O'Brien to Hawker/Mynors, 21 December 1960, C40/614.

[89] Hollom to O'Brien/Cromer/Mynors, 'The Companies Act. Position of exempt and non-exempt private companies', 25 January 1963; Whittome to O'Brien/Cromer/Mynors, Companies Act 1948 – eighth schedule', 8 February 1963; O'Brien, annotation, 8 February 1963, C40/614.

[90] Morse to Cromer/O'Brien, 'Banks and discount companies, exemptions under the Companies' Act', 24 February 1965, C40/614.

[91] Morse, 'Note for the record – Banks and discount companies, exemptions under the Companies' Act', 27 May 1965, C40/614.

[92] Clarke to Hollom, 5 January 1966, C40/1340.

in consultation with the Bank, were working on a new Companies Bill that envisaged continued exemptions for overseas banks, merchant banks, and discount houses but full disclosure for clearers.[93] The clearing banks were opposed to such a move, and their mood was not improved by the announcement of the NBPI investigation. As *The Banker* noted, the clearers faced a difficult summer and autumn.[94]

The CLCB outlined its case against disclosure in October 1966. When Fforde was asked by the Treasury for the Bank's view, he replied that the balance lay with continuing exemptions.[95] Fforde evidently had been swayed by the clearing banks, as had Parsons. Fforde also touched on one of his favoured subjects, the economic efficiency of the banks, reckoning that the NBPI reference gave the authorities an alternative means of surveillance and one that could continue even without disclosure.[96] Subsequently, O'Brien told Goldman that the case for non-disclosure was 'significantly stronger than he had originally thought' and reiterated this in a letter to Armstrong.[97] Hollom still found all this unpersuasive, declaring himself strongly in favour of disclosure. He was also alarmed by the talk of policing efficiency, asking, 'Do we really consider that we (let alone the Board of Trade) should undertake the task ordinarily entrusted to market forces?'[98]

A compromise whereby there would be disclosure but only to the authorities was deemed unacceptable on broad political grounds. They received some backing when the NBPI report called for full disclosure as soon as practicable.[99] As Hollom observed later that year, disclosure had now been

---

[93] Blunden, Note for record – 'Banks' hidden reserves', 10 January 1966; Hollom to Radice, 17 January 1966, C40/1340.

[94] *The Banker* 116(485):429, July 1966. It was not only clearers who were lobbying on this bill. Rothschilds, then a partnership, wanted the new bill to allow additional partners. The Bank was not encouraging because it felt that such forms of business organisation had no part in modern banking. The Rothschilds told the Governor that they were reluctant to become a limited company because their name 'conjured up extravagant ideas of wealth which might be disappointed when the facts were known'; O'Brien, Governor's note – 'N. M. Rothschild and sons', 8 November 1966, C40/1340.

[95] Stirling to O'Brien, 21 October 1966; O'Brien to W. Armstrong and Sir Richard Powell, 24 October 1966, enc. CLCB, 'Companies bill', 21 October 1966, C40/1340.

[96] Fforde to O'Brien/Parsons/Hollom, 'Companies bill: future of schedule VIII', 27 October 1966, and Parson's annotation, 27 October 1966, C40/1340.

[97] 'Extract from Deputy Governor's memo dated 28.10.66 … '; O'Brien to Armstrong, 31 October 1966, enc. 'Companies bill: future of eighth schedule', C40/1340.

[98] Hollom to O'Brien/Parsons, 'New companies bill', 9 November 1966, C40/1340.

[99] Hollom, note for record – 'Companies bill: disclosure', 7 March 1967, C40/1341; NBPI Report, *Bank Charges*, 34, cmnd. 3292, May 1967, pp. 56–58.

conceded and would be difficult to reverse.[100] The matter then went quiet for a while, but in September 1969, to forestall any legislation, the clearers announced, to the surprise of many commentators, that they would voluntarily implement full disclosure by February 1970.[101] At the same time, the Bank was resisting pressure from the Select Committee on Nationalised Industries (SCNI) to publish its own accounts. Questioned by the committee in November 1969, O'Brien denied any similarity, arguing that 'we hold a unique position' and the fact that the clearing banks had changed did not imply that the Bank should.[102] Nonetheless, it subsequently did in 1971.

Money and Monetary Control

In the 1950s, the Bank was still very much the product of Norman's powerful personality, and there was not much room for economic analysis or economists. Some of this was understandable given the nature of the Bank's work, its history, and the limited role there had been for monetary policy. However, it is not entirely understandable, and it was not understandable to Radcliffe – hence the committee's proposals for more data collection and economic analysis, the recruitment of economics graduates, and the secondment of more experienced academic economists. Part of the problem in attracting economics graduates to the Bank was the lack of a clear role, something that was to persist for some time. Nonetheless, the need to obtain such expertise was growing each year, particularly given the developments that were taking place in the academic world. One source of fresh ideas had been the work being done in the United States under Milton Friedman's guidance, where there had been increasing research output in monetary economics in the 1950s. A major event in academic economics was the publication of Friedman and Schwartz's *Monetary History of the United States* in 1963, a book that was widely reviewed, generally extremely favourably, and stimulated enormous discussion. The role of money, which had been out of favour for some time, was being debated again.

The centrepiece of monetary policy in the 1960s was the exchange rate. Containing monetary growth was not on the agenda, perhaps hardly even on the radar, in Britain at this time. Indeed, it was more commonly dismissed. That did not derive from any appreciation of the monetary economics of fixed exchange rates. The world of Radcliffe prevailed. The

---

[100] Hollom to O'Brien, 'Disclosure', 24 October 1967, C40/1341.
[101] *The Banker* 119(524):999–1001, October 1969.
[102] SCNI 1970, 'Evidence', question 1093.

discussion on money that went on in the Bank in the middle of the decade took place largely in relation to the appropriate approach to bank lending, whether it was the liquidity ratio or the cash ratio that was crucial for its control. Writing on the subject to Hollom, then Chief Cashier, de Moubray recalled that Mynors had told him that he still thought the cash ratio was the crucial one. In a short handwritten note to Luce, de Moubray added that he thought that the greatest mistake Radcliffe made was in dismissing 'money supply' and introducing 'liquidity'.[103] But these kinds of reservations were rare at the time. De Moubray and Mynors were a distinct minority.

In the early and mid-1960s, there was also a sustained assault by a minority on the core of the Radcliffe thesis. One early attack was on what was seen as the essence of the new orthodoxy – that there was a strong positive causal relationship between the supply of Treasury bills and the supply of bank deposits. The new orthodox prescription therefore was manipulation of Treasury bills through funding/unfunding and/or retirement of bills with the proceeds of a budget surplus or issuance in order to finance a budget deficit.[104] Crouch argued that control of the supply of bills was not necessary and not sufficient. There were three striking occasions in the previous decade when contraction of Treasury bills was accompanied by an expansion of bank deposits. The orthodox proposition – that control of the supply of cash was sufficient to provide control of bank deposits – had been demonstrated: 'The control of the supply is both necessary and sufficient to provide control of bank deposits.'[105] There were several points of disagreement in this analysis, frequently among people on the same side, and Crouch accepted many of the corrections but insisted that his basic case was unaffected. (Many of the same kinds of criticisms were being made of the working of the gilt-edged market, which is dealt with at greater length later.)

Newlyn said that Crouch 'demonstrates by means of rigorous numerical process analysis that a reduction in the Treasury Bill issue is not a sufficient condition for enforcing a contraction in deposits' and further that he had provided 'irrefutable confirmation of my own verbal exposition'.[106] Tew, in the same issue of the *Economic Journal*, argued that none of the authorities Crouch cited had ever claimed that the volume of bank deposits is

---

[103] De Moubray to Hollom, 'Control of the money supply', 30 April 1964; de Moubray to Luce, 8 May 1964, EID4/196.
[104] Crouch (1963, 1964).
[105] Crouch (1963, p. 92).
[106] Newlyn (1965, pp. 857–859).

determined by the Treasury bill issue.[107] It was rather that the banks' liquid assets ratio simply set a ceiling to the expansion of bank deposits. To this Crouch replied that banks therefore would buy up all the liquid assets in the economy and expand their deposits to match (the marginal costs of deposits always being less than the minimum yield on their lowest-earning asset). The reason banks could not do this was that they had not got, and could not get, the cash reserves to support any more deposits. Crouch returned to the theme in a 1966 paper that applied the same kind of analysis to the use of special deposits and rejected them with the same gusto. However, he seems to have lacked the necessary charm to be a persuasive advocate. He had dismissed Sayers' article on the determination of bank deposits in scathing terms.[108] Moreover, in the 1966 paper he sent to the Governor, he less than tactlfully wrote: 'It would certainly seem from the theoretical discussion and empirical evidence presented in the previous sections that the Bank has shown itself to be technically incompetent to control the money supply generating process', and the Bank's officials 'carried out to the best of their limited abilities their assigned tasks in accordance with received monetary opinion.'[109]

Tony Cramp, who was seconded from University College London in the mid-1960s, commented on much of the academic literature that was appearing. Indeed, he saw this as his principal role. He wrote, 'To ignore outside work would be arrogant. Even to pass over ideas that seem outlandish may be to be miss something of great value – unless they are too outlandish!' And he thought that this was how the recent 'offering' of Professor Victor Morgan should be classified.[110] De Moubray rejected that view immediately. 'You will not, I am afraid, be surprised to hear that I find myself in pretty general agreement with most of what Morgan says. ... I have no doubt that his proposal to limit the increase in the note issue – mentioned only on one page out of fifty pages – will condemn the pamphlet in the eyes of many readers in the Bank.' (This might be seen as an early indication of the antipathy to a cash ratio that persisted or to the monetary-base approach that came later.) He finished by saying, 'We might do well to look a little closer at the money supply, which in recent months has been expanding much more rapidly than for many years past

---

[107] Tew (1965, pp. 859–860).
[108] Crouch (1965, p. 185).
[109] Crouch, 'The special deposits farce'. This paper was sent to the Governor, 1 June 1969, 3A8/4.
[110] Morgan (1964); Cramp to de Moubray, 'Control of the money supply, etc', 15 July 1964, EID4/196.

and more rapidly than the national income.'[111] There also were contributions from other central banks. After attending a SUERF seminar in Paris
in September 1964, Cramp noted that 'continental central banks still tend
to claim, as the Bank of England no longer does, a unique sphere of activity and a set of objectives separate from those of the central government's
general economic policy. They are therefore prone to support theories,
such as the quantity theory, that give them some hope of success.'[112] In the
Bank, voices in support of the control of money supply were few and, when
heard, quietly ignored or put down.

Pressure for change from outside the Bank came first from the IMF's
insistence in 1965 that the letter of intent, following the negotiated standby
agreement, should contain a commitment on monetary growth. The
British authorities had tried then to dismiss the idea, but the IMF was
successful in having it accepted – the commitment that is, not the outcome.
However, the authorities' attitude towards money was at best ambivalent.
In 1965, a Treasury draft document on credit control had explicitly rejected
consideration of the quantity of money and of interest rates.[113] McMahon
recommended that the Bank should do the same, but he suggested giving a
bow in the direction of the recent developments by inserting, 'Much work
has been done in the United States on the relationship between the quantity of money variously defined and total expenditure. Some correlations
have been established for particular periods, but a great deal of uncertainty
remains as to whether the relationship can be regarded as tight enough to
use as a basis for policy.'[114] McMahon's suggestion was not contained in
the final version. On the other hand, and also in 1965, the Treasury sent
two papers to the Bank: 'The Money Supply' in October; and 'Changes in
the Money Supply in the United Kingdom, 1954 to 1964', in November.
The latter was written by two officials in the Economic Section, Geoffrey
Bell and Lawrence Berman. They wanted to see it published in *Economica*,
and Cairncross thought it should go to the Bank for clearance, assuming
that Allen would be the person to do this. There were very few in the Bank
qualified to comment. Allen had responded to the first paper in brief and
general terms. It was fortunate that the monetary economist Andrew Bain
had recently arrived at the Bank from Cambridge and was able to provide

---

[111] De Moubray to Cramp, 'Professor Victor Morgan on monetary policy', 16 July 1964,
EID4/196. De Moubray was influenced by his close relationship with Per Jacobsson.
[112] Cramp to de Moubray, 'S.U.E.R.F. [Societe Universitaire Europeene de Recherches
Financieres] seminar in Paris, 26–27 September 1964', 30 September 1964, EID4/196.
[113] HMT, 'Draft memorandum on credit control', 2 July 1965, C40/1253.
[114] McMahon to Morse, 'Draft report on credit control', 5 August 1965, C40/1253.

a succinct note on the emerging academic debate on money.[115] At about the same time, McMahon asked Bain what determined the money supply, and he quickly replied with a 27-page 'note' plus tables and diagrams! More followed on related topics in quick succession. When Allen told McMahon that he would 'quite like to know what the Friedman/Modigliani et al debate amounted to', McMahon again asked Bain, who came back with a short note on the essence of the debate.[116]

Bain's paper on the money supply was discussed subsequently at an EID meeting in early January 1966, where McMahon asked for the empirical work to be taken back further. A new version was circulated in May, now described as a 'draft bulletin article'.[117] By September, it was scheduled for publication in the December 1966 *Bulletin*.[118] Unfortunately for Bain, the article was dropped. Allen and Fforde decided that the analysis was 'insufficiently general' and did not 'take sufficient account of current controversy'.[119] Looking back on the episode in 1968, McMahon noted that Bain's piece had not been put in the *Bulletin* 'largely, I believe, on the grounds that we had not sorted out a Bank view on this very important topic', and the Bank did not want to enter the field in a 'casual way'. McMahon now argued that a new article should be prepared for early inclusion in the *Bulletin*.[120] It would be another two years before this appeared.

The pressure from the IMF in 1967–68 was much greater, and while there continued to be resistance, there was no escape, and the authorities had to accept that a clear attempt needed to be made, and indeed success achieved,

---

[115] HMT, Draft: 'The money supply', 26 October 1965; Cairncross to Rickett, 29 November 1965; Rickett to Morse, 30 November 1965, enc. 'Changes in the money supply in the United Kingdom, 1954 to 1964'; Allen to Cromer/O'Brien, 'Money supply, 9 November 1965; Andrew Bain (EID) to McMahon, 'The money supply and the level of income', 3 December 1965; Morse to Rickett, 17 December 1965, 6A50/1. The article was subsequently published; see Bell and Berman (1966).

[116] Bain to McMahon, 9 December 1965, enc. Bain 'Some factors affecting the money supply', 9 December 1965; Allen to McMahon, 16 December 1965; Bain to McMahon/Allen, 'The money supply controversy (*American Economic Review*, September 1965)', 30 December 1965, 6A50/1.

[117] Bull, Note for the record [on a meeting held on 3 January 1966], 10 January 1966; interim work was in Bain to Heasman et al, 'The money supply 1952–65', 18 February 1966, 6A50/1; Bain to Heasman et al., 'The money supply, 1952–65: draft *Bulletin* article', 3 May 1966, enc. 'The money supply, 1952–65', 3 May 1966, 6A50/2.

[118] Bull, Note for the record – 'The money supply: 1952–65', 31 May 1966; Bain to Allen, 18 July 1966, enc. 'The monetary liabilities of the U.K. banking sector, 1952–65'; Bain to Heasman et al., 'The monetary liabilities of the U.K. banking sector, 1952–65', 9 September 1966, enc. 'The monetary liabilities of the U.K. banking sector, 1952–65', 6A50/2.

[119] Bain to de Moubray/Heasman, 26 September 1966, 6A50/2.

[120] McMahon to O'Brien, 'Money supply and the *Quarterly Bulletin*', 25 April 1968, 5A175/1.

in containing monetary growth, albeit couched in terms with which they could feel comfortable. In 1969, there was an article in the *Bulletin* on domestic credit expansion (DCE) that has sometimes been interpreted as giving the signal of a new way of thinking.[121] As the Wilson Committee later expressed it, 'At the end of 1967 the government decided at the instigation of the IMF to impose a limit on domestic credit expansion, and monetary aggregates began to play a more important role in the conduct of monetary policy.'[122] Wilson also noted that when the IMF advocated its use as a means of improving the balance of payments in 1969, 'the potential role of monetary policy was then further enhanced.'[123] However, it is not clear that there was any major shift in policy. The *Bulletin* article on DCE reiterated the view that the path of the money stock was not a good indicator of monetary conditions.[124] More important was the 1970 *Bulletin* article, 'The Importance of Money', by Goodhart and Crockett.[125] It might even be described as a watershed in the Bank. It marked the beginning of some monetary economists' influence in the Bank, and there was some move towards watching monetary aggregates as early as 1973. In 1976, explicit monetary targets were used by the Bank. But that is told later in the story.

These exchanges marked the first genuine realisation by the Bank of the need to have their own economists to help interpret the growing academic output on what was increasingly being recognised as important. At this stage, the work was taking place only in the background, but it was there nonetheless, and senior people were aware of it. And it is interesting for the fact that it came as early as it did. The *Bulletin* of June 1979 claimed that 'Since 1966, however, … the main emphasis has shifted to controlling the trend in the growth of the money supply (and in particular, in recent years, the growth of sterling M3)'.[126] There is some ambiguity in this; it was certainly after 1966 that the emphasis shifted but really in 1968 and at the insistence of the IMF.

Early Interest in Monetary Aggregates

As far as concern with a monetary aggregate went, the first serious step along the road was DCE. The account of the acceptance of DCE targets for

---

[121] 'Domestic credit expansion', *BEQB* 9(3):363–382, September 1969.
[122] Wilson Report, p. 79. There is an element here of Wilson claiming credit for the change in direction.
[123] *Ibid.*, p. 16.
[124] 'Domestic credit expansion', p. 363.
[125] Goodhart and Crockett (1970). See also Crockett (1970) for associated work on relationships between movements of monetary and expenditure variables.
[126] 'The gilt-edged market', *BEQB* 19(2):137, June 1979.

the purpose of obtaining IMF assistance has already been told briefly in Chapter 8, but it needs a different examination here from the point of view of its role as the new focus of a monetary aggregate. The Bank saw the need to investigate the role of money even if only to form a view and be prepared to defend a position. Soon after the discussion of DCE was underway, there began to be something of a blurring of the distinction between broad money and DCE. The starting point was the seminar proposed by the IMF in 1968. It finally took place in October, and press reports were frequently of the kind that Keynes was dead and the Chicago School had triumphed.[127] This kind of thing upset the IMF and threatened to upset their client countries.[128] The IMF formed the view that the Treasury was more amenable to the IMF's line than was the Bank, and while this does seem to have been the case, Cairncross recalled that 'even after the IMF seminar in 1968, the Treasury remained sceptical.'[129]

For some time after the seminar, at which the concept of DCE was hammered out, discussion continued on what it meant and how it could and should be used. The Treasury and the Bank developed their ideas separately. Lovell at the Treasury wrote, 'The concept is rather mechanical and is based on certain theoretical concepts of the special contribution of money supply to the generation of real demand which has still to be proven. ... we would need to regard the main purpose of Domestic credit expansion as providing little more than an early warning system that events might be turning sour.'[130] That same week, Goodhart in the Bank got on with the business of calculation. In a note for Maurice Allen, he set out the growth of 'money supply' for 1968.[131] This set off a long series of exchanges in the Bank, and later that month, Goodhart was using the two terms more or less synonymously: 'this implies that changes in the money supply (or credit creation).'[132] A later note by Carlisle described the DCE concept as 'absolute nonsense from beginning to end'. But then, according to Carlisle, this rejection could be extended to any definition of the money supply.[133]

The Bank was still conscious that it did not have a clear grasp of all the issues, and the Governor wanted to determine what the official Bank

---

[127] For example, 'Is Keynes Defunct?', *New York Times*, 6 November 1968.

[128] Polak to Acting Managing Director, 'Publicity on the monetary seminar', 6 November 1968; IMF, Research Department Immediate Office, Director J. Polak, Box 35, Folder 6.

[129] Cairncross (1996, p. 270).

[130] Lovell, 'The IMF concept of total domestic credit', 3 February 1969, 5A177/1.

[131] Goodhart to Allen, 'Quick calculation of net domestic credit creation', 7 February 1969, 5A177/1.

[132] Goodhart, 'Overall credit ceilings', 24 February 1969, 5A177/1.

[133] Carlisle to Goodhart, 16 May 1969, 5A177/2.

attitude on money supply was. Thornton, as Head of the EID, consulted the principal members of his department and then drafted a strong statement claiming that it was the collective view of the EID and all its previous incarnations for more than a decade, and also, he believed, of the Chief Cashier, and it was the philosophy of the *Bulletin* – agnostic.[134] McMahon was a good deal more cautious. He believed the Bank had underplayed the importance of money and indeed may have been negligent. He reminded the Governors about the article on the money supply that had been prepared by Bain for the *Bulletin* in 1966 but had not been used. 'For better or for worse', he wrote, 'the Bank and the Treasury analysis and policy recommendation has hitherto been in a Keynesian framework and has not laid much stress on the money supply. We may, of course, be wrong.' He was, above all, pragmatic:

Simply and rather suddenly to give prominence to the money supply as an important variable might, unless we were clearly able to demonstrate our new views of how the economy worked, be likely to make us look a bit silly, a bit tendentious, a bit reactionary, or a bit of all three. We could well have a fight with the Treasury on our hands and we should have to be prepared to defend our position in depth. The I.M.F. might be pleased, but even they might be a little sceptical about our conversion until they could see exactly why we thought what we thought.

He did believe strongly that the Bank should now do something serious on money that would '"show" willing to the I.M.F. and those observers who feel we have been on the wrong track'.[135] Throughout the summer of 1968, EID prepared figures on money supply and comment on various aspects.

By September, things were warming up. Posner wrote to McMahon about worries over the money supply.[136] Later that month, Peter Jay stirred things up in *The Times* by saying that the Bank was conducting a thorough review of the subject. Thornton wrote, 'We have to accept that everyone is now waiting to hear which side we shall join in a contest, the terms of which have been fixed for us. Peter Jay and those he has alerted will submit whatever the Governor says to microscopic analysis to determine whether he is for or against "Chicago"'. And he felt the need to write to the Governor about his forthcoming Mansion House speech that he should avoid inviting 'the press to label him as being "Chicago"'.[137] In his speech, the Governor

[134] Thornton, 'Money supply', 22 April 1968; Thornton to O'Brien, 22 April 1968, 5A175/1.

[135] McMahon to O'Brien/Parsons, 'Money supply and the quarterly *Bulletin*', 25 April 1968, 5A175/1.

[136] Posner to McMahon, 11 September 1968, 5A175/1.

[137] *The Times*, 19 September 1968, p. 22; Thornton to O'Brien, 'Money supply', 4 October 1968, 5A175/1.

made some brief reference to money and its importance, but the references were in fact close to anodyne:

The money supply cannot become the be-all and end-all of policy. ... I do not accept that controlling the money supply is simply a question of the proper use of central banking techniques, as some appear to believe. Much more fundamental matters are involved.[138]

At the same time, the Treasury was proposing a working party on 'liquidity in the private sector' partly in preparation for the forthcoming IMF seminar. McMahon would be on it, and he, in turn, wanted the recently recruited Goodhart to assist him.[139] McMahon was preparing his own position on the subject and in October sent a note to the Governors, 'Paying attention to the money supply'. His argument was that the Bank was being attacked from all sides. This was due in large part to the poor economic performance of the economy over the post-war years but much more the recent past. Politicians rather than technicians were to blame for this in his view, but there was nevertheless good reason to use something such as money supply as a red light indicator. Even if they did not put great faith in it themselves, it might enable the IMF to exert some pressure on government. He believed that it would be useful to start some work on the effect of money supply on economic activity. The critics were urging a fiercer use of central bank powers to bring home to governments the implications of their policies.[140]

Whatever differences there were between the Bank and the Treasury on the issue, however, they were obliged to respond to the IMF's conditions, and joint Bank-Treasury exercises began that were concerned with practical questions. Early in 1969, McMahon pointed out that work had been under way in the Bank (even before Goodhart came), and while not wanting to prejudge the issue, he thought that what was going to emerge on the basis of the empirical research 'will be sceptical, to say the least, as to the causal role of money supply in the economy'. Allen was by no means so sure: 'I think Goodhart will not disagree with me when I express the view that the "empirical work" in question has been inconclusive.'[141]

---

[138] Governor's Mansion House speech, 17 October 1968; *BEQB* 8(4):410, December 1968. Thornton certainly had a hand in drafting this piece.

[139] McMahon to O'Brien/Parsons, 17 September 1968 and McMahon, Annotation, 18 September 1968, 5A175/1.

[140] McMahon to O'Brien/Parsons, 7 October 1968, enc. McMahon, 'Paying attention to the money supply', 4 October 1968, 5A175/1.

[141] Allen to O'Brien, 'Domestic credit expansion', 20 March 1969, 5A177/1.

How the new concept of DCE was to be communicated to a wider public then became of concern and resulted in something of a farce. In May, the Treasury was well advanced with a piece to be published in *Economic Trends*, and the Bank was contemplating putting an explanatory piece in the June 1969 *Bulletin*. Before anything could be done, though, word came from the Treasury that the Chancellor wanted to make it clear that 'DCE is a UK concept emerging from work done in UK official circles; it is not something which has been foisted on us by the Fund but which we do not ourselves believe in.'[142] This prompted Allen to ask Goodhart where the concept dated from, and Goodhart showed that it had been in the IMF since its founding ('goes right back to the very earliest days of the Fund's operations'), although the highly explicit formulation was that of Polak in 1957.[143] (The trick of turning it into a British concoction left a visitor to the Bank from the Fed perplexed: 'I have not yet determined whether DCE is a JJ Polak notion or something conceived in London.')[144] This need to make it look British set work and publication back, for a different complexion would have to be put on it if a British model were to be achieved. Meanwhile, publication of the proposed Treasury piece for *Economic Trends* was being discussed at the highest levels.[145] Maurice Allen's comments on the final version were not approving. Apart from it trying to make out that DCE had grown out of work done by British officials, he found it 'woolly in its attempts to explain why British officials have cultivated this herb'.[146] The Bank nevertheless was producing figures for DCE, and the idea was that these would be published in the *Bulletin*, although some wanted to distance themselves from the Treasury in defending the concept and wanted to prevent the *Bulletin* from being the main outlet for publication of the figures because 'a loss of editorial freedom and an extension of Treasury interference with the Bulletin – perhaps to a point where a Whitehall line prevails in our pages against our better judgment' was feared.[147]

Very little of this was getting to the nub of the matter. The IMF had more or less demanded that control of DCE be implemented and taken seriously. First, though, there was the silliness over trying to make out it was a British

---

[142] Edwards to Armstrong, 'DCE pamphlet', 10 May 1969, 5A177/2.

[143] Goodhart to Allen, 2 June 1969, 5A177/2.

[144] Stephen Taylor (chief, Flow of Funds and Savings Section, Federal Reserve) to Hillage, 22 July 1969, 5A177/2.

[145] Morse to Allen/O'Brien/Parsons, 'Article on D.C.E. for *Economic Trends*', 20 May 1969, 5A177/2.

[146] Allen to O'Brien, '*Economic Trends* article on D.C.E', 22 May 1969, 5A177/2.

[147] Norman Brodick (EID) to Thornton/Goodhart, 'Publication of DCE figures', 2 July 1969, 5A177/2.

idea; then there was the grudging acceptance of it. The collection of figures followed without any obvious belief that they mattered other than in being used in some way as some kind of indicator but as much as anything to satisfy the IMF. During a meeting at the Treasury at the end of November 1969, Posner asked Goodhart a hypothetical question, 'If we could control the money supply, how should we seek to exercise this control?' It was when reflecting on this 'apparently innocuous question' that Goodhart found that he was drawn into asking, 'How we should choose the DCE target for next year.'[148] In an accompanying note, he expressed some scepticism over the concept and its use. Titled, 'The Future of DCE or What Is to Be Done When the IMF Have Gone', he argued that DCE was being used as an indicator that changed when changes in the economy came about (a bit 'like a thermometer measuring temperature') but whose own movements did not effect changes in the economy – 'a posture which we have taken up for the public benefit'. He argued that it was not a good indicator of developments in the whole economy but was a reasonably good indicator of the general thrust of monetary policy. 'If monetary policy has any important effect in controlling the economy, then taking steps to control DCE will help to control the economy.'[149] Thornton said that they certainly would have to live with DCE for some time 'without the benefit of knowing, and being able to demonstrate, much about it'.[150] By the beginning of January 1970, Goodhart was arguing that DCE was shifting attention towards overall monetary aggregates, that using a DCE target implied 'some acceptance of a quasi-automatic stabilisation and adjustment process, working through monetary changes', and that the rate of change of the money supply should be directed in this manner. He personally doubted the wisdom of this, but he went on to argue that regarding DCE as a major indicator of monetary conditions meant expressing 'the key assumptions for the forecasting round also in terms of monetary aggregates'.[151]

The Bank duly published its piece on DCE, essentially the work of Goodhart, as a supplement to the September 1969 issue of the *Bulletin*. It indirectly colluded in the fiction that it had a domestic origin: 'An account of some recent studies of monetary questions, which led to the adoption of

[148] Goodhart to McMahon/Dicks-Mireaux/Crockett, 'Money supply group. control over D.C.E. and the money supply', 20 November 1969, 5A177/3.

[149] Goodhart, 'The future of D.C.E. or what is to be done when the I.M.F. have gone', nd, 5A177/3.

[150] Thornton to Dicks-Mireaux/McMahon/Goodhart, 'The future of D.C.E.', 25 November 1969, 5A177/3.

[151] Goodhart to Thornton, 'The future of D.C.E.', 9 January 1970, 5A177/3.

this concept as an indicator, was included in the article on "Money Supply and Domestic Credit" in *Economic Trends*, May 1969.'[152] The article in the *Bulletin* was to spark more enquiry and dispute in the Bank and outside. Outsiders such as Gordon Pepper of the stockbrokers Greenwells were trying to make sense of the DCE figures in conjunction with the balance-of-payments figures, not very successfully. And Goodhart had to agree with him that it wasn't easy to follow the figures.[153] Inside the Bank, Clews (EID) asked, 'What does DCE measure?' and could it be consistent with a narrow money measure, and further, why, if DCE was not an indicator, had the *Bulletin* article referred to it as one throughout?[154]

At the practical level, Fforde could not decide if the increases in DCE and money supply in the second quarter of 1970 could be relied on to imply a relaxation, and McMahon shared his distaste for looking at 'magic' numbers. Interestingly, McMahon at this stage began to use the phrase 'monetary targets'.[155] And at the end of July, Goodhart wrote a note headed, 'Monetary Targets' addressed to McMahon. It happened to be about DCE, but by then, the terms were being used interchangeably. There seemed 'to be a need for some reconsideration of policy with respect to overall monetary targets'. He went on to talk about the need to keep monetary policy 'slightly tighter than neutral … which would suggest allowing the money supply to rise by about 8 to 8½ per cent this year in all'.[156] Already, then, there was some suggestion of an implicit monetary target. In fact, slightly earlier in a comment on Andrew Britton's Treasury paper, 'Monetary Policy and Money Supply', Goodhart had written, 'Just a starting point for discussion, but does tend to assume without argument that we should adopt a monetary aggregate target.'[157] Thus some talk of money targets was going on from as early as the beginning of 1970.

There was a follow-up IMF seminar that resumed the London discussions of October 1968 held in Washington in April 1970. Unfortunately, yet again, there are no Bank papers for the seminar, and from Bank records, it is not even possible to tell who from the Bank attended. It was, in fact, Goodhart, Crockett, and Dicks-Mireaux. The Treasury record of

[152] 'Money supply and domestic credit: some recent developments in monetary analysis', *Economic Trends*, pp. xxi–xxv, May 1969.
[153] Goodhart to Dicks-Mireaux, 'Greenwell's fixed interest commentary', 26 May 1970; Goodhart to Gordon Pepper (Greenwell's), 2 June 1970, 5A177/3.
[154] Clews to Goodhart, 'The government/banking nexus', 22 April 1970, 5A177/3.
[155] Fforde annotation on McMahon to O'Brien/Hollom, 'Surveillance of DCE', 17 July 1970; McMahon to O'Brien/Hollom, 'Surveillance of DCE', 21 July 1970, 5A177/3.
[156] Goodhart to McMahon, 'Monetary targets', 31 July 1970, 5A177/3.
[157] See Britton (2001); HMT, Group on Monetary Policy, MP(70)14, 2 March 1970, 6A74/3.

the meeting was said to have been agreed by the Treasury and the Bank. But that was often said without it being the case.[158] And that is the position here. We are left without a clear idea of what the differences between the Bank and the Treasury were or indeed what the Bank's views were. At any rate, at the follow-up seminar, there were three days of meetings, with discussion ranging from the theory of monetary policy to the monitoring of DCE targets.[159] The IMF was now happier. Polak, now economic counsellor, told Schweitzer:

In the first seminar in October 1968, we found it was not easy to reach common ground on any of the major issues. ... A significant development is that the officials now accept without reservation the significance of a total bank credit target in a situation where recovery in the balance of payments is needed. There is little difference between us on the importance of the role of money.[160]

Thus, from at least the middle of 1968, there was quite intensive and extensive discussion in the Bank and the Treasury on DCE and money supply, and this was to continue to be the case for the next decade. We return to the paper on money supply later, but first there was an interesting interlude.

Ten Years after Radcliffe

Inside the Bank, there was some preparedness to discuss monetary aggregates and money supply, but the public stance was much less open, as the following episode reveals. Over the weekend 25–26 October 1969, to mark the occasion of the tenth anniversary of the publication of the Radcliffe Report, a conference was held in Hove, Sussex. Organised by a group of academics led by Harry Johnson, with financial support from the CLCB, 60 people attended, mainly economists from universities and banks, together with five representatives from the Treasury and McMahon, Thornton, Dicks-Mireaux, and Goodhart from the Bank. Such a meeting of experts from differing areas was claimed by the organisers to be the first of its kind to be held in Britain. The Bank presented a paper anonymously,

---

[158] Thornton, annotation on HMT, Group on Monetary Policy, MP(70)18, 'The commercial bill problem – a note by the Secretary', 12 May 1970, 6A74/4.

[159] HMT, Group on Monetary Policy, MP(70)19, 'Report on the United Kingdom/IMF monetary seminar in Washington, April 1970', 1 June 1970, 6A74/4.

[160] Polak to Schweitzer/Southard, 'United Kingdom – monetary seminar', 6 May 1970, IMF, Research Department Immediate Office, Director J. Polak, Box 35, Folder 7; W. A. Beveridge, memorandum for files – 'U.K. Monetary seminar', 7 May 1970, ibid.

'The Operation of Monetary Policy since Radcliffe'.[161] Given all the ongoing discussion surrounding DCE and the money supply, it might have been thought that these would have received some prominence in the paper. In fact, they were mentioned only in passing, and as a public statement, the message appeared to be that there was no real change of view at the Bank. As one of the discussants at the conference remarked, 'Radcliffe is alive, well, and living in Threadneedle Street'.[162]

When the idea of the conference had first been mooted, in August 1968, it was generally welcomed in the Bank. In early 1969, Johnson asked McMahon to deliver a paper with the suggested title, 'The Operation of Monetary Policy since the Radcliffe Report, from the Aspect of the Policy Makers'. McMahon argued in the Bank that presenting such a paper might be a counter to 'some of the nonsense that is bound to get talked', and in any case, if the offer were declined, 'we might look foolish or obsessively secretive'.[163] It was decided that the Chief Cashier's and EID would prepare a draft, whereas O'Brien and Douglas Allen agreed that it would make sense if the final paper was in the joint name of the Bank and the Treasury.[164]

Although the first draft was written by Chris Wiles, Assistant Chief of EID, the paper was mainly the work of McMahon, together with comments from Goodhart.[165] Thornton felt that any joint Bank-Treasury document was certain to be a disappointment to the audience and something that would say non-controversial things about the development of statistics and 'avoid too much apology for the lack of research into monetary policy'. Moreover, he correctly predicted that the conference delegates would put the paper aside after only casual study before questioning the Bank on what it was really doing and thinking.[166] The Treasury was particularly concerned about policy in the gilt-edged market and DCE. Robert Armstrong said that not to make any reference to the latter would be 'as

---

[161] 'The operation of monetary policy since the Radcliffe Report', *BEQB* 9(4): 448–60, December 1969.

[162] Croome and Johnson (1970), p.234. J.R. Winton (Economic Adviser, Lloyds Bank) was the discussant.

[163] Thornton to Allen/Parsons/O'Brien, 18 November 1968; Johnson to McMahon, 22 January 1969; McMahon to Thornton/Fforde/Hollom/Allen/O'Brien/Parsons, 'The question of a Bank of England paper for the post-Radcliffe conference', 12 February 1969, 6A72/1.

[164] O'Brien to Allen, 26 February 1969; Allen to O'Brien, 4 March 1969, 6A72/1.

[165] Wiles to Thornton, 23 July 1969, enc. Draft 'The Radcliffe Report – ten years after', 21 July 1969; McMahon to Thornton, 26 August 1969, enc. Draft 'The Radcliffe Report – ten years after', 6A72/1.

[166] Thornton to McMahon, 1 August 1969, 6A72/1.

significant as the dog that did not bark in the night-time', the more so given that the Bank and the Treasury would both have published pieces on the subject.[167] In an effort to meet this criticism, McMahon added what he called a 'minimal bow' to DCE.[168] With less than a month to go before the conference, the Treasury was attempting to distance itself from the paper. Armstrong told Thornton that 'it is not in every respect written in precisely the words which we should have chosen.'[169] He suggested that instead of a joint attribution, the paper should be presented by the Bank, with a statement that the Treasury had been consulted and are in general agreement with the contents. As McMahon pointed out to O'Brien, when sending him a copy, this, in effect, gave the piece the same status as a *Bulletin* article.[170]

McMahon had presented another paper in 1969, on this occasion signed, when commenting on a paper by Maurice Mann on monetary policies in the United States and the United Kingdom in the 1960s. He summarised very succinctly the Bank's view (also that of Radcliffe and most of the economic establishment) in the following way: In Britain there was, first, an extraordinarily flexible fiscal mechanism; second, a large public sector, 'totally insensitive to interest rates or any other monetary variables'; third, a large national debt that limited the use of open market operations; and fourth, a concentrated banking system. These factors, he argued, had resulted in dirigiste rather than 'market' monetary policies – the imposition of ceilings on lending and consumer credit controls. He noted that in Britain there had been a growing interest recently in the role money supply played in monetary policy. This had been prompted in part by the dissatisfaction with the results of controls. There was a need, he believed, for a major improvement 'in the UK policymaking process'. 'It may well be that this will involve a greater emphasis on monetary policy than in the past', and he was happy to push forward on that front.[171]

As far as the Hove conference went, there was a sting in the tail that resulted in the paper appearing in the *Bulletin* at an earlier date than anticipated. The conference had been a private affair, and so there was

---

[167] Armstrong to McMahon, 19 August 1969, 6A72/1; 'Domestic credit expansion'; HMT, 'Money supply and domestic credit. Some recent developments in monetary analysis', *Economic Trends* 187:xxi–xxv, May 1969.

[168] McMahon to Thornton, 'Ten years after Radcliffe', 26 August 1969; Armstrong to Thornton, 22 September 1969, 6A72/1.

[169] Armstrong to Thornton, 2 October 1969, 6A72/2.

[170] McMahon to O'Brien, 7 October 1969, enc. 'The operation of monetary policy since the Radcliffe Report', 6A72/2.

[171] McMahon (1969, pp. 549–552).

disappointment when an article appeared in the *Observer* under the name of one the academic participants, Brian Griffiths.[172] It seems that Johnson had encouraged Griffiths to write a report of the conference for publication in a newspaper. Johnson travelled back by train from Brighton with Frances Cairncross of the *Observer* and told her this, and she obtained the article from Griffiths. The newspaper's editorial staff then chopped it about and sensationalised the account by picking up a single sentence from the Bank's paper referring to the failure of economic policy over the previous decade.[173] This sentence remained 'troublesome' because the SCNI, then taking its evidence on the Bank, asked to see a copy of the paper. While there was little objection to this, the Treasury wanted the sentence to be replaced. What was at issue were the words, 'In one sense, economic policy may be said quite simply to have failed in that none of the major economic problems facing the United Kingdom in 1959 can be said to have been solved and some of the most important of them have become more severe.' O'Brien was told by McMahon that the Treasury was insisting on 'something more anodyne'.[174] The Treasury view is perhaps not surprising when it is recalled that Sir William Armstrong's Stamp Memorial Lecture of the previous year had claimed that economic policy had been a big success over the previous ten years. In the event, a decision was unnecessary because the Select Committee did not see the paper.

The *Observer* article prompted requests for the Bank's paper from Members of Parliament (MPs) and foreign embassies, requests refused on the basis that the paper would be included in a book of conference proceedings to be published by Oxford University Press. The situation was also complicated because *The Bankers' Magazine*, one of the sponsors of the Hove event, wanted to print exclusive summaries of the papers before the book appeared. This caused great offence at the rival journal *The Banker*, which also had been refused access to the Bank paper, and led its chairman, Lord Robbins, to complain to both Maurice Allen and Douglas Allen about discriminatory behaviour. With the matter now reaching Governor and Chancellor level, it was decided, just as the issue was about to go to press, that the article would be included in the December 1969 *Bulletin*. The book's publishers and *The Banker's Magazine* both accepted this

---

[172] *The Observer*, 2 November 1969, p. 13.
[173] Gordon Costello (Deputy Secretary, Secretary's Department), Note for record – 'The Hove Seminar', 3 November 1969, 3A38/3.
[174] McMahon to O'Brien, 'The Bank's paper for the Hove Conference and the Select Committee', 11 November 1969, G38/3.

reluctantly.[175] McMahon had told the Governor that the conference had been a valuable exercise and that if a similar event were repeated, the Bank should welcome this and even be prepared to offer some finance. However, he also warned Johnson that the *Observer* article and its aftermath had not gone down well in either the Bank or the Treasury and that future assistance might be jeopardised.[176] At some distance, this all seems a trivial matter, but it is indicative of the sensitivities of the authorities and the relations between policymakers and professional academic economists.[177]

Importance of Money

Running more or less in tandem with the work on DCE was the wider-ranging work on money. The IMF clearly had been important in forcing discussion on DCE and was indirectly important in speeding up the more general discussion on money and monetary policy in both the Bank and the Treasury. This had begun in the mid-1960s, but it certainly intensified after 1968–69. At the outset, discussion was in terms of 'the transmission process by which monetary variables have an impact on the real economy' and not on inflation.[178] Crockett's paper was not prepared for the IMF seminar, but Dicks-Mireaux thought it 'useful background and certainly more interesting than many of the papers specifically prepared for the seminar'.[179]

In the middle of October 1968, Fforde reported to the Governors that *The Times* was saying that the Bank was conducting a thorough review into the subject of the money supply. He pointed out that this was not the case, but he thought it should be. This more or less coincided with a paper that Pepper had produced on the money supply and that had come to the Bank's

---

[175] Geoffrey Maynard (editor, *The Bankers' Magazine*) to McMahon, 7 October 1969; Robbins to Maurice Allen, 14 November 1969; Armstrong to McMahon, 18 November 1969; Armstrong to Douglas Allen (copy to McMahon), 19 November 1969; 'Extract from the Deputy Governor's memo dated 21.11.69 … '; Maurice Allen to Robbins, 26 November 1969; McMahon to Maynard, 2 December 1969, 6A72/2.

[176] McMahon to O'Brien, 'The Bank's paper for the Hove Conference and the Select Committee', 11 November 1969, G38/3; McMahon to Johnson, 28 November 1969, 6A72/2.

[177] After the Hove conference the Money Study Group was established as a forum at which participants from academia, the Bank, the banks, and government could discuss specifically monetary matters. Also other conferences were organised in subsequent years to which the Bank sent representatives. One was held in Sheffield in 1970, and another was held in London in 1971; for the proceedings, see Clayton et al. (1971) and Johnson and Nobay (1971).

[178] Crockett to Dicks-Mireaux, 1 October 1968, enc. 'The money supply and expenditure', nd, 2A128/1.

[179] Dicks-Mireaux to Thornton/Allen, 3 October 1968, 2A128/1.

attention.[180] With discussion developing, some formality was given to it with the forming of a small group within the Bank in December 1968 made up of McMahon, Dicks-Mireaux, Goodhart, and Crockett (those who later attended the Hove conference). The first meeting of this 'Money Supply Group' was held on 10 December 1968, at which it was proposed that an article on the money supply be ready for the *Bulletin* in June 1969. (Papers were not to be circulated outside the group except to Thornton.) The return meeting with the IMF was due after the budget, and that injected some urgency to the proceedings. Goodhart agreed to draft a report reviewing the current state of theoretical and empirical knowledge in the United States and the United Kingdom, with the assistance of Crockett. It was this work that would become the article, 'The Importance of Money'.[181]

Several meetings of this group were held within the first few weeks of its formation, discussing some of the academic literature and central bank contributions that were appearing and attracting attention [such as, for example, Alan Walters' *Money in Boom and Slump*, Karl Brunner, in *St. Louis Fed Review* (where he made early use of the word 'monetarist'), and Anderson and Jordan on monetary and fiscal actions in economic stabilisation].[182] By January 1969, Goodhart had produced a report complete with appendices summarising recent empirical results.[183] At this point, the article was planned for the September 1969 issue of the *Bulletin*, and a document was prepared, 'The Importance of Money?'. The question mark would be removed at a later date.[184] McMahon suggested inviting Maurice Allen and Sayers to a future meeting, and Goodhart was asked to prepare some questions that might be put to them. Goodhart expressed some trepidation over putting to Sayers the view that recent econometric research was contradicting the position he had taken at Radcliffe and yet,

---

[180] *The Times*, 15 October 1968, p. 21; Fforde to O'Brien/Parsons, 'The money supply', 15 October 1968; Fforde to Thornton, 'Greenwell & Company', 17 October 1968; Pepper to Wood, 23 October 1968, 2A128/1.

[181] McMahon to Allen/O'Brien/Parsons, 'The money supply', 12 November 1968; Crockett, Note for record – 'Money supply committee', 11 December 1968, 2A128/1.

[182] Goodhart to McMahon/Dicks-Mireaux/Crockett, 'A. A. Walters: Hobart paper on the importance of money', 13 December 1968; Goodhart to McMahon, 'Note on article in F.R.B., St Louis, Review, November 1969', 15 January 1969, 2A128/1; Walters (1969); Brunner (1968); Anderson and Jordan (1968).

[183] Goodhart to McMahon/Dicks-Mireaux/Crockett, 'A background note on the issues involved', 6 January 1969; Crockett to McMahon, 'Money supply group', 17 January 1969, 2A128/1. Crockett's paper on velocity was discussed in March; Goodhart commented that the conclusions were anti-Radcliffe and pro-Friedman. Goodhart had a note on velocity in Canada: 'A stable velocity function for Canada', in *Economica*, 1969, pp. 314–315.

[184] Crockett to McMahon, 'The velocity of circulation of money', March 1969, and 'Money supply group', 25 March 1969, 2A128/1.

as he said, 'the question is really at the epicentre of the whole debate, and cannot be burked.'[185] The questions were put, along with the suggestion that money supply was a better indicator of monetary stance than the nominal interest rate. Sayers was sceptical of the econometric evidence, and his replies were not convincing.

By July, this was the position on money supply: 'An enormous amount of work, almost entirely misguided, has gone into the task of showing that in theory the authorities can control the various bases for the money supply.'[186] 'We do not believe that the evidence warrants the assertion that control over the money supply (or over any other monetary quantity) has been, is, or could be a particularly satisfactory instrument for directly controlling expenditures, especially in the institutional context of market structures as we believe these to be in this country.'[187] This did not survive in the final version, and in the next draft, the question mark was removed from the title. (A Federal Reserve Bank of New York paper had just appeared with the title, 'How Much Does Money Matter?[188]) By this time it was felt that the paper might be presented at the IMF seminar planned for October 1969 and be ready for the March 1970 *Bulletin*. By December, though, the seminar had not taken place, and it still was not clear when the article would be published. In February 1970, Morse was highly approving of the latest version and thought it 'well worthwhile busy Advisers and others in o'seas finding time to look at'.[189] That month, the paper went to the Treasury for the Treasury Group on Monetary Policy.[190]

After the Group on Monetary Policy had submitted its interim report in April 1970, Douglas Allen proposed that it then should 'concentrate mainly on problems involving the relationship of monetary theory to monetary policy, and on how the authorities, given all the uncertainties about this relationship might construct a credible monetary policy'.[191] It was to examine the contribution of monetary policy to monetary management. The work was undertaken against a background of intellectual ferment over monetary theory and policy. It set out to examine key areas where post-war policy might be said to have failed and needed changing. It started from the position that recognised that monetary policy was easier to adjust than

---

[185] Goodhart to McMahon, 'Money supply group', 7 May 1969, 2A128/2.
[186] 'The importance of money', 8 July 1969, p. 6, 2A128/2.
[187] *Ibid.*, p. 11.
[188] Davis (1969).
[189] Morse annotation on McMahon to O'Brien/Parsons, 'The importance of money', 17 February 1970, 2A128/3.
[190] McMahon to Allen, 25 February 1970, 2A128/3.
[191] Allen, 'The next stage of the Group's discussions', MP(70)16, 14 April 1970, 6A74/4.

fiscal policy, although there was uncertainty about its effects and a growing uncertainty about the effects of fiscal policy.

At the May 1970 meeting of the group, Goodhart's paper was discussed. The Treasury minutes recorded Goodhart's summing up as (1) he disagreed with Radcliffe, (2) he thought monetary policy difficult to use because the effect on interest rates could be quite violent and dislocating, but (3) he thought that monetary aggregates might be better indicators of the tightness of monetary policy than interest rates. The ensuing discussion covered a lot of ground. Did the monetary authorities need a target for monetary policy, and if so, should it be interest rates or money supply? It depended on the stability of velocity, but there was a feeling that 'it might be sensible to establish a money supply objective rather than an interest rate objective', although that implied accepting greater variations in nominal interest rates than had obtained in the past. There still was confusion over whether money-supply control 'could prevent a cost-push inflation from developing'. It was decided that that depended on 'the stability of the Phillips curve and perhaps on the financial position of the company sector'. Such a policy, it was noted, raised difficulties for debt management. But the group was content that the prevailing policy on DCE 'had something of the flavour of a money supply objective'.[192]

The final report of the group in March 1971 reflected on 16 months of work.[193] First, it noted the powerful influence on policy that the Radcliffe Report exerted for 10 years after it appeared – the view that there was only a modest role for monetary policy. Then, at the end of the 1960s, DCE appeared, and more attention was given to it. In the course of the 1960s, some of the defects in methods of trying to contain bank lending were becoming clearer, and the group became seriously critical of Radcliffe, coming to argue that money supply had a significant role to play. This did not by any means constitute a conversion to monetarism, and there was continuing debate in the group over most aspects of the money relationships. The report particularly stressed that the monetary authorities could not be indifferent to the level of interest rates nor to too much fluctuation in them. And yet the group was not entirely unsympathetic to the idea of a monetary growth rule. Some time was devoted to associated problems of an open economy – in particular those of a tight monetary stance and the extent to which concomitant capital flows could be countered. DCE was supposed to

---

[192] D. A. Harding (HMT), Group on Monetary Policy, MP(70) 9th meeting (minutes), 21 May 1970, 6A74/4.
[193] HMT, Group on Monetary Policy, MP(71)1 (final), 25 March 1971, 6A74/5.

deal with this, especially so if defined to combine the government's target for the increase in foreign-exchange reserves with a money-supply objective. The group did, however, continue to believe that controls to insulate the domestic system should be examined.

There was general approval of the control measures in the April 1970 budget, including special deposits. Furthermore, the group remained ambivalent about debt management and the gilt-edged market. However, it had reached a stage where the group believed that monetary policy should be defined in an unambiguous way. It was accepted that changes in the money supply 'seemed to provide a sensible means of interpreting changes in monetary stance'.[194] The report went on to envisage a year-to-year money-supply objective but warned that any such scheme should consider the recent trends in money-supply growth and avoid disruptive action. This, it was accepted, would involve moving away from step adjustments in interest rates that had been going on.

Alongside Allen's Group on Monetary Policy, the Treasury was forcing the pace in another way, too. In February and March 1970, Robert Armstrong held meetings to discuss definitions of the money supply; Goodhart, Boulter, and Gilbert Wood (EID) were there from the Bank.[195] A working party was established, and it agreed on a definition and to publish money-supply figures. In September 1970, the *Bulletin* carried a brief article setting out the Bank's ideas on the appropriate definition of the money stock.[196] Quarterly figures on M1, M2, and M3 were provided going back to 1963 and were updated in each *Bulletin* after that. However, it still was not plain sailing, and discussions continued into 1971 as new queries arose – what to do with items in transit, how to regard the Bank float, etc. Then there was a desire on the part of the Treasury to publish monthly rather than quarterly. In December 1972, the *Bulletin* carried another brief article to describe two new tables they were publishing carrying changes in the broad and narrow money series on a monthly and quarterly basis.[197]

Nevertheless, at the beginning of the decade, there was little contemplation of any monetary action on the inflation front. The Governor's Mansion House speech in October 1970 warned of the dangers of inflation becoming established and of the costs of inflation but rejected strict monetary and fiscal policies as the solution. While money supply and domestic credit

---

[194] *Ibid.*, para. 70.
[195] Goodhart, Note for record – 'Definition of money supply and D.C.E.', 25 February 1970; Boulter, Note for record – 'Definition of money supply', 6 March 1970, 5A175/2.
[196] 'The stock of money', *BEQB* 10(3):320–326, September 1970.
[197] 'New money stock tables', *BEQB* 12(4):512–513, December 1972.

had been expanding at a faster rate than was appropriate, 'I do not accept that the monetary authorities can exercise a precise control over the rate of increase in the money supply from month to month ... or that priority should be given to trying to influence movements in this particular magnitude. Real life is too complex and the objectives of policy too many and various for us to be able to rely on any simple rule.'[198] This was certainly representative of the Bank's view and supported by McMahon. He had had a long talk with Friedman at the Sheffield conference of the Money Study Group in September 1970, where Friedman had explained to him what his position was: choose the rate of inflation wanted, add to that the rate of growth of productive potential, and then ensure that the rate of growth of nominal incomes proceeds at this pace. Friedman believed that the simplest and perhaps the only way of doing this was by setting an appropriate money-supply target. Writing to Posner to outline all this, McMahon said: 'All this is neat and logical enough. It simply depends on being able to ensure that a desired rate of growth of nominal incomes is in fact achieved. Since Friedman believes you can do this through the quantity of money, he is happy. Since I don't, I am not.'[199]

When Charles Goodhart joined the Bank in 1968, he was told, as so many other recruits before him had been, 'that the Bank was a bank and not a study group'. However, he seems to have resolved at an early date to change things and certainly was instrumental in setting it on a path to where there were those within the Bank who behaved exactly like study groups. By 1971, there was considerable activity in writing academic-type papers and reading and commenting on outsiders' papers. Proposals were put to academics to join work that was going on in the Bank. Outsiders included Michael Hamburger, Michael Artis, David Laidler, Michael Parkin, Maurice Peston, and so on. Insiders included Lionel Price, John Townend, Leslie Dicks-Mireaux, Crockett, and of course, Goodhart. Some of the monetary econometric work that was going on in the United States was replicated for the United Kingdom – determinants of the money stock, money and income causality, relationship between short and long rates and inflation, and so on.[200]

Gilt and Money Markets

Open market operations undoubtedly were required for any control of monetary aggregates but had not been used for that in the 1960s. If they were to

---

[198] Lord Mayor's dinner speech, *BEQB* 10(4):473–476, December 1970.
[199] McMahon to Posner, 16 September 1970, 2A128/4.
[200] See 2A128/7–9.

be used, changes were going to be needed in the markets, and complicating these was the reaction to events along the way. The first of these was devaluation. In the immediate aftermath of devaluation with Bank Rate at 8 per cent, there was heavy demand for gilts. The markets were closed on Monday, 20 November, but for the following day, Fforde wrote, 'Today has been the most fantastic day in the Gilt Edged Market we remember. By 10:15 we had sold the best part of £400 million stock in the three Tap Stocks.'[201] To put this in context, there were £600 million net sales in the three months ending March 1967, and there were only two previous occasions when as much as £100 million had been sold in a single day. Issue Department stocks were left heavily depleted. The Government Broker had already warned that the long tap stock (6¾ per cent Treasury Loan, 1995–98) could run out, and in order to control the rate, it was essential to put something in its place. He thought that the only solution was to announce an additional tranche of the same stock, priced at the then-prevailing market rate. Consequently, a prospectus was hastily prepared for an issue of a further £600 million at 94½, some 3¼ below the price of the October 1966 issue of the same stock. Given the speed of the issue, there were very few applications, and the Issue Department took up £599.4 million.[202] After that immediate post-devaluation burst, in the last few weeks of 1967, the market was quieter, but for the quarter ending in December, there were net sales of £297 million.

The next two years were something of a roller coaster. After a subdued start to 1968, the Bank bought £500 million of stock in the second quarter of the year. It then sold £413 million in the three months to September and bought £911 million over the next six months. Thereafter, there were net sales of £998 million over the year ending in March 1970. Despite the heavy intervention, for the period October 1967 to March 1970, there were net sales of £283 million. The pattern was of prices falling to the summer of 1969 and then rising over the following 12 months. Yields reached historically high levels in June 1969, and the issue of 9 per cent Treasury Loan 1994 announced the following month was the highest coupon on government borrowing since the 8 per cent loan made when the Bank was established in 1694[203] (albeit in periods with radically different inflation expectations).

---

[201] 'Tuesday, 21 November, 1967', market report initialled by Fforde, C41/5.
[202] Painter (HMT) to Radice (HMT), 20 November 1967; Note to O'Brien, 'New tranche of 6¾ per cent Treasury Stock 1995/98', 21 November 1967; Fforde to Radice, 21 November 1967; Andrews to O'Brien/Parsons, 'Issue of £600 million 6¾ per cent Treasury Loan 1995/98', 24 November 1967, 5A44/44.
[203] Fforde to Armstrong, 2 July 1969; Armstrong to Fforde, 3 July 1969; Fforde to O'Brien, 'Issue of £400 million 9 per cent Treasury Loan 1994', 23 July 1969, 5A44/45; *BEQB* 9(4):287–288, September 1969.

In the summer of 1968, Fforde noted that there was a lot of criticism of the Bank's operations in the gilt-edged market. Some of the doubts emanated from unnamed sources in the Bank who, according to Fforde, argued that the present system put an 'undesirable brake on upward movements of longer-term interest rates, with effects on the money supply contrary to policy while also encouraging (on the other tack) undesirably fast downward movements'. In addition, the IMF was suspicious of the Bank's explanations, and some of the IMF's Directors had expressed the view that there should be no intervention in the gilt-edged market. Finally, 'young turks' at the Treasury also had been inclined to question the Bank's methods. Characteristically, Fforde's response was to demand some logical rigour: it was wrong to criticise the Bank for not doing something under the existing system that could only be done under a different system. There should be a proper assessment, which he went on to provide, of the merits and demerits of the alternatives.[204]

In the system of 'continuous funding', the Bank bought in near-maturing stocks and endeavoured to refinance maturities by sales from the Issue Department, whereas new sales to finance the government's net borrowing requirement were raised through tap stocks. These procedures had 'led us to intervene in the market so that there may be preserved the orderly conditions in which day-to-day refinancing and new borrowing can proceed as smoothly as possible'. This was still the dominant motive. He continued, 'Rightly or wrongly, this willingness to intervene, which has developed into the accepted convention that we will always be prepared to deal *at a price* if the market so requests the Government Broker, has rendered gilt-edged securities much more "marketable" than any other securities in the U.K.' The marketability was underpinned by the fact that the Bank was prepared to deal in very large amounts. Large holders of gilts therefore knew that they could buy or sell in one day without disrupting the market or driving prices against themselves. As a result, Fforde considered that, on average, more gilt-edged stock was held outside official hands and at a lower yield than otherwise would be the case. It was 'virtually inherent' in the system that stock other than near maturities would be bought in when interest rates were moving upwards, and the abolition of day-to-day intervention would in practice change the entire system. The outcome of change would be a higher cost of government borrowing and a reduction in bank and non-

---

[204] Fforde, Aide memoire, 'The Bank of England and the gilt-edged market', 26 July 1968, 3A92/16; Andrews, Annotation, 1 August 1968, 'As handed to Brian Rose (I.M.F.) for use within the mission only'.

bank holdings of gilt-edged stock; he saw very few compensating advantages. With this in mind, critics should be encouraged to examine the likely consequences of altering the system.[205]

Whatever the system, Fforde had little time for Radcliffe-style sales of gilts at prices far below the market level. To offer a tap or new stock at a yield of 7½ or 8 per cent when the market rate was 7 per cent was 'complete nonsense'. The market would not function if 'a dominant borrower is liable, and known to be liable, to make radical changes in the price level of long-dated stocks without warning'. The only result would be 'a series of wholly disorderly situations',[206] and of course, if there was one thing that the Bank disliked intensely, it was disorder. Fforde's rejection of lowering prices in order to sell stock was merely a continuation of Bank policy that had been stated consistently since the evidence given to Radcliffe.

The Bank outlined its operations in the gilt-edged market to the IMF in October 1968 with an explanation and defence of the Bank's general tactics. An unusually active and orderly market was required in order to conduct the large financing and refinancing operations and to maintain the superior marketability of gilts. Without continuous intervention, such operations would be 'difficult and clumsy'. And to ensure that financing techniques were fully effective, it was necessary to intervene over the whole range of maturities. Intervention did not mean support; rather, it entailed 'being prepared to purchase stock, if we judge the prices to be right'. By being present in the market every day, the Bank could enhance the marketability of gilts. If the Bank did not act in such a way, then the market makers, unable to absorb the stock, would have to quote 'very much wider prices'.[207]

Of course, there were dangers. The Bank admitted that intervention could turn into 'a refusal to allow anything but very small price movement over a day', and from this could develop a more generalised official support, possibly in conflict with other policy objectives. Indeed, this is what later occurred. The Bank was 'obliged to behave very carefully and as nearly as possible as if we were not dominant'. Thus the Bank did not, through the Government Broker, ask jobbers to bid for large lines of stock, neither did it go out and offer stocks for sale at below-market prices. Instead, it waited for the jobbers to approach the Government Broker. The prices at which the Bank chose to deal would not necessarily be 'middle market prices'

---

[205] *Ibid.*
[206] *Ibid.*
[207] Bank of England, 'Some observations on official operations in the gilt-edged market', 15 October 1968, 3A92/16.

but were 'at all times consistent with an orderly market'. Occasionally, the Bank entered the market as 'active outright *buyers* of a range of stocks, at the prices ruling', but this practice was claimed to be extremely rare and occurred only where, for exogenous reasons, there would be a 'thoroughly disorderly situation' in the absence of any overt support. The Bank claimed that by changing tactics on its dealing prices it was able to 'assist or resist adjustments depending on whether we think these are necessary and in accordance with wider aims of policy'.[208]

Apart from the Radcliffe evidence, the October 1968 seminar with the IMF was an unusual case of the Bank and Treasury discussing gilt-edged operations with outsiders. The IMF was sceptical about the Bank's case for continuous intervention, pointing out that violent fluctuations in equity markets had not deterred investors. Much of the debate concerned the Bank's power to influence the level of rates and the effects of high rates on the sale of gilts. For example, if the long-term rate could be pushed right up, large sales to the public might be induced. But the Bank argued that while it had a degree of influence to resist or encourage the level desired by the market, it was unable to go beyond this without some external change, such as Bank Rate. The standard Bank line was emphasised: techniques were limited, and dramatic initiatives designed to achieve spectacular sales were not possible.[209]

In mid-November 1968, Fforde worried that all the 'gossip' about money supply and the supposed enthusiasms of IMF staff would mean that the authorities would be obliged to change their tactics and techniques. Phrases such as 'aggressive selling', Fforde complained, cannot but encourage a bearish view of gilts. Adverse trade figures would be likely to cause the market to fall further, and Fforde suggested that the Bank should retreat 'unless and until yields get near to 8 per cent'. The Chief Cashier was reluctant to see rates go higher than this because it was 'uncharted territory'. Above all, he felt that the Bank should try to avoid disorderly conditions and the 'appearance of wild talk that the Chicago School is now in charge', alluding to developments on monetary control. Thus, Fforde concluded, the best policy was to 'wait and see' and the less said in public the better.[210]

As Fforde predicted, the market 'turned sour' after the release of poor trade figures in November, and the Bank felt compelled to buy large amounts

---

[208] *Ibid.*
[209] Monetary seminar (International Monetary Fund), MS(IMF)3rd meeting, 18 October 1968, 7A353/1.
[210] Fforde to Figgures, 12 November 1968, enc. 'Gilt-edged market: prospect for long-term interest rates in the U.K.', 12 November 1968, 3A92/16.

of stock.[211] The market was 'highly nervous and sensitive', and press reports about the Bank having to make a drastic change in tactics did not help.[212] A week later, Hollom was told by Figgures, in what was probably a first, that the Treasury did not want to see a large amount spent in the gilt-edged market without the opportunity to comment and discuss.[213]

The Governor's first letter on market operations for more than five years gave an assessment of the Bank's recent and future tactics in the market. If there was further upward pressure on the long-term rate, the Bank should 'retreat as rapidly as we judge safe', continuing to deal according to normal practice and adjusting tactics in order to minimise purchases of stock. If conditions turned bullish, then the Bank would be prepared 'to sell readily and avoid any abrupt reversal of the recent upward adjustment of yields'. The Governor then addressed an apparent Treasury suggestion that the emergency package should be reinforced by radical changes to the way that the gilt-edged market was managed. He could appreciate the underlying argument that the current arrangements for managing the national debt made it difficult to prevent the public turning a portion of the debt into cash, and it might be better if the arrangements were changed to prevent this. In particular, 'how much easier it would be if the Government Broker never bought stock in the market.' He could appreciate this but not accept it. He adopted Cromeresque tones: 'I must warn you that I regard this wishful thinking as dangerous in the highest degree.' He provided an extensive analysis rejecting any notion that a partial withdrawal would allow the desired adjustments in interest rates without an appreciable monetisation of debt. This was a 'mirage'. It still would result in an irreversible change to the status of the market, with all the grave consequences, and then when the Government Broker reappeared, investors would take the 'heaven-sent opportunity' to sell. O'Brien concluded by saying that he was convinced that the withdrawal of the Government Broker would be a 'catastrophic error of policy'. He conceded that the present system was not perfect, and he was ready to accept any amount of further scrutiny, but 'in the meantime, we should continue market management along the present lines.'[214]

---

[211] Fforde to O'Brien (by hand to Basle), 'Gilt-edged market', 15 November 1968, 3A92/16; *BEQB* 9(1):15, March 1969.

[212] Fforde to O'Brien, 'The gilt-edged market up to lunch time today, 18 November', 18 November 1968, 3A92/16.

[213] Hollom, 'Conversation with Mr. Figgures and Mr. Goldman, 25 November 1968', 26 November 1968, 3A92/16.

[214] O'Brien to Sir Douglas Allen, 28 November 1968, 3A92/16.

In late 1968 and early 1969, the market remained fragile. Yields rose to historically high levels, and there was continued press speculation about official tactics.[215] In the Bank, caution ruled. Hollom felt that the Bank should not peg ('the worst solution') or press the market down, and he attached great importance to retaining maximum room for manoeuvre.[216] A moment of relief came during the debate on the April 1969 budget when it was alleged by one speaker that the Government Broker was unable to distinguish between Milton Friedman and Marty Feldman (a popular comedian of the time).[217] The following month when there was a national newspaper strike, O'Brien confided in representatives of the London Discount Market Association (LDMA), 'what a relief it was not to have to read Peter Jay' (economics editor of *The Times* and one of the principal critics of the Bank). Reportedly, the Governor went on to say that he was 'tired of these long haired economists', and it was difficult to run the gilt-edged market while they were talking and theorising so freely.[218]

O'Brien told Jenkins a week after the 1969 budget that current discussions about the control of the money supply and the visit of the IMF had had a considerable impact on attitudes in the gilts market, and it was widely thought that the Bank would have to stay out of the market entirely. He was against that. One possibility would be to establish a firm floor, but O'Brien argued that that would be rash in the circumstances because there was no certainty that the floor could be maintained. Finally, the authorities could continue edging along with the market as at present, allowing yields to rise while also trying to reverse market expectations. If the Bank was to acquire large sums of gilts, the government would be placed in a difficult negotiating position with the IMF; such purchases should be avoided, even at the expense of substantial increases in interest rates. There was general agreement that in the immediate future, edging along was the only realistic course, although the authorities also should look for any opportunity to create a floor. O'Brien, along with Hollom and Fforde, expressed doubt about the IMF's claim that all the Bank's purchases of gilts were equally harmful to the market. Evidence suggested that many institutional investors were selling gilts in order to get back in at a better price later. The Bank also thought that the effect of its operations was exaggerated because attention

---

[215] HC Deb, 17 December 1968, Vol. 775, c343.

[216] Fforde to Hollom/O'Brien/Parsons, 'The gilt-edged market', 19 December 1968, and Hollom, Annotation, 20 December 1968, 3A92/16.

[217] HC Deb, 15 April 1969, Vol. 781, c1097. Daniell denied making the comparison but did not dispute its validity; see Fforde to O'Brien, 16 April 1969, 3A92/16.

[218] LDMA reports, 2 May 1969, LDMA1/32.

was concentrated on the periods when it was a net seller. In his summing up, Jenkins, who generally was suspicious of the Bank, told the Bank representatives that they should be prepared to let prices drop sharply that week so as to avoid buying large quantities of stock. If the market showed signs of becoming healthier towards the end of April, then a floor might be established to revive confidence and make sales.[219]

The Bank then outlined its operations in the gilt-edged market between April 1968 and April 1969 and sent copies to the Treasury and one to the IMF, in Hollom's words, for its 'education'.[220] It showed at the short end of the market that the Bank had made substantial purchases, although these were mainly of near-maturing stocks. At the long end, in the period between September 1968 and April 1969, there was 'an upward adjustment' of the long-term rate on gilts from just over 7½ per cent to nearly 9 per cent, and such had been the conditions that this had been achieved 'without the Bank being a net purchaser of long dated stocks on any significant scale'.[221] Overall, the paper was optimistic about what could be achieved with continuous funding, even in difficult circumstances.

In April, most of the discussion was about the implications of the budget surplus for the gilt-edged market and the relative importance of the maturity structure of the debt, as opposed to total net sales. Two significant points emerged, both of which can be seen as an erosion of the Bank's traditional freedom in operational matters. Jenkins said that there was a measure of choice in deciding whether to take pressure on the rate or on the amount of support provided, and it therefore would be useful to have agreed general guidelines on policy together with a daily market report. O'Brien undertook to produce the former, while arrangement for the latter had just been put in place, with the Bank agreeing to submit to the Treasury a pro forma return showing data on transactions, including cumulative figures, and yields.[222]

In the guidelines agreed in May 1969, the stated primary objective of official operations was to 'maximise net sales or minimise net purchases (as the case may be) of stock of all maturities'. It was of particular importance 'in the light of the intention to limit domestic credit expansion in 1969–70', and all operations were to be based in pursuit of this objective.

[219] Hancock, 'Note of a meeting … 22 April, 1969', 3A92/16.

[220] Hollom to O'Brien, 'I.M.F', 25 April 1969, 3A92/16.

[221] Bank of England, 'Operations in the gilt-edged market: 1 April 1968 to 19 April 1969', 24 April 1969, 3A92/16.

[222] Armstrong to Fforde, 18 April 1969; Armstrong to Fforde, 24 April 1969, 3A92/16; Andrew Edwards (Principal, HMT), 'Note of a meeting … 28 April 1969, 3A8/3.

In the case of medium- and long-dated stocks, at times of weakness, the Bank would not refuse to bid for stock offered, but 'it will not, however, be an objective of policy to avoid a rise in rate of interest', and the Bank would 'bid at prices sharply below going market levels if it is judged that the primary objective will be best served by their doing so'. If there was a prospect of sustained demand for gilt-edged securities, then the Bank would operate in a manner that would encourage net sales 'at as high a pace as is sustainable'. This was 'unlikely to be consistent with the prevention of any fall at all in yields: demand for stock is not likely to be sustained if the market believes that it is the object of official policy to prevent prices from rising'. The level of yield at which sales of the long tap would resume was a matter for consultation between the Bank and the Treasury. For short-dated stocks, the objective was the same: to minimise net purchases or maximise net sales. However, there were three additional elements: sales to investors in the non-bank sector were desirable, but temporary and speculative sales to banks might not in the longer term serve the primary objective, the attitude to yields at the short end was likely to be seen as an indicator of intentions on Bank Rate, and the smoothing of maturities by purchasing stock in advance of redemption was to continue, but again, in doing this, due weight was to be given to the primary objective.[223] It was the first time that such a document had been compiled, and O'Brien was not keen on the development, describing it as 'an unavoidable innovation'.[224] Daily reports and joint policy formulation were a marked change from the Cobbold and Cromer eras, when exchanges between the Bank and the Treasury about gilts were mainly restricted to the authorisation of new issues.

Some technical changes were made to the way that the Bank operated to improve its room for manoeuvre at the end of the decade. One change related to the buying of stocks close to redemption. The Bank was ready to buy stocks nearing maturity 'at a price that gives, over the remaining life of the stock, the current rate on Treasury bills', a 'widely known practice', under which the Bank might acquire up to three-quarters of a maturing stock.[225] In May 1969, it was announced that the official buying price for stocks within three months of maturity would no longer be tied to the Treasury bill rate. This would give greater control over the timing

---

[223] Fforde to O'Brien, 'Gilt-edged market: "guidelines for official operations"', 14 May 1969, enc. 'Guidelines for official operations in gilt-edged', 3A92/16.

[224] O'Brien, Annotation 28 April 1969 on Fforde to O'Brien/Parsons, 'Draft guidelines for operations in gilt-edged', 28 April 1969, 3A92/16.

[225] 'Official transactions in the gilt edged market', *BEQB* 6(2):144, June 1966.

of purchases, and the new tactic was first employed in August 1969.[226] Shortly afterwards, Fforde claimed that this 'enables us to conduct rather more of an interest rate policy and rather less of a stock sales policy'. The Bank believed that steep rises in long-term interest rates could now be achieved without heavy purchases, and large falls in rates could be made with smaller sales.[227]

In 1952, then Chief Cashier Kenneth Peppiatt had set out how to operate in the gilt-edged market. As Fforde later observed, it was a rare example of such a statement, and as such, he felt it worthy of replicating verbatim in his official history.[228] He went on to deprecate the subsequent intervention from the late 1950s and wished that it had never happened, so it is ironic that such activity should have reached its peak in the period when he himself was Chief Cashier. Yet he was also playing a key role in making gilt-edged operations less interventionist.

In the money markets, devaluation brought a reappraisal of operations. Initially, there were acute difficulties. At the Treasury bill tender on 17 November 1967, the market had bid £98.8s.0d, with an average rate of discount of £6.8s.3.10d (6.43 per cent per annum or 1.6 per cent per quarter); the following day, Bank Rate was raised to 8 per cent. While the markets were closed on the following Monday, LDMA representatives attended three meetings at the Bank. The Governor intervened personally with an offer that the Bank would buy back each house's tender at approximately tender rate. O'Brien put the highest security classification on this and stressed to the LDMA that on no account should any details of the deal be leaked.[229] The next tender saw what was then the lowest-ever acceptance price of £98.2s.1d. There also were severe shortages of money in the market in the immediate aftermath of devaluation as a consequence of the heavy purchases of gilt-edged stock.

The following month, Fforde warned the Governors that the reluctance of the banks and discount houses to sell Treasury bills would cause the Bank difficulties. This situation was a consequence of the low volume of Treasury bills in the market, which had not been accompanied by a reduction in the scale of the Bank's day-to-day operations. Indeed, these had increased because of disturbed conditions in the gilt-edged and foreign-exchange markets. Thus Fforde wrote, 'we are left trying to operate on a larger scale

---

[226] *BEQB* 9(3):288, September 1969; 'Operation of monetary policy', p. 456.

[227] Fforde to O'Brien/Parsons, 'The long term rate of interest', 30 September 1969, 3A92/17.

[228] Fforde (1992, pp. 648–649). Fforde did not give the reference. Peppiatt to Cobbold/Bernard/Mynors, 'Gilt-edged market', 1 January 1952, C42/12.

[229] LDMA, '20 November 1967. Meeting no. 3 held at 5:00 p.m.', LDMA1/16.

but with a stock of Treasury Bills that has declined.'[230] Matters were made worse by the fact that with rates high and expected to fall, Treasury bills were relatively attractive to the discount houses, and they were not inclined to sell them to the Bank or the banks. The clearers also became reluctant sellers to the Bank because of the knowledge that they would have difficulty in replacing their sales by purchases from the market. Fforde observed that as long as the houses received small allotments at the tender, which was likely if they heeded the Bank's desire not to let the tender rate fall too far and too fast, then they would continue to refrain from selling. Thus the Bank could not easily relieve shortages of money through purchasing Treasury bills, and it had to resort to overnight lending at market rates. Overnight lending was already being used heavily by the Bank as part of its strategy to keep the market short of money every day and to maintain short-term rates. This policy itself reinforced the paucity of Treasury bills because it gave the Bank little opportunity to sell those bills and add to the supply available to the market.

Fforde then attempted to find ways to alleviate the problem. It was not easy. Various means of encouragement or sanction were considered. The primary cause, for Fforde, was that some of the participants would not 'play the money market game wholeheartedly. ... In this game Treasury Bills are the principal counter and it is not surprising that the game becomes more difficult if some of the players hoard their counters.'[231] Smooth money-market operations, said Fforde, depended on the free movement of Treasury bills, and a reluctance to accept this could 'greatly impede our operations as a central bank'. This analysis led him to recommend that most favoured of tactics for the Bank – exhortation. To be effective, it would have to be carried out by the Governor. A letter to the clearing banks and the discount houses was drafted, although the request for 'co-operation' was undertaken orally. At a meeting with Stanton and Jessel, Chairman and Deputy Chairman of the LDMA, in December, O'Brien asked the discount market to 'play ball'. As a quid pro quo, he said that the Bank would try to move away from the policy of persistent shortages towards more normal market conditions. The LDMA also were told that the clearers were being asked to sell bills more regularly. O'Brien emphasised that the new policy should receive 'absolutely no publicity'.[232]

---

[230] Fforde to O'Brien/Parsons, 'The money market', 12 December 1967, C40/1466.

[231] *Ibid.*

[232] O'Brien, Annotation, 21 December 1967, on Fforde to O'Brien/Parsons, 'The money market', 12 December 1967; Draft letter to chairmen, clearing banks, and LDMA, 12 December 1967, C40/1466; LDMA notes, 22 December 1967, LDMA1/31.

As promised, the Bank did gradually alter its tactics during 1968. Initially, the market was still unable or unwilling to sell Treasury bills, so the Bank continued to make overnight advances at market rates. The Bank found this level of lending unwelcome, and so two special operations were mounted to attempt to reduce it. In mid-February, £100 million of Treasury bills were bought subject to resale to the market in March. However, this failed to halt the Bank's advances to the market, which rose to a peak of £228 million on 28 March 1968, with a record monthly total of £1,500 million. At the same time, the market had been adding to its gilt holdings – the Bank expressed disapproval of this and engaged in an operation on 11 April to purchase £200 million in short-dated stock. During the remainder of the year, there was further encouragement to reduce gilt holdings, and this proved successful because the Bank was able to eliminate advances to the market by the end of the year. As the Discount Office's annual review of the market explained, the use of overnight lending was deliberately reined back with the intention of employing it only for its original use as a short-term convenience of rolling forward a shortage on one day to remove a surplus in the days immediately following. Lending to the market in 1969 was limited; no advances were made, and shortages were relieved by purchasing commercial bills.[233] All in all, this was a dramatic change compared with the previous year.

In the Bank's 1969 survey of monetary policy since Radcliffe, the development of new parallel financial markets was noted. Foremost was the Eurodollar market, but on the domestic side, there were markets in sterling inter-bank funds and local authority deposits. The use of commercial bills revived, and negotiable sterling certificates of deposits were introduced (Table 9.2). These alternatives had grown up alongside the Treasury bill market, but interest rates in these markets had no fixed or formal relation to the Treasury bill rate.[234] Neither were they subject to the rates fixed by the clearing banks under their 'cartel' arrangements. Although the Bank did not operate in these parallel markets, it had arguably contributed to their growth through its prolonged use of credit restrictions and ceilings and its tacit sanctioning of the cartel.

The local authority temporary money market dated back to the 1950s. In the early 1960s, the funds outstanding were in the region of £1 billion, and this grew steadily to around £2 billion at the end of the decade. Typically, 60 to 70 per cent of this was short-term borrowing of up to seven days. When data were first collected for the inter-bank market towards the end of 1962,

---

[233] Discount Office, 'Discount market annual reviews, 1968 and 1969', C47/40.
[234] Bank of England, 'Operation of monetary policy', p. 451.

Table 9.2. *Parallel money markets, funds outstanding, 1961–70 (£m)*

Month end	Inter-bank market		Negotiable CDs		Local authority Short-term (up to 12 months)		Bills discounted	
	Deposits	Advances	Sterling	Dollar	Total	Up to 7 days	Treasury bills	UK bills
Dec 1961	N/a	N/a	–	–	1,116	716	N/a	N/a
Dec 1962	131	191	–	–	1,178	676	N/a	N/a
Dec 1963	229	298	–	–	1,394	831	1,624	657
Dec 1964	266	333	–	–	1,762	1,152	1,304	800
Dec 1965	366	421	–	–	1,798	1,257	1,389	860
Dec 1966	484	510	–	81	1,807	1,327	1,180	920
Dec 1967	704	684	–	249	1,918	1,468	1,182	949
Dec 1968	1,059	1,123	165	597	1,952	1,496	1,071	1,111
Dec 1969	1,483	1,567	442	1,541	1,982	1,429	820	1,249
Dec 1970	1,694	1,747	1,089	1,650	1,982	1,374	1,370	1,478

Source: BEQB.

the sums involved were small: Sterling deposits were £96 million. There was then rapid growth, and by the end of 1969, deposits totalled £1,438 million. Like the local authority market, inter-bank offered facilities for short-term borrowing, mostly for periods of less than 14 days, with attractive rates of interest and was seen as a buffer against unexpected withdrawals of deposits. It also provided a 'call money type' liquid asset. The main players were the accepting houses and the overseas banks. EID analysis showed that until the end of 1965, the US banks were net lenders in inter-bank funds, whereas from mid-1967, the accepting houses became more regular participants.[235]

Negotiable sterling certificates of deposit (CDs) were first issued in London in 1968.[236] They originated in the United States, where they were used by banks from 1961 to counter the impact of Regulation Q. Dollar CDs appeared in London in May 1966.[237] Initially, the Bank's stance was to disapprove of the CD, instead encouraging the banks to compete for deposits through subsidiaries.[238] Cromer in particular was not enamoured about what he described as the 'importation from the US'.[239] That was in 1963. The question resurfaced four years later when the US-based First National City Bank requested consent for their London office to issue CDs. In Fforde's view, the situation was now entirely different because there was now far greater competition for sterling time deposits, with rates 'somewhat above' the Treasury bill rates. Here he noted the fact that the inter-bank market was now 'flourishing, rather than embryonic', and money rates in general were now 'less subject to close official influence – though that influence remains very strong'. He reckoned that 'very little' had been achieved by disapproving of CDs in 1963 and now recommended that the objection should be withdrawn.[240] Interestingly, O'Brien declared that he had never been happy about the Bank's original ruling, perhaps indicative of the weight of

---

[235] EID, 'The inter-bank sterling market', 4 August 1966, EID4/13; Jennifer Jeffreys (EID) to David Nendick, 'The sterling inter-bank market', 8 October 1969, 6A59/1; *The Banker* 117(495):415, May 1967.

[236] The CDs could be issued in multiples of £10,000 with a minimum of £50,000 and a maximum of £500,000 and with a maturity of not less than three months and not longer than five years. The rate of interest was fixed by the issuing bank. It was a negotiable instrument that could be traded in a secondary market (made by the discount houses). 'Sterling certificates of deposit', *BEQB* 12(4):487–495, December 1972.

[237] Anthony Bushell (EID) to Thornton, 'London dollar certificates of deposit', 10 June 1966, C40/1089; Bank of England, 'The London dollar certificate'.

[238] Fforde to Hollom, 'Sterling negotiable certificates of deposit', 31 March 1967, C40/1322.

[239] Cromer, Annotation, 29 April 1963, on Hollom to O'Brien/Cromer/Mynors, 'Negotiable certificates of deposit', 24 April 1963, C40/1088.

[240] Richard S. Vokey (vice president, First National City Bank) to Hollom, 14 March 1967; Fforde to Hollom, 'Sterling negotiable certificates of deposit', 31 March 1967, C40/1322.

Cromer's opinion at the time. However, his caveat was that 'I am certainly not having an American bank being the first to issue them.'[241] This was in April 1967, and there followed an 18-month period while the Bank gauged interest, consulted, and agreed technical details before the first sterling CDs were issued in October 1968.[242] Initial growth was steady rather than spectacular, from £165 million to £281 million in the first half of 1969, but this was followed by significant expansion. A figure of £1 billion was outstanding in December 1970 and £4.9 billion two years later.

All of this was reflected in the changing asset portfolios of the discount houses. Over the 1960s, their total assets almost doubled (£1 billion to £1.8 billion), but the composition at the end of the decade was markedly different. At the start of the period, holdings of Treasury bills and British government securities formed 80 per cent of the total; this had halved by 1969. Treasury bills fell from 40 to 20 per cent in the same period and then to less than 10 per cent at the end of 1970. Instead, the discount market was making greater use of short bonds, and there was a revival in commercial bill business, the latter increasing from about 10 per cent of discount-market assets to between 30 and 40 per cent. The houses formed the secondary market in CDs, and holdings of these were 10 per cent in 1970. The discount houses were having to adapt to meet the challenge of new and changing money markets, and the same applied to the Bank.

Through a mix of developments in academic economics and pressure from the IMF, the Bank in the 1960s was forced to reach a view on the role of money. Furthermore, it had become increasingly unhappy with the operation of controls on lending, and it was keen to see greater competition in banking. However, if it were to take action on these fronts, there needed to be changes in the money and gilts markets. All these elements were, of course, intensified following devaluation, and the Bank moved at a pace that it judged propitious. There was, of course, the refusal to allow interest rates to rise sufficiently or to tolerate volatility. At the same time, the Bank resented the growing interference from the Treasury that resulted in part from the attention it was giving to monetary aggregates such as DCE and the need to use the gilt market as part of its armoury. The Treasury then took an increasing interest in its operations. The old independence of the 1960s was beginning to come under threat.

---

[241] O'Brien, Governor's note – 'Sterling negotiable certificates of deposit', 10 April 1967, C40/1322.

[242] See material in C40/1322–4; *BEQB* 8(4):347, December 1968.

10

Competition and Credit Control

The 1970s would turn out to be the worst decade of the century in British monetary, financial, and macroeconomic history, as well as that of many other countries in the Organisation for Economic Co-operation and Development (OECD). In Britain, inflation would reach its worst levels ever recorded (wartime or peacetime), serious banking instability would appear for the first time in over a hundred years, there was the largest ever asset price collapse, and the performance of the real economy would be worse than it had been since the late nineteenth century. None of that was obvious as the decade opened, although there were some ominous indicators. The 1967 devaluation had taken longer to work than expected, serious doubts surrounded the effectiveness of lending controls, and inflation was rising. The newly elected Conservative Government of June 1970 seemed set on promoting competition and moving away from the interventionist and planning approach of the 1960s. But there was still the belief that inflation was sensitive to the level of unemployment and that it was essentially a non-monetary phenomenon. In any case, hardly had the new course been set when unemployment started to rise in 1971, and there was an almost immediate reversal of the policies of the 1960s.

At the beginning of the decade, the government believed that they could raise the rate of economic growth, and they set out to do that. In 1973, there was dramatic growth, but in the following two years, it collapsed to negative rates and was negative again in 1980. Unemployment rose from about 2.5 per cent at the beginning of the decade to 7.5 per cent at the end. The dash for growth was reflected in part in monetary growth. M3 jumped dramatically in 1970 to 16 per cent from 2 per cent the previous year. It peaked at 27 per cent in 1973, and while it was brought down sharply almost to single digits in the middle years of the decade, it was back up to 16 per cent at the end. The combination of stagnant/negative output growth and raging inflation became known as 'stagflation'.

The inflation of the late 1960s and 1970s was a worldwide phenomenon, but the British experience was worse than most in the OECD. A monetary explanation was being offered by a small minority: 'the ultimate consequence of an increase in the rate of world monetary expansion' attributable in the main to monetary policy in the United States.[1] Most central banks, however, were slow to accept this and seemed not to know what to do about it. Academic and international institutional pressures may have been building, but deeply entrenched ideas and practices take time to change. In the Bank there had been some action on the monetary front, albeit reactive and reluctant and without conceding much more than the fact that money might be more important than had been thought previously. There was still a long way to go before it was accepted that inflation was a monetary phenomenon, let alone that money could be adjusted to contain it.

Formulating the New Approach

The new government's initial emphasis in 1970 on competition generally gave the Bank the encouragement it needed to press ahead with its 'new approach'. Some clear strands had developed that prepared the way. One was dissatisfaction with controls on lending (ceilings and quantitative controls in particular), one was the desire for greater competition in banking, and another was the need to control monetary growth. And there were related concerns about operations in the money and gilt-edged markets. Through the 1960s, there had been several attempts to think longer term and address some of the issues, but this typically was overtaken by short-term crises. In September 1969, Tony Coleby, then Assistant Chief of the Overseas Department, argued for a banking system free from restraints on competition, with the use of cash deposits, supplemented by an active interest-rate policy, during periods of restraint. Goodhart produced a response that elaborated on the problems of controlling the monetary system.[2] Again, this initiative was overtaken by short-term requirements. Yet Fforde was insistent that this 'longer range exercise' to which Coleby and Goodhart had contributed, 'must *not* be forgotten' (emphasis in original).[3]

---

[1] Johnson (1972, p. 335).

[2] Coleby, 'A new deal for the banks', September 1969; Wood to Fforde, 'A new deal for the banks', 10 October 1969; Goodhart to Fforde, 'A new deal for the Banks', 20 October 1969, 3A8/5.

[3] Fforde, 'Credit control', 28 October 1969, enc. with Fforde to Hollom, 'Credit controls', 28 October 1969, 3A8/5.

Following the 1970 budget, Fforde wanted the 'Group on Monetary Policy' to return to consideration of the clearing banks' cartel.[4] William White, an economist on secondment from Manchester University, argued that any alteration would not have a major impact on the financial system.[5] Fforde responded that it was the apparatus of official control that was the problem, not the existence of the cartel.[6] There were several underlying assumptions – that the desirable developments should be undertaken by the clearing banks; if controls had to be imposed, then ratio controls were preferred, and these would be easiest to operate where there was a small number of and/or homogeneous banks; non-clearing banks and finance houses should not be protected by officially imposed constraints that prevented the clearing banks from competing across the full range of banking services; and any new system should offer member banks the freedom to compete while at the same time enabling the authorities to operate a control of credit that did not require ceilings on individual banks. Fforde suggested that if 75 per cent of banks (by size) were prepared to join, then a scheme should be pursued.

His early sketch had three main elements: first, banks would agree to maintain a minimum 15 per cent liquidity ratio comprising 1½ per cent cash at the Bank and 13½ per cent in other specified liquid assets. (Hollom suggested that 'reserve ratio' might be a more appropriate term.) Second, members would agree to the special deposits scheme, with interest payable at the Treasury bill rate. Finally, there would still be an agreement on rates for some types of deposits. Such a system would offer uniform liquidity ratios and an effective means of varying them, for credit-control purposes, via special deposits. The liquidity rules would impose and preserve 'an efficient money market through which we can work'. A system along these lines would be sufficiently attractive to encourage the clearing banks, outside banks, and finance houses to want to join. Furthermore, it would promote 'parent-subsidiary mergers', that is, between clearers and their various non-clearing interests. Banks that did not join the system would face the prospect of both restrictive controls and greater competition. Of course, Fforde recognised that this would be an imposed solution, but one driven

4   Fforde to Hollom, 'Group on Monetary Policy', 16 April 1970, 3A8/6.
5   William White (Economic Section) to McMahon, 4 May 1970, enc. 'Possibility and implications of a change in the clearing banks' collective agreement', 4 May 1970, 3A8/6. White later became Deputy Governor of the Bank of Canada and then economic adviser and Head of the Monetary and Economic Department at the Bank for International Settlements (BIS).
6   Fforde to McMahon/Hollom, 'Further thoughts on the bankers' cartel (based, inter alia, upon a reading of White's paper of the 4 May)', 13 May 1970, 3A8/6.

by 'the impossibility or ineffectiveness' of alternatives. 'Do you think the idea worth pursuing?' he asked.[7]

It seemed that it was, and work continued in both the Economic Intelligence Department (EID) and the Chief Cashier's Office, culminating in October 1970 with Fforde's paper, 'The Future Control of Credit',[8] a version of which Page, who was now Chief Cashier, sent to the Treasury.[9] The document offered nothing revolutionary, only a gradual and voluntary renegotiation of the cash deposits scheme (not in use but waiting in the wings), with its possible extension to finance houses. This would be a step towards other changes, such as modifications to the cartel and to liquidity ratios. Perhaps more surprising was that restraint could be supported by more frequent and larger variations in short-term interest rates. However, using Bank Rate in this way, it was argued, would have two main disadvantages. First, the 'aura' of Bank Rate as the key monetary weapon would mean that changes, at least to begin with, were seen as having more significance than merely technical adjustments. Second, there could be considerable speculation once it became established that Bank Rate was changing more frequently. The Bank believed that these difficulties would be mitigated if Bank Rate was 'sometimes to follow rather than to lead changes in market short-term interest rates'. For example, the Treasury bill rate could be allowed to move in line with rates in parallel money markets rather than being kept below Bank Rate. These ideas were discussed at length in Douglas Allen's Group on Monetary Policy.[10]

And then, on Christmas Eve 1970, Fforde injected a sense of urgency into the proceedings when he produced, what he called, a 'curious and emotional note' on the subject.[11] It was put together after discussion with McMahon

[7] *Ibid.*
[8] Page to Fforde/O'Brien/Hollom, 'Credit control: finance houses and consumer credit', 1 May 1970, enc. 'Control of finance houses', 1 May 1970; Fforde to Hollom, 22 May 1970; Coleby to Page, 'Control of finance houses', 29 May 1970, enc. Peter Edgley, 'Control of finance houses overseas', 28 May 1970, 3A8/;. Willetts to Cooke, 'The legal basis for credit control', 2 June 1960; Wood to Thornton et al., 'Homogenising the banks', 12 June 1970; Page to Fforde, 3 July 1970, enc. 'Monetary policy: outline paper', 3 July 1970; 'Homogenisation', 15 July 1970; Page to Fforde, 'The future of credit control', 20 August 1970, 3A8/7; Willetts to McMahon et al., enc. Fforde draft, 'The future of credit control', 6 October 1970, 3A8/8.
[9] Page to O'Brien, 'Monetary policy: restraint on bank and finance house lending', 13 October 1970; Page to Allen, 14 October 1970, enc. Bank of England, 'Monetary policy: restraint on bank and finance house lending', 14 October 1970, 3A8/8.
[10] MP(70)16, 19 October 1970, 6A74/5.
[11] Fforde to O'Brien/Hollom, 'Banking system (and credit control)', 24 December 1970, 3A8/9.

and Page, but Fforde alone took responsibility for the specific proposals. He observed that by April 1971 the outside (non-clearing) banks 'will have been subjected to uninterrupted ceiling controls for longer than the second world war', while the clearers would celebrate an anniversary that was 'only slightly less miserable'. This was unacceptable, and the Bank should 'move onto the offensive' in changing the system. The Bank had hoped that Edward Heath's new Conservative Government would be receptive to a fresh approach, but Fforde claimed that the Treasury was 'nervous' and 'hostile' about anything that implied a less strict monetary policy, 'sceptical' about greater freedom of interest-rate policy, and 'anxious' in case their ministers were attracted by the prospect of greater competition. Thus Treasury officials had, according to Fforde, shown little inclination to push matters forward and indeed had made it pretty clear that they were happy to see the Bank's ideas put aside for a future review. From this, he concluded, the 'soft sell', step-by-step approach of the autumn would not suffice, and the Bank must now try a tougher 'hard sell'. Beyond this, he even favoured a public enquiry.[12]

Fforde then embarked on some 'abusive generalities', including the fact that the credibility of the Bank suffered when its repetition of complaints about the damaging effects of ceilings or the banks' cartel was not accompanied by action. Worse still was that the current situation was at odds with the Bank's 'fundamental and correct view' that the shape of the banking sector should not be 'notably subordinated to the requirements of monetary policy'. Banking was a 'legitimate commercial activity' that often 'inconveniences the Government of the day', but the 'temptation to convert the banks into mere slaves of official policy' had to be resisted. A usable defence for the present arrangements was that 'an emergency required emergency methods', but this vanished once it was admitted, and Fforde believed that it should be 'that the so-called emergency is more like the normal state of affairs'. After all, he observed:

> He who argues for fundamental change must, to some degree, be preaching a faith. If one does not believe that competition is capable of stimulating efficiency and innovation, then presumably one ought not to object to a permanent system of ceiling controls on banks. But if competition has any virtue, we ought not to have a system that stifles it.[13]

He then returned to his ideas for a uniform system of control of the banking system, elaborated seven months previously: some relaxation of the

---

[12] *Ibid.*
[13] *Ibid.*

cartel-rate agreements, reductions in the cash and liquidity ratios to 1½ and 12½ per cent, respectively, and use of special deposits.

All of this was in Fforde's highly characteristic style: sweeping, polemical, challenging, and with expansive rhetorical flourishes. It was undoubtedly the most important document he had written since joining the Bank in 1957 and arguably in his entire career. Five months later, a consultation paper was issued, and changes to the management of the gilt-edged market were implemented. Then, after another four months, the new policy – competition and credit control – became a reality. For a cautious institution, this might be considered almost reckless speed.

When Fforde had to turn his attention to the Rolls-Royce crisis (see Chapter 15), Crockett took over the work.[14] His opening premise was that 'Any device which inhibits competition between institutions in the banking system carries with it the danger of a misallocation of resources.' The network of imposed ceilings and the cartel were two such devices. In order to achieve the objective of a 'uniform, competitive banking system', several elements were proposed. First, ceiling controls on advances would end, and official approval of the cartel arrangements would be withdrawn. Second, a uniform 'Reserve Ratio' would apply to all institutions that wished to be regarded as banks, either a cash ratio set to a low level or a liquidity ratio of about 15 per cent. Third, restrictions would be placed on the activities of those institutions that did not want to be regarded as banks. Fourth, credit control would be achieved by variations in reserve ratios through calling special deposits and more flexible operations in the money and gilt-edged markets.[15]

The proposed timetable envisaged a general statement by the Chancellor in the 1971 budget, a period of negotiations with the banks before the prescribed ratios came into operation, and the formal removal of ceilings once it was clear that the new system was working. The 1972 budget was the target for completion of the transition period. Some such as Page were not convinced that this new regime had to be imposed straightaway, preferring instead to allow 'changes in banking practice to flow from changes in our techniques'. He also thought that the cash-deposits scheme was unfairly maligned and that it was 'idle to suppose' that a more competitive banking system and a high degree of restraint on bank lending could be achieved.

---

[14] 'A new approach to credit control and the banking system, draft synopsis', 8 January 1971; Crockett to Fforde/McMahon/Thornton/Page, 22 January 1971; 'Money market interest rates in the New Approach', 25 January 1971, 3A8/10; Fforde to O'Brien/Hollom, '"New approach" (Credit control and the banking sector)', 5 February 1971, enc. 'A new approach to credit control and the banking system', 3A8/11.

[15] 'A new approach to credit control and the banking system', 3A8/11.

Moreover, the possible alteration in technique to bring about changes in short-term interest rates without always moving Bank Rate first was a 'will of the wisp'.[16]

In drafting the paper, Crockett had paid considerable attention to the merits of a cash ratio versus a liquidity ratio. He argued that under the latter, when the authorities were seeking to restrain credit, a shortage of reserve assets would be created that would cause yields on those assets to be bid down. The banks, he thought, might find the prospect of being forced to hold 15 per cent of assets in low-earning form unacceptable. This seems a strange position for Crockett to adopt because special deposits had had that effect on the liquidity ratio since their introduction a decade before. The mechanism had not changed. It was designed to press on the liquidity ratio and so restrict credit and push interest rates upwards. In any case, Crockett preferred a cash ratio because he believed that it would be easier to negotiate with the banks, and he also claimed that it possessed benefits in terms of control. Fforde told the Governors that he and Page were not entirely convinced by Crockett's arguments on the cash ratio, and the version of the paper that was sent to the Treasury talked only of a reserve ratio.[17]

It is not surprising that the new approach was entirely the work of the Bank. It involved, after all, the main areas of its expertise. There was the operation of controls on lending, its knowledge of the City and its understanding of competition, its market skills in the gilt-edged and foreign-exchange markets, and its work on domestic credit expansion (DCE)/ monetary aggregates. There were also elements in the new approach, such as changes to the gilt market, that required complete secrecy (no problem for the Bank there). What is surprising is the lack of discussion with the Treasury. Any proposed changes on this scale might have been expected to have been the subject of close consultation with the Treasury over a long period. But it was not. It was only at a late stage that the Bank saw fit to inform the Treasury of its proposed changes. Indeed, so abrupt was the revelation that many in the Treasury have been left with impression that they knew nothing of the scheme until it was announced – it was simply dropped on them. For example, Lord Croham, who had been permanent Secretary at the Treasury, later recalled that he was not shown the paper before it went to the Chancellor and that none of his staff would have seen it without

---

[16] Page to Fforde, 'Credit control', 2 February 1971, 3A8/11.

[17] Crockett, 'The choice of ratios in the "new approach"', 3A8/10; Fforde to O'Brien/Hollom, "New approach" (Credit control and the banking sector)', 5 February 1971; Fforde to Allen, 12 February 1971, enc. 'A new approach to credit control and the banking system', 3A8/11.

telling him. He knew of no exchange that went on before that. And Frank Cassell, chief economic adviser in Home Finance at the time, wrote, 'I recall the "shock" of Competition and Credit Control in 1971. When the Treasury first received the draft of that document (there had been no prior discussion), we on the Home Finance side were quite thrown.'[18] Yet, from the files, it appears that the Bank had informed Treasury officials in January about the work that was going on, and Allen was sent six copies of the document on 12 February. A few weeks later, Allen said at a meeting with the Bank that a short note on the scheme would be submitted to the Chancellor.[19] Nonetheless, this was all late in the day by normal standards.

It is true that the Treasury was sceptical about certain elements, and it took some persuading. And time for discussion certainly was short: officials held only three recorded meetings on the subject before O'Brien wrote to the Chancellor outlining the proposals on 12 March.[20] The Treasury's main worry was whether control of monetary policy would be lost during the transition period. Indeed, the Bank's own assessment suggested that there would be a greater increase in bank advances than under continuing ceilings and that it might prove necessary to call for special deposits or adopt higher interest rates than were assumed in the financial forecasts. Figgures said that the latter could be 'very awkward for H.M.G.'[21] Critical here was the Bank's work on the stability of the demand for money function. This had not featured in any explicit way in the Fforde/Crockett drafting, but it was now fed into the debate. The paper on the quantitative implications of the new approach, given to the Treasury in early March, said that neither the overall stock of money nor its rate of growth had been affected by the imposition of ceilings. Although this did not mean that the removal of ceilings would have no impact, 'the likelihood is that it would induce a more pronounced change in the components of the money stock than in the aggregate'. McMahon's covering letter to Allen concluded that 'it does not look likely that anything like the theoretical possible expansion of credit under the new approach would occur if it were introduced'.[22] These arguments

[18] Interview with Lord Croham, 17 March 2008; Cassell, Private communication with author, 26 October 2008.
[19] Fforde to O'Brien, 13 January 1971; 'Extract from the Deputy Governor's memo dated 13.1.71 ... ', 3A8/10; Fforde to Allen, 12 February 1971, 3A8/11; D. A. Harding, 'Minutes of a meeting ... 9 February 1971 ... ', 1 March 1971, 3A8/12.
[20] O'Brien to Barber, 12 March 1971, 3A8/12.
[21] Fforde to O'Brien/Hollom, 'Budgetary measures and the "new approach"', 9 March 1971, 3A8/12.
[22] McMahon to Allen, 2 March 1971, enc. 'A new approach to credit control: some quantitative implications'; Harding, 'Minutes of a meeting ... 8 March 1971', 3A8/12.

proved decisive. As Goodhart later wrote, they were used to persuade the Treasury that controls on bank lending were a waste of time and that interest rates could be used instead, so paving the way for competition and credit control (CCC).[23]

Consultations were proposed, and following a meeting between the Governor and the Chancellor, a Treasury note recorded that the Governor had agreed that the Treasury should be 'directly involved in the discussions with the bankers'; alongside 'agreed', O'Brien wrote in 'to keep them (HMT) closely in touch!'[24] The Treasury was evidently keen to secure representation. The following week, O'Brien took exception to the wording in another Whitehall 'note for the record' when he added on the front, 'Kindly note that I did *not* agree to Treasury presence at any of the meetings with the banks.'[25] In these negotiations, there was going to be no dilution of accepted protocol, and O'Brien was a stickler for such things.

In the budget of March 1971, Barber announced that he wanted to see greater flexibility in the techniques of monetary control. There had been preparatory work in this area, he said, and the ideas would now be fully explored by the authorities, the banks, and the finance houses. Barber then referred to the Crowther Report on consumer credit, which had just been published, and rejected its call for the abandonment of hire-purchase controls. Finally, while the new ideas were being discussed, it would still be necessary to retain guidelines on bank lending; he said that this would be allowed to grow at a rate of 2½ per cent per quarter. Further details were given in a notice sent by the Bank to 96 associations and banks. Clearing banks were asked that their lending should not rise in the quarter to June 1971 by more than 7½ per cent of the March 1970 level. The same percentage was applied to finance houses, whereas the figure for other banks was 9½ per cent.[26]

In early March, the Governor was already tipping off Committee of London Clearing Banks (CLCB) representatives Forbes (chairman of Midland) and Eric Faulkner (chairman of Lloyds) that radical changes were possibly in the offing. O'Brien recorded, 'Characteristically, Mr. Faulkner's eyes lit up at the prospect of entering a more competitive era in the banking field.'[27] O'Brien embarked on another round of informal briefings with representatives of the

[23] Goodhart (2003, pp. 25–27).
[24] O'Brien, Annotation on Ryrie, 'Note for record', 16 March 1971, 3A8/12.
[25] O'Brien, Annotation, 26 March 1971, on Ryrie, 'Note for record', 25 March 1971, 3A8/12.
[26] HC Deb, 30 March 1971, Vol. 814, cc.1371–1374; Willetts to Fforde, 'Credit control notices', 29 March 1971; Bank of England, Notice – 'Bank and finance house lending', 30 March 1970, 3A8/12.
[27] O'Brien, Governor's note – 'New style credit control', 3 March 1971, 3A8/12.

various banking organisations, where he set out the nature of the changes that were planned. The day before the budget, O'Brien saw Forbes and Faulkner again. Forbes asked whether there would be implications for the gilt-edged market, but the Governor played a straight bat.[28] During the first two weeks of April, the Governor also met representatives of the Scottish clearers, the chairmen of the London Discount Market Association (LDMA), the Accepting Houses Committee, and the Finance Houses Association (FHA), as well as representatives of various foreign banks.[29] O'Brien's hope was that the Bank would issue its consultative document on 19 April.[30] The first draft was dated 22 March 1971, and it appears to have been the first occasion on which the phrase 'competition and credit control' was used,[31] even if in most correspondence the plans usually were referred to as 'the new approach'. The Bank, with some contribution from the Treasury, produced at least half a dozen versions of the consultation document, but despite O'Brien's intentions, the release was delayed by one month.[32]

Changes in Market Operations

The delay to the consultation paper mainly was a result of trying to settle the gilt-edged market aspect of the proposals. Between April and November 1970, Government Broker Peter Daniell had outlined several possible changes in the management of the gilts market, such as allowing a further widening of prices or rationing the amount of stock that the Issue Department would buy on any one day. None was felt to be workable either from an administrative point of view or because of the likely impact on the marketability of stocks. But Mullens also thought that other more fundamental options also were unattractive, notably removing government securities from the stock exchange and setting up of 'dealer

---

[28] Fforde to O'Brien/Hollom, 'The Governor's conversation with Sir A. Forbes and Mr. Faulkner on Monday, 29 March', 30 March 1971, 3A8/12.

[29] O'Brien, Governor's note – 'Credit control: new look', 1 April 1971; Hollom, Note for record – 'The new approach', 7 April 1971; Fforde, Note for record – '"The new approach" (Finance Houses Association)', 7 April 1971; Fforde, Note for record – '"The new approach" (Accepting Houses Committee)', 7 April 1971; Hollom, Note for record – 'The new approach', 14 April 1971 (two letters), C40/1482.

[30] 'Extract from the Deputy Governor's memo on the Governor's conversation with Sir Douglas Allen 24.3.71'; Fforde to O'Brien/Hollom, 'The Governor's conversation with Sir A. Forbes and Mr. Faulkner on Monday, 29 March', 30 March 1971, 3A8/12.

[31] Page to Fforde/O'Brien/Hollom, 'The new approach', 22 March 1971, 3A8/12.

[32] Harding, 'Minutes of a meeting … 26 March 1971', 30 March 1971, 3A8/12; 'Extract from the Deputy Governor's memo on the Governor's conversation with Mr.Neale 2.4.71', C40/1482.

organisations' along American lines. This, it was predicted, would lead to a drastic shortening of the length of debt.[33] Another concern was the image of the gilt-edged market. Price changes were becoming more 'violent', and the press were describing the market as a 'gambler's paradise'. Explanations included the introduction of capital gains tax (1965), after which insurance companies no longer engaged in 'anomaly switches', previously a stabilising influence on the market. The dealing strategy of the authorities had also played a part. Four main objectives were given by Daniell, of which three, an orderly market, the redemption of stock, and lengthening the maturity of the debt, were familiar enough. The fourth was new – 'to try to avoid increasing the money supply'. Daniell thought that Bank and Treasury sensitivities on this had taken precedence over maintenance of an orderly market. He went on to explain that before December 1968, the Bank normally would have been willing to deal at very close to the middle market price. Since the beginning of 1969, however, bidding had tended to be at a price well below middle market, and this had encouraged sales by institutional investors expecting to repurchase at considerably lower levels. As a result, there had been 'violent price fluctuations in response to comparatively minor occurrences'. Daniell wanted to see tactics modified with the aim of steadying price movements.[34] He recounted that between 1952 and 1958, only short-dated stocks were bought, although occasional bids were made if one of the big banks was a seller. The policy was continued in the period 1959–62, but 'bad bids' for stock were made when the market was 'overloaded'. This is what had happened in February 1960. Since 1962, the tactics of 'always being prepared to buy any stock offered gradually developed'. He argued that it appeared 'reasonable to revert, at any rate in some degree, to the policies prevailing before 1962 so as to avert "orders from on high" to abandon the Gilt Edged Market in toto'. There would be an inevitable contraction in the turnover of the market, but since much of this was speculative, Mullens felt this to be no bad thing. In more detail, various permutations were listed that involved never buying stock outright with a maturity of more than one year, switching freely but only to shorter stock, and being prepared to sell 'when prices were suitable and stock was wanted'. Variations included increasing the maturity limit to five years, buying if the seller was known to be a clearing bank, and switching in either direction but within specified parameters.[35]

[33] Mullens & Co., 'The market in British government stocks', 28 April 1970, 3A8/6.
[34] Peter Daniell to Page, 'Market management', 9 September 1970, 3A8/8.
[35] Mullens, 'Notes for possible alterations in our role in managing the gilt edged market', 6 November 1970, 3A8/9.

These ideas were discussed at a meeting between Fforde, Page, and Mullens in November 1970. Daniell and Gore Browne reiterated their view that fears about money supply and DCE in Whitehall would mean radical alterations to the market. They were determined to head this off rather than wait for the 'inevitable'. However, they were left with the suspicion that the Bank saw their proposals as 'too revolutionary or unnecessary'.[36] This was not the case. Fforde conceded that change in the management of the gilt-edged market might be required. He had in mind 'the restoration of discretionary buying operations, near-maturities excepted, in place of the present obligatory arrangement'. This undoubtedly would reduce marketability, but if the new arrangements were adopted, obligatory buying, at a price of the Bank's choosing, would be difficult to sustain: 'The freer the system … the more damaging would be the customary criticism whenever the gilt-edged market was falling and we were, in the normal course, buying in such stock as we were offered and inflating the money supply.'[37]

The starting point for Page's reassessment of techniques in January 1971 was that the damage done by ceasing to deal in gilts would considerably outweigh any benefits. To back this up, he appended a lengthy extract from O'Brien's November 1968 letter to the Treasury that had warned of the dangers of withdrawing from the market. Page then confessed to 'scepticism about the damage done to the desired course of economic developments which is seen by some to arise from short period changes in the rate of growth in the money supply'. He doubted that much harm was done by institutions 'temporarily liquifying' medium- and long-dated stocks because the Bank usually was able to resell them after quite a short period. However, Page was not dogmatic, admitting that he could be wrong about the money supply and that arguing for staying in the market did not mean that present techniques were 'immutable'. He admitted that the Bank's attempts to frustrate short-term operators through greater flexibility in pricing had, in part, only encouraged speculation because the market was more volatile. Personally, Page did not find this 'intolerable'. But if it was intolerable, and short-run fluctuations in the money supply were important; it did not follow, he argued, that the remedy was the complete abandonment of present technique. Taking Mullen's line, he wanted to 'examine the possibility of reverting to our pre-1962 mode of operation or something close thereto'.[38]

[36] Gore Browne, 'Notes on a meeting yesterday evening between Mr. Fforde, the Chief Cashier, T. A. G. B. and myself with reference to memorandum of the 6 November', 3A8/9.

[37] Fforde to O'Brien/Hollom, 'Banking system (and credit control)', 24 December 1970, 3A8/9.

[38] Page to O'Brien/Hollom, 'The gilt-edged market', 26 January 1971, C40/1481.

Mullens refined their ideas on the management of gilts in February 1971. The stated object was to be able to retain general control of the market so as to enable the present methods of redemption and issue to continue, but at the same time not to have to deal in large quantities of stock because of worries about the money supply, and also to avoid encouraging large-scale operators in the market. There were three elements to the plan. First, there would be no outright purchases of any stock with more than one year to run other than in exceptional circumstances at the discretion of the Bank. Second, outright sales would always be made when the price was suitable. Third, switching could take place in either direction 'always shorter, but longer only within definite maturity brackets'. Suggested bands were 0–5 years, 6–15 years, 16–25 years, 26 and over. Thus, for example, a 30-year stock always could be sold for a 10-year one, and a 10-year stock could always be sold for maturities of up to 9 years. The 10-year stock could also be switched into longer maturities, but only within its band, that is, up to 15 years. Daniell noted that it was hard to predict the impact on the markets, but it was likely that turnover would be reduced, debt held by the public probably would be shorter dated, and it would be more difficult for the Bank to control the rate of interest. Nevertheless, he continued, 'I see no reason why the market should not continue to be a good and active one', and critically, in the Government Broker's view, the buying-in of next maturities and the issue of stock could continue.[39]

Page agreed with Daniell and told the Governors that the proposals inhibited the ability of investors to move out of gilts by switching to near-maturing stocks. If such modifications were to be introduced, Page argued that this would have to happen immediately at the start of the consultation period with the banks on the new approach. On the timetable then envisaged, this meant early April.[40] Page explained that in order to improve the technique of continuous refinancing and to preserve the marketability of gilts, there had been an extension of official operations such that by 1962 'we were prepared to deal at a price whether in outright purchases or sales or by way of exchanges of one stock for another in the whole range of British Government securities.' The principal criticism of this technique was that it 'obliges the authorities to acquiesce in the monetisation of Government debt, thereby weakening domestic monetary policy'.[41] The new proposals were then outlined. Two key questions were raised when Fforde, McMahon, and Page went to the Treasury in March: was there likely

---

[39] Daniell to Page, 'Suggestions for alteration of Issue Department's role in the gilt edged market (with reference to out memorandum of the 6th November 1970', 3A8/11.
[40] Page to O'Brien/Hollom, 'Gilt-edged market', 12 March 1971, 3A8/12.
[41] Page to Painter, 18 March 1971, 3A8/12.

to be an 'undesirable effect' on the marketability of government debt? and would the changes give better control over the money supply? The Treasury also wanted to know if the rest of the new approach could be adopted without implementing the proposals for gilt-edged management. On the likely impact, the Bank took the Government Broker's view that there probably would be a shortening of the average maturity of the debt and that interest rates might well be higher. In terms of the money supply, the main advantage of the scheme was that it would remove the existing 'obligation' on the Bank to buy stock from the clearing banks. It was also essential to the new approach to credit control, which envisaged a more flexible use of special deposits, that the banks could not easily offload their gilts.[42]

In early April, there were some highly secret consultations involving the Bank, the Government Broker, and a few key participants in the market. Reactions ranged from shock to encouragement, and overall, the exercise was felt by the Bank to be invaluable.[43] The most significant discussions were those with the senior partners of the two principal gilt jobbing firms, Wedd Durlacher and Akroyd and Smithers. They found the Bank's proposals 'most disturbing', and they did not think that they would be able to operate for long under the new arrangements without running the risk of bankruptcy unless the authorities provided some form of escape clause. Hugh Merriman (Akroyd and Smithers) suggested a secret 'last resort' agreement under which the Bank would, if asked, take stock off the jobbers' books up to a certain maximum amount. Although Daniell was unconvinced by this particular arrangement, he was sure that it would be necessary to 'prop up the jobbers' in some way during the initial period.[44] O'Brien and Hollom told the Government Broker that they could not agree to the 'Merriman plan' but that the Bank might be prepared to consider some other form of assistance.[45] However, the safety net that followed looks remarkably like this suggestion.

These negotiations had focused attention on whether the Bank should continue to conduct its gilt-edged operations exclusively through jobbers in the stock exchange or make some move towards an American pattern of bond dealing. When consulted about the changes, Harry Goodson of

---

[42] Harding, 'Minutes ... 26 March 1971', 30 March 1971, 3A8/12.

[43] Mullens, 'Possible alteration of our role in the gilt edged market', 2 April 1971; Cooke, 'Official management of the gilt-edged market (Informal consultations about proposed modifications of technique', 5 April 1971; Fforde to O'Brien/Hollom, 'Gilt-edged market', 8 April 1971, C40/1482.

[44] Mullens, 'The gilt edged market', 7 April 1971; Merriman to Gore Browne, 8 April 1971; Fforde to O'Brien/Hollom, 'Gilt-edged market', 8 April 1971, C40/1482.

[45] Daniell, Note, 15 April 1971; Merriman to Daniell, 15 April 1971; Daniell to Gore Browne, 16 April 1971, C40/1482.

the LDMA had asked whether the discount houses would be able to deal directly with the Bank in stocks of less than 12 months. Fforde was enthusiastic, but he realised that it was a 'delicate area', and in any case, 'we cannot go from Stock Exchange to Over-the-Counter in a week.' Perhaps, he suggested, stocks under 12 months could be dealt through both the money market and the stock exchange.[46] Daniell was opposed and told Page that he was 'extremely unhappy' about the idea. Indeed, he thought that the purpose of any new arrangement was to avoid precisely such a thing happening. While there might be some logic in direct dealings for short maturities, he claimed that it would be difficult to restrict this to the discount houses. Denying any self-interest, Daniell insisted that the Bank must 'set their face firmly against direct dealings and should do their best to make the Gilt Edged Market in the Stock Exchange work.'[47] Two days later, Daniell reported that the Governors had 'thrown out any suggestion of an American type market', although he added that significantly Fforde, who was still 'somewhat enamoured of this idea', was not present at the meeting.[48]

When Page briefed the Governors in April, he made five points. First, in general, there was a strong case for a significant change in the scale of intervention in the gilt-edged market. Second, immediate introduction of the proposals would be not so much a modification of technique as 'the creation of a substantially different gilt-edged market'. Third, while a different market might be an advantage, it was not at present an aim of the Bank. Fourth, it appeared that it would be necessary to provide more support to the market than allowed in the original proposals in order to avoid disruption and a restriction of marketability. Finally, he reiterated that Merriman's plan was not acceptable because it limited the Bank's room for manoeuvre each day. However, the Bank did need to provide the two main jobbers with a 'stop-large-loss' arrangement, and Page outlined the basis of an understanding whereby each morning the Bank would indicate the volume of stock and the minimum price that it would, if necessary, be prepared to take outright from the jobbers at the close of business. In addition, there would be a financial facility, either an advance or a sale and repurchase arrangement. Other elements included some discretion on switching, a possible reversion to announced tap prices, and an undertaking by the jobbers to disclose, daily if required, the state of their books to the Bank. All this would be subject to review after a transitional period of three months. Much of this had, in fact, been suggested by the Government Broker. Page wanted to add

---

[46] Fforde to O'Brien/Hollom, 'Gilt-edged market', 8 April 1971, C40/1482.
[47] Daniell to Page, 14 April 1971, C40/1482.
[48] Daniell to Gore Browne, 16 April 1971, C40/1482.

something further to the paragraph on gilts in the consultation document. 'As you know', he told the Governors:

I remain unrepentantly sceptical about some of the monetary policy arguments for changes we propose. I am, however, more and more attracted by the argument that lesser intervention on the part of the authorities in the gilt-edged market is philosophically an appropriate companion to lesser intervention on the part of the authorities in the banking system.

If banks were freer to conduct their business, he continued, then investors also should be freer to carry out their transactions without market interference from the authorities.[49]

On the same day, Hollom, Fforde, Page, and the brokers discussed the paper and generally were content with the line adopted.[50] The next day, Page told the Treasury that the proposals would help to maintain the marketability of gilts. He explained why the consultative document now made reference to the general desirability for the authorities to reduce their intervention in the market, and he hoped that it would entice new traders to enter the market. In something of an admission, Page stated, 'We have some reason for believing that our greater intervention since 1962 has had some atrophying effect on the market and that lessening intervention by us, if orderly and not too abrupt, will encourage others to come in.' A safety net would be offered through 'a confidential indication on our part to the two main jobbers that our withdrawal from outright purchases of stocks other than next maturities was not total'. At least over the next three months, the Bank generally would be prepared to buy small amounts up to a specified limit and at 'very penal prices'. This would provide an escape route for the jobbers if they felt that continuing to deal would expose them to large risks. In addition, jobbers were offered small 'last resort' facilities in the form of borrowing for seven days at Bank Rate.[51]

At the same time, the implications for the discount market were also being considered. In the 1960s, the Bank had seen the arrangements – the syndicate bid and covering the tender – as an administrative convenience and something that gave the Bank influence over the Treasury bill rate. Rodney Galpin, Deputy Principal of the Discount Office, thought

[49] Page to O'Brien/Hollom, 'Gilt-edged market', 19 April 1971, C40/1482.
[50] Hollom to O'Brien, 19 April 1971, C40/1482.
[51] Page to Robert Painter (HMT), 20 April 1971, C40/1482. See also, Draft 'The new approach: the gilt-edged market', 4 May 1971, 3A8/13. For more on borrowing facilities for jobbers, see C40/1410 and 1411.

that it should be possible to continue with this under the new approach.[52] Hollom was not convinced; in fact, he did not think that the Bank should do anything to encourage maintenance of the syndicate.[53] This aside, the proposals for the banks, particularly proposals relating to eligible assets, would have an impact on activities in the discount market, and the Bank wanted to be able to exert some control. Page's suggestion was that the discount houses should observe some form of 'public sector debt ratio'. There would be two elements: (1) 12½ per cent of non-bank funds to be invested in public-sector debt, with an acceptance of special deposits, to be placed with the Bank at whatever rate was called for the rest of the banking system, based on this part of their funds and (2) a certain proportion, say, 50 to 65 per cent, of bank-borrowed funds also to be invested in the same way. It was felt that this would be consistent with the treatment of the rest of the banking system, would counterbalance the inclusion of money at call with the discount houses as an eligible reserve for banks, and would prevent the discount market from employing 100 per cent of any increase in call money in commercial bills or certificates of deposit.[54] These ideas were developed during April and May, again in conjunction with the Treasury, and set out in a document that was presented to the LDMA as a basis for consultation. As part of the negotiating strategy, the percentages that the Bank had in mind for the holdings of public-sector debt were not mentioned.[55]

CCC Unveiled

At 3:30 p.m. on Friday, 14 May 1971, 'Competition and Credit Control' was published. Sometimes referred to as a 'green paper', it actually was a

[52] Galpin to Keogh/Page, 'A new approach to credit control and the banking system. The discount market', 25 March 1971, 7A97/1.

[53] Hollom, Annotation, 30 March 1971, on Page to Fforde/O'Brien/Hollom, '"The new approach": the discount market', 26 March 1971, 3A8/12.

[54] Page to Fforde/O'Brien/Hollom, '"The new approach": the discount market', 26 March 1971, 3A8/12.

[55] Cooke to Painter, 8 April 1971; Page to O'Brien/Hollom, 'The new approach: the discount market', 29 April 1971, C40/1482; Page to Painter, 4 May 1971, enc. Bank of England, 'Competition and credit control: the discount market', May 1971; Douglas Henley (HMT) to Page, 6 May 1971; Page to Fforde/O'Brien/Hollom, 'The new approach: the discount market', 6 May 1971; O'Brien to HF Goodson, 14 May 1971; Bank of England, 'Competition and credit control: the discount market', May 1971, 3A8/13. Public-sector debt: British government Treasury bills, local authority bills and bonds, British government and local authority stocks with not more than five years to maturity.

Bank consultation document and not part of the government legislative process. A meeting of jobbers was also called where the Government Broker explained personally the changes that were to be made to the Bank's dealings in the gilt-edged market. Daniell finished with a plea for co-operation to make the new system work. If not, then he warned that an alternative might be developed, and that, he said, 'cannot be a good thing for us in this room'.[56]

The Bank sent out around 150 letters, enclosing copies of the consultation document, to central banks, banks, and banking organisations.[57] This outlined the proposals whereby existing liquidity and quantitative controls on lending would be replaced and at the same time the clearing banks' agreements on interest rates would be abandoned. It was explained that monetary policy techniques would 'involve less reliance on particular methods of influencing bank and finance house lending and more reliance on changes in interest rates, supported by calls for Special Deposits on the basis of a reserve asset ratio across the whole of the banking system'. Similar arrangements would apply for deposit-taking finance houses. The two key elements were that all banks should 'hold not less than a fixed percentage of their sterling deposit liabilities in certain specified reserves assets', and they should 'place such amount of Special Deposits with the Bank of England as the Bank may call from time to time'. According to the document, the observance of the minimum reserve assets ratio would 'provide the authorities with a known firm base for the operation of monetary policy'. The composition of the reserve ratio, which it was proposed would be set at 12½ per cent, was outlined, and it was noted that there would need to be discussion with the London clearing banks about the level of bankers' balances within this. Changes in gilt-edged operations were to have immediate effect, the Bank would 'no longer be prepared to respond to requests to buy stock outright' apart from those with one year or less to run, the Bank reserved the right to purchase stocks with more than one year to run 'solely at their discretion and initiative', the Bank would be prepared to undertake exchanges of stock 'at prices of their own choosing' except where this would 'unduly shorten the life of the debt', and the Bank be prepared to respond to bids for tap and other stocks that it might wish to sell. These modifications represented a return to the position that the Bank occupied in the market 'some

---

[56] Daniell, 'Announcement to jobbers of proposed new gilt edged methods', 5 May 1971, 3A8/13.
[57] Bank of England, 'Competition and credit control', May 1971; letters to various organisations in 3A8/13.

10 years ago'.[58] O'Brien emphasised that the basic aim of the system was that 'the allocation of credit is primarily determined by its cost'.[59]

The immediate impact on the gilt-edged market, as expected, was some sharp falls in the week following the announcement. Press comment attributed much of this to the market trying to digest the changes – the market was operating 'in the dark, or rather in the grey light of an unpleasant dawn'.[60] On the wider proposals there was apparently little scope for entertaining newspaper headlines. Only the *Sun* with 'Battling Banks to Bid for Your Wallet' and *The Economist*'s 'Yes, at Last, Revolution for the City' injected much excitement into the new era of competition. Although opinion was mixed, there was a consensus that the proposals were a milestone. *The Economist* claimed that British financial history had been made, whereas *The Times* went so far as to suggest that it was 'the most important paper that any banker is likely to read in his working lifetime' and arguably on a par with Radcliffe.[61]

Academics and other economists were given the opportunity to discuss the CCC proposals when 50 were invited to the Bank in June for a seminar of the Money Study Group. One of those present, John Wadsworth, economist at the Midland Bank, commented that this was 'the first time for over 250 years that the Bank had consulted anyone'. An exaggeration maybe, but it was one of the first occasions when external professional economists had debated policy within the Bank. With so many present, views were predictably diverse; it was a step in the right direction, a compromise, a mix of ideas with escape routes for the Bank, strong action would be avoided, ceilings inevitably would reappear, and everyone had their own favoured reserve ratio. Although there was plenty of criticism of the proposals, the seminar was deemed to be a success. For most of the participants, it was the first time they had set foot in the Bank, and McMahon believed that it had created a favourable impression.[62]

Out of all the discussion at the seminar, however, two important subjects can be identified. One was the reserve ratio and the other the gilt market. At one extreme, there were those who would have preferred to do without

58 Bank of England, 'Competition and credit control', May 1971, 3A8/13. Also reproduced in *BEQB* 11(2):189–193, June 1971.
59 O'Brien 'Key issues in monetary and credit policy' address at the International Banking Conference, Munich, 28 May 1971, 3A8/14.
60 *The Daily Telegraph*, 18 May 1971, p. 17.
61 *The Economist*, 22 May 1971, pp. 70–75; *The Times*, 17 May 1971, p. 18.
62 McMahon to O'Brien, 'Seminar on competition and credit control', 1 July 1971; Tony Latter and Lionel Price, 'Money Study Group seminar on competition and credit control, Oak Room, 15 June 1971', 29 June 1971, 3A8/17.

the ratio and rely wholly on open market operations, perhaps with the help of special deposits (most were content with retaining the latter). But if there were to be a ratio, there were those who advocated a narrower one (Griffiths) and those who would have gone for a cash ratio (Newlyn and Parkin). The Bank fully accepted that with any ratio there would be transitional and prudential problems but that the cost and difficulty of getting to a ratio (unspecified) would not be too severe for most banks. However, a cash ratio was out of the question. They knew that it would work but were not prepared to face the upheaval it would entail. It would require huge changes in money-market and discount-house practices. They were not prepared to be that revolutionary and were satisfied that the proposed ratio would work like a cash ratio.

As far as the gilt market was concerned, the strong view was that success hinged on this (Newlyn) but that the system could not survive monetary and fiscal policy pulling in different directions (Oppenheimer) – something that was beyond the ability of the Bank to affect. Pepper argued that the gilt market was going to have to neutralise changes in money supply that resulted from both domestic and overseas transactions. Given the openness of the British economy, this was asking a lot. Furthermore, the market would have to accommodate the whims of the Bank as monopoly issuer of stock. He concluded that the market could not do all this on its own and would need assistance from other techniques. Aggressive open market operations, he said, would produce disorderly markets, something his long experience told him the Bank would not tolerate. The seminar was unlikely to result in any changes to the scheme, but it might have alerted the Bank to some possible dangers that lay ahead.[63]

Between May and September 1971, the Bank also undertook extensive consultations with all the main banking associations and a number of individual banks as well. Agreement with the discount houses was soon concluded. The LDMA would still cover the weekly Treasury bill tender, but the syndicated bid would be abolished. Instead, there would be a minimum underwriting price with houses free to apply for bills at any price above this, and they would also have to tender for at least their allocated quota. The discount-market consultation paper had envisaged that there would be two minimum public-sector debt ratios, but Fforde told market representatives that if the proportions of the market's bank and non-bank borrowed funds remained unchanged, then a single ratio might be acceptable.[64] By the end of

---

[63]   *Ibid.*
[64]   Galpin, Note for record – 'The new approach: the discount market', 20 May 1971; Tom Hohler (King & Shaxson) to Keogh, 26 May 1971, 3A8/14; Goodson to Galpin, 28 June

July, the new arrangements for the discount market had been settled. Each house would agree on a day-to-day basis to hold public-sector debt of not less than 50 per cent of its total borrowed funds. The LDMA would still cover the Treasury bill tender, and in return, the Bank would continue to confine lender-of-last-resort facilities to the discount market. Finally, the houses agreed that they would not knowingly engage in transactions with the banks for the purposes of 'window dressing'. All this was confirmed in an exchange of letters, and it was also made public in a paper issued by the Bank.[65]

Despite assurances from the London clearers that they were anxious to comply, progress was slow, and Forbes proved difficult.[66] The CLCB felt that aspects of the new approach 'discriminated' against them: qualitative guidance still might be given; their ability to compete with building societies and savings banks might be restricted; cash in tills was excluded from reserve assets, as was another currently liquid asset, fixed-rate export and shipbuilding credit; only 2 per cent of eligible bills could be counted as reserve assets; and 2 per cent of eligible liabilities were required to be held at the Bank, interest-free, as bankers' balances. Above all, there was the Bank's proposal to issue government stocks to deal with the existing special deposits and the excess liquidity of the banks.[67]

The Bank was unwilling to widen the definition of the reserve asset ratio, as the clearers wanted, because this would leave liquidity too high: based on the figures for July, the inclusion of cash in tills would add 5.5 per cent and fixed-rate lending another 4.4 per cent.[68] However, it was agreed to reduce the bankers' balances to an average of 1½ per cent of eligible liabilities.[69] The question of funding had the capacity to scupper the entire venture. As O'Brien was told by Page, 'we shall not be able to secure the Treasury's or the

1971, 3A8/16; Page to O'Brien, 'Direct dealings in gilt-edged with the discount market', 15 July 1971, 3A8/17; Page to Goodson, 29 July 1971, 3A8/18.

[65] Page to Goodson, 29 July 1971, 3A8/18; reply 9 August 1971, 3A8/19; Page to Fforde/ O'Brien/Hollom, 'New approach: discount market', 5 July 1971; Galpin to Page/O'Brien/ Hollom, 'Discount market: new arrangements', 1 July 1971, 3A8/17; Page to O'Brien, 'Competition and credit control. The discount market', 20 July 1971, 3A8/18.

[66] Page to O'Brien/Hollom, 'The new approach: clearing banks', 28 May 1971, 3A8/14; 'Extract from Mr. Fforde's memo dated 23.6.71 on the Deputy Governor's conversation with Mr. Rawlinson'; Hollom, Note for record – 'The new approach – clearing banks', 29 June 1971, 3A8/16; Page to O'Brien/Hollom, 'Competition and credit control. Clearing banks', 8 July 1971; 'Extract from Mr. McMahon's note on the Governor's conversation with Mr. Neale 16.7.71', 3A8/17.

[67] Page, Note for record – 'Competition and credit control. Clearing banks', 13 July 1971, 3A8/17.

[68] Page to O'Brien, 'Competition and credit control. Some outstanding points', 16 July 1971, 3A8/17.

[69] Page to O'Brien/Hollom, 'The clearing banks', 3 August 1971, 3A8/19.

Chancellor's agreement to introducing the new arrangements unless we can show that the capacity of the Clearing Banks in the form of reserve assets to expand credit is fairly limited.'[70] But Forbes complained to O'Brien that the funding proposals meant that for the first time the Bank would be intervening directly in the clearers' investment policy in gilts. The Governor disputed this, arguing that the Bank was 'merely seeking to clear the decks for the new deal', as had been done in 1951 (the occasion on which market holdings of Treasury bills were reduced by the issue of £1,000 million of 1¾% Serial Funding Stocks). O'Brien stressed to Forbes that Whitehall would only agree to the new scheme provided that the banks did not 'start out with a mass of excess liquidity'.[71] Data presented by the CLCB showed that compared with the proposed 12½ per cent minimum, reserve assets in July 1971 were 16.6 per cent (£1,752 million). Allowing for other gilts that would move into the reserve asset category during July, it therefore would be necessary to fund some £360 million in order to reduce the reserve asset position to 15 per cent, a figure felt by the Bank to be more acceptable. In addition, special deposits of £392.5 million were outstanding. Thus the Bank and the clearers settled on £750 million as the total amount to be funded.[72] These figures were passed to the Treasury, and it was agreed to put the matter to the Chancellor.[73] When the Governor and the Chancellor met in August, Barber said that he would be in a position to make an announcement on 10 September.[74]

Some questions remained to be resolved with other banks. Scottish clearers argued that their historical development and distinctive features, together with regional economic factors, warranted modifications to the proposals. The main complaints were about the reserve asset ratio and that special deposits were to be universal with no lower rate for the Scots. On eligible assets, the Scots were upset that Bank of England notes held as backing for Scottish notes would not count, and neither would 'cheques in course of collection', usually regarded as liquid in Scotland.[75] The initial response from

---

[70] Page to O'Brien, 'London clearing banks: funding', 27 July 1971, 3A8/18.

[71] Hollom, Note for record – 'The Governor's conversation with Sir Archibald Forbes', 3 August 1971, 3A8/19; Fforde (1992, pp. 402–406); Bank of England, 'Some features of monetary history', para. 7; Radcliffe, 'Memoranda', Vol. 1.

[72] Page to Fforde/O'Brien/Hollom, 'Competition and credit control. Clearing banks: funding', 13 August 1971; 'Extract from Deputy Governor's note for record on the Governor's conversation with Mr. Neale 13.8.71', 3A8/19.

[73] Fforde to Henley, 16 August 1971; HMT, 'Note of a meeting … 17 August [1971] …'; Wood, Note for record – 'New approach: meeting at H.M.T. 17.8.71', 18 August 1971, 3A8/19; Henley to Fforde, 19 August 1971.

[74] Ryrie, Note for the record, 24 August 1971, 3A8/20.

[75] Committee of Scottish Clearing Bankers, 'Note of meeting between the Committee of Scottish Clearing Bankers and the Chief Cashier of the Bank of England held at the Bank of

Page was not encouraging, and this resulted in further pleadings, including a private letter from Lord Polwarth, Governor of the Bank of Scotland, to O'Brien citing the writings of Sir Walter Scott. The Bank was adamant that the fears were exaggerated. Nonetheless, O'Brien did send a slightly placatory letter that held out the prospect of 'some alleviation' in relation to special deposits.[76] The Scots did not let up in their campaign, pressing the Bank to allow some leeway on the one purely Scottish feature, the note issue. They flatly denied being the source of newspaper stories suggesting that the Scottish bank notes were under threat from CCC.[77] One concession examined by the Bank was to allow an increase in the Scottish fiduciary issue, which had remained fixed since the Bank Notes (Scotland) Act of 1845, but this would require specific legislation and might be controversial. A simpler option, and one that Fforde congratulated the Cashier's Department for discovering, was the abolition of stamp duty on the note issue, worth about £600,000 per annum. This could be done with less publicity through a clause in the Finance Act. It proved a sufficient attraction to obtain agreement from the Scottish clearers at the beginning of September.[78]

Similar problems were encountered with the Northern Ireland banks.[79] Admittedly, the political and economic situation in the province was highly sensitive, but Page thought that at the very least the Northern Irish banks should agree in principle that it was appropriate for them to come within the framework.[80] Fforde, who had close Northern Ireland connections, travelled to Belfast in the latter half of August and told representatives of

England, London, on Friday, 11 June 1971', 3A8/15; Page, Note for record – 'Competition and credit control. Scottish banks', 26 July 1971, 3A8/18; Saville (1996, pp. 696–697).

[76] Page to Burke (chairman, CSCB), 6 July 1971, 3A8/17; Lord Polwarth (Governor, Bank of Scotland) to O'Brien, 28 July 1971 (two letters). Polwarth referred to Scott's 'Letters of Malachi Malagrowther', which protested about English plans to withdraw notes below £5 in value in Scotland, 3A8/18; Page to O'Brien/Hollom, 'The Scottish and Northern Irish banks', 4 August 1971; 'Extract from the Deputy Governor's memo dated 4.8.71 on the Governor's conversation with Sir Archibald Forbes and Mr. Faulkner', O'Brien to Polwarth, 5 August 1971 (two letters), 3A8/19.

[77] Polwarth to O'Brien, 10 August 1971; Page, Note for record – 'Competition and credit control. Scottish banks', 13 August 1971; James Ogilvy Blair-Cunynghame (chairman, Royal Bank of Scotland) to O'Brien, 17 August 1971, 3A8/19.

[78] Cooke to O'Brien/Hollom, 'Competition and credit control. Scottish banks', 24 August 1971, with Fforde annotation; enc. on 'Scottish banks' note issue', nd; Cooke to Henley, 25 August 1971, 3A8/20; Cooke to Fforde/O'Brien/Hollom, 'Competition and credit control. Scottish banks', 1 September 1971; CSCB, 'Note of a meeting of chairmen and chief executives of the Scottish clearing banks with the Governor of the Bank of England held at the Bank of England on 2 September, 1971'; Burke to O'Brien, 7 September 1971, 3A8/21.

[79] David Russell (Chairman, NIBA) to O'Brien, 16 July 1971, 3A8/17.

[80] Page to O'Brien/Hollom, 'The Scottish and Northern Irish banks', 4 August 1971, 3A8/18; O'Brien to Russell, 11 August 1971, 3A8/19.

the Northern Ireland Bankers' Association that the Bank recognised the special problems of the area, and it did not want to impose the system on the banks but that they could not be just left out of scheme. He was able to secure agreement to a reserve asset ratio, with the details to be settled after further consideration.[81]

Negotiations with the finance houses were the most protracted, starting almost immediately after publication of the consultation document. The FHA had several objections. It was worried about a uniform application of the 12½ per cent reserve assets ratio to finance houses whose balance sheets may not have to employ the defined assets. There was also wariness about the scheme's emphasis on deposit taking, something that was not applicable to all finance houses. Moreover, if finance houses were to be treated as banks for the purposes of credit control, then they should also be counted as banks for the purposes of the Protection of Depositors Act, with the dispensations this gave. While the Bank was happy to see a move in this direction, the Treasury and the Department of Trade and Industry were reluctant.[82] Some concessions were offered. The arrangements would apply only to FHA members whose total deposit liabilities were greater than £5 million, and notwithstanding 'unresolved problems', these houses would be accorded the status of banks. The level of the reserve ratio also might be up for discussion, although Page warned that the Bank would retain the right to apply special deposits at a different rate as well.[83] The FHA still thought it unreasonable that its members should have to run a loss by holding reserve assets to the same extent as banks and suggested that 7½ per cent would be a more suitable figure. Fforde responded with an offer of 10 per cent.[84] Eventually, 16 finance houses opted to subject themselves to the 10 per cent reserve asset ratio.[85]

[81] Fforde to O'Brien/Hollom, 'New approach: Northern Ireland', 24 August 1971; Fforde to Henley, 26 August 1971, 3A8/20; A. A. Ketley (Secretary, NIBA) to Fforde, 1 September 1971, 3A8/21.

[82] Malcolm Wilcox (chairman, FHA) to O'Brien, 17 May 1971; Fforde to O'Brien/Hollom, 'F.H.A. and the new approach (progress report)', 27 May 1971, 3A8/14; Peter Filmer, 'Meeting with the Finance Houses Association, Friday, 4 June 1971', 11 June 1971; Wilcox to Fforde, 14 June 1971, 3A8/15; Page to O'Brien, 'Competition and credit control. Progress report', 8 July 1971; Henley to Page, 14 July 1971, 3A8/17.

[83] Page to O'Brien, 'Competition and credit control. Finance houses', 30 July 1971; Page to Wilcox, 30 July 1971, 3A8/18.

[84] Wilcox to Page, 6 August 1971, 3A8/19; Stephen Clarke (EID), 'Meeting with the Finance Houses Association. Wednesday, 11 August 1971', 20 August 1971, 3A8/20.

[85] Ryrie, Note for the record, 24 August 1971; Fforde to Wilcox, 27 August 1971, 3A8/20; G. A. Cooke (vice-chairman, FHA) to Fforde, 2 September 1971; J. B. Damer (Secretary, FHA) to Fforde, 23 September 1971, 3A8/21.

The discussions with these other organisations were critical in order that the Bank could secure its desired uniform system. It was largely successful. There may have been grumbles that local peculiarities were of little interest in London, but as Hollom noted in the case of the Scots, they simply could not have freedom of manoeuvre 'whatever may be going on in the rest of the U.K.'[86] Above all, it was vital that the co-operation of the CLCB was gained, and this meant keeping everyone else in line. As O'Brien told Goldman in August, he did not want to make a concession to Scots because the London clearers would want this to be matched for them.[87] However, with agreement finally reached with everyone else, on 7 September 1971, the CLCB sent the letter that contained its own acceptance of the new scheme.[88]

The way then was clear for the scheme to proceed. On 10 September 1971, the Bank issued notices explaining the change in techniques, together with a paper, 'Reserve Ratios and Special Deposits', that clarified the modifications to the basic scheme that had been agreed. The 28 per cent liquidity ratio was replaced by a 12½ per cent minimum reserve asset ratio comprising balances held at the Bank (1½ per cent for the clearers), Treasury bills, company tax reserve certificates, money at call, British government stocks with one year or less to maturity, and local authority and commercial bills eligible for discount at the Bank (the former limited to a maximum of 2 per cent of eligible liabilities). In effect, this amounted to a reduction and re-specification of the previous liquidity ratio: the inclusion of till money and other previously accepted liquid assets would have given a ratio of 22 per cent. The changes came into effect on 16 September 1971.[89] Thus a new regime had been set out in a consultative document and agreed and introduced in a period of only four months – and on an entirely voluntary basis. *The Economist*, while welcoming what it thought was a 'banking revolution', observed, 'It really is worth remarking that this radical change of Britain's whole internal financial system … has not been the subject of a single clause of legislation. Parliament has barely discussed it. It has all been fixed up as a gentlemen's agreement in private conclaves in the City.'[90]

---

[86] Hollom to O'Brien, 'The Scottish banks', 11 August 1971, 3A8/19.
[87] 'Extract from the Deputy Governor's note on the Governor's conversation with Sir Samuel Goldman 11.8.71', 3A8/19.
[88] Forbes to O'Brien, 7 September 1971, 3A8/21.
[89] O'Brien to Barber, 8 September 1971, and reply, 5A148/1; Bank of England, Press notice and notice – 'Credit control – the new approach', both 10 September 1971, 3A8/21; 'Reserve ratios and special deposits', September 1971. Further definitions were given in December 1971, 'Reserve ratios: further definitions', *BEQB* 11(4):482–489, December 1971.
[90] *The Economist*, 18 September 1971, p. 69.

CCC in Operation

In the period following the introduction of CCC, there was much reflection on what had been achieved and how it was working. There was also much more explicit discussion of monetary policy. This would not surprise a modern student of the subject, who would doubtless feel that the proximate cause of the renewed interest would have been the adoption of a floating exchange rate in the middle of 1972 and the new freedom this gave for the pursuit of an independent monetary policy. However, there was no such discussion at the time either in the Treasury or in the Bank. For one thing, it was not clear or accepted that there was a floating rate, and the immediate intention was to return to a fixed/pegged rate. For another, the theoretical position was not one that was widely embraced.

However, attention had shifted to the money stock. As Fforde expressed it, in 1971 they had thrown out the old and the simple. Gone were the ceilings, and controls on consumer credit were suspended. The banking cartel was abolished, and support for the gilt-edged market was largely withdrawn. 'Another feature … was our apparent adoption of the wider-definition money stock (M3, published monthly) as the one new simple aim in substitution for those we had discarded.' He wanted monetary policy to be stated more clearly and to be 'less exclusively related to a particular definition of the money stock itself' but rather to a variety of indicators and other data.[91] He felt that the Deputy Governor's speech to the Lombard Association had made a start in this direction. What Hollom had said, in classic Hollom style, was that while CCC allowed interest rates a greater role and shifted attention to broader monetary aggregates, the relationships that held in the past had broken down in 1972. The previous year's rise in M3 had been 26 per cent. A large rise in M3 could be a cause of inflation or a symptom or perhaps a bit of both, he argued. 'We in the Bank believe that in the circumstances of today, some form of incomes policy may have a part to play.… monetary policy is one of a number of influences.'[92] Thus there was not really much change from the old days there. Fforde went on to argue that selective credit controls therefore must come on the agenda. He finished by complaining about the existing institutional arrangements – the 'curious ladder of contacts between Treasury and Bank, with varying degrees of vertical communication and control at various stages, and varying semblances of group work.' He thought that the Chief Cashier should produce a note on this.[93] Page duly

---

[91] Fforde to O'Brien /Hollom, 'Monetary Policy', 27 March 1973, 6A50/8.
[92] Hollom speech on 11 April 1973, *BEQB* 13(2):201, June 1973.
[93] Fforde to O'Brien/Hollom, 'Monetary policy', 27 March 1973, 6A50/8.

did, agreeing with Fforde's analysis and bemoaning the fact that politicians had been too influential – 'so that the decisions have not always appeared to be rational'.[94] Minimum lending rate (MLR) was adopted to avoid Bank Rate being frozen by ministers. But Treasury officials were complicit in the political presentational requirements placed on them and then left the Bank to take whatever criticism followed.

While the new approach saw a greater role for more flexible use of interest rates, including Bank Rate, with special deposits and open market operations used in support, at the time CCC was introduced, it remained unresolved how this flexibility would be achieved.[95] One difficulty was that since Radcliffe, although the Bank made all the running, alterations in Bank Rate had been made with the formal approval of the Chancellor. The Bank was keen to escape from this, and by the end of 1971, a suggestion was that Bank Rate changes might be divided into two distinct categories: those related to shifts in policy, which would still require involvement of the Chancellor; and technical adjustments judged necessary by the Bank for the purposes of market operations. A danger foreseen was that the Treasury might start to take too much interest in day-to-day money-market operations. There was little progress with the idea, and by the summer of 1972, the Bank regarded the proposal as dead, the Chancellor feeling unable to relinquish any responsibility for Bank Rate changes, however small.[96]

Monetary conditions, however, helped to revive the idea. Money growth in the first half of 1972 was extremely rapid. M3 increased by 4.5 per cent in the first quarter and 7.5 per cent in the second quarter.[97] Bank Rate had been raised from 5 to 6 per cent in June 1972 at the time sterling floated, and the Bank soon was advocating another rise, to 7 per cent. Reportedly, the Prime Minister was completely against such a move. In August, Page came up with two possibilities. The first was for the Bank to operate entirely through its Treasury bill prices, leaving Bank Rate to lapse into disuse, but he discounted this because he was 'very chary of putting Bank Rate in the museum'.[98] The

---

[94] Page to O'Brien /Hollom, 2 April 1973, 6A50/8.
[95] 'Competition and credit control: further developments', *BEQB* 13(1):51–55, March 1973. The Northern Ireland issue was resolved in September 1972; see Hollom to David Russell (chairman, Northern Ireland Bankers' Association), 17 May 1972; Russell to Hollom, 19 June 1972, 3A8/23; Hollom to Russell, 3 July 1972; Russell to Hollom, 19 September 1972, 3A8/24.
[96] Page to Fforde/O'Brien/Hollom, 'Money market management: Bank rate', 22 December 1971; Page to Henley, 26 January 1972; Page to Fforde/O'Brien/Hollom, 'Bank Rate', 17 August 1972, C40/1392.
[97] *BEQB* 13(1):90, March 1973.
[98] Page to Fforde/O'Brien/Hollom, 'Bank rate', 17 August 1972, C40/10.

alternative was for a 'floating' Bank Rate, with the rate linked to a market rate, most obviously that for Treasury bills, and allowed to fluctuate with it, although step changes at the initiative of the Bank were not ruled out. Page professed that at one stage he had found a floating Bank Rate attractive but had since changed his view because it left the market without a guide, and there were the constitutional implications. Overall, he thought that both options were 'little more than devices, without great technical merit, for getting round the problem that Ministers are reluctant to change [the] Bank Rate'.[99] For the moment, he preferred to stick to Bank Rate.

Over the next few months, ministers, and especially the Prime Minister, continued to refuse to countenance a rise to 7 per cent because of the perceived political impact it would have. Inflation was running at an annual rate of 7.2 per cent. The Bank was worried that politicians' fears would result in it being stuck with an inoperative rate. Indeed, in early September 1972, the Treasury bill rate moved above Bank Rate. Treasury officials did accept the need for an increase, and officials held further discussions on a means of 'de-fusing' the significance given to Bank Rate. Despite Page's earlier qualms, floating was back on the agenda, with the rate to be set automatically under a formula based on the average rate of discount for Treasury bills in the most recent tender plus ½ per cent and rounded up to the nearest ¼ per cent. The formula was not completely sacrosanct because there was scope for the Bank, with the approval of the Chancellor, to administer a change in rate if it was felt necessary. In these circumstances, operation of the formula would be suspended temporarily until rates had adjusted to the new level. For presentational reasons, the expression 'Bank Rate' would receive less prominence, and the introduction of ¼ per cent fractions would also assist in underlining the difference between the old and new arrangements. Page hoped that the change could be pushed through in September, but in the event, 'minimum lending rate' (MLR), as the new mechanism was called, was not introduced until October, bringing to an end 270 years of Bank Rate.[100]

MLR was to be made known on each Friday afternoon at the same time as the results of the Treasury bill tender, thus also ending the long-standing tradition of the simultaneous announcement of Bank Rate each Thursday in the front hall of the Bank and on the floor of the stock exchange. For

---

[99] *Ibid.*
[100] Page to O'Brien/Hollom, 'Special deposits and Bank rate', 18 September 1972, C42/10; Treasury/Bank monthly meeting on monetary policy, 15 September 1972; O'Brien to Barber, 3 October 1972, C40/1392. The term 'official Bank rate' was reintroduced in May 2006; Bank of England, *The Framework for the Bank of England's Operations in the Sterling Money Market.* May 2006, p. 3.

public consumption, the official reasons given for the introduction of MLR were that it was in line with the reduced significance of Bank Rate under CCC and that it allowed the increased flexibility that was required in the money market without signifying major shifts in monetary policy. It would also ensure that there was a margin over the Treasury bill rate as a penalty to deter borrowing. While the move generally was well received by the financial press, *The Banker* did ask whether the Bank might later come to regret the 'debunking' of Bank Rate.[101] Whatever its merits, operation of the formula certainly seemed to have an immediate impact. Bank Rate had stood at 6 per cent since June 1972. The first MLR on 13 October 1972 was 7.25 per cent; by the end of the year, it had reached 9 per cent (Table 10.1). Looking back four years later, Page was clear that these rates, which the Bank judged appropriate, would not have been achieved without a change in the system.[102]

When CCC came into operation in September 1971, the outstanding special deposits (3½ per cent for London clearers, 1¾ per cent for Scottish clearers) were repaid in full. New guidelines were agreed with the Chancellor for operation in the future, with the intention that under the new approach special deposits would be used in a more flexible manner.[103] It was not clear what 'flexible' meant. The first call under CCC came towards the end of 1972, although it had already been under discussion for some months. On 7 November, O'Brien wrote to Barber saying that it was clear that the liquidity of the banking system would be eased by the end of the year owing to the large financing requirements of government and because large holdings of 5¼% Treasury Stock 1973 could be treated as a reserve asset, this adding three percentage points to their reserve asset ratio. O'Brien therefore recommended that a call of 1 per cent should be made. Some discussion about timing followed, and on 9 November, the Bank announced that a call would be made on 15 November, with ½ per cent to be paid on 30 November and the remainder on 14 December.[104] This was quickly followed by a call for 2 per cent the following month, to be made in two instalments in January 1973.[105]

---

[101] Bank of England, Press notice, 9 October 1972, 4A139/5; *BEQB* 12(4):442–443, December 1972; press cuttings in ADM38/6; *The Banker*, Vol. 12(2):1365–1366 (November 1972).

[102] Page to Fforde/Richardson/Hollom, 'Bank rate v. minimum lending rate', 31 December 1976, C42/10.

[103] O'Brien to Barber and reply, both 8 September 1971; Bank of England, 'Special deposits. Technical arrangements', September 1971, 5A148/1.

[104] O'Brien to Barber, 7 November 1972; 'Extract from the Deputy Governor's note dated 8.11.72 … '; Barber to O'Brien, 8 November 1972; Bank of England, 'Press announcement', 9 November 1972, 5A148/2.

[105] O'Brien to Barber, 20 December 1972; BoE, press announcement, 21 December 1972, 5A148/2.

Table 10.1. *Changes in Bank Rate/minimum lending rate, 1971–73*

Date	Change (per cent)	New rate (per cent)
Bank rate		
1 April 1971	−1	6
2 September 1971	−1	5
22 June 1972	1	6
Minimum lending rate		
13 October 1972	1.25	7.25
27 October 1972	0.25	7.5
1 December 1972	0.25	7.75
8 December 1972	0.25	8.0
22 December 1972	1.0	9.0
19 January 1973	−0.25	8.75
23 March 1973	−0.25	8.5
13 April 1973	−0.5	8.0
19 April 1973	0.25	8.25
11 May 1973	−0.25	8.0
18 May 1973	−025	7.75
22 June 1973	−0.25	7.5
20 July 1973	1.5	9
27 July 1973	2.5	11.5
19 October 1973	−0.25	11.25
13 November 1973	1.75 (administered)	13

Source: BEQB.

In April and May 1973, the Bank was advocating a reduction of ½ per cent because it would be a good opportunity to demonstrate the flexible use of special deposits, and the cash released might be used by the banks to purchase gilts. The Treasury reportedly advised the Chancellor to agree to a release in mid-May, but in the event, this did not happen, and total special deposits remained at 3 per cent.[106]

---

[106] Cooke to O'Brien, 'Special deposits', 17 April 1973; 'Extract from the Deputy Governor's note on the Governor's conversation with Mr. Littler 25.4.73'; Page to Fforde/O'Brien/Hollom, 'Short-term interest rates', 8 May 1973; 'Extract from Mr. McMahon's note on the Deputy Governor's conversation with Mr. Henley 11.5.73.'; Fforde to O'Brien/Hollom, 'Special deposits (conversation with Mr. Wass)', 14 May 1973, 5A148/2.

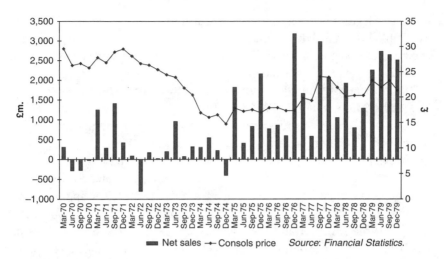

Figure 10.1. Gilt-edged net quarterly sales/purchases and consols price, 1970–79.

The immediate transition following the changes to the way the Bank conducted its operations in the gilt-edged market turned out to be smooth, although the market was reportedly 'thinner' and prices 'more volatile'.[107] From the end of 1971, prices started to fall, something that continued until the end of 1974 (Figure 10.1). Net sales were rather variable, averaging below £1 billion a year, and there were two quarters where there were net purchases, coinciding with the floating of sterling, and generally poor market conditions at the end of 1974. Notwithstanding the declared intentions of the new operational regime, by the summer of 1972, the Prime Minister was asking whether anything could be done to support the market and stem the fall in prices. Heath also wanted to know if it would be possible to intervene through operators other than the Government Broker to try to disguise the operation. The Treasury explained that under CCC the emphasis on money supply meant that there would be greater variations in interest rates than in the past. The rise in yields was due to the fear of inflation, fears heightened by the rapid monetary growth. Large-scale intervention would be expensive: to reduce interest rates by 1 per cent, Heath was told, probably would add £800 million to 1,000 million to the money supply. In addition, an upward movement in rates was required to induce investors to buy government debt. As to intervention through other channels, the Bank was said to be satisfied with the existing arrangements. Discreet operations

[107] Page to Fforde/O'Brien/Hollom, 'Monetary policy', 23 June 1971; Cooke to Page/Fforde, 'Gilt-edged market turnover', 1 July 1971, 3A92/1.

could be disguised, and large operations would, in any event, be identified. The Bank did not feel that the authorities were being hampered in achieving their objectives in the market.[108] Calls for the Bank to change its method of operation were to increase later in the decade.

The monetary turmoil following 1971 led the Prime Minister to request, in March 1973, a reappraisal of CCC. This might encompass whether 'competition' and 'credit control' were compatible, whether ceilings might be a better option, the problems of credit allocation, the use of sanctions, and market management.[109] Page's immediate view of the past 18 months was that decisions on monetary policy had been heavily influenced by political factors and that the Bank had been left on its own.[110] The appraisal was completed in April, and in early May, a simplified version was produced for the Prime Minister and the Chancellor.[111] There was disagreement in the Bank about some of the wording in the review, and in particular, there appeared to be differences over the role of money in the original justification for the new approach. In an annotation O'Brien remarked, 'In my mind the importance of more effective control of the money supply bulked large.'[112] The final version noted that in the years preceding CCC, there had been a shift in emphasis towards (1) changes in the money stock, (2) variations in interest rates as opposed to quantitative restrictions, and (3) the need for competitive efficiency in the banking system. Remembering the genesis of Fforde's ideas from his 1965 paper, this was a complete inversion of how CCC appears to have developed, with competition the driving force.[113]

The reappraisal tackled several of the major criticisms that had been levelled at the new approach. One was that there had been no control over money supply or bank lending, and the rapid inflation since 1972 therefore

---

[108] Letter from Armstrong to Bailey, 'Dictated over the telephone by Mr. Downey, H.M.T.', 12 June 1972; Bailey to Armstrong, 14 June 1972, 3A92/1.

[109] Downey to Wass, 30 March 1973; HMT, 'Note of a meeting … 2 April [1973]', 5 April 1973; Willets to Fforde, 'Review of the new approach', 10 April 1973, 6A50/8; Willetts/ Marcus Miller to O'Brien et al, 'Review of the new approach', 13 April 1973; Dicks-Mireaux to Wass, 27 April 1973, enc. Bank of England, 'Review of the new approach', 27 April 1973, 3A28/25.

[110] Page to O'Brien/Hollom, 'Monetary policy', 2 April 1973, 3A8/25.

[111] 'Extract from Mr. Fforde's memo dated 25.4.73 …; Fforde to Wass, 25 April 1973; O'Brien to Fforde, 25 April 1973, 6A50/9; O'Brien to Barber, 4 May 1973, enc. 'Competition and credit control: a review and reappraisal', 4 May 1973, 6A50/10.

[112] O'Brien, Annotation attached to Dicks-Mireaux to O'Brien et al., 'Review of the new approach', 19 April 1973, 6A50/9.

[113] By 1977, Goodhart wrote that 'the new system was designed to place more weight on the monetary aggregates as measures of the thrust of monetary policy'; Goodhart to GPS, 28 March 1977, enc. 'Monetary control in the UK', 6A50/21.

was a consequence of the new policy. Another was that the authorities did not fully understand the operating characteristics of the new system and that this had reduced the efficiency of monetary policy. Arising from these two points was what the review considered the most serious charge – that the new system made it impossible for the Bank to control the quantity of money or credit. The reappraisal was largely unapologetic about all this, with the defence being that things would have happened anyway or the new approach was not to blame. For example, greater restriction in 1972 would have been counter to general economic policy. The process of re-intermediation, after years of administered ceilings, meant that monetary growth was inevitable, and the rise in house and land prices probably would have occurred whatever system was in place. Overall, the new approach had been operating for only 18 months, and this had been a transitional phase during which distortions to competition were being reversed. The general conclusion was that the principles underlying CCC should not be jeopardised prematurely on the basis of limited experience. Some modifications were required, but 'experience so far can scarcely be regarded as negating the attempt to provide this country with a more competitive and efficient system of financial intermediation.'[114] They did not mention that interest rates, which were said to have been important in CCC, had not risen to what would have been needed to contain monetary growth.

Some concerns, largely put down as technical issues, were highlighted in the reappraisal. One related to control of the discount market, where the Bank conceded that some unforeseen distortions had been created. Indeed, from early 1973, the LDMA had made its concerns known to the Bank and put forward a number of solutions that included ways of creating additional reserve assets. These were rejected by the Bank because it would mean a slackening of pressure on the banking system.[115] The LDMA was also critical of the MLR arrangements, and it found some sympathy in the Bank. Page accepted that the formula was imperfect, but the previous autumn there had been the need 'to move the Bank's lending rate out of the political arena', and it was the best course of action available. He hoped that eventually it would prove possible to make amendments that would allow the Bank some manoeuvre around the formula.[116] The Bank proposed that the existing 50 per cent public-sector debt ratio be replaced by a private-sector lending multiplier, thus giving the

---

[114] Bank of England, 'Review of the new approach', 27 April 1973, 3A28/25.
[115] Page to O'Brien/Hollom, 'The discount market', 15 February 1973, 7A58/5.
[116] Page to Fforde, 'The discount market', 9 April 1973; Fforde to O'Brien/Hollom, 'The discount market', 16 February 1973; 'The London discount market', enc with Page to Fforde/O'Brien/Hollom, 'The discount market', 20 March 1973, 7A58/5.

houses a greater flexibility in managing their books. After some negotiation, it was agreed that the discount houses would observe an upper limit on their private-sector lending (all assets other than those defined as public-sector assets) of 20 times capital and reserves.[117] In early June, Page outlined the scheme to the Treasury. He explained that a paucity of short-dated public-sector debt had pushed down yields, particularly on Treasury bills, relative to other short-term assets and that the houses' holdings of this paper had become less profitable: the existence of the present ratio limited any switch into higher-yielding private-sector debt. The change that had been negotiated would eliminate these distortions without weakening the arrangements put in place in 1971. It also would help to 'eliminate the artificially low yield on Treasury Bills and thus the artificially low level of the minimum lending rate'. However, the Bank judged that the rise in yields (and hence MLR) would not be large if the change was made in the next few weeks.[118]

Other considerations included the fact that short-term rates in London were out of alignment with international rates. In the first half of 1973, MLR had fallen, reaching a low point of 7.5 per cent in June. In other countries, rates had been rising, and by July, the adverse differential was significant: 1½ per cent between the sterling inter-bank rate and the three-month Eurodollar rate. This made London unattractive for short-term funds, and this contributed to pressure on sterling, as did the deteriorating balance-of-payments current account. In addition, bank liquidity was increasing, and money-supply growth was a worry. Consequently, Bank and Treasury officials considered whether changes were required to the direction of monetary policy and recommended that the MLR formula should be suspended (suspension was allowed, but had not so far been used) and the rate 'administered' from 7½ to 8½ per cent, whereas at the same time there would be a 1 per cent call for special deposits. It was also argued that this should be the occasion to introduce the new limit on private-sector lending for the discount houses. Although this was presented as a package, the Treasury was in fact hoping that pressure from external rates would ease and thus that the suspension of the MLR formula would prove unnecessary. Reportedly, the Chancellor, too, was strongly against moving on MLR. The anticipated date for implementation of the measures was Thursday 19 July.[119] In the event, although

---

[117] Roger Barnes (Deputy Principal, Discount Office) to Fforde, 12 and 26 April and 18 May 1973, enc. Notes for record of meetings with LDMA; Galpin to Fforde, 11 and 16 May 1973, enc: notes for record of meetings with LDMA, 7A58/5.

[118] Page to Downey, 8 June 1973; Downey to Page, 11 June 1973, 7A58/5.

[119] Allen to Bailey (HMT), 12 July 1973, enc. HMT, 'Monetary policy'; Note by Treasury and Bank of England officials', 12 July 1973; Hollom to Richardson, 13 July 1973, 3A8/26.

announcements were made that day, these covered only the 1 per cent call for special deposits, taking them to a total of 4 per cent, and the change affecting the discount market. There was no 'administered' rise in MLR, but the discount-market measure resulted, as predicted, in an increase in short-term rates. The discount houses lowered their bids sharply, and the average rate of discount on Treasury bills rose by nearly 1½ per cent, sufficient to push MLR to 9 per cent on 20 July. International rates continued to rise the following week, pressure on sterling continued, and on 27 July, MLR went up another 2½ per cent, taking it to 11½ per cent, a post-war high for the Bank's interest rate. This rate was made effective by the Bank enforcing over-night borrowing on three consecutive days.[120] Two discount houses were left in difficulty owing to the consequent fall in the price of short-dated bonds, and the Bank had to step in secretly with assistance. These transactions were made directly rather than through the market.[121]

In the aftermath of these changes, the Bank reviewed the MLR arrangements. It claimed that under the previous regime the upward movement in December 1972 (1 per cent) and the recent rises in July would have been more difficult to make, and this experience meant that the system had been satisfactory. Certainly it is hard to believe that ministers otherwise would have accepted a 4 per cent point rise in little more than a week. Nevertheless, there were still problems. Bank Rate had given clear guidance on the authorities' view of short-term rates, and without this, the Treasury bill rate had become volatile. Moreover, the Bank did not always want to follow the Treasury bill rate, especially given its volatility, so it had used various means to manipulate the market, and to an increasing extent. In addition, the Bank's degree of influence over the Treasury bill rate was incomplete, especially when it was moving downwards, and thus falls in MLR could not be restrained easily. The Bank believed that it was debatable whether the level of interference 'has become or will soon become so large that the distinction between the new and old arrangements is so fine as to be not worth preserving'. However, further experience was required. In any case, a return to the original means of determining Bank Rate would be difficult to present. Thus it was concluded that at this stage the arrangements should continue, but with a modification that would give the Bank

---

[120] Page to K. H. Whitaker (chairman, LDMA), 19 July 1973 and others; Bank of England, 'Agreements with money market houses', 19 July 1973, 3A8/26; Richardson to Barber, 18 July 1973; Bank of England, Press announcement, 'Special deposits', 19 July 1973, 5A148/2. *BEQB* 13(3):269–279, 289–291, September 1973. 'Competition and credit control: modified arrangements for the discount market', *BEQB* 13(3):306–307, September 1973.

[121] Note by the Government Broker, 30 July 1973, 3A8/26.

the power not to have to follow a fall in Treasury bill rates with an automatic reduction in MLR. It would be mid-1978 before the arrangements finally ended, but it is evident that after less than a year of operation, the Bank harboured substantial reservations about the MLR mechanism.

In the middle of all this, O'Brien had stepped down. After 46 years in the Bank, and only partway through his second term as Governor, he had announced his retirement on 8 February 1973, his sixty-fifth birthday, to take effect on the 30 June. O'Brien says that he had indicated to the Chancellor in 1971 that he would retire at age 65, and two years later Barber reminded him and asked for a leaving date.[122] Cecil King claims that 'O'Brien was sacked ... as he was not felt to fit in sufficiently quickly with Ted's [Heath] financial and commercial ideas'; he 'lost his job for not being subservient enough'.[123] King often overstated things, but it is true that there was increasing friction between O'Brien and Heath and O'Brien and Barber.

Views differ on O'Brien's performance as Governor. For some, he 'made a first-class Governor', even a 'great governor', and one of the Bank's 'leading technicians'.[124] Some felt that after the turbulent relationship between Cromer and the government, O'Brien was seen as being more compliant, but he was not wholly subservient. Obituaries remarked on his calmness and that he was rarely flustered even in a crisis. But he did on occasion explode, particularly when not consulted on matters that he felt he should have been. O'Brien was quick, firm, and decisive in his approach. He often attributed his success to good luck – being in the right place at the right time. He was well respected in the City and by other central bankers. In 1973, O'Brien was made a life peer, becoming Baron O'Brien of Lothbury. On leaving the Bank, he continued to play a prominent role in the City.[125]

O'Brien's successor was Gordon Richardson. Prior to his appointment, he had been chairman of Schroders and also had been a non-Executive Director of the Bank since 1967. He was the one-hundred and sixteenth Governor. At the age of 57, he was not exactly the young man to whom O'Brien thought he should give way, but Richardson had been appointed to the Court with the succession partly in mind, and he was the name that the senior Directors recommended to the Prime Minister. Other candidates were Morse, Eric Faulkner, and Morgan Grenfell's Sir John Stevens (a former Executive Director at the Bank) was also mentioned by tipsters. Richardson was educated at Nottingham High School (where he was

---

[122] O'Brien, Memoir, p. 134.
[123] King (1975, pp. 271, 293).
[124] *The Guardian*, 25 November 1995, p. 32; *The Economist*, 6 July 1973; Middlemas (1994).
[125] O'Brien, Memoir, p. 140.

head boy), read law at Gonville and Caius College, Cambridge, and by the mid-1950s was established as a leading specialist in company law. He joined Schroders in 1957, becoming Deputy chairman in 1962 and chairman in 1965. He was the driving force behind the firm's achievements in London in the 1960s.[126] He had already been tipped by some to succeed Cromer in 1966.[127] Although it was predicted that he would be in sympathy with the Conservative Government's commercial and financial philosophy, he was, in fact, also sympathetic to Labour and enjoyed particularly good relations with the Chancellor Denis Healey.[128] Like his two immediate predecessors, Richardson took over at a difficult time, and as with them, interest rates increased during his first month in office.

However, the appointment of a new Governor and adoption of the new approach did not represent a complete break with the past. There was still provision for 'directional guidance' to the banks. This was first used in the new era in August 1972.[129] In July 1973, Richardson had told the clearing bank chairman that he was most anxious about the increase in bank lending and the corresponding increase in the money supply. He warned that if this trend continued, restrictive action must follow, and this might include direct controls. Although this would be unwelcome, 'it had to be recognised that personal lending, if not controlled, could come to be the Achilles heel of Competition and Credit Control.'[130] Then, in the second week of September 1973, a further Governor's guidance letter was issued. This explained that after two years of active competition, the banking system was 'closer to being fully lent', and banks now were asked to limit their bidding for small deposits. With immediate effect, and until further notice, banks were asked to limit the interest paid on any deposit of less than £10,000 to no more than 9½ per cent. In wording reminiscent of the 1960s letters on ceilings, Richardson asked that finance for exports and industrial investment be given priority, whereas lending to persons or property development should be limited. The limitation of competition for individuals' savings was also extended to building societies, the first time they had been subject to such direction.[131]

---

[126] Roberts (1992, pp. 417, 422–425).
[127] Cutting from *Daily Mail*, 12 January 1966, ADM38/23.
[128] Interview with Lord Healey, 28 February 2006, and Healey (1990), p. 375.
[129] O'Brien to banks, 7 August 1972, *BEQB* 12(3):327, September 1972.
[130] 'Extract from the record of the meeting at Bank of England 25.7.73 between the clearing bank chairmen and the Governors, 6.8.73', 5A148/2.
[131] The interest ceiling was withdrawn on 28 February 1975; Bank of England, *Annual Report*, year ending February 1974, pp. 7–8, year ending February 1975, p. 6.

Richardson's guidance letter also addressed the issue of interest arbitrage activities. Borrowing from banks for the purpose of redeposit was an issue highlighted in the review of CCC. Under such interest arbitrage, known as 'round tripping', borrowers could draw on their unused overdraft facilities and then redeposit the proceeds at higher rates, for example, in certificates of deposit (CDs) and the inter-bank market. The result was an increase in both M3 and interest rates.[132] Richardson welcomed recent efforts by some banks to curtail the activity, but he also warned that it put unnecessary pressure on money markets, and he encouraged all banks to 'be on the watch for, and active in combating, this misuse of their lending facilities'.[133] The Bank also asked the clearers to consider how such arbitrage might be limited, and their response suggested that the central bank should operate in the parallel money markets.[134] By the end of 1973, there were poor trade and money supply figures and the first round of Organisation of Petroleum Exporting Countries (OPEC) oil price increases. There was also serious industrial unrest, notably involving the National Union of Mineworkers, and Heath declared a state of emergency on 13 November. On the same day, the Bank made a call for special deposits of 2 per cent, and at the same time, the first administered change in MLR was made, taking it from 11¼ to 13 per cent. This news took the markets by surprise, and trading in gilts was temporarily suspended as jobbers decided on the appropriate adjustment. The reaction was the biggest fall in gilt-edged securities since the Second World War.[135]

The Chancellor wrote to the Governor on 15 November to relate his concerns about the impact on CCC and the effect of high interest rates. It was a nakedly political intervention in monetary policy. Barber recorded that Heath had, on several occasions, expressed concern that the only effective way to control credit seemed to be 'to jack up interest rates to intolerably high levels'. Heath also reportedly thought that despite the merits of CCC, it had had 'unforeseen and undesirable consequences from the point of view of the Government's overall economic strategy and its political and social priorities'. Thus the Prime Minister wanted to find an alternative that was 'less adverse in both its short-term consequences and long-term implications'. Barber went on to press for the Bank's new ideas on controlling bank

[132] Bank of England, 'Review of the new approach', 27 April 1973, 3A28/25; Fforde to Hollom, 'Managing upward pressures on the parallel rates', 29 August 1973, 3A8/26.
[133] Bank of England, Press notice, 11 September 1973, 3A8/27.
[134] C. E. Trott (chief GM, Midland Bank) to Page, 21 November 1973, enc. 'Report of the working party on overdraft arbitrage', 21 November 1973, 3A8/28.
[135] Richardson to Barber, 13 November 1973; Bank of England, Press notice, 13 November 1973, 5A148/2; *The Times*, November 14 1973, p. 23.

advances, stating that although he was reluctant to overthrow the basic principles of CCC, 'it is a matter of some urgency that we should be able to bring to the Prime Minister's attention possible approaches to this problem which would rely less exclusively on increases of interest rates to control the level of money supply'. Furthermore, Barber was sure that 'we shall have to parade before him the pros and cons of the old methods which, despite their other disadvantages, will seem to many to have produced a degree of control which, however imperfect, did not raise interest rates to levels which were intolerable politically'.[136] But that was the problem.

A new technique was then devised by the Bank initially described as a 'supplementary scheme', that is, additional to the existing CCC arrangements. Under the scheme, banks had to deposit, interest-free, with the Bank a proportion of their interest-bearing deposits beyond a base starting point, with permitted growth related to a target for M3. The origins of the scheme could be found in the CCC review and the subsequent debate, but as Goodhart observed, the underlying philosophy was quite straightforward: 'We wanted to be in a position to exert more control over M3, without pushing interest rates up or going back to ceilings'.[137] There was no link with special deposits, but they quickly became known as the 'supplementary special deposits' (SSDs) and, later, 'the corset'. Whereas special deposits could not be avoided, SSDs were payable only if a bank breached the target growth rate.

Briefing Richardson ahead of a meeting with the CLCB in mid-November, Page said that if additional techniques had to be applied to the banking system as a whole, then 'supplementary deposits ... look to be the most promising possibility'.[138] There was a renewed debate about the impact of credit ceilings, but having done away with them under CCC, there was little appetite in the Bank for their re-introduction. Fforde complained that fiscal expansion had been too rapid. this was a familiar story, but according to Fforde, 'the present manifestation of it is probably the worst example we have yet had' and 'an attempt to cover it up by imposing direct controls on the banking system ... can achieve very little'.[139] Goodhart warned that

---

[136] Barber to Richardson, 15 November 1973, G1/255. In July 1973, there had been worries about getting Heath to agree to a package of monetary measures; Page to Fforde/Richardson/Hollom, 'Monetary policy', 4 July 1973, 6A50/10.

[137] Goodhart to Dow/Fforde, 'The supplementary deposit scheme: a public exposition', 10 January 1974, 5A149/1.

[138] Page to Richardson/Hollom, 'Meeting to-day [*sic*] with the CLCB', 14 November 1973, 3A8/28.

[139] Goodhart to Richardson/Hollom, 'Ceilings on bank credit: some notes', 14 November 1973; Fforde to Richardson/Hollom, 'The case against ceiling controls', 19 November 1973, 3A8/28.

disintermediation would see business diverted from the banks into other credit channels, so the introduction of any controls, as well as being largely cosmetic, would have little measurable impact on the real economy. He argued that the least harmful option probably would be a ratio imposed, in the form of non-interest-bearing supplementary deposits, on the increment of banks' interest-bearing deposits above a rising base. The main reason was that interest-bearing deposits were the fastest-growing and largest element in M3.[140] The scheme was to apply to all banks and deposit-taking finance houses. In essence, up to 50 per cent of the *growth* in an institution's interest-bearing eligible liabilities (IBELs) over a specified rate (initially 8 per cent over six months) would have to be placed as a non-interest-bearing deposit with the Bank.[141] It was to be activated immediately, but no deposits were required for the first six months. As with ceilings in the 1960s, discussions with banks threw up a range of complaints, anomalies, and special pleadings. Two general problems came to light. One was that the growth of new institutions with a small IBEL base would be hampered by the 8 per cent constraint, and the other was that some banks had already made firm commitments to loans at the time the scheme was announced, and honouring them might mean that the permitted growth rate was exceeded. The solutions were to introduce a minimum exemption figure of £3 million (later raised to £5 million) for the former and transitional arrangements for the latter.[142]

Further tightening measures were announced by Barber in December, including tax increases and cuts in public expenditure. Hire-purchase controls were reintroduced for the first time since July 1971, and the minimum monthly repayment on credit cards was raised. SSDs also were unveiled, and because of this, the size of the November call for special deposits was reduced from 2 per cent to 1 per cent.[143]

The ambition had been for CCC to do away with controls as far as possible, introduce competition to the banking sector, and gain a better control over monetary growth. Both open market operations and interest rates were to be used to a greater extent and to greater purpose. Monetary aggregates were to receive more attention partly on the grounds that in inflationary times interest

---

[140] Goodhart to Richardson/Hollom, 'Alternative methods of direct control', 19 November 1973; Goodhart to Richardson/Hollom, 'A brief for the Governor's meeting with the Chancellor at the Treasury on Wednesday, 21 November', 20 November 1973, 6A50/12.

[141] Bank of England, Press notice, 17 December 1973, 3A8/28.

[142] Drake to Coleby/Page, 'Supplementary special deposits', 14 January 1974; Page to Fforde/Richardson/Hollom, 'Supplementary special deposits', 25 January 1974, 5A149/1.

[143] HC Deb, 17 December 1973, Vol. 866, cc952–966; *BEQB* 14(1):3, 37–38, March 1974.

rates were less useful as a guide to the monetary stance. For all this, though, CCC has been judged a 'disaster' (Gowland) and as having 'failed comprehensively' (D. P. O'Brien, one of the most sober of academic judges). It is not easy, however, to disentangle the several causal factors that were present in the monetary explosion. The Bank might have complained more vigorously. There was the general expansionary economic policy, particularly fiscal and monetary expansion, of the Heath Government, about which the Bank could do little. There was, though, the Bank's failure to anticipate the extent of the re-intermediation that would appear following CCC. And there was the failure yet again to use interest rates, some of the blame for which attaches to the Bank and some to the politicians. According to the Bank, the central problem was the breakdown in the stable relationship between interest rates and broad money aggregates after 1971. However, even if the relationship had changed, there surely still was a role for interest rates. Professor O'Brien described the Bank's statements on interest rates as 'intellectually incoherent'. In 1973, the Bank was to argue that with MLR at 13 per cent (unprecedented), the needed rise in interest rates was incalculable. However, it failed to mention that they were operating at that point with negative real interest rates. And Professor O'Brien made the further point that as the Bank's document noted, its willingness to buy gilts of up to one year to maturity would affect the portfolio composition of the financial sector and increase liquidity, 'but this insight was, rather remarkably, not pursued.'[144] The Bank rather proceeded on the basis that the banks would be forced to sell gilts when their liquidity was squeezed, and that would raise interest rates. When it was clear that things were not operating as intended, the new device of SSDs was designed. That was just a return to controls by another name, though, and the Bank seems not to have taken them seriously itself.

At the start of 1974, a three-day working week was implemented. After negotiations to end the miners' industrial action broke down, Heath announced, on 7 February, that there would be a general election in three weeks time. Labour formed a minority government, and Wilson appointed Denis Healey as Chancellor. On top of this, there was the collapse of London and County and Cedar Holdings at the end of 1973, precipitating what became the secondary banking crisis.

[144] Gowland (1982, p. 13); O'Brien (1992, p. 412).

11

The Secondary Banking Crisis

British banking had been enormously stable from the third quarter of the nineteenth century until the 1970s. The stability is frequently explained casually as a consequence of the cartel. But there was no cartel before 1914, and even through the twentieth century, the rate of return on capital in banking was not out of line with that in the rest of the economy, a feature more in keeping with a competitive model than a monopolistic one.[1] Of course, there are many possible explanations for that and many ingredients in the stability. Importantly, the banks had found their own way to the appropriate capital, cash, and liquidity ratios. After the Second World War, the latter two were to change under direction from the authorities. And while it was not spelled out in these terms at the time, the Bank took responsibility for financial stability. The fact that the banking system had been so stable for so long meant that the subject was little discussed. The fact was, though, that the Bank watched over all that went on in the City and gathered intelligence on everything from mood to individual behaviour. The key figure in this in the Bank was the Principal of the Discount Office. That job was becoming more difficult in the world after competition and credit control (CCC) and came under close scrutiny in the secondary banking crisis that broke at the end of 1973, one of the most dramatic events in an eventful decade in which the Bank was involved. The secondary, or 'fringe', banking sector had its origins in the late 1950s and early 1960s with institutions borrowing in the wholesale money markets and lending in the main on property. It grew rapidly under the expansionary economic policy of the years 1971–73 and the impetus of CCC, and it then ran into liquidity difficulties in the course of 1973. The euphoria that had surrounded the growth gave way to an escalating crisis of confidence and led the Bank, together with the clearing banks

[1] Capie and Billings (2001).

and Scottish banks, eventually to launch a support group that came to be known as the 'Lifeboat'. Unilateral assistance later was given by the Bank to other institutions such as Slater Walker and Edward Bates in the later stages of the crisis on the grounds that it was needed to protect the sector. The Bank made comment to the Select Committee on Nationalised Industries (SCNI) in 1976 and gave its official account of the events in its evidence to the Wilson Committee in 1978, the latter reproduced in a *Bulletin* article in the same year.[2] This evidence has formed the basis subsequently of the secondary literature on the crisis, in which Margaret Reid's seminal *The Secondary Banking Crisis, 1973–75* is still the most detailed account. With the bulk of the Bank's archival material on the crisis destroyed, this account of the crisis cannot be as full as desired, having to rely as it does in large part on other sources. However, there is some archival record of the Bank's involvement.

Early Indicators of Trouble

There are several strands in the story of the crisis. The backdrop was the freeing of the banking sector in CCC and the monetary explosion in the preceding three years. There was the development of the fringe banks themselves. A complex ladder of formal and informal recognitions, and legislative provisions had grown up around the banking sector (see Chapter 12). While the main banks in the 1960s were subject to numerous controls, the 'fringe banks', as the term suggests, operated outside these controls, and indeed, the controls help to explain their emergence. They paid higher interest rates and enjoyed profitable growth. The development of the wholesale money markets nourished that growth. Through the newer 'parallel' or 'wholesale' money markets in sterling, they dealt in short-term liquid finance.[3] Their foreign-currency advances grew rapidly, and they offered higher rates on sterling deposits than the clearing banks.

---

[2] In the Commons on 14 December 1977, Dennis Skinner requested an inquiry into the Lifeboat, arguing that the money provided by the Bank had come from the taxpayers (of course, it wasn't taxpayers' money). It was felt that the SCNI's 1976 report had failed to pursue the subject adequately. Committee member Russell Kerr spoke to the press about the need for an inquiry, and *The Guardian* reported on 23 November 1977 that the rescue operation was a suitable area for the Select Committee to investigate. In response to a growing call for more information on the support operations from left-wing members of the Labour Party, it was decided that SCNI Sub-Committee C would take evidence. This took place on 18 and 25 January 1978, with Richardson, Hollom, Blunden, and Taylor appearing.

[3] Revell, *The Banker* 118(511);803, September 1968; 'UK banking sector', *BEQB* 9(2):176, June 1969.

Many of the fringe banks held a Section 123 certificate, something that placed them on a rung towards the bottom of the ladder of banking recognition. By 1970, there were 78 companies holding one of these certificates. Although approximately 30 were subject to ceiling controls on advances, the Bank's view was that Section 123 banks generally were too small to worry about.[4] In a February 1970 report, Richard Hall, Deputy Principal of the Discount Office, noted:

The majority of the fringe banks are small, and it is hardly practicable to attempt to exercise strict control over most of them. As soon, however, as they become sufficiently big to attract attention or to need some favour from us we impose the maximum restraint we can and endeavour to police it. It is probably true to say that the bigger the bank the better the policing is; in the case of the small ones where we have no more than annual balance sheet figures, it must necessarily be very imperfect.... we would have closer control if we were to bring all these institutions within our reporting system and recognise them as 'statistical banks.' We have been reluctant to do so because it would imply a recognition and perhaps a responsibility for their soundness which we are not ready or equipped to assume.[5]

This was before CCC. The new arrangements saw removal of the restraints whose prolonged application to the banks had enabled the fringe to establish itself. The Bank had believed that with the introduction of CCC, 'the fringe would contract to a level of comparative unimportance.'[6] The likelihood that the fringe institutions would survive once other established banks were free to compete for business was believed to be slim.[7] Yet, according to Keogh, it was after CCC that the fringe 'became a menace'.[8] Instead of fading away, the fringe banks prospered. This was aided by an expansionary economic and particularly monetary policy and the fact that finance intended to stimulate industry had ended up in property development.[9] Fear of rising inflation stimulated equity sales and boom. But the stock market peaked in May 1972, and thereafter, the boom transferred to property. The Heath Government's relaxation of controls on property development at the start of the 1970s facilitated that boom. Furthermore, the Land Commission was abolished, a move that restored the whole of the development value of

---

[4]   Hollom to Kirkpatrick, 'Control of fringe institutions', 2 January 1970, 2A70/4.
[5]   Hall to Hollom, 'Credit control – Section 123 companies', 17 February 1970, 2A70/4.
[6]   'The secondary banking crisis and the Bank of England's support operations', *BEQB* 18(2):232, June 1978.
[7]   Keogh, Note for record – 'The Fringe', 5 June 1974, 7A95/1; Dyer (1983, p. 47).
[8]   Keogh, Note for record – 'The Fringe', 5 June 1974, 7A95/1.
[9]   Reid (1978, p. 25). See Congdon (2005) for asset bubbles. Also see 6A328/1.

property to owners, with a subsequent dramatic rise in property shares.[10] New lucrative opportunities were presented to the fringe banks to finance the purchase and development of residential and commercial property.[11] Bank advances to the property sector rose from £362 million in February 1971 to £2,584 million in February 1974, an increase of 614 per cent.[12] This lending was arranged with little or no margin and with funds borrowed short term from the money markets.[13] *The Economist* wondered where was 'the normal business caution that prudent men of affairs usually exercise' and, believing that the property market had 'gone somewhat mad', questioned whether men of property could continue 'turning stone into gold'.[14] Growth in property lending continued and this despite the requests for containment included in the Governor's guidance letters of August 1972 and September 1973.[15] As was later observed, 'With property prices rising rapidly, it looked like a one-way option; it didn't even matter whether the initial cost of borrowing was greater than the rental return on properties purchased, since eventually, it was assumed, rising rents and rising property values would ensure a healthy profit.'[16]

Some of the symptoms that led to the crisis are also evident in the activities of institutions that were not strictly banks. One of these was the Crown Agents. The Crown Agents were founded by the British government in 1833 to act for the colonies as commercial and financial agents in Britain, providing goods, services, and capital. Their role later broadened in the first half of the twentieth century to include work for the governments of independent countries both inside and outside the Commonwealth as well as public corporations.[17] The Agents bought, inspected, and shipped materials and equipment for principals, arranged printing and coin minting, provided specialist advice, supplied personnel services, and arranged various financial services. In 1968, they were acting for 80 governments and more than 160 public authorities and international bodies. From the late 1960s, the Crown Agents, while continuing their traditional activities, also started to engage in banking-related business on their own account. This

---

[10] Reid (1982, p. 62); Scott (1996, p. 184).
[11] Richardson speech to the Institute of Bankers on 5 February 1974, *BEQB* 14(1):54, March 1974; Reid (1982, pp. 66–67).
[12] Scott (1996, p. 183).
[13] Dyer (1983, p. 47); Richardson, 'Fringe banks (speaking notes)', 15 January 1974, 6A395/2.
[14] *The Economist*, 18 March 1972, p. 7.
[15] Bank of England, 'The 1970's property boom', May 1977, 1A179/41.
[16] *The Banker* 124(580):553, June 1974.
[17] Sunderland (2004, p. 13; 2007, p. 1).

diversification was prompted by concerns that business would wither away as colonial territories became independent, and there was a desire to build up their capital and reserves, which were small.[18] The Agents borrowed heavily in the London money market and lent to fringe banks and property developers. The business of the own account dealing arm, Finvest (Finance Department Investment Account), grew rapidly from £58 million at the end of 1968 to £127 million in a year, and 'by the end of 1970, the Crown Agents were running what was in effect a banking operation deploying funds of £403 million.'[19] This had grown to £472 million by 1973.[20] However, they did not possess the necessary skilled staff and expertise to assess the risks of such operations.[21]

In April 1970, a critical article in *The Sunday Times* by Charles Raw drew attention to the Crown Agents' recent involvement in the world of secondary banking. Charles Raw was one of only a few serious financial investigative journalists and the son of Rupert Raw, an Adviser to the Governors at the time. Hollom asked Keogh about the piece. His reply highlighted the unique and anomalous status of the Agents: they were neither a bank and therefore not subject to credit control nor a company and thus not subject to the Companies Acts and not a government department and not formally answerable to Whitehall.[22] Nevertheless, the Bank was concerned about the nature of the financing and investments, and it tried to obtain more information from the Agents.[23] The Bank also raised the issue with the Treasury, but neither side appeared to want to take responsibility.[24] Ultimately, these discussions resulted in the appointment, in 1971, of a committee chaired by retired senior civil servant Sir Matthew Stevenson to consider the status, functions, and financial operations of the Crown Agents. Reporting in March 1972, Stevenson found that there was inadequate accountability for the Crown Agents' banking and investment activities, but the financial management of the Crown Agents was competent, and they should be permitted to continue the 'own account' business. The findings were

---

[18] Hollom, 'The Fay Report', 3A161/182.
[19] *Report of the Tribunal Appointed to Inquire into Certain Issues Arising Out of the Operations of the Crown Agents as Financiers on Own Account in the Years 1967–74* [Croome-Johnson Report], 26 May 1982, HL 149, HC 364, para. 4.85.
[20] *Ibid.*, para. 5.03.
[21] Blunden, Statement for the Tribunal, 9 August 1978, 7A329/12.
[22] Keogh to Hollom, 'The Crown Agents', 7 May 1970, 7A329/1.
[23] *Ibid.*; Hollom, Annotation on Keogh, Note for record – 'Crown Agents', 16 July 1970, 7A329/1.
[24] Hollom, Statement for Tribunal, 31 August 1978, 7A329/12; Page, Annotation on Keogh to Page, 'Crown Agents', 19 November 1970, 7A329/1.

suppressed by the government and not made known until publication of the Fay Report in 1977[25] (see Chapter 12). Officials continued to discuss possible courses of action, including a merger or link with another financial institution.[26] The Bank sought, without success, to secure the appointment of a senior Bank official to manage the Agents' banking operations.[27] They were brought within the CCC regime, and in mid-1973 it was agreed that the Agents would comply with the requirements on prudential banking practice and the application of reserve asset requirements and special deposits. This would be done through the formation of a separate banking subsidiary. Although this was set up, nevertheless, it was overtaken by events and never activated.[28]

Another indication of emerging problems came in the winter of 1972–73 when the Scottish Co-operative Wholesale Society (SCOOP) got into difficulties because of its banking department's 'lunatic commitments' in forward dealings in certificates of deposit (CDs).[29] Lord Diamond, former Member of Parliament (MP) and chief Secretary to the Treasury, had phoned the Bank in February 1973 seeking an urgent meeting with either O'Brien or Hollom without saying why. He had warned that there would be massive unemployment if Bank assistance was not forthcoming, and this led to a quick guessing game with Luce (now an Adviser specialising in industry) suspecting that it might have something to do with Concorde because Diamond's constituency had been Gloucester.[30] But it was not. It was about SCOOP. With the Governor busy, Diamond saw Hollom and explained that SCOOP's banking department was in dire financial straits. It had a portfolio of £90 million of sterling CDs that was mostly financed through the inter-bank market, and the CDs yielded less than the cost of financing them.[31] Furthermore, it had entered into firm forward commitments to take up additional CDs to a total of over £365 million at rates of interest well below the current level. Given the path of interest rates at the time, likely losses were estimated to be somewhere in the region of £25 million. Without assistance, SCOOP faced

---

[25] *Report by the Advisory Committee on the Crown Agents [Stevenson Committee], 24 March 1972*, 1 December 1977, HC 50, 1977–78.
[26] Memorandum by Lord O'Brien, 9 August 1978, 7A329/12.
[27] Hollom, Statement for Tribunal, 31 August 1978, 7A329/12.
[28] Brief for Judge Fay's visit to the Governor on 12 February, 10 February 1976, 7A329/6.
[29] Page to O'Brien/Hollom, 'Scottish C.W.S.', 6 April 1973, C40/1316.
[30] Luce, Annotation on James Noakes (GPS) to O'Brien/Hollom, 22 February 1973, C40/1316.
[31] Hollom, 'The Scottish Co-Operative Wholesale Society Limited', 23 February 1973, C40/1316.

a strong risk of insolvency. Such a failure would disrupt the CD market and also badly damage the co-operative movement.[32]

The Bank ascertained that the major counterparties were the clearing banks, which had entered into the transactions at rates that were almost certainly going to ruin SCOOP.[33] Hollom set to work on possible solutions. He did not want to involve the government because he saw it as a banking-sector problem. The involvement of one or more of the clearers was sought: either Lloyds, as a result of its connection with the National Bank of New Zealand, the largest placer of CDs with SCOOP in the forward list, or National Westminster, the principal bankers to the Co-operative Wholesale Society (CWS).[34] The Bank formed a syndicate with the clearing banks to assist in handling the money-market commitments. This would prop up the banking side of SCOOP, although there was a risk that the trading side would collapse. Thus SCOOP merged with the CWS, and its banking department was transferred to the Co-operative Bank, a wholly owned subsidiary of CWS. All deposits in the SCOOP banking department were guaranteed by the Co-operative Bank.[35]

The clearers wanted the Bank to take some share in the loss. Hollom suggested to Faulkner that this should be divided among the London clearers, the Scots, and the Bank on the basis of pre-tax profits, which would give the Bank a share of 3 per cent in the syndicate. This offer was thought to be 'derisory' and to bear unduly heavily on the Scots. Nevertheless, Hollom thought that since the Bank had not been in the forward CD market, and virtually everyone else had, it was fair that the Bank should carry a disproportionately small share of the loss. This caused some bitterness among the clearers, who still pressed for the Bank to take a larger share and argued that by failing to prevent the difficulties in the CD market from occurring, the Bank had fallen down on its responsibilities.[36] Hollom refused to be drawn into this argument but made a gesture to go to 5 per cent. He certainly would not contribute more than this given the share that the clearing banks had taken in providing the counterpart to SCOOP's forward dealings.[37] Page also noted that some of the main banks had 'behaved with gross irresponsibility ... by

[32] O'Brien to Barber, enc. 'Scottish Co-operative Wholesale Society Limited', 13 March 1973, G3/317.

[33] Interview with Sir Jasper Hollom, 12 October 2007.

[34] Hollom, Note for record – 'Scottish Co-operative Wholesale Society Limited', 9 March 1973, C40/1316.

[35] Draft press release, 'Scottish Co-operative Society Limited', 9 April 1973, G3/317.

[36] Hollom, Note for record – 'Scottish Co-Operative Society – recent developments', 3 April 1973, C40/1316.

[37] Hollom to O'Brien, 'The C.L.C.B and Scottish C.W.S.', 17 April 1973, C40/1316.

"taking the SCOOP name" ... for amounts which were beyond all reason out of proportion to the size of that bank".[38] It was later agreed in May 1973 that losses would be divided in the following way: the first £10 million to fall on the CWS, the next £10 million to fall on the syndicate (with the Bank's 5 per cent), the next £5 million to fall on the CWS, and any loss exceeding £25 million to be for discussion between the Bank, the clearing banks, and the CWS. As the £25 million level approached in May 1974, discussion began again.[39] It was agreed in July 1976 that the syndicate should meet 50 per cent of the SCOOP losses above £25 million, subject to an upper limit of £2 million on this further contribution.

The SCOOP episode is revealing. It showed a certain casualness on the part of the clearing banks, although they might be excused on the grounds that they were simply behaving commercially in the new competitive environment. It also revealed the 'dangers of trading in the unregulated interbank sterling market for unskilled operators'.[40] And it showed one kind of reckless behaviour in the new environment following CCC. *The Daily Mirror* portentously reported on the consortium: 'This is the first operation of its kind, but it may not be the last.'[41]

The Developing Crisis and Launching of the Lifeboat

The problems of SCOOP were largely a consequence of its own actions but not helped by the behaviour of the clearers. They were, however, indicative of the changed environment. The state of the domestic economy in the course of 1973 further served to make life difficult: minimum lending rate (MLR) rose from 7.5 per cent in July to 13 per cent by the end of the year, the balance of payments deteriorated, the first oil-price shock had been announced, and property prices were rising steeply. Then, in late November, London and County Securities, unable to renew deposits taken through the money markets, ran into liquidity difficulties. This marked the real beginning of what became the secondary banking crisis. London and County had been formed as a holding company for a finance company, London and County (Advance and Discount) Ltd., in 1969. In the 1970s, its chairman and Managing Director was Gerald Caplan, a barrister by profession and a

---

[38] Page to O'Brien/Hollom, 'Scottish C.W.S.', 6 April 1973, C40/1316.
[39] Hollom to Richardson, 'SCOOP, note for today's C.L.C.B. meeting', 9 June 1976, C40/1318.
[40] Faulkner to Hobson, 9 February 1983, Lloyds TSB Archive, HO/Ch/Fau/5.
[41] *The Daily Mirror*, 21 April 1973, p. 2.

judo expert, although the latter expertise was not called on. Jeremy Thorpe, leader of the Liberal Party, was appointed a non-executive director in 1971. The group was active in investment and retail banking, the latter through its subsidiary, London and County Securities, which had 21 branches across the country.

London and County Securities was granted a Section 123 certificate in 1967 and became a public company in 1969 with capital of £1 million and £2 million of deposits. Shares first traded on the stock exchange in May 1969 at 25p per share. In the early 1970s, London and County experienced dramatic growth through extensive activity in the short-term money markets. By May 1972, the share price had risen to 400p. Profits swelled from £58,000 in 1969 to £3.6 million in the financial year ending March 1973.[42] Issued and fully paid-up capital had lagged behind, and by the second half of 1973, London and County's success began to turn. In line with a general downturn in the stock market, its share price began to fall. Speculation about its situation began, and matters were not helped when a partner of Harmood Banner, the company's auditors, resigned because of serious differences of opinion over the interpretation of London and County's figures.[43]

Between March 1973 and November 1973, the Bank had kept in touch with London and County through meetings between Keogh and Caplan and other Directors of the company. But the only statistical or balance-sheet information that Keogh received was an estimated and final audited balance sheet for the year ending March 1973. Nothing else was provided.[44] After looking at the ratio of its assets that were either available at call or short notice to its liabilities to the public, the Bank believed that London and County had an adequate liquidity position.[45] The cash position was, in fact, grossly inflated, giving the impression of strong liquidity. Nonetheless, Keogh was nervous about the position of London and County in the summer of 1973, and he secured the appointment to its board of Donald Bardsley from the merchant bank Hill Samuel, in the hope that an experienced banker would be able to reorganise its banking operation. Bardsley kept in close touch with Keogh. He found that the long-term lending had left the group with dangerously low liquidity, and he was not happy with an October 1973 offer document that falsely stated that there had been no

---

[42] Bank of England, 'Secondary banking crisis. Support group operation', draft, 19 October 1977, 1A179/11.

[43] Department of Trade (DoT), *London and County Securities Group Limited*, 1976, p. 227.

[44] Bank of England, draft, 10 July 1980, 8A170/1.

[45] Barnes to S. Silver (Freshfields), 16 September 1980, enc. Galpin, Evidence for London and County, 8A170/1.

material change in the financial or trading position of London and County since 31 March 1973.[46] On 12 November, after a mere four months at the company, Bardsley telephoned Keogh and indicated his intention to resign. He did so 10 days later, citing personal problems.[47] When the resignation was made public on 26 November, it confirmed suspicions that the collapse of London and County was both imminent and unavoidable.[48]

The share price plunged dramatically, and the company encountered difficulties in renewing its money-market deposits, and small depositors also began to withdraw their funds.[49] A meeting was held at the Bank on 28 November to discuss the market rumours of liquidity difficulties, with Keogh, Galpin, Caplan, other Directors and officials of the company, and two representatives from their auditors present. One of the Directors claimed that he was satisfied that the company could clear up its temporary illiquidity, but the Bank suggested that London and County should submit weekly figures.[50] The following evening Keogh attended a late meeting at the merchant bankers Keyser Ullman that had been convened by London and County's principal backers Eagle Star Insurance, to be told that London and County would fail the next day.[51] Keogh then phoned Alex Dibbs, chief executive of National Westminster, London and County's principal clearing bank, in the early hours of Friday, 29 November, and a meeting was convened at 8 a.m. in Dibbs' office. Both Keogh and Dibbs were friends of Pat Matthews, of the secondary bank First National Finance Corporation (FNFC), and he was invited to the meeting at their request.[52]

On 30 November, London and County announced that talks were in place between Eagle Star, United Drapery, National Westminster, and Keyser Ullman 'with a view to seeking means of continuing the viability of the company and the security of its depositors'.[53] With the share price continuing to fall, however, trading in London and County was suspended when the price was 40p per share, having been 200p at the beginning of the month. Supported by advice from Hambros, FNFC was inclined to

---

[46] DoT, *London and County*, pp. 205–219.
[47] The Discount Office diary reveals that Keogh met Bardsley on 23 November, but there is no record of what was discussed, C55/138.
[48] DoT, *London and County*, p. 56.
[49] Bank of England, 'Secondary banking crisis. Support group operation', draft, 19 October 1977, 1A179/11.
[50] Galpin, Evidence for London and County, 16 September 1980, 8A170/1.
[51] *The Sunday Times*, 22 January 1978, p. 63.
[52] The Discount Office diary shows that Keogh had frequent contact with Dibbs and Matthews, C55/138.
[53] *The Times*, 1 December 1973, p. 1

concentrate on its own position and not offer assistance. Nevertheless, on Monday, 3 December, FNFC representatives went to meet Dibbs and his Deputy, Sidney Wild, at National Westminster. Keogh was also there. Both the Bank and National Westminster made it clear that they believed a support operation should be mounted, and FNFC agreed to participate in the rescue. Final agreement on the nature of the consortium was reached at 11 p.m. on the Monday. The consortium agreed to advance a sum of £20 million, with FNFC, Keyser Ullman, Eagle Star, and United Drapery each contributing £5 million. FNFC were to assume the management role of London and County, with Matthews becoming Deputy chairman.[54] Changes in the board were made, and Caplan resigned on 4 December 1973. Thorpe left two weeks later on 17 December.

News of London and County's problems induced a crisis of confidence in the sector at the end of 1973. On 1 December, *The Times* led with a front-page headline, 'City Faces Major Crisis over Banking Group's Difficulties'.[55] An article a few days later advised that 'the big banks would be doing themselves, and the City, a favour if they now took a hard look at the reasons why so many secondary banks have made such rapid progress'.[56] With the withdrawal of deposits from the money market, on which the secondary banks were dependent, many banking groups encountered difficulties in maintaining their liquidity. This situation was further exacerbated by rising interest rates and falling property values that made the quick realisation of assets even more difficult.[57]

Then another bank was in trouble. Cedar Holdings, established in 1958, was involved in second-mortgage lending. It was active in bidding for retail deposits and conducted extensive advertising campaigns, offering interest on current accounts and 'free gifts', such as sherry goblets and sailing dinghies, to those opening time deposits.[58] Between 1969 and December 1973, Cedar's deposits grew from £2.5 million to £75 million, of which about £10 million was retail deposits. It had made loans totalling about £74 million, of which 70 per cent was in medium-term second mortgages. Most of the money was borrowed very short but was lent for periods up to 15 years. Like many fringe banks, much of Cedar's capital and long-term loans were

---

[54] Bank of England, 'Secondary banking crisis. Support group operation', draft, 19 October 1977, 1A179/11.

[55] *The Times*, 1 December 1973, p. 1.

[56] *The Times*, 3 December 1973, p. 21.

[57] Bank of England, 'Secondary banking crisis. Support group operation', draft, 19 October 1977, 1A179/11.

[58] *The Banker* 123(568):729, June 1973.

in property. Not surprisingly, the general crisis of confidence prompted by London and County's problems sparked market worries over Cedar's liquidity position when a large part of its short-term money-market deposits were not renewed. A meeting was called with Phoenix Assurance, the Electricity Council, the National Coal Board, and Unilever pension funds, the four institutions that owned a total of 25 per cent of Cedar. They put in £25 million, but this proved to be insufficient. The share price reflected the drain on funds: from a high of 90p early in the year, to 27p on 30 November (the day London and County's shares were suspended), and subsequently slipping to 10p on 18 December. By this time, the stock exchange was pressing for the shares to be suspended, but Charles Gordon claims that in an unprecedented confrontation the Bank told the stock exchange that nothing should be done until a rescue operation had been agreed. The Bank then called a meeting about Cedar on 19 December.[59]

Following the difficulties of London and County and it becoming evident that a widespread run on the secondary banks had started to develop, Keogh set up the Fringe Banks Standing Committee on 14 December to manage affairs. The committee had a short life (a total of eight meetings were held between 14 and 27 December), but it does seem to have been of some significance. It had representatives from Midland, National Westminster, Barclays, Lloyds, and Williams and Glyn's, and they all met at the Bank to discuss the position of the troubled banks and the extent of assistance that might be given to them. The first meeting was held in Keogh's office on Friday afternoon, 14 December, but the bank representatives had different impressions of the purpose of the meeting. Some thought it was specifically related to the problems of Moorgate Mercantile, a motor hire-purchase group, whereas others thought it was to discuss the more general problems with the smaller banks in the City.[60] At the second meeting, Keogh suggested exchanging the names of companies felt to be experiencing difficulties. Wild was aware of nine such names. Over the course of the meetings, problems at Bowmakers, British Bank of Commerce, Triumph Investment, Medens Trust Limited, Cedar, Twentieth Century Banking, FNFC, and Mercantile Credit were identified, and they were all later taken on by the support group at its first meeting. At the fourth meeting of the Fringe Banks Standing Committee on 19 December 1973, a proposal was put forward by Wild that could have been the template for the one later drawn up by Hollom. Wild suggested the

---

[59] Gordon (1993, pp. 193–208); *The Banker* 124(575):16, January 1974.
[60] 'Meeting held in Mr. Keogh's office at the Bank of England, 3 p.m. Friday, 14 December, 1973', Lloyds TSB Archive, HO/Ch/Fau/5.

establishment of a support fund (of over £1,000 million) to provide large amounts of assistance needed for joint rescue operations.[61] This figure was in fact very close to what was finally agreed in the main support group. The amounts in Wild's scheme were based on the supporting banks' eligible liabilities, and Wild also suggested that the accepting houses and certain other banks with exemption under the Protection of Depositors Act should contribute to the pooling scheme, an element that was absent from Hollom's later 'Heads of Agreement'. The Bank circulated a paper under the heading of the 'Support Fund' based on Wild's suggestions, and the Bank undertook to produce a further paper on this subject for the Fringe Banks Standing Committee's sixth meeting on the 21 December.[62] At that meeting, Keogh announced that the further paper on the support fund would not be circulated because 'the Governor was to talk to the Chairman of the Clearers that afternoon about an all-embracing exercise with a wider scope than immediate liquidity problems.'[63] It is not clear whether Hollom was aware of Wild's proposal, but the general idea of a pool of City contributors certainly was not unknown. After all, it had been the basis of the resolution of the Barings crisis in the late nineteenth century. The last meeting took place on 27 December 1973, when it gave way to the final terms of reference and mechanics of the support system set by the 'higher authority' and confirmed that afternoon between the Governors and the clearers.[64] What is interesting about Keogh's Fringe Bank Standing Committee is the lack of involvement from or consultation with the top. Hollom was not involved and, when later interviewed, could not recall the existence of the Committee.[65]

Wednesday, 19 December 1973 would be a day that many would remember for a long time. Richardson summoned two separate groups to the Bank: Barclays (Cedar's bankers), together with the heads of the four main institutional shareholders, met in the morning, and the chairmen of the big four clearers met in the afternoon. The meeting was a long one. As *The Economist* later wrote, 'a great many arms had to be twisted very hard in Camelot.'[66] Although many thought that the meeting was unlikely to last

[61] Note for record – 'Fringe banking', 19 December 1973, HSBC141/019.

[62] Note for Mr. Trott, Mr. Graham, Mr. Cave, Mr. Kneale from C. W. Linton, Fringe Banks Standing Committee Fifth Meeting, 20 December 1973, HSBC141/019.

[63] Note for record – 'Fringe banking', 21 December 1973, Lloyds TSB Archive, HO/Ch/Fau/5.

[64] Note for Mr. Trott, Mr. Graham, Mr. Cave, Mr. Kneale from C. W. Linton, Fringe Banks Standing Committee Eighth Meeting, 27 December 1973, HSBC141/021.

[65] Interview with Sir Jasper Hollom, 12 October 2007. Barnes also could not recall the existence of the committee; interview with Roger Barnes, 27 September 2007.

[66] *The Economist*, 5 January 1974, p. 79.

beyond lunchtime, it ran from around 10 a.m. until 3 a.m. the following morning.[67] In the meeting, the Bank applied considerable pressure for a rescue package to be provided, making it clear from the outset that the meeting would not end until a solution was agreed on. The next morning, 20 December, Cedar was due to open for business. If it did not, a domino effect was feared. Lord De L'Isle (Phoenix Assurance), Hugh Jenkins (Coal Board), and Burton Johnson (Electricity Supply Industry) all accepted the need to support Cedar. Cob Stenham of Unilever, however, proved harder to convince. Clashing with Hollom on two occasions, Stenham was told by the Deputy Governor at one point that he had half an hour to make up his mind, and at another stage in the day, he threatened to summon Sir Ernest Woodroofe, Unilever's chairman, from his bed. Stenham replied that he would not be treated like a clerk and argued that he was perfectly capable of the task in hand.[68] Stenham eventually agreed, and the financial advisers, lawyers, and stockbrokers were sent to the Bank to negotiate a price. Later that day, the executive directors, led by the Chairman Jack Morrison and his son Michael, who had been waiting all day at Cedar's offices, made the short walk from Fenchurch Street to the Bank and waited anxiously on the ground floor of the Parlours. On hearing the offer, the executive directors refused to sign. Kenneth Cork then was called on to help settle the issue. Cork was a senior partner in W. J. Cork Gulley, the largest insolvency practice in Britain in the 1970s, and it was said that 'the mere mention of Cork's name struck terror into the hearts of business everywhere.'[69] The board was reluctant to agree and needed more time, but Cork, a man who had a 'considerable reputation for winding up failed concerns', made it clear that there was no choice.[70] After redrafting the agreement, Cork managed to persuade a majority, and by the end of the day/early hours, £72 million had been settled, a sum that underwrote the balance sheet.[71] The Bank provided £2 million and Barclays £22 million.[72] On the following day, Cedar's stock market quotation was suspended in the face of heavy withdrawals.

Hope that the £72 million would calm the crisis was misplaced. News of this assistance sparked rumours of problems at other fringe banks, and on 21 December, the front page of *The Times* told how the crisis of confidence had taken a turn for the worse and warned that that 'the current state of emergency

---

[67] Hollom's habit was to get into the Bank at around 9.30 am.
[68] Gordon (1993, pp. 225–227); *The Daily Telegraph*, 6 November 2006.
[69] Pimlott (2004). Cork was later a member of the Wilson Committee.
[70] Interview with Sir Jasper Hollom, 12 October 2007.
[71] For Cork's own account, see Cork (1988, pp. 93–95).
[72] Ackrill and Hannah (2001, p. 207).

in the secondary banking sector must be taken seriously.'[73] Many secondary banks then experienced large-scale withdrawals, and share prices dropped dramatically – what Richardson described as a 'contagion of fear' developed.[74] Friday, 21 December was, coincidentally, the Governor's monthly meeting with the chairmen of the clearers, and Hollom and other senior Bank staff attended. The topic was dictated by events. At this stage, the Bank had no clear idea of what the scale of the crisis might be, but the Governor warned that a total collapse of confidence was possible, and the problems could have spread into the banking sector proper, thereby crippling the entire economy. He later recalled that at this stage the Bank believed that it had 'to stop a potential avalanche before its full potential could be developed'.[75]

There have been some suggestions that initially not all the clearers were entirely supportive of the Governor's suggestion that they should provide aid to the troubled institutions. In particular, the Midland was relatively unexposed, and its chairman, Forbes, was inclined to take a divergent line. Eventually, though, all agreed to cooperate without too much of a struggle. The meeting ended after 90 minutes, and the general concept of the support group, what became known as the 'Lifeboat,' was accepted. That day, a press statement announced:

The Bank of England established, in conjunction with the clearing banks, machinery whereby such cases can be promptly considered, and the situation as a whole kept under continuous review. This machinery, which is working well, is being further strengthened; and in cases where additional support is shown to be necessary and justified, arrangements for reinforcing the liquidity of the deposit-taking companies concerned have been and will be made, in order to protect depositors.[76]

Over Christmas, Hollom sketched out the details of the support operation. His deliberations resulted in a four-page document entitled, 'Rescue Operations: Heads of Agreement'. The general premise was that the Bank and the clearers would 'work together in closest co-operation', and other suitable financial institutions might at some stage join the support group. Lending and losses would be shared by the group. The operation would be co-ordinated by a 'Controlling Committee', with applicants for assistance

---

[73] *The Times*, 21 December 1973, pp. 1, 15.

[74] *The Select Committee on Nationalised Industries (Sub-Committee C). Minutes of Evidence, Session 1977–78, 18 January 1978, Bank of England Report and Accounts for the Year Ended 28 February 1977*, 166-I, question 2, 27.

[75] *Ibid.*, question 2; Kynaston (2001, p. 491) states that the Bank 'was not willing to allow potentially threatened secondary banks to make their own, autonomous arrangements for financial support', which seems an unlikely position.

[76] Bank of England, Press release, 21 December 1973, HSBC ACC141/019.

introduced by the 'related bank', that is, the clearer having the 'closest relationship' with the bank requiring help. The Controlling Committee would classify applications under four categories: A, supported in full by the group on a shared-risk basis; B, supported in full by group funds but with the risk carried by the related bank; C, limited interim support on a shared-risk basis pending further investigation; and D, no support given. If the Controlling Committee agreed to give support, it was free to attach conditions in areas such as the acceptance of new business, the realisation of assets, and the imposition of board and management changes. Details of the scheme's mechanics and accounting also were outlined in this document.

Richardson had proposed to Hollom that a 'bright young man from one of the accepting houses' should be brought in to run the operation, but Hollom was dubious and proposed himself as chairman of the Controlling Committee. He believed that if he as Deputy Governor was in the chair, the clearing banks would 'have to put in more senior representatives than they otherwise would', and in the event of any problems, he could 'switch fairly easily to the CLCB [Committee of London Clearing Banks] themselves and get them to overrule their managers successfully'.[77] On 27 December, Richardson called another meeting with the clearing bank chairmen to discuss the details of the support group. One point of contention was whether the Bank would contribute any money to the rescue operation. Richardson suggested a participation of 7½ per cent and hoped that the clearers would regard this as generous. They did not and suggested 10 per cent. Richardson then said that he wished the Bank to play a proper part in the operation, and if the chairmen 'felt strongly that 10 per cent was the right figure, he would agree'.[78] Thus a 10 per cent share was settled on, coincidently being the same percentage the Bank had put into Cedar Holdings. The remaining 90 per cent was shared by the clearing banks using a formula based on the average of their eligible liabilities over the previous six months. This was subject to periodic recalculation but in the first instance gave the following proportions: National Westminster 25.5 per cent, Barclays 24.7 per cent, Midland 17.1 per cent, Lloyds Bank 12.4 per cent, Royal Bank of Scotland 3.4 per cent, Williams and Glyn's 2.6 per cent, Bank of Scotland 2.6 per cent, and Clydesdale Bank 1.7 per cent.[79] Later, in June 1978, the agreement was formalised.[80]

[77] Interview with Sir Jasper Hollom, 12 October 2007.
[78] CLCB, 'Note of a meeting held at the Bank of England at 3.15 p.m. on Thursday 27 December 1973', Lloyds TSB Archive, HO/Ch/Fau/5.
[79] Draft heads of agreement between Bank of England and the clearing banks, 10 April 1974, HSBC ACC141/030.
[80] Minutes of the Control Committee, 21 and 28 June 1974, 5A197/1; *The Banker* 124(584):1181, October 1974; Reid (1982, p. 17).

Some alternatives to the pooled support operation might have been considered, although details, and more critically, the timing, are uncertain. In an undated note on 'Rescue operations', Hollom laid out three situations that could be dealt with.[81] First was to underpin companies where liquidity was threatened by the withdrawal of deposits (private or market) but the firm appeared to have 'a viable future'. Second was 'to hold the position' on a temporary basis while long-run prospects were investigated. Finally was to take over, for sale or liquidation, of firms where there was no viable prospect other than disposal on at least a break-even basis. The first ought not to involve losses, but the second and third 'certainly might', although with possible offsetting gains in the last case: 'The main argument for intervention would not, of course, be the possibility of gain', wrote Hollom, 'but rather the avoidance of collapses leading to chain reactions which would do major damage to the system.' Where the note then departed from the support scheme that was adopted was in the suggested vehicle to undertake rescue operations. Two possibilities were floated: use of the Finance Corporation for Industry (FCI) or establishing a new company specifically for the purpose. FCI came 'ready made', and the shareholding was in the right hands, that is, the banks. But borrowing powers were limited, and it did not have any institutional investors. Thus Hollom thought it at best an interim device. A new company could be created with a small capital but with 'wide powers to borrow and to take and give guarantees'. The borrowing would be used to channel money-market funds to where 'underpinning seemed desirable'. Shareholders would include clearing banks and major institutional investors. Hollom suggested that any losses would be borne in proportion to the amount of eligible liabilities for the clearers, some measure of size for other institutions, and a 'modest share' for the Bank. Clearly, a scheme of this nature would have taken some time to establish, and time was of the essence at the end of 1973. There is also no indication that it went beyond Hollom's note.

The first meeting of the Controlling Committee took place on 28 December in the Bank's Octagon Room in the Parlours. Chaired by Hollom, the clearing bank representatives were Robert Runciman (Bank of Scotland), Jim Dyson (Barclays), William Smith (Clydesdale), Evan Vaughan (Lloyds), Wild (National Westminster), Stuart Graham (Midland), Alec Ritchie (Williams and Glyn's), and William Lyall (Royal Bank of Scotland). Keogh was also present, and Roger Barnes, from the Discount Office, acted as Secretary. At this inaugural meeting, the names of 20 institutions were put

---

[81] Hollom, 'Rescue operations', nd, but some time in November–December, 7A244/1.

Table 11.1. *Institutions discussed at the first meeting of the Control Committee, 28 December 1973*

Name	Related bank
London & County	National Westminster
Duboff	National Westminster
Cannon Street Acceptances	National Westminster
First National Finance Corporation	National Westminster
Morris Wigram	National Westminster
Burston Finance	National Westminster
Twentieth Century Banking Corporation	National Westminster
Wintrust	National Westminster
Cedar Holdings	Barclays
First Maryland	Barclays
Northern Commercial Trust	Barclays
Guardian Property	Barclays
Mercantile Credit	Barclays
Medens Trust	Midland
Triumph Investment	Lloyds
Bowmaker	Lloyds
Vavasseur	Lloyds
David Samuel Trust	Williams & Glyn's
Cripps Warburg	Williams & Glyn's (not for pool)
British Bank of Commerce	Bank of Scotland

Source: Control Committee minutes, 5A197/1.

forward for consideration. National Westminster was the related bank in eight of the cases and Barclays in five (Table 11.1). At this stage, the figures were highly uncertain, but around £150 million apparently had already been advanced to 12 institutions by the related banks, whereas the 'further possible exposure' totalled more than £300 million. There was apparently little surprise at the extent of the assistance sought. Both Hollom and the banks were confident that 'there would be a lot.'[82]

The Controlling Committee, soon to be known simply as the 'Control Committee,' quickly got into its stride. There had been 12 formally

[82] Interview with Sir Jasper Hollom, 12 October 2007.

minuted meetings by the end of January 1974, eight in February, and another eight in March. After that, the frequency diminished, although there had been over 50 meetings by the end of August 1974. The occasion of the one-hundredth meeting, in June 1975, was marked with a drink.[83] When Hollom chaired his last Control Committee in January 1984, it was the two-hundred and second meeting: after a decade in the chair, he expressed the view, with typical caution, that it was 'too early to talk in terms of the ending of the Lifeboat, though that phase was now perhaps in sight'.[84]

The related bank brought the cases to the Control Committee and was responsible for establishing the facts, gathering and presenting the data, and making recommendations. The Committee then decided what should be done. The related bank also advised as to the security for the support lending, whether it was appropriate and available and, if so, in what form it should be taken. Furthermore, the related bank had to monitor the progress of the company receiving support, reporting back to the Committee, and recommending changes in the facility where necessary.[85] The main criteria were whether the company was solvent and whether it had a reasonable prospect of survival if given liquidity support. The Committee also sought to ascertain whether there were any substantial institutional shareholders who could be pressed to join in each support operation. Support would not be given if the company was insolvent. Aid was provided through the 'recycling of deposits'. Depositors had withdrawn their deposits from the secondary banks and placed them in more secure clearing banks. In effect, the clearers put this money back into the secondary banks. It might be wondered why they needed prompting. They were, after all, their customers, and if they were solvent and viable, it made sense to recycle. Funds were raised and distributed through the 'Money Desk' set up in the Discount Office. 'Money needs', defined as the minimum amount of market money necessary to carry the business of the applicant, were reported by the applicants' related bank by telephone to the Money Desk by 10 a.m. Any funds required beyond those reported on any day were provided by the related bank on an overnight basis and replaced through the Money Desk the following day. The Money Desk aggregated the day's requirements, divided them among the support group, and then telephoned

---

[83] Control Committee minutes, 5A197/1–2; Interview with Sir Jasper Hollom, 12 October 2007.

[84] 'Minutes of the 202nd meeting of the Control Committee held on Tuesday, 24 January 1984', 7A369/5.

[85] Bank of England, 'Secondary banking crisis', pp. 233–234.

to each member of the support group details of the payments to be made. The same afternoon, the Money Desk would issue confirmatory notes to the lending banks setting out details of the transactions that would act as evidence of the borrowings and lendings made.[86] Following the daily decision on the amount needed to be advanced in the next 24 hours, the Money Desk would telephone every clearing bank for its contribution.[87] It was agreed by the Committee that calls on the pool should not be made for individual amounts less that £5 million.[88] 'The aggregate amounts for each recipient were divided between the supporting banks in proportion to each bank's average eligible liabilities, and the banks then made the appropriate advance, repayable at short term to the applicants (normally one month).'[89] Lending was made either for overnight, fixed periods of one week, one month, or three months but did not exceed three months. Interest on support lending was 'charged at a commercial rate, based on the appropriate inter-bank rate, to which a margin was added, which varied according to the Committee's perception of the risk involved (typically 1½ to 2 per cent).'[90] Barnes recalls that relations within the Committee were harmonious, with 'no wrecking tactics'.[91]

On 15 January 1974, Richardson spoke about the crisis at a meeting of the City Liaison Committee. He asserted rather positively that 'the crumbling of confidence which at one time appeared to be developing has been halted, and indeed reversed.'[92] Others also felt that the tide was turning. A few days earlier, *The Sunday Telegraph* expressed 'a note of very cautious optimism', believing 'we are over the immediate hump.'[93] However, during January, five additional names were put forward to the Control Committee, and this resulted in three additions to the support group. At the end of that month, the Lifeboat had lent £331 million to 25 institutions.[94] Two months later, support had increased to £390 million at shared risk (category A), with an additional £96 million of support outstanding 'at own risk' (Table 11.2).

---

[86] Rescue Operations, Heads of Agreement, 27 December 1973, 6A260/1.
[87] Reid (1982, p. 17).
[88] 'Minutes of the second meeting of the Controlling Committee 31 December 1973', 5A197/1.
[89] Bank of England, 'Secondary banking crisis. Support group operation', draft, 19 October 1977, 1A179/11.
[90] Bank of England, 'Secondary banking crisis', p. 233.
[91] Interview with Roger Barnes, 27 September 2007.
[92] Richardson, 'Fringe banks (speaking notes)', 15 January 1974, 6A395/2.
[93] *The Sunday Telegraph*, 13 January 1974, p. 24.
[94] Note for Mr. Trott, Rescue Operations, 25 January 1974, HSBC ACC141/024.

Table 11.2. *Lifeboat, total amounts outstanding, quarterly, March 1974–December 1977 (£m)*

Quarter ending	Support group joint risk	Bank of England risk	Related banks' risk
March 1974	390.2	Nil	96.1
June 1974	443.4	16.0	214.7
September 1974	994.3	25.0	66.3
9 December 1974 (max)	1,189.3	–	–
December 1974	1,181.7	33.7	70.2
March 1975	1,173.4	122.1	67.5
June 1975	1,148.5	121.2	65.4
September 1975	949.9	114.3	59.9
December 1975	913.5	93.3	59.2
March 1976	876.1	56.3	57.1
June 1976	827.2	77.1	56.0
September 1976	774.4	94.9	51.3
December 1976	782.7	153.8	50.4
March 1977	752.1	142.1	50.4
June 1977	731.7	125.2	45.5
September 1977	713.8	113.1	44.4
December 1977	676.5	122.0	45.2

Source: Briefing paper, 13 January 1978, for SCNI hearing, 2A170/1.

Despite some discussion of a crisis in the secondary banking sector in the newspapers before Christmas, press coverage was strangely muted in January. Early in the month, some mention was made of the troubles of Cornhill Consolidated, as well as the drop in share prices of the secondary banks Triumph Investment and J. H. Vavasseur, but it was not until the end of the month that attention was given to the Bank rescue operation. On 28 January, *The Times* highlighted an article that was about to be published by *Barron's*, a weekly financial newspaper in the United States, claiming that 30 fringe banks in England were in difficulty. This prompted *The Times* to write, 'The public has seen only the tip of the iceberg.' The *Barron's* piece also suggested that the Bank had tried to keep the full extent of the crisis secret and had told those involved in the rescue operation to keep quiet 'lest the credit of The City be gravely damaged'. The next day, Margaret Reid gave her account in *The Financial Times* on 'How the "Bankers' Lifeboat" came to the rescue' – the first use of the term 'Lifeboat'.[95] She also described how the clearers along with the Bank had 'acted as secretly as possible in the past two months' to control the crisis. Thus little had been said publicly of the support operation, and even Reid's piece on how the financial crisis was the biggest the City had witnessed for the last 50 years was tucked away on page 12.

The limited reporting at least meant that the press did not exacerbate the crisis. In the 1970s, there was less transparency, and fewer people were involved than would be the case later and, consequently, a much more restricted flow of information. And the Bank's position and its power in the City meant that it could control much of the flow, and it did. Also at that time there were far fewer investigative financial journalists, and they or their papers were generally much more compliant with the wishes of the authorities. And the wishes of the authorities tended to the non-revealing end of the spectrum. The Bank was never slow to reprimand those it felt had stepped out of line. The Governor's summoning of Rees-Mogg was just one earlier example. Thus, in the 1973–74 crisis, there was little coverage to excite. One picture was published in *The Financial Times* of a queue outside London and County in December 1973, but there was little sense of drama. The media were disinclined to do anything that would challenge the law. So little was reported that one financial journalist of the time recalled (incorrectly) 35 years later that the Bank had slapped D-notices on the press to prevent comment. This was impossible, and even impossible to arrange, but it reflects a feeling that the Bank was in a position to do so and was inclined to do so.[96] Reid was a trusted confidante of both Keogh and Blunden and produced the main accounts.[97] They look very much like what the Bank was prepared to reveal.

The Banker reported in February 1974:

Natwest have been caught by many of these cases – 'they had 12 on their books before I had one' commented another banker almost gleefully – because the old Westminster bank had a large City business, to which was added the London business of National Provincial at the time of the merger. There was then a gap of seven days or so (in mid-December) before it became obvious that a widespread run on the secondary banks had developed through the money market.

[95] *The Financial Times*, 29 January 1974, p. 12. It quoted Leonard Mather's (vice-chairman, Midland Bank) reference to the support operation as 'The National Joint Stock Bankers' Lifeboat Institution'.

[96] Tim Congdon, Seminar, Queen Mary College, 30 January 2008.

[97] See Discount Office diaries, 1973 and 1974, C55/138–139. Hollom declined to speak to Reid but approved of her account; interview with Sir Jasper Hollom, 12 October 2007.

The article did end by saying that because of the seriousness of the situation, a journalist 'must exercise extreme reticence.... What can be said is that many institutions still standing today will not survive.'[98] Even this was treading a delicate line as far as the Bank was concerned.

To complete the story of London and County, in January 1974, it was agreed that its affairs would be investigated by the Department of Trade. In February, the Control Committee had been unable to agree on proposals for London and County's future, and the Bank proposed that it should acquire a 50 per cent share in two subsidiaries, London and County Securities (the banking arm) and Overseas Financial Trust (Holding) Ltd., for a nominal amount. The remaining share was taken by FNFC, and the parent company, London and County Securities Group, was to be put into liquidation.[99] By March, the full extent of the company's problems had emerged, and the planned consortium rescue was abandoned. When the report of the investigation into London and County was published in 1976, the corrupt activities of Caplan were exposed. He had maintained accounts under a fictitious name for his own purposes and to purchase London and County shares. A system of 'warehousing', whereby customers and Directors of London and County were asked to purchase its shares with loans provided to them by the company, was also pursued. Substantial sums were lent for the purchase of shares through subsidiaries, also controlled by Caplan. The auditors were actively deceived because Caplan disguised 'not only the extent of his acquisitions but also the source of his finance, which was usually the bank itself'. On top of this, window dressing was used to inflate the amount of cash stated in the annual accounts, and while that had been a common practice, the scale was unacceptable.[100] London and County was taken to Court in 1980 for creating and maintaining a false share price, a fraud of a 'breathtaking magnitude'. Other charges included theft, falsifying a document, passing on a forged letter, and dishonestly obtaining the reduction of debt.[101] By this stage, Caplan had fled the country and successfully avoided extradition from California in 1979. The Bank provided evidence in which Galpin recalled that London and County was not regarded as a bank and fell outside the Bank's non-statutory system

---

[98] The Banker 124(576):87–89, February 1974.

[99] 'Minutes of the nineteenth meeting of the Control Committee on Friday, 22 February', 5A197/1; The Banker 124(577):210, March 1974. Liquidation was in March 1975. FNFC had written off a large part of their support for London and County in October 1974; The Banker 124(584):1179, October 1974.

[100] DoT, London and County, pp. 22–23, 68, 252–253, 258–259.

[101] The Times, 25 February 1981, p. 3; The Times, 28 February 1981, p. 2.

of supervision over UK registered banks.[102] Two employees were found guilty of conspiring with Caplan to defraud and were given 18-month jail sentences, suspended for two years.[103]

The Lifeboat and After

The secondary banking crisis consisted of three stages. The first, from November 1973 to March 1974, was essentially a liquidity problem. This was resolved through recycling deposits. Most of the deposits withdrawn from the fringe banks had been deposited with the banks that were to man the Lifeboat; these were recycled to the supported institutions through the Lifeboat operation.[104] Following the liquidity troubles were solvency problems. This was the second stage, from March to December 1974, and came against a background of the collapse of property values and increasing inflation. The third phase followed in 1975 with the Bank discreetly rescuing firms to avoid a spreading crisis of confidence. The Control Committee minutes of 4 April noted that in view of the impact that the failure of property companies might have on the fringe and other banking institutions, such cases should be mentioned at the Committee. This was not to imply any obligation of support, and there was none, although apparently such action came close.[105] The following month, the multimillion-pound property empire of William Stern ran into trouble. Stern had £200 million outstanding in loans, against which there were assets of £250 million, mainly in industrial and commercial property. Many of the properties could not be sold or let, and the company faced serious illiquidity. The crash of Stern and other property groups induced a rapid growth in Lifeboat support. United Dominions Trust (UDT) and FNFC, for example, were exposed to the Stern Group to the extent of £22 million; they were to be the Lifeboat's biggest borrowers. Both had run into problems in May 1974 when they found it increasingly difficult to maintain their money-market deposits. UDT, the largest finance house in the country, had been in difficulty for some time but did not want to risk adverse publicity if it were to get out that it was on the Committee's list. On the odd difficult day, Barclays and the Bank had been able to make additional facilities

---

[102] Barnes to S. Silver (Freshfields), 16 September 1980, enc. Galpin, Evidence for London and County, 8A170/1.

[103] *The Times*, 18 April 1981, p. 2.

[104] Bank of England, 'The secondary banking crisis', p. 234.

[105] 'Minutes of the twenty-ninth meeting of the Control Committee on 4 April 1974', 5A197/1; interview with Roger Barnes, 27 September 2007.

available.[106] UDT was taken into the Lifeboat under category A in July 1974 and by 16 August had been advanced £320 million.[107]

During this phase, the crisis took on an international dimension. Rumours that I. D. Herstatt, a German private bank, was over-trading in foreign currencies first circulated in the summer of 1973. The German Federal Banking Supervisory Office began to look into Herstatt's affairs, but it was not until the week ending 22 June 1974 that the enormity of Herstatt's foreign-exchange losses became apparent. Emergency meetings took place, but when the rescue attempt fell through, the Supervisory Office took immediate action and closed the bank on 26 June 1974.[108] This, along with the failure of the Israel-British Bank of Tel Aviv, and the foreign-exchange losses of £33 million suffered by the Lugano Branch of Lloyds Bank International caused 'a great deal of nervousness in international banking circles'.[109]

By the end of July 1974, the advances at joint risk to the Lifeboat totalled £674.8 million, of which £565.7 million was shared funds and £109.1 million was lent solely by the related banks.[110] In August, as a result of the collapse of the property market and the capital market, the clearers were concerned by the considerable rise in the amount of Lifeboat assistance, particularly to UDT and FNFC. In addition, Keyser Ullman, a member of the Issuing Houses Association, also ran into difficulties. There were no signs that support would lessen. The recent rapid escalation of UDT's support was thought to signal a possible similar trend for other groups in the Lifeboat, and there was a genuine belief that given UDT's position, overall support lending could rise dangerously high, possibly to over £2,000 million.[111] Anxiety from the clearers also stemmed from the belief in the media and among the general public that the 'integrity of the inner core' of the clearing banks and accepting houses was in question.[112] Thus they were concerned not only over the general health of the City but also over their own position. They felt that exposure had to be limited so that confidence in the clearing banks as recipients

---

[106] 'Minutes of the thirty-seventh meeting of the Control Committee on 30 May 1974'. 5A197/1.

[107] 'Minutes of the fifty-first meeting of the Control Committee Friday, 16 August', 19 August 1974, 5A197/1.

[108] Balfour to McMahon, 'I. D. Herstatt', 4 July 1974, 3A49/2.

[109] Bank of England, 'Secondary banking crisis', p. 235.

[110] Bank of England, 'Secondary banking crisis. Support group operation', draft, 19 October 1977, 1A179/11.

[111] CLCB memorandum – 'The support operation', 16 August 1974, Lloyds TSB Archive, HO/Ch/Fau/5.

[112] Faulkner, 'Memorandum on visit to the Governor on 13 August 1974', Support Group, 16 August 1974, Lloyds TSB Archive, HO/Ch/Fau/5.

of deposits was not endangered and depositors' funds placed in jeopardy and that the distortion of their balance sheet was 'not such as to reduce their capital/deposit ratios to unacceptable levels'.[113] The clearing banks believed that their exposure had to be limited by setting a ceiling on total support. Furthermore, Faulkner later recalled that the clearing banks felt it prudent to limit their contribution because they, and especially Midland, believed that they had to be ready to come to the help of industry, which they felt would be very illiquid as a result of the three-day week.[114] Faulkner and Anthony Tuke (of Barclays) told the Bank of their concern at the extent of support they were being asked to provide and that an overall limit needed to be set.[115] At this stage, the amount committed by the CLCB was £1,000 million. Tuke argued that a limit of £2,000 million should be set; Faulkner wanted £1,500 million.[116] Two days later, Hollom and Fforde met Tuke, Graham, and John Prideaux (chairman of National Westminster). The CLCB had further considered the situation and warned of the considerable strain on continuing to put large amounts into the support operation. 'They could not extend their commitments to a level which might damage their basic business.' A limit of £1,200 million therefore was agreed, a figure that 'represented about half of their banks' shareholders' funds, and was twice the amount of the sum originally envisaged'.[117] The limit applied to group funds as a whole (i.e., including the Bank's contribution) and related to money out at joint risk (i.e., excluding category B cases).[118] An agreement was also reached whereby further companies would be accepted into the Lifeboat only once an investigation was carried out.

The clearers were complaining in 1974 that they could go no further because of the strain on their capital resources (Table 11.3). The banks had found their own way to safety and capital adequacy. In the late nineteenth century, their capital-assets ratio was above 16 per cent. But that fell slowly such that by the interwar years it was less than half that at around 7 per cent. It

[113] CLCB memorandum – 'The support operation', 16 August 1974, Lloyds TSB Archive, HO/Ch/Fau/5.

[114] N. C. H. Falls (Governor's office) to Hollom, 'Wilson Lifeboat paper', 21 April 1978, 1A179/18.

[115] CLCB, 'Informal note of discussion on 15 August 1974', Lloyds TSB Archive, HO/Ch/Fau/5.

[116] Note of a meeting at the Bank of England, The Rescue Operation, 19 August 1974, HSBC ACC141/35.

[117] Note of a meeting at the Bank of England, The Support Operation, 21 August 1974, HSBC ACC141/36.

[118] Barnes, 'Minutes of the fifty-third meeting of the Controlling Committee on 30 August 1974', 2 September 1974, 5A197/1.

Table 11.3. *Clearing banks' share price and balance-sheet details, 1970–75*

Bank/year	Share price			Balance sheet (£m)		
	High	Low	Year ending	Share capital	Total	Capital ratio (per cent)
Barclays						
1970	414	268	334	337.2	3,996.1	8.4
1971	622	327.5	578	423.9	4,356.7	9.7
1972	492	298	455	470.8	5,653.2	8.3
1973	468	277	295	532.3	6,841.6	7.8
1974	340	108	118	554.5	7,423.7	7.5
1975	325	112	293	613.6	7,575.1	8.1
Lloyds						
1970	338	256	318	265.0	2,438.7	10.9
1971	618	310	576	283.9	2,622.3	10.8
1972	850	601	712	308.2	3,070.4	10.0
1973	361	197	222	483.3	3,873.4	12.5
1974	267	92	102	491.5	4,630.5	10.6
1975	265	94	232	517.8	4,947.9	10.5
Midland						
1970	354	238	293	259.5	3,691.5	7.0
1971	552	287.5	514	279.3	4,467.7	6.3
1972	530.5	348	478	314.1	5,896.5	5.3
1973	503	267	295	468.7	8,215.5	5.7
1974	345	115	128	592.4	9,940.2	6.0
1975	308	122	282	714.7	10,364.9	6.9
National Westminster						
1970	398	256	325	355.6	5,544.0	6.4
1971	630	323.75	584	395.2	6,648.5	6.0
1972	492	300.5	455	539.3	8,760.8	6.2
1973	473	257	277	901.3	11,849.6	7.6
1974	312	90	98	947.1	13,585.7	7.0
1975	275	88	240	993.4	14,659.7	6.8

Source: Share prices are taken from *The Economist*. Balance sheets are taken from *Bankers Alamanc*, 1970–75.

would fall further to its lowest level in the 1950s when it reached 2.6 per cent. While this looks dangerously low, it should be remembered that the banks were awash with gilts from the war years, so the capital probably was entirely adequate. Nevertheless, the banks wanted to raise capital but were prevented by the Capital Issues Committee. There was some recovery in these levels, and as their pre-war balance sheets were gradually restored and restrictions on raising new capital removed, the ratios were back to around 6 per cent in the 1960s.[119] Immediately prior to full disclosure in 1969, the ratios were 6 per cent, but disclosure was in part responsible for them rising to 8 per cent. No sooner had that happened, however, than rapid inflation operated to erode the capital base again.[120] Thus it was not surprising that the banks should be nervous about that extra pressure on their capital in the middle of 1974.

Neither was it easy at that point to raise new capital. The stock market had suffered its biggest ever fall in the previous two years. The *Financial Times* (*FT*) Industrial Share Index fell from 533 in May 1972 to 160 in December 1974. Bank shares had fared worse than most. National Westminster was worst of all, with a fall from a high of 630 in 1971 to 90 in 1974 (and 88 in 1975), but the other clearers were not very different. (Strangely, there was little or no comment from the Bank on this collapse in asset prices.) The prospects of raising new capital in these circumstances were not good. The market did not begin to improve until the beginning of 1975. There are competing stories about how the turnaround came about. One is that in December 1974 some big investors decided the fall had gone too far. The two chief investment officers, Peter Moody and Edward Hatchett, at Prudential Assurance invited their counterparts to lunch, where they agreed that they would embark on some aggressive buying up to £20 million. Whether or not they helped remains an open question, but the *FT* Index (FT30) that stood at 162 on 1 January 1975 rose by almost 50 per cent to 240 at the end of January. And it carried on rising. Thereafter, the pressure on raising capital began to ease.[121]

In November 1974, Triumph Investment Trust became insolvent. Triumph had been on the support group list since its inception. Earlier in 1974, the Committee agreed that the group would be run down gradually, and the support group repaid. But this did not happen. Although various other schemes were considered, the Lifeboat withdrew its support.[122] Subsequently, the press reported that the support operation was in danger

---

[119] Billings and Capie (2007).
[120] Wilcox (1979).
[121] Dennett (1998, pp. 338–340); *The Daily Telegraph*, 25 May 1974, p. 23.
[122] Note for the chairman, 'Rescue Operation – Triumph Investment Trust Limited', 21 November 1974, HSBC ACC141/038.

of breaking down.[123] The amount provided at joint risk by November 1974 was £1,141.6 million.[124] Rumours then spread through the City that the large clearing bank National Westminster was on the verge of collapse. Speculative reports in the stock market that National Westminster had arranged a large standby credit facility with the Bank resulted in National Westminster's share price falling to 90p on 29 November against a peak earlier in the year of 312p. The Bank denied the existence of any standby facility, and Prideaux released a press statement asserting that the rumours had 'absolutely no foundation'. Ironically, this came a year to the day after the collapse of London and County.

By mid-December 1974, the total support exceeded £1,200 million, and the Bank assumed £50 million of the lending to UDT for its sole risk. On 20 December, National Westminster, Barclays, Lloyds, and Midland agreed to make £10 million each available on a short-term basis outside the pool. Gordon Downey at the Treasury wrote:

If the situation deteriorated beyond the capacity of the support operation ... direct government intervention would be required, which might, for example, involve an extension of the support arrangements by the clearing banks with a government guarantee against loss. This and other possible measures are being considered in a separate contingency planning exercise.[125]

At the end of 1974, 25 companies had received advances from the support group, and lending at joint risk totalled approximately £1,160 million. Of this, some 80 per cent was accounted for by lending to companies involved in the instalment credit business.[126] Reorganisation plans were made for both FNFC and UDT because liquidation would involve greater losses and possibly have an adverse effect on others in the Lifeboat. FNFC's consumer credit division was still commercially viable and profitable, so it was separated from the other activities of the company and continued to operate normally. The remainder of the business – mostly property interests – was run down over several years. This was perhaps an early intimation of the good bank/bad bank approach. After the reorganisation was accepted, FNFC applied for, and received, authority to relinquish its prime banking status, thus releasing reserve assets and special deposits, which were used to reduce borrowing from the support group

[123] Laurence Airey (HMT) to Fforde, 26 November 1974, TNA T233/2842.
[124] Fforde to Airey, 29 November 1974, TNA T233/2842.
[125] Downey, 'Banking support operation', 20 December 1974, TNA T233/2842.
[126] Bank of England, 'Secondary banking crisis. Support group operation', draft, 19 October 1977, 1A179/11.

and, therefore, the cost of maintaining the loans. In July 1976, a capital reorganisation was agreed for UDT by which a further £10 million of loan stock was subscribed by the two major shareholders, Prudential Assurance and Eagle Star, together with a reorganisation of their shareholding.[127]

Despite the difficulties that the Crown Agents had brought on themselves, when the banking crisis hit, they were encouraged by the Bank to give assistance to certain secondary banks, just as other financial institutions that were either significant shareholders or large depositors were pressed to contribute to any support operations by increasing their lending or, at the very least, not withdrawing their deposits.[128] Although the Bank knew that problems existed in the Agents' loan book and that there were some poor investments, the Bank was still unaware of the true extent of the problem.[129] Towards the end of 1973, G. T. Whyte, the banking subsidiary of Triumph Investment Trust, experienced 'a run on its money-market deposits'. Immediate support was provided, and on 2 January 1974, the Bank arranged a meeting with Triumph's shareholders and depositors. Group deposits totalled £80 million to £90 million, mainly short term, and had been invested in long-term illiquid assets. Early indications were that support of £24 million might be required if all short-term deposits were withdrawn on maturity.[130] The Crown Agents had deposits and loans of £17 million with the group, and under pressure, they agreed to roll over the existing loans and to advance a further £5 million. At the request of the Lifeboat, the Agents also gave indirect support to FNFC, Burston, and Northern Commercial Trust. The total direct and indirect support given by the Agents was later put at £26 million, although the Bank doubted the accuracy of the figure because it included long-term loans made before the crisis broke.[131] A recent history of the Agents claims that the unofficial contribution through both 'passive' and 'active' assistance was probably £110 million.[132]

The Crown Agents got into further trouble as a result of the property crash. They had lent considerable sums to the property sector and invested in their own portfolio, and on 4 April 1974, the Bank became aware of the Agents'

[127] *Ibid.*
[128] Bank of England, 'The secondary banking crisis and the Bank of England's support operations', paper for Wilson Committee, 1A179/18.
[129] Blunden to Jordan (HMT), 14 January 1976, 7A329/6.
[130] Bank of England, 'Triumph Investment Trust Limited', 29 October 1976, 7A329/11.
[131] 'CA part in the Lifeboat operation', November 1977, 7A329/3; *Report by the Committee of Inquiry Appointed by the Minister of Overseas Development into the Circumstances Which Led to the Crown Agents Requesting Financial Assistance from the Government in 1974* [Fay Committee], 1 December 1977, HC 48, paras. 347–354.
[132] Sunderland (2007, p. 231).

involvement in the Stern Group (£35 million had been lent to Stern), realising the severe implications that a collapse of the group would have. According to Sunderland, there was a meeting on 11 April at which Richardson asked the Agents and Barclays to 'nurse Stern into viability again', indicating that the Bank would support them. Consequently, the Crown Agents put a further £3.25 million into the Stern Group.[133] Richardson felt that the only way to deal with the situation was to avoid as much publicity as possible.[134] The Bank was also informed that the Crown Agents had made other large loans to vulnerable companies, but the Bank did not warn the Treasury of the extent of these problems until several weeks later. Galpin and Treasury officials tried to gain a greater understanding on the Agents' position and to discuss possible steps should confidence in the group be so damaged as to result in a widespread withdrawal of deposits.[135] Although the Agents said that they would not be seriously affected by the collapse of Stern, knowledge of their involvement would spark a general crisis of confidence, threatening to cause a run, and in turn, they would call in their deposits with the secondary banks, causing further difficulties for that sector.[136] Hollom later recalled that the Bank approached the meeting believing that the Crown Agents were 'bust or capable of being bust'. Nobody had come prepared with a balance sheet, so one was drawn up on the back of an envelope.[137] The difficulties experienced by the secondary banks and the collapse of the property sector had left the Agents in dire financial trouble. Hollom argued that they were not a bank, and the fact that the Agents had assisted the support group, by increasing lending to fringe banks and by not calling in money deposited, was insufficient justification for the Lifeboat to offer help. Hollom therefore maintained that government support was the only realistic option.[138]

In October 1974, John Cuckney, formerly of the Property Services Agency, took over as chairman of the Crown Agents. He met Hollom that

---

[133] *Ibid.*, p. 232. There is no record of this meeting in the Bank's archive, nor is it mentioned in the official investigations.

[134] Richard King (Ministry for Overseas Development), Note for record, 3 May 1974, 7A329/4. Sunderland argues that this was because the Bank suspected that the new Labour minister, a strong critic of property developers, would block the advances.

[135] Galpin, Note for record – 'Crown Agents', 9 May 1974, 7A329/4.

[136] J. B. Unwin, 'The Crown Agents and property companies: record of meetings held by Mr. Wass at the Treasury on Monday, 13 May 1974', 15 May 1974, 7A329/4.

[137] *The Times*, 2 December 1977, p. 24.

[138] 'The Crown Agents and property companies: record of meetings held by Mr. Wass at the Treasury on Monday, 13 May 1974', 7A329/4. Unconvincingly, Sunderland believes the hesitance from the Bank to assist the Crown Agents was the result of 'a century of disputes', and the Bank 'perhaps sought revenge for the many slights that it had suffered at the hands of the Agency'; Sunderland (2007, p. 237).

month amidst concern over the Agents' property lending and merchant banking businesses and admitted that 'his top people had got quite out of their depth.' Coopers & Lybrand were called in to report on the solvency and liquidity position, especially relating to the banking and money-market operations.[139] The report showed that it was not just a problem of liquidity; the Crown Agents' solvency was in question.[140] When Cuckney talked to Richardson in December, the latter said that the Bank would do whatever it could to help, but it would be difficult to provide interim liquidity support to an organisation whose solvency was in doubt, and the only people who could take action were the government, the effective owners of the Crown Agents.[141] This is what happened, and the government propped up the Agents with a recoverable grant of £85 million in December 1974. To cover the immediate crisis of reserves and liquidity, the Bank also gave a standby facility of £50 million. The Agents then started an orderly and phased withdrawal from property and secondary banking.

The recent history of the Agents places a large amount of blame for their collapse at the feet of the Bank. Sunderland maintains that the Bank deliberately hid the Agents' insolvency from the Ministry for Overseas Development and Treasury and instead gave the impression that they were solvent because it was in the Bank's interest for the Crown Agents to trade as normal. An announcement that the Agents had made considerable losses would affect confidence and further threaten the attempt to stabilise the crisis. A collapse would also place further burden on the Lifeboat, and once the banks had set a limit in August, greater financial burden would be placed on the Bank. Knowing the Agents' dire situation, the Bank should not have pressed them for help, yet the Bank exploited the loyalty of the Agents to the City and encouraged them to help the Lifeboat unofficially. The Agents did not have the strength in management to refuse the Bank's pressure, and when the companies they supported collapsed, the Agents lost a considerable amount of money.[142] From the Bank's perspective, it had told the Treasury in 1976 that the Bank was aware at the time that some problems existed in the Crown Agents' loan book and that they held some poor investments, but the Bank was, like everyone else, unaware of the true seriousness of the overall position. The Bank and the support group therefore regarded the Crown Agents in the same way as any other responsible financial institution. Furthermore, the Crown Agents were not asked to give support to any secondary bank or

---

[139] Hollom, Note for record – 'Crown Agents', 18 October 1974, 7A329/4.
[140] Blunden to Richardson/Hollom, 'Crown Agents', 2 December 1974, 7A329/4.
[141] Blunden, Note for record – 'Crown Agents', 6 December 1974, 7A329/4.
[142] Sunderland (2007, p. 239).

other financial institution to which they had not already got a substantial commitment as lenders and/or shareholders.[143] A subsequent enquiry was more critical of the Bank (see Chapter 12).

Three Rescues

In March 1975, Blunden, then in charge of banking supervision, told the Treasury that the Bank was handling the support operation with much greater control and certainty than in the earlier stages. The Bank now felt that the crisis was stable, but it was still important to rebuild confidence.[144] With this in mind, the Bank took unilateral action to rescue three institutions outside the Lifeboat: Slater Walker, Edward Bates, and Wallace Brothers. This marked the third stage of the crisis. The Bank claimed that its motive in undertaking such operations was 'no different from its motive in setting up the Lifeboat itself: i.e., to protect depositors and to prevent a damaging blow to confidence in the banking system'.[145] In the cases of Slater Walker and Bates, the Bank actually bought the firms. Although unusual, it was not the first time that this had happened. In 1921, the Bank had taken over the Anglo Austrian Bank.[146] The three rescues of the 1970s took up a great deal of the Bank's resources in terms of time and money.

Slater Walker Securities Limited (SWSL) began life as an industrial holding company and later became predominantly an investment and finance group. Jim Slater, the founder, was the son of a builder from Wembley, north London. Born in 1929, Slater left school at age 16 and joined a firm of London Chartered Accountants. After qualifying as an accountant, he gained some experience with accountants Cooper Brothers and other companies until he was appointed Deputy sales Director at Leyland Motors in 1963.[147] By the late 1960s, he was at the peak of his career. Although his social and educational background meant that he was an outsider in the City, Slater was widely known for his talents as an investment analyst and stock market trader and was deemed by some to be a financial genius.[148] Indeed, in 1969, *The City Press* felt that the 'likeable, handsome fellow'

---

[143] Blunden to Jordan, 14 January 1976, 7A329/6.
[144] Unwin to Downey, 4 March 1975, TNA T233/2842.
[145] Brief on support operations, filed 1 March 1978, 1A179/17.
[146] 'Proposals to share and loan stock holders', 3A124/1. The company was merged with the British Trade Corporation to form the Anglo International Bank, in which the Bank had a controlling interest.
[147] Keogh, 'James Derrick Slater, F.C.A', 13 December 1971, 6A70/2.
[148] 'Foreign banks in London annual review', *The Banker* 125(597):1235, November 1975.

should win an Oscar if such awards were made simply for making profits.[149] The Bank, too, looked favourably on Slater. Keogh admired his 'razor sharp mind', 'fantastic memory', and great focus.[150] In the early 1970s, though, Slater's success began to falter, and by 1975, outside help was essential for survival, and the Bank stepped in to save Slater's group. Slater was rarely out of the newspaper headlines.

Formed in 1964 in association with Peter Walker, Conservative MP for Worcester, SWSL was the holding company for a number of property and investment interests, including financial advice and investment banking.[151] Between 1965 and 1975, SWSL underwent significant changes. The group went from being an industrial holding company to a banking and financial services company with large investment stakes in industrial and financial companies. In 1973, SWSL was rated the City's best-performing share of the past decade. However, following the secondary banking crisis, the group was forced into retrenchment, selling most of its overseas investments and a number of British assets.[152]

The Bank's main interest was in the banking subsidiary of SWSL. This was established in April 1965 as Slater Walker Acceptances and changed its name to Slater Walker Limited (SWL) in November 1965. The company operated as bankers to the Slater Walker group and had authorised bank status after acquiring full control of Ralli Brothers in January 1970. Keogh felt in 1971 that SWL had become 'a powerful merchant banking group ... whose stability is not in question'.[153] Indeed, in December 1971, Slater's name was mentioned as a possible candidate for the Court.[154] As late as 1973, the Bank was happy with the way SWL was being run. This changed in 1974. Despite regular discussions with management, as well as with Slater himself, the Bank had difficulty getting sufficiently detailed information to assess the health of SWL. From September 1974 onwards, the Bank started to press SWL, and when Hollom saw Slater in December, he expressed his concern that at several interviews representatives had been unable to explain some of the group's transactions. The Bank knew that the financial affairs of SWL depended on its relationship with SWSL, but

---

[149] *City Press*, 8 May 1969, p. 3.
[150] Keogh, 'James Derrick Slater, F.C.A', 13 December 1971, 6A70/2.
[151] Walker was a member of the Shadow Cabinet in 1965 and held ministerial positions in the Heath and Thatcher administrations. He had left Slater Walker in June 1970.
[152] *The Evening Standard*, 1 August 1973, p. 40; *The Economist*, 1 November 1975, p. 72. For further details, see 6A70/1–3.
[153] Keogh, 'James Derrick Slater, F.C.A', 13 December 1971, 6A70/2.
[154] Erskine, 'The Slater Walker rescue', January 1978, 8A17/1.

the exact relationship was not clear. Galpin later noted that to a certain degree SWL was guilty of deliberate deception because 'the real extent of the in-house nature of the business was not revealed to us, and the banking Directors repeatedly assured us that there were no skeletons either in the Group or in the bank.'[155]

The case illustrated the problems of supervising the banking subsidiary of a large and complex group.[156] Analysis in the Bank already suggested that 24 per cent of SWL's advances were to companies that had bought substantial assets from SWSL. Perhaps this was an 'unfortunate coincidence', but clearly, a close investigation into the SWL's connected activity was required.[157] There also were concerns about the unconnected banking business, where the Bank felt that SWL was over-lent (advances were 95 per cent of deposits). Group liquidity had deteriorated sharply, and there were questions about whether SWSL had the resources to support its bank or survive for long in a major run.[158]

A further worry was SWL's activities in the Far East, notably a £14.5 million loan to Haw Par Brothers International, operating in Singapore, and Spydar, SWL's Hong Kong subsidiary and dealing company set up in 1972. Both these concerns threatened the stability of SWL. Slater had received bad publicity on his affairs with Haw Par, and problems had emerged through a series of questionable share dealings involving SWL. After accusations made by the Singapore Finance Minister that Spydar had been used for share deals for the personal benefit of Directors, the Singapore and Hong Kong authorities began an investigation into the group. Sir Henry Benson, an Adviser to the Governors on industrial finance, certainly was not impressed: 'Instead of carrying into these eastern countries the principles and traditions of the City of London, he [Slater] has used the cheapjack devices to allow Directors to make profits on private account.... If the Bank generally shares my strong views on this subject I hope the Governor will tell Jim Slater so in the firmest terms.'[159] Aware that SWL's involvements in the Far East potentially could put at risk Slater's position as chairman and certainly damage confidence in that

[155] Galpin to Hollom/Richardson, 'Slater Walker/Edward Bates/Wallace Brothers', 25 October 1976, 6A70/17.
[156] Galpin to Richardson/Hollom, 'Slater Walker Securities Limited', 4 September 1975, 6A70/5.
[157] Erskine to Galpin, 'Slater, Walker Securities Ltd', 5 September 1975, 6A70/5.
[158] Galpin to Richardson/Hollom, 'Slater Walker Securities Limited', 4 September 1975, 6A70/5.
[159] Benson to Blunden, 12 September 1975, 6A70/5.

bank, Fforde advocated that a close eye be kept on the situation and a contingency plan devised in case of a crisis.[160]

The Bank made plans to protect SWL's depositors in the event of a run that could have brought down SWSL as well. But they still needed more information on the group. When Slater met Fforde and Blunden in September 1975, they discussed the stability of SWL and matters relating to Spydar and Haw Par. Slater claimed that he had evidence to disprove charges of insider trading and that the group's activities in the Far East were legitimate. When asked about SWL, Slater said that he would provide estimates of the bank's vulnerability along with details of the group's capacity to support the bank. He viewed SWL as a possible drain on the resources of the group and had thought that an agreement could be reached with Rothschilds to take it over. An alternative was an alliance with James 'Jimmy' Goldsmith, the chairman of Cavenham Foods, who was a close friend and business associate of Slater. Goldsmith's associates already had a 10 per cent shareholding in SWL. The Bank wanted to be consulted if any of the proposals developed. Another option that Slater suggested was retirement, claiming that he wanted to devote more time to his family. He had, in fact, been thinking of leaving the City since the failed merger attempt with Hill Samuel in 1973. But the Bank said that Slater's departure would not solve the problem.[161] In September, Slater gave further details of SWL's position. He thought that the assets of the group were sufficient to support SWL but that there could be a problem in terms of cash flow. Support therefore would be needed.[162] For Blunden, Slater was far too complacent about the ability of the group to support the entire deposit book of SWL. Nevertheless, Blunden was happy that the Bank now had a clearer idea of the dimensions of a rescue and thought that considerable help could be given without undue risk because of the availability of SWSL's resources.[163] By the end of September, Slater had provided the Bank with figures on SWL's position. Attempts had been made to measure the anticipated liquidity pressure that a run on SWL would produce, and the Bank also had been provided with details of securities available with SWSL that could be pledged as collateral against a standby facility.[164] In October, Richardson told Slater that he would like to proceed to making formal arrangements for a standby, but more information on the group still was required. Slater,

---

[160] Fforde to Hollom/Richardson, 'Slater Walker Limited', 3 September 1975, 6A70/5.
[161] Blunden, Note for record – 'Slater Walker', 8 September 1975, 6A70/5.
[162] Slater to Blunden, 18 September 1975, 6A70/5.
[163] Blunden to Fforde, 'Slater Walker', 22 September 1975, 6A70/5.
[164] Galpin to Blunden/Fforde/Hollom/Richardson, 'Slater Walker Securities Limited', 30 September 1975, 6A70/18.

seeming nervous about his own and his group's vulnerability, confirmed that he wanted to get out of banking and business and that he was hoping to sell SWL. There had been short-lived interest from American Express, the Bank of America was a remote possibility, and Goldsmith still was considered by Slater to be an option.[165] The Bank was not keen on this solution, and Goldsmith in the end was unwilling to bid.[166]

On 24 October 1975, Slater resigned and nominated Goldsmith as his successor. No objection was raised by the Bank.[167] Yet Goldsmith's credentials were not promising. He had left Eton at age 17 after winning £8,000 on a three-horse accumulator at the races and devoted the next five years to gambling. A Bank note commented on 'his propensity to trade companies as if he was playing Monopoly' and that he was not by temperament a banker.[168] The Treasury was also unsure about the appointment:

Given the history of 'City' characters who have come a cropper, and whom the Bank may have misjudged, I hope the Bank, who are up to their neck in the Slater Walker affair, are fully satisfied that Mr Goldsmith is a proper person.... he is hardly a noted banking figure and indeed his reputation as far as the general public is concerned is that of a playboy and speculator.[169]

He was undoubtedly clever, with Hollom believing that he had one of the fastest minds that he had ever met.[170] With the encouragement of the Bank, Goldsmith's cousin, Lord Rothschild, together with Ivor Kennington of Rothschilds and Charles Hambro and Peter Hill-Wood of Hambros, joined the board. The new board agreed to use group deposits to inject £25 million of additional capital into SWL. Labour MPs called for a government enquiry into SWL in relation to share dealings under the 1948 Companies Act, but the Bank, aware of the effect it would have on confidence, was against it.[171] Instead, the board appointed Peat Marwick Mitchell and Price Waterhouse to investigate the group's financial position, and Goldsmith promised to keep the Department of Trade informed of the findings.[172]

The Bank's main objective was to protect the depositors of SWL, involving a total of £95 million. By 1975, Slater Walker Investments managed

---

[165] Blunden to Fforde/Richardson/Hollom, 'Slater Walker', 7 October 1975, 6A70/6.
[166] Mallett to Galpin, 'Slater Walker Securities Ltd', 2 March 1976, 6A70/10.
[167] Blunden to Fforde/Richardson/Hollom, 'Slater Walker', 21 October 1975, 6A70/18.
[168] Ian Clarke/Erskine, 'James Goldsmith', 17 October 1975, 6A70/6.
[169] Unwin to Bridgeman, 27 October 1975, 6A70/18.
[170] Interview with Sir Jasper Hollom, 12 October 2007.
[171] Raw (1977, p. 346).
[172] Paper for Court, 'Slater Walker Securities Ltd. Background briefing to December 1975 Accounts and circular to shareholders', 14 September 1976, 3A161/190.

£250 million in unit trusts for 300,000 people, and Slater Walker Insurance, a life insurance and a general insurance business, had issued life insurance polices with a liability of £42.5 million. Additionally, there were pension schemes involving 29,000 pensioners with a liability of £13.7 million.[173] To prevent a run on SWL and protect its depositors, the Bank secretly prepared a standby facility of £130 million on 24 October. The facility included £23 million to £30 million to finance the repurchase of SWSL's sterling loan stock, but restrictions in the loan stock trust deeds made this difficult, so in November the standby facility was reduced to £70 million, £61 million of which was to support unconnected depositors.

SWSL had borrowed through issuing £30 million in UK loan stocks with over 24,000 holders and £75 million of loans held by overseas investors. These came with particular covenants, and by December 1975, SWSL was in difficulties in relation to the sterling loan stock obligations. The group needed to pay off certain of its borrowings at the end of the year in order to remove the most onerous of the restrictions. If this was not done, there was a distinct danger that all the loan stocks would have to be repaid at par at a cost of £105 million.[174] The Bank's assessment was that there was little prospect of SWSL raising the funds privately, and the Bank seemed to be the only available source of support.[175] It had to decide whether to provide this support or let the group go into liquidation. After 'considerable heart searching', the Bank could see no other acceptable way of preventing a triggering of repayment of the loan stocks. In December 1975, it therefore guaranteed SWL's loan portfolio up to a maximum principal amount of £40 million.[176] A disorderly collapse in December would have exposed the Bank to losses of £45 million to £55 million.[177] The complexities of the group's affairs, coupled with the uncertainties surrounding its financial position, meant that the Bank was unable to negotiate terms for the guarantee that would ensure full protection against loss.[178] At the same time, the Bank also granted a facility of £14 million to enable SWL to repay the loan stocks that carried the most restrictive conditions. Instead of accepting an obligation to repay amounts called under the guarantee, SWL agreed to make

---

[173] Slater Walker, *Directors' Reports and Accounts 1975*, 2A185/1.
[174] Paper for Court, 'Slater Walker Securities Ltd. Background briefing to December 1975 Accounts and circular to shareholders', 14 September 1976, 3A161/190.
[175] Slater Walker Securities, 4 December 1975, 5A142/1.
[176] Paper for Court, 'Slater Walker Securities Ltd. Background briefing to December 1975 Accounts and circular to shareholders', 14 September 1976, 3A161/190.
[177] Plenderleith (GPS) to Monck, 1 October 1976, enc. 'Slater Walker', 6A70/17.
[178] Richardson to Healey, 13 September 1976, G3/339.

over their profits to the Bank until such time as 125 per cent of the amount called had been repaid, enabling SWS and SWL to produce an end-year balance sheet unburdened by an obligation to repay the Bank.[179] In order to protect the Bank's position as much as possible in respect of the guarantee, SWSL agreed to subscribe fresh capital to SWL, and SWL agreed not to pay dividends without the Bank's approval. On 4 December 1975, when the Governor briefed the Chancellor on Slater Walker, it was agreed that knowledge should be kept to a close circle.[180] The Bank was adamant that their financial involvement was not made public.

In September 1976, the Bank's involvement became public knowledge when Slater Walker's 1975 report and accounts were posted to shareholders. *The Banker* wondered whether the Bank was regretting the speed with which it came in to render financial support to the group, adding that 'it looks as though the Bank will have a long wait before it gets its money back – if at all.'[181] Frank Hooley, MP for Sheffield, certainly was not impressed. Writing to Treasury Permanent Secretary Sir Douglas Wass, he wondered why money was used 'to prop up the activities of a shoddy swindler' and added, 'Why is it that the Bank of England can rescue any lousy City twister while manufacturing companies in difficulties have to beg and plead and argue for the odd couple of million to help them out.'[182]

Throughout 1976 and 1977, the Bank and the board of SWSL were in continual negotiations to settle the future of the group. SWL closed its regional offices and sold three subsidiaries in Jersey, Guernsey, and the Isle of Man in the summer of 1976. Goldsmith devised various schemes of reorganisation, each one proving unacceptable to the Bank because of certain objectionable elements such as an addition to the Bank's capital loss, an immediate payment to shareholders, or the continuance of SWL as an independent banking company. The non-income-producing assets of SWSL created running losses that threatened to breach SWSL's borrowing limits under its loan stock trust deeds. The Bank was concerned mainly with supporting SWL and was not keen to get drawn into the affairs of SWSL; thus debate centred on whether to buy SWL or liquidate. In June 1977, the issue was discussed at Court. Goldsmith had new reconstruction proposals that involved the Bank buying SWL together with two properties: Oyez House, a substantial office block in central London, and 125 acres

---

[179] Paper for Court, 'Slater Walker Securities Ltd. Background briefing to December 1975 Accounts and circular to shareholders', 14 September 1976, 3A161/190.

[180] Blunden, Note for record, 4 December 1975, 6A70/18.

[181] *The Banker* 126(608):1103, October 1976.

[182] Hooley to Healey, 23 September 1976, 6A70/18.

of land at Wokingham, Berkshire – near London. Richardson believed that if liquidation were pursued, then it might give the impression that the Bank had failed to achieve what it had set out to do. Nevertheless, after a long examination of the issues involved, the Court concluded that liquidation would be preferable; the prices asked for the properties were well above the market value.[183] Richardson met the Chancellor to explain that it had not been possible to devise satisfactory reconstruction proposals. Healey accepted that the effect of liquidation on confidence certainly would be smaller than it would have been in 1975.[184]

SWSL's Directors were alarmed by the Court's decision. If SWSL did not receive help from the Bank, it most likely would breach the borrowing limits in its sterling loan stock trust deeds, which, in turn, would trigger demands for repayment of most of the group's other outstanding loans, thereby resulting in liquidation. SWSL submitted a revised set of reconstruction proposals. Richardson went to see Healey on 21 June to discuss these terms and told him that SWSL, in their response, had made it clear that if liquidation of SWSL were pursued, the liquidator might try to include SWL in the liquidation, and that, in turn, might involve litigation for the Bank. If the Bank lost, the cost to the Bank could be greater than the cost of reconstruction. Richardson thus was more inclined to adopt reconstruction and felt that if he had been in a purely commercial situation, he would have gone for this option. The Chancellor and Wass made it clear that ultimate responsibility for the decision lay with the Governor.[185] After considerable discussion at an emergency meeting of Court, it was agreed that it would be in the best interests of the Bank and in the wider public interest to adopt the modified proposals.

Under the agreement, the Bank provided SWSL with liquidity by buying SWL for £3.5 million. This detached the banking business from the rest of the group. In order to provide further liquidity for SWSL, it was agreed that SWL would buy the freehold properties in Fetter Lane and Wokingham for £6.5 million and assume responsibility for repayment of an existing mortgage of £7.5 million on the former. SWL also bought a Convertible Note maturing in 1988 in a US company, Cornwall Equities Limited, at the face value of £10 million, and it paid £3 million to SWSL in settlement of a tax losses claim.[186] The agreements gave SWSL the £14.2 million it needed to redeem its three loan stocks. The two healthy elements of the company, Britannia

---

[183] Formal Court minutes, 16 June 1977, 3A161/190.
[184] Monck, Note for record, 22 June 1977, 6A70/18.
[185] *Ibid.*
[186] Erskine, 'The Slater Walker rescue', January 1978, 8A17/1.

Financial Services and Arrow Life Assurance, merged to become Britannia Arrow Holdings Limited, and Hambros continued its management and collection of the loan book. SWL would be an operational bank but would not undertake new business. Once the transactions had been completed, in September 1977, the Bank, with assistance from Hambros, proceeded to run down SWL. Hollom was its chairman, and Page and Coleby were Directors.

The second notable case of Bank assistance outside the Lifeboat was the merchant (investment) bank Edward Bates. Having experienced problems in the wake of the secondary banking crisis, the difficulties of this company came to a head in 1976. This was largely due to the deteriorating shipping market, an area in which Bates had built up business. The Bank came to the rescue with a standby facility, and restructuring negotiations culminated in the establishment of a new group, Allied Arab Bank, and a Bank-owned realisation company, Edward Bates Investments Limited, which was essentially a vehicle for disposing of the assets.

Edward Bates was founded in Bombay in 1839 and was established in Liverpool in 1848. Until the early twentieth century, the company was interested mainly in East India trading and shipping. Edward Bates then focused its activities on merchant banking during the First World War, but during the interwar period and for some time after the Second World War it was rather inactive. In 1967, a new holding company, Edward Bates Holdings (EBH), was formed with Edward Bates & Sons (EBS) as a wholly owned subsidiary. Also in 1967, EBS had requested authorised bank status. Although the Bank regarded EBS as 'perfectly respectable', it doubted whether the company was 'sufficiently well equipped technically' to meet the criteria. It took another six years for EBS to achieve authorisation, gaining it on 20 December 1973, just as the secondary banking crisis was breaking.[187]

By 1973, EBS was providing a range of banking services, including corporate finance, investment management, and insurance. In the property boom in 1972–73, EBS became heavily involved in property development, and after several members of Brandts bank joined the board of EBS, it also began to undertake shipping finance. Brandts had for some time provided finance to Greek ship owners, and EBS offered loan facilities to build up its shipping portfolio.[188] Between March 1973 and March 1974, advances grew from £17 million to £71 million, and over the same period, deposits increased from £48 million to £131 million.[189]

---

[187] Galpin to Hunter, 'Edward Bates & Sons Ltd', 8 August 1967, 7A260/1.
[188] Price Waterhouse report, Pt. 1, p. 29, 9 July 1976, 7A289/1.
[189] *Ibid.*, p. 12.

When the secondary banking crisis broke in December 1973, EBS Chairman Peter Brandt assured Galpin that it was under no pressure and held ample liquid assets.[190] And yet just seven months later he revealed that £38 million of deposits had been lost in the preceding three months.[191] EBS, it turned out, was not immune to the widespread deterioration of confidence following the difficulties of the fringe institutions. The loss of deposits was accelerated by EBH's problems with Welfare Insurance, which it had bought in August 1973 for approximately £5.5 million. EBH also had put a further £2 million into new shares in order to maintain the insurance company's solvency margin at an acceptable level. Despite this capital injection, Welfare's business continued to decline during 1974, and when the difficulties became public knowledge, they undermined confidence in EBS, and deposits began to drain away.[192] Thus, in September 1974, EBS turned to the Control Committee, and Barclays Bank International refinanced $75 million of EBS' shipping loans portfolio. Welfare Insurance was sold in December 1974 to London and Manchester Assurance Company and National Westminster Bank at a loss of approximately £9.7 million.

EBH then turned to Arab financial institutions as a way of solving its problems. Initial discussions were held in November 1974 with the Cairo-based Arab International Bank, which was interested in forming a consortium of Arab banks and financial institutions with the intention of investing in an authorised British bank.[193] There was also a proposal for the shares to be sold to First Arabian Corporation, a Luxembourg-registered holding company through which a number of prominent Arabs invested their personal wealth. The Bank was non-committal about this. Galpin felt that First Arabian seemed 'an inappropriate vehicle', and he was not keen for the Arabs to take more than a 25 per cent interest.[194] In May 1975, First Arabian, headed by Prince Abdullah Bin Musaid Bin Abdul Rahman, the son of the Saudi Arabian Finance Minister, bought the 25 per cent equity for £1.34 million with an option to buy another 15 per cent within three years. The Bank reluctantly agreed, provided that it received a letter from First Arabian stating that it would accept moral responsibility for supporting EBS. The Bank also agreed to provide EBS with a £5 million short-term advance facility to enable them to build up their reserve assets. Unable to

---

[190] David Tyler, Note for record – 'Edward Bates & Sons Ltd.', 13 May 1976, 7A260/4.
[191] *Ibid.*
[192] Paper for Court, 'Edward Bates & Sons Limited (EBS)', 21 July 1977, 3A161/197.
[193] Barnes to Hollom, 'Edward Bates', 26 November 1974, 7A260/2.
[194] Galpin to Blunden/Hollom, 'Edward Bates', 21 March 1975; Galpin to Hollom, 4 April 1975, 7A260/3.

attract significant deposits, EBS requested renewals of the facility on several occasions until November 1975.[195]

In 1976, the Bank became concerned about the quality of the EBS ship-ping and property portfolios. Shipping lending constituted an unusually high proportion of the total loan book. EBS had £6 million outstanding to a Greek ship owner but also about £4 million to Raglan Property Trust. As the Bank saw it, 'The scale of provisions needed against loans made by EBS to the more speculative end of the property and Greek shipping markets put the solvency of the group in doubt.'[196] Indeed, an investigation conducted by Hambros concluded that it was insolvent. In early May, the share price of EBH fell from 40p to 20p in 10 days, and on 13 May, EBH asked for its shares to be suspended on the stock exchange at 20p 'pending ... clarifi-cation of the company's financial position.'[197] EBS then needed assistance to meet withdrawals of depositors. It had £67 million in deposits, half of which came from Arab sources. Long and intense discussions between the EBS board, First Arabian, and the Bank were held over the weekend. Owing to the complexities and the uncertainties of the financial position of EBS, it was not felt to be an appropriate recipient of Lifeboat funds. Thus, on 17 May, the Bank, in conjunction with First Arabian, granted a standby facility of £80 million to be drawn in tranches of £100,000 to protect unconnected depositors in EBS.[198] First Arabian also agreed to meet 10 per cent of any ultimate deficiency in EBS, subject to a maximum contribution of £6 mil-lion payable over a period of five years.[199] This enabled the board of EBS to continue to trade, despite being technically insolvent, while a proper evalu-ation of their position was carried out. Following suspension of the shares, the Bank and First Arabian asked Price Waterhouse to report on the extent of the losses suffered by EBS and EBH. The findings revealed the need for heavy provisions in both EBH and EBS and that in 1976 EBH had a defi-ciency of assets of £17.2 million (subsequently updated to £28 million in November 1976).[200]

The EBH and EBS reconstruction negotiations were a slow process. The Bank was keen to minimise its loss and to avoid any repercussions for London from the collapse of an authorised bank in which the Arabs had invested.

---

[195] Somerset to Page, 6 October 1975, 7A294/1.
[196] Paper for Court, 'Edward Bates & Sons Limited (EBS)', 21 July 1977, 3A161/197.
[197] Galpin, Note for record – 'Edward Bates & Sons', 13 May 1976, 7A260/4.
[198] 'Edward Bates: draft answers to press enquiries 28.7.77', 7A260/17.
[199] Paper for Court, 'Edward Bates & Sons Limited (EBS)', 21 July 1977, 3A161/197.
[200] R. D. Broadley (Barings), 'Summary of the current situation for information of possible banking investor', 9 November 1976, 7A260/12.

Discussions were held with a number of Arab interests, and the Bank worked on a proposal whereby the balance-sheet deficiency would be eliminated through creation of a realisation company. This achieved, it was planned that EBS would be sold to a third party who would inject fresh capital into the business. An Iraqi-born banker, Sabih Shukri (and former chief manager at the London Branch of the Jordanian-based Arab Bank), told the Bank that he represented certain Arab interests that might be interested in buying EBS. In October 1976, Shukri's advisers put forward some outline proposals, and the Bank required that not less than 10 per cent of the business should be owned by a clearing bank. Barclays was considered originally, but it had been black-listed by the Arab League Boycott Office and therefore was ruled out. Midland was a possibility, but it decided that it was unable to participate because it was already involved with two Arab groups. There was another abortive attempt with the National Bank of Abu Dhabi in January 1977. Mohammed Mahdi Al Tajir, the United Arab Emirates's ambassador in London, said to be the richest man in the world at the time, then became involved.[201] But the Bank found that he 'could not be relied upon to provide solid counsel and banking expertise', and his involvement in banking with the Bank of London and the Middle East had attracted adverse comment.[202] A short biographical note described him as 'intelligent, with a brilliant brain.... can be a good friend or a nasty enemy.... he can be brutally frank or deceptively smooth.'[203]

In April 1977, Shukri proposed that the National Westminster should have 20 per cent for four years and management control, Altajir Bank should have 20 per cent, and the consortium should hold 60 per cent.[204] Galpin made clear that the Bank attached great importance to the participation of an international, well-established Arab bank in the reconstruction and doubted whether Altajir Bank met that requirement. Shukri went on to imply that a breakdown in negotiations over Edward Bates could jeopardise a developing Arab policy of close co-operation, both financial and political, with the United Kingdom.[205] National Westminster, having expressed a willingness to proceed, then drew back. Leigh-Pemberton, the bank's chairman (and a future Governor of the Bank), saw the Governors in early June 1977 to express reluctance about becoming associated with Al Tajir.[206] National Westminster decided to pull out of the reconstruction proposals. However,

---

[201] Galpin, 'Edward Bates', 17 February 1977, 7A260/15.
[202] Galpin to Hollom, 'Edward Bates/National Westminster Bank', 29 March 1977, 7A260/16.
[203] Galpin to Richardson/Hollom, 24 March 1977, enc. 'FCO note on Al Tajir', 7A260/16.
[204] Galpin to Hollom, 'Edward Bates', 7 April 1977, 7A260/16.
[205] Mallett, Note for record – 'Edward Bates & Sons Limited', 28, April 1977, 7A260/16.
[206] Plenderleith, Note for record, 1 June 1977, 7A260/14.

with the Arab boycott on Barclays now lifted, the consortium sought to involve Barclays again.

It was finally agreed in August 1977 that Barclays Bank International would take 20 per cent of the share capital of EBS, and a consortium consisting of Arab and other investors would acquire the remaining 80 per cent. Notwithstanding the Bank's reservations, Altajir Bank was included.[207] The reconstituted bank became Allied Arab Bank (AAB), retaining its authorised status. As well as enhancing 'the attractiveness of the reconstruction proposals', the Bank saw the involvement of Barclays as important in gaining AAB's acceptance in the City and in international financial markets.[208] The Bank's 1976 standby facility committed it to a loss, and thus, before the new shareholders took over EBS, the Bank, through a wholly owned realisation company called EBS Investments (EBSI), acquired certain loans and assets, including the whole of EBS's shipping portfolio. This would help to restore the net worth of EBS to a nominal amount and would enable the consortium to take over the bank with a clean balance sheet.[209] The realisation company was managed by Price Waterhouse, with Directors nominated by the Bank. Somerset became chairman, Barnes Director, and David Mallett an alternate to both. Through EBSI, the Bank also acquired EBH's 83 per cent stake in Banque Pommier, a small and profitable bank, for £1.4 million. The Bank intended to find, in consultation with the French authorities, an appropriate buyer for this bank. In October 1977, EBS sold most of its assets to EBSI, including all its subsidiaries and the loans made to those subsidiaries. The following day, EBS was sold and EBH was put into liquidation.

The third of these special operations and 'the last casualty of the secondary banking crisis' was Wallace Brothers.[210] Like Edward Bates, Wallace Brothers was established in the middle of the nineteenth century (1863) with interests predominantly in trading in India. Its merchant banking activities expanded in the 1960s, and in June 1970, Wallace Brothers & Co. was incorporated as a subsidiary company of Wallace Brothers & Co. (Holdings) (WBH) to take over all the banking activities of the group. Through its various subsidiaries, Wallace Brothers' interests covered merchant banking, financial consultancy, commodity broking, leasing, and insurance broking,

---

[207] The consortium consisted of Al-Mubarakah Finance Holding Company (51 per cent), Sanctuary Investments Ltd. (2.5 per cent), Alhamdoulilah Finance Foundation (6 per cent), and Altajir Bank (20 per cent).

[208] 'Edward Bates: draft answers to press enquiries', 28 July 1977, 7A260/17.

[209] *The Daily Telegraph*, 2 August 1977, p. 15.

[210] Mallett, 'Extension of the indemnity arrangements for Wallace Brothers (London) Limited', 18 December 1985, 7A311/8.

and it had overseas operations in Australia, Jersey, and south east Asia. In March 1972, an authorised bank, E. D. Sassoon Banking Company, was purchased, and the name was changed to Wallace Brothers Sassoon Bank; in 1974, the Sassoon name was dropped, and it became Wallace Brothers Bank (WBB).[211] It was with WBB that most of the problems lay. Jeremy 'Jinx' Grafftey-Smith, WBB's Managing Director until the summer of 1976, kept in close contact with the Discount Office, and Keogh found him to be 'enthusiastic and imaginative'.[212]

One of the major shareholders in WBB was the Crown Agents (they held 27 per cent), and when the difficulties of the Agents came to a head in December 1974, the Bank granted WBB a £5 million unsecured standby to protect against temporary liquidity problems.[213] This was renewed monthly and expired in June 1975. In September, Grafftey-Smith asked for the reinstatement of this facility, but the Bank decided that detailed analysis of WBB's position would be required first.[214] Beginning this process, Murray Erskine (in Banking and Money Market Supervision) wrote 'Like the Tower of Pisa, Wallace Brothers' continued ability to defy the laws of gravity is a wonder to behold', but the indications were that the annual figures would be bad.[215] Heavy provisions were needed against the fall in property values (half of all advances, and over 90 per cent of large ones, were secured against property).[216] Thus the accounts for the financial year to July 1975 included exceptional provisions for loans and advances totalling £2.8 million, resulting in a pre-tax loss of £1.4 million.[217] At the same time as the accounts were published, in December 1975, the Bank somewhat reluctantly agreed to another £5 million unsecured standby for six months. The proviso was that it would be renewed only after further scrutiny; Richardson thought that the situation warranted 'very close watching'.[218]

By the summer of 1976, WBB was on the Bank's list of major problems. The difficulty was that further provisions would be required in the annual

[211] 7A302/1 and 7A302/2.
[212] Keogh to Page/Fforde/Governors, 'Crown Agents', 3 June 1970, 7A388/6.
[213] Galpin to Blunden/Hollom, 'Wallace Brothers', 17 December 1974, 7A302/2.
[214] Galpin to Somerset/Fforde/Richardson/Hollom, 'Wallace Brothers Bank Limited', 23 September 1975 and annotations by Fforde and Hollom, 7A311/1.
[215] Erskine to Mallett/Galpin, 'Wallace Brothers Bank Ltd', 2 October 1975, 7A311/1.
[216] Erskine, Note for record – 'Wallace Brothers Bank Ltd', 20 October 1975, 7A311/1.
[217] Galpin to Page/Fforde/Richardson/Hollom, 'Wallace Brothers Bank Ltd', 5 December 1975, 7A311/1; Wallace Brothers Bank Limited, *Annual Report and Accounts*, 1975, in 7A302/3.
[218] Galpin to Page/Fforde/Richardson Hollom, 'Wallace Brothers Bank Ltd', 5 December 1975 and Richardson annotation, 14 December 1975; Somerset to Grafftey-Smith, 23 December 1975, 7A311/1.

accounts, and this would mean another loss, and it would erode the bank's capital. Page reckoned that since WBB was a recognised bank and a long-standing customer, the Bank would have to support it. Price Waterhouse would be asked to produce a report, and in the meantime, the Crown Agents would be asked to give assistance, for instance, by subscribing to additional loan stock.[219] The Crown Agents refused to offer any form of help until the Price Waterhouse report was produced, and even then, the answer was likely to be negative.[220] That the Crown Agents were themselves in diffi-culties and could only finance an additional subscription to equity by draw-ing on the government did nothing to alter the Bank's view that as a major shareholder it should help WBB.[221] Price Waterhouse's report made gloomy reading but was indicative of the activities of fringe banks. The loan book of £33 million was almost all in property, and provisions of £5.4 million were required against 20 loans with a nominal value of £14 million. There would be capital losses on investments in other companies, again mainly related to property.[222] Cash-flow difficulties also were identified, and as a short-term measure in mid-October, the Bank provided WBB with a £12.5 million facility; unlike previous facilities, this one was secured. There still was some annoyance about the attitude of the Crown Agents, with a feeling that the lack of assistance was incompatible with size of shareholding and that the Agents should live up to their responsibilities.[223]

A long-term solution was needed, and this meant trying to find a buyer. There were several possibilities, but Standard Chartered, a large overseas banking group chaired by former Chancellor Barber, was felt by the Bank to be the most suitable. There were already long-standing connections through overseas trading interests, and Standard Chartered also faced some expo-sure if WBB went into liquidation. Furthermore, Cooke, who had taken over from Blunden in charge of banking supervision, pointed out that up to this point, it had not been involved in any 'lifeboatery'.[224] When the Governors

---

[219] Galpin to Page/Fforde/Richardson, 'Wallace Brothers Bank', 6 July 1976, and Page annota-tion, 6 July 1976; Gill to T. M. Rawcliffe (Price Waterhouse), 19 July 1976, 7A302/4.

[220] Gill, Notes for record – 'Wallace Brothers', 16, 29, and 30 July 1976, 7A302/4.

[221] Fforde/Richardson/Hollom, Note for record – 'Crown Agents and Wallace Brothers', 25 August 1976, 7A302/4.

[222] Alan Savery to Gill/Galpin, 'Wallace Brothers. Price Waterhouse report', 11 October 1976; Galpin to Page/Richardson/Hollom, 'Wallace Brothers Bank Limited', 14 October 1976, 7A302/5.

[223] Margo Ringle, Note for record – 'Wallace Brothers Bank', 18 October; Galpin to Hollom, 'Wallace Brothers Bank Ltd', 20 October 1976, 7A311/1. Cooke to Richardson/Hollom, 'Wallace Brothers Bank Limited', 14 October 1976, 7A302/5.

[224] Cooke to Richardson/Hollom, 'Wallace Brothers Bank Limited', 14 October 1976, 7A302/5.

met Standard Chartered in November, Richardson said that a rapid response was required and that it was desirable to find a solution before the accounts were published. The outcome of the meeting was positive, with a distinct possibility of help.[225] Three days later, Galpin told Standard Chartered that although it would be the main rescuer, the Bank might be prepared to offer 'discreet assistance' if necessary.[226] However, the potential rescuer came to the conclusion that WBB was in a very poor state: 'a net shortfall of £8.3 million; a "dreadful" loan portfolio, requiring provisions of 50 per cent; over-valued assets, including property mortgaged for at least £1 million more than its value; formidable carrying costs; and a top heavy staff'.[227] It was essentially a candidate for liquidation, but Richardson did not want to see this. The secondary banking crisis was now beginning to die down, and the Bank neither wanted to disturb the gradual return of confidence nor to make negotiations for the reconstruction of Slater Walker and Edward Bates more difficult by another public failure.[228] Thus the Bank continued to encourage the acquisition by Standard Chartered.

A complicated plan was developed whereby Standard Chartered, through its subsidiary, Standard Bank, would acquire all the share capital of WBH. This was done for a 'deferred consideration' of not more than £1 million, to be calculated on a formula related to the net worth of WBH in 1982. There was plenty of the promised discreet assistance from the Bank. It would lend Standard Bank the £1 million provisional purchase price, to be held in escrow (the loan and the deposit were interest-free). Standard Bank would guarantee the loan portfolio and contingent liabilities of WBB to the extent that the deficiency of net worth would not rise above £700,000, and a matching indemnity was provided by the Bank to Standard Bank. In addition, the Bank provided a comfort letter that ensured that Standard Chartered would suffer no loss greater than its exposure if WBB had gone into liquidation (the limit was £700,000), and it also granted a secured facility of £30 million to WBB to meet cash-flow requirements. The estimated deficiency was put at £6 million, shared £0.7 million by Standard Chartered and £5.3 million by the Bank.[229] Agreement in principle was announced on

[225] Plenderleith to Galpin, 'Wallace Brothers', 5 November 1976, 7A302/5.
[226] Atkinson, Note for record – 'Wallace Brothers Bank Limited', 8 November 1976, 7A302/5.
[227] Plenderleith, Note for record – 'Lord Barber's call on the Governor', 23 November 1976, 7A302/5.
[228] Wallace Brothers, Speaking notes for the Governor, 23 November 1976, 7A302/5; Mallett, 'Wallace Brothers Bank Limited – indemnities', 2 July 1980, 7A311/3.
[229] Galpin to Page/Richardson/Hollom, 'Wallace Brothers', 29 November 1976, 7A302/5; Galpin to Richardson/Hollom, 'Wallace Brothers', 3 and 5 December 1976; 'Wallace

7 December 1976, although various complications meant that the deal was not completed until the end of March 1977.[230]

At the time of rescue, it was hoped that the rundown would be completed by December 1981. The original indemnity was designed primarily to give protection against the emergence of significant bad-debt losses in WBB. With it proving hard to realise some of the company's assets, the indemnity arrangements to support the group were extended subsequently in 1983, 1985, and 1987, and the realisation programme finally was completed in 1989–90.[231]

Assessment

In total, the Control Committee approved support for 26 companies. Of these, 18 had Section 123 certificates, and five were either authorised banks or Section 127 banks. Eight of the companies that had been taken on by the Lifeboat were placed into receivership or liquidation. Four banks did manage to survive and leave the Lifeboat. A further five institutions were assisted by the Bank at the Bank's sole risk. By the end of 1975, the number receiving assistance from the Lifeboat had declined to eight, and by 1978, there were only four companies, including UDT and FNFC[232] (Tables 11.4 and 11.5).

In the main, Richardson won much praise for his handling of the crisis. 'If he is not careful', said *The Sunday Times,* 'Gordon Richardson will become the model Governor of the Bank of England by whom all future governors will be judged…. the Governor is now an outstanding Central Bank professional.'[233] In Churchillian tones, it was, according to the paper, his 'finest hour'.[234] Kynaston states that Richardson 'deployed all his formidable powers of persuasion to achieve broad acceptance for the principle of a joint support operation'.[235] But Richardson never got involved in the detail of the Lifeboat; as Blunden said, 'it was left to Jasper'. Hollom played the crucial role in managing the crisis, and his calm approach ensured the

Brothers' (handed to Deputy Governor evening 6.12.76), 7A302/6; Atkinson to Galpin, 'Standard Bank Ltd/Wallace Brothers (Holdings) Ltd', 19 April 1977, 7A302/7.

[230] Standard Chartered Bank, News release, nd, filed as 7 December 1976, 7A311/1; Atkinson to Ian Keynes/GPS, 'The Standard Bank/Wallace Brothers & Co. (Holdings) Ltd. Agreement', 29 March 1977, 7A302/7.

[231] Mallett, 'Extension of the indemnity arrangements for Wallace Brothers (London) Limited', 18 December 1985; Mallett to Somerset, 'Wallace Brothers Group', 1 December 1987; Kentfield to Blunden, 'Wallace Brothers', 23 January 1989, 9A208/2.

[232] Reid (1978, p. 30).

[233] *The Sunday Times,* 29, January 1978, p. 53

[234] *Ibid.*

[235] Kynaston (2001, p. 488).

Table 11.4. *Secondary banking crisis, institutions supported through the Lifeboat (£m)*

Name	Date in	Maximum drawing (and date)	Date of support or amount outstanding in January 1978	Notes (as of January 1978)
Category A				
Edward Bates & Sons	Sept. 74	2.5 + US$67.3, DM.7.1 (Nov. 75 to Jan. 76).	Sept. 77	Reorganisation, EBS Investments
Beverley Bentinck	Jan. 74	0.8 (Apr. 74)	Mar. 75	Renamed Britannia Credit Trust and resumed normal credit arrangements
Bowmaker	Jan. 74	89.0 (Dec. 74)	Dec. 75	Resumed normal trading
British Bank of Commerce	Jan. 74	10.0 (Oct. 74 to Nov. 74)	Jan. 75	Takeover by National Grindlays
Burston Finance	Jan. 74	25.5 (Dec. 74 to Aug. 75)	17.1	Placed in receivership in Feb. 75
First Maryland	Jan. 74	5.0 (Jan. 75 to Mar. 75)	Jan. 75	Placed in receivership Jan. 75; Barclays carry additional risk
First National Finance Corporation	Jan. 74	362.0 (Sept.75 to Dec. 75)	241.7	Reorganisation scheme Mar. 1976, implemented retrospectively to Oct. 75
Keyser Ullmann	Sept. 74	65.0 (Mar. 75)	Aug. 76	Resumed normal trading
Knowsley	June 75	33.5 (July 75)	25.5	Absorbed Northern Commercial Trust's property loans on Algemene's takeover

(continued)

Table 11.4 *(continued)*

Name	Date in	Maximum drawing (and date)	Date of support or amount outstanding in January 1978	Notes (as of January 1978)
London and County Securities	Jan. 74	39.8 (Apr. 75 to June 76)	25.2	In voluntary liquidation Mar. 75
Medens Trust	Jan. 74	0.9 (Oct. 74 to Nov. 74)	June 75	Resumed normal trading
Mercantile Credit	Jan. 74	167.0 (Apr. 75 to May 75)	Aug. 75	Takeover by Barclays Bank
Morris Wigram	Jan. 74	7.6 (Dec. 74)	July 75	Acquired and renamed by Schlesingers
Northern Commercial Trust	Jan. 74	34.0 (May 75 to June 75)	June 75	Acquired by Algemene Bank (v. Knowsley)
Sterling Industrial Securities	Oct. 74	2.0 (Nov. 74 to Apr. 75)	Oct. 76	Acquired by Duncan Goodricke Investments
Triumph Investment Trust (G.T. Whyte)	Jan. 74	30.2 (Dec. 74 to Apr. 75)	25.2	In receivership Nov. 74
Twentieth Century Banking Corporation	Jan. 74	31.8 (Aug. 74)	Mar. 74	Takeover by P&O
United Dominions Trust	July 74	430.0 (Dec. 74)	300	Still trading
Vavasseur	Jan. 74	10.2 (Nov. 75)	5.6	Reconstruction under Hambros management
Wagon Finance	Jan. 74	6.0 (Apr. 74 to July 75)	July 76	Resumed normal trading

Name	Date in	Maximum drawing (and date)	Date of support or amount outstanding in January 1978	Notes (as of January 1978)
Category B				
Audley Holdings	Jan. 74	1.7 (Sept. 74 to Feb. 75)	May 75	In receivership May 75
Cannon Street Acceptances	Jan. 74	40.0 (Oct. 74 to Feb. 75)	Sept. 74	In receivership Sept. 74
Cedar Holdings	Jan. 74	21.7 (Mar. 74)	Feb. 75	Reconstruction
Duboff	Jan. 74	4.0 (Nov.77 to date)	4.0	Close to receivership
Guardian Property	Jan. 74	2.8 (Jan. 74 to date)		In receivership June 74
David Samuel Trust	Jan. 74	(Nov. 75 to date)		In receivership May 74

Source: Briefing paper, 13 January 1978, for SCNI hearing, 2A170/1.

smooth running of the Control Committee.[236] He was undoubtedly 'the father figure' throughout and the 'captain of the lifeboat'.[237]

The Bank believed that the rescue operation had been successful, and in its evidence to the Select Committee in 1978, specifically instructed to examine the matter, the decision to launch the Lifeboat was defended. Richardson said that faced with the same circumstances, he would without hesitation take the same strategic decision and would act in the same way.[238] Fundamentally, the Bank felt that it was its duty to prevent the spread of a loss of confidence and so avert a financial crisis. It saw itself as the guardian of the financial system, a role that had evolved in the nineteenth century. Was its decision the right one? The reckless fringe banks might have been left to fail. In October 1974, *The Banker* reported that 'some bankers believe that the operation was misconceived from the start and that more of the bad apples should have been allowed to fall to the ground.'[239] Frank

[236] Reid (1982, p. 194).
[237] *The Sunday Times*, 7 August 1977, p. 45.
[238] *The Select Committee on Nationalised Industries (Sub-Committee C). Minutes of Evidence, Session 1977–78, 18 January 1978, Bank of England Report and Accounts for the Year Ended 28 February 1977*, 166-I, question 3.
[239] *The Banker* 124(584):1181, October 1974.

Table 11.5. *Secondary banking crisis, institutions supported by the Bank at sole risk (£m)*

Name	Date in	Maximum drawing (and date)	Date of support or amount outstanding Jan. 78	Notes
First National Finance Corporation	Jan. 74	10.0 (Jan. 74)	Feb. 74	Transferred to joint-risk A
United Dominions Trust	June 74	100 (Jan. 75 to Sept. 75)	Aug. 76	Banks own lending to keep joint total below 1,200
London & County Securities	Dec. 74	9.9 (Apr. 75)	6.3	Rundown of London & County in-store banks (pre-liquidation)
London & County Securities	–	0.2	0.2 still outstanding	Purchase of assignments (post-liquidation)
Cannon Street Acceptances	–	1.62	Oct. 76 1.62	Purchase of assignments (post-liquidation) (written off Oct. 76)
David Samuel Trust	Apr. 77	2.6	2.6	Special arrangement with National Westminster/ Williams & Glyn's
Slater Walker	Nov. 75	54.8 (Dec. 76)	54.4	Reorganisation
Jacobs Kroll	Nov. 75	1.1 (Sept. 76)	0.7	Purchase of assignments on behalf of Slater Walker Limited

Name	Date in	Maximum drawing (and date)	Date of support or amount outstanding Jan. 78	Notes
Thames Guaranty	Aug. 76	0.5	0.4	Joint purchase of assignments with Portuguese shareholders
Wallace Brothers Bank	Oct. 76	13.0 (Oct. 77 to date)	13.0	See Standard Bank below
Standard Bank	Apr. 77	1.0	1.0	In connection with rundown of Wallace Brothers above
Edward Bates & Sons	May 76	55.1 (Apr. 77)	Oct. 77	Reorganisation and purchase of EBS Investments below
EBS Investments	Oct.77	32.9	32.9	See Edward Bates & Sons above
Ionian Bank	Jan. 77	Nil	Dec. 77	Facility to cover possible liquidity problems during rundown; never utilised

Source: Briefing paper, 13 January 1978, for SCNI hearing, 2A170/1.

Hooley, MP, wrote to Richardson in 1975 reinforcing this view. As far as he was concerned, the 'swindlers' of the fringe banking community could 'go bankrupt and shoot themselves', and he could not see why major banks, let alone the Bank, should worry. Furthermore, the support operations 'appear to indicate to the financial "Smart Alecs" in this country that they need not worry too much in future about incompetent or shady deals since, at the end of the day the Bank of England itself will step in and save any outright scandal.'[240] He had a point.

[240] Hooley to Richardson, 9 October 1975, TNA T233/2842.

Although few dispute the way the Bank handled the crisis, criticism was made of the fact that the Discount Office was far too small to carry out close supervision effectively; 'the Discount Office's administrative resources were quite outstripped by the scale of the banking system: fifteen people overseeing over three hundred banks.'[241] In his account of the secondary banking crisis to the Institute of Bankers in 1974, the Governor announced that 'it has been possible for deposit-taking institutions to flourish without full official recognition as banks and without the supervision that goes with it.'[242] The Bank was more concerned with the overseas banks and the finance houses than with the fringe. As the Bank stated in evidence to the Wilson Committee, it 'did not maintain any formal or regular contact with companies which did not fall within the banking sector proper, seeking to develop such relationships only when a company became a serious contender for full recognition as a bank.'[243] It has thus been assumed that many fringe banks failed as a result of the Bank not subjecting them to the same supervisory regime as the established banking system. 'The Bank's gentlemanly approach to control of the banking system was dangerously inadequate. To exclude the Section 123 banks and finance houses from close financial scrutiny because they did not enjoy the right pedigree seems nonsensical, for such concerns seem implicitly in need of greater supervision.'[244] In retrospect, Keogh argued that the failure of the fringe banks did not lie in the fact that they were not subjected to the same supervisory regime as the established banking system. The Bank, he maintained, attempted to supervise the secondary banking system, but they proved to be 'totally beyond supervision'. Keogh noted, 'It is almost certain that as much of the time of the Discount Office was spent with the "fringe" as with recognised banks.'[245] The Bank became acquainted with all the major fringe banks, along with some of the smaller ones, and contacted the larger fringe institutions to seek their co-operation with the credit-control regime.[246] Indeed, in June 1973, the Bank invited approximately 30 of these 'miscellaneous deposit-taking companies' that were thought to have eligible liabilities of £5 million or over to submit a return in the shape of a summarised balance sheet. From

[241] Moran (1986, p. 94).
[242] Richardson speech to Institute of Bankers at Bristol, 5 February 1974, *BEQB* 14(1):54, March 1974.
[243] 'Supervision of banks and other deposit-taking institutions', *BEQB* 18(3):383, September 1978.
[244] Channon (1977, p. 106).
[245] Keogh, Note for record – 'The Fringe', 5 June 1974, 7A95/1.
[246] *Ibid.*

this the Bank could consider whether credit control should be extended to such institutions.[247] Furthermore, many fringe banks approached the Bank in the hope of moving up the banking ladder. Keogh noted, 'All but the most piratical made sure that we saw their annual balance sheets and all insisted on coming in and talking, just like recognised banks.... we tried to make them think about their balance sheets and made them aware of our formulae, though all of it looked a bit academic in those times.'[248] He maintained that despite the Bank's warnings and advice, the lack of banking experience of those running the companies meant that the advice went unheeded. The Bank tried to improve the management of the fringe banks by talking to experienced and trustworthy figures to manage the fringe but found little success. Reflecting on the events, Keogh felt that the main problem was not so much the lack of monitoring of the fringe but 'the speed with which they grew from being a nuisance into a menace to themselves and to the system'.[249]

Despite Keogh's defence, blame had to lie somewhere, and it fell at his feet as Principal of the Discount Office. Keogh, at age 57, took early retirement and left in December 1974, having been in the Bank for 37 years (including wartime service). According to one financial journalist, he was 'ruthlessly, and arbitrarily ... thrown overboard'. He was the official scapegoat and was forced out of the Bank.[250] When asked by the Select Committee whether the Bank was to blame, Richardson cryptically replied:

It falls ill to me to speak of those who were in positions of relevant authority at the Bank over that period, but I doubt they would deny that the particular manner in which the crisis manifested itself might have been somewhat different had they taken a radically different view of the appropriate limits to their supervisory authority.[251]

When explaining the failure of the fringe banks, Keogh pointed not to other individuals but to factors that were simply out of his control. He argued that 'during the period of the "fringe" growth the rest of the banking system was not on our side and certainly did not care, even though we tried to involve them.' And he also maintained that despite giving warnings to those in charge

---

[247] Bank of England, 'Miscellaneous deposit-taking companies', 28 March 1977, 5A208/1.
[248] Keogh, Note for record – 'The Fringe', 5 June 1974, 7A95/1.
[249] *Ibid.*
[250] Christopher Fildes, *The Spectator*, 18 May 1991, p. 21. Keogh subsequently joined the International Monetary Fund's Panel of Overseas Advisers, spending three years in Singapore to help with work on their new monetary authority.
[251] SCNI, Briefing material, January 1978, 2A170/1.

of the secondary banks, these went unheeded because they were inexperienced 'wheeler/dealer financiers'.[252] But Richardson 'believed positively that Keogh should have foreseen what was going to happen and should have been advising Leslie O'Brien earlier of the dangers of what might be happening'. Richardson was truly convinced that Keogh had failed.[253] This quite possibly stemmed from a poor relationship between the two that dated from the time Richardson was at Schroders.[254] Charles Gordon found Keogh 'an odd person to find in the Bank' and believed that 'though he was castigated somewhat excessively as a scapegoat, he must bear much of the responsibility for the Bank's lack of basic, never mind detailed knowledge of the fringe banks, with whom he was the main Bank of England interface'.[255] While the *Old Lady* wrote, 'Keogh's natural stamina, strong personal character and unequalled knowledge of the individuals involved made him the essential element in preventing catastrophe', Fforde in a note to the Governor recalled that around 1970 an attempt was made to remove Keogh from his position as Principal, although the reason for this is unclear.[256] A colleague reflected that 'Keogh was the only senior officer in the Bank who had a chance of pulling the information strings together, but analysis was not his forte'.[257] Certainly, to place all the blame on one man was too harsh. Also, it might well be felt that there was a failure of structure. And it should be remembered that no one inside the Bank or outside saw the systemic problem coming. Even after the crisis broke in November, some at most risk failed to appreciate the urgency and recognise the speed at which a credit crisis can move. This was a criticism later made by Sir Martin Jacomb, who had been a non-executive director of Mercantile Credit at the time.[258]

Might the Bank have seen trouble brewing in the early 1970s? These years certainly had their share of financial scandal and incident. The explosion of the money stock and the accompanying property boom were clear signals. Some parts of the financial press were expressing concern from the middle of 1973. The judgement of *The Banker* was

The 'mad gushing' of the money supply and the 'permissive' banking climate of 1973 – to both of which *The Banker* drew attention in those very words in July and September

[252] Keogh, Note for record – 'The Fringe', 5 June 1974, 7A95/1.
[253] Coleby interview with Sir George Blunden, 20 March 1997.
[254] Interview with Barnes, 27 September 2007.
[255] Gordon (1993, p. 235).
[256] *The Old Lady*, December 1975, p. 256; Fforde to Richardson, 'Secondary banking: the antecedents', 20 January 1978, 7A149/2.
[257] Private communication with Roger Barnes, September 2008.
[258] Interview with Sir Martin Jacomb, 23 September 2008. He also admitted that he didn't see the crisis coming.

1973 – … were bound to cause speculative excesses. The Bank should have spotted them earlier than it did; it should have kept its ear closer to what was being said by uncouth types in the City's bustling new money market, and where it did know what these new 'banks' were up to it should have used its informal powers (the Governor's eyebrows) to stop them. It should have shouted more loudly about the Crown Agents. There had been warning signals – as evidenced by the Scottish Co-operative Society's problems.… The Bank should have taken them more seriously.[259]

The costs of the support operations during the secondary banking crisis are elusive. Giving evidence to the Select Committee in 1978, Richardson said that the total cost was £1,250 million to £1,300 million; this was made up of the £1,200 million at joint risk (10 per cent contributed by the Bank) and the additional amount put in by the Bank alone. Pressed as to actual losses incurred by the Bank, as opposed to the provisions made, he put the figure at around £5 million.[260] Reid estimates that the total of the Bank's support operations including the Lifeboat, Slater Walker, and Bates came to about £100 million.[261] An internal note written in 1984 estimated that the cost to the Bank would be around the £80 million to £90 million mark.[262] For London and County alone, it was reckoned in 1988 that the cost to the Bank would be 'approximately £4 million, of which about £3 million is attributable to unilateral support and something over £1 million to the Bank's share of the Support Group assistance'. The cost to the other members of the support group was approximately £11 million.[263] According to John Rumins, writing in 1995, the total *provisions* made for the Bank's support operations in the period 1974–80 were approximately £113 million, including £37.9 million for Slater Walker and £32.3 million for Edward Bates. For the main Lifeboat operation, the Bank's own 'share of losses', up to 1980, was £9.2 million. Moreover, 'The total commitment to the support operations was of course much larger than the figures for provisions for losses. A total of £1300 million was advanced through the lifeboat (of which the Bank's share was 10 per cent) and over £300 million was advanced by the Bank for the unilateral cases'.[264] The extent of the provision for losses on support operations is confirmed in other Bank working papers (Table 11.6). Of course, assets continued to be realised and

[259] *The Banker* 128(625):19, March 1978.
[260] *The Select Committee on Nationalised Industries (Sub-Committee C). Minutes of Evidence, Session 1977–78, 18 January 1978, Bank of England Report and Accounts for the Year Ended 28 February 1977*, 166-i, question 43.
[261] Reid (1982, p. 190).
[262] Mallett to Quinn, 'Losses in the secondary banking crisis', 9 November 1984, 7A311/5.
[263] Note for record – 'London & County – Cost to the Bank', 25 August 1988, 7A369/2.
[264] Rumins (1995, pp. 59–60).

Table 11.6. *Bank of England provision for losses on support operations (£m)*

	Support Group[a]	Shared[c]	Unilateral				Unilateral total	Total
			Edward Bates	Wallace Bros	Slater Walker	Others[d]		
February 1974–February 1980								
1974	3.0[b]	0	–	–	–	–	0	3.0
1975	2.8	0.05	–	–	–	10.5	10.5	13.3
1976	1.2	2.4	–	–	20.0	8.6	28.6	32.3
1977	2.3	0.2	20.4	3.8	7.2	(0.6)	30.8	33.3
1978	0.1	0.1	13.3	1.9	9.4	0.7	25.3	25.6
1979	0.2	0	2.0	1.3	1.4	0.8	5.5	5.7
1980	(0.5)	(0.07)	(3.4)	0.9	(0.001)	0.1	(2.6)	(3.2)
Total	9.2	2.7	32.3	7.9	38.0	19.9	98.1	110.0
February 1974–February 1994								
Total provisions	1.3	2.2	25.5	(0.03)	7.8	17.9	51.2	54.7
Written off	(1.3)	(2.2)	(25.5)	0.03	(7.8)	(17.9)	(51.2)	(54.7)
Provision								
At 1 March 1994	0	0	0	0	0	0	0	0

[a] Triumph Investments, Burston Finance, First National Finance Corporation, J. H. Vavasseur, London & County, Knowsley & Co.
[b] General provision.
[c] David Samuel Trust, Scottish Co-operative.
[d] Jacobs Kroll, Israel-British Bank, Canon St. Acceptances, Goulston Banking, G. T. Whyte, Whyte Gasc, London & County, Duboff Brothers.

Source: Working paper on provision for losses, 7A369/1.

money recouped so that by 1994 the provision against 1970s support had been reduced to £55 million, when it was written off. This might be said to represent a loss at that point, at least in accounting terms, although the picture is considerably clouded by the impact of two decades of serious inflation. Unsatisfactory as it may be, it appears that it is not possible to calculate definitive figures for what the secondary banking crisis actually cost the Bank.

Why did the Bank become involved in all these operations? There were several reasons, but the main one used to justify assistance was the fact that they were authorised banks.[265] The Bank had long considered itself as being responsible for the health of the financial system and believed that if an authorised bank carrying the highest banking recognition were left to fail, then the damage to the banking system's reputation could be serious. Financial confidence was fragile, and although the immediate crisis was stabilised relatively quickly, the failure of an authorised bank might have jeopardised the progress made. Turning a blind eye to these banks would have put at risk other support operations and would cast doubt on certain other cases not in support but of which the Bank were aware, so damaging confidence and provoking a run on other weak banks.[266] This was the line adopted by the Bank in its evidence to both the Select Committee and the Wilson Committee, as well as one that some Bank officials maintained when interviewed about the secondary banking crisis 30 years later. And yet, in a speech in 1975, Blunden played down the authorised status: 'In particular, the status of authorised bank is often held to mean more than it does.... it does not imply any broader seal of approval or assumption of responsibility on the part of the Bank or Treasury.'[267] Richardson also downplayed its importance. The credibility of the recently introduced supervisory arrangements was another consideration.[268] Prevention of the failure of an authorised bank was deemed necessary to preserve confidence in the system, but the Bank was anxious, too, that international confidence in London should not be damaged.[269] More specific international ramifications also played their part. EBS, for example, had a significant Arab shareholding, and collapse would have damaged Anglo-Arab relations. In the

---

[265] The Bank also rescued another authorised bank, Johnson Matthey, in 1984.
[266] *The Daily Telegraph*, 18 May 1976, p. 17.
[267] Blunden, 'The supervision of the UK banking system', *BEQB* 15(2):189, June 1975.
[268] Fforde to Richardson/Hollom, 'Slater Walker Limited', 3 September 1975, 6A70/5.
[269] Mallett to Kibble, 'Loss arising from the acquisition of Edward Bates and Sons Holdings Limited unsecured loan stock', 13 August 1981, 7A344/2.

case of Slater Walker, the Bank was keen to prevent the first failure of a British borrower in the Euro-currency market.[270]

The crisis was another of those operations that the Bank handled on its own with its own resources, and the Treasury was content with that. In a Treasury note, reference is made to the fact that 'at one point the Governor sought government involvement in the support operation and the Chancellor indicated that he regarded this as a matter for the banking sector to sort out'.[271] Richardson told the Chancellor about the Control Committee arrangements on 3 January 1974, and the Treasury thereafter wrote to the Bank asking about the state of play, the way in which the Bank saw the situation developing, and the extent of the clearing banks' commitments. Hollom worked on briefing material for the Prime Minister in case of questioning in the House. The extent of the Bank's aid did, of course, depend on its resources, and it was under pressure from the Treasury to provide more information. In September 1977, Wass wrote to the Governor about the need for a more systematic arrangement between the Bank and the Treasury for information about the extent and nature of the Bank's commitments in various support operations. Although the Bank did provide information from time to time, Wass wanted periodic written reports.[272] Blunden was not impressed with these suggestions, believing that the Chancellor had been adequately informed and that he should come directly to the Bank if he needed more information. Wass's suggestions were deemed 'a major assault on our independence which should be resisted to the full'.[273] Cooke shared Blunden's views, believing that written reports would add little to the oral information that the Bank gave to the Treasury.[274] Unsatisfied with the responses from the Governor, Wass continued to press the Bank for more than a year. Richardson finally admitted 'considerable bafflement' to Wass in June 1978. Support operations in his view were the responsibility of the Bank and the Court and 'not of Ministers'.[275] Wass still felt that the Bank should keep the Treasury informed in order to ensure that public funds were not at risk, and the Bank felt Wass's persistence to be troublesome.

---

[270] *The Select Committee on Nationalised Industries (Sub-Committee C). Minutes of Evidence, Session 1977–78, 18 January 1978, Bank of England Report and Accounts for the Year Ended 28 February 1977*, 166-I, question 47.

[271] Downey to Airey, 11 December 1974, TNA T233/2842.

[272] Wass to Richardson, 16 September 1977, 7A244/1.

[273] Blunden to Richardson, 'Support operations', 23 September 1977, 7A244/1.

[274] Cooke to Richardson/Hollom, 'Support operations', 7 October 1977, 7A244/1.

[275] Richardson to Wass, 'Support operations', 9 June 1978, 7A244/1.

The Bank's role as the lender of last resort also might be considered. The Bank had developed in the course of the nineteenth century to a point that might be described as a mature lender of last resort.[276] It had learned through the experience of several financial crises how to respond when a sudden demand for liquidity arose. And the commercial banks, too, had a role to play as they found their own way to the appropriate cash and liquidity ratios that gave acceptable profitability and stability. By the 1870s, that system was in place, and there were no more financial crises. There were occasional bank failures, no more than a healthy part of the process. There were even occasions when the Bank felt the need to organise the rescue of an individual bank – such as Barings in the 1890s – an act that might be called 'crisis management' rather than lender of last resort. On these occasions, the Bank might not lend anything at all. The concept of lender of last resort is best defined in terms of lending to the market as a whole rather than to an individual bank and so avoiding charges of cronyism. The old discount market allowed this to be done in an ideal fashion: a range of self-liquidating assets (essentially high-quality commercial bills and Treasury bills) could be cashed anonymously at the Bank.

It might reasonably be asked, then, why the Bank abandoned the old approach in 1973–74 and spent so much time and money sorting out the affairs of so many individual banks. There are at least three possible answers. The answer that tended to be put at the time, and indeed clung to by many thereafter, was that an authorised bank could not be allowed to fail. That would have reflected badly on the Bank, which had authorised them all either directly or indirectly, a view repeated in recent times.[277] Apart from the moral hazard that involved, however, this overstates the Bank's position. As already noted, both Richardson and Blunden later remarked that authorised status should not be exaggerated. A related part of the answer would have been the Bank's long-running concern with the reputation of the City. Anything that reflected badly on City institutions and on its own authority was to be avoided. But this does not really account for the type of action taken to preserve stability in the sector. A second possibility is that the system had in fact changed considerably following the introduction of CCC. After CCC, there were many more banks, and many or most were competing aggressively for existing and some new kinds of business in property and foreign exchange. With a different system, it might have

---

[276] Capie (2002).

[277] Discussion with David Mallett, 6 November 2007. Interviews with Roger Barnes, 27 September 2007; Sir Jasper Hollom, 12 October 2007; and Rodney Galpin, 10 October 2007.

been thought that different methods might have been required. Neither of these two explanations is terribly convincing. A third that perhaps carries more weight is that monetary growth in the first few years of the 1970s had been extremely rapid, and there was mounting pressure on the Bank to try to contain that growth. Insofar as the lender-of-last-resort action was associated with an injection of liquidity, that was something the authorities wanted to avoid in the prevailing circumstances. They may have decided that a more targeted approach was desirable. An additional part of this explanation might be that their use of the discount window for these purposes had long since disappeared. Nevertheless, it does seem, in retrospect, that while the operation was a success in the sense that no wider panic developed, the same result might have been achieved at much lower cost and without the danger of generating moral hazard.

12

Banking Supervision

In the latter part of the twentieth century, a view developed that while the market economy was superior to alternative models and that competition generally was desirable for promoting optimal outcomes, it did not hold in banking, where 'the social costs of failure outweigh any advantages that untrammelled competition might bring', to cite just one authority.[1] Some regulation therefore is required. The argument for regulation in banking derives in part from the problem of asymmetric information; markets then do not work as well as they might and could benefit from intervention. But there is also an important externality. When an 'ordinary' firm fails, its shareholders lose. When a banking firm fails, however, depositors also lose. If one such failure alarms depositors elsewhere and more generally, then there is a risk of a flight to cash or greater liquidity or quality. And this means that there is a potential threat to the payments system. One means of allaying the fears of depositors is the provision of insurance. However, even if this does not exist, or is seen as inadequate, or is not otherwise trusted, the authorities had a powerful tool at their disposal. The issuer of cash, usually the central bank, can reassure the banks by making it clear in advance that liquidity will always be available, albeit on terms – the role of the lender of last resort.

This is the system that evolved in England in the course of the nineteenth century. The Bank stood ready to cash all good (specified) assets. Once the banks understood this, there was no need to worry for if they kept a well-balanced portfolio, they could be sure of the necessary cash in times of need. Perfectly well behaved banks, through no fault of their own, could be subject to a run but would always be able to satisfy any demand. There was no regulation to speak of and only the lightest touch of informal supervision. The banking system that evolved was a highly concentrated one with

[1]   Grady and Weale (1986, p. 35).

several separate parts doing slightly different business. Retail banking was separate from wholesale and so on. Self-regulatory clubs evolved and looked after the affairs of their members. They restricted entry and limited competition, and the consumer paid a higher price for the product. An argument can be made for such arrangements. At any rate, the system remained in place more or less unchanged in its essential form from the 1920s to the late 1960s. By around then, however, the welfare costs of the arrangements were regarded as being too high and were one of the motivations for introducing greater competition.

While politicians and journalists expressed their views on monetary policy during the 1950s and 1960s, much less was said about the financial system or about banking supervision. Neither was the latter a topic that featured prominently in banking textbooks or academic study. For its part, the Bank maintained a discreet approach. The low profile accorded to supervision by the Bank was one reason why it was little discussed; another was that the financial system had been extremely stable for such a long time. And in historical perspective, the central bank's role in crisis management and adoption of a lender-of-last-resort function 'did not imply any large scale exercise of supervisory or regulatory operations'.[2] Thus supervision as a subject was undeveloped, and there was little discussion on whether it was the function of a central bank to supervise the banking system. By the end of our period, the situation had changed dramatically, and banking supervision had flowered into a discipline in its own right. There was both domestic and international pressure to formalise and codify controls with the aim of improving supervision and protecting depositors. The Bank strongly resisted this and sought to protect its traditional light-touch, informal, and non-statutory approach. In shaping the 1979 Banking Act, the Bank was successful in attaining its main aims. Yet this Act also marked the beginning of the shift towards greater formality, statute, and bureaucracy in banking supervision.

Supervision in the 1950s and 1960s

The word 'supervision' does not appear in the index of the Radcliffe Report, and the subject received scant attention in the report itself. Of course, Radcliffe was concerned mainly with monetary policy, not the stability of the financial system, and in any case, the system was stable. There were occasional examples of fraud or malpractice, but the supervisory regime, such as it was, was seen to work.

---

[2]   Goodhart and Schoenmaker (1995, p. 542).

The Bank's submission to Radcliffe on 'constitution and functions' stated that there was 'no formal control over other banks and no duty of inspection'. The possibility of refusing to maintain an account for a bank historically had been an effective sanction, whereas the 1946 Act allowed the Bank, if it thought it was necessary in the public interest, to request information from bankers and make recommendations to them. This was backed by the power, subject to Treasury authorisation, to issue directions to comply with such requests.[3] These powers were never used. The report did give ample coverage to the relationships between the Bank and the other elements in the financial system, but this was principally in the context of market operations and the pursuit of monetary policy, whether they could be influenced for the purposes of credit control rather than prudential or stability reasons. The Bank kept a close eye on the capital resources, liquidity, and general standing of the accepting houses and had considerable knowledge about the activities of the discount houses. The latter was characterised as 'paternalistic supervision', with the Bank acting as the 'good parent' and doing its best to 'help its children in maintaining the position that they have established, while reserving the right to keep the children in order'.[4] Extending this analogy, the extent to which the Bank could and should discipline other wayward children was less clear.

Banking supervision was a mixture of statutory and non-statutory powers, with the emphasis on informality and flexibility rather than legislation and rigidity. This was in contrast to many other countries, but the Bank was frequently to uphold the advantages of the British approach. This was the world of the 'Governor's eyebrows' and moral suasion, and institutions were by and large responsive to the warnings issued within this informal regime. A close watch was kept on the discount houses, and in the case of one, National Discount, the Bank had raised repeated concerns about performance during the 1960s. Eventually, it encouraged National to merge with Gerrard and Reid.[5] The accepting houses and, to a lesser degree, the clearing banks were subject to a similar regime.[6] As new forms of financial institution developed, both domestically and internationally,

---

[3] Bank of England, 'Constitution and functions', June 1957, Radcliffe, 'Memoranda', Vol. 1, p. 5.

[4] Radcliffe, 'Report', paras. 186–189, 361.

[5] The Gerrard and National Discount Company was formed in 1970. Hollom had told Frank Figgures in 1969 that the company had for some time been 'the lame duck of the market'; Hollom to Figgures, 10 July 1969, 7A233/1. Files C47/11 and 7A233/1 cover the whole story.

[6] Fforde (1992, pp. 749–760). For the clearers, the chairmen of the 'Big Five' were easily brought in to see the Governor.

the Bank's authority faced greater challenges. An important aspect was secrecy; knowledge was restricted to a very small circle of people. Looking back in 1978, Fforde wrote that supervision 'was in practice operated by the two Governors in person, the Principal of the Discount Office and not more than two or three assistants (whose own knowledge of events was circumscribed), together with some limited help from the senior official on the foreign exchange side'.[7] Everyone else was excluded. Information and intelligence were gathered by the Discount Office, the 'eyes and ears' of the Bank. Much of it was garnered in the marketplace, with the Discount Office sounding out views and opinions about the status and reputation of organisations. Judgements could also be obtained from the banking members of Court. The Bank's supervisory interest also extended to other issues; for instance, it was routinely consulted about senior appointments and possible mergers in the City. In 1972, Galpin noted that it was accepted that no British bank would 'make a marriage proposal' to another bank without first consulting the Discount Office.[8]

Privately, and with the benefit of a small degree of hindsight, faults with this system were admitted. Fforde observed that is was difficult for the Principal to criticise financial institutions unless this criticism 'was initiated and supported from within the City "establishment"'. Moreover, 'the Principal had to remain acceptable to his sources of information, or become unable to fulfill his task. If he became "unacceptable", he risked summary and humiliating transfer to another post.' Indeed, Fforde claimed that this had happened to Hilton Clarke's predecessor and that around 1970 there also had been an attempt to remove Keogh.[9] There was also an element of self-regulation in the system, with the Bank partly reliant on the co-operation of one group to bring 'non-conformists' into line. Crucially, Keogh felt that the clearers were not amenable to suggestion and did not care about the fringe, even though the Bank tried to get them involved.[10]

The nature of the statutory control was not something that gave the Bank regulatory powers over the whole banking system: 'The amalgam of the

---

[7]   Fforde to Richardson, 'Secondary banking: the antecedents', 20 January 1978, 7A149/2.

[8]   Galpin to Keogh/Fforde, 'Banking mergers, etc', 4 July 1972, 7A3/3.

[9]   Fforde to Richardson, 'Secondary banking: the antecedents', 20 January 1978, 7A149/2. Fforde did not name the person who was 'banished to the Law Courts Branch'. In fact, it was not Clarke's immediate predecessor but the one before that: Douglas Johns was appointed Principal in 1949 and relinquished the post in July 1952 'at his own request', according to the House list for 1952, E20/156. His obituary in *The Old Lady* noted that Johns resented, as he put it, being 'eased out of the running for Chief Cashier' and, instead, turned out to grass "down the Strand", *The Old Lady*, September 2000, p. 136.

[10] Keogh, Note for record – 'The fringe', 5 June 1974, 7A95/1.

market-based and statutory recognitions resulted in what may be described as a status ladder, with a series of rungs represented by individual recognitions, up which companies could progress as their reputation and expertise developed'; only those 'which had acquired the highest recognitions were regarded by the Bank as banks in the full sense of the word'.[11] An alternative view was that the definition of a bank was what the Principal of the Discount Office said it was.

Apart from the general regulations governing the registration and formation of companies and the requirement to produce annual accounts, there were also more specific pieces of legislation that affected banks.[12] Under the 1947 Exchange Control Act, only 'authorised banks' were entitled to deal in foreign exchange and freely open accounts for non-residents. They also enjoyed a wide range of delegated authority in the administration of exchange control. Interim permissions were also granted, allowing limited participation in foreign-currency markets for a period of six to 12 months before full authorisation.[13] The Treasury, with advice from the Bank, was required to maintain a list of the authorised banks. The Companies Act 1948 included provision for the Board of Trade to establish a list of banks that enjoyed certain accounting privileges, notably the maintenance of hidden reserves. Institutions so treated were called 'Schedule 8 banks'. Names on this list were largely historically determined; no additions were made after 1967, and by the 1970s, some institutions had voluntarily foregone the privilege. The 1948 Act also proscribed the use of company names felt to be undesirable, and in practice, the Board of Trade exercised strict control over the use of 'bank', 'bankers', and 'banking'. This was felt by the Bank to be a useful support to the supervisory system, although there were loopholes, and names containing words such as 'trust' and 'guarantee' were readily allowed.[14]

In addition to the company and exchange-control recognitions, there was legislation relating to the protection of depositors. Raising capital by share issues was regulated by the Companies Act 1948, whereas the Prevention of Fraud (Investments) Act 1958 required a licence before a banking company could deal in securities other than for its own account. The standing of a firm and the reputation of its management were the main criteria for a licence.[15] Neither of these acts, though, covered deposit

---

[11] Bank of England, 'Supervision of banks and other deposit-taking institutions', *BEQB* 18(3):383, September 1978.

[12] For a useful summary, see Allsopp (1975).

[13] Brian Gent to Coleby, 'Overseas banks in London', 20 March 1978, 7A212/4.

[14] Bank of England, 'The supervision of banks', July 1974, 7A222/2.

[15] 'Banking supervision in the United Kingdom', enc. with Galpin to GPS, 'Supervisory function', 31 December 1973, 7A222/1.

taking. Throughout the 1950s, the Bank was uneasy about that, and in the middle of the decade, there were moves to introduce a credit trading bill that would have given powers to control the acceptance of deposits. In a scheme devised by Hollom, institutions, other than some exempted categories, would be required to register with the Board of Trade for an annual licence and demonstrate that they met prescribed financial conditions.[16] Lacking government support in 1957, the idea came to nothing, a missed opportunity in Fforde's opinion.[17] Then, at the end of the 1950s, there were some high-profile cases where small investors lost their money, notably in the collapse of the MIAS property group.[18] This produced the inevitable clamour for action. At this stage, the initiative lay with the Board of Trade, which established an inter-departmental working party. There had also been some expectation that Radcliffe might comment, but in the event, the Committee was silent on the matter.[19] In November 1959, Maudling, who was then president of the Board of Trade, announced that the government was considering new legislation to give protection to the investing public.[20] The Treasury now had assumed responsibility and was, according to O'Brien, 'moved by recent events to a state of near panic on the subject'.[21] A submission to ministers in December recommended that deposit seekers should be treated as public companies and made to publish audited accounts. In addition, the nature and content of advertisements would be prescribed. Beyond this, some form of registration for deposit takers was envisaged, overseen by a registrar. The Chancellor requested that officials consult with interested parties on a possible registration scheme.[22]

---

[16] Hollom to Peppiatt/Cobbold, 'Hire purchase', 16 March 1956, C40/721; Cobbold to Makins, 16 November 1959; O'Brien to Armstrong, 12 May 1959, C40/110; O'Brien to Cobbold, 'Protection of depositors', 26 May 1960, C40/111.

[17] Fforde (1992, p. 777).

[18] Mortgage Investment (Albert Square), Ltd., was founded in 1955, giving loans on mortgage and buying properties for conversion and investment. An investigation into the company was launched in 1958 after it failed to return money to depositors, and by the end of the year, MIAS had collapsed. At a court case the following year, five men were found guilty of defrauding the public to invest in a financially unsound company. MIAS's liabilities were £1 million and its assets less than £250,000. *The Times*, 13 October 1959, p. 6, 23 September 1959, p. 10, and 9 December 1959, p. 8.

[19] O'Brien to Armstrong, 12 May 1959; Whittome to O'Brien/Hollom, 7 July 1959, Anthony Carlisle to Hollom/O'Brien, 'Protection of depositors', 27 October 1959, C40/110; Board of Trade, 'Protection of depositors bill, second reading brief', 28 November 1962, C40/1099.

[20] HC Deb, 26 November 1959, Vol. 614, c570.

[21] O'Brien to Hawker/Cobbold/Mynors, 'Mr. Greaves and hire purchase', 12 November 1959, C40/110.

[22] HMT, 'Protection of depositors', 9 December 1959; Figgures to Hollom, 12 January 1960, C40/111.

Meanwhile, Percy Browne, the Conservative Member of Parliament (MP) for Torrington, introduced a private members' bill to amend the 1948 Companies Act to give protection to investors, primarily by requiring deposit-taking institutions to provide details of their business. At the second reading in March 1960, Economic Secretary Anthony Barber sought to persuade Browne to withdraw his bill because it seemed certain that legislation would be introduced in the next session.[23] When Treasury officials drafted a further submission to ministers in May 1960, they had drawn back from a comprehensive scheme of registration and instead favoured a minimum of control, with the option of greater stringency if required.[24] O'Brien regarded this as 'timorous' and suggested that the Governor should urge the Chancellor to arm the registrar with adequate powers.[25] Accordingly, Cobbold pressed the case in two letters to Amory sent in the space of 17 days.[26] Preparations for a bill began, but the Treasury started to have doubts, and opposition to the scheme was growing among the clearing banks.[27] In November 1960, O'Brien heard from Armstrong that ministers had decided that the promotion of the bill should revert to the Board of Trade.[28] Despite further work, no bill materialised.[29] The Bank undoubtedly was frustrated, the more so because Butler, the Home Secretary and leader of the House, reportedly considered that the bill owed its place more to political than practical factors. O'Brien countered that the avoidance of another MIAS-type episode was 'the most practical of reasons for taking action'. To delay until another scandal had occurred would be short-sighted.[30]

In March 1962, the Treasury asked the Bank whether the possible breakup of the Finance Houses Association (FHA) would increase competition to

---

[23] Companies Act of 1948 (Amendment) Bill, 11 November 1959; HC Deb, 18 March 1960, Vol. 619, cc1631–637; 1681–1686.

[24] Carlisle, 'Note for record – protection of depositors', 12 May 1960; HMT, 'Protection of depositors', 23 May 1960, C40/111.

[25] O'Brien to Cobbold, 'Protection of depositors', 26 May 1960, C40/111.

[26] Cobbold to Amory, 1 June 1960; Cobbold to Amory, 17 June 1960, C40/111.

[27] E. W. Maude (HMT) to Hollom, 5 August 1960; O'Brien to Hawker/Cobbold/Mynors, 'Protection of depositors', 18 August 1960; O'Brien to Hawker/Cobbold/Mynors, 'Protection of depositors', 21 September 1960; Hollom, 'Note for record – Protection of depositors and control of financial institutions', 30 September 1960; HMT, '... meeting ... 29 September, 1960 ...', 5 October 1960, C40/111.

[28] O'Brien, Note for record, 24 November 1960, C40/111.

[29] HC Deb, 16 February 1961, Vol. 634, c177W; 21 February 1961, Vol. 635, cc26–27W; 28 February 1961, Vol. 635, cc1365–1366; 23 March 1961, Vol. 637, c558; 2 May 1961, Vol. 639, c114; 21 November 1961, Vol. 649, c.108–109W; 28 November 1961, Vol. 650, c215–216; Home Affairs Committee, March 1961 HA(61)28; Maude to Hollom, 15 May 1961, C40/1098.

[30] O'Brien to Hawker/Cromer/Mynors, 'Protection of depositors', 26 July 1961, C40/1098.

the extent that a case could be made for bringing forward the bill as soon as possible. Hollom considered the risks low, but O'Brien said that if recent events at the FHA could be used to press for action, then he would actively encourage this.[31] Cromer put suitable emphasis on this aspect in a letter to the Treasury, and his intervention apparently gained the bill higher priority. However, it was not enough to secure a place for the bill in the legislative timetable. In September, Cromer repeated his case, this time to the Chancellor, who replied that he shared the concern.[32] Then on 20 November, Browne, who had continued to champion the cause, asked when legislation was likely to be introduced and got the reply, 'as soon as parliamentary time could be found'.[33] In fact, a bill appeared the following day, and the Protection of Depositors Act received Royal assent on 10 July 1963.

Several questions of principle arose from the lengthy discussions over the contents of the bill. First, to whom should the legislation apply? The 1960 draft instructions assumed that all financial institutions would be covered. This did not please the clearing banks. While supporting its overall aims, they were surprised and concerned to discover that the provisions of the bill were intended to apply to them. The clearers argued that sufficient financial information was already provided, and the registrar's use of powers might compromise bank-customer relations. Further, the banks already were subject to considerable oversight by the authorities, and more might lead to their reputation, at home and abroad, being questioned.[34] While O'Brien recognised the high standing of the clearing banks, he explained that if they were to be exempted, there inevitably would be calls for the same treatment from a host of other financial institutions, making it impossible to draw a line. For this reason, he argued, it was unavoidable that all deposit-taking companies be included.[35] Hilton Clarke was also opposed to exemptions, but he accepted that a satisfactory document was unlikely to emerge without making a concession to the banks. Thus a line was drawn by exempting the Schedule 8 banks. There were over 100 on the list: 20 were clearing banks, 16 merchant banks, 13 discount houses,

---

[31] O'Brien, Annotation on Hollom to O'Brien/Cromer, 'Protection of depositors bill', 20 March 1962, C40/1099.

[32] Cromer to Lee, 5 April 1962; Lee to Cromer, 3 May 1962; Cromer to Maudling, 13 September 1962; Maudling to Cromer, 14 September 1962, C40/1099.

[33] HC Deb, 20 November 1962, Vol. 667, c997.

[34] O'Brien to F. Keighley (chief general manager, National Provincial Bank), 25 August 1960; A. D. Chesterfield (chief general manager, Westminster Bank) to O'Brien, 12 September 1960; O'Brien to Cobbold/Mynors/Hawker, 'Protection of depositors bill', 15 September 1960, C40/111.

[35] O'Brien to Chesterfield, 16 September 1960, C40/111.

and the remainder were overseas banks.[36] Yet blurred edges remained. For example, Rothschilds, clearly a bank, was not on the list because it was a private partnership. Furthermore, only months after declaring itself against special cases, the Bank made an unsuccessful attempt to persuade the Treasury to exempt members of the FHA so as to offer an incentive for others to join the organisation.[37]

The second question was the thorny one of use of the word 'bank' and related words in company names and advertising. It was something of a minefield because there were many examples of banks that did not contain 'bank' in their title and 'non-banks' that did. The former included Coutts and Glyn Mills; there were at least 10 cases of the latter, most notably Lombard Banking.[38] The Board of Trade had powers to prohibit usage by new companies, but it could do nothing where a name had been registered before 1947, as had Lombard Banking, or if used by overseas institutions. Neither could it prevent 'bank' and its derivations being used in a more descriptive way. The Treasury had envisaged that the use of such terms should be reserved for those on Schedule 8, and where necessary, companies would have to change their names. This idea was dropped, although the legislation as introduced in 1963 did prevent the use of 'bank', 'banker', and 'banking' in advertisements.[39]

As finally framed, the Protection of Depositors Act 1963 penalised the 'fraudulent inducement to invest on deposit'. Any person found guilty of making misleading, false, or dishonest statements and promises in order to induce someone to place money on deposit would be liable to a maximum of seven years imprisonment, or a fine, or both. The Act, together with its associated statutory instruments, also introduced restrictions on advertisements, stipulated that audited accounts should be provided, and gave the Board of Trade powers to wind up firms that did not comply with the regulations. All companies that advertised for deposits were covered, but

---

[36] Phelps (HMT) to Rudolf, October 1961, enc. 'Names of companies treated by the Board of Trade as banks and discount companies for the purposes of Paragraph 23(3) of the Eighth Schedule to the Companies Act, 1948'; Clarke to Rudolf, 'Depositors' bill', 27 October 1961; Rudolf to Rhodes (HMT), 3 November 1961; Rhodes to H. Osborne (BoT), 29 November 1961, C40/1098.

[37] Hollom to Radice, 14 December 1962; Radice to Hollom, 19 December 1962, C40/1210.

[38] Lombard Banking made several applications to be included on Schedule 8; see Fforde to Clarke, 'Companies Act, 1948. Protection of Depositors Act, 1963', 1 October 1963, C48/173.

[39] Carlisle to Hollom, 23 February 1960, enc. Figgures to Osborne (BoT), 23 February 1960; Carlisle to Hollom, 'Protection of depositors. Restriction of use of word "bank"', 29 February 1960; HMT, 'Protection of depositors. Use of the words "Banker" and "Banking," etc.', 2 March 1960, C40/111.

Schedule 8 banks were exempt. This exemption, together with the fact that there was no compulsory registration nor a registrar, meant that the final scheme was a somewhat watered-down version of the original proposals.[40] As Hollom had observed, the objectives were modest, and although reducing the dangers of placing money with 'fringe concerns', it would 'seldom give depositors much warning of losses in the pipeline'.[41] The Bank later argued that despite the weaknesses of the Act, there was little danger that the public would not be able to distinguish between a bank and other deposit-taking institutions, and the supervisory apparatus worked to the extent that 'no institution of any importance could in practice, readily and without challenge, deliberately call itself a bank, or be accepted as such, unless it was within the informal supervisory area administered by the Bank.'[42]

There were still 'legal obscurities' about the difference between a bank and a moneylender. This resulted in a Court of Appeal case, *UDT* v. *Kirkwood*, in 1966 that had important implications. The judgement hinged on what was a bona fide banking business and thus exempt from Section 6(f) of the Moneylenders Act of 1900.[43] United Dominions Trust (UDT), a finance house, was ruled to be a bank for this purpose, and the outcome served only to make matters more confusing. Consequently, Section 123 of the 1967 Companies Act created a new recognition that protected a lending company against the accusation of being an unlicensed moneylender. Holders of a Section 123 certificate were described as firms 'bona fide carrying on the business of banking for the purposes of the Moneylenders Acts 1900–1927'.[44] The Board of Trade, in consultation with the Bank, drew up a list of 'objective' criteria for the characteristics of a bank so that it could issue certificates equitably, and if necessary, ministers could defend these decisions in Parliament. Criteria included minimum capital of £250,000 and provision of a range of banking services, such as the issue of cheque books and offering current and deposit account facilities. A detailed questionnaire had to be returned to the Board of Trade indicating the firm's activities, sources of deposits, and spread of lending.[45] At first, certificates were issued without reference to the Bank, although the Discount Office soon came to be consulted on every application. Although the Bank might temper its views

---

[40] Protection of Depositors Act 1963, 10 July 1963: Statutory Instruments 1963, Nos. 1353 and 1397.
[41] Hollom to O'Brien/Cromer, 'Protection of depositors bill', 20 March 1962, C40/1099.
[42] Bank of England, 'The supervision of banks', July 1974, 7A222/2.
[43] Megrah (1968, pp. 490–524).
[44] Discount Office, 'The present system', enc. with Galpin to GPS, 'Supervisory function', 31 December 1973, 7A222/1.
[45] *Ibid.*

based on more subjective information, the Board of Trade apparently found it 'virtually impossible, if all the other criteria are met, to refuse any application on the grounds of poor reputation'.[46] Another major disadvantage was that having issued a certificate, there was no formal procedure for checking that criteria were maintained subsequently, neither in practice were certificates ever revoked. The 1967 Companies Act also extended the scope of exemption from the protection of depositors legislation with the introduction of 'Section 127 banks'. Inclusion on this list, agreed between the Bank and the Board of Trade, depended on a minimum capital of £1 million, a wide range of banking services, adequate liquidity and 'well spread' lending, the quality of management, and a high reputation.[47] A final recognition was Section 54 of the Income and Corporation Taxes Act 1970, which allowed a company to pay and receive interest gross where this was allowed. There were similar though less onerous criteria, as in the Section 123 certificate.[48] While all this entailed bureaucratic checking, it was scarcely supervision.

In terms of timescale, the Discount Office reckoned that a newly established domestic company would have a licence under the Prevention of Fraud Act within six months, and it would take two to three years to gain a Section 123 certificate or Inland Revenue Section 54 recognition. To gain authorised status would take eight to 15 years, and about two years after this would see exemption from the Protection of Depositors Act.[49]

In all these legislative recognitions, it was a government department that was responsible, but the advice of the Bank was sought. It took into account reputation and status, the nature of business and whether this conformed to accepted standards in banking, and various balance-sheet ratios: public liabilities not more than 10 times 'free' resources, acceptances not greater that four times 'free' resources, and readily realisable assets equal to at least one-third of deposits and one-fifth of acceptances.[50] A long-established and reputable firm could be expected to hold all the recognitions, although probably not Section 123, and be aware of, and in many cases observe, the ratios used by the Discount Office.[51] In addition to the statutory recognitions, there

---

[46] *Ibid.*

[47] Discount Office, 'Banking supervision in the United Kingdom', enc. with Galpin to GPS, 'Supervisory function', 31 December 1973, 7A222/1; note on 'Criteria against which applications for exemption from the Protection of Depositors Act 1963 shall be judged', 3A8/28.

[48] 'Banking supervision in the United Kingdom', enc. with Galpin to GPS, 'Supervisory function', 31 December 1973, 7A222/1.

[49] *Ibid.*

[50] *Ibid.*

[51] *Ibid.*

was a number of other indicators that reflected the progress an aspiring company was making up the 'ladder of banking recognitions' and how it was viewed by the banks. These included being allocated a clearing code number by the Committee of London Clearing Banks (CLCB), membership of the British Bankers' Association (BBA), a Drawing Office account at the Bank, inclusion in the *Bankers Almanac*, having their bills taken by the Bank, and members of the Accepting Houses Committee.[52] These prudential criteria, in their many forms, were to prove extremely troublesome when it came to framing legislation in the second half of the 1970s.

For the purposes of compiling banking data, such as those published in the *Bulletin*, the Bank had to decide which institutions should be asked to contribute. Those identified were called the 'statistical banks' and consisted of authorised banks, Schedule 8 banks, and the Section 127 exempt banks. After September 1971, the statistical banks equated to those institutions maintaining a minimum reserve asset ratio under competition and credit control (CCC). In April 1970, there were 229 statistical banks, of which nearly 100 were overseas banks. By October 1972, the figure had risen to 283 and a year later to 323.[53] Much of what happened in the following years was concerned with the institutions that did not appear on this list.

Pressure from the Fringe: Pressure from Europe

During the 1960s, the Bank and the Treasury had several times considered the subject of the control of other financial institutions, notably the hire-purchase finance houses. Although on occasion the protection of depositors was mentioned in this debate, use of the term 'control' had very little to do with supervision and everything to do with monetary policy and restraining credit. This would later prove troublesome because if an institution was recognised by the Bank for the purposes of credit control, it might have implied some degree of banking status. When CCC was under consideration, there was discussion about the inclusion of finance houses and the implications that this would have for their treatment as banks or near banks. CCC was partly intended to embrace the larger non-bank institutions, and there was some expectation that smaller fringe companies might disappear, but again, CCC was about credit control and not supervision.

At the beginning of 1973, there were over 30 Section 123 companies with deposits over £5 million, in total amounting to more than £550 million. Aside

---

[52] Discount Office, 'Other minor banking type recognitions', enc. with Galpin to GPS, 'Supervisory function', 31 December 1973, 7A222/1.

[53] 'U.K. Banking sector', 1 April 1970, 3A8/6; *BEQB* 12(4):573–575, December 1972; *BEQB* 13(4):538–541, December 1973.

from the main question of credit control, there was the issue of how any extension of CCC to embrace the larger fringe banks would be interpreted in terms of banking recognitions. For instance, to subject fringe institutions to the 12½ per cent reserve asset ratio would mean placing them on the statistical list. But that list was reserved for institutions with certain recognitions and listed status provided in the eyes of the market – 'a certain standing'. Practically, this was demonstrated by the fact that listed banks could borrow at lower rates from other listed banks. To admit fringe banks simply because of their size would mean that the Bank thought the statistical list was 'conditioned solely by the requirements of credit control rather than by the standing and reputation of the institutions on it'.[54] The 10 per cent reserve asset ratio applied to finance houses did not offer the advantage of lower borrowing rates and consequently might be less attractive to the fringe banks. This raised the question of the Bank's authority and whether the fringe could be forced to join: Application of Section 4 of the 1946 Act (which allowed directions) was uncertain because a banking undertaking had never been defined in law. Despite this, it was assumed that these institutions would fall into line if pressed because of their desire to attain banking status. Uncertainty remained, but it was evident that concerns about the fringe for the purposes of monetary policy entailed wider considerations about supervision of the banking sector.

In any case, despite some contacts and collection of balance-sheet data, the Bank knew little in detail about the Section 123 companies. When, in June 1973, the Discount Office wrote to 38 fringe banks informing them that a reserve asset requirement might be applied, together with liability for special deposits, the recipients were asked to complete a return that would enable the Bank to gain a better idea of the level of their eligible liabilities.[55] As a result of this exercise, only two were incorporated into the list of statistical banks and asked to observe the 12½ per cent ratio.[56] In November, Page reported that the stage had been reached when companies could be invited to join the 10 per cent arrangement, but since the fringe crisis was developing, the move was postponed.[57]

---

[54] Bank of England, 'Credit control and the fringe', January 1973, 3A8/25.

[55] HMT, 'Note of a meeting held in the Treasury on 27 March 1973 to discuss credit control and the fringe', nd; Wass to Fforde, 16 April 1973, 3A8/25; Drake, Note for record – 'Credit control: fringe banks', 27 March 1973, 6A50/8; Discount Office to various fringe banks (list attached), 19 June 1973, 3A8/26.

[56] Page to Chairman of Wintrust Securities, Ltd., and G. T.Whyte & Co., Ltd., 19 September 1973, 4A116/22.

[57] Page to Richardson/Hollom, 'Section 123 banking companies', 5 November 1973, 3A8/28.

While the fringe was in the Bank's sights, in the period between the introduction of CCC and advent of the crisis, discussions about supervision were driven mainly by the need to respond to a European Economic Community (EEC) directive on banking. The commission's interest in co-ordinating banking legislation went back to the late 1960s. A working group was established in 1969 and continued to meet until the beginning of 1972. The outcome of these deliberations was a document with the daunting title, in translation, 'Draft Directive for the Co-ordination of the Legal and Administrative Provisions for the Taking Up and Exercise of the "Independent Operator" Activities of Credit Institutions'. Running to 41 articles, the draft directive envisaged the authorisation of all credit institutions, with stipulations relating to requisite capital, managerial competence, and legal form. There was also provision for the protection of depositors. Prudential ratios and the reporting of significant items to the authorities, such as large credits to a single borrower, were also covered, as was the exchange of this information among member states. Frank Hall, one of the Bank representatives who attended the meetings, told Fforde that if the text was adopted in anything like its current form, it would establish 'a considerable supervisory apparatus endowed with statutory powers'. It still had to be debated, however, and some aspects were contentious, so Hall thought that it was likely to be a long time before a final text was adopted.[58] The process was bureaucratic: discussion by a panel of experts produced a revised directive that was sent to the Council of Ministers, which, in turn, sent it to the Committee of Permanent Representatives for negotiation. Hall and Galpin, along with Nigel Wicks from the Treasury, attended the experts' group in November 1972. Most of the two days was spent discussing one single article. The British representatives made it plain that there was a fundamental difference between the British system of progressive recognitions and the Continental concept of licensing that underpinned the directive. There appeared no easy way to bridge the differences. What was evident to Hall was that eventually there would be a directive, and the Bank would have to decide on its response and negotiating stance.[59]

---

[58] Commission of the European Communities, 'Draft directive for the co-ordination of the legal and administrative provisions for the taking up and exercise of the "independent operator" activities of credit institutions', July 1972; Frank Hall (Assistant to Chief Cashier) to Fforde, 'Draft directive on the co-ordination of legal and administrative provision relating to credit institutions', 12 September 1972, 7A3/3; Hall to Page/Fforde, 'Draft directive on banking supervision', 20 October 1972, 7A3/4.

[59] Hall to Page/Fforde, 'Group on co-ordination of banking legislation. Meeting of 13–15 November', 20 November 1972, 7A3/4.

There was potential conflict between the general aims of the banking directive and essential characteristics of the British system. Britain was the only country that had difficulties with both the principle of statutory licensing and detailed regulation. No doubt this was also a reflection of the different legal systems of common law and Roman law. In the light of this, three broad options were identified in the Bank: veto the directive, build up the present system, or establish a licensing system. The possibility of a veto was quickly discarded as impractical. In any case, the Bank thought that there were some positive reasons for moving at least partially towards meeting the directive. One was that if Britain remained outside, it might be 'justifiably criticised' for providing a haven for 'low-grade credit institutions' that had been unable to gain licences in other EEC countries. That freedom from regulation might in fact have been an advantage was not recognised. More important was the prospect that domestic pressures might force the authorities to take similar action in the future. Again, the growth of the 'fringe' was mentioned, and the paper stated that some individual institutions accounted for sizeable deposits from the public: 'A failure of one or two among these might well prove embarrassing to the authorities.' Moreover, many of these 'aspirant banks' had called on the Discount Office to discuss their progress towards the banking recognitions, and in these interviews, the Bank often gave advice about the broad shape of their balance sheets. In the event that such an institution failed, 'the Bank might be held implicitly to have assumed and accepted at least *some* responsibility for its soundness.' In addition, the available sanctions over the fringe were tenuous. Thus 'this unsatisfactory position should, the argument would continue, be rectified now by some modest tightening of the authorities' power to supervise the activities of such institutions, before any failures occur to stimulate political pressures, which might result in a more rigid system.' As to the appropriate response thereafter, the Bank was against an exclusive statutory licensing system. Although it might well be introduced in a low-key way at first, it would involve 'the acceptance of some very significant risks and dangers' and in particular the inevitable increase in coverage and complexity. Thus the Bank's opinion was that 'by far the most attractive approach would be to develop our existing system of privileges and recognitions.'[60] In presenting this to the Governors, Fforde said that the main purpose was to open a dialogue with Whitehall. He considered that seeking a compromise over the

---

[60] Bank of England, 'E.E.C. draft directive on the co-ordination of legal and administrative provision governing credit institutions', 29 January 1973; the paper was sent to the Treasury; Fforde to Wass, 29 January 1973, 7A3/16.

directive would have the advantage of 'enabling us to do things … which we are beginning to want to do anyway'. The paper's conclusion about building on the existing machinery was, for Fforde, 'clearly preferable' to new statutory powers, although he conceded that this approach might not in the end prove acceptable to the EEC.[61]

All this was discussed with the Treasury and the Department of Trade and Industry (DTI) in March 1973, but other than agreeing that a veto was untenable, this proved inconclusive. There was exasperation over the attitude of the DTI. Barnes recorded that their representatives displayed a 'lack of comprehension' of the main issues and a 'marked disinclination' to alter their disposition towards forthcoming legislation. This was a reference to the consumer credit bill, arising from the Crowther Report, that would see the repeal of the Moneylenders Acts and mean the end of Section 123 companies. Wass and Fforde both expressed their concerns about this prospect. The former commented that it would leave the UK authorities 'extremely exposed' in negotiations over the banking directive, and the latter explained that the demise of Section 123 firms would pose 'considerable problems for the Bank, both in respect of the ladder of recognitions and also the extension of credit control beyond present limits'. Wass asked whether broad licensing powers could be included in the companies' bill, but the suggestion apparently 'fell on very stony ground', with the DTI arguing that the bill was already too long and controversial.[62]

The following month, Fforde reported that the British representatives on the experts group were arguing for less detail and greater flexibility, particularly for the simplification of the ratios that were proposed, and had gained some support from other delegations. On the Bank's proposals, Fforde warned that the Treasury was coming round to the view that a formal system of licensing ultimately would prove inevitable.[63] Later he confirmed the conclusion that it would not be possible to comply with the directive by building upon existing UK legislation, and the option of a simple licensing bill for deposit-taking institutions was about to be examined.[64] Meanwhile, the banking directive itself had run into trouble. Although as many as five articles had been discussed at the two-day-long working group in September – 'the pace was almost feverish', remarked Hall – any sense of progress was

[61] Fforde to O'Brien/Hollom, 'Draft directive on the harmonisation of banking regulation within the E.E.C.', 12 January 1973, 7A3/16.
[62] Barnes, Note for record – 'E.E.C. Banking Directive', 14 March 1973, 7A3/5.
[63] Fforde to O'Brien/Hollom, 18 April 1973, 7A3/5.
[64] Fforde to Richardson/Hollom, 'E.E.C. draft directive on banking legislation', 16 October 1973, 7A3/7.

'hallucination'.[65] When Henri Simonet, the EEC vice-president, visited London in October, he admitted that the present draft was too complicated, and he asked the United Kingdom, along with other member states, to come forward with constructive counter-proposals.[66] Despite this, Cooke (at this time Adviser to the Governors) felt that 'they [the Commission] have the full panoply of the present coverage still in view as an ultimate objective', albeit achieved in stages. Yet he was convinced that 'if we are to sustain the posture of premier banking nation, we must be prepared to respond positively to the current cri de coeur'.[67] Barnes's idea was that harmonisation should be restricted to broad aims and it be suggested to the commission that the directive was confined to the basic conditions for granting a licence, together with greatly simplified balance-sheet ratios. This would require only nine of the existing articles. But there was a crucial aspect: The proposal implied the acceptance by the UK authorities of the need to introduce some form of legislation on deposit-taking institutions.[68]

As far as a bank licensing bill went, Barnes focussed on the basic aim, which was to provide depositors with 'an adequate level of security for their deposits in any institution in which they chose to place funds'.[69] This would be achieved by a 'competent authority' knowing of and approving all deposit-taking institutions. Subject to exclusions, it would be illegal for any institution that was not known or approved to accept deposits. The competent authority would ensure that approved bodies maintained adequate capital, liquidity, and management. As to who should be the competent authority raised a critical issue relating to the role of the Bank. In one model, the Bank would be concerned only with the supervision of fully recognised banks, while a separate competent authority would look after the other deposit-taking institutions. The alternative model saw the Bank assuming formal responsibility for all institutions. Barnes noted that a risk here would be that deposit takers 'currently more remote from the Bank might not react as constructively as the present group of supervisory institutions and that consequently the delicate balance of the Bank's pragmatic approach might

---

[65] Hall to Page/Fforde, 'Group on co-ordination of banking legislation. Meeting of 12–13 September', 19 September 1973, 7A3/7.

[66] Barnes to Page/Fforde, 'E.E.C. banking directive', 24 October 1973, enc. draft paper 'E.E.C. banking directive', 24 October 1973, 7A3/7.

[67] Cooke to Page/Fforde/Richardson/Hollom, 'EEC banking directive', 16 November 1973, 7A3/7.

[68] No author (but Barnes), 'E.E.C. banking directive', 16 November 1973; Cooke to Downey, 4 December 1973, 7A3/7.

[69] Barnes to Page/Fforde, Bank licensing bill', 15 November 1973, 7A222/1.

be severely put to the test.'[70] However, everything was still tentative at this stage, and no firm conclusions were reached.

Discussion continued in the Bank over the relative merits of single-tier (the Bank supervising all institutions) and two-tier (recognised banks and deposit takers supervised separately) models, with the latter option meaning that the Bank and the DTI were the competent authorities. Fforde explained to the Governors that the purpose of the two-tier system would be to preserve 'at least the appearance' of the relatively informal supervisory arrangements for recognised banks while also 'ensuring that the "fringe" was deprived of all its nuisance value by being subjected to a licensing system and some fairly heavy-handed regulation by Whitehall'.[71] But he wondered whether, in practice, politicians would adopt legislation along these lines or whether a two-tier system would prove durable. One danger, though not something that should be made too much of, was that the failure of an institution within the Bank's informal purview could result in the loss of all supervisory powers to the DTI. A single-tier arrangement administered by the Bank might avoid the difficulties of the alternative model, but it would need far greater resources to be devoted to supervision and 'lead us inevitably closer to the introduction of an inspectorate'.[72] Opinion on all this was divided. Advocates of the single-tier option put great weight on the problems of the current system and considered that a move towards 'less informal methods' would in any case be required by the 'facts of life' in a more aggressive and competitive banking system. On the other hand, those 'who attach the greatest importance to the preservation (through evolution) of our present way of doing things' were inclined to favour the two-tier system and emphasised that its inherent methods made it both acceptable and durable.[73] In the following years, this was to be a central area of debate. Views were split in the Bank, but critically, Richardson was firmly in the two-tier camp.

Thus, towards the end of 1973, but before the secondary banking crisis had broken, there had been slow progress on addressing supervision. Bringing the fringe into CCC presented some problems, but this was not the reason for discussion over legislation to cover deposit takers. It was the need for compromise in Europe, and possible domestic legislation, that was

[70] *Ibid.*
[71] 'The licensing and supervision of deposit-takers', 19 December 1973; also see, 'The supervisory function: one tier or two tier', 31 December 1973, enc. with Galpin to GPS, 'Supervisory function', 31 December 1973, 7A222/1.
[72] 'The licensing and supervision of deposit-takers', 19 December 1973, 7A222/1.
[73] *Ibid.*

nudging the Bank in a direction that it did not really want to go. Thus, while Keogh may have legitimately argued that something was being done, it was at best half-hearted. Of course, things were about to change dramatically. In early December, a further draft rehearsing the need for a licensing scheme noted that the London and County affair had drawn attention to the ambivalent position of sizeable deposit-taking institutions that were not banks.[74] By 19 December it was the crisis in fringe banks that had brought matters to fore. Fforde explained that concern was the result of discussions and meetings that had taken place over the past year, and recent events had brought urgency.[75]

Aftermath of the Crisis

In the last week of 1973, the Governor called a meeting on 'supervisory functions'. Arising from this, the Discount Office set out the origins of the prevailing system of supervision and suggested some possible ways ahead.[76] The starting point was that apart from some minor technical changes, 'there is no need for the Bank to take any further action', the rationale being that 'any person wishing to take advantage of the high deposit rates offered by non-recognised institutions did so entirely at their own risk and that the authorities assumed no responsibility whatsoever for the solvency of such institutions'. It was doubtful, though, that Parliament or the press 'would tolerate such a laissez-faire attitude'. These internal pressures, together with those from Europe, meant that at some stage legislation would be necessary, and there was thus felt to be a strong case for undertaking positive action immediately. This led into a further rehearsal of the form of a possible bill and the respective pros and cons of the one- and two-tier systems.[77]

At the beginning of February 1974, Richardson admitted that it was 'hard to avoid the conclusion that we shall have to extend our present arrangements'. He also conceded that the system of progressive recognitions, while having undoubted merits, had become 'complicated and not easily comprehensible by the public'. Yet he also saw 'no need to rush into some elaborate statutory system of supervision which might only succeed in appearing to render trouble unlikely at the expense of stifling initiative and innovation.

---

[74] 'A licensing bill for deposit takers', draft, 5 December 1973, 7A222/1.
[75] Fforde to Richardson/Hollom, 'The supervisory function', 19 December 1973, enc. 'The licensing and supervision of deposit-takers', 19 December 1973, 7A222/1.
[76] Galpin to Noakes (GPS), 31 December 1973, 7A222/1.
[77] 'The way ahead' enc. with Galpin to Noakes, 'Supervisory function', 31 December 1973, 7A222/1.

Our special strength as a financial centre has lain in the responsiveness of our informal regulation to changing methods of business and I should myself be slow to sacrifice this positive advantage.' Nevertheless, he concluded that some formal framework might in the end be required.[78]

When Richardson met the Chancellor at the beginning of January, Barber had accepted that there should be major reforms to banking legislation, with the aim of being ready to introduce the necessary changes in 1975. Similar views were expressed when Hollom, Fforde, and Keogh saw Geoffrey Howe, the minister for trade and consumer affairs, in mid-January. At the end of the month, Wass proposed to Fforde that a review should be undertaken in conjunction with the DTI as quickly as possible and with Wass himself as chairman.[79] Meanwhile, the Bank had continued its own work with the Discount Office, preparing a note outlining a bill to provide for the licensing of all credit institutions. Galpin sent a copy to Hugh Peppiatt at the Bank's legal advisers, Freshfields, seeking a view on definitions and exemptions. It was a problematic area, and Peppiatt admitted that his response might not be very helpful. As Keogh observed, it was 'a start on a long road'.[80]

The Bank reserved its position on the terms of reference of the Wass group, although its hesitation about the review went beyond those details. In typical style, Fforde navigated the subject. He put forward six propositions: any new arrangements should not maintain the division of the supervisory function between the Bank and the DTI; new arrangements should not preserve 'the barrier we have recently had' between recognised and fringe banks; new arrangements should not enlarge the supervisory powers of a government department (i.e., the DTI); the world would not stand still while new legislation was enacted, and in any case, 'the supervisory function will develop, and should develop, by force of circumstances before legislation can be passed'; it should not be assumed either that the existing fringe would disappear or that no new, unrecognised banking institutions would appear in the future; and the existing level of supervision for the more newly recognised banks should be strengthened. If these

---

[78] 'Richardson speech to the Institute of Bankers, 5 February 1974', *BEQB* 14(1):55, March 1974. In a similar vein, Richardson told Wass in June that he wanted to move 'quietly and steadily since rush and drama would be bad for confidence'; 'Extract from DG's note 28.6.74 ...', 7A222/2.

[79] 'Extract from Mr. Dow's note on the Deputy Governor's conversation with Mrs. Hedley-Miller 16.1.74.'; Wass to Fforde, 28 January 1974, 7A222/2.

[80] Galpin to Fforde, 3 January 1974; Galpin to Hugh Peppiatt [Freshfields], 7 January 1974; Peppiatt to Galpin, 17 January 1974; Keogh, Annotation on Galpin to Keogh/Fforde, 'Bank licencing', 5 February 1974, 7A222/2.

propositions were accepted, said Fforde, then three positive conclusions could be drawn. First, the Bank should 'consolidate and develop the extension of our "jurisdiction" which has arisen de facto from the rôle the Bank has played in the fringe banking exercise'. Fforde saw this as a trade-off with the Bank proceeding to supervise secondary banks in return for the 'relatively benevolent attitude towards them at a time of crisis'. It would accompany the intention to bring the fringe banks into the CCC arrangements. Second, for the time being, the procedures and criteria for recognition as an authorised bank or exemption from Protection of Depositors Act should continue. Finally, the proposed Whitehall working party should be used as a means of ensuring that the extension of jurisdiction was recognised by the government and allowed to persist, or it was given a statutory basis through a licensing act with supervision for all deposit-taking institutions devolved to the Bank. Assent having been given to these conclusions then led Fforde to three practical problems to be dealt with: structuring and equipping the Discount Office to deal with wider responsibilities (Page was preparing a paper on this), defining the nature of the supervision to which fringe banks would be subjected and ensuring its consistency with the treatment of recognised banks, and handling the Treasury and DTI over the working party. Fforde saw little reason for stalling the working party or for concealing the Bank's 'real opinions and intentions'; thus he suggested that the Bank should prepare a full-scale paper on supervision to be used as the basis for discussions. He also thought that deliberations would be easier 'if there were at the start a presumption both that the Bank would for the future undertake full executive responsibility for supervision and that the Bank would become answerable in this respect to the Treasury *if* a new statute were enacted'.[81]

Before any progress could be made, the general election intervened, and with Labour returned to power, it was unclear what the attitude of a new government would be. Reviewing the prospects, Fforde considered that although the legislative outlook was uncertain, the consumer credit bill was to be reintroduced, and thus Section 123, as a recognition, 'must now be regarded as moribund'. Fforde went on to reconsider the options on supervision. On the face of it, he found that the most attractive was to develop the supervisory function as he put it 'within the territory that we now occupy'.[82] That was fully recognised banks determined by the Exchange Control and

---

[81] Fforde to Richardson/Hollom, 'Supervision of deposit-taking institutions', 6 February 1974, 7A222/2.
[82] Fforde to Richardson/Hollom, 'Supervision', 13 March 1974, 7A222/2.

Protection of Depositors Acts and the existing fringe that now had little choice but to accept the Bank's guidance. Adopting this approach would avoid the need for new legislation – always an ambition of the Bank's – and leave the Bank to 'get on with the job'. However, Fforde was less sanguine about this option in the longer term for two reasons. First was the threat that a 'new fringe' might at some stage emerge. Fforde pointed out that 'experience in dealing with fringes as and when they turn up, whether in the credit control or supervisory context, is not entirely encouraging.' In addition, he felt that it would be short-sighted not to use the present opportunity to look at legislation to secure a lasting solution to the problem. Second, the draft banking directive and EEC requirement to introduce a licensing system was some years off, but it could not be ignored forever. And, as Fforde stated, 'one must recognise that our general case in Brussels against closer regulation … has been weakened by the fringe crisis.' These factors pointed towards undertaking a serious study of a licensing bill. Consequently, Fforde recommended that the Bank should both press ahead with the restructuring and extension of existing supervisory arrangements 'at least as far as the new frontier which the fringe crisis has established for us' and an examination of licensing legislation in the Whitehall working party. Fforde ended with a caveat. Wider issues would be raised by these discussions in Whitehall, and the implications for the Bank might be such as to 'inhibit the consideration of desirable legislation confined to the supervisory field'. This was the Bank's familiar worry: Whenever the prospect of legislation in the banking field was mentioned, the relationships established in the 1946 Act would be altered.

During May and June, Barnes and Fforde worked on a note on supervision that Richardson redrafted.[83] It explained that as a result of the crisis, the Bank would be widening the field of supervision to include all the large non-bank deposit-taking companies. The main criterion for becoming a supervised institution simply would be a certain minimum level of deposits, in contrast to the argument in early 1973. As for ensuring compliance, there were vague threats that if a company refused to subject itself to the Bank's supervision or failed to comply with its guidance, then 'the Bank would let it be known and expect market forces to take effect.' Supervision was also to be strengthened through the collection and analysis of more frequent and detailed returns on companies' financial positions. The question of statutory licensing was treated with caution. The positive arguments were played down, and there was no mention of the EEC. On the other

---

[83] Fforde to Richardson/Hollom, 23 May 1974, enc. 'The supervision of banks' (first draft); second draft with Richardson annotations, nd; Fforde to Richardson/Hollom, 6 June 1974, 7A222/2.

hand, with statutory powers, 'our system would soon lose its informal and flexible nature. The position of the Bank would have undergone a decisive and irreversible change such that we would be looked upon as the administrator of statutory powers rather than as the senior member and leader of the banking community.' Moreover, 'the informal and intimate relationship between the Bank and the banking system would have been weakened and self-regulation given way to a lazy acceptance of government authority and government responsibility.' On balance, the Bank saw little need for statutory licensing, and it was apprehensive about the disadvantages that such a system could bring. In addition, the Bank warned that current circumstances were such that it would be harmful to even let it be known that the authorities were considering a new statute.[84]

The most notable Bank casualty of the banking crisis was the Discount Office. In early February 1974, Page was already suggesting that it be wound up. Even before the fringe banking crisis, there had been a steady increase in its workload, and it was likely to continue to grow. In addition, Page worried that existing arrangements concentrated relations between the Bank and banks too much on the Principal himself, and they generated a tendency for the Discount Office to operate as a self-contained entity. To overcome this, he recommended that the Discount Office should cease to exist as a separate administrative entity and most of its ordinary work be transferred to elsewhere within the Cashier's Department. He also proposed the creation of several new posts, including an additional Deputy Chief Cashier who would have responsibility for supervision and relations with the sterling money markets. The historic title of Principal of the Discount Office would disappear, although it was proposed that Keogh should remain as an 'Adviser to the Governors', a suggestion that smacked of being shunted aside. Keogh was due to retire in March 1977, but it was said he 'would welcome some withdrawal from the hurly-burly and could then make a powerful contribution to planning for the future'.[85]

Hollom was in sympathy with Page's general interpretation and accepted 'that wider and closer supervision of the banking system cannot be satisfactorily handled within the existing Discount Office structure'. However, he was not convinced that it was right to add to the Chief Cashier 'already exceedingly wide' field of responsibility and suggested that it might be better to hive off the banking supervisory function: 'Supervision for prudential and allied reasons is not only going to be a rather large-scale operation;

---

[84] Bank of England, 'The supervision of banks (memorandum by the Bank of England)', July 1974, 7A222/2.

[85] Page to Richardson/Hollom, 'Cashier's Department', 6 February 1974, 0A46/2.

its basic justification and the doctrine that it will be building up is clearly separate from considerations of monetary policy, and this separation should desirably be reflected in our administrative structure.' In the longer run, this might justify a separate department reporting primarily to the Executive Director for home finance and, in the short run, a separate office within Cashier's but again reporting directly to the Home Finance Director.[86] Separation also had been favoured by O'Brien, the former Governor. He was firmly of the view that the special position of the Principal, with direct access to the Governor, was not lost in any reorganisation, while accepting that the need for change was 'patently obvious'. The Discount Office had 'performed wonders' with limited resources, but 'the job is now too big for the existing organisation, however much it may be reinforced.' While the work could be done by a suitable office in Cashier's, his preference was for a new department that would demonstrate that the Bank was taking the current problems seriously.[87]

Whatever the precise organisational structure might eventually be, it was evident that the days of the Discount Office were numbered. The end came on 18 July 1974, when the work of the office was split into two separate though closely linked functions: supervision of the banking system and day-to-day dealings with the money market. The latter was in the hands of a new division, Banking and Money Market Supervision (BAMMS), located in the Chief Cashier's and run by Galpin, who was appointed Deputy Chief Cashier. Blunden was put in charge of banking supervision, the first time that a senior member of the Bank was given explicit responsibility in this area, with staff and resources provided by BAMMS. As for Keogh, he had little opportunity to contribute to the new regime and retired at the end of 1974, although his appointments diary is empty from the summer of the year onwards. For public consumption, the Bank claimed that the administrative changes were under consideration long before the secondary banking crisis. There is little evidence to support this, although the arguments about the ability of the Discount Office to deal with an increasing workload were real enough. And while the changes represented a partial move towards a separate supervisory function, they did not denote an alteration in style. As *The Banker* pointed out, the structural reorganisation was 'unlikely to signal any fundamental change in the Bank's traditional approach to control of the banking system.'[88]

---

[86] Hollom to Richardson, 'Cashier's Department. The Chief Cashier's note of 6 February', 21 February 1974, 0A46/2.

[87] O'Brien to Richardson, 11 March 1974, enc. 'The Discount Office and bank supervision', invited comment, 0A46/2.

[88] *The Banker* 124(583):1045, September 1974.

Prudential Returns

With the reorganisation of supervision came additional resources. During the mid-1960s, the Discount Office consisted of the Principal, his Deputy and Assistants, and around 10 staff. Some additional posts were created in the following years, taking the total to 20. After the 1974 reorganisation, the newly established BAMMS had seven senior positions along with a support staff of 30. Five years later, just before the 1979 Banking Act, numbers had increased to 77 (by 1989, there were 200 staff). In percentage terms, this made supervision the fastest growing area in the Bank, albeit from a low base. By contrast, an additional 200 staff were taken on in exchange control from 1970 up to the time of its abolition in 1979.[89]

One reason additional staff were needed was because of improved data collection, the so-called prudential returns, and analysis. Design of this new paperwork began in May 1974 with the assistance of Coopers and Lybrand, who advised on the content and frequency of returns from the banks and on the level of their capitalisation.[90] Progress was fairly rapid, which it had to be with Blunden determined that banks would complete their first returns on 30 September. In the first week of August, Blunden told the Governors that discussions with Coopers had been concluded and the main gaps in prudential information identified. These included the maturity pattern of deposit liabilities and claims in sterling, liabilities and claims that accounted for an appreciable proportion of the total of any category, standby facilities, undrawn overdraft, loan and acceptance facilities granted, and details of shareholders' funds. On tactics, there was not time for negotiation with banking associations over the new requirements, and in any event, negotiation would only result in co-ordinated objections and delay. In addition, rather than going through the associations, which was the normal practice, requests were to be sent to individual banks directly. The three main bodies (CLCB, AHC, and BBA) would be informed of the proposals in general terms. As to coverage, the majority of fringe banks were to be brought in, although each case would be assessed separately.[91]

---

[89] 'The supervision of the UK banking system', a shortened version of a talk given by Blunden to a seminar in London on 17 March 1975 organised by the Institute of European Finance of the University College of North Wales, Bangor, *BEQB* 15(2):190, June 1975; Bank of England, *Annual Report*, various.

[90] Ian Cobbold, Note for record – 'Prudential returns from the banks', 28 May 1974; Galpin to Brandon Gough (junior partner, C&L), 21 June and 16 July 1974; Gough to Galpin, 24 July 1974, enc. paper on banking supervision, 7A222/2.

[91] There was a case for not including fringe banks under the aegis of the control committee, especially if being restructured.

Blunden suggested a number of temporary exceptions that included the clearing banks, members of the FHA, banks operating mainly through a network of overseas branches, and all wholly foreign banks. The Bank had no wish to prejudice forthcoming talks with the clearers on capital ratios, and there was probably no 'urgent need to consider their positions on prudential grounds'. Talks were also going on with the finance houses. Two reasons were given for ignoring foreign banks. The first was a matter of principle that ultimate responsibility for these branches lay 'with the parent bank and the monetary authorities in the country of the parent bank'. The second was a practical issue. So that the new arrangements were not dismissed 'merely as a statistical exercise', it was intended to follow up the receipt of the prudential returns with individual interviews, a task that would be impossible within a reasonable time if all the foreign banks were covered.[92]

The new arrangements were made public in August 1974. In addition to the returns designed primarily to meet statistical and credit-control requirements, the Bank wanted more information for supervisory purposes provided regularly. Thus most banks would be asked to complete new supplementary returns quarterly, whereas other deposit-taking companies, most holding a Section 123 certificate, would be invited to submit similar returns. The Bank also explained that the Banking Supervision Division would be discussing the information contained in the returns with the management of the reporting institutions.[93]

The exercise imposed a heavy workload, with the preparation of analysis and comments sheets prior to the interviews and up to an hour and a half allowed for the interviews with a representative of each bank. The work was shared among Blunden, Galpin, and four of the latter's senior staff (Barnes, Craik, Brearley, and Gill). With nearly 130 institutions making returns in the first round, Blunden expected that the task would take five to six weeks to complete. In this light, Fforde wondered whether there should be a reappraisal of staffing requirements, and Hollom suggested the idea of bringing in 'a bright young accountant' on secondment.[94] Reporting on the outcome at the end of 1974, Galpin thought the exercise had been 'fruitful' and increased the Bank's knowledge about individual companies. With a few

---

[92] Blunden to Richardson/Hollom, 'Prudential returns', 7 August 1974; Blunden, Note for record – 'Prudential returns', 14 August 1974, 7A222/2.

[93] Bank of England, Press notice, 20 August 1974, 7A222/2.

[94] Blunden to Page/Fforde/Richardson/Hollom, 'Prudential returns', 1 October 1974, and Fforde and Hollom annotations, 7A222/2. Subsequently, David Mallett, from William Brandt's, joined as a 'banking supervision accountant' in 1975; discussion with David Mallett, 6 November 2007.

exceptions, it had been welcomed by the banks. Out of 128 banks and fringe companies, four had been asked to provide returns on a monthly basis and three to give regular progress reports, and the returns also had revealed some other potential problems. Blunden expressed himself favourably surprised at how well things had gone and was confident that they would be better informed from then on.[95]

The new returns were to be provided by about 100 of the statistical banks and, in addition, 40 or so of the large miscellaneous deposit-taking companies.[96] The scheme was quickly extended, with 30 members of the FHA asked to make their first returns as at 31 December 1974.[97] In March 1975, information was sought from a dozen or so miscellaneous deposit-taking institutions that had been excluded previously on the grounds of size.[98] Although the clearers did not take part, they were subject to prudential interviews, the first round of these being held during 1976 and 1977, an exercise that yielded few surprises.[99]

A great deal of effort was put into refining the design and technical content of the returns, the analysis of subsequent results, and the administrative process itself.[100] For example, there was work on the type of accounting information and questions that might be asked of fringe banks in order to assess potential insolvency problems.[101] There was also an idea for an early-warning system based on the standardised scoring of responses.[102] At the beginning of 1977, after 10 sets of returns, there was some move towards the formal categorisation of the monitoring procedures on the basis of risk so that not every

---

[95] Galpin to Blunden/Fforde/Richardson/Hollom, 'Prudential returns', 12 December 1974, and Blunden annotation, 16 December 1974, 7A222/2.

[96] Blunden to William Balfour, 'Prudential returns: press briefing: questions and answers', 19 August 1974, 7A222/2.

[97] Blunden, Note for record – 'Prudential returns: F.H.A.', 1 October 1974; Letter to finance houses, 6 November 1974, 7A222/2.

[98] Richard Tyson-Davies to Barnes/Galpin/Blunden, 7 March 1975, 7A222/3.

[99] Wood to Cooke/Page, 'Prudential interviews with the clearing banks 1976/77', 14 April 1977, 7A319/1.

[100] Jeremy Huddle/Alan Savery to Blunden, 'Prudential returns', 17 December 1974, 7A222/2; Huddle/Savery to Barnes/Galpin/Blunden, 7 March 1975; David Mallett to Galpin, 22 August 1975, enc. 'The prudential review and interview', 7A222/3. For a set of forms (titled BS, Q3, S2, Q6, and Q7) with various amendments, see 7A222/5. Ian Kerr, Note for record – 'Prudential analysis and interviews', 16 February 1976, 7A222/4; Noakes (Chief Cashier's) to 'all group leaders', 'Pre-interview notes', 20 October 1976; Noakes to Galpin, 'Prudential analysis: feedback', 21 October 1976, 7A222/5.

[101] Mallett to Galpin/Blunden, 'Secondary bank insolvency – the profit and loss account as a guide to solvency', 3 October 1975, 7A222/3.

[102] Known as the 'Savery test'; Savery to Galpin, 'Prudential statistics', 17 September 1975, 7A222/3; Savery to Gill/Galpin, 'Prudential analysis', 15 March 1976, 7A222/4; Noakes to Gill/Galpin, 'The Savery test', 17 January 1977, 7A222/6.

institution needed to be seen.[103] There was a heavy workload, and the capacity for this supervisory bureaucracy to grow was significant. New elements could be added as thoughts turned to prudential liquidity controls, measures of capital adequacy, operations outside the United Kingdom, and bank exposure to country risk, and much of this was spurred by developments in international supervision.[104] Despite some pressure, the Bank continued to hold that there could be no inviolable figures for such criteria.[105]

When it came to the supervision of overseas banks' branches located in Britain, the Bank's underlying principle was that 'branches and their head office are legally indissoluble and that the primary responsibility for the supervision of the business of the branch and the security of its depositors rests with the supervisory authority of the branch's head office.'[106] There was also an argument, one pressed by some other Group of Ten (G10) members in Basle, that the host country had responsibility for the oversight of branch liquidity and the conduct of local management. There was also a worry in the Bank that guilt by association might harm the reputation of London as a financial centre. In the summer of 1977, Cooke (he had become Head of BAMMS when Blunden was appointed an Executive Director in 1976) pressed for greater contact with the overseas banks' branches. On a practical level alone this presented a challenge because there were some 160 of them. He suggested that the exercise should be undertaken on an informal and voluntary basis, and it should be characterised as a way of improving contacts rather than as overt supervision. It would also be selective rather than comprehensive. No general circular was issued to launch the new discussions, but the *Annual Report* published in July 1978 reiterated that primary responsibility for these branches still rested with the supervisory authorities in the parent bank's home country.[107] The fact that this was in apparent

[103] Noakes to Galpin, 'Interviews', 10 January 1977, 7A222/6.
[104] John Anderson (EID) to William Hawkins/Walter Hillage, 'Country risks', 20 September 1976, 7A222/5; Savery, 'Capital adequacy', 5 November 1976, 7A206/2; Anderson to John Mutch/McMahon, 'Country risks' exercise: BIS consolidated data', 23 June 1977; Paul Allen to Gent/Galpin, 'IRBO report on UK banking supervision', 18 July 1977, 7A222/7; Hall to Fforde, 'Liquidity exercise', 15 June 1978, enc. 'Prudential liquidity controls', nd, 7A222/10; Mutch to McMahon, 'Bank exposure to country risk', 17 July 1978, 7A222/11; Bank of England, 'The capital and liquidity adequacy of banks', *BEQB* 15(3):240–243, September 1975.
[105] Briefing note, 'Banking supervision in the United Kingdom', prepared for use of Advisers travelling abroad, July 1977, 7A222/7. On the origin of this note, see Galpin, Note for record – 'Liaison with the Overseas Department', 14 February 1977, 7A222/6.
[106] Cooke to Galpin/Coleby, 'Discussion with overseas banks' branches', 12 August 1977, 7A222/8.
[107] Noakes to Galpin/Cooke, 'Supervision of overseas bank branches', 3 May 1977, 7A222/7; Cooke to Galpin/Coleby, 'Discussions with overseas banks' branches', 12 August 1977,

conflict with the G10 approach was queried by Dow. Notwithstanding the Bank's stance, there was a developing concept of sharing responsibility, although Cooke had to concede that 'we are somewhere near the bottom of the league in the *extent* of our involvement.'[108]

How to use the information contained in these prudential returns was another matter. Blunden hoped that the analysis of the returns would give a much more comprehensive and up-to-date picture of a bank's business, and he went as far as to claim that if such information had been available earlier, then the troubles of 1973 could have been forestalled.[109] It also offered a form of early warning, with lists compiled of high-risk institutions. These were subdivided into varying categories of actual or potential cause for concern. In December 1976, there were 32 on the list; this had fallen to 29 in July 1977; by September 1979, the figure was 27. Many of the problem institutions were connected with the secondary banking crisis.[110] Nonetheless, Richardson had worried that the difficulties experienced with Slater Walker, Edward Bates, and Wallace Brothers might be attributed to shortcomings in prudential supervision. In fact, all three had been on the 'problem list' since the start.[111] BAMMS also produced monthly summaries of the information that had come to its notice during the period, and in 1978, a monthly supervision meeting was instigated where these reports and other material were discussed. Richardson saw the purpose of these meetings as improving the flow of information, suggestive perhaps that in some ways BAMMS was perceived of as being isolated.[112]

There were negative aspects to the way in which prudential machinery had developed. Even early in the process, at the end of 1974, Galpin had seen some proposed expansion of data collection and wondered whether there was a

---

7A222/8; Cooke to Coleby, 'Discussions with overseas banks' branches', 15 September 1977, 7A212/3; Bank of England, *Annual Report*, year ending 28 February 1978. The first round of discussions with nearly 160 banks was completed in November 1978, with the Bank encouraged by what it found, Michael Lockett (BAMMS) to Nicolle/Cooke, 'Discussions with branches of overseas banks', 24 November 1978, 7A212/5.

[108] Dow to Cooke, 'Supervision of foreign banks', 13 July 1978; Cooke to Dow, 'Supervision of foreign banks', 27 July 1978, 7A212/5.

[109] 'The supervision', p. 191.

[110] Cooke to Richardson/Hollom, 23 July 1976, 7A221/2; Erskine to Galpin, 'High risk list', 22 December 1976, 7A319/1; Gent to Cooke/GPS, 'High risk list', 22 August 1977, 7A222/8; Barry Hoffmann, 'Risk list – end-September 1979', 19 October 1979, 7A222/13.

[111] Noakes to Richardson/Hollom, 'Slater Walker/Edward Bates/Wallace Brothers', 25 October 1976, 7A302/5.

[112] For example, Peter Conoboy (BAMMS) to GPS, 'BAMMS monthly summary – February 1978', 1 March 1978; Coleby to Cooke/Richardson/Hollom, 'Meeting on banking supervision, Monday, 20 March', 16 March 1978, 7A222/9. Papers for period from December 1978 onwards in 7A282/1.

danger of the returns becoming excessively complicated.[113] Six months later, Barnes warned that increasingly detailed requirements could over time lead to inspection of the total records of the supervised institution, with subsequent pressure on resources and a dilution in the quality of analysis. Barnes also noted that examination of the figures and interviews was only part of the process; equally important was getting out and about in the marketplace in order to 'identify rumours about individual names, the emergence of new fads or the development of new techniques'.[114] Although he did not say so, this had, of course, been one of the traditional functions of the Discount Office. Similar concerns about the negative impact of a surfeit of information were expressed by Richard Farrant of BAMMS in the middle of 1978, when he questioned whether 'the routine of full analysis every quarter is not lessening the standards of supervision'. Getting too close could lead to a loss of perspective. This was not a repudiation of past policy because there had been a clear need in the mid-1970s to acquire knowledge. Now this exploratory phase was complete, and practice now should be tailored better to suit current needs.[115]

By 1979, the emphasis was changing. The previous approach had been based on data for banking statistics supplemented by additional returns, but now, greater importance was attached to a consolidated approach to supervision, strongly endorsed by international debate and by the Governor. This meant that the existing statistical base was not felt to be adequate for prudential purposes. At the same time, the needs of credit control focussed only on UK offices, whereas prudential supervision increasingly was concerned with the 'totality' of each business.[116]

Towards Legislation

When the Bank's views on supervision were discussed by the Governor and the Chancellor at the end of July 1974, it was agreed that the Bank would participate in a Whitehall-led working party.[117] At the first meeting, three ambitious and possibly unrealistic objectives were set: to clarify the current structure of banks and financial institutions and the confusion of statutory

---

[113] Galpin, Annotation on Huddle/Savery to Blunden, 'Prudential returns', 17 December 1974, 7A222/2.

[114] Barnes to Galpin/Blunden, 'Banking supervision', 20 June 1975, 7A222/3.

[115] Richard Farrant to Barnes, 'The quarterly round', 23 June 1978, 7A222/10; Mallett to Farrant/Barnes, 'The quarterly round', 7 July 1978, 7A222/11.

[116] Farrant to Barnes, 'BAMMS statistical returns', 19 April 1979, 7A222/12; Farrant to Barnes/Coleby/Cooke, 'The statistical base for prudential supervision', 13 July 1979; Derrick Ware, 'Statistics for prudential supervision', 18 July 1979, 7A222/13.

[117] Mick Folger to Noakes (GPS), 1 August 1974, 7A213/1.

and informal recognitions and to define more precisely what constituted a bank, to establish 'the most efficient supervisory system for both the protection of depositors and the health of the financial system as a whole', and to set down clear lines of departmental responsibility.[118] Thereafter, discussion was based on the Bank's July paper and a note by the Department of Trade on its own responsibilities in relation to deposit-taking companies. After the inaugural meeting, Fforde reckoned that Whitehall was already disposed to some sort of licensing statute not because officials thought that this would result in better supervision but because they were dissatisfied with the existing statutes and the degree of 'responsibility-without-power'. He also noted that the Department of Trade disliked the Protection of Depositors Act and wanted it to be repealed rather than strengthened.[119]

After three meetings, Blunden reported that while Treasury representatives accepted the arguments for a control that 'is flexible, discretionary and participative', the Bank had been unable to persuade them that 'present arrangements would not be strengthened by addition of a simple licensing system for deposit-takers.'[120] He said that the Treasury was greatly influenced by the Board of Trade's view that the Protection of Depositors Act was ineffective and should be replaced with a licensing system and that the Bank should be the sole regulatory authority. Furthermore, Whitehall officials apparently were unconvinced that the Bank would, under the existing arrangement, be able to keep a firm grip on the secondary institutions once the crisis was over and were unduly worried about the need for harmonisation with other EEC countries. They wanted to put a submission to ministers offering a choice between no change other than minor tidying-up measures and an alternative of a simple Bank-administered licensing system in place of the Protection of Depositors Act. The Bank was asked to devise a scheme, giving an undertaking that this would not be regarded as admission that the Bank thought a licensing system was in fact necessary. Blunden agreed, saying, 'I see considerable danger in ceding to the Treasury authorship of what might become the base document for a new system.'[121] As well as being prepared without commitment, Blunden was adamant that 'the legislation would not be a Banking Act, but an extension of the Protection of Depositors Act 1963, which it would supersede.'[122]

---

[118] SBS (74)lst, 7A213/1.
[119] Fforde, Annotation, 4 September 1974 on SBS (74)1st, 7A213/1.
[120] Blunden to Fforde/Richardson/Hollom, 'Banking supervision', 14 October 1974, 7A213/1.
[121] *Ibid.*
[122] Blunden, 'Licensing deposit-takers', 25 November 1974, 7A213/1.

An outline of a scheme was ready by in mid-December 1974. It was one in which no person or institution would be allowed to accept deposits without having been licensed to do so. The granting of licenses would be dependent on meeting certain specified criteria, and licenses also could be refused or withdrawn if these were not met. Other provisions included limiting the use of 'bank' and 'banking' and remaining licensed but undesignated institutions would be required to contribute to a deposit-insurance scheme. The Bank would be the sole licensing authority.[123] This final point raised an awkward question about the relationship between the licensing authority and Parliament and whether it would lead to any erosion of the Bank's independence. In seeking to avoid this, Blunden had proposed a 'deposit-takers licensing commission' with the Chancellor and Governors as the commissioners and the staff, premises, and services all provided by the Bank. The commission would deal with licensing, deposit insurance, and use of the word 'bank' and be liable to parliamentary scrutiny, whereas all other banking supervision would continue to be dealt with by the Bank, thus retaining traditional independence. However, this was dismissed as too elaborate, and instead, it was assumed that the Chancellor would be the responsible minister, although the nature of the relationship was left undefined.[124]

In early 1975, a submission was put to ministers that recommended the establishment of a statutory system for the licensing and supervision of deposit-taking institutions, with legislation to be introduced during the 1975–76 session of Parliament. However, while the Bank had confirmed that such a system could 'feasibly be set up', the Governor would wish to offer separate advice on whether it was desirable.[125] In briefing the Governors, Fforde reiterated that although the Bank had contributed to the drafting of the submission, it was not formally associated with it, and the Governor would need to make his views known to the Chancellor. Notwithstanding the fact that the Bank had been arguing for minimal change to the existing arrangements, Fforde concluded that, on balance, 'it would be unwise to resist the principle of legislation' on the grounds that the pressures to accept statutory licensing – from ministers, from officials, and from the EEC – were considerable.[126] It was not a conclusion with which Richardson could agree.

[123] Blunden to Fforde/Richardson/Hollom, 'Licensing deposit-takers', 25 November 1974; Fforde to Airey, 18 December 1974, enc. Bank of England, 'Licensing deposit-takers', December 1974, 7A213/1.

[124] Blunden 'Licensing deposit-takers', 28 October 1974; Blunden to Richardson, 'Licensing', 2 April 1975, 7A213/1.

[125] Downey to Blunden, 5 February 1975, enc. Airey, 'Supervision of the banking sector', February 1975, 7A213/1.

[126] Fforde to Richardson/Hollom, 'Whitehall working party on the supervision of the banking sector', 26 February 1975, 7A213/1.

The Governor made it clear to the Chancellor at the beginning of April that he was extremely worried about the proposed licensing system. He could see no justification for applying such a control to the central core of British banking in order to address the weakness of the outer fringes, and he wanted the application of licensing limited to non-bank deposit-taking institutions and achieved through a new and tougher Protection of Depositors Act.[127] This approach, which Fforde termed the 'exemption route', did not have unanimous support; the alternative, he called the 'umbrella method'. In a convoluted note, Fforde asserted that although there was a case for preferring the exemption route, it was a rather fine one. He remained deeply exercised about what would happen in the event that the 1946 Act was ever changed. By leaving supervision of banks with the Bank, Fforde felt that the exemption route left it vulnerable to an amendment of the Act, whereas the umbrella method, which gave the Bank a specific statutory responsibility, 'could in practice prove to shield banking supervision from Treasury interference'.[128] Fforde felt strongly about the point, but he had little success in persuading others. McMahon declared himself sympathetic, to which Fforde replied that he was grateful, 'for I have been unable to convince anyone else!'[129]

The Governor remained fundamentally opposed to the proposals to bring licensing and supervision of the entire deposit-taking system under a comprehensive statutory umbrella. He said that he supported many of the aims and objectives contained in the submission, but 'the mischiefs that require correction lie in the licensing and supervision of the secondary sector, the "fringe", and not in the central core of the banking system. To use the same system for both would be inappropriate and damaging.' He went on to claim that the 'adaptable and informal' arrangements gave 'our banking system a security without rigidity that is the envy of many other countries'. In order to 'preserve beyond doubt' the current arrangements and to 'make the distinction between banks and non-banks absolutely clear', he made four proposals. First, there should be a new Protection of Depositors Act. Second, the new Act should include proposals for the licensing, supervision, and insurance of non-bank deposit-taking institutions. Third, as with the 1963 Act, deposit takers, recognised as banks by the Bank, should be exempted

---

[127] Christopher France (PPS to Healey), Note for record (of a meeting on 3 April 1975), 3 April 1975, 7A204/1; Blunden to Richardson/Hollom, 'Licensing', 7 April 1975; Page to Fforde/Richardson/Hollom, 'Supervision'; Blunden to Richardson/Hollom, 'Supervision', 22 April 1975; Blunden to Richardson/Hollom, 'Supervision', 29 April 1975, 7A204/1.

[128] Fforde to Richardson/Hollom, 'The licensing question', 9 April 1975, 7A204/1.

[129] McMahon and Fforde, Annotations on Fforde to Richardson/Hollom, 'The licensing question', 9 April 1975, 7A204/1.

from its provisions. Finally, institutions that were not exempt would not be allowed to describe themselves as banks in any circumstances. As to the operation of the Act, the Governor was adamant that responsibility had to be kept separate from that for supervision of banks. He recognised that the Department of Trade wished to be relieved in this area and accepted the proposal that the Bank should be the statutory licensing authority. Richardson envisaged the establishment of a new division of the Bank to carry out the new functions.[130] He played a pivotal role in drafting this note, and the final version was a firm expression of his own views on banking supervision.

In June, Fforde told the Governor that the Treasury's revised submission now 'satisfies the conditions you have specified as necessary for a licensing statute that [would] meet with [your] approval'. Richardson agreed with the terms, which became known as 'the concordat', with Wass on 13 June 1975.[131] In September, Blunden reported that the prospects of a bill had slipped into the 1976–77 session but that the Treasury was aiming for a planted parliamentary question and a white paper within two months.[132] This would then be two years since the secondary banking crisis had broken.

In the autumn of 1975, some urgency attached to the production of a white paper.[133] Gill, one of the Bank's representatives, thought that the pressure to produce a form of words for the white paper meant that discussion of some elements had been 'rather sketchy and hurried'.[134] By February, there still were three main issues outstanding: a deposit-insurance scheme, parliamentary accountability, and whether Schedule 8 exemption under the 1948 Companies Act should be retained. To this, Fforde added minimum capital requirements and regulation of advertisements.[135] During the subsequent discussions, three of these were settled quickly. It was decided that the white paper should include a deposit-protection scheme, something that the Bank wanted, but covering exempt as well as licensed deposit takers, to be financed by the institutions themselves. In addition, the white paper would not refer to the abolition of Schedule 8, again the Bank's preferred position,

[130] 'Supervision of deposit-taking institutions', 30 April 1975, 7A204/1.
[131] HMT, 'Note of a meeting ... 6 June 1975'; Airey to Fforde, 10 June 1975, enc. 'Banking supervision: possible outline legislative framework'; Fforde and Richardson, Annotations on Airey to Fforde, 10 June 1975, 7A213/1.
[132] Blunden to Richardson/Hollom, 'Banking supervision', 23 June 1975; Blunden, Note for record –'Licensing', 22 September 1975, 7A204/1.
[133] Lawrence Airey (HMT, Deputy Secretary) to Fforde, 10 October 1975, 7A179/1.
[134] Gill to Galpin/Blunden, 'H.M.T. working party on licensing', 4 December 1975, 7A179/1; CSCI(76)1, 14 January 1976 (second revise of draft white paper), 7A179/2.
[135] Couzens to Fforde, 9 February 1976; Fforde to Richardson/Hollom, 'White paper on licensing of deposit-taking institutions', 13 February 1976; Fforde to Couzens, 17 February 1976, 7A213/1.

and the concept of minimum capital requirement would be mentioned, but no figure would be given.[136] This left accountability or, more specifically, whether the granting or revocation of exempt status should be the subject of an appeals procedure and advertising regulations.

The Treasury wanted to include an appeals procedure against any Bank decision on exemption in order to give adequate accountability to Parliament, but Fforde objected that to allow an appeal to the Treasury would mean that they would have to go through the same kind of procedures as the Bank had already gone through. 'This would seem to us not only to be a process with little purpose but one which would substitute the less clearcut and ultimately less responsible judgment of two official bodies for the clear and responsible judgment of the institution primarily concerned.'[137] This was a long way of saying that these subjective matters were for the Bank alone. On advertising, the Bank disliked the idea of legally enforceable regulations, when much of the bill was based on guidelines and the sanction of revocation, not prosecution. The Treasury suggested a compromise whereby the Act instead would contain reserve powers for regulations to be issued, but this then led to a disagreement about whether these would be applied to both the licensed and the exempt sectors. Fforde observed that this showed the tendency on the part of the Treasury to disregard the principle of the two-tier structure and the proposition that the banking sector does not require statutory regulation, an attitude that was to become more apparent.[138]

The Treasury wanted the white paper to 'emphasise the need for, and advantages of, the new system' while playing down 'any suggestion that the old order has its merits'. The Bank's approach tended to be the opposite.[139] After reading the fourth draft, Galpin observed that as a result of the Treasury's drafting, the stage was approaching where 'no real distinctions are drawn between the manner in which we will supervise the licensed institutions and that which we adopt in relation to the exempt category.'[140] Given a free hand, the Bank would have wanted to make more explicit the point that exempt institutions would be outside the statutory provisions of the Act, but overall, they were was reasonably happy with the content.[141] By the end of April, a

---

[136] HMT, 'Note of a meeting ... 20 February 1976, resumed ... 27 February', 12 March 1976, 7A213/1; Fforde to Richardson/Hollom, 'White paper on licensing of deposit-takers', 2 March 1976, 7A185/1.

[137] Fforde to Couzens, 5 March 1976, 7A185/1.

[138] Fforde to Richardson/Hollom, 'White paper on licensing of deposit-takers', 2 March 1976, 7A185/1.

[139] Gill to Cooke, 'White paper on licensing', 22 March 1976, 7A185/1.

[140] Galpin to Cooke/Fforde, 'Licensing white paper', 24 March 1976, 7A185/1.

[141] Draft paper to Galpin/Cooke, 'White Paper on licensing', 1 April 1976, 7A185/1.

submission was being prepared for Treasury ministers.[142] This set out the outstanding issues and also appended the sixth draft of the white paper. When Healey talked to Richardson in the middle of May, he started with the premise that legislation was needed for better regulation of the banking system, but he was concerned that under the agreed two-tier approach it appeared that the exempt category was to be far larger than the licensed sector, and this might make the scheme difficult to sell. He thought that the absence of appeal against refusal to grant exempt status would look like decisions were made by 'the "old boys" group' with no parliamentary accountability. Richardson responded by saying that legislation was not intended to improve the quality of supervision but to extend its coverage, and in addition, it was a convenient way of meeting EEC obligations. There was, he felt, no need to change the existing system, under which there were no appeals. He did not suppose that those hearing such an appeal, a Queen's Counsel (QC), for instance, should be expected to make a better judgement than the Bank, and in any case, if any appeal was upheld, could the Bank then be responsible for an institution that it did not think was trustworthy? The Chancellor accepted these arguments, but he emphasised the political and parliamentary difficulties to be faced: he could not be seen to introduce, in effect, the 'legitimisation of black-balling', and he needed further time for reflection.[143]

During June, intensive rewriting went on.[144] The Bank also attempted to clarify the boundary between exempt and licensed institutions.[145] In July, both the Minister of State and the Governor faced questions about the forthcoming white paper from the Select Committee on Nationalised Industries (SCNI) as part of its inquiry into the Bank.[146] Following further refinements, the definitive draft was completed in the second half of July, and the white paper, 'The Licensing and Supervision of Deposit-Taking Institutions',

---

[142] Jordan to Cooke, 30 April 1976, enc. Jordan, draft – 'Banking supervision: the outstanding issues', 29 April 1976, 7A185/1.

[143] Nick Monck (HMT), 'Note of a meeting held in the Chancellor of the Exchequer's room, H.M. Treasury, at 5:15 p.m. on Thursday, 13 May 1976'; Cooke, Note for record – 'Licensing of deposit-taking institutions. Meeting with the Chancellor, Thursday, 13 May', 14 May 1976, 7A185/2.

[144] Fforde to Richardson/Hollom, 'Licensing: draft white paper', 10 June 1976, enc. 'Draft white paper (amended version of the sixth draft)', 10 June 1976; Bridgeman to Cooke, 22 June 1976, enc. 'Draft white paper: eighth draft, 22 June 1976)'; Bridgeman to Cooke, 28 June 1976, enc. 'Draft white paper: ninth draft (25 June 1976)', 7A185/2; Cooke to Fforde/Richardson, 'Licensing of deposit takers white paper', 2 July 1976, 7A185/3.

[145] Gill to Cooke, 'The boundary between exempt and licensed institutions', 7 June 1976; Cooke to Richardson, 'The boundary between exempt and licensed institutions', 7 June 1976; Cooke to Richardson, 9 June 1976; Plenderleith to Monck (HMT), 11 June 1976, 7A207/4.

[146] SCNI 1976, 'Report', para. 180.

was finally published on 3 August 1976. Only those institutions holding a licence granted by the Bank would be allowed to carry on the business of taking deposits. In order to obtain a licence, companies would have to 'comply with certain general conditions laid down in the legislation and with published prudential criteria which will be determined by the Bank'. The criteria would include minimum capital and reserves figures, managerial experience, and past performance. There would be continuing supervision of these institutions, and the Bank could revoke or suspend a licence if it considered that standards were no longer being met. Appeals against such a decision could be made to the Treasury. The Bank was also able to grant a new statutory recognition as a bank to certain deposit-taking institutions, thus exempting them from the licensing provisions. Again, certain criteria had to be met, but it was expected that most of the current primary banking sector would qualify for the new recognition. The supervisory arrangements for this group would remain unchanged. Other key elements in the legislation related to banking names and a deposit-protection scheme. The former would reserve use of the word 'bank' to recognised banks only; the latter was not fully developed, but it would be mandatory, administered by the Bank, and cover sterling deposits up to £10,000.[147]

The white paper was generally well received, although the clearers expressed disquiet about the compulsory deposit-protection scheme. Their concerns were picked up by *The Economist*, which also found that the proposals were in general lacking in detail; it did not require much percipience on its part to suggest that there would have to be an awful lot of discussion before it became a workable draft for the banking system. Writing in *The Banker*, Jack Revell thought that the paper was successful in conceding the necessary points towards EEC harmonisation while retaining the traditional flexibility of supervision. However, in his opinion, the division between the recognised and licensed groups was too sharp, and he argued for a 'gradual' approach with more than just two categories. He also wondered whether there would be sufficient high-calibre supervisors to operate the system effectively.[148] The SCNI Report on the Bank was published in October 1976, but it had no view on the merits of the proposal.[149]

---

[147] Cooke to Fforde/Richardson/Hollom, 'White paper', 19 July 1976; Cooke to Fforde/Richardson/Hollom, 'Licensing of deposit-taking institutions white paper', 22 July 1976, 7A185/3; Gill, Press briefing, 2 August 1976, 7A186/1; *The Licensing and Supervision of Deposit-Taking Institutions*, cmnd. 6584, August 1976.

[148] Minutes of Court, 5 August 1976; note of 'The licensing and supervision of deposit-taking institutions', G14/348; *The Economist*, 7 August 1976, pp. 56–57; Jack Revell, 'Reforming UK bank supervision', *The Banker* 126(607):1021–1023, September 1976.

[149] SCNI 1976, 'Report', paras. 180–200.

The white paper differed from what the Bank wanted in that the two-tier concept had been watered down in four areas. First, the Bank had acknowledged that membership of the primary sector would have to be on a statutory basis, even though its supervision would be non-statutory in its detailed provisions. Secondly, the Bank had conceded that there should be a right of appeal against a refusal or revocation of a recognition. Thirdly, the deposit-protection scheme would cover both sectors and have a statutory basis. Fourthly, the Treasury would have the power, in consultation with the Bank, to issue regulations governing advertising for deposits. This would apply formally to both sectors but with an understanding that the powers would not be used for the exempt sector.[150] During deliberations, there was a tendency for the two-tier structure to be eroded, something that the Bank increasingly had to fight as the legislation progressed.

While the white paper was being formulated, there had also been some public pronouncements from the Bank about its attitude towards supervision. Most notable was a speech Blunden gave in London in March 1975, which was reproduced subsequently in the *Bulletin*.[151] This ranged over the legislative background, the characteristics of the system, and recent developments. Blunden highlighted the long process of evolution and emphasised that the Bank's approach to supervision remained 'flexible, personal, progressive and participative'.[152] The Bank was not abandoning its old-style personal approach to supervision; indeed, Blunden said that regular discussions with representatives from reporting institutions would be 'by far the most important part of this new exercise'. And discussion was the watchword, with the Bank looking for a 'two-way exchange not for an inquisitorial examination'. Moreover, such dialogues were held by Blunden to be 'more conducive to the maintenance of good banking practices than the technique adopted in many other countries of sending in teams of inspectors to examine banks' books'.[153] Blunden's final topic was prudential ratios, where he made it clear that while such measures could be a valuable tool and an adjunct to other approaches, the Bank did not 'in any way accept the approach which claims that the strength of a bank can be assessed entirely in terms of rigid balance-sheet relationships'.[154] Blunden's speech was a carefully crafted and strong defence of the banking supervision arrangements, with particular importance attached to its flexible nature. Similar

---

[150] Cooke to Fforde/Richardson/Hollom, 'Banking legislation', 7 October 1976, 7A210/1.
[151] 'The supervision of the UK banking system'.
[152] *Ibid.*, p. 190.
[153] *Ibid.*, p. 191.
[154] *Ibid.*, p. 192.

sentiments were expressed by the Governor when reflecting on the appropriate balance between statutory control and self-regulation at a seminar in Luxembourg in November 1975.[155] As the white paper progressed towards a bill and then an Act, the Bank was to have to fight to try and protect its stated beliefs about supervision.

International Supervisory Co-operation

During the mid-1970s, there were several problem cases in international banking where heavy losses were incurred. Examples could be found in Lloyds' Lugano branch, the collapse of the Israel British Bank in Tel Aviv, the Franklin National Bank in New York, and most prominently, the West German Bankhaus Herstatt. These brought calls for international co-operation in banking supervision. As an article in the *Bulletin* was to admit, looking back to the early 1970s, it was evident that banking supervision had not kept pace with the development of new international financial institutions, markets, and centres. Supervisors concentrated largely on domestic issues, and there was very little contact between those responsible for banking supervision in different countries.[156]

The starting point for international co-operation on banking supervision came in 1972, when an informal 'Groupe de contact' was set up to discuss issues in the EEC and to exchange information on particular cases. More significant was the action taken by the Governors of the central banks of the G10 countries in December 1974 to establish a standing committee with membership drawn from the G10 countries plus Switzerland and Luxembourg. Variously called the Standing Committee of Banking Supervisory Authorities, the Committee on Banking Regulations and Supervisory Practices, or the Basle Committee of Supervisors, it usually was known as simply the Blunden Committee, after its first chairman. Despite the fact that Blunden soon moved away from supervision in the Bank, in order to avoid disruption, he remained in the chair until 1977. Cooke, who had the required credentials, was Blunden's successor, and he remained in post until 1988. This gave the Bank an influential position, although the chairman's role on the Committee was supposed to be strictly neutral. Twelve countries each sent two representatives, with one an expert in supervision and the other an expert in foreign exchange, and the

---

[155] Richardson speech 'Given at a seminar on "Banking tomorrow" held in Luxembourg on 27–28 November 1975', *BEQB* 15(4):367–369, December 1975.

[156] Cooke, 'Developments in the co-operation among banking supervisory authorities', *BEQB* 21(2):238, June 1981.

secretariat was provided by the Bank for International Settlements (BIS). The inaugural meeting took place in Basle in February 1975.[157]

In establishing the Committee, the Governors wanted a high priority to be given to the examination of an international early-warning system. This was discussed at the Committee's first three meetings, and a preliminary report was drawn up by Blunden in June. Responsibility for identifying potential dangers, even with an international aspect, should continue to be derived from national supervisory systems, but the Committee noted a number of areas where existing arrangements might be improved. These included increasing the awareness of techniques used in other countries and looking at ways to dismantle barriers to the exchange of information between supervisory authorities. Most important, the Committee thought that it should seek to ensure that no part of the international banking system was left unsupervised. This was a danger resulting from the authorities in a host country not supervising an institution because they thought that the authorities in the parent country were doing so, and vice versa. Detailed work had already started on this, and a report was promised.[158]

That report on the supervision of banks' foreign establishments was completed in September 1975. It set out what the Committee saw as the principal guidelines for co-operation between national authorities. The primary aim was to ensure that no foreign banking establishment escaped supervision, and it was agreed that each country had a duty to ensure that such institutions in its territory were supervised, although the parent country could not be relieved entirely of responsibility. In addition to the desirability of achieving full coverage, it was also important that the supervision be adequate. Co-operation between host and parent supervisors would help to achieve this, and this was one of the main purposes of Blunden's Committee. The division of responsibilities between host and parent authorities was also considered. It was not a clear-cut issue, being dependent on the type of institution, but in general, liquidity was a matter for the host authority, whereas solvency was essentially an issue for the parent country. In order to

---

[157] 'Annotated agenda for meeting of the committee on banking supervision, 6–7 February 1975', 6A115/5. The countries were Belgium, Canada, France, West Germany, Italy, Japan, Luxembourg, Netherlands, Sweden, Switzerland, United Kingdom, and the United States. 'Speaking notes for Basle, December 1975', 6A115/2; Richardson to Zijlstra, 11 March 1977, 6A115/4.

[158] Blunden to Michael Dealtry (BIS), 24 March 1975, enc. 'Discussion draft of a report to the Governors on an international early-warning system', 6A115/5; Blunden to Zijlstra, 24 June 1975, enc. Blunden, 'Preliminary report to the Governors of the Group of Ten countries and Switzerland by the chairman of the committee of banking regulations and supervisory practices on international early-warning systems', 20 June 1975, 6A115/1.

improve supervision and aid co-operation, the Committee called for efforts to be made to reduce restraints on the transfer of information between and on inspections by supervisory authorities.[159] The report was endorsed by the central bank Governors in December 1975 and subsequently received wide circulation in central banks and supervisory authorities.[160] According to a 1981 *Bulletin* article:

The importance of this early agreement cannot be emphasised too much. It represented the first, and a most significant, co-operative step forward, and even if it may have been a step made easier by the pressure of events at the time, it was nonetheless a considerable achievement which laid the foundation for later co-operative efforts.[161]

Later, the guidelines were to become better known as the 'Basle Concordat'.

Meanwhile, work had continued on the draft EEC banking directive. A simplified version was developed from 1974 and this was more of a statement of general principles than the original detailed proposals. The Bank felt that the paper was more attuned to its own philosophy, although it still included the ultimate goal of comprehensive harmonisation.[162] A draft was approved by EEC Commissioners in December 1974, after which it entered the council machinery. It was debated by the European Parliament in May 1975, and the directive on the 'Regulation of Credit Institutions' was adopted in December 1977. Britain was committed to complying by December 1979.[163]

Major areas of work, for what was now known as the Cooke Committee, in the latter part of the 1970s included consolidation and country risk. The Committee first recommended the benefits of a consolidated approach in

---

[159] Blunden to Zijlstra, 26 September 1975, enc. Committee on banking regulations and supervisory practice, 'Report to the Governors on the supervision of banks' foreign establishments', 26 September 1975, 6A115/1; 'Introductory remarks by Mr. Blunden on 13 October to the Group of Ten Governors about the report on supervision of foreign banking establishments', 13 October 1975, 6A115/2.

[160] Dealtry to Blunden, 18 December 1975, 6A115/2.

[161] 'Developments in the co-operation', p. 239.

[162] Barnes to Keogh/Page/Fforde, 'E.E.C. banking harmonisation', 13 March 1974; Cooke, Note for record – 'Talk with Hutton, 18.3.74', 19 March 1974; Barnes to Keogh/Fforde, 'E.E.C. banking harmonisation', 20 March 1974, 7A3/7; Cooke, Note for record – 'Banking harmonisation (a new draft directive)', 15 May 1974, 7A3/8.

[163] Hall, 'EEC banking directive', 5 November 1974; Cooke, Note for record, 6 December 1974, 7A3/8; Fenton to McMahon/Richardson/Hollom, 4 January 1975, enc. 'The current situation in the EEC', 7A3/9; European Parliament, Minutes of proceedings, 15 May 1975 (copy in 7A3/10); 'First Council Directive 77/780/EEC of 12 December 1977 on the coordination of the laws, regulations and administrative provisions relating to the taking up and pursuit of the business of credit institutions', *Official Journal*, L322, 17 December 1977, pp. 30–37.

1978, and the principle was strongly endorsed by the Governors. Under consolidation, a bank's international business, including all its foreign branches, was brought together for supervisory purposes. This gave a clearer picture of a bank's overall exposure to risk and allowed parent supervisors to apply their own standards irrespective of where the business was conducted. Country risk was concerned with the possibility that borrowers in a particular country might be unable or unwilling to repay their loans because of the actions taken by their own government, for instance, to conserve foreign-exchange reserves. At a basic level, this was merely another form of credit risk and a matter of commercial judgement, but the Committee felt that the provision of the best possible data would assist banks with lending decisions. The BIS started to produce half-yearly data on the maturity structures of claims on banks, and the authorities in several countries developed means of evaluating country exposure. Much of this work dovetailed with the Committee's early concern with improving the cross-border flows of information between banks and supervisors.[164]

One indicator of the growing importance of international supervision during the decade was a conference held in London in July 1979. Organised by the Bank in association with the Cooke Committee, it was attended by over 150 banking supervisors from around 80 countries. It was the first event of its kind and was felt to have been a success, particularly in meeting its primary aim of bringing supervisors from across the world together in order to develop co-operation and discuss mutual problems. In the opening address, Richardson commended the 1975 guidelines to his audience (he did not use the term 'concordat') before moving on to a fairly gloomy assessment of prospects for the world economy. He also found room to make reference to the advantages of the British system of participative and flexible supervision. Copies of the concordat had been circulated to all delegates, and in his closing remarks, Cooke said that the Committee would be looking to see if a new version of the paper should be produced and whether a general endorsement of its contents should be sought from supervisory authorities worldwide.[165] Such aspirations were to take some time to achieve.[166]

---

[164] 'Developments in co-operation', pp. 241–243; 'The Basle Committee on banking regulations and supervisory practices', June 1979, 7A341/4.

[165] Cooke, 'Brief for Basle', 7 September 1979; Cooke to Zijlstra, 9 October 1979, enc. with Cooke to GPS, 10 October 1979, 7A341/7; 'International conference of banking supervisors, London, July 5–6 1979. Record of proceedings', 7A341/3; 'International conference of banking supervisors', *BEQB* 10(3):298–301, September 1979; 'A colloquy of custodians', *The Banker* 129(642):17–19, August 1979.

[166] A revised version of the concordat was finalised in 1983 (Principles for the Supervision of Banks' Foreign Establishments), and a supplement to this was issued in 1990. These were reformulated into a set of minimum standards in 1992.

The Banking Act (1979)

The drafting of the bill took nearly two years, during which time there was also a consultation exercise going on with the CLCB, the FHA, and the BBA.[167] The first draft of September 1976 raised so many issues that Gill had difficulty in knowing where to start.[168] Three stood out. First, and a recurring complaint, was that the provisions applied almost equally to the banking and licensed sectors. Gill had assumed that the two would be treated separately, with the provisions for the licensed sector being more detailed. Second was how specific the criteria for recognition or licensing should be on capital, competent management, range of banking services, and reputation. Gill thought that it would be left to the Bank, in agreement with the Treasury, to determine and publish the criteria. Finally, the Bank was unhappy about some of the powers and obligations that the Treasury wanted to include, such as the ability to enter and search premises and regulations about advertising.

In October 1976, Cooke revisited the interpretation of the concordat between the Governor and the Chancellor that established that the bill should prescribe a new statutorily based system for licensing deposit-taking institutions not within the primary banking sector but that institutions that were 'undoubted banks' would be exempt from the statutory provisions and supervised 'on the basis of the Bank's traditional approach through a voluntary system based on moral suasion'. This had been watered down in the white paper, and Cooke warned that the Treasury appeared to be seeking to erode further the differentiation between the two sectors by 'extending the statutory umbrella over a number of other areas of the banking sector's activities'. This had tended to be driven by Treasury judgements on what might prove 'politically acceptable'. Cooke foresaw problems in several areas if the Bank accepted a framework where there were statutory powers to supervise one sector but not the other. There was also 'considerable blurring' over the issue of prudential criteria appearing in the bill. The Treasury's argument was that incorporation of these aspects in the legislation would ease parliamentary acceptance of the wide discretionary powers that would be given to the Bank. Cooke reckoned that the Bank should insist that supervisory criteria for the banking sector should be wholly outside the bill.[169] It was then learned that the ministers had decided not to introduce legislation in the next session of Parliament

---

[167] For the consultations. see papers in 7A200/1.
[168] Gill to Cooke, 'Contents of licensing bill', 23 September 1976, 7A210/1.
[169] Cooke to Fforde/Richardson/Hollom, 'Banking legislation', 7 October 1976, 7A210/1.

and that the bill had been put back to the 1977–78 session.[170] This was just as well given the slow progress, but work continued.

By March 1977, the Treasury had produced a paper in which there was a marked divergence over the treatment of recognised banks.[171] Denzil Davies, the new minister of state at the Treasury was 'an old-fashioned lawyer' who argued that the Act had to be as comprehensive and explicit as possible and that he could not pilot legislation through the House on any other basis. For example, he wanted the Act to define 'high standing and reputation'. In the margin, Fforde asked sceptically, 'By Parliamentary Draughtsmen??'[172] Senior figures in the Bank were disappointed about the way the draft differed from the June 1975 understanding. Fforde considered that the Bank should 'stand firm' and 'only agree to statutory provisions affecting recognised banks when they are necessary to give effect to the terms of the Concordat'. With a tone of irritation, Richardson wrote, 'It does not seem to me that the Minister of State has any notion of my agreement with the Chancellor.' 'Storm clouds ahead', warned Cooke.[173]

On recognised banks, the Treasury's stance was that 'parliamentary sensibilities would not allow discretionary powers ... to be conferred on the Bank unless the basis on which the Bank was to apply its judgment were fully specified in the Act.'[174] Either the Treasury had chosen to ignore the Concordat or 'as they would rather put it, [they] have been impelled in considering the provisions of the Bill to move away from the original concept'.[175] Davies's intervention, and his apparent ignorance of the concordat, had only served to complicate matters. Meanwhile, the latest Treasury drafts made virtually no distinction between the licensed and exempt sectors.

Contentious points remained. The Treasury wanted to confer powers of entry and search, which the Bank was against because it would 'imply a system different from that which we envisage and more akin to inspection'. In any case, it was a role that the Bank felt ill-equipped to perform. On prudential criteria, the details were felt to be too precise. Specific ratios should be resisted; 'otherwise', Gill argued, 'our supervisory procedures will become fossilised, and scope for development will be restricted.'[176] In telling the clearing

---

[170] Cooke to Fforde/Richardson/Hollom, 'Licensing bill', 25 November 1976, 7A210/1.
[171] Gilmore to Cooke, 22 March 1977, enc. draft policy paper, 7A210/2.
[172] Fforde, Annotation on Gill to Cooke, 'Licensing legislation', 29 March 1977, 7A210/2.
[173] Gill to Cooke, 'Licensing legislation', 29 March 1977, and annotations by Cooke, Fforde, and Richardson, 7A210/2.
[174] Chris Thompson, Note for record – 'Licensing: the Treasury policy paper', 13 April 1977, 7A210/2.
[175] Cooke to Richardson/Hollom, 'Banking legislation', 22 April 1977, 7A210/1.
[176] Gill to Cooke, 'Licensing policy paper', 3 May 1977, 7A210/2.

bank chairmen of the position, Richardson said that 'it would be wrong to give up a system of banking supervision which was widely praised abroad and contributed significantly to London's standing as a financial centre.'[177]

The bill was now longer and more complex than the simple licensing bill that the Bank had originally conceived. A highly unsatisfactory aspect was that because of pressure from ministers to push ahead, final drafting was to be based on instructions that were not agreed between the Bank and the Treasury. The outstanding issues included remedial powers, the disclosure of confidential information, fees, and most notably, prudential criteria. On the last of these, Cooke re-stated that the Bank believed that while it was desirable to publish a more detailed explanation of the criteria, they should not be bound by statutory provisions that could only be changed by cumbersome procedures: 'maximum flexibility' needed to be retained in the Bank's conduct of supervision.[178]

Progress still blew hot and cold in the autumn of 1977. During October and November, there was speculation in the Bank about what would happen if the bill were to fall.[179] This seemed a distinct possibility because the measures could not now become law until 1979, and Cooke's psephology was that 'the chance of the current Parliament running that long cannot be very high'. As it transpired, of course, Callaghan was to delay the general election. Various tactics were considered, including deliberately delaying the bill in the hope of getting a 'better bill (in the Bank's terms)' with another government. Although not necessarily arguing for inaction, Cooke maintained that there was no urgent need for legislation to enable effective supervision by the Bank. While there were minor problems, there were 'no major holes in current controls through which coach and horses can be driven by perverse operators', and as far as miscellaneous deposit takers were concerned, 'since 1973–74 they value the status which supervision by the Bank conveys, and they are generally receptive to our advice.'[180] Furthermore, he thought that the Bank's supervisory techniques still could be developed without legislation, and neither was there any need to widen coverage. Indeed, Cooke was more worried about improving knowledge of international banks' branches in London than encompassing more of

[177] 'Extract from minutes of meeting 4.5.77 between the chairmen of the London clearing banks and the Governors', 7A204/1.
[178] Cooke to Richardson/Hollom, 'Banking legislation', 26 August 1977, 7A210/4.
[179] 'Extract from minutes of meeting between the chairmen of the London clearing banks and the Governors 7.9.77', 7A222/8; Barnes to Coleby/Cooke, 'The future of bank supervision', 28 October 1977 and 7 November 1977, 7A204/1.
[180] Cooke to Fforde/Richardson/Hollom, 'Banking supervision', 9 November 1977, 7A204/1.

the fringe. The diminished prospects for legislation may have led Cooke to make these candid admissions, but in any case, in December the bill was back on track again. Responding to a planted parliamentary question, Davies said that he hoped to publish draft clauses later in the session.[181]

Prudential criteria remained the principal outstanding issue, with consensus seemingly some way off.[182] The detail included in the draft legislation was far greater than the Bank had ever envisaged, and they especially objected to the inclusion, in a parliamentary document, of arithmetical ratios. The Bank wanted to see elimination of 'the whole concept of prescribed prudential criteria from the face of the bill'.[183] Hollom explained all this to Davies and argued that 'guidance, indications, or information were acceptable but not formal, published criteria.'[184] Cooke was also worried about how the bill as a whole would be presented to the banks, the press, and the public. There would, he thought, inevitably be questions about the two-tier structure and particularly the 'asymmetry' between treatment of the recognised banks and the licensed sector and why the regime governing the former was apparently less stringent than for the latter. It might be clear enough to the Bank, said Cooke, 'but not necessarily to those looking at the system from the outside'.[185] There still were unresolved points, but in its final form, there were felt to be 'no major differences of principle between the Bank and the Treasury'.[186]

And yet, when Hollom wrote to Davies in July, he reiterated that the Governor could not be taken to be committed to the present text and might want to see modifications to certain clauses; it was 'more complex than it need be'. Richardson also felt that the proposed title 'Banking Act 1978' was 'inappropriate' because it dealt 'extensively with institutions that are not, and may not be called, banks'. It would better be called the 'Deposit Protection Act'. However, Hollom said that the Governor was 'prepared to

[181] Diana Seammen (HMT) to Hall, 11 December 1977, 7A180/1; HC Deb, 16 December 1977, Vol. 941, c550.
[182] HMT, 'Banking legislation: note of a meeting held on 22 December 1977 in the Treasury', 7A204/1; Gilmore to Coleby, 26 January 1978; Hall to Gilmore, 2 March 1978, 7A206/2.
[183] Cooke to Hollom, 'Banking legislation', 10 March 1978, 7A180/2.
[184] R. M. Bent, Note of a meeting – 'Banking legislation: meeting with the Deputy Governor [on 26 April 1978]', 26 April 1978, 7A180/2.
[185] Cooke to Richardson/Hollom, 'Banking legislation', 24 April 1978, 7A180/2; Cooke to Richardson/Hollom, 'Banking legislation', 28 June 1978, 7A180/4.
[186] For drafting, see file series 7A180/1–7; Malcolm Law (BAMMS), Note for record – 'Banking bill: draft clauses', 14 July 1978; Hall to J. M. Romanes (Freshfields), 26 July 1978; Seammen to Hall, 31 July 1978; Law, Note for record – 'Banking bill: draft clauses', 18 August 1978, 7A180/5; Hall to Richardson/Hollom, 'Draft legislation on deposit-taking institutions', 30 June 1978, 7A180/4.

accept the structure envisaged in the bill as a workable basis on which the Bank could carry out the wider functions proposed, without damage to its existing supervision of the banking system proper' and did not oppose early publication of the draft clauses.[187] Davies believed that the bill was concerned with what most people would regard as 'banking' operations, and therefore, he thought 'Banking Bill' was apt.[188] The white paper containing the clauses for the banking bill and the separate credit unions bill was published in July 1978.[189]

Richardson explained to the Court that the need for legislation arose from the obligation of EEC members to introduce prior authorisation for all credit institutions and to bring deposit-taking institutions that were not banks under proper control. Although longer and more complex than originally envisaged, the draft bill met his concerns to protect the close and informal relationship with the banks and to leave operational flexibility unconstrained by a statutory framework. He also made it clear that all this was entirely separate from the [1946] Bank Act and that no cross-reference or any implied connection existed.[190]

Assessing the draft bill against the three Blunden criteria (flexibility, participation, and progressiveness), Farrant thought that with its informal supervision of the recognised sector, the system would still be participative, and he saw the statutory powers as a rarely used 'reserve'. Nevertheless, the reliance on statutes, precedent, and case law might lead to a reduction in operational flexibility. There were also implications for progressions and the danger that if there was no upward mobility, then there would be 'a top tier much of which is moribund and the rest of which may be protected and uncompetitive'. The restrictions on the lower tier verged on 'draconian', especially the ban on banking descriptions. Farrant asked, 'How can one become a bank if one cannot even suggest that one is offering a banking service?' He concluded that the decision on where to draw the line between the two sectors would have important implications for the success of the system in meeting its objectives.[191] Others also measured the bill against the Bank's own criteria, with *The Banker* asking whether a ladder with one rung could be progressive. *The Banker* also carried two articles by 'a leading city banker' that expressed the view that the changing regulatory arrangements

---

[187] Hollom to Davies, 4 July 1978, 7A211/1.
[188] Davies to Hollom, 7 July 1978; 7A211/1.
[189] *Banking and Credit Unions Bills*, cmnd. 7303, July 1978.
[190] Court minutes, 20 July 1978; 'Banking legislation. Speaking note for Court, 20 July', G14/348.
[191] Farrant, 'Banking bill', 8 September 1978, 7A204/1.

could have a deleterious effect on the relationship between the Bank and the banks. All that said, the representations received in response to the white paper from the banks generally were favourable, and subsequent discussions were felt to have gone well.[192]

The banking bill received its first and second readings in the Commons in November 1978, and the committee stage began in December.[193] Cooke told the Governors that on the basis of the amendments put down, there was 'no risk of trouble from the Labour Left'. However, a large number of amendments were tabled by the opposition, who were seeking to harass the ailing Callaghan Government. More seriously, it appeared that the opposition harboured some doubts about the wisdom of the proposed two-tier system and the denial of the use of banking names to the licensed sector, which was seen as limiting competition. Some of this had an antagonistic flavour, with Conservative accusations that parts of the bill equated to the 'creeping paralysis of socialism' and charges of 'nannying and interventionism'. The Bank itself was largely unscathed in these attacks.[194] In the New Year, progress was swift and the tone less political. The Conservatives dropped their opposition to the two-tier system, going so far as to admit that, if in power, they would have introduced the same arrangements.[195] At the end of January, the committee stage was completed, and the bill received an unopposed third reading in the Commons on 14 February 1979 and then proceeded to the Lords.[196] Callaghan lost a vote of confidence on 28 March and called an election for 3 May. The Banking Act received the Royal assent on 4 April 1979. The following day, Richardson told the Court that he believed that the legislation provided a framework within which the Bank could 'operate flexibly and without prejudice to our close relationship with the banks that has contributed so much to the effectiveness of our existing supervisory arrangements'.[197]

---

[192] *The Banker* 128(630):27, August 1978; *The Banker* 128(632):19–27, October 1978; *The Banker* 128(633):25–30, November 1978; Diana Seammen to Hall, 1 November 1978, enc. Seammen to Gilmore, 26 October 1978, 7A183/1; specific representations also contained in 7A183/1.

[193] Hall to Cooke/Richardson/Hollom, 'Draft banking bill', 23 October 1978, listed range of issues still being worked on, 7A180/6.

[194] Law, Note for record – 'Banking bill: committee stage', 1 December 1978; Cooke to Richardson/Hollom, 5 December 1978; Law to Cooke, 'Banking bill – committee stage third sitting – Tuesday, 12 December', 14 December 1978; Law to Cooke/Fforde/Richardson/Hollom, 'Banking bill', 15 December 1978, 7A184/1.

[195] Law to Cooke, 'Banking bill – committee stage fourth sitting – Tuesday, 16 January', 17 January 1979; 'Banking bill – committee stage seventh sitting – Thursday, 25 January', 26 January 1979, 7A184/1.

[196] Law to Cooke, 'Banking bill', 31 January 1979 and 19 February 1979, 7A184/1.

[197] Minutes of Court, 5 April 1979; speaking note 'Banking bill', G14/348.

As finally framed, the Act contained 52 sections in four parts and seven schedules. It required that all institutions accepting deposits had to be authorised by the Bank either as a recognised bank or by obtaining a licence. The Act made provision for continuing supervision of these institutions by the Bank and for the regulation of advertisements for deposits and the use of banking names and descriptions. There was also to be a deposit-protection scheme. This would be administered by a separate board, and the initial fund would total between £5 million and £6 million. A few exceptions aside, all institutions were liable to contribute to the scheme, with the individual size based on a percentage of the deposit base and subject to a minimum of £2,500. The maximum sum protected for depositors was limited to £10,000.[198]

In July it was announced that the Act would operate from 1 October 1979, after which no new deposit-taking business could be established without authorisation of the Bank. Those businesses which were already operating had until 31 March 1980 to apply for authorisation to continue taking deposits. A handbook of banking supervision was put together by the Bank that included a summary of the Act and gave advice to potential applicants about the procedures and the information that would be required. This was issued in September 1979, and around 1,400 copies were distributed to interested parties in the space of a fortnight.[199] Over 600 applications were received, with a large number appearing in the Bank just before the final deadline; many of them the Bank had never heard of. The first published list, in April 1980, revealed 208 recognised banks, 39 licensed institutions, and 365 institutions that were still under consideration. By February 1981, 279 of the original applicants were listed as recognised banks, and 259 had licenses. Authorisation was refused in 11 cases, and 65 withdrew from the process before a final decision had been made.[200]

Just at the time the legislation for the new supervisory framework was being developed and put into effect, the defects of the old informal system of supervision were being put under the spotlight by the investigations into the affairs of the Crown Agents. The Stevenson Committee had already enquired into the earlier activities of the Agents; a new committee was appointed in April 1975 to investigate the circumstances that led to the request for government aid at the end of 1974. Chaired by Judge Edgar Fay, it produced its report in

---

[198] For a detailed commentary on the act, see Vaughan (1987).
[199] Bank of England, Press notice, 20 September 1979; Margaret Peskett (BAMMS) to Barnes, 'Banking supervision handbook', 4 October 1979, 8A8/2; Bank of England, *Handbook of Banking Supervision*, August 1979.
[200] *Banking Act 1979, Annual Report by the Bank of England*, 1979/80 and 1980/81.

December 1977, described by Hollom as a 'horror story of the way the Crown Agents swam out of their depth into every kind of speculative venture'.[201] Fay concluded that the losses of the Agents were due to incompetence rather than misconduct. No one escaped criticism, including the Bank: 'We appreciate that the Bank is independent of government, but it is government's major contact with the City, and we think it would not have been unreasonable for the Bank to have played a greater part in this affair than it did.' Moreover, while the Bank had detected signs of trouble and passed initial warnings to the Treasury, after that, it played a minor role. Although frequently consulted, the Bank remained on the sidelines.[202] Hollom, however, believed that it was not the Bank's responsibility, the Agents being 'a government creature', and Fay's portrayal of the Bank's role therefore was inaccurate.[203]

Following the Fay Committee, a tribunal headed by Justice Croom-Johnson was appointed in February 1978 to inquire into the operations of the Crown Agents as financiers on own account between 1967 and 1974.[204] It was an exercise to apportion blame for the losses incurred by the Crown Agents. The tribunal heard oral testimony for 260 days from 98 witnesses, including Richardson, Hollom, O'Brien, Fforde, Blunden, Galpin, Keogh, Page, and Barnes. A central issue was whether the Bank had any responsibility for monitoring or controlling the Agents' activities and why action by the Bank, Treasury, and Ministry for Overseas Development was not taken sooner. Both Richardson and Hollom were still adamant that responsibility lay with the government, particularly once it had agreed to back the Agents. Nevertheless, the Bank came in for some criticism because it did not alert the Treasury to potential dangers. According to the tribunal, the main responsibility for this rested with Hollom: 'We consider this failure to inform the Treasury promptly of the threat to the Crown Agents' survival amounted to a lapse.' Furthermore, he was also criticised for encouraging the Agents to participate in support operations without ensuring that the government was aware.[205] In the end, the main responsibility for the Agents

---

[201] Hollom, 'The Fay Report', 3A161/182.

[202] *Report by the Committee of Inquiry Appointed by the Minister of Overseas Development into the Circumstances which Led to the Crown Agents Requesting Financial Assistance from the Government in 1974* [Fay Committee], 1 December 1977, HC 48, para. 421; Sunderland (2007, pp. 179–221) maintains that Fay and the subsequent Croom-Johnson enquiry were too harsh on the Crown Agents and that many of the criticisms were unjustified.

[203] Evidence of Sir Jasper Hollom, 9 June 1976, 7A329/6.

[204] *Report of the Tribunal Appointed to Inquire into Certain Issues Arising out of the Operations of the Crown Agents as Financiers on Own Account in the Years 1967–74* [Croom-Johnson Report], 26 May 1982, HL 149, HC 364.

[205] *Ibid.*, paras. 20.86, 20.129, 20.133.

lay with the ministry, although the report also highlighted the confusion of responsibilities between the ministry, the Treasury, and the Bank: there was a great deal of activity and papers passed to and fro that concealed the fact that nothing was being achieved; meetings ended without anything being decided, and no action agreed. Nobody took the lead.[206] While the Crown Agents were not a bank, in some ways the episode epitomised the problems that had been experienced in determining responsibility for banking supervision in this period.

Under the informal structure of banking supervision that had developed, there appears to have been a lack of clarity about where responsibility lay between the different authorities. This allowed the defence 'they were not a bank' to be adopted, whether for the fringe banks or the Crown Agents. With the introduction of greater competition in banking under CCC, more thought might have been given to changes needed in supervision. However, it is far from clear that different arrangements would have prevented the secondary banking crisis. The Bank claimed that it was powerless to act over the fringe banks, and as we have seen, Keogh asserted that the fringe was, for several reasons, 'beyond supervision'.[207] He was, of course, saying this from his position as scapegoat, but Fforde, who was not implicated in the crisis, expressed similar thoughts. Fforde also felt that it was unfair to blame the Bank for not taking action to change the supervisory system at an earlier stage, when such action would have been 'quite out of historical context'. Yet he also conceded that some blame might be attached to the Bank 'for portraying itself in public (or allowing itself to be portrayed) as being responsible for the general health of the financial system when it should have known, if it asked itself frankly, that it did not possess the power to exercise any such responsibility at all closely … until an open crisis occurred'. Fforde went on to say that some of the criticism in the aftermath of the fringe crisis may have been because people thought that appropriate safeguards were in place when they were not and never had been. Moreover, 'Perhaps the Old Lady was too susceptible to flattery, and herself came to believe that she possessed some mysterious influence which was self-exercised without her being fully aware of it.'[208] This was at least some admission that supervisory arrangements were not perfect, but it was one that was shown only to the Governor and the Chief Cashier.

It is usually held that the changes in supervisory arrangements and the 1979 Banking Act were a necessary consequence of the secondary banking

---

[206] *Ibid.*, para. 31.12.
[207] Keogh, Note for record – 'The fringe', 5 June 1974, 7A95/1.
[208] Fforde to Richardson, 'Secondary banking: the antecedents', 20 January 1978, 7A149/2.

crisis. The cause and effect seem obvious. However, the impact of the EEC Banking Directive should also be recognised; this was in any event going to force the Bank to move towards prior authorisation or licensing of deposit takers, and the draft of a simple bill to enact this was already being prepared before the crisis broke at the end of 1973.[209] Politically, too, something had to be seen to be done. Further, in public, the Bank was adamant that the crisis did not show that there was anything seriously wrong with the system of supervision, and use of its resources was simply an extension of the existing arrangements.

In terms of legislation, the Bank largely achieved what it wanted: a two-tier system that retained the existing type of supervision for recognised banks and prudential criteria that were not set in stone. Lord O'Brien, delivering the Ernest Sykes Memorial Lecture in November 1979, felt that 'regulators and the regulated' should both be satisfied with the UK's first general banking Act. He concluded that the Act would ensure order and discipline without impairing 'that freedom to do business under the benevolent if watchful eye of our central bank, on which all of us in the British banking industry set such great store'.[210] This is not the place for a full analysis of the success of the 1979 Act, but suffice to say that it was not that long before changes occurred. In the wake of the Johnson Matthey failure in 1984, there appeared, in 1985, a report by the new Governor, Robin Leigh-Pemberton, and a white paper on banking supervision. New legislation came with the Banking Act of 1987, which, among other things, swept away the two-tier structure that the Bank had been so intent on establishing in the previous decade. Part of the reason for the extension of supervision was the failure of Johnson Matthey, a recognised bank; the report that highlighted this was itself a consequence of the failure.[211]

---

[209] Reid also recognises both the 'dual influence' of the crisis and the EEC directive; Reid (1986).

[210] O'Brien, 'The Banking Act 1979', The Ernest Sykes Memorial Lecture, 1979, Institute of Bankers.

[211] *Report of the Committee Set Up to Consider the System of Banking Supervision*, cmnd. 9550, June 1985. Also see, for example, Hall (1999, pp. 27–39).

Plate 14. 'Taj Mahal' – the Bank of England branch at Newcastle.

Plate 15. Gold vault at the Bank.

Plate 16. The Court of the Bank of England, 1971. *Clockwise from centre, far side:* Leslie O'Brien (Governor), Jasper Hollom (Deputy Governor), Kit McMahon (Executive Director), Sir Sydney Greene, Adrian Cadbury, Leopold de Rothschild, Jack Davies (Executive Director), Sir Val Duncan, Sir Eric Roll, Sir John Stevens, Gordon Richardson, Lord Robens, Jeremy Morse (Executive Director), Sir Maurice Laing, Lord Nelson, Lord Pilkington, William Keswick, Peter Taylor (Secretary). *Absent:* John Fforde (Executive Director).

Plate 17. Kit McMahon (Executive Director 1970–80).

Plate 18. Charles Goodhart (Economic Adviser 1968–85).

Plate 19. The Bank's Foreign Exchange Dealers' Office in the 1970s.

Plate 20. Jim Keogh (Principal of the Discount Office, 1967–74).

Plate 21. Christopher Dow (Executive Director 1973–81).

Plate 22. John Page (Chief Cashier 1970–80).

Plate 23. Gordon Richardson (Governor 1973–83).

13

Monetary Targets and Monetary Control

It was inevitable that competition and credit control (CCC) would be followed by transitional problems, some anticipated and some less so. Monetary conditions were made more difficult when accompanied by the coincidental expansionary policies of the Heath Government. When exogenous shocks such as the oil-price rises and some attendant exchange-rate changes were added, they resulted in turmoil. The need to address monetary control intensified, and talk of monetary aggregates and targets then came increasingly to the fore and were finally made explicit and public in 1976. What was less clear was how firm the belief in them was or how strong the commitment to achieving them was. As far as tackling inflation went, the emphasis still was heavily on incomes policies. It was only after the advent of the new Conservative Government in 1979 that interest rates began to be used more aggressively.

Whereas the monetary variables had been remarkably steady for 100 years, in the 1970s there was wildly different behaviour. The money multiplier (M3) had been stable at close to 4 from 1870 to 1970, but after 1970 it rose abruptly and was almost 10 by 1981. The components of the multiplier that reflect the behaviour of the non-bank public and of the banking sector, respectively, followed different but relatively easily explained paths. There is not much to remark on for the banks' reserve-deposit (R/D) ratio. Since the Second World War, the minimum reserve requirement of 8 per cent imposed on the clearing banks remained until 1971. Following CCC, the new ratio that was introduced allowed the banks a portfolio of short-dated government securities as reserve assets, and within the reserves, a smaller cash element was specified.[1] (In 1981, the reserve-asset ratio was abolished, but a cash requirement was extended to a large number of financial institutions.) The public's cash-deposit ratio also fell. The main part of

---

[1] Capie and Rodrik-Bali (1986).

the explanation undoubtedly lies in the fact that the banks were losing out to other financial institutions. Clearing bank deposits were growing much more slowly than those of roughly comparable institutions such as building societies and the Trustee Savings Banks. Individuals had a greater choice for their portfolios, interest rates were active again, and individuals were increasingly aware of interest-rate differentials. More than this, however, following CCC, the banks began paying interest on current accounts and attracted deposits from other institutions. Another part of the explanation can be found in the accelerating inflation because with the opportunity cost of holding cash rising, the demand can be expected to fall. And sharp revisions in inflationary expectations could be expected to have had a further impact.

Talking about Monetary Targets

A story has developed that there were unpublished monetary targets in use as early as 1973. This is not something that is in evidence in the documents.[2] It was 1976 when something drastic needed to be done and International Monetary Fund (IMF) financing was needed and the knowledge that on this occasion the IMF would demand determined action on containing monetary growth before serious attention to monetary targets took place. The first explicit public talk of monetary targets, albeit in ambiguous terms, came in the Chancellor's measures of July 1976, when he presented a quantitative limit for money-supply growth for 1976–77. This was to be quickly superseded by a domestic credit expansion (DCE) target imposed by the IMF in December 1976 and acknowledged in the 'Letter of Intent'.

The attention that was given to monetary targets at the beginning of the 1970s was partly a consequence of pressure from outside. In June 1971, an American economist who had friends in the Bank sent a paper that argued that to a monetarist economist it was obvious that there had to be a monetary target, but it was equally obvious that central banks had a deep distaste for this view.[3] Distaste was indeed what the Bank felt. The Treasury was perhaps more open. (Most politicians were not. Alan Walters, an Adviser to Heath in 1972, gave up in despair after a few months.) In any event, movement towards a monetary target was slow. In April 1972, the Treasury outlook for 1972–73 accepted that monetary policy would be used as 'an integral part of

---

[2] See, for example, Smith (1987, p. 59); in 1973, 'the BoE [Bank of England] began to set secret internal money supply targets'.
[3] Meigs to McMahon, 21 June 1971, enc. Meigs and Wolman, 'Central banks and the money supply', 2A128/7.

the general management of demand'.[4] And while there were no numerical targets for money supply, the Chancellor nevertheless had accepted the advice of officials that the 'present policy should be directed towards a target rate of growth of money supply of about 20 per cent in the financial year 1972/73, 20 per cent being the growth which the Bank of England's demand-for-money equations suggest will be required, given the outlook for real output and prices, if there is to be no significant rise in interest rates from their present levels'. (A truly extraordinary objective.) If the economy did enter a period of rapid expansion, then the money supply would be contained by selling more public debt to the non-bank sector, and 'the authorities must seek to bring about the necessary upward movement in interest rates through open market operations supported as appropriate by changes in Bank Rate and calls for special deposits'.[5] This simply repeated the aims of CCC. Treasury and Bank officials would meet regularly to look at money-supply statistics and to consider policy. The Bank already had a Monetary Review Committee, established at the time of CCC, that met monthly to survey and report on monetary developments.[6] Goodhart claimed that the Treasury was neither able nor willing 'to review the use of monetary policy at all, let alone regularly and flexibly'.[7] The first of these joint monthly meetings on monetary policy took place in May 1972. Douglas Allen was in the chair, and the intention was to draw any new issues to the attention of the Chancellor and to make policy recommendations.[8] Later, in October 1974, it became a formal committee called the 'Treasury/Bank Monetary Policy Group' (MPG). It would be a mistake, however, to see these arrangements as representing a well-defined mechanism for joint decision making.

In 1973, the Bank was still grappling with the relative turmoil that had followed CCC and how to distinguish between these temporary aspects and more serious underlying growth of money.[9] In the Governor's Mansion House speech in October, Richardson said that 'moderation in the rate of growth of the economy and in the pace of inflation requires moderation in

---

[4] HMT, 'Monetary policy 1972–73', 13 April 1972, 6A50/6. The document was assumed (probably incorrectly by Goodhart) to be the work of Cassell.

[5] HMT, 'Monetary policy 1972–73', 13 April 1972, 6A50/6.

[6] Goodhart to Atkinson et al., 'Surveillance of monetary developments', 17 September 1971, 6A142/1.

[7] Goodhart to McMahon, 'Monetary policy 1972/73', 19 April 1972, 6A50/6.

[8] HMT, 'Monthly meeting on monetary policy', meeting held on 19 May 1972, 23 May 1972, 6A50/6.

[9] Dicks-Mireaux, 'The money supply and its control', 3 September 1973; Fforde, 'The money supply and its control', 19 September 1973; Dow, 'The money supply', 21 September 1973, 6A50/11.

the pace of monetary expansion.[10] Goodhart wanted to follow this up with an article in the December *Bulletin* about how difficult it was to define money. Carlisle found Goodhart's piece interesting and, as he put it, appealing to an elderly cynic like himself who suspected that money could not be measured, and even if it could, it could not be controlled, but if it could be, it would not be clear what effect it was having on anything. Puzzlingly, he added, 'The B/E has no real function to perform anyhow!' Thornton held similar views on money but nonetheless rejected the Goodhart piece for the *Bulletin*.[11]

Discussion of monetary policy does not seem to have been advanced much in the Bank by the recruitment of Christopher Dow in early 1973. Dow had spent all his working life in the Treasury, the National Institute of Economic and Social Research, and the Organisation for Economic Co-operation and Development (OECD), from where he was recruited in March 1973 at the age of 57. He was appointed Executive Director for economics and was the first person from outside the Bank to go straight into an executive position. Dow's position was essentially Keynesian, but frequently it is not easy to be sure what he was saying. In 1973, he felt that it was hard to say whether over the previous 6 to 12 months monetary policy had been expansionary or not – this at a time when M3 was growing at an annual rate of over 20 per cent. In the first half of 1973, he argued, when interest rates were at near-record levels, they were beginning to be a factor entering into investment decisions. But this ignored the fact that real rates were in fact close to zero or negative. He felt that any rise in short rates would damage sales of gilts, but that was harking back to an earlier debate. He wanted short rates to ease to help gilt-edged sales. He was also keen to ease the position of first-time mortgage borrowers on social and political grounds. He favoured giving general guidance to the banks and 'quantitative ceilings on certain categories of borrowing' and wanted to restore hire-purchase controls.[12] Come July, he had slipped further back into the past. After surveying the state of the economy and taking into account the external context, he argued that higher interest rates were needed chiefly for external effects, although they could have domestic effects.[13] He also felt that the Common Agricultural Policy had protected

---

[10] *BEQB* 13(4):476, December 1973.

[11] Goodhart to Thornton, '"What do the monetary aggregates show?": a proposed *Bulletin* article for December', 23 October 1973, and Carlisle, Annotation, 24 October; Thornton to Goodhart, 23 October 1973, 2A128/11.

[12] Dow to Fforde, 16 May 1973, enc. 'The possible future stance of monetary policy', 6A50/10.

[13] Dow to Richardson/Hollom, 25 July 1973, enc. 'The economic background to monetary policy', 6A50/10.

'us for a considerable time from rises in the prices of imported food arising from exchange rate fluctuations'. There was more interventionist talk, too. Resources, he claimed, needed to be shifted to exports and investment.[14]

In September, Dow asked, How fast should the money supply grow? His views, he said, differed from those of the Bank in the past and from the Economic Intelligence Department (EID) at present, and they might be awkward politically. He did not remark on the fact that minimum lending rate (MLR) had moved from 5 per cent in June 1972 to 13 per cent in September 1973; at the time of his writing, though, this was taken to imply a sharp tightening of monetary policy. If, however, inflationary expectations were rising much faster, as seems likely, monetary policy was easing. The rise in nominal rates, though, was not part of his argument, although it may have influenced his thinking. Dow felt that the economic case for drastically slowing down the growth of the money supply was a weak one. And further, he felt that there was a 'neutral' growth rate for money that was faster than the growth of money national income, which at that time he would have as 14 per cent. He went on to ask if growth of M3 of 18 per cent was a sign of permissive policy and concluded that it was not. He saw three possible ways of moderating the rate of monetary expansion: ceilings on lending to the private sector, minimum ratios for financial-sector holding of public-sector debt and tightening by operating on banks' liquidity ratios.[15]

In the course of 1974, with inflation running at more than 16 per cent, work in the Bank and the Treasury ranged over subjects such as housing finance and mortgage rates and on how building societies should be treated. There was also a lot of discussion on the harmonisation of monetary instruments in the European Economic Community (EEC), initiated by the EEC, although how harmonisation was to be achieved when many of the instruments were not being used in many of the countries was not seen as an obstacle.[16] What dominated the discussion in the Bank and the Treasury, however, was what monetary policy was, how it should be described, how it could be presented, and ultimately, how it could be implemented. At the beginning of 1974, hopes of controlling monetary growth were pinned on supplementary special deposits (SSDs). In April it was decided to extend the scheme for a further six months from July, with a monthly growth rate of 1½ per cent allowed.[17]

---

[14] Dow to Richardson/Hollom, 26 July 1973, enc. 'Possible lines of a public statement on monetary policy in the context of the external situation', 6A50/10.

[15] Dow, 'The money supply', September 1973, 2A128/11.

[16] See 6A50/13.

[17] Coleby to Fforde/Richardson/Hollom, 'The supplementary special deposits scheme', 19 April 1974; Bank of England, 'Notice to banks and deposit-taking finance houses. Supplementary special deposits', 30 April 1974, 5A149/2.

The first SSDs deposited in July totalled £6 million, paid by 14 banks. During the remaining seven months of operation, SSDs were much lower, and the number of banks liable halved (Table 13.1). In the early months of 1975, the monetary situation was felt to have eased markedly. Permitted growth in interest-bearing eligible liabilities (IBELs) stood at 18½ per cent above base; the London clearers were only 7¾ per cent above base, giving an ample cushion of 10¾ per cent. Page concluded that the control was presently ineffective and that there was a strong case for suspension of the scheme. Another argument in favour of this was that it would address what was described as the principal defect of the scheme, that individual banks were locked into their relative positions at the base date and could not move in relation to one another. There was little dissention from these points, and the suspension of SSDs was announced at the end of February 1975, although the scheme could be reactivated when required.[18]

An early monetary aggregate was DCE, and while the requirement on that had lapsed in 1970, a new target for 1970–71 was announced in the April 1970 budget. The following year saw the Chancellor drop the objective, saying that it was less relevant when the external position was strong. This explicit rejection led to an annotation by Carlisle, 'DCE died 30 March 1971. R.I.P.' Thereafter, DCE was little discussed by the authorities, although the data continued to be published in the *Bulletin*.[19] At the end of 1974, however, when Samuel Brittan raised questions about DCE in *The Financial Times*, the article attracted the Governor's attention, and Goodhart was asked to provide answers.[20] This went back over old ground, but it was also the beginning of further discussion of monetary aggregates, especially something wider than M3. (The EEC harmonisation group was also favouring a 'concept of primary and secondary liquidity'.)[21]

By the summer of 1975, projections were being made for money supply for the following three years, all set out in terms of the counterparts. The discussion in these years almost always was in terms of what could be achieved given the borrowing requirement. Fforde thought that the pursuit of a cautious monetary policy of the kind they had been following 'during

---

[18] Page to Fforde/Richardson/Hollom, 'Supplementary special deposits', 21 February 1975; Page to Downey, 24 February 1975; Bank of England, 'Notice to banks and deposit-taking finance houses', 28 February 1975, 5A149/5.

[19] HC Deb, 14 April 1970, Vol. 799, c1232; 30 March 1971, Vol. 814, c1373; Tony Carlisle, Annotation on MP(71) 1, 6A74/5.

[20] Richardson, Annotation, 24 December 1974, on cutting from *The Financial Times*, 19 December 1974, 5A175/6.

[21] Goodhart to Fforde, 'D.C.E.', 10 January 1975, enc. 'Domestic credit expansion' (draft), 10 January 1975, 5A175/7.

Table 13.1. *Supplementary special deposits, 1974–78*

	Total		1st tranche		2nd tranche		3rd tranche	
	No. of banks	(£m)						
17 Jul 1974	6	14	–	2	–	–	6	12
21 Aug 1974	1	7	–	2	–	1	1	4
18 Sep 1974	2	5	–	1	–	1	2	–
16 Oct 1974	1	6	–	1	–	1	–	–
20 Nov 1974	2	6	–	–	–	–	2	6
11 Dec 1974	2	6	–	–	–	–	2	6
16 Dec 1974	1	5	–	3	–	–	1	2
15 Jan 1974	2	4	–	–	–	3	2	1
19 Feb 1974	–	3	–	–	–	1	–	2
18 May 1977	1	5	–	3	–	1	1	1
15 Jun 1977	5	–	4	–	–	–	1	
20 Jul 1977	1	4	–	2	–	–	–	2
15 Nov 1978	1	7	–	7	–	2	1	1
13 Dec 1978	2	5	–	5	–	2	1	1
17 Jan 1978	2	4	–	4	–	3	1	1
21 Feb 1978	3	5	–	5	–	4	2	3
21 Mar 1978	2	3						
18 Apr 1978	1	4	–	4	–	2	–	2
16 May 1978	4	4	–	4	1	3	3	2
20 Jun 1978	9	6	–	6	1	3	7	3
18 Jul 1978	2	6	2	6	–	1	–	–
15 Aug 1978	10	14	6	14	3	5	2	3
19 Sep 1978	4	10	3	10	–	2	–	1
17 Oct 1978	1	12	1	12	–	2	–	–
21 Nov 1978	3	8	–	8	–	4	3	3
12 Dec 1978	3	8	–	8	–	4	3	3
17 Dec 1978	19	20	10	20	8	7	2	2

Source: BEQB.

the period of recession' was appropriate and had stood them in good stead; liquidity now had to be restored. Money supply could be used as an indicator of performance.[22] Pressure was building to produce something for

[22] Fforde to Richardson/Hollom, 'Monetary policy 1975/77', 8 July 1975, EID4/200.

discussion with the Treasury before the end of July.[23] In August, Fforde was worrying about the likely path of consumer credit, which had been flat since controls had been re-imposed at the end of 1973.[24]

Much of the debate on inflation taking place outside the Bank revealed little advance on the 1960s. For example, when Aubrey Jones wrote a book with the title, *The New Inflation: The Politics of Prices and Incomes* (1973), he accepted the inadequacies of the prevailing solutions, such as exhortation, leaning on the public sector, or allowing more unemployment. However, he was a long way from accepting monetary control. Instead, he focussed on improvements to the existing prices and incomes policies. These were couched in terms of fairness, anomalies, and the case for exceptions. He argued that there needed to be direct intervention in specific wage settlements and, ideally, that there should be one body to which all wage claims would be submitted. Academic approval followed. Reviewing the book for the *Economic Journal*, G. D. N. Worswick agreed that 'if inflation is to be mastered in a modern mixed economy, an incomes and prices policy, with some continuing adjudicating body, is essential.'[25] Worswick even felt that the argument of the book was so well put that some unbelievers might well be converted.

In mid-1975, when inflation was running at an annual rate of around 25 per cent, a white paper appeared explaining the cause and setting out the cure. According to this, the rise in inflation since 1972 had been rooted in the increases in the prices of imported raw materials and food, and in particular the price of oil. Yet most other countries faced these too but had much lower inflation. The white paper proposed some cures that reflected a continuing belief in both the Phillips curve and the idea that costs drove inflation. It said that government, the Confederation of British Industry (CBI), and the Trades Union Congress (TUC) were in agreement that inflation should be brought down by 'a reduction in the rate of increase in wages, rather than the deliberate creation of mass unemployment'.[26] Price controls were to be continued. But there was also a note that steps would be taken to control public expenditure and control the growth of the money supply. Yet the most revered Government Adviser, Kaldor, was still, at the end of 1976, arguing that 'the basic cause [of inflation]

---

[23] Dicks-Mireaux to Richardson, 15 July 1975, enc. Michael Bridgeman (Under Secretary, HMT) to Airey, 'Counter-inflation and monetary policy', 15 July 1977; Fforde to Richardson/Hollom, 'Monetary policy and the PSBR, etc.', 17 July 1975; Graham Kentfield, Note for record – 'Monetary policy 1975/6–1976/7', 17 July 1975, EID4/200.

[24] Fforde to Richardson/Hollom, 'Consumer credit', 27 August 1975, EID4/200.

[25] Jones (1973); Worswick (1973, p. 1282).

[26] *Attack on Inflation*, cmnd. 6151, July 1975.

was increased trade union militancy'.[27] When A. J. Brown surveyed world inflation from 1950 to the 1980s, a follow-up to his earlier study, *The Great Inflation, 1939 to 1951*, he repeated his earlier thesis: the central cause of inflation was a rise in costs.[28] Money supply accommodated to the rise in costs. These were among the leading academic contributors, and it therefore might be felt that the Bank was not in a position to diverge from such opinion. Major changes would need to await a younger and more challenging generation, and indeed, such contributions were appearing.[29] However, this does open up a lot of questions over how ideas find their way into policy.

There were some within the authorities who saw things differently. For example, at the beginning of 1976, a young economist in the Treasury, Michael Beenstock, wrote a paper on money and inflation that found its way to the Bank. Goodhart told Cassell that all it demonstrated was that the demand-for-money function was relatively stable over the long run. He wondered if that was a 'big deal'.[30] Beenstock replied that the main point was 'that wage costs, like import costs, cannot generate inflation in the long run and that in the long run inflation is essentially a monetary phenomenon.... Trade unions can only cause unemployment ... but they cannot cause inflation. Only the monetary authorities can do that.' He believed that this *was* a 'big deal'.[31] More urgently in need of a reply was Rees-Mogg's piece in *The Times*, 'How a 9.4 Per Cent Excess Money Supply Gave Britain 9.4 Per Cent Inflation'.[32] Goodhart told the Governors that more rigorous work had been done in the Bank and that no strong causal relationships had been found, but insofar as there were any, they went from income to money. However, he pointed out that the work done was on the period up to 1971 and that Rees-Mogg's results in fact got their strength from the years after 1971.[33] There was no discussion of the differing exchange-rate regimes. Close attention was being given to the growing array of models of inflation on the United Kingdom but particularly the London Business School (LBS) 'monetarist' one. In the middle of 1976, there developed a long correspondence with the Prime Minister and the Chancellor, Peter Middleton of the Treasury, and several

[27] Kaldor (1976, p. 710).
[28] Brown (1955, 1985).
[29] For example, Laidler (1975); Laidler and Parkin (1975); Williamson and Wood (1976).
[30] Goodhart to Cassell, 17 March 1976, 6A7/2.
[31] Beenstock to Goodhart, 23 March 1976, 6A7/2.
[32] *The Times*, 13 July 1976, p. 14.
[33] Goodhart to Ian Plenderleith (GPS), 'Money supply and inflation', 13 July 1976, 6A7/2.

Bank economists on deeper technical aspects of the issues.[34] There was discussion, but it was a long time before there was action.

Be that as it may, in 1975, with inflation about to reach its dramatic peak, Dow re-opened some basic discussion on what the Bank believed monetary policy to be and how it worked. He wrote almost entirely about the borrowing requirement.[35] Fforde treated it in his usual complex fashion, but he concluded:

I found myself moving somewhat towards the monetarist position. Or, at least, I find myself sympathetic to the idea that it is a position which the Bank could at least partly adopt, as a means of trying to get what we (and most other people) would want in the prices and incomes and PSBR [public-sector borrowing requirement] areas.[36]

McMahon was unequivocal: fiscal policy was more powerful than monetary policy, the level of public expenditure was much too high, and 'it will only be possible to contain inflation in late twentieth century democratic industrial societies with the aid of more or less continuous incomes policies based broadly on consent'. (These were the policies that had been used without success for the previous 20 years. Incomes policy surely had been tested to destruction.) The only reason he supported tight control of money supply was as a means of exerting pressure on government expenditure. McMahon wrote, 'If we could get a public statement of a target for the growth of money supply, we should have a tighter rope round the Chancellor's neck. For that very reason we are unlikely to persuade him. But we could perhaps try.'[37]

At the beginning of October, Dow sent the Governors a paper, 'What Are the Implications of Adopting a Monetary Target?' that raised a number of questions: What rate of monetary expansion? Should it be a public target? What would be the interest-rate effects? How big an interest-rate rise could be tolerated? What aggregate should be chosen, M1 or M3?

The answers to most of these questions depend on the genuine spirit with which one adopts a monetarist [*sic*] target. (1) At one extreme one could adopt it very cynically, aiming to make the money figures look good, but to avoid any impact if possible on interest rates – which I take it would mean a big expansion of the nearest thing to money, i.e., very short-term and liquid assets to be held by non-banks ('cheating', for shorthand).... (2) I suggest that, in practice, we will not want to decide this general position in advance. In other words, at a certain stage we may

---

[34] Bray to Dow, 11 July 1977, and subsequent correspondence in 6A7/2.
[35] Dow to Fforde, 'Monetary policy', 23 September 1975, EID4/200.
[36] Fforde to Dow, 'Monetary policy (Dialogue des sourds)', 24 September 1975, EID4/200.
[37] McMahon to Dow, 'Monetary policy', 26 September 1975, EID4/200.

feel we have done as much to interest rates as we think we can bear, and will want to go nearer to 'cheating'.[38]

This was a mixture of cynicism and confusion. Dow thought that Goodhart should prepare another paper, which he did, and it recorded that the Bank had become increasingly anxious about prospective monetary developments and felt the need for a review. After a long analysis of the borrowing requirement and the likely monetary growth, the paper simply concluded that no immediate action was needed but that contingency planning should go ahead. Richardson also pressed Healey for an urgent review before the Mansion House dinner. Later that month, at a meeting of the MPG, it was confirmed that a working party had been established under the chairmanship of Michael Bridgeman, an Under Secretary at the Treasury.[39]

While the Bridgeman group was deliberating, the immediate situation had eased because monetary growth had slowed to 9½ per cent; therefore, the review focussed on prospects for the next two years. On the monetary objective, the report noted that the Chancellor had on several occasions repeated his intention that the growth in the money supply should not add to inflationary pressures; this had been taken to mean that the growth of the money supply, as measured by M3, would be kept below the rate of growth of money gross domestic product (GDP).[40] The wisdom of this now was questioned. The Treasury asked what should be targeted, money or interest rates. It was not made explicit, but in some circumstances one would be more stabilising than the other. In practice, however, the Treasury argued that the monetary authorities were unlikely to choose either one exclusively. They could not be indifferent to the rate of growth of money, but equally, they could not be indifferent to the level of interest rates.[41] Bridgeman's main policy conclusion was that the existing objective was vague, it could accommodate almost any increase in GDP, and it was insufficient to ensure that monetary factors did not jeopardise counter-inflation policy. The group recommended that in future the objective should be expressed 'as a

[38] Dow to Richardson/Hollom, 'What are the implications of adopting a monetary target?', 6 October 1975, 6A50/17.

[39] Fforde to Airey, 9 October 1975, enc. Bank of England, 'Monetary policy', October 1975; MPG(75) 6th meeting, 24 October 1976, 1A151/1.

[40] In the April 1975 budget, Healey stated, 'I have aimed to keep the rate of monetary expansion firmly under control and to avoid a repetition of the experience of 1972 and 1973 when excessive monetary growth contributed substantially to inflationary pressures'; HC Deb, 15 April 1975, c279.

[41] Middleton to Bridgeman, 31 October 1975, enc. 'Possible monetary policy objectives', nd, 6A50/17.

particular numerical target for the growth of M3 ... selected as part of the Budget judgement and to be rolled forward thereafter'. It would provide a 'fail-safe' element in monetary policy. As to the question of whether to publish this target, the group was split on where the balance of advantage lay.[42]

When all this was discussed at the MPG in early January 1976, strong divisions emerged, with some participants (Treasury, according to Goodhart) feeling that the role of the money stock was not sufficiently clear for an objective to be expressed in terms of it. And there was virtually no support for publication, which would only lead to criticism for non-adherence.[43] Dow was frustrated, complaining to Fforde that there was a rejection of the present way of stating the aims of monetary policy and a failure to agree on anything else.[44] Goodhart's assessment was slightly more positive. He thought that the most important finding was that 'increases in interest rates, in the present conjuncture of a continuing high PSBR, would not be particularly effective in restraining monetary growth, because the effect of higher debt sales would be largely offset by continuing higher debt interest payments'. Yet the general tone of the discussion was negative, more so than the Bank wished, with no clear sense of what monetary policy objective might be defined or defended, either publicly or in private. Goodhart concluded, 'it is more than ever important for us to develop a "non-monetarist" presentation of policy which both commands intellectual credibility and pays appropriate regard to the monetary aggregates.'[45]

There were clear differences between Dow and Goodhart on several areas of discussion, as was evident in Goodhart's invited response to Dow in January 1976.[46] And later in the month, Goodhart was more outspoken:

You [Dow] suggest that 'a rate of monetary expansion more or less in line with the rise in money national income could, however, still be regarded as a norm'.... Neither I, nor other members of the Bridgeman group, would be prepared to accept this formulation. ... You appear to seek a formulation which will leave money national incomes, determined by other factors such as fiscal policy, prices policy, unaffected by specifically monetary measures. The Bridgeman Group was seeking a more interventionist role for monetary policy.

---

[42] MPG(75) 17, 'Review of monetary policy. Report of the Treasury/Bank working party', December 1975; Bridgeman, 'Note by the chairman of the working party', 23 December 1975, 1A151/1.

[43] MPG(76) 1st, 7 January 1976, 1A92/1.

[44] Dow to Fforde, 'The Bridgeman Report and the aims of monetary policy', 9 January 1976, 6A50/18.

[45] Goodhart, 'The report of the Treasury/Bank (Bridgeman) working party', 12 January 1976, 6A50/18.

[46] Goodhart to Dow, 'A statement of monetary aims', 19 January 1976, 6A50/18.

There was much more of that before, 'Finally you end by stating that "For the time being there therefore appears an advantage in going along with market forces and accepting little growth in the money stock". I do not comprehend what this advantage consists of. Why is it an advantage?'[47]

To give some further indication of the flavour of the debate, it is worth quoting at length a contribution by Fforde to Dow the same day. Fforde could be brilliant in his summaries of important issues, but there was another complex side to him, and on this occasion, he was in more convoluted mode. Headed 'Aims of Monetary Policy (A Contribution to Irritation)', he wrote:

1. In his note of January 19th, CAEG [i.e., Goodhart] says –

    (i) on page 1, 'the really tricky question, which is just *how* do you measure the degree of restrictiveness of monetary policy? ...

    (ii) on page 4, 'How exactly should we measure the stance of monetary policy?'

2. In your note of January 19th, you say –

    Paragraph 3, '... the thrust of monetary policy can in principle be judged either from ...' and later in the same paragraph '... neither indicator is a completely reliable pointer to monetary policy....'

1. I do not think the differences of phraseology are either unimportant or accidental. Measuring something does not seem to be the same thing as judging it. But what actually is the difference? To use a rather laboured and imperfect analogy, one can measure the airspeed and the altitude of an aircraft by reference to instruments that record those quantities. But a pilot, in the final stage of landing a simple aircraft, continuously judges his airspeed (and sometimes his groundspeed), his height above the ground and if necessary, his cross-wind drift by a combination of sight and feel, and with hardly any reference to instruments. The landing will be good or bad according to whether the pilot's judgment is good or bad.

A great deal more followed, extending the analogy to its limits, before concluding:

11. So I suggest there is a sequence or cycle of procedures – measurement, judgment, description, assessment, decision – and that the all-embracing question 'how exactly do you measure/judge the thrust of

---

[47] Goodhart to Dow 'The aims of monetary policy', 21 January 1976, 6A50/18.

policy' disappears under critical examination. It is a non-question, to which there is no answer. So don't worry about it.[48]

When Dow wrote to the Governors two days later, it was to complain that 'Hopkins [*sic*] has all along had misgivings about specifying the aims of monetary policy in terms of the growth of monetary aggregates.' Dow was now playing the monetarist and claiming that he had hoped to persuade Hopkin that monetary aggregates gave a better indication of the aims of monetary policy.[49] When Goodhart returned to the subject at a later date, he supported that position when he said that from 1973, 'The Bank sought to adopt and operate unpublished quantified monetary targets for M3.' But he continued, 'the government resisted the adoption of monetary targets until the end of 1976'.[50] Reflecting on the process at the beginning of the 1980s, Fforde said that after 1973, political and market opinion were sensitive to M3, and it was then that the course of M3 became a strong policy constraint.[51]

Monetary Targets

At the end of March 1976, Richardson alerted Healey to the size of the PSBR and the likely monetary expansion. He asked that the forthcoming budget in April should contain a 'firm statement on monetary policy'.[52] In the event, Healey said in his budget speech that he did not want to see inflation fuelled by the growth of the money supply, and his aim was that 'the growth of the money supply is consistent with my plans for growth and demand expressed in current prices'. This came to be widely interpreted as meaning M3 growth of 12 to 13 per cent in that financial year.

Sterling began to plummet in the spring of 1976, and this contributed to the intensifying discussion and correspondence that continued through to

---

[48] Fforde to Dow, 'Aims of monetary policy (a contribution to irritation)', 21 January 1976, 6A50/18. Page enjoyed the complex analogy. Like Fforde, he had been in the RAF and still 'remained fond of the Tiger Moth'. The reader could be excused for believing this was Henry James rather than Fforde. Page annotation, 22 January 1976, on Fforde to Dow, 'Aims … ', 1A92/1.

[49] Dow to Richardson/Hollom, 'The aims of monetary policy', 23 January 1976, 6A50/18.

[50] Goodhart (1989, p. 357).

[51] Fforde (1983). The paper was presented at a Federal Reserve Bank of New York (FRBNY) conference in May 1982.

[52] Goodhart to Richardson, 'Whither monetary policy?', 26 January 1976; Cassell to Goodhart, 12 February 1976, enc. 'Targets for monetary policy'; Couzens to Fforde, 2 March 1976; Couzens to Fforde, 19 March 1976, enc. 'Operational factors' (of a monetary target), 6A50/18; Richardson to Healey, 30 March 1976, enc. 'Monetary policy: the next two years', 30 March 1976, 6A50/18.

the summer. When Healey announced a $5.3 billion support package for sterling on Monday, 7 June, he also reiterated that growth in the money supply would not be permitted once again to stimulate inflation. This was not enough for *The Economist*, which had just advocated a specific limit of 5 per cent in money-supply growth; it also maintained that the Bank would be busy saying that 'money supply cannot even be counted, let alone controlled'.[53] Nonetheless, a fortnight later, Richardson made some positive noises about the potential advantages of having a monetary target.[54] And another Bridgeman working group recommended setting an internal target for M3.[55] Some thought that it should be published. The Bank argued that there had to be 'an explicit monetary target for this year, with commitment to further and lower target for next year'.[56] To press this home, Richardson emphasised the need for Healey to express his intention to limit money-supply growth to 12 per cent.[57] In his statement the following day, the Chancellor outlined a package that envisaged a £1 billion reduction in the PSBR. He also said that for the financial year as a whole, 'money supply growth should amount to about 12 per cent. Such an outcome would be fully consistent with our objectives for reducing inflation'.[58] Writing to Richardson the same day, Healey said that he had given a great deal of thought to the question of explicit targets and decided against them. He hoped the Governor would be satisfied with the choice of words.

> You may say that there is ambiguity in saying that money supply growth for 1976/77 'should' amount to about 12 per cent. You would be right, and I am not unaware of it. If pressed, I would of course say that this was not a target which carried with it a commitment automatically to take whatever corrective action was needed to validate it.[59]

Having seen a draft of the speech, Goodhart wondered what current monetary policy was and whether the statement implied a shift in stance. Was it a guideline, a target, or a forecast? Fforde tried his best to provide illumination:

[53] *The Economist*, 5 June 1976, pp. 9–10.
[54] Speech given at the annual conference of the Chartered Institute of Public Finance and Accountancy, 18 June 1976, *BEQB* 16(3):325, September 1976.
[55] HMT, 'Policy and the monetary aggregates', nd, filed as 2 June 1976; Goodhart to Fforde, 'Money supply targets', 4 June 1976; Couzens to Fforde, 14 June 1976; Treasury/Bank working group, 'Internal monetary targets', nd, filed as 29 June 1976, 6A50/18; Bridgeman to PPS, 4 June 1976, TNA T386/116.
[56] S. N. Wood (HMT), Note for record, 5 July 1978; Hopkin to Wass, 15 July 1976, TNA T386/116; Bank of England, 'A monetary target', 19 July 1976, 6A50/19.
[57] Richardson to Healey, 21 July 1976, 6A50/19.
[58] HC Deb, 22 July 1976, Vol. 915, cc2018–2019.
[59] Healey to Richardson, 22 July 1976, 6A50/19.

HMT are saying 'it isn't a target but it's more than a forecast'. We are saying it is a 'guideline', for executant purposes, but I don't suppose HMT [would] yet go as far as that. They are only able to say what it isn't, not what it is. Specifically they deny they are committed to taking action '*automatically*' if performance diverges, over an appreciable time, from the more-than-forecast. But they admit that such divergences would cause them concern.[60]

Alongside this talk of objectives and targets was the practical question of which operational techniques had the most effective influence on monetary growth. During the summer of 1976, the only available tool that was thought to work was SSDs, the 'corset'.[61] Work then proceeded on the preparation of the corset, but it was not until November that the garment was donned. It was done in the knowledge that there was about to be a DCE target, and it was intended to have an 'impact' effect.[62] The rate of growth of IBELs was specified at 3 per cent for the first six months and then ½ per cent for a further two months.[63] When details of the SSD scheme were given to the IMF mission in London, they disapproved and sought assurances that SSDs would be phased out reasonably quickly; they saw it as a 'partial rationing scheme' and were concerned about the impact on DCE. During these discussions, David Finch, an Australian economist who was Deputy Director of the IMF's Exchange and Trade Relations Department, had also pressed the case for money-base control, but British officials were antipathetic, saying that it had never been used in the United Kingdom and would raise a large number of questions about the structure of the whole financial system. Certainly, nothing could be done in the timescale of the current drawing, but there was an undertaking to prepare something on it for the next annual consultations in May 1977.[64]

In his July 1976 statement, Healey also had said that there was a risk that monetary restraint might result in industry not receiving essential finance. There was a resort then to guidance issued by the Bank, which emphasised that increases in lending should be to priority areas (manufacturing/

---

[60] Goodhart to Dow, 'The presentation of monetary policy', 22 July 1976, and Fforde, Annotation, 23 July 1976, 6A50/19.

[61] The term 'corset' was coined by Gilbert Wood; see *The Old Lady*, March 1980, p. 44; Goodhart (2003, p. 27).

[62] Coleby to Fforde, '"Corset" preparation', 11 November 1976, 5A149/6; Wood to Page, 'The corset', 11 February 1977, 5A149/7.

[63] Bank of England, 'Notice to banks and deposit-taking finance house. Credit control', 18 November 1976, 5A149/6.

[64] Goodhart, Note for the record – 'IMF discussions: supplementary special deposits (Tuesday, 16 November p.m)', 17 November 1976, 5A149/6; Goodhart, Note for record – 'IMF discussions: monetary performance criteria (Thursday, 18 November a.m.)', 18 November 1976, 6A399/1; Bridgeman to Ryrie (UKTSD), 6 April 1977, 6A50/21.

expanding exports/reducing imports), with restraint exercised elsewhere ('to persons, property companies and for purely financial transactions').[65] This was essentially a restatement of the September 1973 guidance, which had never been lifted, and there followed further reiterations in November 1976 and again in 1977. Although the guidance was supposedly qualitative, it had gradually become an 'unspoken quantitative control' with the character of a ceiling. By 1978, Page found this to be unsatisfactory, and new guidance was issued that removed the request to maintain existing restraint.[66]

Special deposits were also imposed during the 1976 crisis. A call was made in September, an additional 1 per cent in October, and a further 1 per cent in November (i.e., to a total of 5 per cent) (Table 13.2). An administered increase in MLR from 13 to 15 per cent accompanied the October rise, with the stated aim being to moderate monetary growth.[67] It soon appeared that a smaller government borrowing requirement and higher gilt sales were about to 'produce undue pressure on the reserve asset position'.[68] This continued, so by December the Bank wanted to defer the imposition of special deposits until 28 January 1977.[69] Healey and Whittome (who had left the Bank in 1964 to become European Director at the IMF[70]) were both unhappy about the idea, but as Richardson told Whittome, there was the prospect of an 'absolutely massive' shortage in the money market, gilts were firm, and there was a new tap stock available. If the move was not announced now, then a release of special deposits might have to be made later, and this would send the wrong message. Deferral was 'a simple act of good management of the money market'.[71] Whittome finally conceded that 'the Fund could not of course issue an order', and later that day, Richardson indicated that Whittome had acquiesced reluctantly. Richardson then stressed to the Chancellor that further heavy sales of gilts would create pressure to release an even larger amount of special deposits if that day's call was not deferred. In the face of this, Healey relented.[72]

[65] Wass to Richardson, 9 September 1976; Bank of England, Press notice, 22 July 1976, C40/1430.
[66] Page to Richardson/Hollom, 'Directional guidance to banks and finance houses', 29 March 1978; Bank of England, Press notice, 11 April 1978, C40/1436; Peter Ironmonger, Note for record – 'Directional guidance', 10 October 1978, C40/1440.
[67] Bank of England, Press notices, 16 September and 7 October 1976, 5A148/5.
[68] Page to Bridgeman, 4 November 1976; Bank of England, Press notice, 5 November 1976, 5A148/5.
[69] Page to Richardson/Hollom, 'Special deposits', 9 December 1976, 5A148/5.
[70] O'Brien had offered Whittome the post of Chief Cashier in 1969. but he decided to stay at the IMF. Coleby interview with Alan Whittome, 1994.
[71] Plenderleith, Note for record – 'Special deposits', 10 December 1976, 5A148/5.
[72] Bank of England, Press notice, 10 December 1976, 5A148/5.

Table 13.2. *Changes in special deposits, 1972–79*

Date	Call (per cent)	Total (per cent)
Dec 1972	1	1
Jan 1973	2	3
Oct 1973	1	4
Dec 1973	1	5
Feb 1974	−0.5	4.5
Apr 1974	−1	3.5
May 1974	−0.5	3
Jan 1976	−1	2
Feb 1976	1	3
Oct 1976	1	4
Nov 1976	1	5
Jan 1977	−2	3
Feb 1977	−1	2
Mar 1977	1	3
Jun 1978	−1.5	1.5
Jul 1978	0.5	2
Aug 1978	−1	1
Sep 1978	1	2
Oct 1978	1	3
Feb 1979	−2	1
Mar 1979	−1	0
May 1979	2	2
Jul 1979	−2	0
Sep 1979	2	2

Source: BEQB.

The Bank's analysis of the situation proved correct, and in mid-January it was announced that special deposits of 2 per cent would be repaid on the seventeenth, and the additional call for 1 per cent was cancelled; the move was made because the reserve-asset position was of 'exceptional stringency beyond the requirements of present monetary policy.'[73]

[73] Bank of England, Press notice, 13 January 1977, 5A148/5.

Financing a large PSBR, tackling inflation, and dealing with the problems of sterling all presented great challenges to gilt-edged market operations, but the greater emphasis on money and the advent of monetary targets also had implications. There was much comment from practitioners, academics, and journalists, not to mention ministers. For some, the Bank failed; one article in *The Banker* asserted, 'How the Bank has mismanaged monetary policy.'[74] Yet the Bank was unrepentant about its methods and tactics, although such comment and explanation generally were restricted to internal circulation, leaving outsiders to guess at their intentions. On occasion, offenders would be called to the Bank. After writing a piece on interest rates and the money supply in *The Times* that described the Bank's attitude towards a rising market, Tim Congdon was asked in so that Page could issue a correction. The young journalist was unperturbed, suggesting that there remained 'a great deal of muddled thinking in monetary policy.'[75] The criticism even extended to a partner in a firm of stockbrokers breaking protocol and writing directly to the Governor on the subject. The Government Broker declared this an 'extraordinary' incident but symptomatic of the situation where a large number of people 'think they could run the Gilt-Edged Market very much better than we do!'[76] Seemingly impervious to critics, the Bank remained resolute that it knew best how to operate in the market.

Both the number of stocks issued and the total value (nominal) offered during the 1970s exceeded the figures in previous decades (Figure 13.1). Following the long-term decline in yields up to the 1970s, the market began to turn from the beginning of 1975 (Figure 13.2). There were substantial net sales of stock, totalling £33 billion between 1975 and 1979. Some quarters were particularly positive: £3.2 billion in the three months ending December 1976 and £3.0 billion between July and September 1977. There were also troughs, with only £578 million sold in the quarter ending in June 1977 and £793 million in the quarter ending September 1978. This feast and famine was even more apparent in the data showing daily sales of stock (Figure 13.3). It was these fluctuations, especially once monetary targets were adopted, that prompted much of the external criticism of the Bank's market management and increased the interest of Treasury

---

[74] Griffiths (1976, p. 1411).
[75] Cutting from *The Times*, 7 August 1976: 'Come back Peter Jay, all is forgiven' was Quinn's annotation alongside; Congdon to Page, 16 August 1976, C40/1430.
[76] Mullens, Note, 26 October 1976, C40/1430.

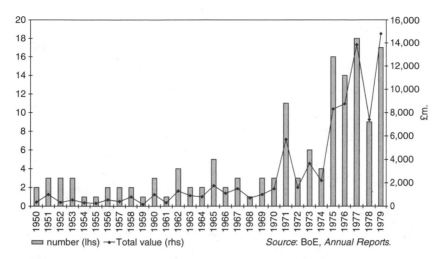

Figure 13.1. Number and total value of new gilt-edged stocks issued, 1950–79.

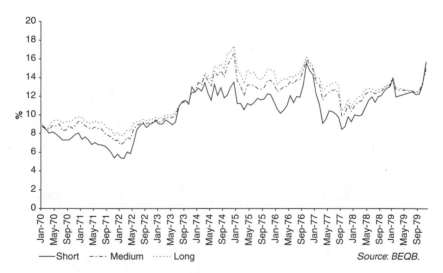

Figure 13.2. Yields on short, medium, and long British government securities, 1970–79.

officials and ministers. This also resulted in far more explicit figuring and assessments on the level of gilt sales required.[77]

---

[77] For example, Price/T. Sweeney to Plenderleith, 'Gilt sales required to meet DCE and £M3 objective', 1 June 1977; Michael Hewitt/Ironmonger, 'Gilt sales required to meet monetary objectives', 21 September 1977, 3A92/6.

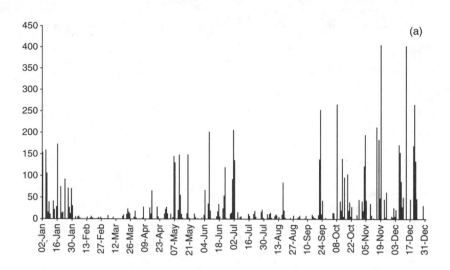

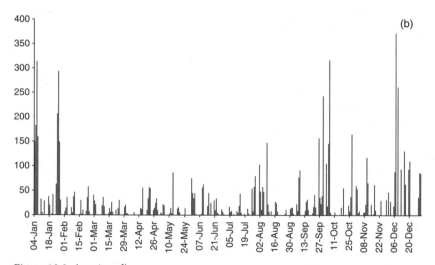

Figure 13.3 *(continued)*

Despite the changes to gilt techniques introduced when CCC had been unveiled, purchases of stocks other than those near maturity were made. The secret safety-net arrangement for jobbers was only intended to be a transitional feature, but it was certainly renewed for a further three months in September 1971 and thereafter remained in place. Its first use, in October 1971, was reported, but after that usage, it proves impossible to identify.

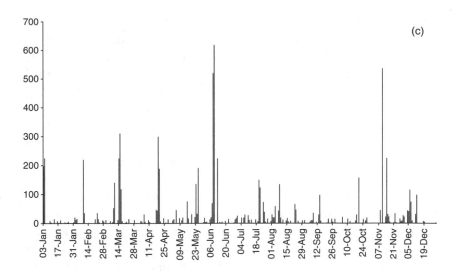

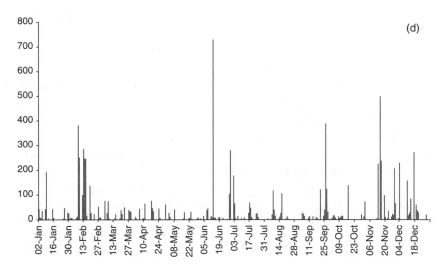

Figure 13.3. Daily sales of gilt-edged stock, (a) 1976; (b) 1977; (c) 1978; (d) 1979.
Source: C11/69–71.

Of course, under CCC, the Bank reserved the right to 'make outright purchases of stock with more than a year to run solely at their discretion and initiative', which it did.[78]

---

[78] Blunden to Page/Fforde/O'Brien/Hollom, 'Loan facilities for gilt-edged jobbers', 15 September 1971; O'Brien/Cooke, Note for record – 'Safety net', 29 October 1971,

One of the frequent criticisms during this period was that the Bank was slow to develop new instruments. This was perhaps unfair because new types of stock were considered, and there were some limited experiments. In 1973, both a convertible stock and a low-coupon stock had been issued. The first of these, the 9 per cent Treasury Convertible Stock 1980, offered holders the option, in 1980, to switch into a stock maturing in 2000. Two years later, the Bridgeman Group suggested that new variable-interest and indexed-linked stocks needed to be examined, and this was endorsed by the MPG.[79] The Bank thought that the variable, or floating-rate, gilt was unlikely to be attractive to investors, and that it would impede sales because it would give the appearance that the authorities were uncertain about the appropriate level of yields, and it was a 'device' – Page did not like such things.[80] Further consideration followed the adoption of monetary targets because such instruments might provide a means of smoothing the path of official sales and avoid barren periods that led to inflated short-term growth in the money stock.[81] However, the Government Broker hoped that in the event of gilts failure, neither a convertible-rate gilt 'or any other unheard of innovations' would have to be introduced.[82]

The Bank was exercised about the capacity of the gilt jobbers, but it was reluctant to see incursions from outside. The London Discount Market Association (LDMA) on several occasions was repelled in its desire for its members to deal directly with the Bank in short-dated gilts. Another potential challenge came from the ARIEL (Automated Real-Time Investments Exchange Limited) system established by the accepting houses in 1972. From February 1974, the company operated a computerised system for trading in securities that provided a service for direct dealings between large investors at very competitive dealing costs. The Bank's view was that fragmentation of the securities market was undesirable but that the stock exchange needed to be stirred up, and the securities industry had to be able to experiment

---

3A92/1; Coleby to Page/Fforde, 'Techniques in the gilt-edged market', 6 October 1976, 3A92/5; *BEQB* 12(3):318, September 1972; Tony Coleby speaking at 'The Old Gilt-edged market', witness seminar, 22 March 2006. www.lombardstreetresearch.com/witness_seminars/2006_gilt-edged.html (accessed 13 November 2009)

[79] MPG(75) 17, 23 December 1975, and annex IV to the main report, MPG(75) 18, 23 December 1975, 1A151/1.

[80] Page, Annotation on Fforde to Richardson/Hollom, 'Monetary policy over the next few weeks', 26 August 1976, 1A92/1.

[81] Mullens to Page, 14 October 1976; Coleby to Page/Fforde/Richardson/Hollom, 'A convertible gilt', 27 October 1976; Fforde to Richardson/Hollom, 'A convertible gilt', 1 November 1976, 3A92/5.

[82] Mullens, Note, 12 October 1976, C40/1430.

in order to adapt itself more effectively to meet modern needs, particularly through automated techniques.[83] In June 1976, Coleby (Deputy Chief Cashier responsible for markets) visited ARIEL and was impressed.[84] But the Bank was less disposed to the idea of ARIEL operating in the gilt-edged market, indeed was consistently opposed to any such development, even in a limited number of stocks for a trial period.[85] The Bank felt that it would result in a structural weakening of the gilt-edged market, which, in turn, would damage the Bank's ability to fund the Government's borrowing and achieve their monetary objectives.[86] Despite the specific concerns about ARIEL, the Bank was not against improving the settlements of transactions in gilt stocks. A study was launched, in conjunction with the stock exchange, in August 1977 that recommended a computer-based system to be maintained in a 'Central Gilts Office'. A joint Bank–stock exchange study group was formed in 1979 that endorsed the principle, and subsequently, the development of a 'real-time' trading system came to fruition with 'Big Bang' in 1986.[87]

Meanwhile, the Bank was preparing responses to their critics for internal consumption. Goodhart noted that ways had to be found of resuming large-scale sales of public-sector debt. Notwithstanding the fact that management of the market since 1945 had been a structural triumph, with a broader and deeper market than existed anywhere else, there were still disadvantages. In particular, it was hard for the authorities to sell gilts when they needed to, and there were periods of 'massive bunched sales broken by months of inactive markets'. Quantified targets for M3 or DCE were likely to exacerbate these difficulties. New instruments to stimulate the market were all very well, but for Goodhart, they did not go to the heart of the problem that 'we wait for investors to approach us to buy bonds when they want to, not when we want them to do so'. His preference was to extend the auction technique beyond the Treasury bill market to the short end of the gilt market to regulate growth of the monetary aggregates. He envisaged weekly auctions of short bonds/bills with the volume on offer related to monetary objectives, and other than an unpublished minimum floor price to prevent a disorderly market, yields would be set in the market, not by the Bank. He accepted that there would be many market objections, that it would take time to develop,

---

[83] Cooke to Richardson/Hollom, 'Securities regulation', 2 December 1975, 6A385/5.

[84] Coleby, Note for record – 'Visit to Ariel', 7 June 1976, 6A385/6.

[85] Cooke, Note for record – 'Ariel', 20 May 1976, 6A385/6.

[86] Cooke to Page, 'Ariel and the gilt-edged market', 25 June 1973, 3A92/2; George to Page/Richardson/Hollom, 'Ariel and gilt edged', 13 October 1978; Bank of England, 'Ariel', enc. with Richardson to John Baring, 22 December 1978, 3A92/8.

[87] Bank of England, *Annual Report*, year ending February 1978, p. 17; year ending February 1979, p. 19; year ending February 1981, p. 12. Also see Michie (1999, Chaps. 11 and 12).

and that it went against current thinking in the Chief Cashier's Office, but it was offered 'in the belief that it would be the generally accepted recommendation of economists on the right way to move forward'.[88]

Coleby argued that the adoption of monetary targets concentrated attention on the volatile nature of gilt-market sales. Existing techniques, he acknowledged, put greater emphasis on moderating volatility of yields rather than volatility of sales, although this emphasis was now nothing compared with the situation up to 1968. Coleby divided the potential innovations into non-aggressive and aggressive. Non-aggressive tactics included the use of new instruments, changes in operating practices (the market allowed to guide itself to higher yields more speedily), and publishing monetary data more promptly and more frequently. Aggressive techniques included the Bank taking the lead in moving yields sharply upwards by cutting tap prices to a level significantly below the market and the Bank pressing the offer of stock by inviting buyers to name their price through sale by tender or negotiated underwriting/placing with a group of institutions. Coleby agreed with Goodhart that any experimentation should be confined to the short end, although he wondered whether the auction technique should be extended beyond maturities of 12 months.[89]

In November, Page tackled the criticisms that the gilt-edged market failed to maximise sales outside the banking system or failed to sell stock as smoothly as possible or both.[90] He suggested remedies under three headings: types of stock offered, techniques of management under the existing arrangements, and fundamental changes to the arrangements. For new securities, Page noted that work on both a variable rate and a convertible stock was progressing. Index-linked instruments were another matter and not greatly favoured in the Bank because they might carry an implication that continuous high inflation was to be accepted. On the alternative techniques of management, the Chief Cashier typically was sure of his opinion. Suggestions for changing the basis for pricing tap stocks and the use of tenders or auctions received short shrift. 'My experience indicates that the assumption on which these two remedies are based is invalid. This is a judgment which some would dispute, but I can do no other than rest on it.' Both would introduce a random and arbitrary element into the market. He had little time too for any proposals that sought to curtail the freedoms of investors. He pointed out that investor behaviour was bound to be volatile

---

[88] Goodhart to Coleby, 'Initiatives in the gilt market', 17 September 1976, 3A92/5.
[89] Coleby to Page/Fforde, 'Techniques in the gilt-edged market', 6 October 1976, 3A92/5.
[90] Page to Bridgeman, 11 November 1976, 3A92/5.

at a time of uncertainty about government policy and the future course of inflation and interest rates. Rather than trying to lessen the causes of the uncertainty, said Page, critics wanted to reduce market volatility by obliging the main investment institutions to negotiate to underwrite issues of stock by tender. He doubted that such an arrangement could be negotiated in practice and that it therefore offered no solution, and he feared that extreme restriction through the statutory direction of investment might follow. The Bank had examined this in the past and reached two principal conclusions. First, a larger take-up of stock was possible only with 'intolerably oppressive regulation', and second, it would be difficult to sell gilts during the 12 to 18 months required to put the required legislation on the statute book.[91]

Some thought was also given to improving relations with the press so that 'ignorant and ill-informed criticism can be deflected' and developing direct contact between the Bank and investment institutions. From recent episodes, Fforde's impression was that journalists were 'not nearly so well-informed as they would like their readers to believe'. On direct contacts, he observed that secret consultations with market participants had been undertaken on two occasions: the first prior to the change in market tactics in 1971, when the safety-net arrangement was made with jobbers, and the second in September 1975, when soundings were taken about the proposed floating-rate bond. There still was an argument, however, for greater contact between the Bank and institutional investors, perhaps in the form of meetings or lunches with the Governors, which would give the opportunity of 'letting off steam' without the Bank having to give much in return.[92]

He also addressed the question of the 'Grand Old Duke of York', the supposed tactic of the Bank to boost flagging sales of gilts by increasing MLR and then hoping that the ensuing rise in yields would attract buyers.[93] A falling trend in short-term rates was then engineered by the Bank to maintain the interest of gilt investors. He asserted that the thesis was a 'travesty of the truth'. Of course, changes in MLR affected gilt yields and sales, but it was 'absurd' to leap from this to the conclusion that rates were habitually raised only for this purpose and in the absence of any other reason for doing so. Analysing events in detail over the previous 15 months, Fforde rejected the 'assiduously fostered myth' that any of the increases in short-term rates had been in support of the Grand Old Duke. 'Rather does this

[91] Page to Fforde/Richardson/Hollom, 'Gilt-edged market management', 4 November 1976, 3A92/5.
[92] Fforde to Richardson/Hollom, 'Gilt-edged market', 26 November 1976, 3A92/5.
[93] It is said that the term originated with John Forsyth of Morgan Grenfell and was used by Anthony Harris in *The Financial Times*.

old soldier take advantage of situations created in support of other people, and who can blame him for that?'[94]

However, from the evidence, it seems that sales were revived by the Grand Old Duke. In early September 1976, Coleby was arguing that to get M3 back onto the 12 per cent guideline, there would have to be substantial sales of gilts and that a rate rise was needed (he suggested MLR up 1½ per cent), although this would not be a sufficient condition.[95] Sales did not improve, and there was what some termed a 'gilts strike', although this was not a phrase ever used by the Bank. Then, under 'operation Draconis', MLR was increased to 15 per cent, supposedly in order to revive sales.[96] At a meeting in October with Healey, Lever (now Chancellor of the Duchy of Lancaster), and a dozen Treasury officials, plus Richardson, Fforde, Dow, Page, Goodhart, and Kirbyshire, monetary measures were discussed in the context of preventing damage to sterling when the next money-supply figures were published on 18 October and the need to meet the July target and the forthcoming negotiations with the IMF. The M3 forecast was 19 per cent and DCE £10.9 billion. Richardson argued that gilt sales were needed on a massive scale, and this could not be done under the present rate structure. Fforde wanted a deliberate increase in MLR of 2 per cent (in fact, alternative packages had been prepared based on rises of 2 and 3 per cent), whereas the Treasury were more inclined to favour fiscal action.[97] The Chancellor accepted that 2 per cent probably would be needed but wondered whether some action on indirect taxation might reduce the severity of the monetary measures.[98] The administered increase was announced on 8 October, apparently taking everyone by surprise.[99] Whatever the reasons behind the rise (Goodhart argued that it was largely occasioned by the collapsing external position), yields did rise to a level where large-scale sales were resumed.[100]

At the Mansion House in October 1976, the Chancellor and the Governor were speaking with one voice, the former stating that a target for sterling

[94] Fforde to Richardson/Hollom, 29 November 1976, 3A92/5.
[95] Coleby to Fforde/Richardson/Hollom, 'Policy action tomorrow', 8 September 1976, C40/1430.
[96] Browning (1986, p. 83). 'Draconis' was the security codeword for a major package of monetary measures.
[97] Bridgeman, 'Monetary measures', 4 October 1976, 7A167/1.
[98] Monck, 'Note of a meeting … 5 October 1976', 6 October 1976, 7A167/1.
[99] Mullens, Note, 12 October 1976, C40/1430. Healey says that he threatened to resign if Jim Callaghan did not accept the 2 per cent rise in interest rates. Healey (1989, pp. 430–431).
[100] Goodhart to Richardson/Hollom/Fforde, 'Debt management and monetary targets', 30 November 1976, C40/1430.

M3 (£M3) would be adopted and the latter endorsing the use of publicly announced monetary targets. The target was 9 to 13 per cent for £M3 in 1976/77, and it was clear that it was now £M3 that mattered.[101] But almost no sooner had this happened than the sterling crisis that had brought the IMF back focussed attention again on DCE.[102] Indeed, from July 1976, Bank and Treasury officials had been discussing DCE in the confident expectation that its control would be one of the main criteria for further assistance.[103] The IMF was clear that it wanted a DCE target but not a monetary target as well.[104] Details were set out in the 'Letter of Intent' (see Chapter 14), with a DCE ceiling of £9 billion for 1976/77. In a briefing for the Governors, Page noted that the money-supply target had been 'deposed' and DCE performance criteria 'imposed with concordant money-supply growth expressed as a range'.[105]

The Bank's public position was not exactly a ringing endorsement of targets. Richardson gave a measured treatment in a speech in early 1977, and similar sentiments were reflected in the *Bulletin* of June the same year: 'Targets may therefore help to focus discussion of monetary policy … and may raise new questions or old questions in new form. It is too soon to make a definitive judgement about the usefulness of monetary targets and how they should be operated.' It went on to say that although monetary growth in the previous three years had been moderate, 'it nevertheless appeared desirable last year to indicate in public the pace of expansion which was being aimed at'.[106] At the same time, a conference paper was being written that Goodhart said was avowedly more positive about the virtues of monetary targeting than the Bank would be in private.[107]

---

[101] Bank of England, 'Monetary targets in the UK', July 1977, 6A50/22. In the files, it seems that references to M3 often mean £M3.

[102] Price, 'Monetary objectives and instruments in the United Kingdom', February 1977, 6A50/20; Bank of England (1984), p. 47.

[103] Goodhart to Dow, 'DCE', 28 July 1976.

[104] Atkinson to Thornton, 'Definition of DCE', 27 September 1976, 5A175/7; Atkinson to Stephen Matthews (HMT), 29 October 1976, enc. draft 'The definition of DCE and money supply in relation to monetary targets', 29 October 1976; Robert Atkinson, Note for record – 'Performance criteria: discussion with the IMF', 12 November 1976; Thornton to Page, 'Publication of DCE', 13 December 1976, 5A175/8; Middleton to Alan Lord/Wass, 2 November 1976, 1A92/2.

[105] Page to Fforde/Richardson/Hollom, 'Publication of DCE and money supply statistics', 29 December 1976, 5A175/8.

[106] Speech given to the Institute of Bankers in Scotland, 17 January 1977, *BEQB* 17(1):48–50, March 1977; *BEQB* 17(2):151, June 1977.

[107] Goodhart to Thornton/Dow, 'SUERF colloquium', 30 June 1977, 6A50/22.

Trying to Influence Monetary Growth

At the end of 1976, published targets for M3 were in place. How deep the commitment was to hitting these targets has been questioned, as has the suitability of the principal tools used for the job. The techniques available were special deposits, supplementary special deposits (SSDs), the reserve-asset ratio, minimum lending rate (MLR), and open market operations. These were not seen as substitutes but as all being needed to differing degrees according to circumstance – one target, five instruments. Defects in them were, however, being acknowledged, and while some refinements and tactical changes were experimented with, the difficulty of hitting the targets persisted.

Despite the claims that under CCC special deposits were to be used flexibly, they were static for most of the period; with the exception of two crises (in 1973 and 1976) and three instances of 'technical smoothing', they were effectively stuck at 3 per cent between early 1973 and the end of 1978 (Figure 13.4). Amid market stringency in January 1977, the Bank had to announce a 'release and recall' of special deposits. It was a tactic that had first been used at the beginning of 1976 when it appeared that the reserve-asset ratio would be pushed below the minimum 12½ per cent, a consequence of high tax receipts and firm gilt sales. As Page warned, banks would take action in the money markets leading to an increase in short-term interest rates. The Bank made a temporary release of special deposits of 1 per cent on 19 January, to be re-deposited on 10 February, when it was expected that heavy government disbursements would add to reserve assets.[108] The 1977 release and recall was a similar exercise; 1 per cent was repaid on 31 January and then recalled on 10 March, and it was undertaken for the same reasons.[109] Further use of the device occurred in the summer of 1978, once again to avoid unnecessarily high rates and facilitate money-market management, and again during 1979.[110]

Yet it seemed that special deposits had not succeeded in restraining the growth of M3, nor did releases accelerate monetary expansion. The explanation was that banks had started to practice liability management rather

---

[108] Page to Richardson/Hollom, 'Special deposits', 14 January 1976; Bank of England, Press notice, 15 January 1976, 5A148/5.

[109] Bank of England, Press notice, 27 January 1977, 5A148/6.

[110] George to Fforde/Richardson/Hollom, 'Release of special deposits' 14 June 1978; George to Page/Fforde/Richardson/Hollom, 'Special deposits', 13 July 1978; Bank of England, Press notices, 17 and 27 July 1978; 'Extract from note of meeting held at 11 Downing Street 26.7.78'; Page to Richardson/Hollom, 'Special deposits', 30 August 1978; George to Hollom, 'Special deposits', 18 September 1978, 5A148/7; Bank of England, Press notices, 15 February, 5, 15, and 26 March, 5 and 27 July 1979, 5A148/8.

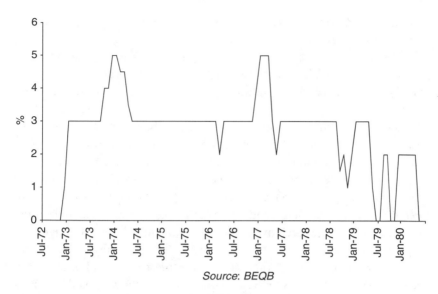

Source: BEQB

Figure 13.4. Special deposits, 1972–80.

than to adjust assets when facing a reserve deficiency; that is, they simply bid for necessary funds in the money, certificate of deposit (CD), and interbank markets. This added considerable complications to the use of special deposits as a policy instrument after 1971. Both Goodhart and Wood asserted that nobody, either inside or outside the Bank, had foreseen the change of emphasis towards liability management at the time CCC was introduced.[111] In 1978, the Treasury accepted the conclusion that special deposits had been ineffective.[112]

Reviewing the position in May 1977, Page noted that since the beginning of the year, the SSD scheme had not been biting. He put this down to factors such as the impact of the sharp rise in interest rates in the autumn of 1976. While he expected demand for bank finance to remain subdued, he did not want to take any risks and therefore concluded, 'perhaps overcautiously', that the scheme should be continued for a further six months with allowed growth of ½ per cent a month.[113] Within three months, Page,

[111] Goodhart to Fforde/Dow/Page/Thornton, 'Provisional *Bulletin* article on special deposits and supplementary special deposits', 31 January 1977, 6A50/20; Wood, 'Money market arrangements and the reserve ratio', draft, 7 July 1977, C40/1433.

[112] HMT, 'The use of special deposits', 28 June 1978, C40/1437.

[113] Page to Richardson/Hollom, 'Supplementary special deposits', 9 May 1977; Page to Couzens (HMT), 11 May 1977; Bank of England, 'Notice to banks and deposit-taking finance houses. Supplementary special deposits', 12 May 1976, 5A149/7.

supported by Goodhart, was recommending that the opportunity should be taken to suspend the scheme. He judged that the reactivation of SSDs had 'at most a quite minor effect on the rate of monetary growth. It may have deterred a few banks from agreeing to new facilities and a few customers from applying for them, but nothing more.'[114] The SSDs paid had been negligible, and only a handful of banks were liable (see Table 13.1). Total IBELs in the banking system were 6½ per cent below the allowable limit, so again there was comfortable headroom, and the scheme was inoperative. The suspension was announced in the second week of August 1977.[115]

There was some ambivalence in assessing the effects. Understandably, there was reluctance to reject measures that had only relatively recently been designed and implemented. For example, Goodhart presented a modest defence of SSDs as a relatively effective instrument in restraining monetary expansion but conceded that it was difficult to disentangle their impact from other factors. One of the latter was interest rates, and another was greater caution by bankers in the aftermath of the secondary banking crisis. The 1976 imposition coincided with higher rates and additional restraining measures. Nonetheless, continued use of the device was felt to be justified, even if it was recognised that SSDs introduced artificial distortions and interfered with competition, while banks could anticipate any re-imposition by rearranging their balance sheets. This meant that the scheme needed to be used sparingly if it was not to become discredited.[116]

Liability management also prompted further deliberations on the Bank's money-market operations. When the authorities had sought to squeeze liquidity, the results had been perverse, at least in the short run, with a tendency for M3 to grow. By 1977, it was generally accepted in the Bank that the reserve ratio of 12½ per cent was 'little, if any, help in controlling banks' activities', and market operations could still continue as at present if the ratio were abolished. Outside observers were also sceptical. At a meeting of the Money Study Group, not one of the 100 people present was in favour of the 12½ per cent ratio.[117] The Treasury was reluctant to abandon it, and Goodhart said that while most in the Bank would accept that dropping the reserve-asset ratio was a necessary step towards gaining the

---

[114] Goodhart to Page, 'The supplementary special deposits scheme', 5 August 1977; Page to Richardson/Hollom, 'Supplementary special deposits', 5 August 1977, 5A149/7.

[115] Bank of England, 'Notice to banks and deposit-taking finance houses', 11 August 1977, 5A149/7.

[116] Goodhart to Fforde/Dow/Page/Thornton, 'Provisional *Bulletin* article on special deposits and supplementary special deposits', 31 January 1977, 6A50/20; Goodhart to Loehnis, 'Wilson questions on monetary policy: redraft', 24 November 1978, 5A203/3.

[117] Price to Fforde, 'Alternative reserve ratios', 21 March 1977, 6A50/21.

ability to smooth the monetary aggregates, it was not sufficient because he felt that banks would still look to inter-bank markets to adjust their positions. One scheme, a variation on quantitative easing, was to place Issue Department deposits with the clearing banks. If the Bank had a good gilt sale and the market was short, the Bank could place the cash as deposits with the banks. These would be used as reverse special deposits, without any fanfare of announcement, and used day-to-day with basic operations shifted closer to the American-type system, something that would represent a major change.[118] Another of Goodhart's proposals was to operate with no reserve ratio at all; although this might appear to outsiders to be a lot looser, he doubted whether the ability to control the system would in fact be lessened.[119] Fforde felt that the reserve ratio arrangements produced 'high profile' central banking but without effective control, and he advocated what he described as a modified version of the pre-1971 position with a lower profile but closer control. This would comprise a small working-balance cash ratio instead of the 'front-line' reserve ratio, Issue Department deposits with banks, bill operations conducted with flexible daily prices rather than linked to the Treasury bill tender rate, and an administered MLR.[120] It was anticipated that the Treasury would not like it, and it might be an embarrassment to alter the system only six years after it had been introduced with such fanfare.[121] However, the debate was moving closer to notions of operating on a cash or money base.

Monetary base control was an idea that had come to prominence, although it was not a new concept, and for some time there had been awareness in the Bank that there ought to be an agreed position. There were three sources of outside pressure: one was academic work, another was the City, and a third was the IMF. It is always difficult to identify accurately where even the proximate beginnings of a proposal originate. Thus it is with the British monetary base debate. The story could be taken back to 1844, but more recently, in early 1976, Nigel Duck and David Sheppard, from the universities of Bristol and Birmingham, respectively, sent a paper to the Bank that advocated something close to a cash base control system

---

[118] Goodhart to Fforde/Richardson/Hollom, 'The Treasury bill market and 'Treasury' (Issue Department) deposits', 29 March 1977, 6A50/21.

[119] Goodhart to Fforde/O'Brien/Hollom, 'Monetary control', 1 March 1977, 6A50/21; Goodhart, Annotations on Page to Goodhart, 'Monetary control', 22 April 1977, C40/1432.

[120] Fforde to Page, 'Money market arrangements', 10 June 1977, C40/1433.

[121] Wood to Fforde/Coleby/George, 'Money market arrangements', 24 June 1977; Wood to Fforde, 'Money market arrangements', 14 July 1977, C40/1433; Fforde to Richardson, 'Monetary control', 27 May 1977, 6A50/22.

(they envisaged control via a specially created reserve asset called 'reserve deposits'). The idea was dismissed by Goodhart.[122] Enthusiasm in the City for a monetary base system was mainly promoted by Greenwells or, more precisely, Gordon Pepper. In January 1977, they circulated one of their bulletins on the subject (which Richardson asked to read), and the following month Pepper spoke about 'mechanisms for controlling the money supply' at a seminar organised by Roger Alford of the London School of Economics (LSE). Goodhart was there and reported a large attendance, including many economists from City and financial institutions. The audience, he noted, revealed little support for the prevailing reserve ratio system.[123] Eighteen months later, when Richardson and Fforde lunched at Greenwell's, Pepper took the opportunity to again express his support for money base control.[124]

Apart from the fact that some other countries (notably Switzerland) practiced a monetary base technique, there had been direct encouragement from the IMF during the November 1976 consultations. However, there were differences in expectations about what would be covered in the forthcoming May 1977 meeting. The British side wanted a more general discussion on methods of monetary control; Finch thought it would be concentrating on base money. In April 1977, Finch gave Ryrie, now economic minister in Washington, some topics for discussion. On seeing this, Goodhart immediately expressed concern because he said that it rested on the assumption 'that we already have a "monetary base" system, and that the issues involved are how to make this work better.... [this] reveals considerable misapprehension about the working of the UK financial system'.[125]

Before the IMF meeting could take place, the Governor wondered whether it would be a good idea to organise a seminar on monetary policy that might build up understanding and sympathy for the Bank's handling of monetary policy. Goodhart did not think it a good idea. It was more likely to polarise views than see them converge. 'The Brown conference on Monetarism, for example, was, at times, something of a punch up (Tobin/Friedman in particular) and changed nobody's views.' The one on CCC had not been a genuine consultation at all because the Bank's mind was already

---

[122] Duck to Goodhart, 28 January 1976, enc. Duck and Sheppard, 'A proposal for the control of the U.K. money supply', November 1975; Goodhart to Duck, 3 February 1976, 6A7/2.

[123] Price to Plenderleith, 'Pepper on a UK "monetary base"', 14 January 1977, 1A92/2; Goodhart to Fforde, 'Gordon Pepper on "Mechanisms for controlling the money supply"', 23 February 1977, 6A151/2.

[124] Fforde, Note for record – 'Greenwell's', 10 July 1978, 3A92/7.

[125] Finch to Ryrie, 6 April 1977; Bridgeman to Ryrie, 6 April 1977; Goodhart to Page, 'Seminar on "base money"', 14 April 1977, 6A50/21; Ryrie to Bridgeman, 9 May 1977, 6A50/22.

made up. But the main point was that it was 'the monetary base argument which is uppermost in the Governor's mind, and he would like a paper soon'.[126]

Goodhart's preparation for the IMF meeting grew into a major survey and statement of the state of play in the Bank. It included suggestions for changes in the gilts market and accepted that while the two applications of SSDs were followed by a slowing of monetary expansion, in neither case could the scheme 'be held solely or even primarily responsible'. Yet Goodhart felt that the record of achievement was not bad. After allowing for a period following CCC for adjustments to take place and the present direction of policy adopted, say, by the end of 1973, comparison with other countries on the average rate of monetary growth had been good.[127] He was sceptical about the introduction of a monetary base system. He believed that the existing structure of the monetary system was not conducive to keeping to smooth monetary growth and that there was considerable dissatisfaction with the operation of the reserve ratio system then in place; he nevertheless rejected the idea that changing to a cash ratio would solve the problems. He thought it worth following up some recent ideas of William Poole (good, 'despite his monetarist leanings') in the United States on an incremental cash ratio.[128]

Comprehensive as it was, the Goodhart paper offered no clear remedies for the deficiencies. It was as a consequence of this that he, Fforde, and Coleby made a trip to North America in the spring of 1977 to see if either Canada or the United States had the answers. In the main, they did not, but after the visit, there was another reconsideration of M1.[129] Fforde again made interesting comments on the state of play. He reflected that the changes of mid-1976 were significant and that they represented a 'substantial move towards the monetarist point of view'. (Dow rejected this.) Fforde saw the rationale as strategic: to put in place a counter-inflationary policy that had little or nothing to do with demand management. Without

[126] Dow to Goodhart, 'The idea of a seminar on monetary policy', 1 February 1977; Goodhart to Dow, 'The idea of a seminar on monetary policy', 3 February 1977, 6A50/20.

[127] Final version of 'Proposals for improving monetary control', section A, p. 13, enc. with Goodhart to Richardson/Hollom, 'Monetary control', 26 April 1977, 6A50/21.

[128] The outcome of this assessment, undertaken by Lionel Price, was essentially negative; Price to Fforde, 'Incremental cash ratios' 16 March 1977, enc. 'Incremental cash ratios: an appraisal', 6A50/21.

[129] Goodhart, Note for record – 'Discussions on monetary control techniques with Bank of Canada and US monetary authorities, 28 April–5 May', 23 May 1977, 6A50/22; Goodhart to Fforde, 'Proposals for improving monetary control: a note on subsequent developments', 27 April 1978, 6A10/1.

such a constraint, the system would remain 'dangerously liable to runaway inflation'. Fforde showed that he could be open minded. He concluded a (typically long) note:

Finally, I would accept the comment that I have changed my mind on many of the issues discussed in this note; and that I have been driven by experience into realising that there may be more to be said for some of the views held by, e.g., *The Times* and *FT* [*Financial Times*] on the status of the Bank than I had previously thought.[130]

For the IMF, Goodhart's thoughts had been distilled into an eight-page paper on the general aims, methods, and problems of monetary control. It was lukewarm on the question of monetary base.[131] Finch insisted that there was information in the monetary base and that it was relatively easy to put the figures together – notes in circulation plus bankers' balances – it could even be done weekly. Movements in the series could give early warning of what was happening to M3. Goodhart and Page strongly doubted if anything could be learned from such movements, although they did offer to carry out empirical work to test the proposition.[132] The econometric results from this work were 'as bad as, or possibly worse than, most of us would have hoped'. Deputy Chief Cashier David Somerset bemoaned the fact that so much effort had been necessary to prove the obvious – 'obvious, at any rate, to anyone who has any practical knowledge of how the note circulation and bankers' balances behave'.[133] (Some work by the EEC harmonisation group, and in particular, Michele Fratianni, an Economic Adviser to the European Commission, on money-stock control was being taken seriously in Europe. But the Bank reported that the results were not good enough to make them reconsider their position in the Bank.[134])

Many countries in the Organisation for Economic Co-operation and Development (OECD) had by the mid-1970s adopted some target for a monetary aggregate. Nonetheless, the arguments would go on for very

---

[130] Fforde, 'The state of the art', 28 April 1977, 6A50/21.
[131] Goodhart to Fforde/Richardson/Hollom, 'Monetary control', 1 March 1977, 6A50/21; Bank of England, 'Monetary control in the United Kingdom', 18 May 1977, 6A50/22.
[132] Price, 'IMF monetary base seminar', 26 May 1977, 6A50/22.
[133] Price to Goodhart, 'Monetary base paper for IMF', 21 October 1977, and Somerset, Annotation, 26 October 1977, 6A50/23; Price to Kent (UKTSD), 3 November 1977, 6A50/24.
[134] Michele Fratianni, 'Speaking notes on money stock control problem: the European experience', given at conference on debt management and monetary control, London, 21–23 November 1977; Goodhart to Price, nd, 6A50/24; Goodhart to Page, 'Monetary base and money stock control in the EEC', 16 January 1978, 6A50/25.

much longer over which aggregate should be used, should it be a point or a range, how often might the target have to be re-set, should it be a rolling or fixed target, and so on. Through 1977, these issues were to the fore in the Bank. Goodhart's April verdict on M1 versus M3 was that although there was a strong argument for putting greater emphasis on the former, on balance, it was better to 'soldier on' with the latter because it would not now be easy to relegate the significance of M3. What tended to dominate in favour of M3 was the ability to link it to its counterparts, PSBR, bank lending, debt sales, and external flows, as a means of co-ordinating fiscal and exchange-rate policies with monetary policy.[135] But partly because of the difficulty there seemed to be in controlling M3, a view developed that there should be targets for more than one aggregate.[136] 'We believe that the case for adopting a dual target, comprising M1 as well as M3, is strong.'[137] Lever disliked the idea and in any case was unconvinced by M1 as a monetary aggregate. (No one seems to have raised the question of the possibility that these two aggregates might move in different directions for some time.) Healey concurred, adding that critics would focus on whichever indicator was performing badly at the time. Wass, too, was sceptical.[138] The Bank and the Treasury agreed that £M3 should remain the target for the coming year, with the caveat that the Treasury wanted to hold in reserve a DCE limit should the balance of payments show weakness.

Interest-Rate Flexibility

While the debate on the appropriate target was running and doubts about the effectiveness of the control techniques continued, there were also doubts over the usefulness of MLR. At the beginning of 1977, Page told the Treasury that the Bank considered that the MLR arrangements should be terminated and replaced by direct and flexible administration of the Rate: 'It is now openly acknowledged that monetary policy aims are defined in terms of quantitative targets for the rate of monetary expansion whether measured by the money supply or by domestic credit expansion....It is a logical consequence that the operation of monetary policy will require flexibility of

---

[135] Price to Atkinson/Hillage/George, 'M2 as a monetary aggregate', 22 December 1977, 5A175/9.
[136] Goodhart to Coleby, 'M1 vs M3', 21 April 1977, and Fforde, Annotation, 26 April 1977, 6A50/21; Goodhart to Fforde, 'Fixing a target for M1', 15 September 1977, 6A50/22; Goodhart to Fforde, 'Monetary targets', 8 November 1977, enc. 'Which M for emphasis'. 6A50/24.
[137] Bank of England, 'Monetary targets, 1978–79', 15 November 1977, 6A50/24.
[138] Tony Battishill, 'Note of a meeting ... [1]7 November 1977', 21 November 1977, 6A50/24.

interest rates.' An administered Bank Rate would recognise this and put short-term interest-rate policy 'in a clear light', confer greater control, and remove periodic strains in the Bank's relationship with the market. What it did not mean was a return to the pre-September 1971 position, where Bank Rate was pre-eminent in setting market rates and acting 'as a barometer of the "state of the nation".'[139]

Since MLR had been introduced, it was scarcely a secret that despite the market nature of the formula, the Bank could influence rates through its own operations, either in the bill market or by manipulation of the tender. An upward push could be attained quite effectively by enlarging the tender or lowering the Bank's dealing prices. Upward movements could be restrained by the Bank tendering itself, something that could be disguised, or by cutting the top off the tender once the bid prices were known. A push down might be achieved by reducing the size of the tender and raising dealing prices, although for real effect, action in the gilt-edged market was required. In order to restrain a downward movement, the tender could be enlarged and dealing prices kept down.[140] According to one discount house, the market liked MLR being linked to the Treasury bill tender because it gave the houses great power. However, as a system by which the Bank could influence money rates, it worked poorly. The problem was that the effectiveness of the Bank's various signals, imparted through its market operations (such as lending overnight or for seven days), had weakened to the extent that it had to issue rather more explicit messages. This had led to the Bank's every word being 'over-analysed'.[141]

Until 1977, there were only two administered MLR changes, in November 1973 from 11.25 to 13 per cent and in October 1976 from 13 to 15 per cent. According to Page, there were also four occasions when the Bank had operated through the market. For example, in July 1975, the Bank engaged in seven-day lending to the market and made it clear what it expected in the following tender; this produced an increase from 10 to 11 per cent on 25 July. Other changes were often presented in the newspapers as if they had been administered as well. The October 1975 rise from 11 to 12 per cent was portrayed in this light, although it was the market that had decided that a rise in Treasury bill rates was appropriate, and this happened to coincide with official views (Table 13.3). Page did concede that the semantic distinction between market forces and positive action by the Bank was a matter

---

[139] Page to Bridgeman, 26 January 1977, C42/10.
[140] Page to O'Brien/Hollom, 'Special deposits and Bank rate', 18 September 1972, C42/10.
[141] Price, Note for record – 'Petherbridge [Senior Managing Director, Union Discount] on monetary control and the discount market', 23 March 1978, 6A50/26.

Table 13.3. *Changes in minimum lending rate, 1974–79*

Date	Change (per cent)	New rate (per cent)
4 Jan 1974	−0.25	12.75
1 Feb 1974	−0.25	12.5
5 Apr 1974	−0.25	12.25
11 Apr 1974	−0.25	12.0
24 May 1974	−0.25	11.75
20 Sep 1974	−0.25	11.5
17 Jan 1975	−0.25	11.25
24 Jan 1975	−0.25	11.0
7 Feb 1975	−0.25	10.75
14 Feb 1975	−0.25	10.5
7 Mar 1975	−0.25	10.25
21 Mar 1975	−0.25	10.0
18 Apr 1975	−0.25	9.75
2 May 1975	0.25	10.0
25 Jul 1975	1.0	11.0
3 Oct 1975	1.0	12.0
14 Nov 1975	−0.25	11.75
28 Nov 1975	−0.25	11.5
24 Dec 1975	−0.25	11.25
2 Jan 1976	−0.25	11.0
16 Jan 1976	−0.25	10.75
23 Jan 1976	−0.25	10.5
30 Jan 1976	−0.5	10.0
6 Feb 1976	−0.5	9.5
27 Feb 1976	−0.25	9.25
5 Mar 1976	−0.25	9.0
23 Apr 1976	1.5	10.5
21 May 1976	1.0	11.5
10 Sep 1976	1.5	13.0
7 Oct 1976	2.0 (administered)	15.0
19 Nov 1976	−0.25	14.75
17 Dec 1976	−0.25	14.5
24 Dec 1976	−0.25	14.25

(continued)

Table 13.3 *(continued)*

Date	Change (per cent)	New rate (per cent)
7 Jan 1977	−0.25	14.0
21 Jan 1977	−0.75	13.25
28 Jan 1977	−1.0	12.25
3 Feb 1977	−0.25 (administered)	12.0
10 Mar 1977	−1.0 (administered)	11.0
18 Mar 1977	−0.5 (formula suspended)	10.5
31 Mar 1977	−1.0 (administered)	9.5
7 Apr 1977	−0.25	9.25
15 Apr 1977	−0.25	9.0
22 Apr 1977	−0.25	8.75
29 Apr 1977	−0.5 (formula suspended)	8.25
13 May 1977	−0.25 (formula suspended)	8.0
5 Aug 1977	−0.5	7.5
12 Aug 1977	−0.5	7.0
9 Sep 1977	−0.5	6.5
16 Sep 1977	−0.5	6.0
7 Oct 1977	−0.5	5.5
14 Oct 1977	−0.5	5.0
25 Nov 1977	2.0	7.0
6 Jan 1978	−0.5	6.5
11 Apr 1978	1.0 (administered)	7.5
5 May 1978	1.25	8.75
12 May 1978	0.25	9.0
MLR formula ends		
9 Jun 1978	1.0	10.0
10 Nov 1978	2.5	12.5
9 Feb 1979	1.5	14.0
2 Mar 1979	−1.0	13.0
6 Apr 1979	−1.0	12.0
15 Jun 1979	2.0	14.0
16 Nov 1979	3.0	17.0

Source: BEQB.

of judgement.[142] Most recently, the 1½ per cent rise in September 1976 was brought about through the market, although newspaper comment was as if it had been administered. While it was convenient for the Bank to 'hide behind the market' when it suited, Page asserted that this represented at least a 'partial abandonment' of initiative by the authorities and 'detracts from our authority as central bank in the marketplace'. Furthermore, there was a clear disadvantage when the Bank's view of the appropriate course of short-term rates differed from that held by the discount market. The Bank was able to make its view prevail, but often by forcing the discount houses to act against their own commercial judgement, thus creating stresses. In addition, the size of the outside tender for Treasury bills had grown, thus diminishing the effectiveness of the Bank's private influence in the market, and they had had to resort to more overt and explicit signals in public to try and get the market to conform. Against this background, Page worried that 'we risk losing control', and he thought that there was a clear choice between continuing with MLR or reverting to an administered Bank Rate. On balance, he favoured the latter, which could be presented positively as the 'restoration to the authorities of full control of one of the instruments of monetary management'.[143]

Typically, the autobiographies of politicians serve to highlight or exaggerate their own critical role. Healey relates how in September 1976, 'I had to raise interest rates' by 1½ per cent to revive gilt sales. But he also claims that the Bank made a major mistake by letting rates fall in March 1976, thus exacerbating the decline of sterling – not mentioning that the fall was only ¼ per cent. Both these instances were during the period of 'automatic' MLR. In fact, Healey did not always welcome involvement in such decisions. At the end of 1975, Wass phoned him to discuss a quarter-point reduction in MLR, and Healey reportedly asked 'why he was being bothered with trivia at Christmas'.[144] Healey later bemoaned that he and Callaghan had, over this period, both been personally involved in time-consuming decisions on the rate.[145]

Aware of the concerns of ministers, Treasury officials were reluctant to move to a fully administered rate, and attention instead was directed towards modifying the formula.[146] On 3 February 1977, there was an

---

[142] Page to Downey, 15 July 1975, C40/1394; Page to Ryrie (UKTSD), 18 June 1976, C40/1395.

[143] Bridgeman to Coleby, 15 November 1976; Page to Fforde/Richardson/Hollom, 'Bank rate v. minimum lending rate', 31 December 1976, C40/1395.

[144] Page to Richardson/Hollom, 'Interest rates', 24 December 1975, 1A151/1.

[145] Healey to Callaghan, 18 May 1978, C40/1397.

[146] Galpin to Page/Fforde/Richardson/Hollom, 'Minimum lending rate', 20 January 1977; Fforde to Richardson/Hollom, 'Minimum lending rate', 1 February 1977; Bridgeman

administered reduction when the Bank sought to prevent rates dropping sharply by reducing MLR from 12¼ to 12 per cent.[147] On 10 March, another administered change was made, from 12 to 11 per cent. The next day it was announced that the MLR mechanism was to be modified so that if the market move was downwards, the Bank reserved the right to leave the rate unchanged or to change it by less than the amount dictated by operation of the formula.[148] These powers were used on 18 and 25 March to moderate MLR at 10.5 per cent, and this was followed by a further administered change to 9.5 per cent at the end of the month. The Bank stepped in again at the end of April and the beginning of May to keep MLR at 8¼ per cent. After that, the rate was allowed to fall through the normal market mechanism, and by October, it was down to 5 per cent, having been 14¼ per cent at the start of the year (see Table 13.3).

One of the influences on falling interest rates was the sharp appreciation of sterling. There was heavy intervention to try to moderate the impact of these inflows on domestic monetary policy. Although the effect was uncertain, the likelihood was that £M3 growth would breach the 13 per cent upper limit of the prevailing target. Indeed, in September and October, the question of the exchange rate, the monetary objective, and MLR were the overriding concerns in policy discussions between the Governor, Chancellor, and senior officials. If interest rates were to be used primarily to achieve domestic monetary targets, then exchange-rate stabilisation would have to be abandoned or another instrument found to influence exchange rates.[149] By this time, they agreed that if there was a conflict between the exchange-rate and money-supply objectives, the latter should have priority.[150] The inflows and falling interest rates had implications for the gilts market. While large sales of gilts had achieved some neutralising effect, it was becoming increasingly hard to maintain this. Richardson told Healey that it would be impossible to meet the monetary target for 1977–78 and that the required average gilts sales of £600 million a month could not be met without discouragement of further inflows. At the end of October it

to Fforde, 1 February 1977, 7A131/2. There was also informal consultation with the discount market; Galpin, Note for record – 'minimum lending rate', 2 February 1977, 7A131/2.

[147] *BEQB* 17(2):162–163, June 1977.

[148] Bank of England, Press notices, 10 and 11 March 1977, 4A139/5. This idea had been suggested previously in 1973; Page to Richardson/Hollom, 'Bank rate', 8 August 1973, C40/1392.

[149] Goodhart to Richardson/Hollom, 'The money supply and exchange inflows', 1 September 1977, C40/1434.

[150] McMahon, 'Exchange rate and inflows', 14 September 1977, C40/1434.

was decided to uncap sterling (see Chapter 14) in order to remove the risk of inflows exerting further expansionary impact on £M3.[151]

MLR then moved up from 5 to 7 per cent on 25 November, albeit in a highly unsatisfactory manner. The Bank wanted an administered rise; the Government did not. Thus the Bank had to operate through the market, giving strong hints to the London Discount Market Association (LDMA) that it wanted to see a 2 per cent increase, but no more. This occurred, and publicly, the Bank was able to say that market forces coincided with the official view. However, the following week, there was much speculation that rates would rise to 8 per cent and perhaps even 9 per cent. Ministers were disturbed, and Callaghan even threatened to intervene by having a parliamentary question planted to enable him to declare that 7 per cent was the right level. The Bank acted by issuing a statement on 30 November saying that there had been an adequate correction and that it did not wish to see any further rise, something that was interpreted as being an ex-post administration of the 2 per cent increase. Richardson had to provide an explanation of these events to the Prime Minister, who asked, as did the Chancellor, for a review of the MLR arrangements. The Bank's preference was still to replace the formula-based system with a fully administered rate, although Fforde warned that care would be needed in putting this case to Whitehall lest it aroused suspicions that the Bank was covertly planning for achieving a greater degree of independence.[152]

At the beginning of 1978, Gordon Richardson inaugurated the series of Mais lectures at City University (named after their sponsor, Lord Mais, a former mayor of the City of London.)[153] His lecture, 'Reflections on the Conduct of Monetary Policy', attracted wide attention and became frequently

[151] 'Exchange inflows and the money stock', 15 September 1977, enc. with Fforde to Richardson, 15 September 1977; HMT, 'Note of a meeting … 20 October 1977', 24 October 1977, C40/1435; *BEQB* 17(3):283, 294–296, September 1977; *BEQB* 17(4):415, 426–428, December 1977.

[152] Fforde to Page/George/Somerset, 5 December 1977, C40/1435; Battishill, Note for record, 23 November 1977; Ian Keynes (Governors' Office), Note for record, 30 November 1977; Healey to Callaghan, 30 November 1977; Richardson to Callaghan, 9 December 1977; Fforde to Richardson/Hollom, 'MLR', 30 December 1977; Page to Richardson/Hollom, 'MLR v. Bank rate. Round 2', 30 December 1977, C40/1396; *The Times*, 30 November 1977, p. 1 and 1 December 1977, pp. 1, 17.

[153] Mais had been instrumental in the establishment of the University's Department of Banking and Finance. Richardson was invited at some point in May 1977. On a note by Fforde suggesting that the Bank prepare a definitive explanation of its intellectual position on monetary control for publication in the *Bulletin*, Richardson wrote 'consider in connection with Prof. Griffiths' invitation to City University'; Richardson, Annotation on Fforde to Richardson, 'Monetary control', 27 May 1977, 6A50/22.

cited in subsequent years. In the lecture he looked at how monetary policy had changed over the course of the 1970s. In doing so, he contributed to the rewriting of history along the lines that had been developed by the Bank. For instance, he said the aims of CCC had been twofold. One was the removal of ineffectual controls. That was true. The other was that 'importance was now attached to the monetary aggregates; their rate of growth was to be controlled by the market instrument of interest rates.'[154] As we have seen, this was less true. That aside, the lecture was an admirable survey of the developments in monetary policy in the course of the decade. This should not surprise because it was written largely by Goodhart, although, as was always the case with Richardson, there was more than one person involved. In this case, the other principal contributor was Dow, and the lecture went through many revisions and accompanying discussion, although the papers have not survived.

In 1978, the economic situation was deteriorating again, and the path of MLR was upward. Remarkably, an administered increase, from 6.5 to 7.5 per cent, was announced by the Chancellor in his April 1978 budget. The rise had been pressed by the Governor in order to restrain money growth and align domestic and external short-term interest rates.[155] The following month, there were two more 'market' increases, taking MLR to 9 per cent. Thereafter, they reverted to an administered regime.[156] The justification was greater emphasis on the need to meet published targets. In reaching this decision, it was recognised that the market had increasingly looked to the authorities for signals on rates and that these had been given in increasingly explicit form. The result was that the rate scarcely could be said to be market-determined, and the Bank accepted that in practice the authorities already bore the main responsibility for MLR. Moving to an administered rate would give greater control over interest rates and make the views of the authorities more open. Thereafter, changes made, as for Bank Rate, would be announced on a Thursday by the Bank. However, to avoid giving the message that all this meant a return to the old inflexible arrangements, the title of MLR was retained. This was insufficient to persuade the press.[157] *The Financial Times* led with 'Bank Rate by another name'; *The Sun*'s title read, 'It's back to the old Bank Rate system'; and *The Sunday Times* explained, 'Why Bank Rate is Back in business'.[158]

---

[154] Capie and Wood (2001, p. 17).
[155] Bridgeman to Wass, 7 April 1978; Michael Williams (HMT), 'Note of meeting ... 10 April 1978', 10 April 1978; Bank of England, Press notice, 11 April 1978, C40/1397.
[156] Battishill, 'Note of a meeting ... 10 May 1978', 11 May 1978, C40/1397.
[157] Bank of England, Press notice, 25 May 1978, 4A139/5.
[158] Press cuttings in ADM38/6.

Quantitative controls also returned to the agenda. The possibility of SSDs being re-imposed was evidently being expected because in the first half of 1978, the Bank had picked up clear evidence of 'padding', that is, the banks increasing IBELs in anticipation of SSDs, and this itself had produced distortions in money markets.[159] The situation was reviewed by Goodhart in May, who again argued that the 'corset' would be able to control the difficult element in £M3, that is, time deposits and CDs, without any large general increase in interest rates. As we have seen, the corset generally hampered competition and individual growth, and these effects worsened the longer the scheme was in place. Artificialities and inefficiencies were also likely if observers perceived that the mechanism was being run on a 'control-on, control-off' basis. Thus Goodhart and Fforde proposed a 'contingent' corset whereby it would be announced that the authorities were thinking about reintroducing the scheme but that it might be removed 'before it was firmly fastened in place'. The outcome, it was hoped, was that the banks would behave as if the corset had been applied. This was a typical piece of Bank psychology. Indeed, Goodhart conceded that the plan was 'really too clever by half', and it was not pursued.[160]

Concerns about the appropriate target also reappeared. Fforde reiterated his contention that £M3 should be scrapped as the target variable and replaced by M1.[161] They had, according to Goodhart, stacked the cards against themselves by choosing £M3 as the centrepiece of monetary policy. Moreover, reforms that were being suggested to debt management would not allow £M3 to be controlled any more effectively. Goodhart now agreed with Fforde that they should move towards an M1 target 'but that we will still need to supplement it with a wider aggregate which enables us, and HMT, to relate the PSBR to financial developments'. He went on to say that if they were forced to reintroduce the 'corset', they could make a virtue out of necessity by noting in public that that reduced the value of £M3 as an indicator, so M1 was a better aggregate to watch.[162]

By early June, talk in the Bank was of the need for a 'severe' monetary package. There still was some unease about use of the corset, in particular,

---

[159] Goodhart to Page, 17 February 1978; Atkinson to Page, 'Padding to IBELs at mid-February', 3 March 1978; Goodhart to Richardson/Hollom, 'Some notes on the corset', 23 May 1978, 5A149/8.

[160] Goodhart to Richardson/Hollom, 'Some notes on the corset', 23 May 1978; Goodhart to Richardson/Hollom, 'A submission on the corset', 24 May 1978, enc. Bank of England, 'The reintroduction of the supplementary special deposits scheme', 24 May 1978, 5A149/8. See also postscript, Fforde to Richardson, 19 May 1978, C40/1436.

[161] Fforde to Richardson/Hollom, 'Money supply', 26 May 1978, C40/1436.

[162] Goodhart to Fforde 'Monetary woes', 30 May 1978, 6A50/27.

because experience prior to 1971 made it conscious of 'drifting into a state of semi-permanent direct controls'. But the situation was felt to be urgent, and the corset would have to be tight enough to bring growth in £M3 to the lower end of the 8 to 10 per cent target. This was not an alternative to MLR, and a rise in that of 2 per cent was advocated. Any qualms about M3 as aggregate would have to wait until a calmer time.[163] The Governor and Chancellor met on successive days (6–7 June) to discuss the package. In Richardson's opinion, the central problem was to persuade the markets of the consistency of the fiscal and monetary targets. This would require the strongest possible statement on the fiscal side, use of the corset, and the increase in MLR to demonstrate that the administered system was not designed to allow authorities to hold down the rate. It transpired that the Prime Minister was uncertain about the package, wanting to have a low-key announcement with little drama and with the monetary measures announced by the Bank in the normal way. Richardson made it clear that the market would not react well to splitting the package in this manner, and he was strongly opposed to it. Neither would he want to proceed with the corset without the MLR rise.[164] The package was announced by Healey in a statement on 8 June 1978. It included an increase in MLR from 9 to 10 per cent and the reintroduction of SSDs. Allowed growth in IBELs was 4 per cent over six months, with subsequent extensions of the scheme specifying 1 per cent per month.[165] Initially, during this third phase, the total deposits involved and the number of banks remained small (see Table 13.1).

There was a change in MLR on 4 April 1979 from 13 to 12 per cent. This is potentially interesting for the light it might throw on how changes were being made at the end of our period. Labour lost a vote of confidence on 28 March, and a general election was called for 3 May. The Bank would have taken the initiative as usual and recommended the change. But could the government in which no confidence had been placed sanction the rise? Should they have consulted the Opposition? The Permanent Secretary could not remember, and there are no papers to tell us.

Monetary base control was still being discussed. In March 1978, the *Economic Journal* published the Duck and Sheppard article. Goodhart was still dismissive: 'I think that this is a silly idea', he told David Walker, Chief

---

[163] Goodhart to Richardson/Hollom, 6 June 1978, enc. Bank of England, 'The financial situation', 6 June 1978, 6A50/27.

[164] Battishill, 9 and 12 June 1978, notes of meetings held at 11 Downing Street on 6 and 7 June 1978, C40/1437.

[165] Bank of England, Press notices, 8 June and 17 August 1978, 5A149/8, 3 April 1979, 5A149/9.

of EID.[166] He wanted to submit a rejoinder but was told that there were more important things to do. Despite this, he and Richard Coghlan (EID) worked in their own time to draft a reply. By May, Goodhart was again writing to Walker, but with a slightly different emphasis:

Monetary base control is an important question. Many outsiders, ranging from the IMF, through the EEC onto Pepper, believe that the adoption of monetary base control would somehow make our operations much easier and more effective. The Governor worries about this; he asked me again about it the other day.

There would, he said, be continuing pressure for the Bank to reveal its thinking.[167] Indeed, the Duck and Sheppard piece was picked up on with approval by Samuel Brittan in *The Financial Times*. Brittan wrote, 'Like most promising proposals, this one is basically simple.... This is basically a cash ratio system with modifications.'[168] Fforde was against a rigid base money control system, but surprisingly, Dow came out in favour, or at least he thought that the case against was not proven, and it should be given serious consideration. He was particularly attracted to the apparently stronger control and the quicker monetary policy adjustments offered.[169] In 1978, EID produced an article on monetary base for the *Bulletin*. The stance was still sceptical. Indeed, Fforde offered 'profound sympathy' for anyone who had to be immersed in the subject for very long.[170]

Open Market Operations

In his 1977 'magnum opus', Goodhart noted that while the authorities had been able to make substantial gilt sales over the years, such sales could not, and had not been intended to, achieve short-term monetary smoothing. This was so because the tap method of selling, the fact that the authorities preferred to follow the lead of the market, and that the Government Broker had to wait to be approached by bidders resulted in periods of intense activity interspersed by slack ones as market expectations changed; expansionary bank lending and PSBR would be likely to lead to expectations of higher interest rates in

---

[166] Goodhart to Walker, 'A proposal for the control of the UK money supply', 28 February 1978, 6A10/1.

[167] Goodhart to Walker, 'The monetary base and other friends', 26 May 1978, 6A10/1.

[168] Duck and Sheppard (1978); *The Financial Times*, 15 June 1978, p. 21.

[169] 'Monetary management: an assessment of the problems and a programme for improvement', nd, but enclosed with Fforde to Richardson/Hollom, 6 July 1978, 6A10/1; Dow, 'Reflections on monetary control', 11 July 1978, C40/1438.

[170] Draft, 'Monetary base control', filed as 25 September 1978; Fforde to Goodhart, 'Monetary base control', 26 September 1978, 6A10/2.

the future, a situation not conducive to gilt sales. As a consequence, there was a 'structural bias' against the authorities because it was 'broadly easiest to sell gilts when there is no need to do so to smooth the course of the monetary aggregates, and vice versa'. The adoption of a publicly announced monetary target would exacerbate the problem because any deviation in the aggregate above the intended path would lead to the view that the authorities would have to raise interest rates/gilt sales to check the upward movement. People thus would be less likely to buy gilts, causing the initial deviation to worsen – 'an automatically destabilising system'. He then considered the catalogue of amendments to operational techniques and new instruments that had been suggested and to sales by tender. He was sceptical on the latter, although he did not rule out an experiment at the short end. The conclusion was firmer in expressing 'serious doubts about adopting the main suggestions advocated, especially that of switching to a tender system, for altering the authorities' methods of operations'. He hoped that the recent innovations would help to smooth and control the pattern of debt sales and that these should be given a chance before embarking on more radical changes.[171] A year later, when reviewing developments, Goodhart found that part-paid issues had been a useful aid but conceded that variable-rate bonds had been less successful as a smoothing mechanism than had been hoped.[172]

Throughout 1977 the authorities continued to worry about gilt sales.[173] Part of the problem was that the market was unsure about exchange-rate policy, but there were also concerns about pay settlements and monetary growth. With such uncertainty, investors were unable to determine the yield at which they should invest. The new instruments and techniques were intended to remove some of these uncertainties.[174] The partly paid stock had part of the subscription paid at the time of application and the balance at times to suit the expected funding needs of government. It was introduced following the heavy oversubscriptions of issues and was intended to smooth the flow of funds from outside the banking system and subsequently proved to be a successful adaptation.[175]

---

[171] Goodhart to Richardson/Hollom, 26 April 1977, enc. 'Proposals for improving monetary control', C40/1432.

[172] Goodhart to Fforde, "Proposals for improving monetary control': a note on subsequent developments", 27 April 1978, C40/1436.

[173] Mullens, Note, 17 June 1977, C40/1433.

[174] George to Fforde/Richardson/Hollom, 'The gilt-edged market', 29 June 1977; Page to Richardson/Hollom, Gilt-edged market', 22 July 1977, 3A92/6; HMT, Notes of meetings held at 10 Downing Street on 5 and 26 July 1977; Bridgeman to PPS, 12 and 25 July 1977; Mullens, Note, 25 July 1977, C40/1433.

[175] Bank of England, *Annual Report*, year ending February 1978, p. 9; *BEQB* 19(2):140, June 1979.

Another feature of this period was the high level of ministerial interest, even interference, in the gilt-edged market. Treasury officials engaged in more detailed briefing about required sales and new issues, and ministers became involved in questions about operations and instruments, and even what statistical information should be published.[176] In particular, there were frequent interventions from Lever. When he discussed gilt-edged with the Bank in November 1977, he accused the Bank of unsettling the market by being over-anxious about the money stock; it should, he said, try and avoid the impression of a nervous cat waiting to pounce.[177] Since the advent of the published target, there certainly was a greater preoccupation with the level of gilt sales necessary to meet the target, and not only in the Bank. The Prime Minister and the Chancellor were both kept informed, and they took a keen interest in what were operational rather than policy matters.

Callaghan wanted to know, in January 1978, why the Bank had not been achieving gilt sales in recent weeks; he was told that uncertainty had put the market in a stupor, and there was no scope for significant sales.[178] By May, Healey was wondering whether the framework of the gilt-edged market could be altered to make public-sector financing more certain. He complained that institutional holders had the freedom to manage their portfolios 'without regard for the national interest'.[179] The concerns were raised because sales had been low (and nothing for five consecutive days), and the latest available monthly figure was more than £100 million below the £500 million average required. The prospect of forcing investors into gilts appalled the Bank, and as Fforde pointed out, it certainly was not what was in mind when the Bank had advocated published monetary targets. The matter was raised again by Healey in early June when he told Richardson that the Prime Minister had expressed disquiet about the failure of institutions to invest in gilts, and he wanted the Governor to intervene with leading brokers and fund managers. Richardson warned that a direct approach

---

[176] For example, Couzens to PPS, 3 November 1976, C40/1430; Bridgeman to Couzens, 15 December 1976, 3A92/5; Battishill to Wicks, 27 October 1977; Bridgeman to PPS, 1 November 1977, 3A92/6. This related to the monthly publication of data; Battishill, 'Note of a meeting … 15 August 1978'; George to Bridgeman, 6 September 1978, C40/1439; George to Fforde/Richardson, 'Monthly publication of central government debt sales', 11 October 1978, C40/1440.

[177] Fforde to Richardson/Hollom, 'Meeting with the Chancellor of the Duchy of Lancaster', 9 November 1977, C40/1435.

[178] Bridgeman to PPS, 13 December 1977, 3A92/6; George to Fforde/Richardson, 'MLR and gilt-edged', 5 January 1978; Bridgeman to PPS, 26 January 1978, 3A92/7.

[179] Battishill, 'Note of a meeting … 17 May at 6.15 p.m.', May 1978; Healey to Wass, 17 May 1978, C40/1436.

would be unprecedented, counter-productive, and a sign of weakness.[180] The Bank remained adamant that innovation in debt management could not alone remedy the situation; reducing the PSBR would be a more convincing sign of the government's intent than any monetary measure.[181] Lever continued to press his own particular views, and another review of operations, including a wider investigation into control of monetary aggregates, was agreed on.[182] The 'Monetary Control Review' would be a major policy reassessment following in line from the Bridgeman Report of 1975 and the Bank's own investigations during 1976–77.[183]

Healey queried whether the present funding arrangements 'are capable of meeting the needs of the situation with the degree of flexibility and sophistication now required' and observed that countries such as the United States, Germany, and France did not appear to have the same institutional and procedural difficulties. He then set out the main areas of concern, which included avoiding swings in the money supply, inflexibility in marketing stocks, the refusal to use tenders, and the reluctance to develop new instruments. Perhaps he was unaware of the paperwork that had already been generated in the Bank and the Treasury on these subjects, but whatever, a new report had to be produced.[184]

While ministers had been getting agitated, Fforde had written one of his classic notes entitled, 'Some Obiter Dicta, Old and New, on Gilt-Edged'. On the present system of debt management, he wrote: 'Awkward though it at times may be, the established selling technique had in practice enabled the continuous and at times huge need of H.M.G., stretching over many years, to be met successfully.' But published commitments on money supply, DCE, and PSBR represented an 'intent to do something' if they were not being met. This brought problems. The stress of the impasse, he argued, produced

---

[180] Fforde to Richardson/Hollom, 'Money supply', 26 May 1978, C40/1436; Battishill, 'Note of meeting … 6th June, 1978', 9 June 1978, C40/1437.

[181] Page, 'The financial situation', 2 June 1978, 3A92/7; Bank of England, 'The financial situation', 6 June 1978, 6A50/27. This was a draft paper intended for the Chancellor that does not appear to have been sent.

[182] Nigel Wicks (HMT) to Jones (HMT), 30 May 1978 (two letters); Bridgeman to Page, 1 June 1978, enc. 'Gilt-edged market. Note by Bank and Treasury officials'; Battishill to Wicks, 2 June 1978; Lever to Healey, 9 June 1978; Wicks to Jones, 12 June 1978, 3A92/7. Lever had long-held misgivings on the way in which the authorities operated in the market; for example, see Fforde to Richardson/Hollom, 'Meeting with the Chancellor of the Duchy of Lancaster', 9 November 1977, 6A50/24.

[183] Wicks to Battishill, 22 June 1978; Bridgeman to Wiggins, 23 June 1978, 3A92/7; Healey to Wass, 28 June 1978; Wass to Richardson, 29 June 1978, C40/1437; Richardson to Wass, 5 July 1978, C40/1438.

[184] Healey to Wass, 28 June 1978, C40/1437.

criticism of the underlying techniques and led to suggestions to introduce new types of stock, lowering prices, and engaging in direct dialogue with large investors. In a typical Fforde analogy, he continued:

> Meantime, the pianists, who are accustomed to being shot but still havn't [*sic*] learnt to enjoy it, urge that it would be wrong to damage or destroy their instrument, to no lasting purpose, for it may be needed again very soon. These pianists cried, 'how please do you think you can dispel uncertainties about your borrowing requirement by either "gimmicks and cosmetics", or "suddenly selling stock for whatever it will fetch", or "creating an expectation that the fight against inflation will in the end be given up" (indexation), or "arm-twisting"?' Moreover, the pianists might suggest to higher authority: 'don't you think that part of the problem is due to your expressing your monetary objective in terms of an erratic and wayward statistic [M3] whose month by month performance relates far too directly to official operations in gilt-edged and is far too prone to upset market nerves?'

But above all, Fforde wanted to avoid an overt political confrontation between the government and institutional investors that might lead to 'de facto "direction" of the institutions "in the public interest" and to "managed financing" of the CGBR (central government borrowing requirement)'. For Fforde, this would be a 'political nightmare that would end in fewer gilts being sold, and at lower prices, than under the present system'.[185]

Prime Ministerial unease continued, and in mid-September, Callaghan again suggested that there should be a seminar.[186] Bank and Treasury officials understood that the Prime Minister's criticisms of gilt-edged tactics actually were those of a young economist and No. 10 Adviser, Gavyn Davies. When Bridgeman and Eddie George (Deputy Chief Cashier with responsibility for the gilt-edged market) met Davies, they discovered that he fully accepted the Bank's general arguments, but what had dissatisfied Callaghan was the feeling that not much could be done to increase and smooth debt sales. Callaghan, said Davies, would be irritated by any further crises in the funding programme and likely to seek some form of external investigation into gilt operations. Bridgeman and George agreed that a public airing of the issues might be useful, perhaps through some sort of 'green paper'. This, they suggested, could be the projected *Bulletin* article, an idea put forward by Fforde in June 1978 and something that he had just reiterated to Richardson.[187] The extended debate on gilts was dropped

---

[185] Fforde to Richardson/Hollom, 'Some obiter dicta, old and new, on gilt-edged', 13 June 1978, 3A92/7.

[186] Wicks to Battishill, 17 October 1978, 3A92/8.

[187] George to Page/Fforde/Richardson/Hollom, 'The Prime Minister's views on gilt-edged instruments and techniques', 31 October 1978; Bridgeman to Page, 31 October 1978;

because of the more pressing matters, notably the need to discuss the extension of the monetary target.[188] In any case, the subsequent increase in MLR, from 10 to 12.5 per cent, restored the market and allowed substantial sales. Nevertheless, it was evident that a significant amount of gilts would still have to be sold for the remainder of the year and beyond.[189]

One feature of the later years of the decade was that tap stocks were, on several occasions, oversubscribed. For example, the early weeks of January 1977 were 'one of the most dramatic' in the history of the market.[190] A new short was almost twice oversubscribed, the long tap was exhausted within four days, and its replacement was offered in the unprecedentedly high quantity of £1,250 million. Two months later, there were applications totalling over £3,000 million for £800 million of 12¼% Exchequer Stock 1992. Other instances followed, but the most infamous occurred in February 1979 in what became known variously as the 'Battle of Watling Street' or the 'New Change Riots'. Two stocks were involved: a medium, £500 million of 13¼% Exchequer Stock 1987 and a long, £800 million of 13¾% Treasury Stock 2000/2003. The respective applications amounted to £3,817 million and £5,212 million. Such was the volume that the doors at New Change were closed at 10.01 a.m., and not everyone was able to lodge their applications, even those who were already in the building. Afterwards, the Bank received a host of complaints from disgruntled brokers, and two firms made an official complaint to the Council for the Securities Industry. This appeal was unsuccessful, and the Bank remained firmly unapologetic about the situation, arguing among other things that it could not be expected to cope with a large number of applicants who wanted to wait until the last minute to submit.[191] Nigel Althaus of gilt-edged brokers Pember and Boyle and later the Government Broker told Page that the Bank was in some sense asking for all that it got; he found it 'difficult to resist [the] impression that you are encouraging speculation to help you float your issues', something he found 'undignified'.[192] More than a decade later, the chaos of the battle came

Fforde to Richardson/Hollom, 'Debt management', 2 November 1978, 3A92/8; Fforde to Richardson/Hollom, 'Some obiter dicta, old and new, on gilt-edged', 13 June 1978, 3A92/7; Bridgeman to Wass, 1 November 1978, 7A174/4.

[188] T. P. Lankester (Callaghan's PS), 'Note of a meeting … 8 November 1978', 10 November 1978, 7A174/4.

[189] Page to Fforde/Richardson/Hollom, 'Issue Department portfolio', 15 November 1978; Bridgeman to Healey PPS, 16 November 1978; David Green to Page, 'Gilt sales for the year October 1978–October 1979', 17 November 1978, 3A92/8.

[190] Mullens, Note, 14 January 1977, C40/1431.

[191] Council for the Securities Industry, Press statement, 15 March 1979, and other papers in 7A356/9.

[192] Althaus to Page, 25 July 1979, 3A92/10.

to be seen by one observer as the inevitable outcome of 25 years of official intervention. In the Bank's attempts to achieve orderly markets, they had frequently acted too late and in the end produced the greatest disorder.[193]

While in public the Bank was unmoved by the furor, privately there was some thinking about the wider implications. Shortly afterwards, Brian Quinn (who succeeded Morgan as press officer) advised Fforde that the episode had been used as a pretext for the press to reopen the debate on a range of questions on monetary control. He wanted the Bank to take a more active approach in these debates and suggested a programme of publishing articles and documents, speeches, and dinners with selected journalists, commentators, and academics.[194] The planned *Bulletin* article on the gilt-edged market duly appeared in June 1979, largely the work of George. In addressing the criticisms of external observers, the article was a defence of existing methods and not an agenda for change.[195]

Monetary Control

In mid-June 1978, Fforde told Richardson that the Bank should be embarking on a wide-ranging review of monetary policy. He highlighted key strands that distilled views that the Bank had been formulating: the phasing out of the existing reserve-asset ratio and its replacement with a small cash ratio for all banks and new prudential guidance on banking liquidity, substitution of M1 for M3 as the main published target (this would distance management of the gilts market from short-run variations in the target aggregate), and public argument for the retention of the present system of marketing gilts but with the possible addition of a new short (6 to 24 months) instrument.[196] Fforde expressed 'the sharp unease and dissatisfaction which we feel with the current state of monetary affairs'. He highlighted that the move to a published target in 1976 had not been thought to imply a marked change in the method of control or in the control variable itself, but 'experience now suggests that this thought was wrong'.

---

[193] Pepper (1991).

[194] Quinn to Fforde, 'The debate on monetary control', 8 March 1979, 3A38/5.

[195] 'The gilt-edged market', *BEQB* 19(2):137–148, June 1979. The Treasury saw a draft and was largely content; Littler to Fforde, 21 May 1979, 3A92/9. Comments on the article were received from City experts on gilt-edged operations; for example, see, Nigel Althaus (Pember and Boyle) to Page, 25 July 1979, 3A92/10; John Forsyth (Morgan Grenfell) to Goodhart, 16 July 1979, C40/1445.

[196] Fforde to Page, 'Domestic monetary arrangements', 16 June 1978; Fforde to Richardson/Hollom, 'Monetary control (your meeting on Wednesday this week)', 22 June 1978, C40/1437.

The Bank, argued Fforde, was well aware of the defects of M3 ('analytic and statistical linkage with other macroeconomic quantities was excellent, but its behavioural characteristics as a control variable were strikingly poor') but had proceeded in the hope that things would improve, the target would be hit, PSBR pressure would be reduced, and the market would live with the erratic behaviour of M3, but it had not proved to be the case. While previous reviews of monetary policy had maintained the status quo, he said that it was now time to change the arrangements. This meant the control variable or the methods of control: the latter could not be solely relied on, so most serious attention had to be given to the former.[197] Fforde still found time to respond to a Goodhart piece advocating a move to M1 that in classic Fforde style ranged over Keynesianism, monetarism, and even pre-Copernican astronomy.[198]

From this developed a programme of work agreed by the Bank and the Treasury as part of the Monetary Control Review. It covered the relevance of respective monetary aggregates; control systems, in particular monetary base, and the future of the reserve-asset ratio system; the implications of a British commitment to move to any European agreement on exchange rates; and technical issues such as developing a broader aggregate for money (to be called M5) that would encompass, for instance, building societies.[199] A synopsis of this work was compiled at the end of 1978. The review had proceeded largely at the instigation of the Bank, with Treasury officials disinclined to present anything to ministers. However, sufficient work was undertaken, mainly with Middleton, to confirm that strong differences of opinion still existed over the rationale for monetary targets and the appropriate choice of aggregate. The Treasury was wedded to £M3; the Bank was suggesting M1 and M5, even though there were definitional and statistical problems outstanding with the latter.[200] Away from this review, the Bank's stance was slightly different, with Richardson telling the Wilson Committee

---

[197] Fforde to Richardson/Hollom, 'Monetary control', 6 July 1978, enc. 'Monetary management: an assessment of the problems and a programme for improvement', C40/1438.

[198] Goodhart to Fforde, 'Justifying M1', 26 June 1978, 6A50/27; Fforde to Goodhart, 'Justifying M1 (further thoughts following your note of 26.6.78)', 28 June 1978, C40/1437.

[199] Michael Foot (EID), 'The Monetary Control Review: The Governor's meeting of 12 July and matters arising', 21 July 1977, 6A10/1; Fforde to Littler, 24 July 1978; Bridgeman to Wass 'Monetary control: The gilts market' 24 July 1978 C40/1438.

[200] Goodhart to Fforde, 'Monetary control review: Treasury papers', 28 September 1978, 6A10/2; Goodhart, Note for record – 'Monetary control review: progress report', 5 October 1978; Foot to Fforde, 'Policy issues arising out of the monetary control review', 20 October 1978; Fforde to Richardson/Hollom, 'The review of monetary control', 20 December 1978; Foot, 'The review of monetary control', 20 December 1978, 6A10/3.

that £M3 was the best general indicator, although not the only one, and that the instruments for monetary control were adequate.[201]

Towards the end of 1978, consideration was turning again to a new monetary target – that for banking year to April 1979 was the range 8 to 12 per cent. The discussion still was in terms of incomes policy tackling inflation and monetary growth being set in relation to these forecasts. However, while monetary growth of 8 to 12 per cent would be consistent with the forecast for nominal incomes, problems might arise in relation to the PSBR and gilt sales. Forecasts were not good for the six months ahead, but it was decided to stay with the 8 to 12 per cent range.[202] This was felt to be credible if supported by immediate monetary measures, and MLR was increased on November 10 from 10 to 12½ per cent, a move explained as reflecting rises in short-term rates overseas and uncertainties about the domestic monetary outlook. Industrial unrest during the 'winter of discontent' also added to pressures. Market rates rose, with the Treasury bill rate actually going above MLR. Richardson warned that not to increase MLR would create the impression that monetary policy was weakening. Accordingly, it went to 14 per cent on 8 February 1979.[203] By now, inflation forecasts for 1979/80 were looking gloomier at 10½ to 12 per cent rather than the 9 per cent of 1978/79. Not only that, but the Bank was pessimistic about gilt sales. However, given the rise in interest rates, a growth of £M3 of 10 per cent was forecast. There was therefore a case for reducing the monetary target from 8 to 12 per cent to perhaps 6½ to 10½ per cent, but this was by no means clear-cut.[204] Short-term rates then quickly began to fall, and only three weeks after the rise to 14 per cent, MLR was reduced to 13 per cent, with the Bank stating that it wanted to see some stability. To reinforce this, it engaged in one-week lending to the discount market. However, the strength of sterling and further downward pressure on short-term rates resulted in another cut, to 12 per cent, in early April.[205] By this time, Callaghan had lost a vote of confidence in the Commons, and an election had been called.

---

[201] Loehnis to Richardson/Hollom, 'Wilson Committee. Transcript of oral evidence', 13 December 1978, 5A203/3.

[202] Goodhart to Richardson/Hollom, 'The roll-over to a new monetary target', 2 November 1978, 6A50/28.

[203] Bridgeman to Page, 3 November 1978; Battishill, 'Note of a meeting ... 6 November, 1978', 7 November 1978, C40/1441; Bank of England, Press notice, 9 November 1978, C40/1397; Richardson to Healey, 5 February 1979; Bank of England, Press notice, 8 February 1979, C40/1398.

[204] Goodhart to Fforde/Richardson/Hollom, 'Monetary policy and the budget', 16 March 1979, 6A50/29.

[205] Bank of England, Press notices, 1 March and 5 April 1979, C40/1398.

Thought was already being given in the Bank to what a Conservative Government might mean for monetary policy. The experience of 1971–73 had left many Conservatives suspicious about the Bank. Furthermore, the fact that they had specialist advisers with expertise in the monetary field (Pepper and Griffiths, for example) might make for a more difficult relationship. But it was thought unlikely that there would be any great difference in macroeconomic policy between a Conservative Government and that of Labour, who, since 1976, were seen as having 'effectively adopted a Conservative-type policy'. One difference was that the Conservatives believed that monetary policy could be used to control inflation, and they were certainly pledged to continuing with monetary targets. There was recognition of the fact that several of the advisers were 'theoretically committed to monetary base control in one version or another', and it was clear that the Bank would have to argue its case on that clearly.[206] Much of that case was already in preparation as draft *Bulletin* articles on gilts (George) and monetary base control (Goodhart, Foot, and Hotson). The latter, which was published in June 1979, was opposed to the monetary-base proposals, although it did tend to attack the more extreme version of the scheme, but Walker's main suggestion was that they could 'drive a further nail into the coffin' by showing that there was no evidence for the view 'that there is a strong causal relationship between high powered money and nominal incomes, adding that causality is almost certainly right-left'.[207] When Professor J. R. Sargent (then group Economic Adviser at Midland Bank) addressed the problems of monetary targeting and advocated monetary-base control, an indication of the antipathy found Goodhart writing to Fforde, 'I had thought Dick Sargent more sensible than this,' and Fforde repling, 'Yes, so did I. But his economics has always been very "mechanistic" – or at least it was when we were contemporaries at Oxford.'[208]

A fortnight after the election, Pepper told Prime Minister Margaret Thatcher that the Bank had been studying monetary base control for some time and was planning an article for the *Bulletin*. Thatcher hoped that the Treasury would give urgent consideration to this work, and she also asked Chancellor Geoffrey Howe for his views.[209] The immediate outcome of this was a high-level seminar, held on 18 July, attended by the Prime Minister,

---

[206] Goodhart to Fforde 'Monetary policy under a Conservative government', 3 April 1979, 6A50/29.

[207] Walker to Goodhart, 'Revised monetary base control paper', 18 May 1979, 6A10/4.

[208] Goodhart to Fforde, 'Yet more on monetary base', 8 May 1979, and Fforde, Annotation, 9 May 1979, 6A10/4.

[209] Lankester to Battishill, 18 May 1979, 6A10/4.

Treasury ministers, senior Whitehall officials, and the Governor and Chief Cashier. In addition to monetary base, monetary objectives and prospects and the gilt-edged market were also discussed. The seminar generated a mountain of paper and on monetary base specifically included the Bank's assessments of the recent contributions on the subject, such as those by Pepper, Griffiths, and Geoffrey Wood.[210] At the seminar, Richardson said that they were proposing the abolition of reserve-asset ratio control. He claimed to have an open mind on monetary base: current methods of controlling the money supply were imperfect, but while monetary base might be better, it would also involve major structural changes. Summing up, the Prime Minister said that the Bank and Treasury should jointly undertake a more detailed study of monetary-base control for possible publication and consultation. This work resulted in a green paper the following year.[211]

It is clear that around the middle of 1979 a greater urgency entered the discussion of hitting the target, doubtless a consequence of the new government's determination to use targets to achieve their inflation objectives. And despite the new government's distaste for such things, there was also a contemplation of returning to a greater use of direct controls in an attempt at ensuring that the monetary target was hit.[212] In June, Howe and Richardson discussed the worrying figures on money-supply growth, bank lending to the private sector, and government borrowing. Richardson and Howe agreed that MLR should be increased by 2 per cent, to 14 per cent, the following day. It was the only possible response to money-supply figures moving outside the target range. In the evening, the Governor and the Chancellor called on the Prime Minister, who was worried about the likely repercussions on mortgage rates. But Richardson and Howe were insistent: 'Our first use of a monetary policy instrument should be effective and unequivocal.' The Prime Minister remained unconvinced but accepted their advice, and the change was announced on 12 June.[213]

[210] Hotson/Foot, 'Pepper on the monetary base', 5 July 1979; Goodhart, Note for the record – 'Monetary base', 6 July 1979; Foot/Hotson to Fforde, 'Wood on the monetary base', 10 July 1979; Goodhart to Fforde, 'Griffiths on the monetary base', 11 July 1979; Fforde to Richardson/Hollom, 'The seminar on monetary policy', 13 July 1979, 6A10/4.

[211] Lankester, 'Note of the seminar ... 18 July in the Prime Minister's room at the House of Commons', 19 July 1979, 6A10/4. See 8A19/1–2 for work on the green paper.

[212] Bridgeman to George, 'Domestic monetary control and exchange control', 24 September 1979, 6A50/30.

[213] Howe to Thatcher, 6 June 1979; Lankester to Battishill, 7 June 1979; Howe to Thatcher, 11 June 1979; Lankester to Battishill, 11 June 1979; Bank of England, Press notice, 12 June 1979, C40/1398.

Special deposits and SSDs continued to be used in 1979 but were not re-imposed after January 1980.[214] It had been apparent for some time that under the reserve-asset ratio, special deposits were not effective in squeezing bank liquidity and in the short run even had perverse effects.[215] A three-month continuation of SSDs had been announced in April 1979. At this stage, the growth in IBELs had been 5.8 per cent, against the penalty-free limit of 9 per cent, but thereafter the 'corset' began to tighten, and for the first time, clearing banks were liable to make deposits.[216] Another extension, for six-months, was announced in November 1979, but operation of the scheme was threatened by the abolition of exchange controls in October, and assurances were sought from the various banking associations that they would not seek to avoid the effects of SSDs by arranging transactions outside the United Kingdom.[217] In the March 1980 budget, Howe announced that the scheme would be terminated when the present period of operation ended that June.[218] In the final month, clearing banks and their subsidiaries accounted for the bulk of SSDs, £438 million out of £456 million.[219]

An examination of the effects of the corset suggested that movements in M1 and overseas sterling deposits seriously undermined the usefulness of controlling IBELS as a way of securing a given £M3. 'This is not to deny the safety net concept, but rather to emphasize the importance in the construction of the corset of elastic rather than stays.' (Someone who knew about these things wondered if 'whalebone' should be preferred to 'stays'.) Higher-than-forecast bank lending and PSBR were precisely offset by larger-than-forecast debt sales and negative external factors. The conclusion was that the corset was not responsible for the success in hitting the target zone; rather, it was down to 'aggressive gilt-edged marketing policies'. When it came to the crunch, the Bank had to rely on interest rates. And yet, towards the end of the year, there was another change of view. [220]

[214] For details on 1980, see 7A324/1.

[215] Rachel Lomax (HMT) to Monck, 21 May 1981, 7A324/2.

[216] P. T. Heard/N. W. Thompson (EID) to Atkinson/Page, 'Interest-bearing eligible liabilities (IBELs) banking, March', 20 April 1979; D. F. Swords to Ecklin/Page, 'Interest-bearing eligible liabilities (IBELs) banking June', 18 July 1979, 5A149/9.

[217] Bank of England, 'Notice to banks and deposit-taking finance houses: supplementary special deposits', 15 November 1979; John Beverly (Governor's Office), Note for record, 15 November 1979; Lord Armstrong (chairman CLCB) to Richardson, 10 December 1979, 5A149/9.

[218] Goodhart to Fforde/Richardson/McMahon, 'The SSD scheme and the £m3 target in 1980–81', 4 March 1980; Bank of England, Press notice, 26 March 1980, 7A317/1.

[219] T. Brasier (FSD) to Gill, 'Operational interest-bearing eligible liabilities (IBELs): banking, June', 10 July 1980, 5A149/10.

[220] Green to Goodhart, 'The corset and money supply', 25 July 1979, 6A50/30; Green to Page, 'Extension of the corset', 7 November 1979, 6A50/31.

Disillusionment with the corset was more or less complete after the abolition of exchange controls in October 1979 and the increased possibilities for avoidance that that allowed. Nevertheless, abandoning it would produce re-intermediation and rising money-supply figures. More important, though, the Government had to be seen to be serious, Howe argued, about getting control of the money supply. They needed to get the gilt market moving again and moving MLR – 'I am strongly advised that anything less than a move to 16 per cent now would be seen as the action of Canute, and call in question our resolve to adhere to our monetary targets.' Interestingly, he added that the second – the MLR rise – was 'a matter for the Governor'.[221] At about the same time, in November, McMahon was arguing that neither the Bank nor the government could afford to lose credibility at this stage and recommended acting toughly and to keep on acting toughly. He proposed going 'for overkill in interest rate terms'. He hoped that this would mean no more than 2 per cent on the following Thursday, but at the same time as that change, an announcement should be made that the corset was being allowed to lapse. He also suggested confessing that monetary growth had been unacceptably high and that new methods of monetary control would be found.[222] MLR went to 17 per cent later that month.

Discussion became more heated and complicated by personnel changes towards the end of the year. A draft of an article in a publication (*Economic Outlook*) of the London Business School was sent to the Treasury in October 1979. The piece went under the name of Alan Budd but was joint work with Terry Burns. The article set out confidently forecasts of inflation, real output growth, and a demand for money function. It included specific numerical targets for future monetary growth based on these. Goodhart objected in the strongest terms, and exchanges followed before the *Economic Outlook* was published on 26 November 1979 after Goodhart had been satisfied that it had been 'successfully neutered'. But this, together with other influences on the Chancellor, marked the beginning of medium-term thinking on inflation and targets.[223]

As Executive Director in the 1970s, Fforde was central to the Bank's position on domestic monetary policy. Having played 'a leading part in British monetary affairs for more than three decades', he retired as Executive Director (Home Finance) in 1982.[224] Pragmatism was perhaps his hallmark. He was forthright in his views and put them across forcefully

---

[221] Howe to Thatcher, 'Monetary policy', 9 November 1979, 6A50/31.
[222] McMahon to Richardson/Hollom, 'Monetary measures', 6 November 1979, 6A50/31.
[223] Draft letter, Goodhart to Budd, 24 October 1979, 6A50/31.
[224] *The Guardian*, 10 May 2000, p. 22.

and stuck to his arguments. His work at the Bank laid the foundations for future advances in the Bank's capacity for economic and monetary analysis. He could at times lose the reader in his over-embellished and complicated writing style. On a personal note, he was a rather reserved man but had a wry sense of humour and helped his younger and less experienced colleagues. As the Governor, Eddie George recalled, he inspired 'not just respect but great affection'.[225] Alongside Fforde in terms of centrality to monetary policy was Charles Goodhart. He was really at the centre of all that the Bank did on monetary policy from the time he joined the Bank in the late 1960s to the end of our period. Across these years he provided the Bank with its main intellectual power and marked the real beginning of the Bank building its own economics team. Although he returned to academic life in the mid-1980s, he remained close to the Bank, acting as an adviser and being a founder member of the Monetary Policy Committee set up in 1997.

Conclusion

Although there was much discussion on the detail of monetary instruments and agonising over what monetary policy was, there is less evidence of a belief that monetary policy mattered. When Wass gave a lecture to the Johnian Society in Cambridge in 1978 on the problems of economic management, he was no more than lukewarm on monetary targeting. He remained sceptical on the relationship between money and prices, but he thought that sensibly applied targets could give assurance to the markets about the authorities' intentions. 'But such targets need to be viewed intelligently by both the authorities and those in the markets reacting to them, if they are to help rather than hinder sensible economic management.'[226] If Wass was sceptical, Healey was cynical. He was fond of saying that the great advantage he took to the Treasury was never having studied economics. On money, he wrote that no one had found an adequate definition of it, and no one knew how to control it. Worse, monetary statistics were unreliable.[227] 'I have never met a private or central banker who believed the monetarist mumbo-jumbo', he went on, but if markets believed it, then you could not ignore it. 'In order to satisfy the markets, I began to publish the monetary forecasts we had always made in private, and then described them as targets.'[228]

---

[225] *The Old Lady*, June 2000, p. 84.
[226] Wass (1978, p. 100).
[227] Healey (1989, p. 382).
[228] *Ibid.*, p. 434.

Given the reluctance with which the Bank accepted the need to adopt targets, a legitimate question is, what did they do to achieve them? Interested parties certainly were not sure that enough was being done. Following the IMF seminar in the Bank in May 1977, two members of their team (Ed Brau and Adalbert Knöbl) told Price that although publicly announced targets were in place, the Bank seemed to have done little or nothing to ensure that they were met. Price countered, somewhat less than convincingly, that a number of innovations had been made such as part-paid and variable-rate issues, and consideration was being given to other unspecified developments. Brau asked Price at what kinds of meetings targets were discussed, who took the decisions, and on what basis were decisions made. Price played the traditional straight bat, giving nothing away, but the IMF team were left believing that Bank procedures were 'very loose'. Fforde reported a similar 'going over' from Finch. Fforde accepted that greater use could be made of M1 but said that weekly figures for bankers' balances had no useful meaning in this context and that note circulation might or might not tell anything of significance. He concluded: 'Over-concentration by monetarists on short-term movements in an unreliable aggregate sometimes causes them to be taken for a ride by enthusiastic non-monetarists.'[229]

At times, it is hard to tell where confusion left off and willful misunderstanding took over. It is not really clear what the Bank's view on monetary control was. There were differences within the Bank and changing positions. Despite a long history of sound money, there was also an anti-monetarism and a determination to resist anything that could be interpreted as being monetarist. There was a growing concern with the path of aggregate money after 1971. However, if the growth of the money supply was the net outcome of the Bank's actions in the money market, the gilt-edged market, and the foreign-exchange market, then there should be some evidence that they were operating in these markets to achieve the desired results. Critics felt that there was insufficient such evidence. Interest rates were supposed to do the bulk of the work, but given that for most of the decade it was politically unacceptable for these to rise above certain nominal levels, SSDs were used to achieve the objectives. As we have shown, they could not succeed.

Despite undoubted progress in the Bank in keeping abreast of developments in academic economics, the discussion on money and inflation still ignored several important elements that were available at the time. The question that frequently crops up is, why were better models not employed

---

[229] Fforde to Page/Goodhart/Price/George, 'IMF: monetary base seminar (LDDP's note of May 26)', 27 May 1977, 6A50/22.

when they were available? For example, Thomas Saving had set out the lexicon for monetary policy more than a decade before: instruments, indicators, proximate objectives (targets), and ultimate objectives.[230] This did not inform the discussion on indicators and targets in the Bank. There was also already quite a substantial literature on what a quantity target meant as opposed to a price target. There was a strong case made that an interest-rate target left the price level indeterminate. Poole had shown that if money markets were more prone to unpredictable shocks than goods markets, the authorities should target interest rates, and if the opposite held, they should target the money stock. But a stronger case than this could be made. If price-level stability, rather than nominal income stability, were the ultimate objective, then given some assumptions about expectations, a money-supply rule gives a determinate course for the price level. And there was also a considerable literature on what fixed- and floating-rate regimes meant for monetary policy. None of this entered the discussion.[231]

When Foot presented a paper on the subject of monetary targeting at the end of the 1970s, he rather gave away the Bank's ambivalence. He opened by saying, 'Undoubtedly the major change this decade *in the presentation – if not the aims –* of monetary policy in many advanced economies has been a move away from the pursuit of an interest rate objective to the formal announcement of a target rate of growth for some monetary aggregate' (emphasis added). This captures the lack of belief and commitment. The paper had been through the usual drafting process in the Bank and had been seen at all stages by Goodhart and Fforde.[232] Foot went on to say that those who introduced targets agreed that the prospect of achieving them (other than DCE) had improved after floating released monetary policy from the exchange-rate commitment, that they were strengthening the stance of long-run anti-inflationary policy, but that they were not trying to achieve short-run control of money. There is not much evidence that any of this was true in either 1973 or 1976. Foot's assessment of performance of targets across the countries he examined was judged by simple observation of the rate of growth of money and output before and after adoption of the targets. Most countries failed. Apart from the weakness of the test, though, a problem was that the Bank was choosing a target based on the forecast of money growth. It could be that the monetary tightening that followed the first targets was largely a consequence of the collapse in

---

[230] Saving (1967).
[231] Poole (1970).
[232] Foot (1981, p. 13).

sterling and that when the pound recovered in 1977, interest in monetary aggregates diminished somewhat. In the closing years of the decade, it was still incomes policy that was being used to attack inflation.

The Treasury was arguing that monetary targets could not be discussed without also discussing the conduct of fiscal policy and exchange-rate policy.[233] While monetary growth was seen as the net outcome of the financing of the PSBR and bank lending to the private sector, they stressed that the PSBR was not fiscal policy. The latter could remain unchanged, while for a host of reasons PSBR could change. The Treasury's large macroeconomic model had been used to carry out a number of simulations to test the relationships. And yet, as a commentator pointed out, if the information needed to carry out these exercises existed then, 'we would also know enough to be able to ensure that the level of aggregate demand was always just where we wanted it.'[234]

There is as yet no body of economic history literature on the 1970s, and yet it is surely a decade that will attract more and more attention from economic historians because it appears increasingly to be a major turning point in economic experience, thought, and policy. However, a start has been made and, in particular, a start on the nature and explanation of the inflationary experience. Much of this, of necessity, is on the United States, where the origins of the great inflation are found, although it did not reach its worst levels there.[235] For Britain, the seventies had opened with a floating/managed exchange rate, money supply growing rapidly, and inflation rising. The exchange rate was sliding, and foreign-exchange reserves were inadequate to protect it. In addition, changes in financial markets were accompanied by financial instability. By mid-decade, there was financial crisis, inflation approaching 30 per cent, and high and rising unemployment. The principal focus had been on growth and employment, and a deep scepticism remained about the potency of monetary policy. There seems to have been an overly optimistic view of the potential of the economy as against its performance.

The 1970s was also marked in the Bank by a growing awareness of, and interest in, theoretical developments in monetary economics and a desire to improve the Bank's technical expertise. For example, it was in the early 1970s that the Economic Section of the EID introduced economic forecasting.

---

[233] Middleton et al. (1981).
[234] Laidler, Comments in Griffiths and Wood (1981, pp. 176–180).
[235] See, for example, Blinder and Rudd (2008); DeLong (1997); Meltzer (2004); Gordon (1977); Velde (2004); and for the United Kingdom, see Nelson (2004).

Initial work began in 1973 when the London Business School made available its model.[236] This allowed the Bank's economists to prepare short-term analyses and forecasts of the economy that helped Bank officials discuss with Whitehall economic prospects and policy decisions. By 1977, seven full-time staff were employed in the economic forecasting group, four of whom were economists, and three ancillary staff prepared the data and programmed and operated the model. There was some minor criticism of the doubling up of economic forecasting in the Bank, and the Treasury and the Select Committee on Nationalised Industries suggested that a single forecasting model should be used.[237] The Bank objected that it would not save on resources; it also believed that 'the joint use of one structure would be a serious impediment to the full testing of the results of Bank research work.'[238]

---

[236] Latter, 'Select committee: the Bank's economic model', 16 January 1978, 4A90/3.

[237] SCNI 1976, 'Report', para. 110.

[238] Dow to Dicks-Mireaux, 'The select committee and the Bank's model', 9 December 1976, 4A90/2; Dicks-Mireaux to Dow, 'Select committee. "The Bank's forecasting model"', 24 January 1977, enc. 'Should the Bank have an independent forecasting model?', 4A90/2.

14

The Bank and Sterling in the 1970s

Although the Bank had long had responsibility for the exchange rate, in a sense since the eighteenth century, and from the 1930s it had managed the Exchange Equalisation Account (EEA) on behalf of the Treasury and was steeped in its roles as adviser, as an operator in the foreign-exchange markets, in the 1970s its task was to become less clear and more difficult. The breakdown of the Bretton Woods arrangements, the accompanying upheaval in currencies, sterling's problems as a reserve currency, and the 'overhang' of sterling balances from which the exchange rate could not easily be separated all contributed. As far as the exchange rate went, the Bank was subordinate to the Treasury, although in terms of what could be achieved and how, it still had some freedom and was central to decision making. It took a long time before anything resembling an exchange-rate policy emerged. For the first years of the decade, it was a case of reacting to events, hastily arranged consultations with the Treasury without a view as to what rate was desired or what reserves were wanted or 'needed'. Efforts were concentrated on holding operations while a new system was designed. However, attempts at reform were abandoned in the wake of the oil-price hike of 1973–74. In rudderless Britain, things came to a head in the crisis of 1976. The wildly expansionist policies had failed. The resolution and subsequent improvement in performance had to wait the slow recognition, acceptance, and implementation of the appropriate monetary and fiscal policies. These, adopted under pressure from the International Monetary Fund (IMF) and together with its assistance, helped to restore some confidence, and sterling gradually recovered as the decade closed.

Across the 1970s, the picture on the exchange rate is as gloomy as might be expected given the monetary, financial, and economic turmoil that prevailed. After the upheavals at the beginning of the decade, the nominal rate had settled in early 1973 to about $2.40. There was volatility through 1973,

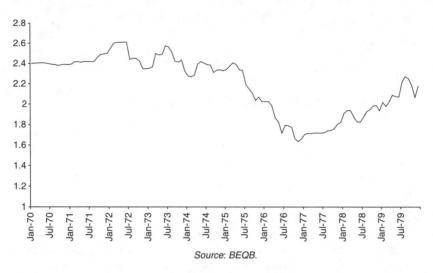

Source: BEQB.

Figure 14.1. £/$ exchange rate, monthly, 1970–79.

but then in 1974 a fairly flat trend of $2.35 occurred. It reached $2.40 again in the first quarter of 1975 before sliding steadily to finish the year just above $2.00. 1976 saw a further slide to a low point of $1.59 in the last week of October. In 1977, it was steady at just above $1.70 until late summer, when it began to rise, and it then surged to over $1.90 in December. There were losses and gains the following year, but it finished the year above $2.00. In 1979, it continued to rise, albeit with greater fluctuations, but finished the period around $2.20 (Figure 14.1). The volatility in the decade was perhaps no more than to be expected from a recently introduced 'floating' regime.

Of course, the story of sterling cannot be told in isolation. The exchange rate is a relative price, and much of what happened can be explained by reference to other currencies and especially to the US dollar. Soon after the float, the Bank began to calculate an effective exchange rate that took account of a basket of major trading partners' currencies on a trade-weighted basis. From the middle of 1973, greater emphasis was placed on this rate, but being a rate that was not observed or traded meant that it had little appeal to the public or the press.[1] The rate was made available three times a day through news agencies, and the series and method of calculation were published in the *Bulletin*.[2] The rate captured the movement (largely a depreciation) since

[1] Hallett to Richardson, 'The dollar/sterling relationship', 15 May 1974, C43/786; Bank of England, *Annual Report*, year ending February 1974, p. 19.
[2] Thornton to Hallett/McMahon, 'Continuous publication of the "effective depreciation"', 4 January 1974; Hallett to Hedley-Miller, 8 March 1974. The Chancellor wanted the

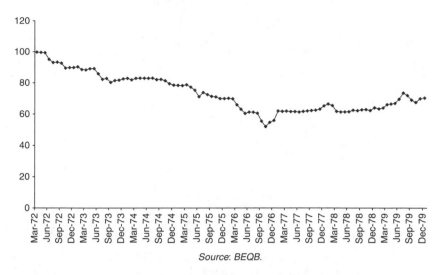

Source: BEQB.

Figure 14.2. Effective exchange rate, monthly, 1972–79.

the Smithsonian Agreement (Figure 14.2), a contentious point because, as Sangster argued, it gave the Smithsonian rate an unwarranted validity.[3] The model used by both the Bank and the Treasury took account of the price elasticities of traded goods and the elasticity of substitution between any two supplying countries.[4] However, it was based solely on visible trade weights, from only 11 countries, and used 1969 data. The calculation was revised in March 1977, with additional countries and new weights derived from 1972 figures, and it was then given as an index number.[5] Across the decade, it moved from 100 in December 1971 to around 70 in 1979, equivalent to a fall of about 4 per cent per annum.

Another way of looking at the exchange rate is to take account of the differential price movements in the respective countries and produce a 'real' exchange rate (rather than the nominal one normally quoted; see Figure 14.3). The trend is more or less flat until 1976 and then distinctly upward for the remainder of the decade. At the end, the nominal pound/dollar (£/$)

published rate to be titled the 'World Value of the Pound'; Middleton to Morgan, 8 January 1974, 3A38/4.

[3] Sangster to Hallett/McMahon, 'The effective exchange rate calculation for sterling', 21 December 1973, C43/129; Sangster to Hallett/McMahon/Dow, 'Exchange rate terminology', 30 May 1974, C43/786.

[4] This drew heavily on the work of J. R. Artus and R. R. Rhomberg at the IMF; see Artus and Rhomberg (1973).

[5] 'The "effective" exchange rate for sterling', *Economic Trends* 248:xxix–xxxi, June 1974; Latter to Thornton et al., 'Effective exchange rate', 23 May 1974, 6A119/3; 'Effective exchange rates – revised calculation', *BEQB* 17(1):46, March 1977.

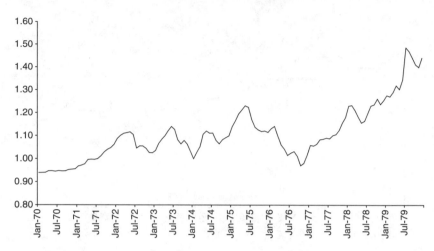

Figure 14.3. £/$ real exchange rate, monthly, 1970–79.
Sources: Bank of England internal calculation.

rate was not far away from its starting point, but British prices had risen much more than those in the United States. The movement in the real £/$ rate was from 1.00 to 1.40; in other words, the deterioration was on the order of 40 per cent in the closing years of the decade.

The Exchange Rate and Exchange-Rate Policy

It is clear in retrospect that the Bretton Woods arrangements had broken down by the beginning of the 1970s. Different dates could be chosen.[6] But there was a reluctance to accept the breakdown at the time, and proposals for reform were circulating that tried to salvage something of the system; some were pursued with greater purpose than others. The Smithsonian Agreement of December 1971 was essentially a holding operation while more serious discussions went on with a view towards reclaiming the system. The meeting of the Group of Ten (G10), plus Switzerland, in Washington on 17–18 December 1971 agreed to a general realignment of currencies. Congressional authority would be sought to raise the dollar value of monetary gold from $35 to $38, an 8 per cent devaluation of the dollar in terms of

---

[6]   Some would put it as early as 1968 and give it a life of only a decade. August 1971 is the strongest candidate, the date when the dollar went off gold. Others put it as late as 1974: 'By March 1974 the structured world of Bretton Woods, with its fixed, if adjustable, exchange rates, was dead' (Dell, 1991, p. 4). The pedantic would place it at April 1978, the date of the second amendment to the Charter allowing the move from fixed to floating rates. See Tew in Kandiah (2002).

gold. The new middle rate for the pound was $2.6057, and the IMF agreed to allow 2.25 per cent fluctuation of a currency against the intervention currency. In late December, the rate for sterling had settled at $2.55/56, but by early February it had risen to $2.61.

Perhaps the Bretton Woods mindset had taken such a hold that policymakers (and others) in the 1970s were gripped by the desire to hold to something like a pegged rate even after the system had gone. An even bolder concept was that of monetary union. The Werner Report of 1969 had carried the idea of monetary union in Europe, and at the beginning of 1972, the principal European countries took a step in that direction when they made the agreement to reduce the fluctuations in their currencies, what became known as the 'snake'. These arrangements quickly unravelled, though. Britain joined the snake on 1 May 1972, membership being seen as showing willingness ahead of joining the European Economic Community (EEC) in January 1973.[7] Membership was a disaster, however. In the second half of 1971, there had been a current account surplus and some optimism, but there was growing concern at the beginning of 1972 that the surplus was disappearing. Even so, through May and into June, the pound remained steady at $2.61. There was, though, persistent industrial strife, and on 15 June when a national dock strike seemed imminent, there was a huge movement out of sterling. There also was the belief that the pound would need to be devalued when Britain officially joined the EEC on 1 January 1973. The outflow of sterling continued over the next week despite huge support. Bank Rate was raised from 5 to 6 per cent on 22 June, but the following morning, Friday, 23 June, an announcement was made that the exchange-rate arrangement was being abandoned.[8] Over the previous week, a total of $2.5 billion had been spent in support. O'Brien was on holiday in Cannes at the time and records, remarkably, how on the day he was planning on returning to London he woke to hear that sterling had been floated the previous day. He was not informed, never mind consulted. It was only later that he learned of the huge losses.[9]

Most of the sterling area countries then severed their exchange-rate links with sterling, and Britain tightened exchange-control measures. It redefined the Scheduled territories to the United Kingdom, the Channel Islands, the Isle of Man, Ireland, and Gibraltar. All others would be treated

[7]   Bank of England, 'Notice to the market', 27 April 1972, 3A38/4.
[8]   HC Deb, 23 June 1972, Vol. 839, cc877–879.
[9]   O'Brien, Memoir, p. 124. Perhaps necessarily, press briefing maintained that the Governor had in fact been kept in touch with developments by telephone. Morgan to Fforde/O'Brien, 30 June 1972, enc. cutting from *Evening Standard*, 3A38/4.

on the same basis as other foreign countries and be subject to the full exchange-control measures. The London foreign-exchange markets were closed and remained so until Tuesday, 27 June. When they re-opened, the pound stood at \$2.41, and at the end of July, it was \$2.44. Thus Britain lasted less than eight weeks in the 'snake'. One factor in the breakdown, as discussed previously, was the preceding monetary expansion in Britain and the United States. US monetary growth powered ahead at the rate of 12 per cent per annum in 1972, and there was little prospect of the new exchange-rate arrangements surviving that. As Meltzer put it, 'The years 1971–73 are among the worst in Federal Reserve history. The Federal Reserve did not "fall into the trap" of excessive expansion under price controls. It entered by choice.'[10]

Following the exit, the Bank stated that 'for the first time since 1939 sterling was floating completely freely.' We will have occasion to consider this assertion more fully in the course of this chapter. The Bank did say that there would be occasional interventions to steady the market.[11] Indeed, a purpose of the EEA was to iron out fluctuations. However, while the pound did float initially, the intention was to return to a fixed or pegged rate when possible. This did not happen.[12] What did evolve was a dirty float for most of the rest of the decade. The 'float' of 1972 was not undertaken as a strategic break with the past. It was simply that there was no other option at the time. There was no clearly thought-out strategy, and as had often been the case, it became simply a matter of reacting to events, but with the underlying intention being to return to a pegged-rate regime before long. The election of a Labour Government less than two years later meant that it would be years before there would be any agreement on what policy should be pursued.

It is fair to say, then, that confusion reigned over exchange-rate policy through much of the 1970s. To some extent, the authorities can be excused on the grounds that the exchange rate was not a prominent policy consideration. In the Keynesian framework, which still predominated, and the elasticity pessimism that derived from the 1930s but still prevailed, exchange-rate adjustments were of doubtful efficacy for employment and the current

---

[10] Meltzer (2009, p. 788).

[11] Bank of England, *Annual Report*, year ending February 1973, pp. 20–21.

[12] Although we say floated, it was really a managed float at best, although one in which it is not clear who was suggesting the rate and why. Nevertheless, it is probably indicative of the way of thinking to note that in the middle of 1973 Dow wrote to McMahon to say that a country such as the United Kingdom should have some idea of what current balance and exchange rate it was aiming at, and 'it should intervene to keep near that rate and not go in for pure floating'; Dow to McMahon, 26 June 1973, 4A112/5.

account.[13] And matters were made worse because the subject was bedevilled by inadequate flows of information, lack of proper discussion within the Bank and between the Bank and the Treasury, and no coherent government policy. The climate in favour of floating was undoubtedly changing at the beginning of the decade, with a vigorous academic debate taking place and widespread discussion in the press. But there was still a strong desire for stability, as was supposedly found in fixed-rate regimes. The 'problem' of sterling continued to be cast in the same old way.[14] Life in the foreign-exchange markets continued as before. The daily foreign-exchange reports carry the same tone – even if they lack the added acid comments of Roy Bridge. The solutions to the 'problem' of sterling are as before: negotiate on sterling balances providing further guarantees and so on; use exchange controls; and continuing discussions on reform of the international monetary system.[15] In the middle of 1972, there was no policy. As the editor of *The Banker* put it at the time, the Bank 'has never put much faith in strategic policy objectives'.[16]

It is useful to bear in mind the structure of the Gold and Foreign-Exchange Office in the Bank and how that might have impinged on operations. The structure was one where the Head of Foreign Exchange had three senior officials immediately beneath him, and below that there was a chief dealer (market-oriented) and a senior dealer (policy-inclined). Below them were the foreign-exchange dealers. Additionally, there was the 'gimlet', who carried policy information from the head/three to the dealers and market information from the dealers back to the heads. In foreign exchange, the head had direct access to the Executive Director and the Governor, bypassing the Chief Cashier. Difficulties arose in terms of communications with the Treasury and was particularly afflicted by the status of those involved, but there was frequent daily contact. The Chancellor and the Governor might well decide on the rate or on how much to spend in support. This would then be communicated to the head, who would then discuss it with one of the three. Tactics then would be discussed, probably involving the chief dealer. The chief dealer would decide how to carry out an operation, say, through brokers or friendly banks, for example. Difficulties could arise, though, at a time of pressure when dealers needed to know what to do from minute to minute.[17] In the Treasury, Peter Harrop felt that they should keep

---

[13] Middleton (2002, pp. 125–126).
[14] *The Banker* 122(557):914–917, July 1972; Solomon (1977, p. 221).
[15] Hallett to Morse, 'Market tactics', 28 October 1971, 3A49/1.
[16] Pringle (1977, p. 30).
[17] Coleby interview with Derrick Byatt, 27 November 1996. I am grateful to former members of these teams for this information.

note of the amount of intervention, but the problem was finding out what it was. 'Although we ask the Bank, we look rather silly if we do so too often as they simply tell us that fresh authority has been given'.[18] This was perhaps another area where the effective rate was of little use.

The intention after June 1972 was to return to some version of the pegged system, and the Committee of Twenty was in the process of being set up to look to a longer horizon. However, soon after the pound came out of the snake, Morse suggested to the Policy Committee in the Bank that there was a need for a study of the strategy and tactics for re-fixing. This was no grand policy design – simply how to get back to the pegged rate, which at that stage stood at $2.45. A working party was duly set up under the chairmanship of Fenton (Chief of Overseas) 'to examine and report on – (1) the advantages and disadvantages of a return to a fixed exchange rate for sterling; (2) the most beneficial circumstances, timing and rate for a return to a fixed rate; (3) the relationship of such a move with other aspects of U.K. policy; and to make recommendations'.[19]

Political factors in favour of re-fixing included forthcoming membership in the EEC and Britain's adherence to the principles of the par value system and its advocacy of monetary reform. External political pressure generally was aimed at keeping the rate above $2.40. There were economic constraints, too, in the high and rising inflation. The working party also considered what to do, having chosen a rate, in terms of influencing the markets prior to a re-fixing.[20] An immediate objection was that an appropriate rate could not be chosen in the absence of a medium-term balance-of-payments objective. In fact, several months earlier, the Bank's 'Sterling Area Working Party' had already settled on a figure for the annual current account surplus of between £200 million and £300 million.[21] A first consideration in relation to the balance of payments was the state of the reserves. Given the huge improvement in reserves (almost a doubling) over 1971–72, even after the sharp losses of June, it was not felt any longer necessary to try to earn additions to the reserves, and it was concluded that the Sterling Area Working Party target remained appropriate.[22]

---

[18] Harrop to Walker, 'The exchange rate: Treasury/Bank relations', 9 May 1975, TNA T358/208.

[19] Morse to O'Brien, 'Working party on the sterling exchange rate', 26 July 1972; Fenton to Page/Thornton, 'Working party on the sterling exchange rate', 27 July 1972, OV44/128.

[20] 'Working party on the sterling exchange rate', 27 July 1972, OV44/128.

[21] Fenton to Morse/O'Brien/Richardson, 7 March 1972, enc. 'Report of the Sterling Area Working Party – March 1972', OV44/122.

[22] Christopher Elston to Goodhart, 'The exchange rate', July 1972; Coleby to Fenton/Morse, 'Balance of payments objectives for the U.K.', 4 August 1972, OV44/128.

Fenton reported in just over a month with the assessment that a rate of $2.40 would not produce a current balance in 1975 anywhere near the £300 million suggested target figure. There was even a great risk that £2.40 would not hold until 1975 without substantial intervention, and they did not wish to recommend substantial use of reserves. They proposed that policies should be implemented that would keep inflation to 5.5 per cent or below. They could see certain attractions in a longer period of floating, but both the political constraints and a deeper lack of belief in the efficacy of long-term floating persuaded them against. They concluded that a rate of $2.30 to $2.25 would meet the targets fully and that the rate of $2.40 that was expected abroad risked being overturned by capital movements. Clearly, much depended on achieving a desired rate of inflation and on what happened elsewhere, not least to the US dollar. They recommended re-fixing at $2.40 on or before 1 January 1973 – 'accepting the risks that a further devaluation may be required well within the next three years'.[23]

Fforde immediately challenged the report on two grounds. The first was on the reduction of inflation and the second on 'the *paramount* [my emphases] importance of refusal by the UK to accept any limitation on its continued freedom to make changes in the parity'. He greatly approved of the focus on inflation but doubted its realisation – doubted the government's ability to achieve any breakthrough on prices and incomes, still the way in which they saw inflation being tackled. He therefore thought that the Bank 'must tactically proceed for the time being on the assumption that domestic inflation is unlikely to be subdued to avoid the problem of a further devaluation in say 1974.' His main point, though, was to provoke discussion on 'how we can effectively secure continued freedom of exchange rate policy. For unless we think we can do this, and know how to do it, we ought not to recommend re-fixing on or before 1 January 1973'. If $2.40 on 1 January 1973 would not hold, then freedom to float again needed to be guaranteed in black and white, he suggested.[24] Floating was not provided for in the IMF rules – it was only through non-objection that the IMF condoned it.[25]

The rate was not fixed on 1 January, and Fforde and McMahon were both concerned that postponing re-fixing was allowing the government to side-

---

[23] 'Working party on the sterling exchange rate', enc. with Fenton to Morse/O'Brien, 5 September 1972, OV44/128.

[24] Fforde to O'Brien/Hollom, 'Report on the working party on the sterling exchange rate', 7 September 1972, OV44/128.

[25] Balfour to Morse/Fforde, 'Freedom of exchange rate policy – Mr. Fforde's note of 8.9.72', 18 September 1972, OV44/128.

step urgent questions of external financial policy. Fforde fretted over the idea of a large IMF standby and the conditions that would likely attach to it, and Hollom agreed, speculating that the strings would include a reduction in the borrowing requirement and in the rate of increase in the money supply. And even if there were a standby of up to twice the size of the quota in light of the previous June's experience, would that be enough?[26] McMahon favoured re-fixing at $2.35 – 'not because we believe that $2.35 will be right indefinitely, but simply because it may be a better way of managing the next couple of years to defend $2.35 for some considerable time and *then* move down from it'.[27] The officials were correct in their fears, although these were not realised for a further two years.

Treasury economists believed that a rate of $2.35 would not hold to the end of 1973 and that the medium-term 'equilibrium' rate was $2.16 – rather precise for such a calculation. The consensus was that they should continue to float for the time being, although it was left unclear what this meant.[28] With the dollar coming under pressure, Richard Hallett, who was Bridge's successor on foreign-exchange matters, told McMahon that it was '… not easy to suggest either a tactical plan for the immediate future or a strategic plan for the next few months'. Nevertheless, Hallett suggested keeping a cap on sterling at $2.40 and, if necessary, taking in large amounts to the reserves and reminding the public that these could be highly volatile.[29]

Fforde argued that there may well be some countries that could afford to sacrifice some element of domestic policy in the interests of international monetary order, but Britain was not one of them. Britain was in dire straits, needing to solve an inflation problem (through a prices and incomes policy) and to increase investment in manufacturing industry. Given that, the overriding requirement was to hold the exchange rate at $2.35. The idea that the pound could be allowed to depreciate by about 10 per cent over a year was wrong. It would not be imperceptible to the public, and it was in any case doubtful that it could be achieved. He therefore suggested a programme of external borrowing alongside a floating rate, together with a further borrowing from the IMF.[30] Their inclination was to go on floating after April, but they needed a strategy for the exchange rate for the longer term.[31]

O'Brien finally wrote to the Chancellor along these lines, setting out the options and concluding, 'Whatever might be accomplished in these ways, a

[26] Hollom to McMahon, 22 January 1973, 7A114/14.
[27] McMahon to O'Brien, 22 January 1973, 7A114/14.
[28] Fenton, Note for record – 'Sterling exchange rate', 1 February 1973, 7A114/15.
[29] Hallett to McMahon, 'The exchange markets', 1 February 1973, 3A49/1.
[30] Fforde to O'Brien/Hollom, 'Policy', 5 February 1973, 7A114/15.
[31] McMahon to Hollom/O'Brien, 'The exchange rate', 6 February 1973, 7A114/15.

strategy for the exchange rate must be decided', and he advocated holding to a rate of $2.30 to $2.35. High interest rates would support this, but O'Brien reckoned that over the next 12 months they might need to spend $2 billion in support. He was against borrowing or arranging a standby from the IMF because he felt that that would make it more difficult to hold to the rate of $2.30.[32] In the end, little of this was to matter much because in the first week of February and into the second, the pressure on the dollar was such that everything changed. It is worth noting, though, from the point of view of the approach to the exchange rate, for it was the kind of approach that continued for much of the rest of the decade.

In January and early February, the turmoil in the foreign-exchange markets prompted the Italians to adopt a two-tier market for rates and led the Swiss to float on 23 January. Publication of the US trade figures for 1972 showed a likely deficit of $6 billion and led to heavy selling of the dollar.[33] Central banks provided huge support for the dollar, and urgent talks followed; the US dollar then was devalued by 10 per cent against gold. On 12 February, the London market was closed (it re-opened on the following day), and the yen floated. After the devaluation of the dollar, the pound stood at $2.50, but it soon fell to $2.42. After that, what happened had more to do with the dollar than anything else. There was no sign of any movement on international monetary reform, and market doubts grew. On 1 March, there was unprecedented selling of the dollar. On 2 March, the London market again was closed and would remain so until the 19 March. At that point, no one was supporting the dollar any longer. After meetings on 10 and 11 March in Brussels and Paris, it was announced that the Deutsche mark (DM) was to be re-valued by 3 per cent against gold, and Germany and five other EEC countries would maintain a 2¼ per cent spread against each other but float against the dollar. Britain, Italy, and Ireland were to float independently.[34]

The Treasury wanted the rate to come down somewhat later on,[35] but apart from that, there was still no sign of any consideration of a broader strategy.[36] However, the Bank was authorised to 'use the proceeds of future borrowing to support the market as and when it seemed appropriate and that up to $300 million might be taken out of the proceeds of past foreign

[32] O'Brien to Barber, 9 February 1973, 7A114/15.
[33] Dealers' reports, February 1973, C8/41.
[34] *BEQB* 13(2):127–130, June 1973.
[35] Hollom to Allen 15 May 1973, 7A136/2; Allen to Hollom 25 May 1973, 7A136/2.
[36] For broad purposes, they thought of a 2.5 cent fall in the dollar rate as being equal to a 1 per cent effective depreciation. Hallett to McMahon, 'Intervention policy', 9 November 1973, 3A49/1.

currency borrowing now in the reserves over the next two or three months with a similar purpose'.[37]

By November, when the sterling rate was $2.4050 but poor trade figures were in the offing and technical factors were less favourable to sterling than hitherto, Hallett (now an Adviser to the Governors) gave his views on how to proceed. It was all couched in terms of feel and what they might get away with. They could let the rate go to $2.36, for example (a 19 per cent effective depreciation from the starting point), without doing anything, but they should hold it there if possible, spending up to $50 million. Between $2.36 and $2.34, they should be prepared to spend up to $200 million. If a really serious attack broke out and $2.34 was not possible, they would need authorisation to spend up to $500 million. But they needed to have in mind 'an ultimate point beyond which sterling will not be allowed to go for the time being, within the bounds of acceptable cost'. Hallett felt that they should try to keep at $2.30 for some weeks at least. Much would depend on the reaction to the measures to be announced on the following Tuesday [November 13, when minimum lending rate (MLR) and special deposits were increased and a state of emergency was declared].[38] When McMahon passed these views to the Governors, he added that it was important that dealers 'keep in touch with the market'. They also would need to get clear authority from the Chancellor in terms of figures for the support allowable on 13 November. His own view was that on that day they should have authority to spend $50 million 'down to 19 per cent effective depreciation', thereafter about $50 million per ½ per cent, but with a ceiling of $200 million. He did say, 'We *are* floating and our policy *is* more or less to let speculative movements blow themselves out'.[39]

By the end of the month, McMahon was expressing a certain frustration. He found it hard to formulate principles on which dealers should be authorised to spend money. Unless they could intervene at their discretion, however, with minimum sums, the markets would believe that the authorities had given up on the exchange rate, and he believed that that would be destabilising. The dealers also needed discretion as to when they should intervene – say, allowed $100 million over the week rather than $20 million per day. Sometimes they had to go 'to the Treasury for sometimes literally hourly authorisations of small sums'.[40] What he suggested, therefore, was that they get authorisation for the next few months for a minimum amount per month – say, $250 million – that could be spent with considerable

[37]   Hallett to Richardson, 16 August 1973, 3A49/1.
[38]   Hallett to McMahon, 'Intervention policy', 9 November 1973, 4A49/1.
[39]   McMahon to Richardson/Hollom, 'Intervention policy', 9 November 1973, 3A49/1.
[40]   McMahon to Richardson, 'Intervention', 28 November 1973, 3A49/1.

discretion but not to defend any particular rate. The Chancellor agreed to the sum when he saw the Governor but thought it should be considered on a monthly basis.[41]

At the end of 1973, the oil-price rise meant a huge increase in foreign-exchange activity. In October, prices were raised by 66 per cent to $5 a barrel and on 1 January to $11.5, a quadrupling in all. Oil producers were forecast to run a balance-of-payments surplus of $60 billion in 1974. The price rises meant that the large oil companies in Britain, notably Shell and British Petroleum (BP), were having to make payments to producers of as much as $800 million per month. They were also receiving large dollar amounts each month, but exchange-control regulations needed altering to allow them to retain these dollars and make payment from that account. The other side of this was that large dollar holdings were building up in the producer countries, and the ambition of some in London was to attract substantial longer-term dollar deposits from the Middle East. However, the exchange-control limit needed to be raised from five years to 10 years for London dollar certificates of deposit (CDs). In response to the oil-price increases, the Managing Director of the IMF Johannes Witteveen, devised a temporary oil facility to assist members in meeting oil-related payments deficits.[42] Devaluation, deflation, and import restraint were not suitable responses to current problems, and he proposed that the IMF borrow from its oil-exporting members with payments surpluses and lend to those with deficits – a recycling scheme.[43] The facility was established in August, and by December, the IMF had borrowing agreements with nine members and a total of a little over 3 billion denominated in special drawing rights (SDRs) was available.[44] It was succeeded by a larger facility in 1975.

As a consequence of the miners' strike, the government announced on 13 December 1973 the introduction of a three-day working week from 1 January as a means of curbing power usage. (A full five-day week was not restored until 9 March.) The current account worsened sharply in the last quarter of 1973 and then again in January 1974, and there were plans to apply to the IMF for a large standby.[45] Interestingly, though, from the point of view of reserves and the exchange rate, there was less to excite than might have been expected. In effective terms, the rate had improved in the last

---

[41] France (PPS to Healey) to Mitchell, 30 November 1973, 3A49/1.
[42] De Vries (1986, p. 140).
[43] De Vries (1985, p. 314).
[44] *Ibid.*, p. 330.
[45] Mitchell, 'Possible IMF standby: brief for talk with Mr. Witteveen', 9 January 1974, TNA T358/128.

quarter, although it did lose all that ground in the following January. Some use was made of reserves, but not much. In the first quarter of 1974, output was slowing around the world, and prices were rising. The current account deficit for the first quarter of 1974 was £1,000 million, mainly financed through overseas investment in the private sector and a rise in official sterling balances – in part a result of bigger sterling receipts of the oil producers. Reserves fell by only £40 million, and in April they rose by £200 million. The £/$ rate rose almost uninterruptedly from January at $2.20 to June when it was over $2.40 before settling back for the remainder of the year to just under $2.35, although more attention was being paid to the effective rate. When Sir Derek Mitchell, second Permanent Secretary (Overseas Finance), put forward a strategy for the rate for 1974, it was couched almost entirely in terms of the effective rate, with the ambition being to keep it between 17 and 21 per cent depreciation on the Smithsonian level.[46] It was 16.9 per cent in July 1974 and 21.4 per cent in December 1974.

In the course of 1974, the £/$ rate remained relatively flat at $2.35; the effective rate was similar, and there was almost no intervention at all until the closing weeks of the year. Reserves rose from $6,178 million in January 1974 to $7,824 million in November before slipping back in December. A large part of the explanation for the moderate performance in 1974 was that the oil-exporting countries were financing a large part of the UK deficit by increasing their sterling holdings by around £2,220 million, roughly $5 billion. Discussions in the Bank were on what the 'right' exchange rate might be and the relationship among interest rates, borrowing, and the exchange rate. Dow's view was to choose an exchange rate that would 'produce the current balance required'. Mysteriously, he added, 'it is very costly to choose a low exchange rate in anticipation of future greater-than-average inflation. A better strategy is to preserve competitivity at the point judged appropriate, that is, offset excess inflation by an equal depreciation of the exchange as we go along.'[47] Derrick Layton, an Adviser in the Economic Intelligence Department (EID), pointed out that depreciation was a method of alleviating the effects of the disease, and it was an expensive one that added to inflation. 'Far better to cure the disease itself.'[48] Later in the month, Dow added on the question of the rate: 'It seems to come down to a question of intelligent hunch (for instance, I would like to see a "clearly competitive" rate maintained, without being able to be sure that the present rate is not a

---

[46] Mitchell, 'Management of the exchange rate', 25 April 1974, 4A112/6.
[47] Dow, 'The level of the exchange rate', 23 April 1974, 4A112/6.
[48] Derrick Layton to Dow, 'Interest rates …', 26 April 1974, 4A112/6.

bit unnecessarily competitive).' He continued, 'There seem firmer grounds for supposing that our exchange rate will/should depreciate gradually compared with other currencies in general, and *still more vis-à-vis the dollar*' (emphasis in original).[49] Some clarity finally came to the discussion when Goodhart said that if you adopt a floating exchange rate, policy instruments should be used to maintain domestic equilibrium – 'the floating exchange rate should buffer the economy from external shocks. To intervene to manage the exchange rate is then both unnecessary and undesirable.' Quite. All the recent papers had rejected this position, going on at some length 'into calculations about desirable current account balances, "equilibrium" long-run exchange rates, *et hoc genus omne,* which in principle are quite out of keeping and unnecessary with a floating exchange rate'. If it were necessary to accept a political imperative for lower rates, it should be admitted that holding the rate up would in due course fail expensively. Tactics should be based on that.[50]

On the basis of the forecasts available for 1974 and 1975 and hints of direction after that, it was estimated in the Treasury that external financing of £10 billion would be needed over the five-year period 1974–79. This could be done in a variety of ways, with foreign-currency borrowing by the public sector among the more favoured means.[51] The effective rate should be kept broadly at recent levels, with support given as necessary to achieve this, and the finance for this should come from foreign-currency borrowing. Reserves had been $6,178 million in January and would be about $6,900 million at the end of April on account of the considerable public-sector borrowing.[52]

Reserves

Since the float was a managed one, the state of the reserves remained a focus, and there continued to be a desire to influence the market's perceptions. The question, 'What reserve figure shall we publish this month?' was one that had been discussed for years by the Governor and his senior officials. The practice of using swaps to window dress the figures developed

[49] Dow to McMahon, 'Interest rates ...', 29 April 1974, 4A112/6.
[50] Goodhart to Dow, 'How do we justify intervention to manage the exchange rate?', 1 May 1974, 4A112/6.
[51] McMahon to Richardson/O'Brien, 'Economic strategy and its financing', 5 June 1974, 4A112/7.
[52] Mitchell to Allen, enc. 'Management of the exchange rate in 1974', 25 April 1974, 4A112/6.

in the 1960s and continued in the 1970s. On occasion, when sterling was rising and reserves were also rising, swaps would be used to transform as much as 30 per cent of foreign-exchange reserves into sterling in order to hide the size of the reserves from those who might put pressure on the Chancellor for some monetary easing.[53] Additionally, 'the Treasury occasionally "doctored" the true reserves figure, either by switching from spot to forward transactions or by timing the drawing on the external loans simply to bolster what might otherwise have been worrying published figures.'[54] It therefore remains close to impossible to construct a true series from the Bank's original figures.

For these reasons, it is not wise to place much confidence in figures for individual years in the official published reserves, although the general trend is probably reliable (Figure 14.4). As the balance of payments improved rapidly in 1970–71, reserves grew and then remained flat at around $6 billion until they began to slip in 1976. There was then a great surge to $20 billion at the end of 1977, and apart from some slippage in two quarters in 1978, the strengthening continued so that reserves finished the period at $30 billion. There can be no mistaking the broad picture. The current account and hence sterling were weak in the first half of the decade, but for a variety of reasons, from monetary and fiscal tightening to the reform of public finances to the expectations attaching to the imminence of North Sea oil coming on stream, the exchange rate improved after 1977. Sterling then bounced back with all the confidence of a Roman consul returning from exile.

Figure 14.5 shows daily movements for intervention in the foreign-exchange markets. In 1970 and 1971, flows were almost entirely inward, and the only really significant support needed was in the last week of the year when the new revalued parity came into being. 1972 is striking, with the third week of June standing out sharply. On just one day, more than $1,200 million was spent. 1973 is again a year of inflows, reflected in the exchange rate, and that pattern continued in 1974 with little intervention in support and generally strong inflows. 1975 was more mixed. The question is often raised as to what the cost of intervention was. Apart from the difficulty of getting hold of the 'right' figures in terms of reserve use, the next problem is deciding where to close the books. Large amounts of reserves might on occasion be used to support, successfully or not, the rate on a particular date. The support might continue over a short or long period. What should

[53] Price (2003, pp. 89–90).
[54] Wass (2008, p. 134).

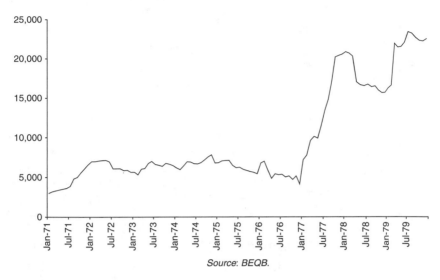

Source: BEQB.

Figure 14.4. UK official reserves, monthly, 1971–79 ($m).

be judged the cost? The effectiveness of the support might be judged in part by what happened to the reserves over the succeeding period, but deciding where the cutoff point should be is not easy.[55]

Financing the external deficit was eased in the mid-1970s with increased oil producers' revenues, and the Bank was central in developing a programme of foreign borrowing of these by the nationalised industries and local authorities. This was done under the exchange-cover scheme, under which foreign-currency loans were converted into sterling by the Bank.[56] Of course, the use of this facility equally could be seen as delaying facing harsher realities. Be that as it may, the Bank, along with the Treasury, embarked on highly secret discussions with the Saudi Arabian Monetary Agency (SAMA) to secure foreign-currency borrowing for the public sector. Saudi Arabia was the third largest oil producer and awash with funds. And relations with the Bank were quite close because senior positions in SAMA often were filled by Bank officials on secondment.[57] By the end of 1975, lending by SAMA to British nationalised industries totalled $775 million. Nationalised industries negotiated loans either directly with the

---

[55] One interesting exercise for the late seventies is 'Intervention, stabilisation, and profits', *BEQB* 23(3):384–391, September 1983.
[56] The exchange cover facilities were announced by Barber in his March 1973 budget; HC Deb, 6 March 1973, Vol 852, c247; Bank of England, *Annual Report*, 1974 onward.
[57] Wass (2008, p. 50).

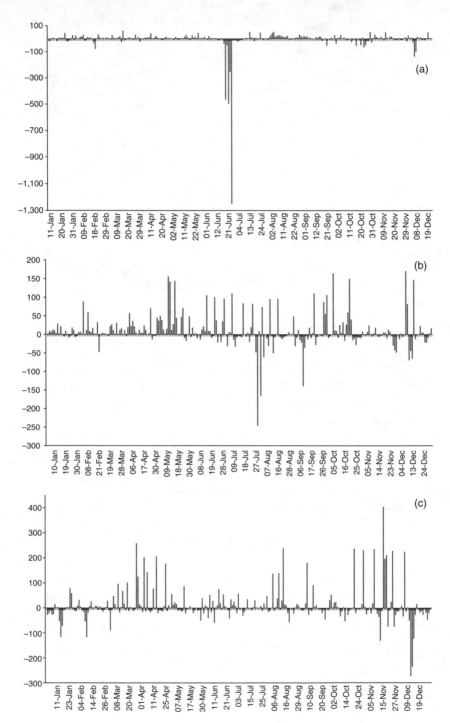

Figure 14.5 *(continued)*

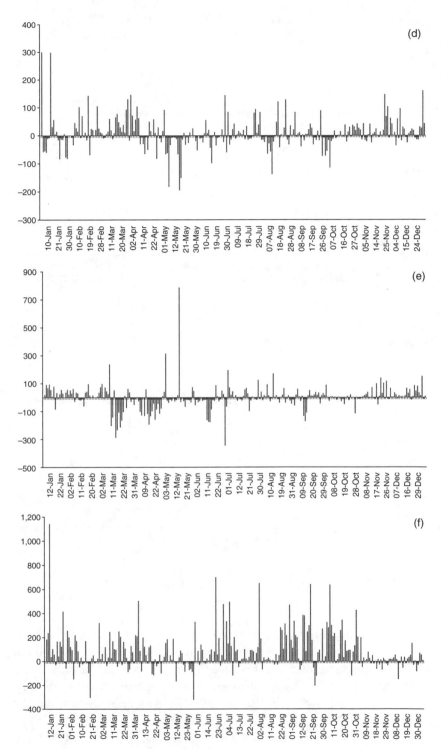

Figure 14.5 *(continued)*

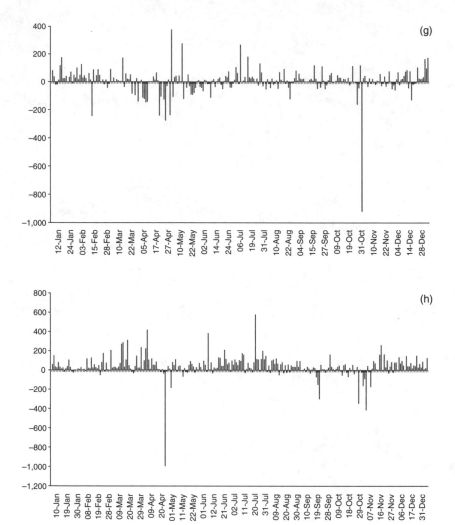

Figure 14.5. Bank of England daily transactions in the foreign-exchange market, (a) 1972; (b) 1973; (c) 1974; (d) 1975; (e) 1976; (f) 1977; (g) 1978; (h) 1979.
Source: Dealers' reports, C8 various.

lenders or through selected banks. In most cases, the transaction took the form of a private issue of bearer notes or bonds, and SAMA's name did not appear in the documentation because the Saudis were intent on keeping the loans secret. However, increasingly, the negotiations were conducted directly with the Bank rather than intermediated by a merchant bank. The first was in 1974 when Richardson and Page met the Governor of SAMA and arranged a loan of $200 million between SAMA and British Steel, available at fixed rates for 7 to 10 years.[58] Further deals were anticipated for the British Gas Corporation and the Electricity Council, but the Bank had a queuing procedure whereby only one public-sector body at a time was allowed to seek funds.[59] In February 1975, McMahon and Mitchell went to Saudi Arabia for meetings to set up a bilateral financing deal under which Saudi Arabia would lend approximately $1 billion for a minimum period of 5 years. With SAMA seemingly content to invest further, Mitchell and McMahon gave them a list of projects that could form a basis of a public-sector borrowing programme. The Saudis were not yet ready to agree to a longer-term commitment but were prepared to consider loans of $150 million to the North of Scotland Hydro Electric Board and $75 million to the National Coal Board.[60] A Bank team revisited Saudi Arabia in April 1975 to arrange the terms. Overall, between 1973 and 1976, Saudi Arabia lent a total of $1,295 million to British nationalised industries in foreign currencies.[61] The authorities also sought to borrow from Iran, and in July 1974, a line of credit of $1.2 billion to be drawn in three tranches over three years was arranged. The National Water Council took up $400 million in October 1974, although difficulties then arose with the second and third tranches when in January 1976 the Iranians announced a shortfall in their oil revenues.

The scale of this activity grew in total from $600 million in March 1973 to $7 billion three years later and $10 billion by the end of 1977 (Table 14.1). In addition to these foreign-currency borrowings, in his budget speech, Healey announced a $2,500 million 10-year Eurodollar loan, the largest loan ever raised in the international capital markets.[62] The clearers were not enthusiastic, concerned as they were for their capital ratios and staggered by the size of the borrowing in relation to their balance sheets.[63] (This was hardly surprising, with the contemporaneous secondary banking crisis requiring the banks to extend loans for the rescue operation, putting further pressure on their capital ratios.) They suggested that the loan consist of two parts: $1.5 billion would be found by the clearers and associates, and

[58] Page to Anwar Ali (governor, SAMA), 5 July 1974, 7A18/1.
[59] France, Note for the record, 8 July 1974, 7A18/1.
[60] Richard Turner (Adviser, Overseas) to Fenton/McMahon, 'Borrowing from Saudi Arabia' enc. draft 'UK borrowing from Saudi Arabia', 28 February 1975, 7A18/2.
[61] C. J. Baker (HMT), 'Visit to Saudi Arabia and attached note for records', 30 January 1976, 7A18/4. The notes of the meetings were written by Paul Tempest, an Arabist in the Bank's Overseas Department.
[62] HC Deb, 26 March 1974, Vol. 871, c286.
[63] *The Times*, 18 February 1974, p. 19; Hallett to McMahon/Richardson, and McMahon annotation, 25 February 1974, 6A374/4.

Table 14.1. *UK total assistance outstanding, quarterly, 1972–79 ($m)*

	IMF	Other borrowing with a sterling counterpart	Foreign-currency deposits placed with the Bank by overseas monetary authorities	Public-sector foreign currency borrowing (net of repayments)		Total
				HMG	Other public sector	
Mar 1972	1,055	0	0	0	366	1,421
Jun 1972	0	2,608	0	0	366	2,974
Sep 1972	0	0	0	0	366	366
Dec 1972	0	0	0	0	366	366
Mar 1973	0	0	0	0	602	602
Jun 1973	0	0	0	0	1,337	1,337
Sep 1973	0	0	0	0	2,257	2,257
Dec 1973	0	0	0	0	2,982	2,982
Mar 1974	0	0	0	0	3,698	3,698
Jun 1974	0	0	0	0	4,737	4,737
Sep 1974	0	0	0	0	5,182	5,182
Dec 1974	0	0	0	1,500	5,592	7,092
Mar 1975	0	0	0	2,500	5,700	8,200
Jun 1975	0	0	0	2,500	6,069	8,569
Sep 1975	0	0	0	2,500	6,159	8,659

Dec 1975	0	0		2,500	6,421	8,921
Mar 1976	1,206	0		2,500	7,000	10,706
Jun 1976	2,051	400	630	2,500	8,059	13,640
Sep 1976	2,051	600	945	2,500	8,904	15,000
Dec 1976	2,051	0	0	2,500	9,609	14,160
Mar 1977	3,257	0	0	3,500	9,639	16,396
Jun 1977	3,643	0	0	3,500	9,695	16,838
Sep 1977	4,029	0	0	4,000	9,896	17,925
Dec 1977	4,029	0	0	4,000	10,013	18,042
Mar 1978	4,029	0	0	4,000	9,585	17,614
Jun 1978	3,109	0	0	4,350	9,230	16,689
Sep 1978	3,062	0	0	4,350	8,989	16,401
Dec 1978	2,152	0	0	4,350	9,345	15,847
Mar 1979	2,300	0	0	4,350	9,901	16,551
Jun 1979	1,209	0	0	4,350	9,545	15,104
Sep 1979	1,128	0	0	4,350	9,305	14,783
Dec 1979	1,048	0	0	4,350	9,187	14,585

Source: BEQB.

the second $1 billion would be spread more widely, but the clearers would underwrite the amount.[64] The loan, finalised in May, was to be repaid in four equal annual instalments of $625 million in the early 1980s.[65]

The beginning of 'floating' also gave rise to considerable commercial demand for forward foreign-exchange activity. Commercial banks and others generally had done well out of the limited business they had done in the currency realignments that had taken place under the pegged-rate system – the one-way bet. After February 1973, many commercial banks set out to profit from the volatility in the rates. The National Westminster, for example, which had one of the largest foreign-exchange divisions in the world, adopted an aggressive policy of going 'out on the road' to help their own customers and recruit others in solving their currency problems.[66] Dealing in forward markets was one aspect of this, and while not completely new, it was to develop on a huge scale.

Over the next few years, users of foreign exchange sought Bank approval for varying the kinds of forward cover they could make use of given the constraints of exchange controls. Commodity traders were prominent among them. Things could go wrong. For example, Hambros warned the Bank in the middle of 1973 that they might be faced with a major default in their foreign-exchange position. They had entered into a massive forward transaction with a customer who had then indicated that they might be unable to deliver.[67] Lord Cromer, who was now British ambassador in Washington, wrote to the Governor to air some related concerns. At a meeting in Washington with the British American Chamber of Commerce, made up mostly of British exporters to the United States, Cromer asked them how they were finding living under a floating regime, and they replied that they had gone heavily into forward markets and had been making profits. Cromer worried about the situation arising in which they were making losses.[68] Richardson had been hearing much the same thing in London, and he too worried about conditions changing.

The middle months of 1974 were dominated by problems in the forward foreign-exchange markets. The failure of the German Bank Herstatt as a consequence of over-trading in the foreign-exchange markets impinged on banks in the United Kingdom and the United States. Herstatt's forward

[64] Hallett to McMahon/Richardson, 25 February 1974, 6A374/4.
[65] Sangster to McMahon/Hollom/Richardson, 'Further meeting of the five main clearers about H.M.G.'s $2.5 bn. Loan', 20 September 1974, 6A374/5.
[66] *The Evening Standard*, 11 April 1972, p. 47.
[67] Hallett, Note for record – 'Hambros Bank Limited', 24 July 1973, 3A49/1.
[68] Cromer to Richardson, 15 October 1973, 3A49/1.

foreign-exchange losses originally were assessed at DM470 million.[69] One British Bank in particular, Hill Samuel, was quite exposed and took the losses badly. Even if the Bank had thought it important to come to the rescue of a Bank with liquidity problems in foreign currency, it would have faced some clear limitations because foreign-exchange resources were strictly limited. Neither was it clear that funds from the EEA could be used in this way. The lines of policy would need to be cleared in advance with the Treasury. Further, speed of action was of the essence in such cases. The Bank would need to be the agent acting, but it would need an indemnity from the Treasury. In any event, such were the concerns that some supervisory thoughts were put together and letters sent to all authorised banks and branches in Britain reminding them of what the dangers were and what behaviour was expected of them. It threatened the possibility of tightening exchange-control measures.[70]

The Bank had carried out forward intervention between 1964 and 1967 on a grand scale, and the experience was a chastening one. During the problems of late 1971, John Sangster (the Adviser in charge of foreign exchange) told Fenton, 'There are no exchange market tactics to delay or disguise the inevitable which do not entail very large losses. We learnt this at very heavy cost, when selling forward dollars massively before devaluation.'[71] As Edward Bradshaw observed:

The suggestion that, at times of pressure on the pound, we should support the rate by buying outright forward sterling would, in my opinion, be the second greatest mistake that we have ever made – the first being the outright and swap operations of pre-1967.... In effect we are saying, 'Come and sell your sterling now and we will subsidise your sales at a nice cheap price for 3 or 6 months' – I appreciate this Government is in favour of subsidies but why should non-residents benefit from these handouts?[72]

McMahon pointed out there were times when they might profit from forward intervention – when they really believed 'that on a relatively short time-scale the prospects for sterling are better than the market thinks'. Otherwise, it was 'rather like taking a ride on a tiger'.[73]

[69] Sangster to Thornton, 'Gold and foreign exchange meeting, Basle: I.D. Herstatt', 11 June 1974, 3A49/2. Reid estimates the overall losses of Herstatt to be in the region of DM 1,200 million; Reid (1982, p. 115).

[70] Sangster to Hallett/McMahon, 'Hill Samuel & Herstatt', 17 July 1974; Hallett to McMahon, 'Rescue action in the Euro-currency markets', 25 July 1974; Sangster to McMahon, 'Control of Overseas Branches of U.K. Banks', 19 September 1974; Blunden to Fforde, 'Foreign exchange operations', 18 November 1974, 3A49/2.

[71] Sangster to Fenton, 'Possible operations in the exchange markets', 7 October 1971, 3A49/1.

[72] Bradshaw to Sangster, 'Operations in the forward market', 28 March 1974, 3A49/2.

[73] McMahon to Richardson/Hollom, 'Forward intervention', 25 January 1974, 3A49/2.

Bradshaw returned to the subject of forward operations from the Bank's perspective at the beginning of 1975, but with a slightly different angle. He pointed out that over the previous five years the Bank had been reasonably successful in countering attacks on sterling through operations in the spot and short-dated forward market. The financial press had praised the Bank for this. But this kind of action would not cope with a full-scale sterling crisis. Nevertheless, a similar type of operation in 3-, 6-, and 12-month swaps along with spot intervention 'would help to deter excessive speculative positions being built up.' The dealers certainly wanted this weapon at their disposal. He thought that it was the words 'forward intervention' that scared the Treasury. It should be explained, he suggested, that the Bank was now proposing borrowing pounds from the market, where in 1964 to 1967 pounds were lent.[74] As Sangster put it to McMahon, in the 1960s, sterling had been supported by buying it forward and spot, predicated on a policy of a fixed rate and very low reserves. This was now different and was designed to raise the cost to bears of funding their sales of spot sterling.[75]

By the middle of 1975, Bradshaw had changed tack. He said that it had become obvious over the first half of the year that the Bank's ability to 'apply squeezes on short £ positions has seriously diminished'. This he attributed to the large sterling balances the oil producers were lending in the Euro-currency markets that found their way into swap markets via specialist banks. He thought that techniques that could be devised to allow them to control the spot rate. He felt that they had gained control of sterling in the foreign-exchange markets in recent years only to have it snatched away in the last few months – 'unless we can devise methods of regaining control we shall have to take a back seat again and let market operators drive our bus.'[76]

Sterling Balances

The question of the exchange rate for sterling was closely tied to the balances of sterling holders. Indeed, sometimes Bank views on sterling balances were close to synonymous with exchange-rate policy. The Basle Agreements of 1968 were regarded as something of a success in that there was no diversifying out of sterling; in fact, there was an almost uninterrupted increase from September 1968 through to May 1972. This came almost entirely from the overseas sterling countries. There had in fact been an outflow from the non-sterling countries to the point where private balances stood at around

---

[74] Bradshaw to Sangster, 7 January 1975, 3A49/3.
[75] Sangster to McMahon, 'Forward intervention', 16 January 1975, 3A49/3.
[76] Bradshaw to Byatt, 'Control of forward margins/Euro £ rates', 24 June 1975, 3A49/3.

£500 million in the early 1970s, reckoned to be the lowest the figure could go to provide essential working balances.

The Sterling Agreements negotiated in September 1968 were for a period of three years, with the provision for a two-year extension. This was duly carried through in September 1971, as was the renewal of the parallel Basle facility. The trigger for the guarantee under the agreements had been set at $2.3760, 1 per cent below the $2.40 rate. By December 1971, the new Smithsonian parities had been established, with sterling at $2.6057. The guarantee rate remained unchanged, and this led to complaints from some holders of sterling in the early months of 1972. In particular, Kuwait and Bahrain made specific requests for the guarantee to be raised, and there was disquiet from others, including Singapore, Malaysia, and Australia. Some in the Bank then started to push for an early renegotiation of the agreements with the ambition of an extension to September 1975, but O'Brien was inclined to delay, and there were sharp divisions within the Treasury. The debate then was thrown into turmoil when sterling left the snake and floated in June 1972.[77]

Following the 'float', the Chancellor proposed a review of the current agreements and their possible revision and extension to beyond 1973. The main response from the overseas sterling area (OSA) was that compensation should be $2.60, and many wanted a 'numeraire' other than the dollar. Nonetheless, there was no great pressure for immediate action, with a preference to wait until sterling was re-fixed within the snake and reform of the international monetary system had been effected. They then decided that the present arrangements should be left as they were.[78]

Under the agreements, the guarantee was triggered when the rate fell to below $2.3760 and remained there for 30 consecutive days. On 25 October 1972, the rate was, for the first time, at that level. (In normal commercial banking, there then surely would have been some incentive to intervene and nudge it above that rate for a day if the cost of doing so were less than the

[77] Stanley Payton to Fenton/O'Brien/Hollom, 'Sterling agreements: exchange guarantee', 1 February 1972; Payton to Morse, 'Sterling agreements', 21 February 1972; Herbert Tomkins to Payton/Fenton, 'Sterling agreements', 6 March 1972; Payton to Fenton, 'Sterling agreements', 7 March 1972, OV44/195; Tomkins to Morse, 'Sterling agreements. SARC meeting of 19 April', 21 April 1972; Payton to Fenton/Morse, 'Sterling agreements', 25 April 1972; 'Extract from the Deputy Governor's note of the Governor's conversation with Mr. Rawlinson 7.6.72.'; Payton, Note for record – 'Treasury meeting: Friday 23 June', 24 June 1972; Barber to Heath, 26 June 1972; I. P. Wilson (HMT), Notes of meetings held in the Treasury on 29 and 30 June 1972, OV44/196.
[78] Barber, 'The sterling arrangements of 1968 (continued), 1973 and 1974', 8 January 1975, OV44/219; Payton to McMahon, 'Sterling agreements: next steps', 12 January 1973, OV44/204. Also see OV44/197–201.

compensation to be paid. But the Bank could hardly do that.) The rate was still below on 24 November, so the guarantee came into effect. Payments amounted to about £59 million.[79] Thereafter, sterling improved, and there were no further calls until 1973, at a new rate. From the autumn of 1972 to the spring of 1973, there was an inflow of sterling, mostly from Middle East oil countries.

Almost as soon as 1973 dawned, the issue of further renewal was back on the agenda. The case against renewal was that the balances were more or less stable, there was nowhere else for them to go, renewal could add to the balances, and the OSA would try to drive a harder bargain.[80] Little progress was made over the first half of the year partly because the Treasury again was unenthusiastic; in fact, both Allen and Mitchell wanted the agreements discontinued.[81] The Bank was in favour of renewal, and the Governor reported that OSA Governors were disappointed that nothing was being done. The crucial element was the rate at which the exchange-value guarantee would work.[82] By July, there were some signs of shift in the Treasury position. There was also the question of whether Basle should be renewed if sterling agreements were. Consideration was given briefly to this at the beginning of September, but by this time the circumstances had so changed – chiefly sterling balances had risen so far above the triggering level – that the Basle facility had been rendered irrelevant, and it was then allowed to lapse.[83]

After much deliberation, it was decided that a unilateral guarantee would be offered to the sterling balances of OSA countries for six months in return for them keeping their existing minimum sterling proportions (MSPs).[84] This was announced on 6 September 1973 and came into effect the day after the 1968 sterling arrangements expired. At that point, the dollar value of eligible sterling balances was guaranteed at $2.4213, being the average rate prevailing over three working days, 4 to 6 September. The balances eligible were official sterling reserves at either 24 September 1973 or the last working day of March 1974, whichever was less.[85] The largest holders at this stage for

[79] Bank of England, *Annual Report*, year ending February 1974, p. 22.
[80] Payton to McMahon, 'Sterling Agreements: next steps', 12 January 1973, OV44/204.
[81] Payton to McMahon/O'Brien/Hollom, 'Sterling agreements', 30 May 1973, OV44/206; Mitchell to D. C. Maughan (Private Secretary to Sir Douglas Allen)/A. M. Bailey, 13 June 1973, OV44/207.
[82] O'Brien to Barber, 21 June 1973; Bailey to O'Brien, 22 June 1973, OV44/207.
[83] McMahon to Fenton, 'Sterling Agreements', 2 July 1973, OV44/208; Payton to McMahon, 'The "Basle facility" and the sterling agreements', 4 September 1973, OV44/211.
[84] Ewbank to Russell Barratt (HMT), 30 July 1973, OV44/208; Payton to Fenton/Richardson/Hollom, 'Sterling agreements', 24 August 1973, OV44/210.
[85] Payton to Richardson/Hollom, 6 September 1973; HMT, Press release, 6 September 1973, OV44/211.

the purposes of the guarantee were Australia, Kuwait, New Zealand, Hong Kong, and Ireland in that order. Together they held £2,393 million out of a total of £3,387 million – more than half of all OSA reserves.[86] Reactions to the unilateral declaration came in slowly in the course of October; at the end of that month there were 16 firm acceptances, including New Zealand and Kuwait. Ireland accepted in November, with Australia and Hong Kong marked down as 'probable' to agree. In the end, 53 countries agreed to participate.[87]

What would happen after March 1974 then had to be addressed almost immediately. Some kind of phased diversification with a more limited guarantee accompanied by a reduction in the required MSPs was one of the possibilities envisaged.[88] A complicating factor was the nature of the reform of the international monetary system that was under discussion. Stanley Payton, Deputy Chief of Overseas, complained that Treasury officials had not thought about the subject as much as they might have. Nonetheless, it was agreed that some stabilisation would be necessary, and it would be best to go for three-year agreements and that ways of financing the necessary phased diversification should be explored. Apparently, Allen wanted to borrow $8 billion 'to get rid of' sterling balances altogether'.[89] At the end of the month, McMahon passed Payton's views to the Governors, telling them, 'We must now develop a Bank view on the appropriate policy towards the sterling balances after next March.'[90] Most of the main holders were looking for greater freedom to diversify. Payton's understanding at the end of 1973 was that the Treasury wanted a phased diversification and, assuming that financing could be arranged, without a guarantee; the Bank's official preference was for phased diversification but with a guarantee. The Foreign Office wanted a unilateral declaration for a further six months, which Payton considered both dangerous and tempting to ministers.[91] Work was also undertaken in the Bank on an effective exchange-rate guarantee. A number of OSA countries had requested a non-dollar-based rate, and an effective exchange rate was a better measure of the value of sterling, and in

---

[86] Barber to Richard Ewbank (Deputy Chief, Overseas)/McMahon, 'Sterling agreements', 10 October 1973, OV44/212.

[87] Raymond Barber, Note for record – 'Sterling guarantees', 27 September 1973, OV44/211; Barber to Payton, 'Sterling guarantees', 19 October 1973, OV44/212; Barber, 'The sterling arrangements of 1968 (continued), 1973 and 1974', 8 January 1975, OV44/219.

[88] Walker (HMT) to Fenton, 2 October 1973, OV44/212.

[89] Payton to McMahon, 'Future arrangements for sterling', 15 November 1973, OV44/213.

[90] McMahon to Richardson/Hollom, 'Future arrangements for Sterling', 28 November 1973, OV44/213.

[91] Payton to McMahon, 'SARC', 12 December 1973, OV44/213.

any case, the effective rate was felt by the Bank to be closer to broader issues of exchange-rate management.[92]

In the course of December and January, a number of other ideas found their way into the discussions, from an extension of the guarantee in some form or other, to IMF finance, to large-scale borrowing in the Eurodollar markets, to the issuing of new sterling bonds that carried a guarantee, to gentlemen's agreements with the principal holders.[93] Although the Chancellor's own preference was for further guarantees, at the beginning of January 1974, some in the Treasury were favouring the gentlemen's agreements, but the Bank did not believe that they would achieve the stability required, and McMahon was worrying that things were in danger of being botched.[94]

Through October and November 1973 with the pound staying at around $2.42, there was no cost accruing. But the rate began to fall in December, and by early January, it had reached $2.28. The cost of the guarantee was beginning to mount. The average daily rate for sterling from September 1973 to March 1974 was $2.3335, so the guarantee was implemented at a cost of £80 million. In early 1974, the calculation as to the wisdom of continuing with the guarantees was a fine one but a complicated one. There was the question of whether guarantees on existing balances would spread to new balances – that cost could be huge – but leaving that aside, the total balances under guarantee were about £1,600 million. If half of this went, the authorities could borrow in the Eurodollar markets. The crude calculation was then the cost of the borrowing against the cost of the guarantee.

In March 1974, the guarantee was extended again, this time until the end of the year. There was a general reduction in MSPs of 10 per cent, but the key change was that it was now to be based on an effective exchange rate of 18.35 per cent (below the Smithsonian). Again, this was a unilateral declaration, and there was no negotiation.[95] The offer was made to 53 holders of sterling, with one, albeit the largest, Australia, declining to participate. Further consideration did not then take place until October 1974, after the general election. The guarantees were now generating less interest, and their importance was diminishing: only 58 per cent of participants' sterling was covered by the 1974 declaration, and 40 per cent of that was

[92] Payton to McMahon, 'Future arrangements for sterling', 18 December 1973; Bank of England, 'An effective exchange rate guarantee', 18 December 1973, OV44/213.

[93] The Sterling Agreements Renewal Committee (SARC), OV44/222.

[94] Payton to McMahon/Richardson/Hollom, 'Sterling arrangements', 3 January 1974; McMahon to Richardson/Hollom, 'Sterling arrangements', 3 January 1974, OV44/214.

[95] HMT, Press release, 15 March 1974, 3A38/4.

held by oil producers. Just £82 million of Nigeria's £977 million sterling was under the guarantee, whereas Saudi Arabia, which had never been party to any agreement, was now the third largest holder.[96] This changing pattern of sterling holdings, the likely costs and limited effectiveness of continuing the guarantees, and their coverage meant that officials were unanimous in deciding that the arrangements should be allowed to lapse at the end of December 1974. The Chancellor accepted this advice and announced it in his budget on 12 November.[97] A Bank assessment in early 1975 concluded that during their six-year life, the guarantees had succeeded in stabilising the official sterling holdings of the OSA over what was a troubled period.[98] This, of course, was not the end of the debate on sterling balances. The oil-price rise had changed the scale and distribution of the balances and their volatility. They would be back in the discussion when IMF assistance was being sought in 1976.

International Monetary Reform: Committee of Twenty

The desire to hold to a fixed/pegged exchange rate was a constant in the period, and it was unsurprising that when the dust settled after June 1972, the IMF Governors established a temporary committee in which negotiations could take place for a reformed international monetary system, but one based on pegged rates. Building on the work that had been done in the 1950s and 1960s, it was envisaged that by 1974 a design for a new system would be reached. The committee's full and cumbersome name was the 'Committee of the Board of Governors of the International Monetary Fund on Reform of the International Monetary System and Related Issues', the 'Committee of Twenty' (C20) for short. The C20 had arisen out of the desire of US officials for reform to be undertaken outside the IMF and the G10. The US Treasury had become frustrated with the G10 because it appeared biased in favour of the EEC. Sensing US dissatisfaction, the IMF pressed for the board of Governors to carry out reform. The US authorities, in particular Volcker, under Secretary for monetary affairs at the US Treasury, were not keen, having become irritated by the IMF's recent behaviour, particularly some public statements by the Managing Director, and feeling that the IMF paid too little attention to US

---

[96] Barber, Note for record – 'Sterling guarantees', 11 October 1974, OV44/218; Barber, 'The sterling arrangements of 1968 (continued), 1973 and 1974', 8 January 1975, OV44/219.

[97] Barber to Payton/Fenton, 'Sterling guarantees', 23 October 1974, OV44/219; HMT, Press release, 12 November 1974.

[98] Barber, 'The sterling arrangements of 1968 (continued), 1973 and 1974', 8 January 1975, OV44/219; 'Overseas sterling balances 1963–1973', *BEQB* 14(2):168–171, June 1974.

problems. They argued that a group of high-level officials independent of the IMF would be more appropriate. A compromise finally was reached in 1972, when it was proposed that the C20 should be temporary. It was agreed that the group should consist of 10 developed and 10 underdeveloped constituencies from the IMF's executive board.[99] The C20 then was structured on two levels: the ministerial level and the deputies level. The C20 reported to the IMF's Board of Governors, and the deputies' role was to present the ministers with recommendations on which they could act. In setting out the key issues in a report, the C20 could then negotiate the final shape of reform.

The Bank was to play a prominent part in the process. Morse, an Executive Director of the Bank, was elected chairman of the deputies. Since 1966, he had been responsible for overseas matters in the Bank but now had to relinquish his executive directorship and handed over his overseas duties to McMahon.[100] A 'bureau' was established made up of Morse and four vice chairmen – Robert Solomon (USA – Adviser to the Federal Reserve Board), Alexandre Kafka (Brazil, Executive Director of the IMF), Hideo Suzuki (former Executive Director of the IMF for Japan), and Jonathan Frimpong-Ansah (former Governor of the central bank of Ghana).[101] Morse chose Eddie George as his Personal Assistant. Since Morse was not keen on moving to the United States and also reluctant to give the impression that the C20 was too closely allied to Washington, he spent most of his time in the Bank, where accommodation and other support were provided. According to Morse, 'without the Bank's help, matching that of the IMF in Washington, we could not possibly have carried through so large an operation'. Morse continued to lunch with the Governor and the Bank's senior colleagues.[102] In the course of the two years, the deputies met in Washington, Paris, Nairobi, and Rome, with meetings every seven or eight weeks. For the United Kingdom, Alan Neale and McMahon were the deputies, with Kirbyshire, Geoffrey Littler, and Anthony Rawlinson as advisers. Mitchell as the UK Executive Director (or Peter Bull as alternate) was also entitled to attend.[103]

The C20 grappled with the exchange-rate mechanism, the role of various reserve assets, the international adjustment process, the role of SDRs, and the problem of capital movements.[104] Progress was slow initially. Mitchell

---

[99] De Vries (1985, pp. 141–155).
[100] *The Times*, 29 September 1972, p. 17.
[101] Solomon (1977, p. 236).
[102] Richardson to Morse, 8 November 1974, OV53/81.
[103] Solomon (1977, p.236); Williamson (1977, p. 68).
[104] Deputies to Committee of Governors, Draft summary of meeting 72/1 (held on 29 September 1972), OV53/66.

told O'Brien that within the bureau, 'only Solomon was really any good'.[105] Morse chaired the technical group working on multi-currency intervention and received strong intellectual support from the Bank.[106] Sangster, for example, devised 'an extremely elegant system' on SDR intervention that had strong support.[107] In Rome in January 1974, the C20 decided that total agreement was no longer possible, and instead, it moved towards 'a more evolutionary process of reform'.[108] External circumstances had changed priorities. The oil crisis and the high and rising levels of inflation and balance-of-payments difficulties had forced a shift of emphasis. Once the C20 had finished its report, a new Council of Governors then would be created to take over the C20's work.

Redrafting of the final 'Outline of Reform' was carried out in the bureau over several months and was presented to the C20 at its last meeting in June 1974.[109] The C20 finally disbanded in October 1974. Morse summarised the main achievement of the Committee's work as fixing 'a broad idea of the reform system sufficiently strongly to govern action in the period ahead, and starting the evolutionary process toward it'.[110] However, the C20 has been remembered as a failure. In June, Morse gave the reasons that ultimately led to its failure. External events, including high inflation, had played their part, but interestingly, Morse also spoke of 'a lack of political will', 'the will to agree and do things together in the common interest even though they may not be precisely what any of the parties would have chosen'.[111] In assessing the C20, De Vries rejected the conventional explanation that the Committee was 'overtaken by events', that is, the high levels of inflation and balance-of-payments difficulties. These were in fact used as an excuse. She maintains that 'even by the time of the 1973 Annual Meeting in Nairobi, the prospect for successful negotiations was already dim'. The unique circumstances that enabled the success of Bretton Woods, she argues, were simply not present in the years 1972–74.[112] Volcker agreed that the oil-price rise was used as an excuse to terminate proceedings.[113]

---

[105] 'Extract from the Deputy Governor's note 28 February … ', OV53/69.
[106] Coleby, interview with Sir Geoffrey Littler, 25 July 1996.
[107] Littler to Mitchell, 'Steering brief for C-XX deputies', 21 March 1974, OV53/77.
[108] Morse, Press conference, 29 March 1974, OV53/77.
[109] 'Report to the board of Governors of the International Monetary Fund by the Committee on Reform of the International Monetary System and related issues', 14 June 1974, OV53/78.
[110] Morse, Press conference, 14 June 1974, OV53/78.
[111] Morse, Speech to International Monetary Conference, 7 June 1974, OV53/78.
[112] De Vries (1985, pp. 264–270).
[113] Samuelson and Barnett (2007, p. 176).

Although unsuccessful, the outcome did not affect Morse's standing. Richardson appreciated all the effort he had put into the Committee: 'It is sad that great political and economic forces prevented the C20's efforts being crowned with the full success which we all hoped for.... Not merely the Bank but the country has cause to be very proud of the reputation you have established for yourself.'[114] Morse did not return to the Bank and took up the chairmanship of Lloyds Bank in 1974, still aged only 45. He would have been a candidate for the Governorship, but with Richardson just appointed, that opportunity had gone.

1976 Crisis

In 1975, the Bank saw two dangers for the year ahead: (1) being unable to finance the forecast deficit by borrowing and (2) experiencing a sudden crisis like 1972 without the necessary resources to meet it. For insurance, they wanted a full IMF standby 'because we may need to make a massive drawing at the drop of a hat', and they wanted all the technical problems ironed out in advance.[115] There was an almost uninterrupted fall in the exchange rate across the year to just above $2.00 in December and a drop in the effective rate from 78.4 at the beginning of the year to 69.9 at the end (–21.6 to –30.1 per cent below the Smithsonian). There was comparatively little intervention, almost suggestive of a policy of allowing the rate to float in an unrestricted way. Other than that, there is no evidence of a policy. The Treasury were coming to the view that defending 22 per cent below the Smithsonian level was not sensible any longer, and it should be let go 'to see what happens'.[116] In April, McMahon was complaining that there was still no exchange-rate policy: 'I do not know whether this is the right occasion to raise with the Chancellor what our strategy for the exchange rate should now be.... at some point we shall certainly need a full scale discussion.'[117] The Treasury was talking of aiming for 25 or 26 per cent effective level and not worrying about the amount spent in doing so. And further, it wanted to impress on the Bank that it did not like 'the present quite rapid downward movement ... and we really must only smooth, not resist'.[118] However, there were some in the Treasury, in particular, David Walker, who were arguing for an effective depreciation of 10 per cent or more in the 12 months from April 1975. In all likelihood, this would take sterling

[114] Richardson to Morse, 8 November 1974, OV53/81.
[115] Hallett to McMahon, 5 February 1975, 4A112/8.
[116] Hedley-Miller to Wass, 28 January 1975, TNA T358/207.
[117] McMahon to Richardson, 3 April 1975, 4A112/8.
[118] Hedley-Miller to Mitchell, 5 May 1975, TNA T358/208.

below the psychological trading level of $2.00, but Walker asserted that it would improve the competitive position.[119] In August, the Prime Minister expressed his 'concern about the Treasury's overt desire to get the rate down', and the Chancellor was unhappy with Treasury advice, much of which, he said, did not stand up to examination, a view former Paymaster General Edmund Dell believed to have been justified. 'Too frequently, advice was brought forward without adequate preparation or for that matter conviction.' And yet, on the other side, it was not clear what the Chancellor wanted: 'he had still not made up his mind between different schools of thought.... he still seemed to lack a policy of his own.'[120]

1975 was a low point in the recession that was widespread around the world, and in the same year, Britain had an inflation rate in excess of 25 per cent, more than double the average for the other Organisation for Economic Co-operation and Development (OECD) countries. Although the deficit on current account was less than half of what it had been in 1974, sterling had fallen in the year to close to the $2.00 mark. There was sufficient concern to begin thinking about a possible IMF drawing. With a view to sounding out the IMF, Lionel Price (Bank) and Frank Cassell (Treasury) were sent off secretly in August 1975 to see what kind of reception such a request was likely to receive. The IMF needed persuading that there was a need, let alone any urgency.[121] In late November, there was a drawing of SDR 1,000 million under the 1975 special oil facility, and a request was made for a standby arrangement for SDR 700 million.[122] Ryrie, the UK Executive Director at the IMF, made the case that Britain would have been able to finance its deficit had it not been for the oil-price rise. The IMF's board wholly supported the application, accepting that the UK was taking action considered appropriate on the inflation front, namely, incomes policy and reducing public expenditure.[123] There still were no revenues from British oil. Indeed, there still was huge expenditure on imports of ships and installation equipment. But there was talk of imminent large revenues.[124]

---

[119] Walker to Mitchell, 11 April 1975, C43/787; Walker to Hedley-Miller, 21 October 1975; Walker to Sangster, 11 November 1975, C43/778; Coleby discussion with Sir David Walker, 19 September 1996, 5A83/45.

[120] Dell (1991, pp.135, 180).

[121] Cassell to Fogarty, 18 August 1975, TNA T354/416.

[122] For the debate on the numbers, see Littler to Fogarty, 22 October 1975, TNA T381/12; and for the drawing, see Mitchell, 'Fund drawing: meeting with Dr. Witteveen', 27 October 1975, TNA T3812/12; and Healey to Witteveen, 18 December 1975, TNA T381/13.

[123] De Vries (1985, pp. 464–466).

[124] This seems to ignore the effect of a new resource on the economy, but at the time, there was no discussion of Stolper-Samuelson.

Even after the setbacks of 1973–75, 1976 stands out as a low point in British economic life – 'looking into the abyss', as one official later put it.[125] After almost four years of a 'floating' exchange rate, there was still no clear-cut policy on the rate. When the Labour Government came to power in March 1974, they arrived without policies of any kind, hopelessly unprepared. According to one of their team, 'There is no comparable example of such intellectual and political incoherence in a party coming into office in the twentieth century history of the United Kingdom.' They had no short-term, no medium-term, and no long-term policies. Nothing appears to have changed in the next two years. They had come to office, 'more divided, more ideological, and more closely tied to the trade unions' apron strings' than in the 1960s.[126] The divisions and the ideology and the strings were all still in place in 1976 when there was another change of Prime Minister. There was no coherent policy, and the government was continually on the defensive.[127]

No one seemed clear on where the responsibility for the exchange rate lay. When the Chancellor of the time, Dennis Healey, was asked who decided on the rate (in this period of floating!), he said that he would have spoken to the Governor, and they would have sorted it out between them.[128] When former Bank officials were asked the same question, they were more inclined to have seen it as a Treasury responsibility.[129] Clearly, someone had to give instructions as to how much support to provide and how much it would tolerate spending to hold a particular rate. There even should have been possibilities for dialogue with dealers able to report on the feeling in the market and so suggest what might be achievable. Such dialogue was handicapped by the poor state of relations that existed between the Treasury and the Bank.[130]

The year had opened with sterling hovering, but apparently stable, at just above $2.00. It remained like that for almost two months. At the beginning of March, though, a number of factors triggered a slide that more or less continued until late in the year when IMF support was organised. On 4 March, pressure first appeared on sterling, and as soon as the market opened on Friday, 5 March, it was under pressure again and within minutes

---

[125] Author's conversation with Wass, 16 April 2008.
[126] Dell (1991, pp. 12, 19).
[127] Sir Geoffrey Littler, CCBH/Churchill College witness seminar, 'The changing climate of opinion: economic policymaking, 1975–9', 28 October 2005.
[128] Interview with Lord Healey, 28 February 2006.
[129] Interview with Sir Kit McMahon, 14 March 2008.
[130] See also Coleby interviews with Sir David Walker, 19 September 1996, and 28 February 1997.

had fallen from \$2.0120 to \$2.0070 and then to \$2.0031 by midmorning. It then slipped below the important psychological barrier of \$2.00 at 1.18 p.m., with the small downward adjustment in MLR of ½ per cent triggering a further decline 'in thin and extremely nervous dealings.' After-hours trading saw sterling sink to \$1.9772. \$200 million had been spent in support.[131] A City theory at the time was that the Nigerians, after a political skirmish with Britain, decided to move out of their recently acquired increased holdings of sterling. The Nigerians did reduce their holdings from £1,800 million in early 1975 to just £800 million in March 1976. On 9 March, the Nigerians announced that they had diversified, although there is no mention of that in the foreign-exchange daily reports. And in the following weeks, the Nigerians themselves then suggested otherwise.[132] In the week's summary report, the judgement was that once the psychological barrier of \$2 was breached, on Friday 5 March it 'weakened further in an acutely nervous market when the cut in MLR was announced amid growing – *but unfounded* – rumours that Nigerian selling had started the fall' (emphases added).[133] The Head of Foreign Exchange, Sangster, explained to the Governors that sterling was fine until lunchtime and even showed signs of strengthening. However, 'Given the increasing stridency of the alarm calls from certain parts of the Treasury at the unwelcome stability of sterling we thought it necessary to prevent the effective depreciation narrowing to 30.0 per cent.' So they bought dollars. But 'it was inevitable that we were seen, and at that stage, the market reversed rather brusquely.' Normally, they would then have bought sterling but were afraid that those 'elements in the Treasury anxious for further depreciation could well have accused us of trying to stabilise the effective depreciation at 30.1 per cent.' It was then too late to do anything because outsiders had decided that the Bank was trying to get a significant fall.[134] Sangster was later to argue that in March the Treasury forced the Bank to change the rules on intervention and 'made us appear to the market as deliberately wishing to force the rate down.' This had destroyed the market's confidence in the authorities' handling of exchange policy thereafter.[135] In a note to the Governor's Private Secretary (GPS) the

---

[131] Market report, 5 March 1976, C8/45.
[132] *The Times*, 9 March 1976, p. 1 and 10 March 1976, p. 17; IED 'Monitoring movements in Miani official sterling holdings', 25 March 1976; Edgley to Payton/McMahon, 'Nigeria: Ciroma speaks out on sterling', 26 March 1976, 8A210/15.
[133] 'Foreign exchange and gold markets (15 December 1975–16 March 1976)', 17 March 1976, C8/45.
[134] Sangster to McMahon/Richardson, 'Events of the afternoon of Thursday 4 March 1976', 5 March 1976, C43/779.
[135] Sangster to Dow, 'Intervention policy', 4 October 1976, C43/781.

following day, he wrote: 'The Treasury are always very concerned that nothing we say or write should suggest any differences between us – and they must be particularly sensitive over the events of 4 March, where we have taken all the blame for the policy change that they forced us to make against all our advice and judgment.'[136]

On the following Monday sterling suffered its largest ever fall in a single day, falling 4 cents against the dollar and losing 1.6 per cent in effective terms. There is no evidence of any one large seller. Official support of $142 million failed to halt the decline, and the pound bottomed out at $1.9287 and closed the day at $1.9445.[137] Tuesday was calm, and sterling 'regained a degree of poise', in the language of the daily report, but on the Wednesday, two large Middle Eastern sales put sterling under pressure yet again, and again despite support of $274 million, the rate fell. Thus, across the quarter from mid-December to mid-March, the story was one of steadiness until 4 March, and that was through a series of cuts in MLR that took the rate from 12 per cent in November to 9 per cent in March. Thereafter, the exchange rate tumbled to $1.9156 on 16 March. Derrick Byatt, then Adviser (Foreign Exchange), would later complain that 'the trouble was that we very often didn't know what was the aim of policy'.[138] As McMahon put it, the experience of March 'demonstrates a fundamental truth that while there are hosts of factors influencing an exchange market, the overwhelmingly most important one at any particular time, is the market's view of what the central bank is up to'.[139]

According to the Chancellor, Healey, the collapse in March was all the fault of the Bank. The Bank made two major mistakes. On 4 March, it sold sterling when the pound was already under pressure, and markets believed that this was part of a policy to push the market down. Then, on the next day, they lowered interest rates (MLR move to 9 per cent) instead of raising them and so appeared to confirm the market's suspicions. This analysis, of course, would mean that the Bank was entirely independent and both set interest rates and decided on an appropriate rate for sterling and took action to achieve that rate. It might have been able to do one, but not both. It is true that there was a certain amount of freedom with MLR, although, as has been shown elsewhere, this was largely a fiction or, more accurately, a fix. Friday was the weekly Treasury bill tender day, and it was clear on

---

[136] Sangster to Noakes, 5 October 1976, C43/781.
[137] Market report, 8 March 1976, C8/45.
[138] Coleby interview with Derrick Byatt, 27 November 1996.
[139] McMahon to Richardson/Hollom, 'Exchange rate policy in the light of events of the past month', 8 April 1976, C43/779.

this occasion that short-term rates were below the prevailing MLR. Thus MLR was simply allowed to fall into line with these rates. Healey believed it a responsibility of central banks to outwit the markets, 'a responsibility in which the Bank of England failed dismally in March 1976'.[140] Callaghan took a different view. He had become Prime Minister on 11 April following Wilson's unexpected resignation on 16 March and recalled in his memoirs:

The Chancellor and the Bank of England had apparently agreed during February that the exchange rate of sterling, which was then about two dollars to the pound, was unrealistically high and the Bank set out to edge it down, but the manoeuvre got out of hand when the foreign exchange dealers realised what was afoot, sterling fell faster and further than was intended, and the Bank of England was forced to spend substantial reserves to hold the rate up.

Callaghan, who had been badly scarred by his experience as Chancellor during sterling's problems in the sixties, culminating in the 1967 devaluation, was now shocked by the scale of support that had been given to the pound since the beginning of the year. He told Healey that he wanted to have meetings with Richardson.[141] Donoughue, a member of the Prime Minister's 'think tank' remembered that the Prime Minister was upset at the 'botched devaluation'.[142] But Dell says that there was no plan. Healey simply had been unable to make up his mind on depreciation.[143]

That is rather supported by the immensely detailed account by Wass, Permanent Secretary in the Treasury through most of the 1970s, which confirms that Treasury policy from the third quarter of 1974 was to engineer a depreciation of sterling. However, in February 1976, Healey was still not persuaded of the case for this, 'but if he were, he would want to go further ... probably on the basis of a step change with an immediate approach to our overseas depositors with proposals for compensation or guarantees'.[144] By late February when he met his advisers, Healey said that he was ready to see a depreciation of sterling to the levels of 1975 but was not ready to accept what the Treasury was advocating at that stage, a depreciation of 10 per cent by June. When he had lunch with the Governor at the Bank on 1 March, he said that he had decided on depreciation but not of how much nor of the method, timing, or political handling.[145] The techniques that the Treasury

---

[140] Healey (1989, p. 427).
[141] Callaghan (1987, pp. 414, 417).
[142] Donoughue (1987, p. 86).
[143] Dell (1991).
[144] Wass (2008, p. 176).
[145] Monck, 'Lunch meeting note for record', 1 March 1976, 7A133/1.

were then considering for bringing about their desired depreciation were rendered redundant by the market in the next week. Wass goes on to say that the Treasury did not understand the sales of 4 March until the Bank informed them that the Nigerian Central Bank had placed a sell order that the Bank duly executed in the normal way. What happened in that first week in March, however, was exactly in line with what the Treasury was seeking in its memorandum of February. At any event, the support of the foreign-exchange markets in March had been at a cost of $1,200 million, roughly one-quarter of Britain's reserves. As usual, at the time, there was wild speculation as to the amount of support given. And even long after the event, the normally sober Dell, speaking of the week in March, wrote that intervention was 'at one point reported to be at the rate of $500 million a day'.[146] On no day did it ever approach that.

Wass claims that the achievement of March was what the Treasury wanted:

The Treasury could hardly believe its luck. It had obtained a course of action it had been advocating for over eighteen months and one about which the Chancellor had always seemed to have misgivings. In the week that followed 4 March sterling fell from $2.0149 to $1.9120, a depreciation of over 5 per cent – not quite as much as the Treasury had been arguing for, but a decided step in the right direction.[147]

As far as the Bank was concerned, the damage done to its reputation was considerable. The idea that it operated with a degree of independence in this area was severely dented. James (Jim) Noakes, an Assistant to the Chief Cashier, remembered visiting the dealing room at Standard Chartered in the first week in March, where the first reaction of their dealers had been that the Bank had induced the fall by clumsy tactics. But 'The older heads could not bring themselves to believe this and greater reflection produced the view that the fall had been deliberately engineered.' Since they were unwilling to accept that the Bank had lost its touch, they concluded that the fall had been ordered by the Treasury against the advice of the Bank. This upset them because it threatened to diminish the importance of the London foreign-exchange market, and the 'loss of caste by the Bank threatened to undermine their ability to maintain an orderly market'.[148]

What had been set running in March by whatever means could not be easily stopped. Despite a desire for stability for at least a few months, in the course of April and May, the £/$ rate plunged further from $1.90 at the

---

[146] Dell (1991, p. 206).
[147] Wass (2008, p. 179).
[148] Noakes to Byatt, 'Taking the cap off', 10 October 1977, C43/791.

end of March to close to $1.72 at the beginning of June. And in these two months, the depreciation captured in the effective rate moved from 33.7 to 39.6 per cent below the Smithsonian rate. There was a fair amount of intervention all through these weeks as the Bank sought to hold to some rate or at least prevent a precipitate fall or perhaps the appearance of a precipitate fall. A total amount of $544 million was spent in support in these two months. The daily market reports stretched the author's ability to find new phrases: 'Market fears that sterling's underlying weakness might develop into further fall were vindicated' (1 April); 'sterling suffered a further disorderly retreat' (2 April); 'sterling continued to drift nervously' (5 April); 'the sharp bout of selling in New York last night cost sterling 13/4 cents' (6 April); more 'disorderly retreats' and 'nervousness' followed with very little 'recovery of poise'.[149]

There was still little sign of evidence on how the rate was to be managed. The Governor met the Chancellor on 21 April and apparently agreed that 'the absolute maximum that could be spent up to the end of May would be of the order of $2 billion', although this was not 'to be construed as a firm expression of view on the amount that should be spent on intervention'. 'But all this figuring was done very much off the cuff'.[150] When they met again on 21 May, it was on whether an interest-rate rise or intervention (support) should be used. The Governor was ambivalent, Wass wanted a ½ per cent rise or more in MLR, and the Chancellor preferred a 1 per cent rise – he left 'whether this should be achieved by administrative action or by persuasion to the Governor and Sir Douglas Wass to sort out'.[151]

On Friday 21 May, the pound fell by 2½ cents, and the 'market divined that no official support was forthcoming'.[152] At the end of May, McMahon was complaining to the Governor again that on exchange-rate policy there was

… an unsatisfactory position as regards both tactics and strategy.… The Prime Minister and the Chancellor appear to have taken a decision to stop intervening. They presumably feel that the $3bn. odd which we have spent since the 4th of March has been largely wasted.… it cannot be right to stop us operating in the exchange markets at all.… Until what appeared to come as a Prime Ministerial edict on Friday [not to intervene], we had always indeed believed that we had operating discretion of up to say £10mn. at any time. I think it imperative that we secure that discretion again explicitly.… Of course it will not follow that if we have discretion

---

[149] Dealer's reports, April and May 1976, C8/45.
[150] Barratt to Monck, 'Exchange rate', 26 April 1976, 3A49/4.
[151] Monck (HMT), Note of meeting – 'The exchange rate and interest rates', 21 May 1976, 3A49/4.
[152] Dealer's report, 21 May 1976, C8/45.

to spend up to, say, $25m. a day that we will do so every day. But even if we do so, we should not, I think, be too frightened of spending $100m. a week for some time to come.[153]

This is the most explicit statement of the general lack of policy and the failure of communication between the Bank and the Treasury on the subject. McMahon wrote to Mitchell along these lines, but it is indicative of the confusion that he began by stating, 'As we understand it, we are at the moment under a ministerial edict to do no intervention in the foreign exchanges at all'. For so fundamental an issue, 'as we understand it' seems vague, particularly in relation to a supposed edict. Mitchell's reply ignored that part of the letter, but he was happy to proceed on McMahon's suggested basis of discretion up to $25 million but wanted further talks and a weekly review.[154] There seems to be no discussion of the rate that sterling might be held to, simply how much they could afford to spend over a period. At any rate, the recently agreed position seems to have broken down again within a couple of weeks, for the Governor telephoned the Chancellor, who was in Puerto Rico, with 'an urgent request for a stay of execution of yesterday's decision to withdraw from the market'.[155]

The annual consultation with the IMF had been planned for the week 17 to 25 May. It was agreed that Finch would lead the negotiations, although Whittome may join any subsequent negotiation. Finch recalls that the mission went well, 'as no immediate crisis was looming'.[156] Apart from their usual concerns about the too rapid growth of domestic credit expansion (DCE) and money, their main concern was over the size of the public-sector borrowing requirement (PSBR), and they pressed for cuts.[157] The Chancellor obstinately resisted this, believing that appropriate policies were in place. The IMF nevertheless went along with the decline of sterling, believing the rate that had evolved after March to be satisfactory. Finch's closing statement concentrated on the need to reduce the PSBR urgently and that the reduction might need to be large. (£3 billion was a figure being bandied about.) There had been a session on the

---

[153] McMahon to Richardson/Hollom, 'Exchange market policy', 24 May 1976, 3A49/4. It was not uncommon to come and go between using dollars and pounds like this, even within the space of a few lines.

[154] McMahon to Mitchell, 24 May 1976; Mitchell to McMahon, 27 May 1976, C43/780.

[155] Plenderleith, Note for record – 'Exchange market intervention', 28 June 1976, 3A49/4.

[156] C. David Finch, 'Werribee to Washington. A career at the International Monetary Fund', unpublished manuscript, 1997, p. 82. Finch says that Karl Otto Pöhl, the German Finance Minister, was critical of the success of the consultation.

[157] A. W. Batchelor, Note for record – 'IMF consultations', 25 May 1976, 6A399/1.

exchange rate at which the possibility of 'improvement' was discussed, and Finch expressed the view that when that came, it would be advisable to re-build reserves.[158] By July, when the IMF's report was being circulated prior to the board considering it, Littler recorded that while there was general satisfaction with the direction being taken in policy generally, 'The fact remains that the IMF are expecting decisive action, that they want it as soon as possible.'[159]

In an effort to stabilise the rate, Richardson approached Arthur Burns, chairman of the Fed, about the possibility of a large drawing on the Federal Reserve Bank of New York (FRBNY) swap facility. They spoke twice on 3 June, when Burns indicated that he was sympathetic. Nevertheless, he warned that it would be difficult to draw the full amount ($3 billion); the United States would be looking for measures on the fiscal front, and there should be an application to the IMF if the swap could not be repaid. Later that day, Richardson suggested to Healey that the aim should be to negotiate $2 billion from the United States and $1 billion from Europe.[160] The following day, Zijlstra, chairman of the Bank for International Settlements (BIS), phoned Richardson and proposed that substantial backing for sterling should be organised in order 'to demonstrate that Central Banks considered the present rate to be ridiculously low'.[161] There were some on both sides of the Atlantic who were keen to see the IMF involved in order to impose some discipline.[162] A suitable package was quickly arranged, and on 7 June, Healey was able to announce a $5.3 billion standby for three months with the possibility of one renewal for a further three months. The United States contributed $2 billion but still insisted on repayment out of reserves or that Britain would have to go to the IMF for longer-term assistance. Thus the unconditional BIS arrangement would become a conditional one. It undoubtedly was an example of central bank co-operation, although Healey claimed, 'I got the credit without difficulty because all the contributors shared my view that the pound was then undervalued.'[163] Following the announcement, the rate rose by 3½ cents. It was by no means plain sailing after that, and some support still was given, but a certain amount of calm

---

[158] *Ibid.*

[159] Littler to Monck, 13 July 1976, 6A399/1.

[160] Plenderleith, Note for record – 'Telephone conversation with Dr. Burns: 3 June 1976', 3 June 1976; Monck, 'Note of a meeting held at No. 11 Downing Street at 7.00 p.m. on Thursday, 3 June 1976', 4 June 1976, 2A77/1.

[161] Plenderleith, 'The Governor's telephone conversation with Dr. Zijlstra: 4 June', 2A77/2.

[162] Dell (1991, p. 219); Wass (2008, pp. 198–203). Also see Keegan and Pennant-Rae (1979, pp. 152–173) for a contemporaneous account of the crisis.

[163] Healey (1989, p. 427).

and even a little recovery seemed to have been effected, and in the course of the summer, the rate rose to the higher $1.70s.

In July and August, most of the attention in the foreign-exchange markets was on the European currencies and the changes in the snake, and sterling remained quietly in a backwater, happy to be out of the limelight. However, there was sufficient concern for British officials and IMF management to be engaged in secret exploratory discussions about a stand-by arrangement, even to a consideration of the possible amounts needed.[164] There is some evidence of renewed support in the last week of August. In a telephone conversation between the Chancellor and the Governor on the morning of 25 August, Healey said that he would come back with firm views on support by 10.30 a.m. He had now agreed that 'a further $100 million, plus another $50 million if the Governor considers it would be really useful, should be available to defend a rate of $1.77'. If these sums were insufficient, then the rate should be allowed to fall. The funds were spent, and the rate stayed close to $1.77 until into September.[165] The markets were quiet when September opened, even if a little unease was being expressed. Although the Bank wanted to try and stay above the $1.77 floor, ministers and the Treasury were worried about the likely costs, and on 8 September, Callaghan and Healey decided that intervention to maintain $1.77 should cease.[166] By now, there was talk of further industrial problems and a possible seaman's strike, and 'A cold wind from the desert chilled sterling as ... selling orders swept out of the Middle East behind the clouds of yesterday's balance of payments revelation of reduction in sterling holdings and the Seaman's Union vote.'[167] On 9 September, there was another burst of selling that drove the rate below the floor. The rate was heading down to the lower $1.70s, and there had been three days when support had been over $100 million. Then the market was surprised when on 27 September the rate fell below $1.70. 'For the first time since the free float started, the absence of any support was deplored rather than accepted as a necessary evil.'[168] The rapid fall continued the next day, 28 September, with the market seeming to panic at one point. The Chancellor and the Governor were preparing to go to the Commonwealth finance ministers' meetings in Hong Kong and the IMF meeting in Manila. The continuing dramatic events resulted in the

---

[164] De Vries (1985, p. 467).
[165] Monck to Plenderleith, 25 August 1976, 7A133/1.
[166] Monck, Notes 3 and 8 September 1976 (of meetings held at 11 Downing Street on 1 and 8 September 1976), C43/781.
[167] Dealer's report, 8 September 1976, C8/45.
[168] Dealer's report, 27 September 1976, C8/45.

Governor cancelling his plans late in the day, and with further news of tumbling sterling, the Chancellor returned from Heathrow airport at the last minute.[169] (McMahon still went as the Governor's representative.) The rate closed that day at $1.6365, a new low point. The pound had fallen 8 cents in four days of trading. The cancellation of the Chancellor's trip apparently brought hopes of a package of economic measures, and some recovery in the rate was detected.

It was then that Callaghan made his 'turning-point' speech at the Labour Party Conference:

... for too long, perhaps ever since the war, we postponed facing up to fundamental changes ... living on borrowed time.... We used to think that you could spend your way out of a recession.... I tell you in all candour that that option no longer exists.... it only worked ... by injecting a bigger dose of inflation ... followed by a higher level of unemployment.[170]

Healey had been determined not to go to the IMF for a conditional loan, and his July measures were in part designed to obviate that need. However, the tumbling exchange rate and the fears that it was on its way to $1.50 changed that. With Callaghan opposed to spending in support of the rate and other measures such as import deposits ruled out, it was announced on 29 September that there would be an application to the IMF for standby facilities.[171] On the following day, rumours of a rise in MLR to 15 per cent pushed the rate up 3 cents in minutes. And yet, the markets remained essentially unconvinced. It was on 7 October that the MLR formula was suspended and the rate administered to 15 per cent as part of operation 'Draconis'. October thereafter was a mix of quiet to uncertain, with the rate staying at around $1.60. Then towards the end of October came the 'Sabbath thunderclap'. A story in *The Sunday Times* by Malcolm Crawford on 24 October attributed to the IMF the view that the appropriate rate for sterling was $1.50 and that that rate would be included in the conditions set by the IMF brought the month of quiet progress to a halt. It did not help that on the same day Milton Friedman, appearing on the US television programme 'Meet the Press', also had expressed the view that Britain was a country on the verge of collapse.[172] At its worst, the rate fell 7½ cents (that

---

[169] Interview with Ian Plenderleith, 21 July 2005; Wass (2008, p. 229).

[170] Callaghan (1987, pp. 426–427). Peter Jay, his son-in-law, takes credit for much of the speech; Dell (1991, p. 236).

[171] The application was made in October. Wass, 'The approach to the IMF', 18 October 1976, TNA T381/15.

[172] *The Times*, 25 October 1976, p. 1.

then becoming the biggest ever one-day fall), and the effective depreciation moved to 48.5 per cent. The rate had gone to $1.5730. It would fall further to $1.5550 on Thursday, 28 October. That day had been 'atypically rumour-free', but on 29 October, the British Broadcasting Corporation (BBC) gave credence and publicity to a story that a £10 billion facility was being negotiated to deal with the sterling balances. Another rumour had it that the application to the IMF had been vetoed.[173]

Much has been written about the Crawford article, some of it citing the IMF denials at the time, but others have clear recollections of papers in which $1.50 was being proposed.[174] Also, just a week later, when Whittome and Finch met McMahon and Pen Kent (UK alternate Director), they said that the IMF saw the rate going down further. On the following day, Ryrie was writing to Hedley-Miller that Finch was keen on an engineered depreciation.[175] What is more, when the IMF began discussions in November, they said that they could accept that a rate of $1.60 'is about right for the purposes of UK competitiveness', but they regarded further depreciation as essential to maintain competitiveness.[176] Thus there might be some substance to the claims of Crawford.

The Crawford article prompted the Governor to write to the Chancellor stressing that it was critical to regain control of the exchange rate, and since intervention alone was unlikely to be enough, a package of measures was necessary, and the Bank had drawn up a programme.[177] The essence of this was to speed up the improvement in the balance of payments and the reduction of the PSBR and to reassure financial markets and prevent further destabilising falls.

The IMF mission, headed by Whittome, arrived in London in November amidst growing fears that the British government was losing its ability to take decisions. There were some positives, though – interest rates had gone up, wage settlements had begun to drop back, and public expenditure was being tackled in a reasonably convincing way. Nevertheless, members of the IMF's team were taken aback by the change that had occurred in the relatively short time since their last visit. The IMF's historian describes the atmosphere

[173] Market reports, 25–29 October 1976; see C8/45.
[174] De Vries (1985, p. 470); Hickson (2005, pp. 116–117); Harman (1997, p. 173); Burk and Cairncross (1992, p. 68). But Bill Allen, for example, recalls being asked to comment on one such paper; 'Conversation with Bill Allen', July 2008.
[175] Kent, Note for record – 'Talk with Whittome and Finch', 7 October 1976, TNA T381/16; Ryrie to Hedley Miller, 'IMF and exchange rate policy', 8 October 1976 TNA T381/16.
[176] Barratt, 'Discussions with the IMF: the exchange rate', 19 November 1976, TNA T381/17.
[177] Richardson to Healey, 25 October 1976, 7A133/1.

in London as tense and 'In order to reduce encounters between the Fund staff and reporters, U.K. officials registered the staff in a hotel under assumed names.'[178] When this was discovered, it was interpreted as a way of the IMF quietly imposing tough policies. The negotiations were never going to be easy, for Healey had already announced that he believed that sufficiently tough policies were already in place. Lord Cromer could not resist pointing out that we were asking for funds from countries that had organised their affairs more prudently than we had, and they were therefore likely to want to impose conditions, and we should be prepared to accept them.[179]

Negotiations indeed were protracted and not helped by Callaghan seeking to enlist President Ford and West German Chancellor Helmut Schmidt to put pressure on the IMF to make conditions as light as possible. Such were the tensions in late 1976 that when the IMF team arrived on 1 November, the Prime Minister, according to Healey, would not allow them to speak to Treasury officials for two weeks after they arrived.[180] In fact, discussions on procedural questions did get underway almost immediately.[181] Finch, who took a leading role in the mission, records that the IMF's desire to see the PSBR reduced was deeply resented by Wass and that 'one under Secretary accused us in an outburst of rage of dismantling the post-war social reforms'.[182] There was at least one difference of opinion in the Treasury, and Derek Mitchell claimed to have been warned to keep away from the IMF team. Mitchell was regarded with great suspicion within the Treasury. Walker later recalled, 'Mitchell represented the Bank, and the IMF, and all that was abhorrent to this particular strand of thinking.'[183] Finch makes another remarkable claim, that he and Allan Whittome were warned by a Bank of England Director that their hotel rooms were bugged.[184] Whether true or not, the climate was apparently sufficiently dangerous and unpleasant for the claim to be made without it seeming wild.

The formal full meeting took place at the Treasury on 18 November, but the talks did not get off to a good start when Whittome queried a number of the forecasts on inflation, unemployment, and the PSBR. Of particular

---

[178] De Vries (1985, p. 469).

[179] HL Deb, 4 October 1976, Vol. 374, cc845–849.

[180] Healey (1989, p. 430); Wass (2008).

[181] Monck, 'Note of a meeting at 9.15 a.m. on Thursday, 4 November at No. 11 Downing Street', 4 November 1976, T381/17.

[182] Finch, *op. cit.*

[183] Coleby interviews with Sir David Walker, 19 September 1996 and 28 February 1997.

[184] Finch, *op. cit.*

concern were rising imports, the DCE forecast in excess of that agreed with the IMF earlier in the year, and the considerable revision of the overall outlook that had taken place since June and July. Was more depreciation of the currency needed?[185] Whittome was so disturbed by the forecasts that he contemplated returning to Washington (by Concorde) to discuss them with Witteveen.[186] Meetings of different groups on all aspects of the economy followed. None was easy.

Apart from the main meetings, there were small unofficial meetings and private dinners ranging over broad strategy down to detailed technical issues. The possibility of introducing base money control was raised by Finch and rejected by Bridgeman. When Goodhart mentioned to Littler that the media would soon pick up on the fact that not everything was going smoothly, Littler replied, 'rather grimly, that if this did come to have an effect on the markets by Wednesday, this might concentrate the minds of the Cabinet wonderfully'.[187]

There were clear differences between the Bank and the government. McMahon complained that the National Institute of Economic and Social Research (NIESR) and the economic establishment were providing support for those in the Cabinet who wished to do very little:

None of the economists who have been writing for the papers, nor the people in the National Institute [NIESR], have any significant experience of or feel for markets. Many of them tend to be deficient in understanding of financial factors more widely conceived. What *we* can see is that the country is at the end of its financial tether unless some radical change is brought about.[188]

He continued in seriously gloomy vein. If we did not accept the full discipline of the IMF and tried to persuade them of less than they wished to impose, the markets would not be convinced, and we would not be able to sell gilts or hold the exchange rate. 'If the markets do not accept that we have done enough and the rate starts to slide, there are no shots left in

---

[185] Dicks-Mireaux, Note for record, 8 November 1976, 6A399/1.

[186] Much rested on the lack of confidence they seemed to put in the Treasury's model. Bill Allen had drawn attention to the fact that there was a defect in the Treasury (MTA) model. It had imports as a function of GDP and exports as a function of world trade, but the elasticities used meant that all was doom – a continuously deteriorating trade balance. At a meeting at the Treasury in March 1976 Allen (in the company of Eddie George) made the point, but Posner dismissed it and appealed successfully to Liesner for support. But Allen was right (and was later supported by Andrew Britton). Allen, Note for record, 22 March 1976, 6A119/5.

[187] Goodhart, Note for record – 'IMF discussions', 25 November 1976, 6A399/1.

[188] McMahon, 'Conversation with the Chancellor on Sunday night', 26 November 1976, 7A133/1.

the locker.' The July package was a warning of how not to do things, 'much agony and all thrown away because of the inadequacy'. With an adequate package, this time financing would be relatively easy.[189]

As late as 5 December it was still not clear whether or not the negotiations would succeed, and some preparation was needed in the event of failure. Wass prepared a paper, at the request of Number 10, on how they might 'minimise financial disruption in the event that the Cabinet decide not to proceed with the application for an IMF standby'. If that happened, the government would have to say that the terms being demanded were too harsh and then put forward a plan that would achieve what was wanted. This would include cutting the PSBR, raising taxes, and selling the BP shares. An import-deposit scheme lasting for six months also should be announced. In addition, it would be useful to team up with the Trades Union Congress (TUC) and the Confederation of British Industry to contain wages and promote exports. Even so, there still would be a great risk that confidence would not be re-established. *In extremis*, some would be prepared to go for a siege economy.[190] This last was resisted strongly in the Bank. It meant 'welshing on our debts' and would destroy sterling's longer-term prospects and the future of the City as an international financial centre.[191]

Be all that as it may, agreement finally was reached by the weekend of 11–12 December. According to Finch, Richardson 'had publicly threatened to resign if any extension was needed'.[192] The IMF's Managing Director complimented Whittome for conducting 'the largest, longest, most difficult, and, perhaps, most momentous negotiation in the history of the Fund'.[193] Healey was able to announce the standby arrangement for SDR 3,360 million (£2.3 billion) for two years, the first of its kind that the IMF had approved, to the House of Commons on 15 December.[194] Conditions included that public-sector borrowing had to come down from a forecasted £10.5 billion in 1977/78 to £8.7 billion and from £11.5 billion in 1978/79 to less than £8.7 billion. These reductions were to be achieved mainly by cuts in expenditure. DCE was to be held at £9 billion in 1976/77 and reduced to £7.7 billion in the following year. Taxes were increased, and the Bank

---

[189] *Ibid.*
[190] Wass to Monck (HMT), 'Plans contingent on a failure of the application for an IMF standby', 5 December 1976, 7A114/17.
[191] Edwin Bennett to McMahon/Richardson, 6 December 1976, 7A114/7.
[192] Finch, *op. cit.*, p. 83.
[193] De Vries (1985, p. 472).
[194] HC Deb, 15 December 1976, Vol. 922, c1535; Healey, 'Letter of intent', 15 December 1976, 6A399/1.

had to sell the BP shares it had acquired – roughly £500 million. Such were the pressures and so great was the crisis of politics that Britain considered withdrawing from its German defence commitments or abandoning its nuclear deterrent as it sought to find ways of reducing expenditure. In addition to the IMF standby, a new BIS facility was organised in support of the sterling balances. And in January 1977, the Bank announced that $1,500 million was being raised on behalf of the Treasury in the capital markets. This helped to convince the markets that different means were being used to finance the external deficit.[195]

As far as the exchange rate went, the 'Letter of Intent' had said that it would be managed so as to maintain the competitiveness of manufacturing industry in home and foreign markets. This was not very precise, and there was nothing to suggest in the letter that the authorities thought the rate was at that time undervalued. However, since British costs were rising faster than those of their 'competitors', the only sensible deduction was that they must intend depreciation. In fact, the rate rose after the letter was published.

The Crisis and the End of Sterling Balances

The successful appeal to the IMF in 1976 is sometimes linked to the renewed attempt to settle the sterling balances question. In fact, it was essentially a separate matter. The oil-price rises in 1973–74 had boosted oil producers' sterling holdings, and Organisation of Petroleum Exporting Countries (OPEC) countries became the largest holders, with more than 70 per cent of the total. These had their uses, but they were volatile, and where they had been £4,862 million in March 1975, they had fallen to £2,379 million in September 1976. Indeed, the withdrawals had been a factor in the crisis. Although official balances at the end of 1976 were greatly reduced from what they had been a few years earlier, they still represented a potential source of pressure on sterling. To neutralise this threat, new arrangements with some similarities to previous ones were sought. Like the 1968 facility, the new one (known as the 'Third Group Arrangements') would be drawn on only when there was a net reduction in the balances. Private holdings were not covered because they were regarded as working balances and held only for trading purposes. In any case, they were widely dispersed, and it would have been impractical to approach individual holders, as could be done with official balances. The facility would be for two years, with a possible third-year renewable. Repayment then

---

[195] Press notice, 24 January 1977, 4A39/23.

would be due over four years from the end of the drawdown period. In January 1977, when the Chancellor was making his statement on this, the technical details were still to be worked out. The determination was to avoid problems of the kind that had arisen after the oil-price hike of 1974 and to achieve in the next two years an 'orderly reduction in the role of sterling as a reserve currency'.[196] Eligibility to draw on the facility was conditional on continuing eligibility to draw on the IMF's standby (effective from 3 January 1977), which, in turn, depended on persevering with the policies introduced.

What was new in the Third Group Arrangements was the agreement that Britain would attempt ('use all reasonable effort') to reduce the official balances in sterling, one means of which was the sale of foreign-currency bonds. These would be 'foreign currency "funding" securities' of five- to ten-year maturity and negotiable, and no more than 75 per cent would be in dollars, a means of getting holders out of gilts and into foreign-currency bonds. Also different was that no explicit guarantees were being offered.[197] Negotiations were far from straightforward, though. US Treasury Under Secretary for Monetary Affairs Edwin Yeo (Volcker was now chairman of the FRNBY) had come to London with a position (which he had worked out with Burns) with limited room for manoeuvre. Agreement was reached, and Yeo left, but then McMahon discovered that the Prime Minister was not satisfied, particularly with the involvement of the IMF and with the repayment schedule. (The Bank bridled at the thought of IMF monitoring.) Later, when Ryrie wrote to Mitchell, he passed on a suggestion of Whittome's that 'we could always stipulate that, besides the Managing Director himself, only a small number of senior people who deal regularly with the U.K. should have access to the information we shall provide.' McMahon caught Yeo at the airport, and he came back. However, when Burns found out, he then cancelled his own trip to Basle 'and there was a period of crisis'.[198]

A key part of the problem was what 'reasonable efforts' should mean.[199] There was some scepticism over what efforts would be made. Governor

[196] HC Deb 11, January 1977, Vol. 923, cc1260–1261.

[197] George/Quinn to Payton/Page/McMahon, 'Sterling balances: foreign currency bond offer', 4A39/22.

[198] Payton, Note for record – 'Facility for supporting sterling balances', 10 January 1977; McMahon, 'Sterling balances negotiations: London and Basle 8–11 January', January 1977, 4A39/22. For the Treasury view, see Monck, 'Note for record', 7 March 1977, TNA T364/110.

[199] Payton, Note for record – 'Facility for supporting sterling balances', 10 January 1977, 4A39/22.

Clappier, of the Banque de France, recalled that five years previously the British had expressed a wish to reduce the balances but that 'the results of their efforts had so far been scanty', and the French declined to participate in the arrangement.[200] As late as 10 January, there was still no agreement on the amount of the facility.[201] The amount was established at $3 billion, but it would not be until the February meeting in Basle that all the details would be settled. The bulk of the $3 billion facility put together by the participating central banks was contributed by the Americans and the Germans ($1.6 billion), on which the British could draw on the condition that official sterling balances did not exceed $6.75 billion net of public-sector foreign-currency borrowing.

The Bank did set to work immediately on the proposal for a foreign-currency bond offer, envisaging selling about £500 million.[202] Permission from the countries whose currencies were to be used also would need to be gained. Some soundings were taken by Bank representatives around the Middle East, and while reception was friendly, there seemed to be no great enthusiasm for the idea.[203] When McMahon met Mitchell in early February, he expressed his own unease that not many foreign-currency bonds would be taken up.[204] At the end of February, after the offer of bonds had been made, the most widely voiced concern seemed to be the question of marketability/negotiability and the related matter of the length of the maturities'.[205] However, the operation was judged a success when 15 holders subscribed to the bonds a total of £395 million, of which just under half were in US dollars and the rest in DM, yen, and Swiss francs. India was the largest buyer by far, with £155 million, and one or two took as little as £2 million.[206]

Private balances had proved more stable and were thought to be for the most part close to normal working levels. With the continual movement of funds, it was difficult to give precise figures for half-yearly (or any other)

[200] Renee Larre (general manager, BIS) to Richardson, 19 January 1977, enc. draft 'Record of meeting of central bank governors, in Basle on 10 January 1977', 13 January 1977', 4A39/22.

[201] Payton, Note for record – 'Sterling balance facility', 10 January 1977, 4A39/22. Alan Holmes was vice-president of the FRBNY.

[202] George/Quinn to Payton/Page/McMahon, 'Sterling balances: foreign currency bond offer', 18 January 1977, 4A39/22.

[203] Richard Turner to Payton/McMahon, 'Visit to Jeddah, Kuwait and Bahrain', 24 January 1977, 4A39/23.

[204] McMahon, Note for record – 'Conversation with Sir Derek Mitchell', 4 February 1977, 4A39/23.

[205] Barber to Payton, 'Offer of bonds', 28 February 1977, 4A39/24.

[206] 'Sterling balances, Basle facility and foreign currency bonds', 23 May 1977, 4A39/27.

points. But in mid-1977 it did seem to be the case that sterling holdings were less than they had been in the previous December. The IMF was not particularly pleased with the monthly information it was given. Witteveen had to make a judgement as to whether reasonable efforts had been made to persuade governments to hold less sterling. He wanted to be briefed more fully than had hitherto been the case, but the Bank resisted this, pointing out that the Managing Director was the 'handmaiden' of the Basle Governors, and the first duty was to the Governors.[207] During the two years, there was no need to make recourse to the $3 billion, and the option to renew was not required, the facility lapsing in February 1979. Although private holdings had increased at the same time (see Figure 8.5), the authorities were satisfied that there had been no shift between the two. Overall, the view was that the Third Group Arrangements had played some part in the restoration of confidence in sterling.[208]

Changing Fortunes

Almost no sooner had the new tighter controls on outflows of sterling been introduced in the crisis of 1976 than consideration started to be given to controls on inflows. 1977 opened with sterling in heavy demand, some of it attributable to need for end-year balances, but more had to do with an apparent reappraisal of Britain's prospects for the year ahead. Not everyone was convinced, and Sangster was of the view that sterling would fall in the course of the year.[209] However, demand for sterling did continue, with only an occasional lull, for some time. Almost $1,200 million was taken in on 13 January. As demand continued through the month, so, too, did official intervention to hold the rate down. 'The intervention is now increasingly obvious to the market ... and subject to comment.... frustration can be sensed in some quarters.'[210] Such was the demand the following day that it required 'increasingly heavy handed intervention by the authorities'. The next week was similar. Even the 1 per cent cut in MLR on Thursday, 27 January, was received quietly. While the authorities wrestled with this new problem in January, something close to a policy was at least articulated. This was that stability was the main objective with a band of $1.60 to $1.72, and there being no intention to lower the rate. Interestingly, Sangster still

---

[207] McMahon to Ryrie, 'Sterling balances', 27 July 1977, 4A39/27.
[208] Mutch, 'Third Group Arrangement', 9 February 1979, 4A39/34; C. A. Enoch to McMahon, 'UK experience in winding down the reserve role of sterling', 22 September 1981, 8A201/21.
[209] Sangster to McMahon, 'Exchange rate policy', 12 January 1977, C43/788.
[210] Foreign exchange reports, 18 January 1977, C8/46.

believed that the rate would fall in the course of 1977, and he raised the idea that they might again engage in swaps.[211]

Even at the beginning of February 1977 it was believed that the large January inflow was probably a one-off. But that certainly was not the case. A major turn-around was beginning to take place. Sterling opened 1977 at $1.70 and then remained stable for many months, and the reserves began to grow rapidly (see Figure 14.4). Reserves that had struggled to stay close to $5 billion over the recent past now jumped from just over $4 billion in December 1976 to just over $7 billion in January 1977 and grew further to $11.5 billion at the end of June. At the end of the year, they stood at over $20 billion. These were huge advances. It seemed that no amount of selling could hold the pound down; the rate rose in the course of 1977 to finish at $1.9185, and at the end of October, they gave up any hope of capping.[212] When the Head of Treasury at Grindlays Bank rang McMahon to express his dismay at the disorderly state of the foreign-exchange markets – 'as volatile as he could ever remember' – McMahon expressed sympathy but said that the market was being left to its own devices and would doubtless take some time to settle down.[213]

In 1977, both Bank and Treasury models led to recommendations that depreciation was necessary to maintain competitiveness of British industry. This was essentially the view that was implicit in the December 1976 'Letter of Intent' to the IMF, and this was the view that most of the press carried. The NIESR tended to go along with this, as did, in a more qualified way, the OECD. Samuel Brittan was seen as the clearest exponent of the monetarist, or international monetarist, position, which saw monetary policy affecting first the exchange rate and then, in turn, the inflation rate. Peter Jay was in this camp, as were London Business School economists Terry Burns and Jim Ball, and support also could be found in the US Treasury.[214] Overall, the weight of argument was that it was unwise to try to engineer depreciation but that downward movements should not be resisted. It probably was wiser to let the rate find its own level once all the other instruments had been set.[215]

In August 1977, when sterling was particularly strong, a number of news agencies reported that there were strong rumours in the stock market that

---

[211] Barnes, Note for record, 17 January 1977, C43/788.
[212] Wicks, 'Exchange rates and monetary policy. Note of a meeting held at 10 Downing Street, at 11.00 am on 28 October', 28 October 1977, TNA PREM16/208.
[213] McMahon, Note for record, 3 January 1977, 3A49/5.
[214] See also Williamson and Wood (1976).
[215] Latter, 'The exchange rate debate', 1 June 1977, 3A38/5.

the Bank had changed its intervention tactics and were allowing sterling to float upward. The agencies wanted some formal word, and as the rumours persisted, the Press Officer George Morgan issued a statement through Reuters, with McMahon's agreement: 'A Bank of England spokesman said that rumours that the Bank had changed its intervention policy in the Foreign Exchange market since the 27th July were utterly unfounded.'[216] This was strong language for the Bank. However, it was only a couple of months later that there was an official change of stance. The scale of the inflows was making life difficult. The attempt through 1977 had been to keep the rate stable, a policy that had its critics but was judged to have commanded general support. This aim was not difficult to achieve when the US dollar was itself stable. Come the summer, though, the stability of sterling had to be expressed in terms of the effective rate. In Whitehall, they were arguing that the inflows were based on an expectation of the rate improving, and the proper response was therefore to lower interest rates, relax exchange controls, repay $2.5 billion of nationalised industry debt, and refrain from drawing the November tranche from the IMF.[217] In the Bank, they were now worrying more about M3 and did not want to see any fall in MLR. They were happy with relaxation of exchange controls and repayment of debt. After that, they would allow the exchange rate to appreciate.[218]

Things worsened at the end of September, and there was a huge outflow of dollars from the United States, and while they would not all arrive in Britain, to the extent that they did, they posed a threat to monetary control. Heavy intervention therefore was to be eschewed and the sterling rate allowed to find its own level. While the Treasury in 1977 had wanted to hold the exchange rate to $1.72, after September, it let it go, and it, too, turned its attention to money.[219] Payton, now Chief of the Overseas Department, worried about this and cautioned that the sterling rate had more to do with the weakness of the dollar and the perceived prospective benefits of North Sea oil. The danger that might develop was that sterling would appreciate, making it more attractive, for instance, to Middle East oil producers who were holding large sums on deposit in the United States. Payton therefore favoured staying with the current policy of intervention.[220] Byatt, too, was apprehensive and complained to Sangster, 'I

---

[216] Morgan, Note for record, 16 August 1977, 3A38/5.
[217] Wicks, 'Note of a meeting ... 5 September, 1977', 15 September 1977, TNA T364/111.
[218] Richardson to Healey, 16 September 1977, TNA T364/111.
[219] Sir Geoffrey Littler, CCBH/Churchill College witness seminar – 'The changing climate of opinion: economic policymaking, 1975–79', 28 October 2005.
[220] Payton to Richardson/Hollom, 7 October 1977, 7A114/17.

find it almost unbelievable, after the traumas which we have been through in the past 18 months or so, that policies are still being advocated which completely ignore our experience of the market-place.' He was prepared for the rate to move in the direction the market wanted but feared disorderly markets.[221] There was little alternative to uncapping given the inflows, and there were also sound reasons for allowing some appreciation of the rate. Complete freedom was not anticipated, but an appreciation of around 5 per cent could be tolerated. Berrill worried about damaging competitiveness, and Wass agreed with him.[222] At base, of course, the reason for the decision was that the inflows were making it impossible to keep to the agreed monetary targets for the IMF.

Ahead of the recovery in sterling and the considerable buildup in reserves, at the beginning of 1977, the Bank negotiated on behalf of the government a syndicated credit of $1.5 billion. Led by a group of major British, American, and German banks, the loan was the result of a desire to strengthen the official reserves on a secure basis. The Bank saw the government's Eurodollar borrowing as 'an opportunity to obtain the support of the international banking community in meeting our medium term external financial requirements at a time when the UK's credit status is showing a marked improvement'.[223] The $1.5 billion was needed to cover the balance-of-payments financing gap in 1977 over and above the initial IMF borrowings, which had itself been largely offset by repayment of the 1976 G10 drawings.[224] Jurgen Ponto, chairman of Dresdner Bank, first expressed an interest in providing funds in November 1976, and when the decision was taken to proceed with the government borrowing in January, the Bank took up Ponto's earlier suggestion.[225] From there, the loan was arranged swiftly. In January 1977, Richardson called in the clearing bank chairmen and proposed that they contribute $325 million – $25 million from Williams and Glyn's and $75 million each from the others. Barclays were concerned 'at the political consequences of government being seen to raise yet another international loan', but Richardson explained that given the prospect of a further payments deficit in the coming year, it

---

[221] Byatt to Sangster, 'Taking the cap off', 7 October 1977, 7A114/17.

[222] Wicks, 'Exchange rates and monetary policy, Note of a meeting held at 10 Downing Street', 28 October 1977, C43/791. Keegan and Pennant-Rae (1979, p. 69) claimed close to the time that in a discussion, presumably this one, to let the pound float, Wass was present and opposed the move.

[223] Quinn, 'HMG's Euro-dollar borrowing', 14 January 1977, 6A374/9.

[224] Plenderleith (GPS), Note for record – 'Dr Leutwiler's call on the Governor 4 February', 4 February 1977, 6A374/8.

[225] Quinn to Plenderleith, 'Dresdner Bank A. G', 28 January 1977, 6A374/9.

seemed right to take steps to raise finance in an orderly manner by taking advantage of favourable market conditions. The clearers were reluctant but eventually agreed to co-operate with the scheme.[226] McMahon praised Quinn (then working in Chief Cashier's) for the success of the operation: 'He conceived its broad outline; was endlessly thorough in following through the detailed implications of his conception; and anticipated all the problems which arose. Perhaps most important, he never lost his courage (and often stiffened mine) when things looked to be going badly, as at one or two points they certainly did.' Richardson thanked McMahon and also praised him for the success of the 'excellently conceived and conducted operation'.[227]

For the last two years of the decade, the external indicators looked healthy. The £/$ rate finished 1977 at close to $2.00. The effective rate remained essentially flat through 1977 and again in 1978, and then in 1979 it rose to be within about 30 per cent of its Smithsonian value. The official reserves also went up hugely. In 1977, they rose from around $5 billion to $20 billion. They slipped back slightly in 1978 before rising strongly again to finish 1979 at $22.5 billion and to go on to rise to close to $30 billion in 1980, a colossal turn-around from just a few years before. Figure 14.5 shows how intervention had changed from heavy buying of sterling to heavy selling across the last three years of the decade. (The figure of $980 million in October 1978 is an IMF repurchase, and that for April 1979 is another.)

As far as exchange-rate policy went, though, there had not been much progress. At the beginning of 1978, the Executive Director for economics wrote, 'My ideas about exchange rate policy are at the moment somewhat unclear.' He believed that what was needed was 'sufficient depreciation', although he did not say sufficient for what. The prime objective of economic policy was to maintain a 'competitive' rate. This implied that 'we *can* alter the real exchange rate: On this I stick to the September Bulletin doctrine'. It is a puzzle to see what that might have been: there was discussion about the benefits of an appreciating exchange rate being rather less than might be anticipated, but nothing so strong as a doctrine. Since Dow wanted depreciation, he suggested monetary growth of 11 to 15 per cent for 1978 'in order to undermine confidence a bit, but not too much'. As far

[226] Quinn, Note for record – 'HMG rollover credit: meeting with clearing banks', 17 January 1977, 6A374/9.

[227] McMahon to Richardson/Hollom, 'HMG loan'; Richardson, Annotation, 24 January 1977, 6A374/9.

as intervention went, he was in favour of keeping the market guessing as to when and where they would act – 'Let us call this "fuzzy rate-oriented" intervention.'[228] He did not elaborate on his view that money could affect the exchange rate but not inflation.

As 1979 opened, there was discussion over whether there should be a target exchange rate or a rate band and what criteria might be used for judging the target and moving towards it. With sterling strengthening, the Bank worried about competitiveness worsening. Walker, who had now moved from the Treasury to the Bank, wondered if a strong exchange rate could be used as a means of reducing inflation and suggested to Dow that Panic should prepare a paper on the subject, and Dow commented to McMahon, 'I would I think be content with a paper which was not too definite in any conclusions it came to, but talked round some main issues.'[229] In April, Walker continued to fret over the strong pound and the likelihood, as he saw it, that it would continue to rise through the election period. He was influenced by reports that came from industrial contacts. He favoured 'a steady and, if necessary, substantial programme of intervention to counter upward pressure on the rate'. He further wondered if it might be a good idea to warn the markets that 'further appreciation would be regarded as unwelcome and excessive.[230]

A briefing paper for the incoming government in May began by asserting that the scepticism that had developed recently over the possibilities of managing an exchange rate was not entirely justified. Since the beginning of 1977, the United Kingdom had been leaning against short-run market trends but always ready to let the rate move if 'underlying pressures prove too strong'. The view was that sterling was too strong and, because of North Sea oil, was likely to remain so. Further, the United Kingdom 'would be better off with a somewhat lower exchange rate than is likely to emerge as a result of market forces'. Yet, there was in practice relatively little room for manoeuvre. The possibility of joining the European Monetary System (EMS) was put but just as quickly set aside.[231]

When the Governor gave the inaugural Henry Thornton Lecture at City University in 1979 (not to be confused with the inaugural Mais Lecture,

[228] Dow to Walker, 'Exchange rate policy', 10 January 1978, 4A112/13; *BEQB* 17(3):298–299, September 1977.

[229] Walker to Dow, 'Paper on the exchange rate', 3 January 1979; Dow to McMahon 'Project of a paper on the exchange rate', 4 January 1979, 4A112/17.

[230] Walker to Richardson, 'Exchange rate and money', 4 April 1979, 4A112/17.

[231] 'Exchange rate policy', 4 May 1979, enc. with Richardson to Howe, 4 May 1979, 4A112/17.

which he gave in the previous year), he chose the subject of the international monetary system and reflected on the problems in the 1970s. It was exaggerated, he said, to claim that floating offered all the answers. There could be no disagreement there. Critics argued that central banks should leave the rates alone completely, but this, to his mind, brought adjustment not in 'the form that policymakers tend to seek'. He conceded that the early experience of 1971–73 was hampered by the massive monetary stimulus from the United States. But that aside, he felt that the next six years were unsatisfactory and that there was widespread disillusion with floating. His own inclination was a fixed rate. He advocated that the authorities 'use exchange rate and domestic monetary policies in a complementary rather than a competitive manner'. He approved of 'pragmatic, but above all, collaborative' efforts to ameliorate our problems and regarded the snake as a particularly successful illustration of such a regime.[232]

The continuing desire for fixity in the exchange rate can be found again in the efforts to revamp the snake at the end of the seventies. The improvements in sterling in 1977–78 coincided with these proposals, and there was fairly general acceptance in Britain that that was the right direction to take. The snake of 1972 hardly could have been judged a success. What had worked was an arrangement between Germany and some small and closely related trading partners whose policies and interests were closely connected. For others, the snake had proved more difficult, and for some, impossible. Yet there was still widespread political support in Britain quite apart from Europe for a fixed exchange-rate regime. Thus, when in early 1978 a new snake proposal was made, the British seemed ready to take it seriously.[233] As Howe, the shadow Chancellor at the time, later put it, there was the desire to return to the order that they believed went with a pegged-rate regime.[234]

The early form of the new proposal, made by Schmidt, was not regarded with enthusiasm in the Bank, although Dow felt that 'rejoining the snake might give us a lower rate than would happen without.... It is not clear to me that rejoining the snake is not a tenable possibility.' But he often put the counter case as well, and in the end, he concluded that it would be better not to join the snake because 'we could do better than just keep the exchange rate stable', and yet, again he looked 'longingly again at the snake'.[235] Some weeks

[232] Richardson (1989, pp. 21–39).
[233] Wood (HMT), 'Minutes of meeting ... 11 January 1978', 16 January 1978, 4A112/13.
[234] Kandiah (2008, p. 23).
[235] Dow to Walker, 'Exchange rate policy', 10 January 1978, 4A112/13.

later when McMahon was briefing the Governor, he noted, 'when nothing comes out, it may be put about that it was the British who stopped it and though this obviously has some substance in relation to EMU [Economic and Monetary Union] … it was also pointed out that we can no longer hold back on EMU on the grounds that it might be anti-American. The Americans are, in both public and private, blessing the idea (even though they do not quite know what it is).'[236] McMahon met Karl Otto Pöhl, vice-president of the Bundesbank, in Luxembourg later in June, and Zijlstra just happened to be there and was encouraged to stay. Pöhl asked if Britain was not interested in joining some kind of European monetary arrangement. McMahon said that the British government were, but it depended on 'the symmetry of obligations'. Pöhl professed not to know what that meant. His main fear was that Giscard and Schmidt and possibly Callaghan would agree to some scheme in principle that the Bundesbank might not like. At the close, McMahon 'called his bluff' and asked what his reaction would be if Britain announced that they were joining an unamended snake, and Pöhl admitted that he would not welcome it.[237] At Bremen in July 1978, the EMS was announced – designed to be at least as strict as the original snake had been but with countries not participating in the snake allowed wider bands initially.

The End of Exchange Controls

Exchange controls had been part of exchange-rate management, and they were still used extensively in the 1970s as an emergency means of supporting whatever else was being done to protect the sterling rate. They were continually being adjusted. In fact, in the 1970s, numbers employed in exchange control rose from 490 in 1970 to 750 in 1978. However, such was the turnaround in the exchanges at the end of the 1970s that discussion was of increasing controls to deter inflows rather than outflows. At the beginning of May 1979, there was a proposal to introduce some downward pressure on the sterling rate by relaxing exchange controls.[238]

In the Bank, there was a tradition of hostility to controls, perhaps particularly exchange controls.[239] There were many influential voices going back to Cobbold and Cromer who were passionately opposed. The case against grew stronger when the fixed parity was abandoned in the early 1970s, as

---

[236] McMahon to Richardson, 'Sherpa briefing', 6 June 1978, 7A155/2.
[237] McMahon, 'Conversation with Poehl in Luxembourg 19 June 1978', 28 June 1978, 7A155/2.
[238] McMahon to Richardson/Hollom, 3 May 1979, 4A112/17.
[239] Lawson (1992, p. 39).

Cairncross, by then retired from the Treasury, pointed out in a paper he sent to the Bank in 1972.[240] In the middle of 1977, Goodhart had advocated getting rid of as much exchange control as possible, and work was going on in both the Treasury and the Bank on the effects of removing the controls.[241] Both McMahon and Douglas Dawkins (Chief of Exchange Control) were opposed, too, although timing was seen as a problem:

The sequence of events culminating in the removal of exchange controls began in 1977.... In October there were relaxations in the rules affecting inward direct investment, travel, cash gifts and emigration. More relaxations were made with effect from 1 January 1978 including certain concessions for UK direct and portfolio investment in the EEC.[242]

It was not, however, until August 1979 that the decision was finally made to go all the way and remove the remainder of the controls. Relaxation had been one thing; abolition was another.

Thus the rising exchange rate in 1977 and large-scale intervention to keep it down prompted thoughts on relaxing or removing controls. In that month, the Bank became aware, through a story in a German newspaper, of a swap technique that was being used to escape exchange control. Continental Illinois had arranged a 10-year foreign-currency swap for $25 million at fixed rates of exchange between British and American firms. According to the paper, 'the procedure is a new one and in no way contravenes UK Exchange Control regulations'. Consolidated Goldfields wished to acquire Hydro Conduit Corp in the United States. It received $25 million and deposited the same amount in sterling at Continental Illinois. Continental then found an American company that wanted the equivalent of $25 million in sterling and arranged a similar swap in the other direction. Since British interest rates were higher than American rates, the American firm had agreed to pay an annual charge of 2 per cent to go to Consolidated Goldfields. Penal rates of interest thus were avoided.[243]

An influential pamphlet that attracted a lot of attention appeared in February 1979 advocating the abolition of exchange controls, but it was

---

[240] See Geoffrey Wood (EID) to Dicks-Mireaux, 'U.K. capital controls', 3 November 1972, 4A112/5. Cairncross's paper was published the following year; see Cairncross (1973).

[241] Goodhart to Richardson/Hollom, 'The inter-relationship of monetary and external policies', 28 July 1977, 6A50/22; Peter A. Bull to Rachel Lomax, 'Effects of removing exchange controls', 4 January 1978, 4A112/13.

[242] Buxton, 'UK exchange control', 20 October 1989, 4A165/9.

[243] Translation from *Handelsblatt*, 6 October 1977; 'Swap operation provides a way round exchange control', 13 October 1977, 3A49/5.

only after the return to power of a Conservative Government in May 1979 that serious proposals emerged.[244] Nigel Lawson, Financial Secretary to the Treasury, set up a small team headed by David Hancock from the Treasury and Dawkins from the Bank. On 12 June 1979, new Chancellor Geoffrey Howe announced in his budget statement the intention to dismantle exchange controls progressively.[245] The pace of relaxation would be influenced by sterling's strength, as well as the speed with which economic problems could be solved. The first package announced in the budget concentrated on greatly liberalising outward direct investment and increasing limits on certain personal transactions, with only minor moves on outward portfolio investment. By the middle of July 1979, McMahon was opposed to 'further major relaxations, or indeed abolition until the autumn when we have been able to review carefully the implications of total abolition, particularly for our prudential controls over banks, commodity markets, etc.'[246]

Although Richardson was also opposed to controls, caution as ever asserted itself, and he said that 'he thought it would be hard to go all the way in one step in a tidy and satisfactory manner'. Wass, on the other hand, wanted to go faster and believed that they were in 'a sufficiently strong position to dispense with Exchange Control altogether', and Howe looked at October as his target for further changes.[247] With the continued strength of sterling, a further package of exchange-control relaxations was released on 18 July that included the removal of all restrictions on the financing of direct investment overseas and also made significant portfolio relaxations.[248] The Financial Times felt that the new relaxation 'goes so far as to bring the whole future of the exchange control apparatus into question'.[249]

In late August, Lawson asked for proposals for further exchange-control relaxations to be released towards the end of October, with complete removal of all restrictions no later than in the budget the following April. Dawkins noted:

If our experience of the last forty years has taught us anything, it is that exchange control restrictions do not cure problems. It has also shown that restrictive systems

[244] Miller and Wood (1979).
[245] HC Deb, 12 June 1979, Vol. 968, cc244–245.
[246] McMahon to Richardson, 'Some points to make this afternoon', 13 July 1979, 7A133/1.
[247] Hollom, Note for record – 'Exchange control relaxations', 10 July 1979, EC5/645.
[248] John Townend to Dawkins/Willetts/Mutch, 'Outward direct investment', 2 April 1981, enc. 'Outward direct investment and the abolition of exchange control', 4A79/6; HC Deb, 18 July 1979, Vol. 970, c720W.
[249] The Financial Times, 19 July 1979, EC5/685.

usually have a bias towards becoming more restrictive.... I am therefore much in favour of dispensing with controls and the associated machinery entirely.[250]

Bank and Treasury officials concluded that there was no practicable halfway house and that the next step should be complete abolition. However, the timing of the abolition still was uncertain. The choice was either in October or six months later in the budget. McMahon felt that early action could increase confidence and would leave the government with the initiative.[251] Further arguments for action sooner rather than later could be found in the possibility of joining the EMS, which could not be done with exchange controls still in place; 'the removal meant that the UK would at last be meeting in full her obligations on capital movements under the EEC Treaty and also OECD Code on Capital Movements'[252] – although both France and Italy still had restrictions on payments in respect of capital transactions.[253]

A perceived problem was that liberalisation would make certain direct controls on the money supply such as the 'corset' less effective, but the SSD scheme was deemed to be nearing the ending of its life anyway. McMahon wrote:

I am satisfied that it would be wrong, and indeed self-deceiving, for us to believe that we would be able to rely on exchange controls for any lasting help in managing our monetary policy. None of the most important central banks abroad does so; and we should be on very weak ground in relation to the markets and commentators in claiming that we were prolonging the life of exchange control in order to maintain our monetary policies.[254]

There were other factors at work, too. One was North Sea oil. The benefits meant that there was no longer the same need to discourage capital outflows. The Treasury certainly believed that North Sea oil enhanced the arguments for abolition and probably made the process of removing controls quicker than it otherwise would have been. A second was that with part of the government's overall economic policy to cut public expenditure, the removal of controls was estimated to produce a saving of around £14½ million simply in staff costs at the Bank and the Treasury. Every little bit helped.

---

[250] Dawkins, 'The future of exchange control', 20 August 1979, EC5/647.

[251] N. J. Ilett, 'Note of a meeting ... 9 October 1979', 10 October 1979, EC5/652.

[252] Norman to Porter, 'Exchange control', 13 October 1980, 4A79/6.

[253] MF, *Annual Report on Exchange Arrangements and Exchange Restrictions*, Washington, D.C, 1980.

[254] McMahon, Draft letter to the Prime Minister – 'Exchange control liberalisation', 12 October 1979, EC5/652. The sale of BP shares was also a factor.

On Tuesday, 23 October 1979, Howe announced that all remaining restrictions would be removed from midnight except those necessary for economic sanctions against Rhodesia.[255] Thus, after a period of 40 years, exchange controls were brought to an end. At the time, approximately 750 people worked in the Bank on exchange control, including 100 at the branches and the Glasgow Agency. After the June relaxation, the Bank started contingency planning in the event that all restrictions were removed. In July it withdrew offers to 200 new recruits who had not yet started at the Bank: given the short notice, these people were offered three months' salary as compensation. Coinciding with the Chancellor's October announcement, staff assembled in the lecture theatre at New Change to be told by Dawkins that controls were to be abolished. Rather than make compulsory redundancies, there was a voluntary severance scheme with generous terms. Over 700 across the Bank took advantage of the severance scheme, including 300 from Exchange Control. Looking back a year later, Dawkins concluded, 'All in all, the Bank appears to have survived one of the most traumatic upheavals in its long history relatively unscathed.' Employees at the branches had greater difficulty, with few of the employment opportunities that were available in London, and the same article acknowledged that 'the Bank's reputation in the recruitment market had suffered severely and will take some years to repair'.[256]

The abolition of exchange controls that came in October 1979 is sometimes presented as a dramatic gesture by the new Conservative Government that took the markets completely by surprise. The new Chancellor made his 'historic, and totally unexpected, announcement', and it was greeted with 'cheers and whistles of incredulity'.[257] It was the end of an era, and the City could hardly believe it. Few even at the Bank had expected a move so soon after the election. For Peter Norman of *The Financial Times*, it was 'one of the great turning points in Britain's post-war economic history'.[258] Nigel Lawson remarked, 'It's hardly possible to overstate the critical importance of our decision.'[259] It might be wondered why it took so long for the controls to be removed. Certainly, it was unlikely that a Labour Government would push the case. This was still a government with elements at least in favour of a National Enterprise Board, one that would not only limit the export

---

[255] HC Deb, 23 October 1979, Vol. 972, cc202–214.
[256] *The Old Lady*, January 1980, pp. 7–8.
[257] Kynaston (2001, p. 585).
[258] Press cuttings in 3A152/21.
[259] Kynaston, 'Exchange controls', CASS Business School Conference, October 1999.

of capital but also rather be inclined to repatriate already exported capital for channelling back into British industry. There were even those who, soon after abolition, were advocating their reinstatement as soon as a Labour Government returned to power. Was there a lack of enthusiasm even in less expected places, too? Kynaston says that there was an 'instinctive attachment in some quarters of the Bank of England to exchange controls as a key source of authority'.[260] This is harder to sustain. The Bank enjoyed the exercise of power in the City, perhaps particularly so when its power over monetary policy and the exchange rate were severely circumscribed, but its distaste of controls would over-ride that.

There appears to have been great rejoicing in the City and more widely on the announcement of abolition. And yet is there not a puzzle, for there was a remarkable absence of effort on the part of prospective beneficiaries directed at getting the controls removed. It could be that this was still not the 'British way' of doing things. Aggressive lobbying was an American practice that had not yet developed in Britain in the 1950s and 1960s. And in the city there was the additional tendency to keep heads down, particularly so when, as some have suggested, there were many ways around the controls and even that the Bank was complicit in some of these so that by nods and winks they could be evaded at least to a tolerable level. Also, the extensive regulations were both difficult to interpret and sometimes not readily available, and this could be another means by which the Bank could operate to make them as lenient as it thought desirable.

Any assessment of the removal would take us far beyond our period, but a brief observation might be made. There had been some fears that removal would result in wholesale flight of sterling into foreign assets. There was a flow of funds abroad, but it was largely a once-for-all portfolio shift. At the end of 1979, the stock of net external assets was roughly £12.6 billion. Within five years, this had risen to £70 billion, although the great bulk of the increase came from the changing value of the assets rather than new investment.

The 1970s witnessed the greatest economic and financial turmoil of any decade in the century, and this was reflected in the exchange rate and the reserves. The breakdown of Bretton Woods at the beginning of the decade was followed by years of uncertainty as to what could or should be done. The result was a dirty/managed float. In the absence of any clear strategy, the Bank was frustrated as it handled persistent difficulties for sterling and

---

[260] Kynaston (2001, p. 562).

sterling balances. Only after matters had come to a head in the crisis of 1976 and after more appropriate monetary and fiscal policies were put in place did things improve. Then they improved quite quickly in 1977, only for some further slippage to occur before the end of the decade. Even with exchange controls abolished and reserves hugely built up and most debt repaid, the pound was at $2.27 in January 1980.

At the end of the decade, the Bank reflected on what had happened to the rate over the course of the 1970s and attempted some explanation.[261] There was no complaint over monetary expansion. They felt that in the circumstances of 1973 there was a fear that if the market was left to itself, there could be damaging movements in the rate, and that was then exacerbated by the oil-price rises at the end of 1973. Intervention was used to avoid dramatic movements. By March 1976, the rate was thought to be appropriate, and the authorities intervened to hold it there but only succeeded in triggering a fall. When the rate began to recover at the beginning of 1977, the authorities again tried to peg it. But that proved impossible, and following the large buildup in reserves in the course of 1977, there was an abandonment of the cap at $1.72 in October, and the rate was at last allowed to float comparatively freely.

However, it was really the election of the Conservative Government in May 1979 that marked the turnaround. Just as they made it clear that monetary policy would be used to contain inflation, so on the external side they pursued greater freedom and fewer controls.

[261] I. D. Saville, 'The sterling dollar exchange rate', draft, 26 May 1978, 6A119/6.

15

The Bank's Freedom to Operate

From the 1950s to 1979, across a broad range of its activities, the Bank operated with considerable freedom. It had, of course, been independent since its foundation, and even though, in the late nineteenth century, its public responsibilities took precedence over its obligations to shareholders, it still operated independently. A major test of that independence came with the outbreak of war in 1914, but a face-saving arrangement was devised. It is true that Norman complained in the 1930s that he was no more than an instrument of the Treasury, but in fact, the Bank continued to operate with a great degree of autonomy. Nationalisation did not make much difference to its operations, and neither did Radcliffe. After the Second World War, the Bank continued to regard itself as in many ways independent, and frequent appeals to its independence were made. Throughout the 1950s and 1960s, it was left pretty much alone to manage the exchange rate, manage the government debt, administer exchange controls, take the initiative in monetary policy, look after the City, and so on. As Cobbold put it in 1962, central bankers could not carry out their responsibilities unless they had a large measure of independence from government 'both in operations and in policy'.[1]

In the 1960s, in effect, there was a target (the exchange rate), and it is clear from the evidence that the Bank was free to pursue the target in its own way, which meant, among other things, organising swaps and credits and engaging in forward intervention on a massive scale in order to protect the rate. At the beginning of our period, Bank Rate was regarded as primarily for use for external purposes, and movements in Bank Rate were driven by the Bank. In monetary policy, controls were designed by the Bank, and their implementation was largely at the Bank's initiative. It was the Bank that had devised special deposits for the control of bank lending. It had been sold

[1] Lord Cobbold, 'Some thoughts on central banking', Stamp Memorial Lecture, 1962.

to the clearers on the basis that the alternative was legislation: Voluntarism suited the Bank and the banks. In the money and gilt-edged markets, the Bank encouraged the idea of mystery and complexity and made much of its special expertise. Its 'feel' for the market gave it freedom to operate. Likewise, supervision of the mainstream banking sector, informally pursued, remained the preserve of the Bank. The method of financing the Bank (a levy on financial institutions) implicitly gave it greater freedom than would have been the case had it been financed out of taxation. Not having to publish accounts also helped, as did the curious situation whereby 'profits' grew at the same time as agency work was being charged at a 'loss' to avoid having to reveal too much information to the Treasury. The position was relatively unchallenged from outside, and some notable exceptions aside, the financial press reported rather than investigated events.

Much of this continued in the 1970s. Competition and credit control (CCC) was a Bank exercise, and some former senior Treasury officials maintain that they knew nothing about it until the last moment. Supplementary special deposits (SSDs) were yet another Bank device for the control of bank lending. The Bank was left to sort out the secondary banking crisis using its own resources. Some of these operations left its resources depleted just at a time when a struggle with the Treasury over the 'dividend payment' was intensifying. Wass's interest in the Bank's commitments in the fringe crisis had been described by Blunden as 'a major assault on our independence'. The legislation for the two-tier supervision that was introduced as a result of the banking crisis was very much the Bank's or, more accurately, Richardson's preferred model.

Another aspect of this independence was that the Bank engaged in all sorts of activities that might not be thought to have been part of a central bank's role. The promotion of London as an international financial centre might have been understandable. Yet the Bank strayed beyond the City and into industry, providing finance and even rescuing companies. Of course, such interests went back to Norman's time, but during the 1970s, concerns were renewed. In particular, Richardson had a record of close involvement in industrial finance, and this gave further impetus within the Bank. The Bank played a central role when two major industrial companies, Rolls-Royce and Burmah Oil, got into difficulties and was also instrumental in discussions about industrial finance. It promoted the creation of a number of bodies to assist in this area, and it established a new Industrial Finance Unit in the Bank. It was its freedom of action that allowed the Bank to do a number of things that were far removed from what were, before the war and became again in the twenty-first century, its core purposes.

There were, however, the beginnings of change in the 1970s. After 1972, there was no longer an exchange-rate target of the same kind. The dirty float meant that there was continuing discussion with the Treasury. A number of pressures, such as questioning by the Select Committee on Nationalised Industries (SCNI), brought scrutiny, as did publication of the Bank's accounts. The most visible aspect of this change was the growing politicisation of monetary policy, something epitomised by the issue of monetary targets (which the Bank had endorsed). Targets simplified things and gave politicians an easy object on which to focus. It was perhaps inevitable that ministers soon would take an interest in the factors influencing the target, such as sales of gilts, and from there begin to question the Bank's view on appropriate techniques and instruments. On the external side, without a pegged rate, ministers and the Treasury became more influential in dictating the appropriate level to be defended and the resources available to achieve this. Comment in the press and from academics had also become more informed and strident. All this obviously affected the Bank's independent stance.

In the Bank in the latter part of the 1970s, senior figures tried to counter these moves by redefining, if not reasserting, independence. This debate was conducted spasmodically and had no obvious conclusions, but it does reveal what they thought a central bank should do, its relation with government, and its perception in the public eye. In fact, after 1979, the Bank's freedoms were to be even more severely eroded. A measure of operational independence was restored in 1997, when, once again, there was a target, set by government, and the Bank was left to achieve it. Arguably, this is not so far away from the sort of operational independence that the Bank had enjoyed in the 1950s and 1960s.

In April 1976, the Governor asked Dow to set down some ideas on what the Bank should be doing. Principal among them was that the Bank should be more active in providing policy advice to the Chancellor; indeed, there should be 'parity of esteem' with the Treasury in this area. The 'post-Radcliffe settlement', as he termed it, with the Bank sitting on some Whitehall committees, fell short of what was required and gave the Bank a subordinate role. Dow's views reflected those in an Organisation for Economic Co-operation and Development (OECD) report he had co-authored that envisaged a key role for central banks in providing a second opinion for governments on monetary policy. He also wanted the Bank to take a more prominent part in the public debate on economic issues by increasing the number of major speeches made each year. When it came to the Bank's public image, the phrase that came to Dow's mind was 'discreet ostentation and extravagance'. Even relatively minor matters of appearance might benefit from some modernisation. Dow wondered if the Court Room was really a suitable place for business meetings and even whether messengers should continue to wear their traditional pink coats. He saw similarities with the Royal Family, 'a decorative and dispensable branch of government, as the Bank can appear to be'. Both institutions had attempted to enhance their image by producing films, although, in Dow's opinion, the Royal Family's was better than the Bank's. As for the Court, Dow supposed that it had no great role now, and its position might have to be reformulated. A more explicitly 'advisory council' was proposed, with membership drawn equally from the City and business, across the whole political spectrum. The main task would be to consider policy papers, with ritual discarded and other business (e.g., promotions and pensions) dealt with elsewhere under delegated authority. Any moves along these lines would have implications for the internal organisation of the Bank, although Dow put these to one side.[2] There is no evidence of any subsequent comment or discussion. This is not surprising given the events in the remainder of 1976 and the fact that only Richardson received a copy. However, some of the suggestions were distinctly radical; there would undoubtedly have been a furore had the SCNI proposed anything comparable. Yet this was a document produced in the Bank by someone close to the Governor.

A little more than a year later, the Governor, Dow, Quinn, Plenderleith Governor's Private Secretary (GPS), and David Walker from the Treasury (but shortly to join the Bank) met. Also present was Anthony Loehnis, a Director of Schroders, who had been seconded to advise Richardson. (He had been his Personal Assistant at Schroders in the late 1960s.) The record of the meeting was headed 'Externalising the Bank'. What this meant was that the Bank should take a more active role in explaining its policies and operations at a number of different levels, with the short-term aim of preventing and countering ignorant and misplaced criticism of the Bank and in the longer term to establish 'a more distinctive and recognised position for the Bank as an independent and intellectually sound source of advice on monetary policy and thus increasing the visible role of the Bank in the formulation and direction of national economic policy'.[3] This was clearly in line with the views Dow had expressed. The means of achieving these ends included speeches (again), publications, seminars, and relations with the

---

[2]   Dow to Richardson, 'Possible lines of development for the Bank', 7 April 1976, enc. Dow, 'Possible future lines of development for the Bank', 6 April 1976, 7A127/1.

[3]   Loehnis to Richardson, 'Externalising the Bank', 13 May 1977, enc. draft 'Externalising the Bank', 7A127/1.

press. The last traditionally had been a low-key activity in the Bank. There was a press officer, and financial journalists were seen by the Governors, Executive Directors, and senior officials as appropriate, but in general, the Bank was a reluctant partner and tended to react to events. Loehnis noted that there was little specific briefing of journalists by the experts involved, a Bank spokesman was rarely produced for radio or television coverage, and the holding of press conferences was rare. The Bank still disliked any exposure.

Some responses were elicited over the summer of 1977.[4] Page was wary that if the Bank spoke out publicly on policy, then there might be a resulting loss of influence with governments. He also took great exception to the contrast that Loehnis drew between actions based on 'seat of the pants hunch' and 'academically and intellectually respectable analytic work'.[5] In fact, Page might have misinterpreted what Loehnis meant, but the defence was revealing. The key to the Bank's reputation and influence lay in 'maintaining the highest possible professional competence and efficiency in all our operations; informing our actions with the fullest possible understanding of the behaviour of markets and the business of financial institutions, especially banks; and being seen to exercise clear and good judgment (an apparently unfashionable quality nowadays described as a hunch, or words to that effect) based on knowledge and experience'. Fforde had similar qualms. He also addressed public relations, arguing that it was the style with which it was conducted that was important. He saw dangers in a strategy that succeeded only in 'planting the image of an agitated Old Lady resorting to PR tricks'.[6]

For his part, McMahon agreed with most of what was being suggested by Loehnis, especially the desirability of being, or at least being seen to be, more open. To this end, he wanted to see more seminars and conferences involving outside economists to enable the Bank to explain its attitudes and also to demonstrate the dilemmas encountered in policy formulation. Of course, there was bound to be academic crossfire, but this would offer 'edifying enjoyment' for participants from the Bank. In fact, Richardson asked for this to be pursued, and the 'Panel of Academic Consultants', based on similar arrangements at the Fed, was established and first met in October 1977.[7] McMahon also felt that on occasion the Governor's speeches might

---

[4] Loehnis to Hollom, 'Externalising the Bank', 18 May 1977, 7A127/1.
[5] Page to Loehnis, 'Externalising the Bank', 23 May 1977, 7A127/1.
[6] Fforde to Loehnis, 'The public relations of the Bank', 30 May 1977, 7A127/1.
[7] The panel was chaired by Professor R. C. O. Matthews. Meeting four times a year, it covered a wide range of topics, and the academics attending varied according to the expertise required. For origins and record of meetings up to December 1979, see EID19/1.

contain statements that were 'clearly unwelcome to the Government and their political supporters'. This could achieve 'big headlines' and transform comment about the Bank. More covertly, McMahon wondered about news management and the fact that the Bank tended to play this 'extremely straight'. There were, he conceded, arguments for continuing with this, but perhaps if the Bank was more calculating and political in its off-the-record comments, it might be possible 'to change our image and get ourselves more space in the press and more respect as a motive power in policy; we might also enhance our ability actually to influence policy'.[8]

Something that featured in much of this discussion was the extent to which the Bank could or should be looking to be 'independent'. It was accepted that no central bank could ever be entirely autonomous, and in any case, it was not clear what 'independent' meant. Loehnis thought that this was far too emotive a word and preferred 'different'.[9] Nevertheless, Dow said that there were 'a number of ways along which the Bank might hope to see a strengthening of its degree of independence'. He then reiterated his earlier views and repeated his OECD work, that the Bank should provide a second opinion on economic policy issues and not just act as executant. Drawing on the US example, Dow also saw advantages in some accountability, such as the Bank having to appear before a parliamentary committee and to provide it with periodic reports on monetary policy. This would, he felt, give public emphasis to the new role.[10]

McMahon was forthright on the matter, having a 'strong disposition in favour of greater independence for the Bank, both actual and apparent. I believe this would be not only in our interest but in the interests of the economic management of the country; and I should be prepared for us to pay some price (as I think we should have to do) to achieve it'. He was attracted to Dow's idea of reporting to a parliamentary committee and stressed that it should not be considered a disaster if the Bank and the Treasury disagreed in this forum. Indeed, it should be welcomed and would add to credibility. On a related issue, McMahon envisaged submissions and memoranda being prepared by individuals at different levels in the Bank. As we have seen, throughout our period, this had not been the case, and as McMahon said, 'we have tended to deliver to the Treasury only very carefully considered views and at the very highest levels'. What of the costs that McMahon mentioned? The area that he had in mind was in the City, where some reduction

[8]   McMahon to Loehnis, 'Externalising the Bank', 24 June 1977, 7A127/1.
[9]   Loehnis to Richardson, 'Externalising the Bank', 21 June 1977, 7A127/1.
[10] Dow, 'The position of the Bank', 12 July 1977, 7A127/1.

in the Bank's traditional role as exclusive representative might have to be accepted. Similarly, the Treasury might seek to increase its contacts in the City. In McMahon's view, the tide was running in the Bank's favour. He said that economists, by no means all monetarists, had suggested to him the idea of greater independence, and the Conservatives were apparently giving the matter serious consideration. Even under the present administration, McMahon thought that there were plenty of small steps that could be taken, and he did not believe that the Bank should simply wait, 'a prisoner of our own inhibitions'.[11]

From this concern with the Bank's ability to express its views more freely and publicly developed other strands in independence. One of these was related to market operations. This was an issue that went back to Radcliffe. We have seen that in our period the Treasury had begun to encroach on some operating areas. The day-to-day management of both external and domestic monetary affairs had come to the front of the political stage in the mid-1970s, and Treasury officials and ministers had increased their participation in tactical decisions. Officials also developed 'a habit of making central-banking judgements and an imagined capability to take central-banking decisions'.[12] Fforde described meetings with the Chancellor to decide what action the Bank should take in the money market or what stock should be issued, where it sounded as if two central banks were offering competing advice to the same government. He did admit that the Bank reacted to this by widening the scope of its arguments so that in some discussions sounded as if there were two Treasuries. This was clearly an unsatisfactory position, but the general feeling was that changing market circumstances eventually would enable the Bank to re-establish operational freedoms.[13]

Other strands in the discussion related to the constitution of the Bank and the freedom to manage its internal affairs, notably finances, on which both Page and Fforde wrote to the Governors at length. The Chief Cashier outlined the elements in the constitution and warned that any radical changes would require legislation and general political endorsement. It appeared as if he

[11] McMahon to Richardson/Hollom, 'The position of the Bank', 16 August 1977, 7A127/1. Later that year, the Bow Group advocated greater independence for the Bank, including the repeal of Section 4(1) of the 1946 act that gave the Treasury authority over the Bank. Bow Group, *Britain's Money Puzzle*, December 1977; Goodhart to GPS, 'Bow Group paper on Conservative monetary policy', 16 December 1977, 6A50/24.

[12] Fforde to Richardson/Hollom, 'The Treasury, the Bank and the constitution', 25 August 1977, 7A127/1.

[13] McMahon to Richardson/Hollom, 'The position of the Bank', 16 August 1977; Blunden to Richardson/Hollom, 'The position of the Bank and the constitution', 7 September 1977, 7A127/1.

was raising obstacles, and since he commented that 'governments come and governments go and governments change their mind, and I would rather the Bank stayed as they were than go through sharp changes in their position at unpredictable intervals', he was probably hoping that nothing would happen.[14] Fforde always could be relied on to warm to this sort of subject, and he took 10 days to produce 'a flight of emotive fancy'. This was a characteristic tour de force that ranged widely over the constitution, the 1946 Act, and relations between the Bank and the Treasury. Its distillation was that without having to alter the existing constitution, an accord would give the Bank new responsibilities to present the Chancellor with monetary assessments, forecasts, and proposals for tactical monetary action. However, the determination and presentation of monetary objectives to ministers would continue to rest largely with the Treasury. Disarmingly, Fforde then added in a postscript, 'I am none too confident that what I now think, as written in these pages, is what I will continue to think.'[15]

London as an International Financial Centre

One area in which the Bank had for long been engaged was the promotion of London as an international financial centre.[16] London's highly developed financial markets, expertise, and openness to foreigners all attracted business. By the end of the 1960s, 'the City had once more become a truly cosmopolitan centre of finance, as it had been before the catastrophe of 1914.... in 1960 there were 77 foreign banks (14 of them American) with branches in London; by 1970 there were 159 (of which 37 were American).'[17] In February 1971, O'Brien's annual speech at the Overseas Bankers Club at Guildhall highlighted the 'international character of the London banking community'.[18] He welcomed the influx of foreign banks that came to London to operate in the Euro-currency markets, the driving force behind the growth of London as an international financial centre. O'Brien hailed the innovations in the City and praised 'the cross fertilisation of ideas between banks of many different national backgrounds in this process of invention and development'. Such ideas included the development of the inter-bank

---

[14] Page to Richardson/Hollom, 'The constitution', 24 August 1977, 7A127/1.
[15] Fforde to Richardson/Hollom, 'The Treasury, the Bank and the constitution', 25 August 1977, 7A127/1.
[16] For a survey of international financial centres, see Cassis (2005).
[17] Kynaston (2001, p. 401).
[18] O'Brien, Speech to the Overseas Bankers Club, 1 February 1971, *BEQB* 11(1):83–84, March 1971.

and local authority markets and new fields such as factoring and leasing, all of which broadened and deepened London's role as a financial centre. Also operating in London's favour was its 'open, flexible and individual system of regulation'. Indeed, Blunden claimed that most looked to London for leadership in this area.[19] *The Banker* also found the Bank's 'intelligent attitude' to enforcing the regulatory controls as of 'paramount importance'.[20] The Bank argued that 'the maintenance and development of London's role as an international financial centre depends on the continued presence here of foreign organisations'.[21] The number of foreign banks in London continued to rise, and when *The Banker* published its survey of the field in November 1978, there was a total of 395 foreign banks. The 1979 edition estimated over 400. There were then roughly twice as many banks represented in London as in any other centre, ensuring, on that criterion, that London remained 'overwhelmingly the world's major financial centre'.[22]

Towards the end of 1971, the Central Policy Review Staff (CPRS) expressed a desire to look into the restraints on growth in the City. The Bank was rather sceptical about the apparent vagueness of the project but assisted by organising informal meetings with interested parties.[23] By the middle of 1972, the CPRS had commissioned the Inter-Bank Research Organisation (IBRO) to produce a study on London's future as a financial centre that would 'identify action which the UK Government might take to promote London's future development and to identify obstacles that government action could help to remove'.[24] The Bank was not involved in this work, and it was keen to make clear that the report did not represent its views. Hollom deemed the project to be 'impossibly ambitious'.[25] The main report, available at the end of the year, was concerned largely with the nature of communications between the City and Whitehall and how government intervention might help London's development in the future. In particular, it recommended that a focal authority should be charged with the tasks of co-ordinating, sponsoring, and promoting. The Bank and Government Departments were

[19] Draft, 'Supervision of deposit-taking institutions', enc. with Blunden to Richardson/ Hollom, 'Licensing', 7 April 1975, 7A204/1.
[20] *The Banker* 129(636):57, February 1979.
[21] Nigel Carter (Overseas Department), draft 'London's position as an international financial centre', 10 March 1977, 7A88/1.
[22] *The Banker* 129(636):55, February 1979.
[23] Fforde to O'Brien/Hollom, 'The growth of the City', 7 October 1971; Page to Fforde/ O'Brien/Hollom, 'The growth of the City', 7 December 1971, 7A13/1.
[24] James Robertson (director, IBRO) to Blunden, 30 June 1972, enc. 'The future of London as an international financial centre', 7A13/1.
[25] Cooke to Robertson, 7 July 1972; 'Extract from the Deputy Governor's memo on his conversation with Mr. Faulkner and Mr. Prideaux on the C.L.C.B. agenda, 5.7.72', 7A13/1.

considered for this job but rejected in favour of establishing a separate 'task force'. Cooke bemoaned the report's paucity of analysis about the Bank's current role. Indeed, he pointed out that the first reference to the Bank was a comment that it had been unwilling to discuss the study. Overall, the report 'paints a picture which, while never saying so, envisages a very substantially reduced role for the Bank in the future'.[26] This possibility was unlikely to be accepted in Threadneedle Street, and a subsequent 'Governor's note' made a strong defence of the status quo. Unsurprisingly, the Bank did not want to see the report published, and it was not.[27]

In February 1973, a small working group met under Sir Antony Part [Permanent Secretary at the Department of Trade and Industry (DTI)] to consider the official response to the report. The most pressing issue was publication, with the DTI, CPRS, and Inland Revenue supporting this; Fforde and Wass (who was strongly critical of the study) were outnumbered.[28] The Bank was also aware of politicking by the DTI. Its Permanent Secretary had courted the clearing-bank chairmen to ask them not to veto publication, and he tried to entice them to join a Whitehall standing committee on City affairs. The clearers replied that they had no wish to erode the Bank's position. O'Brien complained to Wass that the DTI was trying to enhance its own position 'rather too hard'.[29] The Treasury judged that this was part of an operation to test the opposition and expose itself and the Bank as 'old and blinkered institutions resisting adjustment to the facts of contemporary life'. There were also worries that the Prime Minister would latch onto the DTI's scheme. Counter-proposals were thus developed in which the idea of an autonomous task force was abandoned, with an inter-departmental co-ordinating committee in its place, and some strengthening and enlargement of the City Liaison Committee was also envisaged.[30] This was broadly accepted in the working group, although Fforde remained wary of the suggestion that the DTI's Permanent Secretary should chair the co-ordinating

---

[26] Cooke to Page/Fforde/O'Brien/Hollom, 'The I.B.R.O. study for the C.P.R.S. on the future role of the City of London', 11 December 1972, 7A13/1.

[27] Bank of England, 'The City and Whitehall', 23 January 1973; Page to John Burgh (CPRS), 22 December 1972; 'Extract from the Deputy Governor's note 17.1.73. on the Governor's conversation with Mr. Fogarty', 7A13/1.

[28] O'Brien, Governor's note – 'I.B.R.O. report', 30 January 1973; Fforde to O'Brien/Hollom, 'Committee on the future of London as a financial centre', 21 February 1973, 7A13/1.

[29] 'Extract from a record of a meeting at the Bank of England between the chairmen of the London clearing banks and the Governors 28.2.73'; 'Extract from Mr. Fforde's note on the Governor's conversation with Mr. Wass 14.3.73', 7A13/1.

[30] Downey to Page, 26 March 1973; Fforde to O'Brien/Hollom, 'The City and Whitehall', 30 March 1973; 'Extract from the Deputy Governor's note 11.4.73 on the Governor's conversation with Mr. Wass', 7A13/1.

committee. It would, he argued, put too much power over City matters in the hands of a senior official at an aggressive department who over time would 'come to rival the position of the Governor of the Bank at the centre of the financial system'.[31] The Bank may have sought to promote London's international standing, but it was as much concerned with trying to maintain its own pre-eminent role in the City.

Further studies of London as an international financial centre were undertaken in 1977 by both the Bank and the Committee of London Clearing Banks (CLCB).[32] The Bank explained the similarities and differences between these. It was easy to agree that London's role in international finance was of great value to the economy, that this position was being eroded, and that measures were required to halt and reverse this in the future. The Bank and the CLCB maintained that London had to guard against losing business to other financial centres and feared that lost business would not be readily recaptured. Foreign-owned institutions were susceptible to tax and exchange-control changes and could move easily to other centres. With high UK corporation tax, American international banks had the incentive to shift their international business to low- or zero-tax centres such as the Bahamas and Cayman Islands. Other factors undermining London's position were higher rents and labour costs. Both highlighted the fact that since the Second World War London had increasingly become reliant on foreign-currency business, in particular, the US dollar, and the diminished role of sterling had weakened London's claims as a natural centre for international finance. This highlighted the key difference between the two studies: the Bank recognised that London could not pursue an international banking role based on sterling; the CLCB argued for a return to a situation where London could conduct international business in its own internationally acceptable currency. The Bank's view was surely the more realistic. Official policy towards the City always had been 'explicitly and convincedly liberal'. Rather than the grandiose interventionist plans of the Inter-Bank Research Organisation IRBO study, the way forward was now seen to be through maintaining a flexible regulatory framework, along with action to reduce tax disincentives and the impact of exchange controls.[33] In the summer of 1977, such moves remained some way off.

---

[31] Fforde to O'Brien/Richardson, 'The future of London as a financial centre', 27 April 1973, 7A13/1.

[32] Bank of England, 'London's role as an international financial centre', 31 March 1977; CLCB, 'The future of London as an international financial centre', May 1977, 7A88/1.

[33] Richardson to Healey, 29 July 1977, enc. 'Covering note to Bank and CLCB papers on the future of London as a financial centre', 7A88/1.

During the 1970s, the Bank continued to seek to exert its influence within the City and to represent the views of the City. The Bank established and provided the secretariat for various committees intended to co-ordinate views, including the City Liaison Committee and specialist groups covering areas such as Europe, capital markets, company law, taxation, and telecommunications.[34] It also sought order in foreign-exchange and sterling markets. This was not a new ambition. When Britain left the gold standard in September 1931, the commercial banks established a Committee of Foreign Exchange Managers. It was an informal and not totally representative body, but it continued to function on that basis until the summer of 1936, when Norman suggested that it should be replaced. Although the new Foreign Exchange Committee (FEC) was a formal body, its banking constituency remained unchanged, and despite Norman's role, the Bank was not a member.[35] During the war, the FEC became moribund, with any issues related to exchange regulations handled by a Foreign Exchange Sub-Committee. This arrangement was clarified in 1942, with the FEC meeting only infrequently and mainly in order to appoint the sub-committee.[36] Radcliffe was told that the London foreign-exchange market had no constitution or rules and was regulated by custom, whereas the FEC was concerned largely with exchange-control matters.[37] Membership comprised clearers, accepting houses, and various foreign banks. After the war, a new body, the Foreign Exchange Brokers' Association, was formed, made up of the eight large broking firms. By the latter half of the 1960s, the market had expanded greatly, and the use of foreign-currency deposits also had grown. This led to the body being re-formed, in February 1968, as the Foreign Exchange and Currency Deposit Brokers' Association (FECDBA). Subsequent developments in the foreign-exchange and currency-deposit markets led to the establishment of a Joint Standing Committee (JSC) at the end of 1973. It was intended to facilitate regular and smooth communication between the market participants: the banks on the FEC, on the one hand, and the brokers in the FECDBA, on the other. The JSC consisted of four bankers and four brokers. From time to time, with the approval of both the FEC and the FECDBA, the JSC issued guidelines on the proper practices to be

---

[34] Bank of England, *Annual Report*, year ending February 1976, p. 16, year ending February 1978, p. 18.
[35] 'Report on Committee of Foreign Exchange Managers by the executive officers of clearing banks, 13 July 1936'; FEC minutes, 27 August 1936, G1/246.
[36] Cobbold to Norman, 29 December 1941; FEC minutes, 12 February 1942, G1/207.
[37] Bank of England, 'The British monetary system: institutional framework', Radcliffe, 'Memoranda', Vol. 1, p. 8.

adopted in the market. It also investigated serious breaches of confidentiality and the rules of conduct and considered membership applications for the FECDBA and other market issues and disputes raised by banks and/or brokers. The Bank provided a Chairman and Secretary, and the meetings took place at the Bank. No doubt the Bank was happy to support an initiative that might assist in promoting an orderly market.[38] However, there was some disquiet when the structure of the foreign-exchange market was challenged by Sarabex, Ltd., a firm of brokers that was not a member of the FECDBA. The case was taken to the European Commission, which found that competition rules were not being breached because the Bank had since accepted responsibility for setting brokerage scales and the admission of new brokers to the market.[39]

The arrangements in the foreign-exchange market acted as a model in the sterling money markets. Largely as a consequence of the Scottish Co-Operative Wholesale Society (SCOOP) episode and the Bank's desire to broaden its market knowledge, a working party consisting of clearers and discount and accepting houses was established in September 1973 to review the organisation and procedures of the sterling inter-bank and certificate of deposit (CD) markets. It recommended the creation of a body for sterling brokers that would be broadly along the lines of the FECDBA. There then followed several years of discussions before formation of the Sterling Brokers' Association was announced in July 1979. As with the JSC, the chairman was provided by the Bank. At the same time, a code of conduct for transactions in the sterling deposit market was issued.[40]

The Rolls-Royce Crisis

The Bank did not restrict itself to promoting or even saving financial institutions. It extended its activities to industry and the rescue of individual companies. One such was Rolls-Royce. At the beginning of the 1970s, Rolls-

---

[38] D. A. Stirling (chairman FEC) to all authorised banks, 6 December 1967; FEC, draft letter to authorised banks, February 1975, 5A150/1; Giddings (secretary FEC), 29 October 1973; Terry Smeaton to Byatt, 'Joint standing committee', July 1974, C163/1; 'Joint standing committee of representatives of banks and of the F.E.C.D.B.A.', periodic report no. 8, September 1978, C163/5.

[39] Bank of England, *Annual Report*, year ending February 1978, p. 17, year ending February 1979, p. 18.

[40] Bank of England, 'Report of the working party on the sterling inter-bank and certificate of deposit market', April 1974, C40/1551; Barnes, 'Sterling Brokers' Association: press briefing', 26 July 1979; Bank of England, 'Sterling Deposit Market: press notice', 31 July 1979, 7A65/8; Bank of England, *Annual Report*, year ending February 1980, pp. 17–18.

Royce, one of the most illustrious companies in modern British history, collapsed. The event shocked the City and was seen by some as a national tragedy; in one view, the company had been 'regarded by the man in the street as being "as safe as the Bank of England"'. For others, in the student revolutionary fervour of the time, the collapse was an early indicator of the last throes of capitalism.[41]

Rolls-Royce's difficulties began in the 1960s when the world aircraft market became increasingly competitive. The company needed to succeed in the United States to survive, and in 1966, with government support, it began the development of the RB 211 engine, the largest and most complex the company had ever undertaken, in an attempt to rival its American competitors, Pratt & Whitney and General Electric.[42] In March 1968, Rolls-Royce won the contract for the Lockheed 1011 aircraft. However, it soon faced problems in financing the engine's development, having been 'allowed to indulge its technological ambitions well beyond the limits of financial safety'.[43] Both the development time and the costs involved had been underestimated.[44] Changes were made to the engine in response to alterations in the design of the aircraft, which sent costs spiralling. When the difficulties became apparent in 1969, the government asked the Industrial Reorganisation Corporation (IRC) to look into Rolls-Royce's finances. The IRC believed that there would be a loss of £5.1 million in 1970 and £4.3 million in 1971, and it decided to lend the company £10 million in 1970 (and a further £10 million in 1971 on condition that an IRC Director would be on the Rolls-Royce board) in order to relieve the immediate cash crisis so that Rolls-Royce could proceed with its work under much tighter financial control.[45]

By July 1970, the situation had reached crisis point and was brought to O'Brien's attention.[46] The essence of the problem lay in the fact that the original estimated cost was £74.9 million, and the government had promised £47.13 million, about 72 per cent. This, however, was a fixed sum, so when technical problems pushed the cost to £137.5 million, the government share

---

[41] The Credit Insurance Association, Ltd., 'The Rolls-Royce affair, p. 1, 5A161/3; HC Deb, 4 Feb 1971, Vol. 810, c1923; Pugh (2001, p. 148).

[42] For greater detail on the development of the RB 211, see Pugh (2001, pp. 108–113, 141); Cownie (1989); Lazards/Rolls-Royce, 'Rolls-Royce Limited', 12 October 1970, 5A161/1.

[43] *The Banker* 121(541):235, March 1971.

[44] Bowden (2002, p. 36).

[45] IRC, 'Report on Rolls Royce', 7 January 1970, 5A161/1. The second £10 million was never received because the IRC was abolished by the 1970 Conservative Government.

[46] Pugh (2001, p. 136); O'Brien, Memoir, p. 106.

dropped to about 34 per cent, leaving Rolls-Royce needing £90 million.[47] At this stage, the company had overdraft facilities amounting to £50 million (£25 million each from its bankers Midland and Lloyds) and a £20 million acceptance facility from a syndicate of 13 accepting houses. In late September, the minister of technology proposed that there should be additional assistance in the form of £25 million each from the public and private sectors.[48] Given the company's prestige and status, Hollom felt that it was right for the Bank to take a hand in Rolls-Royce's affairs.[49] A failure might produce some loss of confidence overseas and even a temporary unsettling effect on sterling. And there were other elements to Rolls-Royce, notably the importance of its military aeroengine activities to the UK defence programme.[50] When the Chancellor asked the Governor what might be done to mount a 'minimum salvage operation', O'Brien agreed to cooperate but warned that the banks and insurance companies were reluctant to become involved.[51] O'Brien later recalled that 'Mr Heath, perhaps more than half seriously, offered me a peerage if I could rid him of one clearing banker who, in his opinion, was being particularly unhelpful.'[52] Meetings involving the Bank, City institutions, and government continued throughout October 1970. The government seemed reluctant to offer aid, and Fforde asked, 'Do they want ... the enforced bankruptcy of the most prestigious name in British industry whose products are regarded as prime evidence that our indigenous industrial skills are still front rank?'[53] O'Brien told the Chancellor that institutions might put in £30 million, and the Bank was willing to offer £10 million, but that all this was conditional on the government providing a further £20 million and giving assurances that it would continue to support Rolls-Royce. Barber responded that it was not practical for the government to give an open-ended commitment.[54] Then, in November, the government said that it was prepared to put up £42 million of the £60 million that was estimated to be required, and O'Brien met Forbes and Faulkner to discuss the remaining sum. Forbes was extremely reluctant and said that if the banks were to provide further money, they certainly would

[47] Hollom, Note for record – 'Rolls Royce', 29 September 1970, 5A161/1.
[48] Barratt (HMT) to Ryrie, 1 October 1970, T225/3629. The private sector would provide £15 million in long-term capital and £10 million in additional overdraft facilities.
[49] Hollom to O'Brien, 'Rolls Royce', 24 September 1970, 5A161/1.
[50] Note of a meeting, 2 October 1970, TNA T225/3629.
[51] Ryrie, 'Record of a meeting ... 6 October 1970', 5A161/1.
[52] O'Brien, Memoir, p. 108.
[53] Fforde to O'Brien, 'Rolls-Royce Limited (meeting held in the Bank on 12 October, J.S.Ff. in the chair)', 12 October 1970, 5A161/1.
[54] Ryrie, 'Record of a meeting ... 15 October 1970', 15 October 1970, 5A161/1.

never do such a thing again for anyone. (It was only three years later when they were being called on again to contribute to the 'Lifeboat'.) The Prime Minister was unhappy: 'The tough, not to say obstructive, attitude adopted by the banks, was entirely attributable to Sir Archibald Forbes, and … the other bankers concerned were prepared to take a more constructive and reasonable attitude.'[55] O'Brien suggested that £5 million was not unreasonable a sum that both Midland and Lloyds agreed to provide, although only on stiff conditions, particularly in relation to repayment arrangements. The Bank itself would offer an advance of £8 million. The availability of the government money was also conditional on the satisfactory outcome to an investigation into Rolls-Royce by the accountants Cooper Brothers. Also at this stage, the accepting houses syndicate agreed to continue their existing facility to accept up to £20 million of Rolls-Royce's commercial bills when these came up to renewal in April 1971. Looking back, O'Brien wrote, 'maybe I did press too hard on the City institutions involved at the behest of an angry and forceful Prime Minister, but thankfully not hard enough to bring about what would have proved a disastrously wrong result.'[56] Knowledge that the Bank had had a hand in the operation was not made public until late November. Until that point it had been assumed that all the £18 million, being the difference between the government's £42 million and the required £60 million, had been provided by Lloyds and Midland.[57]

By the beginning of 1971, the situation had worsened. The Rolls-Royce board felt that it could no longer fulfill its contract with Lockheed except at a loss, and it would be best to discontinue the RB 211 programme. O'Brien, Fforde (who had temporarily stopped working on the CCC proposals), Page, Hallett, and Keogh met at the beginning of February and concluded that the banking system could take the strain but that it would be better not to make a statement that the Bank stood ready to provide credit. It was also accepted that the news would have an adverse effect on the pound, and thus the rate should not be allowed to plummet and that support should be given if necessary.[58] A draft press statement was prepared explaining the abandonment of the project, but the announcement was delayed until Nixon had discussed it with Heath. At a meeting with the accepting houses syndicate, the Governor gave assurances that the Bank would give help to any house that encountered serious difficulties as a result of Rolls-Royce.[59] The

---

[55] HMT, Note for record, 5 November 1970, TNA T225/3379.
[56] O'Brien, Memoir, p. 108.
[57] *The Times*, 26 November 1970, p. 27.
[58] Gill, Note for record, 1 February 1971, 5A161/2.
[59] Keogh, Note for record, 3 February 1971, 5A161/2.

company was placed in receivership on 4 February 1971. The government's £42 million was not required, nor had there been drawings on the clearers' £10 million or the Bank's £8 million advance, whereas the accepting houses' November commitment to renew their facility to Rolls-Royce after April 1971 did not become operative. Rolls-Royce Limited (1971), a new, government-owned company, was formed to take control of the assets of Rolls-Royce.[60]

Cromer, who had just become British ambassador in Washington, also intervened. He was reportedly unhappy about the lack of consultation before the public announcement of Rolls-Royce's collapse, and he felt that there was insufficient appreciation in London of the repercussions in the United States if the RB 211 fell through. The former Governor believed that the contract must be renegotiated in order to preserve Britain's reputation in the United States, and he wanted O'Brien to see if there was any role that the City could play in this. O'Brien thought that responsibility for this rested primarily with the government.[61] This is what happened: Lord Carrington, the Minister of Defence, commissioned a technical and cost study of the RB 211 that concluded that the engine could be resurrected and problems resolved with a six-month delay and cash-flow injection of a further £120 million. After negotiations involving the British and US governments, Rolls-Royce Limited and Lockheed signed a new contract for the completion of the RB 211.[62]

There were subsequent complaints from the accepting houses about the exact status of the government support. The syndicate was bothered by the fact that they had believed the money put up in November 1970 had been unconditional, whereas they were now told that it was in fact conditional. Articles soon appeared in the press revealing the connection between the government's £42 million and the report by Cooper Brothers.[63] The Bank stayed in the background, refusing to comment. O'Brien told the accepting houses that he was ready to receive representations if they thought that they had not been fully informed and if they had suffered material damage as a result.[64] Nevertheless, the Bank's view in November was that when the accepting houses gave their agreement, they had not been misled as they

---

[60] Lazonick and Prencipe (2003, p. 8).
[61] Gill, Note for record – 'Rolls-Royce', 16 February 1971, 5A161/2.
[62] Lazonick and Prencipe (2003, p. 8).
[63] Hollom, Draft, 'Rolls-Royce. Catalogue of main events in the negotiations with the banks', 9 March 1971, 5A161/3.
[64] R. L. Gregson (No. 10) to R. J. Priddle (Ministry of Aviation Supply), 8 March 1971, 5A161/3.

claimed.[65] Collaborating with Lloyds and Midland, the Bank prepared a response explaining that the syndicate had been told everything that was known about the 'conditionality'.[66] O'Brien sent a draft of the response to Barber, who reportedly found it 'unwelcome, owing to its inconsistency with his own statement in the House'.[67] The Accepting Houses remained unhappy about the response to their grievances, but after meeting two of their representatives in early September 1971, O'Brien managed to reach agreement that the issue should no longer be pursued.[68] The crisis had damaging effects on relations between the City and government, and it was awkward for the Bank. O'Brien commented that the affair was 'not among my more agreeable experiences while in office', and he felt that he had 'earned no thanks from anyone for the part I played in achieving it [the final result]'.[69] Certainly, his efforts to assist Rolls-Royce seem to have damaged his standing among bankers. While there may have been no financial cost to the Bank, its reputation does appear to have suffered.[70]

The Bank was also concerned about some other enterprises that got into financial difficulties in the 1970s. The Mersey Docks and Harbour Board (MDHB), the acting authority for the port of Liverpool, ran into serious trouble in the late 1960s with an overall deficit of £1.8 million in 1969. The situation worsened in 1970, and the board experienced difficulties in covering its operating expenses and meeting rising interest repayments.[71] MDHB approached the government seeking a loan of £20 million, but this was refused. The board went into receivership, and in 1971 it was reconstituted as the Mersey Docks and Harbour Company. This might have been thought to have little to do with the Bank, but the Bank had acted as a financial adviser to MDHB, as it did for other statutory authorities. In the 1960s, the Bank had advised the board to borrow through short-term bonds rather than by long-term debenture issues on which it had formerly relied. The higher interest on these short-term loans was thought by some to have

---

[65] Hollom, Draft, 'Rolls-Royce, Ltd. and the Acceptance Syndicate', 25 March 1971, 5A161/3.

[66] 'Extract from Mr. Fforde's memo on the Deputy Governor's conversation with Mr. Neale, 21.4.71', 5A161/3.

[67] 'Extract from Mr. Fforde's memo dated 26.4.71 on the Deputy Governor's conversation with Sir Douglas Allen 23.4.71', 5A161/3.

[68] Hollom, Note for record – 'Rolls-Royce', 3 September 1971; 'Extract from the Deputy Governor's memo dated 3.9.71 on the Governor's conversation with Sir Douglas Allen', 5A161/3.

[69] O'Brien, Memoir, p. 108.

[70] King (1975, p. 54); Kynaston (2001, p. 431).

[71] Cooke to Fforde/O'Brien/Hollom, 15 September 1970; Mersey Docks and Harbour Board, Press announcement, 24 September 1970, 5A172/1.

contributed to the board's problems.[72] Another reason was the Bank's desire to maintain market confidence in the stocks of statutory bodies. Thus it had favoured some limited support for MDHB. Both Hollom and Fforde were worried about the effects on the market if the board defaulted on its debts because such bodies were regarded as virtually free from credit risk.[73] None of this entailed any cost to the Bank, but the episode was indicative of the abiding concern with orderly markets.

There was also a peripheral interest in the vehicle manufacturer British Leyland Motor Corporation (BLMC), another company in severe financial trouble in the mid-1970s. In the final quarter of 1974, BLMC had sought a loan of £150 million from the 'Big Four' clearers, but the banks were reluctant to extend additional facilities without some assurance of government backing. The Bank was involved in discussions with the representatives of the banks, Treasury officials, and the Chancellor. A statement was made in the Commons on 6 December 1974 that the government would stand behind BLMC in the form of both a short-term guarantee and longer-term financing.[74] The company was nationalised the following year. In this case, the Bank simply held a watching brief and acted as the link between the various parties. However, the experience was used by Richardson to illustrate the need to monitor companies in difficulties and be ready to act in support.

Burmah Oil

One of the Bank's biggest and best-known operations in the mid-1970s was its involvement in the rescue of Burmah Oil, Britain's twenty-fifth largest company. Between 1975 and 1980, the Bank supported Burmah by guaranteeing loans and offering standby facilities. More controversially, it also injected cash into the company by purchasing Burmah's 21.6 per cent stake in British Petroleum (BP) for £179 million. Burmah's shareholders took legal action for the return of the shares, but they lost their case in 1981, and the shares were transferred from the Bank to the Treasury.

Burmah was incorporated in 1902, and BP (originally the Anglo Persian Oil Company) was its wholly owned subsidiary until 1918, when the

---

72 The Bank's advice reflected its view that the possibility of nationalisation would make it hard for MDHB to float a long-term loan.

73 Shelley to Page/Fforde/O'Brien/Hollom, 'Mersey Docks and Harbour Board', 9 February 1970; 'Extract from Mr. Fforde's memo on the Deputy Governor's conversation with Mr. R. J. Painter 18.9.70', 5A172/1.

74 Fforde to Richardson/Hollom, 'B.L.M.C.', 4 September 1974, 6A333/1; Fforde to Richardson/Hollom, 'B.L.M.C. (Chief Cashier's note of 3 October)', 7 October 1974, 5A37/1; HC Deb, 6 December 1974, Vol. 882, cc2115–2124.

government acquired a 51 per cent interest in BP, and Burmah's holding was reduced to 25 per cent. In the early 1970s, Burmah embarked on a series of ambitious ventures, including transportation of liquefied natural gas, the building of a trans-shipment terminal in the Bahamas, tanker chartering on a large scale, and a stake in the North Sea. At the beginning of 1974, Burmah acquired Signal Oil and Gas for $420 million, giving it access to oil production in the United States and the North Sea and exploration activities in other areas. Burmah's expansion programme involved heavy borrowing with a high degree of risk. Dollar borrowings were $625 million: $420 million was from a consortium led by Chase Manhattan and Orion, $150 million from one led by Morgan Guaranty, and $55 million from another led by the Royal Bank of Canada. There was also £54 million of 8½ per cent loan stock outstanding. In all, the borrowing was spread over some 30 banks, mostly overseas. The myriad interlocking agreements and guarantees rested substantially on the rising value of the parent company's holdings of marketable shares in BP and Shell. The oil crisis and the drop in value of BP shares, coupled with a forecast of losses from Burmah's tanker fleet, produced serious financial difficulties for Burmah. At the end of 1973, BP shares stood at 534.5p, but by December 1974, the price had fallen to around 200p. The contraction in the value of Burmah's assets meant that the company could no longer meet the terms of certain loan agreements, and in October 1974, Burmah renegotiated the terms of the Signal Oil loan agreements. Burmah accepted certain new conditions, including a covenant requiring that the net interest costs of the group should not exceed a certain proportion of operating profits. The deteriorating trading position of the tanker operations threatened to cause an infringement of the Signal loan, which, in turn, would affect other agreements. If Burmah became liable for accelerated repayment of a massive burden of debt, then it could not survive without outside help.[75]

On the morning of 23 December 1974, representatives of Barings and Fleming and Co., Burmah's financial advisers, went to the Bank to tell Richardson and Hollom about the company's problems. The Governors immediately arranged to see Burmah's representatives later that afternoon, and in the evening, they reported the situation to the Chancellor. Healey wondered whether an arrangement with BP or Shell should be explored and said

---

[75] Alastair Down (chairman) to Burmah shareholders, 12 February 1975, 7A197/1; Bank of England, 'Revision of Burmah support operation', 19 November 1975; Paymaster General's Office, 'Revision of Burmah support operations. Report by officials', nd, but filed 25 November 1975, 7A175/7.

that he did not like the idea of direct government involvement.[76] During the next week, there was a series of meetings, including ones on Christmas Eve and Boxing Day, involving Hollom, the Treasury, the Department of Energy, Burmah, and its financial advisers.[77] Hollom proposed that the Bank guarantee the dollar borrowings for a period of 12 months to allow renegotiation. Through the Issue Department, it would subscribe up to £54 million of new redeemable loan stock in Burmah to enable the firm to repay the money owing on the loan stock. Finally, the Bank would give temporary assistance if difficulties arose with Burmah's short-term money-market borrowing. As collateral, Burmah would offer its unpledged holdings in BP and Shell Transport and Trading, and the Bank would be free to sell those stocks to repay the loans and advances. Burmah also would sell its North American investments, excluding the Signal interests in the Thistle Field, so that the loans guaranteed by the Bank could be repaid no later than the end of 1975, and it had to transfer 51 per cent of its interest in commercial oil fields on the Continental Shelf to the government when required. There also would be changes at board and senior management level, with the Bank having a say in the appointment of replacements.[78]

It quickly became apparent that the December arrangements would have to be renegotiated. New information showed that owing to Burmah's complex network of cross-guarantees on other borrowings, a pledge of the BP and Shell shares could not be made without causing breaches of other borrowing agreements, which would, in turn, bring Burmah down. The Bank's intention to take BP shares as security would trigger demands for repayment of a large number of other loans. Furthermore, the viability of the tanker business was doubtful. Barings proposed a revised package, but this was felt unacceptable because neither the Bank nor the government would put up any unsecured money for Burmah while it had a saleable asset, namely, the BP stock. Thus attention turned to a scheme whereby Burmah would sell its BP shares to the Bank outright, at market price, and the cash generated would allow the company to continue to develop its North Sea interests and to finance its tanker operations. It was suggested that any subsequent profit on resale should be split between the Bank and Burmah.[79]

---

[76] France (PPS to Healey), Note for record (of a meeting held on 23 December), 24 December 1974, 7A175/1.

[77] See 7A175/1 *et seq.*

[78] Hollom to J. A. Lumsden (chairman, Burmah), 31 December 1974, enc. 'The Burmah Oil Co., Ltd. Outline proposals', 7A175/1.

[79] Somerset to Page, 8 January 1975; Quinn, Note for record – 'Burmah Oil Company Limited', 8 January 1975; 'Note of a meeting on Friday, 10 January at 6 pm'; M. C. S.

Hollom also recommended that the offer price for the BP shares 'should not be too harsh'. However, Sir Douglas Henley (Treasury) argued that, given the risks, there was a case for paying the lowest price (190p), and he also thought that any profit should go to taxpayers and not the shareholders. Sir Jack Rampton (Permanent Secretary at the Department of Energy) agreed that Burmah should not be entitled to benefit from any profit.[80] Hollom favoured buying at the prevailing market price, but he did not want it to be thought that the Bank was taking advantage of Burmah's weak position. A low price might suggest that Burmah's position was bad, which would, in turn, undermine confidence in the company's future viability. However, the government argued that Burmah had brought its troubles on itself, and the government was taking substantial risk in mounting the rescue operation. Dell, paymaster general, suggested an averaging formula that met protestations from Burmah, but Dell was adamant on the terms of the sale in light of the risks they were taking.[81]

On 23 January 1975, Burmah sold its 77,817,507 BP shares to the Bank, through the Issue Department, at a price of 230p per share, a total £178,980,226. The price was based on an average of prevailing market prices from 31 December 1974 to 22 January 1975. The Bank undertook that while it held the stock it would not exercise the votes attached, and any profits from the shares were to be paid over to the government. In place of the charge on the share capital in BP and Shell, the Bank took as security a charge on all the share capital of the Burmah Oil and Gas Company and of Burmah Oil Development, Inc. (both owned by Burmah Oil, Inc., Burmah's subsidiary in the United States). The Bank also made available a 12-month £75 million standby facility, and the Bank guaranteed the existing long-term dollar borrowings of $650 million up to 31 December 1975. On 27 January, Alastair Down, Deputy Chairman and Managing Director of BP, became Burmah's new Chairman and Managing Director. To emphasise the importance that the government attached to the matter, it provided the Bank with a 'comfort letter' protecting it against any loss on the operation.[82]

Why did the Bank get so deeply involved? According to the press briefing, the government and Bank judged it 'in the national interest'. Burmah was

Aitchison (Department of Energy), 'Note of a meeting to discuss Burmah … 15 January 1975', 16 January 1975, 7A175/2.

[80] Aitchison, 'Note of PUS' meeting to discuss Burmah, 17 January 1975', 20 January 1975, 7A175/3.

[81] J. S. Beastall, Note for record (summarising events of 21–23 January), 24 January 1975, 7A197/1.

[82] Burmah, Press releases, 23 January 1975; 'Memorandum of agreement between Burmah Oil Company Limited and the Bank of England', 23 January 1975, 7A175/3.

a major British company operating internationally.[83] During the discussions on Christmas Eve, Hollom had argued that the position of the pound would be weakened if Burmah was allowed to default on such a large dollar loan, and Somerset later recalled that 'it would be a very bad mark for the City of London' if this had happened.[84] Thus the Bank had concerns about the implications for sterling and London as an international financial centre. The other factor, though probably of less interest to the Bank, was that Burmah had a critical role in the development of North Sea oil. While the rescue was effectively guaranteed by the government, it was nevertheless a Bank-organised operation, contrary to what has been commonly portrayed in the secondary literature.[85] The use of the Issue Department also should be noted. In the aftermath of the secondary banking crisis, Hollom was reluctant to put the balance sheet of the Banking Department under further pressure – reserves were not much over £100 million. The Issue Department had assets of more than £5 billion. In fact, it was not quite the first time that the Issue Department had been used to provide assistance: under pressure from government, advances had been made from Issue to two port authorities in 1971.[86] Nevertheless, the magnitude in the case of Burmah was completely different.

The disposal of Burmah assets began in February 1975, with the proceeds used to repay debt. Despite the sales, a substantial proportion of the Bank's £75 million standby facility was used. In October 1975, Burmah put forward revised support proposals, seeking to roll over the guarantees of the borrowings and to increase the standby from £75 million to £125 million to £150 million.[87] So bleak was the outlook that the question of liquidation was explored. Somerset felt that if some share of the profit made on the BP shares had been available to the company, Burmah's financial position would have been better. He also argued that morally the government could not let Burmah go into liquidation while sitting on this potential profit.[88] Hollom felt the situation to be 'discouraging but not hopeless' and favoured an extension of the guarantees as opposed to liquidation.[89]

[83] Press briefing, attached to Aitchison, Note for record, 31 December 1974, 7A175/1.

[84] Aitchison, 'Meeting to discuss Burmah Oil 24 December 1974', 24 December 1974, 7A175/1; interview with David Somerset, 25 May 2005.

[85] See, for example, Dell (1991, p. 129).

[86] The two bodies were the Clyde Port Authority (£2.9 million facility) and Forth Ports Authority (£0.5 million facility). See 7A160/1 and 7A161/1.

[87] Down to Hollom, 13 October 1975, 7A175/6; Bank of England, 'Burmah support operations. Burmah's revised proposals', 16 October 1975, 7A175/7.

[88] Somerset to Hollom, 'Burmah', 20 October 1975, 7A175/7.

[89] Aitchison, 'Note of PUS' meeting to discuss Burmah support operation, Monday, 20 October 1975', 22 October 1975, 7A175/7.

Concern focussed on the implications of further assistance in the light of Section 332 of the Companies Act 1948, designed to 'prevent a company from continuing to trade at a time when, to the knowledge of those responsible, there is no reasonable prospect of the company ever being in a position to satisfy its creditors'.[90] However, it was agreed that the risk of attack under Section 332 was low, and the Governor argued that the Bank should renew the guarantee on Burmah's dollar obligations and increase the standby for nine months.[91] On 18 December 1975, the Bank extended the guarantees up until 30 September 1976 to enable sale of US assets without pressure from potential purchasers and to allow for greater flexibility in any disposal strategy. The standby remained unchanged at £75 million (though now split £55 million to Burmah and £20 million to Manchester Oil Refinery Holdings).[92]

Burmah's US businesses (Burmah Oil and Gas Company and Burmah Oil Development, Inc.) were sold in the summer of 1976 for approximately $520 million, and $480 million was used to reduce the dollar borrowings guaranteed by the Bank. Thus, by September 1976, Burmah had disposed of its American assets, and from the proceeds, it had repaid most of its $650 million borrowing. Burmah had, it seemed, made a significant recovery since the end of 1974. Nevertheless, it still faced uncertainties, and there was also the prospect of continuing tanker losses.[93] Tanker operations proved to be a severe drain on the company's limited resources, and in September, the Bank agreed to provide a new guarantee for a $100 million term loan from a consortium of banks. This was secured by a charge over the shares in two subsidiary companies, Castrol and Burmah Oil Trading Limited. The loan would replace the existing $74 million guaranteed by the Bank, which was due to be repaid at that time. In addition, the amount of the standby facility was increased to £85 million, until June 1977, thereafter continuing at £60 million until June 1982, when it would terminate.[94] The Department of Energy undertook to reimburse the Bank for any loss it might suffer. Burmah finally dispensed with financial support from the Bank

[90] Bank of England, 'Revision of Burmah support operation', 19 November 1975, 7A175/7.
[91] France, Note for the record, 28 November 1975; Richardson to Healey, 1 December 1975, 7A175/8.
[92] Somerset to Hollom, 'Burmah', 12 December 1975; Page to Burmah/Manchester Oil Refinery (Holdings), 23 December 1975, 7A175/9.
[93] M. H. Atkinson (BoE) to E. Ferguson (HMT), enc. draft, 'Review of Burmah Support Operation: November 1977', 8 December 1977, 7A176/1.
[94] Hollom to Down, 23 September 1976; extracts from minutes of the Committee of Treasury, 30 September 1976, 3A161/189.

in December 1980 when it repaid £19.2 million drawn under the standby and said that it would no longer need to use the credit arrangement.

The government held 48 per cent of BP stock and the Bank 20 per cent. In December 1976, Healey announced that as part of the package related to the International Monetary Fund (IMF) borrowing, some of the Bank's stock would be sold in order to reduce the public-sector borrowing requirement (PSBR). Sufficient would be disposed of to lower the combined government-Bank holding from 68 per cent to 51 per cent.[95] The Bank's BP shares had never been regarded as a long-term portfolio investment, and it was originally hoped that they would be sold along with some of the government's BP stock. However, Burmah's threat of legal action against the Bank was a serious barrier. Government officials discussed with Burmah the possibility of an arrangement to remove the blocking effect of its action, but the conditions that the company wanted to impose proved unacceptable, and the government decided that 17.3 per cent of its own holding would be sold. The Bank would sell its holding to the government at a later date.[96]

The sale of 66,785,591 BP shares was expected to yield £500 million to £600 million, and the proceeds were required in the financial year 1977/78. Some consideration was given to dividing the sale into separate offerings in a variety of financial centres, but the preferred option was for a single offer split between London and New York.[97] Given that it would be the largest equity offering that had been made so far in world markets, it was not surprising that the Bank was heavily lobbied by various financial institutions offering advice and assistance. After ministerial clearance finally was given, Hollom called a meeting of merchant banks and brokers on 20 May and outlined the plan, which involved an announcement ('impact day') on 14 June, lists opened and closed on 24 June, and allotment on 27 June. Hollom asked David Scholey from Warburgs to speak for all the banks.[98] There then followed a huge amount of work on all sides to prepare. On 13 June, the Prime Minister approved the offer price of 845p, and this was announced the following day. The UK issue was 4.7 times oversubscribed, so the US share was reduced from a maximum of 25 per cent to 20 per cent. Gross proceeds from the sale were £571 million, and costs were around £11 million.[99]

[95]   HC Deb, 15 December 1976, Vol. 922, c1532.
[96]   Alan Lord (HMT) to Hollom, 23 February 1977, enc. 'Sale of BP stock, note by officials', 7A164/2.
[97]   Bank of England, 'Sale of BP stock', 10 February 1977, 7A164/2.
[98]   Christopher Elston, Note for record – 'Sale of BP Shares' (note of meeting held with bankers and brokers on 20 May 1977), 25 May 1977, 7A164/4.
[99]   Plenderleith, Note for record – 'Sale of BP shares', 13 June 1977; Bank of England, Press notice, 14 June 1977, 7A164/7; Bank of England, Press notice, 27 June 1977, 7A164/8.

From the other side, Michael Valentine recalls that Scholey was summoned by the Governor and given six weeks to organise the sale. He also claims that having initiated the process, the Bank's officials were 'remarkably reluctant to involve themselves at all, some muttering about their annual leave, conveniently early, so that in the absence of anyone there taking active responsibility the whole weight of their necessary part fell on their lawyer, Peter Peddie'. Peddie, from Freshfields, undoubtedly played a critical role for the Bank, but there was also a great deal of effort on the part of many others to make the sale a success, notably BP's brokers, Scrimgeours. According to Valentine, Warburgs and the merchant bankers worked flat out to pull off the sale but only had a 'paltry sum' from the Bank for their efforts.[100] They did, of course, share the underwriting commissions, which amounted to more than £8 million: Warburgs received £75,000 to cover expenses and services.[101]

A further sale of the government's BP stock took place in November 1979 when the Chancellor announced that he planned to reduce the PSBR by sales of public-sector assets amounting to £1 billion. It was also part of the government's long-term programme for promoting wider share ownership.[102] The intention was to reduce the combined holding of the government and Bank to 46 per cent. The sale, again arranged by the Bank, was considerably smaller than the 1977 operation, and the offer was made only in London. A total of 80 million ordinary shares of 25p each were offered at £3.63 per share, of which £1.50 was payable on application and the balance on or before 6 February 1980. The issue again was oversubscribed.[103]

The Bank's purchase of the BP shares caused much disquiet among Burmah's shareholders, and this eventually culminated in a legal action against the Bank. A group representing shareholders claimed that the renegotiation of the loans agreements 'constituted a suicide deal for Burmah'.[104] They also asserted that the Bank's acquisition of the BP shares was unfair because it had been done without their consent, but it is difficult to see how this argument had much force. Furthermore, it was argued that averaging the market price over the three-week period from 31 December was unfair because oil shares had been depressed even more than the market in

---

[100] Valentine (2006, pp. 95, 97, 99).
[101] Hollom to Airey (HMT), 28 March 1978; Hollom to Scholey, 5 April 1978, 7A164/10. Scholey deliberately excluded his own time from the estimate of costs; Elston to Page/Hollom, 'Expenses of the BP sale', 12 August 1977, 7A164/9.
[102] Plenderleith to George, 'BP sale: press briefing', 7A208/23.
[103] Bank of England, *Annual Report*, year ending February 1980, p. 15.
[104] *The Financial Times*, 11 May 1978, p. 24.

general. Politicians also had their say. In February 1975, Shadow Secretary of State for Energy Patrick Jenkin told the Commons that the terms of the rescue were such that 'lasting damage' had been done 'to the credibility and independence of the Bank of England as a lender of last resort', revealing a lack of grasp of both concepts.[105]

The Bank was inundated with letters from angry shareholders complaining that they had been treated poorly. Typical was this letter to Fforde: 'Before the Burmah Oil affair the Bank of England had a reputation for straight dealing; ... unless something is done shareholders will continue to feel that they have been cheated by the Bank of England and will continue to press for justice.'[106] One irate complainant telephoned the Bank and was put through to Hollom, who listened patiently. On realising that he was talking to the Deputy Governor, the caller apologised and said that he wanted to speak to someone 'at the working level'. 'I think that you will find that I am the working level', replied Hollom.[107] Hollom was pivotal in the story. The Bank's response to these grievances was unapologetic. Speed, according to Hollom, was essential, and there had not been time to consult shareholders. In the circumstances, it was 'the best scheme in the interests of the Company that could be devised', and delay would have 'place[d] the Group's entire net worth in jeopardy'.[108] Certainly, without this support, the shareholders would have been in a much worse position.

At the Burmah annual general meeting in June 1976, shareholders were told that there were grounds for a claim against the Bank. Jonathan Stone, a lawyer and treasurer of the Burmah Shareholders Action Group, described the sale dramatically as 'the greatest financial scandal ever' and rashly asserted 'Burmah had been raped by the Bank at the behest of the Government.'[109] By July 1976, the BP stock bought for £179 million was valued at £465 million. When Down, Burmah's chairman, visited Richardson in July, he said that while he was personally opposed to litigation, there was pressure from his lawyers and the 'hawks' on his board.[110] Down then wrote to Hollom stating that unless the Bank agreed, by 5 October, to enter negotiations on the question of meeting the claim, Burmah would have to initiate proceedings. Hollom could offer no such

---

[105] HC Deb, 25 February 1975, Vol. 887, c313.
[106] C. D. Sills to Fforde, 13 February 1975, 3A161/189; K. Weinberg to Richardson, 12 March 1975; Smith to Richardson, 28 January 1975, 7A197/2.
[107] Interview with Roger Barnes, 27 September 2007.
[108] Hollom to C. D. Sills, 20 February 1975, 3A161/189; Hollom to Cutler, 13 June 1975, 7A197/2.
[109] *The Times*, 5 June 1976, p. 17.
[110] Plenderleith, Note for record – 'Mr. Down's call on the Governor', 1 July 1976, 7A175/15.

guarantee. Yet the prospect of legal action troubled Richardson: 'Win or lose, the actual conduct of a case in Court for return of the stock could involve considerable awkwardness', he told Healey.[111] On 6 October 1976, Burmah issued a writ in the High Court for an order that the BP stock be transferred back to Burmah against repayment on the purchase price less any dividends received. The company argued that the acquisition of the BP stock was 'unconscionable, inequitable and unreasonable and that the Bank, in breach of its duty of fair dealing, took unfair advantage of Burmah, wrongfully deprived Burmah of the right to redeem the stock and obtained an improper collateral advantage in connection with the taking of security'.[112] In 1978, Burmah attempted to gain access to government documents to support its case for the return of the shareholding. These included letters that the company believed would throw light on whether the government had pressured the Bank into taking unfair advantage of Burmah.[113] The application was rejected on the grounds that release would be 'injurious to the public interest'.[114] After losing an appeal, Burmah took the case to the House of Lords, where it was unanimously rejected in November 1979.

In April 1980, Hollom sought a secret meeting with Burmah's chairman. Down was willing to settle if a reasonable offer was made. Hollom saw little wrong with exploratory talks, arguing that 'it still seems clear that it was inequitable to deny Burmah a share in a potential profit ... and it is further obviously undesirable to drag such an action through the Courts, at great cost, if it can be avoided'.[115] Nevertheless, Hollom conceded that reaching acceptable terms would be difficult and likely to involve a considerable sum, around £75 million to £100 million.[116] The Chancellor was adamant that such a meeting would not take place.[117] Instead, the case went to Court in June 1981, at the time one of the biggest civil cases ever brought by a British company. As Somerset put it, 'in the light of the serious consequences of an adverse decision we considered that every effort should be made to mount the best possible defence, whatever the cost'.[118] Burmah's argument in the High Court was that the Bank had taken advantage of the company's weak financial position to get

[111] Richardson to Healey, 13 September 1976, G3/339.
[112] Down, Chairman's statement to stockholders, 14 September 1977, 7A175/29.
[113] *The Financial Times*, 2 November 1979, p. 6.
[114] *The Times*, 20 July 1978, p. 20.
[115] Hollom, 'The Burmah action against the Bank of England', 4 January 1980, 7A149/2.
[116] *Ibid.*
[117] Howe to Hollom, 8 April 1980, 7A149/2.
[118] Somerset to Blunden/Hollom, 18 February 1981, 7A197/12.

the BP shares considerably below their value.[119] The case was rejected. The hearing finished on 3 July with Justice Walton concluding:

One cannot help feeling great feelings of sympathy for the unfortunate shareholders in Burmah.... they have every right to feel aggrieved. But their real quarrel is not with the Bank ... but for the action of the Bank in coming to the rescue of Burmah in December and January, there would have been a liquidation of Burmah, in which they would have got absolutely nothing whatsoever.... There may very well be targets against whom the shareholders should direct their wrath; the Bank is not one of them.[120]

Burmah decided not to appeal and paid £375,000 to cover the Bank's costs. In August 1981, discussion turned to the transfer of the Bank's 311,270,028 BP shares from the Issue Department to the Treasury, and this was carried out in December for the sum of £1,033 million (based on the November 1981 quarterly revaluation and equal to 332p per share).[121] After seven years, the Bank's involvement had come to an end.

Industrial Finance

In light of the failure of Rolls-Royce and against the possibility of similar occurrences, the Bank identified the need for a body that could look into companies whose future seemed to be under threat. The argument was that industrial weaknesses might not have been so severe or might have been avoided if there had been a close and more effective relationship between companies and their bankers and major shareholders.[122] The Bank therefore felt that it should improve its industrial intelligence and awareness of industry's need for finance, and it devoted a good deal of effort to doing so.

Following a series of informal consultations in early 1972, a working party on 'Industrial Management and the Institutional Investor' was established, chaired by Hollom, to report on the possible structure and operation of a central organisation through which institutional investors could stimulate action to improve efficiency in industrial and commercial companies.[123] The idea found little support. Instead, the Bank's compromise proposal was adopted, whereby the four major institutional

---

[119] *The Financial Times*, 3 June 1981, p. 8.
[120] Transcript of Justice Walton's judgement, 3 July 1981, C40/1424.
[121] HMT, Press release, 21 October 1981; Somerset to McMahon, 'BP shares', 27 November 1981; A. B. Milligan (HMT) to S. N. Wood (HMT), 30 November 1981, 9A58/1.
[122] 'Speech delivered by Cooke in Fforde's stead: no final copy of speech', to the Graduate Business Centre, City University, 29 November 1973, 6A233/2.
[123] Terms of reference for the working party, 1972, 7A112/1.

investors' associations sat on the Institutional Shareholders Committee (ISC).[124] The ISC was supposed to co-ordinate and extend the existing 'investment protection activities' of institutional investors with a view to encouraging action by companies to improve their efficiency. Between 1973 and the end of 1979, the ISC considered 37 cases and set up ad hoc case committees to deal with seven of these.[125] It is doubtful that much was achieved.

Under Richardson, the Bank's work on industrial finance gathered momentum. He had a genuine interest. He had worked at the Industrial and Commercial Finance Corporation (ICFC), been a board member of Rolls-Royce and ICI, and in 1972 was appointed chairman of the newly created Industrial Development Advisory Board, designed to promote direct government investment in industry. In his first Mansion House speech in October 1973, Richardson said that relations between the City and industry 'could be much improved with advantage to both the City and the country', and he spoke of a predominant sense of wariness, a 'gap of sympathy and understanding', and his desire 'to make an extra contribution to the financing of industry'.[126] Improvements in collecting, analysing, and using financial data to ensure that the financial system was providing industry with the finance it needed would, it was hoped, further the Bank's and City's relationship with industry. Outside London, there had been for a long time Regional Agents based at the Bank's branches who kept head office informed about industrial conditions in their areas.[127]

There were several ideas, such as creating a central body in the City to which industry could turn and the establishment of a think tank, or a 'diagnostic unit', that would attract and seek out 'industrial patients' and then try to mobilise shareholders and bankers to devise and administer appropriate remedies.[128] Richardson thought that the Bank could provide 'a neutral focal point' for companies to discuss financial difficulties.[129] Assured trust and confidentiality meant that the Bank appealed to industrialists as a place where they could talk about their problems. Unlike government ministries,

---

[124] Bank of England, *Annual Report*, year ending February 1973, p. 8.
[125] Wilson Report, para. 912.
[126] Richardson, Speech at the Lord Mayor's dinner, 18 October 1973, *BEQB* 13(4):479, December 1973.
[127] For example, see Bank of England, *Annual Report*, year ending February 1971, p. 37.
[128] Luce to Fforde, 'Finance for Industry – but what sort of industry do we want?', 17 October 1974; Fforde to Richardson/Hollom, 'A place in the City where one can go and talk about one's problems', 11 February 1975, 6A135/1.
[129] Fforde, Note for record – 'Finance for Investment', 25 April 1975, 6A135/1.

the Bank had 'the privileged position of being able to give dispassionate and non-political advice'.[130]

In March 1975, Dow proposed an Industrial Finance Unit (IFU) that he envisaged as 'a centre for intelligence about firms' needs for finance'.[131] Sir Henry Benson, a senior partner with Coopers and Lybrand, who had over 50 years of involvement with industry as an accountant, was appointed by Richardson as an Adviser on industrial finance.[132] He had worked closely with Richardson at Schroders and was clearly one of Richardson's 'inner circle'. The Bank's decision to set up the IFU was welcomed by the City, and it became the focal point in the Bank on matters relating to investment for industry.

The principal aim of the IFU was to 'obtain a more systematic flow of financial intelligence from industry and assist in identifying the financial problems of particular [firms or] industries, and to establish a closer liaison on these matters with the financial community'.[133] The Bank was anxious to learn of problems before they reached crisis point and to identify cases of financial difficulty and indicate whether any action or assistance was justified, and if so, what sort.[134] By 1978, the IFU had been built up to a 20-strong team and was collecting data on different industries and developing the Bank's knowledge on financial ratios that could be used to highlight companies that were deviating from the norm.[135] In such affairs, the Bank liked to keep a low profile, and close observers described its activities as analogous to a 'fire-engine without bells'.[136] With or without bells sounding, it is difficult to assess what was achieved by the IFU in this period.

Since the Second Word War, the Bank had connections with FCI and ICFC, both institutions created to finance industry. FCI's future had been in doubt at the end of the 1960s because of a lack of business, and its original functions essentially had been taken over by the IRC.[137] In early 1969, a proposal to merge FCI with ICFC came to nothing because the clearers, who

---

[130] Alan Watson (Press Office), Note for record – 'Press interview, Mr. Walker/Miss Reid *Financial Times*, 21 September 1978', 6A233/6.

[131] Dow to Richardson/Hollom, 'Industrial Finance Unit', 18 April 1975, 6A135/1.

[132] Bank of England, Press notice, 24 April 1975, 6A135/1.

[133] Draft press notice, 15 April 1975, 6A135/1.

[134] Dow, Draft – 'Industrial intelligence. The proposal for an Industrial Finance Unit', 17 March 1975, 6A135/1.

[135] Alan Watson (Press Office), Note for record – 'Press interview, Mr. Walker/Miss Reid *Financial Times*, 21 September 1978', 6A233/6.

[136] *The Financial Times*, 3 October 1978, p. 21.

[137] Blunden, 'Finance Corporation for Industry and Industrial and Commercial Finance Corporation', 7 September 1970, C40/1423.

had long been wary of FCI, refused to buy out the existing shareholders.[138] A year later, Humphrey Mynors, FCI's chairman, remained pessimistic about the future. He did not demur either from Hollom's suggestion that the organisation be put into mothballs or O'Brien's conclusion that the time has come for FCI to be wound up.[139] However, the atmosphere quickly changed with the election of the Heath Government. The Conservatives wanted to do away with the IRC, and the idea of merging FCI and ICFC was revived.[140] O'Brien now backed the union. Furthermore, he told the Chancellor that the Bank ought to be seen to be contributing towards the efforts to encourage industrial investment and that the acquisition of a substantial shareholding in the merged institution would be one way to do this.[141] In Richardson's first Mansion House speech, he had followed his predecessor's line by stressing the importance of the relationship between City and industry. The new Governor said that the merger between FCI and ICFC would be 'tangible evidence' that the Bank and the clearing banks wanted to make an extra contribution to the financing of industry.[142] Agreement for the merger was reached in November 1973 with the creation of a new holding company called 'Finance for Industry Limited' (FFI). The Bank took 15 per cent of the issued nominal capital of £60 million, with the rest shared between the London and Scottish clearing banks.[143] In November 1974, it was announced that FFI planned to make up to £1 billion of medium-term loans available over a period of two years, funded by additional resources from the shareholding banks. By the end of March 1978, some £660 million had been lent or committed by the group since its formation in 1973. From 1983 on, FFI became known as '3i'.[144]

Another manifestation of the Bank's concerns in this field was its support of Equity Capital for Industry Limited (ECI), an organisation for

---

[138] Hollom, FCI/ICFC, 11 February 1969; Hollom, 21 February 1969; Gill to Page/Fforde, 'Whither F.C.I.?', 14 August 1970, C40/1423.

[139] Hollom, 'Finance Corporation for Industry', 17 March 1970; Hollom, Note for record – 'FCI', 23 March 1970; Hollom, Note for record – 'Finance Corporation for Industry', 1 April 1970, C40/1423.

[140] Coopey and Clarke (1995, p. 110).

[141] O'Brien to Barber, 'Finance for industrial investment', 22 June 1973, 6A310/1; O'Brien, Governor's note – 'I.C.F.C/ F.C.I', 10 July 1970, C40/1423.

[142] 'Speech by the Governor of the Bank of England given at the Lord Mayor's dinner to the bankers and merchants of the City of London on 18 October 1973', *BEQB* 13(4):479, December 1973.

[143] *The Times*, 8 November 1973, p. 29; Coopey and Clarke (1995, p. 112).

[144] Bank of England, *Annual Report*, year ending February 1975, p. 8; year ending February 1978, p. 20; Coopey and Clarke (1995, p. 135). The Bank eventually sold its stake after the floatation of 3i in 1994. It also received profits of £119.5 million from the float; Bank of England, *Annual Report*, year ending February 1994, p. 11; 1996, pp. 42–43.

channelling institutional funds into industry. In the summer of 1975, the chairman of the British Insurance Association expressed his anxiety to the Bank about criticisms that were being voiced about the lack of investment in industry. Richardson asked Benson to investigate the matter. Benson found a general view that something along the lines of a new equity fund was needed. Predictably, a working party was established. At Richardson's suggestion, this group comprised experienced representatives drawn from all the major sectors of the City concerned with the placing of funds. It was to consider whether the existing machinery of the capital markets needed to be supplemented to improve the availability of equity capital for industry and to recommend how the City could contribute.[145] The first meeting was at the Bank in October 1975. Richardson made it clear that he was anxious that the Bank should be seen as a catalyst only, and he did not want to force the institutions into participating.[146] Furthermore, at a CLCB meeting in January 1976, the Governor, sensitive to the fact that opinions were sharply divided, said that while he believed that ECI was a scheme worth supporting, 'there was no pressure on potential subscribers to take on a commitment for which they had no liking'.[147] There were divisions. When the first proposals were submitted in January 1976, only about one-third of the working party supported them. The working party's report of 1976 concluded that a new source of funds should be established to make equity capital available to industry that would supplement the normal working of capital markets.

The report sparked much critical comment, and the press enjoyed exposing the discontent and disagreement.[148] *The Observer* could 'not recall a single issue on which the City has been more divided'. *The Sunday Telegraph* reported that since the institutions were badly split over the draft proposals, Richardson had to call some of them in to get them to toe the line.[149] According to *The Observer*, it was only because of the persuasive arguments of Richardson and Benson that ECI was not stillborn. Indeed, ECI was nicknamed 'the Bastard Child of the Bank of England' and the 'Benson Bank'.[150]

---

[145] 'Equity capital for industry', May 1976 (covering memo to draft report), 6A265/4.

[146] Lomax, Note for record – 'Equity Fund, note of a meeting held in the Court Room on Thursday, 9 October 1975 at 4:30 pm', 14 October 1975; Smith, 'Note of a meeting held in the committee room (1st floor) Bank of England on 15 October 1975'; Lomax, Note for record – 'Equity Fund, meeting held in First Floor Committee Room on Wednesday, 15 October 1975 at 2.45 pm', 22 October 1975, 6A265/1.

[147] 'Extract from minutes of CLCB meeting, 26 January 1976', 6A265/3.

[148] Benson to Hollom/Richardson, 'ECI (next steps)', 19 February 1976, 6A265/3.

[149] *The Sunday Telegraph*, 2 January 1976, 6A265/3.

[150] *The Observer*, 25 January 1976, p. 15; *The Daily Express*, 4 February 1976, p. 13.

The working party was criticised for not conducting adequate research, and some, including Ian Fraser of Lazards and Harold Lever, asserted that the existence of an investment gap in the market had not even been proven.

Despite the disagreements and tensions, ECI was formally established in May 1976. Its primary role was to provide equity capital for industry for companies unable to obtain it through the capital markets. The Bank was keen to make clear that no pressure had come from government to set up the fund. ECI would take funds from pension funds, insurance companies, and unit and investment trusts and place them directly in industrial equity capital that could not be obtained through the stock exchange.[151] The May 1976 prospectus invited institutions to subscribe for a minimum of £30 million. In the event, applications were received and allotted for £41 million spread among 360 members. Although ECI began to receive enquiries and some applications soon after, it was not until February 1977 that it really became fully operational. By June 1977, it had considered 100 cases, but only three resulted in firm commitments totalling £5.8 million.[152] ECI can hardly be judged a success. One episode, the involvement in Bond Worth, was a disaster, with the company collapsing only four months after a share issue. *The Observer* wrote that ECI 'now needs nothing short of a miracle if its original aspirations are not to be completely shattered.... the Bond Worth fiasco has made even ECI's few supporters wince.'[153] Indeed, even Fforde felt that ECI had failed to get off the ground.[154]

The many attempts by the Bank to improve the means of financing industry did not impress a government that generally was sceptical of City motives. In September 1976, Callaghan announced at the Labour Party conference in Blackpool that he would be setting up a committee to review the functioning of financial institutions. This was to be the first full-scale analysis of the financial system since Radcliffe, although its focus was different, but like many such enquiries, it was essentially a political move. In this case, Callaghan wanted to defuse calls from the Labour Left for the nationalisation of banks and insurance companies.[155] (It was not the first occasion such a proposal had been made, Labour having previously wanted nationalisation of banks, and the Bank, in 1932.[156]) The committee was to 'enquire

[151] *The Financial Times*, 26 January 1976, p. 32.
[152] Lomax to Richardson, 'Equity capital for industry', 2 September 1977, 6A265/5.
[153] *The Observer*, 16 October 1977, 6A265/5.
[154] Lomax to Thornton, 'ECI', 20 October 1977, 6A265/5.
[155] A statement by the National Executive Committee called for nationalisation of the big four clearing banks and the seven largest insurance companies; see 7A123/1.
[156] Howson (1993, p. 65).

into the role and functioning, at home and abroad, of financial institutions in the United Kingdom and their value to the economy; to review in particular the provision of funds for industry and trade; to consider what changes are required in the existing arrangements for the supervision of these institutions, including the possible extension of the public sector, and to make recommendations'. Lord Plowden and Lord Robens were among possible names to chair the enquiry, but it was Harold Wilson who was appointed, something that was met with outcry in some quarters. He was felt to be too political, and having spent 'a life-time making snide remarks about the City', ill-suited.[157] But Wilson had mellowed, and the former Prime Minister made it clear that he would 'not be taking a bloodhound into the City'.[158] Richardson hoped that the investigation would be done carefully by an experienced committee free of extreme views, and he welcomed the enquiry as providing an opportunity for rebutting hostile opinions.[159] Hollom thought that the committee would need to 'adopt a most rigorous approach to its work if it is not to be regarded as a mere piece of political gimmickry'.[160]

Consisting of 18 members, including the Director of the London School of Economics (LSE), Ralf Dahrendorf, Wilson's former Policy Adviser, Andrew Graham, and a former economist at the Bank, Andrew Bain, as well as other figures drawn from business, the City, and trade unions, the Committee began its work in January 1977. The enquiry had two elements: the first related to the provision of funds to industry, and the second on the functioning of financial institutions more broadly, including their supervision and regulation, and questions of public ownership. The Committee consulted representative bodies, academics, and prominent individuals with relevant experience in 55 meetings (the majority of which were held near the Bank in the Guildhall). Richardson, Hollom, Fforde, McMahon, Thornton, and Goodhart all gave evidence in December 1977.

After more than three and a half years, the final report was published in June 1980. In answer to the central question, Wilson found that British industry had not been starved of investment funds by the financial system and that there was no great imbalance between the demand for funds and the supply from the capital market. The price of finance in relation to expected profitability, argued Wilson, was the major financial constraint

---

[157] *The Financial Times*, 8 October 1976, p. 44, and 11 October 1976, p. 7.
[158] *The Times*, 19 January 1977, p. 18.
[159] 'Extract from the minutes of the City Liaison Committee meeting, 4 November 1976', 1A179/1.
[160] Hollom to Richardson, 3 November 1976, enc. 'Committee on Financial Institutions', 3 November 1976, 1A179/1.

on real investment. Most of Britain's industrial problems had little or nothing to do with the availability of finance. The Committee was split on the issue of how to channel more finance into industry. The majority believed that there were enough institutions trying to lend to industry and that there was little point in creating another. Nevertheless, Wilson, along with the trade unionists, wanted a new fund of £1 billion to £2 billion that would channel a portion of institutional funds and of North Sea oil revenue into manufacturing. Part of the Committee's terms of reference was to investigate the extension of public ownership. The Labour Party National Executive had argued that greater public ownership was necessary to ensure that the required volume of finance was available to sustain an increase in industrial investment, but the Wilson Committee was united in opposing nationalisation of the banks and insurance companies.[161] The Committee concluded that the Bank had taken an active and formal role in discussions on industrial finance, although it wondered whether there had been sufficient steps on the part of the Bank to equip itself 'adequately with staff experience and qualifications to match its increased responsibilities', particularly in capital markets supervision and industrial finance. It recommended that the Governor give further consideration to such areas.[162]

The report was met with mixed reactions. Although *The Banker* adopted a positive view, noting that 'even if none of the detailed Wilson recommendations were to be implemented, ... the committee would have served a valuable purpose [because] its mere presence has undoubtedly acted as a powerful catalyst to City thinking.' *The Evening News* remarked that the report was 'long on words but rather short on ideas' and was a 'waste of time and money'.[163] Asked for its reaction, the Bank said that it was in broad agreement with some of the main themes.

The Bank under Scrutiny

Although concerned primarily with the financing of industry, the Wilson Committee also looked at the Bank more generally. The Bank had submitted its own written evidence, and Richardson, Hollom, and Page all appeared before the Committee in December 1978. Some evidence, for example,

---

[161] Wilson Report, para. 1316.

[162] *Ibid.*, para. 1286.

[163] *The Banker* 130(653):12, July 1980; *Evening News*, 25 June 1980, and copy of 'Reuter tape', 25 June 1980, 2A159/2.

from the Fabian Society, was highly critical of the Bank but was not evident in the final report.[164] The chapter on the Bank covered the relationship with government, the City, accountability, the role of non-Executive Directors, and supervision. It noted that the Bank was 'well regarded in financial services' but also noted the criticism that had been made over the Bank's role in the rapid monetary expansion of 1972–73, its supervisory shortcomings leading to the secondary banking crisis, and the methods used to issue gilt-edged stock.[165] It acknowledged that the Bank had become less secretive in light of more informative *Annual Reports*, the *Bulletin*, and speeches by the Governors and Executive Directors, and according to Wilson, the considerable strengthening of statistical and economic expertise and a greater analytic capability meant that the Bank's authority and influence had increased significantly in the 20 years since Radcliffe.

A little earlier and of more significance, however, was the follow-up investigation of the SCNI. In November 1974, it was announced that the SCNI would conduct a short investigation into the Bank as an update on its 1970 report. As was the case with the original enquiry, the Bank's role in monetary and financial policy; the gilt-edged, money, and foreign-exchange markets; its exchange-control activities; and its role as banker to other banks all were supposed to be out of bounds. Oral evidence was taken between February and July 1976, with Richardson, Hollom, Page, Taylor, Andrews, and Rumins all appearing for the Bank. The report, published in October 1976, was significantly less critical than its predecessor. It asserted that many of the charges levelled against the Bank were 'emotive and uninformed' and concluded, 'Within the restricted area of our terms of reference we have few, if any, faults to find with the way in which the Bank discharges its responsibilities and manages its own affairs.' From the evidence presented, the Committee found that on both domestic and foreign activities, the Bank was held in high regard. Indeed, 'No other country has a system as good.'[166] Areas that had previously caused concern to the Committee were re-addressed, and the Bank was congratulated on its improvement. The Report said that the Bank could 'no longer be held secretive and aloof except in matters of policy direction by the Government, on which it must remain silent'.[167] The conclusion re-emphasised that the Bank was the agent of the government and argued that 'the Bank does what it is instructed to

---

[164] Fabian Society, Statement of evidence to the Wilson Committee, December 1978, OV197/1.
[165] Wilson Report, para. 1262.
[166] SCNI 1976, 'Report', paras. 98, 204.
[167] *Ibid.*, para. 206.

do, whether it likes it or not.'[168] Given that the investigation was limited in effect to the Bank's agency work, it is difficult to see what other conclusion might have been reached. It also argued that the Bank did not speak for the City, and although it was useful as a channel for transmitting information from the City to Whitehall, Government Departments could be approached directly by financial institutions. This surprised the Bank, and there is not much evidence that it was the case.

Thus the report's criticisms were of relatively minor significance for the Bank. The restrictions on its terms of reference meant that controversial topics were left untouched, thereby leaving a favourable a picture of the Bank. This was simply not good enough for the critics. Brian Griffiths, in *The Banker*, picked apart the way the Committee conducted its affairs. For Griffiths, the report merely reproduced the views of the witnesses, who naturally had the defence of the Bank in their interest. It was a mere collection of opinions rather than a systematic look at what happened based on the Committee's own judgement of facts. Furthermore, the restrictive terms of reference led Griffiths to advocate a more focused and specific 'Select Committee on Monetary Affairs' that would examine 'the techniques, instruments and objectives of the control of money and credit and the supervision and regulation of the financial system'.[169]

The SCNI conducted a further enquiry into the Bank in January 1978, the main purpose of which was to meet calls for greater detail on the support operations during the secondary banking crisis. Unlike the previous two enquiries, there was no formal report, although the minutes of evidence were published. The Bank appeared before the committee twice, with Richardson, Hollom, Blunden, and Taylor attending both sessions. At the first session, focussed mainly on the fringe bank crisis, no details of individual cases were given owing to rules of banking confidentiality, and in any case, they lay outside the Committee's terms of reference. The Governor believed that the current stability of the financial system was due to the improvements made in banking supervision. The second session incorporated a wider set of questioning on nationalised industry foreign-currency borrowing, finance for industry, the Bank's capital and current expenditure, exchange control, and administrative matters. The Committee was content with the information provided by the Bank.

The SCNI had showed some interest in the financing of the Bank, which continued to be done through earnings on bankers' balances, although the

[168] *Ibid.,* para. 204.
[169] Griffiths (1977, p. 113).

system was formalised following the introduction of CCC. At that point, the banks agreed to hold 1.5 per cent of their eligible liabilities with the Bank as non-interest-bearing balances.[170] One possible way to have bolstered finances would have been to use the Issue Department, where the profits were substantial (over £500 million in 1975). Indeed, in 1977, Page had floated the idea that the Banking and Issue Departments could be merged, with the Bank given first access to the total profits.[171] That it would have required amendment to the 1844 Bank Charter Act was only one reason why it was a completely unrealistic proposition. According to Blunden, it would stir up a hornet's nest: 'It is inconceivable that in present circumstances any Government could hand over to an independent body control over a major source of revenue which has accrued to the Government for a century and a half.' Even if such a move were allowed, Blunden was sure that it would come at the price of a greater Whitehall say in how the money was used by the Bank, thus hastening the loss of financial independence instead of retarding or reversing it.[172] While income in the form of earnings on bankers' balances may not always have given a sufficient margin over non-government-related expenditure to provide adequately for provisions and additions to reserves, it was undoubtedly an independent income that remained substantial.

In contrast with the previous decades of secrecy, stability, and the comfortable accumulation of reserves, the finances of the Bank in the 1970s were slightly more open, certainly more volatile, but much less comfortable for the Bank, and reserves were depleted. The impact of inflation, the effects of the secondary banking crisis, the need for pension provisions, and falls in the value of government securities all had an effect, and in one presentation, the retained profit figure for 1973/74 actually was negative, the first occasion that this had occurred. On top of this, the data are also complicated by accounting changes, notably the treatment of certain provisions. The first

---

[170] This ratio then fell on several occasions: to 0.5 per cent in 1981, to 0.45 per cent in 1986, and to 0.15 per cent in 1998. The definition of eligible liabilities also has been changed so that, for example, in 1981 the 0.5 per cent was levied on a much larger base. The Bank of England Act 1998 put the arrangements on a statutory basis, with the ratio set by government and provision for a periodic review. A review in 2003 resulted in slight amendments to take account of the growth of financial intermediation, and some perceived injustices in the incidence of the burden; Bank of England, *Annual Report*, 1999, pp. 7, 39–40, and 2006, p. 27.

[171] Age to Richardson/Hollom, 'The constitution', 24 August 1977, and appendix IV, 7A127/1. The profits of Issue were (£m): 145.6 (1971), 170.2 (1972), 202.8 (1973), 370.2 (1974), 555.2 (1975), 445.4 (1976), and 681.4 (1977).

[172] Blunden to Richardson/Hollom, 'The position of the Bank and the constitution', 7 September 1977, 7A127/1.

Select Committee Report on the Bank had some important implications for finances, with a number of specific recommendations made: capital expenditure should be subjected to the same test and scrutiny as other nationalised industries, annual accounts should be published, the Bank should charge the full costs of services performed for government, and the Bank should pay over the profits of the Banking Department after an agreed provision for reserves and working capital.[173] Since this report appeared in the month before the June 1970 general election, it was not a particularly high priority for either the outgoing Labour Government or the new Conservative administration.[174] Nonetheless, one issue was dealt with quickly. O'Brien told the Court that accountability could not be 'shrugged aside' and that in future accounts would have to be published. The Governor hoped that this could be done without new legislation and without jeopardising independence.[175] The *Annual Report* for the year ending February 1970, which appeared in July 1970, stated that preparations were being made for publication of accounts, although no timescale was given. It was a move welcomed by the Treasury.[176]

The government's formal response to the SCNI came in a white paper in March 1971. This had been drafted with the full involvement of the Bank and addressed the four key issues: accounts, capital expenditure, charges, and profits. On the first of these it was noted that a set of accounts would be included in the Bank's *Annual Report* for the year ended 28 February 1971. In the future, five-year capital expenditure plans would be submitted to the Treasury and subject to the same methods of investment appraisal as used elsewhere in the public sector. Reimbursement of the full costs of administering exchange control and the management of the national debt and Exchange Equalisation Account (EEA) was accepted. Finally, the Bank would pass the statutory payment in lieu of dividend to the Treasury in accordance with the committee's recommendation.[177] The Treasury suggested

---

[173] SCNI 1970, 'Report', paras. 191–193, 237–238, 242, 262.

[174] 'Extract from the Deputy Governor's memo on the Governor's conversation with Sir Douglas Allen 4.6.70'; Hollom, Note for record – 'The Governor's conversation with Sir Douglas Allen', 22 June 1970, G38/5.

[175] 'Court: 4 June 1970, Select Committee on Nationalised Industries'; Note by Taylor, G38/5.

[176] Bank of England, *Annual Report*, year ending 28 February 1970, p. 24; Hollom, Note for record – 'The Governor's conversation with Sir Douglas Allen', 22 June 1970, G38/5.

[177] Painter to Taylor, 10 November 1970 and 14 January 1971; Taylor to Painter, 18 February 1971, G38/5. *Report from the Select Committee on Nationalised Industries in Session 1969–70. Bank of England. Observations by the Chancellor of the Exchequer*, March 1971, cmnd. 4633.

that it would be helpful to exchange a 'memorandum of understanding' detailing the principles that were laid out in the white paper. The resulting document was not completed and agreed until July 1972.[178]

Between the financial years 1970/71 and 1979/80, the Bank's total income increased from £26.5 million to £116.5 million in nominal terms (Table 15.1). The internal accounts showed the sources of income in a different format from the 1950s and 1960s, differentiating between what was termed 'fixed' income and 'variable' income. The former included interest on British government stocks (derived from the bankers' balances) and miscellaneous securities, commissions, fees, rents, and other receipts. The latter comprised interest on Treasury bills, bills discounted, and advances. Treasury bills, generally the largest component of variable income, had previously been included with British government stocks. The makeup of bills discounted varied over time but included local authority paper and, at the very end of the period, commercial bills. Reflecting the operations during the secondary banking crisis, interest on advances jumped from around £2.0 million per annum in the early 1970s to more than £25 million a year in the middle of the decade.

The key difference compared with the previous periods was the fact that the cost of work undertaken for government was recouped in full. Much of this work had been performed at a loss, with the Bank reluctant to act because it would mean revealing details of true income and expenditure to the Treasury. For the financial year 1969/70, only £4 million out of identified costs of £9.5 million had been recovered, and the 'subsidy' because of undercharging between 1959/60 and 1969/70 totalled £33 million.[179] Under the new arrangements, the Bank prepared five-year estimates of the full costs of agency work. These were submitted to the Treasury, with the Bank then claiming a quarter of these costs at intervals of three months, with an adjustment made after the end of the financial year to take account of the actual figures. The first estimates, covering the years 1972–76, were submitted in February 1971, and £14 million was recovered for 1971–72, the first year of operation.[180] In the event, the projections were somewhat wide of the mark. For example, the costs of managing government securities were expected to fall from £5.2 million in

---

[178] Painter to Taylor, 11 March 1971; Nigel Wicks (HMT) to Ronald Fairbairn, 7 July 1972, enc. 'Memorandum of understanding between the Treasury and the Bank of England about the white paper on the Bank of England', cmnd. 4633, 4A7/1; Taylor to Hollom, 1 August 1972, G38/5.

[179] Taylor, Note for record – 'Select Committee on Nationalised Industries', 9 March 1971, 5A19/1.

[180] Fairbairn to Aphra Maunsell, 'Service performed for H. M. Government', 13 October 1970; David Best (Accounts and Costing Office), Note for record – 'Recovery of costs

Table 15.1. *Bank of England sources of income, 1971–80 (£m)*

Year ending	Fixed income		Variable income	Recovery from HMG for services performed	Profit/(loss) on sales (3)	Total income
	Interest on British Government securities	Other[a]	Interest on Treasury bills, bills discounted, and advances[b]			
Feb 1971	10.4	2.4	9.1	5.0	(0.4)	26.5
Feb 1972	11.7	2.2	9.1	14.0	2.1	39.1
Feb 1973	12.7	2.8	12.0	15.7	(0.1)	43.1
Feb 1974	13.3	2.8	23.3	17.4	(4.8)	52.0
Feb 1975	14.7	3.9	30.5	27.0	(6.2)	69.9
Feb 1976	16.4	6.5	24.8	35.0	(6.4)	76.3
Feb 1977	17.1	7.3	26.9	35.0	(7.2)	79.1
Feb 1978	18.4	6.8	21.6	35.7	2.2	84.7
Feb 1979	18.6	6.9	31.8	37.5	(4.8)	90.0
Feb 1980	24.0	7.6	52.6	39.7	(7.5)	116.4

[a] Interest on miscellaneous securities, commissions, fees, rents, and other receipts.
[b] Less interest paid on deposits.
[c] Sales of British government securities and other assets.
Source: 'Blue book' accounts, 7A299 and 7A325.

1972 to £4.5 million by 1976: the actual figures were £6.4 million and £16.0 million. Even in real terms, costs increased up to the mid-1970s. Thereafter, there was a real reduction, and taking financial years 1971/72 and 1979/80, the amount recovered from government was static (Tables 15.2 and 15.3). Part of the reason was pressure from the Treasury to cut costs and the impact of 'cash limits' introduced in 1976 as an attempt to control public expenditure. The costs of exchange control were placed within the cash-limits regime during 1976/77, and the remaining services were embraced in 1977/78.[181]

from H.M.G., 4 January 1971; Fairbairn to Len Taylor (HMT), 23 February 1971; Taylor to Hollom, 'Charges to H.M.G.', 10 August 1971, ADM6/209.
[181] Taylor to heads of departments, 'Cash limits', 10 February 1976; Taylor to Jordan (HMT), 11 March 1976, 5A29/1; Unwin (HMT) to Taylor, 21 November 1975; Rumins to Blunden/

Table 15.2. *Bank of England amount recovered from government for services performed, 1971–80 (£m)*

Year ending	Stock and bonds	Note issue	Exchange control	EEA	Other[a]	Total recovered	Total recovered (constant 1970 prices)
Feb 1971	1.8	1.7	0.1	–	1.4	5.0	5.0
Feb 1972	6.4	2.3	3.3	0.4	1.6	14.0	12.8
Feb 1973	7.4	2.1	3.6	0.5	2.1	15.7	13.3
Feb 1974	7.6	2.6	5.3	0.4	1.5	17.4	13.7
Feb 1975	9.9	3.2	5.7	1.0	7.2	27.0	18.6
Feb 1976	16.0	4.8	10.6	1.8	1.8	35.0	18.9
Feb 1977	15.5	5.2	10.8	1.4	2.1	35.0	16.4
Feb 1978	14.4	5.6	11.4	1.5	2.8	35.7	14.7
Feb 1979	15.2	5.4	12.4	1.6	2.9	37.5	13.9
Feb 1980	18.7	6.5	9.1	2.3	3.1	39.7	12.8

[a] Mainly recoveries in relation to Printing Works. 1975 includes a special pension recovery of £5.5 million.

Source: 'Blue book accounts', 7A299 and 7A325.

The Bank's total expenditure grew from £20 million to £65 million over the decade (Table 15.4), although in real terms the increase was around only 4 per cent. Personnel costs remained the largest item of expenditure, with salaries, wages, and pensions amounting to 68 per cent of total spending. Yet the number of staff had remained fairly constant. Relating the expenditure figures to the monies reclaimed from the government shows that following the implementation of the new policy, some 60 to 70 per cent of the Bank's total costs were recovered. This still left many millions spent on the remaining central banking functions, such as monetary policy, economic intelligence, banking services, overseas work, and other unallocated costs of running the institution.

Capital expenditure in this period averaged £3.6 million per year, with a peak of £7 million in 1973/74, and this was split roughly 50–50 between premises and equipment. The latter included new computer centres at

Hollom, 'Cash limits', 21 October 1976, 5A21/1; Blunden to budget centre managers, 'Cash limits 1978/79', 31 January 1978, 5A21/2.

Table 15.3. *Bank of England main financial indicators, constant prices,*
index 1971 = 100

Year ending	Total income	Total expenditure	Operating profit	Retained profit	Free reserves	GDP at market prices implied deflator (1971 = 100)
Feb 1971	100	100	100	100	100	100
Feb 1972	135	93	258	78	94	109.1
Feb 1973	138	96	266	97	90	118.2
Feb 1974	154	103	160	84	72	127.3
Feb 1975	181	118	142	87	66	145.5
Feb 1976	156	123	137	64	54	184.8
Feb 1977	140	115	97	109	50	213.1
Feb 1978	132	109	135	148	48	242.4
Feb 1979	125	98	164	205	50	270.7
Feb 1980	142	104	131	134	50	310.1

Source: Derived from Tables 15.1 and 15.2 and 15.4 and 15.6.

Threadneedle Street and New Change and additional machinery at Debden.[182] Another O'Brien initiative was the new reference library, authorised in 1969 at a cost of £250,000 and opened in 1971.[183] After criticism over the Bank's lavish 'Taj Mahal' branches, spending on branches in the 1970s was relatively subdued. There were extensions to the Bristol and Southampton branches and a new agency in Glasgow. One of the branches, the Law Courts in the strand, was closed and sold. It had served the legal profession for almost a century. The number of accounts had dropped from 487 in 1925 to 131 in 1965 and still further by the 1970s. Furthermore, under the new Supreme Court Fund Rules introduced in December 1975, all cash lodgements into Court were made at the Court Funds Office, and the provision of banking facilities immediately adjacent to the Courts was no longer necessary.[184] The branch's accounts were transferred to head office in December 1975, and the

[182] For example, see Bank of England, *Annual Reports*, year ending February 1972, pp. 46–47 and year ending February 1975, p. 28.
[183] Committee of Treasury, Minutes, 15 January 1969, G8/84; *The Old Lady*, June 1971, p. 75.
[184] Bank of England, *Annual Report*, year ending February 1976, p. 20.

Table 15.4. *Bank of England gross expenditure, 1971–80 (£m)*

Year ending	Personnel[a]	General[b] expenditure	Total	Recovered per cent	Not recovered per cent
Feb 1971	13.5	6.8	20.3	5.0 (25)	15.3 (75)
Feb 1972	14.3	6.4	20.7	14.0 (68)	6.7 (32)
Feb 1973	16.1	7.0	23.1	15.7 (62)	7.4 (38)
Feb 1974	17.4	9.2	26.6	17.4 (65)	9.2 (35)
Feb 1975	22.7	12.2	34.9	27.0 (69)	7.9 (31)
Feb 1976	30.2	15.9	46.1	35.0 (76)	11.1 (24)
Feb 1977	33.3	16.5	49.8	35.0 (70)	14.8 (30)
Feb 1978	35.4	18.4	53.8	35.7 (66)	18.1 (34)
Feb 1979	38.1	15.7	53.8	37.5 (70)	16.3 (30)
Feb 1980	45.4	20.0	65.4	39.7 (61)	25.7 (39)

[a] Includes salaries and wages, national insurance and other payments, pension contributions, and Governors' and Directors' remuneration.

[b] Operating costs, maintenance, and depreciation.

Source: 'Blue book' accounts, 7A299 and 7A325.

Law Courts' staff were guaranteed jobs elsewhere in the Bank.[185] The building was sold in 1979 for £0.8 million.

What then happened to Bank 'profits' in the 1970s (Table 15.5)? Gross profit is the difference between total normal income, including the recovery from the Treasury, and total expenditure. Changes in accounting standards meant that from the financial year 1974/75 provisions for losses and pensions were charged to the profit and loss account, whereas previously provisions for losses could be charged to reserves.[186] Up to the end of February 1980, provisions totalling £38 million were made for pensions and £70 million for losses. In the published accounts, the provision for losses was shown as a net figure comprising sums related to the Bank's share in the support operations, offset by reductions in a provision that had been made against a large fall in the value of British government and other securities during 1973/74.[187] Thus provisions for losses on support operations were partially

---

[185] For more on closure of the law courts branch, see 0A30/1.

[186] This was required to comply with the Statements of Standard Accounting Practice, SSAP 6.

[187] See 7A325/1 and 2. For example, the published provision in 1976–77 was £16.1 million; it consisted of bad debts £28.5 million, miscellaneous securities £5.5 million, and British government securities £6.9 million.

Table 15.5. *Bank of England gross and net profits, 1970–80 (£m)*

Year ending	Gross profit[a]	Provisions losses	Pensions	Pre-tax (operating) profit	Tax	Dividend payment to Treasury	Additional pensions provision	Profit after tax and dividend
Feb 1971	6.3	–	–	6.3	1.9	1.7	–	2.7
Feb 1972	18.4	–	–	17.7	5.0	5.5	4.9	2.3
Feb 1973	19.6	–	–	19.8	4.9	7.0	4.8	3.1
Feb 1974	25.4	–	–	24.7	9.9	6.0	5.9	2.9
Restated								
Feb 1974	25.4	–	11.9	12.8	3.9	6.0	–	2.9
Feb 1975	35.0	9.8	12.2	13.0	3.6	6.0	–	3.4
Feb 1976	30.2	14.3	–	15.9	6.7	6.0	–	3.2
Feb 1977	29.2	16.2	–	13.0	3.7	3.0	–	6.3
Feb 1978	30.9	10.3	–	20.6	5.4	5.5	–	9.7
Feb 1979	36.1	8.1	–	28.0	5.5	7.5	–	15.0
Feb 1980	51.0	11.4	14.0	25.6	7.9	6.5	–	11.2

[a] Normal income plus amount recovered from HMG, less normal expenditure.

Source: 'Blue book' accounts, 7A299 and 7A325.

obscured in the public accounts; the total figure was actually more than £100 million. These provisions resulted in significant reductions in profits, both in nominal and in real terms (see Table 15.5). In particular, the pre-tax figure in the restated accounts for 1973/74 was halved from £24.7 million to £12.8 million and after a further re-working showed a loss of £7.4 million. All this had an impact on reserves. In real terms, 'free' capital and reserves (i.e., after deducting premises and equipment) fell by 50 per cent (Table 15.6).

The unpredictability of the Bank's profits had implications for the size of the dividend that was paid to the Treasury. Following the recommendations of the SCNI, the Bank considered ways in which the payment might be altered. A formula was put forward to the Treasury at the beginning of March 1971 that each year the Bank would claim an addition to its reserves (after tax) equivalent to 5 per cent of the previous year-end total of capital and general reserves, and thereafter any remaining pre-tax profits would be split 10 per cent to the Bank and 90 per cent to the Treasury.[188] There followed some uneasy negotiations in which the Bank still refused to reveal its accounts for the 1960s, leading to Treasury complaints that it could not judge whether the buildup of reserves had been reasonable. Taylor took the impression away from one meeting that some in the Treasury saw the white paper as an opportunity to become more closely involved in the affairs of the Bank. However, in June 1971, Taylor was told that the ministers had decided to put the matter to one side for time being, and the question was again dropped in 1973.[189] With no agreement over a formula, the issue was left to twice-yearly horse trading over the amount that would be handed over in lieu of the dividend. This did not stop the Treasury continuing to press for more detail. For example, in 1972, it had attempted to identify the specific needs for reserves, but this approach was strongly discouraged by Taylor. He asserted that it would undermine the philosophy of the Bank as an independent institution, able to respond and react to events and decide the timing and extent of its interventions and initiatives.[190] All this argument over profits was exactly what the Bank had sought to avoid in the 1950s and 1960s.

Revisiting the issue in the mid-1970s, the SCNI was told that payments to the Treasury in lieu of dividend in the four years 1971/72 to 1974/75

---

[188] Somerset to John Rumins, 'Retention of profits', 10 January 1971, C40/1363; Taylor to Hollom, 'Profit formula', 1 February 1971; Taylor to Painter, 1 March 1971, 4A7/1.

[189] Fairbairn, Note for record, 7 April 1971; Taylor to O'Brien/Hollom, 7 April 1971; Peter Kitcatt (assistant secretary, HMT) to Taylor, 18 June 1971; Rumins, Note for record – 'Meeting at the Treasury on 22 February 1973', 4A7/1.

[190] Gordon Downey to Taylor, 30 March 1972; Fairbairn to Taylor, 7 April 1972; Taylor to Downey, 14 April 1972, 4A7/1.

Table 15.6. *Bank of England reserves, 1971–80 (£m)*

Year ending	General reserve	Capital and reserves	Less premises/ equipment	Free capital/ reserves	Free capital/ reserves (constant 1971 prices)
Feb 1971	101.1	115.7	31.6	84.1	84.1
Feb 1972	104.4	118.9	32.6	86.3	79.1
Feb 1973	107.6	122.1	33.1	89.0	75.3
Feb 1974	100.1	114.7	37.9	76.8	60.3
Feb 1975	103.6	118.2	37.2	81.0	55.7
Feb 1976	106.8	121.4	37.2	84.2	45.6
Feb 1977	120.4	187.4	97.7	89.7	42.1
Feb 1978	130.2	197.2	98.5	98.7	40.7
Feb 1979	145.8	212.3	99.2	113.1	41.8
Feb 1980	164.0	230.4	99.9	130.5	42.1

Note: Figures from year ending February 1977 onwards reflect a revaluation of property that produced a revaluation surplus of £52.4 million.
Source: 'Blue book' accounts, 7A299 and 7A325; Rumins, 'The Bank's accounts and budgetary control'.

had totalled £24.5 million, whereas capital and reserves had increased by only £5.1 million. Questioned by the committee, Hollom said that he regarded the reserves as 'unduly low' and that they should be seen against the standards that the Bank imposed on others: 'We should not be preaching what we ourselves do not practice.' Thus, argued Hollom, capital and reserves had to have a 'sensible relationship' to the business that the Bank carried out. While capital adequacy cannot apply in the same way to a central bank, Hollom continued, 'We certainly expect other banks to approach the question of capital adequacy in that way.' Whatever he had hoped to achieve with this evidence, it certainly had an effect. In its October 1976 report, the committee concluded that the additions to the reserves had not been adequate or appropriate, and it recommended that full weight should be given in future negotiations to ensuring that the 'capital adequacy of the Bank of England' did not fall below the standard that was imposed on other banks.[191] The next set of negotiations with the Treasury, for the six months ending 5 April 1977, resulted in no dividend being paid owing to

[191] SCNI 1976, 'Report', paras. 154–157, p. lxxxiii.

the provision for support operations. It was the first break in the sequence since the 1946 Act.[192]

In January 1978, when the SCNI questioned the Bank about its *Annual Report* and accounts, Hollom was again asked whether the level of reserves was satisfactory. His typically careful response was, 'I think, really, that all reserves, particularly in the case of an institution like our own, need to be evidently more than adequate rather than no more than just adequate.' When pressed further, Hollom said that while he had no anxiety about the current level of reserves, he would like 'a higher figure bearing a better relationship to our obligations'.[193] Given these sentiments, it is not a surprise to find that five months later Hollom issued an instruction that not more than £4 million was to be offered to the Treasury in negotiations. It cut little ice with the Treasury. Assistant Secretary Rosalind Gilmore warned that £7 million was the minimum figure acceptable. She argued that even at this level, reserves would be increased by more than in previous years, which in any case were at comparatively high levels. This produced a robust defence from John Rumins, who doubted whether the arguments would lead to a change in the views of Court. The matter then moved to higher levels. While Deputy Secretary Geoffrey Littler did not quite issue an explicit threat, Hollom was urged to 'reflect' on what had been said. Consequently, the Bank relented, although Richardson expressed in writing the Court's concerns about the level of the reserves.[194]

Calculations made in the Bank showed that total operating profits for the 10 financial years 1970/71 to 1979/80 were £135 million: £55 million was paid to the Treasury plus another £29 million in tax; £51 million was retained by the Bank. Over the same period, free capital and reserves increased from £84 million to £130 million. In real terms, however, the figure fell to £40.5 million, and there were only two years (1978 and 1979) when retained profit was sufficient to avoid drawing on reserves.[195] When Rumins looked back over the history of the negotiations in the 1970s, he

---

[192] Taylor to Hollom, 'The Bank's accounts', 21 March 1977; Hollom to Wass, 31 March 1977; Wass to Hollom, 3 April 1977, 4A7/1.

[193] *The Select Committee on Nationalised Industries (Sub-Committee C). Minutes of Evidence, Session 1977–78, 25 January 1978, Bank of England Report and Accounts for the Year Ended 28 February 1977*, 166-i., questions 117–120.

[194] Hollom to Taylor, 25 May 1978; Rosalind Gilmore (assistant secretary, HMT) to Taylor, 13 June 1978; Rumins to Gilmore, 16 June 1978; Geoffrey Littler (deputy secretary, HMT) to Hollom, 26 June 1978; Richardson to Wass, 16 August 1978, 4A7/1; Hollom to Richardson, 10 July 1978, 7A149/2.

[195] Rumins to McMahon, 'Dividend discussions', 29 May 1981, 4A7/2; Rumins, 'The Bank's accounts and budgetary control 1969–1994', September 1995, pp. 48–64.

observed that 'although this has not appeared openly in the Bank-Treasury discussions', financial independence was the 'crux of the whole discourse'.[196] Of course, this wish for financial independence was not merely an aim in itself but a matter of what was consistent with the Bank's ability and desire to perform what it saw as the tasks of a central bank without recourse to its ultimate shareholder.

[196] Rumins to Hollom et al., 'Retention of profits', 24 October 1978, 5A19/2.

16

Epilogue

From its foundation in 1694 until the second half of the twentieth century, the Bank's basic structure had remained essentially unchanged with many of the departments, offices, and functions easily identifiable across the centuries. Nationalisation had done little to alter this, and neither had subsequent changes such as the creation of Central Banking Information Department/ Economic Intelligence Department (EID) or even the end of the Discount Office. However, in the 1970s, there was a feeling that the structure was no longer suitable. In March 1980, the Bank implemented what it claimed was 'the most radical restructuring ... since 1694'.[1]

The immediate origins are found in the summer of 1978, when Richardson discussed the subject with Blunden. Blunden identified several defects in the existing organisation: the administration was outdated, and on many matters the Governor and Executive Directors had to rely on the 'grapevine' to keep themselves informed. All this was 'a relic of the pre-1914 Bank'. Blunden felt that the Chief Cashier's role ranged too widely (whether or not he also meant that Page himself was too powerful was left unsaid); one man could not be expected to be deeply involved in credit and monetary policy and market operations while at the same time acting as the Bank's chief administrator. Again, this was an historical relic. The four Executive Directors had never been properly integrated into the structure of the Bank, and their number was determined by the 1946 Act and based on historical influences rather than organisational needs. One of these posts, in fact, Blunden's, was concerned with administration and routine operations. He argued that it should bear the burden of the internal management, but its extension was frustrated by the role of the Chief Cashier. The other three had heavy commitments in policy but possessed no clear executive roles,

---

[1] *Financial Weekly*, 18 January 1980, attributed this to a senior Bank official, 6A262/1.

nor were they effectively involved in management, and when they were, it tended to be disruptive. Finally, the career structure was designed to ensure a supply of people to run the Bank machine, but it failed to provide enough top-quality people to perform in the limited areas of policymaking or market operations.[2]

Blunden suggested some remedies for these defects, although change might have to wait until Page's retirement (due in 1983). The first proposal was that the full-time Directors should have proper job titles that fitted into the hierarchy of the Bank. In fact, anyone looking at the *Annual Report* prior to 1980 would not even be able to identify who the executives were, let alone what they did. Next came a fundamental proposal: the Cashier's Department should be divided into two. One, the Banking Department, could deal with the routine areas. In charge would be someone still called the Chief Cashier, but as a normal head of department. It would be staffed by people who would expect to spend their entire career at the Bank. The remainder of the Cashier's empire would become a new department that Blunden suggested might be called 'Central Banking', or 'Supervision and Operations'. It would comprise three divisions: gold and foreign exchange, supervision, and sterling operations, that is, money and gilt-edged markets. Blunden did not expect that this department would normally be the domain of 'career staff', and he thought that in the future appointments would come increasingly from outside the Bank.[3] This was also in line with earlier views about the recruitment and retention of specialists for EID.[4] While the precise details were to change, in essence, the reorganisation that was implemented followed Blunden's prescription. When Richardson garnered other opinions, they provided only minor variations on the Blunden agenda.[5]

The next stage, in 1979, was an organisational review undertaken by Lord Croham (formerly Sir Douglas Allen), who had joined the Bank the previous year as an Adviser to Richardson. By early April, Croham had completed a draft report that was sent to Richardson on a strictly personal basis. Considerable space was devoted to the Executive Directors, who tended to regard their role 'as that of policy co-ordinators without managerial responsibilities'.[6] Croham believed that there should be lines of command

---

[2] Blunden to Richardson, 'Organisation', 8 August 1978, G1/567.

[3] *Ibid.*

[4] See George, 'Review of E.I.D.' (George Report), 29 September 1975; Drake to Blunden/ Dow, 'Recruitment and development of specialist E.I.D. staff', 24 June 1976, 7A152/1.

[5] Taylor to Richardson, 15 December 1978; Benson, 'Organisation', 13 December 1978, G1/567.

[6] Croham to Richardson, nd, enc. draft report, 2 April 1979, 7A127/1.

running through the Executive Directors into the areas for which they were responsible. He also saw no reason why their number should be limited to four, and the Bank should be free to create additional posts as required. In placing the emphasis on Directors rather than departments, two alternative organisational structures were presented. Both divided the Bank into three: 'management and executive operations', 'policy and strategy', and 'supervision'. Under the first option, many areas, such as Cashiers, would be largely unchanged. The second would involve breaking up the Cashiers. Either option, argued Croham, would mean the 'elimination of all doubt about who was in command'.[7] He later wrote that the Governors (though presumably this really meant Richardson) favoured implementing the more radical approach straightaway, and Croham redrafted the report to present the single option.[8] It bore a striking resemblance to Blunden's initial views.

Over the following months, these ideas were discussed within a limited circle (Richardson, Dow, McMahon, Blunden, and Croham). The decision to press ahead appears to have been taken at a meeting held at the end of May 1979. This took place at New Change rather than in Threadneedle Street, and Richardson expressly asked that the Chief Cashier not be invited. Afterwards, Blunden wrote a personal note for the Governor that stated, 'In the light of the meeting at New Change I have assumed that you wish broadly to adopt its [Croham's report] recommendations.'[9] Thereafter, a range of questions was addressed relating to the basic structure, the allocation of responsibilities, and the appropriate titles of the various posts and divisions. Practical transitional matters also were addressed, notably which post could be offered to Page so that he could 'be moved without a loss of face'. With some retirements due, there was also an element of succession planning. Blunden began putting names against the senior positions, with some possible candidates coming from outside the Bank: one was Loehnis, who had returned to Schroders; another was Alberto Weissmuller, an international banker identified as a suitable Adviser on supervision.[10] There was a great deal of speculation and gossip in the Bank about the new structure and its justification, with some saying that the changes would be 'divisive'

[7] *Ibid.*
[8] Croham to Richardson, 19 April 1979, enc. 'The Bank of England. A proposal for a revised directing structure', 20 April 1979, 7A127/1; Croham to Blunden, 31 January 1980, 6A262/1.
[9] Molly Abraham (Richardson's personal Secretary) to Richardson, 22 May 1979; Blunden to Richardson, 'The Croham report', 15 June 1979, 7A127/1.
[10] Blunden to Richardson, 'The Croham report', 15 June 1979; Blunden to Richardson, 'Supervision and financial structure', 30 July 1979, 7A127/1. Weissmuller's relative was Johnny Weissmuller of Tarzan fame.

and amounted to an 'economists' charter'. This referred to the feeling that the routine departments were being relegated to an inferior position. Allied to the redundancies following the demise of Exchange Control, Galpin, now Head of Corporate Services, reckoned that morale in the Bank was low, and the presentation of the restructuring would require careful handling.[11]

At the end of 1979, events moved quickly, with Richardson wanting to tie in the announcement with changes to the membership of the Court. By then, it was confirmed that Hollom would be standing down as Deputy Governor. Even at a late stage there was plenty of room for manoeuvre, and last-minute changes included the merging of 'Monetary and Credit Policy' into Economics, whereas the 'Deputy Directors' were renamed as 'Assistant Directors'.[12] In the final scheme, there was also only a single Associate Director, and rather than assisting either Dow or Fforde, the post-holder was to be in charge of the overseas side. This role was to be taken by Loehnis. The new structure, with its three areas of operation, was unveiled to staff on 16 January 1980 (Figure 16.1). 'Policy and Markets' was concerned with domestic and external monetary policy, research, and market operations and would work closely with the Governor and Deputy Governor. Under Fforde (Home Finance Director) were three Assistant Directors: Coleby (money markets), George (gilt-edged market), and Goodhart (Chief Adviser on monetary policy). Dow (Economics Director) was assisted by Walker (industrial finance and financial statistics) and John Flemming, a leading macroeconomist who had spent a year in the Bank in 1975 on secondment from Nuffield College.[13] As Associate Director (Overseas), Loehnis was assisted by Balfour and Holland on general matters and Sangster on foreign-exchange operations. Page was the Executive Director in charge of 'Financial Structure and Supervision'. Under him, Cooke continued as Head of Banking Supervision, Weissmuller as an Adviser, and Dawkins was responsible for surveillance and development work. Finally, there was 'Operations and Services'. Blunden was the Executive Director, with four departments below him: the Banking Department, led by Somerset, who also held the traditional title of Chief Cashier; the former Accountant's Department, now renamed Registrar's; the Printing Works; and the

[11] Galpin to Blunden/Richardson/Hollom, 'Senior management structures', 8 January 1980, G1/567.

[12] Blunden to Richardson, 27 December 1979, with Richardson amendments; McMahon to Richardson, 'Management structure', 2 January 1980; Blunden to Richardson, 4 January 1980, 6A262/1.

[13] Goodhart (2007, pp.1, 26–28). After his secondment, Flemming had continued to work one day per week at the Bank.

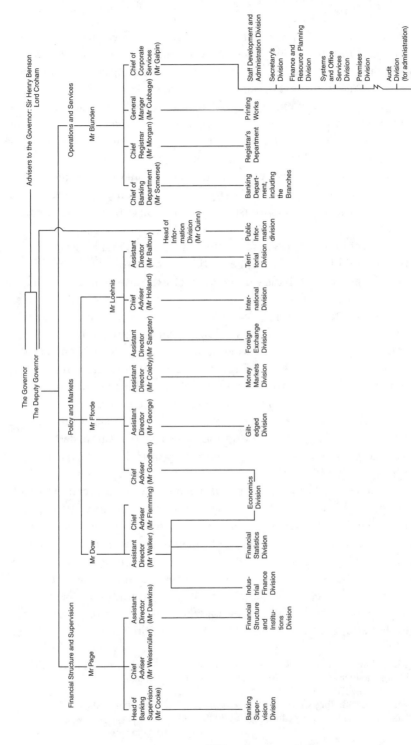

Figure 16.1. Bank of England organisation structure, 1980.

Corporate Services Department. Lying outside the three areas was Quinn, as the Head of Information Division, who reported directly to the Deputy Governor.[14] The new structure elevated some of the key people who would head the Bank in the next decade and beyond.

Copies of the announcement were sent to former Governors, and Cromer quickly responded, telling Richardson that the new structure was much more in line with the present needs of the Bank. He was also glad that 'as I did in my day' [with Morse], an outsider had been brought in at a senior position; 'however excellent the professional staff of the Bank is, there is always a danger of the "ivory tower" syndrome'.[15] He was neither the first nor the last person to use the phrase 'ivory tower' where the Bank was concerned.

The downgrading of the Chief Cashier's role meant that Page was the last person to hold the position while it still retained all its traditional levers of power and was the Bank's de facto chief executive officer. He was the longest-serving Chief Cashier in our period (and the second longest serving in the twentieth century). As such, he was widely known and respected in the City for his grasp of the working of financial markets.[16] Yet Page's term in office not only coincided with the increasing use of monetary theory but also theory for which Page had little time. Reserved in character and quiet, he was not a strong communicator. But his post had undoubted power, and he could express his views forcibly enough – certainly enough to irritate Richardson.[17] Whether the 1980 moves were designed to deal with the post or the post-holder, they undoubtedly left Page emasculated.

The reorganisation also saw the retirement of Hollom. He was in a relatively senior position in all the major events and policies covered in this history. Hollom was always unruffled; losing his composure amounted to peering over his dark-rimmed glasses. He was guarded, something some attributed to his experience as a prisoner of war, but he was measured and 'decisive, firm and clear in a very mild mannered way'.[18] Hollom's modest nature and lack of ego meant that he had the respect of those who worked for him, and he got on with most. Richardson described Hollom as 'a rock and wholly reliable, … a colleague and deputy beyond price'. He went on to say, 'speaking of the difficult period since 1973, I am sure that – apart from Jasper himself … – no-one but me knows the full extent of what he

---

[14]   Richardson, 'A message to the staff from the Governor', 16 January 1980, 7A127/1.
[15]   Cromer to Richardson, 17 January 1980, 7A127/1.
[16]   *The Old Lady*, June 2005, p. 72.
[17]   Interviews with Tony Coleby, 2 October 2007 and Brian Quinn, 27 February 2008.
[18]   Interview with Sir Jeremy Morse, 1 June 2005.

contributed to the good of the Bank and the good of the country.' Hollom stayed on the Court as a non-executive until 1984 and also continued to give advice on support operations and Burmah Oil. By the time he left the Bank, he had been there for almost 50 years.

Hollom was replaced by McMahon. As an economist with experience on both the domestic and the international scenes, still relatively young (age 52), and in the Richardson circle, he was the obvious, and probably the only, candidate from within the Bank. He also might have seemed to be the natural successor to Richardson, but his colleagues were not surprised when he was passed over for the Governorship.[19] Thatcher was opposed, apparently stemming from a brusque rebuff by McMahon when she was leader of the Opposition.[20] Leaving the Bank in 1985, he went on to join Midland Bank as chairman and chief executive. In this respect, similarities can be drawn with Morse. Both were drafted in by Cromer to give the Bank intellectual muscle. Both rose effortlessly through the Bank. Both were tipped as future Governors, and each left to run a clearing bank. Throughout the hectic 1970s, as Overseas Director, 'nothing daunted him', and one employee recalled that 'the greater the difficulties the more buoyant and positive was his response'.[21]

Richardson continued as Governor until 1983. Bank Governors had for long been treated like Eastern potentates, and while this was waning, Richardson was perhaps the last to which it might be applied. The idea of kingship is medieval in origin, and central to it is the taking of counsel; the wider counsel was sought, the better. It is perhaps of interest that it developed under Richards I, II, and III, but it seems to have reached some kind of apotheosis in Richardson. This was certainly Richardson's approach, and he did have good Advisers in the main. Yet, the more counsel he took, the harder it was for him to make up his mind. His greatest weakness was indecision, something that could cause havoc when it came to writing speeches. Every option would be looked at, considered, and analysed from every possible angle, what one former Bank employee called 'paralysis by analysis'.[22] His professional background was tax barrister and merchant banker, so it is perhaps not surprising that he was much more comfortable with City matters than economics. And his close relationship with Healey ensured that the Bank went some way towards restoring its relationship with government, which had been under strain in the days of Cromer and during the final stages of

[19] *The Independent*, 13 May 1990, 'Business on Sunday', p. 8.
[20] *The Sunday Times*, 29 September 1985.
[21] *The Old Lady*, December 1985, p. 190.
[22] Discussion with David Mallett, 6 November 2007.

O'Brien's governorship. His detractors often refer to his vanity, but neutrals would speak of his quality. Even Harold Wilson said, 'I've known them all, and most of them have been very, very high quality; he [is] certainly of the highest quality.'[23] To McMahon, he was a man of 'great intelligence and flexibility of mind'. Richardson undoubtedly was suave, but many Bank staff did not warm to him. He could appear arrogant, and it was often said that he would keep people waiting unnecessarily. For Richardson, you either belonged or you did not. Both Page and Keogh suffered from not belonging.

As far as the financing of the Bank went, the possibility of moving to a formula was raised again by the Treasury in the early 1980s. Initially, the Bank was unreceptive, but by September 1983, attitudes had shifted, and it was finally agreed that one-third of pre-tax profits would be passed to the Treasury, leaving about the same proportions retained and paid in tax. This arrangement was to be reviewed after five years, or *in extremis*. The two main reasons given for accepting a formula now were that it would allow the *Annual Report* to be published earlier because there would be no need for protracted negotiations over the dividend, and it also would eliminate what it was admitted had been a major source of conflict and poor relations with the Treasury.[24]

An important change, and a welcome one from the historian's point of view, was the change to record keeping (if not preserving) that came after heavy criticism. The report of the Croom-Johnson tribunal, which was published in 1982, found that the Bank had failed to inform adequately both the Treasury and the Stevenson Committee of its concerns over the Crown Agents, and after Stevenson, the Bank gave less help to the government than it should and could have done. One of the reasons was the way in which the Bank conducted work informally and orally. This certainly contrasted with civil service practice: when Gill was seconded to the Treasury in 1977, he was struck by the fact that it operated on paper, and everything was recorded.[25]

---

[23] Transcript of BBC's 'The Money Programme 29 November, 1978', filed as 29 November 1979, OV197/4.

[24] Rumins to Nick Monck (HMT), 9 December 1981; McMahon to Richardson, 'Bank dividend', 29 March 1982; McMahon to Richardson, 16 June 1982; Committee of Treasury, 17 June 1982; Rumins to McMahon, 'Dividend', 10 May 1983; Rumins to McMahon, 31 August 1983, enc. 'Speaking note on dividend for the Governor – 1.9.83'; Committee of Treasury, 1 September 1983; Leigh-Pemberton to Nigel Lawson (Chancellor), 7 September 1983. Changes in corporation tax in the 1984 budget resulted in an agreement to modify the formula so that profits were shared on a 50–50 basis; see Minutes of Court, 3 and 10 May 1984; McMahon to Peter Middleton (permanent Secretary, HMT), 18 May 1984; Middleton to McMahon, 24 May 1984, 4A7/2.

[25] Interview with Malcolm Gill, 14 February 2006; *The Old Lady*, June 1980, pp. 55–56.

Croom-Johnson found that the failure to record discussions and decisions taken as a result of internal meetings led to confusion within the Bank. The organisation of the Bank meant that the relevant information was dispersed among many people, each of whom had only a partial picture.[26] The failure of different departments within the bank to communicate effectively all elements of information about the Crown Agents and the Bank's tendency to send inappropriate and insufficiently briefed spokesmen to important meetings also were factors. The over-reliance of the Bank on oral methods of reporting was also highlighted, and McMahon conceded that the Bank should go further in making sure that decisions were recorded.[27] However, Richardson was satisfied that the 1980 reorganisation had gone a long way towards meeting many of the criticisms.[28]

As well as the changes to the Bank's structure, leading personnel, record keeping, and financing, the monetary policy environment was also on the point of changing. An important part of this was that the exchange rate was, at least for some years, allowed to float freely, and the resources devoted to attending to it could be channelled elsewhere. The genuinely floating rate allowed an independent monetary policy, and the Bank's main efforts then could concentrate on that. In some respects, the changes can be seen from a current perspective as the culmination of a very long discussion going on over a number of years and leading to a new concern with monetary aggregates. It had begun in a serious way with the imposition of domestic credit expansion targets by the International Monetary Fund in the late 1960s and again in the mid-1970s. Although there was some work going on in both the Treasury and the Bank on the subject, there was still a clinging to some old ideas. Intense discussion was provoked by the new Conservative Government, one of whose priorities was the control of inflation and whose belief was that monetary control was an essential part of that.

In June 1979, the Treasury and Civil Service Select Committee was established by the new government. It had powers to question the Bank in all the areas from which the Select Committee on Nationalised Industries was debarred, notably monetary, exchange-rate, and exchange-control policy. Old habits die hard: considering the new committee, Croham believed that 'the art will be to convey the impression of openness while being relatively non-commital [*sic*] on delicate issues'.[29] The Committee set to work on an

---

[26] Croom-Johnson Report, para. 16.39.
[27] McMahon to Richardson, 23 August 1982, 8A32/1.
[28] Richardson to executive directors et al., 4 October 1982, 3A161/182.
[29] Croham to Richardson/Hollom, 'Select committee on the Treasury', 3 October 1979, 3A19/1.

investigation that resulted in a less than ringing endorsement of monetary policy published in March 1981.

Meanwhile, in March 1980, the government published the green paper, 'Monetary control'.[30] This had been announced by Howe in November 1979 when he set in place a formal review of the methods of controlling the money supply. The consultative paper, produced jointly by the Bank and the Treasury, stated that the government believed that 'a progressive reduction in the rate of growth of the money stock is essential to achieving a permanent reduction in inflation'.[31] The paper repeated the views of the Bank and the Treasury on the difficulty of measuring money, advising that a range of measures was needed. However, it did state unequivocally that 'The Government believes that its monetary policy can best be formulated if it sets targets for the growth of one of the aggregates against which progress can be assessed.'[32] There was considerable agreement that £M3 was the best measure for British circumstances at the time. The main conclusions of the paper were that the supplementary special deposits scheme had come to the end of its useful life; the 12½ per cent reserve-asset ratio was no longer necessary, although some cash requirement was; and the special deposit scheme needed to be retained to combat any excess liquidity that developed in the banking system. In August 1981, new arrangements for monetary control took effect. These included abolition of the reserve-asset ratio, the Bank ceased to post minimum lending rate continuously, and the need for the London clearing banks to hold 1½ per cent of eligible liabilities at the Bank was replaced by a requirement for a ½ per cent cash ratio for all recognised banks.[33] This marked the formal end of competition and credit control (CCC), almost exactly 10 years after it was introduced.

The other significant change taking place was the move from the light touch and informal supervision to the statutory and more concentrated supervision. After 1980, the Banking Supervision Division grew steadily and substantially from around 80 in 1979 to 200 in 1989 as the Bank began taking an ever-closer interest in the activities of all sizes of banks even before any signs of stress appeared.

Thus this period ends on the cusp of major changes across the Bank's business and probably marks an intellectual transformation that had moved the Bank somewhat along the spectrum from being a bank to something closer to a study group. It might not have pleased Norman or Cobbold, but

---

[30] Green paper, 'Monetary Control', cmnd 7858, March 1980.
[31] 'Monetary Control', p. iii, para. 2.
[32] *Ibid.,* p. iv, para. 8.
[33] 'Monetary control – provisions', *BEQB* 21(3):347–349, September 1981.

there probably was a clearer conception of monetary policy and the Bank's role in executing it, together with a clearer picture of what the Bank need not be doing. A comment on the Bank across the third quarter of the twentieth century could be expressed in a paraphrase of the *Book of Common Prayer*: the Old Lady left undone those things she ought to have done and did those things she ought not to have done.

Bibliography

Abramson, D. M. 2006. *Building the Bank of England: Money, Architecture, Society 1694–1942*. New Haven, CT: Yale University Press.

Ackrill, M. and L. Hannah. 2001. *Barclays: The Business of Banking, 1690–1996*. Cambridge: Cambridge University Press.

Alford, R. F. G. 1972. 'Indicators of direct controls on the United Kingdom capital market, 1951–69', in M. Peston and B. Corry (eds.), *Essays in Honour of Lord Robbins*. London: Weidenfeld & Nicolson, pp. 324–355.

Alford, R. F. G. and H. B. Rose. 1959. 'The Radcliffe Report and domestic monetary policy', *London and Cambridge Economic Bulletin* 109(403):ii–v.

Aliber, R. Z. 1962. 'Counter-speculation and the forward exchange market: a comment', *Journal of Political Economy* 70(6):609–613.

1972. 'The Commission on Money and Credit', *Journal of Money, Credit and Banking* 4(4):915–929.

Allsopp, C. and D. G. Mayes. 1985. 'Demand management in practice', in D. Morris (ed.), *The Economic System in the UK*. Oxford: Oxford University Press, pp. 398–443.

Allsopp, P. W. 1975. 'Prudential regulation of banks in the United Kingdom', Inter Bank Research Organisation, Report No. 274 (November).

Althaus, N. 1969. 'The market view', *The Banker* 119(525):1175–1179.

Anderson, L. C. and J. L. Jordan. 1968. 'Monetary and fiscal actions: a test of the relative importance in economic stabilization', *St. Louis Federal Reserve Bank Review* 50(11):11–24.

Armstrong, W. 1968. *Some Practical Problems in Demand Management: The Stamp Memorial Lecture Delivered Before the University of London on 26 November 1968*. London: Athlone Press.

Arnon, A. and W. L. Young, eds. 2002. *The Open Economy Macromodel: Past, Present and Future*. Boston, MA: Kulwer Academic Press.

Atkin, J. 2004. *The Foreign Exchange Market of London, Development since 1900*. London: Routledge.

Artus, J. R. and R. R. Rhomberg. 1973. 'A multilateral exchange rate model', *International Monetary Fund Staff Papers* 20(3):591–611.

Bacon, R. and W. Eltis. 1976. *Britain's Economic Problem: Too Few Producers*. London: Macmillan.

Bain, A. D. 1965. 'The Treasury bill tender in the UK', *Journal of Economic Studies* 1(1):62–71.

Bagehot, W. 1873. *Lombard Street: A Description of the Money Market*. London.

Bank of England. 1984. *The Development and Operation of Monetary Policy 1960–83: A Selection of Material from Quarterly Bulletin of the Bank of England*. Oxford: Clarendon Press.

Balogh, T. 1956. 'Debate on monetary control: dangers of the new orthodoxy', *The Banker* 106(365):347–353.

Bank for International Settlements. 1963. *Eight European Central Banks: Organisation and Activities; a Descriptive Study*. London: Allen & Unwin.

Batini, N. and E. Nelson. 2005. 'The UK's rocky road to stability', *Federal Reserve Bank of St. Louis Working Paper 2005–020A*, (March); *http://research.stlouisfed.org/wp/2005/2005-020.pdf*.

Bean, C. and N. Crafts. 1996. 'British economic growth since 1945: relative economic decline … and renaissance?' in N. Crafts and G. Toniolo (eds.), *Economic Growth in Europe since 1945*. Cambridge: Cambridge University Press, pp. 131–172.

Beckerman, W. and A. A. Walters. 1966. 'The British economy in 1975', *Journal of the Royal Statistical Society*, Series A (general), 129(2):275–280.

Beenstock, M., F. H. Capie, and B. Griffiths. 1984. 'Economic recovery in the United Kingdom in the 1930s', Panel Paper No. 23 in Bank of England, Panel of Academic Consultants (eds.), *The UK Economic Recovery in the 1930s*. London, April, pp. 57–85.

Bell, G. 1964. 'Credit creation through Euro-dollars?', *The Banker* 114(462):494–502.

1973. *The Eurodollar Market*. London: Macmillan.

Bell, G. and L. S. Berman. 1966. 'Changes in the money supply in the United Kingdom, 1954 to 1964', *Economica* 33(133):148–165.

Bernholz, P. 2007. 'From 1945 to 1982: the transition from inward exchange controls to money supply management under floating exchange rates', in Swiss National Bank (ed.), *The Swiss National Bank 1907–2007*. Zurich, Swiss National Bank, pp.109–199.

Besomi, D. 1998. 'Roy Harrod and the Oxford Economists' Research Group's inquiry on prices and interest rates, 1936–39', *Oxford Economic Papers* 50(4):534–562.

Billings, M. and F. H. Capie. 2004. 'The development of management accounting in UK clearing banks, 1920–70', *Accounting, Business and Financial History* 14(3):317–338.

2007. 'Capital in British banking, 1920 to 1970', *Business History* 49(2):139–162.

2009. 'Transparency and financial reporting in mid-20th century British banking', *Accounting Forum* 33(1):38–53.

Bindseil, U. 2004. *Monetary Policy Implementation: Theory, Past and Present*. Oxford: Oxford University Press.

Blackaby, F. T., ed. 1978. *British Economic Policy 1960–74: Demand Mangement*. Cambridge: Cambridge University Press.

1978. 'Narrative, 1960–74', in Blackaby (1978, pp. 11–76).

Blinder, A. S. and J. B. Rudd. 2008. 'The supply-shock explanation of the great stagflation revisited', NBER Working Paper No. w14563, December.

Bloomfield, A. I. 1959. 'An American impression', *Westminster Bank Review*, November:15–20.

Bond, A. J. N. and M. O. H. Doughty. 1984. *The House: A History of the Bank of England Sports Club 1908–1983*. Roehampton: Bank of England Sports Club.

Bootle, R. 1997. *The Death of Inflation: Surviving and Thriving in the Zero Era*. London: Nicholas Brealey Publishing.

Bordo, M. D. and B. J. Eichengreen, eds. 1993. *A Retrospective on the Bretton Woods System: Lessons for International Monetary Reform*. Chicago: The University of Chicago Press.

Bordo, M. D. 2003. 'Exchange-rate regime choice in historical perspective', NBER IMF Working Paper No. 03/160.

Bordo, M. D. and M. Flandreau. 2003 'Core, periphery, exchange rates regimes, and globalization', in M. D. Bordo , A. M. Taylor, and J. G. Williamson (eds.), *Globalization in Historical Perspective*. Chicago: The University of Chicago Press, pp. 417–468.

Bordo, M. D., O. F. Humpage, and A. J. Schwartz. 2006. 'Bretton Woods and the U.S. decision to intervene in the foreign-exchange market, 1957–1962', Working Paper No. 0609, Federal Reserve Bank of Cleveland.

Bordo, M. D. and F. E. Kydland. 1995. 'The gold standard as a rule: an essay in exploration', *Explorations in Economic History* 32(4):423–464.

Bordo, M. D. and H. Rockoff. 1996. 'The gold standard as a "Good Housekeeping Seal of Approval"', *Journal of Economic History* 56(2):389–428.

Bordo, M. D., R. MacDonald, and M. J. Oliver. In press. 'Sterling in crisis: 1964–1969', *European Review of Economic History*.

Borio, C. and G. Toniolo. 2005. 'Central bank cooperation and the BIS: an insider's perspective', Fourth BIS Annual Conference, June 2005, Basel, Switzerland.

Bowden, S. 2002. 'Ownership responsibilities and corporate governance: the crisis at Rolls-Royce, 1968–71', *Business History* 44(3):31–62.

Boyle, E. 1979. 'The economist in government', in J. K. Bowers (ed.), *Inflation, Development and Integration: Essays in Honour of A. J. Brown*. Leeds: Leeds University Press, pp.1–26.

Brandon, H. 1966. *In the Red: The Struggle for Sterling, 1964–66*. London: Andre Deutsch.

Bretherton, R. 1999. *The Control of Demand, 1958–1964*. London: Institute for Contemporary Business History.

Britton, A. J. C. 1986. *The Trade Cycle in Britain, 1958–1982*. Cambridge: Cambridge University Press.

2001. *Monetary Regimes of the Twentieth Century*. Cambridge: Cambridge University Press.

Brittan, S. 1964. *The Treasury under the Tories, 1951–1964*. Harmondsworth: Penguin. A later version appears as Brittan, S. 1969. *Steering the Economy: The Role of the Treasury*. London: Secker & Warburg.

1970. *The Price of Economic Freedom; A Guide to Flexible Exchange Rates*. London: Macmillan.

Broadberry, S. and N. Crafts. 2003. 'UK productivity performance from 1950 to 1979: a restatement of the Broadberry-Crafts view', *Economic History Review* 56(4):718–735.

Brown, A. J. 1955. *The Great Inflation, 1939–1951*. London: Oxford University Press.

1985. *World Inflation since 1950: An International Comparative Study*. Cambridge: Cambridge University Press.

Browning, P. 1986. *The Treasury and Economic Policy, 1964–85.* London: Longman.

Brunner, K. 1968. 'The role of money and monetary policy', *Federal Reserve Bank of St. Louis Review* 50(7):9–24.

Brunner, K., ed. 1981. *The Great Depression Revisited.* Boston: Martinus Nijhoff.

Brunner, K. and R. L. Crouch. 1967. 'Money supply theory and British monetary experience', *Methods of Operations Research* 3(1):77–112.

Burk, K. and A. Cairncross. 1992. *Goodbye, Great Britain: The 1976 IMF Crisis.* New Haven, CT: Yale University Press.

Burnham, P. 2003. *Remaking the Postwar World Economy: Robot and British Policy in the 1950s.* New York: Palgrave Macmillan.

Butler, R. A. 1971. *The Art of the Possible: The Memoirs of Lord Butler, KG, CH.* London: Hamilton.

Buyst, E., I. Maes, W. Pluym, and M. Daneel. 2005. *The Bank, the Franc and the Euro: A History of the National Bank of Belgium.* Brussels: Lanoo Publishers.

Byatt, D. 1994. *Promised to Pay: The First Three Hundred Years of Bank of England Notes.* London: Spink & Son.

Cagan, P. 1956. 'The monetary dynamics of hyperinflation', in Milton Friedman (ed.), *Studies in the Quantity Theory of Money.* Chicago: The University of Chicago Press.

1965. *Determinants and Effects of Changes in the Stock of Money, 1875–1960.* Columbia, NC: National Bureau of Economic Research.

Cairncross, A. 1973. *Control of Long-Term Capital Movements: A Staff Paper.* Washington: Brookings Institution.

1985a. 'One hundred issues of the *Quarterly Bulletin*', *BEQB* 23(3):381–387.

1985b. *Years of Recovery, British Economic Policy, 1945–51.* London: Methuen.

1987. 'Prelude to Radcliffe: monetary policy in the United Kingdom, 1948–57', *Rivista de Storia Economica* 4(2):2–20.

1991a. 'Richard Sidney Sayers, 1908–1989', *Proceedings of the British Academy* 76:545–561.

ed. 1991b. *The Robert Hall Diaries, 1954–61.* London: Unwin Hyman.

1995. 'The Bank of England and the British economy', in Roberts and Kynaston (1995, pp. 56–82).

1996. *Managing the British Economy in the 1960s: A Treasury Perspective.* Oxford: Macmillan, in association with St Anthony's College, Oxford.

1997. *The Wilson Years: A Treasury Diary, 1964–69.* London: Historian's Press.

1999. *Diaries of Sir Alec Cairncross: The Radcliffe Committee, Economic Adviser to HMG, 1961–64.* London: Institute of Contemporary British History.

Cairncross, A. and B. Eichengreen. 1983. *Sterling in Decline: The Devaluations of 1931, 1949 and 1967.* Oxford: Blackwell.

Callaghan, J. 1987. *Time and Chance.* London: Collins.

Capie, F. H. 1983. *Depression and Protectionism: Britain Between the Wars.* London: Allen & Unwin.

1986. 'Conditions in which very rapid inflation appears', Carnegie Rochester Conference Series on Public Policy, No. 24, pp. 115–168.

1990. 'The evolving regulatory framework in British banking in the twentieth century', in M. Chick (ed.), *Governments, Industries and Markets: Aspects of Government-Industry Relations in the UK, Japan, West Germany and the USA since 1945.* Aldershot: Elgar.

ed. 1991. *Major Inflations in History.* Aldershot: Elgar.

2002. 'The emergence of the Bank of England as a mature central bank', in D. Winch and P. O 'Brien (eds.), *The Political Economy of British Historical Experience, 1688–1914.* London: Oxford University Press for British Academy.

Capie, F. H. and M. Billings. 2001a. 'Accounting issues and the measurement of profits – English banks – 1920–68', *Accounting, Business & Financial History* 11(2):225–251.

2001b. 'Profitability in English banking in the twentieth century', *European Review of Economic History* 5(3):367–401.

Capie, F. H. and M. Collins. 1983. *The inter-war British economy: a statistical abstract.* Manchester: Manchester University Press.

Capie, F. H. and G. Rodrik-Bali. 1986. 'The behaviour of the money multiplier and its components since 1870', *City University Business School Economic Review* (UK) 4(1).

Capie, F. H. and A. Webber. 1985. *A Monetary History of the United Kingdom, 1870–1982,* Vol. 1. London: Allen & Unwin.

Capie, F. H. and G. E. Wood. 2001. *Policy Makers on Policy; The Mais Lectures.* London: Routledge.

2002a. 'Price controls in war and peace: a Marshallian conclusion', *Scottish Journal of Political Economy* 49(1):39–60.

2002b. 'The international financial architecture in the second half of the twentieth century', in M. J. Oliver (ed.), *Studies in Economic and Social History: Essays in Honour of Derek H. Aldcroft.* Aldershot: Ashgate.

Capie, F. H., C. A. E. Goodhart, and N. Schnadt. 1995. 'The development of central banking', in F. H. Capie , C. A. E. Goodhart , S. Fischer, and N. Schnadt (eds.), *The Future of Central Banking: The Tercentenary Symposium of the Bank of England.* Cambridge: Cambridge University Press.

Capie, F. H., T. C . Mills, and G. E. Wood. 1986. 'Debt management and interest rates: the British stock conversion of 1932', *Applied Economics* 18(10):1111–1126.

Cassell, G. 1922. *Money and Foreign Exchange after 1914.* London: Constable.

Cassis, Y. 2005. *Capitals of Capital: A History of International Financial Centres, 1780–2005.* Geneva: Pictet & Cie.

Castle, B. 1984. *The Castle Diaries 1964–70.* London: Weidenfeld & Nicolson.

Chadha, J. S. and N. H. Dimsdale. 1999. 'A long view of real interest rates', *Oxford Review of Economic Policy* 15(2):17–45.

Chalmers, E., ed. 1967. *The Gilt-Edged Market: A Study of the Background Factors.* London: W.P. Griffith & Sons.

1968. *Monetary Policy in the Sixties: UK, USA and W. Germany.* London: W.P. Griffith and Sons.

Channon, D. F. 1977. *British Banking Strategy and the International Challenge.* London: Macmillan.

Chester, N. 1975. *The Nationalisation of British Industry, 1945–51.* London: HMSO.

Chrystal, A. and P. Mizen. 2003. 'Goodhart's law: origins, meaning, and implications for monetary policy', in Mizen (2003, pp. 221–244).

Clapham, J. 1944. *The Bank of England: A History,* Vol. 2: *1797–1914: With an Epilogue, the Bank as It Is.* Cambridge: Cambridge University Press.

Clarke, S. V. O. 1977. *Exchange Rate Stabilization in the Mid-1930s: Negotiating the Tripartite Agreement.* Princeton, NJ: Princeton Studies in International Finance.

Clayton, G., J. C. Gilbert, and R. Sedgwick, eds. 1971. *Monetary Theory and Monetary Policy in the 1970's: Proceedings of the Sheffield Money Seminar.* London: Oxford University Press.

Clendenning, E. W. 1970. *The Euro-Dollar Market.* Oxford: Clarendon Press.

Cobham, D. 1992. 'The Radcliffe Committee', in Newman, Milgate, and Eatwell (1992, vol. 3, pp. 265–266).

Congdon, T. 2005. *Money and Asset Prices in Boom and Bust.* London: Institute of Economic Affairs.

Coombs, C. C. 1969. 'Treasury and Federal Reserve foreign exchange operations', *Federal Reserve Monthly Review* 51(3):43–56.

Coombs, C. A . 1976. *The Arena of International Finance.* London: Wiley.

Cooper, R. N. 1968. 'The balance of payments', in R. E Caves (ed.), *Britain's Economic Prospects.* Washington: Brookings Institution.

     2008. 'Almost a century of central bank cooperation', in C. Borio, G. Toniolo, and P. Clement (eds.), *The Past and Future of Central Bank Cooperation.* Oxford: Oxford University Press, pp. 76–101.

Coopey, R. and D. Clarke. 1995. *3i: Fifty Years of Investing in Industry.* Oxford: Oxford University Press.

Cork, K. 1988. *Cork on Cork, Sir Kenneth Cork Takes Stock.* London: Macmillan.

Courtney, C. and P. Thompson, eds. 1996. *City Lives: The Changing Voice of British Finance.* London: Methuen.

Cownie, J. R. 1989. 'Success through perseverance: the Rolls-Royce RB.211 engine', *Putnam Aeronautical Review* 4:230–239.

Crafts, N. F. R. 1993. *Can De-industrialisation Seriously Damage Your Wealth? A Review of Why Growth Rates Differ and How to Improve Economic Performance.* London: Institute of Economics Affairs.

Crafts, N. F. R. and C. K. Harley. 1992. 'Output growth and the British industrial revolution: a restatement of the Crafts-Harley view', *Economic History Review* 45(4):703–730.

Crafts, N. F. R. and G. Toniolo, eds. 1996. *Economic Growth in Europe since 1945.* Cambridge: Cambridge University Press.

Cramp, A. B . 1966. 'Control of the money supply', *Economic Journal* 76(302):278–287.

     1968. 'Financial theory and control of bank deposits', *Oxford Economic Papers*, New Series, 20(1):98–108.

Crockett, A. D. 1970. 'Timing relationships between movements of monetary and national income variables', *BEQB* 10(4):459–472.

Croham, Lord. 1992. 'Were the instruments of control for domestic economic policy adequate?' in F. Cairncross and A. Cairncross (eds.), *The Legacy of the Golden Age: The 1960s and Their Economic Consequences.* London: Routledge, pp. 81–109.

Croome, D. R. and H. G. Johnson, eds. 1970. *Money in Britain 1959–69.* Oxford: Oxford University Press.

Crouch, R. L. 1963. 'A re-examination of open-market operations', *Oxford Economic Papers*, New Series, 15(2):81–94.

     1964. 'The inadequacy of "new orthodox" methods of monetary control', *Economic Journal* 74(296):916–934.

     1965.'The genesis of bank deposits: new English version', *Bulletin of Oxford University Institute of Economics & Statistics* 27(3):185–199.

Dacey, W. M. 1951, 1958. *The British Banking Mechanism*. London: Hutchison.

Dalton, H. 1962. *High Tide and After: Memoirs 1945–1960*. London: Muller.

Davenport-Hines, R., ed. 2006. *Letters from Oxford: Hugh Trevor-Roper to Bernard Berenson: Letters from Hugh Trevor-Roper to Bernard Berenson*. London: Weidenfeld & Nicolson.

Davis, R. G. 1969. 'How much does money matter? A look at some recent evidence', *Federal Reserve Bank of New York Monthly Review* 51(6):119–131.

Day, A. C. L. 1956. *The Future of Sterling*. Oxford: Clarendon Press.

DeLong, J. B. 1997. 'America's peacetime inflation: the 1970s', in C. Romer and D. Romer (eds.), *Reducing Inflation: Motivation and Strategy*. Chicago: The University of Chicago Press.

Dell, E. 1991. *A Hard Pounding: Politics and Economic Crisis, 1974–76*. Oxford: Oxford University Press.

Dell, S. 1981. 'On being grandmotherly: the evolution of IMF conditionality', *Princeton Essay in International Finance* 144:1–34.

De Moubray, G. 2005. *City of Human Memories*. Stanhope: The Memoir Club.

Dennett, L. 1998. *A Sense of Security: 150 Years of Prudential*. Cambridge: Granta Editions.

Department of Trade. 1976. *London and County Securities Group Limited Investigation under Sections 165(b) and 172 of the Companies Act 1948*. London: HMSO.

Devons, E. 1959. 'An economist's view of the Bank Rate Tribunal evidence', *Manchester School of Economic and Social Studies* 27(1):1–16.

De Vries, M. G. 1985. *The International Monetary Fund 1972–1978: Cooperation on Trial.*, Washington: International Monetary Fund.

1986. *IMF in a Changing World, 1945–85*. Washington: International Monetary Fund.

Donoughue, B. 1987. *Prime Minister: The Conduct of Policy under Harold Wilson and James Callaghan*. London: Cape.

Dorey, P. 2001. *Wage Politics in Britain: The Rise and Fall of Incomes Policies since 1945*. Brighton: Sussex Academic Press.

Dow, J. C. R. 1964. *The Management of the British Economy, 1945–60*. Cambridge: Cambridge University Press.

Downton, C. V. 1977. 'The trend of the national debt in relation to national income', *BEQB* 17(3):319–324.

Duck, N. W. and D. K. Sheppard. 1978. 'A proposal for the control of the UK money supply', *Economic Journal* 88(349):1–17.

Duggleby, V. 1994. *English Paper Money: 300 Years of Treasury and Bank of England Notes Design 1694–1994*, 5th ed. London: Spink & Son.

Dyer, L. S. 1983. 'The secondary banking crisis', *Journal of the Institute of Bankers* 104:46–48.

Economic, Financial and Transit Department (League of Nations), mainly by R. Nurkse. 1944. *International Currency Experience: Lessons of the Inter-war Period*. Princeton, NJ: Economic, Financial and Transit Department, League of Nations.

Eichengreen, B. J. 1992. *Golden Fetters: The Gold Standard and the Great Depression, 1919–1939*. New York: Oxford University Press.

2004. 'The dollar and the new Bretton Woods system', Henry Thornton Lecture, Cass Business School.

(2007), *Global imbalances and the lessons of Bretton woods*, Cambridge, Mass.: MIT Press.

Eichengreen, B. J. and J. Sachs. 1985. 'Exchange rates and economic recovery in the 1930s', *Journal of Economic History* 45(4):925–946.

Eichengreen, B. J. 1995. 'Central bank cooperation and exchange rate commitments: the classical and interwar gold standards compared', *Financial History Review* 2(2):99–117.

Einzig, P. 1964. *The Euro-dollar System: Practice and Theory of International Interest Rates*. London: Macmillan.

    1967. 'Forward exchange intervention', *Westminster Bank Review*, February:2–13.

Fausten, D. K. 1975. *The Consistency of British Balance of Payments Policies*. London: Macmillan.

Fay, S., and Lord O' Brien of Lothbury and Lord Richardson of Duntisbourne. 1987. *Portrait of an Old Lady: Turmoil at the Bank of England*. London: Viking.

Feldstein, C. H. 1993. 'Lessons of the Bretton Woods experience', in Bordo and Eichengreen (1993), pp. 613–18.

Fels, A. 1972. *The British Prices and Incomes Board*. London: Cambridge University Press.

Fforde, J. S. 1954. *The Federal Reserve System, 1945–49*. Oxford: Clarendon Press.

    1983. 'Setting monetary objectives', *BEQB* 23(2):200–208.

    1992. *The Bank of England and Public Policy, 1941–1958*. Cambridge: Cambridge University Press.

Fisher, I. 1896. *Appreciation and Interest: A Study of the Influence of Monetary Appreciation and Depreciation on the Rate of Interest*. New York: Macmillan.

    1911. *The Purchasing Power of Money: Its Determination and Relation to Credit Interest and Crises*. New York: Macmillan.

Flandreau, M. 1997. 'Central bank cooperation in historical perspective: a sceptical view', *Economic History Review* 50(4):735–763.

Fletcher, G. A. 1976. *The Discount Houses in London*. London: Macmillan.

Fogel, R. W. 2005. *Reconsidering Expectations of Economic Growth after World War II from the Perspective of 2004*. Cambridge, MA: National Bureau of Economic Research.

Foot, M. D. K. W. 1981. 'Monetary targets: their nature and record in the major economies', in B. Griffiths and G. E. Wood (eds.), *Monetary Targets*. London: Macmillan.

Friedman, M. 1956. *Studies in the Quantity Theory of Money*. Chicago: The University of Chicago Press.

    1960. *A Program for Monetary Stability*. New York: Fordham University Press.

    1968a. *Dollars and Deficits: Inflation, Monetary Policy and the Balance of Payments*. Englewood Cliffs, NJ: Prentice-Hall.

    1968b. 'The case for flexible exchange rates', reprinted in Milton Friedman, *Essays in Positive Economics*. Chicago: The University of Chicago Press.

    1968c. 'The role of monetary policy', *American Economic Review* 58(1):1–17.

    1970. 'The Eurodollar market: some first principles', in Herbert V. Prochnow (ed.), *The Eurodollar*. Chicago: Rand, McNally and Co.

Friedman, M. and A. J. Schwartz. 1963. *A Monetary History of the United States, 1867–1960*. Princeton, NJ: Princeton University Press.

Fry, R., ed. 1970. *A Banker's World: The Revival of the City 1957–1970; the Speeches and Writings of Sir George Bolton*. London: Hutchinson.

Gardener, E. P. M., ed. 1986a. *UK Banking Supervision: Evolution, Practice and Issues.* London: Allen & Unwin.

1986b. 'Supervision in the United Kingdom', in Gardener (1986, pp. 70–85).

Garvin, S. 1970. 'Should the Bank be subject to scrutiny?', *The Banker* 120(537):1186–1188.

Gavin, F. J. 2004. *Gold, Dollars, and Power: The Politics of International Monetary Relations, 1958–1971.* Chapel Hill: University of North Carolina Press.

Gilbert, M. 1968. 'The gold-dollar system: conditions of equilibrium and the price of gold', in *Princeton Essays in International Economics.* Princeton, NJ: Princeton University Press.

Goodhart, C. A. E 1973. 'Monetary policy in the United Kingdom', in Holbik (1973, pp. 465–524).

1989. *Money, Information and Uncertainty.* London: Macmillan Palgrave.

1999. 'Monetary policy – demand management', in K. A. Chrystal (ed.), *Government Debt Structure and Monetary Conditions: A Conference Organised by the Bank of England, 18–19 June 1998.* London: Bank of England, pp. 25–36.

2003. 'A central bank economist', in Mizen (2003, pp. 13–62).

2004. On Sayers, in D.Rutherford (ed.), *The Biographical Dictionary of British Economists,* Vol. 2. Bristol: Thoemmes Continuum.

2007. *John Flemming 1941–2003: A Biography.* Wilton: Windsor.

Goodhart, C. A. E. and A. D. Crockett. 1970. 'The importance of money', *BEQB* 10(2):159–198.

Goodhart, C. A. E. and D. Schoenmaker. 1995. 'Should the functions of monetary policy and banking supervision be separated?', *Oxford Economic Papers* 47(4):539–560.

Gordon, C. 1993. *The Cedar Story: The Night the City Was Saved.* London: Sinclair-Stevenson.

Gordon, R. 1977. 'Can the inflation of the 1970s be explained?', *Brookings Papers on Economic Activity* 8:253–277.

Gowland, D. 1982. *Controlling the Money Supply.* London: Croom Helm.

Grady, J. and M. Weale. 1986. *British Banking 1960–1985.* London: Macmillan.

Green, E. 1979. *The Making of a Modern Banking Group: A History of the Midland Bank since 1900.* London: St George Press.

Griffiths, B. 1970. *Competition in Banking,* Hobart Papers No. 51. London: Institute of Economic Affairs.

1971. 'The determination of the Treasury bill tender rate', in *Economica,* New Series, 38(150):180–191.

1976. 'How the Bank has mismanaged monetary policy', *The Banker* 126(610):1411–1419.

1977. 'The Bank under scrutiny', *The Banker* 127(612):111–117.

Griffiths, B. and G. E. Wood, eds. 1981. *Monetary Targets.* London: Macmillan.

Hague, D. and G. Wilkinson. 1983. *The IRC: An Experiment in Industrial Intervention. A History of the Industrial Reorganisation Corporation.* London: Allen & Unwin.

Hall, M. J. B. 1999. *Handbook of Banking Regulation and Supervision in the United Kingdom.* Cheltenham: Edward Elgar.

Hall, N. F. 1935. *The Exchange Equalization Account.* London: Macmillan.

Hanham, H. J. 1959. 'A political scientist's view', *Manchester School of Economic and Social Studies* 27(1):17–29.

Hansen, A. H. 1938. *Full Recovery or Stagnation?* London: A & C Black.

Hargrave, J. 1937. *Professor Skinner Alias Montagu Norman.* London: Wells Gardner, Darton and Co.

Harman, M. D. 1997. *The British Labour Government and the 1976 IMF Crisis.* London: Macmillan.

Harrod, R. 1959. 'Is the money supply important?', *Westminster Bank Review*, November:3–7.

   1965. *Reforming the World's Money.* New York: St. Martin's Press.

   1969. *Money.* New York: St. Martin's Press.

Hawtrey, R. 1959. 'The Radcliffe Report on the working of the monetary system: a preliminary survey', *The Bankers' Magazine* 109(404):172.

Hayek, F. A. 2005. *The Road to Serfdom.* London: Institute of Economic Affairs.

Healey, D. 1989. *The Time of My Life.* London: Michael Joseph.

Henderson, D. 1986. *Innocence and Design: The Influence of Economic Ideas on Policy.* Oxford: Blackwell.

Hennessy, E. 1992. *A Domestic History of the Bank Of England, 1930–60.* Cambridge: Cambridge University Press.

Hetzel, R. L. 2008. *The Monetary Policy of the Federal Reserve.* New York: Cambridge University Press.

Heward, E. 1994. *The Great and the Good – A Life of Lord Radcliffe.* Chichester: Barry Rose.

Hewitt, V. H. and J. M. Keyworth. 1987. *As Good as Gold: 300 Years of British Note Design.* London: British Museum Publications in association with the Bank of England.

Hickson, K. 2005. *The IMF Crisis of 1976 and British Politics.* London: Tauris.

Hirsch, F. 1965. *The Pound Sterling.* London: Victor Gollancz.

Hodgman, D. R. 1971. 'British techniques of monetary policy: a critical review', *Journal of Money Credit and Banking* 3(4):760–779.

Holbik, K., ed. 1973. *Monetary Policy in Twelve Industrial Countries.* Boston: Federal Reserve Bank of Boston.

Holmes, A. R. and F. H. Klopstock. 1960. 'The market for dollar deposits in Europe', *Federal Reserve Bank of New York Monthly Review* 42(11):197–202.

Holtfrerich, C. L. 1999. 'Monetary policy under fixed exchange rates, 1948–1970', in Deutsche Bundesbank (ed.), *Fifty Years of the Deutsche Mark: Central Bank and the Currency in Germany since 1948.* Oxford: Oxford University Press.

Holtrop, M. W. 1957. 'Method of monetary analysis used by De Nederlandsche Bank', *IMF Staff Papers* 5(3):303–316.

Homes, A. R. and E. Green. 1986. *Midland: 150 Years of Banking Business.* London: B. T. Batsford.

Horsefield, J. K., ed. 1969. *The International Monetary Fund, 1945–1965: Twenty Years of International Monetary Cooperation.* Washington: International Monetary Fund.

Horne, A. 1989. *Macmillan,* Vol 2: *1957–1986.* London: Macmillan.

Howson, S. 1975., *Domestic Monetary Management in Britain, 1919–38.* Cambridge: Cambridge University Press.

   1993. *British Monetary Policy 1945–51.* Oxford: Clarendon Press.

Jacobsson, P. 1964. *International Monetary Problems, 1957–63*. Washington: International Monetary Fund.

James, H. 1996. *International Monetary Co-operation since Bretton Woods*. New York: Oxford University Press.

2002. *End of Globalization: Lessons from the Great Depression*. Cambridge, MA.: Harvard University Press.

Jay, D. 1980. *Change and Fortune: A Political Record*. London: Hutchinson.

Jenkins, R. 1991. *A Life at the Centre*. London: Macmillan.

Johnson, H. G. 1956. 'The revival of monetary policy in Britain', *Three Banks Review* 8(30):1–20.

1969. 'The case for flexible exchange rates, 1969', in *UK and Floating Exchanges*, Hobart Papers No. 46. London: Institute of Economic Affairs.

1970. 'Monetary theory and monetary policy', *Euromoney* 2:16–20.

1971. 'Harking back to Radcliffe', *The Bankers' Magazine* 203(1530):115–120.

1972. *Further Essays in Monetary Economics*. London: Allen & Unwin.

Johnson, H. G. and A. R. Nobay, eds. 1971. *The Current Inflation: Proceedings of a Conference Held at the London School of Economics on 22 February 1971*. London, Macmillan.

Jones, A. 1973. *The New Inflation: The Politics of Prices and Incomes*. London: Deutsch.

Jones, G. 2004. 'Bolton, Sir George Lewis French (1900–1982)', *Oxford Dictionary of National Biography*. Oxford: Oxford University Press; online edition, May 2008; *www.oxforddnb.com/view/article/46639*; accessed 8 January 2009.

Kaldor, N. 1976. 'Inflation and recession in the world economy', *Economic Journal* 86(344):703–714.

1982. *The Scourge of Monetarism*. Oxford: Oxford University Press.

Kandiah, M., ed. 2002. *Debates about the Rise and Fall of the Bretton Woods Agreement*. Witness Seminar, 30 September 1994. London: CCBH.

Kandiah, M., ed. 2008. *Exchange Rate Mechanism: Black Wednesday and the Rebirth of the British Economy*, Witness Seminar, 14 November 2007. London: CCBH.

Keegan, W., and R. Pennant-Rae. 1979. *Who Runs the Economy*. London: Maurice Temple Smith.

King, C. 1972. *The Cecil King Diary, 1965–1970*. London: Jonathan Cape.

1975. *The Cecil King Diary, 1970–1974*. London: Jonathan Cape.

King, M. A. 1994. 'Monetary policy instruments: the UK experience', *BEQB* 34(3):268–276.

King, W. T . C. 1936. *History of the London Discount Market*. London: George Routledge and Sons.

1958. 'The new monetary weapon', *The Banker* 108(391):493–506.

Kinsey, S. and E. Green. 2004. *The Good Companions: Wives and Families in the History of the HSBC Group*. Cambridge: Cambridge University Press.

Kirby, M. W. 1981. *The Decline of British Economic Power since 1870*. London: Allen & Unwin.

Klopstock, F. H. 1968. 'The Euro-dollar market: some unresolved issues', *Princeton Essays in International Finance* 65:1–28.

Klug, A. and G. W. Smith. 1999. 'Suez and sterling, 1956', *Explorations in Economic History* 36(3):181–203.

Kynaston, D. 2001. *The City of London*, Vol. 4: *A Club No More, 1945–2000*. London: Chatto & Windus.

Laidler, D. E. W. 1975. *Essays on Money and Inflation*. Manchester: Manchester University Press.

Laidler, D. 2000. 'Phillips in retrospect', in R. Leeson (ed.), *AWH Phillips: Collected Works in Contemporary Perspective*. Cambridge: Cambridge University Press.

Laidler, D. E. W. and J. M. Parkin. 1975. 'Inflation – a survey', *Economic Journal* 85(340):741–809.

Lawson, N. 1992. *The View from No.11. Memoirs of a Tory Radical*. London: Bantam Press.

Lazonick, W. and A. Prencipe. 2003. 'Sustaining the innovation process: the case of Rolls-Royce plc', paper given on 2 December at University of Urbino, Faculty of Economics, International Workshop: Empirical Studies on innovation in Europe; *www.econ.uniurb.it/siepi/dec03/papers/lazonick.pdf*.

McCallum, B. 1995. 'Two fallacies concerning central bank independence', *American Economic Review* 85(2):207–211.

    1997. 'Crucial issues concerning central bank independence', *Journal of Monetary Economics* 39(1):99–112.

MacDougall, D. 1987. *Don and Mandarin: Memoirs of an Economist*. London: Murray.

McKenna, C. D. 2006. *The World's Newest Profession: Management Consulting in the Twentieth Century*. New York: Cambridge University Press.

McKinnon, R. I. 1993. 'Bretton Woods, the Marshall Plan, and the postwar dollar standard', in Bordo and Eichengreen (1993, pp. 597–600).

McMahon, C. W. 1964. *Sterling in the Sixties*. London, Oxford University Press.

    1969. 'Monetary policies in the United States and the United Kingdom [comment]', *Journal of Money Credit and Banking* 1(38):549–552.

Macmillan, H. 1972. *Pointing the Way, 1959–1961*. London: Macmillan.

Maddison, A. 2006. *The World Economy: Historical Statistics*. Paris: OECD.

Manser, W. A. P. 1971. *Britain in Balance: The Myth of Failure*. Harlow: Longman.

Matthews, R. C. O., C. H. Feinstein, and J. C. Odling-Smee. 1982. *British Economic Growth, 1856–1973*. Stanford, CA: Stanford University Press.

Mayer, T. 1999. *Monetary Policy and the Great Inflation in the United States: The Federal Reserve and the Failure of Macroeconomic Policy 1965–79*. Cheltenham: Edward Elgar.

Meade, J. E. 1951. *The Theory of International Economic Policy*, Vol. 1: *The Balance of Payments*. London: Macmillan.

    1955. 'The case for variable exchange rates', *Three Banks Review* 27:3–27.

Megrah, M., ed. 1968. *Legal Decisions Affecting Bankers*, Vol. 8: *1962–1966*. London: Institute of Bankers, pp. 490–524.

Meltzer, A. H. 1998. *Keynes's Monetary Theory: A Different Interpretation*. Cambridge: Cambridge University Press.

    2002. *A History of the Federal Reserve*, Vol. 1: *1913–1951*. Chicago: The University of Chicago Press.

    2005. 'Origins of the Great Inflation', *Federal Reserve Bank of St. Louis Review* 87(2):145–176.

    2009. *A History of the Federal Reserve*, Vol. 2: Book One 1951–1969, Book Two 1970–1986. Chicago: University of Chicago Press.

Michie, R. 1999. *The London Stock Exchange: A History*. Oxford: Oxford University Press.

Middlemas, K. 1990. *Power, Competition and the State*, Vol. 2: *Threats to the Post-war Settlement, Britain: 1961–74*. Basingstoke: Macmillan.

  1994. 'O'Brien, Leslie Kenneth, Baron O'Brien of Lothbury (1908–1995)', *Oxford Dictionary of National Biography*. London: Oxford University Press; online edition May 2006; *www.oxforddnb.com/view/article/60373*; accessed 18 February 2009.

Middleton, P. 1989. 'Economic policy formulation in the Treasury in the post-war period', *National Institute Economic Review*, February:46–51.

Middleton, P. E, C. J. Mowl, J. C. Odling-Smee, and C. J. Riley. 1981. 'Monetary targets and the public sector borrowing requirement', in B. Griffiths and G. E. Wood (eds.), *Monetary Targets*. London: Macmillan, pp. 135–176.

Middleton, R. 1996. *Government versus the Market: The Growth of the Public Sector, Economic Management and the British Economic Performance, c.1890–1979*. Cheltenham: Elgar.

  2002. 'Struggling with the impossible: sterling, the balance of payments and British economic policy, 1949–72', in Arnon and Young (2002, pp. 103–154).

Miller, R. and J. B. Wood. 1979. *Exchange Control Forever?* London: Institute for Economic Affairs.

Mishkin, F. S. 2004. *Can Central Bank Transparency Go Too Far?* Cambridge, MA: National Bureau of Economic Research (NBER).

Mitchell, B. R . 1988. *British Historical Statistics*. Cambridge: Cambridge University Press.

Mizen, P., ed. 2003. *Central Banking, Monetary Theory and Practice: Essays in Honour of Charles Goodhart*, Vol. 1. Cheltenham: Edward Elgar.

Moore, N. E. A. 1973. *The Decimalisation of Britain's Currency*. London: HMSO.

Moran, M. 1986. *The Politics of Banking: The Strange Case of Competition and Credit Control*, 2nd ed. Basingstoke: Macmillan.

Morgan, E. V . 1964. *Monetary Policy for Stable Growth*. London: Institute of Economic Affairs.

  1966. 'Is inflation inevitable?', *Economic Journal* 76(301):1–15.

Morgan, K. O. 1997. *Callaghan: A Life*. Oxford: Oxford University Press.

Mottershead, P. 1978. 'Industrial policy', in Blackaby (1978, pp. 418–483).

Mundell, R. A 2000. 'A reconsideration of the twentieth century', *American Economic Review* 90(3):327–341.

Murphy, B. 1979. *A History of the British Economy, 1740–1970*. London: Longman.

Nelson, E. 2004. 'The great inflation of the seventies: What really happened?', Federal Reserve Bank of St. Louis WP2004–001.

Nevin, E. 1955. *The Mechanism of Cheap Money: A Story of British Monetary Policy, 1931–1939*. Cardiff: University of Wales Press.

Newlyn, W. T. 1964. 'The supply of money and its control', *Economic Journal* 74(294):327–346.

  1965. 'Mr. Crouch on "new orthodox" methods of monetary control – comment (1)', *Economic Journal* 75(300):857–859.

Newman P., M. Milgate, and J. Eatwell, eds. 1992. *New Palgrave Dictionary of Money and Finance*. London: Macmillan.

Nurkse, R. 1944. *International Currency Experience: Lessons of the Inter-war Period.* Princeton, NJ: Economic, Financial and Transit Department, League of Nations.

O'Brien, D. P. 1992. 'Competition and credit control', in Newman, Milgate, and Eatwell (1992, Vol. 1, pp. 412–413).

Oliver, M. J. and A. Hamilton. 2007. 'Downhill from devaluation: the battle for sterling, 1968–72', *Economic History Review* 60(3):486–512.

Oppenheimer, P. 1966. 'Forward market intervention: the official view', *Westminster Bank Review*, February:2–14.

Orbell, J. 2004a. 'Baring, (George) Rowland Stanley, Third Earl of Cromer (1918–1991)', *Oxford Dictionary of National Biography.* London: Oxford University Press, online edition January 2008; *www.oxforddnb.com/view/article/49616*; accessed 14 January 2009.

    2004b. 'Kindersley, Hugh Kenyon Molesworth, Second Baron Kindersley (1899–1976)', *Oxford Dictionary of National Biography.* London: Oxford University Press; *www.oxforddnb.com/view/article/31312*; accessed 8 January 2009.

Paish, F. W. 1959. 'What is this liquidity?', *The Banker* 109(4):590–597.

    1962. 'Monetary policy and the control of the post-war British inflation', in F. W. Paish (ed.), *Studies in an Inflationary Economy: The United Kingdom 1948–1961.* London: Macmillan.

Parkin, M. and M. T. Summer,   eds. 1972. *Incomes Policy and Inflation.* Manchester: Manchester University Press.

Pepper, G. 1991. 'Official order – real chaos', *Economic Affairs* 11(2):48–51.

Phelps, E. 1967. 'Phillips curves, expectations of inflation and optimal unemployment over time', *Economica* 34(135):254–281.

Phillips, A. W. 1958. 'The relationship between unemployment and the rate of change of money wage rates in the United Kingdom, 1861–1957', *Economica* 25(100):283–299.

Phillips, C. A. 1926. *Bank Credit: A Study of the Principles and Factors Underlying Advances Made by Banks to Borrowers.* New York: Macmillan.

Pimlott, B. 1992. *Harold Wilson.* London: HarperCollins.

Pimlott Baker, A. 2004. 'Cork, Sir Kenneth Russell (1913–1991)', *Oxford Dictionary of National Biography.* London: Oxford University Press; online edition January 2009; *www.oxforddnb.com/view/article/49613*; accessed 21 January 2009.

Pliatzky, L. 1982. *Getting and Spending: Public Expenditure, Employment and Inflation.* Oxford: Blackwell.

Polak, J. J. 1957. 'Monetary analysis of income formation and payments problems', *International Monetary Fund Staff Papers* 6; reprinted in IMF. *The Monetary Approach to the Balance of Payments.* Washington: IMF, 1977.

    2006. 'Two British initiatives for IMF lending to its members, 1960–62', *World Economics* 7(1):11–19.

Pollard, S., ed. 1970. *The Gold Standard and Employment Policies Between the Wars.* London: Methuen.

    1982. *The Wasting of the British Economy: British Economic Policy 1945 to the Present.* London: Croom Helm.

Poole, W. 1970. 'Optimal choice of monetary policy instruments in a simple stochastic exploration model', *Quarterly Journal of Economics* 84(2):197–216.

Pressnell, L. S. 1956. *Country Banking in the Industrial Revolution.* Oxford: Clarendon Press.

1970. 'Cartels and competition in British banking: a background study', *Banca Nazionale del Lavoro Quarterly Review* 95:373–406.

1978. '1925: the burden of sterling', *Economic History Review* 31(1):67–88.

1986. *External Economic Policy since the War,* Vol. 1: *The Post-war Financial Settlement.* London: HMSO.

1997. 'What went wrong? The evolution of the IMF 1941–1961', *Banca Nazionale del Lavoro Quarterly Review* 201:213–239.

Price, L. 2003. 'Reporting reserves – a market view', in N. Courtis and B. Mander (eds.), *Accounting Standards for Central Banks.* London: Central Banking Publications.

Price, R. W. R. 1978. *'Budgetary policy',* in Blackaby (1978, pp. 135–217).

Pringle, R. 1977. *The Growth Merchants: Economic Consequences of Wishful Thinking.* London: Centre for Policy Studies.

Proctor, S. J. 1993. 'Floating convertibility: the emergence of the Robot Plan, 1951–2', *Contemporary Record* 7(1):22–43.

Pugh, P. 2001. *The Magic of a Name: The Rolls-Royce Story Part Two: The Power Behind the Jets, 1945–1987.* Cambridge: Icon Books.

Raw, C. 1977. *Slater Walker: An Investigation of a Financial Phenomenon.* London: Andre Deutsch.

Reid, M. 1978. 'The secondary banking crisis-five years on', *The Banker* 128(634):21–30.

1982. *The Secondary Banking Crisis, 1973–75: Its Causes and Course.* London: Macmillan.

1986. 'Lessons for bank supervision from the secondary-banking crises', in Gardener (1986, pp. 99–108).

Revell, J. 1966. 'The wealth of the nation', *Moorgate and Wall Street Review,* Spring:72.

Richardson, G. 1989. 'The prospects for an international monetary system', in F. H. Capie and G. E. Wood (eds.), *Monetary Economics in the 1980s.* London: Macmillan, pp. 21–39.

Ringe, A. and N. Rollings. 2000. 'Domesticating the "market animal"? The Treasury and the Bank of England, 1955–60', in R. A. W. Rhodes (ed.), *Transforming British Government,* Vol. 1: *Changing Whitehall.* London: Macmillan.

Robbins, L. 1958. 'Thoughts on the crisis', *Lloyds Bank Review,* New Series, 48:1–26.

Robbins, L. C. 1971a. *Autobiography of an Economist.* London: Macmillan.

1971b. 'Monetary theory and the Radcliffe Report', in Lord Robbins (ed.), *Money Trade and International Relations.* London: Macmillan, pp. 90–119.

Roberts, R. 1992. *Schroders. Merchants and Bankers.* Basingstoke: Macmillan.

Roberts, R. and D. Kynaston, eds. 1995. *The Bank of England. Money, Power and Influence, 1694–1994.* Oxford: Clarendon Press.

Robertson, D. H . 1954. *Britain in the World's Economy: The Page-Barbour Lectures for 1953.* London: Allen & Unwin.

Robertson, D. 1959. 'Radcliffe under scrutiny – a squeak from Aunt Sally' *The Banker* 109(406):718–722.

Roosa, R. V. 1965. *Monetary Reform and the World Economy.* New York: Harper & Row.

Rumins, J. S. 1995. *The Bank's Accounts and Budgetary Control, 1969–1994.* London: Bank of England.

Samuelson, P. A. and R. M. Solow. 1960. 'Problem of achieving and maintaining a stable price level-analytical aspects of anti-inflation policy', *American Economic Review* 50(2):177–194.

Samuelson, P. A. and W. A. Barnett. 2007. *Inside the Economist's Mind: Conversations with Eminent Economists.* Oxford: Blackwell.

Sargent, J. 1954. 'Convertibility', *Oxford Economic Papers* 6(1):55–68.

Saville, R. 1996. *Bank of Scotland: A History, 1695–1995.* Edinburgh: Edinburgh University Press.

Saving, T. R. 1967. 'Monetary-policy targets and indicators', *Journal of Political Economy* 75(4):446–456.

Sayers, R. S. 1938. *Modern Banking,* 1st ed. Oxford: Oxford University Press.

  1956. *Financial Policy 1939–45.* London: HMSO.

  1957. *Central Banking after Bagehot.* Oxford: Clarendon Press.

  1958. *Modern Banking,* 4th ed. Oxford: Clarendon Press.

  1960. 'Monetary thought and monetary policy in England', *Economic Journal* 70(280):710–724.

  1963. *Modern Banking,* 6th ed. Oxford: Clarendon Press.

  1972. 'The background of ratio control by central banks', in M. Peston and B. Corry (eds.), *Essays in Honour of Lord Robbins.* London: Weidenfeld & Nicolson, pp. 215–223.

  1976. *The Bank of England, 1891–1944.* Cambridge: Cambridge University Press.

Scammell, W. M. 1968. *The London Discount Market.* London: Elek.

Schenk, C. R. 1998. 'The origins of the Eurodollar market in London, 1955–1963', *Explorations in Economic History* 35(2):221–238.

  2004. 'The Empire strikes back: Hong Kong and decline of sterling in the 1960s', *Economic History Review* 57(3):551–580.

  2010. *The Decline of Sterling Managing the Retreat of Sterling as an International Currency: 1945–1992.* Cambridge: Cambridge University Press.

Schwartz, A. J. 1985. 'Where the Bank went wrong', *The Banker* 135(708):100–101.

Scott, P. 1996. *The Property Masters: A History of the British Commercial Property Sector.* London: E & FN Spon.

Seldon, A. and F. G. Pennance. 1965. *Everyman's Dictionary of Economics.* London: J. M. Dent.

Seldon, A. and P. Thorneycroft. 1960. *Not Unanimous: A Rival Verdict to Radcliffe's on Money.* London: Institute of Economic Affairs.

Siklos, P. L. 2002. *The Changing Face of Central Banking: Evolutionary Trends since World War II.* Cambridge: Cambridge University Press.

Sked, A. 1987. *Britain's Decline: Problems and Perspectives.* Oxford: Basil Blackwell.

Skidelsky, R. 2000. *John Maynard Keynes,* Vol. 3: *Fighting for Britain 1937–46.* London: Macmillan.

Smith, A. H. 1949. 'Evolution of the exchange control', *Economica* 16(63):243–248.

Smith, W. L. and R. Mikesell. 1957. 'The effectiveness of monetary policy: British experience', *Journal of Political Economy* 65(1):18–39.

Smith, D. 1987. *The Rise and Fall of monetarism: The Theory and Politics of an Economic Experiment.* London: Penguin.

Solomon, R. 1977. *The International Monetary System, 1946–76: An Insider's View.* New York: Harper & Row.

1982. *The International Monetary System, 1945–1981* (an updated and expanded version of *The international monetary system, 1945–1976*). New York: Harper & Row.

Sorensen, T. C. 1965. *Kennedy.* London: Hodder and Stoughton.

Strange, S. 1971. *Sterling and British Policy: A Political Study of an International Currency in Decline.* Oxford: Oxford University Press for the Royal Institute of International Affairs.

Stewart, M. 1977. *The Jekyll and Hyde Years: Politics and Economic Policy since 1964.* London: Dent.

Sunderland, D. 2004. *Managing the British Empire: The Crown Agents, 1833–1914.* Woodbridge: Boydell Press.

2007. *Managing British Colonial and Post-colonial Development: The Crown Agents, 1914–1974.* Woodbridge: Boydell Press.

Taylor, P. 2004. 'Cobbold, Cameron Fromanteel, First Baron Cobbold (1904–1987)', Oxford Dictionary of National Biography. London: Oxford University Press; online edition May 2005; *www.oxforddnb.com/view/article/40108*; accessed 8 January 2009.

Tempest, P. 2008. *The Bank of England Bedside Book: A Thread of Gold: 1694–2008,* Vol. 1: *Adventures, Escapades and Memories.* London: Stacey International.

Tether, G. C. 1961. 'Dollars – hard, soft, and euro', *The Banker* 111(424):395–404.

Tew, B. 1965. 'Mr. Crouch on "new orthodox" methods of monetary control – comment (2)', *Economic Journal* 75(300):859–860.

1970. *International Monetary Cooperation 1945–70.* London: Hutchinson.

1977. *The Evolution of the International Monetary System 1945–77.* New York: John Wiley & Sons.

1978a. 'Monetary policy' in Blackaby (1978, pp. 218–257).

1978b. 'Policies aimed at improving the balance of payments' in Blackaby (1978, pp. 304–360).

Toniolo, G. 2005. *Central Bank Cooperation at the Bank for International Settlements, 1930–1973.* New York: Cambridge University Press.

Thirlwall, A. P. and H. D. Gibson, 1994. *Balance-of-Payments Theory and the United Kingdom Experience.* London: Macmillan.

Thornton, H. P. 1802. *An Enquiry into the Nature and Effects of the Paper Credit of Great Britain.* London.

Triffin, R. 1961. *Gold and the Dollar Crisis: The Future of Convertibility.* New Haven, CT: Yale University Press.

Tuke, A. W. and R. J. H. Gillman. 1972. *Barclays Bank Limited 1926–1969.* London: Oxford University Press.

Turner, D. and C. Williams. 1987. *An Investment Bank for the UK,* Fabian Tract No. 518. London: Fabian Society.

Valentine, M. 2006. *Free Range Ego.* London: Antony Rowe.

Vaughan, J. W. 1987. *Banking Act 1979.* London: Lloyd's of London Press.

Velde, F. 2004. 'Poor hand or poor play: rise and fall of inflation in the US', *Economic Perspectives (Federal Reserve Bank Chicago)* 28:35–51.

Volcker, P. and T. Gyohten. 1992. *Changing Fortunes: The World's Money and the Threat to American Leadership*. New York: Times Books.

Wadsworth, J. E. 1973. *The Banks and the Monetary System in the United Kingdom, 1959–71*. London: Methuen.

Waight, L. 1939. *The History and Mechanism of the Exchange Equalization Account*. Cambridge: Cambridge University Press.

Walters, A. A. 1969. *Money in Boom and Slump: An Empirical Inquiry into British Experience since the 1880s*. London: Institute of Economic Affairs.

1986. *Britain's Economic Renaissance: Margaret Thatcher's Reforms, 1979–84*. Oxford: Oxford University Press.

Wass, D. 1978. 'The changing problems of economic management', *Economic Trends* 293:97–105.

2008. *Decline to Fall: The Making of British Macro-economic Policy and the 1976 IMF Crisis*. Oxford: Oxford University Press.

Wee, H. van der. 1986. *Prosperity and Upheaval: The World Economy 1945–1980*. London: Viking.

Weiner, M. J. 1982. *English Culture and the Decline of the Industrial Spirit, 1850–1980*. Cambridge: Cambridge University Press.

Wilcox, M. G. 1979. 'Capital in banking: an historical survey', *Journal of the Institute of Bankers*, June:96–101.

Williamson, J. 1965. *The Crawling Peg*. Princeton Essays in International Finance No. 50.

Williamson, J. and G. E. Wood. 1976. 'The British inflation: indigenous or imported?', *American Economic Review* 66(4):520–531.

Williamson, J. 1977. *The Failure of World Monetary Reform, 1971–74*. Southampton: Thomas Nelson and Sons.

Wilson, H. 1971. *Labour Government 1964–70*. London: Weidenfeld & Nicolson.

Wilson, S. C. and T. Lupton. 1959. 'The social background and connections of "top decision makers"', *Manchester School of Economic and Social Studies* 27(1):30–51.

Winder, G. H. 1955. *The Free Convertibility of Sterling*. London: Batchworth Press.

Winton, J. R. 1982. *Lloyds Bank 1918–1969*. Oxford: Oxford University Press.

Wood, G. E. 2003. 'International financial stability: a meaningful concept?', in J. J. Norton and M. Andenas (eds.), *International Monetary and Financial Law upon Entering the New Millennium*. London: London Institute of International Banking.

Wood, G. E. and D. R. Mudd. 1977. 'Do foreigners control the US money supply?', *Federal Reserve Bank of St. Louis Review* 59(12):8–11.

Wormell, J. 1985. *The Gilt-Edged Market*. London: Allen & Unwin.

Worswick, G. D. N. 1973. 'Review of the new inflation: the politics of prices and incomes by Aubrey Jones', *Economic Journal* 83(332):1281–1282.

Zawadzki, K. K. F. 1981. *Competition and Credit Control*. Oxford: Blackwell.

Ziegler, P. 1993. *Wilson: The Authorised Life of Lord Wilson of Rievaulx*. London: Weidenfeld & Nicolson.

Index